D0203189

INVESTMENTS
Analysis and Management

CANADIAN EDITION

INVESTMENTS

Analysis and Management

W. Sean Cleary
Saint Mary's University

Charles P. Jones
North Carolina State University

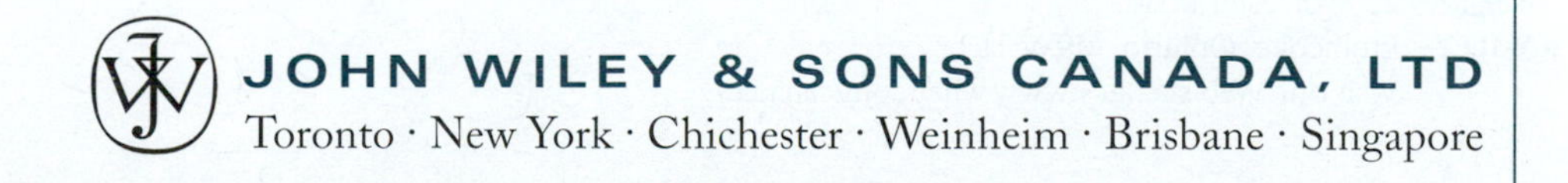
JOHN WILEY & SONS CANADA, LTD
Toronto · New York · Chichester · Weinheim · Brisbane · Singapore

John Wiley & Sons Canada, Ltd gratefully acknowledges the Canadian Securities Institute for permission to reprint material from the Canadian Securities Course™ (CSC) and the CSI logo throughout this textbook. This material is owned by the CSI and is used here only with permission. The CSI's willingness to grant permission does not constitute an endorsement of this textbook.

Statistics Canada information is used with the permission of the Minister of Industry, as Minister responsible for Statistics Canada. Information on the availability of the wide range of data from Statistics Canada can be obtained from Statistics Canada's Regional Offices, its World Wide Web site at <http://www.statcan.ca>, and its toll-free access number 1-800-263-1136.

Canadian Cataloguing in Publication Data

Cleary, W. Sean (William Sean), 1962-

Investments: analysis and management

Canadian ed.

Includes bibliographical references and index.

ISBN 0-471-64530-3

1. Investments. 2. Investment analysis. I. Jones, Charles, Parker, 1943- .

II. title.

HG4521.C523 1999 332.6 C99-931963-9

Production Credits

Acquisitions Editor: John Horne

Publishing Services Director: Karen Bryan

Developmental Editor: Margaret Williams

Assistant Editor: Elsa Passera

Senior Marketing Manager: Carolyn Wells

Copy Editor: Focus Strategic Communications

Proofreader: Focus Strategic Communications

Designer: Interrobang Graphic Design Inc.

Printing and Binding: Tri-Graphic Printing Limited

Printed and bound in Canada

10 9 8 7 6 5 4 3 2 1

John Wiley & Sons Canada, Ltd

22 Worcester Road

Etobicoke, Ontario M9W 1L1

Visit our Web site at: <www.wiley.com/canada>

ABOUT THE AUTHORS

W. Sean Cleary is Assistant Professor of Finance at Saint Mary's University in Halifax, Nova Scotia. Dr. Cleary graduated with his MBA from Saint Mary's University, and with his PhD in finance from the University of Toronto. He has recently completed level II of the Chartered Financial Analyst (CFA) program. He has also completed the Canadian Securities Course (CSC) as well as the Investment Funds Institute of Canada (IFIC) Mutual Fund Course.

Dr. Cleary has taught numerous university finance courses, including Investments, Introductory Finance, and Corporate Finance at Saint Mary's University, the University of Toronto, Ryerson Polytechnic University, and the University of Lethbridge over the past eight years. He has also taught seminars preparing students to write the Canadian Securities Course for the past four years.

Dr. Cleary has recently published articles in *The Journal of Finance,* the *Canadian Journal of Administrative Sciences*, and the *Canadian Investment Review*, in addition to receiving research funding from the Social Sciences and Humanities Research Council of Canada (SSHRC). He has also prepared chapters for professional courses offered by the Canadian Securities Institute.

Charles P. Jones is Edwin Gill Professor of Finance in the College of Management, North Carolina State University. A graduate of UNC-Chapel Hill, he has taught investments, managerial finance, risk management, and financial institutions and capital markets courses for almost 30 years. Dr. Jones has published numerous articles in the leading finance journals, including *The Journal of Finance*, *The Journal of Financial Economics*, *The Journal of Financial and Quantitative Analysis*, *The Journal of Business*, *The Journal of Portfolio Management*, and *The Financial Analysts Journal* as well as several other journals.

Dr. Jones is a Chartered Financial Analyst. He has served as a consultant in several capacities and is currently helping Union Bank of Switzerland in developing the expertise of their employees in the area of portfolio management. Dr. Jones has also received an outstanding teaching award from his university.

PREFACE

GOALS AND FEATURES

This book is designed to provide a solid foundation in the theory of investments plus the practical application that students require to make real-life investment decisions. It is also intended to serve as a useful resource for students intending to pursue a career in the financial services industry. With these objectives in mind, much attention has been devoted to describing the investment environment that presently exists in Canada, as well as globally, with particular emphasis on the United States, since this represents an important and readily accessible market for Canadian investors. In addition, we place great emphasis on topics that are included in professional courses such as the Canadian Securities Course™ (CSC) and the Chartered Financial Analysts (CFA) program.

Students should benefit from the intuitive approach applied to topics throughout. Descriptive material is first covered thoroughly. Then, the analytics of investments are presented throughout every discussion to help students reason out investment issues for themselves. To improve topic flow, more technical or rigorous material is covered in footnotes and appendixes. This also allows instructors to increase the level of the course, if desired. The analytics are applied in illustrative examples to actual Canadian companies or financial instruments to the greatest extent possible. Real-world examples are included from various publications such as *The Globe and Mail*, the *National Post*, and *The Wall Street Journal*, to reinforce the application aspects of the concepts. Finally, an abundance of review questions and problem material is included at the end of every chapter.

The book has several distinct features that contribute to achieving the above objectives:

- It brings a clear accessible approach that focuses on the more applied/practical aspects of investments.
- It provides up-to-date information regarding the Canadian and global investment environments, with a strong emphasis on Canada.
- Many real-world examples are used to apply concepts discussed in the text to Canadian companies. These can be found in the illustrative examples found throughout the text, as well as in the "Real-World Returns" boxes described below.
- There is a strong tie to professional associations throughout the book. While many investments texts have included past CFA examination questions, none have emphasized CSC material. We acknowledge the importance of CFA material, which is included throughout the text and in the end-of-chapter problems; however, we have also placed considerable emphasis on CSC-related material. We feel the inclusion of CSC material is of great importance, since the majority of students pursuing a career in finance in Canada will be required to take the CSC. On the other hand, only a minority will go on to pursue a CFA designation, in most cases after having first completed the CSC.

The book is written for the first course in investments at universities and colleges, and is a useful supplement for students planning to enroll in the CSC. Standard prerequisites include basic accounting, economics, and introductory finance. A course in statistics is very useful but not absolutely essential. We have sought to minimize formulas and to simplify difficult material, consistent with a presentation of the subject that takes into account current ideas and practices. Relevant, state-of-the-art material has been simplified and structured specifically for the benefit of the student.

Organization of the Text

The text is divided into seven parts organized around background, portfolio and capital market theory, the analysis of different types of securities, and portfolio management.

Part 1 provides the needed background for students before encountering the specifics of security analysis and portfolio management. The goal of this section is to acquaint beginners with an overview of what investing is all about. After a general discussion of the subject in Chapter 1, the next five chapters describe the variety of securities available when investing directly and indirectly (investment funds), the markets in which they are traded, the mechanics of securities trading, and a careful and complete analysis of the important concepts of risk and return that dominate any discussion of investments.

Part 2 is concerned with portfolio management, capital market theory, and the concept of efficient markets. Chapter 7 contains a complete discussion of modern portfolio concepts, centring on expected return and risk. The primary emphasis is on the essentials of Markowitz portfolio theory and the single-index model. Chapter 8 continues the discussion of portfolio concepts by concentrating on portfolio selection, based on the concept of efficient portfolios. The separation theorem and systematic and non-systematic risk are discussed. Chapter 9 discusses capital market theory, a natural extension of portfolio theory. This discussion focuses on the Capital Asset Pricing Model, and, to a lesser extent, on the Arbitrage Pricing Theory. Part 2 concludes with a discussion of Market Efficiency in Chapter 10, which provides some insight into the controversy and investing implications that arise from discussion of this topic.

Parts 3 and 4 focus on the basic approach to security analysis and valuation by presenting "how-to" tools and techniques for bonds and stocks, respectively. Part 3 examines the analysis, valuation, and management of bonds, a logical starting point in learning how to value securities. Part 4 builds on these concepts in discussing the analysis, valuation, and management of common stocks.

Parts 4 and 5 are devoted to common stocks, a reasonable allocation given investor interest in common stocks. Part 5 covers fundamental analysis, the heart of security analysis. Because of its scope and complexity, three chapters are required to adequately cover the fundamental approach. The sequencing of these chapters — market, industry, and company — reflects the belief that the top-down approach to fundamental analysis is the preferable one for students to learn, although the bottom-up approach is also discussed. Part 5 also discusses the other approach to common stock selection — technical analysis. Technical analysis is a well-known technique for analyzing stocks that goes back many years.

Part 6 discusses the other major category of securities available to investors — derivative securities. Chapter 19 analyzes call and put options, which are popular investment alternatives in recent years. Stock-index options are also covered. Chapter 20 is devoted to financial futures, an important topic in investments. Similar to options, investors can use these securities to hedge their positions and reduce the risk of investing.

Part 7 concludes the text with a discussion of portfolio management and the issue of evaluating portfolio performance. Chapter 21 is structured around the Association for Investment Management and Research's (AIMR) approach to portfolio management as a process and concludes with some case studies similar to those found in Chapter 12 of the CSC. Chapter 22 discusses portfolio evaluation, which is a logical conclusion to the text, because all investors are keenly interested in how well their investments have performed. Actual Canadian mutual funds are used as examples of how to apply these portfolio performance measures and how to interpret the results.

Pedagogical Features

- **Learning Objectives** identify what students should know after reading each chapter. They are reviewed in the **Summary** at the end of the chapter.
- **Key Terms** are defined in the margin and are listed at the end of each chapter.
- **Real-World Returns** boxes feature articles from the business news media and demonstrate how points discussed in the book are applied in the real world.
- **Investing Tips** help students understand the logic behind important investment concepts.
- The **Additional Resources** section at the end of most chapters points students to important books and articles.
- **Review Questions** help students check that they have understood the concepts discussed in each chapter. **Demonstration Problems** and **Problems** give students the opportunity to apply what they have learned.
- A unique **Preparing for Your Professional Exams** section includes a Special Note to Canadian Securities Course Students that identifies CSC-related material in each chapter, CSC registration questions, and questions from past Chartered Financial Analyst exams. Throughout the book, **CSC Notes** boxes highlight material that is covered by the Canadian Securities Course and that is of practical relevance to Canadian investors but not usually included in investments textbooks.

Website

The ***Investments: Analysis and Management*** website at www.wiley.com/canada/cleary provides a wealth of online resources to maximize the student learning experience. The latest developments in the investment world are made available through direct links to company websites, investment news, weekly financial and economic reports, and much more. As well, on-line cases require students to do research on the Internet, encouraging hands-on learning and providing the most up-to-date material on the market.

ACKNOWLEDGEMENTS

CANADIAN EDITION

I would like to thank my wife Helen, my parents (Bill and Beryl), and my children (Jason, Brennan, Brigid, and Siobhan), for their support and patience during this endeavour. I would like to thank Laurence Booth at the University of Toronto for all he has done for me. Special thanks also goes out to Gordon Dixon (University of Lethbridge), for his tax expertise and to David Copp (Mount Allison University), and Mohamed Jalloh (Saint Mary's University), for their work on the Instructor's and Solutions Manual, as well as for their valuable comments regarding textbook material. Finally, thanks to Mike Inglis (Ryerson Polytechnic University), John Schmitz (Financial Concept Group), and Greg MacKinnon, Francis Boabang, and George Ye (all from Saint Mary's University) for various comments and suggestions.

In addition, I am grateful to the following reviewers whose thoughtful comments contributed to the quality, relevancy, and accuracy of this text:

Ben Amoako-Adu,
Wilfrid Laurier University

Tov Assogbavi,
Laurentian University

Glen Baigent,
Dalhousie University

Steve Beveridge,
University of Alberta

Abraham Brodt,
Concordia University

Wayne Campbell,
Sheridan College

Carol Edwards,
British Columbia Institute of Technology

Lowell Epp,
University of Regina

Carmine Fabiilli,
Algonquin College

Alex Faseruk,
Memorial University

Ibrahim Fooladi,
Dalhousie University

Larry Gould,

University of Manitoba

Richard Grant,
University of Lethbridge

Yunke He,
University College of Cape Breton

Sean Hennessey,
University of Prince Edward Island

Mike Inglis,
Ryerson Polytechnic University

Gene Karlik,
Red River Community College

Andrew King,
Southern Alberta Institute of Technology and RBC Dominion Securities

Patrick Latham,
Northern Alberta Institute of Technology

Michael Leonard,
Midland Walwyn Capital Inc.

Howard Nemiroff,
Saint Mary's University

Peter Ostrowski,
University of Northern British Columbia

Eben Ottuteye,
University of New Brunswick

Geoffrey Poitras,
Simon Fraser University

Ganesh Vaidyanathan,
Brandon College

Marie Zukowski,
George Brown College

W. Sean Cleary
Saint Mary's University
August 1999

BRIEF CONTENTS

CONTENTS

PART ONE • BACKGROUND

PART FOUR • COMMON STOCKS: ANALYSIS, VALUATION, AND MANAGEMENT

UNDERSTANDING INVESTMENTS

LEARNING OBJECTIVES

After reading this chapter, you will be able to

1. Define investment and discuss what it means to study investments.
2. Explain why risk and return are the two critical components of all investing decisions.
3. Outline the two-step investment decision process.
4. Discuss key factors that affect the investment decision process.

CHAPTER PREVIEW

This chapter lays the foundation for the study of investments. You will learn what an investment is and why it is important to study the investment process. We introduce the concept of a trade-off between expected return and risk — the basis for all investment decisions — and outline the two-step investment decision process of security analysis and portfolio management. Finally, we discuss some of the key factors that affect the investment decision process such as global markets and institutional investors.

THE PURPOSE OF THIS TEXTBOOK

The objective of this text is to help you understand the investments field as it is currently understood, discussed, and practiced so that you can make sound investment decisions that will enhance your economic welfare. Key concepts are presented to provide an appreciation of the theory and practice of investments. After reading this text, you will be able to intelligently answer questions such as the following:

- On October 27, 1997, the Dow Jones Industrial Average (DIJA) dropped 554 points (or 7.2 per cent) and the Toronto Stock Exchange 300 Composite Index (TSE 300) dropped 434 points (or 6.2 per cent) in response to turmoil in Asian currency and equity markets. The next day the DJIA regained 337 points and the TSE 300 137 points. Why was the fall and subsequent recovery of greater magnitude in the United States than in Canada? With volatility like this, should most investors avoid common stocks, particularly for their retirement plans?
- The average return on Canadian equity mutual funds was 10.5 per cent for the ten-year period ending January 31, 1998.[1] This is below the 11.3 per cent return achieved over this period by both the TSE 300 and the Scotia McLeod Universe Bond Total Return Index. Why?
- In 1997 the stock markets in Mexico and Brazil experienced gains of 55.6 per cent and 44.8 per cent while that of the TSE 300 was approximately 13 per cent. Should Canadian investors be participating in "emerging" stock markets and, if so, how should they go about it? Should most investors have some part of their funds in international assets?
- Is it possible to have earned 30 per cent or more investing in low-risk Treasury bills in a single year?
- How can futures contracts, with a reputation for being extremely risky, be used to reduce an investor's risk?
- What is the historical average annual rate of return on common stocks and what can an investor reasonably expect to earn from stocks in the future?

Both descriptive and quantitative materials on investing are readily available in a variety of forms. Some of this material is very enlightening, much of it is entertaining but debatable because of the many controversies in investments, and some of it is simply worthless. This text seeks to cover what is particularly useful and relevant for today's investment climate. It offers some ideas about what you can reasonably expect to accomplish by using what you learn

[1] *The Globe and Mail / Report on Mutual Funds*, February 19, 1998.

and therefore what you can realistically expect to achieve as an investor in today's investment world. Many investors have unrealistic expectations, which ultimately leads to disappointment or worse.

Learning to avoid the many pitfalls awaiting you as an investor by clearly understanding what you can reasonably expect from investing your money may be the single most important benefit to be derived from this text. For example, would you entrust your money to someone offering 36 per cent annual return on riskless US government Treasury securities? Some 600 investors did and lost approximately $10 million to a former Sunday school teacher. Intelligent investors learn to say no and to avoid many of the mistakes that can thus be prevented.

THE NATURE OF INVESTMENTS

Some Definitions

The term investing can cover a wide range of activities. It often refers to putting money in GICs, bonds, common stocks, or mutual funds. More knowledgeable investors would include other paper assets, such as warrants, puts and calls, futures contracts, and convertible securities, as well as tangible assets, such as gold, real estate, and collectibles. Investing can range from very conservative to aggressive speculation. Whether you are a university graduate starting out in the workplace or a senior citizen concerned with how to get by in retirement, investing decisions will be very important to you.

An **investment** can be defined as the commitment of funds to one or more assets that will be held over some future time period. The field of **investments**, therefore, involves the study of the investment process. The study of investments is concerned with the management of an investor's wealth, which is the sum of current income and the present value of all future income. (This is why present value and compound interest concepts have an important role in the investment process.) Although the field of investments encompasses many aspects, it can be thought of in terms of two primary functions: analysis and management.

Investment
The commitment of funds to one or more assets that will be held over some future time period.

Investments
The study of the investments process.

In this text the term investments refers in general to **financial assets** and in particular to marketable securities. Financial assets are paper (or electronic) claims on some issuer such as the federal or provincial government or a corporation; on the other hand, **real assets** are tangible physical assets such as precious metals (gold, silver), gems (diamonds), art, and real estate. **Marketable securities** are financial assets that are easily and cheaply traded in organized markets. Technically, investments include both financial and real assets, and both marketable and non-marketable assets. Because of the vast scope of investment opportunities available to investors, our primary emphasis is on marketable securities; however, the basic principles and techniques discussed in this text are applicable to real assets as well.

Financial Assets
Paper or electronic claims on some issuer such as the federal or provincial government or a corporation.

Real Assets
Physical assets, such as gold or real estate.

Marketable Securities
Financial assets that are easily and cheaply traded in organized markets.

The Real-World Returns box below indicates that North American investors are increasingly allocating a higher percentage of their wealth to financial assets. No one can be certain whether or not this trend will continue, but the importance of understanding the underlying nature of various financial assets is obvious.

REAL-WORLD RETURNS

North American Investors Taking on More Risk

What Canadians and Americans own has been undergoing a revolution, fuelled by a craze for mutual funds and rising stock markets. Earlier this month, *The New York Times* ran a front-page story announcing that Americans now have more of their assets invested in stocks than at any time in the past half century, or perhaps ever. Even more compelling was the revelation that the bedrock of most people's assets, their home, had fallen to second place.

According to the *Times*' analysis, which was based on Federal Reserve Board data, in 1997 stocks made up 28 per cent of household assets, edging out real estate at 27 per cent, a sea of change from just a few years ago.

In 1990, Americans had 33 per cent in real estate assets and a measly 12 per cent in stocks. The difference can largely be explained by the huge flow of funds into stocks, particularly through equity mutual funds, and the phenomenal performance of the stock markets.

Though comparable numbers are hard to come by, could we some time see a similar story in *The Globe and Mail* announcing that Canadians had more assets in stocks than in real estate?

Certainly, the real estate versus stocks switch has not yet happened in Canada. According to Investor Economics, a Toronto-based consultant to the financial services industry, Canadians' household balance sheet for 1996 listed assets of $1.165-billion for real estate (36 per cent of total), and $418-billion for stocks (13 per cent). But during the 1990s, Canadians have narrowed what was a large gap with Americans on the ownership of long-term risky financial assets such as stocks and other securities whose value changes with fluctuations in the market.

Here's the background. The household balance sheets of the two countries diverged in the 1980s. The reason is simple. In Canada, high inflation and high interest rates made it advantageous to own real estate, which greatly increased in value. At the same time, Canada's stock markets held little appeal, performing poorly compared with markets abroad and with those in the United States. Deposits were treasured because interest rates were so high.

But the 1990s have turned out differently. Inflation has fallen, and with it interest rates, with the result that real estate has lost much of its lustre. Unlike the 1980s, few people now buy a house as an investment. And Canada's stock markets have finally performed well.

Canadians' switch from real assets, including real estate and durables (everything from cars to fridges), to financial assets (particularly riskier ones), continues to lag behind Americans'.

Take mutual funds. You would expect the Canadian industry to be a bit less than tenth the size of the US industry. But Investor Economics pegs the Canadian industry at 4.5 per cent of the American. While that number is low, it is a substantial improvement from the 3.9 per cent level of 1995.

The stock market has made people feel richer, which is good and bad. It means they are likely to spend more, which is good for the economy. But they are also likely to take on more debt, which will eventually cut into spending and can lead to bankruptcy. And, of course, stock market values can plunge more abruptly than real estate values, leaving investors poorer — and feeling poorer — and in some cases in trouble. Stock market corrections or crashes can lead to panic selling, which doesn't happen with real estate because it is too illiquid.

What all this boils down to is that Americans, and Canadians in their wake, are taking more risks. An increasing percentage of their assets are financial, and an increasing percentage of those assets are higher risk. The trend appears likely to continue, unless a severe correction or a prolonged bear market changes the equation.

Excerpted from Douglas Goold, "Why We're Taking On More Risk," The Globe and Mail / Report on Business, *February 28, 1998, p. B22. Reprinted with permission from* The Globe and Mail.

Even when we limit our discussion primarily to financial assets, it is difficult to keep up with the proliferation of new products. Two such assets that did not exist a few years ago are junk bonds (discussed in Chapter 12) and stock-index futures (discussed in Chapter 20). Junk bonds became a $200 billion market by the end of the 1980s before undergoing a severe crisis and then rebounding significantly, whereas stock-index futures have grown at such a rate that their trading often has an impact on the stock market.

Investing as Part of Personal Financial Planning

The investment of funds in various assets is only part of the overall financial decision making and planning that most individuals must do. Before investing, each individual should develop a financial plan that should include the decision on whether to purchase a house, a major investment for most individuals. In addition, decisions must be made about insurance of various types — life, health, disability, and protection of business and property. Finally, the plan should provide for emergency reserve funds.[2]

This text assumes that investors have established their overall financial plan and are now interested in managing and enhancing their wealth by investing in an optimal combination of financial assets. The idea of an "optimal combination" is important because our wealth, which we hold in the form of various assets, should be evaluated and managed as a unified whole. Wealth should be evaluated and managed within the context of a **portfolio**, which is made up of the asset holdings of an investor.

Portfolio
The securities held by an investor taken as a unit.

Why Do We Invest?

Although everyone would agree that we invest to make money, we need to be more precise. We invest to improve our welfare, which for our purposes can be defined as monetary wealth, both current and future. Funds to be invested come from assets already owned, such as savings or inheritances, borrowed money, or "foregone consumption." By foregoing consumption today and investing the savings, investors expect to enhance their future consumption possibilities by increasing their wealth.

Investors also seek to manage their wealth effectively, obtaining the most from it while protecting it from inflation, taxes, and other factors. There are three primary investment objectives:

1. Safety
2. Income
3. Growth of capital.

These objectives are mutually exclusive in the sense that a single security cannot maximize two or more of these primary objectives. In other words, trade-offs exist, so that, if you wish to maximize safety, you have to be willing to make some sacrifices with respect to income and growth potential.

Secondary investment objectives include liquidity or marketability and tax minimization. They are considered secondary in the sense that investors should not allow them to dominate primary investment considerations. For example, it would be imprudent to alter an

[2] Personal finance decisions of this type are discussed in personal finance texts.

investment portfolio designed to maximize safety, simply to avoid taxes. On the other hand, it makes good sense to devise and follow tax avoidance strategies within the context of any investment plan. The point is that they should not be the overriding factor determining investment decisions.

Investors face several constraints that will affect the objectives of their investment policy and determine how effectively these objectives can be attained. The most obvious factors are the level and stability of income and the level of financial obligations faced by an investor both now and in the future. The individual's level of investment knowledge and general tolerance for risk should also play an important role in the design of an investment policy. Some investors will be constrained by legal, moral, and ethical considerations. In addition, miscellaneous factors such as illness or a pending divorce may become an overriding factor in the investment decision.

THE IMPORTANCE OF STUDYING INVESTMENTS

The Personal Aspects

It is important to remember that all individuals have wealth of some kind; if nothing else, they have the value of their services in the marketplace. Most individuals must make investment decisions sometime in their lives. These include day-to-day decisions such as how to improve the return from savings accounts by investing funds in alternative financial instruments. In fact, the decision to enrol at a post-secondary educational institution represents a significant investment decision, since it requires a large sacrifice of your time and money. The future benefits are uncertain, although they include an increase in earnings potential; intangible benefits include the sense of accomplishment individuals feel as they learn and/or achieve academic success.

A good example of the critical importance of making good investment decisions is deciding how much to contribute to a Registered Retirement Savings Plan (RRSP), and what types of assets these should include.[3] Working taxpayers can make tax-deductible contributions up to specified limits per year (depending on their income and their contributions to other registered plans). The earnings on the contributions are not taxed until they are withdrawn, as long as the assets are RRSP-eligible and the plan satisfies the 80 per cent Canadian content requirements.

RRSP funds can be invested in a wide range of assets, from the very safe to the very speculative. Since these funds may be invested for long periods of time, good investment decisions are critical. Over many years, the differences in the investment returns earned can be staggering. Table 1-1 demonstrates how $4,000 invested every year for 40 years will grow to over $7 million if the funds earn 15 per cent per year; they will earn $1.78 million at 10 per cent and $483,200 at 5 per cent — quite a large variation in final wealth.

[3] RRSPs are discussed in detail in the CSC Notes box on page 65 of Chapter 3.

Table 1-1

Possible Payoffs from Long-Term Investing

Amount Invested per Year	Number of Years	Final Wealth if Funds Are Invested at 5%	10%	15%
$4,000	20	$132,264	$229,100	$409,760
$4,000	30	$265,756	$657,960	$1,739,000
$4,000	40	$483,200	$1,770,360	$7,116,400

With so much individual investor money flowing into mutual funds, and with individual investors owning a large percentage of all stocks outstanding, the study of investments is more important than ever. After being net sellers of stocks from 1968 through 1990, individual investors have swarmed into the financial markets. Individual investor interest in the stock market in the 1990s is best expressed by the power of mutual funds (explained in Chapter 3), their favourite investment vehicle. Mutual funds, pension funds, and other institutional investors are now the driving forces in the marketplace and over half of all trades on the Toronto Stock Exchange (TSE) and on the New York Stock Exchange (NYSE) are block trades by institutional investors. In fact, the total assets in mutual funds in Canada grew from $24.9 billion at the end of 1990, to $326.6 billion by the end of 1998.[4]

In the final analysis, we study investments in the hope of earning better returns in relation to the risk we assume when we invest. A careful study of investment analysis and portfolio management principles can provide a sound framework for both managing and increasing wealth. Furthermore, this knowledge will allow you to sift through and properly evaluate the many articles on investing that appear daily in newspapers and magazines, which in turn will increase your chances of reaching your financial goals.

Investments as a Profession

In addition to the above reasons for studying investments, the world of investments offers several rewarding careers, both professionally and financially. At the end of 1997 there were 187 firms in the securities industry in Canada employing 32,990 individuals.[5] This number is significant but it pales in comparison to the numbers employed by the big Canadian banks. For example, the **Royal Bank of Canada** alone employed over 48,000 people in 1996. A study of investments is an essential part of becoming a professional in these fields.

Investment professionals who arrange the sale of new securities and assist in mergers and acquisitions enjoyed phenomenal financial rewards in the booming 1980s and in the later part of the 1990s. The total value of mergers in Canada reached an all-time high of $148 billion in 1998, while there were over $2.3 trillion US in mergers worldwide. An experienced merger and acquisition specialist can earn around a million dollars a year, and even someone with just a few years experience can earn $200,000 to $400,000 in this area.

---

4 The Investment Funds Institute of Canada (IFIC).

5 *Canadian Securities Course Textbook* (Toronto: Canadian Securities Institute, August 1998), p. 1-39.

Top security traders and registered representatives (investment advisors) commonly earn six-figure salaries, which escalate during periods of strong market activity, such as that displayed during the mid-1990s. Bond traders can also commonly earn in the six-figure range, with the salaries increasing with experience. A relatively inexperienced bond salesperson selling to institutional investors can earn $200,000 or more and, if experienced, the figure rises to the $600,000 to $700,000 range.

EXAMPLE: JUNK BOND TRADERS

In mid-1996 the demand for traders and salespersons in the junk bond (lower quality debt issues) market exploded, with the result that many individuals, including relative newcomers, were doubling their earnings, and pay of $1.5 to $2 million was not unusual among experienced people.

Although less glamorous and less profitable for the firms involved, there are good paying jobs on Bay Street and Wall Street in research. Analysts with a few years of experience can earn well over $100,000, while those with 10 years or more of experience can earn up to $500,000. A range of financial institutions — including securities firms, banks, investment companies, and insurance companies — need the services of investment analysts. Securities firms need them to support their registered representatives who in turn serve the public, for example, by preparing the research reports provided to customers. They also need analysts to assist in the sale of new securities and in the valuation of firms as possible merger or acquisition candidates. Banks, insurance companies, and investment companies need analysts to evaluate securities for possible purchase or sale from their investment portfolios.

The firms mentioned above all need portfolio managers to manage the portfolios of securities handled by these organizations. Portfolio managers are responsible for making the actual portfolio buy and sell decisions — what to buy and sell, when to buy and sell, and so forth. Portfolio performance is calculated for these managers, and their jobs typically depend on their performance relative to other managed portfolios and to market averages.

Finally, the number of financial planners continues to grow. It has been an unregulated profession until recently, without any minimum standards regarding professional qualifications, capital requirements, or ethical behaviour. In November of 1995, the Financial Planners Standards Council (FPSC) was formed to develop a set of minimum standards for financial planners in terms of education, experience, and ethical and moral conduct. Refer to Appendix 1-A for more details regarding FPSC requirements for financial planners.

UNDERSTANDING THE INVESTMENT DECISION PROCESS

An organized view of the investment process involves analyzing the basic nature of investment decisions and organizing the activities in the decision process.

Common stocks have produced, on average, significantly larger returns over the years than savings accounts or bonds, but these higher returns mean larger risks. Underlying all investment decisions is the trade-off between expected return and risk. Therefore, we first consider these two basic parameters that are of critical importance to all investors and the trade-off that exists between expected return and risk.

Given the foundation for making investment decisions — the trade-off between expected return and risk — we next consider the decision process in investments as it is practiced today. Although numerous separate decisions must be made, for organizational purposes this decision process has traditionally been divided into a two-step process: security analysis and portfolio management. Security analysis involves the valuation of securities, whereas portfolio management involves the management of an investor's investment selections as a portfolio (package of assets), with its own unique characteristics.

The Basis of Investment Decisions

Return

Stated in simplest terms, investors wish to earn a return on their money. Cash has an opportunity cost. By holding cash, you forego the opportunity to earn a return on that cash. Furthermore, in an inflationary environment, the purchasing power of cash diminishes, with high rates of inflation (such as that in 1980) bringing a rapid decline in purchasing power.

In investments it is critical to distinguish between an **expected return** (the anticipated return for some future period) and a **realized return** (the actual return over some past period). Investors invest for the future — for the returns they expect to earn — but when the investing period is over, they are left with their realized returns. What investors actually earn from their holdings may turn out to be more or less than what they expected when they first made the investment. This point is the essence of the investments process: investors must always consider the risk involved in investing.

Expected Return
The anticipated return by investors for some future period.

Realized Return
Actual return on an investment for some previous period of time.

Risk

Investors would like their returns to be as large as possible; however, this objective is subject to constraints, primarily risk. The Toronto Stock Exchange had an excellent year in 1996, with total returns for the TSE 300, a broad cross-section of common stocks, in excess of 28 per cent. During the same period, the returns earned by professionally managed Canadian equity mutual funds varied from as low as 1.5 per cent to as high as 89.1 per cent.[6] This demonstrates the riskiness associated with marketable securities that offer variable rates of return. The investment decision, therefore, must always be considered in terms of both risk and return. The two are inseparable.

There are different types, and therefore different definitions, of risk. We define **risk** as the chance that the actual return on an investment will be different from its expected return.[7] Using the term risk in this manner, the nominal (current dollar) return on a long-term Government of Canada bond can be considered free of default risk, since it is virtually assured that the government will redeem these obligations as they mature. On the other hand, there is

Risk
The chance that the actual return on an investment will be different from the expected return.

[6] "Mutual Fund 15-Year Review," *The Financial Post*, February 22, 1997.

[7] As we shall see in Chapter 7, expected return is a precise statistical term, not simply the return the investor expects. As indicated in our definition, risk involves chances or probabilities, which will also be discussed in Chapter 7 along with measures of the dispersion in the expected return.

some risk, however small, that the Royal Bank or BCE will be unable to redeem an issue of long-term bonds when they mature. And there is a very substantial risk of not realizing the expected return on any particular common stock over some future holding period.

Do investors dislike risk? In economics in general, and investments in particular, the standard assumption is that investors are rational and prefer certainty to uncertainty. It is easy to say that investors dislike risk, but more precisely, we should say that investors are risk averse. A **risk-averse investor** is one who will not assume risk simply for its own sake and will not incur any given level of risk unless there is an expectation of adequate compensation for having done so. Note carefully that it is not irrational to assume risk, even very large risk, as long as we expect to be compensated for it. In fact, investors cannot reasonably expect to earn larger returns without assuming larger risks.

Risk-Averse Investor An investor who will not assume a given level of risk unless there is an expectation of adequate compensation for having done so.

Investors deal with risk by choosing (implicitly or explicitly) the amount of risk they are willing to incur. Some investors choose high levels of risk with the expectation of high levels of return. Other investors are unwilling to assume much risk at all, and they should not expect to earn large returns.

We have said that investors would like to maximize their returns. Can we also say that investors, in general, will choose to minimize their risks? No! The reason is that there are costs to minimizing the risk — specifically a lower expected return. Taken to its logical conclusion, the minimization of risk would result in everyone holding risk-free assets such as savings accounts, CSBs, and Treasury bills. Thus, we need to think in terms of the expected risk-return trade-off that results from the direct relationship between the risk and the expected return of an investment.

The Expected Return–Risk Trade-Off

Within the realm of financial assets, investors can achieve virtually any position on an expected risk-return spectrum such as that depicted in Figure 1-1. The line RF to B is the assumed trade-off between expected return and risk that exists for all investors interested in financial assets. This trade-off always slopes upward, because the vertical axis is *expected* return, and rational investors will not assume more risk unless they expect to be compensated for doing so. The expected return must be large enough to compensate for taking the additional risk.

Figure 1-1
The Expected Return–Risk Trade-Off Available to Investors

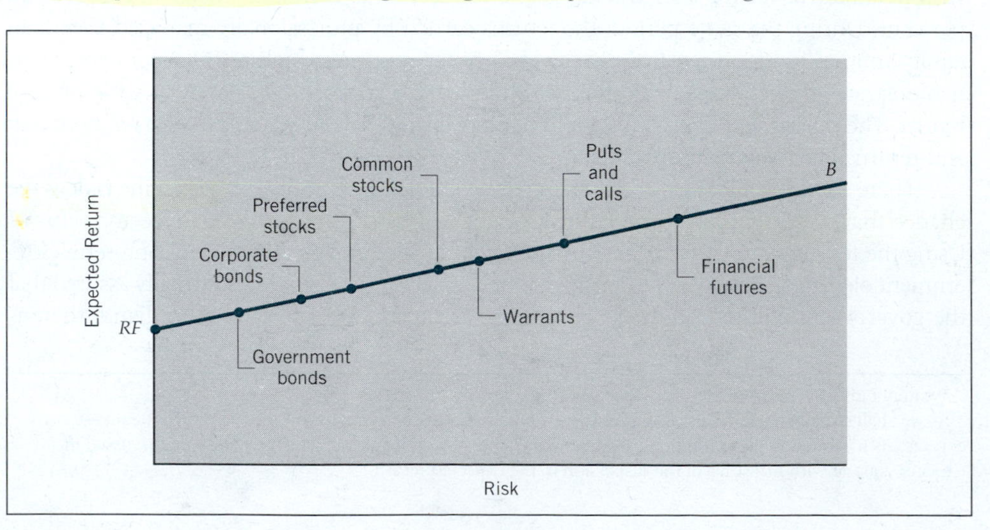

RF in Figure 1-1 is the return on a riskless asset such as Government of Canada T-bills. Since these assets have no risk, the expected return will equal (approximately) the realized return, which equals the current rate of return offered by these assets. This **risk-free rate of return**, which is available to all investors, will be designated as RF throughout the text. Using this as a starting point, we can say the following relationship will hold for expected returns on risky assets:

Risk-Free Rate of Return
The return on a riskless asset, often proxied by the rate of return on Treasury securities.

Expected return = Risk-free rate (RF) + Expected risk premium

This figure shows the relative positions for some of the financial assets that will be discussed in Chapter 2. As we move from riskless securities to more risky corporate bonds, equities, and so forth, we assume more risk in the expectation of earning a larger return. Common stocks are quite risky in relation to bonds, but they are not as risky as uncovered positions in options or futures contracts. (All of these terms are defined in Chapter 2.)

Obviously, we are using broad categories here. Within a particular category, such as common stocks, a wide range of expected return and risk opportunities exists at any time. The important point is that it is the trade-off between expected return and risk that should prevail in a rational environment. Investors unwilling to assume risk must be satisfied with the risk-free rate of return, RF. If they wish to try to earn a larger rate of return, they must be willing to assume a larger risk as represented by moving up the expected risk-return trade-off into the wide range of financial assets available to investors. Although all rational investors like returns and dislike risk, they are satisfied by quite different levels of expected return and risk. Put differently, investors have different limits on the amount of risk they are willing to assume and, therefore, the amount of return that can realistically be expected. In economic terms, the explanation for these differences in preferences is that rational investors strive to maximize their utility, the perception of which varies among investors.[8]

It is important to remember that the risk-return trade-off depicted in Figure 1-1 is *ex ante*, meaning "before the fact." That is, before the investment is actually made, the investor expects higher returns from assets that have a higher risk, and the expected risk premium is positive. This is the only sensible expectation for risk-averse investors, who are assumed to constitute the majority of all investors. *Ex post* (meaning "after the fact" or when it is known what has occurred), for a given period of time, such as a month or a year or even longer, the trade-off may turn out to be flat or even negative. For example, the 1998 return on Canadian stocks as measured by the TSE 300 Composite Index was 3.2 per cent, while the return on long-term Government of Canada bonds that year was 14.1 per cent. This implies that the actual (*ex post*) returns on the riskier common stocks were well below the realized returns on the relatively safer bonds. Such is the nature of risky investments!

[8] Utility theory is a complex subject; however, for our purposes we can equate maximization of utility with maximization of welfare. Because welfare is a function of present and future wealth, and wealth in turn is a function of current and future income discounted (reduced) for the amount of risk involved, in effect, investors maximize their welfare by optimizing the expected risk-return trade-off. In the final analysis, expected return and risk constitute the foundation of all investment decisions.

Structuring the Decision Process

Investors can choose from a wide range of securities in their attempt to maximize the expected returns from these opportunities. They face constraints, the most pervasive of which is risk. Traditionally, investors have analyzed and managed securities using a broad two-step process: security analysis and portfolio management.

Security Analysis

Security Analysis
The first part of the investment decision process, involving the valuation and analysis of individual securities.

The first part of the investment decision process involves the valuation and analysis of individual securities, which is referred to as **security analysis**. Institutional investors usually employ professional security analysts. Of course, there are also millions of amateur security analysts in the form of individual investors.

The valuation of securities is a time-consuming and difficult job. First of all, it is necessary to understand the characteristics of the various securities and the factors that affect them. Second, a valuation model must be applied to these securities to estimate their price or value. Value is a combination of the expected future returns on a security and the risk attached. Both of these parameters must be estimated and then brought together in a model.

For bonds the valuation process is relatively straightforward because the returns are known and the risk can be approximated from currently available data. This does not mean, however, that all the problems of bond analysis are easily resolved. Interest rates are the primary factor affecting bond prices, and no one can consistently forecast changes in these rates.

The valuation process is much more difficult for common stocks than for bonds. The investor must take into account the overall economy, the industry, and the individual company. With common stocks, estimating the expected return and the risk is not easy, but despite the difficulties, investors serious about their portfolios must perform some type of analysis. Unless this is done, one has to rely on personal hunches, suggestions from friends, and recommendations from brokers — all of which may be dangerous to one's financial health.

Portfolio Management

Portfolio Management
The second step in the investment decision process, involving the management of a group of assets (i.e., a portfolio) as a unit.

The second major component of the decision process is **portfolio management**. After securities have been evaluated, portfolio composition must be determined. The concepts associated with building a portfolio are well known and are discussed at some length in Chapters 7 to10.

Having built a portfolio, the astute investor must consider how and when to revise it. This raises a number of important questions. Portfolios must be managed, regardless of whether an investor is active or passive. If the investor pursues an active strategy, the issue of market efficiency must be considered. If prices reflect information quickly and fully, investors should consider how this would affect their buy and sell decisions. Even if investors follow a passive strategy (which involves designing or purchasing a portfolio that mirrors the performance of some market benchmark), questions to be considered include taxes, transaction costs, maintenance of the desired risk level, and so on.

Finally, all investors are interested in how well their portfolio performs. This is the bottom line of the investment process, but measuring portfolio performance is an inexact procedure and needs to be carefully considered.

IMPORTANT CONSIDERATIONS IN THE INVESTMENT DECISION PROCESS

Intelligent investors should recognize that the investment decision process described above can be lengthy and involved. Regardless of individual actions, certain factors in the investment environment affect everyone. Investors should be aware of these factors as they work through the investment decision process.

The Great Unknown

The paramount factor that all investors must come to grips with is uncertainty. Investors buy various financial assets, expecting to earn certain returns over some future holding period. These returns are only what can be expected; they may never be realized. The simple fact that dominates investing is that the realized return on a risky asset is likely to be different from what was expected — sometimes, quite different.

At best, estimates are imprecise; at worst, they are completely wrong. Some investors try to handle uncertainty by building elaborate quantitative models, and others simply keep it in the back of their mind. All investors, however, are affected by it, and the best they can do is make the most informed return and risk estimates they can, act on them, and be prepared for changing circumstances. Regardless of how careful and informed investors are, the future is uncertain, and mistakes will be made. This will always be true for everyone involved with financial markets and in fact for anyone at all, since life itself is uncertain. For example, many experts predicted the Canadian dollar would remain stable or increase during 1998, yet by the end of that year the value of the dollar had declined 6.7 per cent from $0.6991 US to $0.6522 US and had reached levels close to $0.63 during the year.

Investors often use historical data to make their estimates and modify this to incorporate what they believe is most likely to happen. It is important to remember that basing investment decisions solely on the past may lead to serious errors. Just because stocks had a 10 per cent average return over the last ten years is no guarantee of the same return next year, or ten years from now.

Anyone can tell you what you should have bought or sold in the past — it's a matter of record. For example, the **Trimark** Canadian equity mutual fund produced a 15-year compound return of 14.6 per cent for the period ending January 31, 1997, well above the 10.7 per cent average for Canadian equity funds over the same period. However, that same fund returned only 4.5 per cent between January 31 of 1997 and January 31 of 1998, compared to the average Canadian equity fund return of 8.8 per cent. The point is that while the past provides important information, no one can guarantee you a successful portfolio for next year or any other specified period of time. Unanticipated events will affect financial markets. No one can consistently forecast what will happen with interest rates or in financial markets, including the professionals who are paid to make recommendations.

Although uncertainty is always present, all is not lost. It is often possible to make reasonable and informed judgments about the outcomes of many investment opportunities. Investment decisions are both an art and a science. To succeed, we must think in terms of what we expect to happen. We know what has happened, but the past may or may not repeat itself. Although the future is uncertain, investors can attempt to manage it intelligently by developing a thorough understanding of the basic principles of investing. In addition, new tools and techniques are constantly being developed that may help investors to make better decisions.

The Global Investments Arena

Now more than ever, investors must think of investments in a global context. Although foreign investments have been possible for a number of years, many investors have not bought and sold on an international basis. However, astute investors can no longer afford to limit themselves to domestic investment only.

Emerging Markets
Markets of less developed countries characterized by high risks but potentially large returns.

A hot investment concept of the 1990s is the potential rewards of investing in **emerging markets**.[9] Several Asian markets, such as Singapore, Indonesia, and Thailand displayed rapid growth during the 1990s, before collapsing in 1997. Examples of volatility in these markets are plentiful. For example, during 1997 the stock markets in Mexico and Brazil provided returns of 55.6 per cent and 44.8 per cent — well above North American returns, but the very next year returns for these two markets fell to –29.7 and –40.0 per cent. The returns on the Morgan Stanley Emerging Markets Index (which includes over 1,400 stocks from 23 emerging market economies) over the 1988–96 period confirm the substantial volatility (or risk) associated with these markets. The annual returns ranged from a high of 72.1 per cent in 1993 to a low of –32.9 per cent in 1990. During the same period, North American markets displayed much lower volatility. The returns on the TSE 300 ranged from a high of 32.5 per cent in 1993 to a low of –14.8 percent in 1990, while the DJIA ranged from a high of 29.9 per cent in 1995 to a low of –6.4 per cent in 1990.

An international perspective is becoming increasingly important to all investors as we find ourselves operating in a global marketplace of round-the-clock investing. Since the Canadian stock and bond markets comprise only about 2 per cent of their respective world markets, Canadian investors who ignore these markets will be cutting themselves off from a large number of investment alternatives.

The impact of the US economy for Canadian investors is apparent on a daily basis, as we routinely observe large swings in Canadian bond and stock price levels in response to announcements by the US Federal Reserve Board, or the release of other US economic statistics. Given that the United States accounts for well over 70 per cent of Canadian exports and imports, it is not surprising that the returns on Canadian stock markets are tightly tied to those on US markets.[10] However, the performance of Canadian investment assets is also greatly affected by global economic activity outside North America. This point is highlighted by the large volatility caused in domestic markets by international events such as the recent Asian currency crisis or the concerns over the ability of Russia to meet its external debt payments in 1998.

---

[9] The World Bank classifies a stock market as "emerging" if its country's economy had less than $7,910 in US dollars per capita gross domestic product (GDP) in 1991.

[10] For example, Schmitz and Cleary document a correlation coefficient of 0.77 between quarterly Canadian market risk premiums and those of the United States. The market risk premium refers to the return on the market equity index minus the return on three-month government Treasury bills. See: John Schmitz and Sean Cleary, "Are US Variables Good Predictors of Foreign Equity Risk Premiums?," working paper, University of Western Ontario, 1997.

There are several reasons why global events have such a significant impact on Canadian investors. One is the very nature of Canada's economy, which consists of a relatively large proportion of commodity-based industries such as oil, mining, and forestry. Since the price of these commodities is determined in the global marketplace, our economy is greatly influenced by global supply and demand. In addition, many Canadian firms (even those that are not commodity-based), derive a large proportion of their revenues from abroad. As a result, adverse movements in foreign exchange rates can have unhappy consequences for Canadian multinational companies whose foreign currency profits are translated into fewer Canadian dollars. On the other hand, many Canadian companies benefit from a decline in the value of the dollar because their products become relatively less expensive in foreign markets, which increases demand for their products abroad.

Another important reason for Canadian investors to think in a global context is that the rates of return available in foreign securities are often higher than those available from Canadian markets. For example, over the 1989–98 period, the ten-year compound return on the Canadian market was 10.3 per cent, versus 22.9 per cent for the US market, and 14.1 per cent for the Morgan Stanley World Index (which is a market-valued index that includes more than 2,700 stocks from 22 developed market countries).

Finally, the addition of foreign securities allows investors to achieve beneficial risk reduction, since many foreign markets move differently from Canada's. For example, when Canadian stocks are doing poorly, some foreign stocks may be doing well, which would help offset the poor domestic performance. This risk reduction is a result of diversification. The simple point is that if domestic diversification in a portfolio reduces risk, which it clearly does, foreign diversification should provide even greater risk reduction — and it does![11]

Given the increased attention paid to international investing, it is not surprising that an analysis of international equity investing over a recent 20-year period concludes that, "global portfolio diversification is no longer a new route to higher returns and lower risks, as it was two decades ago.... However, thoughtful international equity diversification can improve the risk/return characteristics of investors' portfolios."[12]

Thus, we should consider foreign markets as well as the domestic financial environment. We will do so throughout this text as an integral part of the discussion, rather than in a separate chapter, because although the details may vary, the principles of investing are applicable to financial assets and markets wherever they exist.

Institutional Investors

There are two broad categories of investors: individual and **institutional investors**. The latter group, consisting of banks, pension funds, investment companies, insurance companies, and so forth, includes professional money managers who are frequently publicized in the popular press. The amount of money managed by these institutions is staggering. For example, by February 1999, **Investors Group**, the largest mutual fund company in Canada, managed total net assets exceeding $35 billion, while **Royal Mutual Funds Inc.**, a subsidiary of the Royal Bank of Canada, was the second largest company with total net assets exceeding

Institutional Investors
Pension funds, investment companies, bank trust departments, life insurance companies, and so forth that manage huge portfolios of securities.

[11] The benefits of diversification are discussed at some length in Chapter 7.

[12] Both quotes from Richard O. Michaud, Gary L. Bergstrom, Ronald D. Frashure, and Brian K. Wolahan, "Twenty Years of International Investing," *The Journal of Portfolio Management* 32 (Fall 1996), p. 20.

$29 billion. At this time Investors Group offered investors a choice of over 50 funds to choose from, while Royal offered over 40 funds.

By the beginning of the 1990s, institutional investors in the United States held almost $6 trillion in assets, and the numbers have continued to escalate in both Canada and the United States. In addition to the rapid growth in mutual fund assets in Canada in recent years (to $326.6 billion by the end of 1998), banks, pension funds, and life insurance companies are important participants in Canadian (and international) financial markets. These institutional investors do not constitute a monolithic bloc of investors but are comprised of thousands of different organizations, most of which have multiple money managers.

The first issue to note about institutional investors is that their relative importance has changed. Mutual funds have become the primary buying force in North American stock markets in the 1990s, due to the large growth in popularity of these investment vehicles.[13] The role of pension funds has also changed significantly in both Canada and the United States in recent years. Canadian pension funds have historically invested very conservatively, primarily in fixed income securities such as bonds and money market instruments. However, in recent years, they have become more aggressive and have become more important players in Canadian and foreign equity and derivative security markets (although they face foreign content restrictions and are limited in the amount they can invest in a particular company).

EXAMPLE: THE ONTARIO TEACHERS' PENSION PLAN

The change in the composition of the assets of the Ontario Teachers' Pension Plan (Canada's second largest pension fund — behind the Caisse de Dépôts et Placements du Québec — with assets over $55 billion in 1997) provides a good illustration of the change in Canadian pension fund investment management. This fund consisted entirely of fixed income securities in 1989, but by the end of 1995, fixed income securities accounted for only 35 per cent of their asset mix. The remaining 65 per cent consisted of 31 per cent in Canadian equities, 13 per cent in US equities, 18 per cent in non-North American equities, and 3 per cent in real estate investments. Over 75 per cent of the Canadian equity holdings consisted of a Canadian index fund, designed to mirror the movements of the TSE 35, TSE 100, and TSE 200 stock indexes.[14] In addition, approximately 75 per cent of their foreign investments represent index investments through the use of derivative securities.[15]

In the United States the importance of pension funds has also changed, but for very different reasons. For 30 or more years up to the 1990s, the pension funds and corporate raiders had the big impact on Wall Street. Although pension funds remain the primary institutional owner of common stocks, with about one-quarter of all stock, their importance has declined because many plans have either been terminated or converted into self-directed plans. The private pension plans bought all of the net equities available in the 1960s and 1970s, while in

---

[13] We will analyze mutual funds in detail in Chapter 3.

[14] These indexes will be described in Chapter 4.

[15] Ontario Teachers' Pension Plan, *Annual Report*, 1995.

the 1980s corporate restructurings — mergers, acquisitions, and stock buybacks — took one-half trillion dollars of equity out of the market.

The second issue to note about institutional investors is their dual relationship to individual investors. On the one hand, individuals are the indirect beneficiaries of institutional investor actions, because they own or benefit from these institutions' portfolios. On a daily basis, however, they are competing with these institutions in the sense that both are managing portfolios of securities and attempting to do well financially. Both groups are trying to make intelligent trading decisions about securities. Can individual investors hope to compete fairly with institutions, and how do these large portfolios affect the individual investor's decision process?

Institutional investors are indeed the professional investors, with vast resources at their command. They generally pay minimal commission fees on security transactions, much less than those paid by retail investors. In addition, there is evidence to suggest that some companies disclose important information selectively to some institutional investors. According to a survey by the National Investor Relations Institute (an association for investor-relations professionals), perhaps one-third of public companies disclose sensitive information concerning their stock that may put individual investors at a disadvantage.[16]

Another advantage that institutional investors have is that they can trade in the "aftermarket" (negotiated trades conducted electronically among institutions) following exchange closings. (The TSE closes at 4 p.m. Eastern Time.) By the time a stock opens the next morning, the price may have adjusted significantly.

EXAMPLE: AFTERMARKET ADVANTAGE ON INTEL

On July 16, 1996, **Intel** closed at $70 and then announced better than expected earnings. The stock opened the next morning at $74. Individual investors were unable to participate in this movement.

Does the average investor, then, have a reasonable chance in the market? Yes, in the sense that he or she can generally expect to earn a fair return for the risk taken. On average, the individual investor may do just as well as the big institutional investors, because markets are usually quite efficient and securities fairly priced.

Some individual investors do even better than professionals due to superior skill, insight, or luck. Furthermore, some opportunities can more easily be exploited by individual investors, who have greater flexibility in adjusting their portfolio composition, than by institutional investors.

For example, individual investors can exploit a spinoff (a division of a company that is turned into a separate publicly held company) better than institutional investors in some cases.[17] Some institutional investors do not purchase stock of new companies because they often pay no dividends immediately after spinoff, or they are too small to be held by some institutions. Also, these companies often look unattractive at the time of spinoff because they had problems as a division. However, these problems often are solved by a new, proactive management, and these companies become attractive as takeover candidates.

[16] This discussion and the following example is based on Toddi Gutner, "How To Keep the Little Guy in the Loop," *Business Week*, July 24, 1996, p. 32.

[17] "Personal Investing," ***Fortune***, April 18, 1994, pp. 31–32.

A study of 150 spinoffs found that the average three-year total return was about 75 per cent, 30 percentage points higher than a comparable group of companies. Investors are advised to defer purchases of spinoff IPOs until they have been trading for a few weeks because some institutions may sell the shares they received in the spinoff, and prices are often lower weeks later than at the time trading begins in the new companies.

The question of how well individual investors do relative to institutional investors raises the issue of market efficiency, which we consider next. All intelligent investors who seek to do well when investing must ultimately come to grips with the issue of market efficiency.

The Issue of Market Efficiency

One of the most profound ideas affecting the investment decision process, and indeed all of finance, is the idea that the securities markets, particularly the equity markets, are efficient. In an efficient market, the prices of securities do not depart for any length of time from the justified economic values that investors calculate for them. Economic values for securities are determined by investor expectations about earnings, risks, and so on, as investors grapple with the uncertain future. If the market price of a security does differ from its estimated economic value, investors act to bring the two values together. Thus, as new information arrives in an efficient marketplace, causing a revision in the estimated economic value of a security, its price adjusts to this information quickly and, on balance, correctly. In other words, securities are efficiently priced on a continuous basis. We discuss the full implications of this statement in Chapter 10.

INVESTING *tip*

An efficient market does not have to be perfectly efficient to have a profound impact on investors. All that is required is that the market be economically efficient. That is, after acting on information to trade securities and subtracting all costs (transaction costs and taxes, to name two), the investor would have been as well off with a simple buy-and-hold strategy. If the market is economically efficient, securities could depart somewhat from their true economic values, but it would not pay investors to take advantage of these small discrepancies.

Obviously, the possibility that the stock market is efficient has significant implications for investors. In fact, one's knowledge of and belief in this idea, known as the **Efficient Market Hypothesis (EMH)**, will directly affect how one views the investment process and makes investment decisions. Those who are strong believers in the EMH may adopt, to varying degrees, a passive investment strategy, because of the likelihood that they will not be able to find underpriced securities. These investors will seek to minimize transaction costs and taxes, as well as the time and resources devoted to analyzing securities, which, if the EMH is correct, should be correctly priced to begin with.

Efficient Market Hypothesis (EMH)
The proposition that securities markets are efficient, with the prices of securities reflecting their economic value.

Investors who do not accept the EMH, or have serious doubts, pursue active investment strategies, believing they can identify mispriced securities and/or lags that exist in the market's adjustment of securities' prices to new information. These investors generate more search costs (both in time and money) and more transaction costs but believe the marginal benefits outweigh the marginal costs incurred.

REAL-WORLD RETURNS
Applying the Efficient Market Hypothesis

At the outset of their study of investments, all investors should be aware of the EMH and its potential implications. A tremendous amount of research has been done on the EMH over the last 20 years, and much evidence has been accumulated showing that North American financial markets are quite efficient. Certainly, the idea cannot be dismissed out of hand. For example, data on Canadian equity funds shows that 84 per cent of actively managed funds failed to match the 17.8 per cent annual return offered by the TSE 300 over the five-year period ended January 31, 1998.[18] This suggests that easy opportunities do not abound. On the other hand, evidence of market inefficiencies has been accumulating recently. Possibilities for astute investors appear to exist and have been documented. In the final analysis, the issue remains open.

The point to keep in mind at this stage is that investors should learn as fully and carefully as possible about the actual environment that exists in today's investment world. The EMH cannot be quickly dismissed and the intelligent course of action is to understand the situation, employ what is useful, disregard or use the remainder sparingly, and make the best decisions possible. Only by understanding the investment process and the issues involved in the efficient markets controversy can one hope to answer the question, "How efficient is the market?" and design an investment strategy consistent with that answer.

SUMMARY

The following summary relates to the learning objectives provided on page 1.

1. **Define investment and discuss what it means to study investments.**
   An investment is the commitment of funds to one or more assets that will be held over some future time period. The field of investments involves the study of the investment process and is concerned with the management of an investor's wealth. We study investments for both personal and professional reasons.
2. **Explain why risk and return are the two critical components of all investing decisions.**
   Risk is defined as the chance that what you expect to gain from an investment will differ from its actual return. The basis of all investment decisions is the trade-off between expected return and risk. Expected return and risk are directly related; the greater the risk, the greater the expected return, and the smaller the risk the smaller the expected return. Rational investors are risk averse, meaning they are unwilling to assume risk unless they expect to be adequately compensated.
3. **Outline the two-step investment decision process.**
   The investment decision process is generally divided into two categories: securities analysis and portfolio management. Security analysis involves the valuation and analysis of

[18] Duff Young, "Why Mutual Fund Substitutes are the Rage," *The Globe and Mail / Report on Business*, February 28, 1998.

individual securities. Portfolio management involves building a portfolio of individual securities after they have been evaluated and maintaining that portfolio.

4. **Discuss key factors that affect the investment decision process.**
Major factors affecting the investment decision process include uncertainty, the global nature of investing, the role played by institutional investors, and the efficiency of markets. Investors should consider these factors carefully as they evaluate information and claims and make decisions.

KEY TERMS

Canadian Securities Course (CSC) (Appendix 1-A)
Chartered Financial Analyst (CFA) (Appendix 1-A)
Efficient Market Hypothesis (EMH)
Emerging markets
Expected return
Financial assets
Institutional investors
Investment
Investments
Marketable securities
Portfolio
Portfolio management
Real assets
Realized return
Risk
Risk-averse investor
Risk-free rate of return
Security analysis

ADDITIONAL RESOURCES

A strongly recommended book for today's investor that is very enlightening, as well as highly entertaining is: Malkiel, Burton G. *A Random Walk Down Wall Street*. New York: W. W. Norton & Company, 1995.

One of Canada's best selling books of all time that provides investors with an entertaining look at the basics of financial planning is: Chilton, David. *The Wealthy Barber*. Updated Third Edition. Toronto: Prima Publishing, 1998.

A very popular book on investing by a former mutual fund manager who achieved great success and notoriety is: Lynch, Peter. *One Up on Wall Street*. New York: Penguin Books, 1989.

A book many consider to be one of the important stock market books of the 1990s, involving the well-known investor Warren Buffet is: Hagstrom, Robert G. Jr. *The Warren Buffet Way*. New York: John Wiley & Sons, 1994.

INVESTMENTS ON THE WEB

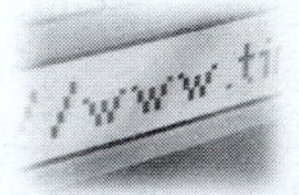

The Canadian Securities Institute (CSI): <http://www.csi.ca>

The Association for Investment Management and Research (AIMR) — for information on the Chartered Financial Analyst (CFA) program: <http://www.aimr.org/knowledge/cfaprogram>

REVIEW QUESTIONS

1. Define the term investments.
2. Distinguish between a financial asset and a real asset. Give two examples of each.
3. List three primary investing objectives and two secondary investing objectives.
4. Briefly describe three constraints that have an impact on the design of an investment policy.
5. With respect to Figure 1-1, when would an investor expect to earn the risk-free rate of return?
6. Distinguish between expected return and realized return.
7. Why should the required rate of return be different for a corporate bond and a Government of Canada bond?
8. A marketable security is said to be liquid if it can be easily and cheaply traded. Why is the liquidity of a marketable security an important thing for investors to consider?
9. Differentiate between an active investment strategy and a passive investment strategy.
10. List at least four categories of institutional investors. Give examples of Canadian corporations that fit in each category.
11. Describe the broad two-step process involved in making investment decisions.
12. Why is the study of investments important to most individuals?
13. Carefully describe the risk-return trade-off faced by all investors.
14. "A risk-averse investor will not assume risk." Do you agree or disagree with this statement? Why?
15. Summarize the basic nature of the investment decision in one sentence.
16. Are all rational investors risk averse? Do they all have the same degree of risk aversion?
17. How are individual investors likely to be affected by institutional investors?
18. What is meant by the expression efficient markets?
19. Of what significance is an efficient market to investors?
20. Discuss some reasons why Canadian investors should be concerned with global investing. Do you think the exchange rate value of the Canadian dollar will have any effect on the decision to invest globally?
21. Although a Treasury bill is said to be "risk free," there actually is some risk associated with investing in one. What do you think the risk (or risks) would be?
22. Define risk. How many specific types can you think of?
23. What other constraints besides risk do investors face?
24. What are four external factors that affect the decision process? Which do you think is the most important, and why?

PREPARING FOR YOUR PROFESSIONAL EXAMS

Special Note to Canadian Securities Course Students

Ensure that you have read and understood the following topics covered in this chapter:*

**Reading these CSC-related topics should provide you with additional understanding of CSC material. However, it should not be seen as a substitute for reading the CSC textbook itself, which is the basis for the CSC exam.*

CSC REGISTRATION QUESTIONS

The Canadian Securities Institute issued the following sample questions in the 1997 CSC registration package as a means for students to self-assess their understanding of CSC-related material.

1. Long-term bonds issued by which of the following issuers would ordinarily have the lowest yield?
   a. Large blue chip corporation AAA
   b. Province of Prince Edward Island
   c. Government of Canada
   d. Municipality of Toronto
2. The primary investment goals of bond funds are ____________ and safety of principal.
3. Which of the following is not usually considered a primary investment objective?
   a. Tax minimization
   b. Growth
   c. Safety
   d. Income

APPENDIX 1-A

PROFESSIONAL EDUCATIONAL ALTERNATIVES

The Canadian Securities Institute (CSI)

The Canadian Securities Institute (CSI) is a not-for-profit, self-funded organization created in 1970 to develop and offer high quality investment education programs for both industry professionals and the general public. CSI serves the broad financial services industry with an emphasis on securities. CSI courses, seminars and specialized programs are recognized by regulators as the proficiency benchmarks for all levels of industry professionals.

The **Canadian Securities Course™ (CSC)**[19] (explained in detail in Appendix 1-B) is a prerequisite for many other CSI courses and is a starting point for earning sought-after professional designations. Completion of certain CSI courses is mandatory to meet the requirements for various registration categories. Individuals who wish to become licensed to sell securities must pass the CSC as well as the Conduct and Practices Handbook (CPH) (explained further in Appendix 1-B). Completion of the CSC also allows individuals to become registered to sell mutual funds.

Canadian Securities Course™ (CSC)
This course is offered by the Canadian Securities Institute (CSI) and is a mandatory requirement for individuals who wish to become licensed to sell financial securities in Canada and to register to sell mutual funds.

CSI's approach to professional investment education is based on extensive research and consultation with the financial services industry, regulators, and end-users. Rather than single-course offerings, CSI programs focus on career streams that lead students to specialized designations.

- CSI's portfolio management stream leads to the Canadian Investment Manager (CIM) designation. Courses in this stream are CSC, Investment Management Techniques (IMT), and Portfolio Management Techniques (PMT).
- CSI's advanced financial planning/wealth management stream leads to the Financial Management Advisor (FMA) designation. Courses in this stream are CSC, Professional Financial Planning Course (PFPC), and Wealth Management Techniques (WMT). Upon successful completion of PFPC, individuals are qualified to take the exam to earn the Certified Financial Planner (CFP) designation administered by the Financial Planners Standards Council.
- Other CSI courses include Derivatives Fundamentals Course (DFC), Options Licensing Course (OLC), Futures Licensing Course (FLC), Trader Training Course (TTC), Partners, Directors and Senior Officers Qualifying Examination (PDO), and more.

Over the past three decades, some 400,000 professionals have relied on CSI for sound, relevant, high quality education. For more information about CSI and its programs, call the office nearest you: Toronto (416) 364-9130; Montreal (514) 878-3591; Calgary (403) 292-1791; Vancouver (604) 683-1338, or visit their Web site <http://www.csi.ca>.

---

[19] The Canadian Securities Course™ (CSC) and other courses discussed here are trademarks of the Canadian Securities Institute.

The Association for Investment Management and Research (AIMR)

The Association for Investment Management and Research (AIMR) is a non-profit professional organization of investment practitioners and academics formed in 1990 from a merger of the Financial Analysts Federation and the Institute of Chartered Financial Analysts (ICFA). AIMR, an autonomous, self-regulatory organization, seeks to maintain a professional organization with high ethical, professional, and educational standards for the investment community, broadly defined. By 1994 approximately 25,000 investment professionals were active members.

Chartered Financial Analyst (CFA) A professional designation for people in the investments field.

Since 1963 the ICFA has offered the **Chartered Financial Analyst (CFA)** program, involving the study of a body of knowledge that encompasses a range of topics important to those in the investment business. Details of the CFA program are included in Appendix 1-C.

Financial Planners

The Financial Planners Standards Council (FPSC) has developed a set of minimum standards for financial planners in terms of education, experience, and ethical and moral conduct. The FPSC is also responsible for monitoring the activities of financial planners and enforcing basic professional requirements of these individuals. Original members of the FPSC included the CSI, the Credit Union Institute of Canada, the Canadian Institute of Chartered Accountants (CICA), the Canadian Association of Insurance and Financial Advisors (CAIFA) (formerly the Life Underwriters' Association of Canada (LUAC)), the Canadian Association of Financial Planners (CAFP), the Institute of Canadian Bankers (ICB), the Society of Management Accountants of Canada (CMA), the Canadian Institute of Financial Planning (CIFP), and the Certified General Accountants Association of Canada (CGA — Canada). The CSI and the ICB withdrew in 1998.

The FPSC has the exclusive right to grant the Certified Financial Planner (CFP) designation in Canada. Educational requirements are satisfied through courses offered by several regulatory and educational organizations including the CSI, CIFP, CAIFA, BC Institute of Technology, Laval University, Wilfrid Laurier University, and Seneca College of Applied Arts & Technology. Candidates who successfully complete the education requirement become eligible to write the Professional Proficiency Examination (PPE) that is administered by the FPSC. In the spring of 1999, the Ontario Securities Commission announced its intention to regulate financial planning. The other securities regulators are also expected to insist that planners become licensed. At this time, the licensing requirements have not yet been announced.

APPENDIX 1-B

THE CANADIAN SECURITIES COURSE (CSC)

The Canadian Securities Course (CSC) is offered by the Canadian Securities Institute (CSI) and is a mandatory requirement for individuals who wish to become licensed to sell financial securities in Canada. It also allows one to register to sell mutual funds, although this can also be achieved by taking courses through IFIC or ICB.

The 1999 enrolment fee for the CSC is $415 for non-industry candidates and $260 for industry candidates. Candidates are required to complete two assignments, pass the final examination (60 per cent or better), and obtain a final mark (based on the exam mark and assignment average) above 60 per cent.

The first assignment is due within three months of registration. The second is due within six months. Examinations are written six times a year (approximately every two months). Individuals may write the CSC exam free of charge (at regular sittings) within one year of enrolment in the CSC. However, they must pay a $70 examination fee if they write in the subsequent two-year period. Enrolment in the CSC expires after three years. Rewrites (at regular sittings) cost $70, while special examination sittings can be arranged for $125.

In order to become licensed to sell securities, individuals must also pass the Conduct and Practices Handbook for Securities Industry Professionals (CPH), in addition to the CSC. This course is much shorter than the CSC, but it covers important practical concerns for licensed representatives including standards of conduct, regulations, securities legislation, and operational procedures to be used when working with clients. It costs $150 for industry students and $260 for non-industry students.

Individuals who are registered in the investment industry and leave it for a period of three years or longer, must rewrite and pass the CPH. Registered investment professionals who leave the industry for five years or longer must rewrite and pass both the CSC and CPH. Finally, a person who has never registered must rewrite and pass the CSC if it has been more than three years and four months since the original date of passing, and must rewrite the CPH if it has been more than two years since the original passing date.

Aside from the practical relevance of the material covered in the CSC, there are very specific career-related benefits for students who wish to pursue careers in the financial services industry in Canada. At one time students who were able to complete the CSC prior to graduation from a post-secondary institution had a competitive advantage, but today most graduating students will have completed the course, and those who have not done so are at a competitive disadvantage.

The CSI estimates that the average time to complete *each* of the assignments is 35 to 40 hours. The CSC examination covers four major subject areas:

1. Understanding and interpreting financial statements
2. Bonds
3. Stocks
4. Other subject areas including derivative securities, taxation and portfolio management, the Canadian regulatory environment, and the Canadian macroeconomy.

At least half of the test consists of a variety of styles of short-answer questions (no more than a three-sentence response), while there are also a significant number of calculation questions. There are no essay-type questions.

This text makes reference to numerous relevant components of the CSC and CFA curriculum, procedures, and philosophy because they represent a significant part of any study of investments. In addition, we have included questions from the CSC registration package as well as questions and problems from past CFA exams at the end of most chapters.

APPENDIX 1-C

THE CHARTERED FINANCIAL ANALYST PROGRAM

Individuals interested in careers in the investment analysis field should consider seeking a Chartered Financial Analyst (CFA) designation, which is, for people in the investment area, not unlike the CA, CGA, or CMA for accountants. The CFA is widely recognized in the investments industry today.

Candidates enrolled in the CFA program must show that they have mastered important material in economics, quantitative analysis, ethical and professional standards, financial accounting, fixed income securities, equity securities analysis, and portfolio management. Candidates must successfully complete three examinations, referred to as Level I, Level II, and Level III, in order to be awarded a CFA designation.

The basis of the CFA study and examination program is a body of knowledge (BOK). The BOK is organized along functional rather than topical lines and is structured around the investment decision-making process. The BOK functional areas are ethics and professional standards, investment tools, asset valuation, and portfolio management.

For each level of the exam, the curriculum is organized around a functional area:

Level I study program — emphasizes tools and inputs

Level II study program — emphasizes asset valuation

Level III study program — emphasizes portfolio management

Ethical and professional standards are considered an integral part of all three functional areas and are included in all levels of the curriculum.

These six-hour examinations are given throughout Canada, the United States, and around the world once a year, around June 1, and must be completed in sequence. Because a candidate may sit for only one exam each year, completion of the CFA program requires a minimum of three years.

By 1997 over 24,000 investment professionals had earned the CFA charter since it was first awarded in 1963. In 1997, 58 per cent of all CFA candidates were from the United States, 13 per cent from Canada, while the remaining 29 per cent were from outside North America, which indicates the global nature of investments and the distinctions to be earned within the investment profession. Over 20 per cent of CFA candidates are female, more than two-thirds are aged 26 to 35, and over 95 per cent hold a bachelor's degree or higher.

What does it mean to be awarded the CFA charter? Increasingly, employers are recognizing the value of this designation and the potential benefits that an employee with it can offer a company. The CFA charter represents a combination of academic achievement and professional experience along with a commitment to a stringent code of professional and ethical standards. CFAs must renew their pledge to abide by the code every year and violations can carry severe sanctions.

The investments profession, like many others, involves lifelong learning. After receiving the CFA designation, investment professionals can participate in the CFA accreditation program in order to remain current on investment issues. This program allows them to earn continuing education credits a number of ways including workshops, seminars, and reading on their own.

For more information about the CFA program, call their toll-free numbers at 1-800-247-8132 or 1-804-980-3668, or visit their Web site <http://www.aimr.org/aimr/cfa/cfaregister. html>.

CHAPTER 2

INVESTMENT ALTERNATIVES

LEARNING OBJECTIVES

After reading this chapter, you will be able to

1. Describe the major types of financial assets and how they are organized.
2. Explain what non-marketable financial assets are.
3. Describe the important features of money market and capital market securities.
4. Distinguish between preferred stock and common stock.
5. Understand the basics of options and futures.

CHAPTER PREVIEW

Changes in the securities field occur so rapidly that investors are regularly confronted with new developments. However, if investors understand the basic characteristics of the major existing securities, they will likely be able to understand new securities as they appear. This chapter explains the most important investment alternatives available to investors, ranging from non-marketable financial assets to marketable investments in money market, capital market, and derivative securities. You will learn the basic features of securities that are of primary interest to most investors, particularly bonds and stocks. We also discuss recent trends such as "securitization" and international investing.

ORGANIZING FINANCIAL ASSETS

The emphasis in this chapter (and in the text in general) is on financial assets, which, as explained in Chapter 1, are financial claims on the issuers of securities. We focus in particular on marketable securities, which are claims that are negotiable, or saleable, in various marketplaces, as discussed in Chapter 4.

This chapter concentrates on investment alternatives available through direct investing, which involves securities that investors buy and sell themselves, primarily capital market securities and derivative securities. The taxation of income earned from these financial assets in Canada is discussed in Appendix 2-A at the end of the chapter. In Chapter 3 we examine **indirect investing**. Rather than invest directly in securities, investors can invest in a portfolio of securities by purchasing the units of a financial intermediary that invests in various types of securities on behalf of its shareowners. Perhaps the most common method of indirect investing involves mutual funds. Indirect investing is a very important alternative for all investors to consider and has become tremendously popular in the last few years with individual investors.

Indirect Investing
The buying and selling of the shares of investment companies that themselves hold portfolios of securities.

People who invest directly in financial markets have a wide variety of assets from which to choose. Non-marketable investment opportunities, such as savings accounts at financial institutions, are discussed briefly at the beginning of the chapter since investors often own these assets and are familiar with them. Henceforth, we will consider only marketable securities, which may be classified into one of three categories:

1. The money market
2. The capital market
3. The derivatives market.

Investors should understand money market securities, particularly Treasury bills, but they typically will not own these securities directly, choosing instead to own them through the money market funds explained in Chapter 3. Within the capital market, securities can be classified as either fixed-income or equity. Finally, investors may choose to use derivative securities in their portfolios. The market value of these securities is derived from underlying securities such as common stock.

Figure 2-1 organizes the types of financial assets to be analyzed in this chapter (under the heading of direct investing) using the above classifications. It also indicates various indirect investment alternatives, which will be discussed in more depth in Chapter 3. Although we cover direct investing and indirect investing in separate chapters, it is important to understand that investors can, and often do, both. Many individuals invest directly through the use of a brokerage account and indirectly in one or more investment companies. Furthermore, brokerage accounts that accommodate the ownership of investment company shares are becoming increasingly popular, thereby combining direct and indirect investing into one account.

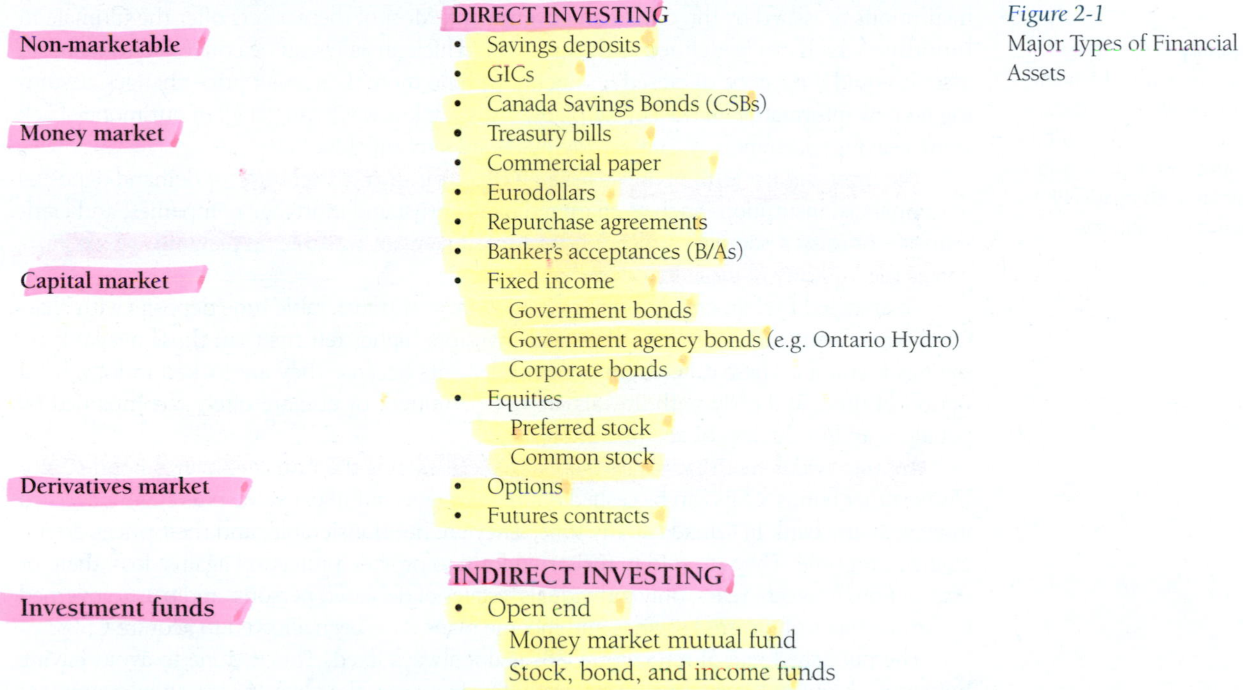

Figure 2-1
Major Types of Financial Assets

An International Perspective

As noted in Chapter 1, investors should adopt an international perspective in making their investment decisions. The investment alternatives analyzed in this chapter, in particular some money market assets, bonds, and stocks, are available to Canadian investors from many foreign markets. Thus, the characteristics of these basic securities are relevant if we invest in domestic or foreign financial assets, or both. Canadian investors usually invest internationally indirectly through investment companies, many of which offer a wide variety of global asset funds.

NON-MARKETABLE FINANCIAL ASSETS

We begin our discussion of investment alternatives by mentioning those that are non-marketable because most individuals will own one or more of these assets regardless of what else they do in the investing arena. Furthermore, these assets represent useful contrasts to the marketable securities we will concentrate on throughout the text.

A distinguishing characteristic of these assets is that they represent personal transactions between the owner and the issuer. That is, as the owner of a savings account at a bank, you must open the account personally and deal with the bank in maintaining the account or in closing it. In contrast, marketable securities trade in impersonal markets where the buyer and seller do not know one another and do not care.

Most non-marketable instruments are safe investments available from insured financial institutions or issued by the Canadian government. Most of these assets offer the ultimate in **liquidity**, which can be defined as the ease with which an asset can be converted to cash. An asset is liquid if it can be disposed of quickly with no more than small price changes, assuming no new information in the marketplace. Thus, we know we can get all of our money back from a savings account or a Canada Savings Bond very quickly.

Liquidity
The ease with which an asset can be converted to cash. An asset is liquid if it can be bought or sold quickly with relatively small price changes.

The most familiar form of non-marketable assets is savings accounts (or demand deposits) with financial institutions such as chartered banks, trust and mortgage companies, and credit unions or caisses populaires. The funds invested here are available on demand, which guarantees the liquidity of these investments.

Guaranteed Investment Certificates (GICs) are non-transferable time deposits with chartered banks and trust companies that offer investors higher returns than those available on savings accounts. These differ from demand deposits because they are locked in for a fixed period of time, and early withdrawals are not permitted, or else are often accompanied by penalties and/or the loss of accrued interest.

Another widely used non-marketable financial asset is the Canada Savings Bond (CSB). Unlike other bonds, CSBs can be cashed out by the owner at full par value plus eligible accrued interest at any bank in Canada at any time. They are not transferable, and their prices do not change over time. They are sold in registered form to provide protection against loss, theft, or destruction. In recent years, only individuals, estates of deceased persons, and trusts governed by certain types of deferred savings and income plans have been allowed to acquire CSBs.

The published rate of return on CSBs is not always fixed. This is done to avoid having holders cash out in times of rising interest rates. However, the government often guarantees minimum rates for the future. For example, 1996 CSBs guaranteed minimum rates for ten years. An effective program for selling CSBs is administered through the payroll savings plans of over 18,000 organizations, which reaches approximately 1.25 million employees. Since 1977 they have been available in two forms: (1) regular interest, which pays annual interest to the holder, and (2) compound interest, which reinvests the interest, so that even more interest is earned. In February 1997 the government introduced RRSP bonds, which are similar to CSBs, except that they can only be purchased for RRSPs and are redeemable only on the anniversary date of their issue.

MONEY MARKET SECURITIES

Money Market
The market for short-term, highly liquid, low-risk debt instruments sold by governments, financial institutions, and corporations. Canadian government Treasury bills are an example.

Money markets include short-term, highly liquid, relatively low-risk debt instruments sold by governments, financial institutions, and corporations to investors with temporary excess funds to invest. The returns on these instruments exceed those offered by savings accounts; however, the size of transactions is generally large ($100,000 or more). On the other hand, several financial institutions purchase large blocks of these instruments and break them up into smaller denominations (as low as $1,000) in order to make them available for their retail

REAL-WORLD RETURNS

Protecting Canadian Investors

Most chartered banks and trust companies are members of the Canadian Deposit Insurance Corporation (CDIC), an agency of the federal government. The CDIC insures qualifying deposits with member institutions, up to a maximum of $60,000 of total deposits with one financial institution. Individuals wishing to have more than $60,000 in insured deposits must maintain deposits with several institutions and ensure the total deposits with any particular institution do not exceed $60,000.

Insurance companies, credit unions and caisses populaires, and investment dealers are not eligible for CDIC membership, but generally provide other forms of protection for their clients. Credit unions generally offer protection through provincial deposit insurance or guarantee programs. For example, deposits with credit unions in British Columbia are protected through the Credit Union Deposit Insurance Corporation of BC. This corporation guarantees the total savings, chequing, and term deposits by an individual with one credit union up to a maximum of $100,000. The $100,000 maximum per individual per credit union also applies to both RRSP and RRIF plans, in addition to the $100,000 limit for savings accounts.

The maximum deposit protection and the qualifying criteria for investment protection varies across the provinces but is similar to the protection offered by the CDIC. The maximum protection per individual per institution is $60,000 of the total of savings, chequing, and term deposits in Nova Scotia, Newfoundland, Ontario, and Prince Edward Island. The caisses populaires in Quebec offer $60,000 coverage per institution for *each* of savings accounts, chequing accounts, and term deposits, for total coverage of $180,000 per institution. Alberta, Manitoba, New Brunswick, and Saskatchewan all offer unlimited protection.

The Canadian Life and Health Compensation Corporation (CompCorp) came into existence in 1990 to provide protection for customers of companies that sell life and/or health insurance to the Canadian public. The Property and Casualty Insurance Compensation Corporation (PACICC) performs a similar function for customers of property and casualty insurance companies. Finally, customers of investment dealers are afforded protection by the Canadian Investor Protection Fund (CIPF), which is discussed in greater detail in Chapter 5. For more details regarding the coverage provided by these three regulatory organizations, refer to their Web sites that are listed at the end of this chapter.

customers. The rates on these smaller denominations will be lower than those available on the larger blocks, which is how the intermediaries make their profits.

The money market is dominated by financial institutions, particularly banks, and governments. The maturities of money market instruments range from one day to one year and are often less than 90 days. Table 2-1 indicates that Canadian trading in money market securities reached $6.7 trillion in 1996, which eclipses the $4.9 trillion traded in Canadian bond markets during the same period. Perhaps even more surprisingly to the average person (given all of the attention devoted to stock market activity in the media), is that this amount is almost 20 times the 1996 volume of trading activity in all Canadian stock markets, which was a mere $369 billion in 1996.

Table 2-1

Secondary Market Trading in Canada

($ Billions)	1997	1996	1995	1994	1993	1992
Debt Securities						
Money Market	5,923.1	6,696.4	6,751.8	6,707.2	1,520.0	1,516.9
Bond Market	5,545.0	4,913.1	3,595.6	3,370.0	1,402.9	1,036.5
Total Debt	11,468.1	11,609.5	10,347.4	9,914.2	2,922.9	2,553.4
Equities						
Stock Market	497.7	369.4	256.3	222.7	186.3	101.8
Total Trading	$11,965.8	$11,978.9	$10,603.7	$10,136.9	$3,109.1	$2,655.2

Data Source: IDA Industry Statistics

*1996 debt trading as of 1994 not comparable to prior years. Data after 1993 reflects total market activity (investment dealers plus banks) and both sides of a trade. 1993 and prior data reflects investment dealer activity and only one side of a trade.

Source: *Canadian Securities Course Textbook* (Toronto: Canadian Securities Institute, August 1998), p. 1-40.© 1998 Canadian Securities Institutue. Reprinted with permission.

Some of these instruments are negotiable and actively traded, and others are not. Most of them are sold on a discount basis. For example, 91-day Treasury bills with a face (or maturity) value of $100,000 may be sold to investors for $98,500. The investor receives $100,000 at maturity, which means they have earned $1,500 in interest on their original investment of $98,500.[1] Investors may invest directly in some of these securities, but more often they do so indirectly through money market mutual funds, offered by investment companies.

Treasury Bill A short-term money market instrument sold at discount by Canadian governments.

Another reason that knowledge of these securities is important is the use of government **Treasury bills** (T-bills) as a benchmark asset. Although in some pure sense there is no such thing as a risk-free financial asset, on a practical basis Government of Canada Treasury bills are risk free since there is virtually no chance of default by the federal government, and the length of the investment period is very short. The T-bill rate, denoted RF, is used throughout the text as a proxy for the nominal risk-free rate of return available to investors (e.g., the RF shown and discussed in Figure 1-1 on page 10).

In summary, money market instruments are characterized as short-term, highly marketable investments, with an extremely low probability of default. Because the minimum investment is generally large, money market securities are normally owned by individual investors indirectly in the form of investment funds known as money market mutual funds, or, as they are usually called, money market funds.

Money market rates tend to move together and most rates are very close to each other for the same maturity, as can be seen in the Real-World Returns box below. Notice that T-bill rates are lower than those for other money market securities because of their risk-free nature.

The following are the major money market securities of most interest to individual investors.

[1] A discussion of price and yield calculations for T-bills is presented in the CSC Notes box in Appendix 11-A at the end of Chapter 11.

REAL-WORLD RETURNS

Money Rates[2]

ADMINISTERED RATES

Bank of Canada	5.00%
Central bank call range	4.50–5.00%
Canadian prime	6.50%

MONEY MARKET RATES

(for transactions of $1-million or more)

3-month T-bill (when issued)	4.65%
1-month Treasury bills	4.52%
2-month Treasury bills	4.60%
3-month Treasury bills	4.66%
6 month Treasury bills	4.90%
1-year Treasury bills	5.11%
10-year Canada bonds	5.60%
30-year Canada bonds	5.93%
1-month banker's accept.	4.83%
2-month banker's accept.	4.87%
3-month banker's accept.	4.93%

Commerical paper (R-1 Low)	
1-month	4.88%
2-month	4.93%
3-month	4.98%
Call money	4.69%

Dow Jones Markets
UNITED STATES

NEW YORK (AP) — Money rates for Wednesday as reported by Dow Jones markets as of 4 p.m.:

DJ Markets interest rate index: 5.500

Prime rate: 8.50

Discount rate: 5.00

Broker call loan rate: 7.25

Federal funds market rate:

High 5.5625; low 5.4375; last 5.4375

Dealers commercial paper:

30–180 days: 5.55–5.45

Commerical paper by finance company: 30–270 days: 5.54–5.35

Bankers acceptances dealer indications: 30 days, 5.56; 60 days, 5.52; 90 days, 5.50; 120 days, 5.50; 150 days, 5.49; 180 days, 5.47

Certificates of deposit primary: 30 days, 4.71; 90 days, 5.02; 180 days, 5.24

Certificates of deposit by dealer: 30 days, 5.58; 60 days, 5.58; 90 days, 5.59; 120 days, 5.62; 150 days, 5.62; 180 days, 5.62

Eurodollar rates: Overnight, 5.4375–5.5625; 1 month, 5.50–5.625; 3 months, 5.5625–5.625; 6 months, 5.5625–5.625; 1 year, 5.6875–5.75

London Interbank Offered Rate: 3 months, 5.69; 6 months, 5.72; 1 year, 5.84

Treasury bill auction results: average discount rate: 3-month as of Mar. 2, 5.120; 6-month as of Mar. 2, 5.125; 52-week as of Jan. 29, 4.965

Treasury bill annualized rate on weekly average basis, yield adjusted for constant maturity, 1-year as of Mar. 2, 5.42

Treasury bill market rate: 1-year, 5.14–5.12

Treasury bond market rate: 30-year, 6.04

Source: The Globe and Mail / Report on Business, *March 5, 1998. Reprinted with permission from* The Globe and Mail.

1. *Treasury bills*. The premier money market instrument, a fully guaranteed, very liquid IOU from the Government of Canada or provincial governments. Government of Canada Treasury bills are sold by auction every two weeks at a discount from face value in denominations of $5,000, $25,000, $100,000, and $1 million. The greater the discount at the time of purchase the higher the return earned by investors. Standard maturities are 91, 182, and 364 days, although shorter maturities are also offered. New bills can be purchased by investors on a competitive or non-competitive bid basis. Outstanding (i.e., already issued) bills can be purchased and sold in the secondary market, an extremely efficient market where government securities dealers stand ready to buy and sell these securities.

2. *Commercial paper*. A short-term, unsecured promissory note issued by large, well-known, and financially strong corporations (including finance companies). Denominations start at $100,000 with maturities of 30 to 365 days. Commercial paper is usually sold at a discount either directly by the issuer or indirectly through a dealer, with rates slightly above T-bills. Although a secondary market exists for commercial paper, it is weak and most of it is held to maturity. Similar to bonds, commercial paper is rated by a rating service as to quality (relative probability of default by the issuer).

[2] The reported rates in this box are auction rates that are available mainly to institutional investors.

3. *Eurodollars*. Dollar-denominated deposits held in foreign banks or in offices of Canadian banks located abroad. Although this market originally developed in Europe (hence the name), dollar-denominated deposits can now be made in many countries, such as those of Asia. Eurodollar deposits consist of both time deposits and certificates of deposit (CDs), with the latter constituting the largest component of the Eurodollar markets. Maturities are mostly short-term, often less than six months. The Eurodollar market is primarily a wholesale market, with large deposits and large loans. Major international banks transact among themselves with other participants including multinational corporations and governments. Although relatively safe, Eurodollar yields exceed those of other money market assets because of the lesser regulation for Eurodollar banks. In addition, Eurodollar CDs are not covered by CDIC.

4. *Repurchase agreement (RP)*. An agreement between a borrower and lender (generally institutions) to sell and repurchase money market securities. The borrower initiates an RP by contracting to sell securities to a lender and agreeing to repurchase these securities at a prespecified (higher) price on a stated future date. The effective interest rate is given by the difference between the repurchase price and the sale price. The annual interest rate implied by these transactions is referred to as the repo rate. The maturity of RPs is generally very short, from three to 14 days, and sometimes overnight. The minimum denomination is typically $100,000.

5. *Banker's acceptance (B/A)*. A time draft drawn on a bank by a customer, whereby the bank agrees to guarantee payment of a particular amount at a specified future date. B/As are negotiable instruments that are sold for less than face value (i.e., at a discount) in the money market. They are traded on a discount basis, with a minimum denomination of $100,000. Maturities range from 30 to 180 days, with 90 days being the most common.

CAPITAL MARKET SECURITIES

Capital Markets
The markets for long-term securities such as bonds and stocks.

Capital markets encompass fixed-income and equity securities with maturities greater than one year. Risk is generally much higher than in the money market because of the time to maturity and the very nature of the securities sold in the capital markets. Marketability is poorer in some cases. The capital market includes both debt and equity securities, with equity securities having no maturity date.

Fixed-Income Securities

Fixed-Income Securities
Securities such as bonds with specified payment dates and amounts.

We begin our review of the principal types of capital market securities owned directly by individual investors with **fixed-income securities**. All of these have a specified payment schedule and, in most cases, such as with a traditional bond, the amount and date of each payment are known in advance. Some of these securities deviate from this format, but all fixed-income securities have a specified payment or repayment schedule — they must mature at some future date.

Bonds

Bonds can be described simply as long-term debt instruments representing the issuer's contractual obligation or IOU. The buyer of a newly issued coupon bond is lending money to the issuer who, in turn, agrees to pay interest on this loan and repay the principal at a stated maturity date.

Bonds
Long-term debt instruments representing the issuer's contractual obligation or IOU.

Bonds are fixed-income securities because the interest payments (if any) and the principal repayment for most bonds are specified at the time the bond is issued and fixed for its life. At the time of purchase, the bond buyer knows the future stream of cash flows to be received from buying and holding the bond to maturity. Barring default by the issuer, these payments will be received at specified intervals until maturity, at which time the principal will be repaid. However, if the buyer decides to sell the bond before maturity, the price received will depend on the interest rates at that time.

Bond Characteristics

The **par value (face value)** of most bonds is $1,000, and we will use this number as the amount to be repaid at maturity.[3] The bond generally matures (terminates) on a specified date and is technically known as a term bond.[4] Most bonds are coupon bonds, where coupon refers to the periodic interest that the issuer pays to the holder of the bonds.[5] Interest on bonds is generally paid semi-annually.

Par Value (Face Value)
The redemption value of a bond paid at maturity, generally $1,000.

EXAMPLE: GOVERNMENT OF CANADA COUPON BOND

A four-year, 11.75 per cent Government of Canada coupon bond was listed in *The Globe and Mail* on January 27, 1999. Assuming the bond has a par value of $1,000, it has a dollar coupon of $117.50 (11.75 per cent of $1,000); therefore, knowing the percentage coupon rate is the same as knowing the coupon payment in dollars.[6] If the interest on the bond is paid semi-annually, this bond would pay interest (the coupons) of $58.75 on a specified date every six months. The $1,000 principal would be repaid four years hence at the maturity date (hence we say the term-to-maturity is four years).

An important innovation in the format of traditional bonds is the **zero coupon bond** (or strip bond), which does not pay any coupons, or interest, during its life. The purchaser pays less than par value for "zeroes" and receives par value at maturity. The difference in these two amounts generates an effective interest rate or rate of return. Similar to Treasury bills, the lower the price paid for the coupon bond, the higher the effective return.

Zero Coupon Bond
A bond sold with no coupons at a discount and redeemed for face value at maturity. Also known as a strip bond.

---

[3] The par value is almost never less than $1,000, although it easily can be more.

[4] The phrase term-to-maturity is used to denote how much longer the bond will be in existence. In contrast, a serial bond has a series of maturity dates. Thus, one issue of serial bonds may mature in specified amounts year after year, and each specified amount could carry a different coupon.

[5] The terms interest income and coupon income are interchangeable.

[6] The coupon rate on a traditional, standard bond is fixed at the bond's issuance and cannot vary.

Zeroes are created when financial intermediaries purchase traditional bonds, strip the cash flows from them, and sell the cash flows separately. These bonds first appeared in Canada in 1982. In the United States, the US Treasury created STRIPS, or Separate Trading of Registered Interest and Principal of Securities, in 1985. Under this program, all new **Treasury bonds** (i.e., bonds issued by the US government) and notes with maturities greater than ten years are eligible to be stripped to create zero coupon Treasury securities that are direct obligations of the US Treasury Department.

Treasury Bond
Long-term bonds sold by the US government.

By convention, bond prices are quoted as a proportion of par value using 100 as par rather than 1,000. Therefore, a price of 90 represents $900, and a price of 55 represents $550, using the normal assumption of a par value of $1,000. The easiest way to convert quoted bond prices to actual prices is to remember that they are quoted in percentages, with the common assumption of a $1,000 par value.

EXAMPLE: PRICE OF A GOVERNMENT OF CANADA COUPON BOND

The closing price of a four-year 11.75 per cent Government of Canada coupon bond was 124.70 on January 26, 1999. This quoted price represents 124.70 per cent of $1,000, or $1,247.00.

The above example suggests that an investor could purchase the bond for $1,247.00 on that day. Actually, bonds trade on an accrued interest basis. That is, the bond buyer must pay the bond seller the price of the bond as well as the interest that has been earned (accrued) on the bond since the last interest payment. This allows an investor to sell a bond any time without losing the interest that has accrued. Bond buyers should remember this additional cost when buying a bond because prices are quoted in the paper without the accrued interest.[7]

The price of the bond in the above example is above 100 (i.e., $1,000) because market yields on bonds of this type were below the stated coupon rate of 11.75 per cent on this bond (in fact the yield associated with this price for this bond is 4.89 per cent). The coupon on this particular bond became more than competitive with the going market interest rate for comparable newly issued bonds, and the price increased to reflect this fact. At any point in time some bonds are selling at premiums (above par value), reflecting a decline in market rates after that particular bond was sold. Others are selling at discounts (below par value), because the stated coupons are less than the prevailing interest rate on a comparable new issue.

Call Provision
Gives the issuer the right to call in a security and retire it by paying off the obligation.

The **call provision** gives the issuer the right to "call in" the bonds, thereby depriving investors of that particular fixed-income security. Exercising the call provision becomes attractive to the issuer when market interest rates drop sufficiently below the coupon rate on the outstanding bonds for the issuer to save money. Costs are incurred to call the bonds, such as a "call premium" and administrative expenses. However, issuers expect to sell new bonds at a lower interest cost, thereby replacing existing higher interest-cost bonds with new, lower interest-cost bonds.

Callable bonds give the issuer the option to call or repurchase outstanding bonds at predetermined "call prices" (generally at a premium over par) at specified times. This feature is detrimental to the bondholders who are willing to pay less for them (i.e., they demand a higher return) than for similar non-callable bonds. Generally, the issuer agrees to give 30 or more

[7] The invoice or cash price is the price the bond buyer must pay and will include the accrued interest.

days notice that the issue will be redeemed. Most callables have a time period (referred to as call protection) prior to the first call date during which they cannot be called. The redemption price often declines on a graduated scale, reflecting the fact that the hardship to the investor of having an issue called is reduced as the time to maturity declines. Most Government of Canada and US Treasury bonds are non-callable.[8] Provincial bonds are usually callable at 100 plus accrued interest. Usually corporate issues have a mandatory call feature for sinking fund purposes.

INVESTING *tip*

The call feature is a risk to investors who must give up the higher yielding bonds. Consistent with our discussion of risk and return in Chapter 1, we generally observe that callable bonds offer investors a higher yield than similar non-callable bonds as compensation for this risk. The wise bond investor will note the bond issue's provisions concerning the call, carefully determining the earliest date at which the bond can be called, and the bond's yield if it is called at the earliest date possible. This calculation is shown in Chapter 11.

Retractable bonds allow the bondholder to sell the bonds back to the issuer at predetermined prices at specified times, while **extendible bonds** allow the bondholder to extend the maturity date of the bond. Both of these bonds offer investors an additional privilege, which implies they will pay more for these bonds (i.e., accept a lower return). They both tend to trade similar to short-term bonds during periods of rising interest rates, as it is likely that they will be redeemed (or not extended). Similarly, they tend to behave like long-term bonds during periods of decreasing interest rates. The holders generally must state their intentions to extend or redeem during the election period (which occurs six to 12 months prior to the extendible or retractable dates).

A sinking fund provision provides for the orderly retirement of the bond issue during its life. The provisions of a sinking fund vary widely. For example, it can be stated as a fixed or variable amount and as a percentage of the particular issue outstanding or the total debt of the issuer outstanding. All or part of the bond issue may be retired through the sinking fund by the maturity date. One procedure for carrying out the sinking fund requirement is simply to buy the required amount of bonds on the open market each year. A second alternative is to call the bonds randomly. Again, investors should be aware of such provisions for their protection.

Retractable Bonds
Bonds that allow the bondholder to sell the bonds back to the issuer at predetermined prices at specified times.

Extendible Bonds
Bonds that allow investors to extend the maturity date of the bond.

Convertible bonds may be converted into common shares at predetermined conversion prices. This privilege is afforded to the investor in order to make the issue more saleable and to reduce the interest rate that must be offered to purchasers. The conversion price is often graduated upward through time to encourage early conversion. Most convertibles are callable. Certain convertibles include a forced conversion clause, which forces conversion by affording the issuer the right to redeem the issue once the common share price goes above prespecified levels. Convertibles typically trade similar to straight debentures when the conversion price is well below the market price of the common shares. A "premium" appears as market price approaches conversion price, and it is said to "sell off the stock" once market price exceeds the conversion price.

Convertible Bonds
Bonds that are convertible, at the holder's option, into shares of common stock of the same corporation at predetermined prices.

Floating rate bonds (or floaters) are an alternative to traditional fixed coupon bonds. They have adjustable coupons that are generally tied to T-bill rates or some other short-term interest rate. They are attractive for the protection offered in times of volatile interest rates (and/or during inflationary periods) and behave like money market securities in an investment portfolio. An example of a floating-rate bond that provides protection against increases in inflation (which is generally accompanied by an increase in interest rates) is Government of Canada Real Return Bonds. These were introduced in 1991 to provide investors with a real yield of about 4.25 per cent. This is

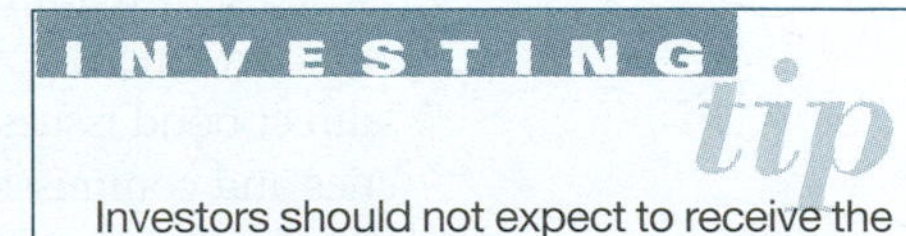

Investors should not expect to receive the conversion option free. The issue sells convertible bonds at a lower interest rate than would otherwise be paid, resulting in a lower interest return to investors.

[8] US Treasury bonds issued after February 1985 cannot be called.

achieved by pegging the face value to the Consumer Price Index (CPI) and having the coupon rate of 4.25 per cent apply to the inflation-adjusted face value.

Types of Bonds

Bond certificates may be in either bearer or registered forms. Bearer bonds are presumed to be owned by the party holding them. Coupons are numbered and dated and may be clipped and redeemed for cash. Registered bonds have the name of the owner on their face and interest is paid to the registered owner by the issuer. If lost or stolen, it is difficult for anyone other than the owner to cash them. Most bonds are traded through dealers in the over-the-counter market which is described in Chapter 4.

Bonds may be classified as domestic, foreign, or Eurobonds. Domestic bonds are issued in the currency and country of the issuer, while foreign bonds are issued primarily in a currency and country other than the issuer's. Eurobonds are issued in any number of currencies in the Euromarket or the international bond market (if issued in Canadian dollars they would be called EuroCanadian bonds, and if issued in US dollars they would be called Eurodollar bonds).

While government bonds constitute the majority of the bond market in Canada, corporate bonds are growing in importance. For example, at the end of 1995 there was $452 billion US in Canadian government bonds outstanding versus $50 billion US outstanding in Canadian corporate bonds (approximately 10 per cent of the Canadian total). However, by 1997, the corporate bond market grew in size to $75 billion US (or 15 per cent of the total Canadian bond market) while the amount of Canadian government bonds outstanding actually shrank from its 1995 level to $432 billion in response to improving fiscal positions of Canadian governments.

Government Bonds

The Government of Canada is the largest single issuer of bonds in Canada and had about $290 billion in bonds outstanding by the end of 1996. Like Treasury bills, they are sold at competitive auctions, but unlike bills, they are sold at approximately face value with investors submitting bids on yields (for example, 5.2 per cent). Interest payments (coupons) are usually paid semi-annually. Face value denominations are $1,000, $5,000, $10,000, $100,000, $500,000, and $1 million. These bonds are considered an extremely safe credit risk because the government's ability to print money and increase taxes implies the risk of default is minimal for these securities. An investor purchases them with the expectation of earning a steady stream of interest payments and with full assurance of receiving the par value of the bonds when they mature.

Provincial governments also participate in Canadian and global bond markets through direct bond issues as well as by guaranteeing bond issues of provincially appointed authorities and commissions (e.g., Ontario Hydro may have outstanding bonds that are guaranteed by the Province of Ontario). Finally, municipal governments also raise debt capital through bond markets. In recent years, municipalities have relied primarily on instalment debentures or serial bonds (described in footnote 4) to raise debt capital from the markets.

US government agencies are the largest issuers/guarantors of bonds in the world, with over $7.3 trillion US in outstanding debt securities by the end of 1997. The US federal government issues numerous notes and bonds with maturities greater than one year through the Treasury Department (hence the name Treasury notes or Treasury bonds).[9] Various US credit agencies also compete for funds in the marketplace by selling government agency securities. Securities issued by federal agencies that are legally part of the federal government are fully guaranteed by the Treasury. The most important agency for investors is the Government National Mortgage Association (often nicknamed "Ginnie Mae"). In addition to these federal agencies, there exist several other federally sponsored credit agencies in the United States, which are privately owned institutions that sell their own securities in the marketplace. They have the right to draw on Treasury funds up to some approved amount; however, their securities are not guaranteed by the government. Some of the more important federally sponsored credit agencies include the Federal Home Loan Mortgage Corporation ("Freddie Mac"), the Federal Home Loan Bank, the Farm Credit System, and the Student Loan Marketing Association. Perhaps the best known of these federally sponsored agencies is the Federal National Mortgage Association (FNMA, referred to as "Fannie Mae"), which is designed to help the mortgage markets.

Corporate Bonds

Several of the larger corporations issue **corporate bonds** to help finance their operations. An investor can find a wide range of maturities, coupons, and special features available from corporate bonds. The average corporate bond pays semi-annual interest, is callable, carries a sinking fund provision, and is sold originally at a price close to par value which is usually $1,000.[10]

Corporate bonds are **senior securities**. That is, they are senior to any preferred stock and to the common stock of a corporation in terms of priority of payment and in case of bankruptcy and liquidation. However, within the bond category itself there are various degrees of security. Mortgage bonds are secured by real assets which means that holders have legal claim to specific assets of the issuer. **Debentures** are generally unsecured and are backed only by the issuer's overall financial soundness. In addition, debentures can be "subordinated," resulting in a claim on income that stands below (subordinate to) the claim of the other debentures.[11]

Corporate bonds carry a greater risk of default by the issuer than government bonds, and as a result, their indentures (or contracts) often include protective covenants which are clauses that restrict the actions of the issuer. Negative covenants prohibit certain actions (e.g., restrict dividend payments or prevent pledging of any assets to lenders). Positive covenants specify actions that the firm agrees to undertake (e.g., furnish quarterly financial statements or maintain certain working capital levels).

Rating services perform detailed analysis of bond issuers to determine their ability to maintain uninterrupted payments of interest and repayment of principal. The Dominion Bond Rating Service (DBRS) and the Canadian Bond Rating Service (CBRS) are the two major Canadian **bond rating** services. Standard & Poor's (S&P) Corporation and Moody's Investors

Corporate Bonds
Long-term debt securities of various types sold by corporations.

Senior Securities
Those securities that are senior, because they are ahead of common and preferred stock in terms of payment in case of liquidation or bankruptcy.

Debenture
An unsecured bond backed by the general financial worthiness of the firm.

Bond Rating
Letters assigned to bonds by rating agencies to express the relative probability of default.

[9] US Treasury securities with maturities greater than one year and less than ten years technically are referred to as Treasury notes, while those with maturities greater than ten years are referred to as Treasury bonds.

[10] There are various exceptions to this generalization, of course, including bonds with warrants attached, mortgage-backed bonds, collateral trust bonds (which are backed by financial assets), and zero coupon bonds.

[11] Other types of corporate bonds exist, including collateral trust bonds, which are backed by other securities. For example, a parent firm may pledge the securities of one of its subsidiaries as collateral. Equipment obligations (or equipment trust certificates) are backed by specific real assets such as railway engines or airplanes. A trustee is used to hold the assets involved with both collateral trust bonds and equipment obligations.

Service Inc. are two major US rating agencies that rate bond issuers (both government and corporate) across the world.

The following are the debt ratings categories for CBRS and DBRS:

CBRS		DBRS	
A++	highest quality	AAA	highest credit quality
A+	very good quality	AA	superior credit quality
A	good quality	A	upper medium grade credit quality
B++	medium quality	BBB	medium grade credit quality
B+	lower medium quality	BB	lower medium grade credit quality
B	poor quality	B	speculative credit quality
C	speculative quality	CCC	highly speculative credit quality
D	default	CC	in default
Suspended	rating suspended	C	second tier of debt of an entity in default

Ratings of both services may also be modified by *high* or *low* to indicate the relative ranking or the trend within the category such as high A+ or low A+. Investment grade bonds are defined as those with bond ratings of BBB (DBRS and S&P), B++ (CBRS), or Baa (Moody's), or higher. Generally, institutional investors must confine themselves to investment grade bonds. Other things being equal, bond ratings and bond coupon rates are inversely related. Junk (or high-yield or low-grade) bonds have bond ratings below these. These bonds are regarded as speculative securities in terms of the issuer's ability to meet its contractual obligations.

Despite their widespread acceptance, bond ratings have some limitations. For example, the different agencies may not be able to agree on their evaluations. Furthermore, because most bonds are in the top four categories, it seems safe to argue that not all issues in a single category (such as A) can be equally risky. Finally, it is extremely important to remember that bond ratings are a reflection of the probability of default relative to other corporate bond issues, which may say little about the absolute probability of default by a particular bond issue.

We conclude by noting that while the Canadian market for corporate bonds has grown in importance in recent years, it is still quite small relative to the Canadian government bond market, as discussed above. In addition, the $75 million US in Canadian corporate bonds outstanding at the end of 1997 is very small relative to corporate bond markets in other countries. For example, the United States, Japan, and Germany had $5.1 trillion, $1.3 trillion, and $952 billion US of corporate debt outstanding at the end of 1997. In fact, the Canadian figure accounts for less than 1 per cent of the world corporate debt market.

Asset-Backed Securities

Asset-Backed Securities (ABS)
Securities issued against some type of asset-linked debts bundled together, such as credit card receivables or mortgages.

The money and capital markets are constantly adapting to meet new requirements and conditions. This has given rise to new types of securities that were not previously available. "Securitization" refers to the transformation of illiquid, risky individual loans into more liquid, less risky securities referred to as **asset-backed securities (ABS)**. The best example of this process is mortgage-backed securities (MBS). These are created when a financial institution purchases (or originates) a number of mortgage loans that are then repackaged and sold to investors as mortgage pools. Investors in MBSs are, in effect, purchasing a piece of a mortgage pool. MBS investors assume little default risk because most mortgages are guaranteed by a federal government agency, as described below.

The Canadian Mortgage and Housing Corporation (CMHC) introduced MBSs in Canada in 1987. Similar to the GNMA in the United States (which fully supports Ginnie Mae issues), the CMHC issues fully guaranteed securities in support of the mortgage market. These securities have attracted considerable attention in recent years because the principal and interest payments on the underlying mortgages used as collateral are "passed through" to the bondholder monthly as the mortgages are repaid. However, these securities are not completely riskless because they can receive varying amounts of monthly payments depending on how quickly homeowners pay off their mortgages. Although the stated maturity can be as long as 40 years, the average life of these securities has actually been much shorter.

ABSs are created when an underwriter, such as a bank, bundles some type of asset-linked debt (usually consumer oriented) and sells investors the right to receive payments made on that debt. As a result of the trend to securitization, other asset-backed securities have proliferated as financial institutions have rushed to securitize various types of loans.

Marketable securities have been backed by car loans, credit-card receivables, railway car leases, small-business loans, leases for photocopiers or aircraft, and so forth. The assets that can be securitized seem to be limited only by the imagination of the packagers, as evidenced by the fact that by 1996 new asset types included royalty streams from films, student loans, mutual fund fees, tax liens, monthly hydro bills, and delinquent child support payments!

EXAMPLE: CANADIAN COMPANIES SELL OFF ABSs

Several Canadian companies have sold off many of their assets in the form of ABSs including **CIBC's Smart Trust** (multi-asset pools), **Co-op Trust's Secure Trust** (credit card receivables), and **Eaton's** (credit card receivables that were protected despite the bankruptcy of the parent company).

Why do investors like these asset-backed securities? The attractions are relatively high yields and relatively short maturities (often five years) combined with investment-grade credit ratings, typically the highest two ratings available.[12] Investors are often protected by a bond insurer. Institutional investors, such as pension funds and life insurance companies, have become increasingly attracted to these securities because of the higher yields; the same is true of foreign investors.

As for risk, securitization works best when packaged loans are homogeneous, so that income streams and risks are more predictable. This is clearly the case for home mortgages, for example, which must adhere to strict guidelines, but for some of the newer loans being considered for packaging — such as loans for boats and motorcycles — the smaller amount of information results in a larger risk from unanticipated factors.

Rates on Fixed-Income Securities

Interest rates on fixed-income securities have fluctuated widely over the years as inflationary expectations as well as supply and demand conditions for long-term funds change. As one would expect on the basis of the return–risk trade-off explained in Chapter 1, corpo-

[12] To date, some 75 per cent of ABSs have been rated AAA.

rate rates generally exceed government rates because of the higher risk, and lower-rated corporate securities yield more than do higher-rated ones.

Equity Securities

Unlike their fixed-income counterparts, equity securities represent an ownership interest in a corporation. These securities provide a residual claim — after payment of all fixed-income obligations — on the income and assets of a corporation. There are two forms of equities — preferred stock and common stock, but investors are usually more interested in common stocks.

Preferred Stock

Preferred Stock
A hybrid security that is part equity and part fixed-income because it increases in value but also pays a fixed dividend.

Most preferred shares in Canada are traded on the TSE and in the United States on the NYSE. They generally offer fixed monthly or quarterly dividends and are rated as to credit risk (similar to bonds and commercial paper). Although technically an equity security, **preferred stock** is often referred to as a hybrid, because it resembles both equity and fixed-income instruments.

As an equity security, preferred stock has an infinite life and pays dividends. It resembles fixed-income securities in that the amount of the dividend is fixed and known in advance, providing a stream of income very similar to that of a bond. The difference is that the stream continues forever, unless the issue is called or otherwise retired. Similar to bonds, the prices of preferreds are very sensitive to interest rates, but their price fluctuations often exceed those in bonds due to their long-term nature.

Preferred shareholders rank below creditors but above common shareholders in terms of priority of payment of income and in case the corporation is liquidated. While payment of preferred dividends is not obligatory like interest payments, payment to common shareholders has to wait until preferred shareholders receive full payment of the dividends to which they are entitled. Most preferred shares are non-voting, however, once a stated number of dividend payments have been omitted, it is common practice to assign voting privileges to the preferred. In addition, failure to pay anticipated preferred dividends weakens investor confidence in the issuer which has an impact on its general credit and borrowing power. Finally, preferred shares usually have a "cumulative" feature associated with their dividends. This requires the firm to pay all preferred dividends (both current and arrears) before paying any dividends to common shareholders, and that makes the preferred less risky than common shares from the investor's point of view.

Preferred dividends are paid from after-tax earnings, and, unlike interest payments, they do not provide the issuer with a tax-deductible expense. However, individual investors receive relief in the form of a dividend tax credit, which implies they will pay lower taxes on a dollar of dividend income than on interest income. In addition, dividends received by one Canadian corporation from another Canadian corporation are not taxable. As a result of this tax incentive many Canadian financial institutions (banks and insurance companies, in particular) used to be large participants in the market for preferred shares. However, tax laws were changed in 1987, which required specified financial institutions (including banks and insurance companies) to treat preferred dividend payments as the equivalent to interest (which is fully taxable). The result of this change in tax laws is that fewer new issues of preferred shares have occurred since then.

Companies issue preferred shares as a compromise between the demands created by debt, and the dilution of common equity caused by the issuance of additional common shares, or when market conditions are unfavourable for new common share issues. Investors may be attracted to them if they want dividend income which offers tax advantages over interest income. In addition, some issues have special features that make them attractive to investors. For example, some preferred issues are convertible into common stock at the owner's option. Similar to convertible debt, most convertible preferred shares are callable at a premium over par value.

Other types of preferred shares include:

1. Retractable preferreds which can be tendered by the holder to the issuer for redemption
2. Variable-rate or floating-rate preferreds which have the dividend rate tied to current market interest rates
3. Participating preferreds which have certain pre-specified rights to a share in company earnings over and above their specified rate.

In addition, some preferreds require the company to purchase a specified amount in the open market if they are available at or below the stipulated price. This provides built-in market support for these shares. Sinking fund provisions are less common for preferred share issues. They have the potential disadvantage to investors that the required purchases may be called in by lot at the sinking fund price plus accrued and unpaid dividends if the fund's open market operations are unsuccessful.

Common Stock

Common Stock
An equity security representing the ownership interest in a corporation.

Common stock represents the ownership interest of corporations or the equity of the shareholders, and we can use the term equity securities interchangeably. If a firm's shares are owned by only a few individuals, the firm is said to be closely held. Most companies choose to go public, or they sell common stock to the general public, primarily to let them raise additional capital more easily. If a corporation meets certain requirements, it may choose to be listed on one or more exchanges such as the TSE. Otherwise, it will be listed in the over-the-counter market (this process is discussed in Chapter 4).

As the residual claimants of the corporation, shareholders are entitled to income remaining after the fixed-income claimants such as the preferred shareholders have been paid; also, in case of liquidation of the corporation, they are entitled to the remaining assets after all other claims (including preferred stock) are satisfied.

As owners, the holders of common stock are entitled to elect the directors of the corporation and vote on major issues.[13] Each shareholder is allowed to cast votes equal to the number of shares owned when such votes take place at the annual meeting of the corporation which each shareholder is allowed to attend.[14] Most stockholders vote by proxy, meaning that they authorize someone else (most often management) to vote their shares. Sometimes

---

[13] The voting rights of the shareholders give them legal control of the corporation. In theory, the board of directors controls the management of the corporation, but in many cases the effective result is the opposite. Shareholders can regain control if they are sufficiently dissatisfied.

[14] Most shareholders do not attend, often allowing management to vote their proxy. Therefore, although technically more than 50 per cent of the outstanding shares are needed for control of a firm, effective control can often be exercised with considerably less because not all of the shares are voted.

proxy battles occur, whereby one or more groups unhappy with corporate policies seek to bring about changes.

There often exists a clause in a corporation's charter which grants existing shareholders the first or pre-emptive right to purchase any new common stock sold by the corporation. The right is a piece of paper giving each stockholder the option to buy a specified number of new shares, usually at a discount, during a specified short period of time. These rights are valuable and can be sold in the market.

Finally, shareholders also have limited liability, meaning they cannot be held responsible for the debts of the company or lose more than their original investment. In the event of financial difficulties, creditors have recourse only to the assets of the corporation, leaving the stockholders protected. This is perhaps the greatest advantage of the corporation and the reason why it has been so successful.

Characteristics of Common Stocks

The par value for a common stock, unlike that of a bond or preferred stock, is generally not a significant economic variable. Corporations can make the par value any number they choose and an often-used par value is $1. New stock is usually sold for more than par value, with the difference recorded on the balance sheet as "capital in excess of par value" or "additional paid-in capital." Canadian corporations incorporated under the Canadian Business Corporation Act (CBCA) and under most provincial acts can no longer issue shares with par value.

Book Value
The accounting value of common equity as shown on the balance sheet.

The **book value** of a corporation is the accounting value of the common equity as shown on the books (i.e., balance sheet). It is the total value of common equity for a corporation, represented by the sum of common stock outstanding, capital in excess of par value and/or contributed surplus, and retained earnings. Dividing this sum — total book value — by the number of common shares outstanding, produces the book value per share. In effect, book value is the accounting value of the stockholders' equity. Although book value per share plays a role in making investment decisions, market value per share is the critical item of interest to investors.

EXAMPLE: BOOK VALUE FOR BOMBARDIER INC.

Bombardier Inc. reported $2.0294 billion in common shareholders' equity for fiscal year-end 1997. This is the book value of common equity. Based on average common shares outstanding of 337.6 million for that year (a figure obtained from a company's annual report), the book value per share was $6.01.

The market value or price of the equity is the variable of concern to investors. The aggregate market value for a corporation is calculated by multiplying the market price per share of the stock by the number of shares outstanding. This represents the total value of the firm as determined in the marketplace. The market value of one share of stock, of course, is simply the "observed" current market price. At the time the observation for Bombardier Inc.'s book value was recorded, the market price was in the $26 range. This implies that Bombardier's market-to-book ratio (discussed in Chapter 13) is $26.00/$6.01 = 4.33.

Dividends
Cash payments declared and paid by corporations to stockholders.

Dividends are the only cash payments regularly made by corporations to their stockholders. They are decided upon and declared by the board of directors quarterly and can range from zero to virtually any amount the corporation can afford to pay (up to 100 per cent of present and past net earnings). Roughly half of the companies listed on the TSE (and three-fourths of the companies listed on the NYSE) pay dividends. However, the common stockholder has no specific promises to receive any cash from the corporation since the stock never matures and dividends do not have to be paid. Therefore, common stocks involve substantial risk because the dividend is at the company's discretion and stock prices can fluctuate sharply, which means that the value of investors' claims may rise and fall rapidly over relatively short periods of time.

The two dividend terms dividend yield and payout ratio are important considerations for investors.

The **dividend yield** is the income component of a stock's return stated on a percentage basis. It is one of the two components of total return, which is discussed in Chapter 6. Dividend yield is commonly calculated as the most recent annual dividend amount divided by the current market price.

Dividend Yield
The income component of a stock's return, generally calculated by dividing the current annual dividend by the prevailing market price.

The **payout ratio** is the ratio of dividends to earnings. It indicates the percentage of a firm's earnings paid out in cash to its stockholders. The complement of the payout ratio is the retention ratio, and it indicates the percentage of a firm's current earnings retained by it for reinvestment purposes.

Payout Ratio
The percentage of a firm's earnings paid out in cash to its stockholders, calculated by dividing dividends by earnings.

EXAMPLE: PAYOUT RATIO FOR BOMBARDIER INC.

Bombardier Inc.'s 1997 earnings were $0.87 per share, and it paid an annual dividend on its class B shares of $0.20625 per share. Assuming a price for Bombardier of $26, the dividend yield would be $0.20625/$26.00, or 0.79 per cent. The payout ratio was $0.20625/$0.87, or 23.71 per cent, and the retention ratio was 76.29 per cent (i.e., 100 per cent – 23.71 per cent).

Dividends are declared and paid quarterly, but to receive a declared dividend, an investor must be a holder of record on the specified date that a company closes its stock transfer books and compiles the list of stockholders to be paid (which is generally done two to four weeks before the payment date). The ex dividend date is set at the second business day before the record date, and shares trade without the right to the associated dividend on and after this date. Since stock trades settle on the third business day after a trade, a purchaser of the share two days before the record date would not settle until the day after the record date, and would thus not be entitled to receive the dividend. Shares are said to trade cum dividend up to the ex dividend date, and trade ex dividend thereafter. This will be reflected in the share price, which typically falls by an amount close to the dividend amount on the ex rights date.

EXAMPLE: ANNOUNCING DIVIDENDS FOR BOMBARDIER INC.

Assume that the board of directors of **Bombardier Inc.** meets on May 24 and declares a quarterly dividend, payable on July 31. May 24 is called the declaration date. The board will declare a holder-of-record date, say, July 9. The books close on this date, but Bombardier goes ex-dividend on July 7 (assuming July 7 and July 8 are regular business days). To receive this dividend, an investor must purchase the stock by July 6. The dividend will be mailed to the stockholders of record on the payment date, July 31.

Stock Dividend
A payment by a corporation of a dividend in shares of stock rather than cash.

Stock Split
The division of a corporation's stock by issuing a specified number of new shares while simultaneously lowering the face value of outstanding shares.

Stock dividends and stock splits attract considerable investor attention. A **stock dividend** is a payment by a corporation in shares of stock instead of cash.[15] A **stock split** involves the division of a corporation's stock by issuing a specified number of new shares while simultaneously lowering the face value of outstanding shares. With a stock split, the book value and par value of the equity are changed; for example, each would be cut in half with a 2-for-1 split. However, on a practical basis, there is little difference between a stock dividend and a stock split since the net result of both actions is an increase in the number of shares outstanding.

EXAMPLE: SPLITTING STOCK 2-FOR-1

A 5 per cent stock dividend would entitle an owner of 100 shares of a particular stock to an additional five shares. A 2-for-1 stock split would double the number of shares of the stock outstanding, double an individual owner's number of shares (e.g., from 100 shares to 200 shares), and cut the price in half at the time of the split.

Stock data, as reported to investors in most investment information sources and in the company's reports to stockholders are adjusted for all stock dividends and stock splits. These adjustments must be made when splits or dividends occur in order for legitimate comparisons to be made for the data.

The important question to investors is the value of the distribution, whether a dividend or a split. It is clear that the recipient has more shares (i.e., more pieces of paper), but has anything of real value been received? Other things being equal, these additional shares do not represent additional value because proportional ownership has not changed. Quite simply, the pieces of paper — stock certificates — have been repackaged. For example, if you own 1,000 shares of a corporation that has 100,000 shares of stock outstanding, your proportional ownership is 1 per cent; with a 2-for-1 stock split, you now own 2,000 shares out of a total of 200,000 shares outstanding, but your proportional ownership is still 1 per cent.

Regardless of the above, some evidence does suggest that the stock price receives a boost following a split. A recent study by a university professor, David Ikenberry, finds that such stocks tend to outperform the market in the first year following a split by an average eight percentage points and that the effect continues for some three years following the split. According to S&P data, split shares tend to outperform the market for some 18 months following the split. Typically, the dividend is raised at the time of the split, which would have a positive effect by itself. If the above findings are correct, it suggests that management signals with splits and dividends that they are confident about future prospects, which in turn should boost investor confidence.

P/E Ratio
The ratio of stock price to earnings, using historical, current, or estimated data. Also known as earnings multiplier. (See also E/P Ratio)

The **P/E ratio**, also referred to as the earnings multiplier, is generally calculated as the ratio of the current market price to the firm's most recent earnings although it can also be based on expected future earnings. It is an indication of how much the market as a whole is willing to pay per dollar of earnings. It is standard investing practice to refer to stocks as selling at, say, 10 or 15 times earnings. Investors have traditionally used such a classification to categorize stocks. Growth stocks, for example, generally sell at high multiples, compared to the average stock, because of their expected higher earnings growth.

[15] The amount of the stock dividend received by an investor equals the number of shares he or she receives, times the prevailing market price per share. This amount is taxable in the same manner as a cash dividend for this dollar amount.

The P/E ratio is a widely reported variable, appearing in daily newspapers carrying stock information, in brokerage reports covering particular stocks, in magazine articles recommending various companies, and so forth. It is usually reported daily in newspapers and in most other sources as the current price divided by the latest 12-month earnings. For example, the P/E ratio for Bombardier based on the information above would be $26.00/$0.87 = 29.89. However, variations of this ratio are often used in the valuation of common stocks. In fact, the P/E ratio in its various forms is one of the best-known and most often cited variables in security analysis and is familiar to almost all investors.[16] The P/E ratio is discussed in great detail in Chapters 13 through 17, which deal with common stock valuation.

Investing Internationally in Equities

Canadians can invest internationally in a variety of ways. First, they may purchase shares of foreign companies that list directly on Canadian exchanges or in the Canadian over-the-counter market. Alternatively, they may purchase shares of foreign companies in the country of origin or purchase options or futures contracts on foreign stock indexes. Finally, they can purchase foreign securities indirectly by purchasing units (or shares) of investment companies (mutual funds or closed-end funds) specializing in foreign securities, as discussed in Chapter 3. The later method is the approach used by the vast majority of Canadians wishing to invest globally.

DERIVATIVE SECURITIES

We focus our attention here on the two types of derivative securities that are of interest to most investors. Options and futures contracts are **derivative securities**, so named because their value is derived from their connected underlying security. Numerous types of options and futures are traded in world markets. Furthermore, there are different types of options other than the puts and calls discussed here. For example, a **warrant** is a corporate-created, long-term option on the underlying common stock of the company. It gives the holder the right to buy the stock from the company at a stated price within a stated period of time, often several years.

Derivative Securities
Securities that derive their value in whole or in part by having a claim on some underlying security.

Warrant
An option created by a corporation to purchase a stated number of common shares at a specified price within a specified time (often several years).

Options and futures contracts share some common characteristics. Both have standardized features that allow them to be traded quickly and cheaply on organized exchanges. In addition to facilitating the trading of these securities, the exchange guarantees the performance of these contracts and its clearing house allows an investor to reverse his or her original position before maturity. For example, a seller of a futures contract can buy the contract and cancel the obligation that the contract carries. The exchanges and associated clearing houses for both options and futures contracts have worked extremely well.

[16] In calculating P/E ratios, on the basis of either the latest reported earnings or the expected earnings, problems can arise when comparing P/E ratios among companies if some of them are experiencing, or are expected to experience, abnormally high or low earnings. To avoid this problem, some market participants calculate a normalized earnings estimate. Normalized earnings are intended to reflect the "normal" level of a company's earnings; that is, transitory effects are presumably excluded, thus providing the user with a more accurate estimate of "true" earnings.

Options and futures contracts are important to investors because they provide a way for them to manage portfolio risk. For example, investors may incur the risk of adverse currency fluctuations if they invest in foreign securities, or they may incur the risk that interest rates will adversely affect their fixed-income securities. Options and futures contracts can be used to limit some, or all, of these risks, thereby providing risk-control possibilities.

Options and futures contracts have important differences in their trading, the assets they can affect, their risk factor, and so forth. Perhaps the biggest difference to note now is that a futures contract is an obligation to buy or sell, but an options contract is only the right as opposed to an obligation to do so. The buyer of an option has limited liability, but the buyer of a futures contract does not.

Options

Options
Rights to buy or sell a stated number of shares of stock within a specified period at a specified price.

Puts
Options to sell a specified number of shares of stock at a stated price within a specified period.

Calls
Options to buy a specified number of shares of stock at a stated price within a specified period.

LEAPs
Options to buy (calls) or sell (puts) securities with longer maturity dates of up to several years, also known as long-term options.

In today's investing world, the word **options** refers to **puts** and **calls**. Options are created not by corporations but by investors seeking to trade in claims on a particular common stock, stock index, or futures contract. A standard equity call (put) option gives the buyer the right to purchase (sell) 100 shares of a particular stock at a specified price (called the exercise price) within a specified time.[17] The maturities on most new puts and calls are available up to several months away, although a newer version of puts and calls called **LEAPs** has maturity dates of several years. Many exercise prices are created for each underlying common stock, giving investors a choice in both the maturity and the price they will pay or receive.

Buyers of calls receive the right to purchase a specified number of shares at a specified price. These investors are betting that the price of the underlying common stock will rise, making the call option more valuable. Put buyers receive the right to sell a specified number of shares at a specified price. They are betting that the price of the underlying common stock will decline, making the put option more valuable. Both put and call options are written (created) by other investors who are betting the opposite of their respective purchasers. The sellers (writers) receive an option premium for selling each new contract while the buyer pays this option premium.

Once the option is created and the writer receives the premium from the buyer, it can be traded repeatedly in the secondary market. The premium is simply the market price of the contract as determined by investors. The price will fluctuate constantly, just as the price of the underlying common stock changes. This makes sense, because the option is affected directly by the price of the stock that gives it value. In addition, the option's value is affected by the time remaining to maturity, current interest rates, the volatility of the stock, and the price at which the option can be exercised.

Puts and calls allow both buyers and sellers (writers) to speculate on the short-term movements of certain common stocks. Buyers obtain an option on the common stock for a small, known premium which is the maximum that the buyer can lose. If the buyer is correct about the price movements on the underlying assets, gains are magnified in relation to having bought (or sold short) the assets because a smaller investment is required. However, the buyer has only a short time in which to be correct. Writers (sellers) earn the premium as income, based on their beliefs about a stock. They win or lose, depending on whether their beliefs are correct or incorrect.

[17] Option expiry dates are expressed in terms of the month in which they expire. Option contracts expire on the Saturday following the third Friday of the month, so the third Friday is the last trading day for these instruments.

Options can be used in a variety of strategies, giving investors opportunities to manage their portfolios in ways that would be unavailable in the absence of such instruments. For example, since the most a buyer of a put or call can lose is the cost of the option, the buyer is able to truncate the distribution of potential returns. That is, after a certain point, no matter how much the underlying stock price changes, the buyer's position does not change. Some basic options strategies are discussed in Chapter 19.

Futures Contracts

Futures contracts have been available on commodities such as corn and wheat for a long time. Today, they are also readily available on several financial instruments, including stock market indexes, currencies, Treasury bills, banker's acceptances, and government bonds.

A **futures contract** is an agreement that provides for the future exchange of a particular asset between a buyer and a seller. The seller contracts to deliver the asset at a specified delivery date in exchange for a specified amount of cash from the buyer. Although the cash is not required until the delivery date, a "good faith deposit," called the margin, is required to reduce the chance of default by either party. The margin is small compared to the value of the contract.

Futures Contract
Agreement providing for the future exchange of a particular asset between a buyer and seller at a specified date for a specified amount.

Most futures contracts are not exercised. Instead, they are "offset" by taking a position opposite to the one initially undertaken. For example, a purchaser of a May Government of Canada bond futures contract can close out the position by selling an identical May contract before the delivery date, while a seller can close out the same position by purchasing that contract.

Most participants in futures are either hedgers or speculators. Hedgers seek to reduce price uncertainty over some future period. For example, by purchasing a futures contract, a hedger can lock in a specific price for the asset and be protected from adverse price movements. Similarly, sellers can protect themselves from downward price movements. Speculators, on the other hand, seek to profit from the uncertainty that will occur in the future. If prices are expected to rise, contracts will be purchased, and if prices are expected to fall, contracts will be sold. Correct anticipations can result in very large profits because only a small margin is required. Futures are discussed at length in Chapter 20.

In addition to traditional options and futures contracts, there also exist options on futures. Calls on futures give the buyer the right, but not the obligation, to assume the futures position.

SUMMARY

This summary relates to the learning objectives provided on page 27.

1. **Describe the major types of financial assets and how they are organized.**
Investors may invest either directly in non-marketable assets, money market instruments, capital market securities (divided into fixed-income and equity securities), and derivative securities, or indirectly in the form of investment company shares (e.g. mutual funds).

2. **Explain what non-marketable financial assets are.**
   Non-marketable financial assets are highly liquid, safe investments available from insured financial institutions or issued by the Canadian government. In contrast to marketable securities, these assets represent personal transactions between the owner and the issuer. Non-marketable financial assets are widely owned by investors and include savings deposits, GICs, and Canada Savings Bonds.
3. **Describe the important features of money market and capital market securities.**
   Money market investments are characterized as short-term, highly liquid, very safe investments. These include (but are not limited to) Treasury bills, commercial paper, Eurodollars, repurchase agreements, and banker's acceptances. Capital market investments have maturities in excess of one year and are of two types: fixed-income securities and equity securities. Fixed-income securities have a specified payment and/or repayment schedule and are issued by governments and corporations. Equity securities represent an ownership interest in a corporation and are of two forms: preferred stock and common stock.
4. **Distinguish between preferred stock and common stock.**
   Preferred stock, while technically an equity security, is often regarded by investors as a fixed-income type of security because of its stated (and fixed) dividend. Preferred stock has no maturity date but may be retired by calls or other means. Common stock (equity) represents the ownership of the corporation. The stockholder is the residual claimant in terms of both income and assets.
5. **Understand the basics of options and futures.**
   Options allow both buyers and sellers (writers) to speculate on and/or hedge the price movements of stocks for which these claims are available. Calls are multiple-month rights to purchase a common stock at a specified price, while puts are the same rights to sell. Futures contracts provide for the future exchange of a particular asset between a buyer and a seller. A recent innovation is options on futures.

KEY TERMS

Asset-backed securities (ABS)
Bonds
Bond rating
Book value
Calls
Call provision
Capital markets
Common stock
Convertible bonds
Corporate bonds
Debenture
Derivative securities
Dividends
Dividend yield
Extendible bonds
Fixed-income securities
Futures contract
Indirect investing
LEAPS
Liquidity
Money market
Options
Par value (Face value)
Payout ratio
P/E ratio
Preferred stock
Puts
Retractable bonds
Senior securities
Stock dividend
Stock split
Treasury bill
Treasury bond
Warrant
Zero coupon bond

ADDITIONAL RESOURCES

The best sources of information about the financial assets available to investors, changes in their characteristics, and new financial assets that become available are the financial press, including, but not limited to:

The Globe and Mail / Report on Business
National Post (Financial Post)
The Canadian Investment Review
Canadian Money Saver
Canadian Business
PROFIT
The Wall Street Journal
Business Week
Financial World
Forbes
Fortune
Kiplinger's Personal Finance Magazine
Money
Smart Money
Worth

In addition, the book *How to Invest in Canadian Securities*, published by the Canadian Securities Institute for the Investor Learning Centre of Canada (1997), provides an excellent overview of basic investment alternatives available to the average Canadian investor.

INVESTMENTS ON THE WEB

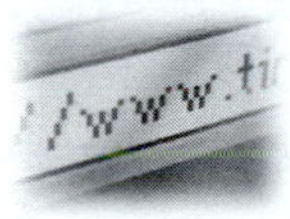

Canada Deposit Insurance Corporation (CDIC): <http://www.cdic.ca>
The Canadian Life and Health Compensation Corporation (CompCorp): <http://www.compcorp.ca>
The Property and Casualty Insurance Compensation Corporation (PACICC): <http://www.ibc.ca/english/pacicc.htm>
The Canadian Investor Protection Fund (CIPF): <http://www.cipf.ca>

REVIEW QUESTIONS

1. Outline the classification scheme for marketable securities used in the chapter. Explain each of the terms involved.
2. What is the difference between a savings deposit and a GIC?
3. What does it mean for Treasury bills to be sold at a discount?
4. Why is the common stockholder referred to as a "residual claimant"?
5. Do all common stocks pay dividends? Who decides?
6. Distinguish between a serial bond and a term bond.
7. What is meant by "indirect" investing?
8. Why should we expect that the six-month Treasury bill rate will be less than the six-month commercial paper rate?

9. What types of securities are traded on the money markets? What types are traded on the capital markets? Give examples of each type obtained from a daily business newspaper.
10. From the investor's perspective, what is the difference between a warrant and a call option?
11. What are the advantages and disadvantages of investing in Government of Canada bonds versus corporate bonds?
12. What are the differences between a Canada Savings Bond and a Government of Canada long-term bond?
13. Why is preferred stock referred to as a "hybrid" security?
14. What is meant by the term derivative security? What is the major determinant of the price of a derivative security?
15. What is meant by the term securitization? Give at least two examples of asset-backed securities.
16. Why are convertible and retractable features generally advantageous for bondholders? How do they pay for these privileges?
17. What is the value to investors of stock dividends and splits?
18. What are the advantages and disadvantages of being a holder of the common stock of Bombardier Inc. as opposed to owning a Bombardier bond?
19. Assume that a company whose stock you are interested in will pay regular quarterly dividends soon. Looking in *The Globe and Mail / Report on Business*, you see a dividend figure of $3.20 listed for this stock. The board of directors has declared the dividend payable on September 1, with a holder-of-record date of August 15. When must you buy the stock to receive the dividend, and how much will you receive if you buy 150 shares?
20. List three types of derivative securities. Explain the difference between each type.
21. Under what conditions might a bondholder utilize the *convertible* feature of a bond?
22. Under what conditions might a bondholder utilize the *retractable* feature of a bond?
23. How is it possible that an investor who buys shares in a company may make a profit even if the share price drops?
24. Do you think that a stock with a high dividend yield will be more or less risky than a stock that does not pay any dividend? Why?
25. Is the call provision on a bond an advantage to the investor or an advantage to the issuing corporation? Given your knowledge of risk and return, what effect should the call feature have on the pricing of a bond; in other words, will the bond offer a higher or lower rate of interest? Why?
26. From the corporation's perspective, what are the differences between a warrant and a call option? If the call option is exercised, what will happen to the share price of the underlying company? If the warrant is exercised, what might happen to the share price of the underlying company?
27. What do you think some of the contributing factors might be when a company's management determines what the dividend payout ratio will be?

PREPARING FOR YOUR PROFESSIONAL EXAMS

Special Note to Canadian Securities Course Students

Ensure that you have read and understood the following topics covered in this chapter:

Organizing financial assets, pp. 28–29
An international perspective, p. 29
Non-marketable financial assets, pp. 29–30
Money market securities, pp. 30–34
Capital market securities, pp. 34–47
Derivative securities, pp. 47–49
Taxation of interest, dividends, and capital gains income, pp. 55–56 (Appendix 2-A)

**Reading these CSC-related topics should provide you with additional understanding of CSC material. However, it should not be seen as a substitute for reading the CSC textbook itself, which is the basis for the CSC exam.*

CSC REGISTRATION QUESTIONS

The Canadian Securities Institute issued the following sample questions in the 1997 CSC registration package as a means for students to self-assess their understanding of CSC-related material.

1. The Canada Deposit Insurance Corporation is designed to protect ______________.
   a. owners of securities held by the Canadian Depository for Securities
   b. clients of eligible Canadian banks and trust companies
   c. clients of Canadian stock exchange member firms
   d. policyholders of Canadian life insurance companies
2. High yield bonds that are not investment grade are often called ________________.
   a. redeemable bonds
   b. junk bonds
   c. callable bonds
   d. municipal bonds
3. A 9.5 per cent bond has a yield of 9.75 per cent. The bond is selling at a price that is _________ par.
   a. higher than
   b. lower than
   c. the same as
4. If a convertible bond is said to be "selling off the stock," its price is __________ its stated par value.
   a. higher than
   b. lower than
   c. the same as

5. Two major types of participants in the futures markets are hedgers and ______.
6. A ______ is a deposit instrument that is usually non-redeemable.
7. (Refer to Appendix 2-A for this question.) Cash dividends from taxable Canadian corporations are grossed up by ______ for individual income tax purposes.
   a. the investor's federal tax rate
   b. 33 per cent
   c. 25 per cent
   d. 66 per cent
8. The main difference between a corporate bond and a corporate debenture is ______.
   a. price
   b. coupon
   c. yield
   d. security
9. Government of Canada Treasury bills are auctioned ______.
   a. at par
   b. on every second Thursday
   c. in three different maturities
   d. at a premium
10. Minimum denominations of Government Treasury bills are ______ those of CSB's.
    a. higher than
    b. lower than
    c. the same as
11. Briefly describe the chief difference between a bond and a debenture.
12. Briefly describe the chief difference between a call option and a put option.

APPENDIX 2-A

TAXATION OF INVESTMENT INCOME IN CANADA

General Information

The basic federal income tax rates (as of 1998) are:

1. 17 per cent for taxable income up to $29,590
2. $5,030 + 26 per cent on the next $29,590 up to $59,180
3. $12,724 + 29 per cent on any amount above $59,180.

In all provinces except Quebec, the provincial tax rate is levied as a percentage of the basic federal tax. For example, a BC resident in the 17 per cent bracket is also subject to a 50.5 per cent provincial tax resulting in a combined marginal tax rate of 17 per cent + [0.505 ÷ 17] = 25.585 per cent. The marginal tax rate is of importance in determining which investments offer higher after-tax yields.

Interest, Dividend, and Capital Gains Income

Interest income from debt securities (including bonds and money market securities) is taxable at the full marginal rate, however dividends and capital gains afford investors a tax break. Dividends (whether they are cash, stock, or reinvested dividends) received from Canadian corporations are taxable in the following manner for all provinces except Quebec. First, the amount of the dividend is "grossed-up" by 25 per cent to obtain the taxable amount of dividend which is used in determining net income. The taxpayer is then able to claim a tax credit (reduction in taxes payable) in the amount of 13.33 per cent of the taxable amount of dividend. Finally, the provincial tax is calculated after the tax credit is claimed.

For example, if an Ontario investor receives $100 in dividends, the grossed up amount of $125 would be added to taxable income. If the investor is in the 26 per cent bracket, this produces a federal tax figure of $125 × 0.26 or $32.50. This amount is then reduced by $16.66 (13.33 per cent of $125) to arrive at the federal taxes payable figure of $15.84. The 1998 Ontario provincial tax would be 45 per cent of $15.84 or $7.13, and total taxes payable would be $22.97, so the net dividend amount would be $77.03, which is well below this investor's combined marginal tax rate.[18] The marginal tax rates on dividends are lower than on interest and are often marginally lower than on capital gains, which enhances the investor's after-tax return.

Foreign dividends are usually taxed by the source country and there is an allowable credit which is essentially the lower of the foreign tax paid and the Canadian tax payable on foreign income subject to certain adjustments.

[18] Quebec calculates taxes payable on dividends differently. In particular, the federal tax payable is reduced further by a standard federal tax abatement (currently 16.5 per cent). For the example above, this amount would be 0.165 × $15.84 = $2.61, leaving federal taxes payable at $15.84 × $2.61 = $13.23. The provincial tax rate (assume 26 per cent) and provincial tax credit (rate is currently 8.87 per cent) are both applied to the grossed up amount of $125 which implies provincial tax of 0.26 × $125 = $32.50 less the credit of 0.0887 × $125 = $11.09, which leaves provincial taxes payable of $21.41 and total taxes payable of $13.23 + $21.41 = $34.64.

A capital gain arises from the disposition of capital assets for proceeds in excess of their cost. Only 75 per cent of the capital gain is taxable, provided the transaction involved a taxpayer whose ordinary business does not involve the trading of securities, or that Revenue Canada did not determine the trading to be speculative in nature. The general rule is that capital gains equal the proceeds from distribution minus the adjusted cost base (which includes commission costs, etc.) plus any costs of disposing of assets.

The adjusted cost base is complicated when shares were purchased at different prices and is based on the average cost method. For example, if 200 shares were purchased for $5 (including commission) and an additional 300 shares were purchased for $6 (including commission), then the average adjusted cost per share would be ($1,000 + $1,800)/500 = $5.60 per share. Taxes on disposition of debt securities are applied as above, however, the accrued interest portion of a bond purchase price is not included as part of the adjusted cost base and is treated as taxable income in the hands of the bond seller.

Capital losses cannot be claimed by the security holder unless ownership is transferred in writing to another person. One exception to this rule is where the security becomes worthless due to bankruptcy of the underlying company. Superficial losses are those that result from the sale and purchase of the same security within a given time frame and are not tax deductible. However, the taxpayer eventually receives the tax benefit since the amount of the superficial loss is added to the cost base of the repurchased shares, which lowers the ultimate capital gain. A superficial loss occurs when securities are sold at a loss but are repurchased and still held 30 days after the sale. They do not apply to losses resulting from leaving Canada, death of a taxpayer, expiry of an option, or a deemed disposition of securities by a trust or to a controlled corporation.

Certain items related to investment income are tax deductible including carrying charges such as interest on borrowed funds, investment counselling fees, fees paid for administration or safe custody of investments, safety deposit box charges, and accounting fees paid for recording investment income. Interest on borrowed funds is deductible only if the investor had a legal obligation to pay the interest, the purpose of the borrowing was to earn income and the income earned from the investment is not tax exempt. (Note: it does not need to be an arms-length transaction.) In addition, the interest charge:

1. Cannot exceed the amount of interest earned on debt securities unless they are convertible
2. Is disallowed as a deduction if it exceeds the grossed-up amount of preferred dividends
3. Is for the most part deductible if it is for the purchase of common shares.

Derivative Securities

When convertible features are exercised, it is not deemed to be a disposition of property, so no capital gain or loss is recorded. Instead, the adjusted cost base of the new shares will be that of the original securities. For example, if 100 preferred shares are purchased for a total cost of $5,000 and each share is convertible into ten common shares, the adjusted cost base of one common share (after conversion), will be $5,000 ÷ 100 or $50 ÷ 10 = $5 per share.

Warrants and rights may be acquired through direct purchase, by owning shares, or by purchasing units with rights or warrants attached. When they are purchased they are treated the same as convertibles, however, if they are the result of owning underlying shares, the adjusted cost base of the original shares is altered. When warrants or rights are not exercised, a capital gain or loss may result, unless they were acquired at zero cost.

There are two basic types of options — calls and puts. At the time of the sale of either option, the seller receives consideration for the option and has disposed of a right. This sale of a right generates a capital gain calculated as the cost of the option, which is nil or zero subtracted from the consideration received. As with all capital gains, only three quarters of it is included in income. The buyer or purchaser of either option has acquired a right with a cost equal to the amount of consideration paid. There are no further tax consequences to the buyer until the option is either exercised or allowed to expire.

If either option expires, then the buyer has disposed of it for no consideration. Since the disposition has occurred, the selling price is zero and the buyer has a capital loss equal to the amount paid to acquire the option subtracted from the selling price, which is zero.

If a call option is exercised, then the price paid to acquire the option is added to the price paid to acquire the underlying asset. The option holder now owns the underlying asset with a cost calculated as the price paid for the underlying asset plus the price paid for the option to acquire the asset. The seller of the underlying asset through the call option contract (the call seller) must add the price received for the option to the selling price of the asset that was sold. This increased selling price becomes the proceeds of disposition of the asset and a capital gain (or loss) is calculated by subtracting the original cost of the asset from these increased proceeds of disposition. When the original option was sold, the seller included a capital gain in their income as described by the above paragraph. This seller must now file an amended tax return if the option was sold in a year previous to the year the actual underlying asset was sold.

If a put option is exercised, the tax consequences are similar to the above. The purchaser of the asset (the put seller) has received consideration for the put option. Therefore the purchaser of the underlying asset deducts the amount received for the option and the cost of the underlying asset is calculated as the actual consideration paid to acquire the asset minus the amount received for the option to sell. Since the buyer of the asset through the put option (the put seller) has already reported a capital gain on the sale of the put option, an amended tax return must be filed to remove this income from the previous year. The seller of the underlying asset (the put buyer) has paid an amount for the put option and has received consideration for the actual sale of the asset. The selling price of the asset is reduced by the amount paid for the option. The seller calculates a capital gain (or loss) equal to the selling price of the asset minus the amount paid for the option minus the purchase price of the asset through exercise of the put option.

Profits or losses on hedging futures contracts, which is normally part of risk management for businesses, are considered normal business income or loss and are included, or deductible, in the annual financial statements.

For the general investor, speculating in futures contracts can generate either capital gains or losses or normal income. The choice of which approach to take is left open to the speculator. The only requirement is that once a choice has been made, that selection must be adhered to in the future. One of the main considerations in this selection is that if the investor is using borrowed funds for the purpose of speculating in futures contracts, the interest on the borrowed funds is deductible against the income that is being generated. Therefore, the normal investor must select income treatment for speculation purposes. If capital gains treatment was selected, and the investor was using borrowed funds, the interest on these funds is not deductible.

INVESTMENT FUNDS

LEARNING OBJECTIVES

After reading this chapter, you will be able to

1. Distinguish between direct and indirect investing.
2. Define open-end and closed-end investment funds.
3. State the major types of mutual funds and give their features.
4. Explain the transactions behind indirect investments.
5. Understand how the performance of investment funds is measured.
6. Discuss the opportunities for investing indirectly internationally.

CHAPTER PREVIEW

Investors may choose to invest either directly or indirectly in the instruments that we described in Chapter 2. In this chapter, we focus on investing indirectly through investment funds, chiefly through the buying and selling of mutual funds. You will learn about the two major types of investment funds (open-end and closed-end), the transactions behind them, and how we measure the performance of these funds. Finally, we turn to opportunities for investing indirectly internationally and explore recent trends such as "supermarkets" and the World Wide Web.

INVESTING INDIRECTLY

Basically, households have three choices with regard to savings:

1. Hold the liabilities of traditional intermediaries, such as banks, trust companies, and insurance companies. These include savings accounts, GICs, and so forth.
2. Hold securities directly by purchasing stocks and bonds through brokers and other intermediaries.
3. Hold securities indirectly through investment companies and pension funds.

There has been a pronounced shift toward indirect investing in North America in recent years.[1] Households have increasingly turned away from the direct holding of securities and the liabilities of traditional intermediaries and toward indirect holdings of assets through pension funds and mutual funds.

Figure 3-1
Net Assets — Canadian Mutual Funds ($billions) December 31st, 1987–98

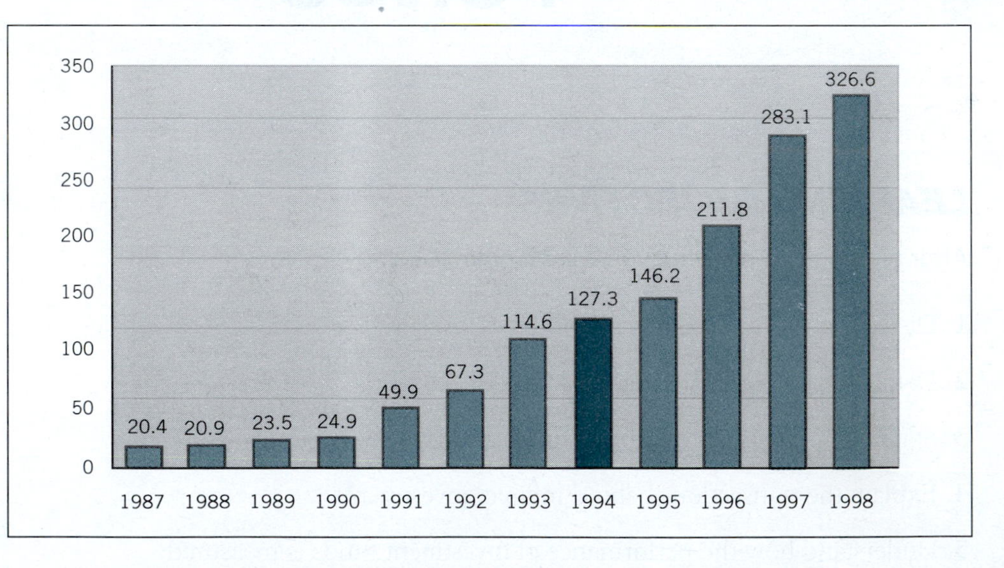

Source: The Investment Funds Institute of Canada (IFIC)

[1] For the purposes of this text, we refer to indirect investing in the sense of indirect investments in financial assets through the use of investment funds. We would note that of the Canadian Securities Course refers to indirect investment as the purchase of financial securities that are issued by entities (such as corporations or governments) to fund "direct" investment in real assets such as purchasing land or acquiring new machinery.

Over 25 per cent of Canadian families now own investment funds of some type. Net sales of mutual funds totalled $35.4 billion in 1998, down from $51.9 billion in the previous year. However, mutual fund assets increased to $326.6 billion by the end of 1998 from $283.3 billion at the end of 1997. In fact, mutual fund assets in Canada have increased approximately sixteenfold over the 12-year period ending December 31, 1998 — from $20.4 billion in 1987. In the United States, mutual funds grew tenfold during the 1980s to $1 trillion, and by early 1997 the amount approximated $3 trillion. The dramatic growth in mutual fund assets in Canada is clearly demonstrated in Figure 3-1. This may well be the most important trend in the 1990s affecting the average household with regard to their investing activities and programs.

The rising ownership of pension fund assets and mutual fund shares, an alternative to the direct investing methods discussed in Chapter 2, is very important to every investor in accomplishing his or her investing goals. Investors now rely heavily on indirect investing. A significant contributor to the growth in investment fund assets in Canada has been the steady increase in contributions to Registered Retirement Savings Plans (RRSPs) by Canadian investors, as demonstrated in the Real-World Returns box below. In 1997, Canadians contributed $27.4 billion to RRSPs, representing a 71 per cent increase over 1991, but RRSP contributions were expected to decline in 1998. The article suggests the 1998 decline is due partly to investor apprehension in response to the extreme volatility displayed by stock markets during that year. The nature of RRSPs is discussed in detail in the CSC Notes box later in this chapter.

There are several advantages associated with RRSPs. First, they allow taxpayers to reduce taxable income during high taxation years. Second, they allow investors to shelter certain types of income from taxation by transferring them into an RRSP. Third, RRSPs are tax efficient mechanisms for accumulation of retirement funds, with the funds earning income on a tax-free basis, thus allowing deferment of some taxes. Finally, they provide investors with an opportunity to split retirement income (through spousal RRSPs), which may result in lower total tax payments.

INVESTING INDIRECTLY THROUGH INVESTMENT FUNDS

An investment fund such as a mutual fund is a clear alternative for an investor seeking to own stocks and bonds. Rather than purchase securities and manage a portfolio, investors can, in effect, indirectly invest by putting their money into an investment fund, and allowing their investment advisor to do all the work and make all the decisions (for a fee, of course). Investment funds are ideal for investors:

- With small capital bases who cannot properly diversify on their own
- Who do not have adequate time to manage their own investments
- Who do not wish to manage their own portfolio.

Indirect investing in this discussion refers to the buying and selling of the units of investment funds that consist of portfolios of securities. Investors who purchase units of a particular fund managed by an investment company are buying an ownership interest in the fund portfolio and are entitled to a portion of the dividends, interest, and capital gains generated.

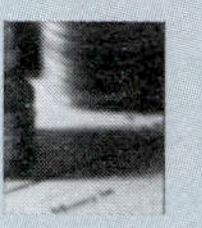

REAL-WORLD RETURNS

Fewer Canadians Contributing to RRSPs

Registered retirement savings plan contributions were expected to fall in 1999 for the first time this decade. Stock market volatility and falling real incomes are expected to put a damper on what is usually an annual spree in advance of the February 28 deadline.

In the 1997 tax year, 6.1 million of us socked away a combined $27.4-billion for our golden years. However, that was up only 2 per cent from $26.8-billion in 1996, the smallest increase in a decade marked by several double-digit jumps. In 1999 some expect to see the first decline in RRSP contributions since 1990.

"An awful lot of Canadians are looking now at their RRSP options, and they don't like any of them," said Dan Richards, president of Toronto consulting firm Marketing Solutions. Stocks, he said, are considered too pricey, while low interest rates make other options, such as guaranteed income certificates, less than appealing.

RRSP Contributions

Year	# of Potential Contributors (millions)	% Contributing	Total Contributions ($ billions)	% Change from Previous Year
1991	14.4	32%	$16.0	+23.5%
1992	15.5	31	17.3	+8.0
1993	16.3	30	20.3	+17.7
1994	16.9	31	22.0	+8.4
1995	17.5	32	23.7	+7.8
1996	18.0	33	26.8	+12.9
1997	19.1	n/a	27.4	+2.4

The number of contributors relates to nominal contributions and excludes rollovers. Dollar amounts are in 1997 figures.

Source: Statistics Canada

But there are some other factors at play, Mr. Richards said. One is the decline in disposable incomes in the country. In 1990, before the most recent recession, the average Canadian had roughly $18,600 in after-tax pay. That number fell by almost $1,200, to just more than $17,400 in 1997.

The savings rate — the share of our incomes we tuck away — has fallen to zero from about 10 per cent at the end of the 1980s.

Mr. Richards said that he expects more and more people to exploit the carry-forward provision introduced in 1991, allowing those who don't maximize their contributions to use that room in future years. Before the rule existed, people had to either use all their contribution room every year, or lose it forever.

The problem is that the rule encourages many to postpone contributing year after year. "And the fact is the vast majority of people who say they'll catch up next year never catch up," Mr. Richards said. Canadians, he said, simply don't plan to meet RRSP targets the way they plan to pay their mortgage or rent.

The unused contribution room continues to pile up. In 1991, Canadians collectively had $45.3-billion worth of space and used 27 per cent of it that tax year. By 1996, the available space had exploded to nearly $190-billion, only 12 per cent of which was used.

But this year's numbers are expected to be down for another reason: the wild time the stock markets have had. Bewildered by the volatility, Canadians are thinking twice before handing large sums over to a fund manager.

Mutual fund sales tumbled by nearly a third in 1998, to $35.4-billion from a record $51.9-billion in 1997. Global markets took the blame, as financial troubles in Asia and Russia whacked North American equities around like ping-pong balls.

"The August/September volatility in 1998 has really caused people to question where they're putting their money," said Mark Tiffen, vice-president of marketing at Mackenzie Financial Corp. Mr. Tiffen said many investors are taking their time and seeking out funds that have been consistent performers.

A survey taken by Royal Trust showed the same trend: fewer Canadians are planning to make an RRSP contribution in 1999. Forty-four per cent of the survey's 1,200 respondents said they were planning to make a contribution in 1999, down from 48 per cent in last year's survey.

But perhaps the biggest sign that the RRSP machine is a little off the tracks is that spending on advertising by RRSP sellers is also expected to fall in 1999 from 1998's estimated $70-million.

"The TV advertising has subsided quite a bit," said FundMonitor.com's Dan Hallett. People were bombarded a year ago, but at some point it doesn't have an effect any more.

Source: Excerpted from Mark MacKinnon, "RRSP Contributions Expected to Fall this Year," The Globe and Mail / Report on Business, *February 15, 1999, p. B7. Reprinted with permission from* The Globe and Mail.

Shareholders must also pay a share of the fund expenses and its management fee, which will be deducted from the portfolio's earnings as it flows back to the shareholders.

The contrast between direct and indirect investing is illustrated in Figure 3-2, which shows that indirect investing essentially accomplishes the same thing as direct investing. The difference is that the investment companies that manage and sell the fund units stand between investors and the portfolio of securities. Although technical qualifications exist, the point about indirect investing is that investors gain and lose through the investment fund's activities in the same manner that they would gain and lose from holding a portfolio directly. The differences are the costs (any sales charges plus the management fee) and the additional services gained from the investment fund, such as record-keeping and cheque-writing privileges.

The choice between direct or indirect investing is very important to all investors. Since each has advantages and disadvantages, the choice may not be straightforward. Investors can be classified as active (those who are interested in participating in managing their portfolios), or passive (those who do not get involved in managing their portfolios). Moreover, it is possible to have both classes of investors invest directly or indirectly.

The line between direct and indirect investing is becoming blurred. For example, investors can invest in investment funds directly through their brokerage accounts, generally at no additional expense. In addition, brokerage firms offer alternatives to mutual funds in several forms, which will be discussed in Chapter 5.

Figure 3-2 Direct Versus Indirect Investing

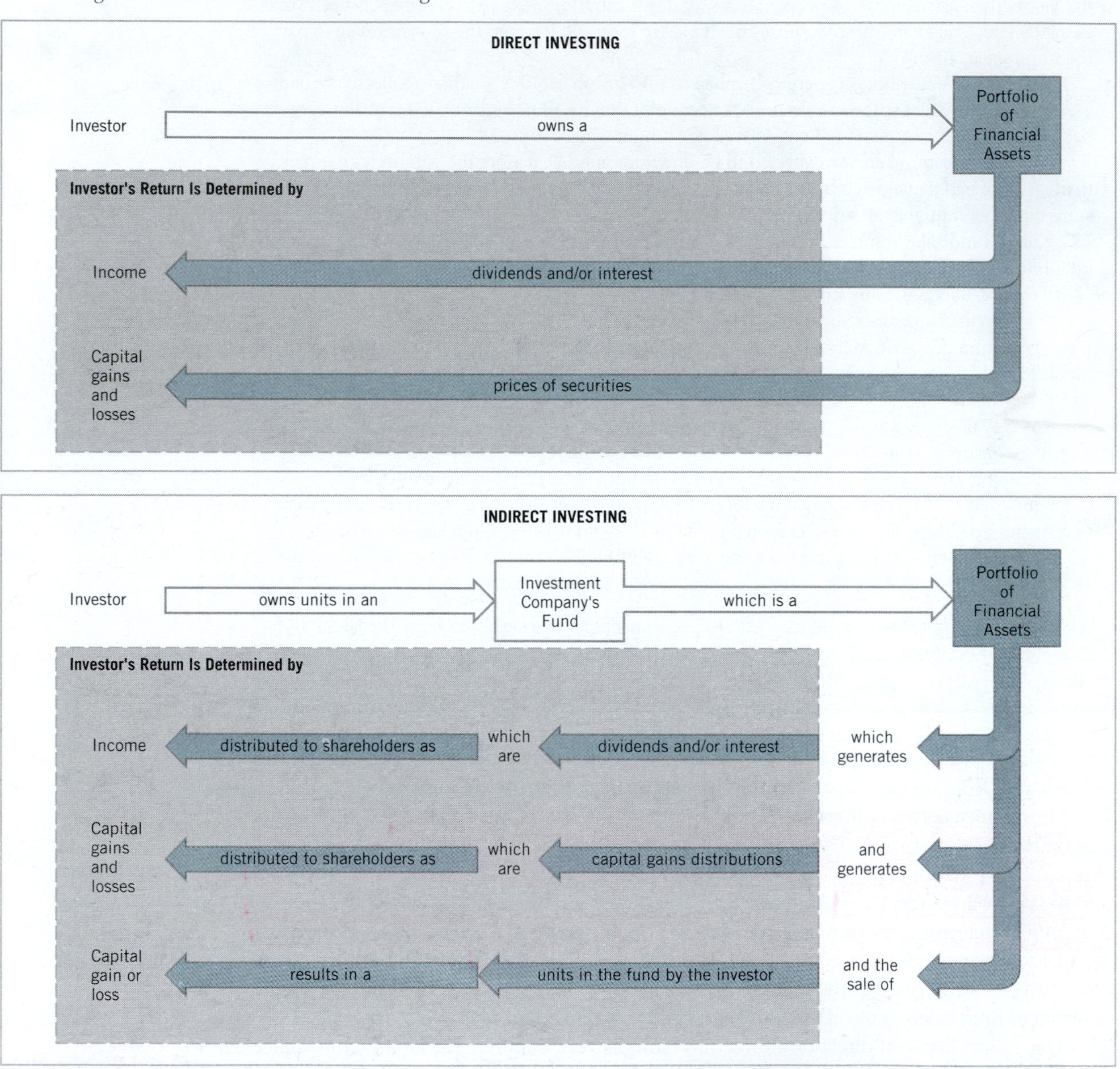

Investment Fund
A financial company or trust fund that sells shares in itself or units of the trust fund to the public and uses the funds to invest in a portfolio of securities such as money market instruments, stocks, and bonds.

WHAT IS AN INVESTMENT FUND?

An **investment fund** sells shares or units in a trust fund to the public and invests these funds in a portfolio of securities such as money market instruments, stocks, and bonds. By pooling the funds of thousands of investors, a widely diversified portfolio of financial assets can be purchased. Investment companies usually manage several funds simultaneously and offer their customers a variety of services.

CSC NOTES

Registered Retirement Savings Plans (RRSPs)

Registered Retirement Savings Plans (RRSPs) are important tax deferral investments that allow Canadian taxpayers to make annual tax-deductible contributions up to predetermined limits. The income earned is tax-free as long as it remains in a plan that is registered with Revenue Canada and meets the 80 per cent Canadian content requirement.

Most individuals contribute to their RRSPs by purchasing one or more mutual funds that are directed by fund managers. Some investors prefer self-directed RRSPs, which allow them to contribute certain acceptable securities into registered plans that are administered for a fee, but investors direct the investment transactions themselves.

RRSPs are trust accounts held for the investor's benefit for use upon retirement and the funds cannot be withdrawn prior to retirement without paying a withholding tax. In addition, RRSPs cannot be used as collateral for loans. RRSP contributions must be made within 60 days of year end and are limited to $13,500 (at present) or 18 per cent of the previous year's earnings, whichever is less (i.e., the dollar limit [presently $13,500] less the previous year's pension adjustment and past service pension adjustment plus the unused RRSP deduction room).

A penalty tax of 1 per cent per month is levied on "over-contributions" of $2,000 or more — this amount was $8,000 prior to 1996. When a plan holder contributes securities already owned to an RRSP (referred to as a "contribution in kind"), it is considered to be a deemed disposition. The taxpayer pays taxes on any capital gains but is unable to claim any capital losses that result.

Married taxpayers may contribute to RRSPs for their spouses to the extent that they have not used up their maximum contribution to their plans and this does not affect the contribution limits of the spouse. For example, if a wife contributes $9,000 of her $12,000 limit to her own plan, she may also contribute $3,000 to her husband's plan, without affecting his contribution limits. The proceeds from de-registering a spousal plan are taxable income for the spouse (not the contributor), except for contributions made in the year of de-registration and the two previous calendar years.

Some pension income can be transferred to RRSPs tax free and without affecting contribution limits:

1. Direct lump sum transfers from Registered Pension Plans (RPPs) and other RRSPs
2. Payments made to an RRSP when a person receives a retiring allowance are subject to limits of $2,000 for each year of service after 1988 ($3,500 limit for service before 1989, reduced to $2,000 for each year the employee contributed to an RPP)
3. Direct or indirect annual transfers of up to $6,000 from RPPs to spousal RRSPs for 1989 to 1994; however, the RPP income is added to the taxpayer's income and a deduction is claimed for the amount transferred to the spousal RRSP.

An RRSP holder may de-register the plan at any time, but mandatory de-registration is required at the age of 69 (which was reduced from 71 in 1996). There are several available options for de-registering RRSPs upon retirement. The least desirable from a tax perspective is to withdraw the full amount, which is then fully taxable as income in that year. To spread out the taxes paid on withdrawn funds, the proceeds from the plan may be used to purchase a life annuity with a guaranteed term or a fixed-term annuity that provides annual benefits to age 90. Similarly, the funds may be used to purchase a Registered Retirement Income Fund (RRIF) that provides annual income to age 90 or life.

Subsequent to retirement, if a plan owner dies, remaining benefits on an annuity or RRIF can be transferred to a spouse or child, or else the value is included in the deceased's income in the year of death and is fully taxable.

RRIF holders must withdraw and pay income tax on a set fraction of the total assets in the fund (the annual minimum amount). The annual fraction is determined by a formula designed to provide benefits for a desired term. However, the owner may choose to increase the payout. A taxpayer may own more than one RRIF and they may be self-directed if desired.

EXAMPLE: FIDELITY INVESTMENTS

Fidelity Investments is the largest mutual fund company in the world; among its more than 200 funds is the Equity-Income Fund. As stated in its prospectus, "Equity-Income is a mutual fund: an investment that pools shareholders' money and invests it toward a specified goal. The fund is governed by a board of trustees, which is responsible for protecting the interests of shareholders."

An investment fund acts as a conduit, flowing dividends, interest, and realized capital gains through to its unit holders who pay taxes on this income at their own marginal tax rates. In effect, fund owners are treated as if they held the securities in the fund's portfolio. During the year funds make capital gains and losses when they sell securities. These gains are taxable in the hands of the investor. Therefore, investors should determine if a capital gains distribution is pending before purchasing a fund, since this will result in a decline in the fund's value corresponding to the amount of the tax liability incurred.

In addition to taxes on income earned by the investment fund, when a fund owner redeems the shares or units in a fund, the transaction is considered a disposition for tax purposes, and is subject to capital gains or losses. A complication arises due to the reinvestment of interest and dividends, which implies that investors (or their investment advisors) must keep track of the actual purchase prices of all units in a fund.

Most Canadian investment funds fall under the jurisdiction of the securities acts of the provinces in which they operate. Since most funds continually issue new shares, they are in a continuous state of primary distribution, and must annually file a prospectus or simplified prospectus. Usually, funds file simplified prospectuses if they comply with National Policy Statement No. 39, which concerns restrictions on the fund's investments. The prospectus must contain all material information and must be amended when material changes occur. Fund buyers must receive copies of this document no later than two business days after an agreement of purchase has been made.

Investment fund managers, distributors, and their sales personnel must be registered with the securities commissions in which they do business, and must adhere to industry code of practice guidelines. Salespeople must have successfully completed the CSC or the education program offered by the Investment Funds Institute of Canada (IFIC).

INVESTING *tip*

Investors who purchase plans through large one-time (lump sum) payments have 48 hours from the time of receipt of confirmation, or two business days after receipt of the prospectus, to rescind the transaction. Investors entering into contractual plans, which require contributions at regular time intervals, have 60 days after receipt of the prospectus or confirmation to rescind their purchase. Rescission investors are entitled to receive the net asset value (NAV) of securities purchased as well as sales charges levied. Rescission is only available on amounts under statutory limits — for example, in Ontario under $50,000 — and the investor must notify the dealer in writing.

TYPES OF INVESTMENT FUNDS

All investment funds begin by selling shares or units in the associated trust fund to the public. Most are managed by investment companies which offer professional supervision of the portfolio as one of the benefits.

Closed-End Investment Funds

A **closed-end investment fund** usually sells no additional shares after the initial public offering (IPO). Therefore, the fund capitalization is fixed unless a new public offering is made. The shares of a closed-end fund trade in the secondary markets — that is, on the exchanges — exactly like any other stock. To buy and sell, investors use their brokers, paying the current price at which the shares are selling plus brokerage commissions, or receiving that price less the commissions.

Closed-End Investment Fund
An investment fund with a fixed capitalization whose shares trade on exchanges and over-the-counter (OTC) markets.

Because shares of closed-end funds trade on stock exchanges, their prices are determined by the forces of supply and demand. Interestingly, however, the market price is seldom equal to the actual per-share value of the closed-end shares. We examine the issue of closed-end discounts and premiums later in the chapter.

Closed-end funds have been around for a long time; in fact, they were a popular investment before the great crash of 1929. After that they lost favour and were relatively unimportant until they started to attract significant investor interest again following the crash of 1987. Since 1986, for example, the number of closed-end funds in the US grew fourfold, exceeding 300 by 1992, and assets amounted to $133 billion by mid-1996. However, only five new closed-end funds of any type were launched in 1995, and none in the first half of 1996. There were only 17 closed-end funds in Canada by the end of 1997.

Open-End Investment Funds (Mutual Funds)

Open-end investment funds (or **mutual funds**) account for over 90 per cent of aggregate funds invested in Canada. As stated earlier, the growth in mutual funds and their assets has been one of the important developments in recent years. The number of mutual funds has grown rapidly as well. At the beginning of 1988, there were 294 Canadian mutual funds, with assets totalling $20.4 billion, and by the end of 1997 there were 1,023 funds, with total assets of $283 billion. Growth in the United States was even more spectacular, where the number of mutual funds increased from 564 in 1980 to approximately 7,000 with total assets exceeding $3 trillion by the beginning of 1997.

Open-End Investment Fund
An investment fund whose capitalization constantly changes as new shares or trust units are sold and outstanding units are redeemed. Popularly known as mutual funds.

As mentioned above, mutual funds are formed either by creating a mutual fund company and selling shares in it, or by creating a mutual fund trust and selling "units" in the mutual fund trust. Mutual funds continue to sell their treasury shares or units to investors after the initial sale that starts the fund. The capitalization of an open-end investment fund is continually changing as it continually issues and redeems shares or units on demand. This right of redemption is the hallmark of open-end funds. In fact, that is what makes it open-ended. As new investors buy additional shares or units and owners cash in by selling their shares or units back to the company.

Mutual Funds
The popular name for open-end investment funds whose capitalization constantly changes as new shares are sold and outstanding shares are redeemed.

Mutual funds are purchased in two ways:

1. Directly from a fund company by mail, telephone, or at office locations
2. Indirectly from a sales agent, including securities firms, banks, life insurance companies, and financial planners.

Mutual funds may be affiliated with an underwriter, who usually has an exclusive right to distribute shares to investors. Most underwriters distribute shares through broker/dealer firms.

Most mutual funds are corporations or trusts formed by an investment advisory firm that selects the board of trustees (directors) for the company. In turn, the trustees hire a separate management company, normally the investment advisory firm, to manage the fund. The management company is contracted by the investment company to perform necessary research and to manage the portfolio, as well as to handle the administrative chores. For that it receives a fee.

There are economies of scale in managing portfolios — expenses rise as assets under management increase but not at the same rate as revenues. Because investment managers can oversee various amounts of money with few additional costs, management companies seek to increase the size of the fund(s) being managed. Most investment companies operate several different funds simultaneously. Investors can choose from a large number of mutual fund complexes. A fund complex is a group or family of funds managed by the same fund management company.

EXAMPLE: INVESTORS GROUP AND ROYAL MUTUAL FUNDS INC.

As of February 1999, **Investors Group** was the largest mutual fund company in Canada with total net assets exceeding $35 billion. **Royal Mutual Funds Inc.**, a subsidiary of the Royal Bank of Canada, was the second largest company, with assets of over $29 billion. At that time Investors Group offered investors a choice of over 50 funds, while Royal offered over 40. These included a variety of the categories of funds described in the subsequent sections of this chapter.

Mutual funds are the most popular form of investment funds for the average investor. One reason is the small minimum investment requirements. Most funds require a minimum initial investment of $1,000 to get started, although some larger funds only need as little as $200. In addition, most funds that are RRSP eligible have a lower required initial investment for RRSP contributions. After the initial investment minimum contributions are typically much lower.

EXAMPLE: INVESTORS GROWTH PLUS PORTFOLIO

Investors Group's Investors Growth Plus Portfolio requires a minimum initial investment of $1,000, but only $500 if the fund is purchased for an RRSP. Subsequent contributions must be in amounts of $50 or more (whether for an RRSP or not).

Net Asset Value (NAV)
The total market value of the securities in an investment company's portfolio divided by the number of investment fund units currently outstanding.

Owners of fund units can sell them back to the company any time they choose; the mutual fund is legally obligated to redeem them. Investors purchase new units and redeem their existing ones at the **net asset value (NAV)** plus (less) commission fees. The NAV for any investment fund unit is computed by calculating the total market value of the securities in the portfolio, subtracting any accounts payable, and dividing by the number of fund shares or units currently outstanding.[2]

[2] Total market value of the portfolio is equal to the sum of the product of each security's current market price multiplied by the number of shares of that security owned by the fund.

EXAMPLE: NAV OF FIDELITY'S EQUITY-INCOME FUND

Using the numbers for **Fidelity**'s Equity-Income Fund for the year 1996,[3] the NAV is calculated as:

NAV, year-end 1995	$30.89
Income from investment operations	
net investment income	.93
net realized and unrealized gain	9.65
Total from investment operations	$10.58
Less Distributions	
from net investment income	(.96)
from net realized gain	(1.36)
Total distribution	(2.32)
NAV, end of period	$39.15

As this example shows, the net asset value is the per unit value of the portfolio of securities held by the investment fund. Over the course of the year this will change as the value of the securities held changes and as income from the securities is received.

MAJOR TYPES OF MUTUAL FUNDS

There are two major types of mutual funds:

1. Money market mutual funds (short-term funds)
2. Equity and bond & income funds (long-term funds).

These two types of funds parallel our discussion in Chapter 2 of money markets and capital markets. Money market funds concentrate on short-term investing by holding portfolios of money market assets, whereas equity and bond & income funds concentrate on longer term investing by holding mostly capital market assets. We will discuss each of these types of mutual funds in turn.

Money Market Funds

A major innovation in the investment company industry has been the creation, and subsequent phenomenal growth, of **money market funds (MMFs)**, which are open-end investment funds whose portfolios consist of money market instruments. Created in 1974, when interest rates were at record-high levels, MMFs grew tremendously in 1981–82 when short-term interest rates were again at record levels. Investors seeking to earn these high short-term rates found they generally could not do so directly because money market securities were

Money Market Funds (MMFs)
Open-end investment (mutual) funds that invest in short-term money market instruments such as Treasury bills, commercial paper, and short-term government bonds.

3 Equity-Income data is based on January 31 as the year end. Therefore, 1995 covers February 1995 through January 1996.

only available in large denominations, and so they turned to MMFs. By June 30 of 1997, the total assets of Canadian MMFs was $31.7 billion, accounting for 12.3 per cent of the total assets of all Canadian mutual fund assets.

The objective of MMFs is to achieve a high level of income and liquidity through investment in short-term money market instruments such as Treasury bills, commercial paper, and short-term government bonds. These funds are attractive to investors seeking low risk and high liquidity. The average maturity of money market portfolios ranges from one to three months.

Investors in money market funds earn and are credited with interest daily. The shares can be redeemed at any time by phone or wire. Money market funds (MMFs) provide investors with a chance to earn the going rates in the money market while enjoying broad diversification and great liquidity. The rates have varied as market conditions changed. The important point is that their yields correspond to current market conditions. Although investors may assume little risk because of the diversification and quality of these instruments, money market funds are not insured. Banks and other financial institutions have emphasized this point in competing with money market funds for the savings of investors.

Equity and Bond & Income Funds

The board of directors (or trustees) of an investment fund must specify the objective that the fund will pursue in its investment policy. The companies try to follow a consistent investment policy, according to their specified objective(s), which may have a great deal of influence on the typical investor's purchase decision.

EXAMPLE: INVESTMENT POLICY AT ROYAL DIVIDEND FUND

The objective of the **Royal Bank of Canada**'s Royal Dividend Fund is to invest primarily in common and preferred shares of major Canadian companies with above average dividend yields. It seeks to strike a balance between regular dividend income that benefits from the preferential tax treatment given to dividends, and modest long-term capital growth. Given these objectives it is not surprising to see the fund's top ten holdings as of June 30, 1998 consisted of several large financial and utility companies, since organizations in both of these industries have traditionally maintained relatively high dividend payments to shareholders. In particular the fund's top ten holdings included five large Canadian financial companies (Bank of Montreal, the Canadian Imperial Bank of Commerce, the Toronto Dominion Bank, the Bank of Nova Scotia, and Power Corporation), as well as two large utility companies (BCE Incorporated and Telus Corporation).

EXAMPLE: BALANCING GROWTH AND INCOME AT INVESTORS GROUP

The investment objective for **Investors Group**'s Investor Growth Plus Portfolio mutual fund is to achieve a balanced portfolio seeking long-term capital growth combined with a modest level of current income. It provides income and balanced growth by holding a portfolio of six of Investors Group's fixed-income and growth-oriented equity funds. It also offers international diversification and potential foreign currency gains. It may be suitable for investors looking for moderate to high growth, who can accept some variability in returns.

The holdings of this fund at the end of 1998 reflected this objective of balancing growth and income. At that time the portfolio was comprised of a mixture of growth-oriented assets (Investors Canadian Equity Fund [15 per cent], Investors US Growth Fund [15 per cent]), and income-oriented assets (Investors Global Bond Fund [30 per cent], Investors Government Bond Fund [20 per cent], Investors Corporate Bond Fund [10 per cent], Investors Real Property Fund [10 per cent]). The holdings also reflect the international diversification referred to in the fund objectives.

The following list identifies and describes several of the major categories of investment objectives, most of which relate to equity and bond & income funds. Investors in these funds have a wide range of investment objectives from which to choose. Traditionally, investors have favoured growth funds, which strive for capital appreciation, or balanced funds, which seek both income and capital appreciation. Today's investors can choose from global funds (either bonds or stocks), precious metal funds, mortgage funds, bond funds, and so forth.

- **Money Market Funds:** Objective is to achieve a high level of income and liquidity through investment in short-term money market instruments such as T-bills, commercial paper, and short-term government bonds. These funds will be attractive to investors seeking low risk and high liquidity.
- **Mortgage Funds:** Riskier than money market funds since terms of investments may be five years or greater, so there is more interest rate risk (although it is less than most bond funds which have longer maturities).
- **Bond Funds:** Primary goals are income and safety. However, they are still subject to capital gains and losses due to inherent interest rate risk.
- **Dividend Funds:** Objective is to benefit from the tax advantage afforded by dividends. Therefore, they are not that appropriate for RRSPs or RRIFs where the credit cannot be applied. Price changes tend to be driven by changes in interest rates and general market trends.
- **Balanced Funds:** Main objective is to provide a mixture of safety, income, and capital appreciation. Usually, the prospectus stipulates minimum and maximum weighting in each asset class.
- **Asset Allocation Funds:** Similar objectives to balanced funds, but they are usually not restricted to holding specified minimum percentages in any class of investment.

- **Equity or Common Stock Funds:** Primary objective is capital gains. The bulk of assets are in common shares, although they maintain limited amounts of other assets for liquidity, income, and diversification purposes. Equity funds may vary greatly in degree of risk and growth objectives.
- **Specialty Funds:** These funds seek capital gains and are willing to forego broad diversification benefits in the hopes of achieving them. They typically concentrate on companies in one industry, one segment of the capital market, or in one geographical location.
- **International or Global Funds:** These can be considered subsets of the specialty finds, and invest in markets that offer the best prospects, regardless of location. They carry the additional risk of foreign exposure.
- **Real Estate Funds:** Invest in income-producing property in order to achieve long-term growth through capital appreciation and the reinvestment of income. The valuation of real estate funds is done infrequently (monthly or quarterly) and is based on appraisals of properties in the portfolio. They are less liquid than other funds and may require investors to give advance notice of redemption.
- **Ethical Funds:** These funds are relatively new and are guided by moral criteria that may prevent the funds from investing in companies that produce tobacco, for example.

Figure 3-3 shows that Canadian and foreign equity funds constitute over 50 per cent of the assets of Canadian mutual funds in June 1997. The nature of these equity funds can vary significantly and it is common to categorize equity funds based on investment objectives such as "growth" and "growth and income." These categorizations may change in the future as many observers believe it is more important to describe a fund's investment style and actual portfolio holdings rather than state that the fund is seeking "growth of capital," which could be accomplished in several different ways. As part of this new trend, Morningstar, Inc., a Chicago mutual fund research firm, decided at the end of 1996 to use only nine categories for US stock funds. These categories, such as large cap, mid cap, small cap, value, and growth, are intended to describe investment styles.[4]

Most stock funds can be divided into two categories based on their approach to selecting stocks — value funds and growth funds. A value fund generally looks for stocks that are cheap on the basis of standard fundamental analysis yardsticks, such as earnings, book value, and dividend yield. Growth funds, on the other hand, seek companies that are expected to show rapid future growth in earnings, even if current earnings are poor or even non-existent.

Value funds and growth funds tend to perform well at different times. Therefore, fund investors should distinguish between the two types, which is not always easy to do. A more risk-averse investor worrying about a market decline may wish to emphasize value funds, while more aggressive investors seeking good performance in an expected market rise might favour growth funds. Given the evidence on efficient markets, the best strategy could be to buy both types of funds. However, there is some evidence to suggest that value stocks outperform growth stocks over the long run. These and other issues relating to market efficiency are considered in Chapter 10.

---

[4] "Cap" refers to capitalization, or market value for a company, calculated as the price of the stock times the total number of shares outstanding. A mutual fund that invests in stocks with large market capitalizations would be a large cap fund, while a small cap fund is one that invests in companies with small market capitalizations.

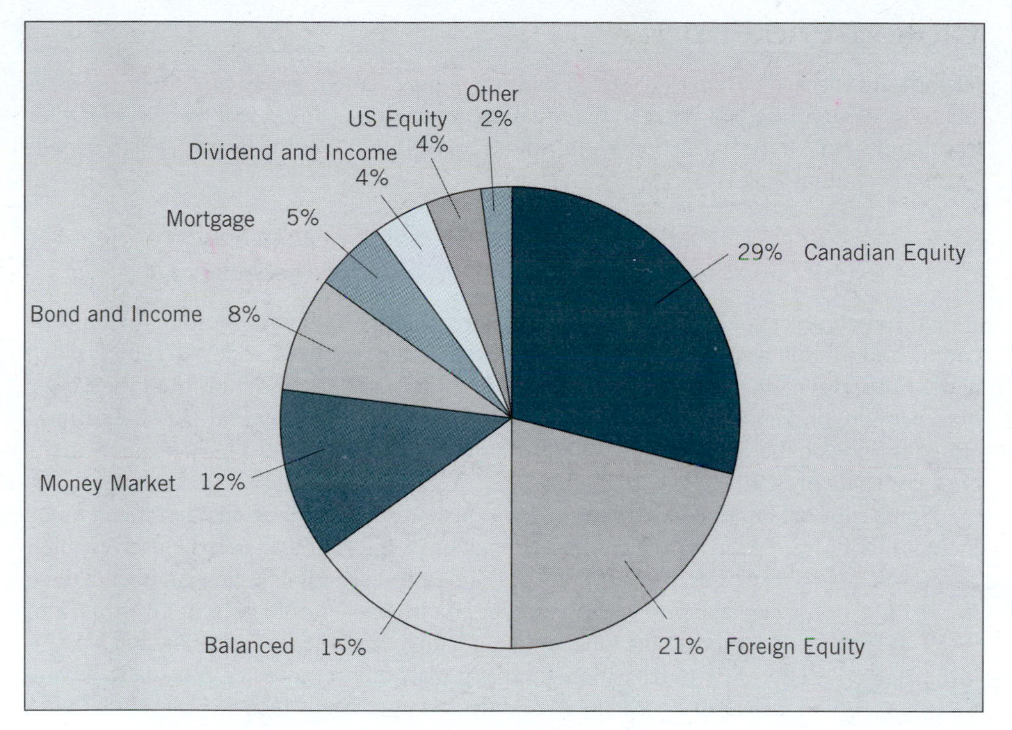

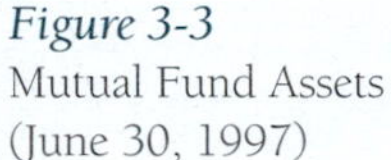
Figure 3-3
Mutual Fund Assets
(June 30, 1997)

Source: Investment Funds Institute of Canada (IFIC).

While Figure 3-3 and the discussion above provide some useful guidelines for investors regarding what particular types of funds are all about, one must be wary of reading too much into the classification of a fund into a particular category. For example, it may be surprising to some readers to observe that two of the top ten holdings of the Royal Dividend Fund referred to in the example "Investment Policy at Royal Dividend Fund" above consisted of Government of Canada bonds (which pay interest and not dividends). This is not uncommon among funds and it is typical to see funds comprised of securities that do not appear to be obvious choices for inclusion in that portfolio based upon the fund name or objectives. This illustrates two important points regarding mutual funds and other professionally managed portfolios:

1. The name of the fund does not always provide a sufficient description of the nature of the securities that are found within the portfolio
2. There is a great deal of variation in the composition of the portfolio holdings across funds, even when they are classified within the same fund category.

INDIRECT INVESTMENT TRANSACTIONS

Investors transact indirectly via investment companies by buying, holding, and selling shares of closed-end funds, mutual funds, segregated funds, and Labour Sponsored Venture Capital Corporations (LSVCCs). In this section, we analyze some of the details involved in these transactions.

Closed-End Funds

Historically, the market prices of closed-end funds have varied widely from their net asset values (NAVs). A discount refers to the situation in which the closed-end fund is selling for less than its NAV. If the market price of the fund exceeds the NAV the fund is said to be selling at a premium. That is,

If NAV > market price, the fund is selling at a discount.
If NAV < market price, the fund is selling at a premium.

Although several studies have addressed the question of why these funds sell at discounts and premiums, no totally satisfactory explanation has been widely accepted by all market observers. On average, closed-end funds tend to sell at a discount from their NAV. For example, on February 1, 1999 the shares of the **Canadian General** closed-end fund closed trading on the TSE at $13.40, which represented a discount of 11.7 per cent from its NAV per share of $15.18.

Some explanations that have been cited to explain discounts in various closed-end funds include illiquidity, either for the fund's holdings or in the fund's shares themselves, high expenses, poor performance, and unrealized capital gains. Another of these explanations — anti-takeover provisions — would prevent investors from taking over the fund and liquidating it in order to realize the full NAV.[5]

By purchasing a fund at a discount, an investor is actually buying shares in a portfolio of securities at a price below their market value. Therefore, even if the value of the portfolio remains unchanged, an investor can gain or lose if the discount narrows or widens over time. That is, a difference exists between the portfolio's return, based on net asset values, and the shareholder's return, based on closing prices.

Funds trade at premiums as well as discounts across time, and the variance between funds is great. In a recent year, a number of closed-end funds were trading at discounts as large as 16 per cent, while a US closed-end fund (the **Korea Fund**) was trading at an astounding premium of approximately 87 per cent, an increase from the previous year's premium of 63 per cent. In other words, investors buying the shares of Korea Fund were willing to pay about 87 per cent more than the net asset value of the fund to obtain the shares.

INVESTING tip

Initial public offerings (IPOs) of closed-end funds typically involve brokerage commissions of 6 or 7 per cent. Brokers often support the price in the after-market temporarily but then the price drops to NAV or below. Many small investors would do well not to purchase the IPOs of closed-end funds.

Mutual Funds

Some mutual funds use a sales force to reach investors, with shares or units available from brokers and financial planners. In an alternative form of distribution called direct marketing, the company uses advertising and direct mailing to appeal to investors.

Most mutual funds permit purchase of fractional shares or units. Purchase methods include lump sum cash purchases, accumulation purchase plans, and buying by reinvesting dividends. Lump sum purchases generally involve initial and subsequent minimum purchase

[5] As for premiums, such as those enjoyed by several US closed-end funds that held municipal bonds in 1992, it is hard to short these funds because of the difficulty in borrowing the shares to do so. Thus, they end up selling at premiums.

amounts as discussed above. Accumulation purchase plans may be voluntary or contractual arrangements, although the latter have declined in popularity due to their restrictive nature. In addition, many funds automatically reinvest dividends and interest to acquire new shares or units, unless instructed otherwise.

Mutual funds can be subdivided into load funds (those that charge a sales fee) and no-load funds (those that do not). Load funds charge investors a sales fee for the costs involved in selling the fund. Investors either pay the fee initially when the fund units are purchased (front-end sales charges), or in the future when the shares are redeemed by the investors (back-end or redemption charges). When an investor purchases units in a fund that charges an upfront sales charge, the offering or purchase price relates the sales charge to the net asset value (NAV) in the following manner:

Offering or purchase price = (NAV) ÷ (100 per cent less the sales charge).

EXAMPLE: CALCULATING OFFERING PRICE

For example, the offering price for a fund that has a NAV of $10 and a 5 per cent upfront sales charge is

$$\text{Offering price} = \$10/(1.0 - 0.05) = \$10.53.$$

Notice that $0.53 is 5.3 per cent of the NAV (or net amount invested). Regulators require that firms report sales charges in prospectuses as both the percentage of amount paid by investor (i.e., 5 per cent), and the percentage of net amount invested (i.e., 5.3 per cent).

The load or sales charge goes to the marketing organization selling the shares, which could be the investment company itself or brokers. The fee is split between the salesperson and the company employing that person. The load fee percentage usually declines with the size of the purchase. The old adage in the investment company business is that "mutual fund shares are sold, not bought," meaning that the sales force aggressively sells the shares to investors. Historically sales charges have been in the range of 9 per cent of offering price, but the current norm for front-end loads is 5 per cent or less as a result of increased competitiveness.

Figure 3-4 shows that 57 per cent of Canadian mutual funds (for a total of 582) charged loads in 1997. Of these, 107 (or 18 per cent) had front-end sales charges, 70 (or 12 per cent) had back-end (redemption) charges, and the remaining 405 (or 70 per cent) gave the investor the option of front- or back-end loads. The other 43 per cent of funds were no-loads (totaling 441), which did not charge direct selling charges. However, no-load funds typically levy modest administration fees and charge other management fees that may add up. Investors should read the prospectus carefully to determine the net cost of these services. In addition, some funds are subject to an early redemption fee (often 2 per cent) if the funds are redeemed within 90 days of purchase. Finally, some funds charge a distribution charge to pay commissioned salespeople, while trailer fees (or service fees) are those paid by a manager to the selling organization.

Figure 3-4
Load Versus No-Load Funds (1997)

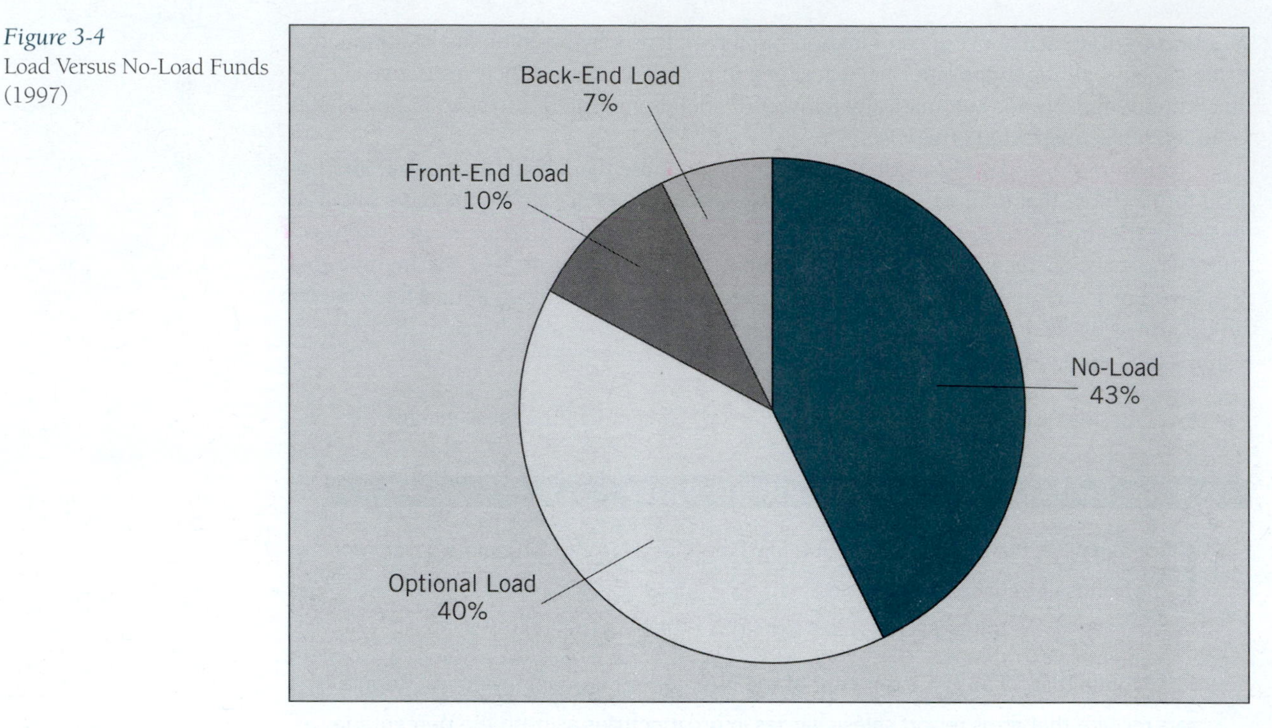

Source: Investment Funds Institute of Canada (IFIC).

The level of management fees paid to compensate mutual fund managers in Canada varies widely depending on the fund from 1 per cent for some money market and index funds to 3 per cent for some equity funds. It is normally expressed as a percentage of fund assets. Other fund expenses such as brokerage fees, audit, legal, safekeeping and custodial, and informational fees are also included in the management expense ratio calculation. These expenses decrease the returns to fund holders and both management fees and expense ratios for the past five years must be included in the fund prospectus. Generally, sales charges are higher for mutual funds than for a bond or stock, but they offer much more in the package.

Mutual funds redeem their shares or units on written request at a price that is either equal or close to the fund's net asset value per share (NAVPS). All funds must compute the NAVPS at least once a month (once a week for equity funds and once a year for real estate funds), and most of the larger ones do so on a daily basis (quarterly for real estate funds). Payment must be made for redeemed shares within five business days from the determination of NAVPS, although most funds reserve the right to suspend redemptions under certain highly unusual or emergency conditions — for example, if trading is suspended on securities comprising more than 50 per cent of portfolio value.

There is normally no charge to redeem funds unless they are back-end loads, in which case the charge is usually a stated percentage of market value at the time of redemption (although some funds charge a percentage of the original amount invested). Systematic withdrawal plans may be arranged to meet investors' cash flow requirements. There are four general types of withdrawal plans:

1. Ratio withdrawal plan — a specified percentage of fund shares are redeemed at fixed intervals (amounts will vary according to prevailing market values)
2. Fixed dollar withdrawal plan — a specified dollar amount is withdrawn at regular intervals
3. Fixed period withdrawal plan — a specified amount is withdrawn over a predetermined period of time with the intent that all capital will be exhausted when the plan ends
4. Life expectancy adjusted withdrawal plan — a variation of number 3 designed to provide as high an income as possible during the holder's expected life; the amounts withdrawn vary in relation to the amount of capital remaining in the plan and the plan holder's revised life expectancy.

Segregated Funds

Segregated funds are offered by insurance companies as alternatives to conventional mutual funds. They are legally considered to be insurance products and the funds must be separated from other assets of the insurance company. They have the unique feature of guaranteeing that, regardless of how poorly the fund performs, investors are entitled to at least a minimum percentage of their total contributions to the fund after a certain period of time. The minimum required by law is 75 per cent after ten years, although most funds guarantee 100 per cent. They may also be structured so that the assets within the fund cannot be seized by creditors if the investor declares bankruptcy.

These funds have grown in popularity in recent years in response to investor concerns about growing volatility in financial markets. As a result of this demand, investment companies and banks have begun to offer similar products referred to as guaranteed funds or protected funds. While these funds represent attractive alternatives to the risk-averse investor who wishes to participate in increasing stock market prices without exposing themselves to an undue amount of risk, there are a couple of things investors should keep in mind. The first point to recognize is that the guarantee is only good after a certain period of time, and if investors sell their fund units before this date they could end up receiving less than the guaranteed percentage of their investment. The second important point is that segregated funds (as well as the similar funds offered by investment companies and banks) tend to have higher load fees and some firms insist they be purchased through a contractual purchase plan.

Labour Sponsored Venture Capital Corporations (LSVCCs)

Labour Sponsored Venture Capital Corporations (LSVCCs) offer investors a tax credit and are usually provincially based. They must be sponsored by labour organizations and their specific mandate is to invest in small to medium-size businesses. Their main purposes are to create and protect jobs, promote economic growth and diversification, increase the supply of venture capital, and encourage greater participation in share ownership and business development. Eligible investments for LSVCCs include shares, ownership interests, or certain debt securities of eligible corporations or partnerships. Eligibility is restricted to taxable Canadian businesses that are active in Canada and meet specific criteria. These investments may be considered hybrid securities since they are speculative investments that also provide tax benefits.

Sales of LSVCCs grew rapidly until 1995, totalling $1.2 billion in that year, and as a result by the end of the first quarter of that year, the funds had only been able to invest approximately 31 per cent of their total assets in qualifying companies. This created a problem, since legislation requires that LSVCCs invest a certain percentage of their equity capital within a specified time frame, usually a year or two after it is received. Federal legislation stipulates that at least 60 per cent of the capital be invested, while provincial legislation may require even higher percentages.

LSVCC sales declined dramatically in 1996 (to $650 million) and in 1997 (to $505 million). The rapid decline in LSVCC sales was mainly attributed to the introduction of new tax rules in 1996 that reduced the tax incentives associated with these assets. While there is no maximum amount an individual may invest in an LSVCC, the federal tax credit applied up to a maximum investment of $5,000 before 1996. The maximum allowable tax credit was 20 per cent federally and 20 per cent in provinces that offered the credit, for a total available credit of 40 per cent. Thus investors had the opportunity to receive a total tax credit of $2,000 (40 per cent of $5,000). However, the maximum amount available for tax credits was decreased to $3,500 in 1996, and the allowable tax credits were reduced to 15 per cent at the federal and provincial level. As a result, the maximum tax credit available to investors was $1,050 (30 per cent of $3,500).

The 1996 tax changes also subjected tax credits to recapture by tax authorities if they are redeemed before they have been held for eight years (if purchased after May 6, 1996). This represents an increase from the previous required holding period of five years. However, the redemption charge was reduced to 15 per cent of the lessor of the redemption proceeds and the original purchase price of the shares (if purchased after May 6, 1996), down from the previous charge of 20 per cent.

In August 1998, the tax rules were changed once again, increasing the maximum investment eligible for federal tax credits back to its former level of $5,000. However, the maximum available tax credits remained at 15 per cent. The net effect is that investors now have the opportunity to achieve a $1,500 tax credit (30 per cent of $5,000). In addition to this change, two additional changes were made to the treatment of LSVCCs. First, unit holders who redeem their units are now eligible to reinvest funds withdrawn from these investments immediately, without the two-year waiting period that previously applied. In addition, RRSPs including LSVCCs are now allowed to hold double the 20 per cent foreign content allowance. This could be an important selling point to investors, especially given the lacklustre performance of Canadian stocks relative to global ones in recent years.

Aside from the available tax credits and foreign content advantages, LSVCCs provide other advantages to investors. In particular, most LSVCCs are RRSP and RRIF eligible, which implies the potential for a double tax advantage. For example, an investor in the 50 per cent tax bracket who purchases $5,000 worth of LSVCCs for RRSP purposes can deduct $2,500 (50 per cent of $5,000) from their taxable income, in addition to receiving the $1,500 in federal and provincial tax credits (as described above). Hence, an investor could potentially invest $5,000 in LSVCCs, at a net after-tax cost of $1,000.

The potential for higher after-tax returns offered by these investments does not come without the assumption of additional risk. Investors must be aware of the highly speculative and illiquid nature of these investments, which make them suitable only for investors with a high-risk tolerance. The portfolios are generally not well diversified geographically and/or across industries and are composed of venture capital investments in small to medium-size companies that often lack an established track record. The companies are typically private companies that may not have been analyzed by a large number of outsiders, and they are not subject to the disclosure requirements of public companies. In fact, their financial statements may not even be audited. The nature of these investments implies that not only are they speculative in nature, but since the companies likely do not trade publicly, there is a great deal of illiquidity associated with the investments.

Investors should be aware that corporate law may require that an LSVCC refuse to retire its shares if the redemption would decrease the realizable value of its assets to a level that would be less than the aggregate of its liabilities plus the amount it would be required to pay other shareholders of equal or greater standing. In addition, most provinces restrict the transfer of LSVCC shares unless they are being moved to an RRSP (for the original purchaser or spouse) or the original purchaser dies.

Disclosure requirements for LSVCCs are similar to those for mutual funds, through a prospectus offering, since shares are continually being issued. Registered salespeople must have passed the CSC exam and follow the IFIC Code of Conduct guidelines. However, LSVCCs differ from mutual funds in several ways. Unlike mutual funds, LSVCCs:

1. Are not restricted to 10 per cent ownership in given companies (in fact, they may exceed 20 per cent)
2. Have restrictions on transferability and redemption
3. May not be valued based exclusively on the market, but rather, may require valuation by independent qualified persons which are to be updated by management.

In short, LSVCCs are only suitable as long-term investments due to their speculative and illiquid nature, as well as to restrictions regarding the provision of tax credit benefits.

INVESTMENT FUNDS PERFORMANCE

Few topics in investments are as well reported on a regular basis as the performance of investment funds, and in particular mutual funds. *The Globe and Mail*, *National Post*, *Business Week*, *Forbes*, and *Money*, among other popular publications, regularly cover the performance of mutual funds, emphasizing their returns and risks. The Real-World Returns box below provides an example of the weekly survey of fund performance found in the *National Post*.

We will discuss the calculation of investment returns in much more detail in Chapter 6, but the primary focus in that chapter is on individual securities and indexes of securities and the actual mechanics involved. Furthermore, we discuss the evaluation of portfolio performance in detail in Chapter 22 and therefore do not consider the evaluation of mutual fund performance in depth now. Nevertheless, it is instructive at this point to consider some of the basic points about mutual fund returns.

Throughout this text we will use total return (explained in detail in Chapter 6) to measure the return from any financial asset, including a mutual fund. Total return for a mutual fund includes reinvested dividends, interest payments and/or capital gains, and therefore includes all of the ways investors make money from financial assets. It is stated as a percentage and can cover any time period — one day, one month, one year, or several years.

A cumulative total return measures the actual performance over a stated period of time, such as the past three, five, or ten years.

REAL-WORLD RETURNS

Mutual Fund Performance Survey

52W	52W					— Friday data —			— Rate of Return † —				— Weekly Data —				
high	low	Fund	Specifics	Assets †	Vty †	cls	$ chg	% chg	1mo	1yr	3yr	5yr	high	low	cls	$ chg	% chg
Canadian Equity																	
16.73	14.50	20/20 Canadian Growth	*FD	194	4	16.62	−0.06	−0.36	4.0	6.3	10.0	7.9	16.73	16.62	16.62	0.01	0.06
4.74	3.92	20/20 RSP Aggressive Equ	*FD	58		4.70	0.01	0.21	3.5	3.5	...	...	4.74	4.67	4.70	0.03	0.64
10.29	8.77	ABC Fundamental-Value	V*N	109	6	9.49	...	...	0.7	2.6	33.2	25.4	9.49	9.49	9.49	...	...
11.27	10.14	AGF Canadian Equity Ser A	*F	118	4	11.13	−0.04	−0.36	3.6	1.3	8.4	4.8	11.27	11.13	11.13	−0.04	−0.36
11.23	10.12	AGF Canadian Equity Ser B	*D	253		11.08	−0.05	−0.45	3.6	...	...	...	11.23	11.08	11.08	−0.05	−0.45
11.26	10.15	AGF Canadian Equity Ser C	*N	2		11.11	−0.05	−0.45	3.5	...	...	...	11.26	11.11	11.11	−0.05	−0.45
19.64	16.58	AGF Growth Equity Ser A	*F	166	5	18.70	−0.01	−0.05	3.6	−7.1	17.5	13.8	18.74	18.68	18.70	0.03	0.16
18.91	16.55	AGF Growth Equity Ser B	*D	308	...	18.64	−0.01	0.05	3.5	...	...	...	18.68	18.62	18.64	0.03	0.16
18.91	16.60	AGF Growth Equity Ser C	*N	4	...	18.68	−0.01	−0.05	3.5	...	...	...	18.72	18.66	18.68	0.03	0.16
9.10	8.02	AGF Resource Cap Ser P	*ZD	7	...	9.10	−0.02	−0.22	3.7	...	...	...	9.12	8.95	9.10	0.15	1.68
9.27	8.02	AGF Resource Capital	*F	!	...	9.09	−0.01	0.11	3.7	...	...	...	9.10	8.93	9.09	0.16	1.79
23.18	19.11	AIC Advantage	*FD	188	5	23.18	0.11	0.48	7.3	5.9	18.8	17.1	23.18	23.05	23.18	0.04	0.17
11.13	9.82	AIC Diversified Canada	*FD	2	...	11.06	0.00	0.00	2.9	...	...	...	11.13	11.05	11.06	0.05	0.45
13.19	11.92	AMI Private Cap Equity	Y*N	2	3	13.19	...	...	3.6	3.4	10.0	4.7	13.19	13.19	13.19	0.17	1.30
6.19	5.56	Admax Cdn Performance	*FR	9	4	6.16	−0.03	−0.50	4.0	2.2	9.4	5.3	6.19	6.16	6.16	0.00	0.05
12.89	11.21	All-Canadian Capital	*F	15	4	12.56	−0.03	−0.24	5.9	9.4	14.8	9.3	12.59	12.37	12.56	0.15	1.21
17.56	14.81	All-Canadian Compound	*Z	14	4	16.46	−0.03	−0.18	5.5	9.1	14.6	9.2	16.49	16.23	16.46	0.19	1.17
3.73	3.26	All-Canadian Consumer	*F	1	...	3.45	−0.03	−0.86	0.6	3.9	...	...	3.48	3.45	3.45	−0.01	−0.29
18.18	14.52	AltaFund Investment	*N	124	5	16.68	0.01	0.06	4.0	6.4	16.4	...	16.71	16.5	16.68	0.16	0.97
14.15	12.37	Altamira Capital Growth	*N	158	4	14.07	−0.06	−0.42	3.0	5.9	12.5	12.3	14.15	14.05	14.07	0.09	0.64
30.25	25.97	Altamira Equity	*N	1851	4	29.52	−0.02	−0.07	4.3	5.4	19.4	22.2	29.56	29.40	29.52	0.19	0.65
12.23	10.81	Altamira n.A. Recovery	*N	90	...	11.61	0.03	0.26	2.8	−2.1	...	...	11.67	11.56	11.61	0.08	0.69
15.95	13.13	Altamira Special Growth	*N	288	5	14.42	0.06	0.42	3.4	−12.7	8.9	14.7	14.42	14.31	14.42	0.15	1.05
4.84	4.30	Apex Equity Growth	*FD	10	...	4.77	−0.03	−0.66	3.9	0.1	...	...	4.84	4.77	4.77	−0.04	−0.75
7.48	6.88	Associate Investors	*N	8	3	7.31	−0.04	−0.54	0.5	4.7	8.2	6.7	7.35	7.30	7.31	0.02	0.27
10.58	9.98	Atlas Canadian Value	*N	2	...	10.54	−0.05	−0.47	3.6	...	...	...	10.59	10.53	10.54	0.05	0.48
11.86	9.83	Atlas Cdn Emerging Growth	*N	10	...	11.86	0.01	0.08	1.6	...	...	...	11.86	11.79	11.86	0.11	0.94
10.48	9.17	Atlas Cdn Emerging Value	*N	2	...	10.48	0.05	0.48	1.0	...	...	...	10.48	10.28	10.48	0.24	2.34
12.30	10.73	Atlas large Cap Cdn Frth	*N	10	3	12.20	−0.07	−0.57	4.2	6.2	6.8	4.5	12.30	12.20	12.20	0.00	0.00
31.56	28.06	BNP (Canada) Equity	Y*N	9	3	31.56	...	...	3.5	4.8	8.6	...	31.56	31.56	31.56	0.15	0.48
6.85	6.00	BPI Canadian Equity Value	*FR	169	3	6.58	−0.01	−0.15	5.5	−4.8	8.2	7.5	6.59	6.56	6.58	0.04	0.61
7.95	6.94	BPI Cdn Small Companies	*FR	90	4	7.95	0.06	0.76	3.6	−0.4	16.5	13.5	7.95	7.81	7.95	0.15	1.92
12.92	11.20	Beutel Goodman Cdn Euity	*F	17	4	12.48	−0.07	−0,59	4.0	8.4	11.1	...	12.59	12.48	12.48	0.01	0.04
5.59	4.76	Beutel Goodman Small Cap	*F	!	...	5.56	−0.01	−0.23	9.8	...	...	...	5.59	5.56	5.56	0.01	0.14
22.36	19.72	Bissett Canadian Equity	Y*N	9	3	22.36	0.3	1.41	3.7	5.6	14.5	10.9	22.36	22.36	22.36	0.31	1.41
20.03	17.79	Bissett Small Cap	Y*N	6	6	19.72	0.12	0.61	2.3	−5.5	29.4	...	19.72	19.72	19.72	0.12	0.61
3.67	3.25	Bullock Growth A	*F	!	...	3.67	0.02	0.55	3.7	...	...	...	3.67	3.63	3.67	0.04	1.10
3.63	3.23	Bullock Growth B	*D	7	...	3.63	0.01	0.28	3.5	...	...	...	3.63	3.60	3.63	0.03	0.83
3.65	3.25	Bullock Growth C	*N	!	...	3.65	0.01	0.27	3.4	...	...	...	3.65	3.62	3.65	0.03	0.83
3.66	3.25	Bullock Growth D	*FD	168	4	3.66	0.01	0.27	3.7	−2.7	14.1	10.9	3.66	3.63	3.66	0.03	0.83
6.79	5.95	C.I. Canadian Growth	*FD	648	...	6.67	−0.03	−0.45	4.7	4.7	...	...	6.71	6.67	6.67	−0.02	−0.30
5.60	4.89	C.I. Sector Canadian	FD	30	4	5.56	−0.03	−0.54	4.5	4.5	15.5	6.0	5.60	5.56	5.56	−0.02	−0.36

Source: © 1997 *The Financial Post*. Reprinted with permission.

EXAMPLE: CUMULATIVE TOTAL RETURNS FOR INVESTORS GROWTH PLUS PORTFOLIO FUND

For the period ending on February 28, 1998, the cumulative total returns for the **Investors Group**'s Investors Growth Plus Portfolio fund, as well as the TSE 300 Composite Index, were:

	Past 1 Year	Past 3 Years	Past 5 Years
Investors Growth Plus Portfolio	17.01%	56.70%	91.70%
TSE 300	21.18%	57.43%	107.69%

This means that an investor who had put $10,000 into the Investors Growth Plus Portfolio mutual fund on February 28, 1993 would have $19,170 on February 28, 1998, consisting of the cumulative total return of 91.70 per cent of $10,000, or $9,170 plus the original $10,000 investment.

Standard practice in the mutual fund industry is to calculate and present the average annual return, a hypothetical rate of return that, if achieved annually, would have produced the same cumulative total return if performance had been constant over the entire period. The average annual return is a geometric mean (discussed in Chapter 6) and reflects the compound rate of growth at which money grew over time. As noted in the Fidelity Investments' prospectus for the Equity-Income Fund, "Average annual total returns smooth out variations in performance; they are not the same as actual year-by-year results."

EXAMPLE: AVERAGE ANNUAL TOTAL RETURNS FOR INVESTORS GROWTH PLUS PORTFOLIO FUND

The average annual total returns for the year ended February 28, 1998 for the **Investors Group**'s Investors Growth Plus Portfolio as well as the TSE 300 Composite Index, were:

	Past 1 Year	Past 3 Years	Past 5 Years
Investors Growth Plus Portfolio	17.01%	16.15%	13.90%
TSE 300	21.18%	16.33%	15.74%

Therefore, investing $10,000 in the Investors Growth Plus Portfolio and compounding at the rate of 13.90 per cent each year for five years would produce a final wealth of $29,170, which corresponds to the number in the previous example.

Average annual total returns allow investors to make direct comparisons among funds as to their performance, assuming they do so legitimately, as explained in Chapter 22 when we discuss the evaluation of performance. In particular, the risk of the funds being compared should be equivalent, and the funds should have the same general objectives. For example, we expect equity funds to outperform bond funds and money market funds on average. Another complexity arising in the comparison of fund performance is that, as discussed above, funds with the same stated objectives often have significant variation in the nature of the assets included in their portfolios.

Consistency of Performance

Can the returns numbers above, widely available for mutual funds, help investors choose this year's, or next year's, winner? The consistency of performance of mutual funds has long been a controversy, and this continues to be true. Early studies tended to find no consistency in fund performance, but some recent studies did find some. For example, in the 1990s, Grinblatt and Titman found persistence in differences between funds over time. More recently Elton, Gruber, and Blake also found evidence of performance differences.[6]

Princeton University professor Burton Malkiel has also found evidence of such differences, although he found that the historical period had an effect, with differences persisting in the 1970s but not in the 1980s.[7] Malkiel, famous for many years as a strong believer in market efficiency, would have a difficult time saying past performance matters in selecting a fund. However, the Real-World Returns box below describes an interview with Malkiel in which he suggests that investors may gain when selecting funds by relying on recent good performance. As the article notes, there are no guarantees when investing, but a possible advantage is to be appreciated.

Before you get your hopes up on selecting funds based on their records, consider some recent work by Droms and Walker, who examine the 151 funds in existence for the entire 20 years ended in 1990. Only 40 of these funds beat a well-known market index in more than ten of these 20 years, and no funds beat the market index in all four of the five-year sub-periods of the 20-year stretch. Funds that did well in the first ten years were no more likely than other funds to do well in the next ten years.[8] This supports the evidence provided by Bogle, who concludes that picking winning funds using past performance is virtually impossible.[9]

A recent study by MPL Communications Inc. of Toronto also documents a lack of persistence in Canadian mutual fund performance. They find that none of the 76 Canadian equity funds that were in existence for the ten-year period ended September 30, 1997 were able to surpass the category average for all ten years. Further, only one fund was able to beat the average nine times, only three beat the average eight times, while only four could beat the average seven times. In fact, less than half (34) of the funds were able to beat the average in five or more years.[10]

In conclusion, although past fund performance provides useful information to investors, strong past performance is no guarantee of strong future performance.

[6] Mark Grinblatt and Sheridan Titman, "The Persistence of Mutual Fund Performance," *The Journal of Finance* 47 (December 1992), pp. 1977–1984; Edwin Elton, Martin J. Gruber, and Christopher Blake, "The Persistence of Risk-Adjusted Mutual Fund Performance," *Journal of Business* 69 (April 1996), pp. 133–157; and Martin J. Gruber, "Another Puzzle: The Growth in Actively Managed Mutual Funds," *The Journal of Finance* 51 (July 1996), pp. 783–810.

[7] Burton G. Malkiel, "Returns from Investing in Equity Mutual Funds: 1971 to 1991," *The Journal of Finance* 50 (June 1995), pp. 549–572.

[8] Jonathan Clements, "By the Numbers: What the Researchers Are Digging Up on Fund Performance," *The Wall Street Journal*, December 24, 1996, p. C1.

[9] John Bogle, "Selecting Equity Mutual Funds," *The Journal of Portfolio Management* 18 (Winter), pp. 94–100.

[10] Peter Brewster, "Better than Average: Not Very Often," *The Globe and Mail / Report on Mutual Funds*, November 6, 1997, p. C1.

REAL-WORLD RETURNS

Does Past Performance Really Matter?

You see the disclaimer in most mutual fund ads: "Past performance is not a guarantee of future results." Yet you want to believe that the portfolio managers with proven track records — the "hot hands" — will continue to provide their shareholders with spectacular gains in the coming years.

A new study by Princeton University professor Burton G. Malkiel indicates that hot hands play an important part in a fund's continued success — despite Malkiel's waffling on the subject (more on that later).

The study, which examined all diversified domestic stock funds from 1973 through 1991, reveals that the top ten funds of one year returned, on average, 15.6% the following year. In contrast, the popular mutual fund benchmark, the S&P 500, averaged 11.5% per annum. Result: A $10,000 investment in the benchmark grew to $79,100 in this period, while the same investment in the top 10 funds nearly doubled that, reaching $157,100. A similar success pattern held true for the top 20 and top 40 funds.

Interestingly, if you ask Malkiel if he has proved that past performance does, indeed, matter, he'll deny it. Yes, he admits, the hot hands approach "shows just a remarkable amount of persistency in the '70s, no question about it." But, he adds, "there wasn't any in the 1980s."

Malkiel bases his arguments on results in four sub-periods of the study. Between 1973 and 1977, the top 10 funds easily beat the S&P 500, averaging a 4% annual return versus a loss of 0.2% for the S&P. Between 1978 and 1981, the top ten averaged a whopping 27% per year versus only 12% for the S&P. The advantage for the top ten shrank between 1982 and 1986, 20% to 19.8%. And between 1987 and 1991, the top ten slightly underperformed the S&P, 14.6% to 15.3%.

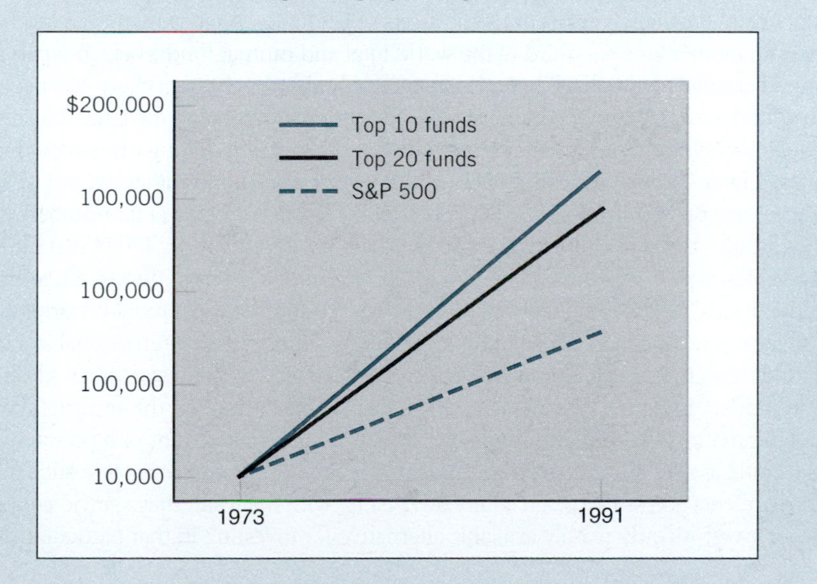

We asked the professor if these weren't precisely the kinds of returns most investors hoped for — beating the market handily in good periods without losing to it in the poor ones.

After much hedging, he answered: "If you want to put the best face on it that you possible could, you could argue that the funds that have done particularly well in some periods continued to do well, and when you did lose by that strategy, you didn't lose by very much."

"So I guess if you pushed me to the wall and said, 'Look, I've got some no-load funds here with low expense ratios and you're a betting man, what would you do, would you buy the ones with the best performance?' I'd say, 'Sure, I probably would.' But if you asked me, 'Can you count on that to produce first-rate returns in the future?' I'd say, 'Absolutely not.' If you're counting on that, that's the will of the wisp."

Of course, investors know that they can never *count* on anything; they're just looking for an advantage based on probabilities. And Malkiel's study shows that following the hot hands does just that. Still, Malkiel would rather place his bet on an unmanaged index fund with very low expenses. He also subscribes to the strategy of buying closed-end funds that are trading at steep discounts below their net asset values.

Though he stubbornly clings to the notion that "there is no evidence of consistent hot handedness," his figures seem to prove otherwise. "There's no question about the fact that there are a few funds with 20-year records that have outperformed the market," he says. "There's no doubt about that. The problem is, could you have identified them 20 years ago?"

Fortunately, Malkiel's study shows you only need to identify the hot hands one year at a time.

Source: "Does Performance Really Matter?" Mutual Funds, *November 1995, pp. 97–98. Reprinted with permission.*

INVESTING INTERNATIONALLY THROUGH INVESTMENT FUNDS

The mutual fund industry has become a global industry. Open-end funds around the world have grown rapidly, including those in emerging market economies. Worldwide assets more than doubled in the five-year period ending in 1995 to approximately US $5.3 trillion, with over half of this total (or $2.8 trillion) representing the assets of US funds. Aggregate mutual fund assets in Europe amount to about one-third of the world total and mutual fund assets in Japan approximate one-half trillion US dollars. In Latin America only about one out of every 200 people owns a mutual fund compared to one in four in Canada and one in three in the United States.

Canadian investors can invest internationally by buying and selling investment funds that specialize in international securities. These funds have become both numerous and well-known in recent years. By March of 1998, Canadians could choose from a large number of foreign funds including: 164 US equity funds; 176 International equity funds; 47 US and International balanced funds; 77 Asia and Pacific Rim funds; 43 European equity funds; 51 Latin/Emerging Market funds; 75 International bond funds; and 20 International money market funds.

So-called international funds tend to concentrate primarily on international stocks, while global funds tend to keep a minimum percentage of their total in domestic assets. Another alternative in indirect investing, the single-country funds, concentrate on the securities of a single country. International closed-end funds usually sell at either a discount or a premium to their net asset value as do their domestic counterparts. Some developing countries, such as Taiwan and Korea, restrict access to foreign equity ownership, with the result that a single-country fund may be an investor's only readily available alternative for investing in that particular country.

New Developments in International Investing

Wright Investor's Services, a small fund company in the United States, has started new open-end country funds concentrating on each of several different countries. Each of these funds is actively managed, in contrast to the typical single-country fund, which is closed-end.

An important new trend in international investing via investment companies is passively managed country funds geared to match a major stock index of a particular country. Each of these offerings will typically be almost fully invested, have little turnover, and offer significantly reduced expenses to shareholders.

Morgan Stanley has created World Equity Benchmark Shares (WEBS), which track a predesignated index (one of Morgan Stanley's international capital indices) for each of 17 countries. These are closed-end funds and trade on the American Stock Exchange.

Deutsche Morgan Grenfell has created Country Baskets, designed to replicate the *Financial Times/Standard & Poor's Actuaries World Indices*. These are available for each of nine countries. Unlike WEBS, which attempts to match the performance of a particular index without owning all of the stocks in the index, Country Baskets own every stock in the index for that country.

THE FUTURE OF INDIRECT INVESTING

One of the hottest new movements concerning indirect investing is the fund "supermarket" in which investors can buy the funds of various mutual fund families through one source, such as a brokerage firm. Supermarket refers to the fact that an investor has hundreds of choices available through one source and does not have to go to other sources to obtain his or her choices. The funds participating in the supermarket pay the firms offering the funds distribution fees (0.25 per cent to 0.40 per cent of assets per year).

The Internet will have a substantial impact on investors who buy and sell mutual funds. Already, major US investment companies such as Fidelity and Vanguard offer extensive Web sites with much information. One estimate is that by the year 2000, individuals will be managing $30 billion in mutual fund assets on-line.

SUMMARY

This summary relates to the learning objectives provided on page 59.

1. **Distinguish between direct and indirect investing.**
   As an alternative to purchasing financial assets themselves, all investors can invest indirectly, which involves the purchase of shares (or trust units) of an investment fund.
2. **Define open-end and closed-end investment funds.**
   Investment funds are comprised of portfolios of securities that are held on behalf of their shareholders. Investment funds are classified as either open-end or closed-end, depending on whether their own capitalization (number of shares or units outstanding) is constantly changing or relatively fixed.
3. **State the major types of mutual funds and give their features.**
   Open-end funds, or mutual funds, can be divided into two categories: money market funds and stock and bond & income funds. Money market mutual funds concentrate on portfolios of money market securities, providing investors with a way to own these high face value securities indirectly. Stock, bond, and income funds own portfolios of stocks and/or bonds, allowing investors to participate in these markets without having to purchase these securities directly.
4. **Explain the transactions behind indirect investments.**
   Investors transacting indirectly in closed-end funds encounter discounts and premiums,

meaning that the price of these funds is unequal to their net asset values. Mutual funds can be load or no-load funds, depending on whether they have a sales charge (load) or not. All investment companies charge a management fee.

5. **Understand how the performance of investment funds is measured.**
   Total return for a mutual fund includes reinvested dividends, interest payments, and/or capital gains. A cumulative total return measures the actual performance over a stated period of time, such as the past three, five, or ten years. The average annual return is a hypothetical rate of return that, if achieved annually, would have produced the same cumulative total return if performance had been constant over the entire period.
6. **Discuss the opportunities for investing indirectly in international funds.**
   International funds concentrate primarily on international stocks, while global funds keep a minimum percentage of their total in domestic assets. Single-country funds concentrate on the securities in a single country.

KEY TERMS

Closed-end investment fund
Investment fund
Money market funds (MMFs)
Mutual funds
Net asset value (NAV)
Open-end investment fund

ADDITIONAL RESOURCES

An excellent source of information regarding Canadian mutual funds can be found at the following Web site, which is maintained by GLOBEfund: <http://www.globefund.com>. This Web site provides a great deal of information about Canadian mutual funds, including performance charts and profiles of investment companies and individual funds.

For daily results on investment companies, Canadian investors may consult *The Globe and Mail / Report on Business* or the *National Post (Financial Post)*, while US investors may refer to *The Wall Street Journal*. *The Globe and Mail* and the *National Post* also publish regular special reports on mutual funds at various intervals (i.e., monthly and/or annually).

REVIEW QUESTIONS

1. What is meant by indirect investing?
2. What is a money market fund? Why would it appeal to investors?
3. Distinguish between a value fund and a growth fund.
4. Distinguish between the direct and indirect methods by which mutual fund units are typically purchased.
5. What are passively managed country funds?
6. What is the difference between the management fee and the management expense ratio for a mutual fund?
7. What is an investment fund? Distinguish between an open-end and a closed-end fund.

8. It has been said that many closed-end funds are worth more dead than alive. What is meant by this expression?
9. What is meant by an investment fund's objective? What are some of the objectives pursued by an equity, bond, and income fund?
10. What is the difference between the average annual return for a fund and the cumulative total return?
11. How would the owner of some units of Investor Group's Investor Growth Plus Portfolio fund "cash out" when he or she was ready to sell the shares?
12. Who owns a mutual fund? Who determines investment policies and objectives?
13. What does it mean when someone says "Mutual funds involve investment risk"?
14. What is the difference between a load fund and a no-load fund?
15. Distinguish between segregated funds and mutual funds.
16. Identify three ways in which LSVCCs differ from other mutual funds.
17. How does the NAVPS affect the price of an open-end investment fund (mutual fund) as compared to the price of a closed-end fund? Explain.
18. As a small investor, what are the major benefits of indirect investing (in a mutual fund, for example) as compared to investing directly in stocks or bonds? What are the drawbacks?
19. The Crabtree Canadian Equity Fund has 500,000 units issued to investors. The fund currently has liabilities of $100,000. If the fund's portfolio is composed of the three securities listed below, calculate the fund's NAVPS.

Security	# of Shares	Price / Share
Evergreen Inc.	100,000	$10
Atlantic Fisheries Ltd.	500,000	8
Great Northern Gas Inc.	1,000,000	1.10

20. How is the net asset value for a mutual fund calculated?
21. Identify the risks associated with investments in LSVCCs.
22. Does a closed-end fund normally trade at a discount or a premium from its NAVPS?
23. List at least four reasons why it is believed that the situation in Question 22 occurs. How does this phenomenon impact on the concept of market efficiency ?
24. Although most closed-end funds trade at a discount to their NAVPS, this is not always the case. Why do you think that some closed-end funds trade at a premium (sometimes a substantial premium) to their NAVPS?

PREPARING FOR YOUR PROFESSIONAL EXAMS

Special Note to Canadian Securities Course Students

Ensure that you have read and understood the following topics:*

Investing indirectly through investment funds, pp. 61–64

What is an investment fund?, pp. 64–66

CSC Notes: Registered Retirement Savings Plans (RRSPs), pp. 65
Types of investment funds, pp. 66–69
Major types of mutual funds, pp. 69–73
Indirect investment transactions, pp. 73–79
Investment funds performance, pp. 79–82

**Reading these CSC-related topics should provide you with additional understanding of CSC material. However, it should not be seen as a substitute for reading the CSC textbook itself, which is the basis for the CSC exam.*

CSC REGISTRATION QUESTIONS

The Canadian Securities Institute issued the following sample questions in the 1997 CSC registration package as a means for students to self-assess their understanding of CSC-related material.

1. The market price of equities of closed-end investment funds generally trade ________ the break-up value of the portfolio.
   a. higher than
   b. lower than
   c. the same as
2. The ______________ is the price of a mutual fund.
3. Why are LSVCCs described as "hybrid" securities ?
4. What are two reasons that LSVCCs are considered to be long-term investments ?
5. A self-employed person who did not belong to a pension plan and had "earned income" of $40,000 could contribute what maximum annual dollar amount to an RRSP in 1995.
6. Which of the following is not a type of mutual fund withdrawal plan?
   a. front-end load plan
   b. fixed dollar plan
   c. fixed period plan
   d. life expectancy adjusted plan
7. At any given time, the redemption price of most mutual funds is __________ their offering price.
   a. higher than
   b. lower than
   c. the same as
8. Investors in LSVCCs may be entitled to a combined federal and provincial tax credit that cannot exceed ________.
9. Briefly describe the chief difference between a closed-end investment fund and an open-end mutual fund.

CHAPTER 4

SECURITIES MARKETS

LEARNING OBJECTIVES

After reading this chapter, you will be able to

1. Distinguish between primary and secondary markets.
2. Describe how the equity markets are organized and how they operate.
3. Explain what we mean by the third and fourth markets.
4. State the major stock market indicators.
5. Describe, briefly, the bond and derivatives markets.
6. Discuss the factors behind rapid change in the securities markets.

CHAPTER PREVIEW

Whether you choose to invest directly or indirectly through investment funds, you need to understand the structure of the markets where securities are bought and sold. Financial markets are of two types: primary markets (new securities are issued, often through investment dealers) and secondary markets (existing securities are traded among investors). In this chapter, we focus on secondary markets in Canada and the United States, as Canadian investors are active mostly in these markets. Secondary markets include the equity, bond, and derivatives markets. We concentrate on equities, because these are the securities that investors most often buy and sell. Bond and derivatives markets are discussed in greater detail in later chapters. We close this chapter with a look at how the structure and operating mechanisms of the securities markets have changed drastically in the past 20 years. Notably, we consider the dramatic changes to the structure of Canadian stock markets that have recently been proposed.

THE IMPORTANCE OF FINANCIAL MARKETS

In order to finance their operations as well as expand, business firms must invest capital in amounts that are beyond their capacity to save in any reasonable period of time. Similarly, governments must borrow large amounts of money to provide the goods and services that the people demand of them. Financial markets permit both business and government to raise the needed funds by selling securities. Simultaneously, investors with excess funds are able to invest and earn a return, enhancing their welfare.

Financial markets are absolutely vital for the proper functioning of capitalistic economies, since they serve to channel funds from savers to borrowers. Furthermore, they provide an important allocative function by channelling the funds to those who can make the best use of them — presumably, the most productive users of these funds. In fact, the chief function of a capital market is to allocate resources optimally.[1]

The existence of well-functioning secondary markets, where investors come together to trade existing securities, assures the purchasers that they can quickly sell their securities if the need arises. Of course, such sales may involve a loss, because there are no guarantees in the financial markets. A loss, however, may be much preferred to having no cash at all if the securities cannot be sold readily.

In summary, secondary markets are indispensable to the proper functioning of the primary markets, which are, in turn, indispensable to the proper functioning of the economy.

Primary Market
The market for new issues of securities, such as government Treasury bills or a corporation's stocks or bonds, often involving investment dealers. The issuers of the securities receive cash from the buyers who, in turn, receive financial claims on the issuing organization.

THE PRIMARY MARKETS

A **primary market** is one in which a borrower issues new securities in exchange for cash from an investor (buyer or lender). New sales of, for example, T-bills, Bank of Montreal common stock, or Ontario Hydro bonds all take place in the primary markets. The issuers of these securities — the Canadian government, the Bank of Montreal, and Ontario Hydro —

[1] A securities market with this characteristic is said to be allocationally efficient. An operationally efficient market, on the other hand, is one with the lowest possible prices for transactions services.

receive cash from the buyers of these new securities, who, in turn, receive financial claims that previously did not exist. Note that in all three examples, each of these organizations already had outstanding securities before the latest new sales occurred. In other words, these were offerings of *new* securities but they were *not* initial public offerings (IPOs).

Corporate bonds are issued through public offerings or private placements, which are described in the following section. Federal government debt securities are issued in the primary market by the minister of finance through the Bank of Canada using the competitive tender system, which is described in the CSC Notes box below.

Sales of common stock of a publicly traded company are called "seasoned" new issues. If the issuer is selling securities for the first time, this is referred to as an **initial public offering (IPO)**. Once the original purchasers sell the securities, they trade in secondary markets. New securities may trade repeatedly in the secondary market, but the original issuers will be unaffected in the sense that they receive no additional cash from these transactions.

Initial Public Offering (IPO) Common stock shares of a company being sold for the first time.

It is generally argued that firms would want to issue securities when they have good uses for the funds and when market prices are high. The latter observation is consistent with the observed record levels of IPOs on the TSE in 1997, in response to high stock market price levels. During 1997, the TSE set a record of $14 billion raised by 102 IPOs. On the other hand, IPO activity declined more than 70 per cent to $4 billion in 1998 in response to falling equity prices and extreme market volatility.

Pricing of initial offerings is an extremely important and complex decision. Firms do not want to set their offering price too low, since the higher the price obtained by the firm per share, the less shares have to be issued to raise the same amount of money. However, they do not want to overprice the issue and have it "undersubscribed," thus not raising the required funds. The following well-known example of IPO underpricing illustrates the difficulties associated with determining a fair issue price for companies with no previous trading history.

EXAMPLE: NETSCAPE

During the summer of 1995, **Netscape** went public at $28 a share. The company had originally planned to go to market at $12 to $14 per share but had raised the price as a result of the substantial interest shown in the issue by prospective investors. The share closed its first day of trading on the Nasdaq market in the $57 range after reaching levels as high as $72 during the day.

This example indicates the complexity and high degree of uncertainty involved in the pricing of some IPOs, particularly for companies with new products, or those operating in rapidly changing industries. Other IPOs for well-known companies in well-defined industries are easier to price with relative accuracy.

There is substantial Canadian, US, and global evidence that, on average, IPOs are underpriced. Underpricing is generally measured as the difference between the first trading day closing price minus the issue price, divided by the issue price. For the Netscape example, this implies underpricing of $(57 - 28) / 28 = 103.57\%$. Loughran, Ritter, and Rydqvist provide summary evidence for international IPOs and find that average underpricing ranged from a low of 4.2 per cent in France to highs of 78.5 per cent in Brazil and 166.6 per cent in Malayasia

CSC NOTES

Government Finance and the Competitive Tender System

The auction or competitive tender system is used for most issues by the federal government. Primary distributors that are eligible to tender include: Schedule I and II banks (who may only tender for trading accounts and client orders and not for head office accounts such as pension funds); investment dealers; and active foreign dealers.[2] Competitive bids may consist of one or more bids in multiples of $50,000 (minimum $250,000 per individual bid), which are submitted (usually electronically) by 12:30 p.m. on the date of the auction. The bid must state the yield to maturity to three decimal places. A primary distributor may also submit one non-competitive tender, in multiples of $5,000, which is subject to a $25,000 minimum and a $500,000 maximum. This bid will be executed at the average price or yield of the accepted competitive tenders.

If a new maturity of bond is being offered, the coupon rate is set to within 25 basis points of the average yield of the accepted competitive tenders, which produces an average issue price at or below par (100). Where an existing issue is being increased in size, successful bidders are allotted bonds at the price equivalents of the bid yields plus accrued interest if applicable.

In addition to bidding for its own requirements, the Bank of Canada stands ready to absorb the entire tender if required, which implies the bank could theoretically set the yield at each tender. At about 2:00 p.m. on the day of tender, the bank releases complete information about the tender so that bidders can determine their net position. No commissions are paid to dealers who purchase the bonds, and there are no selling price restrictions for the successful buyers.

Two- to five-year government bonds are offered by quarterly auctions in denominations of $1,000, $5,000, $100,000, and $1 million. Treasury bills have traditionally been offered every Tuesday by the Bank of Canada through a competitive tender system. However, in 1997 they switched to auctions every other Tuesday. The maturities are 91, 182, and 364 days.

Canada Savings Bonds are sold every October through investment dealers, banks, and trusts, who act as distribution agents for the Bank of Canada. There is no set limit on the size of the issue. However, investors are restricted in the number they can purchase. Since these instruments are medium-term maturity but are cashable at any time, the rates are generally set in accordance with prevailing short-term rates.

New issues of provincial direct and guaranteed bonds are usually sold at a negotiated price through a fiscal agent, such as an underwriting syndicate. Direct bonds are issued directly by the government (e.g., Province of Manitoba bonds), while guaranteed bonds are issued in the name of a Crown corporation but are guaranteed by the provincial government (e.g., Ontario Hydro).

Municipal bond and debenture issues are more likely to be placed in institutional portfolios and pension accounts. Non-market sources of investment capital that purchase municipal securities include:

1. The Canada Pension Plan (CPP) and Quebec Pension Plans (QPP) that commit a pro-rata portion of each province's obligation to the purchase of municipal securities
2. Provincial and municipal pension funds that directly invest in municipal securities
3. Funds that the federal government often loans to municipalities for specific projects.

(during the 1970s and 1980s).[3] Loughran et al. also show that average underpricing in Germany (1978–92), the United Kingdom (1959–90), the US (1960–92), and Japan (1970–91) was 11.1 per cent, 12.0 per cent, 15.3 per cent, and 32.5 per cent respectively.

---

[2] Schedule I banks must have widely held voting shares with no one investor holding more than 10 per cent, and foreign ownership is limited to 25 per cent. Schedule II banks may be wholly owned by residents or non-residents. The majority of Canadian-based banks are Canadian-owned Schedule I banks. Most Schedule II banks are foreign-owned subsidiaries. For example, 41 out of 45 Schedule II banks in Canada as of April 1997 were foreign subsidiaries, while the remaining four were Canadian owned.

[3] Loughran T., J. Ritter and K. Rydqvist, "Initial Public Offerings: International Insights," *Pacific-Basin Finance Journal* 2 (May 1994), p.165–200.

Jog and Riding provide Canadian evidence for 100 IPOs over the 1971–83 period and find average underpricing of 11.0 per cent. However, the degree of underpricing varied significantly and approximately 40 per cent of the new issues were actually overpriced.[4] Jog and Srivastava extend Canadian evidence to the 1984–92 period and find that average underpricing falls to 5.67 per cent during this period, with only 47.4 per cent of the issues being underpriced.[5] It is important to note that not all IPOs are underpriced — some are overpriced. There is also substantial Canadian and US evidence that the subsequent performance of IPOs is below average, which implies that investors could lose any short-term gains in the long run.

Investment Dealers

In the course of selling new securities, issuers often rely on an **investment dealer** (or an investment banker in the US) for the necessary expertise as well as the ability to reach widely dispersed suppliers of capital. Along with performing activities such as helping corporations in mergers and acquisitions, investment dealers specialize in the design and sale of securities in the primary market while operating simultaneously in the secondary markets. For example, **RBC Dominion Securities** offers investment services while operating a large retail brokerage operation throughout the country.

Investment Dealer
An organization specializing in the sale of new securities, usually by purchasing the issue and reselling it to the public. Known as investment bankers in the US.

Investment dealers act as intermediaries between issuers and investors. For firms seeking to raise long-term funds, the investment dealer can provide important advice to their clients during the planning stage preceding the issuance of new securities. This advice includes providing information about the type of security to be sold, the features to be offered with the security, the price, and the timing of the sale.

Investment dealers participate in primary markets as principals when they take on the task of **underwriting** new issues by purchasing the securities (once the details of the issue have been negotiated) and assuming the risk of reselling them to investors. Investment dealers provide a valuable service to the issuers at this stage. The issuer receives its cheque and can spend the proceeds for the purposes for which the funds are being raised. The investment dealers own the securities until they are resold. Although many issues are sold out quickly — sometimes on the first day they are offered to the public — others may not be sold for days or even weeks. Investment dealers are compensated by a spread, which is the difference between what they pay the issuer for the securities and what they sell them for to the public. The securities are purchased from the issuer at a discount.

Underwriting
The process by which investment dealers purchase an issue of securities from a firm and resell it to the public.

In addition to having expertise in these matters and closely scrutinizing any potential issue of securities, investment dealers often protect themselves by forming an underwriting syndicate or group of investment dealers. This allows them to diversify their risk and enhance the marketability of the issue. One investment dealer serves as the lead underwriter overseeing the underwriting syndicate. This syndicate becomes part of a larger group that sells the securities. A primary offering of securities through this process is referred to as a syndicated offering.

Investment dealers may also assume the role of agents in primary markets when they market newly issued securities on a "best efforts" basis. Under these arrangements, they receive compensation in the form of a commission, and it is the issuer that assumes the risk of the issue

[4] Jog V., and A. Riding, "Underpricing in Canadian IPOs," *Financial Analysts Journal* 43 (Nov–Dec 1987), p. 48–55.
[5] Jog V., and A. Srivastava, "Underpricing in Canadian IPOs 1971–1992 — An Update," 3 *FINECO* (November 1995).

not selling. This arrangement is more common for issues of smaller or more speculative companies, or for "private placements" (discussed below) for large companies with good credit ratings where the risk of the issue not selling is negligible.

All public offerings are regulated by the Canadian Business Corporations Act (CBCA) and provincial securities regulations. They require that a **prospectus** be prepared which includes "full, true, and plain disclosure of all material facts relating to the securities offered." A material fact is one that significantly affects, or would reasonably be expected to have a significant effect on, the securities' market price.

Prospectus
Legal documents that contain relevant financial statements about the proposed use of the funds raised by the stock issue, future growth plan, and other relevant information regarding the share issue. Provides information about a public offering of securities to potential buyers.

Prospectuses are lengthy, legal documents which contain relevant financial statements, proposed use of funds from the issue, future growth plans, and the relevant information regarding the share issue. Normally, before a final prospectus may be issued, it is necessary to prepare and distribute copies of a "preliminary prospectus" to the securities commission and prospective investors. This contains most of the information to be included in the final prospectus except the price to the dealers and public, and sometimes the auditor's report. Because the prospectus is for information only and does not solicit the selling of securities, it is often referred to as a "red herring." A statement, in red, must be displayed on the front page to the effect that it is not final and is subject to completion or amendment before shares can be issued. The dealer may also prepare a "greensheet," which is an information circular, for in-house use only. It includes salient features of the issue, both pro and con, and would be used by the sales department to solicit interest in the new issue.

Figure 4-1
The Underwriting Process

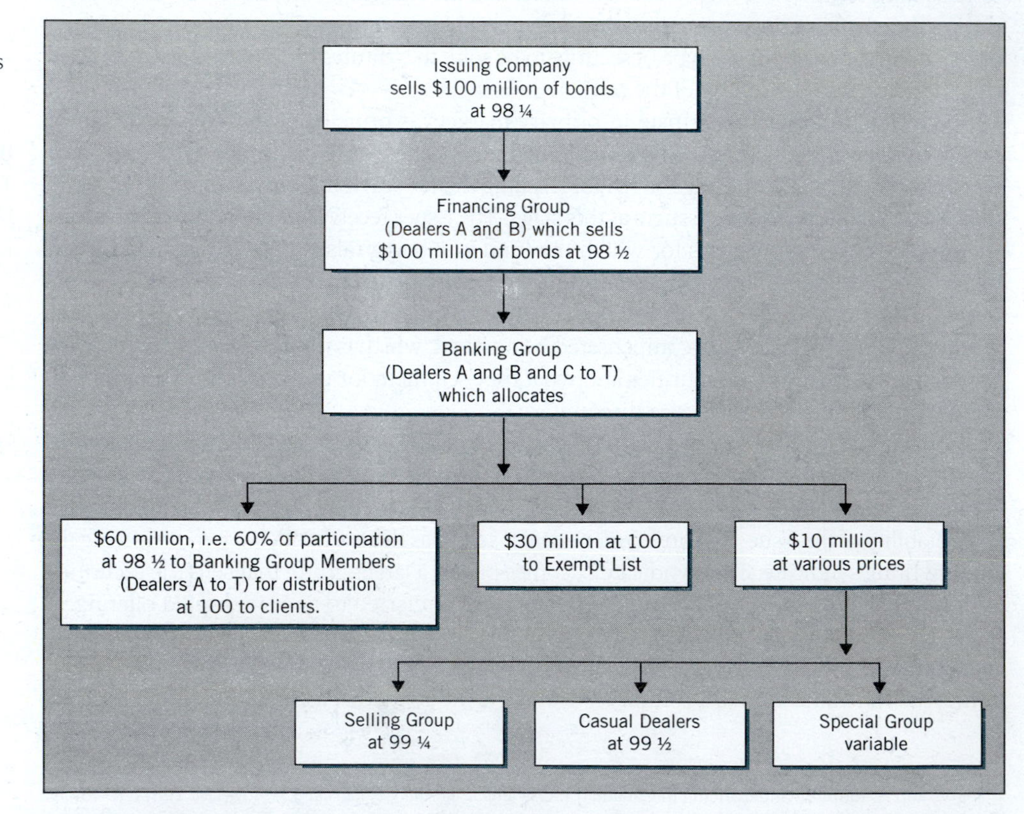

Source: Canadian Securities Course Textbook. *(Toronto: Canadian Securities Institute, August 1998), p. 10-17. © 1998 Canadian Securities Institute. Reprinted with permission.*

During the waiting period (between the issuance of red herrings and the receipt of final prospectuses), dealers are prohibited from activities considered to be furthering the issuance of securities (such as entering into purchase and sale agreements), other than solicitation of expressions of interest. However, the dealer will proceed along other lines, attempting to formalize the details of items such as: the trust deed or indenture (for debt issues); the underwriting or agency agreement between issuer and distributor; the banking group agreement; the selling group agreement; and final price to the public and to the dealer.

Once the prospectus has been prepared, it will be filed with the relevant securities commissions, and approval generally takes three weeks. Any changes must be agreed upon with the issuers before final approval. The issue is then "blue skied" and may be distributed to the public. It must be accompanied by the consent of all experts whose opinions are referred to in the prospectus. This process prevents investors from investing in companies with few or no assets — that is, from purchasing "the blue sky." The prospectus must be mailed or delivered to all purchasers of the securities, not later than midnight on the second business day after the trade.

The Underwriting Process

A typical example of the underwriting process is depicted in Figure 4-1 (above). The first step in the process has the issuing company selling the securities to the financing group (also

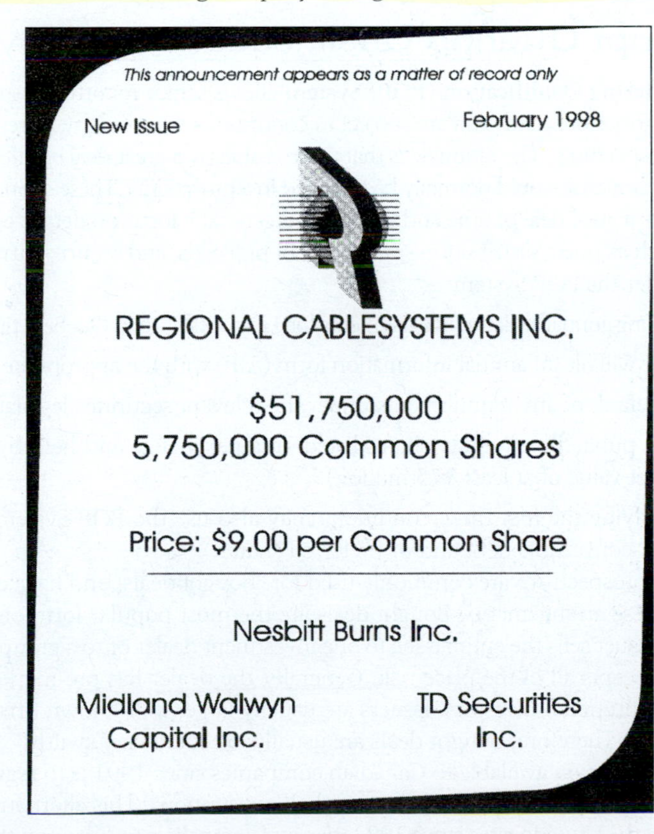

Figure 4-2
Tombstone Advertising

Source: The Globe and Mail / Report on Businesss, *March 3, 1998. Reprinted with permission from Regional Cablesystems Inc.*

known as managing underwriters or syndicate managers) which consists of one or two firms. The financing group accepts the liability of the issue on behalf of the banking group members, which includes themselves, as well as other dealers who have agreed to participate based on certain terms.

Secondly, the financing group sells the securities to the marketing group at a "draw down" price which provides a differential that enables the financing group to recover expenditures undertaken on behalf of the entire banking group. At this point "tombstone advertisements" (such as that depicted in Figure 4-2 above, so named for their resemblance to a tombstone) begin in newspapers, which indicate all members of the banking group selling the issue.

Thirdly, the securities are distributed for sale to the public, with a certain proportion being allocated to:

1. The banking group (the largest proportion)
2. The exempt list, which usually includes only large professional buyers, mostly financial institutions, who are exempt from prospectus requirements
3. The selling group, which consists of other dealers who are not part of the banking group
4. Casual dealers, who are not members of the banking or selling groups, and may be brokers, broker dealers, foreign dealers, banks, etc.
5. Special groups, which may include the issuer's banker or dealer, etc.

The Prompt Offering Qualification (POP) System

Prompt Offering Qualification (POP) System
Allows qualifying senior reporting issuers to put out short form prospectuses in lieu of full ones.

The **Prompt Offering Qualification (POP) System** allows senior reporting issuers, who have made public distributions, and who are subject to continuous disclosure requirements, to issue "short form" prospectuses. The rationale is that there is already a great deal of information available on the company that would normally be included in a prospectus. These short form prospectuses save issuers a great deal of time and money, and generally focus on details of the securities being issued such as price, distribution spread, use of proceeds, and security attributes.

Issuers under the POP System:

1. Have been filing annual and interim statements for 12 months (36 in Quebec) prior to the issue
2. Have filed or will file an annual information form (AIF) with the appropriate administrator
3. Are not in default of any requirements under the relevant securities legislation
4. Have a large public float (equity shares listed on an exchange and held by non-insiders with a market value of at least $75 million).

Issuers satisfying the first three conditions may also use the POP System for issues of high quality non-convertible debt and/or preferred shares.

Short form prospectuses are commonly used for "bought deals" and have contributed to the growth of these arrangements. Bought deals are the most popular form of underwriting in Canada. The issuer sells the entire issue to one investment dealer or to a group that attempts to resell it and accepts all of the price risk. Generally, the dealer has pre-marketed the issue to a few large institutional investors. Issuers are usually large, well-known firms that qualify for the use of POP. Therefore, bought deals are usually executed very swiftly.

An additional option available to Canadian companies since 1991 is to register securities in advance of issuance, which is referred to as "shelf registration." This alternative, which has been available in the United States since 1982, permits companies to "place on the shelf" securities to be sold. The issuing company can sell the new securities over time by auctioning pieces of the issue, which provides flexibility and savings.

The Listing Process

New share issues are usually initially traded over-the-counter (OTC) and are considered for listing on an exchange only after proof of satisfactory distribution is available. Often, the underwriting agreement will require the underwriters to provide some market support for the new security issue for a specified time period. Sometimes a market develops for new issues prior to their actual listing, and trading is handled by dealers in what is known as the "grey market." This is an unofficial OTC market comprised of dealers wishing to execute customers' orders and support an issue until official listing occurs.

Global Security Issues

The global perspective now in place allows companies in various countries to raise new capital in amounts that would have been impossible only a few years earlier because these companies were often limited to selling new securities in their own domestic markets. The global equity offering has changed all that. An important new development for investment dealers is the emphasis on managing the global offerings of securities.

A lead investment dealer can act as a "global coordinator," linking separate underwriting syndicates throughout the world in selling equity issues. For example, **Wellcome PLC**, a British pharmaceutical company, raised $4 billion in new equity recently through a global offering, and **General Motors** sold equity shares around the world to raise over $2 billion.[6]

A number of Canadian companies are "interlisted" on more than one stock market, primarily markets in the United States, such as Nasdaq or the New York Stock Exchange (NYSE). The motivation for Canadian firms to interlist on US markets is to increase the stock's potential market and enhance its visibility. However, empirical evidence is inconclusive regarding share price benefits obtained from interlisting in the United States.[7]

Private Placements

In recent years an increasing number of corporations have executed private placements, whereby new securities issues (typically, debt securities) are sold directly to financial institutions, such as life insurance companies and pension funds, bypassing the open market. One advantage is that the firm does not have to prepare a full prospectus, only a specific contract (or offering memorandum).[8] Investment dealer fees are also reduced because the dealer usually acts as an agent for the issuer for a finders fee, which is well below normal underwriting spreads. The disadvantages of private placements include a higher interest cost, because the financial

6 This discussion is based on "Stock Issues Heard Around the World," *Business Week*, August 31, 1992, p. 54–55 .

7 In particular, Mittoo shows that a portfolio of TSE 35 interlisted stocks had higher returns, lower volatility, and had higher trading volume over the 1977–86 period, than a similar, highly correlated US portfolio of stocks. Foerster and Karolyi have recently demonstrated that Canadian firms interlisting on the US over the 1976–92 period displayed positive abnormal returns during the week of interlisting, as well as the prior 50-week period, but displayed inferior return performance in the subsequent 50-week period. Sources: U. Mittoo, "How Companies Win by Interlisting Shares on US Exchanges," *Canadian Investment Review* 6 (Winter 1994) p. 40–44; and, S. Foerster and A. Karolyi, "The Effects of Market Segmentation and Illiquidity on Asset Prices: Evidence from Foreign Stocks Listing in the US," *Journal of Finance* 54 (June 1999), p. 981–1013.

8 The savings in time can sometimes be important, for market conditions can change rapidly between the time an issue is registered and sold.

institutions usually require a higher return than would be required from a public subscription, and possible restrictive provisions on the borrower's activities.[9]

THE SECONDARY MARKETS

Secondary Markets
Markets where existing securities are traded among investors; the TSE is the largest stock market in Canada.

Once new securities have been sold in the primary market, an efficient mechanism must exist for their resale if investors are to view securities as attractive opportunities. Secondary markets give investors the means to trade existing securities.[10]

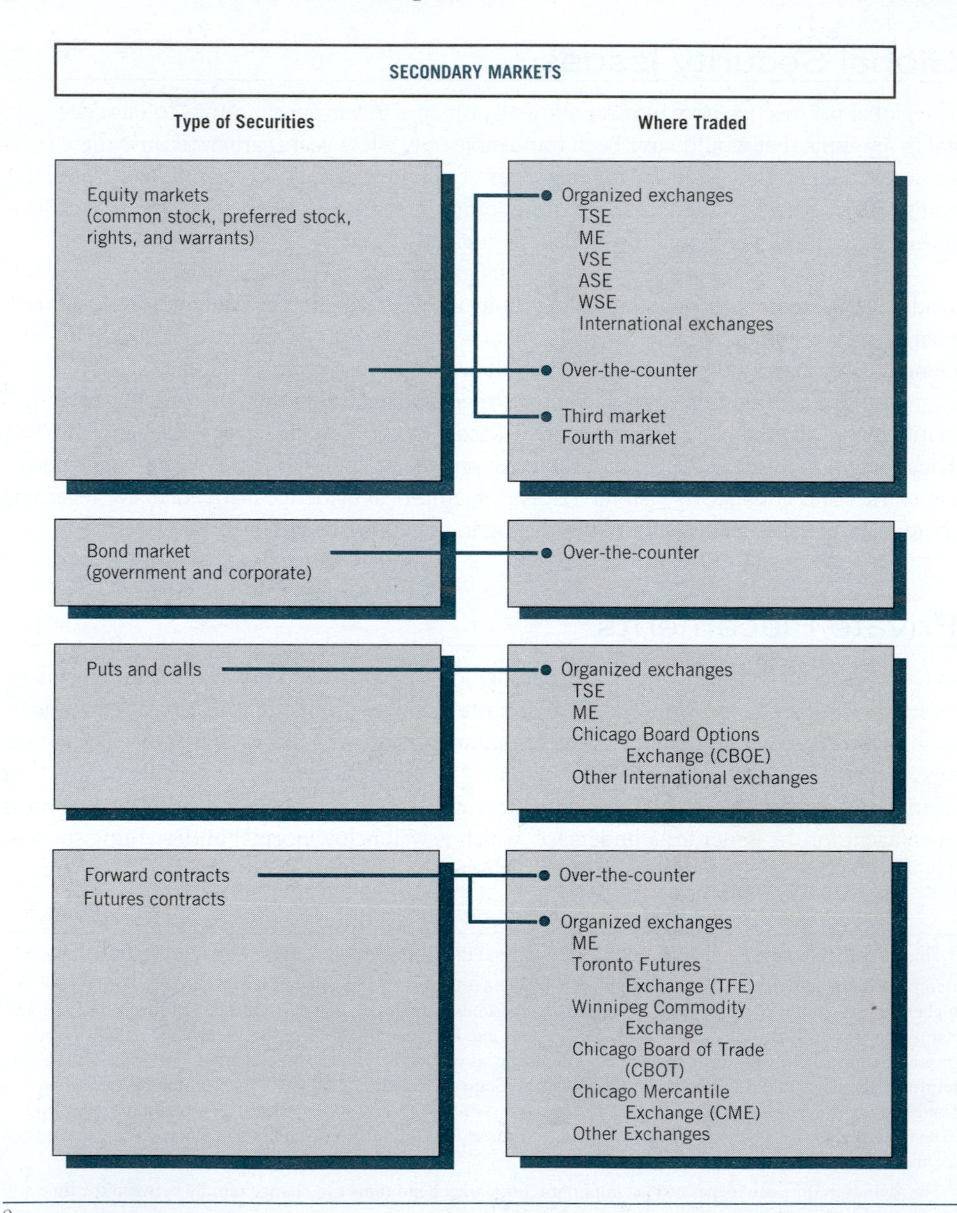

Figure 4-3
The Structure of Secondary Markets

[9] In addition, a lack of marketability exists because the issue is unregistered. Therefore, the buyer may demand additional compensation from the lender in the form of a higher yield.

[10] Again, this does not directly affect the issuer, who sells new securities in the primary market in order to raise funds.

Secondary markets exist for the trading of common and preferred stock, rights, warrants, bonds, and puts and calls. Figure 4-3 diagrams the structure of Canadian secondary markets at the beginning of 1999, which is discussed below in the following order: equities, bonds, and derivative securities.

Equity Securities — Auction Markets

Common stocks, preferred stocks, and warrants are traded in the equity markets. Some secondary equity markets are **auction markets**, involving an auction (bidding) process in a specific physical location. Investors are represented by **brokers**, intermediaries who represent both buyers and sellers and attempt to obtain the best price possible for either party in a transaction. Brokers collect commissions for their efforts and generally have no vested interest in whether a customer places a buy order or a sell order, or, in most cases, in what is bought or sold (holding constant the value of the transaction).

Auction Market
A securities market with a physical location, such as the Toronto Stock Exchange, where the prices of securities are determined by the bidding (auction) actions of buyers and sellers.

Brokers
Intermediaries who represent both buyers and sellers and attempt to obtain the best price possible for either party securities transactions; they receive a commission for this service.

Canadian Exchanges

At the beginning of 1999, there were five stock exchanges in Canada: the **Toronto Stock Exchange (TSE)**, the Montreal Exchange (ME), the Vancouver Stock Exchange (VSE), the Winnipeg Stock Exchange (WSE), and the Alberta Stock Exchange (ASE). In March 1999, a complete overhaul of the present structure was proposed (see the Real-World Returns box below).

Toronto Stock Exchange (TSE)
The largest Canadian stock market, which exchanges accounts for nearly 90 per cent of all transactions in the country.

The new structure would see the TSE take over all trading for stocks of large companies or those with a strong history of profitability (referred to as "senior" stocks). The ME would no longer handle stock trades but would assume the role of a national exchange for derivative securities such as options and futures contracts. In addition to these changes, a new national "junior" stock market would be created for trading shares in smaller companies that do not qualify to trade on the TSE. This national market, which is to be called the Canadian Venture Exchange, will be operated jointly by the ASE and VSE, and most shares trading on these markets would be traded through the newly created national market. The Canadian Dealing Network (CDN), which was the operating authority for the Canadian over-the-counter market (discussed later in this chapter) will also join the new stock market, as will the WSE.

As of June 1999 (at the time this textbook was written), there are several matters to be finalized before the proposed new structure can be introduced. In our remaining discussion, we focus on the structure that has existed in Canada until 1999, rather than speculate how the new system will evolve. By understanding the existing structure, you will gain some insight into the magnitude of the proposed changes, and understand the impetus behind them.

One contributing factor to the proposed changes has been the growth in importance of the TSE, which grew from approximately 80 per cent of all transactions in 1992 to approximately 89 per cent in 1998, as shown in Table 4-1. This growth has come at great expense to the other exchanges, which have seen their percentage of Canadian stock trading activity dwindle in recent years. For example, Table 4-1 also shows the decline of the ME to approximately 10 per cent of all 1998 transactions, while the VSE, ASE, and WSE combined accounted for only 1 per cent of Canadian stock exchange transactions. Whether or not the proposed changes go through, the TSE will obviously remain the dominant stock exchange in Canada.

REAL-WORLD RETURNS

Restructuring of Canadian Stock Exchanges

THE FOUR BIG EXCHANGES

Toronto: Specializes in large-capital Canadian stocks, particularly resources-based companies. Value of trades (1998): $493.2-billion.

Montreal: Mainly derivatives, options, and futures contracts. Value of trades (1998): $55.7-billion.

Vancouver: Focuses on raising venture capital for junior companies. Value of trades (1997): $8.9-billion.

Alberta: Primarily resources, junior capital pools, and technology. Value of trades (1998): $1.8-billion.

Faced with intense competition from foreign stock markets and skyrocketing costs for new technology, Canada's stock exchanges want to reinvent themselves by swapping parts of their business with each other.

The plan, proposed yesterday in a rare common front among the four biggest Canadian exchanges, would see the Toronto Stock Exchange take over all trading of senior stocks — big companies or those with solid histories of profit.

The 125-year old Montreal Exchange would give up stock trading to handle all Canadian trading in derivatives — securities such as futures and options that are linked to the underlying value of a stock or currency.

The TSE's market for small firms, the Canadian Dealing Network, would become part of a national junior stock market to be operated jointly by the Alberta and Vancouver stock exchanges.

To assuage regional concerns, the TSE would have an office in Montreal to handle listings of Quebec-based companies, and the junior exchange would have a presence in Montreal, Ottawa, London and other places where start-up firms abound.

The revamping will save the industry roughly $20-million a year, according to former TSE president Rowland Fleming. It may also cost some jobs and force some stock-exchange employees to move if they want to keep them.

While the exchanges still appear to be squabbling over the details of their proposals, the fact that they've come this far is seen as a major accomplishment.

Market players have talked of reorganizing the Canadian exchanges for years, but regional differences have always scuttled talks. In the past, progress was blocked when Vancouver and Calgary couldn't agree on common goals, and Quebec politicians have fiercely opposed giving up trading of stocks — especially of companies based in the province.

All that changed when the senior Canadian stock-exchange executives met at an international conference in Malaysia late last year. When we sat down together "we recognized the risk of inaction," Mr. Fleming said.

Canadian exchanges have been hit by the fact that more and more domestic companies have been listing on US exchanges, where the high volume of trading means shares move quickly.

Mergers among big exchanges in the United States and Europe have also made it clear that splintered Canadian markets have only a marginal role in the world. Canada's exchanges currently account for only about 2 per cent of trading on international markets.

"When foreign investors look at Canada, they see competing exchanges, lack of focus, and lack of direction," Mr. Fleming said. "When they look at us tomorrow, they'll see one senior market, one derivative market, and one junior market."

Source: Excerpted from Richard Blackwell, "TSE to Take Over All Major Stock Trading," The Globe and Mail, *March 16, 1999, pp. A1, A12. Reprinted with permission from* The Globe and Mail.

Table 4-1

Canadian Stock Exchanges, 1996–98

Exchange	Dollar Volume of Transactions (billions of dollars)			Percentage		
	1996	1997	1998	1996	1997	1998
Toronto	301.299	423.170	493.212	81.56	85.04	88.96
Montreal	50.166	61.911	55.647	13.58	12.44	10.04
Vancouver	12.003	8.670	3.791	3.25	1.74	0.68
Alberta	5.971	3.872	1.780	1.62	0.78	0.32
Winnipeg	0.001	0.035	0.006	0.00	0.00	0.00

Source: Montreal Exchange Web site <www.me.org>.

The TSE, which was incorporated in 1878, is one of the ten largest stock exchanges in the world, and is the third largest stock market in North America, behind the New York Stock Exchange (NYSE) and Nasdaq-Amex stock market. The total dollar value of trading reached a record level of $493 billion in 1998, averaging over $2 billion per day.[11] There were more than 1,400 listed companies on the TSE in 1998. Listing requirements (shown in Table 4-2) are much more stringent for the TSE than for the other Canadian exchanges. These restrictions tend to preclude smaller companies, which has resulted in most of the largest Canadian corporations being listed on the TSE.

The Montreal Exchange was the second largest in Canada as of December 31, 1998 when there were 579 companies listed on it, with a trading volume of approximately $55.6 billion, or an average of $220 million per day. Approximately one half (289) of the listed companies were Quebec-based, while about two thirds (368) of the firms were also listed on the TSE. In addition, 58 of the companies were also listed on the NYSE, 50 on the VSE, and nine on the ASE.[12]

While the VSE, ASE, and WSE are extremely small relative to the TSE and ME, they have served as important sources of capital to start-up firms, primarily in the resource sector. The Vancouver Stock Exchange was established in 1907 to act as a central market for raising venture capital for the emerging resource industries in Western Canada. Their mission statement is "To be an honest, fair, and efficient market for venture capital." In 1997 there were over 1,400 listed companies on the exchange, and it was the fourth largest exchange in North America, in terms of number of shares traded. Listings are predominantly small- and medium-size companies. Over 52 per cent of the listed companies are natural resource-related, while oil and gas companies represent another significant and growing category on the VSE.

The VSE's policies are designed to attract quality companies that are still in their formative stages, as well as those that are more established. Consistent with this objective, the VSE introduced a new Venture Capital Pool (VCP) program on July 1, 1998. This program is designed to help seasoned management groups with a strong track record raise new financing

[11] The TSE Web site: <http://www.tse.com>.

[12] The ME Web site: <http://www.me.org>.

for new business projects and acquisitions. This provides entrepreneurs with an alternative to traditional processes of raising seed capital privately before an initial public offering (IPO). This program requires that the management group forms a company and contributes a minimum of $100,000, before undertaking a VCP/IPO on the exchange with the intention of raising between $300,000 and $700,000. This pool of funds can then be used to invest in qualified business opportunities that are suitable for full listing on the exchange.[13] Unlike the Junior Capital Pool program of the ASE there is no restriction on the location of the business or asset to be acquired.[14]

The Alberta Stock Exchange had 999 listed companies during 1997. Approximately one third of these (325) were industrial companies, 26 per cent were oil and gas companies, 17 per cent were mining companies, 7 per cent were TSE interlisted companies, and 15 per cent were Junior Capital Pool (JCP) companies. The JCP is a forerunner to the VSE's VCP program discussed above. It represents an important source of finance for many high-risk junior mining and oil companies. The JCP program is designed to provide junior start-up companies with a better opportunity of becoming listed on the ASE, and it has been successful in this objective. In particular, the majority of the 793 new listings on the ASE over the 1993–1997 period consisted of companies that were originally Junior Capital Pool issuers. Investors often invest in JCP companies on a purely speculative basis, since most of these companies have no earnings record, and very few assets that would qualify as collateral for traditional credit sources such as bank loans or government grants.

Only issuers who do no not have significant non-cash operating assets or agreements in place to acquire operating assets are eligible to apply for listing under the JCP program. The directors and officers of the applicant issuer must invest at least $100,000 into the issuer at a price per share greater than or equal to 50 per cent of the public offering price. The maximum total value of funds that can be raised is $500,000, while the minimum gross proceeds from the public issue is $200,000 and the maximum is $300,000. The funds raised by this process can then be used to acquire qualifying operating assets, which cannot involve foreign assets or management. In addition, the majority of the directors and officers must be Canadian residents and the public offering must be made through an investment dealer who is a member of the ASE.[15]

The WSE is primarily a regional exchange that provides new Manitoba enterprises with the opportunity to list their shares. Many of these companies have become interlisted on larger exchanges as they have grown. Since investment dealers are required to obtain the best execution price for their clients, much of the trading in the shares of the larger WSE listed companies occurs on other exchanges. This has resulted in minimal trading activity on the WSE, as evidenced by the total of only $6 million in trading activity in 1998. This figure seems low relative to the 1997 trading volume of $35 million but is well above the volumes for 1995 ($524,000) and 1996 ($576,000).[16]

All of the exchanges rely heavily on computerized trading systems. The TSE closed its trading floor on April 23, 1997 and trading is now completely computerized. The other exchanges have followed suit. Stock exchange memberships in the form of stock exchange

---

13 The VSE Web site: <http://www.vse.ca>.

14 Junior Capital Pool is a registered trademark of the ASE.

15 The ASE Web site: <http://www.ase.ca>.

16 The WSE Web site: <http://www.wse.ca>.

seats are sold to individuals, which permits them to trade on the exchange. These seats are valuable assets that may be sold, subject to certain exchange conditions. The number of seats is limited for the TSE, VSE, and ASE. However, the ME provides an unlimited number.

Exchange member firms must be publicly owned, maintain adequate capital requirements, and key personnel must complete required courses of study. Exchanges are governed by bodies that consist of at least one permanent exchange official (e.g., the president), plus governors selected from member firms, as well as two to six highly qualified public governors appointed or elected from outside the brokerage community. Exchanges qualify as non-profit associations and are not subject to corporate income tax.

Exchanges have the power to suspend the trading or listing privileges of an individual security temporarily or permanently. Temporary withdrawals of trading and/or listing privileges include:

1. Delayed opening (which may arise if there exist a large number of buy and/or sell orders)
2. Halt in trading (to allow significant news such as merger activity to be reported)
3. Suspension of trading may occur for more than one session until an identified problem is rectified by the company to the exchange's satisfaction (if the company fails to meet requirements for continued trading or does not comply with listing requirements)

A listed security can be cancelled or delisted for a variety of reasons such as:

1. It no longer exists (e.g., a preferred share issue that has been redeemed)
2. The company has no assets or is bankrupt
3. Public distribution of the security is no longer sufficient
4. The company has failed to comply with the terms of its listing agreement

US Exchanges

The US auction markets include two national exchanges and several regional ones. The national exchanges include the **New York Stock Exchange (NYSE)** and the American Stock Exchange (Amex) (which merged with the Nasdaq Stock Market in 1998 to form the Nasdaq-Amex Market Group). The NYSE was founded in 1792 and is the oldest and most prominent secondary market in the United States. By 1992 it had firmly regained its place as the world's largest secondary market, following the decline of the Tokyo Stock Exchange, which had temporarily overtaken the NYSE in 1987–89. It is generally regarded as the best regulated exchange in the world and has proven its ability to function in crisis. On Black Monday in October 1987, for example, this exchange handled some 600 million shares when other exchanges were experiencing significant problems.

New York Stock Exchange (NYSE)
The largest secondary market for the trading of equity securities in the world.

Similar to the Canadian exchanges, the NYSE is a not-for-profit corporation and had 424 members as of 1998. Most of the members are partners or directors of stockbrokerage houses and many of them own more than one seat.[17] Members may transfer seats, by sale or lease, subject to the approval of the exchange. The number of seats has not changed through the years. However, their price has varied sharply. The value of a seat was less than $100,000 in the mid-1970s but had increased to $1,750,000 by January 1998, before eventually falling to $1,225,000 by the end of that year.

[17] For example, Merrill Lynch, the largest retail stockbrokerage firm, owns over 20 seats.

Specialists
Members of an organized exchange who are charged with maintaining an orderly market in one or more stocks by buying or selling for their own accounts.

Members of the exchange can combine with others to operate as a member organization and do business with the public. By January 1999, 296 NYSE firms, out of a total of 463 member organizations, were doing business with the public. Market **specialists**, who own roughly one third of all the seats on the NYSE, are assigned to each trading post on the floor of the NYSE, where they handle one or more of the stocks traded at that post. Specialists are exchange members who are responsible for maintaining an orderly market in one or more stocks by buying or selling shares for his or her own account. Some specialists firms are part of well-known brokerage operations, while many others are virtually unknown to the public. (Specialists are discussed in more detail in Chapter 5.)

As mentioned above, a number of Canadian companies are interlisted on the NYSE. Table 4-2 shows that the qualifying criteria for TSE-listed companies (which were revised in

Table 4-2

TSE versus NYSE Listing Requirements (1998)*

Criteria	TSE (Cdn $)	NYSE (US $)
Net Tangible Assets	>= $2m	>= $40m
Pre-Tax Income	>= $200,000 in most recent year	(1) >= $2.5m in most recent year and >= $2m in the preceding two years, OR (2) Aggregate of previous three years >= $6.5m and most recent year >= $4.5m (where pre-tax income is positive in all three years)
Pre-Tax Cash Flow	>= $500,000 in previous year	N/A
Market Value of Publicly Held Shares	>= $4m	>= $40m
Number of Outstanding Shares	1m	1.1m
Number of shareholders of "board" (Can.) or "round" (US) lots (generally 100 shares)	300	2,000
Working Capital (W/C) Requirements	Adequate W/C and capitalization to carry on the business	N/A

Source: Toronto Stock Exchange <http://www.tse.com> and New York Stock Exchange <http://www.nyse.com> Web sites. Reprinted with permission from the Toronto Stock Exchange.

*The TSE requirements are for Canadian industrial companies. They were introduced on November 3, 1998 and are effective subsequent to that date subject to Ontario Securities Commission (OCS) approval. Requirements are different for mining, oil and gas, and non-Canadian companies, as well as for junior companies.

November of 1998) pale in comparison to those that must be satisfied by NYSE-listed companies.[18] As a result, only the largest Canadian companies are able to list their shares on this exchange.

The NYSE is the dominant capital market in the world based on trading volume and on the market capitalization of its firms (which is defined as the total number of shares outstanding multiplied by the market price per share). During 1998 the NYSE had 3,114 listed companies and trading volume reached $7.3 trillion. By January 1999, the market capitalization of the NYSE was $10.9 trillion, and the global market value of NYSE-listed companies (including shares listed on other exchanges) was $14 trillion.[19]

A new trend of potential significance that is often discussed in the popular press is **program trading**, which may be defined as the computer-generated trading of large blocks of securities. It is used to accomplish certain trading strategies, such as arbitrage against futures contracts and portfolio accumulation and liquidation strategies. The NYSE published its first report on program trading activities in 1988. By the end of 1998, program trading volume accounted for approximately 17 per cent of total NYSE volume and averaged some 117 million shares daily.

Program Trading
The computer-generated trading of large blocks of securities. It is often implemented to take advantage of price discrepancies between markets (arbitrage opportunities).

The American Stock Exchange (Amex) is the only other national organized exchange in the United States. As mentioned, it merged with the Nasdaq Stock Market in 1998 to form the Nasdaq-Amex Market Group to create the first financial market that brings together the central auction process of stock exchanges with the multiple market maker systems associated with dealer markets (described in the section below). The Amex's organization and procedures resemble those of the NYSE, most notably in being a specialist-based system.

Relative to the NYSE, the Amex is much smaller, with market capitalization of approximately $152 billion for the 770 companies listed there at the end of 1998.[20] The listing requirements for stocks on the Amex are less stringent than the NYSE. While trading volume is significantly below that of the NYSE (the NYSE generally does more trading in the first hour than the Amex does during the entire day), the Amex does a large business in options and derivative securities, with almost 30 per cent of the market in stock-option trading.

The United States also has several regional exchanges patterned after the NYSE, although their listing requirements are considerably more lenient. Some of the largest of these are the Midwest Stock Exchange, the Pacific Stock Exchange, the Philadelphia-Baltimore-Washington (PBW) Exchange, the Boston Stock Exchange, and the Cincinnati Stock Exchange.

Regional exchanges list small companies that may have limited geographic interest. In addition, they engage in dual listing; that is, they list securities that are also listed on the NYSE and the Amex.[21] This allows local brokerage firms that are not members of a national exchange to purchase a seat on a regional exchange and trade in dual-listed securities. Regional exchanges accounted for 4.4 per cent of both share volume and dollar volume in the United States in 1995.

Today's institutional investors are aggressively seeking lower trading costs. One way for Wall Street firms to accommodate these demands by their institutional clients is to take some trades to the regional exchanges where commissions are often lower. In one recent year, only

---

[18] Continuing listing requirements must also be met, or a firm could be delisted from the exchange.

[19] The NYSE Web site: <http://www.nyse.com>.

[20] Nasdaq-Amex Web site: <http://www.nasdaq-amex.com>.

[21] In fact, most of the securities traded on the regional exchanges are also traded on the NYSE or the Amex.

70 per cent of the trades in NYSE-listed stocks were executed on the NYSE, the lowest percentage in the history of the exchange. The NYSE continues to have an advantage in handling big block trades, due to superior liquidity.

Global Exchanges

There are about 200 stock exchanges in over 60 nations in the world, including 15 in North America. The New York, Tokyo, London, and Osaka exchanges are the largest, and the TSE is one of the top ten in terms of market capitalization.

As noted, investors have become increasingly interested in equity markets around the world. Important global equity markets exist in developed countries including the United Kingdom, France, Germany, Italy, Switzerland, Japan, Hong Kong, and Australia. Investors are also interested in emerging markets such as Mexico, Brazil, and Indonesia.[22] Because of the large number and variety of foreign markets, we will consider only a few highlights here.

Western Europe has several mature markets, including (in addition to those mentioned above) Belgium, Finland, Spain, and Sweden. The London Stock Exchange (LSE) is an important equity market that handles listed equities and bonds, as well as unlisted securities. Germany has Continental Europe's largest stock market. Switzerland is home to some of the largest global companies in the world, including Nestlé (food and beverage) and Hoffman La Roche (drugs).

Interestingly, analysts now refer to Europe's emerging markets. These include the Czech Republic, Hungary, and Poland where potential profits are great but risks are also. Illiquidity is a common problem, corporate information is difficult to obtain, and political risk can be an important factor. Turkey is another example of an emerging market.

The Far East is the fastest growing region in the world, with recent growth rates twice that of Canada and the United States. North American investors have been particularly active in the Far Eastern markets in recent years. These markets also have been very volatile, with large gains and losses because of illiquidity (a scarcity of buyers at times) as well as political and currency risks.

Japan, the dominant Asian economic power, has the second-largest stock market in the world. Although Japan has eight stock exchanges, the Tokyo Stock Exchange dominates that country's equity markets. Both domestic and foreign stocks are listed on the Tokyo Exchange, and among domestic issues, relatively few are traded on the floor of the exchange; the rest (as well as foreign stocks) are handled by computer.

Hong Kong is the second-largest Asian market in terms of market capitalization. Other Asian markets include India, Indonesia, Japan, South Korea, Malaysia, Pakistan, the Philippines, Singapore, Sri Lanka, Taiwan, and Thailand. Of course, some of these markets are quite small. The Four Dragons — Hong Kong, Singapore, South Korea, and Taiwan — dominate these markets when Japan is excluded.

The big unknown in Asian markets is, of course, China. An emerging economy of potentially great importance, China is booming as an economy but with great risks, for politics strongly affects investments in China. Its financial markets are still tiny by other countries' standards. Chinese companies do trade on the Hong Kong exchange as well as on exchanges in China such as Shanghai.

[22] There is no precise definition of an emerging market, but generally it involves a stable political system, fewer regulations, and less standardization in trading activity.

Latin America is the remaining emerging marketplace that has been of great interest to investors recently. The markets in Latin America include Argentina, Brazil, Chile, Colombia, Mexico, Peru, and Venezuela. Mexico's market is the largest, followed by Brazil, with the others small by comparison in terms of market capitalization. As we would expect in emerging markets, profit potentials are large, but so are risks — volatile prices, liquidity problems, and political risks such as the assassination of Mexico's leading presidential candidate in 1994.

Mexico's Bolsa has enjoyed popularity as a result of the North American Free Trade Agreement (NAFTA) and a general strengthening of the Mexican economy. Although Mexico is the largest Latin American stock market, one well-known stock, Telefonos de Mexico, accounts for about 20 per cent of the entire market's capitalization.

Equity Securities — Negotiated Markets

Unlike the exchanges, **over-the-counter (OTC) markets** or dealer markets do not have a physical location but consist of a network of dealers who trade with each other over the phone or over a computer network. It is a **negotiated market**, where only the **dealers** bid and ask quotations are entered by those dealers acting as "market makers" in a particular security. Market makers execute trades from their inventories of securities in which they have agreed to "make a market" (discussed in Chapter 5). This market essentially handles securities that are not listed on a stock exchange, although some listed securities are now traded in this market.

Over-the-Counter (OTC) Market
A network of securities dealers linked together by phone and computer to make markets in securities.

Negotiated Market
A market involving dealers, such as the OTC.

Dealer
An individual or firm who makes a market in a stock by buying from and selling to investors.

The Canadian OTC Market

Part of negotiated market

The volume of unlisted, over-the-counter (OTC) equity trading in Canada is much smaller compared to exchange-traded equity transactions. While the exact size of Canadian OTC market activity is difficult to measure due to lack of complete statistics, we do know it has grown in importance in recent years. In 1994, it accounted for 6.4 per cent of total Canadian equity trading, representing an increase from 1.9 per cent in 1992, partially in response to the introduction of trading in foreign shares in the fall of 1992. Reported trading volume has grown from 281 million shares in 1991 to 3 billion in 1997.

Canadian OTC trading takes place using the Canadian Over-the-Counter Automated Trading System (COATS) which is an electronic quotation and regulated trade reporting system for unlisted securities trading. Since 1991 operating authority for COATS lies with the Canadian Dealing Network (CDN). The CDN is now a subsidiary of the TSE. However, the proposed changes to the structure of Canadian stock markets would see the CDN become part of the national junior stock market. The CDN presently consists of a large network that links dealers across Canada, where trading goes on beyond exchange hours. The CDN also provides bid/ask prices together with high, low, and closing prices, and trading volume from the previous day.

The CDN does not have listing requirements for stocks traded on its system, hence these stocks are referred to as "unlisted" securities. It does not attempt to regulate the companies whose securities are traded on its system. As a result, the shares of a number of junior and emerging companies that cannot satisfy the listing requirements of the exchanges, trade in the OTC market. The market is more speculative in nature than the exchanges and is also generally referred to as a "thin" or illiquid market, since it is characterized by low trading volume and relatively few bids or offers.

Nasdaq Stock Market (Nasdaq)
A national and international OTC stock market consisting of communication networks for the trading of thousands of stocks.

National Association of Securities Dealers (NASD)
A self-regulating body of brokers and dealers overseeing OTC practices.

Nasdaq National Market System (Nasdaq/NMS)
The largest secondary market for the trading of equity securities in the world.

The US OTC Market

Roughly 35,000 stocks trade in the OTC market in the United States. Many of these are small, thinly traded stocks that do not generate much interest.[23] The most important part of the negotiated market is the **Nasdaq Stock Market**, or **Nasdaq**, which merged with the Amex in 1998 to form the Nasdaq-Amex Market Group. Nasdaq represents a national and international stock market consisting of communications networks for the trading of thousands of stocks. Nasdaq has insisted for several years that its market is technically not synonymous with the OTC market.[24] This market is a wholly owned subsidiary of the **National Association of Securities Dealers (NASD)**, a self-regulating body of brokers and dealers that oversees OTC practices, much as the TSE or NYSE supervise their members.

The Nasdaq Stock Market consists of a network of market makers or dealers linked together by communications devices who compete freely with each other through an electronic network of terminals, rather than on the floor of an exchange. These dealers conduct transactions directly with each other and with customers. Each Nasdaq company has a number of competing dealers who make a market in the stock, with a minimum of two and an average of 11 dealers. (Some large Nasdaq companies have 40 or more dealers.)

Nasdaq features an electronic trading system as the centrepiece of its operations. This system provides instantaneous transactions as Nasdaq market makers compete for investor orders. An investor who places an order with his or her broker for a Nasdaq security will have this order executed in one of two ways:

1. If the broker's firm makes a market in the security, the order will be executed internally at a price equal to, or better than, the best price quoted by all competing market makers
2. If the broker's firm is not a market maker in this security, the firm will buy from or sell to a market maker at another firm. SelectNet is a screen-based negotiation service that member firms use to quickly obtain efficient execution of orders in Nasdaq securities.

A significant development occurred on April 1, 1982, with the start-up of the **Nasdaq National Market System (Nasdaq/NMS)**, a component of the Nasdaq market. The NMS is a combination of the competing market makers in OTC stocks and the up-to-the-minute reporting of trades. The system uses data similar to that shown for the exchanges (specifically, high, low, and closing quotations, volume, and the net change from one day to the next). By the end of 1997, 4,386 securities traded on Nasdaq/NMS, out of a total of 6,208 active Nasdaq securities. However, on a volume basis NMS issues accounted for well over 90 per cent of all Nasdaq volume.

The Nasdaq Stock Market has become a major player in the securities markets and in all likelihood will continue to gain in importance. In 1998 there were more companies listed on Nasdaq (5,126) than on the NYSE (3,114), and the dollar volume of trading ($5.8 trillion) was fast approaching that of the NYSE ($7.3 trillion). However, the market capitalization of $2.6 trillion, well below the $10.9 trillion of NYSE firms.[25]

An important trend in the OTC market is the emergence of institutional investors as dominant players. Traditionally, the OTC market has been known as the market for mostly

---

[23] Traditionally, the prices of these stocks were reported only once a day on what are called Pink Sheets. Current prices on these stocks are now available electronically.

[24] Nasdaq traditionally was the acronym for the National Association of Securities Dealers Automated Quotation system. Nasdaq now states that the word is not an acronym.

[25] Nasdaq-Amex Web site: <http://www.nasdaq-amex.com>.

small and less well-known companies, where individual investors trade. Since 1982, the institutions have assumed an increasingly larger role and by year-end 1993 were the largest single group, a position they have maintained. At year-end 1995 institutions accounted for 39 per cent of the shares held and for 49 per cent of the market value of the holdings, surpassing individual investors in both categories. Investment firms and mutual funds account for about three-fourths of both shares held and the market value of holdings.

In summary, the common stock issues traded on Nasdaq vary widely in size, price, quality, and trading activity. These stocks range from small start-up companies to huge successes such as Microsoft and Intel, who have chosen to remain Nasdaq companies rather than move on to the NYSE.

The Third and Fourth Markets

The **third market** is an OTC market for the trading of securities that are listed on organized exchanges. This market has traditionally been important in the United States for block trades or extremely large transactions. This is done in order to avoid minimum exchange-regulated commission fees. The use of third markets for block trading has not been essential in Canada because commission fees on large trades are negotiable.

Third Market
An OTC market for the trading of securities that are listed on organized exchanges. Traditionally important in the US for block trades of extremely large transactions.

By the beginning of the 1990s, the third market had become the third largest trader of NYSE-listed stocks, behind the NYSE and the Midwest Stock Exchange. Today a few third-market brokers provide investors with the flexibility to trade when regular exchanges are closed. For example, Jeffries & Company, a leading third-market broker in Los Angeles, specializes in trading big blocks off the floor of major exchanges, particularly when the NYSE is not open. Generally, it makes a market in a stock by matching buyers and sellers (and collecting commissions), but Jeffries often takes positions in stocks to facilitate trading.[26]

The **fourth market** refers to transactions made directly between large institutions (and wealthy individuals), bypassing brokers and dealers. Essentially, the fourth market is a communications network among investors interested in trading large blocks of stock. Several different privately owned automated systems exist to provide current information on specific securities that the participants are willing to buy or sell.

Fourth Market
Transactions made directly between large institutions or wealthy individuals bypassing brokers and dealers. It is a communications network among these large institutional investors.

Instinet (Institutional Network), owned by Reuters, the news agency, is an electronic trading network that has become the largest computerized brokerage. It is a system designed only for brokers and institutions who pay to use proprietary terminals. Instinet Corporation is a New York-based registered broker that is a member of 17 exchanges around the world, including the Toronto Stock Exchange. Instinet is always open for trading stocks on the exchanges to which it belongs.

Instinet (Institutional Network)
An electronic trading network that has become the largest computerized brokerage. It is part of the fourth market and only open to those brokers and institutions who pay to use it.

Instinet offers anonymous trading, allowing large traders to bypass brokers and avoid information leaks regarding who is transacting. Trades are often less than 10,000 shares each, and an institution can do multiple trades to get in or out of a position in a stock without others knowing. Much of Instinet's volume is coming at the expense of Nasdaq. Some estimates are that Instinet's trades account for 20 per cent of Nasdaq's volume on some days. Instinet volume amounted to roughly 100 million shares daily by mid-1996.

Commissions can be as low as one cent a share, compared with perhaps six cents on the organized markets. Furthermore, traders can split the spread between what was bid and what

[26] Another third-market firm, Madoff Investment Securities, pays brokers to execute orders through its system, thereby providing very aggressive competition for both the NYSE and the regional exchanges.

was asked among themselves, thereby saving the dealer spreads that would be paid on the exchanges. Given the small differences in results that often distinguish mediocre from good performance, such savings can be significant to a money manager trying to outperform the market. Not surprisingly, by 1998 over 90 per cent of the US institutional funds under management were Instinet clients. The prospect is for these electronic networks to grow because of institutional trader frustration with the inability of the exchanges to handle large blocks of securities. Organized exchanges have expressed concerns because this type of activity fragments the market and decreases the liquidity on the exchanges.

Comparison of International Equity Markets

Figure 4-4 shows the market capitalization for the top ten major world stock markets for 1996 and 1997. As we can see by this measure, New York was by far the largest market, followed by Tokyo, London, Nasdaq, and so forth. The Toronto Stock Exchange ranked seventh in 1996 and eighth in 1997. Based on market capitalization (and on trading volumes), the TSE is the dominant Canadian stock market, while the NYSE remains the dominant market in the United States, followed by Nasdaq.

Figure 4-4
The Ten Biggest Stock Markets in the World by Market Capitalization (in Millions of US Dollars) 1996–97

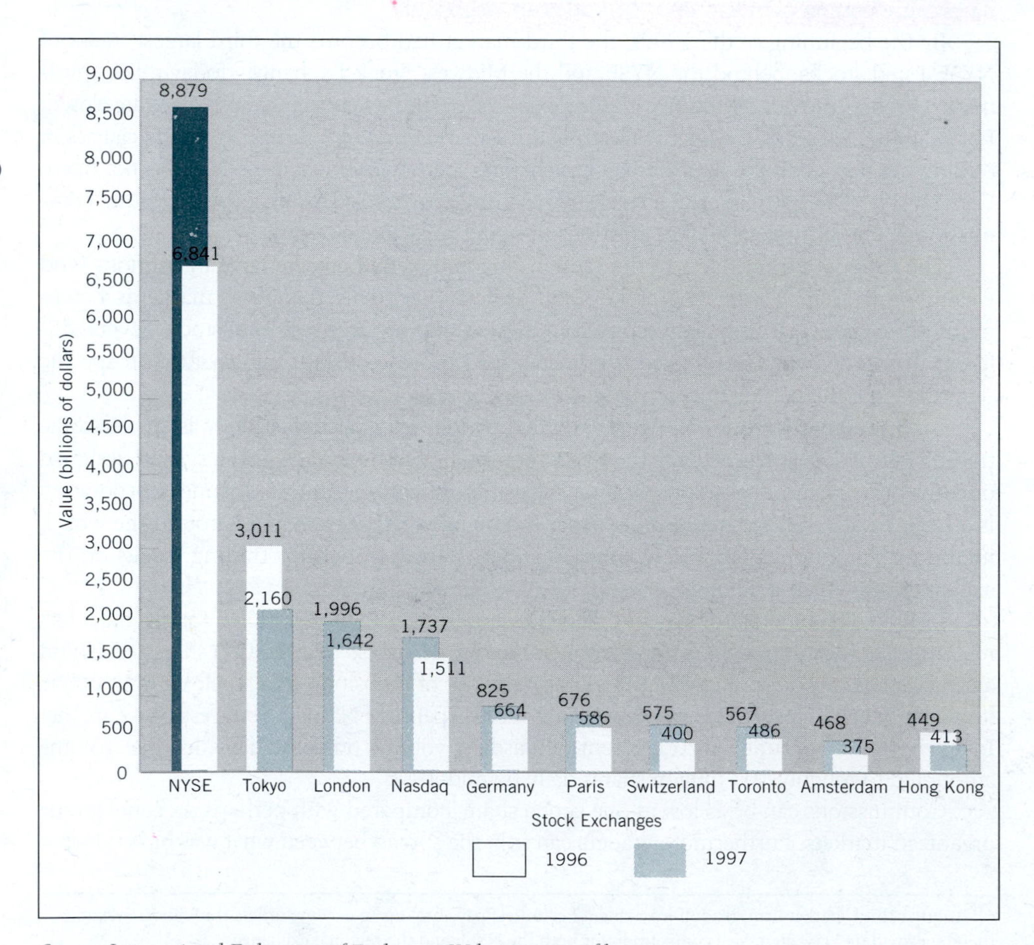

Source: International Federation of Exchanges Web site: <www.fibv.com>.

Stock Market Indicators

The most popular question asked about stock markets is probably, "What did the market do today?" To answer this question, we need a composite report on market performance, which is what stock market averages and indexes are designed to provide. Because of the large number of equity markets, both domestic and foreign, there are numerous stock market indicators.

An index is a series of numbers that represent a combination of stock prices in such a manner that percentage changes in this series may be calculated over time. They are used primarily for performance comparisons and to gauge the overall direction of movements in the stock market. An average is used in the same manner as an index but differs from it because it is composed of equally-weighted items. In this section, we outline only some basic information on these averages and indexes, with subsequent chapters containing more analysis and discussion as needed. The appendix at the end of this chapter provides additional details on these indicators, including composition and construction details.

Canadian Market Indexes

The present TSE 300 Composite Index System was introduced in 1977, with historical series dating back to 1956. The **Toronto Stock Exchange (TSE) 300 Composite Index** measures variations in market values of a portfolio of 300 Canadian stocks due to changes in the total market capitalization (the number of common shares outstanding multiplied by the market price per share) of these stocks. Thus, a stock's weight varies in response to changes in share price and/or the number of shares outstanding. The actual stocks composing the TSE 300 is reviewed annually, and stocks that no longer satisfy the criteria are replaced by others that do. The 300 stocks included in the TSE 300 are classified by industry to form 14 major group indexes, and 40 subgroups are also tracked. The base value of 1,000 was set for the TSE 300 Index and related indexes for the base year of 1975.

Toronto Stock Exchange (TSE) 300 Composite Index
The TSE 300 measures changes in market values of a portfolio of 300 Canadian stocks due to alterations in the total market capitalization (the number of common shares outstanding multiplied by the market price per share) of these stocks.

There are several other TSE indexes whose values are determined in the same manner as the TSE 300. One of the most important of these over the past few years has been the TSE 35 stock index. Introduced in 1987, it has been used for stock index futures and options products. The TSE 100 and TSE 200 were introduced in 1993 and were designed primarily for institutional investors as an instrument for passive management. The TSE 100 includes the 100 largest and most liquid TSE stocks such as consumer, industrial, interest sensitive, and resource sectors. The TSE 200 includes the remaining 200 stocks from the TSE 300 and is used as a proxy for returns on small-cap stocks. Total return indexes were introduced in 1980 and measure the return on the indexes if all dividends had been reinvested. As such, they demonstrate the compound return available from investing in stocks on a continuing basis.

On December 31, 1998, the TSE introduced a new index, the S&P/TSE 60 Index. It will eventually replace the TSE 35 and the TSE 100 as the basis for derivative products including index funds and index-linked GICs, and these two indexes will be phased out over the 1999-2000 period. The S&P/TSE 60 was developed in conjunction with Standard & Poor's Corporation (S&P) who maintain several major market indexes including the S&P 500 Composite Index (which is discussed below).

The S&P/TSE 60 Index is designed to mimic the performance of the TSE 300, which will remain in place as the broad stock market benchmark for Canada. In addition to designing the new index, S&P will assume management responsibilities for all TSE indexes and the

REAL-WORLD RETURNS

The S&P/TSE 60 Index

The Toronto Stock Exchange's new 60-stock blue chip index is heavy on financial services, technology firms, and core resource companies, especially in the oil and gas sector.

The exchange released the list of stocks yesterday that will be included in the new S&P/TSE 60 index, developed in conjunction with Standard & Poor's Corp. of New York. The new index will come into effect on December 31 1998, eventually replacing the TSE 35 and TSE 100 indexes, which will be phased out over the next couple of years.

Selection criteria for membership in the new index, like that of the S&P 500, take into account market capitalization, the size of the public float, liquidity, the health of the firm, and what sector it comes from. The index designers also looked at each company's leadership role in its industry, and financial fundamentals such as its earnings history.

The S&P/TSE 60

1. Abitibi-Consolidated Inc.
2. Agrium Inc.
3. Alberta Energy Co.
4. Alcan Aluminum Ltd.
5. Anderson Exploration Ltd.
6. ATI Technologies Inc.
7. Bank of Montreal
8. Bank of Nova Scotia
9. Barrick Gold Corp.
10. BCE Inc.
11. BioChem Pharma Inc.
12. Bombardier Inc.
13. CIBC
14. Cdn. National Railway Co.
15. Cdn. Natural Resources Ltd.
16. Canadian Pacific Ltd.
17. Cdn. Occidental Petroleum
18. Canadian Tire Corp.
19. Dofasco Inc.
20. EdperBrascan Corp.
21. Enbridge Inc.
22. Euro-Nevada Mining Corp.
23. Falconbridge Ltd.
24. Geac Computer Corp. Ltd.
25. Gulf Canada Resources Ltd.
26. Hudson's Bay Co.
27. Imasco Ltd.
28. Imperial Oil Ltd.
29. Inco Ltd.
30. Laidlaw Inc.
31. Loblaw Cos. Ltd.
32. MacMillan Bloedel ltd.
33. Magna International Inc.
34. Mitel Corp.
35. Moore Corp. Ltd.
36. National Bank of Canada
37. Newbridge Networks Corp.
38. Newcourt Credit Group
39. Noranda Inc.
40. Northern Telecom Ltd.
41. Nova Corp.
42. Petro-Canada
43. Placer Dome Inc.
44. Poco petroleums Ltd.
45. Potash Corp.
46. Renaissance Energy Ltd.
47. Royal Bank of Canada
48. Seagram Co. Ltd.
49. Shaw Cablesystems Ltd.
50. Suncor Energy Inc.
51. Talisman Energy inc.
52. Teck Corp.
53. Teleglobe Inc.
54. Telus Corp.
55. Thomson Corp.
56. Toronto-Dominion Bank
57. TransAlta Corp.
58. TransCanada PipeLines Ltd.
59. United Dominion Industries
60. Westcoast Energy Inc.

Stocks that are included in the S&P/TSE 60 are expected to rise in price as investors start buying to replicate the new index. Those in the TSE 100 that aren't included in the S&P/TSE 60 are expected to fall somewhat.

The TSE 35 and 100 stock indexes are currently used as the basis for a number of derivative products, index funds, and index-linked GICs. The S&P/TSE 60 will take over that function at year-end, although the 35, the 100, and the small-capitalization TSE 200, will continue to be calculated for months, or even years, to allow a transition period.

As existing futures and options contracts expire, they will be replaced by new ones based on the S&P/TSE 60.

To understand what the past performance of the new index would have been if it had already existed, the TSE will create a "synthetic history" dating back to the beginning of 1982.

Next year new small- and mid-cap indexes will be created to fill the gap between the blue-chip 60 stock index and the TSE 300.

The new index was created because the TSE 35 was too small to give index funds enough diversity, was not liquid enough, and didn't closely track the performance of the TSE 300. The TSE 100 was too large for institutions to use for complex hedging strategies, and had too many marginal stocks.

S&P was brought in to set up the new structure because of its strong reputation for fund management. Its participation also means more foreign investors should be attracted to TSE-listed stocks.

The new index has been enthusiastically welcomed by critics of the TSE, which in the past included notorious companies such as Bre-X Minerals Ltd. and YBM Magnex International Inc. in its benchmark TSE 300 index because their stock market value and trading volume met the TSE's numerical thresholds. Bre-X collapsed in a spectacular fraud. YBM is mired in controversy, and trading in its shares has been suspended since May.

S&P will not only help choose the constituents of the new index, it will also take over management of all the TSE's indexes and the marketing and management of derivative products based on them.

The 60 stocks in the new index will also become part of a huge 1,200-stock global index that S&P is expected to launch next fall.

Source: Excerpted from Richard Blackwell, "Nothing Shocking about S&P/TSE 60 Stocks," The Globe and Mail/Report on Business, *December 8, 1998, p. B1. Reprinted with permission from* The Globe and Mail.

marketing and management of related derivative products. The index base value was set equal to 100 as of January 29, 1982 (the base year for the TSE 300 Index is 1975). This base period was chosen due to concerns regarding data reliability prior to that date. The index closing value was reported as 375.98 on December 31, 1998 — its inception date. The stocks included initially in this index are discussed in the Real-World Returns box above.

In addition to the new S&P/TSE 60 Index, the TSE introduced the S&P/TSE Mid-Cap Index and the S&P/TSE Small-Cap Index in 1999. The Mid-Cap Index will consist of 60 mid-cap TSE 300 stocks, while the Small-Cap Index will contain the remaining 180 small-cap stocks in the TSE 300 and will replace the TSE 200 as a small-cap index.

The Canadian Market Portfolio Index (XXM) was introduced by the Montreal Exchange in 1984 with base value of 1,000 as of 1983. It consists of 25 widely held, highly capitalized interlisted Canadian stocks from a variety of economic sectors. The ME also maintains six Canadian market sectoral indexes. These are non-weighted price indexes.

The VSE publishes the VSE Composite Index (based on over 1,400 VSE listed companies that trade at least 50 per cent of their market volume on the VSE) and three subindexes. The Resource Index and the Commercial/Industrial Index track price changes by the "senior board" companies, while the Venture Index tracks junior companies (over 1,200). These indexes are value-weighted.

US Market Indexes

Dow Jones Industrial Average (DJIA)
A price-weighted series of 30 leading industrial stocks that trade on the NYSE, used as a measure of stock market activity and of changes in the economy in general.

Blue Chip Stocks
The stocks of large, well-established, and well-known companies that have long records of earnings and dividends.

Standard & Poor's 500 Composite Index (S&P 500)
Broadly based, market-weighted index of US stock market activity covering 500 stocks. It is generally the measure of the market preferred by institutional investors.

The **Dow Jones Industrial Average (DJIA)** is the most widely quoted measure of NYSE stock performance, despite the fact that it includes only 30 of the 3,700-plus stocks that trade on the NYSE. The DJIA is computed from 30 leading industrial stocks whose composition changes slowly over time to reflect changes in the economy. This average is said to be composed of **blue chip stocks**, meaning large, well-established, and well-known companies.

The DJIA is price-weighted and is therefore affected more by changes in higher priced stocks. It is calculated by adding the prices of the 30 stocks together and dividing by a divisor. The divisor was initially 30, but has been revised downward through the years to reflect the impact of stock splits, and is now below 1.0. The DJIA includes only blue chip stocks with a low-risk profile and it tends to underperform broader based indexes in the long term as a result of this lower risk. Other Dow Jones indexes include the Transportation Average (20 companies), a Utility Average (15 companies), and a Composite Average (65 companies), which are all price-weighted.

There are several other US indexes, of which the **Standard & Poor's 500 Composite Index (S&P 500)** is the most important. The S&P 500 Index is a broadly based market-weighted index, which measures US stock performance. The S&P 500 is obviously a much broader measure than the Dow, and it should be more representative of the general market. However, it consists primarily of NYSE stocks, and it is clearly dominated by the largest corporations.[27] Nevertheless, the S&P 500 Index is typically the measure of the market preferred by institutional investors who most often compare their performance to this market index.

Other US indexes include NYSE-maintained market-valued indexes that include all listed equities for a given group: composite, industrials, transportation, finance, real estate, and utilities. The Amex Index includes all stocks (about 800) that trade on the American Stock Exchange and is value-weighted. The Nasdaq Composite Index includes over 3,700 OTC stocks and is market-valued. The Value Line Composite Index is an average percentage change in about 1,700 stocks that are mainly second-tier issues. Finally, the Wilshire 5,000 Equity Index is a market-valued index that attempts to measure all stocks for which quotations are available; it is the most broadly based US index.

Foreign Stock Market Indicators

Stock market indexes are available for most foreign markets, but the composition, weighting, and computational procedures vary widely from index to index. This makes it difficult to make comparisons. To deal with these problems, some organizations have constructed their own set of indexes on a consistent basis to facilitate international market performance comparisons. The largest provider of international indexes is Morgan Stanley Capital International (MSCI). They

[27] The S&P 500 contains some bank and insurance company stocks traded in the OTC market.

maintain several global indexes including the MSCI World Index, which is a market-valued index that includes more than 2,200 stocks from 22 developed countries. MSCI also maintains 45 country and 18 regional indexes including the **EAFE Index** (the Europe, Australia, and Far East Index), the Emerging Markets Index, and several others.

EAFE Index
The Europe, Australia, and Far East Index is a value-weighted index of the equity performance of major foreign markets.

Similar to the MSCI World Index, the Dow Jones World Stock Index covers Canada, Mexico, and the United States, as well as the Pacific Region and Europe. It is designed to be a comprehensive measure and represents approximately 80 per cent of the world's stock markets. Unlike the DJIA, the World Stock Index is a capitalization-weighted index.

The best-known measure of the Japanese stock market is the Nikkei 225 Average, an arithmetic average of prices for 225 actively traded stocks on the Tokyo Stock Exchange. Similar to the Dow Jones Average, it traditionally has been a price-weighted series. In contrast, the Financial Times Actuaries Share Indexes are market value indexes covering stocks on the London Stock Exchange, the most widely followed being the FT London FT-SE 100 Index. These indexes, as well as those for other foreign markets, can be seen daily in Canadian financial newspapers.

Bond Markets

Just as stockholders need good secondary markets to be able to trade stocks and thus preserve their flexibility, bondholders need a viable market in order to sell before maturity. Otherwise, many investors would be reluctant to tie up their funds for up to 30 years. At the very least, they would demand higher initial yields on bonds, which would hinder raising funds by those who wish to invest productively.

Investors can purchase either new bonds being issued in the primary market or existing bonds outstanding in the secondary market. Yields for the two must be in equilibrium. If, for example, **Seagram**'s existing bonds are trading to provide a 9 per cent yield over a 20-year period, comparable, new Seagram bonds will be sold with approximately the same yield.

Although some bonds trade on the exchanges (convertible bonds only on the TSE), the secondary bond market is primarily an OTC market, with a large network of dealers making markets in the various bonds. Investors can buy and sell bonds through their brokers, who, in turn, trade with bond dealers. The volume of bond trading in the OTC market in Canada dwarfs the volume of bonds traded on all the exchanges combined. The situation is similar in the United States where OTC trading of bonds dominates, although a few thousand bonds are traded on the NYSE and a very few on the Amex.

The Canadian bond market represents a relatively small percentage of the global bond market. For example, in 1997, there was approximately $506 billion US in outstanding debt or 2 per cent of the global market. The size of the Canadian market pales in comparison to several international bond markets such as those in the US and Japan, where there was $12.4 and $4.4 trillion US in outstanding debt in 1997.

Government bonds comprise well over 80 per cent of the Canadian bond market and the major component is Government of Canada bonds. These are widely purchased, held, and traded, resulting in a broad and deep market, with a large volume of transactions. The market is not as deep for provincial or municipal bonds and is even thinner for corporate bonds. Corporate issues account for less than 20 per cent of the total bonds outstanding in Canada in 1997. Despite an increase in trading in corporate issues over the past few years, the market is relatively thin in comparison to the market for government bonds in Canada and in relation to international corporate bond markets. For example, in 1997 the amount of Canadian corporate bonds outstanding was $75 billion US, accounting for a mere 0.8 per cent of the world corporate market. At the same time, there was over $5 trillion US in outstanding corporate bonds in the United States.

Corporate issues are not traded as actively as government issues, which is likely attributable to the fact that over 40 per cent of these bonds are held by institutional investors. Most corporate bond trades by institutions involve large amounts. As a result, liquidity is not always good for small transactions in corporate bonds, with delays occurring in the trade, and price concessions often have to be made. Investors should be careful in trading small amounts of corporate bonds and be prepared for delays and costs. Interestingly, 53 per cent of corporate issues are held by non-residents.

Derivatives Markets

We discuss the details of derivatives markets in their respective chapters. However, at this point we note that options can be bought or sold through an exchange facility or privately arranged (OTC options). All exchange-traded options in Canada are presently traded on the TSE and the ME, since the VSE ceased option trading in 1997. As discussed above, proposed changes to Canadian markets would mean that all exchange trading in derivatives would occur on the ME.

In 1973 the Chicago Board of Options Exchange (CBOE) was formed to begin trading in options. It is the best-known options market in the world and operates using a system of market makers. Bid and ask prices are quoted by the market maker, and floor brokers can trade with the market maker or with other floor brokers. Liquidity problems, which had plagued the OTC options markets were overcome by:

1. Standardizing option contracts
2. Introducing a clearing corporation which would guarantee the performance of the seller of an options contract (it effectively becomes the buyer and seller for each option contract).

In Canada, all equity, bond, and stock index positions are issued and guaranteed by a single clearing corporation, the Canadian Derivatives Clearing Corporation (CDCC), formerly Trans Canada Options Inc. (TCO), which is jointly owned by the TSE and the ME. In the US all listed options are cleared through the Options Clearing Corporation (OCC). Exercise of options is accomplished by submitting an exercise notice to the clearing corporation, which assigns it to a member firm, which then assigns it to one of its accounts.

In contrast to options, futures contracts are traded on exchanges in designated "pits," using an open-outcry process as a trading mechanism. Under this system, the pit trader offers to buy or sell contracts at an offered price and other pit traders are free to transact if they wish. This open-outcry system is unique in securities trading. There are few sights in the financial system that can rival frenzied trading activity in a futures market pit. Another unique feature of these markets is that the delivery time period can vary from four to six weeks for commodities such as corn or wheat to one day for an index contract.

In Canada, the only commodity exchange is the Winnipeg Commodity Exchange where canola futures are by far the most active (1.27 million contracts 1995–96). The ME trades contracts on one and three-month bankers' acceptances (which call for cash delivery), as well as on Government of Canada bonds. The 1997 volumes for Canadian bankers' acceptances was 4.14 million contracts, while the volume for Canada Government bonds was 1.32 million contracts. The Toronto Futures Exchange (TFE) is a subsidiary of the TSE that trades several futures contracts, including one based on 500 times the TSE 35 Index value and another based on 500 times the TSE 100 Index value. Both call for cash delivery. The 1997 trading volumes in contracts for the TSE 100 Index Futures and the TSE 35 Index Futures were 19,317 and 317,372, respectively.

The centre of commodity futures trading in North America is the Chicago Board of Trade (CBOT) and the Chicago Mercantile Exchange (CME). However, there are several other important exchanges in New York including the Commodity Exchange, the New York Mercantile Exchange, the New York Coffee, Sugar, and Cocoa Exchange, the New York Cotton Exchange, and the New York Futures Exchange.

THE CHANGING SECURITIES MARKETS

For the last 15 to 20 years the securities markets have been changing rapidly, with more of the same expected over the coming years. In Canada, a massive restructuring of the security exchanges has recently been proposed, which will result in drastic changes to Canadian secondary markets, if implemented. Several factors explain why markets have undergone such rapid changes. First, institutional investors have different requirements and often different views from individual investors, and their emergence as the dominant force in the market has necessitated significant shifts in market structure and operation.

Institutional investors often trade in large **blocks**. Large-block activity is an indicator of institutional participation, and the average size of trades on the TSE and NYSE has grown sharply over the years. In fact, block trading now accounts for more than half of all TSE and NYSE trading volume.

Blocks
Transactions involving at least 10,000 shares or $100,000 in value; block trades are usually executed by institutional investors.

Another factor stimulating changes in our markets is the growth of computerized trading of securities, which has made possible the inter-market trading of securities. Inter-market trading permits brokerage houses to electronically route orders to whatever market is offering the best price to a buyer or a seller. This system should enhance market efficiency, by promoting competition and lowering bid-ask spreads, because the dealers with the most attractive prices would automatically receive the orders.

Most of the world's major stock exchanges have moved to computerized trading (including the TSE), the most notable exception being the largest exchange in the world, the NYSE. It continues to justify its nearly 200-year-old specialist system, despite criticisms that it is not attuned to the needs of the modern market. The NYSE defends the specialist system vigorously, citing such evidence as the 1987 market crash, when the specialists stayed at their posts to handle orders while many over-the-counter dealers refused to answer the phone. Finally, the global nature of security markets in today's world has put extreme pressure on all markets to compete aggressively for security listings.

The Globalization of Securities Markets

While after-hours trading is not presently permitted for Canadian securities, the move toward around-the-clock trading — which many expected to be the wave of the future — began in the early 1990s. In 1991, the Nasdaq International Market started trading OTC stocks early in the morning during regular trading hours in London. Evening sessions for futures trading were started on the Chicago Board of Trade. That same year, the NYSE began two after-hours "crossing sessions" which last from 4:15 p.m. to 5:30 p.m. One session is for individual stocks, and the other is for baskets of stocks. The Pacific Stock Exchange now has an expanded-hours session that lasts until 4:50 p.m. EST.

None of the above marketplaces offering extended-hour trading has matched the success of Instinet. As mentioned earlier, this electronic trading mechanism allows large investors (primarily institutions) to trade with each other electronically at any hour.[28] While Instinet trading of Canadian stocks outside of trading hours is not presently permitted, Canadian investors may trade foreign securities through Instinet. The Instinet system offers investors privacy and low trading costs because regular brokerage fees do not have to be paid. In addition, institutions are able to negotiate prices electronically with each other.

Through such sources as Instinet, stock prices can change quickly even though the exchanges themselves are closed. The after-hours trading is particularly important when significant news events occur, or when an institutional investor is simply anxious to trade a position. Such activity could, in a few years, lead to the 24-hour trading of stocks, just as currency trading now does.

What about bonds? In today's world, bonds increasingly are being traded at all hours around the globe, more so than stocks. The emergence of global offerings means that bonds are traded around the clock and around the world. The result of this global trading in bonds is that bond dealers and investors are having to adapt to the new demands of the marketplace, being available to react and trade at all hours of the day and night. This includes new employees in various locales, expanded hours, and computer terminals in the home.

SUMMARY

This summary relates to the learning objectives provided on page 89.

1. **Distinguish between primary and secondary markets.**
   Financial markets include primary markets, where new securities are sold, and secondary markets, where existing securities are traded. Primary markets involve investment dealers who specialize in selling new securities. They offer the issuer several functions, including advisory, underwriting, and marketing services. Secondary markets consist of equity, bond, and derivative markets. The Toronto Stock Exchange (TSE) is the largest stock market in Canada, and trading on it has been completely computerized since April 1997. The New York Stock Exchange (NYSE) is the world's premier stock market and operates using a specialist system.

2. **Describe how the equity markets are organized and how they operate.**
   The equity markets consist of auction markets (exchanges) and negotiated markets (over-the-counter — OTC — markets). Brokers act as intermediaries, representing both buyers and sellers; dealers make markets in securities, buying and selling for their own account. The OTC market is a network of dealers making markets in unlisted securities. Canadian OTC trading takes place using the Canadian Over-the-Counter Automated Trading System (COATS) which is an electronic quotation and regulated trade reporting system for unlisted securities trading. Since 1991 operating authority for COATS lies with the Canadian Dealing Network Inc. (CDN), a subsidiary of the TSE. Most OTC trading in the

[28] Instinet also offers the Crossing Network, which allows large investors to trade blocks of stock at daily closing prices.

United States takes place on the Nasdaq Stock Market, an electronic network of terminals linking together hundreds of market makers who compete for investor orders by buying and selling for their own account. Investors have become increasingly interested in the many equity markets that exist all over the world.

3. **Explain what we mean by the third and fourth markets.**
   The third market is an OTC market for the trading of securities that are listed on exchanges. This market has traditionally been important in the United States for block trades, or extremely large transactions. The fourth market refers to transactions made directly between large institutions, bypassing brokers and dealers.
4. **State the major stock market indicators.**
   The best-known market indicator in Canada is the TSE 300 Composite Index, a market-weighted index. The best-known stock market indicator in the United States is the Dow Jones Industrial Average (DJIA), a price-weighted average computed from 30 leading industrial stocks. The S&P 500 Composite Index (which is value-weighted, similar to the TSE 300), is carried in the popular press, and investors often refer to it as a good measure of what the overall US stock markets are doing, at least for large NYSE stocks.
5. **Describe, briefly, the bond and derivatives markets.**
   Although some bonds are traded on the exchanges, most bond trading occurs in the OTC market. Federal government bonds enjoy broad markets, but the markets for provincial, municipal, and corporate bonds are often less liquid. Derivatives markets involve options and futures contracts. Puts and calls are traded on option exchanges using market makers or on the OTC market, while futures contracts are traded in pits using an open-outcry system.
6. **Discuss the factors behind rapid change in the securities markets.**
   The securities markets are changing rapidly, stimulated by the demands of institutional investors and by computerized and inter-market trading of securities. The markets are increasingly linked globally.

KEY TERMS

Auction markets
Blocks
Blue chip stocks
Brokers
Dealer
Dow Jones Industrial Average (DJIA)
EAFE Index
Fourth market
Initial public offerings (IPOs)
Instinet (Institutional Network)
Investment dealer
Nasdaq National Market System (Nasdaq/NMS)
National Association of Securities Dealers (NASD)
Nasdaq Stock Market (Nasdaq)
Negotiated market
New York Stock Exchange (NYSE)
Over-the-counter (OTC) market
Primary market
Program trading
Prompt offering qualification (POP) system
Prospectus
Secondary markets
Specialists
Standard & Poor's 500 Composite Index (S&P 500)
Third market
Toronto Stock Exchange (TSE)
Toronto Stock Exchange (TSE) 300 Composite Index
Underwriting

ADDITIONAL RESOURCES

Factual information concerning major secondary markets can be found in:

The Toronto Stock Exchange Review. Annual. Toronto: The Toronto Stock Exchange.

Nasdaq Fact Book. Annual. Washington, DC: National Association of Securities Dealers, Inc.

New York Stock Exchange Fact Book. Annual. New York: New York Stock Exchange, Inc.

INVESTMENTS ON THE WEB

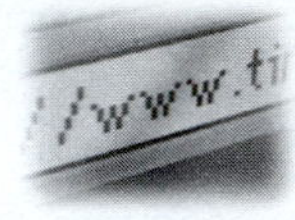

Web sites for the various stock exchanges include:
Toronto Stock Exchange: <http://www.tse.com>
Montreal Exchange: <http://www.me.org>
Vancouver Stock Exchange: <http://www.vse.ca>
Alberta Stock Exchange: <http://www.ase.ca>
Winnipeg Stock Exchange: <http://www.wse.ca>
New York Stock Exchange: <http://www.nyse.com>
Nasdaq-Amex Market Group: <http://www.nasdaq-amex.com>
Nasdaq Stock Market: <http://www.nasdaq.com>
American Stock Exchange: <http://www.amex.com>

REVIEW QUESTIONS

1. Distinguish between the third market and the fourth market.
2. What are two primary factors accounting for the rapid changes in securities markets?
3. What is the TSE 300 Composite Index?
4. What is the Dow Jones Industrial Average? How does it differ from the S&P 500 Composite Index?
5. What is meant by the term blue chip stocks? Cite three examples.
6. What is the EAFE Index?
7. What is meant by block activity? How important is it on the TSE and NYSE?
8. What is meant by the statement "The bond market is primarily an OTC market"?
9. What does it mean to say an IPO has been underwritten by RBC Dominion Securities?
10. Briefly describe the POP system. What kind of companies qualify to use this system?
11. What are "bought deals"?
12. What are the advantages and disadvantages of private placements?
13. What might cause an investment dealer to market newly issued securities on a "best efforts" basis instead of underwriting them?
14. What is the chief function of a capital market?
15. Why do some large Canadian firms want to be interlisted on US stock exchanges?
16. Discuss the importance of financial markets to the Canadian economy. Can primary markets exist without secondary markets?

17. Discuss the functions of an investment dealer. How do they serve as principals and how do they serve as agents in primary markets?
18. Outline the process for a primary offering of securities involving investment dealers.
19. Outline the structure of equity markets in Canada. Distinguish between auction markets and negotiated markets.
20. What is Instinet? How does it affect the over-the-counter market?
21. What is a prospectus?
22. What are some of the concerns that the issuing company takes into account when deciding on the pricing of an initial public offering (IPO)?
23. Comment on the recent global evidence of underpricing in IPOs. How is underpricing measured? Why do you think this phenomenon exists, given your understanding of efficient markets?
24. Explain the difference between a price-weighted index and a market-weighted index.

PREPARING FOR YOUR PROFESSIONAL EXAMS

Special Note to Canadian Securities Course Students

Ensure that you have read and understood the following topics:*

The importance of financial markets, p. 90
The primary markets, pp. 90–98
CSC Notes: Government Finance and the Competitive Tender System, p. 92
The secondary markets, pp. 98–109
The third and fourth markets, pp. 109–110
Comparison of international equity markets, p. 110
Stock market indicators, pp. 111–115
Bond markets, pp. 115–116
Derivatives markets, pp. 116–117
The changing securities markets, pp. 117–118

* *Reading these CSC-related topics should provide you with additional understanding of CSC material. However, it should not be seen as a substitute for reading the CSC textbook itself, which is the basis for the CSC exam.*

CSC REGISTRATION QUESTIONS

The Canadian Securities Institute issued the following sample questions in the 1997 CSC registration package as a means for students to self-assess their understanding of CSC-related material.

CANADIAN SECURITIES INSTITUTE

1. All of the following must be included in a preliminary prospectus except the ___________.

   a. current earnings statement

   b. purpose of the funds being raised

c. issuer's history and current status

d. net proceeds to the issuer

2. To test investor interest in a planned new issue of securities, a company usually issues ________.

a. an information circular

b. statement of material facts

c. a red herring prospectus

d. a request for tenders

3. When there are only a few bids or offers on a particular security the market is said to be a ________.

a. mixed market

b. best efforts market

c. thin market

d. subject market

4. New issue purchasers, for whom a prospectus is not required, are said to be ________.

5. The ________ market is a market for securities that is also known as the "unlisted market."

6. The sale of an entire new security issue directly to an institutional investor is called a ________.

a. private placement

b. fixed price offering

c. flow-through deal

d. farm-out distribution

7. A computerized trading strategy designed to profit from price discrepancies between equity and futures markets is called ________.

a. formula investing

b. program trading

c. market surveillance

d. efficient market trading

8. Another name for a preliminary prospectus is a(n) ________.

APPENDIX 4-A

STOCK MARKET INDEXES

Several issues must be dealt with in the construction of a stock market index or average. The most important involve its composition, the weighting procedure used, and the method of calculation.

What is the composition of the market measure? Is it a sample of one exchange to be used or a sample from the major exchanges? Should a sample from the over-the-counter (OTC) market be included? Alternatively, should every stock on an exchange(s), be used, and if so, how should OTC stocks be handled? (Do you include every active OTC stock or just those for which daily quotes are available?)

If investors need a broad measure of stock performance, several markets (TSE, ME, VSE, ASE, and OTC) need to be included. If investors want to know the performance of the largest stocks, a measure of TSE performance may be sufficient. Some market measures use subsamples of one or more markets, whereas others use every stock on one or more markets. It is important to be aware of compositional differences among the various market measures.

A second issue involves the weighting procedure used in constructing the index or average. Does each stock receive equal weight or is each weighted by its market value (i.e., market price multiplied by shares outstanding)? Alternatively, the measure could be price weighted, resulting in higher priced stocks carrying more weight than lower priced ones.

The third issue is the calculation procedures used. The primary question here is whether an index or an average is being used. A market average is an arithmetic mean of the prices for the sample of securities being used, showing the arithmetic average of the prices at a given time.

A market index measures the current price behaviour of the sample in relation to a base period established for a previous time. Indexes, therefore, are expressed in relative numbers, whereas averages are simply arithmetic means (weighted or unweighted). The use of an index allows for more meaningful comparisons over long periods of time because current values can be related to established base period values.

The Dow Jones Averages are arithmetic averages, but virtually all the other market measures are indexes.

The TSE 300 Composite Index

To determine the index, the market value of all firms is calculated (current market price multiplied by number of shares), and this total value is divided by the market value of the 300 securities for the base period. This relative value is multiplied by 1,000, representing the base period value.[29] In equation form, the TSE 300 is calculated as:

$$\text{TSE 300} = \frac{\Sigma P_{it} Q_{it}}{\Sigma P_{ib} Q_{ib}}(k) \tag{4-1}$$

P_{it} = the price of a stock i at time t
Q_{it} = number of shares of stock i at time t
P_{ib} = the price of a stock i at the base period time b

[29] Before multiplying by 1000, the TSE 300 at any point can be thought of as the price, in relation to the beginning price of $1, of all stocks in the index weighted by their proportionate total market values.

Q_{ib} = number of shares of stock i at the base period time b
b = the base period
k = the base number

A current value of 6,500 for the TSE 300 indicates that the average price of the 300 stocks in the index has increased by a factor of 6.5 in relation to the base period. If the Royal Bank of Canada was included in the TSE 300 and had a market value that was seven times as great as that of the National Bank of Canada, a 1 per cent change in Royal's price would have more than seven times the impact of a 1 per cent change in National's price.

The Dow Jones Industrial Average

In principle, calculation of the DJIA involves adding up the prices of the 30 stocks and dividing by 30 to obtain the average, but it is not that simple because of stock splits and dividends. Instead, the number is adjusted to reflect the stock splits and dividends that have occurred and today is much less than 1.0. As a result, a one-point change in the DJIA does not represent a change of $1 in the value of an average share; rather, the change amounts to only a few cents. You should keep this in mind the next time someone gets excited about a 10- or 20-point rise in one day in the DJIA.

The DJIA is calculated as:

$$DJIA_t = \Sigma P_{it}/n^* \tag{4-2}$$

where P is the price of a stock i at time t and n^* indicates an adjusted divisor.

Other Indexes

The Value Line Investment Survey, perhaps the best-known investment advisory service in the world, publishes several indexes of stock prices.[30] Since Value Line is a well-known investment advisory service, its indexes receive attention. Investors, however, should be aware of how these unique indexes differ from the others.

The Value Line Composite Index is unique in that it is an equally-weighted geometric average of stock prices.[31] It is based on the roughly 1,700 companies in more than 90 industries that Value Line chooses to cover in its reports. June 1961 is assigned the base index of 100.

Since a daily net percentage change in price is computed for the stocks, each stock in the index has the same percentage weight.[32] Therefore, a 20 per cent movement in a stock's price has the same impact on the index, whether 10 million or 100 million shares are outstanding. Neither a stock's market value nor its absolute price level will impact the index. The small,

---

[30] Specifically, Value Line publishes an Industrial, Rail, Utility, and Composite Index. More than 80 per cent of these stocks are listed on the NYSE.

[31] Geometric Averages are discussed in greater detail in Chapter 6.

[32] To compute the VL Index, the closing price of each stock for a given day is divided by the preceding day's close (which is set at an index of 100). The geometric average of these indexes of change is calculated by finding the nth root of the product of the n changes (where n is approximately 1,700). Finally, the geometric average of change for the day is multiplied by the preceding value of the average to obtain the new value.

low-priced stocks covered by Value Line will have the same impact as the larger stocks. In effect, the Value Line Composite is an unweighted index covering a broad cross-section of stocks. Some market observers feel that because it is unweighted, it is more reflective of general market trends.

In March 1988, Value Line introduced a new index, the Value Line Arithmetic Index (VLA). The change in this arithmetically averaged index is the sum of the price changes for all stocks in the index divided by the number of stocks. Value Line sees the arithmetic index as a good estimate of the price performance of an equal dollar portfolio of stocks, whereas changes in the geometric index provide a good estimate of the median price changes of the stocks covered.

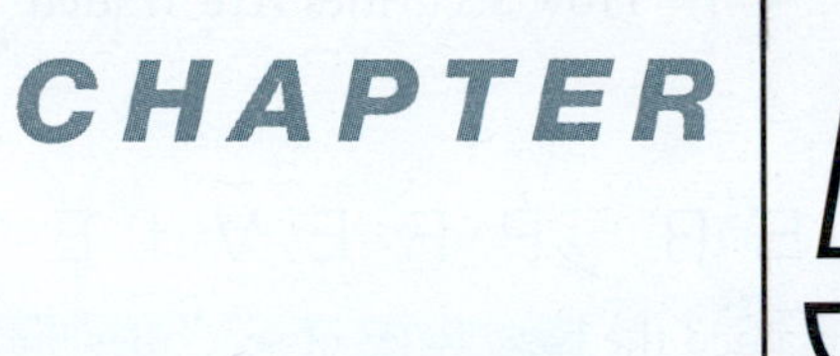

CHAPTER 5

HOW SECURITIES ARE TRADED

LEARNING OBJECTIVES

After reading this chapter, you will be able to

1. Explain the role of brokerage firms and stockbrokers.
2. Describe how brokerage firms operate.
3. Outline how orders to buy and sell securities are executed.
4. Discuss the regulation of the Canadian securities industry.
5. Explain the importance of margin trading and short selling to investors.

CHAPTER PREVIEW

Now that we have explained the basic types of securities and the markets where they are traded, we turn to the mechanics of trading — that is, what actually happens when a trade takes place. Similar to the organization of securities markets, the details of trading continue to evolve, but the basic procedures remain the same. In this chapter, you will learn about brokerage firms and stockbrokers and how they operate. We introduce the three major types of orders — market orders, limit orders, and stop orders — and explain how they are executed on the exchanges and in the Over-the-Counter market. (Appendix 5-A features the specialist system used by the NYSE.) We discuss the regulation of the Canadian securities industry and its role in protecting investors (Appendix 5-B considers regulation in the United States). Finally, you will learn about the importance of margin trading and short selling to investors.

BROKERAGE TRANSACTIONS

Brokerage Firms

In general, it is quite easy for any responsible person to open a brokerage account. An investor selects a broker or brokerage house by personal contact, referral, reputation, and so forth. Member firms of the exchanges are supposed to learn certain basic facts about potential customers, but only minimal information is normally required. Actually, personal contact between broker and customer seldom occurs, with transactions carried out by telephone, in writing, or increasingly by computer.

Full-Service Brokers
Brokerage firms offering a full range of services, including information and advice.

Customers can choose the type of broker they wish to use and brokers can be classified according to the services offered and fees charged. **Full-service brokers** offer a variety of services to investors, particularly information and advice. Thus, investors can obtain a wide variety of information about the economy, particular industries, individual companies, and the bond market, for example. Full-service brokers in Canada are primarily owned by the large Schedule I banks, in response to recent deregulation in the financial services industry, which allowed banks to take over securities firms. Familiar names include RBC Dominion Securities, Scotia Capital Markets, CIBC World Markets (formerly CIBC Wood Gundy), Merrill Lynch Canada, and Nesbitt-Burns.

Discount Brokers
Brokerage firms offering execution services for buying and selling securities at prices significantly less than full-service brokerage firms. They provide little, if any, investing information and give no advice.

In contrast to the full-service brokers, **discount brokers** concentrate on executing orders and are able to charge lower fees. Most offer services frequently used by investors in a manner similar to the full-service brokers, but they provide little, if any, investing information and give no advice. Thus, investors pay less and receive less. Most of the full service brokerage firms also maintain discount brokerage operations. Familiar names include Bank of Montreal Investor Line, Scotia Bank Discount Brokerage, Royal Bank Action Direct Discount Brokerage, TD Waterhouse (formerly TD Greenline), and CIBC Investor's Edge Discount Brokerage.

In addition, there are brokerage firms — including E*TRADE Canada, a service of VERSUS Brokerage Service, Inc., and most discount brokerage firms — that allow reduced commissions for trading of securities using the Internet.

Stockbrokers or Financial Consultants?

Traditionally, investors dealt with stockbrokers at large retail brokerage firms who executed their customers' orders, provided advice, and sent them publications about individual stocks, industries, bonds, and so forth. These brokers earned most of their income from their share of the commissions generated by their customers. The key to being a successful broker was to build a client base and to service the accounts, making money as customers traded.

As noted above, investors can now choose to use a discount broker who will provide virtually all of the same services except advice and publications and will charge less for the execution of trades. Smart investors choose the alternative that is best for them in terms of their own needs. Some investors need and want personal attention and research publications and are willing to pay higher brokerage commissions. Others, however, prefer to do their own research and to pay only for order execution.

What about today's full-service stockbrokers? In the first place, they go by different titles, such as financial consultants or investment advisors (or simply registered representatives). This change in title reflects the significant changes that have occurred in the industry. Brokerage firms now derive a smaller percentage of their revenues from commissions paid by individual investors than in the past. And the typical full-service stockbroker, whatever he or she is called, now derives less of their income from customer commissions.

How do brokers earn the rest of their income? One alternative is to sell mutual funds owned by their own firms. These funds carry a load or sales charge, and the broker selling shares in these funds earns part of this sales charge. Although a large brokerage firm may sell dozens or hundreds of different funds, there is evidence that brokers are pressured to put their customers into the in-house funds.

Another alternative involves "principal transactions," or brokerage firms trading for their own accounts. When these firms want to sell some shares from their own account, brokers are often encouraged to sell these securities to their customers, with some additional financial incentives provided. Smart investors, when given a recommendation to buy a security by their broker, ask if the firm has issued a public buy recommendation or if the broker is being compensated to sell this security. This activity now accounts for an increasingly important source of income for brokerage firms.

Yet another source of income is the sale of new issues of securities (IPOs), discussed in Chapter 4. Underwriting new issues is a profitable activity for brokerage firms, and brokers may have an incentive to steer their customers into the new issues.

Other sources of revenue today that were non-existent or much smaller in the past include administrative fees resulting from imposing charges on customer accounts. For example, fees for inactive accounts, transfers, and maintenance may be imposed on customers. Obviously, commissions on products sold by brokers will vary depending on the product. Government bonds or T-bills may carry commissions of less than 1 per cent, whereas limited partnerships, which are more complicated instruments, may carry commissions of 8 per cent or more.

Types of Brokerage Accounts

The most basic type of account is the **cash account**, whereby the customer pays the brokerage house the full price for any securities purchased. Many customers open a **margin account**, which allows the customer to borrow from the brokerage firm to purchase securities. (Margin

Cash Account
The most common type of brokerage account in which the customer pays the brokerage house the full price of any securities purchased.

Margin Account
A brokerage account that allows the customer to borrow from the brokerage firm to purchase securities.

is explained in some detail later in this chapter.) An alternative to these accounts is for clients of investment dealers to maintain discretionary or managed accounts. Managed accounts are client portfolios that are managed on a continuing basis by the dealer, usually for a management fee. Discretionary accounts are similar but are generally opened as a convenience to clients who are unwilling or unable to attend to their own accounts (for example, if they are seriously ill or are out of the country). Managed accounts may be solicited, whereas discretionary accounts may not. Both accounts require written consent of the client, and the authorization must include investment objectives. These accounts generally require minimum account balances of $100,000 or $200,000 and charge management fees in the 2 per cent range.

Wrap Account
A new type of brokerage account where all costs are wrapped in one fee.

In an important development in brokerage accounts, brokers now act as middlemen, matching clients with independent money managers.[1] Brokerage houses offer **wrap accounts** to investors with a minimum of $100,000 to commit. Using the broker as a consultant, the client chooses one or more outside money managers from a list provided by the broker. Under this wrap account, all costs — the cost of the broker-consultant and money manager, transactions costs, custody fees, and the cost of detailed performance reports — are wrapped in one fee. For stocks, fees are typically in the 2 to 3 per cent range of the assets managed, dropping as the size of the account gets larger.[2]

Commissions

For most of their long history, North American exchanges have required their members to charge fixed (and minimum) commissions, although on transactions involving more than $500,000 they were negotiable in Canada. In the United States, the requirement of fixed commissions applied to all trades and fuelled the growth of the third market for block trading, as discussed in Chapter 4. The United States eliminated fixed commissions requirements in 1975, and Canada followed suit in 1983. The result of these changes is that in today's environment, fees are supposed to be negotiated, with each firm free to act independently.

These changes have lead to lower commission fees, as well as the growth of discount brokerage firms. Today's investors can attempt to negotiate with their brokers, and different brokers charge different commissions. In practice, the larger full-service brokerage houses have specified commission rates for the small investor. However, the overall competition in the industry has an effect on the rates that are set. Customers are free to shop around, and smart ones do so because differences in commissions among major firms can be substantial in some cases.

In contrast, negotiated rates are the norm for institutional customers, who deal in large blocks of stock. The rates charged institutional investors have declined drastically, from an average of 25 cents a share in 1975 to only a few cents a share for exchange-listed stocks. Institutional investors also receive a better deal when trading in OTC stocks. The spread — the difference between the bid and the ask price — averages about 23 cents a share for individuals but only 6 to13 cents a share for institutional investors.

[1] This discussion is based on James A. White, "Stockbrokers Turning into 'Consultants,'" *The Wall Street Journal*, March 1, 1990, p. C1.

[2] Fees are generally lower for bond portfolios or combinations of stocks and bonds.

Electronic Trading and the Internet

Obviously, we are now in the age of electronic trading. In addition to contacting brokerages firms the traditional way by phone, many investors now trade with dedicated software using their personal computer. For example, **RBC Dominion Securities** now offers NETACTION for its customers to obtain quotes (up to 75 quotes for free), place orders, and update their accounts when they choose and as often as they choose.

In 1992 E*TRADE (and **E*TRADE Canada**, a service of VERSUS Brokerage Service Inc.) became the first brokerage service to offer on-line trading, and by December of 1998 Canadian investors could make equity trades for as low as $27.00 (for a transaction involving less than 1,000 shares trading at $3.01 and above). As we would expect, other firms are rushing to offer their services on the Internet.

While discount brokerages offer on-line trading, full-service firms do not. Such firms do not want to give up their higher commissions, nor break the direct link between broker and client that currently exists. Full-service brokers claim that regardless of the information investors can obtain on the Internet, "Technology can't replace advice." Time will tell.

Individual investors now have three choices when executing trades:

1. Full-service brokers — example, Nesbitt Burns
2. Large discount brokers — example, TD Waterhouse (formerly TD Greenline)
3. Internet discount brokers — example, E*TRADE Canada.

Brokerage costs have changed rapidly because of competition and the rise of the Internet. The following example is only one illustration, and fees are continually changing. Investors need to check out various brokers themselves for brokerage and other costs and the services provided.

EXAMPLE: DISCOUNT BROKERS

The average full-service broker in Canada in September 1996, charged $529 for the purchase of 500 shares of an $85 stock ($42, 500), or slightly over 1 per cent. **Royal Bank Action Direct Discount Brokerage**, a well-known discount broker, would charge $65 (less than two-tenths of a per cent) for the same transaction if executed through a broker, according to 1998 commission schedules.[3] You could make the same trade through Royal Bank Action Direct using their PCAction service at a flat rate of $29 (up to 1,000 shares) (less than one-tenth of 1 per cent) for this transaction. **E*TRADE Canada**, the Internet-based discount broker, would charge $27.00 for the same trade, according to rates effective as of December 1, 1998.[4]

---

[3] Royal Bank Action Direct Web site: <http://www.royalbank.com/english/actiondirect>.

[4] E*Trade Canada Web site: <http://www.canada.etrade.com>.

Investing without a Broker

Dividend Reinvestment Plan (DRIPs)
A plan offered by a company that allows shareholders to reinvest dividends to purchase additional shares of stock at no additional cost.

Hundreds of North American companies now offer **dividend reinvestment plans (DRIPs)**. There are about 80 in Canada. For investors, the company uses the dividends paid on shares owned by investors enrolled in these plans to purchase more of the company's shares, and there is usually no brokerage or administrative fees. One of the advantages of such plans is dollar cost averaging, whereby more shares are purchased when the stock price is low than when it is high. In addition, some of the plans (approximately 25 per cent of the Canadian plans) offer a 5 per cent discount for share purchases.[5]

In order to be in a company's dividend reinvestment plan, investors buy the stock through their brokers, although some companies do sell directly to individuals. On becoming shareholders, investors can join the dividend reinvestment program and invest additional cash at specified intervals. DRIPs are starting to resemble brokerage accounts. Investors can purchase additional shares by having money withdrawn from bank accounts periodically, and shares can even be redeemed by phone at many companies.

It is possible to invest in the market without a stockbroker or a brokerage account in the traditional sense. As an outgrowth of their dividend reinvestment plans, a number of companies now offer no-load stock purchase programs to first-time investors. By early 1998 more than 40 Canadian companies offered direct stock purchase programs; that is about half of all Canadian companies offering DRIPs.

EXAMPLE: TRANSCANADA PIPELINES

TransCanada PipeLines permits investors to buy, each quarter, up to $10,000 ($7,000 US) worth of their common or preferred stock from the company itself by reinvesting their cash dividend, with no brokerage commissions or administrative charges. Some other well-known Canadian companies offering similar plans in 1997 included Maritime Tel & Tel, CIBC, Molson's, and Hudson's Bay Company.

Investors make their initial purchase of stock directly from the company for purchase fees ranging from zero to about 7 cents a share. The price paid is normally based on the closing price of the stock on designated dates, and no limit orders are allowed. The companies selling stock by this method view it as a way to raise capital without underwriting fees and as a way to build goodwill with investors.

HOW ORDERS WORK

Figure 5-1 provides an overview of how securities are traded on organized exchanges and through the OTC market. The details are discussed below.

5 Norman Rothery, "Directions—An Investor's Guide to North American Equities: DRIPs and SPPs." Personal Web site: <http://www.ndir.com/stocks/drips.html>.

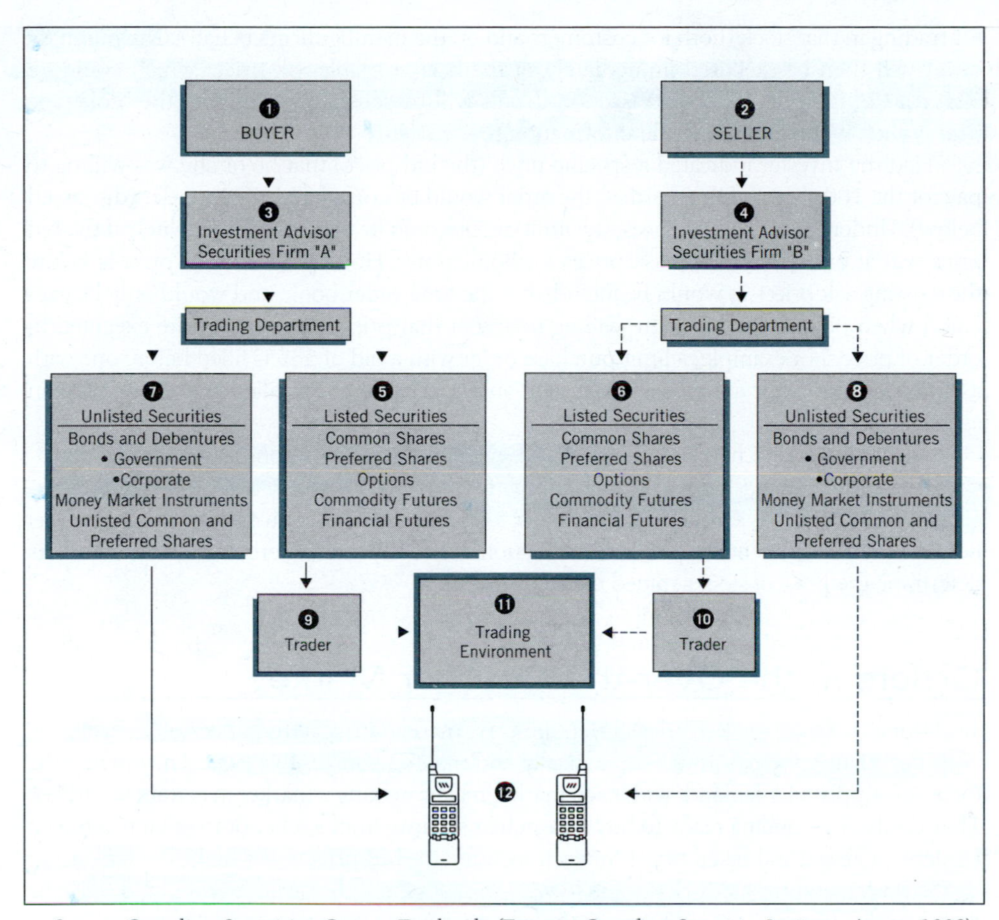

Figure 5-1
A Traditional Retail Securities Transaction

Source: Canadian Securities Course Textbook *(Toronto: Canadian Securities Institute, August 1998); p. 1-36. © 1998 Canadian Securities Institute. Reprinted with permission.*

Orders on the Organized Exchanges

The TSE introduced the world's first computer-assisted trading system (CATS) in 1977, and most exchanges in the world have followed in its footsteps. On April 23, 1997 the TSE closed all floor trading, and all TSE trades are now handled electronically. TOREX is the registered trade name for the TSE's new trading system. It consists of a central computer terminal that links traders from member firms with the TSE. The central terminal processes, records, and monitors all trades.

An order from an investor for 100 shares of **Bombardier** might be handled as follows. The investor phones his or her broker and asks how Bombardier is doing. The broker has immediate access to information regarding the last trade for Bombardier, as well as other information such as the high and low for the day and the number of shares traded.

Assuming that the investor is willing to pay the last trade price or a price close to that, the broker can be instructed to buy 100 shares of Bombardier "at the market." For example, if the last trade price was $22.10 and the investor placed a market order for 100 shares of Bombardier, the order will be transmitted to the firm's registered trader who is responsible for trading in that stock (both for customers and on the member firm's behalf). The purchase order will then be executed immediately, at the best available ask price, which could be $22.20. Confirmation of the transaction details will be sent immediately to the brokerage firm, which will then convey the information to the client.

Had the investor indicated a specific price (the bid price) that he or she was willing to pay for the 100 shares of Bombardier, the order would be considered a limit order (discussed below). Under these circumstances, the limit order would be executed immediately if the bid price was at or above existing ask prices for Bombardier. However, if the bid price is below the existing ask prices, it would be included in the limit order book, and would only be executed when potential sellers were willing to accept that price. Limit orders are executed in order of price. For example, a limit purchase order with a bid of $35 is filled before one with a bid of $34.50, while a limit sell order with an ask price of $36 is filled before one with an ask price of $36.50.

As mentioned in Chapter 4, the NYSE has resisted the move to complete trading automation. The NYSE continues to carry on trading activity on the floor of the exchange using its specialist system, which is described in Appendix 5-A. It is often called an agency auction market because agents represent the public at an auction where the interactions of buyers and sellers determine the price of stocks traded on the NYSE.

Orders in the Over-the-Counter Market

Bid Price
The price at which the specialist or dealer offers to buy shares.

Ask Price
The price at which the specialist or dealer offers to sell shares.

Traditionally, market makers (dealers) in the OTC market arrive at the prices of securities by both negotiating with customers specifically and making competitive bids. They match the forces of supply and demand, with each market maker making a market in certain securities. They do this by standing ready to buy a particular security from a seller or to sell it to a buyer. Dealers quote bid and asked prices for each security; the **bid price** is the highest price offered by the dealer, and the **ask price** is the lowest price at which the dealer is willing to sell. The dealer profits from the spread between these two prices.

The Canadian Dealer Network (CDN) is Canada's only organized OTC equities market and has been the operating authority for OTC trading in Canada since 1991. CDN is a subsidiary of the TSE that provides an electronic quotation and trade reporting system for OTC stocks. It provides bid and ask prices, high, low, and closing prices, as well as trading volumes for the previous days. Market makers on the CDN are required to provide continuous bid and ask quotations throughout the trading day (from 9:30 a.m. to 5:00 p.m.), and there may be more than one market maker for any particular stock. OTC stocks in the United States trade primarily on the Nasdaq market.

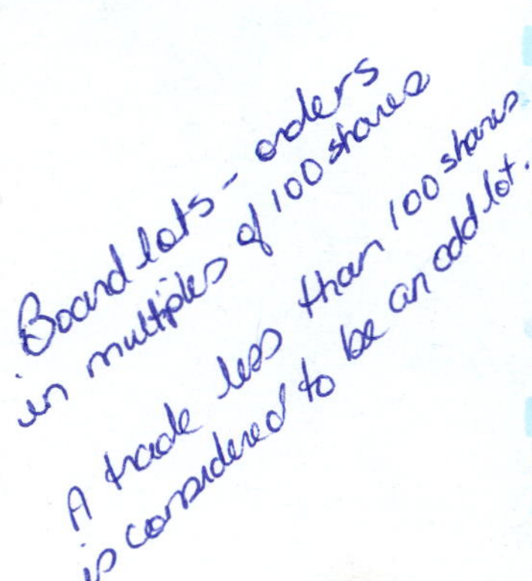

Types of Orders

Investors can buy or sell stocks in "board lots" ("round lots" in the United States) or "odd lots," or a combination of both. Canadian exchanges define board lots as orders in multiples of 100 shares in most cases. A trade for less than 100 shares is considered to be an odd lot. Thus, an order for 356 shares would be for three board lots and one odd lot of 56 shares.

Investors use three basic types of orders: market orders, limit orders, and stop orders.

1. **Market orders**, the most common type of order, instruct the broker to buy or sell the securities immediately at the best price available. As a representative of the buyer or seller, it is incumbent upon the broker to obtain the best price possible. A market order ensures that the transaction will be carried out, but the exact price at which it will occur is not known until its execution and subsequent confirmation to the customer.

Market Order
An order to buy or sell at the best price when the order reaches the trading floor.

2. **Limit orders** specify a particular price to be met or bettered. They may result in the customer obtaining a better price than with a market order or in no purchase or sale occurring because the market price never reaches the specified limit. The purchase or sale will occur only if the broker obtains that price or betters it (lower for a purchase, higher for a sale). Limit orders can be tried immediately or left with the broker for a specific time or indefinitely. In turn, the broker leaves the order with the specialist who enters it in the limit book.

   EXAMPLE: Assume the current market price of a stock is $50. An investor might enter a buy limit order at $47; if the stock declines in price to $47, this limit order, which is on the specialist's book, will then be executed. Similarly, another investor might enter a sell limit order for this stock at $55; if the price of this stock rises to $55, this investor's shares will be sold.

Limit Order
An order that is executed only if the buyer (seller) obtains the stated sell (ask) price.

3. **Stop orders** specify a certain price at which a market order takes effect. For example, a stop order to sell at $50 becomes a market order to sell as soon as the market price reaches (or declines to) $50. However, the order may not be filled exactly at $50 because the closest price at which the stock trades may be $49⅞. The exact price specified in the stop order is therefore not guaranteed and may not be realized.

   EXAMPLE 1: A sell stop order can be used to protect a profit in the case of a price decline. Assume, for example, that a stock bought at $32 currently trades at $50. The investor does not want to limit additonal gains, but may wish to protect against a price decline. To lock in most of the profit, a sell stop order could be placed at $47.

   EXAMPLE 2: A buy order could be used to protect a profit from a short sale. Assume an investor sold short at $50, and the current market price of the stock is $32. A buy stop order placed at, say, $36 would protect most of the profit from the short sale.

Stop Order
An order specifying a certain price at which a market order takes effect.

Because market orders specify the buying or selling of a certain number of shares at the best price available, investors are often advised to enter limit orders that name a particular price whenever possible in order to avoid the range of prices that may result from a market order. Investors can enter limit orders as day orders, which are effective for only one day.[6] Alternatively, they may enter good-until-cancelled (GTC) orders or open orders, which remain in effect unless cancelled or renewed.[7] "Good through" orders are good for a specified number of days and then are automatically cancelled if unfilled. There is no guarantee that all orders will be filled at a particular price limit when that price is reached because orders are filled in a sequence determined by the rules of the various exchanges.

[6] A market order remains in effect only for the day.

[7] Many firms limit GTC orders for a specified time period such as 30, 60, or 90 days.

Limit orders can be filled in whole or in part until completed (involving more than one trading day) in several ways. All or none (AON) orders are only executed if the total number of shares specified in the order can be obtained or sold, and are often referred to as "fill or kill" orders. An order may be given under this heading that states the minimum number of shares that is acceptable to the client. The advantage of this type of order is that it prevents accumulation of odd lots, which can be more expensive to trade and/or less marketable since most investors prefer to purchase shares in board lots. Any part orders are the opposite of AON orders, and may be more costly to execute since they may entail the purchase of all stock in odd, broken, or board lots.

Stop orders are used to buy and sell after a stock reaches a certain price level. A buy stop order is placed above the current market price, while a sell stop order is placed below the current price. Stop loss orders are orders to sell (as market orders) if the price drops below a certain level. They are used to limit losses on long positions. Stop buy orders are the opposite of stop loss orders. A market buy order is generated if the price rises above a certain level to limit losses on short positions.

Clearing Procedures

Clients who do not wish to or are unable to obtain credit from the securities firm open cash accounts and are expected to make full payment for purchases by the settlement date. The settlement date is the same day for government T-bills; two business days after for other Government of Canada direct liabilities and guarantees up to three years; and three business days after for all other securities (including long-term government bonds and common shares). On the settlement date the customer becomes the legal owner of any securities bought (or gives them up if sold) and must settle with the brokerage firm by that time.[8]

Street Name
When customers' securities are held by a brokerage firm in its own name.

Most customers allow their brokerage firm to keep their securities in a **street name** — that is, the name of the brokerage firm. If the certificate is in registered form, the seller must properly endorse and deliver it. Customers receive monthly statements showing the position of their accounts in cash, securities held, any funds borrowed from the broker, and so on.

Brokerage houses must settle all transactions with the other party to the transaction, who may be another brokerage house, a market specialist, or market maker. A clearinghouse facilitates this process by taking the records of all transactions made by its members during a day, verifying both sides of the trades, and netting out the securities and money due or to be paid each member. Members of clearing houses include brokerage houses, banks, and others involved with securities. Once the transaction is completed on the floor (or electronically), the details of the trade are reported to the exchange, and the buying and selling firms are provided with specific details of the trade such as price, time, and the identity of the other party. The firms phone their clients to confirm the transaction and then mail written confirmation to them.

Today, in Canada, most stock and bond certificates are cleared through the Canadian Depository for Securities (CDS). The CDS is a clearing corporation that electronically settles all

---

[8] The purchaser of securities usually will not be able to take physical delivery of the securities on the settlement date because they will not be available by then.

transactions between members on a daily basis without physically moving the certificates. When an investment dealer trades from its own account, the trade occurs at current market value as determined by the exchange. There are detailed regulations which member firms must observe to avoid potential conflicts of interest. In the United States, the National Securities Clearing Corporation operates a central clearinghouse for trades on the New York and American stock exchanges and in the OTC markets.

Use of stock certificates as part of the settlement process is dying out in both Canada and the United States, since computers handle most transactions. Members (brokers and dealers) who own certificates (in street name) deposit them in an account and can then deliver securities to each other in the form of a bookkeeping entry. This book-entry system, as opposed to the actual physical possession of securities in either registered or "bearer" form, is essential to minimize the tremendous amount of paperwork that would otherwise occur with stock certificates. Such a system also reduces the potential for securities to be lost or stolen.

INVESTOR PROTECTION IN THE SECURITIES MARKETS

Investors should be concerned that securities markets are properly regulated for their protection. Our financial system depends heavily on confidence in that system. In the late nineteenth and early twentieth centuries, significant abuses in securities trading did occur; at the same time there was a lack of information disclosure, and trading procedures were not always sound. The market crash in 1929 and the Great Depression served as catalysts for reforms that effectively began in the 1930s.

Investor protection can be divided into government regulation, at the federal and provincial level, and self-regulation by the industry.

The Canadian Regulatory Environment

The Office of the Superintendent of Financial Institutions was established in 1987 by legislation that amalgamated the Department of Insurance and the Office of the Inspector General of Banks. It regulates and supervises banks, insurance, trust, loan and investment companies, and cooperative credit associations that are chartered federally. It also supervises over 900 federally regulated pension plans. However, it does *not* regulate the Canadian securities industry.

The 1987 legislation also established the Financial Supervisory Committee, which is composed of the superintendent (the committee chair), the governor of the Bank of Canada, the deputy minister of finance, and the chairman of the Canada Deposit Insurance Corporation (CDIC). Its purpose is to simplify the confidential exchange of information among its members on all matters relating to supervising financial institutions.

Figure 5-2 provides an overview of the regulatory environment in the Canadian securities industry, discussed below.

Figure 5-2
Securities Industry Flowchart

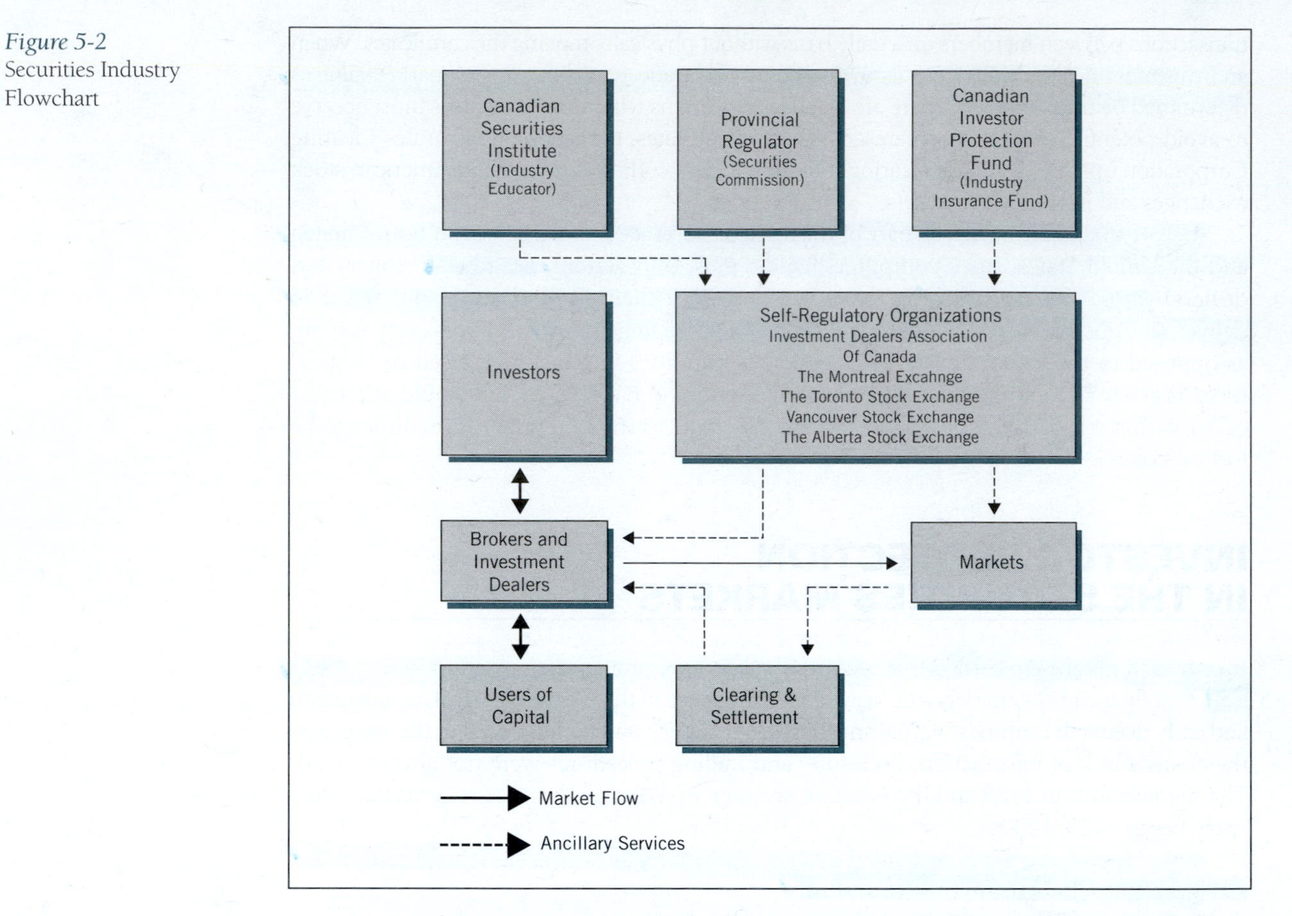

Source: Canadian Securities Course Textbook *(Toronto: Canadian Securities Institute, August 1998); p. 1-31.© 1998 Canadian Securities Institute. Reprinted with permission.*

The Provincial Regulators

Self-Regulatory Organizations (SROs)
Organization in the Canadian securities industry that regulate their own activities. They include the Investment Dealers Association of Canada (IDA), TSE, ME, VSE, ASE, and TFE.

Canada has no central federal regulatory agency for the securities industry, unlike the Securities and Exchange Commission (SEC) in the United States. (US regulators are discussed in Appendix 5-B.) This is because regulation of the securities business is a provincial responsibility that is delegated to securities commissions in most provinces and is handled by appointed securities administrators in others. The provincial regulators work closely with the Canadian Investor Protection Fund and self-regulatory organizations to maintain high standards.

Due to the dominance of the TSE for Canadian stock trading activity, the Ontario Securities Commission (OSC) is one provincial regulatory body of particular importance. The OSC's mandate is "to protect investors from unfair, improper, or fraudulent practices and to foster fair and efficient capital markets and confidence in their integrity." Part of their responsibility in this context is the oversight of the **self-regulatory organizations (SROs)** that are discussed below.[9]

[9] OSC Web site: <http://www.osc.gov.on.ca>.

Canadian Investor Protection Fund (CIPF)

The **Canadian Investor Protection Fund (CIPF)** was established to protect investors in the event of insolvency of a member of any of the sponsoring self-regulatory organizations (SSROs) which include the Investment Dealers Association of Canada (IDA), TSE, ME, VSE, ASE, and Toronto Futures Exchange (TFE). The fund is administered by a nine-member board of governors which includes one representative from each of the SSROs, and three governors representing the general investing public. The president and chief executive officer of the fund is also a governor.

Canadian Investor Protection Fund (CIPF)
A fund established by the Canadian stock exchanges and other organizations to protect investors in the event of the insolvency of any of its members.

The role of this fund is to anticipate and solve financial difficulties of member firms in order to minimize the risk of insolvency, and to attempt to bring about an orderly wind-down of a business if necessary. Fund assets are funded by contributions from the securities industry, as well as an operating line that is provided by a chartered bank.

From the moment an investor becomes a customer of any of the SSROs, the accounts are automatically covered by the fund. The fund covers separate accounts for individuals provided they are not held for the same purpose. For example, the accounts of a customer maintaining two personal holding corporation accounts, would be combined into one. The coverage limit is $500,000 for losses related to securities holdings and cash balances combined. However, the cash balance coverage cannot exceed $60,000. The fund does not cover losses that result from changing market values, and rejects claims from parties that are not dealing at arm's length with the insolvent firm or those whose dealings contributed to the insolvency.

The Self-Regulatory Organizations (SROs)

SROs deal with member regulation, listing requirements, and trading regulation.

The **Investment Dealers Association of Canada (IDA)** is the Canadian investment industry's national trade association and self-regulatory organization. It represents about 180 firms employing more than 29,000 people across Canada. Its mission is to "foster efficient capital markets by encouraging participation in the savings and investment process, and by ensuring the integrity of the marketplace." These dual roles as both industry regulator and trade association are complementary.

Investment Dealers Association of Canada (IDA)
The Canadian investment industry's national trade association and self-regulatory organization, representing 182 firms across the country.

The responsibilities of the IDA include monitoring member firms for capital adequacy and business conduct, as well as regulating the qualifying and registration process of these firms. As Canada's only national SRO, it has the additional responsibility of ensuring that national policies and rules reflect the various perspectives of people in all parts of the country. In its efforts to foster more efficient capital markets, the IDA serves as a market regulator by:

1. Playing a key role in formulating policies and standards for primary debt and equity markets
2. Monitoring activities of member firms, and developing trading and sales practices for fixed-income markets.

The IDA also serves as an international representative and as a public policy advocate by striving to provide accurate information and practical advice to government agencies on matters related to the securities industry.

The IDA strives to ensure the integrity of the marketplace and protection of investors. This requires that member firms maintain financial standards and conduct their business within appropriate guidelines. The IDA's compliance department monitors financial compliance while their investigations department monitors conduct of business compliance.

The Canadian Securities Institute (CSI)

The Canadian Securities Institute (CSI)
The national educational body of the Canadian securities industry.

The **Canadian Securities Institute (CSI)** is a not-for-profit organization that was created in 1970 as the national educator of the Canadian securities industry. Its two goals are to increase the competency levels of people working in the financial services industry and to promote wider knowledge and appreciation of investing among Canadians. It is overseen by a board of governors from the securities industry's SROs. Completion of CSI courses is mandatory to meet the requirements for various registration categories and there were approximately 35,000 industry and non-industry people enrolled in CSI courses in 1997.[10]

MARGIN

As previously noted, accounts at brokerage houses can be either cash accounts or margin accounts. Opening a margin account requires some deposit of cash or securities such as T-bills, bonds, or other equity securities. With a margin account, the customer can pay part of the total amount due and borrow the remainder from the broker, who charges the customer the "margin interest rate." The rate charged to the customer is usually based on the prime lending rate plus a percentage added on by the brokerage firm.[11] For example, in 1998 **Royal Bank Action Direct Discount Brokerage** charged customers Royal Bank Prime Rate plus 1 per cent. Investment firms are allowed the use of customers' free credit balances but must give them written notice to this effect.

A margin account can be used to purchase additional securities by leveraging the value of the eligible shares to buy more. They also permit investors to borrow money from a brokerage account for personal purposes, at the margin interest rate, which is comparable to a bank's prime rate.

Margin
The part of the total value of a sale of securities that a customer must pay to initiate the transaction, with the other part being borrowed from the broker.

The **margin** is that part of the total value of a security transaction that a customer must pay to initiate the transaction; that is, the part that cannot be borrowed from the broker. Cash has 100 per cent loan value, which means that $100,000 in cash deposits constitutes a $100,000 margin. Other assets such as stock securities may have 50 per cent (or lower) loan value because of potential fluctuations in their market value. This means you would have to deposit $200,000 (market value) of common stocks to satisfy a $100,000 margin requirement.

Margin requirements for stocks traded in Canada with exchange and IDA member firms range from 30 per cent to 100 per cent, depending on the price at which the stock is selling.[12] The margin requirements increase as the stock price decreases, reflecting the additional risk associated with lower-priced stocks. The specific details are included in the CSC Notes box at the end of this section. Initial margin requirements for stocks trading in the US, has historically ranged between 40 and 100 per cent, with a current level of 50 per cent since 1974.[13]

---

[10] Refer to Chapter 1 for more details regarding the courses offered by the CSI.

[11] The prime lending rate is the rate at which banks will lend short-term funds to their best customers. It is usually set at a rate slightly above the bank rate, which is the rate the Bank of Canada lends short-term funds to the chartered banks.

[12] Securities firms can demand more initial margin than required by the SROs if they wish.

[13] In addition, US margin purchases require investors to sustain a "maintenance margin," below which the actual margin cannot go. Maintenance margin requirements for NYSE firms require an investor to maintain equity of 25 per cent of the market value of any securities held (and in practice brokers usually require 30 per cent or more) on long positions.

EXAMPLE: MEETING MARGIN REQUIREMENT

If the margin requirement is 30 per cent on a $10,000 transaction (100 shares at $100 per share), the customer must put up $3,000, borrowing $7,000 from the broker.[14] The customer could satisfy their margin requirement by putting up $3,000 in cash or by depositing $6,000 in marginable securities that qualify for 50 per cent loan value.

Market value = current price x number of shares

As the stock price changes, so does the investor's equity. This is calculated as the market value of the collateral stock minus the amount borrowed. The market value of the stock is equal to the current market price multiplied by the number of shares. Securities firms calculate the actual margin in their customers' accounts daily to determine whether a "margin call" is required. This is known as having the brokerage accounts "marked to market." If the investor's equity exceeds the required margin, the excess margin can be withdrawn from the account or used to purchase more stock. Conversely, if the investor's equity declines below the required margin, an investor may receive a margin call (described below).[15]

A margin call (or maintenance call) occurs when the market value of the margined securities less the debit balance (amount owed) of the margin account, declines below the required margin. This type of call is payable on demand, and the brokerage house may reserve the right to take action without notice if market conditions are deteriorating badly enough. In other words, the firm may sell enough shares from the margin account to satisfy the margin requirements.

Margin Call
A demand from the broker for additional cash or securities as a result of the actual margin declining below the margin requirement.

EXAMPLE: CALCULATING MARGIN

Assume that the required margin is 30 per cent, and that the price of the 100 shares of stock (from the previous example) declines from $100 to $95 per share. The following equation is used to calculate actual margin:

$$\text{Actual Margin} = \frac{\text{Market value of securities} - \text{Amount borrowed}}{\text{Market value of securities}}$$

$$26.32\% = (\$9{,}500 - \$7{,}000)/\$9{,}500$$

Notice that the investor's equity position is now $2,500 (down from $3,000), while the dealer's loan is still for $7,000. The actual margin is now below the required 30 per cent and the customer will receive a margin call to restore the investor's equity to the required margin. Thus, the investor should have an equity position of 30 per cent of $9,500 (or $2,850), and the broker's maximum loan value is only 70 per cent of $9,500 (or $6,650). In order to restore the margin, the investor can contribute $350, which will reduce the loan from $7,000 to the required $6,650, and increase the equity position from $2,500 to the required $2,850.

---

[14] If the margin requirement was 50 per cent, the customer would have to initially put up $5,000.

[15] In the United States, investors would only be able to withdraw funds if the actual margin exceeded the initial margin requirement — not just the maintenance margin. On the other hand, they would only receive a margin call when the actual margin fell below the maintenance margin — not the initial margin.

CSC NOTES

Margin Requirements for Canadian Stocks

The word margin refers to the amount of funds the investor must personally provide in a margin account, with the balance being provided by the investment dealer in the form of a loan. Maximum loan values by exchange and IDA members for long positions in securities other than bonds and debentures, expressed as maximum percentages of market value, are:

- 70 per cent for option eligible securities that sell for more than $5, trade on a Canadian stock exchange, and meet other eligibility criteria
- 50 per cent for stocks selling at or above $2
- 40 per cent for stocks selling between $1.75 and $1.99
- 20 per cent for stocks selling between $1.50 and $1.74
- No loan value for stocks selling below $1.50

ILLUSTRATIVE EXAMPLE

An investor purchases common shares of two companies on margin. The first share (A) is option eligible and is presently trading for $10, while the second share (B) is trading at $2.

a. What is the total margin requirement if the investor purchases 1,000 shares of A and 1,000 shares of B?

b. If the price of A immediately increases to $11 and the price of B falls rapidly to $1.50, how much (if any) will be the required deposit in your margin account?

Solution:

a.

Total cost A = $10 × 1,000	=	$10,000	Total cost B = $2 × 1,000	=	$2,000
Less: Maximum loan (@70%)	=	$ 7,000	Less: Maximum loan (@50%)	=	$1,000
Equals: Margin requirement (A)	=	$ 3,000	Equals: Margin requirement (B)	=	$1,000

Total margin requirement (A + B) = $3,000 + $1,000 = $4,000

b.

Original cost A	=	$10,000	Original cost B	=	$2,000
Less: Revised maximum loan A (@70%)			Less: Revised maximum loan B (@ 20%)		
= 0.70 × $11 × 1,000	=	$ 7,700	= 0.20 × $1.50 × 1,000	=	$300
Gross Margin Requirement	=	$ 2,300			$1,700
Margin deficit (surplus)		surplus ($700)			deficit $700

Therefore, the net required deposit is zero, since your margin surplus in one account ($700) offsets your deficit in the other.

While margin requirements for common stocks may be as low as 30 per cent, the margin option does not have to be fully employed. That is, investors could limit their borrowing to less than 70 per cent to reduce the volatility of the investment returns, as well as reducing the probability of ever encountering a margin call.

The traditional appeal of margin trading to investors is that it magnifies any gains on a transaction by the reciprocal of the margin requirement (i.e., 1/margin percentage). Unfortunately, the use of margin also magnifies any losses. This magnification is generally referred to as creating "leverage."

We refer to the example "Meeting Margin Requirement" on page 143 to demonstrate this relationship. Commission fees and interest costs on margin loans are ignored for the sake of simplicity. In the example, the margin requirement is 30 per cent (which magnifies gains or losses by a factor of 1/0.3 = 3.33). First, let's consider the profits to an investor who purchased 100 shares for $100 each, for a total investment of $10,000. If the share price increased (decreased) 10 per cent to $110 ($90), that investor would have gained (lost) $1,000 ($10 per share price change multiplied by 100 shares). This gain (loss) represents 10 per cent of the original investment. Consider another investor who purchased 100 shares at $100 per share on margin, at the 30 per cent margin rate. This investor's initial investment was $3,000 (30 per cent of the $10,000 total cost). If the share price increased (decreased) by $10 to $110 ($90), the total gain (loss) would still be $1,000. However, since the original cash outlay was only $3,000, the investor's gain (loss) is 3.33 times greater, at 33.3 per cent of the original investment (or $1,000/$3,000).

Regardless of what happens, the margin trader must pay the interest costs on the margin account. An investor considering a margined stock purchase should remember that the stock price can go up, remain the same, or go down. In two of these three cases, the investor loses. Even if the stock rises, the break-even point is higher by the amount of the interest charges.

SHORT SALES

The purchase of a security technically results in the investor being "long" in the security. The security is bought and owned because the investor believes the price is likely to rise. But what if the investor thinks that the price of a security will decline? If he or she owns it, it would be wise to sell. If the security is not owned, the investor wishing to profit from the expected decline in price can sell the security short. Short sales are a normal part of market transactions.

Short Sales
The sale of a stock not owned by the investor but borrowed from a third party in order to take advantage of an expected decline in the price of the stock.

How can an investor sell short, which is to say sell something he or she does not own? Not owning the security to begin with, the investor will have to borrow from a third party. The broker, on being instructed to sell short, will make these arrangements for this investor by borrowing the security from those held in street-name margin accounts and, in effect, lending it to the short seller.[16]

The short seller's broker sells the borrowed security in the open market, exactly like any other sale, to some investor who wishes to own it. The short seller expects the price of the security to decline. Assume that it does. The short seller instructs the broker to repurchase the security at the currently lower price and cancel the short position (by replacing the borrowed security). The investor profits by the difference between the price at which the borrowed stock was sold and the price at which it was repurchased.

[16] The securities could be borrowed from another broker. If the lending firm calls back the stock loan, the broker may be forced to close the short position. Also, individuals sometimes agree to lend securities to short sellers in exchange for interest-free loans equal to the collateral value of the securities sold short. Collateral value equals the amount of funds borrowed in a margin transaction.

EXAMPLE: SELLING SHORT ON NEWBRIDGE NETWORKS

An investor named Helen believes that the price of **Newbridge Networks (NNC)** will decline over the next few months and wants to profit from her conviction. She calls her broker with instructions to sell 100 shares of NNC short (she does not own NNC) at its current market price of $36 per share. The broker borrows 100 shares of NNC from another client, Kellie, who has a brokerage account with the firm and currently owns NNC ("long"). The broker sells the 100 shares at $36 per share, crediting the $3,600 proceeds (less commissions, which we will ignore for this example) to Helen's account.[17]

Six months later the price of NNC has declined, as Helen predicted, and is now $30 per share. Satisfied with this drop in the price of NNC, she instructs the broker to purchase 100 shares of NNC and close out the short position. Her profit is $3,600 minus $3,000, or $600 (again, ignoring commissions). The broker replaces Kellie's missing stock with the just-purchased 100 shares, and the transaction is complete.[18]

Several technicalities are involved in a short sale, which are outlined in Table 5-1. Keep in mind that to sell short an investor must be approved for a margin account because short positions involve the potential for margin calls. The margins are expressed in terms of the liability arising from the "borrowing" of the securities from another investor, as outlined in the example "Margin Requirement for Selling Short on Newbridge Networks (NNC)" below. Margin requirements for short sales in Canada are described in detail in the CSC Notes box at the end of this section.

Table 5-1

The Details of Short Selling

1. Dividends declared on any stock sold short must be covered by the short seller. After all, the person from whom the shares were borrowed still owns the stock and expects all dividends paid on it.
2. Short sellers must have a margin account to sell short and must put up margin as if they had gone long. The margin can consist of cash or any restricted securities held long.
3. The net proceeds from a short sale, plus the required margin, are held by the broker; thus, no funds are immediately received by the short seller. The lender must be fully protected. To do this, the account is marked-to-the-market (as mentioned earlier in connection with margin

---

[17] Note that Kellie knows nothing about this transaction, nor is she really affected. Kellie receives a monthly statement from the broker showing ownership of 100 shares of NNC. Should Kellie wish to sell the NNC stock while Helen is short, the broker will simply borrow 100 shares from Elizabeth, a third investor who deals with this firm and owns NNC stock, to cover the sale. It is important to note that all of these transactions are book entries and do not involve the actual stock certificates.

[18] Notice that two trades are required to complete a transaction or "round trip." Investors who purchase securities plan to sell them eventually. Investors who sell short plan to buy back eventually; they have simply reversed the normal buy-sell procedure by selling and then buying.

accounts.) If the price of the stock declines as expected by the short seller, he or she can draw out the difference between the sale price and the current market price. If the price of the stock rises, however, the short seller will have to put up more funds.

4. There is no time limit on a short sale. Short sellers can remain short indefinitely. The only protection arises when the lender of the securities wants them back. In most cases the broker can borrow elsewhere, but in some situations, such as a thinly capitalized stock, this may not be possible.
5. Short sales are permitted only on rising prices or an uptick. A short seller can sell short at the last trade price only if that price exceeded the last different price before it. Otherwise, they must wait for an uptick. Although the order to the broker can be placed at any time, it will not be executed until an uptick occurs.

EXAMPLE: MARGIN REQUIREMENT FOR SELLING SHORT ON NEWBRIDGE NETWORKS

Suppose **Newbridge Networks (NNC)** is an option eligible security that requires a margin of 130 per cent. When Helen short sells the 100 shares of NNC for $36 each, the sale proceeds of $3,600 (which represent 100 per cent of Helen's liability at that time) will remain in an account with her securities firm. In addition, she will be required to deposit 30 per cent of her liability (or $1,080) with the firm, in order to bring the margin account up to 130 per cent (with a total of $4,680).

Should the price of NNC rise to $42, Helen's liability increases to $4,200 ($42/share × 100 shares), and she would be required to have 130 per cent of $4,200, or $5,460, in the account. Since there was only $4,680 in the account, Helen would be required to deposit an additional $780 ($5,460 − $4,680) to restore the margin. Alternatively, if the price of NNC fell to $30, her liability would be $3,000, and her required margin would be $3,900 (1.30 × $3,000). Hence, Helen would find herself in an excess margin position and be able to withdraw $780.

There is no time limit on the maintenance of a short position. However, the client must buy the necessary shares to cover the position if the broker is unable to borrow sufficient shares to do so. Because of this potential problem, many experienced traders confine short sales activities to stocks that are actively traded. Members are required to disclose which trades are short sales, and the TSE, ME, and ASE compile and publicly report total short positions twice a month, while the VSE does so on a weekly basis.

Difficulties and hazards of short selling include: problems in borrowing a sufficient number of shares; responsibility of maintaining an adequate margin; liability for any dividends paid; threat of being required to purchase shares at undesirable prices if the margin is not maintained and/or if originally borrowed stock is called by its owners and cannot be replaced; difficulty in obtaining up-to-date information on total short sales; possibility of volatile prices should a rush to cover occur; and unlimited potential loss.

CSC NOTES

Short Sales in Canada

Short selling is defined as the sale of securities that the seller does not own. The investor is said to be in a short position since he or she must repay it in the future (hopefully it can be repurchased after prices have fallen). The investor must leave the proceeds of the short sale with the dealer (who then has free use of these funds), and deposit a certain portion of the market value in addition to the proceeds.

Required margin amounts for trades with IDA and exchange members in Canada, expressed as percentages of market value, are:

- 130 per cent for option eligible securities
- 150 per cent for stocks with prices of $2 and over
- $3 per share for shares trading between $1.50 and $1.99
- 200 per cent of market value for shares trading between $0.25 to $1.49
- 100 per cent of market price per share plus $0.25 per share for shares trading under $0.25

ILLUSTRATIVE EXAMPLE

a. What amount must an investor put in a margin account, if he or she short sells 1,000 shares of an option eligible security trading for $10?

b. What will happen if the price of the shares, which were sold short immediately, increases to $12?

Solution:

a.	Minimum account balance (@130%)	=	1.30 × $10 × 1,000	=	$13,000
	Less: Proceeds from short sale	=	$10 × 1,000	=	$10,000
	Equals: Minimum margin requirement			=	$ 3,000
b.	Minimum account balance (@130%)	=	1.30 × $12 × 1,000	=	$15,600
	Less: Proceeds from short sale	=	$10 × 1,000	=	$10,000
	Equals: Minimum margin requirement			=	$ 5,600
	Required deposit = margin deficit = $5,600 − $3,000			=	$ 2,600

SUMMARY

This summary relates to the learning objectives provided on page 127.

1. **Explain the role of brokerage firms and stockbrokers.**
   Brokerage firms consist of full-service brokers, discount brokers, and/or Internet brokers who execute stock trades for clients. Full-service stockbrokers earn their incomes from a variety of sources including individuals' trades, in-house mutual fund sales, principal transactions, new issues, and fees.
2. **Describe how brokerage firms operate.**
   With a cash brokerage account, the customer pays in full on the settlement date, whereas with a margin account money can be borrowed from the broker to finance purchases. Wrap accounts, where all costs are wrapped in one fee, are becoming increasingly popular. Brokerage commissions are negotiable. Full-line brokerage houses charge more than discount brokers but offer advice and recommendations, while Internet brokers tend to charge the

least. Investors can also invest without a broker through dividend reinvestment plans (DRIPs), whereby companies sell shares directly to investors through share purchase plans.

3. **Outline how orders to buy and sell securities are executed.**
The TSE was the first stock exchange in the world to go electronic and now handles all trades electronically. Most exchanges are now highly automated, although the NYSE still handles orders using its specialist system. Specialists on the NYSE are charged with maintaining a continuous, orderly market in their assigned stocks. Market orders are executed at the best price available, whereas limit orders specify a particular price to be met or bettered. Stop orders specify a certain price at which a market order is to take over.

4. **Discuss the regulation of the Canadian securities industry.**
Investor protection includes government regulation primarily at the provincial level, and self-regulation by the industry. Self-regulatory organizations (SROs) deal with member regulation, listing requirements, and trading regulation. SROs include the Investment Dealers Association of Canada (IDA), TSE, ME, VSE, ASE, and Toronto Futures Exchange (TFE). The IDA is the Canadian investment industry's national trade association and self-regulatory organization.

5. **Explain the importance of margin trading and short selling to investors.**
Margin is the equity an investor has in a transaction. Required margins are set by the appropriate SROs. The appeal of margin to investors is that it can magnify any gains on a transaction, but it can also magnify losses. An investor sells short if a security's price is expected to decline. The investor borrows the securities sold short from the broker, hoping to replace them through a later purchase at a lower price.

KEY TERMS

Ask price
Bid price
Canadian Investor Protection Fund (CIPF)
Canadian Securities Institute (CSI)
Cash account
Discount broker
Dividend reinvestment plan (DRIPs)
Full-service broker
Investment Dealers Association of Canada (IDA)
Limit order
Margin
Margin account
Margin call
Market order
Self-regulatory organizations (SROs)
Short sales
Stop order
Street name
Wrap account

ADDITIONAL RESOURCES

Information on the mechanics of trading appears in most popular press magazines and newspapers, including:

National Post (Financial Post)
The Globe and Mail / Report on Business
IE: Money

Canadian Business
PROFIT
Barron's
Business Week
Forbes
Fortune
Money
Smart Money
The Wall Street Journal
Worth

INVESTMENTS ON THE WEB

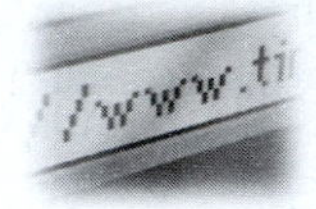

Canadian Securities Administrators, through the Canadian Depository for Securities (CDS), has maintained SEDAR, (System for Electronic Document Analysis and Retrieval). This system has been used since January 1, 1997 to file securities-related information electronically. Investors can obtain public securities filings and company/mutual fund profiles at the following Web site: <http://www.sedar.com>.

The Ontario Securities Commission (OSC) Web site: <http://www.osc.gov.on.ca>.

In the United States, the SEC maintains a well-known database called EDGAR. The SEC requires all filings made by public domestic companies as of May 6, 1996 to be placed in EDGAR, and the SEC posts filings within 24 hours of receipt. Information can be found at the following Web site: <www.sec.gov/edgarhp.htm>.

REVIEW QUESTIONS

1. What is the normal settlement date for common stocks? For long-term government bonds? For T-bills?
2. What are the maximum loan values applicable to IDA and exchange member firms in establishing margin accounts for clients who wish to purchase common shares at various price levels?
3. What conditions result in a margin call?
4. How can an investor sell a security that is not currently owned?
5. What is a wrap account? How does it involve a change in the traditional role of the broker?
6. Distinguish between a full-service broker and a discount broker.
7. How can investors invest without a broker?
8. What is the difference between a day order and an open order?
9. Why are investors interested in having margin accounts? What risk do such accounts involve?

10. Given the lower brokerage costs charged by discount brokers and Internet brokers, why might an investor choose to use a full-service broker?
11. Explain the role of the specialists on the NYSE, describing the two roles they perform. How do they act to maintain an orderly market?
12. Is there any similarity between an over-the-counter dealer and a specialist on an exchange?
13. Discuss the advantages and disadvantages of a limit order versus a market order.
14. How does a stop order differ from a limit order?
15. What is the role of SROs in the regulation of securities markets?
16. What are the risks associated with short selling?
17. What role is performed by the Canadian Investor Protection Fund (CIPF)? What losses does it cover, and what losses does it not cover?
18. Contrast trading on the TSE with the dealer system associated with the OTC market.
19. What conditions must be met for an investor to sell short?
20. Explain the difference, relative to the current market price of a stock, between the following types of orders: sell limit, buy limit, buy stop, and sell stop.

PREPARING FOR YOUR PROFESSIONAL EXAMS

Special Note to Canadian Securities Course Students

Ensure that you have read and understood the following topics:*

Brokerage transactions, pp. 128–132
How orders work, pp. 132–137
Investor protection in the securities markets, pp. 137–140
Margin, pp. 140–143
CSC Notes: Margin Requirements for Canadian Stocks, p. 142
Short sales, pp. 143–145
CSC Notes: Short Sales in Canada, p. 146

**Reading these CSC-related topics should provide you with additional understanding of CSC material. However, it should not be seen as a substitute for reading the CSC textbook itself, which is the basis for the CSC exam.*

CSC REGISTRATION QUESTIONS

The Canadian Securities Institute issued the following sample questions in the 1997 CSC registration package as a means for students to self-assess their understanding of CSC-related material.

1. A(n) __________ certificate is registered in the name of an investment dealer or stock broker but beneficially owned by someone else.

   a. guaranteed investment

   b. definitive

c. street

d. interim

2. A number of shares less than a board lot is called a(n) ________ lot.
3. An order in which the client will accept all stock in odd, broken, or board lots up to the full amount of his order is called a(n) ________ order.
4. A person who sells ABC shares short ____________.

   a. believes that the price of ABC shares will rise

   b. will receive dividends paid on ABC shares

   c. faces a maximum loss of the entire sale price of the stock

   d. must purchase ABC shares in order to realize a profit
5. The number of days between the purchase date and the settlement date of a provincial bond transaction is ________ for a corporate bond transaction.

   a. higher than

   b. lower than

   c. the same as
6. An order to buy or sell no less than a specified number of shares is called a(n) ________ order.
7. A buy or sell order that is valid for a specified number of days is called a(n) ________ order.
8. An order in which the buyer pays the current offer is called a(n) ________ order.
9. The full details of each security transaction must be sent directly to a client promptly in a(n) __________.
10. Investor X buys 2,000 shares of DOY, a non-option eligible security traded on the TSE, at $1.50 a share. What is the minimum amount of margin required of Investor X?
11. Investor W sells short four board lots of EDG, an option eligible security trading on the ME at $5.50.

    a. What minimum amount of margin is required of Investor W?

    b. What type of order could Investor W use to protect his short position?

    c. The price of EDG shares rises to $6.50. Investor W decides to cover his short position. What amount of profit or loss (state which) will result?

    d. What time limit, if any, is there on how long a short sale position can be maintained?

    e. As an alternative to short selling shares, what type of exchange-traded equity option on the same underlying stock could Investor W have considered?
12. An account where a client has authorized a partner of a brokerage firm to use his or her best judgement in buying and selling securities on behalf of the client is called a(n) ______________ account.

PROBLEMS

1. a. Consider an investor who purchased a stock at $100 per share. The current market price is $125. At what price would a limit order be placed to ensure a profit of $30 per share?

   b. What type of stop order would be placed to ensure a profit of at least $20 per share?

2. Assume an investor sells short 200 shares of stock at $75 per share. At what price must the investor cover the short sale in order to realize a gross profit of $5,000? Of $1,000?

3. Assume that an investor buys 100 shares of stock at $50 per share and the stock rises to $60 per share. What is the gross profit, assuming a margin requirement of 30 per cent? Of 50 per cent? Of 60 per cent?

4. An investor buys 100 shares of an option eligible stock on margin at $60 per share. The price of the stock subsequently drops to $50.

   a. What is the actual margin at $50? Is there a margin call?

   b. If the price declines to $45, what is the amount of the margin call? At $35?

   c. If the price increased to $70, how much, if any, funds would the investor have available to them from this account?

5. An investor short sells 200 shares of a stock trading at $3. How much must he or she deposit in order to complete the transaction? Suppose the price subsequently falls to $2. How much money can the investor withdraw? If the price rises to $4.50, how much must the investor deposit?

APPENDIX 5-A

TRADING ON THE NYSE

The Specialist System

Most trading activity on the NYSE is carried out using its specialist system, which works in the following manner.

Customer orders are transmitted from the broker to the broker's New York office and then to the member partner on the exchange floor (or the broker may work through some other exchange member). The representative on the floor will go to the trading post where the specialist handling a particular stock is located. The specialist is charged with maintaining a fair and orderly market in certain stocks. The specialist knows the current quotes for these stocks because he or she keeps a record of all limit orders for the stock.

Assuming no other member partner has come to the post to sell the ordered stock, the specialist will quote a current bid and ask price for the number of shares ordered. The partner then indicates that there is a purchase order to be filled (at the asking price). A confirmation is relayed back to the investor's broker, who notifies the investor. The trade will appear on the NYSE consolidated tape, which prints transactions for all NYSE-listed securities on participating markets. This involves six stock exchanges (in addition to the NYSE), the over-the-counter market, and Instinet.

The role of the specialist is critical in auction markets such as the NYSE. They act as both brokers and dealers. As brokers, specialists maintain the limit book, which records all limit orders, or orders that investors have placed to buy or sell a security at a specific price (or better) and that will not be executed until that price is reached. The commission brokers leave the limit orders with the specialist to be filled when possible; therefore, the specialist receives part of the broker's fee.

As dealers, specialists buy and sell shares of their assigned stock(s) to maintain an orderly market. The stock exchanges function essentially as a continuous market, assuring investors that they can almost always buy and sell a particular security at some price. Assuming that public orders do not arrive at the same time, so that they can be matched, the specialist will buy from commission brokers with orders to sell and sell to those with orders to buy, hoping to profit by a favourable spread between the two sides.

Since specialists are charged by the NYSE with maintaining a continuous, orderly market in their assigned stocks, they often must go "against the market," which requires adequate capital. The NYSE demands that specialists be able to assume a position of 5,000 shares in their assigned stocks.[19] However, the NYSE does not require specialists to fund all the liquidity for the market at a particular time, and these stabilization trades are only a small part of total trading.

Most of the NYSE volume results from public orders interacting directly with other public orders. For example, in 1995, specialist participation (measured as the total shares bought and sold by specialists divided by the total shares traded) accounted for about 17 per cent of

[19] Specialists must be approved by the board of governors of the NYSE and must have experience, ability as dealers, and specified minimum capital.

the share volume traded. This implies that 83 per cent of share volume resulted from public and member firm orders meeting directly in the NYSE market.[20] It is important to note that specialists are not on both sides of any trade.

NYSE Automation

In actuality, the NYSE has become highly automated.[21] An electronic system matches buy and sell orders entered before the market opens, setting the opening price of a stock. The NYSE has SuperDot, an electronic order routing system for NYSE-listed securities. Member firms send orders directly to the specialist post where the securities are traded, and confirmation of trading is returned directly to the member firm over the same system.

In 1995 an average of 304,400 orders per day were processed on SuperDot, and volume totalled some 59 billion shares. The system's peak capacity has been increased to an order processing capability of 2 billion shares per day. As part of SuperDot, the Opening Automated Report Service (OARS) automatically and continuously scans the member firms' pre-opening buy and sell orders, pairing buy and sell orders and presenting the imbalance to the specialist up to the opening of a stock. This helps the specialist to determine the opening price.

SuperDot also includes a post-opening market order system designed to accept orders of up to 2,099 shares. These market orders are executed and reported back to the member firm sending the order within 25 seconds, on average. The specialist's volume-handling and -processing capabilities have been enhanced electronically by creating the Specialist's Electronic Book, which is yet another part of the SuperDot system. This database system assists in recording and reporting limit and market orders.

APPENDIX 5-B

SECURITIES REGULATION IN THE UNITED STATES

Since many Canadian institutional and individual investors transact in securities that are traded in US markets, and since many Canadian companies list their securities in US markets, it is important for Canadians to be familiar with US regulatory practice. The Securities and Exchange Commission (SEC) was created by the US Congress in 1934. It is an independent, quasi-judicial agency of the US government. Its mission is to administer laws in the securities field and to protect investors and the public in securities transactions. The commission consists of five members appointed by the SEC president for five-year terms. Its staff consists of lawyers, accountants, security analysts, and others divided into divisions and offices (including nine regional offices). The SEC has approximately 200 examiners.

[20] This paragraph is based on the *NYSE Fact Book*, which contains many facts and figures about the operations of the NYSE.

[21] The same is true for the Amex.

The SEC is required to investigate complaints or indications of violations in securities transactions. In general, the SEC administers all securities laws. Thus, under the Securities Act of 1933, the SEC ensures that new securities being offered for public sale are registered with the commission, and under the 1934 Act it does the same for securities trading on national exchanges. The registration of securities in no way ensures that investors purchasing them will not lose money. Registration means only that the issuer has made adequate disclosure. In fact, the SEC has no power to disapprove securities for lack of merit.

Investment advisors and companies must also register with the SEC and disclose certain information. The SEC ensures that these two groups will meet the requirements of the laws affecting them.

Similar to Canada, self-regulation is a defining characteristic of the US securities industry. Stock exchanges regulate and monitor trading for the benefit of investors and the protection of the financial system. The NYSE in particular has a stringent set of self-regulations and declares that it "provides the most meaningful market regulation in the world." The NYSE regulates itself as part of a combined effort involving the SEC, itself, and member firms, and NYSE rules and regulations are self-imposed and approved by the SEC. Together, this triad enforces federal legislation and self-regulation for the benefit of the investing public.

The National Association of Securities Dealers (NASD) is a trade association established to enhance the self-regulation of the securities industry. Virtually all securities firms are members. The SEC can revoke the NASD's registration, giving the SEC power over this organization comparable to its powers over exchanges.

The NASD has significantly improved the functioning of the OTC market, developing Nasdaq, for example. It also regulates brokers and dealers, thereby protecting investors. All brokers must register with the NASD in order to trade securities, and the NASD keeps records of disciplinary actions taken against stockbrokers and securities firms.

Similar to the CIPF in Canada, the Securities Investor Protection Corporation (SIPC), a quasi-government agency, ensures each customer account of member brokers against brokerage firm failure. Each account is covered for as much as $500,000. (Coverage of cash maintained in accounts with the firm is limited to $100,000).[22] From 1970 to 1990 SIPC paid out in excess of $180 million in helping some 200,000 investors recover over $1 billion from failed brokers with SIPC insurance.

[22] In addition, many brokerage firms carry additional insurance, often for several million dollars, to provide even more protection for customers.

CHAPTER

THE RETURNS AND RISKS FROM INVESTING

LEARNING OBJECTIVES

After reading this chapter, you will be able to

1. Define "return" and state its two components.
2. Explain the relationship between return and risk.
3. Identify the sources of risk.
4. Describe the different methods of measuring returns.
5. Describe the different methods of measuring risk.
6. Discuss the returns and risks from investing in major financial assets in the past.

CHAPTER PREVIEW

Before you can begin to build a portfolio of investments, you must have a good understanding of the returns and risks from investing that have been experienced to date. Return and risk are described, measured, and estimated throughout this text in relation to the various securities. Our goal in this chapter is to give you a basic working knowledge of these concepts. You will learn about the components of return and risk, and how to measure them. You will have the opportunity to examine *realized* returns on major Canadian financial assets based on the historical record. (In Part II, we turn our attention to *expected* return, which is subject to uncertainty and may or may not occur over some future period.) As you read this chapter, keep in mind that what has occurred in the past should be viewed as a useful, but not guaranteed, guide to the future.

RETURN

As noted in Chapter 1, the objective of investors is to maximize expected returns, although they are subject to constraints — primarily risk. Return is the motivating force in the investment process. It is the reward for undertaking the investment.

Returns from investing are crucial to investors; they are what the game of investments is all about. An assessment of return is the only rational way (after allowing for risk) for investors to compare alternative investments that differ in what they promise. The measurement of realized (historical) returns is necessary for investors to assess how well they have done or how well investment managers have done on their behalf. Furthermore, the historical return plays a large part in estimating future, unknown returns.

The Components of Return

Return on a typical investment consists of two components: yield and capital gain (loss).

Yield

Yield
The income component of a security's return.

The basic component that usually comes to mind when discussing investing returns is the periodic cash flows (or income) on the investment, either interest or dividends. The distinguishing feature of these payments is that the issuer makes the payments in cash to the holder of the asset. **Yield** measures relate these cash flows to a price for the security, such as the purchase price or the current market price.

Capital Gain (Loss)

Capital Gain (Loss)
The change in price on a security over some period of time.

The second component is also important, particularly for common stocks but also for long-term bonds and other fixed-income securities. This component, commonly called the **capital gain (loss)**, is the appreciation (or depreciation) in the price of the asset. We will refer to it simply as the price change. In the case of a long position, it is the difference between the purchase price and the price at which the asset can be, or is, sold. For a short position, it is the difference between the sale price and the subsequent price at which the short position is closed out. In either case, a gain or a loss may occur.[1]

Given the two components of a security's return, we need to add them together (algebraically) to form the total return, which for any security is defined as

$$\text{Total return} = \text{Yield} + \text{Price change} \quad \textbf{(6-1)}$$

where
The yield component can be 0 or +
The price change component can be 0, +, or −

Equation 6-1 is a conceptual statement for the total return for any security. The important point here is that a security's total return consists of the sum of two components — yield and price change. Investor returns from assets can come only from these two components — an income component (the yield) and/or a price change component, regardless of the asset.

EXAMPLE: CALCULATING YIELDS AND PRICE CHANGES

A regular coupon bond purchased at par and held to maturity provides a yield in the form of a stream of cash flows or interest payments. A bond with a maturity value of $1,000 that is purchased for $800 and held to maturity provides both a yield (the interest payments) and a price change. The purchase of a non-dividend-paying stock that is sold six months later produces either a capital gain or loss but no income. A dividend-paying stock produces both a yield component and a price change component (a realized or unrealized capital gain or loss).

RISK

It is not sensible to talk about investment returns without talking about risk because investment decisions involve a trade-off between the two. Investors must constantly be aware of the risk they are assuming, know what it can do to their investment decisions, and be prepared for the consequences.

Risk was defined in Chapter 1 as the chance that the actual outcome from an investment will differ from the expected outcome. Specifically, most investors are concerned that the actual outcome will be less than the expected outcome. The more variable the possible outcomes that can occur (i.e., the broader the range of possible outcomes), the greater the risk.

Investors should be willing to purchase a particular asset if the expected return is adequate to compensate for the risk, but they must understand that their expectation about the asset's return may not materialize. If not, the realized return will differ from the expected return. In fact, realized returns on securities show considerable variability. Although investors may receive on average their expected returns on risky securities in the long-run, they often fail to do so in the short-run.

[1] This component involves only the difference between the beginning price and the ending price in the transaction. An investor can purchase or short an asset and close out the position one day, one hour, or one minute later for a capital gain or loss. Furthermore, gains can be realized or unrealized. See Appendix 2-A: Taxation of Investment Income in Canada at the end of Chapter 2 for a more detailed discussion of capital gains and losses and their taxation.

INVESTING tip

It is important to remember how risk and return go together when investing. An investor cannot reasonably expect larger returns without being willing to assume larger risks. Consider the investor who wishes to avoid any risk (on a practical basis). Such an investor can deposit money in an insured savings account, thereby earning a guaranteed return of a known amount. However, this return will be fixed, and the investor cannot earn more than this rate. Although risk is effectively eliminated, the chance of earning a larger return is also removed. To have the opportunity to earn a larger return, investors must be willing to assume larger risks.

Sources of Risk

What makes a financial asset risky? Traditionally, investors have talked about several sources of total risk, such as interest rate risk and market risk, which are explained below because these terms are used so widely. Following this discussion, we will define the modern portfolio sources of risk, which will be used in Part II when we discuss portfolio and capital market theory.

Interest Rate Risk

The variability in a security's return resulting from changes in the level of interest rates is referred to as **interest rate risk**. Such changes generally affect securities inversely; that is, other things being equal, security prices move inversely to interest rates. The reason for this movement is tied up with the valuation of securities. Interest rate risk affects bonds more directly than common stocks and is a major risk faced by all bondholders. As interest rates change, bond prices change in an inverse direction.

Interest Rate Risk The variability in a security's returns resulting from changes in interest rates. primarily affects bonds

Market Risk The variability in a security's returns resulting from fluctuations in the aggregate market. primarily affects common stock

Market Risk

The variability in returns resulting from fluctuations in the overall market — that is, the aggregate stock market — is referred to as **market risk**. All securities are exposed to market risk, although it primarily affects common stocks.

Market risk includes a wide range of factors exogenous to securities themselves, including recessions, wars, structural changes in the economy, and changes in consumer preferences.

Inflation Risk

A factor affecting all securities is purchasing power risk, or the chance that the purchasing power of invested dollars will decline. With uncertain inflation, the real (inflation-adjusted) return involves risk even if the nominal return is safe (e.g., a T-bill). This risk is related to interest rate risk since interest rates generally rise as inflation increases because lenders demand additional inflation premiums to compensate for the loss of purchasing power.

Business Risk

The risk of doing business in a particular industry or environment is called business risk. For example, as one of Canada's largest steel producers, Dofasco faces unique problems. Similarly, Shell Canada faces unique problems as a result of developments in the global oil situation.

Financial Risk

Financial risk is associated with the use of debt financing by companies. The larger the proportion of assets financed by debt (as opposed to equity), the larger the variability in the returns, other things being equal. Financial risk involves the concept of financial leverage.

Liquidity Risk

Liquidity risk is the risk associated with the particular secondary market in which a security trades. An investment that can be bought or sold quickly and without significant price concession is considered liquid. The more uncertainty about the time element and the price concession, the greater the liquidity risk. A T-bill has little or no liquidity risk, whereas a small OTC stock may have substantial liquidity risk.

EXAMPLE: LIQUIDITY RISK AND LIMITED PARTNERSHIPS

A good illustration of liquidity risk is limited partnerships, which have highly illiquid secondary markets. Limited partnerships have been established to invest in commercial real estate or oil and gas, and they enjoy some tax benefits not available to corporations such as passing tax write-offs through to investors (thereby constituting a "tax shelter"). As of February 12, 1999, there were only 15 limited partnerships trading on the TSE. Four of the 15 did not trade at all on February 12, while two of them did not trade during the entire week. Weekly trading for the 13 that did trade ranged from 600 units to 47,300, with average trading of 11,830 units per week, or 2,366 units per day. Similar illiquidity is displayed by US public limited partnerships, where less than 1,000 of the over 3,000 in existence trade each year and only 200 to 300 trade with any frequency.

Exchange Rate Risk

All investors who invest internationally in today's increasingly global investment arena face the prospect of uncertainty in the returns after they convert the foreign gains back to their own currency. Unlike the past when most investors ignored international investing alternatives, investors today must recognize and understand **exchange rate risk**, which can be defined as the variability in returns on securities caused by currency fluctuations. Exchange rate risk is sometimes called currency risk.

Exchange Rate Risk
The variability in returns on securities caused by currency fluctuations.

also called currency risk

For example, a Canadian investor who buys a German stock denominated in marks must ultimately convert the returns from this stock back to dollars. If the exchange rate has moved against the investor, losses from these exchange rate movements can partially or totally negate the original return earned.

Canadian investors who invest only in Canadian stocks on Canadian markets do not face this risk directly; however, many Canadian companies are multinational corporations that derive large amounts of their profits from foreign countries. As a result, even these investors must be concerned with fluctuations in the value of the local currency. In addition, currency risk affects international mutual funds, global mutual funds, closed-end single country funds, foreign stocks, and foreign bonds.

Country Risk

also referred to as political risk

Country risk, sometimes referred to as political risk, is an important risk for investors today. With more investors investing internationally, both directly and indirectly, the political, and therefore economic, stability and viability of a country's economy need to be considered. Countries are often judged on a relative basis using the United States as a benchmark, and they require careful monitoring of country risk, which changes continuously.

Types of Risk

Thus far, our discussion has concerned the total risk of an asset, which is one important consideration in investment analysis. However, modern investment analysis categorizes the traditional sources of risk identified previously as causing variability in returns into two general types: those that are pervasive in nature, such as market risk or interest rate risk, and those that are specific to a particular security issue, such as business or financial risk. Therefore, we must consider these two categories of total risk. The following discussion introduces these terms. We discuss these two sources of risk in more detail in Chapters 8 and 9.

Dividing total risk into its two components — a general (market) component and a specific (issuer) component — we have systematic risk and non-systematic risk, which are additive:

$$\begin{aligned} \text{Total risk} &= \text{General risk} + \text{Specific risk} \\ &= \text{Market risk} + \text{Issuer risk} \\ &= \text{Systematic risk} + \text{Non-systematic risk} \end{aligned} \tag{6-2}$$

Systematic Risk

Systematic (Market) Risk Risk attributable to broad macro-factors affecting all securities.

As is shown in Part II dealing with portfolio management, an investor can construct a diversified portfolio and eliminate part of the total risk — the diversifiable or non-market part. What is left is the non-diversifiable portion or the market risk. Variability in a security's total returns that is directly associated with overall movements in the general market or economy is called **systematic (market) risk**.

Virtually all securities have some systematic risk — whether bonds or stocks — because systematic risk directly encompasses interest rate, market, and inflation risks. The investor cannot escape this part of the risk because no matter how well he or she diversifies, the risk of the overall market cannot be avoided. If the stock market declines sharply, most stocks will be adversely affected; if it rises strongly, as it did between 1995 and 1997, most stocks will appreciate in value. These movements occur regardless of what any single investor does. Clearly, market risk is critical to all investors.

Non-Systematic Risk

Non-Systematic (Non-Market) Risk Risk attributable to factors unique to a security.

The variability in a security's total returns not related to overall market variability is called the **non-systematic (non-market) risk**. This risk is unique to a particular security and is associated with such factors as business and financial risk as well as liquidity risk. Although all securities tend to have some non-systematic risk, it is generally connected with common stocks.

MEASURING RETURNS

Total Return

A correct return measure must incorporate the two components of return, as discussed earlier: yield and price change. Returns across time or from different securities can be measured and compared using the total return concept. Formally, the **total return (TR)** for a given holding period is a decimal (or percentage) number relating all the cash flows received by an investor during any designated time period to the purchase price of the asset. Total return is defined as

Total Return (TR) Percentage measure relating all cash flows on a security for a given time period to its purchase price.

$$TR = \frac{\text{Any cash payments received} + \text{Price changes over the period}}{\text{Price at which the asset is purchased}} \tag{6-3}$$

All the items in Equation 6-3 are measured in dollars. The dollar price change over the period — defined as the difference between the beginning (or purchase) price and the ending (or sale) price — can be either positive (sales price exceeds purchase price), negative (purchase price exceeds sales price), or zero. The cash payments can be either positive or zero. Netting the two items in the numerator together and dividing by the purchase price results in a decimal return figure that can easily be converted into percentage form. Note that in using TR, the two components of return — yield and price change — have been measured.[2]

The general equation for calculating TR is

$$TR = \frac{CF_t + (P_E - P_B)}{P_B} = \frac{CF_t + PC}{P_B} \tag{6-4}$$

where

CF_t = cash flows during the measurement period t
P_E = price at the end of period t or sale price
P_B = purchase price of the asset or price at the beginning of the period
PC = change in price during the period, or P_E minus P_B

The cash flow for a bond comes from the interest payments received, and for a stock, it comes from the dividends received. For some assets, such as a warrant, there is only a price change. Part A of Figure 6-1 illustrates the calculation of TR for a bond, a common stock, and a warrant. Although one year is often used for convenience, this calculation can be applied to periods of any length.

In summary, the total return concept is valuable as a measure of return because it is all-inclusive, measuring the total return per dollar of original investment. It facilitates the

[2] This can be seen more easily by rewriting Equation 6-3 to show specifically its income and price change components.

$$TR = \frac{\text{Cash payments received}}{\text{Purchase price}} + \frac{\text{Price change over the period}}{\text{Purchase price}}$$

The first term is the yield component, while the second term measures the price change.

comparison of asset returns over a specified period, whether the comparison is of different assets such as stocks versus bonds or different securities within the same asset category such as several common stocks. Remember that using this concept does not mean that the securities have to be sold and the gains or losses actually realized.

Table 6-1 shows the TSE 300 Composite Index for the years 1986 through 1997. Included in the table are end-of-year values for the index, from which capital gains and losses can be computed, and dividends on the index, which constitute the income component.

A. TOTAL RETURN (TR) CALCULATIONS

I. Bond TR

$$\text{Bond TR} = \frac{I_t + (P_E - P_B)}{P_B} = \frac{I_t + PC}{P_B}$$

I_t = the interest payment(s) received during the period
P_B and P_E = the beginning and ending prices, respectively
PC = the change in price during the period

Example: Assume the purchase of a 10 per cent-coupon government bond at a price of $960, held one year, and sold for $1020. The TR is

$$\text{Bond TR} = \frac{100 + (1020 - 960)}{960} = \frac{100 + 60}{960} = 0.1667 \text{ or } 16.67\%$$

II. Stock TR

$$\text{Stock TR} = \frac{D_t + (P_E - P_B)}{P_B} = \frac{D_t + PC}{P_B}$$

D_t = the dividend(s) paid during the period

Example: 100 shares of **DataShield** are purchased at $30 per share and sold one year later at $26 per share. A dividend of $2 per share is paid.

$$\text{Stock TR} = \frac{2 + (26 - 30)}{30} = \frac{2 + (-4)}{30} = -0.0667 \text{ or } -6.67\%$$

III. Warrant TR

$$\text{Warrant TR} = \frac{C_t + (P_E - P_B)}{P_B} = \frac{C_t + PC}{P_B} = \frac{PC}{P_B}$$

Where C_t = any cash payment received by the warrant holder during the period. Because warrants pay no dividends, the only return to an investor from owning a warrant is the change in price during the period.

Example: Assume the purchase of warrants of **DataShield** at $3 per share, a holding period of six months, and the sale of $3.75 per share.

$$\text{Warrant TR} = \frac{0 + (3.75 - 3.00)}{3.00} = \frac{0.75}{3.00} = 0.25 \text{ or } 25\%$$

B. RETURN RELATIVE CALCULATIONS

The return relative for the preceding bond example shown is

$$\text{Bond return relative} = \frac{100 + 1020}{960} = 1.1667$$

The return relative for the stock example is

$$\text{Stock return relative} = \frac{2 + 26}{30} = 0.9333$$

The return relative for the warrant example is

$$\text{Warrant return relative} = \frac{3.75}{3.00} = 1.25$$

To convert from a return relative to a TR, subtract 1.0 from the return relative.

Figure 6-1
Examples of Total Return and Price Relative Calculations

Table 6-1

TSE 300 Composite Index, Dividends in Index Form and Total Returns (TRs), 1986–97, End-of-Year Values

Year	Index Value	Dividends	TR %
1986	3066.18	91.67	—
1987	3160.05	97.32	6.23545
1988	3381.75	113.96	10.62198
1989	3969.79	129.01	21.20352
1990	3256.75	124.90	−14.81539
1991	3512.36	111.98	11.28702
1992	3350.44	102.34	−1.69630
1993	4321.43	97.81	31.90029
1994	4213.61	100.76	−0.16337
1995	4713.54	107.44	14.41448
1996	5927.03	108.63	28.04941
1997	6699.44	110.27	14.89245

To calculate TR: $$TR\% = \frac{(P_t - P_{t-1}) + D_t}{P_{t-1}} \times 100$$

Example: $$\text{For 1997 TR\%} = \frac{(6699.44 - 5927.03) + 110.27}{5927.03} \times 100 = 14.89245\%$$

Note: These TRs will be slightly different than those reported for the TSE Total Return Index, since the Total Return Index assumes the dividends are reinvested as soon as they are received, not at year end as the calculations above assume. For example, the TSE 300 Total Return Index for 1997 was 14.97759%.

Source: *TSE Annual Review*, 1986–97. Reprinted with permission from the Toronto Stock Exchange.

EXAMPLE: TOTAL RETURN CALCULATIONS

The TRs for each year can be calculated as shown at the bottom of Table 6-1, where, as a demonstration of these calculations, the TR for 1997 is calculated. In 1997, the market, as measured by the TSE 300 Composite Index, had a TR of 14.89 per cent. In contrast, in 1990, the same market index showed a TR of −14.81 per cent.

Return Relative

Return Relative
The total return for an investment for a given time period plus 1.0.

It is often necessary to measure returns on a slightly different basis than total returns. This is particularly true when calculating either a cumulative wealth index or a geometric mean (both of which are explained below) because negative returns cannot be used in the calculation. The **return relative** solves this problem by adding 1.0 to the total return. Although return relatives may be less than 1.0, they will be greater than zero, thereby eliminating negative numbers.

Equation 6-4 can be modified to calculate return relatives directly by using the price at the end of the holding period in the numerator rather than the change in price, as in Equation 6-5.

(6-5)

$$\text{Return relative} = \frac{CF_t + P_E}{P_B}$$

Notice that this is equivalent to adding 1.0 to the total return, since:

$$TR + 1 = \frac{CF_t + (P_E - P_B)}{P_B} + 1 = \frac{CF_t + (P_E - P_B)}{P_B} + \frac{P_B}{P_B} = \frac{CF_t + P_E - P_B + P_B}{P_B} = \frac{CF_t + P_E}{P_B}$$

Examples of return relative calculations for the same three assets as the preceding are shown in Part B of Figure 6-1.

EXAMPLE: CALCULATING RETURN RELATIVE

A TR of 0.10 for some holding period is equivalent to a return relative of 1.10, and a TR of −0.15 is equivalent to a return relative of 0.85.

Cumulative Wealth Index

Cumulative Wealth Index
Cumulative wealth over time, given an initial amount and a series of returns on some asset.

Return measures such as TRs measure changes in the level of wealth. At times, however, it is more desirable to measure levels of wealth (or prices) rather than changes. In other words, we measure the cumulative effect of returns over time given some stated beginning amount, such as $1. To capture the cumulative effect of returns, we use index values. The value of the **cumulative wealth index**, CWI_n, is computed as

(6-6)

$$CWI_n = WI_0\,(1 + TR_1)\,(1 + TR_2)\ldots(1 + TR_n)$$

where

CWI_n = the cumulative wealth index as of the end of period n
WI_0 = the beginning index value, typically $1
TR_1 = the periodic TRs in decimal form (when added to 1.0 as in Equation 6-6, they become return relatives)

EXAMPLE: CALCULATING THE CUMULATIVE WEALTH INDEX

For the TSE 300 total returns in Table 6-1, the cumulative wealth index for the period 1989–93 would be, using return relatives,

$$CWI_{1993} = 1.00\,(1.2120352)\,(0.8518461)\,(1.1128702)\,(0.9830370)\,(1.3190029)$$
$$= 1.4898293$$

Thus, $1 invested at the end of 1988 (the beginning of 1989) would have been worth approximately $1.4898 by the end of 1993.

Note that the values for the cumulative wealth index can be used to calculate the rate of return for a given period, using Equation 6-7.

$$TR_n = \frac{CWI_n}{CWI_{n-1}} - 1 \qquad (6\text{-}7)$$

where
TR_n = the total return for period n
CWI = the cumulative wealth index

EXAMPLE: USING THE CUMULATIVE WEALTH INDEX TO CALCULATE TOTAL RETURN

Using the total returns illustrated above for the years 1989–93, we can make the following calculations.

$$CWI_{1993} = 1.00\,(1.2120352)\,(0.8518461)\,(1.1128702)\,(0.9830370)\,(1.3190029)$$
$$= 1.4898293$$

$$CWI_{1992} = 1.00\,(1.2120352)\,(0.8518461)\,(1.1128702)\,(0.9830370)$$
$$= 1.1295117$$

$$TR_{1993} = (1.4898293/1.1295117) - 1$$
$$= 0.3190030$$

Thus, the total return for 1993 was 0.3190030, or 0.32 rounded.

International Returns

When investors buy and sell assets in other countries, they must consider exchange rate risk. This risk can convert a gain from an investment into a loss or a loss from an investment into a gain. An investment denominated in an appreciating currency relative to the investor's domestic currency will lead to a gain from the currency movement, while an investment in a currency that depreciates relative to the investor's own will mean a decrease in the return.

To calculate the return from an investment in a foreign country, we use Equation 6-8. The foreign currency is stated in domestic terms — that is, the amount of domestic currency necessary to purchase one unit of the foreign currency.

$$\text{Total return in domestic terms} = \frac{[\,\text{RR} \times \text{Ending value of foreign currency}\,]}{\text{Beginning value of foreign currency}} - 1.0 \qquad \text{(6-8)}$$

EXAMPLE: INTERNATIONAL RETURN ON US STEEL

Consider a Canadian investor who invests in **US Steel** (which trades on the New York Stock Exchange) at $35 US when the value of the US dollar stated in Canadian dollars is $1.40. One year later, US Steel is at $41 US and the stock paid a dividend of $1.00 US. The US dollar is now at $1.43, which means that the Canadian dollar depreciated against it.

Return relative for US Steel = (1 + 41) / 35 = 1.20

Total return to the Canadian investor after currency adjustment is

TR denominated in Canadian $ = [1.20 × ($1.43 / $1.40)] − 1.0
= [1.20 × 1.0214] − 1.0
= 1.2257 − 1.0
= .2257 or 22.57%

In this example, the Canadian investor earned a 20 per cent total return in US currency, and earned 22.57 per cent in Canadian dollars because the US dollar increased in value against the Canadian dollar. With the weakening of the Canadian dollar, the US dollars from the investment in US Steel buy more Canadian dollars when the investment is converted back from US dollars, driving up the return an investor would earn from 20 to 22.57 per cent.

Summary Statistics for Returns

The total return, return relative, and wealth index are useful measures of return for a specified period of time. Also needed in investment analysis are statistics to describe a series of returns. For example, investing in a particular stock for ten years or a different stock in each of ten years could result in ten TRs, which must be described by one or more statistics. Two such measures used with returns data are described below.

Arithmetic Mean

The best-known statistic to most people is the arithmetic mean. Therefore, the word mean will refer to the arithmetic mean unless otherwise specified. The arithmetic mean, customarily designated by the symbol $\overline{X}$ (X-bar), is

$$\overline{X} = \frac{\Sigma X}{n} \tag{6-9}$$

or the sum of each of the values being considered divided by the total number of values n.

EXAMPLE: CALCULATING THE ARITHMETIC MEAN

Based on data from Table 6-2 for the 11 years from 1987 to 1997, the arithmetic mean is calculated in Table 6-2.

$$\begin{aligned}\overline{X} &= [6.23 + 10.62 + 21.20 + (-14.81) \ldots + 14.89]/11 \\ &= 121.91/11 \\ &= 11.08\%\end{aligned}$$

Table 6-2

Calculation of the Arithmetic and Geometric Means for the Years 1987–97 for the TSE 300 Composite Index

Year	TSE 300 TRs (%)	TSE 300 Return Relatives
1987	6.23	1.0623
1988	10.62	1.1062
1989	21.20	1.2120
1990	−14.81	0.8519
1991	11.28	1.1128
1992	−1.70	0.9830
1993	31.90	1.3190
1994	−0.16	0.9984
1995	14.41	1.1441
1996	28.05	1.2805
1997	14.89	1.1489

Arithmetic mean $= \dfrac{6.23 + 10.62 + 21.20 + \ldots + 14.89}{11} = 11.08\%$

$$\begin{aligned}\text{Geometric mean} &= [(1.0623)(1.1062)(1.2120)\ldots(1.1489)]^{1/11} - 1 \\ &= (2.941832)^{1/11} - 1 \\ &= 1.1031 - 1 \\ &= 0.1031 \text{ or } 10.31\%\end{aligned}$$

Source: *TSE Annual Review 1987–97.*

Geometric Mean

The arithmetic mean return is an appropriate measure of the central tendency of a distribution consisting of returns calculated for a particular time period, such as a year. However, when percentage changes in value over time are involved, the arithmetic mean of these changes can be misleading. A different mean, the geometric mean, is needed to describe accurately the "true" average rate of return over multiple periods. The geometric mean return measures the compound rate of growth over time. It is often used in investments and finance to reflect the steady growth rate of invested funds over some past period — that is, the uniform rate at which money actually grew over time, per period. Therefore, it measures the realized change in wealth over multiple periods.

Geometric Mean
The compound rate of return over time.

The geometric mean (G) is defined as the *n*th root of the product resulting from multiplying a series of return relatives together, as in Equation 6-10.[3]

$$G = [(1 + TR_1)(1 + TR_2) \ldots (1 + TR_n)]^{1/n} - 1 \quad (6\text{-}10)$$

where TR is a series of total returns in decimal form. Note that adding 1.0 to each total return produces a return relative. Return relatives are used in calculating geometric mean returns because TRs, which can be negative, cannot be used.[4]

EXAMPLE: CALCULATING THE GEOMETRIC MEAN

Continuing the example from Table 6-2, consisting of the eleven years of data ending in 1997 for the TSE 300, we find that the geometric mean would be as shown in Table 6-2:

$$\begin{aligned} G &= [(1.0623)(1.1062)(1.2120)(0.8519) \ldots (1.1489)]^{1/11} - 1 \\ &= (2.941832)^{1/11} - 1 \\ &= 1.1031 - 1 \\ &= 0.1031 \text{ or } 10.31\% \end{aligned}$$

The geometric mean reflects compound, cumulative returns over more than one period. Thus, $1 invested in the TSE 300 Composite Index would have compounded at an average annual rate of 10.31 per cent over the period 1987–97, producing a cumulative ending wealth of $2.94. In other words, the 1987–97 cumulative wealth index equals $(1.1031)^{11}$ or 2.94. Notice that the geometric average rate of return in the example above is lower than the arithmetic average rate of return of 11.08 per cent because it reflects the variability of the returns. The geometric mean will always be less than the arithmetic mean unless the values being considered are identical. The spread between the two depends on the dispersion of the distribution: the greater the dispersion, the greater the spread between the two means.

---

[3] Obviously, in most situations a calculator or computer is needed to calculate the geometric mean. Calculators with power functions can be used to calculate roots.

[4] An alternative method of calculating the geometric mean is to find the log of each return relative, add them, divide by n, and take the antilog.

Arithmetic Mean versus Geometric Mean

When should we use the arithmetic mean, and when should we use the geometric mean to describe the returns from financial assets? The answer depends on the investor's objective:

- The arithmetic mean is a better measure of average (typical) performance over single periods.
- The geometric mean is a better measure of the change in wealth over time (multiple periods).

EXAMPLE: CONTRASTING THE ARITHMETIC AND GEOMETRIC MEANS

As an illustration of how the arithmetic mean can be misleading in describing returns over multiple periods, consider the data in Table 6-3, which shows the movements in price for two stocks over two successive holding periods. Both stocks have a beginning price of $10. Stock A rises to $20 in Period 1 and then declines to $10 in Period 2. Stock B falls to $8 in Period 1 and then rises 50 per cent to $12 in Period 2. For stock A, the indicated annual average arithmetic rate of change in price is 25 per cent. This is clearly not sensible because the price of stock A at the end of Period 2 is $10, the same as the beginning price. The geometric mean calculation gives the correct annual average rate of change in price of 0 per cent per year.

For stock B, the arithmetic average of the annual percentage changes in price is 15 per cent. However, if the price actually increased 15 per cent each period, the ending price in Period 2 would be $10 (1.15) (1.15) = $13.23. We know that this is not correct because the price at the end of Period 2 is $12. The annual geometric rate of return, 9.54 per cent, produces the correct price at the end of Period 2: $10(1.0954)(1.0954) = $12.

Table 6-3

Contrasting the Arithmetic and Geometric Means

Stock	Period 0	Period 1	Period 2	Annual Arithmetic Rate of Return	Annual Geometric Rate of Return
A	$10	$20	$10	$[100\% + (-50\%)]/2 = 25\%$	$[2.0(0.5)]^{1/2} - 1 = 0\%$
B	$10	$8	$12	$[-20\% + (50\%)]/2 = 15\%$	$[.8(1.5)]^{1/2} - 1 = 9.54\%$

As these simple examples demonstrate, over multiple periods, the geometric mean shows the true average compound rate of growth that actually occurred — that is, the rate at which an invested dollar has grown. On the other hand, we should use the arithmetic mean to represent the likely or typical performance for a single period. Consider the TR data for the TSE 300 Index for the years 1987–97 as described earlier. Our best representation of any one year's performance would be the arithmetic mean of 11.08 per cent because it was necessary to average this rate of return for a particular year, given the wide spread in the yearly numbers, in order to realize an actual growth rate of 10.31 per cent after the fact. Thus, the average annual return of 12.68 per cent for the three years 1987–89 was offset to a large extent by the annual return of –14.81 per cent for the year 1990.

EXAMPLE: CONTRASTING THE ARITHMETIC AND GEOMETRIC MEANS (CONTINUED)

Assume that the returns for two consecutive years for a particular stock were 16.76 per cent and −2.0 per cent. The arithmetic mean return for these two years would be exactly 7.38 per cent; however, $1 invested at these rates of return would have grown to $\$1 \times 1.1676 \times 0.98 = \$1.1442$, a geometric mean rate of return of only 6.97 per cent. Based only on these two observations, our best estimate of the average return for next year would be 7.38 per cent, not 6.97 per cent.

Inflation-Adjusted Returns

All of the returns discussed above are nominal, or money returns. They measure dollar amounts or changes but say nothing about the purchasing power of these dollars. To capture this dimension, we need to consider real returns, or inflation-adjusted returns. To calculate inflation-adjusted returns, we divide 1 + total nominal return, by 1 + the inflation rate, as shown in Equation 6-11. This calculation is sometimes simplified by subtracting rather than dividing, producing a close approximation.

$$TR_{IA} = \frac{(1 + TR)}{(1 + IF)} - 1 \quad (6\text{-}11)$$

where

TR_{IA} = the inflation-adjusted total return

IF = the rate of inflation

This equation applies to both individual years and average total returns.

EXAMPLE: INFLATION-ADJUSTED RETURN FOR CANADIAN SMALL-CAP COMMON STOCKS

The total return for Canadian small-cap common stocks in 1996 was 28.7 per cent. The rate of inflation was 2.2 per cent. Therefore, the real (inflation-adjusted) total return for small-cap common stocks in 1996 was:

$$1.287 / 1.022 = 1.2593$$

$$1.2593 - 1.0 = .2593 \text{ or } 25.93\ \%$$

Now consider the period 1987–96. The geometric mean for small-cap Canadian common stocks for the entire period was 8.6 per cent, and for inflation, 3.0 per cent. Therefore, the real (inflation-adjusted) geometric mean rate of return for small-cap common stocks for the period 1987–96 was:

$$1.086 / 1.030 = 1.0544$$
$$1.0544 - 1.0 = .0544 \text{ or } 5.44\%$$

The Consumer Price Index (CPI) typically is used as the measure of inflation. The resulting total returns are in real or constant purchasing-power terms. The compound annual rate of inflation over the period 1987–96 was 3.0 per cent. This means that a basket of consumer goods purchased for $1 at the beginning of 1987 would cost approximately $1.3439 at year-end 1996. This is calculated as $(1.030)^{10}$ (the 3.0 per cent inflation rate is rounded, making the $1.3439 approximate).

EXAMPLE: REAL CUMULATIVE WEALTH INDEX FOR CANADIAN SMALL-CAP COMMON STOCKS

For the period 1987–96, the cumulative wealth index for Canadian small-cap common stocks was $2.2861, while inflation had a total index of $1.3439. Therefore, the real total return index, or equivalently, the real cumulative wealth index, was

$$\$2.2861 / \$1.3439 = \$1.7011$$

MEASURING RISK

Risk is often associated with the dispersion in the likely outcomes. Dispersion refers to variability. Risk is assumed to arise out of variability, which is consistent with our definition of risk as the chance that the actual outcome of an investment will differ from the expected outcome. If an asset's return has no variability it has, in effect, no risk. Thus, a one-year T-bill purchased to yield 6 per cent and held to maturity will, in fact, yield (a nominal) 6 per cent. No other outcome is possible, barring default by the Canadian government, which is not considered a reasonable possibility.

Consider an investor analyzing a series of returns (TRs) for the major types of financial assets over some period of years. Knowing the mean of this series is not enough; the investor also needs to know something about the variability in the returns. A histogram presents a frequency distribution pictorially, using a vertical bar for each class in a frequency distribution. The vertical axis shows the frequency (or relative frequency), and the horizontal axis represents the value of the class.

Histograms (distributions) of returns for major financial assets for the period 1938–97 are shown later in this chapter in Table 6-5. Relative to the other assets, common stocks show the largest variability (dispersion) in returns. Long-term bonds have a smaller variability and therefore a more compact distribution, while T-bills are the least risky assets.

Standard Deviation

Standard Deviation
A measure of the dispersion in outcomes around the expected value.

The risk of distributions can be measured with an absolute measure of dispersion or variability. The most commonly used measure of dispersion over some period of years is the **standard deviation**, which measures the deviation of each observation from the arithmetic mean of the observations. It is considered to be a reliable measure of variability because all the information in a sample is used.[5]

The standard deviation is a measure of the total risk of an asset or a portfolio. It captures the total variability in asset or portfolio return, whatever the source(s) of that variability. The standard deviation can be calculated as

$$s = \sqrt{\frac{\Sigma (X - \overline{X})^2}{n - 1}} \quad (6\text{-}12)$$

where

s = standard deviation
X = each observation in the sample
$\overline{X}$ = the mean of the observations
n = the number of returns in the sample

Knowing the returns from the sample, we can calculate the standard deviation fairly easily.

EXAMPLE: CALCULATING THE STANDARD DEVIATION

The standard deviation of the 11 TRs (1987–97) for the TSE 300 Composite Index, as shown in Table 6-2, can be calculated as shown in Table 6-4.

ble 6-4

Calculating the Historical Standard Deviation

Year	TSE 300 TRs (%), X	$X - \overline{X}$	$(X - \overline{X})^2$
1987	6.23	−4.85	23.52
1988	10.62	−0.46	0.21
1989	21.20	10.12	102.41
1990	−14.81	−25.89	670.29
1991	11.28	0.20	0.04
1992	−1.70	−12.78	163.33
1993	31.90	20.82	433.47
1994	−0.16	−11.24	126.34
1995	14.41	3.33	11.09
1996	28.05	16.97	287.98
1997	14.89	3.81	14.52

$$\Sigma (X - \overline{X})^2 = 1833.20$$

$$\frac{1833.20}{11 - 1} = 183.32$$

$$(183.32)^{1/2} = 13.54\%$$

[5] The variance is the standard deviation squared. The variance and the standard deviation are similar and can be used for the same purposes; specifically, in investment analysis, both are used as measures of risk. The standard deviation, however, is used more often.

In summary, the standard deviation of return measures the total risk of one security or a portfolio of securities. The historical standard deviation can be calculated for individual securities or portfolios of securities using TRs for some specified period of time. This *ex post* value is useful in evaluating the total risk for a particular historical period and in estimating the total risk that is expected to prevail over some future period.

The standard deviation, combined with the normal distribution, can provide some useful information about the dispersion or variation in returns. In a normal distribution, the probability that a particular outcome will be above (or below) a specified value can be determined. For normal distributions, within one standard deviation on either side of the arithmetic mean of the distribution, 68.3 per cent of the outcomes will be encompassed; that is, there is a 68.3 per cent probability that the actual outcome will be within one (plus or minus) standard deviation of the arithmetic mean. The probabilities are 95 per cent and 99 per cent that the actual outcome will be within two or three standard deviations, respectively, of the arithmetic mean.

Risk Premiums

A **risk premium** is the additional return that investors expect to receive, or actually do receive, by taking on increasing amounts of risk. It measures the payoff for taking various types of risk. Such premiums can be calculated between any two classes of securities. Two well-known risk premiums are:

Risk Premium
That part of a security's return above the risk-free rate of return.

1. The difference between stocks and a risk-free rate (proxied by the return on T-bills), referred to as the **equity risk premium**.
2. The difference between long-term government bonds and the risk-free rate as measured by the return on T-bills, referred to as the bond horizon premium.

Equity Risk Premium
The difference between stock returns and the risk-free rate (measured as the return on T-bills).

In order to maintain consistency with our other series, these risk premiums are measured as the geometric differences between pairs of return series. Therefore:

$$ERP = \frac{(1 + TR_{CS})}{(1 + RF)} - 1 \quad \textbf{(6-13)}$$

where
ERP = the equity risk premium
TR_{CS} = the total return on stocks
RF = the risk-free rate (the T-bill rate)

and,

$$BHP = \frac{(1 + TR_{GB})}{(1 + TR_{TB})} - 1 \quad \textbf{(6-14)}$$

where
BHP = the bond horizon premium
TR_{GB} = the total return on long-term government bonds
TR_{TB} = the total return on T-bills

Other risk premiums can also be calculated. For example, the bond default premium is measured by the difference between the return on long-term corporate bonds and on long-term government bonds. This premium reflects the additional compensation for investing in risky corporate bonds, which have some probability of default, rather than government bonds, which do not.

REALIZED RETURNS AND RISKS FROM INVESTING

We can now proceed to examine the returns and risks from investing in major financial assets that have occurred in Canada. We also will see how the preceding return and risk measures are typically used in presenting realized return and risk data of interest to virtually all financial market participants.

Table 6-5 shows the average annual geometric and arithmetic returns, as well as standard deviations, for major financial assets for the 1938–97 period.

Total Returns and Standard Deviations

Table 6-5 indicates that Canadian common stocks had a geometric mean annual return over this 60-year period of 10.9 per cent. Hence, $1 invested in the market index at the beginning of 1938 would have grown at an average annual compound rate of 10.9 per cent over this period. In contrast, the arithmetic mean annual return for stocks was 12.1 per cent. The best estimate of the "average" return for stocks in any one year, using only this information, would be 12.1 per cent, not the 10.9 per cent geometric mean return.

Table 6-5

Summary Statistics of Annual Total Returns for Major Financial Assets, 1938–97

Series	Geometric Mean	Arithmetic Mean	Standard Deviation	Distribution
Canadian Common Stocks	10.9%	12.1%	16.2%	
US Common Stocks	13.1%	14.4%	17.1%	
Long-Term Government of Canada Bonds	5.9%	6.4%	9.6%	
91-Day Government of Canada T-bills	5.2%	5.4%	4.5%	
Inflation (CPI)	4.0%	4.2%	3.8%	

Source: The Canadian Institute of Actuaries (CIA) Web site: <http://www.actuaries.ca>. Reprinted with permission from the Canadian Institute of Actuaries.

The difference between these two means is related to the variability of the stock return series. Given the data in Table 6-5, the linkage between the geometric mean and the arithmetic mean is approximated by Equation 6-15:

$$(1 + G)^2 \approx (1 + AM)^2 - (SD)^2 \quad \text{(6-15)}$$

where
G = the geometric mean of a series of asset returns
AM = the arithmetic mean of a series of asset returns
SD = the standard deviation of the arithmetic series of returns

Using the data in Table 6-5 for common stocks:

$$(1.109)^2 \approx (1.121)^2 - (0.162)^2$$
$$1.230 \approx 1.257 - 0.026$$
$$1.230 \approx 1.231 \text{ (difference due to rounding)}$$

Thus, if we know the arithmetic mean of a series of asset returns and the standard deviation of the series, we can approximate the geometric mean for this series. As the standard deviation of the series increases, holding the arithmetic mean constant, the geometric mean decreases.

Table 6-5 also reports statistics for US stocks, long-term Government of Canada bonds, as well as 91-day T-bills, and the inflation rate. As we would expect, the returns are lower for bonds and T-bills than for stocks. Notice the smaller differences between the geometric and arithmetic means for bonds, T-bills and inflation, reflecting the much lower levels of variability in these series.

The standard deviations for each of the major financial assets in Table 6-5 reflect the dispersion of the returns over the 60-year period covered in the data. The standard deviations clearly show the wide dispersion in the returns from common stocks compared with bonds and T-bills. Canadian common stocks had a standard deviation of returns of 16.2 per cent, about 1.7 times that of long-term bonds and about 3.6 times that of T-bills. Therefore, common stocks were riskier, with more variable returns (greater dispersion), as reflected in their standard deviation.

Cumulative Wealth Indexes

Figure 6-2 shows the cumulative wealth indexes for the major financial assets and the corresponding index number for inflation, as measured by the Consumer Price Index. The series starts at the end of 1938 and shows the cumulative results of starting with $1 in each of these series and going through the end of 1997.

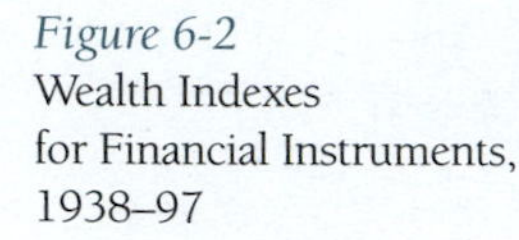
Figure 6-2
Wealth Indexes for Financial Instruments, 1938–97

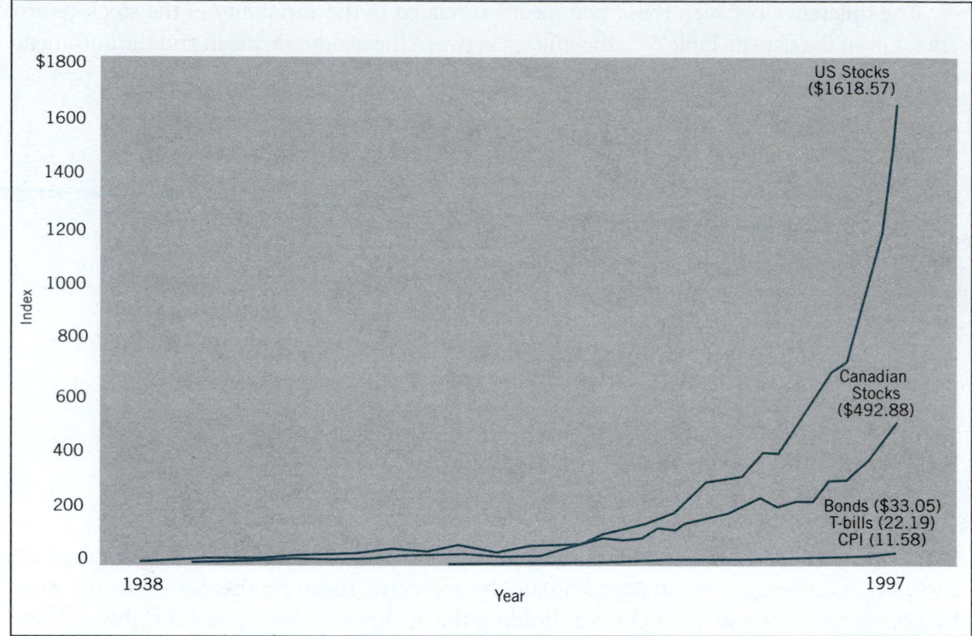

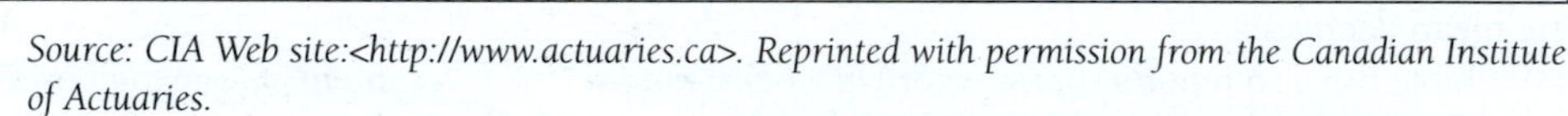
Source: CIA Web site:<http://www.actuaries.ca>. Reprinted with permission from the Canadian Institute of Actuaries.

As Figure 6-2 shows, the returns on Canadian stocks dominated the returns on long-term Government of Canada bonds over this period. In the example below, we use the geometric mean for 1938–97 from Table 6-5 (carried out to five decimal places to 10.88657 per cent) to calculate cumulative ending wealth for common stocks that is shown in Figure 6-2.

EXAMPLE: CALCULATING CUMULATIVE ENDING WEALTH FOR COMMON STOCKS

The ending wealth value of $492.88 for common stocks in Figure 6-2 is the result of compounding at 10.88657 per cent for 60 years, or

$$CWI_{1997} = WI_0\,(1.1088657)^{60} = \$1.00\,(492.88) = \$492.88$$

The large cumulative wealth index value for US common stocks (as measured by the Canadian dollar return on US stocks) is also presented in Figure 6-2. One Canadian dollar invested in these stocks would have grown to $1618.57, which is calculated in the manner demonstrated in the example above. Notice the large difference in ending wealth as a result of the additional 2.2 per cent in annual geometric average returns offered by US stocks (i.e., 13.1 per cent for US stocks versus 10.9 per cent for Canadian stocks).

On an inflation-adjusted basis, the cumulative ending wealth for any of the series can be calculated as

$$CWI_{IA} = \frac{CWI}{CI_{INF}} \quad \text{(6-16)}$$

where

CWI_{IA} = the cumulative wealth index value for any asset on an inflation-adjusted basis
CWI = the cumulative wealth index value for any asset on a nominal basis
CI_{INF} = the ending index value for inflation, calculated as (1 + geometric rate of inflation)^n, where n is the number of periods considered

EXAMPLE: ADJUSTING COMMON STOCK CUMULATIVE WEALTH INDEX FOR INFLATION

The cumulative wealth index for common stocks for the period 1938–97 was $492.88. The geometric average annual rate of inflation over this period was 4.17 per cent. The ending index number for inflation was, therefore, $(1.0417)^{60} = 11.60$. On an inflation-adjusted basis, the common stock cumulative wealth index value as of 1997 was

$$CWI_{IA} = \frac{\$492.88}{11.60} = \$42.49$$

This number indicates that, on an inflation-adjusted basis, an investor in common stocks would have multiplied his or her real wealth by a factor of about 42.5 during the period 1938–97.

Also note that the cumulative wealth index is equivalent to a cumulative total return index and, as such, can be decomposed into the two components of total return: the yield component and the price change component. Because the CWI is a multiplicative relationship, these two components are multiplicative. To solve for either one, we divide the CWI by the other, as in Equation 6-17.

$$CPC = \frac{CWI}{YI} \quad \text{(6-17)}$$

$$YI = \frac{CWI}{CPC} \quad \text{(6-18)}$$

where

CPC = the cumulative price change component of total return on an index number basis
CWI = the cumulative wealth index or total return index for a series
YI = the yield component of total return on an index number basis

Of course, the single most striking feature of Figure 6-2 is the tremendous difference in ending wealth between US stocks, Canadian stocks, bonds, and T-bills. This difference reflects the impact of compounding substantially different mean returns over long periods of time, which produces a dramatic difference in ending results.

Compounding and Discounting

The use of compounding in the previous section points out the importance of this concept and of its complement — discounting. Both are important in investment analysis and are used often. Compounding involves determining the future values resulting from compound interest — earning interest on interest. As we saw, the calculation of wealth indexes involves compounding at the geometric mean return over some historical period.

Present value (discounting) is the value today of a dollar to be received in the future. Such dollars are not comparable because of the time value of money. In order to be comparable, they must be discounted back to the present. Present value concepts are used extensively in Chapters 11 and 13 and in other chapters as needed. Students who do not feel comfortable with these concepts would be well advised to refer to the appropriate section of their introductory finance textbooks.

Tables are readily available for both compounding and discounting, and calculators and computers make these calculations a simple matter. These tables are available at the end of this text.

SUMMARY

This summary relates to the learning objectives provided on p. 155.

1. **Define return and state its two components.**
   The term return can be used in different ways. It is important to distinguish between realized (*ex post*, or historical) return and expected (*ex ante*, or anticipated) return. The two components of return are yield and price change (capital gain or loss).
2. **Explain the relationship between return and risk.**
   Risk and expected return should always be considered together. An investor cannot reasonably expect to earn larger returns without assuming greater risks.
3. **Identify the sources of risk.**
   The general components of risk have traditionally been categorized into interest rate, market, inflation, business, financial, and liquidity risks. Investors today must also consider exchange rate risk and country risk. Modern analysis divides these sources into two categories: systematic (market) risk and non-systematic (non-market) risk.
4. **Describe the different methods of measuring returns.**
   The total return is a percentage return concept that can be used to measure correctly the return for any security. The return relative, which adds 1.0 to the total return, is used when

calculating the geometric mean of a series of returns. The cumulative wealth index is used to measure the cumulative wealth over time, given some initial starting wealth (typically $1) and a series of returns for some asset. Return relatives, along with the beginning and ending values of the foreign currency, can be used to convert the return on a foreign investment into a domestic return. The geometric mean measures the compound rate of return over time. The arithmetic mean, on the other hand, is simply the average return for a series and is used to measure the typical performance for a single period. Inflation-adjusted returns can be calculated by dividing 1 + the nominal return, by 1 + the inflation rate (as measured by the CPI).

5. **Describe the different methods of measuring risk.**
   Historical returns can be described in terms of a frequency distribution and their variability measured by use of the standard deviation. The standard deviation provides useful information about the distribution of returns and aids investors in assessing the possible outcomes of an investment.

6. **Discuss the returns and risks from investing in major financial assets in the past.**
   Canadian common stocks over the period 1938–97 had an annualized geometric mean total return of 10.9 per cent, compared to 6.0 per cent for long-term bonds and 5.3 per cent for T-bills. Over the same period, common stocks had a standard deviation of returns of approximately 16.2 per cent, about 1.7 times that of long-term bonds and 3.6 times that of T-bills.

KEY TERMS

Capital gain (loss)
Cumulative wealth index
Equity risk premium
Exchange rate risk
Geometric mean
Interest rate risk
Market risk
Non-systematic (non-market) risk
Return relative
Risk premium
Standard deviation
Systematic (market) risk
Total return (TR)
Yield

ADDITIONAL RESOURCES

Two excellent sources of data regarding the returns and risks of Canadian financial assets are:

The Canadian Institute of Actuaries (CIA) Web site: <http://www.actuaries.ca>

Scotia McLeod's Handbook of Canadian Debt Market Indices. Annual. Toronto: Scotia Capital Markets.

Other sources of information include: CANSIM database; Statistics Canada; *The Toronto Stock Exchange Annual Review*; Datastream; Frank Russell Canada; and most of the major securities firms.

The best known source for the returns and risk of major financial assets in the United States is:

Ibbotson Associates, Inc., *Stocks, Bonds, Bills and Inflation: Yearbook*. Annual. Chicago: Ibbotson Associates.

REVIEW QUESTIONS

1. Distinguish between historical return and expected return.
2. How long must an asset be held to calculate a TR?
3. Define the components of total return. Can any of these components be negative?
4. When should the arithmetic mean be used when talking about stock returns?
5. What is an equity risk premium?
6. Distinguish between TR and holding period return.
7. According to Table 6-5, common stocks have generally returned more than bonds. How, then, can they be considered more risky?
8. Distinguish between market risk and business risk. How is interest rate risk related to inflation risk?
9. Explain what is meant by country risk. How would you evaluate the country risk of Canada and Mexico?
10. Assume that you purchase a stock in yen on a Japanese market. During the period you hold the stock, the yen weakens relative to the Canadian dollar. Assume you sell at a profit on the Japanese market. How will your return, when converted to dollars, be affected?
11. Define risk. How does the use of the standard deviation as a measure of risk relate to this definition of risk?
12. Explain how the geometric mean annual average inflation rate can be used to calculate inflation-adjusted stock returns over the 1938–97 period.
13. Explain the two components of the cumulative wealth index for common stocks. If we know one of these components on a cumulative wealth basis, how can the other be calculated?
14. Common stocks have returned close to twice the compound annual rate of return for bonds over long periods of time. Does this mean that common stocks are about twice as risky as bonds?
15. When should the geometric mean return be used to measure returns? Why will it always be less than the arithmetic mean (unless the numbers are identical)?
16. What is the mathematical linkage between the arithmetic mean and the geometric mean for a set of security returns?
17. Classify the traditional sources of risk as general sources or specific sources of risk.
18. Explain verbally the relationship between the geometric mean and a cumulative wealth index.

19. As Table 6-5 shows, the geometric mean return for Canadian stocks over a 60-year period has been around 10.9 per cent. The returns on bonds over a recent 15-year period (1983–97) has averaged approximately 12.6 per cent, leading some to recommend that investors avoid stocks and purchase bonds because the returns are similar (or even better on bonds) and the risk is far less. Critique this argument.
20. What does it mean if the cumulative wealth index for government bonds over a long period is 0.85?

PREPARING FOR YOUR PROFESSIONAL EXAMS

Special Note to Canadian Securities Course Students

Ensure that you have read and understood the following topics:*

Return, pp. 156–157
Risk, pp. 157–160
Total return, pp. 161–163

**Reading these CSC-related topics should provide you with additional understanding of CSC material. However, it should not be seen as a substitute for reading the CSC textbook itself, which is the basis for the CSC exam.*

CSC REGISTRATION QUESTIONS

The Canadian Securities Institute issued the following sample questions in the 1997 CSC registration package as a means for students to self-assess their understanding of CSC-related material.

1. Market risk refers to the risk that ____________________.
   a. a security might not be negotiable
   b. a security might not be marketable
   c. can be completely avoided
   d. can be reduced but not eliminated
2. Yields on growth stocks are usually ______ yields on blue chip stocks.
   a. higher than
   b. lower than
   c. the same as
3. Briefly describe the chief difference between the *nominal interest rate* and the *real interest rate*.

PAST CFA EXAM QUESTION

The following question was asked on the 1990 CFA Level I examination:

1. Fundamental to investing is the control of investment risk while maximizing total investment return. Identify four primary sources of risk faced by investors, and explain the possible impact on investment returns.

DEMONSTRATION PROBLEMS

1. **Calculation of Total Return:** Calculate total returns using the following information for XPO, a hypothetical company.

Year	(1) End-of-Year Price (P_t)	(2) Calendar-Year Dividends (D_t)	(3) Capital Gain ($P_t - P_{t-1}$)	(4) Total Return in \$ (2) + (3) = TR	(5) TR% [100 (4) / P_{t-1}]
19X1	$24.70	$1.105	—	—	—
19X2	27.20	1.26	$2.50	$3.76	15.22
19X3	36.30	1.42	9.10	10.52	38.68
19X4	35.75	1.58	−0.55	1.03	2.84
19X5	38.25	1.62			

The 19X5 income or yield component is the calendar-year dividend of \$1.62. The 19X5 capital gain (loss) is the end-of-year price in 19X5 minus the end-of-year 19X4 price — \$38.25 − \$35.75 = \$2.50. The total dollar return for calendar-year 19X5 is equal to income + capital gain = \$1.62 + \$2.50 = \$4.12.

The total return (r) in percentage form (r%) for 19X5 was

$$TR = \frac{\$TR}{P_{t-1}} = \frac{\$4.12}{\$35.75} = 0.1152 = 11.52\%$$

The same result is obtained as

$$r = \frac{D_t}{P_{t-1}} + \frac{PC}{P_{t-1}} = \frac{\$1.62}{\$35.75} + \frac{\$2.50}{\$35.75} = 0.0453147 + 0.069930 \approx 0.1152 = r,$$

$r\% = 11.52$

With the additional information that the price at the end of calendar-year 19X0 was \$25.50, we can calculate the values for 19X1 as capital gain = −\$0.80, and total return is \$0.31. The TR per cent is equal to 1.216 per cent.

2. **Calculation of Arithmetic Mean and Geometric Mean:**

Year(t)	(1) End-of-Year Price (P_t)	(2) Calendar-Year Dividends (D_t)	TR%
19X0	$ 74.60	$2.88	—
19X1	64.30	3.44	−9.2%
19X2	67.70	3.44	10.6
19X3	56.70	3.44	−11.2
19X4	96.25	3.44	75.8
19X5	122.00	3.71	30.6

The arithmetic mean of the holding period for IBM, 19X1–19X5:

$$\frac{\Sigma(\text{TR\%})}{n} = \frac{96.6}{5} = 19.32\%$$

The geometric mean in this example is the fifth root of the product of the $(1 + r)$ version of the TR per cent. We formed the TR per cent by multiplying the decimal by 100 to get r per cent. Now back up to the $(1 + r)$:

Year	TR% = r%	r	$(1 + r)$
19X1	−9.2%	−0.092	0.908
19X2	10.6	0.106	1.106
19X3	−11.2	−0.112	0.888
19X4	75.8	0.758	1.758
19X5	−30.6	0.306	1.306

The geometric mean is $\text{GM} = [(1 + R_1)(1 + R_2) \ldots (1 + R_n)]^{1/n} - 1$. Therefore, take the fifth root of the product

$(0.908)(1.106)(0.888)(1.758)(1.306) = 2.047462654$, and

$(2.047462654)^{1/5} = 1.1541 = (1 + r), r = 0.1541 = 15.41\%$

3. **The Effects of Reinvesting Returns:** The difference in meaning of the arithmetic and geometric mean, holding IBM stock over the period January 1, 19X1 through December 31, 19X5 for two different investment strategies, is as follows:

Strategy A — keep a fixed amount (say, $1,000) invested and do not reinvest returns.

Strategy B — reinvest returns and allow compounding.

First, take IBM's TRs and convert them to decimal form (r) for Strategy A, and then to $(1 + r)$ form for Strategy B.

Strategy A				Strategy B			
Jan. 1 Year	Amt. Inv. ×	r_i =	Return	Jan. 1 Year	Amt. Inv. ×	$(1 + r_t)$ =	Terminal Amt.
19X1	$1000	−0.092	−92.00	19X1	$1000.00	0.908	$908.00
19X2	1000	0.106	106.00	19X2	908.00	1.106	1004.25
19X3	1000	−0.112	−112.00	19X3	1004.25	0.888	891.77
19X4	1000	0.758	758.00	19X4	891.77	1.758	1567.74
19X5	1000	0.306	306.00	19X5	1567.74	1.306	2047.46
19X6	1000			19X6	2047.45		

Using Strategy A, keeping $1,000 invested at the beginning of the year, total returns for the years 19X1–19X5 were $966, or $193.20 per year average ($966/5), which on a $1,000 investment is $193.20/1000 = 0.1932, or 19.32 per cent per year — the same value as the arithmetic mean in Demonstration Problem 2 earlier.

Using strategy B, compounding gains and losses, total return was $1,047.46 (the terminal amount $2,047.46 minus the initial $1,000). The average annual rate of return in this situation can be found by taking the nth root of the terminal/initial amount:

$$[2047.46/1000]^{1/5} = (2.04746)^{1/5} = 1.1541 = (1 + r),\ r\% = 15.41\%$$

which is exactly the set of values we ended up with in Problem 2 when calculating the geometric mean.

4. **Calculating the Standard Deviation:** Using the TR values for IBM for the five-years 19X1–19X5, we can illustrate the deviation of the values from the mean (Y) graphically:

Figure 6-3

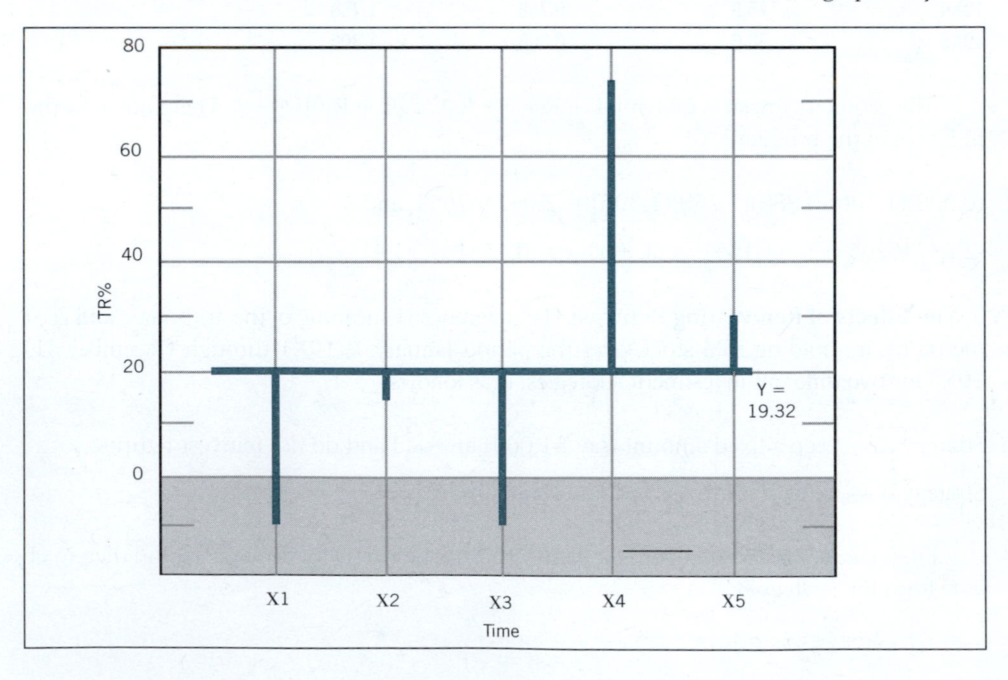

The numerator for the formula for the variance of these Y_t values is $\Sigma(Y_t - Y)^2$, which we will call SS_y, the sum of the squared deviations of the Y_t around $\overline{Y}$. Algebraically, there is a simpler alternative formula.

$$SS_y = \Sigma(Y_t - \overline{Y})^2 = \Sigma Y_t{}^2 - \frac{(\Sigma Y_t)^2}{n}$$

Using IBM's annual total returns, we will calculate the SS_y both ways.

Year	Y_t = TR	$(Y_t - \overline{Y})$	$(Y_t - \overline{Y})^2$	$Y_t{}^2$
19X1	−9.2%	28.52	813.3904	84.64
19X2	10.6	−8.72	76.0384	112.36
19X3	−11.2	−30.52	931.4704	125.44
19X4	75.8	56.48	3189.9904	5745.64
19X5	30.6	11.28	127.2384	936.36
Sum	96.6	-0-	5138.1280	7004.44

$$\overline{Y} = 19.32\%$$

$$SS_y = \Sigma(Y_t - \overline{Y})^2 = 5138.128, \text{ and also}$$

$$SS_y = \Sigma Y^2 - \frac{(\Sigma \overline{Y})^2}{n} = 7004.44 - \frac{(96.6)^2}{5} = 5138.128$$

The variance is the "average" squared deviation from the mean:

$$s^2 = \frac{SS_y}{(n-1)} = \frac{5138.128}{4} = 1284.532 \text{ "squared per cent"}$$

The standard deviation is the square root of the variance:

$$s = (s^2)^{1/2} = (1284.532)^{1/2} = 35.84\%$$

The standard deviation is the same units of measurement as the original observations, as is the arithmetic mean.

5. **Calculation of Cumulative Wealth Index and Geometric Mean:** By using the geometric mean annual average rate of return for a particular financial asset, the cumulative wealth index can be found by converting the TR on a geometric mean basis to a return relative by adding 1.0, and raising this return relative to the power representing the number of years involved. Consider the geometric mean of 6.0 per cent for long-term Government of Canada bonds for the 1938–97 period. The cumulative wealth index, using a starting index value of \$1, is, for the 60 years involved here,

$$\$1\,(1.060)^{60} = \$32.99$$

Conversely, if we know the cumulative wealth index value, we can solve for the geometric mean by taking the nth root and subtracting out 1.0.

$$(\$32.99)^{1/60} - 1.0 = 1.060 - 1.0 = 6.0\%$$

6. **Calculation of Inflation-Adjusted Returns:** Knowing the geometric mean for inflation for some time period, we can add 1.0 and raise it to the nth power. We then divide the cumulative wealth index on a nominal basis by the ending value for inflation to obtain inflation-adjusted returns. For example, given a cumulative wealth index of $32.99 for long-term Canada bonds for the 1938–97 period, and a geometric mean inflation rate of 4.17 per cent, the inflation-adjusted cumulative wealth index for this 60-year period is calculated as

$$\$32.99/(1.0417)^{60} = \$32.99/11.603 = \$2.84$$

PROBLEMS

1. Using the data for IBM from Demonstration Problem 2, calculate the capital gain (loss) and total return for the years 19X1–19X5 and confirm the 19X3 and 19X4 TRs.
2. Assume that an investor in a 28 per cent marginal tax bracket buys 100 shares of a stock for $40, holds it for five months, and sells it at $50. What tax, in dollars, will be paid on the gain?
3. Calculate the future value of $100 at the end of five, ten, 20, and 30 years, given an interest rate of 12 per cent. Calculate the present value of $1 to be received at the end of those same periods, given the same interest rate.
4. Calculate the TR and the return relative for the following assets:
   a. A preferred stock bought for $70 per share, held one year during which $5 per share dividends are collected, and sold for $63.
   b. A warrant bought for $11 and sold three months later for $13.
   c. A 12 per cent bond bought for $870, held two years during which interest is collected, and sold for $930.
5. Show that the geometric mean return for XPO (Demonstration Problem 1) for the five years 19X1 to 19X5 is 13.15 per cent.
6. a. Using a calculator, calculate the arithmetic and geometric mean rate of return for the TSE 300 Composite Index (Table 6-1) for the years 1990–95.
   b. Using a calculator, calculate the standard deviation of TRs (from Table 6-1) for the years 1990 through 1995.
7. Calculate the index value for the TSE 300 (Table 6-2) assuming a $1 investment at the beginning of 1990 and extending through the end of 1995. Using only these index values, calculate the geometric mean for these years.
8. Replicate Demonstration Problem 3 for the XPO data, showing Strategy A (not investing returns) and Strategy B (reinvest returns and allow compounding).
9. Show that the standard deviation for XPO's five annual TRs is equal to 15.042 per cent.
10. Calculate the cumulative wealth index for government bonds for the period 1926–93 assuming a geometric mean annual average rate of return of 5 per cent.

11. Given a cumulative wealth index for corporate bonds of $38.14 for the period 1926–93, calculate the geometric mean annual average rate of return.

12. Given an inflation rate of 3.13 per cent over the period 1926–93 (geometric mean annual average), calculate the inflation-adjusted cumulative wealth index for "small" common stocks as of year-end 1993, assuming that the nominal cumulative wealth index for this asset class was $2,757.15.

13. If a basket of consumer goods cost $1 at the end of 1925 and $9 at the end of 1994, calculate the geometric mean annual average rate of inflation over this period.

14. Using the TRs for the years 1987–97 from Table 6-1, determine the geometric mean for this period.

15. Using data for three periods, construct a set of TRs that will produce a geometric mean equal to the arithmetic mean.

16. According to Table 6-5, the standard deviation for common stocks for the period 1938–97 was 16.2 per cent. Using data from Table 6-1, calculate the standard deviation for the years 1987–91 and compare your results.

Problems 17 through 24 are part of a comprehensive problem set using the information on rates of return as given below:

We will use hypothetical but realistic data for major financial assets starting at the end of December 1925. The following summarizes the data discussed in Chapter 6. Assume the period covered is the 67 years, 1926–92.

	Geometric Mean	Arithmetic Mean	Standard Deviation
Common stocks	10.5%	12.5%	20.6%
Small company stocks	12.5	17.6	35.0
Long-term corporate bonds	5.4	5.8	8.5
Long-term government bonds	5.0	5.2	8.6
Intermediate-term government bonds	5.2	5.3	5.6
Treasury bills	3.7	3.8	3.3
Inflation	3.1	3.2	4.7

17. Calculate the cumulative wealth index from an investment of $1 in common stocks at the end of 1925. There are 67 years involved.

18. Compare this with the corresponding ending wealth for long-term corporates.

19. Calculate the cumulative wealth index from an investment of $1 in small common stocks at the end of 1925. How do you explain the large difference in ending wealth between common stocks and small common stocks given only a 2 percentage point difference in the geometric means?

20. Calculate the ending index number for inflation as of 1992. How can this value be interpreted?

21. Now consider real returns — that is, inflation-adjusted returns. Based on the previous numbers given for the cumulative wealth index for common stocks and the ending index number for inflation, calculate the real (inflation-adjusted) cumulative wealth index for common stocks at the end of 1992.
22. Calculate the geometric mean annual average real return for stocks.
23. Given a geometric mean inflation-adjusted corporate bond annual return of 2.3 per cent, calculate the cumulative wealth index for corporate bonds and compare this number to that of stocks.
24. Compare the arithmetic and geometric means in the preceding table. What factor(s) do you think account for the difference between the two for any given asset, such as for stocks or government bonds? Assume you could invest in a new category of high-risk common stocks with an expected arithmetic mean annual return over the December 1925–92 period of 15 per cent, with a standard deviation of 50 per cent. Estimate the geometric mean rate of return for this new category of stocks.

CHAPTER 7

EXPECTED RETURN AND RISK

LEARNING OBJECTIVES

After reading this chapter, you will be able to

1. Explain how expected return and risk for securities are determined.
2. Explain how expected return and risk for portfolios are determined.
3. Describe the Markowitz diversification model for calculating portfolio risk.
4. Simplify Markowitz's calculations by using the single-index model.

CHAPTER PREVIEW

In Chapter 6, we discussed the returns and risks from financial assets that investors have realized in the past. In this chapter, we consider how investors estimate and manage the expected returns and risks from future investments. You will learn how to estimate return and risk for both individual securities and portfolios. We introduce the Markowitz diversification model for calculating portfolio risk, focusing primarily on the concepts of the correlation coefficient and covariance. Finally, we present the single-index model, which simplifies Markowitz's calculations.

FUTURE RETURN AND RISK

As stated in Chapter 1, this text is concerned primarily with investing in marketable securities. An investment in financial assets represents the current commitment of an investor's funds (wealth) for a future period of time in order to earn a flow of funds that compensates for two factors: the time the funds are committed and the risk involved. In effect, investors are trading a known present value for some expected future value that is not known with certainty.

When we invest, we defer current consumption in order to increase our expected future consumption. We are concerned with the increase in wealth from our investments, and this increase is typically measured as a rate of return in order to adjust for differing dollar amounts of investment.

Risk is the chance that the actual return from an investment will differ from its expected return. In an uncertain world, risk is the opposite side of the coin from return. Investors are concerned primarily with how to achieve the highest possible returns without bearing unacceptable risk.

In this chapter, we outline the nature of risk and return as it applies to investment decisions. Unlike Chapter 6, we are talking about the future, which involves expected returns and not the past, which involves realized returns. Investors must estimate and manage the returns and risk from their investments. They reduce risk to the extent possible without affecting returns by building portfolios. Therefore, we must be concerned with the investor's total portfolio and analyze investment risk accordingly. As we shall see, diversification is the key to effective risk management.

At the conclusion of this analysis, we will be able to understand the two key characteristics of every investment decision — its expected return and risk — on both an individual security basis and, more importantly, on a portfolio basis. This will allow us to concentrate on the selection of optimal portfolios in Chapter 8 using Markowitz portfolio theory, a very well-known investment concept.

ESTIMATING SECURITY RETURN AND RISK

In Chapter 6, we discussed the average returns — both arithmetic and geometric — that investors have experienced over the years from investing in the major financial assets available to them. We also considered the risk of these asset returns as measured by the standard deviation. Analysts often refer to the realized returns for a security, or class of securities, over time using these measures, as well as others such as the wealth index.

Realized returns are important for several reasons. For example, they can show investors how their portfolios have performed, and they can also be important in helping investors form expectations about future returns. How do we go about estimating returns, which is what investors must actually do in managing their portfolios? First of all, note that we will use the return and risk measures developed in Chapter 6. The total return measure (TR) is applicable whether one is measuring realized returns or estimating future (expected) returns. Because it includes everything the investor can expect to receive over any specified future period, the TR is useful in conceptualizing the estimated returns from securities.

Similarly, the variance, or its square root — the standard deviation — is the accepted measure of variability for both realized and expected returns. We will calculate both the variance and the standard deviation below and use them interchangeably as the situation dictates. Sometimes it is preferable to use one and sometimes the other.

To estimate the returns from various securities, investors must estimate the cash flows these securities are likely to provide. The basis for doing so for bonds and stocks will be covered in their respective chapters. For now, it is sufficient to remind ourselves of the uncertainty of estimates of the future, a problem emphasized at the outset of Chapter 1.

Dealing with Uncertainty

The return an investor will earn is not known and must be estimated. Future return is an expected one that may or may not actually be realized. An investor may expect the TR on a particular security to be 0.10 for the coming year, but in truth, this is only a "point estimate." Risk, or the chance of an unexpected return, is involved whenever investment decisions are made.

Probability Distributions

To deal with the uncertainty of returns, investors need to think explicitly about a security's distribution of probable TRs. In other words, investors need to keep in mind that, although they may expect a security to return 10 per cent, this is only a one-point estimate of the entire range of possibilities. Given that investors must deal with the uncertain future, a number of possible returns can, and will, occur.

In the case of a Government of Canada bond paying a fixed rate of interest, the interest payment will be made with virtual certainty barring a complete collapse of the economy. This implies that the probability for receiving those fixed payments is 1.0 — that is, 100 per cent — or very close to it.

With two or more possible outcomes, the norm for common stocks, each one must be considered and its probability assessed. The result of considering these outcomes and their probabilities together is a probability distribution consisting of the specification of the likely returns that may occur and the probabilities associated with these likely returns. Probabilities represent the likelihood of various outcomes and are typically expressed as decimals or fractions. The sum of the probabilities of all possible outcomes must be 1.0 because they must completely describe all the (perceived) likely occurrences.

How are these probabilities and associated outcomes determined? In the final analysis, investing for some future period involves uncertainty and therefore subjective estimates. While past occurrences and historical frequency distributions may be useful for estimating probabilities, there is no guarantee the past will repeat itself. Hence, it is important to monitor current economic and company variables that affect security returns and forecast the future values of these variables.

Probability distributions can be either discrete or continuous. With a discrete probability distribution, a probability is assigned to each possible outcome. In Figure 7-1a, five possible TRs are assumed for a stock for next year. Each of these five possible outcomes has an associated probability, with the sum of the probabilities equal to 1.0. With a continuous probability distribution, as shown in Figure 7-1b, an infinite number of possible outcomes exist. Because probability is now measured as the area under the curve in Figure 7-1b, the emphasis is on the probability that a particular outcome is within some range of values.

The most familiar continuous distribution is the normal distribution depicted in Figure 7-1b. This is the well-known bell-shaped curve often used in statistics. It is a two-parameter distribution in that the mean and the variance (or standard deviation) fully describe it. In other words, if we know the mean and variance of any normal distribution, we can draw its graph accurately without any additional information.

Figure 7-1
(a) A Discrete Probability Distribution
(b) A Continuous Probability Distribution

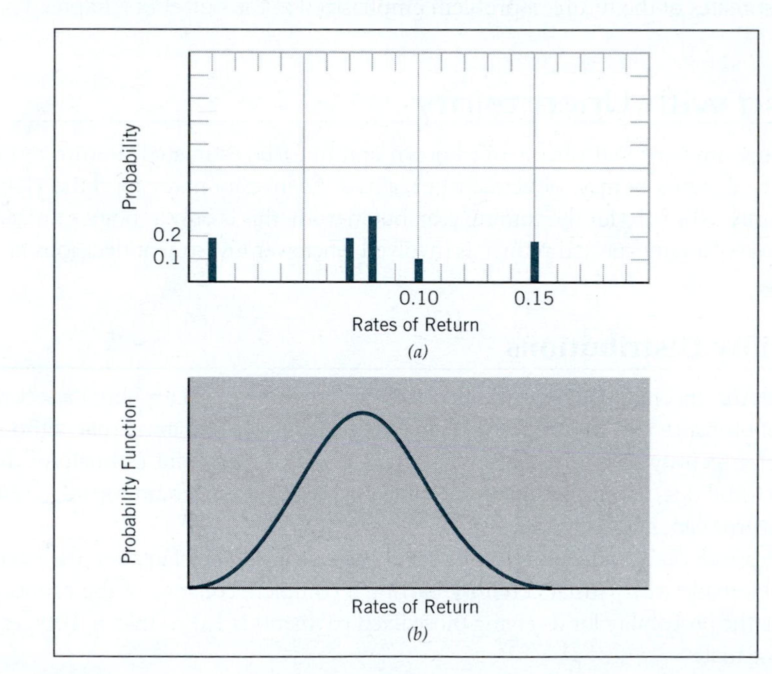

Calculating Expected Return

Expected Return
The *ex ante* return expected by investors over some future holding period.

To describe the single most likely outcome from a particular probability distribution, it is necessary to calculate its expected value. The expected value is the average of all possible return outcomes, where each is weighted by its respective probability of occurrence. Since investors are interested in returns, we will call this expected value the expected rate of return, or simply **expected return**, and for any security, it is calculated as

$$E(R) = \sum_{i=1}^{m} R_i pr_i \tag{7-1}$$

where

$E(R)$ = the expected return on a security
R_i = the ith possible return
pr_i = the probability of the ith return R_i
m = the number of possible returns

The expected return associated with the discrete probability distribution depicted in Figure 7-1a is 0.08. Refer to columns two and three of Table 7-1 for calculations.

Calculating Risk

Investors must be able to quantify and measure risk. To calculate the total risk associated with the expected return, the variance or standard deviation is used. As we know from Chapter 6, the variance and its square root, standard deviation, are measures of the spread or dispersion in the probability distribution; that is, they measure the dispersion of a random variable around its mean. The larger this dispersion, the larger the variance or standard deviation.

To calculate the variance or standard deviation from the probability distribution, we must first calculate the expected return of the distribution using Equation 7-1. Essentially, the same procedure used in Chapter 6 to measure historical risk applies here, but now the probabilities associated with the outcomes must be included, as in Equation 7-2.

$$\text{the variance of returns} = \sigma^2 = \sum_{i=1}^{m} [R_i - E(R)]^2 pr_i \tag{7-2}$$

and

$$\text{the standard deviation of returns} = \sigma = (\sigma^2)^{1/2} \tag{7-3}$$

where all terms are as defined previously.

Calculating a standard deviation using probability distributions involves making subjective estimates of the probabilities and the likely returns. We cannot avoid making estimates because future returns are uncertain since the prices of securities are based on investors' expectations about the future. The relevant standard deviation in this situation is the *ex ante* standard deviation and not the *ex post* based on realized returns. In other words, we are interested in the variability associated with future expected returns.

Although standard deviations based on realized returns are often used as proxies for *ex ante* standard deviations, investors should be careful to remember that the past cannot always be extrapolated into the future without modifications since standard deviations change through time. Hence, while *ex post* standard deviations provide convenient proxies, they should not be relied upon exclusively to estimate future risk.

The variance and standard deviation of the hypothetical stock returns shown in Figure 7-1a are calculated in columns four, five, and six of Table 7-1.

One important point about the estimation of standard deviation is the distinction between individual securities and portfolios. Standard deviations for well-diversified portfolios are reasonably steady across time, and therefore historical values may be fairly reliable in projecting

Table 7-1

Calculating the Standard Deviation Using Expected Data

(1) Possible Return	(2) Probability	(3) (1) × (2)	(4) $R_i - E(R)$	(5) $(R_i - E(R))^2$	(6) $(R_i - E(R))^2pr_i$
0.01	0.2	0.002	−0.070	0.0049	0.00098
0.07	0.2	0.014	−0.010	0.0001	0.00002
0.08	0.3	0.024	0.000	0.0000	0.00000
0.10	0.1	0.010	0.020	0.0004	0.00004
0.15	0.2	0.030	0.070	0.0049	0.00098
	1.0	0.080 = E(R)			0.00202

$s = (0.00202)^{1/2} = 0.0449 = 4.49\%$

future values. However, when we move from well-diversified portfolios to individual securities, historical calculations become much less reliable. For example, the monthly standard deviation of returns on the TSE 300 Composite Index (which is a well-diversified portfolio by construction) was 3.23 per cent over the 1988–92 period and was 3.56 per cent over the 1993–97 period. Thus, the *ex post* value over the 1988–92 period provided a reasonable estimate for the subsequent five-year period. However, if we applied the same approach to estimate the monthly standard deviation for **Abitibi Consolidated Inc.**, a large Canadian producer of newsprint, we would have obtained a very inaccurate estimate. Over the 1988–92 period, the monthly standard deviation for Abitibi was 5.48 per cent, but it increased over 56 per cent to 8.59 per cent during the subsequent five-year period, 1993–97.

Fortunately, the number one rule of portfolio management is to diversify and hold a portfolio of securities, and the standard deviations of well-diversified portfolios may be relatively stable. Therefore, we focus most of our discussion on the expected return and risk for portfolios.

PORTFOLIO RETURN AND RISK

When we analyze investment returns and risks, we must be concerned with the total portfolio held by an investor. Individual security returns and risks are important, but it is the investor's total portfolio that ultimately matters because investment opportunities can be enhanced by packaging them together to form portfolios.

As we will see, portfolio risk is a unique characteristic and not simply the sum of individual security risks. A security that has a large risk if held by itself may have much less risk when held in a portfolio. Since investors are concerned primarily with the risk of their total wealth position, as represented by their overall investment portfolio, individual stocks are risky only to the extent that they add risk to the total portfolio.

Portfolio Expected Return

The expected return on any portfolio is easily calculated as a weighted average of the individual securities' expected returns. The percentages of a portfolio's total value that are invested in each portfolio asset are referred to as **portfolio weights**, which we will denote by *w*. The combined portfolio weights are assumed to add up to 100 per cent of total investable funds, or 1.0, indicating that all portfolio funds are invested.[1]

Portfolio Weights The percentages of portfolio funds invested in each individual security. These will add up to 1.0, representing the total value of the portfolio.

EXAMPLE: DETERMINING PORTFOLIO WEIGHTS

With equal dollar amounts in three securities, the portfolio weights are 0.333, 0.333, and 0.333. An equally weighted portfolio of five securities would have portfolio weights of 0.20 in each security. Of course, dollar amounts are often not equal, and a five-stock portfolio might have weights of .40, .10, .15, .25, and .10, or .18, .33, .11, .22, and .16.

The expected return on any portfolio, p, can be calculated as

$$E(R_p) = \sum_{i=1}^{n} w_i E(R_i) \tag{7-4}$$

where

$E(R_p)$ = the expected return on the portfolio

w_i = the portfolio weight for the *i*th security

$\sum w_i$ = 1.0

$E(R_i)$ = the expected return on the *i*th security

n = the number of different securities in the portfolio

EXAMPLE: CALCULATING PORTFOLIO EXPECTED RETURN

Consider a three-stock portfolio consisting of stocks G, H, and I with expected returns of 12, 20, and 17 per cent, respectively. Assume that 50 per cent of investable funds is invested in security G, 30 per cent in H, and 20 per cent in I. The expected return on this portfolio is:

$$E(R_p) = 0.5(12\%) + 0.3(20\%) + 0.2(17\%) = 15.4\%$$

Regardless of the number of assets held in a portfolio, or the proportion of total investable funds placed in each asset, the expected return on the portfolio is always a weighted average of the expected returns for individual assets in the portfolio.

[1] For now, we ignore the possibility of short-selling, which can create negative weights in securities. In other words, we assume that all of the weights are positive, which implies we are talking about long positions in the individual securities. This assumption can be relaxed without affecting our results.

INVESTING tip

The expected return for a portfolio with positive (long) positions in all of the underlying securities must fall between the highest and lowest expected returns for the individual securities making up the portfolio. Exactly where it falls is determined by the percentages of investable funds placed in each of the individual securities in the portfolio.

Portfolio Risk

The remaining computation in investment analysis is that of the risk of the portfolio. We measure risk as the variance (or standard deviation) of the portfolio's return, exactly as in the case of each individual security.

It is at this point that the basis of modern portfolio theory emerges, which can be stated as follows: *Although the expected return of a portfolio is a weighted average of its expected returns, portfolio risk (as measured by the variance or standard deviation) is less than the weighted average of the risk of the individual securities in a portfolio of risky securities.* Symbolically,

$$E(R_p) = \sum_{i=1}^{n} w_i E(R_i)$$

But

$$\sigma_p < \sum_{i=1}^{n} w_i \sigma_i \tag{7-5}$$

Precisely because Equation 7-5 is an inequality, investors can reduce the risk of a portfolio below the weighted average of the individual securities' risk. We will now analyze portfolio risk in detail in order to see how this risk reduction can be accomplished.

ANALYZING PORTFOLIO RISK

Risk Reduction in Stock Portfolios

To begin our analysis, let's first assume that all risk sources in a portfolio of securities are independent. As we add securities to this portfolio, the exposure to any particular source of risk becomes small. Risk reduction in this manner represents an application of the insurance principle, named for the idea that an insurance company reduces its risk by writing many policies against many independent sources of risk.

If we assume that rates of return on individual securities are statistically independent such that any one security's rate of return is unaffected by another's rate of return and also assume each of these individual securities has the same level of risk (as measured by standard deviation), the standard deviation of the portfolio is given by

$$\sigma_p = \frac{\sigma_i}{n^{1/2}} \tag{7-6}$$

Notice that the risk of the portfolio will quickly decline as more securities are added since the denominator of Equation 7-6 gets larger as n increases.

EXAMPLE: CALCULATING PORTFOLIO RISK

If we combine several securities that each have a standard deviation of 0.20, the risk of the portfolio will quickly decline as more and more of these securities are added. Equation 7-6 indicates that for the case of 100 securities, the risk of the portfolio is reduced to 0.02:

$$\sigma = \frac{0.20}{(100)^{1/2}} = .02$$

Unfortunately, the assumption of statistically independent returns on stocks is not representative of the real world. Going back to the definition of market risk in Chapter 6, we find that most stocks are positively correlated with each other; that is, the movements in their returns are related. Most stocks have a significant level of co-movement with the overall market of stocks, as measured by market indexes such as the TSE 300 Composite Index. Risk cannot be eliminated because common sources of risk affect all firms.

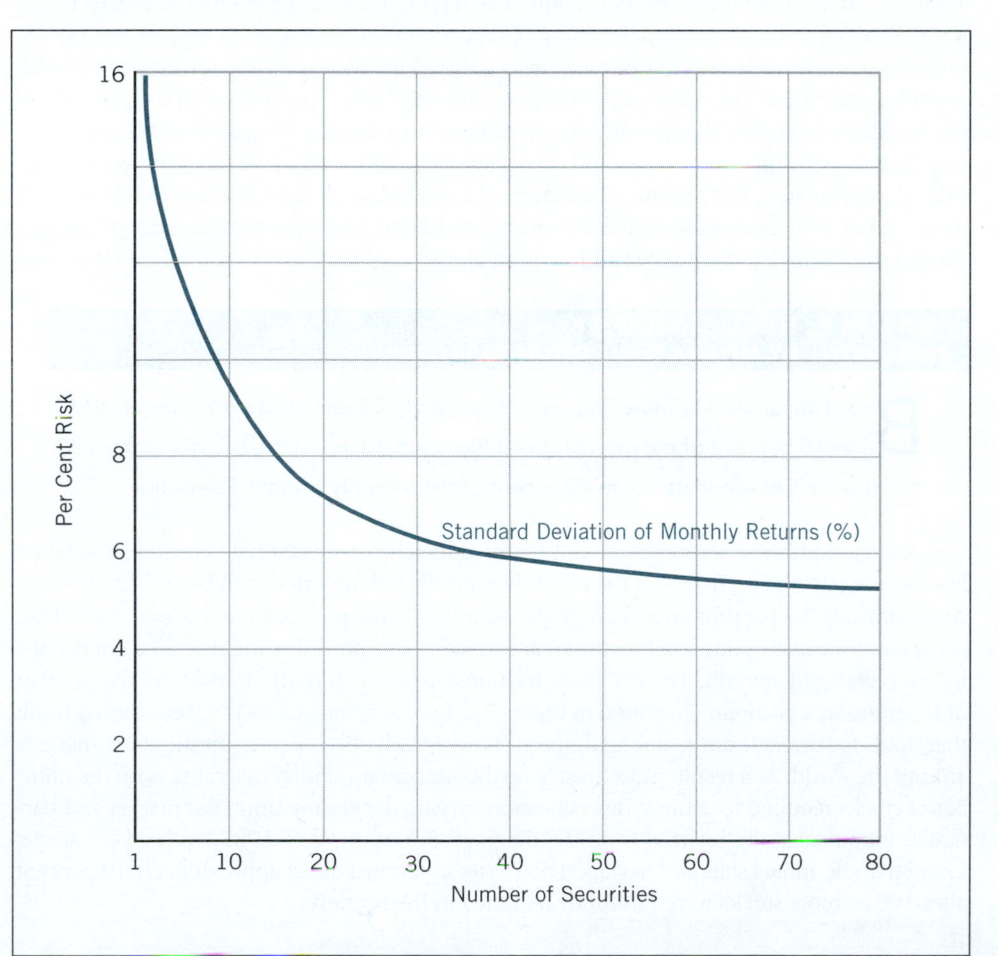

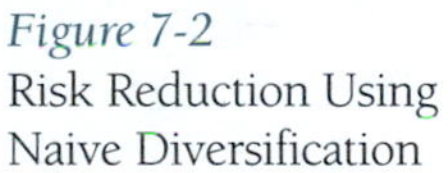
Figure 7-2
Risk Reduction Using Naive Diversification

Diversification

The insurance principle illustrates the concept of attempting to diversify the risk involved in a portfolio of assets (or liabilities). In fact, diversification is the key to the management of portfolio risk because it allows investors to minimize risk without adversely affecting return. Throughout our discussion in both this chapter and the next, we will be focusing on the diversification principle. We begin with random diversification and move to efficient diversification.

Random Diversification

Random or naive diversification refers to the act of randomly diversifying without regard to relevant investment characteristics such as expected return and industry classification. An investor simply selects a relatively large number of securities randomly (i.e., the proverbial "throwing a dart at the newspaper page containing the stock quotes"). For simplicity, we assume equal dollar amounts are invested in each stock.

Figure 7-2 plots the actual monthly data for Canadian stocks for 1993–97 as reported in Table 7-2 to illustrate naive diversification. The reported results are average standard deviations obtained from randomly selecting 5,000 portfolios of each size. As we can see, portfolio risk for a randomly selected portfolio was reduced below 5 per cent per month over this period. As securities are added to the portfolio, the total risk associated with the portfolio of stocks declines rapidly. The first few stocks cause a large decrease in portfolio risk. Based on this data, 47 per cent of portfolio standard deviation is eliminated as we go from 1 to 10 securities. Unfortunately, the benefits of random diversification do not continue indefinitely. As more and more securities are added, the marginal risk reduction per security added becomes progressively smaller, eventually producing an almost negligible effect on total portfolio risk.

EXAMPLE: REDUCING RISK THROUGH RANDOM DIVERSIFICATION

Based on the data in Table 7-2, going from ten to 20 securities eliminates an additional 8 per cent of the monthly portfolio standard deviation, but going from 20 to 30 securities eliminates only 4 per cent of the monthly standard deviation.

A large number of securities are not required to achieve substantial diversification benefits. On the other hand, note that the monthly portfolio risk reported in Table 7-2 levels out at approximately 5.5 per cent once there are 80 securities in the portfolio and beyond. Therefore, no matter how many additional securities are added to this portfolio, the risk does not decline by any significant amount. The declining relationship between portfolio risk and the number of securities in a portfolio illustrated in Figure 7-2 for Canadian stocks is a well-known result that holds for diversification among domestic stocks in all developed domestic stock markets around the world. As a result, most finance textbooks contain similar diagrams, with the number of stocks required to achieve diversification varying depending upon the market and particular empirical study referred to in the diagram. For example, a 1987 study of US stocks found that the annual standard deviation of US stocks levelled out at approximately 19 per cent after 100 or more stocks were randomly included in the portfolio.[2]

[2] Meir Statman, "How Many Stocks Make a Diversified Portfolio?" *Journal of Financial and Quantitative Analysis* 22 (September 1987), pp. 353–363.

Table 7-2

Standard Deviations of Monthly Portfolio Returns (1993–97)

Number of Stocks in Portfolio	Standard Deviation of Monthly Portfolio Returns	Ratio of Portfolio Standard Deviation Standard Deviation of a Single Stock
1	15.97	1.00
2	13.10	0.82
4	10.94	0.69
6	9.76	0.61
8	8.98	0.56
10	8.44	0.53
12	8.03	0.50
14	7.74	0.49
16	7.50	0.47
18	7.29	0.46
20	7.12	0.45
25	6.78	0.42
30	6.52	0.41
35	6.35	0.40
40	6.18	0.39
45	6.06	0.38
50	5.95	0.37
60	5.77	0.36
70	5.64	0.35
80	5.53	0.35
90	5.45	0.34
100	5.37	0.34
150	5.09	0.32
200	4.95	0.31
250	4.86	0.30
300	4.79	0.30
400	4.70	0.29
481	4.66	0.29

Source: Sean Cleary and David Copp, "Diversification with Canadian Stocks: How Much Is Enough?," working paper, Saint Mary's University, 1999.

Figure 7-2 highlights the benefits of holding a well-diversified portfolio in terms of risk reduction when diversification is achieved by random security selection. Not surprisingly, we will see that diversification can be achieved more efficiently when we take a more structured approach to forming portfolios.

International Diversification

Our discussion above assumed random diversification in domestic securities such as stocks traded on the TSE or NYSE. However, we have learned about the importance of taking a global approach to investing. What effect would this have on our diversification analysis?

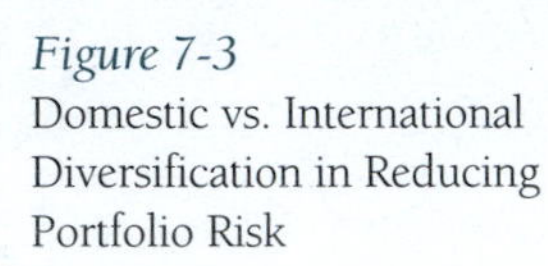

Figure 7-3
Domestic vs. International Diversification in Reducing Portfolio Risk

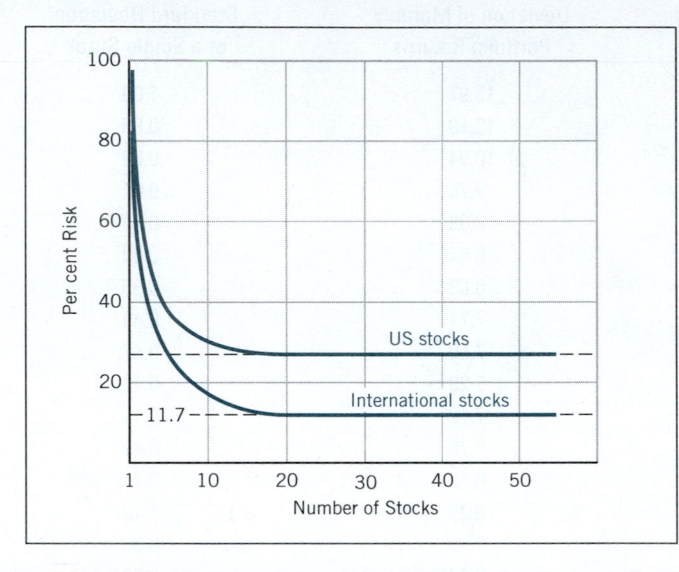

Source: Bruno Solnik, "Why Not Diversify Internationally Rather than Domestically?" Reprinted with permission from *Financial Analysts Journal* July/August 1974, © 1974. Association for Investment Management and Research, Charlottesville, VA. All rights reserved.

Considering only the potential for risk reduction and ignoring the additional hazards of foreign investing such as currency risk, we could reasonably conclude that if domestic diversification is good, international diversification must be better. Figure 7-3, which illustrates the benefits of international diversification in reducing portfolio risk, is taken from a classic article by a noted researcher Bruno Solnik. Throughout the entire range of portfolio sizes, the risk is reduced when international investing is compared to investing in only domestic stocks (US stocks in this example), and the difference is dramatic — about one-third less. Marmer documents similar risk reduction benefits for Canadian investors who diversify internationally.[3] For additional evidence regarding how Canadian investors can benefit significantly by diversifying internationally, refer to the Real-World Returns box in Chapter 8.

MARKOWITZ DIVERSIFICATION

Now that we have an understanding of how random diversification works, we need to be more sophisticated and take advantage of information that we can calculate, such as the expected return and risk for individual securities and measures of how stock returns move together. This will provide us with a better understanding of the true nature of portfolio risk and why Equation 7-5 is an inequality.

[3] H.S. Marmer, "International Investing: A New Canadian Perspective," *Canadian Investment Review* 4 (Spring 1991), pp. 47–53.

Harry Markowitz, the father of modern portfolio theory, was awarded the 1990 Nobel Prize in Economics as a result of his work in this field. In the 1950s, he originated the basic portfolio model that underlies modern portfolio theory. Before Markowitz, investors dealt loosely with the concepts of return and risk. Investors have known intuitively for many years that it is smart to diversify, that is, not to put all of your eggs in one basket. However, Markowitz was the first to develop the concept of portfolio diversification in a formal way. He showed quantitatively why and how portfolio diversification works to reduce the risk of a portfolio to an investor.

Markowitz sought to organize the existing thoughts and practices into a more formal framework and to answer a basic question: Is the risk of a portfolio equal to the sum of the risks of the individual securities comprising it? Markowitz was the first to develop a specific measure of portfolio risk and to derive the expected return and risk for a portfolio based on covariance relationships, which we consider in detail in the discussion below.

Measuring Co-Movements in Security Returns

In order to develop an equation that will calculate the risk of a portfolio as measured by the variance or standard deviation, we must account for two factors:

1. Weighted individual security risks (i.e., the variance of each individual security, weighted by the percentage of investable funds placed in each individual security).
2. Weighted co-movements between securities' returns as measured by the covariance between the securities' returns, again weighted by the percentage of investable funds placed in each security.

Covariance is a measure of the co-movements between security returns used in the calculation of portfolio risk. Before considering covariance, however, we first analyze how security returns move together by considering the correlation coefficient — a measure of association learned in statistics.

The Correlation Coefficient

As used in portfolio theory, the **correlation coefficient** (ρ_{AB} pronounced "rho") is a statistical measure of the relative co-movements between the returns on securities A and B. It measures the extent to which the returns on any two securities are related; however, it denotes only association, not causation. In other words, it measures how security returns move in relation to one another but does not provide information regarding the cause of this relationship. It is a relative measure of association that is bounded by +1.0 and −1.0, with

Correlation Coefficient
A statistical measure of the extent to which two variables, such as the returns on two securities, are associated.

$$\rho_{AB} = +1.0$$
$$= \text{perfect positive correlation}$$
$$\rho_{AB} = -1.0$$
$$= \text{perfect negative (inverse) correlation}$$
$$\rho_{AB} = 0.0$$
$$= \text{zero correlation.}$$

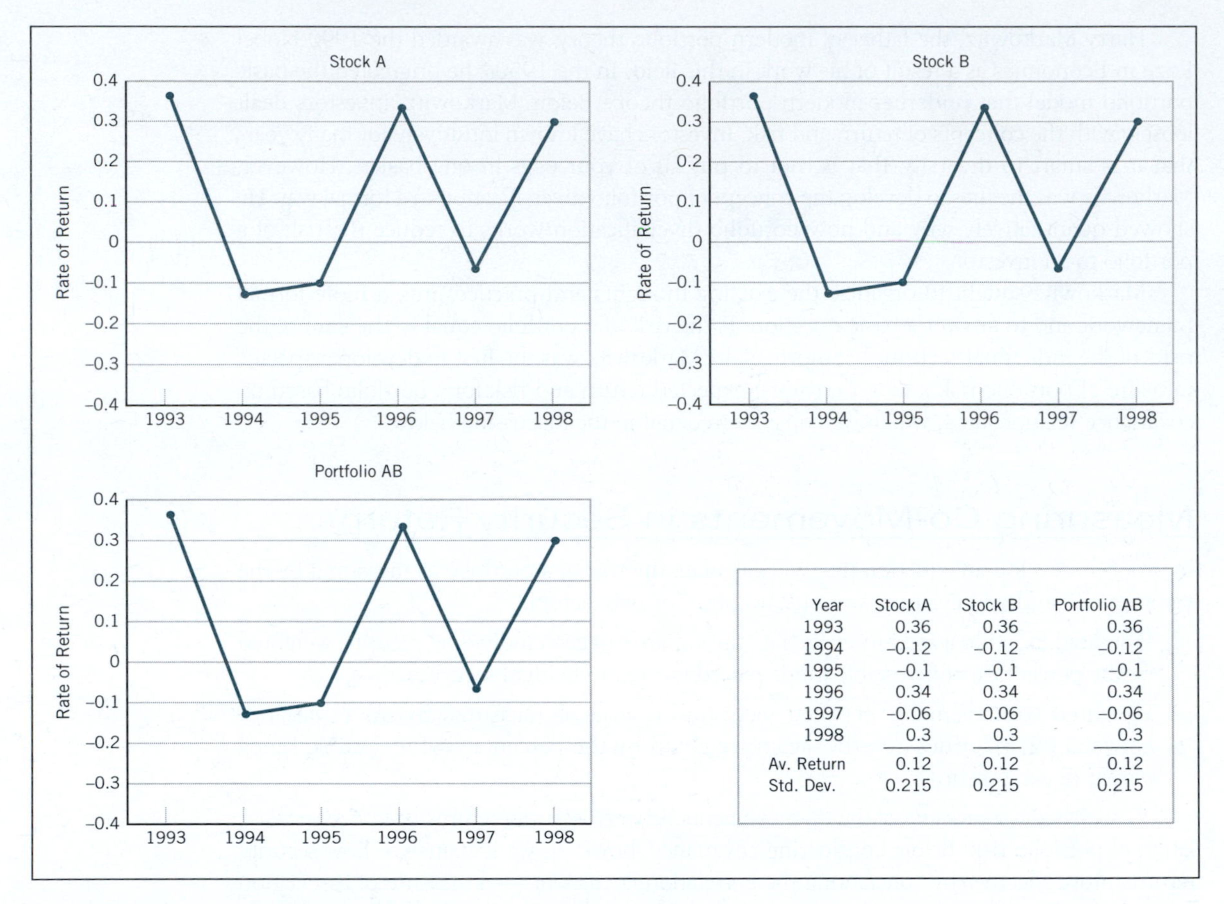

Year	Stock A	Stock B	Portfolio AB
1993	0.36	0.36	0.36
1994	−0.12	−0.12	−0.12
1995	−0.1	−0.1	−0.1
1996	0.34	0.34	0.34
1997	−0.06	−0.06	−0.06
1998	0.3	0.3	0.3
Av. Return	0.12	0.12	0.12
Std. Dev.	0.215	0.215	0.215

Figure 7-4

Returns for the Years 1993–98 on Two Stocks, A and B, and a Portfolio Consisting of 50% A and 50% B, When the Correlation Coefficient is +1.0

With perfect positive correlation, the returns have a perfect direct linear relationship. Knowing what the return on one security will do allows an investor to forecast perfectly what the other will do. In Figure 7-4, stocks A and B have identical return patterns over the six-year period 1993–98. When stock A's return goes up, stock B's does also; when stock A's return goes down, stock B's does also.

Consider the return and standard deviation information in Figure 7-4. Notice that a portfolio combining stocks A and B, with 50 per cent invested in each, has exactly the same return as does either stock by itself since the returns are identical. The risk of the portfolio, as measured by the standard deviation, is identical to the standard deviation of either stock by itself. There is no variation in this return series.

With perfect negative correlation, the securities' returns have an inverse linear relationship to each other. Therefore, knowing the return on one security provides full knowledge about the return on the other. When one security's return is high, the other is low.

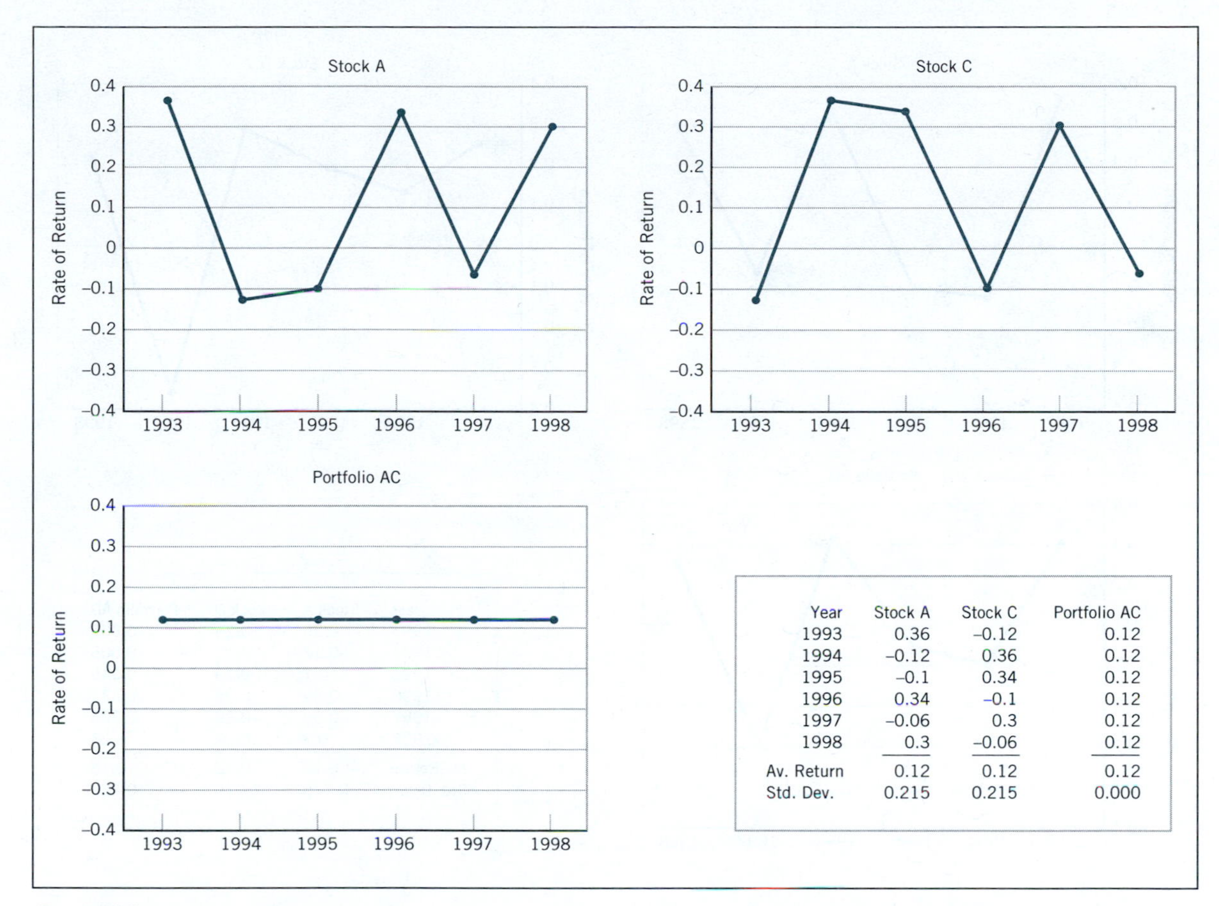

Year	Stock A	Stock C	Portfolio AC
1993	0.36	–0.12	0.12
1994	–0.12	0.36	0.12
1995	–0.1	0.34	0.12
1996	0.34	–0.1	0.12
1997	–0.06	0.3	0.12
1998	0.3	–0.06	0.12
Av. Return	0.12	0.12	0.12
Std. Dev.	0.215	0.215	0.000

Figure 7-5
Returns for the Years 1993–98 on Two Stocks, A and B, and a Portfolio Consisting of 50% A and 50% B, When the Correlation Coefficient is −1.0

In Figure 7-5, stocks A and C are perfectly negatively correlated with each other. Notice that the information given for these two stocks states that each stock has exactly the same return and standard deviation. When combined, however, the deviations in the returns on these stocks around their average return of 12 per cent cancel out, resulting in a portfolio return of 12 per cent. This portfolio has no risk. It will earn 12 per cent each year over the period measured, and the average return will be 12 per cent.

With zero correlation, there is no relationship between the returns on the two securities. Knowledge of the return on one security is of no value in predicting the return of the second security.

When does diversification pay?

1. Combining securities with perfect positive correlation with each other provides no reduction in portfolio risk. The risk of the resulting portfolio is simply a weighted average of the individual risks of the securities. As more securities are added under the condition of perfect positive correlation, portfolio risk remains a weighted average. There is no risk reduction.

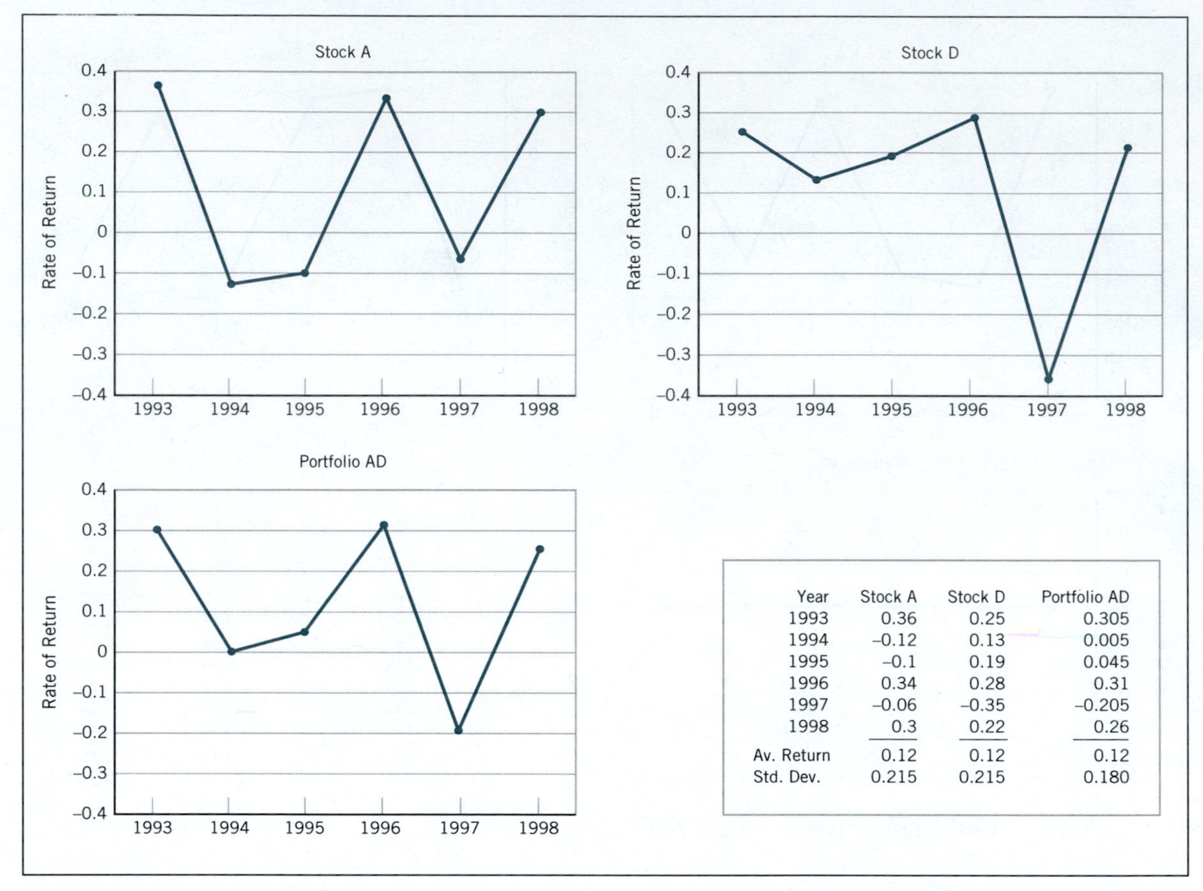

Year	Stock A	Stock D	Portfolio AD
1993	0.36	0.25	0.305
1994	−0.12	0.13	0.005
1995	−0.1	0.19	0.045
1996	0.34	0.28	0.31
1997	−0.06	−0.35	−0.205
1998	0.3	0.22	0.26
Av. Return	0.12	0.12	0.12
Std. Dev.	0.215	0.215	0.180

Figure 7-6
Returns for the Years 1993–98 on Two Stocks, A and B, and a Portfolio Consisting of 50% A and 50% B, When the Correlation Coefficient is +0.55

2. Combining two securities with zero correlation (statistical independence) with each other reduces the risk of the portfolio, which is the foundation for the insurance principle discussed above. If more securities with uncorrelated returns are added to the portfolio, significant risk reduction can be achieved. However, portfolio risk cannot be eliminated in this case.
3. Combining two securities with perfect negative correlation with each other could eliminate risk altogether if the correct portfolio weights are chosen. This is the principle behind hedging strategies, some of which are discussed in Chapter 20.
4. Finally, we must understand that in the real world, these extreme correlations are rare. Rather, securities typically have some positive correlation with each other. Thus, although risk can be reduced, it usually cannot be eliminated. Other things being equal, investors wish to find securities with the least positive correlation possible. Ideally, they would like securities with negative correlation or low positive correlation, but they generally will be faced with positively correlated security returns since all security prices tend to move with changes in the overall economy.

Figure 7-6 illustrates the more normal case of stocks A and D positively correlated with each other at a level of $\rho = +0.55$. This is typical of the correlations displayed by domestic common stocks listed on the TSE, the NYSE, or other domestic exchanges, and it thereby represents the "normal" situation encountered by investors. Note that the standard deviation of each security is still .215, with an average return of .12, but when combined with equal weights of .50 into the portfolio AD, the average return remains the same but the risk is reduced to a level of .18. Any reduction in risk that does not adversely affect return has to be considered beneficial.

EXAMPLE: COMBINING ABITIBI-CONSOLIDATED AND AIR CANADA

Over the 1993–97 period the average monthly return on **Abitibi-Consolidated** (A) common stock was 1.01 per cent, and the standard deviation of monthly returns was 8.59 per cent. During the same period, the average monthly and standard deviation for **Air Canada**'s (AC) common stock returns were 3.37 per cent and 12.21 per cent. The correlation between the returns on A and AC was 0.30 over this period. If we had formed an equally weighted portfolio of these two securities, the return would have been 2.19 per cent, exactly halfway between the 1.01 per cent return on A and the 3.37 per cent return on AC. However, the standard deviation for this portfolio would have been 8.45 per cent, which is below the standard deviation of each of the individual stocks, and well below the weighted average of the individual standard deviations.

In general, we would expect correlations to be higher between stock returns for companies that are similar in nature and lower among stock returns for companies that have greater dissimilarities. Over the 1993–97 period, for example, the correlation coefficient between the monthly returns for **Bank of Montreal** (BMO) common stock and **Abitibi-Consolidated** stock was 0.33. Over the same period, the correlation between BMO returns and those on **Bank of Nova Scotia** common stock was 0.80.

Covariance

Given the significant amount of correlation among security returns, we must measure the amount of co-movement and incorporate it into any measure of portfolio risk because such co-movements affect the portfolio's variance (or standard deviation).

The covariance is an absolute measure of the degree of association between the returns for a pair of securities. **Covariance** is defined as the extent to which two random variables covary, or move together, over time. As is true throughout our discussion, the variables in question are the returns (TRs) on two securities. Similar to the correlation coefficient, the covariance can be:

Covariance
An absolute measure of the extent to which two random variables, such as the returns on two securities, tend to covary, or move together, over time.

1. Positive, indicating that the returns on the two securities tend to move in the same direction at the same time; when one increases (decreases), the other tends to do the same.

2. Negative, indicating that the returns on the two securities tend to move inversely; when one increases (decreases), the other tends to decrease (increase).
3. Zero, indicating that the returns on two securities are independent and have no tendency to move in the same or opposite directions together.

The formula for calculating covariance is[4]

(7-7)
$$\sigma_{AB} = \sum_{i=1}^{m} [R_{A,i} - E(R_A)]\,[R_{B,i} - E(R_B)]\,pr_i$$

where

σAB = the covariance between securities A and B
$R_{A,i}$ = one estimated possible return on security A
$E(R_A)$ = the most likely outcome (or expected return) for security A for the period
m = the number of likely outcomes for a security for the period
pr_i = the probability of attaining a given return $R_{A,i}$

Relating the Correlation Coefficient and the Covariance

The covariance and the correlation coefficient can be related in the following manner:

(7-8)
$$\rho_{AB} = \frac{\sigma_{AB}}{\sigma_A \sigma_B}$$

This equation shows that the correlation coefficient is simply the covariance standardized by dividing by the product of the two standard deviations of returns.

Given this definition of the correlation coefficient, the covariance can be rewritten as

(7-9)
$$\sigma_{AB} = \rho_{AB}\,\sigma_A \sigma_B$$

Therefore, knowing the correlation coefficient, we can calculate the covariance because the standard deviations of the assets' rates of return will already be available. Knowing the covariance, we can easily calculate the correlation coefficient.

CALCULATING PORTFOLIO RISK

Now that we know how to estimate the covariances that account for the co-movements in security returns, we are ready to calculate portfolio risk. First, we will consider the simplest possible case, using only two securities in order to examine what is happening in the portfolio risk equation. We will then consider the case of many securities, where the calculations soon become too large and complex to analyze with any means other than a computer.

[4] Notice the similarity of this equation with Equation 7-2, which estimates the variance of returns on a security. For example, the variance for some security A could be calculated as

$$\sigma_A^2 = \sum_{i=1}^{m}[R_{A,i} - E(R_A)]^2 pr_i = \sum_{i=1}^{m}[R_{A,i} - E(R_A)]\,[R_{A,i} - E(R_A)]pr_i$$

If we replace the As with Bs in the second term of this expression, we have Equation 7-7.

The Two-Security Case

The risk of a portfolio, as measured by the standard deviation of returns, for the case of two securities, A and B, is

$$\sigma_P = \sqrt{w_A^2\sigma_A^2 + w_B^2\sigma_B^2 + 2w_Aw_B\sigma_{AB}} \quad (7\text{-}10)$$

Equation 7-10 shows us that the risk for a portfolio encompasses not only the individual security risks but also the covariance between these two securities and that three factors, not two, determine portfolio risk:

1. The variance of each security
2. The covariances between securities
3. The portfolio weights for each security.

Noting that $\sigma_{AB} = \sigma_A\sigma_B\rho_{AB}$, we can re-express Equation 7-10 as

$$\sigma_P = \sqrt{w_A^2\sigma_A^2 + w_B^2\sigma_B^2 + 2w_Aw_B\rho_{AB}\sigma_A\sigma_B} \quad (7\text{-}11)$$

Equation 7-11 shows that the standard deviation of the portfolio will be directly related to the correlation between the two stocks, as discussed previously. The only case where there are no risk reduction benefits to be obtained from two-security diversification occurs when the correlation coefficient is +1.0. For this case only, the portfolio standard deviation will be a weighted average of the standard deviations of the individual securities.[5] Since $\sigma_P = w_A\sigma_A + w_B\sigma_B$ when $\rho_{AB} = +1$, and since +1 is the maximum value for the correlation coefficient, it must be the case that for all other possible correlation coefficients $\sigma_P < w_A\sigma_A + w_B\sigma_B$, which implies there will be benefits from diversification as long as $\rho_{AB} < +1$. The benefits will be greater as the correlation coefficient approaches −1.

EXAMPLE: RELATING THE CORRELATION COEFFICIENT TO RISK

Assume we have some data for two companies, A and B, and that the estimated TRs are 26.3 per cent and 11.6 per cent, respectively, with standard deviations of 37.3 per cent and 23.3 per cent. To see the effects of changing the correlation coefficient, assume weights of 0.5 each (i.e., 50 per cent of investable funds is to be placed in each security). With this data, the standard deviation, or risk, for this portfolio is

$$\sigma_P = [(0.5)^2(0.373)^2 + (0.5)^2(0.233)^2 + 2(0.5)(0.5)(0.373)(0.233)\,\rho_{A,B}]^{1/2}$$
$$= [0.0348 + 0.0136 + 0.0435\,\rho_{A,B}]^{1/2}$$

since $2(0.5)(0.5)(0.373)(0.233) = 0.0435$.

[5] This fact is easy to show. Using Equation 7-11 and substituting +1 for ρ_{AB}, we obtain

$$\sigma_P = \sqrt{w_A^2\sigma_A^2 + w_B^2\sigma_B^2 + 2w_Aw_B(1)\sigma_A\sigma_B} = \sqrt{(w_A\sigma_A + w_B\sigma_B)^2} = w_A\sigma_A + w_B\sigma_B$$

which represents the weighted average of the individual standard deviations.

The risk of this portfolio clearly depends heavily on the value of the third term, which, in turn, depends on the correlation coefficient between the returns for A and B. To assess the potential impact of the correlation, consider the following cases: $\rho_{A,B}$ of +1, +0.5, +0.15, 0, −0.5, and −1.0. Calculating portfolio risk under each of these scenarios produces the following portfolio risks:

$$\rho = +1.0: \sigma_P = [\,0.0348 + 0.0136 + 0.0435(1)]^{1/2} = 30.3\%$$

Notice that for this case only the portfolio standard deviation is a weighted average of the individual standard deviations (i.e., 0.303 = [0.50][0.373] + [0.50][0.233]).

$$\rho = +0.5: \sigma_P = [0.0348 + 0.0136 + 0.0435(0.5)]^{1/2} = 26.5\%$$

$$\rho = +0.15: \sigma_P = [0.0348 + 0.0136 + 0.0435(0.15)]^{1/2} = 23.4\%$$

$$\rho = +\,0.0: \sigma_P = [0.0348 + 0.0136]^{1/2} = 22.0\%$$

$$\rho = -0.5: \sigma_P = [0.0348 + 0.0136 + 0.0435(-0.5)]^{1/2} = 16.3\%$$

$$\rho = -1.0\ \sigma_P = [0.0348 + 0.0136 + 0.0435(-1.0)]^{1/2} = 7.0\%$$

Notice that for all of these values of $\rho < +1$, the standard deviation is less than the weighted average of the individual standard deviations.

These calculations clearly show the impact that combining securities with less than perfect positive correlation will have on portfolio risk. In general, we can see there will always be risk reduction benefits from diversification as long as the correlation coefficient between the returns is less than one, and the lower the correlation coefficient, the greater the benefits. The risk of the portfolio steadily decreases from 30.3 per cent to 7 per cent as the correlation coefficient declines from +1.0 to −1.0.

We must also recognize the importance of the portfolio weights in the calculation of portfolio risk. Clearly, the proportion of total portfolio funds invested in one security as opposed to another has an effect on portfolio risk. In order to minimize portfolio risk, we must find the minimum variance combination given a level of expected return.

EXAMPLE: DETERMINING MINIMUM VARIANCE WITH PORTFOLIO WEIGHTS

Assume we have two stocks C and D with the same expected returns. The standard deviations for C and D are .20 and .30, respectively. Figure 7-7 shows the effects of portfolio weights on the standard deviation of the portfolio for four different correlations of the pattern of returns over time. If ρ is 1.0, the minimum variance is achieved with 100 per cent of funds placed in C. If ρ is −0.5, the minimum variance is achieved with a portfolio weight for C of .6, and the same is true if ρ is 0.0. On the other hand, if ρ is 0.5, the minimum variance combination involves a portfolio weight for C of .80.

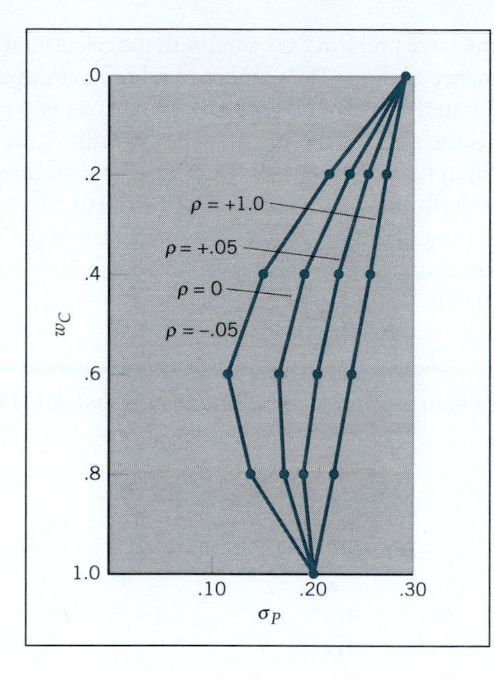

Figure 7-7
The Effects of Portfolio Weights on the Standard Deviation of the Portfolio

The *n*-Security Case

The two-security case can be generalized to the *n*-security case. Portfolio risk can be reduced by combining assets with less than perfect positive correlation. Furthermore, the smaller the positive correlation, the better.

Portfolio risk is a function of each individual security's risk and the covariances between the returns on the individual securities. Stated in terms of variance, portfolio risk for a portfolio comprised of "n" securities is

$$\sigma_p^2 = \sum_{i=1}^{n} w_i^2 \sigma_i^2 + \sum_{i=1}^{n} \sum_{j=1}^{n} w_i w_j \sigma_{ij}, \; (i \neq j) \quad \text{(7-12)}$$

where

σ_p^2 = the variance of the return on the portfolio
σ_i^2 = the variance of return for security *i*
σ_{ij} = the covariance between the returns for securities *i* and *j*
w_i = the portfolio weights or percentage of investable funds invested in security *i*
n = the number of securities in the portfolio
$\sum_{i=1}^{n} \sum_{j=1}^{n}$ = a double summation sign indicating that n^2 numbers are to be added together (i.e., all possible pairs of values for *i* and *j*)

Equation 7-12 illustrates the problem associated with the calculation of portfolio risk using the Markowitz mean-variance analysis. The number of relevant covariances for an n-security portfolio equals $n(n - 1)$. In the case of two securities, there are two covariances. Since the covariance of A with B is the same as the covariance of B with A, we simply multiply the weighted covariance term in Equation 7-10 by two. In the case of three securities, there are six covariances; with four securities, 12 covariances; and so forth. The number of covariances grows quickly based on the calculation of $n(n - 1)$, where n is the number of securities involved. For example, the number of relevant covariances in a 100-security portfolio would equal 100(100 − 1) = 9,900.

Table 7-3

The Variance–Covariance Matrix Involved in Calculating the Standard Deviation of a Portfolio

Two securities:

$\sigma_{1,1}$	$\sigma_{1,2}$
$\sigma_{2,1}$	$\sigma_{2,2}$

Four securities:

$\sigma_{1,1}$	$\sigma_{1,2}$	$\sigma_{1,3}$	$\sigma_{1,4}$
$\sigma_{2,1}$	$\sigma_{2,2}$	$\sigma_{2,3}$	$\sigma_{2,4}$
$\sigma_{3,1}$	$\sigma_{3,2}$	$\sigma_{3,3}$	$\sigma_{3,4}$
$\sigma_{4,1}$	$\sigma_{4,2}$	$\sigma_{4,3}$	$\sigma_{4,4}$

Table 7-3 illustrates the variance-covariance matrix associated with these calculations. For the case of two securities, there are four terms in the matrix — two variances and two covariances. For the case of four securities, there are 16 terms in the matrix — four variances and 12 covariances. The variance terms are on the diagonal of the matrix (i.e., along the grey line) and represent the covariance of a security with itself.

One of Markowitz's major contributions to portfolio theory was his insight about the relative importance of the variances and covariances. As the number of securities held in a portfolio increases, the importance of each individual security's risk (variance) decreases, while the importance of the covariance relationships increases. In portfolios consisting of a large number of securities, the contribution of each security's own risk to the total portfolio risk will be extremely small, and portfolio risk will consist almost entirely of the covariance risk between securities. For example, in a 100-security portfolio, there will be 9,900 weighted covariance terms and only 100 weighted variance terms.

To see this, consider the first term in Equation 7-12:

$$\sum_{i=1}^{n} w_i^2 \sigma_i^2$$

If we assume equal amounts are invested in each security, the proportions, or weights, will be 1/n. For example, in a two-security portfolio, the weights will be ½ or 0.50 in each security. Rewriting this term produces

$$\sum_{i=1}^{n} (1/n)^2 \sigma_i^2 = \frac{1}{n} \sum_{i=1}^{n} (\sigma_i^2 / n)$$

The term in brackets represents an average variance for the stocks in the portfolio. As n becomes larger, this average variance becomes smaller, approaching zero for large values of n (since $1/n$ approaches zero as n approaches infinity). Therefore, the risk of a well-diversified portfolio will be largely attributable to the impact of the second term in Equation 7-12 representing the covariance relationships.

We can rewrite Equation 7-12 into a shorter format:

$$\sigma_p^2 = \sum_{i=1}^{n}\sum_{j=1}^{n} w_i w_j \sigma_{ij} \quad (7\text{-}13)$$

or

$$\sigma_p^2 = \sum_{i=1}^{n}\sum_{j=1}^{n} w_i w_j \rho_{ij} \sigma_i \sigma_j \quad (7\text{-}14)$$

These equations account for both the variance and the covariances because when $i = j$, the variance is calculated; when $i \neq j$, the covariance is calculated.

To calculate portfolio risk using either Equation 7-13 or Equation 7-14, we need estimates of the variance for each security and estimates of the correlation coefficients or covariances. Both variances and correlation coefficients can be (and are) calculated using either *ex post* or *ex ante* data. If an analyst uses *ex post* data to calculate the correlation coefficient or the covariance and then uses these estimates in the Markowitz model, the implicit assumption is that the relationship that existed in the past will continue into the future. The same is true of the variances for individual securities. If the historical variance is thought to be the best estimate of the expected variance, it should be used. However, it must be remembered that an individual security's variance and the correlation coefficient between securities can change over time (and usually does).

SIMPLIFYING THE MARKOWITZ CALCULATIONS

The Markowitz model described above allows us to calculate portfolio expected return and risk. It can also be used to determine optimal portfolio combinations, which is demonstrated in Chapter 8. Hence, this model has the ability to generate the correct solution to the portfolio selection problem. It does so, however, at considerable cost. The major problem with the Markowitz full-covariance model is its complexity. It requires a full set of covariances between the returns of all securities being considered in order to calculate portfolio variance. There are $[n(n - 1)]/2$ unique covariances for a set of n securities.[6]

EXAMPLE: ESTIMATING LARGE NUMBERS OF COVARIANCES WITH THE MARKOWITZ MODEL

An analyst considering 100 securities must estimate [100(99)]/2 = 4,950 unique covariances. For 250 securities, the total number is [250(249)]/2 = 31,125 covariances.

[6] Although for n securities there are $n(n - 1)$ total covariances, $\sigma_{ij} = \sigma_{ji}$; therefore, there are only one-half as many unique covariances.

Obviously, estimating large numbers of covariances quickly becomes a major problem for model users. Since many institutional investors follow as many as 250 or 300 securities, the number of inputs required may become unmanageable. In fact, until the basic Markowitz model was simplified in terms of the covariance inputs, it remained primarily of academic interest.

On a practical basis, analysts are unlikely to be able to estimate directly the large number of correlations necessary for a complete Markowitz analysis. In his original work, Markowitz suggested using an index to which securities are related as a means of generating covariances. The section below describes one frequently used model that employs this strategy.

The Single-Index Model

Single-Index Model A model that relates returns on each security to the returns on a broad market index of common stock returns.

Another Nobel laureate, William Sharpe developed the **single-index model**, which relates returns on each security to the returns on a common index.[7] A broad market index of common stock returns is generally used for this purpose.[8] For example, in Canada, the TSE 300 Composite Index is commonly used, while in the US, the S&P 500 is often employed.

The single-index model can be expressed using the following equation:

$$R_{it} = \alpha_i + \beta_i R_{Mt} + e_{it} \tag{7-15}$$

where

R_{it} = the return (TR) on security i at time t

R_{Mt} = the return (TR) on the market index at time t

α_i = that part of security i's return independent of market performance (commonly referred to as the intercept coefficient, since it represents the expected value of R_{it} when $R_{Mt} = 0$)

β_i = a coefficient that measures the expected change in the dependent variable, R_{it}, given a change in the independent variable, R_{Mt} (generally referred to as the slope coefficient)

e_{it} = the random residual error at time t

The coefficients α_i and β_i in Equation 7-15 are generally estimated using a time series of observations for the returns on a stock or portfolio and regressing these returns on the market index returns over the same time period. Based on this regression, α_i is the intercept term, while β_i is the estimated slope coefficient, which measures the average change in R_{it} for a given change in R_{Mt}. For example, a β_i estimate of 1.5 implies that a 1 per cent increase in R_{Mt} causes a 1.5 per cent increase in R_{it} on average.

The single-index model divides a security's return into two components: a unique part, represented by α_i, and a market-related part, represented by $\beta_i R_{Mt}$. The unique part is a micro-event, affecting an individual company but not all companies in general. Examples include the discovery of new ore reserves, a fire, a strike, or the resignation of a key company figure.

[7] W. Sharpe, "A Simplified Model for Portfolio Analysis," *Management Science* 9 (January 1963), pp. 277–293.

[8] There is no requirement that the index be a stock index. It could be any variable thought to be the dominant influence on stock returns.

The market-related part, on the other hand, is a macro-event that is broad-based and affects all (or most) firms. Examples include a Bank of Canada announcement about the bank rate, a change in oil prices, or an unexpected increase in inflation.

Given these values, the error term is the difference between the left-hand side of the equation (the return on security i) and the right-hand side of the equation (the sum of the two components of return). Since the single-index model is, by definition, an equality, the two sides must be the same.

EXAMPLE: USING THE SINGLE-INDEX MODEL TO CALCULATE RETURN

Assume the return for the market index for period t is 12 per cent, with $\alpha_i = 3$ per cent, and $\beta_i = 1.5$. The single-index model estimate for stock *i* for time *t* is

$$R_{it} = 3\% + 1.5\ R_{Mt} + e_{it}$$

$$R_{it} = 3\% + (1.5)(12\%) = 21\%$$

If the market index return is 12 per cent, the likely return for stock i is 21 per cent.

However, no model is going to explain security returns perfectly. The error term e_{it} captures the difference between the return that actually occurs and the return expected to occur given a particular market index return.

EXAMPLE: CAPTURING THE DIFFERENCE BETWEEN ACTUAL RETURN AND EXPECTED RETURN

Assume in the previous example that the actual return on stock *i* for period *t* is 19 per cent. The error term in this case $e_{it} = 19\% - 21\% = -2\%$.

This illustrates what we said earlier about the error term. For any period, it represents the difference between the actual return and the return predicted by the parameters of the model on the right-hand side of the equation. The β term, or beta, is important. It measures the sensitivity of a stock to market movements. To use the single-index model, we need estimates of the beta for each stock we are considering. Subjective estimates could be obtained from analysts, or the future beta could be estimated from historical data. We consider the estimation of beta in Chapter 9.

R_{Mt} and e_{it} are random variables, and the single-index model assumes that the market index is unrelated to the residual error. As mentioned above, one way to estimate the parameters of this model is by performing time series regression analysis. Use of this technique ensures that these two variables are uncorrelated. We will use σ_{ei} to denote the standard deviation of the error term for stock i. The mean of the probability distribution of this error term is zero, which implies the equality will hold on average.

The single-index model also assumes that securities are related only in their common response to the return on the market. That is, the residual errors for security i are uncorrelated with those of security j, so that the covariance of their returns is zero, which can be expressed as COV $(e_i, e_j) = 0$. This is the key assumption of the single-index model because it implies that stocks covary together only because of their common relationship to the market index. In other words, there are no influences on stocks beyond the market, such as industry effects. Therefore

$$R_{it} = \alpha_i + \beta_i R_{Mt} + e_{it} \text{ for stock } i \text{ at time } t$$

and

$$R_{jt} = \alpha_j + \beta_j R_{Mt} + e_{jt} \text{ for stock } j \text{ at time } t$$

It is critical to recognize that this is a simplifying assumption, and if it is not a good description of reality, the model will be inaccurate.[9]

In the single-index model, all the covariance terms can be accounted for by reference to their common responses to the market index. In other words, the covariance depends only on market risk. Therefore, the covariance between any two securities can be written as

$$\sigma_{ij} = \beta_i \beta_j \sigma_M^2 \quad (7\text{-}16)$$

Once again, this simplification rests on the assumption about the error terms being uncorrelated. Alternative models have been derived that consider more than one index.

In the Markowitz model we must consider all of the covariance terms in the variance–covariance matrix. The single-index model splits the risk of an individual security into two components, similar to its division of security return into two components. This simplifies the covariance calculations and greatly simplifies the calculation of total risk for a security and for a portfolio. The total risk of a security, as measured by its variance, consists of two components: market risk and unique risk.

$$\sigma_i^2 = \beta_i^2 [\sigma_M^2] + \sigma_{ei}^2 \quad (7\text{-}17)$$

$$= \text{Market risk} + \text{Unique risk}$$

The market risk accounts for that part of a security's variance that cannot be diversified away. This part of the variability occurs when the security responds to the market moving up and down. The second term is the security's residual variance, which accounts for that part of the variability due to deviations from the fitted relationship between security return and market return.

This simplification also holds for portfolios, providing an expression to use in finding the minimum variance set of portfolios.

$$\sigma_p^2 = \beta_p^2 [\sigma_M^2] + \sigma_{ep}^2 \quad (7\text{-}18)$$

Total portfolio variance = Portfolio market risk + Portfolio residual variance

[9] The use of regression analysis does not guarantee that this will be true. Instead, it is a specific simplifying assumption that, in fact, may or may not be true.

Some Conclusions about the Single-Index Model

The single-index model greatly simplifies the calculation of the portfolio variance. However, this model makes a specific assumption about the process that generates portfolio returns: the residuals for different securities are uncorrelated. Thus, the accuracy of the estimate of the portfolio variance depends on the accuracy of that key assumption. For example, if the covariance between the residuals for different securities is positive, not zero as assumed, the true residual variance of the portfolio will be underestimated.

The end objective of the single-index model is the same as that of the Markowitz analysis, tracing the efficient frontier (set) of portfolios from which an investor would choose an optimal portfolio. Its purpose is to simplify the calculations necessary to do this. In Chapter 8, we will learn how to derive the efficient frontier.

SUMMARY

This summary relates to the learning objectives provided on page 189.

1. **Explain how expected return and risk for securities are determined.**
   The expected return from a security must be estimated and may not be realized. Probability distributions are involved in the calculation of expected return. The standard deviation or variance of expected return for a security is a measure of the risk involved in the expected return; therefore, it also incorporates probabilities.
2. **Explain how expected return and risk for portfolios are determined.**
   Portfolio weights, designated w_i, are the percentages of a portfolio's total funds that are invested in each security, where the weights add up to 1.0. Portfolio risk is less than a weighted average of the individual security risks as long as the correlation coefficient among the individual returns is less than $+1$. To calculate portfolio risk, we must take into account the relationships between the individual securities' returns. The expected return for a portfolio is the weighted average of the individual security expected returns.
3. **Describe the Markowitz diversification model for calculating portfolio risk.**
   Two primary concepts in the Markowitz diversification model are the correlation coefficient and the covariance. The correlation coefficient is a relative measure of the association between security returns. It is bounded by $+1.0$ and -1.0, with zero representing no association. The covariance is an absolute measure of association between security returns and is used in the calculation of portfolio risk. Portfolio risk is a function of security variances, covariances, and portfolio weights. The covariance term captures the correlations between security returns and determines how much portfolio risk can be reduced through diversification. The risk of a well-diversified portfolio is largely attributable to the impact of the covariances.

4. **Simplify Markowitz's calculations by using the single-index model.**
The major problem with the Markowitz model is the computational burden that arises because it requires a full set of covariances between the returns of all securities being considered in order to calculate portfolio variance. The single-index model simplifies the calculation of portfolio variance by relating the returns on a stock to the returns on a market index. The key assumption of the single-index model is that stocks covary together only because of their common relationship to the market index. The single-index model greatly simplifies the calculation of the portfolio variance.

KEY TERMS

Correlation coefficient
Covariance
Expected return
Portfolio weights
Single-index model

REVIEW QUESTIONS

1. Distinguish between historical return and expected return.
2. How is expected return for one security determined? For a portfolio?
3. How would the expected return for a portfolio of 500 securities be calculated?
4. What does it mean to say that portfolio weights add up to 1.0 or 100 per cent?
5. What are the boundaries for the expected return of a portfolio?
6. What is meant by naive diversification?
7. What is the key assumption underlying the single-index model?
8. Evaluate this statement: With regard to portfolio risk, the whole is not equal to the sum of the parts.
9. How many factors determine portfolio risk and what are they?
10. When, if ever, would a stock with a large risk (standard deviation) be desirable in building a portfolio?
11. Many investors have known for years that they should not put all of their eggs in one basket. How does the Markowitz analysis shed light on this old principle?
12. What type of risk tells us that the assumption of statistically independent returns on stocks is unrealistic?
13. When, if ever, would a stock with a large risk (standard deviation) be desirable as the only position in a portfolio?
14. Consider the following information for Shell Canada and Imperial Oil:

    Annual expected return for each stock is 15 per cent.
    Annual standard deviation for each stock is 22 per cent.
    Covariances with other securities varies.

    Everything else being equal, would the prices of these two stocks be expected to be the same? Why or why not?

15. Select the true statement from among the following:
    a. The risk for a portfolio is a weighted average of individual security risks.
    b. Two factors determine portfolio risk.
    c. Having established the portfolio weights, the calculation of the expected return on the portfolio is independent of the calculation of portfolio risk.
    d. When adding a security to a portfolio, the average covariance between it and the other securities in the portfolio is less important than the security's own risk.
16. Select the correct statement from among the following:
    a. The risk of a portfolio of two securities, as measured by the standard deviation, would consist of two terms.
    b. The standard deviation of returns on a portfolio is a weighted average of the standard deviations of the individual assets in the portfolio.
    c. The risk of a portfolio of four securities, as measured by the standard deviation, would consist of 16 covariances and four variances.
    d. Combining two securities with perfect negative correlation could eliminate risk altogether.
17. Select the correct statement from the following statements regarding the Markowitz model:
    a. As the number of securities held in a portfolio increases, the importance of each individual security's risk also increases.
    b. As the number of securities held in a portfolio increases, the importance of the covariance relationships increases.
    c. In a large portfolio, portfolio risk will consist almost entirely of each security's own risk contribution to the total portfolio risk.
    d. In a large portfolio, the covariance term can be driven almost to zero.
18. The Markowitz approach is often referred to as a mean-variance approach. Why?
19. What is the relationship between the correlation coefficient and the covariance both qualitatively and quantitatively?
20. How many covariance terms in total would exist for a portfolio of ten securities. How many unique covariances?
21. How many terms would exist in the variance–covariance matrix for a portfolio of 30 securities? How many of these are variances and how many covariances?
22. In explaining diversification concepts and the analysis of risk, why is the correlation coefficient usually more informative than the covariance?
23. Should investors expect positive correlations between stocks and bonds? Bonds and T-bills? Stocks and real estate? Stocks and gold?
24. Calculate the number of covariances needed for an evaluation of 500 securities using the Markowitz model. Also, calculate the total number of pieces of information needed.
25. Using the Sharpe model, how many covariances would be needed to evaluate 500 securities? How many total pieces of information?
26. The Markowitz approach is often referred to as a single-period approach. Why?

27. Select the false statement from among the following:
    a. Under the Markowitz formulation, a portfolio of 30 securities would have 870 covariances.
    b. Under the Sharpe formulation, a portfolio of 30 securities would require 92 pieces of data to implement.
    c. Under the Markowitz formulation, a portfolio of 30 securities would have 870 terms in the variance–covariance matrix.
    d. Under the Markowitz formulation, a portfolio of 30 securities would require 435 unique covariances to calculate portfolio risk.
28. Concerning the riskiness of a portfolio of two securities using the Markowitz model, select the true statements from among the following set:
    a. The riskiness depends on the variability of the securities in the portfolio.
    b. The riskiness depends on the percentage of portfolio assets invested in each security.
    c. The riskiness depends on the expected return of each security.
    d. The riskiness depends on the amount of correlation among the security returns.
    e. The riskiness depends on the beta of each security.

PREPARING FOR YOUR PROFESSIONAL EXAMS

PAST CFA EXAM QUESTIONS AND PROBLEMS

AIMR℠

The following questions were asked on the 1991 CFA Level I examination:

1. Given the following:

   Stock A standard deviation = 0.45

   Stock B standard deviation = 0.32

   If stock A and stock B have perfect positive correlation, which portfolio combination represents the minimum variance portfolio?

   a. 100% stock A

   b. 50% stock A/50% stock B

   c. 100% stock B

   d. 30% stock A/70% stock B
2. Which statement about portfolio diversification is correct?
   a. Proper diversification can reduce or eliminate systematic risk.
   b. The risk-reducing benefits of diversification do not occur meaningfully until at least 10–15 individual securities have been purchased.
   c. Because diversification reduces a portfolio's total risk, it necessarily reduces the portfolio's expected return.
   d. Typically, as more securities are added to a portfolio, total risk is expected to fall at a decreasing rate.

The following question was asked on the 1992 CFA Level I examination:

3. Given $100,000 to invest, what is the expected risk premium in dollars of investing in equities versus risk-free T-bills (US Treasury bills) based on the following table?

Action	Probability	Expected Return
Invest in	.6	$50,000
equities	.4	−$30,000
Invest in		
risk-free T-bill	1.0	$ 5,000

a. $13,000

b. $15,000

c. $18,000

d. $20,000

Reprinted, with permission, from the Level I 1994 CFA Study Guide. *Copyright 1994, Association for Investment Management and Research, Charlottesville, VA.*

PROBLEMS

1. Four securities have the following expected returns:

$$A = 15\%,\ B = 12\%,\ C = 30\%,\ \text{and}\ D = 22\%$$

Calculate the expected returns for a portfolio consisting of all four securities under the following conditions:

a. The portfolio weights are 25 per cent each.

b. The portfolio weights are 10 per cent in A, with the remainder equally divided among the other three stocks.

c. The portfolio weights are 10 per cent each in A and B, and 40 per cent each in C and D.

2. Calculate the expected return and risk (standard deviation) for Falconbridge for 1999, given the following information:

Probabilities: 0.15, 0.20, 0.40, 0.10, 0.15

Expected returns: 0.20, 0.16, 0.12, 0.05, −0.05

3. Assume the additional information provided below for the four stocks in Problem 1

		Correlations with			
	σ(%)	A	B	C	D
A	10	1.0			
B	8	0.6	1.0		
C	20	0.2	−1.0	1.0	
D	16	0.5	0.3	0.8	1.0

a. Assuming equal weights for each stock, what are the standard deviations for the following portfolios?

A, B, and C

B and C

B and D

C and D

b. Calculate the standard deviation for a portfolio consisting of stocks B and C, assuming the following weights: (1) 40 per cent in B and 60 per cent in C; (2) 60 per cent in B and 40 per cent in C.

c. In part a, which portfolio(s) would an investor prefer?

The following data apply to Problems 4 through 7.

Assume expected returns and standard deviations as follows:

	EG&G	GF
Return (%)	25	23
Standard deviation (%)	30	25
Covariance (%)	112.5	

The correlation coefficient, ρ is +.15.

Proportion in EG&G w_i	GF $w_j = (1 - w_i)$	(1) Portfolio Expected Returns (%)	(2) Variance	(3) Standard Deviation
1.0	0.0	25.0	900	30.0
0.8	0.2	24.6	637	25.2
0.6	0.4	24.2	478	21.9
0.2	0.8	23.4	472	21.7
0.0	1.0	23.0	625	25.0

4. Confirm the expected portfolio returns in column 1.
5. Confirm the expected portfolio variances in column 2.
6. Confirm the expected standard deviations in column 3.
7. On the basis of these data, determine the lowest risk portfolio.

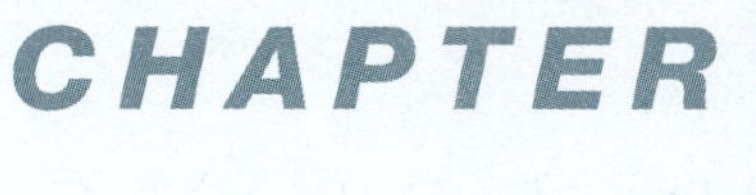

CHAPTER 8

PORTFOLIO SELECTION

LEARNING OBJECTIVES

After reading this chapter, you will be able to

1. State three steps involved in building a portfolio.
2. Apply the Markowitz efficient portfolio selection model.
3. Describe the effect of risk-free borrowing and lending on the efficient frontier.
4. Discuss the separation theorem and its importance to modern investment theory.
5. Separate total risk into systematic and non-systematic risk.

CHAPTER PREVIEW

In Chapter 7, we demonstrated how to evaluate risky assets and calculate portfolio risk using the Markowitz diversification model. In this chapter, we establish three steps to building a portfolio. First, we consider the Markowitz portfolio selection model, which involves the important concept of efficient portfolios. Second, we analyze the impact of risk-free assets on Markowitz's efficient frontier. Third, we discuss how to select the final portfolio based on risk preferences. We conclude the chapter with a discussion of the separation theorem and the concepts of systematic and non-systematic risk.

INTRODUCING RISKLESS ASSETS

In Chapter 7, we learned that risky assets should be evaluated on the basis of their expected returns and risk, as measured by the standard deviation, and that portfolio expected return and risk can be calculated based on these inputs and the covariances involved. Calculation of portfolio risk is the key issue. The complete Markowitz variance–covariance analysis can be used to calculate portfolio risk, or the single-index model can be used to simplify the calculations, subject to the assumptions of the model.

We analyzed basic portfolio principles, such as diversification, and determined that investors should hold portfolios of financial assets in order to reduce their risk when investing. Clearly, risk reduction through diversification is a very important concept. In fact, diversification is the number one rule of portfolio management and the key to optimal risk management. Every intelligent investor will diversify his or her portfolio of risky assets.

Despite the importance of the diversification principle, our analysis is incomplete because an infinite number of potential portfolios of risky assets exist. Furthermore, investors can invest in both risky and riskless assets and buy assets on margin or with borrowed funds. This chapter completes our portfolio analysis by analyzing how investors select optimal risky portfolios and how the use of a risk-free asset changes the investor's ultimate portfolio position. In effect, we are analyzing the optimal trade-off that exists between risk and expected return. This will allow us in the next chapter to analyze asset pricing and market equilibrium.

BUILDING A PORTFOLIO

To build a portfolio of financial assets, investors should follow certain steps. Specifically, they should:

1. *Use the Markowitz portfolio selection model.* Identify optimal risk-return combinations available from the set of risky assets being considered by using the Markowitz efficient frontier analysis. This step uses the inputs from Chapter 7, the expected returns, variances and covariances for a set of securities.
2. *Consider borrowing and lending possibilities.* What is the impact of a risk-free asset on the Markowitz efficient frontier? The introduction of borrowing and lending possibilities leads to an optimal portfolio of risky assets and has a significant impact on the way investors think about the investment process.
3. *Choose the final portfolio based on risk preferences.* It should consist of the risk-free asset and the optimal portfolio of risky assets, based on an investor's preferences.

In this chapter, we follow these steps. We first consider the Markowitz analysis, which is used to identify the efficient set of portfolios, and then we discuss the impact of a risk-free asset on this analysis. We show how investors can construct a final portfolio consisting of the risk-free asset and a portfolio of risky assets that is optimal for them.

STEP 1: USE THE MARKOWITZ PORTFOLIO SELECTION MODEL

As we saw in Chapter 7, even if portfolios are selected arbitrarily, some diversification benefits are gained. This results in a reduction of portfolio risk. However, random diversification does not use the entire information set available to investors and does not always lead to optimal diversification.

To take the full information set into account, we use an alternative approach based on portfolio theory as developed by Markowitz. Portfolio theory is normative, meaning that it tells investors how they should act to diversify optimally. It is based on a small set of assumptions, including:

1. A single investment period — for example, one year
2. Liquidity of positions — for example, there are no transaction costs
3. Investor preferences based only on a portfolio's expected return and risk, as measured by variance or standard deviation.

Efficient Portfolios

Markowitz's approach to portfolio selection is that an investor should evaluate portfolios on the basis of their expected returns and risk as measured by the standard deviation. He was the first to derive the concept of an **efficient portfolio**, defined as one that has the smallest portfolio risk for a given level of expected return or the largest expected return for a given level of risk.

Efficient Portfolio
A portfolio with the highest level of expected return for a given level of risk or a portfolio with the lowest risk for a given level of expected return.

In economics in general, and finance in particular, we assume investors are risk averse. This means that investors will require additional expected return in return for assuming additional risk. Based on this assumption, we can see that rational, risk-averse investors will prefer efficient portfolios because they offer a higher expected return for a given level of risk, or lower risk for a given level of expected return.

Investors can identify efficient portfolios by specifying an expected portfolio return and minimizing the portfolio risk at this level of return. Alternatively, they can specify a portfolio risk level that they are willing to assume and maximize the expected return on the portfolio for this level of risk. Rational, risk-averse investors will seek efficient portfolios because they are optimized on the two dimensions of most importance to investors: expected return and risk.

To begin our analysis, we must first determine the risk–return opportunities available to an investor from a given set of securities. Figure 8-1 illustrates the opportunities available from a given set of securities. A large number of possible portfolios exist when we realize that varying percentages of an investor's wealth can be invested in each of the assets under consideration. Is it necessary to evaluate all the possible portfolios illustrated in Figure 8-1? Fortunately, the answer is no, because investors should be interested in only that subset of the available portfolios known as the efficient set.

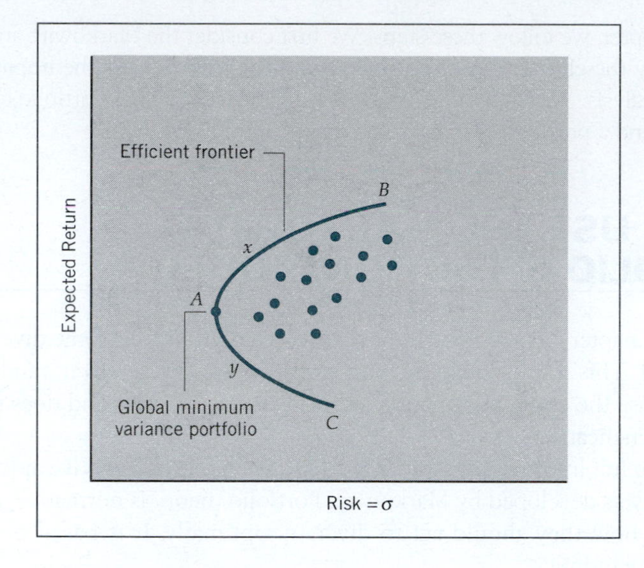

Figure 8-1
The Attainable Set and the Efficient Set of Portfolios

The assets in Figure 8-1 generate the attainable set of portfolios, or the opportunity set. The attainable set is the entire set of all portfolios that could be formed using a group of *n* securities. However, risk-averse investors should be interested only in those portfolios with the lowest possible risk for any given level of return. All other portfolios in the attainable set are dominated by efficient portfolios.

Using the inputs described in Chapter 7 — expected returns, variances, and covariances — we can calculate the portfolio with the smallest variance, or risk, for a given level of expected return based on these inputs.[1] Given the minimum variance portfolios, we can plot the minimum variance frontier, which is represented by the entire parabola-shaped curved line in Figure 8-1. Point A represents the global minimum variance portfolio because no other minimum variance portfolio has a smaller risk. Portfolios on the bottom segment of the minimum variance frontier (AC) are dominated by portfolios on the upper segment (AB). For example, since portfolio X has a larger return than portfolio Y for the same level of risk, investors would not want to own portfolio Y.

The segment of the minimum variance frontier above the global minimum variance portfolio, AB, offers the best risk–return combinations available to investors from this particular set of inputs. This segment is referred to as the **efficient set** or efficient frontier of portfolios. This efficient set is determined by the principle of dominance.

Efficient Set (Frontier)
The set of efficient portfolios composed entirely of risky securities generated by the Markowitz portfolio model.

Technically, the basic Markowitz model is solved by a complex technique called quadratic programming.[2] Since the model is easily solved by computer, we do not expand on the details. However, we note that the solution involves the determination of optimal portfolio weights or percentages of investable funds to be invested in each security. Because the expected returns, standard deviations, and correlation coefficients for the securities being considered

[1] Each investor doing this may use a different set of inputs, and therefore the outputs will differ.

[2] In particular, the problem is to choose optimal weights in the available securities in order to minimize the risk of the portfolio for a given level of expected return. This optimization problem is subject to a wealth constraint (i.e., the sum of the weights in the individual securities must equal total wealth, or 1.0) and is also constrained by the return-risk characteristics of the available set of securities.

are inputs in the Markowitz analysis, the portfolio weights are the only variable that can be manipulated to solve the portfolio problem of determining efficient portfolios.

Think of efficient portfolios as being derived in the following manner. The inputs are obtained, and a level of desired expected return for a portfolio is specified — for example, 10 per cent. Then all combinations of securities that can be combined to form a portfolio with an expected return of 10 per cent are determined, and the one with the smallest variance of return is selected as the efficient portfolio. Next, a new level of portfolio expected return is specified, and the process is repeated. This continues until the feasible range of expected returns is processed. Of course, the problem could also be solved by specifying levels of portfolio risk and choosing that portfolio with the largest expected return for the specified level of risk.

Selecting an Optimal Portfolio of Risky Assets

Once the efficient set of portfolios is determined using the Markowitz model, investors must select from this set the portfolio most appropriate for them. The Markowitz model does not specify a single optimum portfolio. It generates the efficient set of portfolios that provide the minimum risk portfolios that are attainable for given levels of expected return, or the maximum expected returns that are attainable for given levels of risk.

The assumption of risk-averse investors means that, if given a choice, they will not take a fair gamble — one with an expected payoff of zero and equal probabilities of a gain or a loss. In effect, with a fair gamble, the disutility from the potential loss is greater than the utility from the potential gain. The greater the risk aversion, the greater the disutility from the potential loss.

To select the expected return–risk combination that will satisfy an individual investor's personal preferences, **indifference curves** (which are assumed to be known for an investor) are used. These curves, shown in Figure 8-2 for a risk-averse investor, describe investor preferences for risk and return.[3] Each indifference curve represents all combinations of portfolios that are equally desirable to a particular investor.

Indifference Curves Curves describing investor preferences for risk and return.

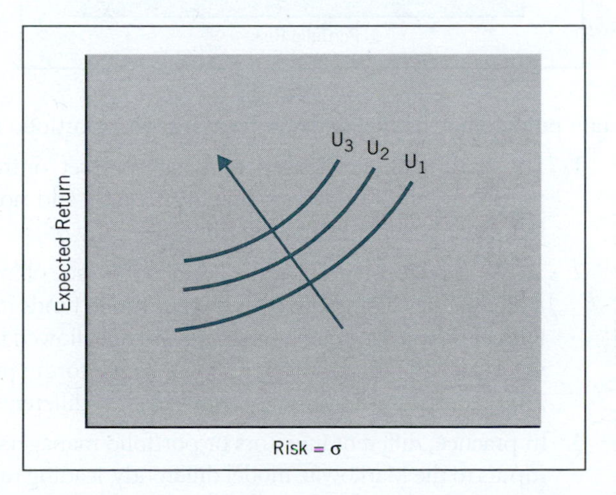

Figure 8-2
Indifference Curves

[3] Although not shown, investors could also be risk-neutral (the risk is unimportant in evaluating portfolios) or risk seekers. A risk-seeking investor will want to take a fair gamble, and larger gambles are preferable to smaller gambles.

A few important points about indifference curves should be noted. They cannot intersect since they represent different levels of desirability. Investors have an infinite number of indifference curves. The curves for all risk-averse investors will be upward sloping, but the shapes of the curves can vary depending on risk preferences. Higher indifference curves are more desirable than lower indifference curves. The greater the slope of the indifference curves, the greater the risk aversion of investors.

The optimal portfolio for a risk-averse investor occurs at the point of tangency between the investor's highest indifference curve and the efficient set of portfolios. In Figure 8-3, this occurs at point 0.[4] This portfolio maximizes investor utility because the indifference curves reflect investor preferences, while the efficient set represents portfolio possibilities. Notice that curves U_2 and U_1 are unattainable and that U_3 is the highest indifference curve for this investor that is tangent to the efficient frontier. On the other hand, U_4, though attainable, is inferior to U_3, which offers a higher expected return for the same risk (and therefore more utility).

Figure 8-3
Selecting a Portfolio on the Efficient Frontier

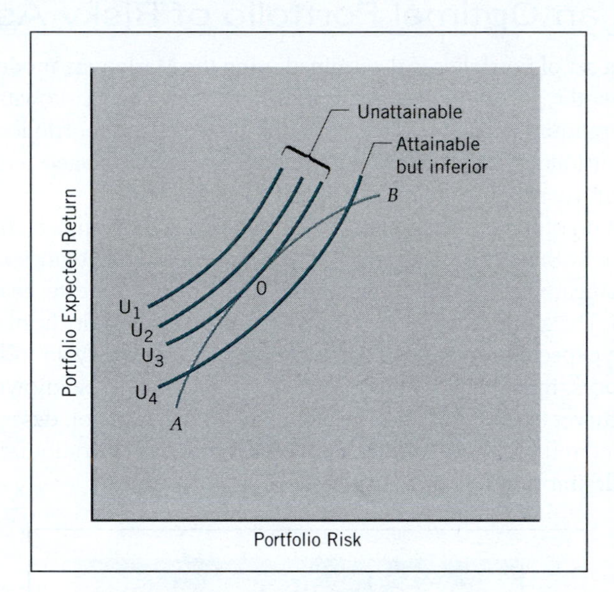

Three important points must be noted about the Markowitz portfolio selection model:

1. The Markowitz analysis generates an entire set, or frontier, of efficient portfolios, all of which are equally "good," and none of these portfolios on the efficient frontier dominates any other.
2. The Markowitz model does not address the issue of investors using borrowed money along with their own portfolio funds to purchase a portfolio of risky assets; that is, investors are not allowed to use leverage. As we will see later in the chapter, allowing investors to purchase a risk-free asset increases investor utility and leads to a different efficient set.
3. In practice, different investors or portfolio managers will estimate the inputs to the Markowitz model differently, leading to different efficient frontiers. This results from the uncertainty inherent in the security analysis part of investments as described in Chapter 1.

INVESTING tip

Stated on a practical basis, conservative investors would select portfolios on the left end of the efficient set AB in Figure 8-3 because these have less risk (and, of course, less expected return). Conversely, aggressive investors would choose portfolios toward point B because these offer higher expected returns (along with higher levels of risk).

[4] The investor is selecting the portfolio with the indifference curve furthest northwest.

Alternative Methods of Obtaining the Efficient Frontier

As we saw in Chapter 7, the single-index model provides an alternative expression for portfolio variance, which is easier to calculate than in the case of the Markowitz analysis. This approach can also be used to determine the efficient set of portfolios, but it requires considerably fewer calculations. In the case of the Markowitz analysis, 250 stocks require calculating 31,125 covariances and 250 variances. Using the single-index model as specified in Equation 7-16, we would need 250 estimates of beta (β_i), 250 estimates of the intercept term (σ_i), 250 estimates of residual variance, one estimate of the expected return on the market portfolio, and one estimate for the variance of the market portfolio.[5] In short, the single-index model is a valuable simplification of the full variance–covariance matrix needed for the Markowitz model.[6]

An obvious question to ask is how it performs in relation to the Markowitz model. In his original paper developing the single-index model, Sharpe found that two sets of efficient portfolios — one using the full Markowitz model and the other using his simplification — generated from a sample of stocks were very much alike.[7] Subsequent studies have confirmed the performance of the Sharpe model.

Selecting Optimal Asset Classes

The Markowitz model is generally thought of in terms of selecting portfolios of individual securities; indeed, that is how Markowitz expected his model to be used. As we know, however, it is a cumbersome model to employ because of the number of covariance estimates needed when dealing with a large number of individual securities.

An alternative way to use the Markowitz model as a selection technique is to think in terms of asset classes, such as domestic stocks, foreign stocks of industrialized countries, the stocks of emerging markets, bonds, and so forth. Using the model in this manner, investors decide what asset classes to own and what proportions of the asset classes to hold.

The **asset allocation decision** refers to the allocation of portfolio assets to broad asset markets — in other words, how much of the portfolio's funds is to be invested in stocks, how much in bonds, money market assets, and so forth. The weights must add up to 100 per cent, representing the total amount of investable funds for an investor. Each weight can range from zero per cent to 100 per cent if we assume that no short selling of securities is allowed.[8] Extending the asset allocation decision to a global setting leads us to ask the following questions:

Asset Allocation Decision
The allocation of a portfolio's funds to classes of assets, such as cash equivalents, bonds, and equities.

5 The single-index model requires 3n + 2 total pieces of data to implement, where n is the number of securities being considered.

Example:

The 250 securities mentioned earlier would require 3n + 2 = 3 (250) + 2 + 752 estimates, consisting of 250 estimates of α_i; 250 estimates of β_i; 250 variances of the residual errors σ^2_{ei}; an estimate of the expected return on the market index; and, an estimate of the expected variance on the market index.

In contrast, the full variance–covariance model of Markowitz requires [n (n + 3)]/2 estimates for *n* securities.

In the case of the 250 securities, [250 (253)]/2 = 31,625 total pieces of data, or

250 expected returns + 250 variances + [250(249)]/ 2 unique covariances = 31,625 total pieces of data.

6 The single-index model can be used to estimate directly the expected return and risk for a portfolio.

7 W. Sharpe, "A Simplified Model for Portfolio Analysis," *Management Science* 9 (January 1963), pp. 277–293.

8 As we shall see, when short-selling is permitted, the weights in the securities sold short will be negative; however, the total weights must still add up to 100 per cent.

1. What percentage of portfolio funds is to be invested in each of the countries for which financial markets are available to investors?
2. Within each country, what percentage of portfolio funds is to be invested in stocks, bonds, bills, and other assets?
3. Within each of the major asset classes, what percentage of portfolio funds is to go to various types of bonds, exchange-listed stocks versus over-the-counter stocks, and so forth?

Many knowledgeable market observers agree that the asset allocation decision is the most important decision made by an investor. According to some studies, for example, the asset allocation decision accounts for more than 90 per cent of the variance in quarterly returns for a typical large pension fund.[9]

EXAMPLE: ASSET MIX AND PORTFOLIO PERFORMANCE

Consider the performance of two Canadian portfolio managers, A and B, between 1993 and 1997. Manager A maintained an equally weighted portfolio with respect to T-bills, long-term government bonds, and common stocks, while manager B was more conservative and allocated 20 per cent of funds to each of bonds and stocks, with the remaining 60 per cent to T-bills. Assume each manager matched the risk–return performance on the relevant asset class benchmark index for the proportion of their portfolio invested in each of the three asset classes. Over the period, the average annual return and standard deviations for the asset classes were:

	Average Annual Return (%)	Annual Standard Deviation (%)
T-bills	7.86	3.60
Government bonds	13.80	10.96
Common stocks	11.85	13.27

Based on the asset allocation decisions presented above, the annual return earned by manager A would have been 11.17 per cent, and the standard deviation of the portfolio would have been 7.29 per cent. Over the same period, manager B would have earned 9.85 per cent annual return, with a standard deviation of 4.41 per cent. In this example, the lower risk and return of manager B's portfolio is completely attributable to her asset allocation decision since we assumed that both managers performed equally well in the management of assets within a given asset class.

The rationale behind the asset allocation approach is that different asset classes offer various potential returns and various levels of risk, and the correlation coefficients may be quite low. As with the Markowitz analysis applied to individual securities, inputs remain a problem

[9] Gary P. Brinson, L. Randolph Hood, and Gilbert L. Beebower, "Determinants of Portfolio Performance," *Financial Analysts Review* 42 (July/August 1986), pp. 39–44.

because they must be estimated for some uncertain future period. However, the use of diversified portfolios to represent different asset classes requires fewer estimates. In addition, portfolio estimates of expected return and risk are generally much more reliable than those for individual securities, since there will be less unique or company-specific risk involved. Programs exist to calculate efficient frontiers using asset classes. These programs allow for a variety of constraints, such as minimum yield and no short selling. A variety of asset allocation strategies are discussed in Chapters 14 and 22.

Global Diversification

Chapter 7 demonstrated that diversification worked the best when the returns for securities being combined in a portfolio displayed low correlations. Due to differences in overall market performance, economic activity, and industrial structure, the correlation between domestic stock returns and those on stocks trading in other countries will be low in comparison to returns displayed among only domestic stock. Therefore, it is not surprising that diversifying internationally has substantial benefits in terms of risk reduction, which was depicted in Figure 7-3. The Real-World Returns box below demonstrates how Canadian investors can expand the efficient frontier significantly by diversifying internationally. The article suggests that Canadian investors could have minimized risk over the 1993–98 period by holding 75 per cent in foreign securities, with the remaining 25 per cent in domestic assets.

STEP 2: CONSIDER BORROWING AND LENDING POSSIBILITIES

As we saw above, investors can use the Markowitz analysis as a portfolio optimizer. This analysis determines the best combinations of expected return and risk for a given set of inputs for risky assets. However, investors always have the option of buying a risk-free asset such as T-bills. The portfolio selection question remains the same. Given any set of assets under consideration, what is the best portfolio of assets to hold? To answer this question, as before, we will determine the possibilities and then match them with investor preferences.

A risk-free asset can be defined as one with a certain return and a variance of return of zero. (Note, however, that this is a nominal return and not a real return, which is uncertain because inflation is uncertain.) Since the variance = 0, the nominal risk-free rate in each period will be equal to its expected value. Furthermore, the covariance between the risk-free asset and any risky asset i will be zero, because

$$\begin{aligned}\sigma_{RF,i} &= \rho_{RF,i}\sigma_i\sigma_{RF} \\ &= \rho_{RF,i}\sigma_i(0) \\ &= 0\end{aligned}$$

ρ denotes the correlation coefficient and σ the respective standard deviation of asset i or the risk-free asset. Therefore, the risk-free asset will have no correlation with risky assets.[10]

[10] Alternatively, one could arrive at the conclusion that $\sigma_{RF,i} = 0$ because $\rho_{RF,i} = 0$ since RF is a constant, which by nature has no correlation with the changing returns on risky security i.

REAL-WORLD RETURNS

International Diversification — More Return, Less Risk

Last year, Canadians invested about $22-billion in foreign stocks, more than double the amount we sent abroad in 1997. Roughly 75 per cent of that amount was purchased through Canadian mutual funds.

Because their registered retirement savings plans are hemmed in by restrictive foreign content rules and Canadian stocks have lagged other countries' exchanges, fund buyers are heading offshore in record numbers.

So, what is the ideal blend of foreign and domestic stocks? History suggests it's likely the foreign component is higher than people think.

Imagine a world in which investors can invest in only two asset classes: Canadian stocks represented by the Toronto Stock Exchange 300-stock composite index, or large foreign stocks represented by Morgan Stanley Capital International's World Index.

Even with only these two choices, you can devise an infinite number of portfolios, one of which will give you the maximum rate of return at each risk level. If you connect all the points that have the optimum risk/return blend, you form a line called the efficient frontier.

Believers will tell you that the additional return available without additional risk is as close to a free lunch as investing will ever provide.

If you start with an all-Canadian portfolio and gradually add foreign stocks, the portfolio's rate of return rises, but its risk decreases because the underlying countries don't zigzag in unison. The portfolio's risk reaches its lowest point between a 20- and 30- per cent TSE weighting. From there, as you add still more foreign stocks, the rate of return increases, but so does the risk.

Over the past 25 years, roughly 75 per cent foreign content has turned out to be the optimal mix, assuming you look at these two asset classes. In the real world, you have multiple asset classes, countries and currencies, so the optimal percentage of foreign to domestic may shift considerably — just as the actual basket of foreign stocks represented by the MSCI World index has changed.

While more foreign stocks have been good, country selection and currency management have been equally important.

The US stock market has enjoyed an almost unprecedented bull run for several years, but you will recall that in the late 1980s, the size of the Japanese market actually surpassed the US market in terms of market capitalization. Similarly, European markets have grown to 35 per cent of the global market capitalization from approximately 20 per cent, while the US share of the global pie has grown to 51 per cent from 29 per cent. Simply put, buying the world index hasn't produced the same country breakdown over the years.

RRSP investors looking to diversify beyond our borders, but content to mimic these gradual shifts, can opt for one of several derivative-based foreign index funds offered by no-load vendors.

Despite this recent interest in foreign markets, Canadian investors still have too much money tied up in Canada. Given the prospects for a revitalized Canadian dollar (remember as our currency gets stronger, the relative value of your global investments is going to fall), 75 per cent foreign stocks may well be too much for even the most aggressive investor.

But it's still a good target to work toward.

Source: Excerpted from Gordon Powers, "About 75% Foreign Content Seems Ideal for Equity Portfolios," The Globe and Mail, *March 6, 1999, p. B7. © Affinity Group.*

The true risk-free asset is best thought of as a government security, which has no risk of default and has a term to maturity matching the holding period of the investor. In this case, the amount of money to be received at the end of the holding period is known with certainty at the beginning of the period.[11] Short-term T-bills are typically taken to be the risk-free asset, and the associated rate of return is referred to here as RF.

Although the introduction of a risk-free asset appears to be a simple step to take in the evolution of portfolio and capital market theory, it is a very significant step. Investors can now invest part of their wealth in this asset and the remainder in any of the risky portfolios in the Markowitz efficient set. It allows Markowitz portfolio theory to be extended in such a way that the efficient frontier is completely changed. This, in turn, leads to a general theory for pricing assets under uncertainty, as discussed in the next chapter.

Risk-Free Borrowing and Lending

Assume that the efficient frontier, as shown by the arc AB in Figure 8-4, has been derived by an investor. The arc AB delineates the efficient set of portfolios comprised entirely of risky assets. (For simplicity, we assume these are portfolios of common stocks.) We now introduce a risk-free asset with return RF and standard deviation of zero.

As shown in Figure 8-4, the return on the risk-free asset (RF) will plot on the vertical axis because the risk is zero. Investors can combine this riskless asset with the efficient set of portfolios on the efficient frontier. The section below demonstrates that we can draw a line between RF and any risky portfolio on the efficient frontier to represent obtainable combinations of risk–return possibilities that did not exist previously.

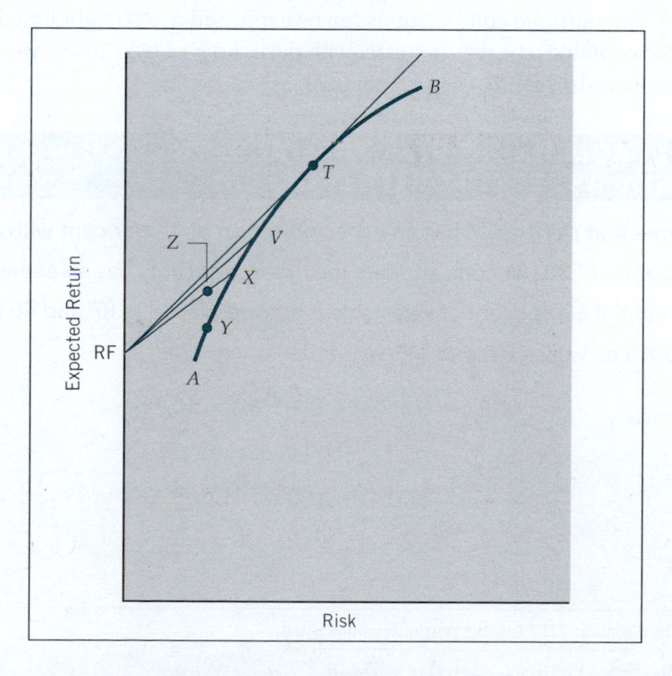

Figure 8-4
The Markowitz Efficient Frontier and the Possibilities Resulting from Introducing a Risk-Free Asset

[11] If there is no uncertainty about the terminal value of the asset, the standard deviation must be zero and the asset must, therefore, be riskless.

Risk-Free Lending

Consider an arbitrary point on the efficient frontier depicted in Figure 8-4 — risky portfolio X. Assume this investor places w_{RF} of investable funds in the risk-free asset and the remainder $(1 - w_{RF})$ in portfolio X. The expected return on this combined portfolio p would be

$$E(R_p) = w_{RF}RF + (1 - w_{RF})\, E(R_X) \tag{8-1}$$

As always, the expected return of a portfolio is a weighted average of the expected returns of the individual assets. Since portfolio X, consisting of risky assets, would always be assumed to have a larger expected return than the return on the risk-free asset (RF), the greater the percentage of an investor's funds committed to X, $(1 - w_{RF})$, the larger the expected return on the portfolio.

The standard deviation of this portfolio is

$$\sigma_p = (1 - w_{RF})\sigma_X \tag{8-2}$$

because $\sigma_{RF} = 0$ and the correlation between RF and any risky portfolio is zero, which eliminates the second and third terms of Equation 7-11.[12] Thus, the standard deviation of a portfolio combining the risk-free asset with a risky asset (portfolio) is simply the weighted standard deviation of the risky portfolio. This confirms what one would expect, as a higher proportion of wealth is invested in the risky asset, the portfolio risk increases.

Since both the expected return and standard deviation of a portfolio comprised of any portfolio of risky assets X and the riskless asset RF are linear functions of the weights invested in RF and X, the portfolio combinations can be expressed as a straight line. In other words, an investor who combines the risk-free asset with portfolio X of risky assets would have a portfolio somewhere on the line RF-X (e.g., point Z).

EXAMPLE: COMBINING RISK-FREE ASSETS WITH RISKY ASSETS (PORTFOLIO)

Assume that portfolio X has an expected return of 15 per cent with a standard deviation of 30 per cent, and that the risk-free security has an expected return of 7 per cent. If 60 per cent of investable funds are placed in RF and 40 per cent in portfolio X (i.e., $w_{RF} = 0.6$ and $1 - w_{RF} = 0.4$), then

$$E(R_p) = 0.6(7\%) + 0.4(15\%) = 10.2\%$$

and

$$\sigma_p = (1.0 - 0.6)\ 30\% = 12\%$$

[12] More formally, Equation 7-11 for this portfolio would equal

$$\sigma_p = \sqrt{(1 - w_{RF})^2\sigma_X^2 + w_{RF}^2\,\sigma_{RF}^2 + (1 - w_{RF})w_{RF}\rho_{RF,X}\,\sigma_X\,\sigma_{RF}}$$

$$= \sqrt{(1 - w_{RF})^2\sigma_X^2 + w_{RF}^2(0) + (1 - w_{RF})w_{RF}(0)\sigma_X(0)} = \sqrt{(1 - w_{RF})^2\sigma_X^2 + 0 + 0} = (1 - w_{RF})\sigma_X$$

An investor could change positions on the line RF-X by varying w_{RF}, and hence $1 - w_{RF}$. As more of the investable funds are placed in the risk-free asset, both the expected return and the risk of the portfolio decline.

It is apparent that the segment of the efficient frontier below X (i.e., A to X) in Figure 8-4 is now dominated by the line RF-X. For example, at point Z on the straight line, the investor has the same risk as portfolio Y on the Markowitz efficient frontier, but Z has a larger expected return. Hence, the ability to invest in RF provides investors with a more efficient set of portfolios from which to choose.

In Figure 8-4, a new line could be drawn between RF and the Markowitz efficient frontier above point X, for example, connecting RF to point V. Each successively higher line will dominate the preceding set of portfolios because it will offer higher expected returns for any given level of risk (i.e., they lie northwest of the other lines). This process ends when a line is drawn tangent to the efficient set of risky portfolios, given a vertical intercept of RF. In Figure 8-4, we will call this tangency point T. The portfolio opportunities on this line (RF to T) dominate all portfolios below them.

Portfolio T is important in this analysis. The Markowitz efficient set consists of portfolios of risky assets. In Figure 8-4, no other portfolio connected to the risk-free rate (RF) lies northwest of the straight line connecting RF and portfolio T. This line has the greatest slope (and thereby provides the highest reward per unit of risk).

The straight line from RF to the efficient frontier at point T (RF-T) dominates all straight lines below it and contains the superior lending portfolios given the Markowitz efficient set depicted in Figure 8-4. The term lending portfolios arises in reference to the fact that purchasing riskless assets such as T-bills to combine with some risky asset is a form of the investor lending money to the issuer of the securities — the federal government. We can think of this risk-free lending simply as risk-free investing.

Through a combination of risk-free investing (investing funds at a rate of RF) and investing in a risky portfolio of securities, T, an investor can improve upon the opportunity set available from the Markowitz efficient frontier, which consists only of portfolios of risky assets. The set of efficient portfolios available to any investor with the introduction of the possibility of risk-free investing now lies along line RF-T.

Borrowing Possibilities

What if we extend this analysis to allow investors to borrow money? The investor is no longer restricted to his or her initial wealth when investing in risky assets. One way to accomplish this borrowing is to buy stocks on margin, which may have margin requirements as low as 30 per cent. Of course, investors must pay interest on borrowed money. We will assume initially that investors can also borrow at the risk-free rate RF. Technically, borrowing at the riskless rate can be viewed as short-selling the riskless asset. We will remove the assumption that funds can be invested at the riskless rate later.

Borrowing additional investable funds and investing them together with the investor's own wealth allows investors to seek higher expected returns while assuming greater risk. These borrowed funds can be used to lever the portfolio position beyond the tangency point T, which represents 100 per cent of an investor's wealth in the risky asset portfolio T. The straight line RF-T is now extended upward, as shown in Figure 8-5, and can be designated RF-T-L.

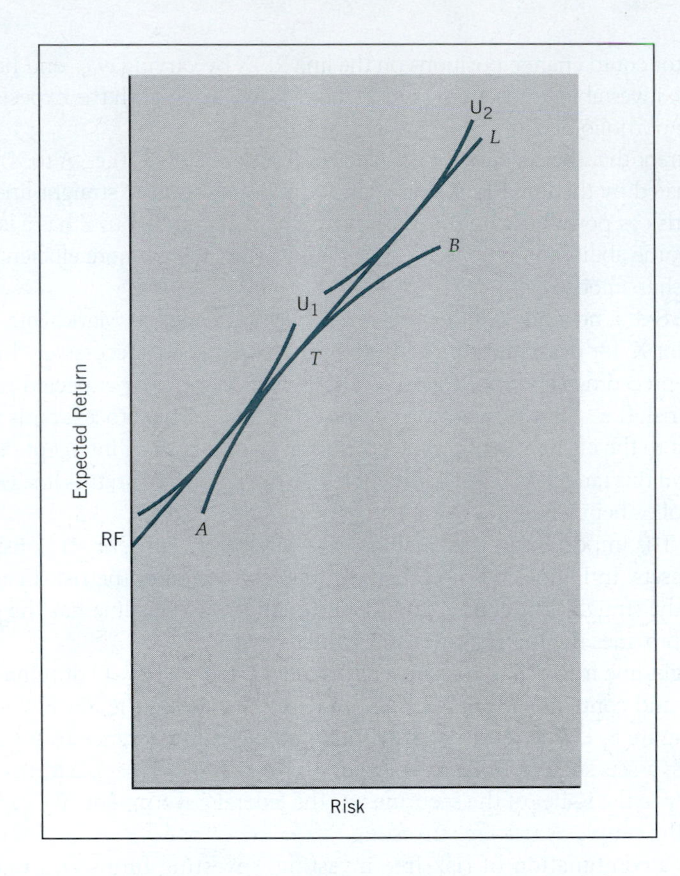

Figure 8-5
The Efficient Frontier when Lending and Borrowing Possibilities Are Allowed

What effect does borrowing have on the expected return and risk for a portfolio? These parameters can be calculated in the usual manner. However, the proportions to be invested are now stated differently. Since the proportions to be invested in the alternatives are stated as percentages of an investor's total investable funds, various combinations must add up to 1.0 (i.e., 100 per cent, representing an investor's total wealth). Therefore, the proportion to be borrowed at RF is stated as a negative figure, so that $w_{RF} + (1 - w_{RF}) = 1.0 = 100$ per cent of investor wealth.

Assume an investor can borrow an amount equal to all of his or her investable wealth, which, together with that wealth itself, will be invested in risky-asset portfolio T (i.e., 200 per cent of investable wealth is invested in portfolio T). The $1 - w_{RF}$ weight must now equal 2.0 to represent the sum of original wealth plus borrowed funds. To obtain this result, the proportion of investable funds associated with w_{RF} is negative; specifically, it is -1.0, representing borrowed funds at the rate RF. Therefore, the proportion to be invested in portfolio T is $[1 - (-1)] = 2$.

Overall, the combined weights are still equal to 1.0, since

$$w_{RF} + (1 - w_{RF}) = 1.0$$
$$-1 + [1 - (-1)] = 1.0$$

The expected return on the investor's portfolio P, consisting of investable wealth plus borrowed funds invested in portfolio T, is now

$$E(R_p) = w_{RF}\ RF + (1 - w_{RF})\ E(R_T) = -1(RF) + 2\ E(R_T)$$

The expected return increases linearly as the borrowing increases. The standard deviation of this portfolio is

$$\begin{aligned}\sigma_p &= (1 - w_{RF})\sigma_T \\ &= 2\sigma_T\end{aligned}$$

Risk will increase as the amount of borrowing increases.

Borrowing possibilities (i.e., leverage) are illustrated by the following example.

EXAMPLE: BORROWING AND RISK

Assume that the expected return on portfolio T is 20 per cent, with σ_T = 40 per cent. The expected risk-free rate, RF, is still 7 per cent, as earlier. However, it now represents the borrowing rate, or the rate at which the investor must pay interest on funds borrowed and invested in the risky asset T. The expected return on this portfolio would be

$$\begin{aligned}E(R_p) &= -1(7\%) + 2(20\%) \\ &= -7\% + 40\% \\ &= 33\%\end{aligned}$$

The standard deviation of this leveraged portfolio would be

$$\begin{aligned}\sigma_p &= (1 - w_{RF})\sigma_T \\ &= [1.0 - (-1.0)]\sigma_T \\ &= 2\ (40\%) \\ &= 80\%\end{aligned}$$

The New Efficient Set

The end result of introducing risk-free investing and borrowing into the analysis is to create lending and borrowing possibilities and a set of expected return–risk possibilities that did not exist previously. As shown in Figure 8-5, the new risk–return trade-off can be represented by a straight line that is tangent to the efficient frontier at point T and that has a vertical intercept RF.

The introduction of the risk-free asset significantly changes the Markowitz efficient set of portfolios. Specifically, the following points emerge:

1. The new efficient set is no longer a curve, or arc, as in the Markowitz analysis. It is now linear.
2. Borrowing and lending possibilities, combined with one portfolio of risky assets, T, offer an investor whatever risk-expected return combination he or she seeks; that is, investors can be anywhere they choose on this line, depending on their risk–return preferences.

The critical reader may point out that it is unlikely that the typical investor can borrow at the same rate as that offered by riskless securities because borrowing rates generally exceed lending rates. As a result, the borrowing rate that must be paid to construct the portfolios lying beyond point T in Figure 8-5 will be higher than RF. Obviously, this will make these portfolios less desirable than before. For example, if we recalculate the expected return and standard deviation for the portfolio described in the example "Borrowing and Risk" above, but increase the borrowing rate to 8 per cent instead of 7 per cent, we would find the expected return for the portfolio would fall to 32 per cent, while the standard deviation would remain at 80 per cent. Nonetheless it is obvious that these portfolios will still dominate those formed using risky portfolios only, but the line depicted in Figure 8-5 will be transformed into a line with a "kink" at point T since the borrowing rate exceeds RF. This new line is depicted in Figure 8-6 below.

Figure 8-6
When Borrowing Rate (R_B) Exceeds RF

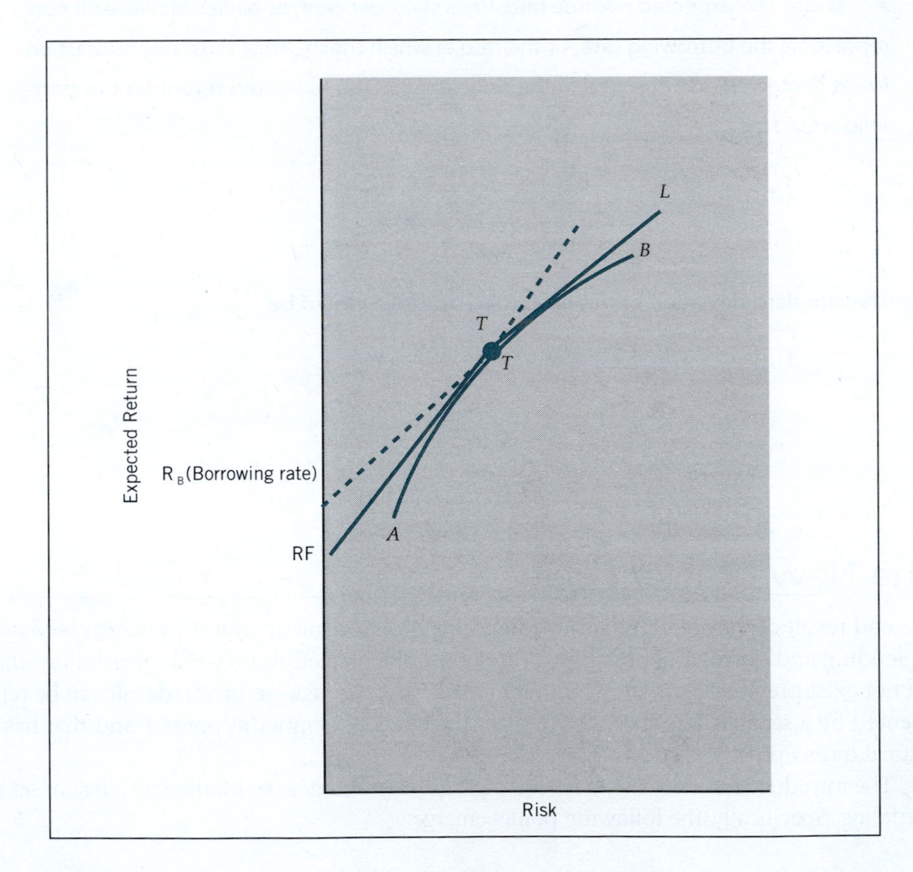

STEP 3: CHOOSE THE FINAL PORTFOLIO BASED ON PREFERENCES

Each investor can choose the point on the efficient-set line that corresponds to his or her risk preferences. Formally, this would be where the investor's highest indifference curve is tangent to the straight line RF-T-L in Figure 8-5 (or the kinked line in Figure 8-6). In practical terms, this means that more conservative investors would be closer to the risk-free asset designated by the vertical intercept RF. More aggressive investors would be closer to, or on, point T, representing full investment in a portfolio of risky assets. Even more aggressive investors could go beyond point T by using leverage to move up the line. In order to simplify the following discussion, we assume we can lend and borrow at RF, so Figure 8-5 provides the basis for our analysis. The general conclusions will not be affected materially by the existence of borrowing rates above RF.

THE SEPARATION THEOREM

We have established that each investor will benefit from holding combinations of the risk-free asset (either lending or borrowing) and the tangency portfolio from the efficient frontier. By combining these two assets into various portfolios, an investor can form efficient portfolios along the line RF-T-L in Figure 8-5. Given the assets under consideration, investors cannot reach a higher risk–return trade-off.

Consider now the case of an investment firm with multiple clients. (Alternatively, we could assume that all investors have identical forecasts of expected returns, standard deviations, and covariances and select the same optimal portfolio of risky assets.) The investment firm, having determined the Markowitz efficient frontier from the set of securities it analyzes for investment purposes, will offer the same portfolio of risky assets to each of its clients. This portfolio is determined as above, where the ray from RF is tangent to the efficient frontier as its highest point.

Unlike the case where we considered the availability of risky assets, it is not necessary to match each client's indifference curves with a particular efficient portfolio because only one efficient portfolio is held by all investors. Rather, each client will use his or her indifference curves to determine where along the new efficient frontier RF-T-L he or she should be. In effect, each client must determine how much of investable funds should be lent or borrowed at RF and how much should be invested in portfolio T. This result is referred to as a separation property.

Separation Theorem The idea that the decision of which portfolio of risky assets to hold is separate from the decision of how to allocate investable funds between the risk-free asset and the risky asset.

The **separation theorem** states that the investment decision (which portfolio of risky assets to hold) is separate from the financing decision (how to allocate investable funds between the risk-free asset and the risky asset). The risky portfolio T is optimal for every investor regardless of that investor's utility function; that is, T's optimality is determined separately from knowledge of any investor's risk–return preferences and is not affected by investor risk preferences. All investors, by investing in the same portfolio of risky assets (T) and either borrowing or lending at the rate RF, can achieve any point on the straight line RF-T-L in Figure 8-5. Each point on that line represents a different expected return–risk trade-off. A more conservative investor with utility curve U_1 will be at the lower end of the line, representing a combination of lending and investment in T. On the other hand, utility curve U_2 represents a more aggressive investor who borrows at the rate RF to invest in risky portfolio T.

The concept of the riskless asset–risky-asset (portfolio) dichotomy is an important one in investments, with several different applications. As we have seen, using the two in combination allows investors to achieve any point on the expected return-risk trade-off that all investors face. This is in sharp contrast to the traditional investing approach where investment firms and money managers tailored a portfolio of stocks to each individual client because of their unique preferences. For example, a retiree living off the income from a stock portfolio would be guided to a portfolio of relatively conservative stocks with an emphasis on their dividend yields. A 35-year-old investor doing well in his or her profession, on the other hand, might be guided to a portfolio with considerably more risk and expected return.

The separation theorem argues that this tailoring process is inappropriate. All investors should hold the same portfolio of risky assets and achieve their own position on the risk–return trade-off through borrowing and lending. The opportunity set is the same because it accommodates investors with different preferences.

Furthermore, some of the new techniques in investments utilize the same two assets. For example, portfolio insurance (see Chapter 19) can be regarded as an asset allocation strategy that seeks to rebalance a portfolio between a risky component and a riskless component in order to keep the portfolio return from declining below some specified minimum return.

CSC NOTES

Toronto 35 Index Participation Units (TIPs) and TSE 100 Index Participation Units (HIPs)

Chapters 7 and 8 spend a great deal of time talking about the investment benefits of holding a well-diversified portfolio. While it is relatively straightforward for professional money managers to construct such portfolios, diversification may pose a problem to the average individual investor. In particular, small investors may lack the financial resources and/or investment knowledge required to design so-called efficient portfolios.

One alternative for individual investors is to purchase shares of investment companies (as discussed in Chapter 3), thereby investing indirectly in a variety of well-diversified portfolios. Another option for Canadian investors is to purchase Toronto 35 Index Participation units (TIPs) or TSE 100 Index Participation units (HIPs).

In March 1990, the TSE introduced TIPs, which were units of a trust called the Toronto 35 Index Participation Fund. The trust holds a basket of stocks representing the TSE 35 Index, which consists of large Canadian corporations from the major sectors of the Canadian economy. The TSE 35 Index closely mirrors the TSE 300 — for example, the TSE 35 Index displayed a 99 per cent correlation with the TSE 300 over the 1982–89 period. HIPs are virtually identical to TIPs except that their trading prices are based upon the value of the TSE 100 Index (which was discussed in Chapter 4). The TSE 100 Index consists of the 100 largest stocks included in the TSE 300 Composite Index and is also highly correlated with the TSE 300.

The value of each TIPs (and HIPs) unit is one-tenth of the index value plus accrued dividends, and they trade in board lots of 100. For example, the closing value of the TSE 35 Index on June 1, 1998 was 410.39, while the closing price for TIPs was $41.25 per unit. TIPs and HIPs are both listed on the TSE and may be bought on margin or sold short. Prices are quoted daily as on other equities, and dividends are sent to holders of record four times a year.

Similar to mutual funds, TIPs and HIPs are eligible for RRSPs, DPSPs, and RRIFs. However, unlike mutual funds, there are no management fees, and the funds are financed through income earned on the investment of dividends before distribution as well as from securities lending activities. Since brokerage commissions are generally lower than management fees for mutual funds (especially for discount or Internet brokerage firms), these instruments offer individual investors a cost-effective method of holding a well-diversified portfolio of equities.

THE IMPLICATIONS OF PORTFOLIO SELECTION

The construction and selection of optimal portfolios for each investor has implications for the pricing of financial assets. Over one half of the riskiness of the average stock can be eliminated by holding a well-diversified portfolio. This means that part of the risk of the average stock can be eliminated, but part cannot. Investors need to focus on that part of the risk that cannot be eliminated by diversification because this is the risk that should be priced in the financial markets.

Systematic and Non-Systematic Risk

As Equations 7-17 and 7-18 showed, the single-index model allows us to divide the risk associated with common stocks into two types: (1) a general component, representing that portion in the variability of a stock's total returns that is directly associated with overall movements in general economic (or stock market) activity; and (2) a specific (issuer) component, representing that portion in the variability of a stock's total return that is not related to the variability in general economic (market) activity. These two components, referred to in investment analysis as systematic and non-systematic risk (or by the alternative names shown below), are additive:

$$\begin{aligned}\text{Total risk} &= \text{Systematic risk} + \text{Non-systematic risk}\\ &= \text{Market risk} + \text{Non-market risk}\\ &= \text{Non-diversifiable risk} + \text{Diversifiable risk}\end{aligned}$$

Variability in a security's total returns that is directly associated with overall movements in the general market or economy is called systematic (market) risk. Whether bonds or stocks, virtually all securities have some systematic risk because it directly encompasses interest rate risk, market risk, and inflation risk. We are concerned here with the systematic risk of common stocks.

The non-systematic risk is the part of the total risk that can be eliminated through diversification. After the non-systematic risk is eliminated, what is left is the non-diversifiable portion, or the market risk (systematic part). Market risk is unavoidable because no matter how well an investor diversifies, the risk of the overall market cannot be avoided. If the stock market declines sharply, most stocks will be adversely affected; if it rises strongly, most stocks will appreciate in value. These movements occur regardless of what any single investor does.

Figure 8-7 illustrates this concept of declining non-systematic risk in a portfolio of securities. As more securities are added, the non-systematic risk becomes smaller and smaller, and the total risk for the portfolio approaches its systematic risk. Since diversification cannot reduce systematic risk, total portfolio risk can be reduced no lower than the total market risk of the portfolio.[13]

How many securities does it take to eliminate most or all of the non-systematic risk? It has become commonplace to say that approximately 30 to 40 securities will provide a

[13] Notice the resemblance of Figure 8-7 to Figure 7-2 of Chapter 7, which was constructed using actual monthly data for Canadian common stocks over the 1993–97 period.

diversified portfolio; however this is largely based on US evidence.[14] Recent Canadian research suggests that 70 or more stocks are required to obtain a well-diversified portfolio.

Figure 8-7
Systematic and Non–Systematic Risk

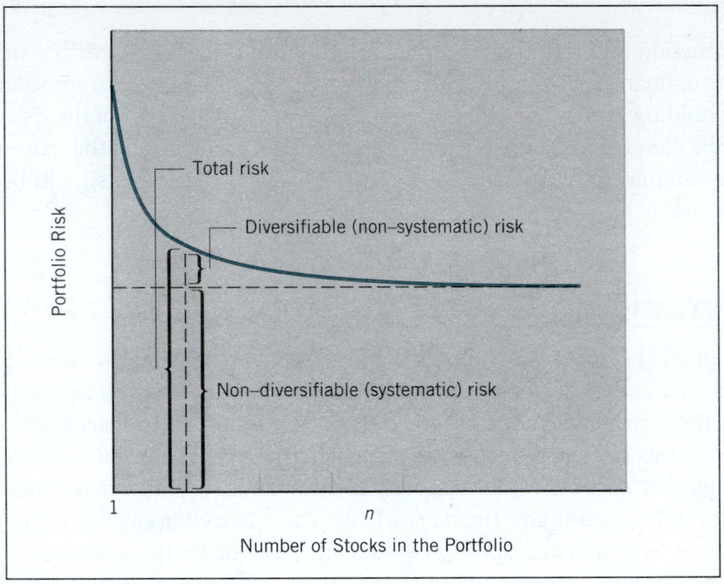

Diversification can substantially reduce the unique risk of a portfolio. However, Figure 8-7 indicates that no matter how much we diversify, we cannot eliminate systematic risk. The declining total risk curve in that figure levels off and becomes asymptotic to the systematic risk. Clearly, market risk is critical to all investors. It plays a central role in asset pricing because investors can expect a reward for taking that risk.

We know that the basic premise of investing is that investors demand a premium for bearing risk. However, we now know the importance of selecting portfolios of financial assets rather than holding individual securities. The relevant risk of an individual stock is its contribution to the riskiness of a well-diversified portfolio. The return that should be expected on the basis of this contribution can be estimated by the capital asset pricing model, which is discussed in the next chapter.

SUMMARY

This summary relates to the learning objectives provided on page 221.

1. **State three steps involved in building a portfolio.**
   To build a portfolio, we first use the Markowitz portfolio selection model to identify optimal risk-return combinations available from the set of risky assets being considered.

[14] Meir Statman, "How Many Stocks Make a Diversified Portfolio?" *Journal of Financial and Quantitative Analysis* 2 (September 1987), pp. 353–363.

Second, we consider the impact of borrowing and lending possibilities on the Markowitz efficient frontier. Third, we choose the final portfolio based on our risk preferences.

2. **Apply the Markowitz efficient portfolio selection model.**
Markowitz portfolio theory provides the way to select optimal portfolios based on using the full information set about securities. According to this theory, an efficient portfolio has the highest expected return for a given level of risk or the lowest level of risk for a given level of expected return. The Markowitz analysis determines the efficient set (frontier) of portfolios composed entirely of risky securities, all of which are equally desirable. The efficient set is an arc in expected return–standard deviation space. The efficient frontier captures the possibilities that exist from a given set of risky securities, while indifference curves can be used to express investor preferences. The optimal portfolio for a risk-averse investor occurs at the *point of tangency* between the investor's highest indifference curve and the efficient set of portfolios.

3. **Describe the effect of risk-free borrowing and lending on the efficient frontier.**
In addition to owning risky assets, investors can also buy risk-free assets, earning the riskless rate RF. We also assume that borrowing is permitted. Risk-free borrowing and lending changes the efficient set to a straight line that intersects the efficient frontier arc at one point (the tangency point).

4. **Discuss the separation theorem and its importance to modern investment theory.**
The separation theorem states that the investment decision (what portfolio of risky assets to buy) can be separated from the financing decision (how much of investable funds should be put in risky assets and how much in the risk-free asset). Under the separation theorem, all investors should hold the same portfolio of risky assets and achieve their own position on the return-risk trade-off through borrowing and lending.

5. **Separate total risk into systematic and non-systematic risk.**
Total risk can be divided into systematic and non-systematic risk. Non-systematic risk, also called diversifiable risk, can be eliminated by diversification. Market risk cannot be eliminated by diversification and is the relevant risk for the pricing of financial assets in the market.

KEY TERMS

Asset allocation decision
Efficient set (Frontier)
Efficient portfolio
Indifference curves
Separation theorem

ADDITIONAL RESOURCE

A good discussion of the intricacies of portfolio theory can be found in:

Elton, Edwin J., and Gruber, Martin J., *Modern Portfolio Theory and Investment Analysis*. Fifth Edition. New York: John Wiley & Sons, 1995.

REVIEW QUESTIONS

1. Using the Markowitz analysis, how does an investor select an optimal portfolio?
2. Why do rational, risk-averse investors seek efficient portfolios?
3. How is an investor's risk aversion indicated in an indifference curve? Are all indifference curves upward sloping?
4. What is meant by the term lending portfolios?
5. What is the difference between non-systematic and systematic risk? Explain why proper diversification of a stock portfolio effectively eliminates non-systematic risk but does not reduce systematic risk.
6. Given a set of inputs, explain conceptually how efficient portfolios are determined.
7. How does the introduction of a risk-free asset change the Markowitz efficient frontier?
8. What does the separation theorem imply about the tailored approach to portfolio selection?
9. Given the availability of risk-free borrowing and risk-free lending, how would your personal optimal portfolio change if you became very risk-tolerant? In contrast, what would be the composition of your optimal portfolio if you were a very conservative, risk-averse investor? Use a diagram(s) to help illustrate your answer.
10. Why would the covariance between a risk-free asset and any risky asset be zero?
11. With the Markowitz portfolio selection model, why is it impossible for the efficient frontier to have any "kinks" in it? Phrased another way, why must the efficient frontier be concave rather than convex?
12. Most stock returns have positive correlations. Give examples of stocks that you think might have high positive correlations, low positive correlations, or negative ones.
13. As an investor's personal level of risk tolerance changes, how (if at all) does the efficient set change? How (if at all) does the investor's indifference curve change? Use diagrams to help illustrate your answer.
14. Explain the separation theorem. What are its implications for portfolio managers? For investors?
15. In a real-world setting, your cost of borrowing is higher than the interest rate that you can earn on government securities ("risk-free lending"). What effect would this real-world condition have on the efficient set.
16. Given your new-found knowledge of stock portfolios and the efficient frontier, it appears that computers could select the most efficient portfolio(s) for investors to invest in. If this is the case, why do investors pay professional money managers to manage their money? Discuss.
17. Select the correct statement concerning the Markowitz model:
    a. The Markowitz model determines the optimal portfolio for each investor.
    b. The efficient frontier expresses preferences while indifference curves express possibilities.
    c. All conservative investors would have the same optimal portfolio.
    d. An investor's optimal portfolio can be found where his or her highest indifference curve is tangent to the efficient frontier.

18. Choose the portfolio from the following set that is not on the efficient frontier.
    a. Portfolio A: expected return of 10 per cent and standard deviation of 8 per cent.
    b. Portfolio B: expected return of 18 per cent and standard deviation of 13 per cent.
    c. Portfolio C: expected return of 38 per cent and standard deviation of 32 per cent.
    d. Portfolio D: expected return of 15 per cent and standard deviation of 14 per cent.
    e. Portfolio E: expected return of 26 per cent and standard deviation of 20 per cent.
19. Select the correct statement from among the following:
    a. Knowing the covariance between two securities and the standard deviation of each, the correlation coefficient can be calculated.
    b. When the total returns for a security are plotted against the total returns for a market index and a regression line is fitted, this line is referred to as the capital market line.
    c. With perfect negative correlation, two securities' returns have a perfect direct linear relationship to each other.
    d. The optimal portfolio for any investor occurs at the point of tangency between the investor's lowest indifference curve and the efficient frontier.
20. Choose the statement below that is most closely associated with the work of Markowitz:
    a. Risk-free borrowing and lending can change the efficient frontier.
    b. Non-systematic risk can be identified and assessed.
    c. The efficient frontier can be changed from an arc to a straight line.
    d. Efficient portfolios can be calculated and chosen.
21. Select the correct statement concerning the Markowitz model:
    a. The Markowitz model determines the optimal portfolio for each investor.
    b. The efficient frontier expresses possibilities while indifference curves express preferences.
    c. All conservative investors would have the same optimal portfolio.
    d. An investor's optimal portfolio can be found where his or her lowest indifference curve is tangent to the efficient frontier.

PREPARING FOR YOUR PROFESSIONAL EXAMS

Special Note to Canadian Securities Course Students

Ensure that you have read and understood the following topics:*

The asset allocation decision, pp. 227–229

CSC Notes: Toronto 35 Index Participation Units (TIPs) and TSE 100 Index Participation Units (HIPs), p. 238

The Implications of Portfolio Selection, pp. 239–240

* *Reading these CCS related topics should provide you with additional understanding of CSC material. However, it should not be seen as a substitute for reading the CSC textbook itself, which is the basis for the CSC exam.*

PAST CFA EXAM QUESTION

AIMR[SM]

The following question was asked on the 1992 CFA Level I examination:

1. Which one of the following portfolios cannot lie on the efficient frontier as described by Markowitz?

Portfolio	Expected Return	Standard Deviation
a. W	9%	21%
b. X	5%	7%
c. Y	15%	36%
d. Z	12%	15%

PROBLEMS

1. Based on the information in the table below, determine which of these portfolio(s) would constitute the efficient set.

Portfolio	Expected Return (%)	Standard Deviation (%)
1	10	20
2	12	24
3	8	16
4	6	12
5	9	21
6	20	40
7	18	36
8	8	15
9	11	19
10	12	22
11	14	26

2. Given the following information:

   Standard deviation for stock X = 12%
   Standard deviation for stock Y = 20%
   Expected return for stock X = 16%
   Expected return for stock Y = 22%
   Correlation coefficient between X and Y = 0.30
   The covariance between stock X and Y is

   a. 0.048
   b. 72.00
   c. 3.60
   d. 105.6

3. Given the information in Problem 2 regarding risk, the expected return for a portfolio consisting of 50 per cent invested in X and 50 per cent invested in Y can be seen to be
   a. 19%
   b. 16%
   c. less than 16%
   d. more than 22%
4. Given the information in Problem 2, assume now that the correlation coefficient between stocks X and Y is +1.0. Choose the investment below that represents the minimum risk portfolio.
   a. 100% investment in stock Y
   b. 100% investment in stock X
   c. 50% investment in stock X and 50% investment in stock Y
   d. 80% investment in stock Y and 20% investment in stock X
5. Given the following information for four securities:

Security	1	2	3	4
E(R) %	10	12	14	18
σ^2	300	350	400	450

$\rho(1,2) = 0.2$; $\rho(1,3) = 0.4$; $\rho(1,4) = 0.6$; $\rho(2,3) = 0.1$; $\rho(3,4) = 0.9$; $\rho(2,4) = 0.5$.

Calculate five efficient portfolios using the Markowitz analysis, an upper boundary of 50 per cent, and a lower boundary of 10 per cent for the weights invested in each portfolio.
   a. What is the highest expected return from these four portfolios?
   b. What is the lowest standard deviation from these four portfolios?
   c. Which portfolios involve short sales?
   d. Which portfolio should be preferred by an investor?
6. Using the information in Problem 5, determine the effects of changing the correlation coefficient between securities 1 and 2 from 0.20 to −0.20.
   a. What is the effect on the expected return of the portfolios?
   b. What is the effect on the variance of the portfolios?

APPENDIX 8-A

MODERN PORTFOLIO THEORY AND THE PORTFOLIO MANAGEMENT PROCESS

The practical relevance of portfolio theory and diversification is demonstrated by its impact on regulations governing the investment behaviour of professional money managers. Guidelines for North American professional money managers require them to adhere to "prudence, loyalty, reasonable administrative cost, and diversification," which alludes to the importance of diversification.

The duty of prudence referred to in the passage above requires fiduciaries to perform their duties "with the care, skill, prudence, and diligence under the circumstances then prevailing that a prudent man acting in a like capacity and familiar with such matters would use in the conduct of an enterprise of a like character and with like aims." The term "familiar with such matters" refers to "the prudent expert rule." This implies the manager's behaviour must meet the standard for trained and experienced investment professionals rather than just that of a "prudent man." This definition of prudence suggests that managers should be responsible for managing the risk of the portfolio as a whole, as opposed to managing the risks associated with each individual investment within the portfolio (which is implied by "the prudent man rule"). This represents an important innovation that can be directly attributable to the concepts underlying modern portfolio theory.

Not surprisingly, the importance attached to taking a portfolio approach to investing is incorporated in educational courses provided for investment professionals. For example, both the CSC and the CFA courses discuss the importance of the portfolio management process. This process stresses the selection of securities based on that security's contribution to the portfolio as a whole, in addition to its individual merit. Security selection and market timing decisions are made within the context of the effect on the whole portfolio. An important feature of portfolio formation (discussed in Chapters 7 and 8) is that portfolio returns will be an average of the returns on all securities within the portfolio, but the risk will be lower than the weighted average of risks as long as the securities are not perfectly correlated. This implies that risk can be eliminated by forming portfolios of securities.

Portfolio management is a continuous process consisting of four parts:

1. Designing an investment policy
2. Developing and implementing an asset mix
3. Monitoring the economy, the markets, and the client
4. Adjusting the portfolio and measuring performance.

We defer an in-depth discussion of the portfolio management process until Chapter 21.

CHAPTER 9

CAPITAL MARKET THEORY

LEARNING OBJECTIVES

After reading this chapter, you will be able to

1. Explain capital market theory and the Capital Asset Pricing Model.
2. Discuss the importance and composition of the market portfolio.
3. Describe two important relationships in CAPM as represented by the capital market line and the security market line.
4. Describe how betas are estimated and how beta is used.
5. Discuss the Arbitrage Pricing Theory as an alternative to the Capital Asset Pricing Model.

CHAPTER PREVIEW

Our discussion of portfolio theory in the last chapter described how to select an optimal portfolio of securities under normal market conditions. In this chapter, we consider capital market theory, which seeks to explain security pricing under conditions of market equilibrium. We focus on the well-known Capital Asset Pricing Model (CAPM) and its application. We conclude the chapter by discussing some of the shortcomings of this model and an alternative model known as the Arbitrage Pricing Theory.

INTRODUCTION TO CAPITAL MARKET THEORY

Capital Market Theory Describes the pricing of capital assets in financial markets.

In this chapter we consider **capital market theory**. What happens if all investors seek portfolios of risky securities using the Markowitz framework under idealized conditions? How will this affect equilibrium security prices and returns? In other words, how does optimal diversification affect the market prices of securities? Under these idealized conditions, what is the risk–return trade-off that investors face? In effect, we wish to examine models that explain security prices under conditions of market equilibrium.

One equilibrium model discussed in this chapter is known as the Capital Asset Pricing Model (CAPM). It allows us to measure the relevant risk of an individual security as well as to assess the relationship between risk and the returns expected from investing.

The CAPM is attractive as an equilibrium model because of its simplicity and its implications, but because of serious challenges to the model, alternatives have been developed. An important alternative to the CAPM is Arbitrage Pricing Theory (APT), which allows for multiple sources of risk. Therefore, we conclude the chapter with a discussion of the APT.

The Assumptions of the CAPM

Capital Asset Pricing Model (CAPM) Relates the required rate of return for any security with the market risk for that security as measured by beta.

The **Capital Asset Pricing Model (CAPM)** is concerned with the equilibrium relationship between the risk and the expected return on risky assets. The traditional CAPM was derived independently by Sharpe and by Lintner and Mossin in the mid-1960s.[1] Although several extensions of this model have been proposed, the original CAPM remains a central tenet of modern financial economics.

The CAPM involves a set of predictions concerning equilibrium expected returns on risky assets. It is derived by making some simplifying assumptions in order to facilitate the analysis and help us to understand the arguments without fundamentally changing the predictions of asset pricing theory.

Capital market theory builds on Markowitz portfolio theory. Each investor is assumed to diversify his or her portfolio according to the Markowitz model, choosing a location on the efficient frontier that matches his or her return-risk preferences. Because of the complexity of the real world, additional assumptions are made to make individuals more alike:

[1] Much of this analysis is attributable to the work of Sharpe. See W. Sharpe, "Capital Asset Prices: A Theory of Market Equilibrium under Conditions of Risk," *The Journal of Finance* 19 (September 1964), pp. 425–442. Lintner and Mossin developed a similar analysis.

1. All investors have identical probability distributions for future rates of return; they have identical (or homogeneous) expectations with respect to the three inputs of the portfolio model explained in Chapter 7: expected returns, the variance of returns, and the correlation matrix. Therefore, given a set of security prices and a risk-free rate, all investors use the same information to generate an efficient frontier.
2. All investors have the same one-period time horizon.
3. All investors can borrow or lend money at the risk-free rate of return (designated RF in this text).
4. There are no transaction costs.
5. There are no personal income taxes — investors are indifferent between capital gains and dividends.
6. There is no inflation.
7. There are many investors, and no single investor can affect the price of a stock through his or her buying and selling decisions. Investors are price-takers and act as if prices are unaffected by their own trades.
8. Capital markets are in equilibrium.

These assumptions appear unrealistic and often disturb individuals encountering capital market theory for the first time. However, the important issue is how well the theory predicts or describes reality. If capital market theory does a good job of explaining the returns on risky assets, it is very useful and the assumptions made in deriving the theory are of less importance. In addition, most of these assumptions can be relaxed without significant effects on the capital asset pricing model or its implications; in other words, the CAPM is robust.[2] Although the results from such a relaxation of the assumptions may be less clear-cut and precise, no significant damage is done. Many conclusions of the basic model still hold.

Most investors recognize that all of the assumptions of the CAPM are not unrealistic. For example, some institutional investors are tax-exempt, and their brokerage costs, as a percentage of the transaction, are quite small. The ability for individual investors to trade through discount brokers and/or the Internet has also reduced their trading costs to extremely low levels. Nor is it too unreasonable to assume that for the one-period horizon of the model, inflation may be fully (or mostly) anticipated and, therefore, not a major factor.

Equilibrium in the Capital Markets

If the assumptions listed above hold, what is the equilibrium situation that will prevail in the capital markets? In Chapter 8, we demonstrated that rational, risk-averse investors will strive to obtain the highest possible expected return for a given level of risk, or the lowest risk for a given level of expected return. When we introduced the assumption that they could borrow and lend at the risk-free rate, we concluded that investors would all desire to hold some portion of their wealth in one optimal portfolio of risky assets. This optimal portfolio was

[2] For a discussion of changing these assumptions, see E. Elton and M. Gruber, *Modern Portfolio Theory and Investment Analysis*, Fifth Edition (New York: John Wiley & Sons, 1995), Chapter 11.

shown to be the one that is tangent to a line drawn from the risk-free asset to the efficient frontier of risky securities, as depicted in Figure 8-5. By assuming that all investors have the same time horizon and have homogeneous expectations regarding the expected returns and risks for any given risky asset, we imply they all use identical information for the same time period to determine the composition of the optimal portfolio. As a result, the optimal risky portfolio will be identical for all investors.

Having established that the optimal portfolio will be identical for all investors, we now demonstrate that it will be the aggregate market portfolio, which contains all assets in existence. The value of this portfolio will equal the aggregate of the market values of all the individual assets comprising it. Therefore, the weights of these assets in the market portfolio will be represented by their proportionate weight in the total value of it. We have assumed the existence of market equilibrium, which occurs when prices are at levels that provide no incentive for speculative trading. This implies that markets clear — in other words all assets are assumed to be bought and sold at an equilibrium price that is established by the forces of supply and demand.[3] Since all assets trade, it must mean that they are correctly priced to adequately compensate investors for the associated risks. For example, if an asset was priced too high, then demand would fall, and the price would decline as a result. Market clearing implies that the price would eventually fall to an equilibrium level that would result in the asset being traded.

Since the market consists of all available assets, which are assumed to be priced correctly to reflect adequate compensation for the associated risk, the market portfolio will be the most efficient (or optimal) portfolio with respect to the weights attached to the individual securities comprising it. For example, consider a market that consists of only two risky assets (A and B) and two investors, each with $1,000 invested in risky assets. This implies the total value of the market would be $2,000. Since each investor will hold the same (optimal) proportions in each of the two assets (say $w_A = 0.80$, and $w_B = 0.20$), these must be the weights for these assets in the market portfolio. In other words, investors A and B, will both have $0.80 \times \$1,000 = \$800$ invested in asset A, representing a total of $1,600. This will be the market value of asset A. Each investor will also hold $200 worth of asset B, for a total of $400, which will be its market value. Thus, the market portfolio weights for assets A and B will be 0.80 ($1,600/$2,000) and 0.20 ($400/$2,000). This example produces the same basic result when extended to many investors and many assets.

The implications of this discussion are:

1. All investors will choose to hold the risky portion of their portfolio in the aggregate market portfolio, which includes all assets in existence.
2. This market portfolio will be on the Markowitz efficient frontier and will be the optimal risky portfolio to hold.
3. All efficient portfolios will lie along the straight line drawn from the risk-free asset that passes through the point represented by the market portfolio, since this line will represent the optimal trade-off between standard deviation and expected return available from the set of available assets.

We will consider these implications below.

---

[3] Markets could not be in equilibrium if markets did not clear since this would imply some assets did not trade because buyers and sellers could not agree upon a trading price.

THE MARKET PORTFOLIO

In the preceding section, we demonstrated that the market portfolio will be the optimal combination of risky assets available to investors and that all efficient portfolios will lie along the straight line drawn from the risk-free asset that passes through the point represented by the market portfolio. This relationship is depicted graphically in Figure 9-1, which is the same as Figure 8-5 except the point of tangency has been changed from T to M. Portfolio M in Figure 9-1 is called the **market portfolio** of risky securities. It is the highest point of tangency between RF and the efficient frontier and is the optimal risky portfolio. This optimal risky portfolio from the Markowitz efficient set is found by determining which efficient portfolio offers the highest risk premium, given the existence of a risk-free asset. Because this line produces the highest attainable return for any given risk level, all rational investors will seek to be on this line.

Market Portfolio
The portfolio of all risky assets, with each asset weighted by the ratio of its market value to the market value of all risky assets.

The Importance of the Market Portfolio

All investors would want to be on the optimal line RF-M-L, and, unless they invested 100 per cent of their wealth in the risk-free asset, they would own portfolio M with some portion of their investable wealth or they would invest their own wealth plus borrowed funds in portfolio M.[4] This portfolio is the optimal portfolio of risky assets.

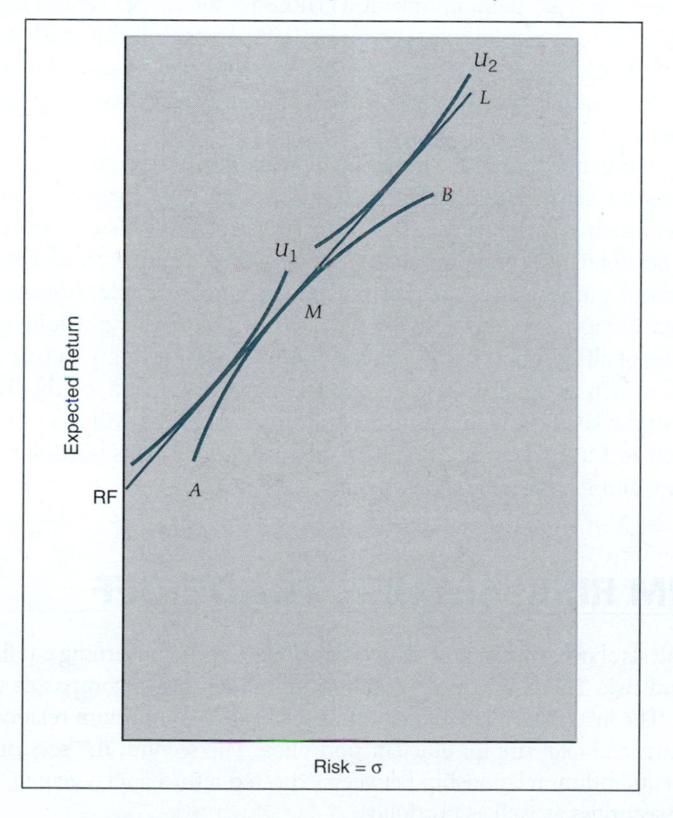

Figure 9-1
The Efficient Frontier with Borrowing and Lending

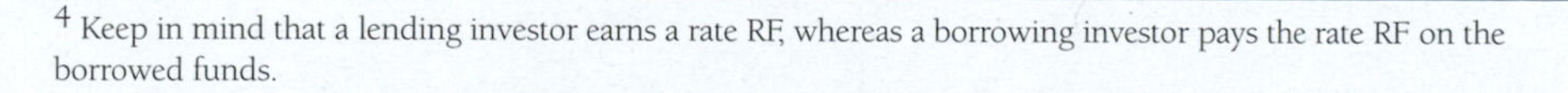

[4] Keep in mind that a lending investor earns a rate RF, whereas a borrowing investor pays the rate RF on the borrowed funds.

All investors hold identical risky portfolios, use the same Markowitz analysis on the same set of securities, have the same expected returns and covariances, and have an identical time horizon. Therefore, they will arrive at the same optimal risky portfolio, and it will be the market portfolio, designated M.

It is critical to note that although investors take different positions on the straight-line efficient set in Figure 9-1, all investors are investing in portfolio M, the same portfolio of risky assets. This portfolio will always consist of all risky assets in existence. The emergence of the market portfolio as the optimal efficient portfolio is the most important implication of the CAPM. In essence, the CAPM states that portfolio M is the optimal risky portfolio.

Composition of the Market Portfolio

In equilibrium, all risky assets must be included in portfolio M because all investors are assumed to arrive at, and hold, the same risky portfolio. Because the market portfolio includes all risky assets, *portfolio M is completely diversified*. Portfolio M contains only systematic risk that cannot be eliminated, even with perfect diversification, because it is the result of macroeconomic factors that affect the value of all securities.

All assets are included in portfolio M in proportion to their market value. For example, if the market value of **Bombardier** common stock constitutes 1.8 per cent of the market value of all risky assets at a given point in time, it will account for 1.8 per cent of the market value of portfolio M. Therefore, it will also comprise 1.8 per cent of the market value of each investor's portfolio of risky assets. As a result, we can state that security i's percentage in the risky portfolio M is equal to the total market value of security i relative to the total market value of all securities.

In theory, the market portfolio should include all risky assets worldwide, both financial (bonds, options, futures, etc.) and real (gold, real estate, etc.), in their proper proportions. The global aspects of such a portfolio imply that international diversification is very important, and a worldwide portfolio, if it could be constructed, would be completely diversified.

For practical purposes, the market portfolio is unobservable, however, we can use proxies to measure its behaviour. Usually, we measure the market portfolio using the portfolio consisting of all common stocks. This common stock portfolio, in turn, is proxied by a market index such as the TSE 300 Composite Index in Canada, or the S&P 500 Composite Index in the US. For the remainder of our discussion, we will refer to portfolio M as a broad market index such as the TSE 300 Composite Index. This portfolio is, of course, a risky portfolio, and its risk will be designated σ_M.

THE EQUILIBRIUM RISK–RETURN TRADE-OFF

Given the analysis above, we can now derive some predictions concerning equilibrium expected returns and risk. The CAPM is an equilibrium model that encompasses two important relationships. The first, the capital market line, specifies the equilibrium relationship between expected return and *total risk* for efficient portfolios. The second, the security market line, specifies the equilibrium relationship between expected return and *systematic risk*. It applies to individual securities as well as portfolios.

The Capital Market Line

The straight line shown in Figure 9-1 traces out the risk–return trade-off for efficient portfolios, is tangent to the Markowitz efficient frontier at point M, and has a vertical intercept RF. We now know that portfolio M is the tangency point to a straight line drawn from RF to the efficient frontier, and that this straight line is the best obtainable efficient-set line. All investors will hold portfolio M as their optimal risky portfolio, and will be somewhere on this steepest trade-off line between expected return and risk because it represents those combinations of risk-free investing/borrowing and portfolio M that yield the highest return obtainable for a given pool of risk. Investors will differ only in the amount of their funds invested in RF versus portfolio M.

This straight line is usually referred to as the **capital market line (CML)**. It depicts the equilibrium conditions that prevail in the market for efficient portfolios consisting of the optimal portfolio of risky assets and the risk-free asset. All combinations of risky and risk-free portfolios are bounded by the CML, and, in equilibrium, all investors will end up with efficient portfolios, which must lie somewhere on the CML.

Capital Market Line (CML) The trade-off between expected return and total risk for efficient portfolios.

The CML is shown as a straight line in Figure 9-2 without the now-dominated Markowitz frontier. We know that this line has an intercept of RF. If investors are to invest in risky assets, they must be compensated for this additional risk with a risk premium. The vertical distance between the risk-free rate and the CML at point M in Figure 9-2 is the amount of return expected for bearing the risk of the market portfolio, that is, the excess return above the risk-free rate. At that point, the amount of risk for the market portfolio is given by the horizontal dotted line between RF and σ_M. Therefore,

$$\frac{E(R_M) - RF}{\sigma_M} = \text{Slope of the CML}$$

$$= \text{Expected return–risk trade-off for efficient portfolios}$$

The slope of the CML is the *market price of risk* for efficient portfolios or the equilibrium price of risk in the market.[5] It indicates the additional expected return that the market demands for each percentage increase in a portfolio's risk, as measured by its standard deviation of return.

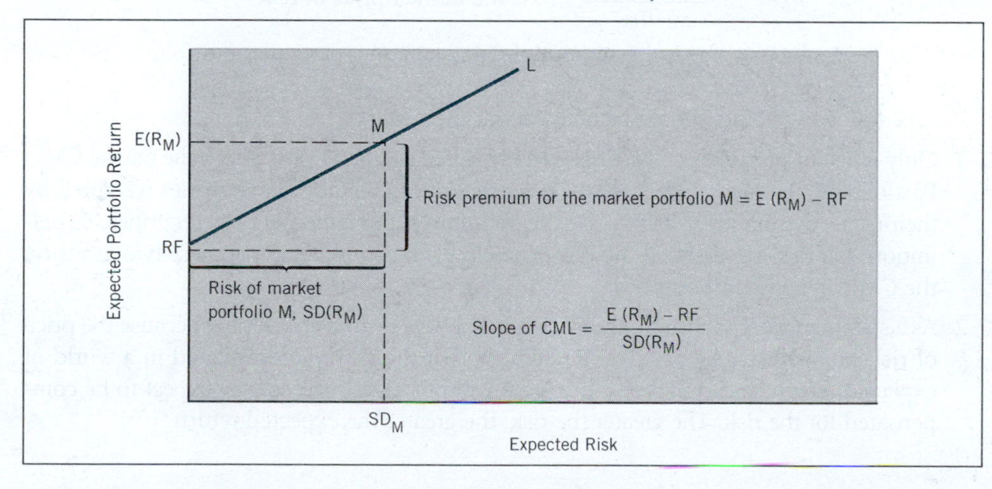

Figure 9-2
The Capital Market Line and the Components of Its Slope

[5] The assumption throughout this discussion is that $E(R_M)$ is greater than RF. This is the only reasonable assumption to make, because the CAPM is concerned with expected returns (i.e., *ex ante* returns). After the fact, this assumption may not hold for particular periods, that is, over historical periods such as a year RF has exceeded R_M, which is sometimes negative.

EXAMPLE: ESTIMATING THE SLOPE OF THE CML

Assume that the expected return on portfolio M is 13 per cent, with a standard deviation of 25 per cent, and that RF is 7 per cent. The slope of the CML would be

$$(0.13 - 0.07)/0.25 = 0.24$$

In our example a risk premium of 0.24 indicates that the market demands 0.24 per cent of return for each one percentage increase in a portfolio's risk.

We now know the intercept and slope of the CML. Since the CML is the trade-off between expected return and risk for efficient portfolios, and risk is being measured by the standard deviation, the equation for the CML is

$$E(R_p) = RF + \frac{E(R_M) - RF}{\sigma_M}\sigma_p \tag{9-1}$$

where

$E(R_p)$ = the expected return on any efficient portfolio on the CML
RF = the rate of return on the risk-free asset
$E(R_M)$ = the expected return on the market portfolio M
σ_M = the standard deviation of returns on the market portfolio
σ_p = the standard deviation of returns on the efficient portfolio being considered

In other words, the expected return for any portfolio on the CML is equal to the price necessary to induce investors to forego consumption plus the product of the market price of risk and the amount of risk on the portfolio being considered. Note that:

RF is the price of foregone consumption

$\frac{E(R_M) - RF}{\sigma_M}$ is the market price of risk

σ_p is the amount of risk taken on a particular portfolio

The following points should be noted about the CML:

1. Only efficient portfolios consisting of the risk-free asset and portfolio M lie on the CML. Portfolio M, the market portfolio of risky securities, contains all securities weighted by their respective market values — it is the optimum combination of risky securities. By definition, the risk-free asset has no risk. Therefore, all combinations of these two assets on the CML are efficient portfolios.
2. As a statement of equilibrium, the CML must always be upward sloping because the price of risk must always be positive. Remember that the CML is formulated in a world of expected return, and risk-averse investors will not invest unless they expect to be compensated for the risk. The greater the risk, the greater the expected return.

3. On a historical basis, for some particular period of time such as four consecutive quarters, or a year or two, the CML can be downward sloping; that is, the return on RF exceeds the return on the market portfolio. This does not negate the validity of the CML; it merely indicates that returns actually realized differed from those that were expected. Obviously, investor expectations are not always realized. (If they were, there would be no risk.) Thus, although the CML must be upward sloping *ex ante* (before the fact), it can be, and sometimes is, downward sloping *ex post* (after the fact).
4. The CML can be used to determine the optimal expected returns associated with different portfolio risk levels. Therefore, the CML indicates the required return for each portfolio risk level.[6]

The Security Market Line

The capital market line depicts the risk–return trade-off in financial markets in equilibrium. However, it applies only to efficient portfolios and cannot be used to assess the equilibrium expected return on individual securities or inefficient portfolios. Since all investors will hold the risky portion of their portfolio in the market portfolio, the important issue with regards to individual securities is how they contribute to the risk of the market portfolio.

We know from Chapter 7 that the equation for portfolio standard deviation consists of many variance and covariance terms. With respect to the market portfolio, each security in the market portfolio (consisting of n securities) will have a variance term and $n - 1$ covariance terms multiplied by two (since we know that Cov (1, 2) = Cov (2, 1) for securities 1 and 2). Chapter 7 also shows that for a well-diversified portfolio consisting of a large number of securities, the covariance terms will be the relevant risk factors, with the individual variance terms having little impact on the overall portfolio risk. Based on this observation, the complex variance and covariance terms associated with estimating the risk of the market portfolio can be simplified to the following equation for the standard deviation of the market portfolio:

$$\begin{aligned}\sigma_M &= [w_1 \text{ Cov }(R_1, R_M) + w_2 \text{ Cov }(R_2, R_M) + \ldots +]^{1/2} \\ &= [\text{security 1's contribution to portfolio variance + security 2's} \\ &\quad \text{contribution to portfolio variance + } \ldots.]^{1/2}\end{aligned} \tag{9-2}$$

Equation 9-2 shows that the contribution of each security to the standard deviation of the market portfolio depends on the size of its covariance with the market portfolio. Therefore, investors should consider the relevant measure of risk for any security to be its covariance with the market portfolio. As a result, we can say that in order for market equilibrium to exist, investors will require that the excess reward per unit of covariance risk be equal for all securities. Thus for any two assets i and j, we can say

$$\frac{E(R_i) - RF}{\sigma_{i,M}} = \frac{E(R_j) - RF}{\sigma_{j,M}} \tag{9-3}$$

[6] This assumes that we can readily compute a portfolio's standard deviation, which is difficult to do in practice.

Since the covariance of the market portfolio with itself is its variance (i.e., $\sigma_{M,M} = \sigma_M^2$), we can express the market price of covariance risk as

$$\frac{E(R_M) - RF}{\sigma_{M,M}} \text{ or } \frac{E(R_M) - RF}{\sigma_M^2}$$

Recognizing that the market portfolio is efficient and is held by all investors, this market price of covariance risk must offer adequate compensation for risk and is the excess reward per unit risk required by investors for any asset. Formally, for any asset *i*, we can say

$$\frac{E(R_i) - RF}{\sigma_{i,M}} = \frac{E(R_M) - RF}{\sigma_M^2} \tag{9-4}$$

Equation 9-4 can easily be rearranged to solve for $E(R_i)$, which produces the following equation that shows the expected return on any risky asset is directly proportional to its covariance with the market portfolio

$$E(R_i) = RF + [E(R_M) - RF]\frac{\sigma_{i,M}}{\sigma_M^2} \tag{9-5}$$

From Equation 7-9 of Chapter 7, we know that $\sigma_{i,M} = \rho_{i,M}\sigma_i\sigma_M$, which implies we could alternatively express Equation 9-5 as

$$E(R_i) = RF + [E(R_M) - RF]\frac{\rho_{i,M}\sigma_i}{\sigma_M} \tag{9-6}$$

We now define a new term, the beta coefficient (β_i) or beta, as

$$\beta_i = \frac{\sigma_{i,M}}{\sigma_M^2} = \frac{\rho_{i,M}\sigma_i}{\sigma_M} \tag{9-7}$$

Substituting beta into the last term of Equation 9-5 or Equation 9-6, we obtain the following expression for determining the expected return of a risky asset

$$E(R_i) = RF + [E(R_M) - RF]\beta_i \tag{9-8}$$

Security Market Line (SML)
The graphical depiction of the CAPM, which relates the expected return on an individual security or portfolio to its market risk as measured by beta.

This equation is referred to as the **security market line (SML)**, which is the key contribution of the CAPM to asset pricing theory.[7] It is depicted as the line RF-Z in Figure 9-3. In this diagram, beta is plotted on the horizontal axis and expected return on the vertical axis, with the intercept on the vertical axis occurring at the risk-free rate of return, RF. The SML

7 Several alternative derivations of the SML are possible. The one presented in this text would be considered non-technical in nature. For a more rigorous derivation refer to: Edwin Elton and Martin Gruber, *Modern Portfolio Theory and Portfolio Analysis*, Fifth Edition (New York: John Wiley & Sons, 1995).

represents the trade-off between systematic risk (as measured by beta) and expected return for all assets, whether individual securities, inefficient portfolios, or efficient portfolios.

The SML implies we measure systematic or market risk by a security's beta, which is simply a standardized measure of the security's covariance with the market portfolio. The reason that it is standardized in this manner reflects the fact that beta measures the sensitivity or responsiveness of the stock's returns compared to the returns on the chosen market portfolio. The reasons for measuring the relationship in this manner will be discussed later.

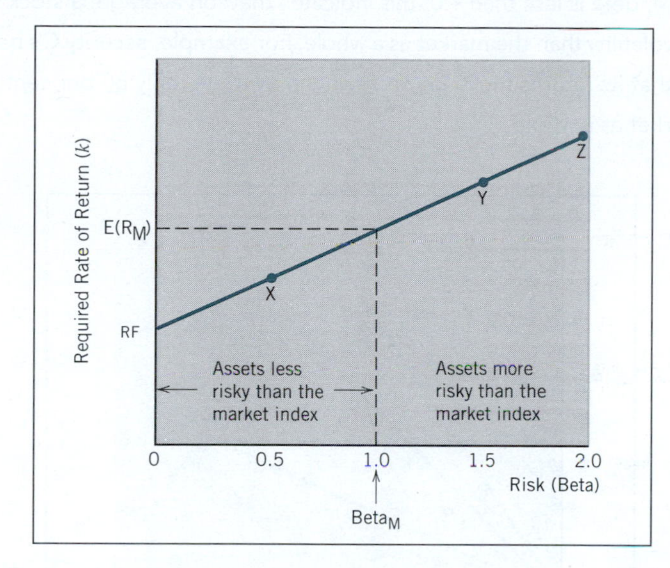

Figure 9-3
The Security Market Line (SML)

Beta
A measure of volatility for stock or portfolio returns. It is the relative market or systematic risk, measured as the sensitivity of returns to that on a chosen market proxy.

Beta

Beta is a measure of the systematic risk of a security that cannot be avoided through diversification. Beta is a *relative measure* of risk — the risk of an individual stock relative to the market portfolio of all stocks. If the security's returns move more (less) than the market's returns as the latter changes, the security's returns have more (less) *volatility* (fluctuations in price) than those of the market. It is important to note that beta measures a security's volatility, or fluctuations in price, relative to a benchmark, the chosen market portfolio of all stocks.

Securities with different slopes have different sensitivities to the returns of the market index. If the slope of this relationship for a particular security is a 45-degree angle, as shown for security B in Figure 9-4, the beta is 1.0. This means that for every 1 per cent change in the market's return, on average this security's returns change 1 per cent.

The riskless asset has a beta of 0, since its return is assumed to be known with certainty. The market portfolio has a beta of 1.0, which is intuitive since it moves exactly with itself. It is also obvious computationally, since if we let $i = M$ in Equation 9-7, we obtain

$$\beta_M = \frac{\sigma_{M,M}}{\sigma^2_M} = \frac{\sigma^2_M}{\sigma^2_M} = 1.0$$

INVESTING tip

As we would expect, Figure 9-3 again demonstrates that if investors are to seek higher expected returns, they must assume a larger risk as measured by beta, the relative measure of systematic risk. The trade-off between expected return and risk must always be positive. In Figure 9-3 the vertical axis can be thought of as the expected return for an asset. In equilibrium, investors require a minimum expected return before they will invest in a particular security. That is, given its risk, a security must offer some minimum expected return before an investor can be persuaded to purchase it. Thus, in discussing the SML concept, we are simultaneously talking about the required and expected rate of return.

EXAMPLE: BETAS OF SECURITIES

In Figure 9-4 security A's beta of 1.5 indicates that, on average, its returns are 1.5 times as volatile as market returns, both up and down. A security whose returns rise or fall on average 15 per cent when the market return rises or falls 10 per cent is said to be an aggressive, or volatile, security. If the line is less steep than the 45-degree line, beta is less than 1.0; this indicates that, on average, a stock's returns have less volatility than the market as a whole. For example, security C's beta of 0.6 indicates that its returns move up or down, on average, only 60 per cent as much as the market as a whole.

Figure 9-4
Illustrative Betas of 1.5 (A), 1.0 (B), and 0.6 (C)

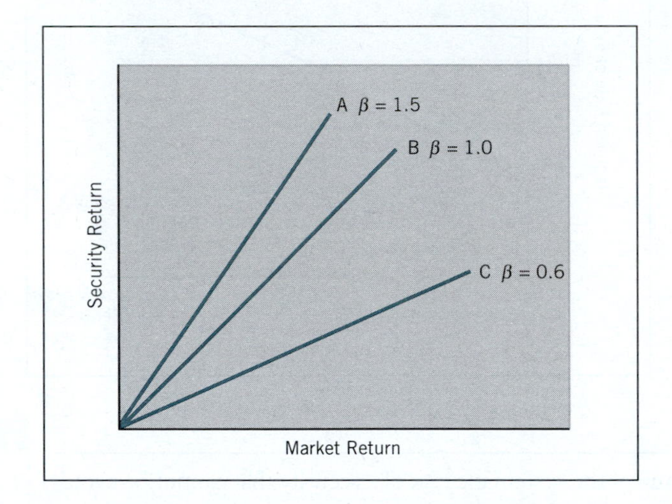

In summary, the aggregate market has a beta of 1.0. More volatile (risky) stocks have betas larger than 1.0, and less volatile (risky) stocks have betas smaller than 1.0, while the riskless asset has a beta of 0. As a *relative* measure of risk, beta is very convenient. Beta is useful for comparing the relative systematic risk of different stocks and, in practice, is used by investors to judge a stock's riskiness. Stocks can be ranked by their betas. Because the variance of the market is a constant across all securities for a particular period, ranking stocks by beta is the same as ranking them by their absolute systematic risk.[8]

Stocks with high (low) betas are said to be high- (low-) risk securities. Betas may vary widely across companies in different industries and within a given industry. They also change through time as the risk characteristics of the underlying security or portfolio change. Table 9-1 below shows beta estimates for some Canadian common stocks at the beginning of 1999, which provide the reader with some insight into the nature of real-world betas.

[8] The absolute measure of systematic risk for a stock is the product of the stock's beta squared and the variance of the return for the overall market.

Table 9-1

Canadian Betas

Company	Industry Classification	Beta
Breakwater Resources	Mining (zinc)	1.8614
Cominco Ltd.	Integrated Mining	1.067
Falconbridge Ltd.	Integrated Mining (nickel)	1.2558
Inco Limited	Integrated Mining (nickel)	1.0507
Barrick Gold Corp.	Gold Producer	1.3183
Homestake Mining	Gold Producer	0.8525
TVX Gold Inc.	Gold Producer	1.5164
Eldorado Gold Corp.	Gold Producer	2.1543
Molson Cos.	Consumer Products	0.5621
Seagram Co. Ltd.	Consumer Products	0.8192
Second Cup	Consumer Products	0.4199
Bombardier Inc.	Industrial Products	0.8531
Moore Corp. Ltd.	Industrial Products	0.7597
Cogeco Cable Inc.	Telecommunications — Cable	0.758
Shaw Communications	Telecommunications — Cable	0.919
Videotron	Telecommunications — Cable	0.5526
Bank of Montreal	Banks	0.9973
Bank of Nova Scotia	Banks	1.2417
Canadian Imperial Bank of Commerce	Banks	1.2243
Royal Bank	Banks	0.9778
Toronto Dominion Bank	Banks	1.267

Source: *Nesbitt Burns Research Red Book*, Third Quarter, 1999.

Intuitively, we might expect the stocks of mining companies such as gold producers to be riskier than other types of firms, since the cash flows generated by these companies are relatively volatile due to several factors including fluctuations in world commodity prices. Table 9-1 confirms that the betas for companies in these industries do tend to be higher than others presented in the table, however, we also note there are significant variations within a given industry. For example, there is a large difference in betas within the firms categorized as gold producers, which range from 0.74 for **Homestake Mining** to 2.17 for **Eldorado Gold Corp.** In this case, the discrepancy in betas is largely attributable to differences at the firm rather than industry level. In particular, while both firms operate in the same industry, Homestake is a senior gold producer whose stock is considered to be large-cap, while Eldorado is small-cap stock with more volatile returns as measured by beta.

Some other trends that are obvious in the table are the low betas displayed by consumer product companies and cable companies, with industrial products firms exhibiting slightly higher betas. Finally, we notice that the big five Canadian banks have betas between 0.99 and 1.26, which implies they display average to above-average volatility with respect to market prices as a whole.

The CAPM's Expected Return-Beta Relationship

The Capital Asset Pricing Model formally relates the expected rate of return for any security or portfolio with the relevant risk measure. The CAPM's *expected return-beta relationship* is the most-often cited form of the relationship. Beta is the relevant measure of risk that cannot be diversified away in a portfolio of securities and, as such, is the measure that investors should consider in their portfolio management decision process.

Required Rate of Return
The minimum expected rate of return necessary to induce an investor to purchase a security.

The CAPM in its expected return-beta relationship form is a simple but elegant statement. It says that the expected rate of return on an asset is a linear function of the two components of the **required rate of return** — the risk-free rate and the risk premium. Thus,

(9-9)

$$k_i = \text{Risk-free rate} + \text{Risk premium}$$
$$= \text{RF} + \beta_i[\text{E}(\text{R}_\text{M}) - \text{RF}]$$

where

k_i = the required rate of return on asset i

$\text{E}(\text{R}_\text{M})$ = the expected rate of return on the market portfolio

β_i = the beta coefficient for asset i

Market Risk Premium
The difference between the expected return for the equities market and the risk-free rate of return.

This relationship provides an explicit measure of the risk premium. It is the product of the beta for a particular security i and the **market risk premium**, $\text{E}(\text{R}_\text{M}) - \text{RF}$. Thus,

$$\text{Risk premium for security } i$$
$$= \beta_i(\text{market risk premium})$$
$$= \beta_i[\text{E}(\text{R}_\text{M}) - \text{RF}]$$

The CAPM's expected return-beta relationship formalizes the basis of investments, which is that the greater the risk assumed, the greater the expected (required) return should be. This relationship states that an investor requires (expects) a return on a risky asset equal to the return on a risk-free asset plus a risk premium, and the greater the risk assumed, the greater the risk premium.

EXAMPLE: REQUIRED RETURN FOR FALCONBRIDGE LTD.

Table 9-1 provides a 1999 beta estimate for **Falconbridge Ltd.**'s common stock of 1.23. If RF was 0.05 at that time while the expected return on the market was estimated to be 0.12, the required return for Falconbridge would be estimated as

$$k_{\text{Falconbridge}} = 0.05 + 1.23(0.12 - 0.05)$$
$$= 13.61\%$$

The required (or expected) return for Falconbridge is, as it should be, larger than that of the market because Falconbridge's beta is larger — once again, the greater the risk assumed, the larger the required return.

Over- and Undervalued Securities

The SML has important implications for security prices. In equilibrium, each security should lie on the SML because its expected return should be what is needed to compensate investors for the systematic risk. What happens if investors believe that a security does not lie on the SML? To make this determination, they must employ a separate methodology to estimate the expected returns for securities. In other words, an existing SML can be applied to a sample of securities to determine the expected (required) return–risk trade-off that exists. Knowing the beta for any stock, we can determine the required return from the SML. Then, estimating the expected return from an alternative approach, say, fundamental analysis (discussed in Chapter 14), an investor can assess a security in relation to the SML and determine whether it is under- or overvalued.

INVESTING tip

Equation 9-9 indicates that securities with betas greater than the market beta of 1.0 should have larger risk premiums than that of the average stock and therefore, when added to RF, larger required rates of return. This is exactly what investors should expect, since beta is a measure of risk, and greater risk should be accompanied by greater return. Conversely, securities with betas less than that of the market average are less risky and should have required rates of return lower than that for the market as a whole. This will be the indicated result from the CAPM, because the risk premium for the security will be less than the market risk premium and, when added to RF, will produce a lower required rate of return for the security.[9]

EXAMPLE: THE SML AND THE VALUATION OF SECURITIES

In Figure 9-5, two securities are plotted around the SML. Security X has a high expected return derived from fundamental analysis and plots above the SML; security Y has a low expected return and plots below the SML. Which is undervalued?

Security X, plotting above the SML, is undervalued because it offers more expected return than investors require, given its level of systematic risk, as measured by beta. Investors require a minimum expected return of $E(R_X)$, but security X, according to fundamental analysis, is offering $E(R_X')$. If investors recognize this, they will purchase security X, because it offers more return than required. This demand will drive up the price of X, as more of it is purchased. The return will be driven down, until it is at the level indicated by the SML.

Security Y, according to fundamental analysis, does not offer enough expected return given its level of systematic risk. Investors require $E(R_Y)$ for security Y, based on the SML, but Y offers only $E(R_Y')$. As investors recognize this, they will sell security Y (or perhaps sell it short), because it offers less than the required return. This increase in the supply of Y will drive down its price. The return will be driven up for new buyers because any dividends paid are now relative to a lower price, as is any expected price appreciation. The price will fall until the expected return rises enough to reach the SML, and the security is once again in equilibrium.

[9] The risk premium on the security will be less than the market risk premium, because we are multiplying by a beta less than 1.0.

Figure 9-5
Overvalued and Undervalued Securities Using the SML

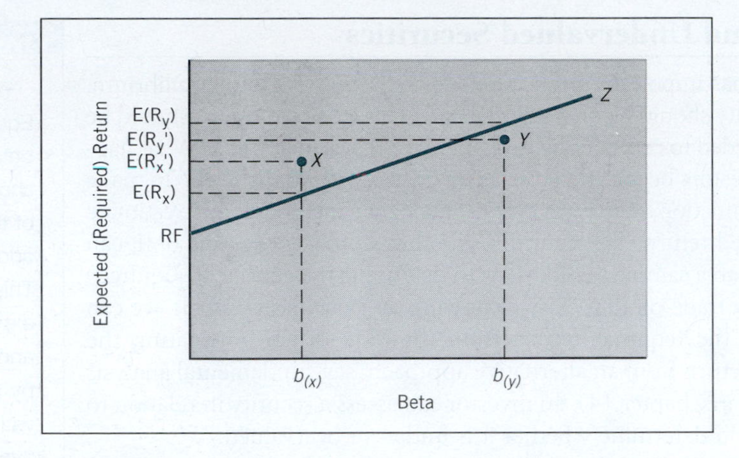

ESTIMATING THE SML

To use the SML to estimate the required return on an asset, an investor needs estimates of the return on the risk-free asset, the expected return on the market index, and the beta for an individual security. How difficult are these to obtain?

The return on a risk-free asset, RF, should be the easiest of the three variables to obtain. In estimating RF, the investor can use the return on government Treasury bills for the coming period. Estimating the market return is more difficult because the expected return for the market index is not observable. Furthermore, several different market indexes could be used. Estimates of the market return could be derived from a study of previous market returns (such as the TSE 300 Composite Index data in Table 6-1). Alternatively, expected future market returns could be determined by calculating probability estimates of market returns based on current market conditions and expectations of future market conditions. This would provide an estimate of both the expected return and the standard deviation for the market.

Finally, it is necessary to estimate the betas for individual securities. This is a crucial part of the CAPM estimation process. The estimates of RF and the expected return on the market are the same for each security being evaluated. Since beta is unique with respect to a chosen market proxy, it brings together the investor's expectations of returns for the stock with those for the market. Beta is the only company-specific factor in the CAPM; therefore, risk is the only asset-specific forecast that must be made in the CAPM.

Estimating Beta

Market Model
Relates the return on each stock to the return on the market, using a linear relationship with intercept and slope.

A less restrictive form of single-index model, which was introduced in Chapter 7, is known as the **Market Model**. It is identical to the single-index model except that it does not make the assumption that the error terms of the different securities are uncorrelated. The Market Model equation is the same as Equation 7-15 for the single-index model (again, without the restrictive assumption)

$$R_{it} = \alpha_i + \beta_i R_{Mt} + e_{it} \tag{7-15}$$

where
R_{it} = the return (TR) on security i at time t
R_{Mt} = the return (TR) on the market index at time t
α_i = the intercept term for security i
β_i = the slope term for security i
e_{it} = the random residual error for security i at time t

The Market Model produces an estimate of return for any stock.

To estimate the Market Model, the TRs for stock i can be regressed on the corresponding TRs for the market index. Estimates will be obtained of α_i (the constant return on security i that is earned regardless of the level of market returns) and β_i (the slope coefficient that indicates the expected increase in a security's return for a 1 per cent increase in market return). This is how the estimate of a stock's beta is often derived.

EXAMPLE: USING THE MARKET MODEL TO ESTIMATE BETA

This example estimates the beta for **Abitibi-Consolidated Inc.** to be 1.305 using the Market Model. Total return data for Abitibi-Consolidated corresponds to the following regression equation estimate using 60 months of return data for 1993–97, along with corresponding TRs for the TSE 300 Composite Index:

$$R_{Abitibi} = -0.832 + 1.305\, R_{TSE\ 300}$$

Characteristic Line
A regression equation used to estimate beta by regressing stock returns on market returns.

When the TRs for a stock are plotted against the market index TRs, the regression line fitted to these points is referred to as **the characteristic line**. Figure 9-6 depicts an example of a characteristic line, based on the monthly return data used in the Abitibi example above.

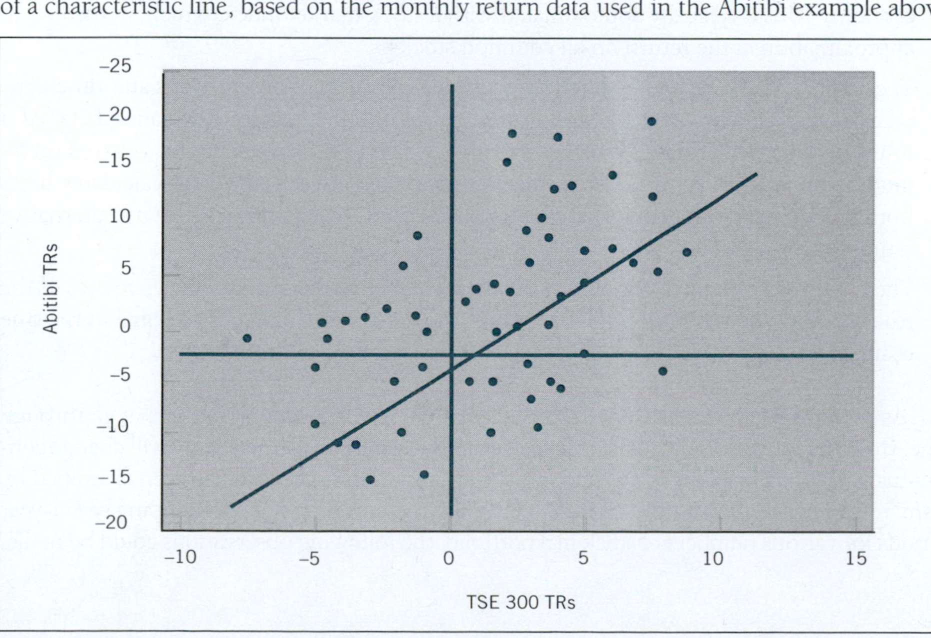

Figure 9-6
A Typical Characteristic Line Based on Monthly Data

The characteristic line is often fitted using *excess returns*. The excess return is calculated by subtracting the risk-free rate, RF, from both the return on the stock and the return on the market. In excess return form, the same analysis as before applies. The alpha is the intercept of the characteristic line on the vertical axis, which in theory should be zero for any stock. It measures the excess return for a stock when the excess return for the market portfolio is zero. The beta remains the slope of the characteristic line. It measures the sensitivity of a stock's excess return to that of the market portfolio. The variance of the error term measures the variability of a stock's excess return not associated with movements in the market's excess return. Diversification can reduce this variability.

Many brokerage houses and investment advisory services report betas as part of the total information given for individual stocks. For example, the betas reported in Table 9-1 were obtained from the *Nesbitt Burns Research Red Book* for the first quarter of 1999. *The Value Line Investment Survey* also reports the beta for each stock covered, as do other brokerage firms. Both measures of risk discussed above, standard deviation and beta, are widely known and discussed by investors.

Whether we use the single-index model or the Market Model, beta can be estimated using regression analysis. However, the values of α_i and β_i obtained in this manner are *estimates* of the true parameters and are subject to error. Furthermore, beta can shift over time as a company's situation changes. A legitimate question, therefore, is how accurate are the estimates of beta?

As noted, beta is usually estimated by fitting a characteristic line to the data. However, this is an estimate of the beta called for in the CAPM. The market proxy used in the equations for estimating beta may not fully reflect the market portfolio specified in the CAPM. Furthermore, several points should be kept in mind:

1. We are trying to estimate the future beta for a security, which may differ from the historical beta, since betas change through time as the risk of the underlying common stock changes.
2. In theory, the independent variable R_M represents the total of all marketable assets in the economy. This is typically approximated with a stock market index, which, in turn, is an approximation of the return on all common stocks.
3. The characteristic line can be fitted over varying numbers of observations and time periods. There is no one correct period or number of observations for calculating beta. As a result, estimates of beta will vary. For example, Nesbitt Burns estimates betas based on 54 months of monthly return data, while *The Value Line Investment Survey* calculates betas from weekly rates of return for 60 months (five years). Other analysts may use alternative estimation approaches.
4. The regression estimates of α and β from the characteristic line are only estimates of the true α and β and are subject to error. Thus, these estimates may not be equal to the true α and β.

As mentioned above, it is not surprising that we would find that betas change through time, since the fundamental variables (e.g., earnings, cash flow) of a company will change continuously. The fact that beta is not stationary is an important issue that has been examined by many researchers. For example, Blume found that in comparing non-overlapping seven-year periods for various numbers of stock in a portfolio, the following observations could be made:

1. Betas estimated for individual securities are unstable; that is, they contain relatively little information about future betas.
2. Betas estimated for large portfolios are stable; that is, they contain much information about future betas.[10]

In effect, a large portfolio (e.g., 50 stocks) provides stability because of the averaging effect. Although the betas of some stocks in the portfolio go up from period to period, others go down, and these two movements tend to cancel each other. Furthermore, the errors involved in estimating betas tend to cancel out in a portfolio. Therefore, estimates of portfolio betas show less change from period to period and are much more reliable than are the estimates for individual securities. This discussion parallels the one in Chapter 7 about using historical standard deviations to proxy for future standard deviations. At that time, we suggested that historical portfolio standard deviations would provide much better proxies than would individual security standard deviations.

Researchers have found that betas in the forecast period are, on average, closer to 1.0 than the estimate using historical data. This would imply that we can improve the estimates of beta by measuring the adjustment in one period and using it as an estimate for the next period. For example, we could adjust each beta toward the average beta by taking half the historical beta and adding it to half of the average beta. Merrill Lynch, the world's largest brokerage firm, reports adjusted betas based on a technique such as this. Other methods have also been proposed, including a Bayesian estimation technique.

TESTS OF THE CAPM

The conclusions of the CAPM are entirely sensible:

1. Return and risk are positively related — greater risk should carry greater return
2. The relevant risk for a security is a measure of its effect on portfolio risk.

The question, therefore, is how well the theory works, despite all of the assumptions on which it is based. To assess the validity of this or any other theory, empirical tests must be performed. If the CAPM is valid, and the market tends to balance out so that realized security returns average out to equal expected returns, equations of the following type can be estimated:

$$R_i = a_1 + a_2\beta_i \qquad \textbf{(9-10)}$$

where
R_i = the average return on security *i* over some number of periods
β_i = the estimated beta for security *i*

When Equation 9-10 is estimated, a_1 should approximate the average risk-free rate during the periods studied, and a_2 should approximate the average market risk premium during the periods studied.

[10] M. Blume, "Betas and Their Regression Tendencies," *Journal of Finance* 10 (June 1975), pp. 785–795; R. Levy, "On the Short-Term Stationarity of Beta Coefficients," *Financial Analysts Journal* 27 (December 1971), pp. 55–62.

An extensive literature exists involving tests of capital market theory in general, and the CAPM in particular. Although it is not possible to summarize the scope of this literature entirely and to reconcile findings from different studies that seem to be in disagreement, the following points represent a reasonable consensus of previous empirical results:

1. The SML appears to be linear; that is, the trade-off between expected (required) return and risk is an upward-sloping straight line.
2. The intercept term, a_1, is generally found to be higher than RF.
3. The slope of the CAPM, a_2, is generally found to be less steep than posited by the theory. This implies that CAPM systematically "overpredicts" realized returns for low-beta stocks and "underpredicts" for high-beta stocks.
4. Although the evidence is mixed, no persuasive case has been made that non-systematic risk commands a risk premium. In other words, investors are rewarded only for assuming systematic risk.[11]

The Fama and French Studies

Recent evidence by Fama and French contradicts the linear relationship between expected return and beta. They demonstrate that CAPM's sole risk factor, the market risk beta, possesses no explanatory power whatsoever in discriminating among the cross-sectional returns of US stocks.[12]

Fama and French contend that two simple and observable variables, common market equity (ME) and the ratio of book equity to market equity (BE/ME) combine to explain the cross-section of expected returns. Their analysis leads them to propose a three-factor pricing model, which has gathered much attention in recent years. Specifically, Fama and French suggest that an overall market factor, and factors related to firm size and the book equity to market equity ratio explain cross-sectional differences in average returns of stocks.[13]

To account for stock return Fama and French's three-factor model includes the following factors:

1. The expected return to a portfolio of small market capitalization stocks less the return of a portfolio of large market capitalization stocks
2. The expected return to a portfolio of high book-to-market stocks less the return of a portfolio of low book-to-market stocks
3. The expected return on the market index.

The Fama and French model has gained increasing acceptance in recent years. Its potential importance is evidenced by the fact that Ibbotson Associates (a major provider of financial information) now provides estimates of the required return on equity for companies based on this model, in addition to estimates determined by the more widely recognized CAPM.

---

[11] For a more detailed discussion of empirical tests of the CAPM, see Elton and Gruber (1995), *Modern Portfolio Theory*.

[12] E. Fama and K. French, "The Cross Section of Expected Stock Returns," *Journal of Finance* 47 (June 1992), pp. 427–465.

[13] E. Fama and K. French, "Size and Book-to-Market Factors in Earnings and Returns," *Journal of Finance* 50 (March 1995), pp. 131–155.

The major problem in testing capital market theory is that it is formulated on an *ex ante* basis but can be tested only on an ex post basis. We can never know investor expectations with certainty. Therefore, it should come as no surprise that tests of the model have produced conflicting results in some cases and that the empirical results diverge from the predictions of the model.

Difficulties in Testing CAPM

Tests of return predictability over a long period of time using a model such as CAPM, inevitably must deal with the "joint-hypothesis problem." This refers to the fact that we can only test whether the asset pricing model (CAPM in this case) fits the data well, if we also assume that assets are priced correctly in the market (i.e., if we assume that markets are efficient). Thus we have two hypotheses that are being tested simultaneously. Evidence that rejects our overall hypothesis may imply a rejection of CAPM, or of market efficiency, or both.

Another important problem with attempting to test CAPM was identified by Richard Roll in his seminal 1977 article.[14] His argument is commonly referred to as Roll's Critique. He argued that CAPM has not been proven empirically, nor will it be. This is because CAPM is untestable since the market portfolio, which consists of all risky assets, is unobservable. This forces researchers or users of CAPM to choose a market proxy that may or may not be mean-variance efficient. In effect, Roll argues that tests of the CAPM are actually tests of the mean-variance efficiency of the chosen market portfolio. He shows that the basic CAPM results will hold whenever the chosen proxy is mean-variance efficient and will not hold if the converse is true.

Despite these and other criticisms, the CAPM remains a logical way to view the expected return–risk trade-off.

ARBITRAGE PRICING THEORY

Another model of security pricing that has received a great deal of attention is based on **Arbitrage Pricing Theory (APT)** as developed by Roll and enhanced by others. APT represents an alternative theory of asset pricing that it is more general than the CAPM, with less restrictive assumptions. However, like the CAPM, it has limitations, and like the CAPM, it is not the final word in asset pricing.

Arbitrage Pricing Theory (APT)
An equilibrium theory that suggests expected returns for securities are based on their relationship with several underlying risk factors.

Similar to the CAPM, or any other asset pricing model, APT posits a relationship between expected return and risk. It does so, however, using different assumptions and procedures. Very importantly, APT is not critically dependent on an underlying market portfolio as is the CAPM, which predicts that only market risk influences expected returns. Instead, APT recognizes that several types of systematic risk may affect security returns.

APT is based on the *law of one price*, which states that two otherwise identical assets cannot sell at different prices. APT assumes that asset returns are linearly related to a set of indexes, where each index represents a risk factor that influences the return on an asset.

[14] R. Roll, "A Critique of the Asset Pricing Theory's Tests; Part I: On Past and Potential Testability of the Theory," *Journal of Financial Economics* 4 (March 1977), pp. 129–176.

Market participants develop expectations about the sensitivities of assets to the factors. They buy and sell securities so that, given the law of one price, securities affected equally by the same factors will have equal expected returns. This buying and selling is the arbitrage process, which determines the prices of securities.

APT states that equilibrium market prices will adjust to eliminate any arbitrage opportunities, which refer to situations where a *zero investment, zero-risk portfolio* can be constructed that will yield a risk-free profit. If arbitrage opportunities arise, a relatively few investors can act to restore equilibrium.

Unlike the CAPM, APT does not assume:

1. A single-period investment horizon
2. The absence of taxes
3. Borrowing and lending at the rate RF
4. Investors select portfolios on the basis of expected return and variance.

APT, like the CAPM, does assume:

1. Investors have homogeneous beliefs
2. Investors are risk-averse utility maximizers
3. Markets are perfect
4. Returns are generated by a factor model.

Also similar to CAPM, APT works much better for well-diversified portfolios than for individual securities.

Factor Model
Used to depict the behaviour of security prices by identifying major factors in the economy that affect large numbers of securities.

A **factor model** is based on the view that there are *underlying risk factors* that affect realized and expected security returns. These risk factors represent broad economic forces and not company-specific characteristics and, by definition, they represent the element of surprise in the risk factor — the difference between the actual value for the factor and its expected value.

The factors must possess three characteristics:

1. Each risk factor must have a pervasive influence on stock returns. Firm-specific events are not APT risk factors.
2. These risk factors must influence expected return, which means they must have non-zero prices. This issue must be determined empirically, by statistically analyzing stock returns to see which factors pervasively affect returns.
3. At the beginning of each period, the risk factors must be unpredictable for the market as a whole.[15]

The last characteristic above raises an important point. In our example below, we use unexpected inflation and unexpected changes in the economy's output as the two factors affecting portfolio returns. The rate of inflation or economic output per se, are not APT risk factors because they are at least partially predictable. In a reasonably stable economy where the quarterly rate of inflation has averaged 1 per cent, we can reasonably assume that next quarter's inflation rate will not be 10 per cent. On the other hand, unexpected inflation — the difference between actual and expected inflation — is an APT risk factor. By definition, it cannot be predicted since it is unexpected.

[15] M. A. Berry, E. Burmeister, and M. B. McElroy, "Sorting Out Risks Using Known APT Factors," *Financial Analysts Journal* 44 (March–April 1988), pp. 29–41.

What really matters are the *deviations* of the factors from their expected values. For example, if the expected value of inflation is 5 per cent and the actual rate for a specific period is only 4 per cent, this 1 per cent deviation will affect the actual return for the period.

EXAMPLE: DEVIATION OF FACTORS FROM EXPECTED VALUES

An investor holds a portfolio of stocks that he or she thinks is influenced by only two basic economic factors, inflation surprises and the unexpected changes in the economy's output. Diversification once again plays a role because the portfolio's sensitivity to all other factors can be eliminated by diversification.

Portfolio return varies directly with output and inversely with inflation. Each of these factors has an expected value, and the portfolio has an expected return when the factors are at their expected values. If either or both of the factors deviates from expected value, the portfolio return will be affected. We must measure the sensitivity of each stock in our investor's portfolio to changes in each of the two factors. Each stock will have its own sensitivity to each of the factors. For example, stock 1 (a mortgage company) may be particularly sensitive to inflation and have a sensitivity of 2.0 to deviations of actual inflation from its expected level. On the other hand, stock 2 (a food manufacturer) may have a sensitivity to unexpected inflation of only 1.0.

Understanding the APT Model

Based on this analysis, we can now understand the APT model. It assumes that investors believe that asset returns are randomly generated according to an n-factor model.[16] For security *i*, the actual return can be formally stated as:

$$R_{it} = E(R_{it}) + b_{i1}f_{1t} + b_{i2}f_{2t} + \ldots + b_{in}f_{nt} + e_{it} \qquad \text{(9-11)}$$

where

R_{it} = the actual (random) rate of return on security *i* in any given period *t*
$E(R_{it})$ = the expected return on security *i* for a given period *t*
f_{nt} = the deviation of a systematic factor F_n from its expected value during period *t*
b_i = sensitivity of security *i* to a factor
e_{it} = random error term, unique to security *i* during period *t*

It is important to note that the expected value of each factor (F) is zero. Therefore, the f's in Equation 9-11 are measuring the deviation of each factor from its expected value. Notice in Equation 9-11 that the actual return for a security in a given period will be at the expected or required rate of return if the factors are at expected levels (e.g., $F_1 - E(F_1) = 0$, $F_2 - E(F_2) = 0$, and so forth) and if the chance element represented by the error term is at zero.

[16] It is assumed that all covariances between returns on securities are attributable to the effects of the factors; therefore, the error terms are uncorrelated.

A factor model makes no statement about equilibrium. If we transform Equation 9-11 into an equilibrium model, we are saying something about expected returns across securities. APT is an equilibrium theory of *expected* returns that requires a factor model such as Equation 9-11. The equation for expected return on a security is given by Equation 9-12.

$$E(R_{it}) = a_0 + b_{i1}F_{1t} + b_{i2}F_{2t} + \ldots + b_{in}F_{nt} \quad (9\text{-}12)$$

where

$E(R_{it})$ = the expected return on security *i* during period *t*

a_0 = the expected return on a security with zero systematic risk

F = the risk premium for a factor (for example, the risk premium for F_1 is equal to $E(F_1) - a_0$).

With APT, risk is defined in terms of a stock's sensitivity to basic economic factors, while expected return is directly related to sensitivity. As always, expected return increases with risk. The expected return–risk relationship for the CAPM is $E(R_i) = RF + \beta_i$ (market risk premium). The CAPM assumes that the only required measure of risk is the sensitivity to the market. The risk premium for a stock depends on this sensitivity and the market risk premium (the difference between the expected return on the market and the risk-free rate).

The expected return–risk relationship for the APT can be described as: $E(R_{it}) = RF + b_{i1}$ (risk premium for factor 1) + b_{i2} (risk premium for factor 2) + ... + b_{in} (risk premium for factor n). Note that the sensitivity measures (β_i and b_i) have similar interpretations. They are measures of the relative sensitivity of a security's return to a particular risk premium. Also notice that we are dealing with risk premiums in both cases. Finally, notice that the CAPM relationship is the same as would be provided by APT if there were only one pervasive factor influencing returns. For this reason and the others outlined above, APT is more general than CAPM.

The problem with APT is that the factors are not well specified, at least *ex ante*. To implement the APT model, we need to know the factors that account for the differences among security returns. The APT makes no statements about the number of risk factors, or the size or sign of the F_is. Both the factor model and these values must be identified empirically. In contrast, with the CAPM the factor that matters is the market portfolio, a concept that is well understood conceptually. However, as noted earlier, Roll has argued that the market portfolio is unobservable.

Most empirical work suggests that three to five factors influence security returns and are priced in the market. For example, Roll and Ross identify five systematic factors:

1. Changes in expected inflation
2. Unanticipated changes in inflation
3. Unanticipated changes in industrial production
4. Unanticipated changes in the default-risk premium
5. Unanticipated changes in the term structure of interest rates.[17]

These factors are related to the components of a valuation model. The first three affect the cash flows of a company while the first two and the last two affect the discount rate. According to this model, different securities have different sensitivities to these systematic

[17] Richard Roll and Stephen Ross, "An Empirical Investigation of the Arbitrage Pricing Theory," *Journal of Finance* 35 (December 1980), pp. 1073–1103.

factors, and investor risk preferences are characterized by these dimensions. Each investor has different risk attitudes. Investors could construct a portfolio depending upon desired risk exposure to each of these factors. Knowing the market prices of these risk factors and the sensitivities of securities to changes in the factors, the expected returns for various stocks could be estimated.

Another study has suggested that an APT model that incorporates unanticipated changes in five macroeconomic variables is superior to the CAPM. These five variables are:

1. Default risk
2. The term structure of interest rates
3. Inflation or deflation
4. The long-run expected growth rate of profits for the economy
5. Residual market risk.[18]

Using APT in Investment Decisions

Roll and Ross have argued that APT offers an approach to strategic portfolio planning. The idea is to recognize that a few systematic factors affect long-term average returns. Investors should seek to identify the few factors affecting most assets in order to appreciate their influence on portfolio returns. Based on this knowledge, they should seek to structure the portfolio in such a way as to improve its design and performance.

Some researchers have identified and measured, for both economic sectors and industries, the risk exposures associated with APT risk factors such as the five identified above (default risk, and so forth). These "risk exposure profiles" vary widely. For example, the financial and transportation sectors were found to be particularly sensitive to default risk, while the utility sector was relatively insensitive to both unexpected inflation and the unexpected change in the growth rate of profits.

An analysis of 82 different industry classifications showed the same result — exposure to different types of risk varies widely. For example, some industries were particularly sensitive to unexpected inflation risk, such as the mobile home building industry, retailers, hotels and motels, toys, and eating places. The industries least sensitive to this risk factor included foods, tires and rubber goods, shoes, and breweries. Several industries showed no significant sensitivity to unexpected inflation risk, such as corn and soybean producers and sugar refiners.

Portfolio managers could design strategies that would expose them to one or more types of these risk factors, or "sterilize" a portfolio such that its exposure to the unexpected change in the growth rate of profits matched that of the market as a whole. Taking an active approach, a portfolio manager who believes that he or she can forecast a factor realization can build a portfolio that enhances or reduces sensitivity to that factor. In doing so, the manager will select stocks that have exposures to the remaining risk factors that are exactly proportional to the market. If the manager is accurate with the forecast — and remember that such a manager must forecast the unexpected component of the risk factor — he or she can outperform the market for that period.

---

[18] These factors are based on Berry et al., "Sorting Out Risks."

SOME CONCLUSIONS ABOUT ASSET PRICING

The question of how security prices and equilibrium returns are established — whether as described by the CAPM, or APT, or some other model — remains open. Some researchers are convinced that the APT model is superior to the CAPM. The CAPM relies on the observation of the market portfolio which, in actuality, cannot be observed. On the other hand, APT offers no clues as to the identity of the factors that are priced in the factor structure.

In the final analysis, neither model has been proven superior. Both rely on expectations which are not directly observable. Additional testing is needed.

SUMMARY

This summary relates to the learning objectives provided on page 247.

1. **Explain capital market theory and the Capital Asset Pricing Model.**
   Capital market theory, based on the concept of efficient diversification, describes the pricing of capital assets in the marketplace. Capital market theory is derived from several assumptions that may appear unrealistic; however, the important issue is the ability of the theory to predict. In addition, relaxation of most of the assumptions does not change the major implications of capital market theory. The Capital Asset Pricing Model (CAPM) is concerned with the equilibrium relationship between the risk and the expected return on risky assets and is considered a cornerstone of modern financial economics.
2. **Discuss the importance and composition of the market portfolio.**
   Given risk-free borrowing and lending, the new efficient frontier has a vertical intercept of RF and is tangent to the old efficient frontier at point M, the market portfolio. In theory, the market portfolio, M, should include all risky assets, although in practice it is typically proxied by a stock market index such as the TSE 300 Composite Index. All investors can achieve an optimal point on the new efficient frontier by investing in portfolio M and either borrowing or lending at the risk-free rate RF.
3. **Describe two important relationships in CAPM as represented by the capital market line and the security market line.**
   The new efficient frontier is called the capital market line (CML), and its slope indicates the equilibrium price of risk in the market, where risk is measured as the standard deviation of returns. In effect, it is the expected return–risk trade-off for efficient portfolios. *Ex ante*, the CML must always be upward sloping, although *ex post* it may be downward sloping for certain periods. Based on the separation of risk into its systematic and non-systematic components, the security market line (SML) can be constructed for individual securities (and portfolios). What is important is each security's contribution to the total risk of the portfolio as measured by beta. Using beta as the measure of risk, the SML depicts the trade-off between required return and risk for securities.

4. **Describe how betas are estimated and how beta is used.**
The Market Model can be used to estimate the alpha and beta for a security by regressing total returns for a security against total returns for a market index. The characteristic line is a graph of the regression involved in the Market Model. Beta, the slope of the characteristic line, is a relative measure of risk. It indicates the volatility of a stock, relative to a market index. If the expected returns for securities can be estimated from security analysis and plotted against the SML, undervalued and overvalued securities can be identified. Problems exist in estimating the SML, in particular, estimating the betas for securities. While all betas change through time, betas for large portfolios are much more stable than those for individual stocks.

5. **Discuss the Arbitrage Pricing Theory as an alternative to the Capital Asset Pricing Model.**
Tests of the CAPM are inconclusive, which is not surprising since it is an *ex ante* model that makes predictions about the uncertain future, and it is tested with *ex post* data. It has not been proven empirically, nor is it likely to be, but its basic implications seem to be supported. Alternative theories of asset pricing, such as the Arbitrage Pricing Theory (APT), also exist but remain unproven. APT is not critically dependent on an underlying market portfolio as is the CAPM, which predicts that only market risk influences expected returns. Instead, APT — as a risk factor model — recognizes that several types of risk may affect security returns. These risk factors represent broad economic forces and not company-specific characteristics, and, by definition, they represent the element of surprise in the risk factor. APT is more general than the CAPM. If only one factor exists, the two models can be shown to be identical. The problem with APT is that the factors are not well specified, at least *ex ante*. Most empirical work involving APT suggests that three to five factors influence security returns and are priced in the market.

KEY TERMS

Arbitrage Pricing Theory (APT)
Beta
Capital Asset Pricing Model (CAPM)
Capital market line (CML)
Capital market theory
Characteristic line
Factor model
Market Model
Market portfolio
Market risk premium
Required rate of return
Security market line (SML)

ADDITIONAL RESOURCE

A good discussion of capital market theory can be found in:

Elton, Edwin and Martin Gruber. *Modern Portfolio Theory and Portfolio Analysis*. Fifth Edition. New York: John Wiley & Sons, 1995.

REVIEW QUESTIONS

1. In terms of their appearance as a graph, what is the difference between the CML and the SML?
2. What is the market portfolio?
3. What is the major problem in testing capital market theory?
4. Why does Roll argue that the CAPM is untestable?
5. What is the relationship between the CML and the Markowitz efficient frontier?
6. The CML can be described as representing a trade-off. What is this trade-off? Be specific.
7. Based on empirical work, how many factors are thought to influence security returns? Name some of these likely factors.
8. What does a factor model say about equilibrium in the marketplace?
9. What role does the market portfolio play in the APT model?
10. What are the three factors included in Fama and French's multifactor model?
11. Differentiate between the CML and the SML. What can the SML be used for that the CML cannot be used for?
12. How do lending possibilities change the Markowitz model? Borrowing possibilities?
13. According to the CAPM, why do all investors hold identical risky portfolios?
14. What is the slope of the CML? What does it measure?
15. Why does the CML contain only efficient portfolios?
16. How can we measure a security's contribution to the risk of the market portfolio?
17. How can the SML be used to identify over- and undervalued securities?
18. What happens to the price and return of a security when investors recognize it as undervalued?
19. The CAPM provides required returns for individual securities or portfolios. What uses can you see for such a model?
20. How does an investor decide where to be on the new efficient frontier represented by the CML?
21. Draw a diagram of the SML. Label the axes and the intercept.
    a. Assume the risk-free rate shifts upward. Draw the new SML.
    b. Assume that the risk-free rate remains the same as before the change in (a) but that investors become more pessimistic about the stock market. Draw the new SML.
22. What common assumptions do the CAPM and APT share? How do they differ in assumptions?
23. What is a factor model?
24. What characteristics must the factors in a factor model possess?
25. How can APT be used in investment decisions?

26. What is meant by an "arbitrage profit?" What ensures that investors could act quickly to take advantage of such opportunities?
27. Why is the standard deviation of a security's returns an inadequate measure of the contribution of that security to the risk of a portfolio that is well diversified?
28. Given the parameters of CAPM, how is it possible that some stocks in a given year actually have negative returns. Why would an investor have bought these stocks, considering the purchase of the risk-free asset would have presented them with a "guaranteed" positive return with no risk?
29. What are some of the difficulties involved in estimating a security's beta?
30. How can the CAPM be tested empirically? What are the expected results of regressing average returns on betas?

PREPARING FOR YOUR PROFESSIONAL EXAMS

PAST CFA EXAM QUESTIONS AND PROBLEMS

The following question was asked on the 1993 CFA Level I examination:

1. Briefly explain whether investors should expect a higher return from holding Portfolio A versus Portfolio B under Capital Asset Pricing Theory (CAPM). Assume that both portfolios are fully diversified.

	Portfolio A	Portfolio B
Systematic risk (beta)	1.0	1.0
Specific risk for each individual security	High	Low

The following question was asked on the 1989 CFA Level II Examination:

2. You ask John Statdud, your research assistant, to analyze the relationship between the return on Coca-Cola Enterprises (CCE) common stock and the return on the market using the Standard & Poor's 500 Stock Index as a proxy for the market. The data include monthly returns for both CCE and the S&P 500 over a recent five-year period. The results of the regression are:

$$R_{CCE} = 0.59 + \underset{(3.10)}{0.94}\, R_{S\&P\ 500}$$

The number in parentheses is the t-statistic (the 0.01 critical value is 2.66). The coefficient of determination (R^2) for the regression is .215.

Statdud wrote the following summary of the regression results:

1. The regression statistics indicate that during the five-year period under study, when the annual return on the S&P 500 was zero, CCE had an average annual return of 0.59 per cent.
2. The alpha value of .59 is a measure of the variability of the return on the market.
3. The coefficient of .94 indicates CCE's sensitivity to the return on the S&P 500 and suggests that the return on CCE's common stock is less sensitive to market movements than the average stock.
4. The t-statistic of 3.10 for the slope coefficient indicates the coefficient is not statistically significant at the .01 level.
5. The R^2 for the regression of .215 indicates the average estimate deviates from the actual observation by an average of 21.5 per cent.
6. There is no concern that the slope coefficient lacks statistical significance since beta values tend to be less stable (and therefore less useful) than alpha values.
7. The regression should be rerun using ten years of data. This would improve the reliability of the estimated coefficients while not sacrificing anything.

Identify which of the seven statements made by Statdud are incorrect and justify your answer(s).

The following question was asked on the 1993 CFA Level I Examination.

3. Within the context of the Capital Asset Pricing Model (CAPM), assume:

   Expected return on the market = 15 per cent
   Risk free rate = 8 per cent
   Expected rate of return on XYZ security = 17 per cent
   Beta of XYZ security = 1.25
   Which one of the following is correct?

   a. XYZ is overpriced.
   b. XYZ is fairly priced.
   c. XYZ's alpha is −0.25 per cent.
   d. XYZ's alpha is 0.25 per cent.

PROBLEMS

1. The expected return for the market is 12 per cent, with a standard deviation of 20 per cent. The expected risk-free rate is 8 per cent. Information is available for five mutual funds, all assumed to be efficient, as follows:

Mutual Funds	SD (%)
Scotia Excelsior Balanced	7
PHN Canadian Equity	12
AGF Canadian Equity	16
Marathon Equity	20
Royal Precious Metals	33

a. Calculate the slope of the CML.

b. Calculate the expected return for each portfolio.

c. Rank the portfolios in increasing order of expected return.

d. Do any of the portfolios have the same expected return as the market? Why?

2. Given the market data in Problem 1, and the following information for each of five stocks.

Stock	Beta	R_i
1	0.9	12
2	1.3	13
3	0.5	11
4	1.1	12.5
5	1.0	12

a. Calculate the expected return for each stock.

b. With these expected returns and betas, think of a line connecting them — what is this line?

c. Assume that an investor, using fundamental analysis, develops the estimates labeled R_i for these stocks. Determine which are undervalued and which overvalued.

d. What is the market's risk premium?

3. Assume that RF is 7 per cent, the estimated return on the market is 12 per cent, and the standard deviation of the market's expected return is 21 per cent. Calculate the expected return and risk (standard deviation) for the following portfolios:

a. 60 per cent of investable wealth in riskless assets, 40 per cent in the market portfolio

b. 150 per cent of investable wealth in the market portfolio

c. 100 per cent of investable wealth in the market portfolio

4. Assume that the risk-free rate is 7 per cent and the expected market return is 13 per cent. Show that the security market line is

$$E(R_i) = 7.0 + 6.0\beta_i$$

Assume that an investor has estimated the following values for six different corporations:

Corporation	β_i	R_i(%)
Hollinger Inc.	0.67	12
Bombardier	0.87	13
Trimac Corp.	1.15	14
Newport Petroleum	1.34	11
Abitibi-Consolidated	1.33	21
Dofasco Inc.	1.35	10

Calculate the $E(R_i)$ for each corporation using the SML, and evaluate which securities are overvalued and which are undervalued.

5. Assume that Canadian Tire is priced under equilibrium conditions. Its expected return next year is 12 per cent, and its beta is 0.96. The risk-free rate is 6 per cent.

   a. Calculate the slope of the SML.

   b. Calculate the expected return on the market.

6. Given the following information:

   Expected return for the market, 12 per cent
   Standard deviation of market return, 21 per cent
   Risk-free rate, 8 per cent
   Correlation coefficient between
   Stock A and the market, 0.8
   Stock B and the market, 0.6
   Standard deviation for stock A, 25 per cent
   Standard deviation for stock B, 30 per cent

   a. Calculate the beta for stock A and stock B.

   b. Calculate the required return for each stock.

CHAPTER 10

MARKET EFFICIENCY

LEARNING OBJECTIVES

After reading this chapter, you will be able to

1. Explain the concept of efficient markets.
2. Describe the three forms of market efficiency — weak, semi-strong, and strong.
3. Discuss the evidence regarding the Efficient Market Hypothesis.
4. State the implications of market efficiency for investors.
5. Outline major exceptions to the Efficient Market Hypothesis.

CHAPTER PREVIEW

Now that we understand how securities are priced under conditions of market equilibrium, we consider the effects of informational efficiency — that is, how quickly and accurately information about securities is disseminated in financial markets — on the equilibrium relationship. We begin this chapter by discussing the concept of market efficiency and its three forms — weak, semi-strong, and strong. We examine the evidence that supports the Efficient Market Hypothesis as well as major exceptions to it.

THE CONCEPT OF AN EFFICIENT MARKET

In Chapter 9, we considered capital market theory, or how asset prices and returns are determined in equilibrium. The CAPM formulates the equilibrium relationship that should exist between expected return and risk. How markets respond to new information is a very important part of obtaining the equilibrium relationship predicted by capital market theory. Therefore, a direct relationship exists between capital market theory, which specifies the equilibrium relationship, and the concept of informationally efficient markets, which involves how well markets process new information that moves prices toward a new equilibrium.[1]

As an investor, should you care if the market is efficient? In an informationally efficient market, many traditional investing activities are suspect at best and useless at worst. Why? Because in a truly efficient market, the expected probability of a portfolio manager "beating" the market is small, while the value of the product of a typical security analyst may be close to zero. Therefore, you need to carefully consider your investing activities.

The idea of an efficient market has generated tremendous controversy, which continues today, and a number of participants refuse to accept it. This is not surprising in view of the enormous implications that an efficient market has for everyone concerned with securities. Some market participants' jobs and reputations are at stake, and they are not going to accept this concept readily.

Because of its significant impact and implications, the idea that markets are efficient deserves careful thought and study. Beginners should approach it with an open mind. The fact that some well-known market observers and participants reject or disparage this idea does not necessarily reduce its validity. Furthermore, the argument that the stock market is efficient is not going to disappear because too much evidence exists to support it regardless of the counter-arguments and exceptions to market efficiency that continue to remain unexplained. The intelligent approach for investors, therefore, is to learn about it and from it.

WHAT IS AN EFFICIENT MARKET?

Investors determine stock prices on the basis of the expected cash flows to be received from a stock and the risk involved. Rational investors should use all the information they have available or can readily obtain. This information set consists of both known information and beliefs about the future (i.e., information that can be reasonably inferred). Regardless of its

[1] Operational efficiency is concerned with how smoothly orders are transmitted to securities markets and processed. We are concerned here with informational efficiency, or how market prices respond to new information.

form, information is the key to the determination of stock prices and therefore is the central issue of the efficient markets concept.

An **efficient market** is one in which the prices of all securities quickly and fully reflect all available information about the assets. This concept postulates that investors will assimilate all relevant information into prices in making their buy-and-sell decisions. Therefore, the current price of a stock reflects:

Efficient Market
A market in which prices of securities quickly and fully reflect all available information.

1. All known information, including:
   - Past information (e.g., last year's or last quarter's earnings)
   - Current information as well as events that have been announced but are still forthcoming (such as a stock split or a dividend).
2. Information that can be reasonably inferred; for example, if many investors believe that interest rates will decline soon, prices will reflect this belief before the actual decline occurs.

The early literature on market efficiency made the assumption that market prices incorporated new information instantaneously. The modern version of this concept does not require that the adjustment be literally instantaneous, only that it occur very quickly as information becomes known. Given the extremely rapid dissemination of information in developed countries through electronic means, information is spread very quickly, almost instantaneously, to market participants with access to these sources. For individual investors without this access, important information can be received almost instantaneously on radio, television, and on the Internet, or, at the latest, the following day in such sources as *The Globe and Mail* or the *National Post*.

The concept that markets are efficient does not claim, or require, a perfect adjustment in price following the new information. Rather, the correct statement involved with this concept is that the adjustment in prices resulting from information is "unbiased."[2] The new price does not have to be the new equilibrium price but only an unbiased estimate of the final equilibrium price that will be established after investors have fully assessed the impact of the information.

Figure 10-1 illustrates the concept of market efficiency for one company for which a significant event occurs that has an effect on its expected profitability. The stock is trading at $50 on the announcement date of the significant event — day 0 in Figure 10-1 is the announcement date for the event. If the market is fully efficient, the price of a stock always reflects all available information. Investors will very quickly adjust a stock's price to its *fair value*. Assume that the new fair value for the stock is $52. In an efficient market, an immediate increase in the price of the stock to $52 will occur, as represented by the solid line in Figure 10-1. Since, in our example, no additional new information occurs, the price of the stock will continue at $52.

If the market adjustment process is inefficient, a lag in the adjustment of the stock prices to the new information will occur, and it is represented by the dotted line. The price eventually adjusts to the new fair value of $52 as brokerage houses disseminate the new information and investors revise their estimates of the stock's fair value. Note that the time it would take for the price to adjust is not known ahead of time — the dotted line is only illustrative.

[2] This means that the expected value of the adjustment error is zero — sometimes too large and at other times too small, but on average balancing out and correct.

Figure 10-1
The Adjustment of Stock Prices to Information: (*a*) If the Market Is Efficient; (*b*) One Possibility if the Market is Inefficient

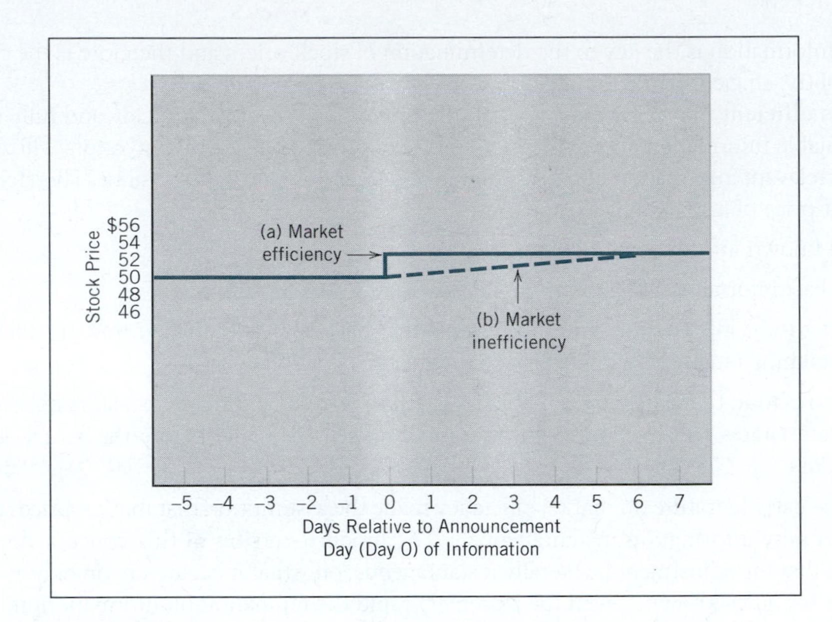

Why the Market Can Be Expected to Be Efficient

If the type of market adjustment described above seems too much to expect, consider the situation from the following standpoint. It can be shown that an efficient market can exist if the following events occur:

1. A large number of rational, profit-maximizing investors exist who actively participate in the market by analyzing, valuing, and trading stocks. These investors are price takers; that is, one participant alone cannot affect the price of a security.
2. Information is costless and widely available to market participants at approximately the same time.
3. Information is generated in a random fashion such that announcements are basically independent of one another.
4. Investors react quickly and fully to the new information, causing stock prices to adjust accordingly.

These conditions may seem strict, and in some sense they are. Nevertheless, consider how closely they parallel the actual investments environment. There is no question that a large number of investors are constantly "playing the game." Both individuals and institutions follow the market closely on a daily basis, standing ready to buy or sell when they think it is appropriate. The total amount of money at their disposal at any one time is more than enough to adjust prices at the margin.

Although the production of information is not really costless, for institutions in the investments business, generating various types of information is a necessary cost of business, and many participants receive it "free" (obviously, investors pay for such items in their brokerage costs and other fees). It is widely available to many participants at approximately the same time as information is reported on the Internet, radio, television, and specialized communications devices now available to any investor willing to pay for such services.

Information is largely generated in a random fashion in the sense that most investors cannot predict when companies will announce significant new developments — when wars will break out, when strikes will occur, when currencies will be devalued, when important leaders will suddenly suffer a heart attack, and so forth. Although there is some relationship between information events over time, by and large, announcements are independent and occur more or less randomly.

If these conditions are generally met in practice, the result is a market in which investors adjust security prices very quickly to reflect random information coming into the market. Prices reflect fully all available information. Furthermore, price changes are independent of one another and move in a random fashion. Today's price change is independent of the one yesterday because it is based on investors' reactions to new, independent information coming into the market today.

Forms of Market Efficiency

If, as discussed, the conditions necessary to produce market efficiency exist, exactly how efficient is the market, and what does this imply for investors? We have defined an efficient market as one in which all information is reflected in stock prices quickly and fully. Thus, the key to assessing market efficiency is information. In a perfectly efficient market, security prices always reflect immediately all available information, and investors are not able to use available information to earn abnormal returns because it already is impounded in prices. In such a market, every security's price is equal to its intrinsic (investment) value, which reflects all information about that security's prospects.

If some types of information are not fully reflected in prices or lags exist, the market is less than perfectly efficient. In fact, the market is not perfectly efficient any more than it is perfectly inefficient, so it is a question of degree. Therefore, we can think of market efficiency with respect to specific sets of information and ask if investors, on average, can earn abnormal returns using a set of information to buy and sell securities — in other words, exactly how efficient is the market?

Standard practice since Eugene Fama's classic 1970 article reviewing the topic is to discuss the market efficiency concept in the form of the **Efficient Market Hypothesis (EMH)**, which is simply the formal statement of market efficiency previously discussed.[3] The EMH is concerned with the extent to which security prices quickly and fully reflect the different types of available information, which can be divided into the three *cumulative* types as illustrated in Figure 10-2.

Efficient Market Hypothesis (EMH)
The proposition that securities markets are efficient, with the prices of securities reflecting their true economic value.

1. *Weak form*. One of the most traditional types of information used in assessing security values is **market data**, which refers to all past price (and volume) information. If security prices are determined in a market that is **weak form** efficient, historical price and volume data should already be reflected in current prices and should be of no value in predicting future price changes. Technical analysis, which relies primarily on the past history of price information, will therefore be of little or no value in markets that are weak-form efficient.

Market Data
Price and volume information for stocks or indexes.

Weak Form
That part of the Efficient Market Hypothesis stating that prices reflect all price and volume data.

[3] E. Fama, "Efficient Capital Markets: A Review of Theory and Empirical Work," *Journal of Finance* 25 (May 1970), pp. 383–417. In a sequel some 20 years later, entitled "Efficient Capital Markets: II," Fama refers to a "weaker and economically more sensible version of the efficiency hypothesis" that deals with prices reflecting information to the extent that it is not financially worthwhile to act on any information. See E. Fama, "Efficient Capital Markets: II," *Journal of Finance* 46 (December 1991), pp. 1575–1617.

Tests of the usefulness of price data are called *weak-form tests* of the EMH. If the weak form of the EMH is true, past price changes should be unrelated to future price changes. In other words, a market can be said to be weakly efficient if the current price reflects all past market data. The correct implication of a weak-form efficient market is that the past history of price information is of no value in assessing future changes in price.[4]

2. *Semi-strong form*. A more comprehensive level of market efficiency involves not only known and publicly available market data, but all publicly known and available data, such as earnings, dividends, stock split announcements, new product developments, financing difficulties, and accounting changes. A market that quickly incorporates all such information into prices is said to show efficiency in a **semi-strong form**. Thus, a market can be said to be "efficient in the semi-strong sense" if current prices reflect all publicly available information. Notice that a semi-strong efficient market encompasses the weak form of the hypothesis because market data are part of the larger set of all publicly available information.

Semi-Strong Form That part of the Efficient Market Hypothesis stating that prices reflect all publicly available information.

Tests of the semi-strong EMH are tests of the speed of adjustment of stock prices to announcements of new information. A semi-strong efficient market implies that investors cannot act on new public information after its announcement and expect to earn above-average risk-adjusted returns. If lags exist in the adjustment of stock prices to certain announcements and investors can exploit these lags and earn abnormal returns, the market is not fully efficient in the semi-strong sense.

3. *Strong form*. The most stringent form of market efficiency is the **strong form**, which asserts that stock prices fully reflect *all* information — public and non-public. If the market is strong-form efficient, no group of investors should be able to earn, over a reasonable period of time, abnormal rates of return by using information in a superior manner. This applies in particular to all non-public information, including information that may be restricted to certain groups such as corporate insiders and specialists on the exchanges.

Strong Form That part of the Efficient Market Hypothesis stating that prices reflect all information, public and private.

In effect, the strong form of the EMH refers to the successful use of a monopolistic access to information by certain market participants. Strong-form efficiency encompasses the weak and semi-strong forms and represents the highest level of market efficiency.

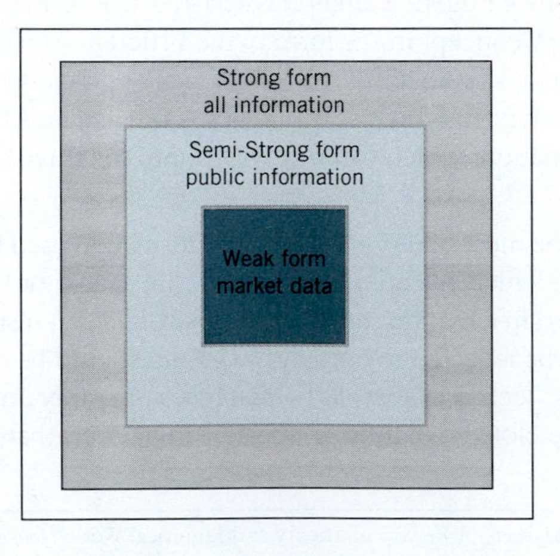

Figure 10-2 Cumulative Levels of Market Efficiency and the Information Associated with Each

[4] It is not correct to state, as is sometimes done, that the best estimate of price at time $t+1$ is the current (time t) price, because this implies an expected return of zero. The efficient market in no way implies that the expected return on any security is zero.

EVIDENCE ON MARKET EFFICIENCY

Because of the significance of the efficient markets hypothesis to all investors, and because of the controversy that surrounds the EMH, we will examine some empirical evidence on market efficiency. Many studies have been conducted over the years and continue to be done. Obviously, we cannot begin to discuss them all, nor is it necessarily desirable to look at several in detail. Our purpose here is to present an idea of how these tests are done, the scope of what has been done, and some results. The empirical evidence will be separated into tests of the three forms of market efficiency previously discussed.

The key to testing the validity of any of the three forms of market efficiency is the consistency with which investors can earn returns in excess of those commensurate with the risk involved. Short-lived inefficiencies appearing on a random basis do not constitute evidence of market inefficiencies, at least in an economic (as opposed to a statistical) sense. Therefore, it makes sense to talk about an economically efficient market, in which assets are priced in such a manner that investors cannot exploit any discrepancies and earn unusual returns after consideration of all transaction costs. In such a market, some securities could be priced slightly above their intrinsic values and others slightly below, and lags can exist in the processing of information, but again not in such a way that the differences can be exploited.

What about the time period involved? In the short run, investors may earn unusual returns even if the market is efficient. After all, you could buy a stock today, and tomorrow a major discovery could be announced that would cause its price to increase significantly. Does this mean the market is inefficient? Obviously not; it means you are either very skilful or, more likely, very lucky. The question is, can you and enough other investors do this a sufficient number of times in the long run to earn abnormal profits? Even in the long run, some people will be lucky given the total number of investors.

INVESTING tip

It should be apparent upon reflection that we are talking about price changes and not about the level of price itself. Obviously, a $60 stock has a price on any given day that will be related closely to its price tomorrow since it is unlikely on a typical day to go much above or below $60. In addition, we are not concerned with whether the change in today's price, say +1/2, is related to the change in tomorrow's price, say −1/4. Dollar price changes such as these are also related. The issue centres on percentage price changes over time — are they related or not?

Weak-Form Evidence

As noted, weak-form efficiency means that price data are incorporated into current stock prices. If prices follow non-random trends, stock price changes are dependent; otherwise, they are independent. Therefore, weak-form tests involve the question of whether all information contained in the sequence of past prices is fully reflected in the current price.

The weak-form EMH is related to, but not identical with, an idea from the 1960s called the *random walk hypothesis*. If prices follow a random walk, price changes over time are random (independent).[5] The price change for today is unrelated to the price change yesterday, or the day before, or any other day. This is a result of the scenario described at the outset of the chapter. If new information arrives randomly in the market and investors react to it immediately, changes in prices will also be random.

[5] Technically, the random walk hypothesis is more restrictive than the weak-form EMH. Stock prices can conform to weak-form efficiency without meeting the conditions of a random walk.

One way to test for weak-form efficiency is to test statistically the independence of stock price changes. If the statistical tests suggest that price changes are independent, the implication is that knowing and using the past sequence of price information is of no value to an investor. In other words, trends in price changes do not exist.

A second way to test for weak-form efficiency, after testing the pure statistical nature of price changes, is to test specific trading rules that attempt to use past price data. If such tests legitimately produce risk-adjusted returns beyond that available from simply buying a portfolio of stocks and holding it until a common liquidation date, after deducting all costs, it would suggest that the market is not weak-form efficient.

Statistical Tests of Price Changes

Stock price changes in an efficient market should be independent. Two simple statistical tests of independence are the serial correlation test and the signs test. The serial correlation test involves measuring the correlation between price changes for various lags, such as one day, two days, and so on, whereas the signs test involves classifying each price change by its sign, which means whether it was +, 0, or − (regardless of amount). Then the "runs" in the series of signs can be counted and compared to known information about a random series. If there are persistent price changes, the length of the runs will indicate it.

Fama studied the daily returns on the 30 Dow Jones Industrial stocks and found that only a very small percentage of any successive price change could be explained by a prior change.[6] Serial correlation tests by other researchers invariably reached the same conclusion.

The signs test also supports independence. Although some "runs" do occur, they fall within the limits of randomness since a truly random series exhibits some runs (several + or − observations in succession).

Technical Trading Rules

The statistical tests described above demonstrate that trends, other than those consistent with a random series, do not appear to exist in stock prices. However, technical analysts believe that such trends not only exist but can also be used successfully. They argue that statistical tests do not detect more sophisticated or realistic strategies. Because an almost unlimited number of possible technical trading rules exist, not all of them can be examined; however, if a sufficient number are examined and found to be ineffective, the burden of proof shifts to those who argue that such techniques have value. This is exactly the situation that prevails. Little evidence exists that a technical trading rule based solely on past price and volume data can, after all proper adjustments have been made, outperform a simple buy-and-hold strategy.

Again, it is important to emphasize the difference between *statistical dependence* and *economic dependence* in stock price changes. Most of the statistical tests discussed earlier detected some small amount of dependence in price changes.[7] Not all of the series could be said to be completely independent statistically. However, they were economically independent

---

[6] E. Fama, "The Behavior of Stock Market Prices," *Journal of Finance* 38 (January 1965), pp. 34–105.

[7] Stock returns tend to exhibit a slight positive correlation.

in that one could not exploit the small statistical dependence that existed. After brokerage costs, excess returns disappear. After all, this is the bottom line for investors — can excess returns be earned with a technical trading rule after all costs are deducted?[8]

Weak-Form Counter-Evidence

DeBondt and Thaler have tested an "overreaction hypothesis," which states that people overreact to unexpected and dramatic news events.[9] As applied to stock prices, the hypothesis states that, as a result of overreactions, "loser" portfolios outperform the market after their formation. DeBondt and Thaler classify stocks as "winners" and "losers" based on their total returns over the previous three- to five-year period. They find that over a half-century, the loser portfolios of 35 stocks outperformed the market by an average of almost 20 per cent for a 36-month period after portfolio formation, while the winner portfolios earned about 5 per cent less than the market. Their results, expressed in terms of the cumulative average residual (described on page 291), are depicted below in Figure 10-3.

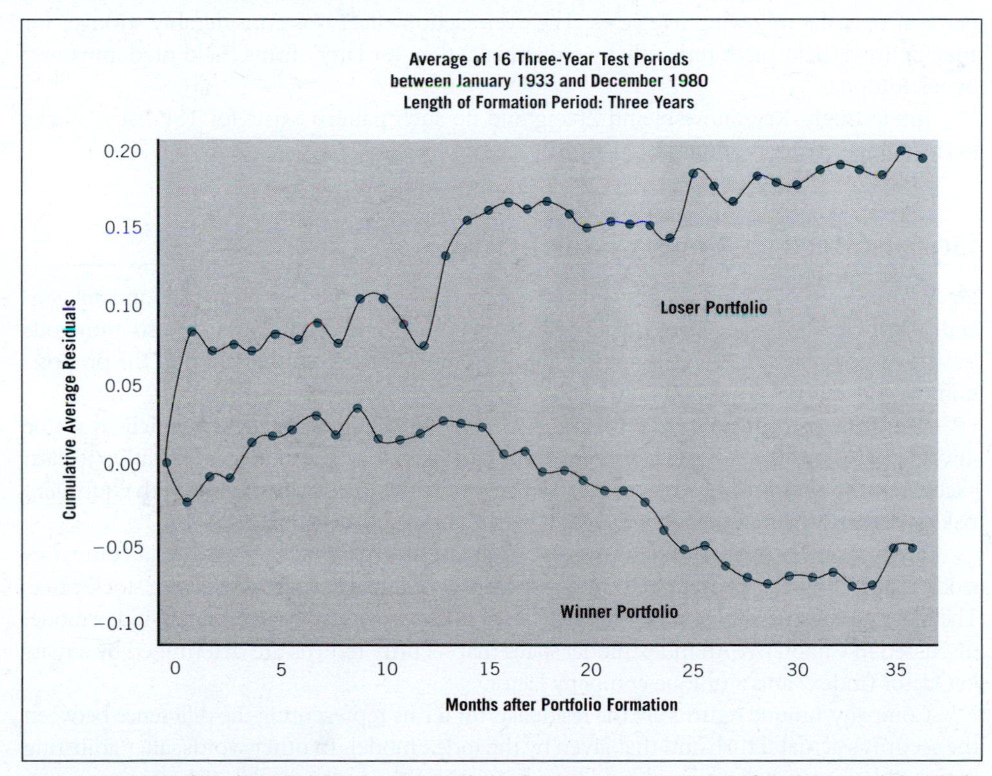

Figure 10-3
DeBondt and Thaler Results

Source: W. DeBondt and R. Thaler, "Does the Stock Market Overreact?" Journal of Finance *40 (July 1985), p. 800.*

[8] Some studies have indicated that trading rules can produce profits after making the necessary adjustments. For a study that argues that trading rules may not be so readily implemented under actual conditions, see R. Ball, S. P. Kothari, and C. Wasley, "Can We Implement Research on Stock Trading Rules?" *Journal of Portfolio Management* 21 (Winter 1995), pp. 54–63.

[9] W. DeBondt and R. Thaler, "Does the Stock Market Overreact?" *Journal of Finance* 40 (July 1985), pp. 793–808.

Interestingly, the overreaction seems to occur mostly during the second and third year of the test period. DeBondt and Thaler interpreted this evidence as indicative of irrational behaviour by investors, or overreaction. Trading strategies designed to exploit this pattern are commonly referred to as "contrarian strategies" since the underlying rationale is to purchase or sell stocks in anticipation of achieving future results that are contrary to their past performance record.

This tendency for stocks that experience extreme returns to go through subsequent return reversals after portfolios are formed, and for the effect to be observed years after portfolio formation, has implications for market efficiency. Specifically, it indicates substantial weak-form inefficiencies because DeBondt and Thaler are testing whether the overreaction hypothesis is *predictive*. In other words, according to their research, knowing past stock returns appears to help significantly in predicting future stock returns.

A recent study of the overreaction hypothesis, which adjusts for several potential problems, found an "economically important overreaction effect" even after adjusting for time variations in beta and for size effects.[10] Using five-year periods to form portfolios, the study revealed that extreme prior losers outperformed extreme prior winners by 5 to 10 per cent per year over the following five years. The overreaction effect was considerably stronger for smaller firms (held predominantly by individuals) than for larger firms (held predominantly by institutions).

Interestingly, Kryzanowski and Zhang find no such pattern exists for TSE-listed stocks over a similar period of time (1950–88).[11]

Semi-Strong-Form Evidence

Weak-form tests, of both the statistical and the trading rule types, are numerous and are generally supportive of weak-form efficient capital markets. Semi-strong tests are also numerous but are more diverse in their findings.[12] Although most of these studies support the proposition that the market adjusts to new public information rapidly, some do not.

Semi-strong-form tests are tests of the speed of price adjustments to publicly available information. The question is whether investors can use publicly available information to earn excess returns after proper adjustments. We can use a buy-and-hold strategy with equivalent risk or perhaps the market as a whole as a benchmark.

Event Study
An empirical analysis of stock price behaviour surrounding a particular event.

Abnormal Return
Return on a security beyond that expected on the basis of its risk.

This empirical research often involves an **event study**, which means that a company's stock returns are examined to determine the impact of a particular event on the stock price. The methodology usually uses an index model of stock returns such as the single-index model discussed in Chapter 7. An index model states that security returns are determined by a market factor (index) and a unique company factor.

Company-unique returns are the residual error terms representing the difference between the security's actual return and that given by the index model. In other words, after adjusting for what the company's return should have been, given the index model, any remaining portion of the actual return is an **abnormal return** representing the impact of a particular event.

[10] N. Chopra, J. Lakonishok, and J. R. Ritter, "Measuring Abnormal Performance: Do Stocks Overreact?" *Journal of Financial Economics* 31 (1992), pp. 235–268.

[11] L. Kryzanowski and H. Zhang, "The Contrarian Strategy Does Not Work in Canadian Markets," *Journal of Financial and Quantitative Analysis* 27 (September 1992), pp. 389–395.

[12] In his more recent (1991) survey of efficient capital markets, Fama uses the "now common title, event studies," instead of semi-strong form tests. See Fama, "Efficient Capital Markets II."

$$\text{Abnormal return} = AR_{it} = R_{it} - E(R_{it})$$

where

AR_{it} = the abnormal rate of return for security i during period t

R_{it} = the actual rate of return on security i during period t

$E(R_{it})$ = the expected rate of return for security i during period t, based on the equilibrium model relationship[13]

Cumulative Abnormal Return (CAR)
The sum of the individual abnormal returns over the time period under examination.

The **cumulative abnormal return (CAR)** is the sum of the individual abnormal returns over the period of time under examination and is calculated as

$$\text{Cumulative abnormal returns } (CAR_i) = \sum_{t=1}^{n} AR_{it}$$

where

CAR_i = the cumulative abnormal return for stock i

Below, we consider a sampling of often-cited studies of semi-strong efficiency without developing them in detail. It is important to obtain a feel for the wide variety of information tested and the logic behind these tests. The methodology and a detailed discussion of the results are not essential for our purposes. At this point, we consider evidence that tends to support semi-strong efficiency.

1. *Stock splits.* An often-cited study of the long-run effects of stock splits on returns was performed by Fama, Fisher, Jensen, and Roll (FFJR), which was the first event study.[14] Theoretically, a stock split adds nothing of value to a company and, therefore, should have no effect on the company's total market value. The FFJR results are depicted in Figure 10-4, which is a diagram format that is frequently used to express the results of any event study. Their results indicate that although the stocks examined displayed sharp increases in price prior to the split announcement, abnormal (i.e., risk-adjusted) returns after the split announcement were very stable. Thus, the split itself did not affect prices. These results indicate that any implications of a stock split appear to be reflected in price immediately following the *announcement* and not the event itself. This supports the semi-strong form of market efficiency because investors could not have earned abnormal returns after the information was made public.[15]
2. *Accounting changes.* Several studies have examined the effects on stock prices of announcements of accounting changes. The accounting changes include depreciation, the investment tax credit, inventory reporting (LIFO versus FIFO), and other items. Essentially, two different types of changes are involved:

[13] For example, according to CAPM, we can express the expected return as $E(R_{it}) = RF_t + [E(R_{Mt}) - RF_t]\beta_i$. Thus, if we used CAPM to determine the expected return on a security, we could express the abnormal return as $AR_{it} = R_{it} - [RF_t + [E(R_{Mt}) - RF_t]\beta_i]$.

[14] E. Fama, L. Fisher, M. Jensen, and R. Roll, "The Adjustment of Stock Prices to New Information," *International Economics Review* 10 (February 1969), pp. 2–21.

[15] A later study provided a very extensive analysis of a sample of stock splits in order to determine stock-price reactions. Effects such as dividend announcements and cash dividends were controlled for. The findings of this study suggest that the price reactions extend several days beyond the announcement date of the stock split or dividend. These results imply that there must be some information associated with such distributions. See M. Grinblatt, R. Masulis, and S. Titman, "The Valuation Effects of Stock Splits and Stock Dividends," *Journal of Financial Economics* 13 (December 1984), pp. 461–490.

a. The change may affect only the manner in which earnings are reported to stockholders, and therefore should not affect stock prices. The reason for this is that such changes do not affect the firm's cash flows and thus its real economic value.

b. The change may affect the firm's economic value by affecting its cash flows. This is a true change and should therefore generate a change in market prices. In an efficient market, stock prices should adjust quickly to the announcement of this type of change.

In general, the studies indicate that the market is able to distinguish the superficial changes described in the first type from the real changes described in the second type.

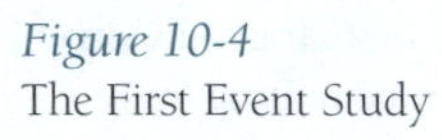
Figure 10-4
The First Event Study

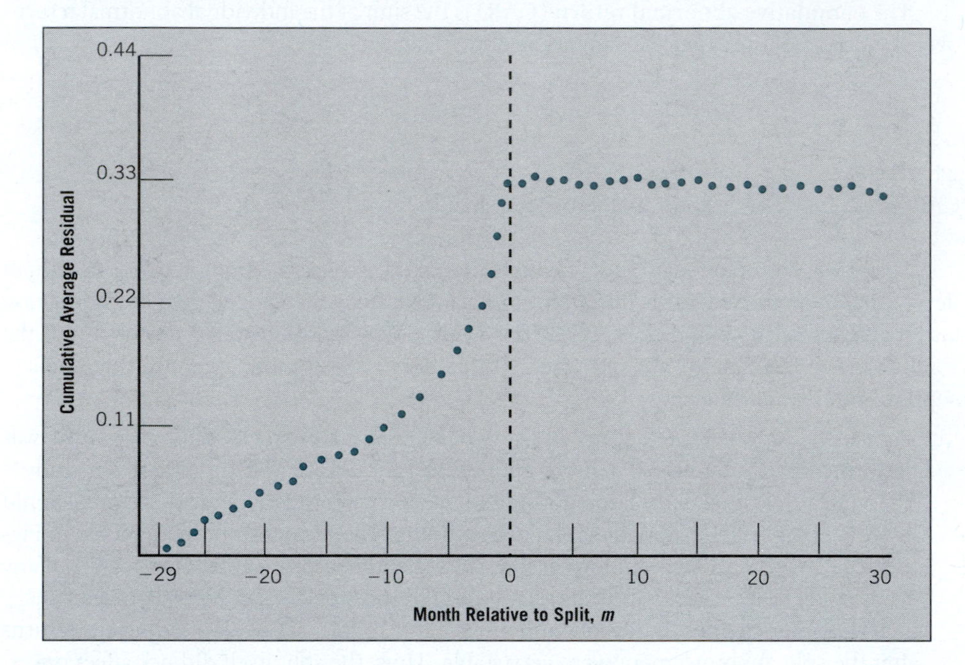

Source: E.Fama, L.Fisher, M. Jensen and R.Roll, "The Adjustment of Stock Prices to New Information," International Economic Review, *February 1969, pp. 2–21.*

3. *Initial public offerings*. A company that goes public creates an initial public offering, or IPO. Given the risk the underwriters face in trying to sell a new issue in which the true price is unknown, they may underprice the new issue to ensure its rapid sale. The investors who are able to buy the IPO at its offering price may be able to earn abnormal profits, but if prices adjust quickly, investors buying the new issues shortly after their issuance should not benefit.

    Empirical evidence indicates that new issues purchased at their offering price yield abnormal returns to the fortunate investors who are allowed to buy the initial offering.[16] This is attributed to underpricing by the underwriters. Investors buying shortly after the initial offering, however, are not able to earn abnormal profits because prices adjust very quickly to the "true" values.

[16] For a review of early IPO literature, see R. Ibbotson, J. Sindelar, and J. Ritter, "Initial Public Offerings," *Journal of Applied Corporate Finance* 1 (Summer 1988), pp. 37–45. Recent international evidence can be found in T. Loughran, J. Ritter, and K. Rydqvist, "Initial Public Offerings: International Insights," *Pacific-Basin Finance Journal* 2 (May 1994), pp. 165–200. Canadian evidence is documented by V. Jog and A. Riding, "Underpricing of Canadian IPOs," *Financial Analysts Journal* 43 (Nov–Dec 1987), pp. 48–55; and, more recently by V. Jog and A. Srivastava, "Underpricing of Canadian IPOs 1971–1992 — An Update," working paper, Carleton University, 1994.

4. *Reactions to announcements and news*. Investors are constantly given a wide range of information concerning both large-scale events and items about particular companies. Each of these types of announcements has been examined for the effects on stock prices.

   One form of announcement involves economic news such as money supply, real economic activity, inflation, and the Bank of Canada rate. A study of these types of announcements found no impact on stock prices that lasted beyond the announcement day.[17] Even an analysis of hourly stock price reactions to surprise announcements of money supply and industrial production found that any impact was accounted for within one hour.[18]

   The "Heard in the Street" column in *The Wall Street Journal* is a daily feature highlighting particular companies and analysts' opinions on stocks. A recent study of public takeover rumours from the "Heard on the Street" column found that the market is efficient at responding to published takeover rumours.[19] Excess returns could not be earned on average by buying or selling rumoured takeover targets at the time the rumour appeared. No significant excess returns occurred on the day the takeover rumour in *The Wall Street Journal* was published, although a positive cumulative excess return of approximately 7 per cent occurs in the calendar month before the rumour appears in the "Heard on the Street" column.

Professional Portfolio Manager Performance

Perhaps the strongest evidence of semi-strong market efficiency is the fact that the average professional fund manager does not outperform the market benchmark on a risk-adjusted basis. The most abundant type of managed portfolios examined in the performance literature is US-based equity mutual funds. This category of fund type includes mutual funds with any or all of the following objectives: aggressive growth, growth, growth and income, balanced, income, and venture. The evidence does not support the hypothesis that the average manager outperforms the appropriate equity market indexes.[20] There are also several US studies regarding the performance of pension funds that indicate that these managers consistently underperform the appropriate benchmark.

The Real-World Returns box below suggests that very few Canadian equity funds have been able to outperform the average fund performance on a consistent basis. Unfortunately, there are very few rigorous empirical studies of the performance of Canadian mutual or pension funds. In addition, the existing studies deal with small numbers of funds over relatively short time periods. Overall, the available Canadian evidence is mixed; however, there is some evidence of superior performance by professionally managed funds in Canada.[21]

---

[17] D. Pearce and V. Roley, "Stock Prices and Economic News," *Journal of Business* 59 (Summer 1985), pp. 49–67.

[18] P. C. Jain, "Response of Hourly Stock Prices and Trading Volume to Economic News," *Journal of Business* 61 (April 1988), pp. 219–231.

[19] J. Pound and R. Zeckhauser, "Clearly Heard on the Street: The Effect of Takeover Rumors on Stock Prices," *Journal of Business* 63 (July 1990), pp. 291–308.

[20] M. Grinblatt and S. Titman, "Mutual Fund Performance: An Analysis of Quarterly Portfolio Holdings," *Journal of Business* 62 (July 1989), pp. 393–416; B. Malkiel, "Returns From Investing in Equity Mutual Funds 1971 to 1991," *Journal of Finance* 50 (June 1995), pp. 549–572.

[21] E. Couture, "Investment's Smart Bomb: Passive Management With Style," *Canadian Investment Review* 5 (December 1992), pp. 43–48; R. Heinkel and R. Quick, "The Relative Performance of Canadian Institutional Portfolios and Canadian Indexes," *Canadian Investment Review* 6 (Fall 1993), pp. 33–39. For an extensive review of the literature on the performance of Canadian and US professional money managers refer to John Schmitz, "The Performance and Consistency of Professional Portfolio Managers: A Review and Synthesis," unpublished manuscript, Financial Concept Group, Toronto, 1999.

REAL-WORLD RETURNS

Few Funds Consistently Beat the Average

On a visit to Canada just last week, famed US investment superstar Peter Lynch made an interesting observation. "If you're right six or seven times out of 10," said the former portfolio manager of the worlds' largest mutual fund, "that's a terrific score."

Of course, Mr. Lynch, vice-chairman of Boston-based Fidelity Management & Research Co., was talking about picking stocks, a job he performed exceptionally well at the top-performing **Fidelity Magellan Fund** from 1977 to 1990.

But a detailed examination of the year-by-year returns of Canadian equity funds suggests that Mr. Lynch's words apply equally to picking mutual funds.

For a fund to perform merely better than the average in its category in a single year hardly seems worth of mention. But what's so surprising is how few funds manage to perform this feat more often.

In fact, according to our examination of Canadian equity funds with ten years under their belt, fewer than half of funds can do it even half the time. So doing so six or seven times out of ten does indeed constitute a terrific score.

Among the 76 Canadian equity funds in existence for the decade to September 30, 1997, not a single one managed to beat the category average in all ten years. And just one managed to beat the category average nine times. That fund — the $159-million **Bissett Canadian Equity Fund** — might well be called the consistency king of Canadian stock funds.

Possibly just as startling, only three funds managed to beat the average in eight years, and four more bested the average seven times. Just another seven managed to outperform in six out of 10 years — in other words, more than half the time. And another 14 outperformed five out of ten years, or exactly half the time.

The overall score: 34 of the 76 funds — fewer than half — beat the average at least five out of ten years. So beating the category average more than half the time really is a performance standard too few mutual funds ever meet.

What does this mean to you, the fund investor? Quite simply, these remarkable statistics reinforce the advice you've no doubt grown tired of hearing — invest for the long term. All funds and portfolio managers — the best and all the rest — go through periods when they simply fail to excel. So don't judge your funds harshly when they've suffered a single year of sub-average returns.

Year after year of consistently superior performance may be the most desirable trait any mutual fund can offer. That's because those few funds that manage to excel according to our criteria also exhibit relatively strong compound annual rates of return over time.

In fact, all four of the funds that beat the average at least eight times out of ten also turned in ten-year compound returns in the top ten per cent of their category.

These statistics may not seem to add much to the fund-selection process. After all, why not just pick the funds with the best long-term returns?

But they tell you a lot about why advisers constantly recommend staying with your existing investments. A year or two of below-average performance simply does not imply a poor fund. Even the best suffer periodic but temporary setbacks.

If you hold a fund that seems to be falling behind its peer group, by all means look for explanations. There may be something worng, such as a change of manager or a wandering of the manager's style. These reasons may suggest that a change in your portfolio is in order.

However, your fund may just be going through a temporary period when its style of stock-picking doesn't lead the charts. If you redeem and move on for that reason alone, you may find yourself selling low just before your fund begins to recover.

What's more, moving into another fund that's been hot recently may mean buying just before it suffers one of its inevitable setbacks.

When a fund's ten-year compound average annual growth rate places it firmly in the top 10 per cent of its category, it usually means the fund performed better than average more than half the time.

So the next time you're wondering how one of your funds could do so poorly, take a look at how many times it beat its category average. After all, even the best funds have a few off years.

Source: Excerpted from Peter Brewster, "Better than Average: Not Very Often," The Globe and Mail, A 15-Year Review, Mutual Funds, *November 6, 1997, pp. C1–C2. © Peter Brewster.*

On aggregate, the results indicate that the net performance of the average active portfolio manager (after management expenses) is substantially worse than the performance of the standard passive portfolio benchmarks. In fact, the average active portfolio manager may underperform the market index by 50 to 200 basis points. This implies that the gross performance (before management expenses) of the average active portfolio manager at best equals the performance of standard passive benchmarks and is likely marginally lower than these benchmarks.

Strong-Form Evidence

The strong form of the EMH states that stock prices immediately adjust to and reflect all information, including private information.[22] Thus, no group of investors has information that allows them to earn abnormal profits *consistently*, even those investors with monopolistic access to information. Note that investors are prohibited not from possessing monopolistic information but from profiting from it. This is an important point in light of the studies of insider trading reported below.

One way to test for strong-form efficiency is to examine the performance of groups presumed to have access to "true" non-public information. If such groups can consistently earn above-average risk-adjusted returns, the strong form will not be supported. We will consider corporate insiders, a group that presumably falls into the category of having monopolistic access to information.

Corporate Insiders

A corporate insider is an officer, director, or major stockholder of a corporation who might be expected to have valuable inside information. The Ontario Securities Commission (OSC) requires insiders (officers, directors, and owners of more than 10 per cent of a company's stock) whose securities trade on the Toronto Stock Exchange to report their monthly purchase or sale transactions to the OSC by the tenth day of the next month. This information is made public in the OSC's weekly publication, the *OSC Bulletin*. Other provinces such as Quebec and Alberta are more demanding and require insiders to report their activity within ten days of

[22] In his 1991 paper, Fama refers to these tests as "tests for private information" instead of strong-form tests. See Fama, "Efficient Capital Markets II."

making a trade. In the United States, the Securities and Exchange Commission (SEC) follows an identical procedure to the OSC, except that the information is made public in the SEC's monthly publication, *Official Summary of Security Transactions and Holdings (Official Summary)*.

Insiders have access to privileged information and are able to act on it and profit before the information is made public. Therefore, it is not surprising that several studies of corporate insiders found they consistently earned abnormal returns on their stock transactions.[23] Other studies, however, have found that insiders do only slightly better than chance alone in predicting the direction of a company's stock.

A recent study of insider trades by chairpersons, presidents, and other top officials of firms over the period 1975–89 found that these groups substantially outperformed the market when they made large trades. Trades by top executives of 1,000 shares or more were "abnormally profitable" for insiders.[24] On the other hand, most insiders did only slightly better than a coin toss. Canadian evidence also suggests that insiders are able to earn abnormal profits.[25]

Profitable insider trading is a violation of strong-form efficiency, which requires a market in which no investor can consistently earn abnormal profits. Furthermore, successful use of this information by outsiders (the general public) would be a violation of semi-strong efficiency. Investors without access to this private information can observe what the insiders are doing by studying the publicly available reports that appear in the *OSC Bulletin*. Several investment information services compile this information and sell it to the public in the form of regularly issued reports, and it is available in *The Globe and Mail* and the *National Post*. Furthermore, services such as The Value Line Investment Survey report insider transactions for each company they cover.

In their 1988 study, Rozeff and Zaman used the typical abnormal return methodology of previous studies and found that outsiders could earn profits by acting on the publicly available information concerning insider transactions.[26] However, when Rozeff and Zaman used an abnormal returns measure that took into account size and earnings/price-ratio effects, the profits decreased substantially and disappeared altogether when transactions cost of 2 per cent were included. Furthermore, imposition of a 2 per cent transactions cost on corporate insiders reduced their abnormal returns to an average of 3 to 3.5 per cent per year. Therefore, this study reaffirms semi-strong market efficiency with respect to insider trading and also suggests that corporate insiders do not earn substantial profits from using inside information directly, which in effect supports strong-form efficiency. The Canadian evidence of Lee and Bishara suggests that outsiders can earn abnormal returns based on insider trading information.[27]

There are several reasons why insider transactions can be very misleading or simply of no value as an indicator of where the stock price is likely to go. Selling shares acquired by key executives through options has become commonplace — they need the cash, and they sell

---

[23] J. Jaffe, "Special Information and Insider Trading," *Journal of Business* 47 (July 1974), pp. 410–428; K. Nunn, G. P. Madden, and M. Gombola, "Are Some Investors More 'Inside' Than Others?" *Journal of Portfolio Management* 9 (Spring 1983), pp. 18–22.

[24] See A. Peers, "Insiders Reap Big Gains from Big Trades," *The Wall Street Journal*, September 23, 1992, pp. C1, C12.

[25] D. J. Fowler and C.H. Rorke, "Insider Trading Profits on the Toronto Stock Exchange, 1967-1977," *Canadian Journal of Administrative Sciences* 5 (March 1988), pp. 13–24.

[26] M. S. Rozeff and M. A. Zaman, "Market Efficiency and Insider Trading: New Evidence," *Journal of Business* 61 (January 1988), pp. 25–45.

[27] M.H. Lee and H. Bishara, "Recent Canadian Experiences on the Profitability of Insider Trades," *Financial Review* 24 (May 1989), pp. 235–249.

shares acquired as part of their compensation. Similarly, acquiring shares through the exercise of options can simply represent an investment decision by the executive.

IMPLICATIONS OF THE EFFICIENT MARKET HYPOTHESIS

The non-exhaustive evidence on market efficiency presented here is impressive in its support of market efficiency. What are the implications to investors if this evidence is descriptive of the actual situation? How should investors analyze and select securities and manage their portfolios if the market is efficient?

For Technical Analysis

As mentioned earlier, technical analysis and the EMH directly conflict with each other. Technicians believe that stock prices exhibit trends that persist across time, whereas the weak-form EMH states that price (and volume) data are already reflected in stock prices. EMH proponents believe that information is disseminated rapidly and that prices adjust rapidly to this new information. If prices fully reflect the available information, technical trading systems that rely on knowledge and use of past trading data cannot be of value.

Although technical analysis cannot be categorically refuted because of its many variations and interpretations, the evidence accumulated to date overwhelmingly favours the weak-form EMH and casts doubt on technical analysis. The evidence is such that the burden of proof has shifted to the proponents of technical analysis to demonstrate, using a properly designed test procedure (e.g., adjusting for transaction costs, risk, and any other factors necessary to make a fair comparison), that technical analysis outperforms a buy-and-hold strategy.

For Fundamental Analysis

The EMH also has implications for fundamental analysis, which seeks to estimate the intrinsic value of a security and provide buy-and-sell decisions depending on whether the current market price is less or greater than the intrinsic value. If the semi-strong form is true, no form of "standard" security analysis based on publicly available information will be useful. In this situation, since stock prices reflect all relevant publicly available information, gaining access to information others already have is of no value.

Given the evidence on market efficiency, clearly superior fundamental analysis becomes necessary. For example, an investor's estimates of future variables such as earnings must be better, or at least more consistent, than those of other investors. This investor must also derive more and better insights from information that is publicly available to all investors. There is no theoretical reason why an investor could not do a superior job of analysis and profit thereby. However, the EMH suggests that investors who use the same data and make the same interpretations as other investors will experience only average results. The evidence of below-average performance displayed by the average professional money manager supports this notion.

For Money Management

What about money management activities? Assume for a moment that the market is efficient. What would this mean to the money management process, that is, to professional money managers? The most important effect would be a reduction in the resources devoted to assessing individual securities. For the manager to act in this respect, he or she would have to believe that an analyst had come up with some superior insights, and passive strategies would become the norm. One passive investment strategy that is becoming increasingly popular is indexing, as discussed in the Real-World Returns box below. Indexing involves the construction of portfolios designed to mimic the performance of a chosen market benchmark portfolio such as the TSE 300 or TSE 35 Index.

Even with passive management, portfolio managers have certain tasks to perform including the following:

1. *Diversification*. As we saw in Chapter 8, the basic tenet of good portfolio management is to diversify the portfolio. The manager would have to be certain that the correct amount of diversification had been achieved.
2. *Portfolio risk*. Depending on the type of portfolio being managed and its objectives, the manager must achieve a level of risk appropriate for that portfolio as well as maintain the desired risk level.
3. *Taxes*. Investors are interested in the amount of return they are allowed to keep after taxes. Accordingly, their tax situation should be kept in mind as investment alternatives are considered. Tax-exempt portfolios have their own needs and interests.
4. *Transaction costs*. Trading costs can have a significant impact on the final performance of the portfolio. Managers should seek to reduce these costs to the extent possible and practical. The index funds mentioned above provide managers with one alternative.

Before deciding that these tasks may be all that is left to do in the portfolio management process in the face of an efficient market, we should examine some evidence that suggests possibilities for investors interested in selecting stocks. This evidence is in contrast with that discussed thus far and constitutes a good conclusion for our discussion by indicating that, regardless of how persuasive the case for market efficiency is, debate of this issue is likely to persist.

EVIDENCE OF MARKET ANOMALIES

Market Anomalies
Techniques or strategies that appear to be contrary to an efficient market.

Having considered the type of evidence supporting market efficiency, we now can appropriately consider some **market anomalies**. By definition, an anomaly is an exception to a rule, or model. In other words, the results from these anomalies are in contrast to what would be expected in a totally efficient market, and they cannot be easily explained away.

We will examine several anomalies that have generated much attention and have yet to be satisfactorily explained. However, investors must be cautious in viewing any of these anomalies as a stock selection device guaranteed to outperform the market. There is no such guarantee because empirical tests of these anomalies may not approximate actual trading strategies that would be followed by investors. Furthermore, if anomalies exist and can be identified, investors should still hold a portfolio of stocks rather than concentrating on just a few identified by one of these methods. As we saw in Chapter 8, diversification is crucial for all investors.

REAL-WORLD RETURNS

Indexing Catching on with Fund Managers

For years, Barbara Palk was a lonely missionary for passive money management, preaching the gospel of indexation as vice-chairwoman of **Toronto-Dominion Bank**'s asset management arm.

In 1991, Ms. Palk began extolling the wisdom of buying an entire index — the TSE 300, ScotiaMcLeod's universe of bonds or Morgan Stanley's world of foreign equities — rather than trying to outguess the market. Armed with charts that showed this approach would yield better-than-average returns with far lower fees, Ms. Palk began to pick up clients. TD Quantitative Capital, the bank's passive management arm, finished 1991 with $400-million in assets.

As recently as four years ago, Ms. Palk could still count the converted on her fingers and toes — assets had grown to $2.5-billion. But since 1995, a whole lot of Canadian pension plan sponsors have got religious when it comes to passive investing.

A recent study by **Greenwich Associates** shows that four years ago, just 9 per cent of Canadian pension funds took a passive approach to any of their domestic equity holdings. Last year, 21 per cent were doing so.

The same trend applies to the bond market. In 1995, 5 per cent of funds were indexing at least part of their Canadian-bought indexes. Last year, 17 per cent of funds were doing it.

Statisticians won't be surprised by Ms. Palk's progress: They see the money management industry as a classic example of regression to the mean.

In simple English, Greenwich Associates partner John Webster summed up the Catch-22 of fund management this way: "With more and more very able, intelligent, hard-working people, using more and more sophisticated technology, doing everything in their power to beat the market, it is becoming more and more difficult to do so."

If pension plans can't beat the index, they might as well buy it. Over the past four years, a flood of passive money has found a home at Ms. Palk's firm. Recent big-ticket wins include getting the mandate for the Canada Pension Plan's domestic equities.

At the end of last year, TD Quantitative Capital's assets were up to $22.8-billion. Its chief competitors are international players — Barclays Global Investors Canada, which has $16.2-billion in assets, and State Street Global Advisors at $15-billion.

There's every indication that the flood will pick up strength. Lea Hansen, a Toronto-based principal in Greenwich Associates, said an additional 50 pension plans will start using some form of indexation this year.

Ms. Palk agrees. She's still hitting the road to sell pension plan sponsors on TD Quantitative Capital, but these days, she doesn't have to explain what an index is quite as often. Ms. Palk said: "The momentum towards passive investing continues to be very strong in domestic, US, and international markets."

Fees remain a compelling argument — at a minimum, a passive manager is likely to be one-third the price of an active fund manager.

And Ms. Hansen noted that the Canadian market is moving to passive investing despite the fact that fees in this country are relatively high, compared with what our neighbours in the United States pay.

Passive managers are being paid 10 to 12 basis points for building a Canadian equity index fund — there are 100 basis points in a percentage point. In contrast, a US fund manager would likely earn less than five basis points.

Source: "Indexing Catching on with Fund Managers," The Globe and Mail / Report on Business, *March 9, 1999, p. C1. Reprinted with permission from* The Globe and Mail.

Persistence in Stock Returns

The short-term persistence in stock returns is a pattern in historical stock returns that has received a great deal of attention in finance literature in recent years. Several recent studies have documented the success attainable by using momentum (or relative strength) indicators. The evidence suggests that stocks that have been top performers over the past six to 12 months will continue to provide superior investment performance in the subsequent six to 12 months. While these results may be surprising to financial economists, it substantiates an old market motto: "the trend is your friend." These sentiments were echoed recently by John Silva, chief economist at Kemper Financial Services of Chicago, who stated "financial markets are driven by expectations and not the real world." Mr. Silva went on to note that North American traders are momentum players.[28]

There is a substantial amount of supporting empirical evidence for the success of momentum trading strategies. One of the most commonly cited studies was performed by Jegadeesh and Titman in 1993, who examined the returns of portfolios formed by ranking stocks based on their past three to 12 month returns.[29] They demonstrated that buying the top-performing decile of NYSE and AMEX stocks and selling the bottom-performing decile of stocks produces very significant positive abnormal returns. It is interesting to note that the persistence in short-term (six to 12 months) returns contrasts sharply with the longer-term (three to five years) reversals in return performance documented by DeBondt and Thaler.

Foerster, Prihar, and Schmitz, as well as Cleary and Inglis show that a similar pattern exists in Canadian stock returns.[30] The Cleary and Inglis results, which cover the 1978–90 period, are depicted graphically in Figure 10-5. In this diagram, the line for the "winner" portfolio represents the wealth that would have been accumulated over their sample period by investing in a portfolio of stocks that displayed the best return performance over the previous 12-month period. The other line represents the cumulative wealth that would have been achieved by investing in the TSE 300 Index, which is well below that for the winner portfolio. Cleary and Inglis also demonstrate that the abnormal returns generated from momentum trading cannot be accounted for by transactions costs, size effects, or underlying risk characteristics. Finally, Rouwenhorst demonstrates that momentum performs well in 12 other international markets.[31]

Earnings Announcements

The adjustment of stock prices to earnings announcements has been studied in several papers, opening up some interesting questions and possibilities. The information found in such announcements does affect stock prices, as it should. Two questions need to be answered:

1. How much of the earnings announcement is new information, and how much has been anticipated by the market. In other words, how much of the announcement is a "surprise"?

[28] Bud Jorgensen, "Avoiding Shoals as the Tide Turns," *Financial Post*, Thursday, October 13, 1995, p. 13.

[29] N. Jegadeesh and S. Titman, "Returns to Buying Winners and Selling Losers: Implications for Stock Market Efficiency," *Journal of Finance* 48 (March 1993), pp. 65–91.

[30] S. Foerster, A. Prihar, and J. Schmitz, "Back to the Future: Price Momentum Models and How They Beat the Canadian Equity Markets," *Canadian Investment Review* 7 (Winter 1994/95), pp.9–13; S. Cleary and M. Inglis, "Momentum in Canadian Stock Returns," *Canadian Journal of Administrative Sciences* 15 (September 1998), pp. 279–291.

[31] K.G. Rouwenhorst, "International Momentum Strategies," *Journal of Finance* 53 (February 1998), pp. 267–284.

2. How quickly is the "surprise" portion of the announcement reflected in the price of the stock? Is it immediate, as would be expected in an efficient market, or is there a lag in the adjustment process? If a lag occurs, investors have a chance to realize excess returns by quickly acting on the publicly available earnings announcements.

To assess the earnings announcement issue properly, we must separate a particular announcement into *expected* and *unexpected* parts. The expected part is that portion anticipated by investors by the time the announcement is made and that requires no adjustment in stock prices. The unexpected part is unanticipated by investors and requires a price adjustment.

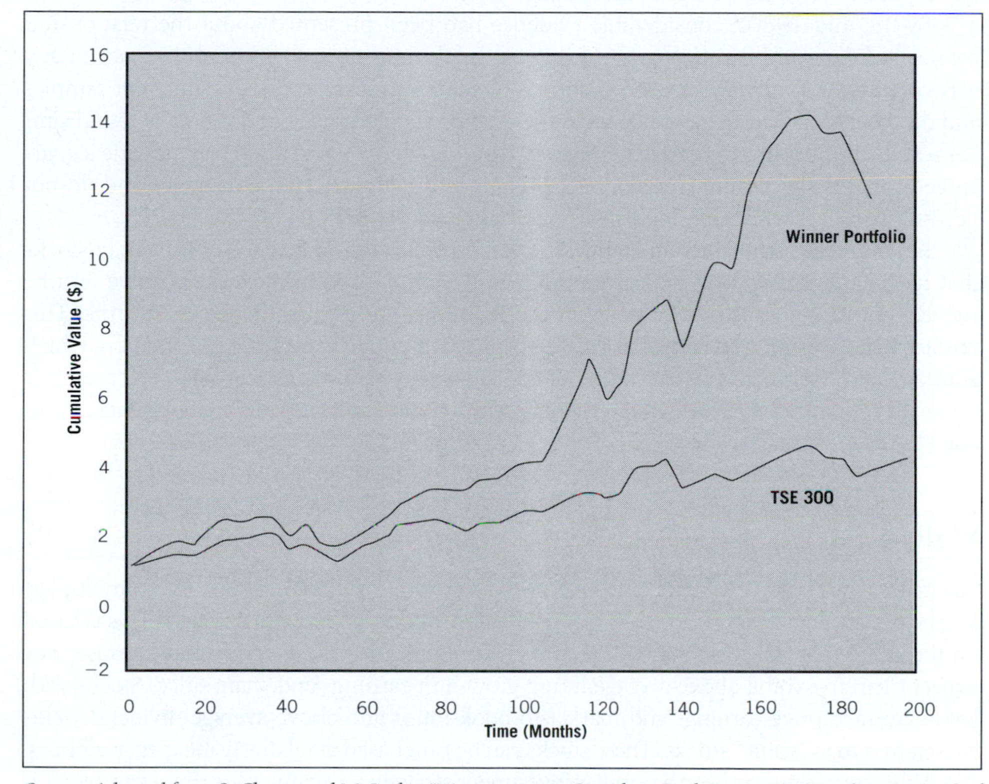

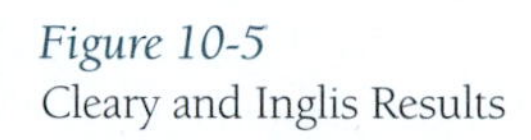
Figure 10-5
Cleary and Inglis Results

Source: Adapted from S. Cleary and M. Inglis, "Momemtum in Canadian Stock Returns," Canadian Journal of Administrative Sciences *15 (September 1998), p. 282. Reproduced by permission of the* Canadian Journal of Administrative Sciences.

Latané, Tuttle, and Jones and many subsequent studies have confirmed that earnings announcements are correlated with subsequent short-term price movements.[32] These findings indicate a lag in the adjustment of stock prices to the information in these reports. In 1974, Latané, Jones, and Rieke investigated the earnings surprises in quarterly earnings data.[33] They devised a method for estimating the unexpected part of the earnings announcement, which is commonly referred to as the "earnings surprise." They hypothesized that companies with high (low) unexpected earnings would have a positive (negative) price response.

[32] H. A. Latané, D. L. Tuttle, and C. P. Jones, "E/P Ratios vs. Changes in Earnings in Forecasting Future Price Changes," *Financial Analysts Journal* 25 (January–February 1969), pp. 117–120, 123.

[33] For a discussion of much of this literature, see O. Joy and C. P. Jones, "Earnings Reports and Market Efficiencies: An Analysis of Contrary Evidence," *Journal of Financial Research* 2 (Spring 1979), pp. 51–64.

Latané and Jones have documented the performance of earnings surprises in a series of papers.[34] These surprises were shown to have a definite relationship with subsequent excess holding period returns. Companies displaying the largest positive earnings surprises had superior subsequent performance, while poor subsequent performance was displayed by companies with low or negative earnings surprises. The studies also showed that while a substantial adjustment to the forthcoming earnings announcements occurs before the actual announcement, there is also a substantial adjustment after the announcement. This is the unexplained part of the earnings surprise puzzle. In an efficient market, prices should adjust quickly to earnings rather than with a lag.

By the mid-1980s, considerable evidence had been presented about the relationship between unexpected earnings and subsequent stock returns, and although it is not in any way conclusive, it cannot be easily dismissed. Different researchers, using different samples and different techniques, have examined the unexpected earnings issue and have found similar results. It must be emphasized, however, that these techniques in no way provide a guarantee of major success for investors. The relationships discussed are averages and do not necessarily reflect what any single investor would experience.

In two recent studies, Sean Hennessey demonstrates that portfolios of Canadian stocks that have experienced positive earnings forecast revisions produce excess positive returns subsequent to the revision.[35] The larger the revisions, the greater the excess returns. This implies that investors can earn abnormal returns using publicly available information, which contradicts the semi-strong form of the EMH. Hennessey also shows that this effect is greater for small capitalization firms, which is consistent with less information being publicly available for these stocks.

Value Stocks

Stocks that carry above-average price-earnings (P/E) ratios, market-to-book (M/B) multiples, and below-average dividend yields (DY) are often referred to as "growth" stocks.[36] This is based on the belief that investors are willing to pay a premium for these companies because they expect them to exhibit above-average future growth in earnings and share price. Stocks with below-average price-earnings and market-to-book ratios and above-average dividend yields are referred to as "value" stocks. These stocks can be purchased at relatively inexpensive prices.

Value investing has been a popular investment strategy for many years. For example, this approach was advocated by Graham and Dodd in their 1934 book *Security Analysis*, which remains the cornerstone of investment policy for several investment professionals to this day. They argued that future growth was difficult to predict; therefore, investors should concern themselves with demonstrated performance. Based on this philosophy, they demonstrate how analysts can identify bargain stocks by analyzing company financial statements.[37]

---

[34] For example: C. P. Jones, R. J. Rendleman, and H. A. Latané, "Stock Returns and SUEs during the 1970s," *Journal of Portfolio Management* 10 (Winter 1984), pp. 18–22.

[35] S. Hennessey, "Can Active Managers Profit from Earnings Forecast Revisions?" *Canadian Investment Review* 6 (Spring 1993), pp. 39–45; S. Hennessey, "Get the Drift," *Canadian Investment Review* 8 (Winter 1995/96), pp. 23–28.

[36] Notice that market price is the numerator in both the P/E and M/B multiples, but is the denominator in dividend yield, defined as dividend per share divided by market price per share. Hence, all else being equal, higher market prices lead to higher P/E and M/B ratios and lower dividend yields.

[37] Benjamin Graham and David L. Dodd, *Security Analysis: Principles and Technique* (New York: McGraw-Hill, 1934).

Several academic studies have shown that value stocks tend to outperform growth stocks. For example, Basu, Ball, and Fama and French find that stocks with low P/E ratios outperform those with high P/E multiples.[38] Similarly, Rosenberg, Reid, and Lanstein, as well as Fama and French find that stocks with low M/B values outperform those with high M/B values.[39] Fama and French demonstrate that this relationship exists for stock portfolios of various sizes (i.e., small-, medium- and large cap stocks). Fama and French and Lakonishok, Shleifer, and Vishny also demonstrate that stocks with low price-to-cash flow ratios display superior investment performance.[40] Finally, Blume and Keim find that stocks with high dividend yields outperform stocks with low dividend yields.[41]

Bourgeois and Lussier demonstrate that in Canada, low P/E stocks outperform high P/E stocks and the market as a whole on a risk-adjusted basis, while Chan, Hamao, and Lakonishok find that most of these value measures produce excess returns in the Japanese market.[42] Capaul, Rowley, and Sharpe, as well as Fama and French demonstrate that the book-to-price effect is strong within other international markets.[43] Lakonishok, Shleifer, and Vishny combine several of the value measures and find even higher average performance.

This evidence seems to contradict the EMH, unless the superior performance of the value portfolios is attributable to greater associated risk levels. However, the results of Fama and French suggest this is not the case. In fact, the exact opposite result arises — value portfolios appear to be less risky than the growth portfolios according to market betas. A recent study by Bauman and Miller also documents superior performance by value stock portfolios. In addition, their results indicate that the standard deviation of these portfolios is slightly lower than that of the growth portfolios.[44] All of this suggests that value investing is no riskier than growth investing, according to traditional risk measures. These results have lead many to adopt extreme views about market efficiency. For example, Haugen argues that the true risk–return relationship is negative — lower risk stocks actually provide higher returns, while riskier stocks provide lower returns.[45]

---

[38] S. Basu, "The Investment Performance of Common Stocks in Relation to Their Price-Earnings Ratios: A Test of the Efficient Market Hypothesis," *Journal of Finance* 32 (June 1977), pp. 663–682; S. Basu, "The Relationship Between Earnings' Yield, Market Value and Return for NYSE Common Stocks: Further Evidence," *Journal of Financial Economics* 12 (June 1983), pp. 129–156; R. Ball, "Anomalies in Relationships Between Securities' Yields and Yield Surrogates," *Journal of Financial Economics* 6 (June–Sept 1978), pp. 103–126; E. Fama and K. French, "The Cross Section of Expected Stock Returns," *Journal of Finance* 47 (June 1992), pp. 427–465.

[39] B. Rosenberg, K. Reid, and R. Lanstein, "Persuasive Evidence of Market Inefficiency," *Journal of Portfolio Management* 11 (Spring 1985), pp. 9–16.

[40] J. Lakonishok, A. Shleifer, and R. Vishny, "Contrarian Investment, Extrapolation and Risk," *Journal of Finance* 49 (December 1994), pp. 1541–1578.

[41] M. Blume, "The Relative Efficiency of Various Portfolios: Some Further Evidence," *Journal of Finance* 35 (May 1980), pp. 269–281; D. Keim, "Dividend Yields and Stock Returns: Implications of Abnormal January Returns," *Journal of Financial Economics* 14 (September 1985), pp. 473–489.

[42] J. Bourgeois and J. Lussier, "P/Es and Performance in the Canadian Market," *Canadian Investment Review* 7 (Spring 1994), pp. 33–39; L. Chan, Y. Hamao, and J. Lakonishok, "Fundamentals and Stock Returns in Japan," *Journal of Finance* 46 (December 1991), pp. 1739–1764.

[43] C. Capaul, I. Rowley, and William Sharpe, "International Value and Growth Stock Returns," *Financial Analysts Journal* 49 (Jan–Feb 1993), pp. 27–36; Eugene Fama and Kenneth French, "Value Versus Growth: The International Evidence," *Journal of Finance* 53(December 1998), pp. 1975–1999.

[44] S. Bauman and R. Miller, "Investor Expectations and the Performance of Value versus Growth Stocks," *The Journal of Portfolio Management* 23 (Spring 1997), pp. 57–68.

[45] R. Haugen, *The New Finance: The Case Against Market Efficiency* (Toronto: Prentice Hall, 1995).

These observations seem to contradict the notion of market efficiency at the semi-strong level since all of the ratios above are publicly available and should not allow investors to obtain abnormal profits through their use. It is even more surprising that the pattern has not disappeared in response to its widespread recognition by the investment community, particularly in recent years. In other words, if investors recognize this pattern and create excess demand for value stocks, their prices will increase, and the excess returns will disappear. Similarly, one would expect investors to reduce demand for growth stocks, which would exert downward pressure on their prices, resulting in increased returns. However, these patterns have persisted for several years, despite their widespread recognition.

In fact, several well-known commentators continue to advocate investing in low P/E stocks. For example, David Dreman recommends that investors ignore professional investment advice and select stocks with low P/E ratios. His hypothesis is that low P/E stocks may currently be unwanted, but if they have strong finances, high yields, and good earnings records, they almost always do well eventually.

Investors need to be careful when following the low P/E strategy. Although a diversified portfolio, as always, is critical, rigid adherence to a low P/E strategy could result in an inadequately diversified portfolio. Dreman has indicated that he takes a minimum of 25 stocks in 15 to 18 industries and that "most [low P/E stocks] have significant problems or very good reasons why you don't want to own them."[46] Only about one in ten candidates on the basis of low P/E passes his additional screens, such as dividend yields higher than average and accelerating earnings growth over the past. Dreman also suggests an emphasis on large stocks as opposed to small-company stocks.

According to some evidence, the low P/E strategy does well neither in turbulent markets nor in periods of slow economic growth. However, these stocks may perform well in a "full-blown" bear market because of their higher dividend yields. Overall, the low P/E strategy should be viewed as a long-run strategy, to be pursued through both good and bad markets.

The Size Effect

Size Effect
The observed tendency for smaller firms to have higher stock returns than large firms.

The **size effect** is one of the most prominent anomalies documented in the finance literature. The firm size effect literature blossomed in the early 1980s with notable contributions by Banz, Reinganum, and Keim.[47] These authors found that small market capitalization stocks tended to outperform large capitalization stocks, even after adjusting for CAPM market risk. Keim found that 50 per cent of the firm size effect occurs in January. Fama and French confirmed the persistence of this pattern for US stocks over the 1963–90 period.

Tinic, Barone-Adesi, and West, as well as Foerster and Porter confirmed the existence of a size effect for Canadian stock returns. Similar to US studies, market betas could not account for the returns, and a large portion of the return accrued during the month of January. Foerster and Porter also demonstrated that bid-ask spreads, which are higher for smaller stocks, could not account for the abnormal returns. They suggest that "when trading on the TSE, the

[46] David Dreman, "Emotion Versus Logic," *Forbes*, November 7, 1994, p. 351.

[47] R. Banz, "The Relationship Between Return and Market Value of Common Stocks," *Journal of Financial Economics* 9 (March 1981), pp. 3–18; M. Reinganum, "Misspecification of Capital Asset Pricing: Empirical Anomalies Based on Earnings Yields and Market Values," *Journal of Financial Economics* 9 (March 1981), pp. 19–46; D. Keim, " Size-Related Anomalies and Stock Return Seasonality," *Journal of Financial Economics* 12 (June 1983), pp. 13–32.

small-firm strategy may be a viable strategy for increasing portfolio returns without an offsetting increase in risk."[48]

Seasonality in Stock Returns

Evidence of seasonal patterns in stock returns has grown out of studies of the size anomaly explained in the previous section. Keim studied the month-to-month stability of the size effect for all NYSE and AMEX firms with data for 1963–79.[49] His findings supported the existence of a significant size effect (a 30.5 per cent small-size premium). However, roughly half of this size effect occurred in January, and more than half of the excess January returns occurred during the first five trading days of that month. The first trading day of the year showed a high small-firm premium for every year of the period studied. The strong performance in January by small-company stocks has become known as the **January effect**.[50]

January Effect
The observed tendency for returns of small-cap stocks to be higher in January than in other months.

The January effect is often referred to as the "small firm in January effect" because it is most prevalent for the returns of small-cap stocks. For example, the average US monthly return for January during the 1941–81 period was 1.34 per cent for the S&P 500 Index versus an average monthly return of 0.92 per cent for the remaining 11 months. During the same period, the average January return was 8.06 per cent for the smallest quintile of NYSE stocks, versus 0.88 per cent for the other 11 months. During the 1982–90 period, the average January return was 3.20 per cent for the S&P 500 Index versus 1.23 per cent for the other 11 months, while the January return for the smallest NYSE quintile was 5.32 per cent versus 0.17 per cent for the remaining 11 months.

Canadian studies have supported the existence of a January effect for Canadian stock returns.[51] For example, Vijay Jog showed that the average January return for the TSE 300 over the 1972–86 period was 3.13 per cent, versus an average monthly return of 0.82 per cent for the other 11 months over the same time period. The difference in returns was even more pronounced for smaller stocks.

There are several other seasonal effects including the day-of-the-week effect, which was first identified by Cross in the US.[52] He found the average Monday return to be negative and significantly different from the average returns for the other four days, which were all positive. Jaffe and Westerfield have confirmed these results for several international markets, including Canada.[53] Ariel identified a day-of-the-month effect in US stock returns, where

[48] S. Tinic, G. Barone-Adesi, and R. West, "Seasonality in Canadian Stock Prices: A Test of the Tax-Loss-Selling Hypothesis," *Journal of Financial and Quantitative Analysis* 22 (March 1987), pp. 51–63; S. Foerster and D. Porter, "Calender and Size-Based Anomalies in Canadian Stock Returns," In Michael Robinson and Brian Smith, eds., *Canadian Capital Markets* (London, ON: Western School of Business, 1993), pp. 133–140.

[49] Donald B. Keim, "Size-Related Anomalies and Stock Return Seasonality," *Journal of Financial Economics* 12 (June 1983), pp. 13–32.

[50] See Richard Roll, "Vas ist das? The Turn of the Year Effect and the Return Premia of Small Firms," *The Journal of Portfolio Management* 9 (Winter 1983), pp. 18–28. Roll also found a turn-of-the-year effect with abnormal returns for small firms on the last trading day in December.

[51] Tinic et al (1987); V. Jog, "Stock Pricing Anomalies: Canadian Experience," *Canadian Investment Review*, vol 1 (1988), pp. 55–62.

[52] F. Cross, "Price Movements on Fridays and Mondays," *Financial Analysts Journal* 29 (Nov–Dec 1973), pp. 67–69.

[53] J. Jaffe and R. Westerfield, "The Week-End Effect in Common Stock Returns: International Evidence," *Journal of Finance* 40 (June 1985), pp. 433–454.

returns tend to be higher on the last trading day of each month.[54] The Canadian results of Jog and Riding support the existence of a similar pattern in Canadian stock returns.[55]

The Value Line Ranking System

The Value Line Investment Survey is the largest, and perhaps best known, investment advisory service in the world. Value Line ranks each of the roughly 1,700 stocks it covers from 1 (best) to 5 (worst) as to its "timeliness" — probable relative price performance within the next 12 months. These timeliness ranks, updated weekly, have been available since 1965.

The performance of the five rankings categories has been very strong, based on Value Line's calculations. For example, the complete record of Value Line rankings for timeliness from 1965 shows that the ranking system clearly discriminates in a monotonic order. Without allowing for changes in ranks (equal amounts are invested in each stock in each grouping at the beginning of the year and held for 12 months without allowing for subsequent changes in ranking), Group 3 stocks performed in an average manner (using the average of the stocks covered by Value Line), whereas Groups 1 and 2 performed much better than either the average or the two market measures reported. On the other hand, short-selling Groups 4 and 5 would have been unsuccessful. Allowing for changes in ranks produced spectacular results. However, such a procedure would have resulted in a prohibitively high portfolio turnover rate.

According to available evidence, for the period from mid-1980 through 1993, Group 1 stocks showed an annualized return of 19.3 per cent. According to Mark Hulbert, who tracks the performance of investment letters for his *Hulbert Financial Digest*, this made Value Line the best overall performer for this period of all the investment letters tracked.

The Value Line Investment Survey now regularly reports a comparison of the performance of its Group 1 stocks with four other strategies: low-P/E, low-cap (small-size), low-price/book value, and low-price/sales. These results provide some information on two of the strategies discussed earlier — low-P/E and the size-effect — as well as two valuation techniques that are discussed in Chapter 13 — price/book value and price/sales.

Several studies of the success of Value Line's rankings have been made. It appears that the rankings, and changes in the rankings, do contain useful information. However, there is evidence that the market adjusts quickly to this information (one or two trading days following the Friday release) and that true transaction costs can negate much of the price changes that occur as a result of adjustments to this information.[56]

Other Anomalies

The above list of anomalies is not exhaustive. Many others have been reported and discussed. Because it is consistent with the common-sense notion that market efficiency is most likely

[54] R. Ariel, "A Monthly Effect in Stock Returns," *Journal of Financial Economics* 18 (March 1987), pp. 161–174.

[55] V. Jog and A. Riding, "The Month-End Effect in Canadian Stock Prices: Some Anomalous Findings," *Canadian Journal of Administrative Sciences* 6 (December 1989), pp. 7–17.

[56] S. Stickel, "The Effect of Value Line Investment Survey Changes on Common Stock Prices," *Journal of Financial Economics* 14 (March 1985), pp. 121–143. A good review that attempts to reconcile the various findings about Value Line can be found in G. Huberman and S. Kandel, "Market Efficiency and Value Line's Record," *Journal of Business* 63 (April 1990), pp. 187–216.

applied to larger, well-known stocks as opposed to all stocks, one interesting anomaly is the *neglected firm effect*. In this case, neglect means that few analysts follow the stock or that few institutions own it. The area of neglected stocks would appear to be a good opportunity for small investors interested in security analysis and stock selection.

SOME CONCLUSIONS ABOUT MARKET EFFICIENCY

Given all of the evidence about market efficiency discussed previously — the studies supporting it as well as the anomalies — what conclusions can be drawn? In truth, no definitive conclusion about market efficiency can be stated. The evidence in support of market efficiency is persuasive because of the large amount of research done over many years by numerous investigators. Nevertheless, the evidence of anomalies has yet to be explained satisfactorily. Moreover, many technicians and fundamentalists are convinced that they can outperform the market, or at least provide more benefits than cost. Paradoxically, this belief helps to make the market efficient because it implies there will be many analysts, both amateur and professional, simultaneously scrutinizing the factors that affect any given stock price.

> **INVESTING tip**
>
> The paradox of efficient markets and active investors is that investors, in an attempt to uncover and use important information about security prices, help to make the market efficient. In other words, in the course of searching out undervalued and overvalued stocks, investors discover information and act on it as quickly as possible. If the information is favourable, the discoverers will buy immediately, and if it is unfavourable, they will sell immediately. As investors scramble for information and attempt to be the first to act, they make the market more efficient. If enough of this activity occurs, all information will be reflected in prices. Thus, the fact that a number of investors do not believe in the EMH results in actions that help to make the market efficient.

In the final analysis, it is probably best to accept the idea that the market is quite efficient but not totally. Most of the research done to date suggests that information is received and acted on quickly, and generally the correct adjustments are made. In order to outperform the market, superior fundamental analysis must be accomplished. The fundamental analysis that is routinely done every day is already reflected in stock prices. The marginal value of one more investor performing the same calculations that have been done by other investors is zero. Until more evidence to the contrary is forthcoming, the benefits of technical analysis remain questionable at best.

Simon Keane has argued that investors must choose between a belief in operational efficiency and inefficiency.[57] In an operationally efficient market, some investors with the skill to detect a divergence between price and semi-strong value earn economic rents. For the majority of investors, however, such opportunities are not available. An operationally inefficient market, on the other hand, contains inefficiencies that the average investor can spot. The evidence to date suggests that investors face an operationally efficient market.

Some anomalies do seem to exist, and since the late 1970s the flow of research reporting on anomalies has accelerated. These anomalies require considerable work to document scientifically and do not represent a guarantee of investment riches. Although they do appear to offer opportunities to astute investors, the reasons why they exist remain unsettled. The quantity and quality of the research in this area has undermined the extreme view that the market is so perfectly efficient that no opportunities for excess returns could possibly exist.

[57] Simon Keane, "The Efficient Market Hypothesis on Trial," *Financial Analysts Journal* 42 (March–April 1986), pp. 58–63.

One difficult problem for those who believe in efficient markets is the crash of October 1987. The TSE 300 Composite Index lost over 11 per cent and the S&P 500 Index over 20 per cent in one day. Is it really reasonable to argue that investors, efficiently discounting information, decided in one day that the market should be valued some 20 per cent less? Not many people, including efficient market proponents, are comfortable making this argument.

In addition to the above challenges to the concept of market efficiency, mathematicians are helping a new kind of trader to justify the position that the market is not very efficient, using leading-edge ideas such as chaos theory, neural networks, and genetic algorithms.

The controversy about market efficiency remains, and every investor is faced with the choice between active and passive investment strategies or some combination of the two.

SUMMARY

This summary relates to the learning objectives provided on page 279.

1. **Explain the concept of efficient markets.**
   An efficient market is defined as one in which the prices of securities fully reflect all known information quickly and accurately. The conditions that guarantee an efficient market can be shown to hold to a large extent: many investors are competing, information is widely available and generated more or less randomly, and investors react quickly to this information.
2. **Describe the three forms of market efficiency — weak, semi-strong, and strong.**
   To assess market efficiency, three cumulative forms (or degrees) of efficiency are discussed: the weak, semi-strong, and strong form. The weak form involves market data, whereas the semi-strong and strong form involve the assimilation of all public and private information, respectively.
3. **Discuss the evidence regarding the Efficient Market Hypothesis.**
   The weak-form evidence generally supports the hypothesis. Many tests of semi-strong efficiency have been conducted, including stock splits, money supply changes, accounting changes, dividend announcements, and reactions to other announcements, among others. In addition, the performance of professional money managers as a whole has not been better than passive market benchmarks. Although all the studies do not agree, the majority support semi-strong efficiency. Strong-form evidence generally tests the ability of groups presumed to have "private" information to outperform the market. Insiders apparently are able to do well, although the decisions of the managers of mutual funds have not been found to add value. Most knowledgeable observers accept weak-form efficiency, reject strong-form efficiency, and feel that the market is, to a large degree, semi-strong efficient. This casts doubt on the value of both technical analysis and conventional fundamental analysis.
4. **State the implications of market efficiency for investors.**
   Although the EMH does not preclude investors from outperforming the market, it does suggest that this is quite difficult to accomplish and that the investor must do more than

the norm. Even if the market is efficient, money managers still have activities to perform, including diversifying the portfolio, choosing and maintaining some degree of risk, and assessing taxes and transaction costs.

5. **Outline major exceptions to the Efficient Market Hypothesis.**
Several major anomalies that have appeared over the last several years have yet to be satisfactorily explained. These anomalies, which would not be expected in a totally efficient market, include the following:
    1. *Persistence in stock returns*. Historical evidence indicates a recurring pattern in stock returns. In particular, stocks that have been top performers over the past six to 12 months will continue to provide superior investment performance in similar, subsequent periods.
    2. *Unexpected earnings*. The market appears to adjust a lag with earnings surprises contained in earnings announcements.
    3. *Value stocks*. Value stocks (with low P/E ratios, low market-to-book values, and high dividend yields) appear to outperform growth stocks (with high P/E ratios, high market-to-book values, and low dividend yields) over annual periods, even after adjustment for risk and size.
    4. *The size effect*. Small firms have been shown to outperform large firms, on a risk-adjusted basis, over a period of many years.
    5. *The January effect*. Much of the abnormal return for small firms occurs in the month of January.
    6. *Value Line's performance*. The Value Line rankings for timeliness have performed extremely well over time and appear to offer the average investor a chance to outperform the averages.

KEY TERMS

Abnormal return
Cumulative abnormal return (CAR)
Efficient market (EM)
Efficient Market Hypothesis (EMH)
Event study
January effect
Market anomalies
Market data
Semi-strong form
Size effect
Strong form
Weak form

ADDITIONAL RESOURCES

An interesting discussion of the efficient market hypothesis can be found in:

Burton, Malkiel. *A Random Walk Down Wall Street*. Fifth Edition. New York: W.W. Norton & Co., 1996.

An interesting argument against market efficiency can be found in:

Haugen, Robert. *The New Finance: The Case Against Market Efficiency*. Toronto: Prentice Hall, 1995.

REVIEW QUESTIONS

1. What is meant by an efficient market?
2. Why is a weak-form efficient market in direct opposition to technical analysis?
3. Distinguish between economic significance and statistical significance.
4. If the EMH is true, what are the implications for investors?
5. What types of events or information, other than those discussed in this chapter, could be used in semi-strong-form tests?
6. Do security analysts have a role in an efficient market?
7. What is meant by an operationally efficient market?
8. Describe the three forms of market efficiency.
9. What are the conditions for an efficient market? How closely are they met in reality?
10. What do semi-strong market efficiency tests attempt to test for?
11. Describe two different ways to test for weak-form efficiency.
12. Why could the performance of mutual fund managers be considered a test of semi-strong efficiency?
13. Describe the money management activities of a portfolio manager who believes that the market is efficient.
14. What are market anomalies? Describe four.
15. What is the relationship between earnings surprises and fundamental analysis?
16. What are the benefits to society of an efficient market?
17. If the market moves in an upward trend over a period of years, would this be inconsistent with weak-form efficiency?
18. Evaluate the following statement: "My mutual fund has outperformed the market for the last four years. How can the market be efficient?"
19. What are the necessary conditions for a scientific test of a trading rule?
20. Assume that you analyze the activities of specialists on the NYSE and find that they are able to realize consistently above-average rates of return. What form of the EMH are you testing?
21. How can data on corporate insiders be used to test both the semi-strong and the strong forms of the EMH?
22. Assume that the price of a stock remains constant from time period 0 to time period 1, at which time a significant piece of information about the stock becomes available. Draw a diagram that depicts the situation if

    a. the market is semi-strong efficient and

    b. there is a lag in the adjustment of the price to this information.
23. What would the slope of the demand curve be for stocks in a perfectly efficient market?
24. If all investors believe that the market is efficient, could that eventually lead to less efficiency in the market?

25. What are some possible explanations for the size anomaly?
26. An investment consulting firm has developed and marketed a sophisticated computerized stock trading program. It has been tested using stock market returns for the past 15 years and would have generated economically significant risk-adjusted excess returns after all transaction costs if it had been utilized during those 15 years. Is this consistent with the concept of market efficiency? Explain.

PREPARING FOR YOUR PROFESSIONAL EXAMS

Special Note to CSC Students

Ensure that you have read and understood the following topics:*
What is an efficient market?, pp. 280–285

**Reading these CSC-related topics should provide you with additional understanding of CSC material. However, it should not be seen as a substitute for reading the CSC textbook itself, which is the basis for the CSC exam questions.*

PAST CFA EXAM QUESTION

The following question was asked on the 1992 CFA Level I examination:

1. a. List and briefly define the three forms of the Efficient Market Hypothesis.
   b. Discuss the role of a portfolio manager in a perfectly efficient market.

CHAPTER 11

BOND YIELDS AND PRICES

LEARNING OBJECTIVES

After reading this chapter, you will be able to

1. Calculate the price of a bond.
2. Explain the bond valuation process.
3. Calculate major bond yield measures, including yield to maturity, yield to call, and horizon return.
4. Account for changes in bond prices.
5. Explain and apply the concept of duration.

CHAPTER PREVIEW

This chapter builds on the background developed in Part I. Having introduced the characteristics of bonds in Chapter 2, we can now examine bond yields and prices. In addition to calculating bond price, in this chapter we lay out the basic principles of valuation, which we will use again when considering other investing alternatives, particularly common stocks (Chapter 13). As part of valuation, you will learn to calculate major bond yield measures such as yield to maturity, yield to call, and horizon return. You will also learn about the factors that affect bond price changes, notably changes in interest rates. Finally, we discuss duration, a concept used by investors to deal with the effect of yield changes.

BOND PRICES

In addition to the total return concept considered in Chapter 6, which is applicable to any security, bond investors must also understand specific measures of bond yields. It is traditional in the bond markets to use various yield measures and to quote potential returns to investors on the basis of these measures. However, these gauges can mislead unwary investors who fail to understand the basis on which they are constructed. Investors must understand that bond yields shown daily in sources such as *The Globe and Mail* and the *National Post* do not necessarily represent the true yield an investor will achieve when he or she buys bonds in the marketplace and holds them to maturity.

The Valuation Principle

What determines the price of a security? The answer is that a security's estimated value determines the price that investors place on it in the open market.

Intrinsic Value The estimated value of a security.

A security's **intrinsic value**, or estimated value, is the present value of the expected cash flows from that asset. Any security purchased is expected to provide one or more cash flows some time in the future. These could be periodic, such as interest or dividends, or simply a final price or redemption value, or a combination of these. Since these cash flows occur in the future, they must be discounted at an appropriate rate to determine their present value. The sum of these discounted cash flows is the estimated intrinsic value of the asset. Calculating that value, therefore, requires the use of present value techniques. Equation 11-1 expresses the concept:

(11-1)

$$\text{Value}_{t=0} = \sum_{t=1}^{n} \frac{\text{Cash flow (at time } t)}{(1 + k)^t}$$

where

$\text{Value}_{t=0}$ = the value of the asset now (time period 0)

Cash flow (at time t) = the future cash flow (at time t) that results from ownership of the asset

k = the appropriate discount rate or rate of return required by an investor for an investment of this type

n = number of periods over which the cash flows are expected

To solve Equation 11-1 and derive the intrinsic value of a security, it is necessary to determine the following:

1. The *expected cash flows* from the security. This includes the size and type of cash flows, such as dividends, interest, face value expected to be received at maturity, or the expected price of the security at some point in the future.
2. The *timing* of the expected cash flows. Since the returns to be generated from a security occur at various times in the future, they must be properly documented for discounting back to time period 0 (today). Money has a time value, and the timing of future cash flows significantly affects the value of the asset today.
3. The *discount rate* or required rate of return demanded by investors will reflect the time value of money and the risk of the security. It is an opportunity cost, representing the rate foregone by an investor in the next best alternative investment with comparable risk.

Bond Valuation

The intrinsic value of any asset is calculated from the present value of its expected cash flows. This is true for short-term instruments such as T-bills, as well as for long-term ones such as bonds or common stocks. The CSC Notes box at the end of this chapter discusses the valuation of T-bills, and we focus here on the valuation of traditional bonds.

The interest payments (coupons) and the principal repayment for bonds are known in advance — coupons are paid at regular intervals (either annually or semi-annually) and the principal repayment occurs at the maturity date. The coupons are all for the same amount, which is determined by multiplying the coupon rate (which is stated on an annual basis) by the maturity value of the bond (MV). For example, a bond with a coupon rate of 10 per cent and a maturity value of $1,000 would pay annual coupons of $100 ($50 if paid semi-annually). Hence, the fundamental value of a bond is determined by discounting these future payments from the issuer at an appropriate required yield, *r*, for the issue. Equation 11-2 is used to solve for the value of a coupon bond.[1]

$$P = \sum_{t=1}^{n} \frac{C_t}{(1 + r)^t} + \frac{MV}{(1 + r)^n} \quad \textbf{(11-2)}$$

where

P = the price of the bond today (time period 0)

C = the regular coupons or interest payments (paid annually or semi-annually)

MV = the maturity value (or par value) of the bond

n = the number of periods to maturity of the bond (the periods may be for a full year or for six months, depending on payment interval)

r = the appropriate period discount rate or market yield (which may be an annual or semi-annual rate depending on how frequently coupons are paid)

[1] This formulation is nothing new; John Burr Williams stated it in a book in 1938. See J. B. Williams, *The Theory of Investment Value* (Cambridge, MA: Harvard University Press, 1938).

Finance students should immediately realize that the stream of interest income to be received in the form of coupons represents an annuity. This is because it represents a series of cash flows that provide the same payment at the same interval (every year or six months), and we are determining the present value of these cash flows using the same discount rate. Recalling some introductory mathematics of finance concepts, we can use the present value annuity (PVA) factor to determine the present value of any cash stream that represents an annuity. Combining this result with the fact that $\frac{1}{(1+r)^n}$ is generally referred to as the discount or present value factor for a discount rate of r for n periods ($PV_{r,n}$), we can rewrite Equation 11-2 as

$$P = C \times (PVA_{r,n}) + MV \times (PV_{r,n}) \tag{11-3}$$

where

$PVA_{r,n}$ = the present value annuity factor for an n period annuity using a discount rate of r

$PV_{r,n}$ = the present value or discount factor for discounting an amount to be received at time n, using a discount rate of r

For expositional purposes, we will illustrate the calculation of bond prices by referring to the PV and PVA tables at the end of the textbook; in actuality, a calculator or computer is used. The present value process for a typical coupon-bearing bond involves three steps, given the dollar coupon on the bond, the face value, and the current market yield applicable to a particular bond:

1. Using the present value of an annuity (PVA) table (Table A-4 in the appendix at the back of the book), determine the present value of the coupons (interest payments).
2. Using the present value (PV) table (Table A-2 in the appendix at the back of the book), determine the present value of the maturity (par) value of the bond; for our purposes, the maturity value will usually be $1,000.
3. Add the present values determined in steps 1 and 2 together.

EXAMPLE: CALCULATING BOND PRICES — ANNUAL COUPONS

To determine the price of a three-year bond with a maturity value of $1,000 that paid annual coupons at a rate of 10 per cent when the appropriate discount rate was 12 per cent, we would input the following information into Equation 11-3: C = $100; MV = $1,000; $n = 3$; and $r = 12$ per cent.

$$P = C \times (PVA_{r,n}) + MV \times (PV_{r,n}) = \$100 \times (PVA_{12\%,3}) + \$1{,}000 \times (PV_{12\%,3})$$

$$= \$100 \times (2.402) + \$1{,}000 \times (0.712) = \$240.20 + \$712.00 = \$952.20$$

Notice that these bonds sell below their maturity value (at a discount from par), which is always the case when the discount rate exceeds the stated coupon rate. We will talk about this result in greater detail later in this chapter.

Generally bonds pay interest semi-annually rather than annually, so the discount rate is calculated by dividing the annual discount rate by two, while the number of semi-annual periods to maturity is determined by multiplying the number of years to maturity by two.

EXAMPLE: CALCULATING BOND PRICES — SEMI-ANNUAL COUPONS

Assume the three-year bond in the example above paid semi-annual coupons instead of annual ones and that all the other information above remained the same. To determine its value we would input the following information into Equation 11-3: C = \$50; $n = 6$; and $r = 6$ per cent.

$$P = \$50 \times (PVA_{6\%,6}) + \$1{,}000 \times (PV_{6\%,6})$$

$$= \$50 \times (4.917) + \$1{,}000 \times (0.705) = \$245.85 + \$705.00 = \$950.85$$

Thus, while we can see the results are similar, they do differ slightly, and it is essential to use the correct equation to obtain the correct answer.

While the PV and PVA factors for various discount rates and periods are found in Appendices A-2 and A-4 at the end of the book, it is often necessary to use the equations provided at the top of these appendices, which are given below:

$$PV = \frac{1}{(1+r)^n} \text{ and,}$$

$$PVA_{r,n} = \frac{1 - \dfrac{1}{(1+r)^n}}{r}$$

EXAMPLE: CALCULATING BOND PRICES

A bond with 10 years to maturity has a 8 per cent coupon rate, with coupons being paid semi-annually. If it maturity value is \$1,000 and the appropriate discount rate is 6.52 per cent, we can determine it value as follows:

$$P = \$40 \times (PVA_{3.26\%,20}) + \$1{,}000 \times (PV_{3.26\%,20}) = \$40 \times \left[\frac{1 - \dfrac{1}{(1.0326)^{20}}}{0326}\right] + \frac{\$1{,}000}{(1+.0326)^{20}}$$

$$= \$40 \times (14.526) + \frac{\$1{,}000}{(1.900)} = \$581.04 + \$526.32 = \$1{,}107.36$$

Notice that these bonds sell above their maturity value (at a premium over par), which is always the case when the discount rate is less than the stated coupon rate. As with the example above in which we calculated the price for a three-year bond that paid annual coupons, we defer our discussion of this result until later.

Notice that for zero-coupon bonds, the first term of Equation 11-2 is zero, so we are left with the following equation that can be used to determine the price of these bonds:

(11-4)
$$P = \frac{MV}{(1 + r)^n}$$

In the examples above, the bonds are valued, as are any other assets, on the basis of their future stream of expected benefits (cash flows), using an appropriate market yield. Since the numerator is always specified for coupon-bearing bonds at the time of issue, the only problem in valuing a typical bond is to determine the denominator or discount rate. The appropriate discount rate is the bond's required yield.

The required yield, r, in Equations 11-3 and 11-4 is specific for each particular bond. It is the current market rate being earned by investors on comparable bonds with the same maturity and the same credit quality. (In other words, it is an opportunity cost.) Thus, market interest rates are incorporated directly into the discount rate used to establish the fundamental value of a bond.

Since market interest rates fluctuate constantly, required yields do also. When calculating a bond price it is customary to use the yield to maturity (YTM), which is discussed in the next section, as the appropriate discount rate. If the YTM is used, we can restate Equation 11-3 as

(11-5)
$$P = C \times (PVA_{YTM,n}) + MV \times (PV_{YTM,n})$$

The Real-World Returns box below contains a list of bond quotations reported daily in the *The Globe and Mail / Report on Business*. The closing bid prices and corresponding yields are for June 29, 1998, therefore the government of Canada bonds that mature on July 1, 2000 have a term to maturity of almost exactly two years.[2] These bonds have a 10.5 per cent coupon rate, and the reported yield is 5.33 per cent (which refers to the yield to maturity). These bonds are selling at a premium over their maturity value since the coupon rate exceeds the yield. If we assume coupons are paid semi-annually, and use Equation 11-3, the quoted yield of 5.33 per cent for this bond, and assuming a maturity (or par) value of \$100 (since bond prices are usually reported per \$100 of face value), we can determine that the price will equal:

$$P = \$5.25 \times \left[\frac{1 - \frac{1}{(1.02665)^4}}{.02665}\right] + \frac{\$100}{(1.02665)^4} = \$5.25 \times (3.747) + \$100 \times (0.900) = \$109.67$$

This is exactly the price reported for this bond, because the reported yields are determined based on the day's closing bond prices (or closing bid prices, which are the reported prices in this case). In other words, once we are given the yields (and the coupon rate and term to maturity), we can determine the corresponding price and vice versa. We deal with the issue of estimating the implied yield from a given price in the next section.

Calculating the price of a bond is an easy procedure in today's financial world using either a financial calculator or personal computer. For example, by using a basic financial calculator, price can be determined after entering the cash flows and required yield.

---

[2] The quoted prices are the bid prices at 5 p.m. the previous day, which implies they are the highest price at which an offer to purchase the bonds has been made. Therefore, a potential bond purchaser may have to pay more than this price to buy the bonds, since the closing ask price was likely higher.

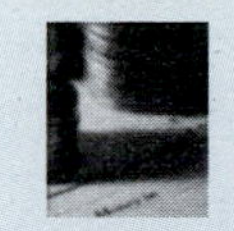

REAL-WORLD RETURNS

Canadian Bonds — Provided by RBC Dominion Securities

Selected quotations, with changes since the previous day, on actively traded bond issues yesterday. Yields are calculated to full maturity. Price is the final bid-side price as of 5 pm yesterday.

Issuer	Coupon	Maturity	Price	Yield	Price $ Chg
GOVERNMENT OF CANADA					
Canada	6.500	Aug 01/99	101.28	5.26	−0.02
Canada	7.750	Sep 01/99	102.74	5.29	−0.03
Canada	4.750	Sep 15/99	99.42	5.25	−0.03
Canada	9.250	Dec 01/99	105.30	5.31	−0.04
Canada	5.500	Feb 01/00	100.30	5.30	−0.04
Canada	8.500	Mar 01/00	105.02	5.30	−0.05
Canada	5.000	Mar 15/00	99.64	5.22	−0.04
Canada	10.500	Jul 01/00	109.67	5.33	−0.07
Canada	7.500	Sep 01/00	104.38	5.33	−0.06
Canada	10.500	Mar 01/01	112.64	5.34	−0.09
Canada	7.500	Mar 01/01	105.30	5.34	−0.07
Canada	9.750	Jun 01/01	111.75	5.34	−0.08
Canada	7.000	Sep 01/01	104.77	5.34	−0.07
Canada	9.750	Dec 01/01	113.57	5.34	−0.08
Canada	8.500	Apr 01/02	110.61	5.33	−0.08
Canada	5.500	Sep01/02	100.71	5.31	−0.08
Canada	11.750	Feb 01/03	125.70	5.35	−0.10
Canada	7.250	Jun 01/03	108.12	5.35	−0.09
Canada	5.250	Sep 01/03	99.76	5.30	−0.10
Canada	7.500	Dec 01/03	109.98	5.35	−0.10
Canada	10.250	Feb 01/04	123.32	5.36	−0.11
Canada	6.500	Jun 01/04	105.77	5.35	−0.08
Canada	9.000	Dec 01/04	119.59	5.35	−0.10
Canada	8.750	Dec 01/05	120.51	5.36	−0.07
Canada	14.000	Oct 01/06	156.79	5.38	−0.15
Canada	7.000	Dec 01/06	110.98	5.36	−0.06
Canada	7.250	Jun 01/07	113.20	5.37	−0.05
Canada	6.000	Jun 01/08	104.86	5.36	−0.04
Canada	10.000	Jun 01/08	135.12	5.38	−0.05
Canada	9.500	Jun 01/10	135.59	5.41	−0.02
Canada	9.000	Mar 01/11	132.44	5.42	−0.02
Canada	10.250	Mar 15/14	150.27	5.44	0.04
Canada	9.750	Jun 01/21	154.42	5.53	0.11
Canada	8.000	Jun 01/23	133.25	5.53	0.10
Canada	9.000	Jun 01/25	148.27	5.53	0.11
Canada	8.000	Jun 01/27	135.61	5.52	0.09
Canada	5.750	Jun 01/29	104.49	5.45	0.09
CMHC	5.500	Sep 03/02	100.38	5.40	−0.08
PROVINCIAL					
Alberta	6.250	Mar 01/01	102.18	5.36	−0.06
Alberta	6.375	Jun 01/04	104.76	5.42	−0.08
BC	9.000	Jan 09/02	111.09	5.49	−0.10
BC	7.750	Jun 16/03	109.67	5.49	−0.09
BC	9.000	Jun 21/04	117.56	5.51	−0.09
BC	6.000	Jun 09/08	103.12	5.59	−0.04
BC	8.500	Aug 23/13	128.04	5.71	−0.02
BC	6.150	Nov 19/27	104.09	5.86	0.09
BC Mun Fin	7.750	Dec 01/05	112.99	5.58	−0.07
BC Mun Fin	5.500	Mar 24/08	99.35	5.59	−0.04
Hydro Quebec	10.875	Jul 25/01	114.89	5.52	−0.09
Hydro Quebec	5.500	May 15/03	99.70	5.57	−0.10
Hydro Quebec	7.000	Jun 01/04	106.92	5.61	−0.08
Hydro Quebec	10.250	Jul 16/12	141.76	5.85	−0.14
Hydro Quebec	9.625	Jul 15/22	146.15	5.98	0.15
Manitoba	7.875	Apr 07/03	110.01	5.46	−0.09
Manitoba	5.750	Jun 02/08	101.46	5.56	−0.04
Manitoba	7.750	Dec 22/25	127.35	5.76	0.10
New Brunswic	8.000	Mar 17/03	110.28	5.49	−0.09
New Brunswic	5.700	Jun 02/08	101.16	5.55	−0.04
New Brunswic	6.000	Dec 27/17	103.14	5.73	0.04
Newfoundland	6.150	Apr 17/28	102.26	5.99	0.09
Nova Scotia	5.250	Jun 02/03	98.94	5.50	−0.08
Nova Scotia	6.600	Jun 01/27	109.56	5.91	0.09
Ontario	10.875	Jan 10/01	112.60	5.45	−0.08
Ontario	8.000	Mar 11/03	110.25	5.49	−0.09
Ontario	8.750	Apr 22/03	113.55	5.50	−0.09
Ontario	7.750	Dec 08/03	110.51	5.49	−0.10
Ontario	9.000	Sep 15/04	118.19	5.50	−0.09
Ontario	8.250	Dec 01/05	116.37	5.53	−0.07
Ontario	7.500	Jan 19/06	112.02	5.53	−0.07
Ontario	7.750	Jul 24/06	114.19	5.54	−0.07
Ontario	6.125	Sep 12/07	104.13	5.54	−0.05
Ontario	9.500	Jul 13/22	147.02	5.84	0.10
Ontario	7.600	Jun 02/27	124.33	5.85	0.10
Ontario	6.500	Mar 08/29	109.24	5.85	0.09
Ontario Hyd	10.000	Mar 19/01	111.29	5.46	−0.09
Ontario Hyd	8.625	Feb 06/02	110.13	5.48	−0.10
Ontario Hyd	9.000	Jun 24/02	112.41	5.48	−0.11
Ontario Hyd	5.375	Jun 02/03	99.54	5.48	−0.08
Ontario Hyd	7.750	Nov 03/05	113.24	5.53	−0.07
Ontario Hyd	5.600	Jun 02/08	100.25	5.57	−0.04
Ontario Hyd	8.250	Jun 22/26	132.91	5.85	0.10
Quebec	10.000	Apr 26/00	107.73	5.46	−0.06
Quebec	10.250	Oct 15/01	114.00	5.52	−0.10
Quebec	5.250	Apr 01/02	99.05	5.53	−0.05
Quebec	7.500	Dec 01/03	108.81	5.59	−0.09
Quebec	7.750	Mar 30/06	112.85	5.67	−0.05
Quebec	6.500	Oct 01/07	105.65	5.70	−0.05
Quebec	11.000	Apr 01/09	141.70	5.74	−0.05
Quebec	9.375	Jan 16/23	143.20	5.99	0.15
Quebec	8.500	Apr 01/26	133.65	6.00	0.15
Quebec	6.000	Oct 01/29	100.00	6.00	0.10
Saskatchewan	6.125	Oct 10/01	102.03	5.44	−0.07
Saskatchewan	5.500	Jun 02/08	99.76	5.53	−0.04
Saskatchewan	8.750	May 30/25	139.55	5.82	0.10
Toronto -Met	6.100	Aug 15/07	103.39	5.62	−0.06
Toronto -Met	6.100	Dec 12/17	102.94	5.84	0.04
Corporate					
AGT Limited	8.800	Sep 22/25	136.12	6.07	0.10
Associates	5.400	Sep 04/01	99.23	5.67	−0.06
Avco Fin	5.750	Jun 02/03	99.88	5.78	−0.13
Bank of Mont	6.900	Oct 16/01	103.85	5.60	−0.07
Bank of Mont	6.400	Apr 09/02	102.69	5.59	−0.08
Bank of Mont	5.550	Aug 27/02	99.72	5.63	−0.08
Bank of Mont	5.650	Dec 01/03	100.01	5.65	−0.09
Bank of Mont	8.150	May 09/06	115.19	5.72	−0.07
Bank of NS	6.000	Dec 04/01	101.18	5.61	−0.07
Bank of NS	6.250	Jun 12/02	102.18	5.62	−0.11
Bank of NS	8.100	Mar 24/03	110.08	5.64	−0.09
Bank of NS	5.400	Apr 01/03	98.97	5.65	−0.12
Bank of NS	7.400	Feb 08/06	110.24	5.72	−0.20
Bank of NS	6.250	Jul 16/07	103.51	5.75	−0.19
Bell Cda Ent	8.950	Apr 01/02	111.05	5.68	−0.08
Bell Cda Ent	6.200	Aug 28/07	103.40	5.72	−0.05
Can Cred Tst	5.625	Mar 24/05	99.52	5.71	−0.06
Can Trust M	5.450	Dec 03/01	99.37	5.65	−0.07
Can Trust M	5.650	Sep 13/02	99.98	5.65	−0.08
Cards Trust	5.420	Sep 21/01	99.40	5.63	−0.05
Cards Trust	5.510	Jul 21/03	99.32	5.67	−0.07
Cards Trust	5.630	Dec 21/05	99.52	5.71	−0.10
Cdn Imp Bank	4.500	Dec 06/99	98.70	5.46	−0.02
Cdn Occ Pet	6.300	Jun 02/08	98.47	6.51	−0.04
Crestar En	6.450	Oct 01/07	98.17	6.72	−0.04
Domtar Inc.	10.000	Apr 15/11	120.23	7.51	−0.02
Grtr TTO Air	5.400	Dec 03/02	99.20	5.61	−0.08
Grtr TTO Air	5.950	Dec 03/07	101.68	5.72	−0.05
Grtr TTO Air	6.450	Dec 03/27	106.32	5.99	0.07
Gtc Trans	6.200	Jun 01/07	101.32	6.01	−0.04
Imperial Oil	9.875	Dec 15/99	105.91	5.58	−0.04
Interprv Pip	8.200	Feb 15/24	127.96	6.04	0.09
Legacy	5.930	Nov 15/02	99.44	6.08	−0.08
Loblaws Co	6.650	Nov 08/27	106.89	6.14	0.07
Loewen	6.100	Oct 01/02	97.78	6.71	−0.08
London Ins	9.375	Jan 08/02	111.74	5.64	-0.08
Macmillan Bl	10.125	Jan 23/02	112.81	6.06	-0.01
Milit - Air	5.750	Jun 30/19	100.91	5.67	0.04
Morguard Ret	6.600	Oct 09/07	98.18	6.87	−0.04
Mstr Cr Trus	5.760	Aug 21/02	100.34	5.66	−0.06
Mstr Cr Trus	5.700	Nov 21/03	100.20	5.66	−0.05
Mstr Cr Trus	6.150	Dec 21/04	102.57	5.67	−0.06
Nav Canada	7.560	Mar 01/27	119.09	6.14	0.09
Oxford	6.860	Jul 21/04	97.98	7.28	−0.07
Renaissance	6.850	Feb 06/07	104.88	6.11	−0.06
Rogers Cable	8.750	Jul 15/07	101.13	8.57	−0.04
Rogers Cant	10.500	Jun 01/06	112.41	8.32	−0.07
Royal Bank	11.000	Jan 11/02	116.99	5.61	−0.09
Royal Bank	5.400	Sep 03/02	99.16	5.63	−0.08
Royal Bank	5.400	Apr 07/03	99.09	5.62	−0.08
Royal Bank	6.500	Sep 12/06	105.03	5.72	−0.05
Royal Bank	6.750	Jun 04/07	107.00	5.74	−0.05
Royal Bank	5.600	Apr 22/08	99.24	5.70	−0.04
Sask Wheat	6.600	Jul 18/07	101.79	6.34	−0.04
TD Bank	5.600	Sep 05/01	100.00	5.60	−0.06
TD Bank	6.450	Oct 17/01	102.49	5.61	−0.07
Trizec Hahn	7.950	Jun 01/07	103.43	7.42	−0.04
Union Gas	8.650	Nov 10/25	133.04	6.14	0.10
West Fraser	6.800	Nov 19/07	100.22	6.77	−0.04
Weston Geo	7.450	Feb 09/04	108.40	5.68	−0.08
Wstcoast Ene	6.750	Dec 15/27	108.40	6.13	0.07
Real Return	4.250	Dec 01/21	105.55	3.89	0.00
Real Return	4.250	Dec 01/26	106.40	3.88	0.00

DS Barra indexes

Index	Level	Daily Total Return % Chg	Daily Price Return % Chg	MTD Total Return % Chg
Market	310.16	0.02	−0.04	0.28
Short	261.80	0.00	−0.06	0.11
Intermed	314.12	−0.01	−0.06	0.04
Long	387.93	0.09	0.04	0.83
Govts	308.16	0.02	−0.03	0.29
Canadas	299.82	0.02	−0.04	0.27
Provs	330.16	0.04	−0.02	0.34
Munis	113.73	0.03	−0.03	0.28
Corps	330.62	0.02	−0.04	0.25

Scotia Capital Markets indexes

Index	Close	% chg	Yield	Chg	52 wk High	52 wk Low
Short	312.10	0.00	5.365	0.02	312.15	295.95
Mid	374.02	−0.00	5.492	0.01	375.53	339.56
Long	462.60	0.06	5.696	0.00	465.61	384.43
Universe	373.65	0.92	5.491	0.01	374.77	337.76

Benchmarks

Issuer	Coupon	Maturity	Price	Yield	$ chg
US Treasury	61/8	Dec/27 106	27/32	5.64	−6/32
British guilt	7.25	Dec/07 109	26/32	5.87	−4/32
German	5.25	Jan/08	103.71	4.75	+0.0
Japan #182	3.0	Sept/05	111.39	1.275	−0.34

Source: "Canadian Bonds," *The Globe and Mail / Report on Business*, June 30, 1998, p. B20. Reprinted with permission from RBC Dominion Securities.

Before proceeding to the next topic, we would point out that the prices discussed in this section are typically referred to as "quoted" prices. These differ from the actual prices investors pay for bonds whenever bonds are sold at a date other than the one of a coupon. The reason is that interest will accrue to bondholders in between such payment dates, although they will have not actually received the portion of the next coupon to which they are rightfully entitled. As a result, bond purchasers must pay the bond seller the quoted price plus the accrued interest on the bond. This amount is referred to as the cash price of the bond.

EXAMPLE: CASH VERSUS QUOTED PRICES

Consider a bond with a $1,000 maturity value and an 8 per cent coupon rate that is sold on July 15 at a quoted price of $980. If interest payments on this bond are made annually on July 1, the purchaser would have to pay the seller the cash price, equal to $980 plus 15 days of accrued interest at the coupon rate of 8 per cent, or

$$\text{Cash price} = \text{Quoted price} + \text{Accrued interest}$$

$$\text{Cash price} = \$980 + [(\$1{,}000) \times (0.08) \times (15/365)] = \$980 + \$3.29 = \$983.29$$

BOND YIELDS

Bond yields and interest rates refer to the same concept. Therefore, we begin our discussion of the former with a brief consideration of the latter. Interest rates measure the price paid by a borrower to a lender for the use of resources over some time period — that is, interest rates are the price for the funds loaned. The price differs from case to case, based on the supply and demand for these funds, resulting in a wide variety of interest rates. The spread between the lowest and highest rates at any time could be as much as 10 to 15 percentage points. In bond parlance, this would be equivalent to 1,000 to 1,500 basis points, since one percentage point equals 100 **basis points**.

Basis Points
100 basis points is equal to one percentage point.

It is convenient to focus on the one interest rate that provides the foundation for other rates. This rate is referred to as the short-term riskless rate (designated RF in this text) and is typically proxied by the rate on short-term government Treasury bills. All other rates differ from RF because of two factors: maturity differentials and risk premiums.

The Basic Components of Interest Rates

Explaining interest rates is a complex task that involves substantial economics reasoning and study, and it is not feasible in this text; however, Appendix 11-B at the end of the chapter provides a brief discussion of the way in which the Government of Canada can affect interest rate levels through its monetary policy, as conducted by the Bank of Canada. In this chapter, we analyze the basic determinants of nominal (current) interest rates with an eye toward recognizing the factors that affect such rates and cause them to fluctuate. The bond investor who understands the foundations of market rates can then rely on expert help for more details and be in a better position to interpret and evaluate such help.

The basic foundation of market interest rates is the opportunity cost of foregoing consumption, representing the rate that must be offered to individuals to persuade them to save rather than consume. This rate is sometimes called the **real risk-free rate of interest**, because it is not affected by price changes or risk factors.[3] We will refer to it simply as the *real rate* and designate it RR in this discussion.

Real Risk-Free Rate of Interest
The opportunity cost of foregoing consumption, given no inflation.

Nominal interest rates on T-bills consist of the RR plus an adjustment for inflation. A lender who lends $100 for a year at 10 per cent will be repaid $110. But if inflation is 12 per cent a year, that $110 that the lender receives upon repayment of the loan is worth only $98.21(1/1.12) ($110) in today's dollars. Lenders therefore expect to be compensated for the *expected* rate of price change in order to leave the real purchasing power of wealth unchanged or improved. As an approximation for discussion purposes, this inflation adjustment can be added to the real risk-free rate of interest. Unlike RR, which is often assumed by market participants to be reasonably stable over time, adjustments for expected inflation vary widely.

Thus, for short-term, risk-free securities, such as T-bills, the nominal interest rate is a function of the real rate of interest and the *expected* inflationary premium. This is expressed as Equation 11-6, which is an approximation:[4]

$$RF \approx RR + EI \qquad (11\text{-}6)$$

where
RF = short-term T-bill rate
RR = the real risk-free rate of interest
EI = the expected rate of inflation over the term of the instrument

Equation 11-6 is known as the Fisher hypothesis (named after economist Irving Fisher). It implies that the nominal rate on short-term risk-free securities rises point-for-point with anticipated inflation, with the real rate of interest remaining unaffected.[5] Turning Equation 11-6 around, estimates of the real risk-free rate of interest can be approximated by subtracting

---

[3] The real rate of interest cannot be measured directly. It is often estimated by dividing (1.0 + MIR) by (1.0 + EI), where MIR is the market interest rate and EI is expected inflation. This result can be approximated by subtracting estimates of inflation from nominal (market) interest rates (on either a realized or expected basis).

[4] The precisely correct procedure is to multiply (1 + the real rate) by (1 + the expected rate of inflation), and subtract 1.0. For purposes of our discussion, the additive relationship is satisfactory, provided that levels of inflation are relatively low.

[5] Fisher believed that inflation expectations were based on past observations as well as information about the future and that inflation expectations were slow to develop and slow to disappear.

the expected inflation rate from the observed nominal interest rate.[6] The expected rate of inflation can be determined by reference to various economic projections from the government, banks, and securities firms.

All market interest rates are affected by a time factor that leads to maturity differentials. That is, although long-term government bonds are virtually free from default risk in the same manner as government T-bills, they generally yield more than medium-term bonds, which, in turn, yield more than T-bills. This typical relationship between bond maturity and yield applies to all types of bonds, whether they are corporate, or federal, provincial, municipal government debt securities. The term structure of interest rates, discussed in Chapter 12, accounts for the relationship between time and yield — that is, the maturity differentials.

Market interest rates, other than those for riskless government securities, are also affected by a third factor, a risk premium, which lenders require as compensation for the risk involved. This risk premium is associated with the issuer's own particular situation or with a particular market factor. The risk premium is often referred to as the yield spread or yield differential.

Measuring Bond Yields

Several measures of the yield on a bond are used by investors. It is very important for bond investors to understand which yield measure is being discussed and what the underlying assumptions of any particular measure are.

Current Yield

Current Yield
A bond's annual coupon divided by the current market price.

Current yield is defined as the ratio of the coupon interest to the current market price. The current yield is clearly superior to simply citing the coupon rate on a bond because it uses the current market price as opposed to the face amount of a bond (almost always, $1,000). However, current yield is not a true measure of the return to a bond purchaser because it does not account for the difference between the bond's purchase price and its eventual redemption at par value. In effect, it is a one-period rate of return that measures the interest payment return relative to the initial investment.

Yield to Maturity

Yield to Maturity (YTM)
The promised compounded rate of return on a bond purchased at the current market price and held to maturity.

The rate of return on bonds most often quoted for investors is the **yield to maturity (YTM)**, which is defined as the *promised* compounded rate of return an investor will receive from a bond purchased at the current market price and held to maturity. This is the yield that was referred to in the Real-World Returns box in the previous section. It captures the coupon income to be received on the bond as well as any capital gains and losses realized by purchasing the bond for a price different from face value and holding to maturity. Similar to the internal rate of return (IRR) in financial management, the yield to maturity is the periodic interest rate that equates the present value of the expected future cash flows (both coupons and maturity value) to be received on the bond to the initial investment in the bond, which is its current price.

[6] While estimates of the real rate associated with government funds can be made by subtracting actual inflation for the same quarter because government funds are of very short duration, estimates of real rates on instruments with longer maturities require measures of expected inflation over the term of the instrument.

To calculate the yield to maturity for a bond, we use Equation 11-5 where the market price, the coupon, the number of years to maturity, and the face value of the bond are known, and the discount rate or yield to maturity is the variable to be determined.[7]

$$P = C \times (PVA_{YTM,n}) + MV \times (PV_{YTM,n}) \qquad \textbf{(11-5)}$$

Since both the left-hand side of Equation 11-5 and the numerator values (cash flows) on the right side are known, the equation can be solved for YTM. When the bond pays semi-annual coupons all terms are expressed in terms of six-month periods. (The resulting semi-annual rate must be doubled to obtain the annual YTM.)

To estimate the YTM requires a trial-and-error process to find the discount rate that equates the inflows from the bond (coupons plus maturity value) with its current price (cost). Different rates are tried until the left-hand and right-hand sides are equal. It is relatively easy today to find financial calculators or computer programs to solve YTM problems. We illustrate a simple example of the trial-and-error process involved in a yield-to-maturity calculation by referring to the present value tables at the end of the text. The purpose is simply to demonstrate conceptually how to calculate the YTM. Investors will normally use a calculator, computer, or the approximation formula described below to do computations such as these.

EXAMPLE: CALCULATING YIELD TO MATURITY

A 10 per cent coupon bond has five years remaining to maturity and pays coupons semi-annually. Assume the bond is selling at a premium over par with a current market price of $1,081.00. Because of the inverse relation between bond prices and market yields, it is clear that yields have fallen since the bond was originally issued, because the price is greater than $1,000. Using Equation 11-5 to determine yield to maturity,

$\$1,081 = \$50 \times (PVA_{YTM,10}) + \$1,000 \times (PV_{YTM,10})$

Trying a semi-annual rate of 4 per cent for YTM, we get

$\$1,081 = \$50 \times (PVA_{4\%,10}) + \$1,000 \times (PV_{4\%,10})$

$\$1,081 = \$50(8.111) + \$1,000(0.676)$

$\$1,081.00 \approx \$1.081.50$ (difference due to rounding error)

In this example, the solution is approximately 4 per cent on a semi-annual basis, which by convention is doubled to obtain the annual YTM of 8 per cent.

---

[7] A traditional method for calculating YTM, used by bond traders and others, is the use of bond tables. These tables provide investors with a YTM, given the coupon rate, the price of the bond, and the time to maturity. They can also be used to determine the price of a bond when the yield (and the other factors) are known.

To find the YTM on a bond using these tables, follow these three steps:

1. Choose the page in the bond table corresponding to the appropriate coupon rate. There is a page for each different coupon.
2. Select the column with the appropriate maturity date.
3. Find the price of the bond in the appropriate maturity column and read across this row to the left column which contains the resulting YTM.

The example above was simplistic because we were able to find a discount rate that equated the present value of the future cash flows almost exactly with its price. In practice, the trial-and-error process will be much more complicated and time consuming.[8] In order to estimate the YTM in a relatively straightforward manner, an approximation formula exists. It relates the net annual effective cash flow from the bond to the average amount of money invested in it during the ownership period. Effectively, the investor is assumed to have an average investment of this amount in the bond as the price gradually converges to $1,000, as it must by the maturity date.

$$\text{Approximate YTM} = \frac{\text{Annual coupon interest} +/- \text{Average annual amortization of the discount (or premium)}}{(\text{Maturity value} + \text{Current market price})/2} \tag{11-7}$$

or,

$$\text{Approximate YTM} = \frac{\text{Annual coupons} + \left[\dfrac{\text{MV} - \text{P}}{n}\right]}{\dfrac{\text{MV} + \text{P}}{2}} \tag{11-8}$$

where,
P = current market price of the bond
n = number of years to maturity

EXAMPLE: CALCULATING APPROXIMATE YTM

Consider the bond in the previous example with a 10 per cent coupon and a term to maturity of five years. Thus, the annual coupons are $100, and at the current market price of $1,081.00, the approximate YTM is 8.05 per cent, which is close to the estimate arrived at by trial and error.

Approximate YTM =

$$\frac{\$100 + \dfrac{(\$1{,}000 - \$1{,}081.00)}{5}}{\dfrac{(\$1{,}000 + \$1{,}081.00)}{2}} = \frac{\$100 + (-\$16.20)}{\$1{,}040.50} = \frac{\$83.80}{\$1{,}040.50} = 0.0805 = 8.05\%$$

The YTM calculation for a zero-coupon bond is based on the same process shown in Equation 11-5 — equating the current price to the future cash flows. Because there are no coupons, the process reduces to Equation 11-9, with all terms as previously defined, and n is generally expressed in semi-annual periods, producing an estimate for the semi-annual YTM:

$$\text{YTM} = [\text{MV/P}]^{1/n} - 1 \tag{11-9}$$

[8] One commonly used approach for estimating the appropriate rate involves the use of an estimation technique referred to as linear interpolation, which students may have come across in other quantitative courses.

EXAMPLE: CALCULATING YTM FOR ZERO-COUPON BONDS

A zero-coupon bond has 12 years to maturity and is sold for $300. Given the 24 semi-annual periods to maturity, the power to be used in raising the ratio of $1,000/$300, or 3.333, is 0.04167 (calculated as 1/24). Using a calculator with a power function produces a value of 1.0514. Subtracting the 1.0 and multiplying by 100 leaves a semi-annual yield of 5.145 per cent. Because YTM numbers are usually stated on an annual basis, this figure is doubled, which produces an annual yield of 10.29 per cent.

It is important to understand that YTM is a promised yield, because investors earn the indicated yield only if the bond is held to maturity and the coupons are reinvested at the calculated YTM. Obviously, no trading can be done for a particular bond if the YTM is to be earned. The investor simply buys and holds. What is not so obvious to many investors, however, is the reinvestment implications of the YTM measure. Because of the importance of the reinvestment rate, we consider it in more detail by analyzing the reinvestment risk.

Interest on Interest
The process by which bond coupons are reinvested to earn interest.

Reinvestment Rate Risk
That part of interest rate risk resulting from uncertainty about the rate at which future interest coupons can be reinvested.

Reinvestment Risk

The YTM calculation assumes that the investor reinvests all coupons received from a bond at a rate equal to the computed YTM on that bond, thereby earning **interest on interest** over the life of the bond at the computed YTM rate. In effect, this calculation assumes that the reinvestment rate is the yield to maturity.

If the investor spends the coupons, or reinvests them at a rate different from the assumed reinvestment rate, the realized yield that will actually be earned at the end of the investment in the bond will differ from the promised YTM. And, in fact, coupons almost always will be reinvested at rates higher or lower than the computed YTM, resulting in a realized yield that differs from the promised yield. This gives rise to **reinvestment rate risk**.

This interest-on-interest concept significantly affects the potential total dollar return. The exact impact is a function of coupon and time to maturity, with reinvestment becoming more important as either coupon or time to maturity, or both, rises. Holding everything else constant:

- The longer the maturity of a bond, the greater the reinvestment risk
- The higher the coupon rate, the greater the dependence of the total dollar return from the bond on the reinvestment of the coupon payments.

To illustrate the importance of interest on interest in YTM calculations, Table 11-1 shows the realized yields under different assumed reinvestment rates for a 10 per cent non-callable 20-year bond purchased at face value of $1,000. If the reinvestment rate exactly equals the YTM of 10

INVESTING tip

Consider what happens when investors purchase bonds at high YTMs, such as when interest rates reached exceptionally high levels in the summer of 1982. Unless they reinvested the coupons at the promised YTMs, investors did not actually realize these high promised yields. For that to happen, coupons had to be reinvested at the record rates existing at that time, an unlikely situation especially for a high-YTM bond with a long maturity. The subsequent decline in interest rates during the fall of 1982 illustrates the fallacy of believing that one has "locked up" record yields during a relatively brief period of very high interest rates. On the other hand, if the investor chose to sell the bond before maturity, it would sell at a premium as a result of falling interest rates, resulting in capital gains.

per cent, the investor would realize a 10 per cent compound return when the bond is held to maturity, with $4,040 of the total dollar return from the bond attributable to interest on interest. At a 12 per cent reinvestment rate, the investor would realize a 11.14 per cent compound return, with almost 75 per cent of the total return coming from interest on interest ($5,738/$7,738). With no reinvestment of coupons (spending them as received), the investor would achieve only a 5.57 per cent return. In all cases, the bond is held to maturity.

Clearly, the reinvestment portion of the YTM concept is critical. In fact, for long-term bonds the interest-on-interest component of the total realized yield may account for more than three-quarters of the bond's total dollar return.

Table 11-1

Realized Yields, Using Different Reinvestment Rate Assumptions, for a 10 Per Cent 20-Year Bond Purchased at Face Value of $1,000

Coupon Income[a] ($)	Assumed Reinvestment Rate (%)	Amount Attributable to Reinvestment[b] ($)	Total Return[c] ($)	Realized Yields[d] (%)
2000	0	0	2000	5.57
2000	5	1370	3370	7.51
2000	8	2751	4751	8.94
2000	9	3352	5352	9.46
2000	10	4040	6040	10.00
2000	11	4830	6830	10.56
2000	12	5738	7738	11.14

[a]Coupon income = $50 coupon received *semi-annually* for 20 years = $50 × 40 periods.

[b]Amount attributable to reinvestment = total return minus coupon income. This is also known as the interest on interest.

[c]Total return = sum of an annuity for 40 periods, $50 semi-annual coupons (Example: at 10 per cent reinvestment rate, $50 × [5 per cent, 40 period factor of 120.80] = $6,040.)

[d]Realized yield = [Future Value per Dollar Invested]$^{1/N}$ − 1, where future value per dollar invested = (total return + the cost of bond) / cost of the bond. The result of this calculation is the potential yield on a semi-annual basis. To put this on an annual basis, this figure must be doubled. This has been done for the yields in Table 11-1.

The realized yield (RY) shown in Table 11-1 can be calculated using the following formula: (Note that RY assumes a constant reinvestment rate.)

$$\text{RY} = \left[\frac{\text{Total future dollars}}{\text{Purchase price of bond}}\right]^{1/n} - 1.0 \quad \text{(11-10)}$$

EXAMPLE: CALCULATING REALIZED YIELD

For the bond calculations shown in Table 11-1, consider the yield an investor would achieve at an assumed reinvestment rate of 12 per cent. The total future dollars equals the total dollar return shown in Table 11-1, \$7,738, plus the cost of the bond, \$1,000, or \$8,738. Therefore,

$$\begin{aligned} RY &= [\$8{,}738/1{,}000]^{1/40} - 1.0 \\ &= [8.738]^{.025} - 1 = 1.05569 - 1.0 \\ &= 0.05569, \text{ or } 5.569\% \text{ on a semi-annual basis} \\ &(= 11.14\% \text{ on an annual basis}). \end{aligned}$$

One advantage of a zero-coupon bond is the elimination of reinvestment rate risk because there are no coupons to be reinvested. At the time of purchase investors know the YTM that will be realized when the bond is held to maturity.

Horizon Return

Bond investors today often make specific assumptions about future reinvestment rates in order to cope with the reinvestment rate problem illustrated earlier. This is sometimes referred to as horizon analysis. Given their explicit assumption about the reinvestment rate, investors can calculate the **horizon return** to be earned if that assumption turns out to be accurate.

Horizon Return Bond returns to be earned based on assumptions about future reinvestment rates.

The investor makes an assumption about the reinvestment rate expected to prevail over the planned investment horizon. The investor may also make an assumption about the yield to maturity expected to prevail at the end of the planned investment horizon, which in turn is used to estimate the price of the bond at that time. Based on these assumptions, the total future dollars expected to be available at the end of the planned investment horizon can be determined. The horizon return is then calculated as the interest rate that equates the total future dollars to the purchase price of the bond.

Yield to Call

Most corporate, as well as some government bonds, are callable by the issuers after some deferred call period. For bonds likely to be called, the yield-to-maturity calculation is an inappropriate measure of its expected return. A better measure in such situations is the promised **yield to call**. The end of the period when a bond can first be called is often used for the yield-to-call calculation. This yield is particularly appropriate for bonds selling at a premium (i.e., high-coupon bonds with market prices above par value) since they are highly likely to be called by the issuer at the first available call date.[9]

Yield to Call The promised return on a bond from the present to the date that the bond is first eligible to be called.

To calculate the yield to first call, the YTM formula (Equation 11-5) is used, but with the number of periods until the first call date substituted for the number of periods until maturity and the call price substituted for face value. These changes are shown in Equation 11-11.

[9] That is, bonds with high coupons (and high yields) are prime candidates to be called.

(11-11)
$$P = C \times (PVA_{YTC,c}) + CP \times (PV_{YTC,c})$$

where
c = the number of periods until the first call date
YTC = the yield to first call
CP = the call price to be paid if the bond is called

Bond prices are calculated on the basis of the lowest yield measure. Therefore, for premium bonds selling above a certain level, yield to call replaces yield to maturity, because it produces the lowest (and most appropriate) measure of yield.[10]

BOND PRICE CHANGES

Bond Price Changes Over Time

We know how to calculate the price of a bond using the cash flows to be received and the YTM as the discount rate. Assume that we calculate the price of a 20-year bond issued five years ago and discover that it is $910. The bond still has 15 years to maturity. What can we say about its price over the next 15 years?

When everything else is held constant, including market interest rates, any bond price that differs from the bond's face value (assumed to be $1,000) must change over time. Why? On a bond's specified maturity date, it must be worth its par or maturity value. Therefore, over time, holding all other factors constant, a bond's price must converge to $1,000 on the maturity date. In other words, the bond's price is "pulled to par."

After bonds are issued, they sell at discounts from par (prices less than $1,000) and premiums over par (prices greater than $1,000) during their lifetimes. Therefore, holding all other factors constant, a bond selling at a discount will experience a rise in price over time, and a bond selling at a premium will experience a decline in price over time as the bond's remaining life approaches the maturity date.

Figure 11-1 illustrates bond price movements over time, assuming constant yields. Bond 2 depicts a 10 per cent coupon, 30-year bond assuming that yields remain constant at 10 per cent. The price of this bond does not change, beginning and ending at $1,000. Bond 1, on the other hand, depicts an 8 per cent coupon, 30-year bond assuming that required yields start, and remain constant, at 10 per cent. The price starts below $1,000 because bond 1 is selling at a discount as a result of its coupon of 8 per cent being less than the required yield of 10 per cent. Bond 3 illustrates a 30-year bond with a 12 per cent coupon, assuming that required yields start and remain constant at 10 per cent. The price of bond 3 begins above $1,000 because it is selling at a premium (12 per cent is greater than the required yield of 10 per cent).

If all other factors are held constant, the price of all three bonds must converge to $1,000 on the maturity date. In actuality, however, other factors do *not* remain constant. In

[10] The technical name for the point at which yield to call comes into play is the "crossover point," which is a price and is approximately the sum of par value and one year's interest. For a discussion of this point, see S. Homer and M. Leibowitz, *Inside the Yield Book* (Englewood Cliffs, NJ: Prentice Hall, 1972), Chapter 4.

particular interest rates or yields to maturity change constantly as do bond prices. Furthermore, the sensitivity of the price change is a function of certain variables, especially coupon and maturity. We now examine these variables.

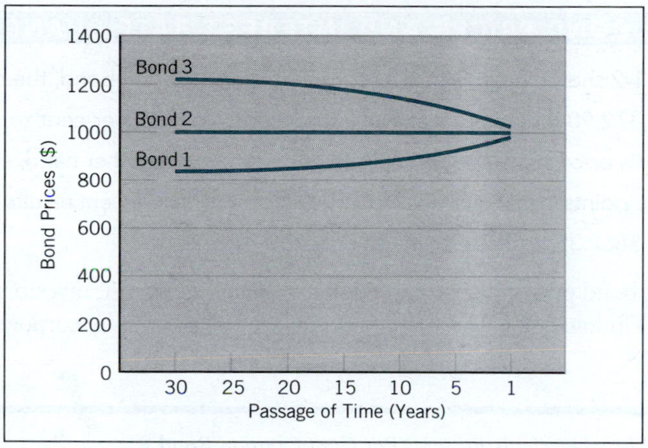

Figure 11-1
Bond Price Movements Over Time Assuming Constant Yields of 10 Per Cent for Three 30-Year Bonds

Bond Price Changes as a Result of Interest Rate Changes

Bond prices change with interest rates and required yields. Understanding how bond prices change in relation to interest rates is critical to successful bond management. The basics of bond price movements as a result of interest rate changes have been known for many years. For example, over 30 years ago Burton Malkiel derived five theorems about the relationship between bond prices and yields.[11] Using the bond valuation model, he showed the changes that occur in the price of a bond (i.e., its volatility), given a change in yields, as a result of bond variables such as time to maturity and coupon. We will use Malkiel's bond theorems to illustrate how interest rate changes affect bond prices.

Bond Prices Move Inversely to Interest Rates

Investors must always keep in mind a fundamental fact about the relationship between bond prices and bond yields: Bond prices move inversely to market yields. When the level of required yields demanded by investors on new bond issues changes, the required yields on all bonds already outstanding will also change. For these yields to change, the prices of these bonds must change since the coupon and maturity payments are fixed when the bond is originally issued. This inverse relationship, which was evident in the bond valuation examples presented earlier in the chapter, is the basis for understanding, valuing, and managing bonds.

Table 11-2 shows prices for a 10 per cent coupon bond for market yields from 6 to 14 per cent and for maturity dates from one to 30 years. For any given maturity, the price of the bond declines as the required yield increases and increases as the required yield declines from the 10 per cent level. Figure 11-2 shows this relationship using data from Table 11-2.

[11] B. G. Malkiel, "Expectations, Bond Prices, and the Term Structure of Interest Rates," *Quarterly Journal of Economics*, May 1962, pp. 197–218.

An interesting corollary of the inverse relationship between bond prices and interest rates is as follows: *Holding maturity constant, a decrease in rates will raise bond prices on a percentage basis more than a corresponding increase in rates will lower bond prices.*

EXAMPLE: BOND PRICES AND INTEREST RATE CHANGES

Table 11-2 shows that for the 15-year 10 per cent coupon bond, the price would be $1,172.90 if market rates were to decline from 10 per cent to 8 per cent, resulting in a price appreciation of 17.29 per cent. On the other hand, a rise of two percentage points in market rates from 10 per cent to 12 per cent results in a change in price to $862.35, a price decline of only 13.77 per cent.

Obviously, bond price volatility can work for, as well as against, investors. Money can be made (and lost) in low-risk government bonds as well as more risky corporate bonds.

Table 11-2

Bond Price and Market Yields for a 10 Per Cent Coupon Bond

Years to Maturity	Bond Prices at Difference Market Yields and Maturities				
	6%	8%	10%	12%	14%
1	$1,038.27	$1,018.86	$1000	$981.67	$963.84
5	1,170.60	1,081.11	1000	926.40	859.53
10	1,297.55	1,135.90	1000	885.30	788.12
15	1,392.01	1,172.92	1000	862.35	751.82
20	1,462.30	1,197.93	1000	849.54	733.37
25	1,514.60	1,214.82	1000	842.38	723.99
30	1,553.51	1,226.23	1000	838.39	719.22

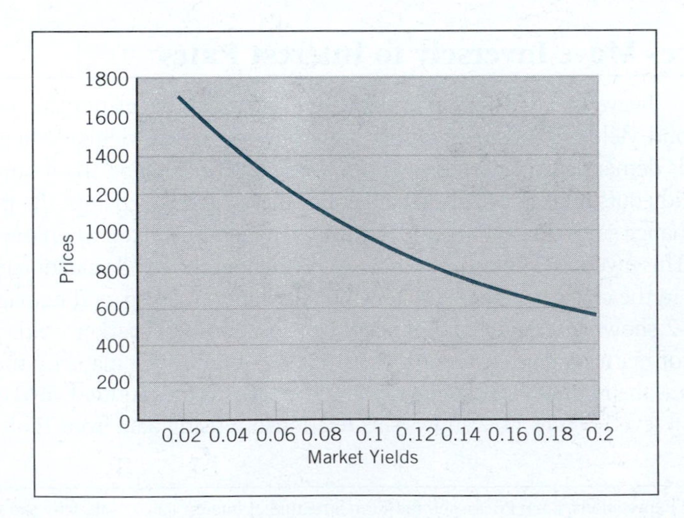

Figure 11-2
The Relationship between Bond Prices and Market Yields

Although the inverse relationship between bond prices and interest rates is the basis of all bond analysis, a complete understanding of that relationship requires additional information. An increase in interest rates will cause bond prices to decline, but the exact amount of decline will depend on important variables unique to each bond such as time to maturity and coupon. We will examine each of these in turn.

The Effects of Maturity

The effect of a change in yields on bond prices depends on the maturity of the bond. An important principle is that for a given change in market yields, changes in bond prices are directly related to time to maturity. Therefore, as interest rates change, the prices of longer-term bonds will change more than the prices of shorter-term ones, everything else being equal.

EXAMPLE: MATURITY AND BOND PRICES

Given two 10 per cent coupon bonds and a drop in market yields from 10 to 8 per cent, we can see from Table 11-2 that the price of the 15-year bond will be $1,172.92, while that of the 30-year bond will be $1,226.23.

The principle illustrated here is simple but important. Other things being equal, bond price volatility is a function of maturity. Long-term bond prices fluctuate more than short-term ones. A related principle regarding maturity is: *The percentage price change that occurs as a result of the direct relationship between a bond's maturity and its price volatility increases at a diminishing rate as the time to maturity increases.*

EXAMPLE: MATURITY AND PRICE VOLATILITY

As we saw above, a two percentage point drop in market yields (from 10 to 8 per cent) increased the price of the 15-year bond to $1,172.92, a 17.29 per cent change, while the price of the 30-year bond changed to $1,226.23, a 26.23 per cent change.

This example shows that the percentage of price change resulting from an increase in time to maturity increases but at a decreasing rate. Put simply, a doubling of the time to maturity will not result in a doubling of the percentage price change resulting from a change in market yields.

The Effects of Coupon

In addition to the maturity effect, the change in the price of a bond as a result of a change in interest rates depends on the coupon rate of the bond. We can state this principle as (other things being equal): *Bond price fluctuations (volatility) and bond coupon rates are inversely related.* Note that we are talking about percentage price fluctuations; this relationship does not necessarily hold if we measure volatility in terms of dollar price changes rather than percentage price changes. This result is intuitive since a greater proportion of total income on higher coupon bonds is received in earlier periods, therefore the discount rate effect is lower for such bonds.

The Implications of Malkiel's Theorems for Investors

Malkiel's derivations for bond investors lead to the practical conclusion that the two bond variables of major importance in assessing the change in the price of a bond, given a change in interest rates, are its coupon and its maturity. This conclusion can be summarized as follows: A decline in interest rates will cause a rise in bond prices (and vice versa), with the most volatility in bond prices occurring in longer maturity bonds and bonds with low coupons. Therefore:

1. A bond buyer, in order to receive the maximum price impact for an expected change in interest rates, should purchase low-coupon, long-maturity bonds.
2. If an increase in interest rates is expected (or feared), an investor contemplating their purchase should consider bonds with large coupons, short maturities, or both.

These relationships provide useful information for bond investors by demonstrating how the price of a bond changes with interest rates. Although investors have no control over the change and direction in market rates, they can exercise control over the coupon and maturity, both of which have significant effects on bond price changes. Nevertheless, it is cumbersome to calculate various possible price changes on the basis of these theorems. Furthermore, maturity is an inadequate measure of the sensitivity of a bond's price change to changes in yields, because it ignores the coupon payments and the principal repayment.

Investors managing bond portfolios need a measure of time designed to more accurately portray a bond's "average" life, taking into account all of the bond's cash flows, including both coupons and the return of principal at maturity. Such a measure — called duration — is available and is widely used.

Measuring Bond Price Volatility: Duration

In managing a bond portfolio, perhaps the most important consideration is the effect of yield changes on the prices and rates of return for different bonds. The problem is that a given change in interest rates can result in very different percentage price changes for the various bonds that investors hold. We saw earlier that both maturity and coupon affect bond price changes for a given change in yields.

Although maturity is the traditional measure of a bond's lifetime, it is inadequate, because it focuses only on the return of principal at the maturity date. Two 20-year bonds, one with an 8 per cent coupon and the other with a 15 per cent coupon, do not have identical economic lifetimes. An investor will recover the original purchase price much sooner with the 15 per cent coupon bond. Therefore, a measure is needed that accounts for the entire pattern (both size and timing) of the cash flows over the life of the bond — the effective maturity of the bond. Such a concept, called duration, was conceived over 50 years ago by Frederick Macaulay.[12] Duration is very useful for bond management purposes because it combines the properties of maturity and coupon.

[12] F. R. Macaulay, *Some Theoretical Problems Suggested by the Movement of Interest Rates, Bond Yields and Stock Prices in the United States Since 1856* (New York: National Bureau of Economic Research, 1938).

Duration Defined

Duration measures the weighted average maturity of a bond's cash flows on a present value basis; that is, the present values of the cash flows are used as the weights in calculating the weighted average maturity. Thus,

Duration
A measure of a bond's economic lifetime based on the weighted present value of expected cash flows over the life of the bond.

Duration = number of years needed to fully recover purchase price of a bond, given present values of its future cash flows
= weighted average time to recovery of all interest payments plus principal

Figure 11-3 illustrates the concepts of both time to maturity and duration for a bond with five years to maturity, a 10 per cent coupon, and selling for $1,000. As the figure indicates, the stream of cash flows generated by this bond over the term to maturity consists of $50 every six months, or $100 per year, plus the return of principal of $1,000 at the end of the five years. The last cash flow combines the interest payment of $50 with the principal repayment of $1,000 that occurs at the maturity date.

Although the term to maturity for the bond illustrated in Figure 11-3 is five years, its duration is only 4.17 years as indicated by the arrow. This means that the weighted average maturity of the bond's cash flows is 4.17 years from the beginning date. It is important that we understand how this duration value is calculated.

Calculating Duration

To calculate duration, it is necessary to consider a weighted time period. The time periods at which the cash flows are received are expressed in terms of years and denoted by CF_t in this discussion. When all of these cash flows (CF_ts) have been weighted and added together, the result is the duration, stated in years.

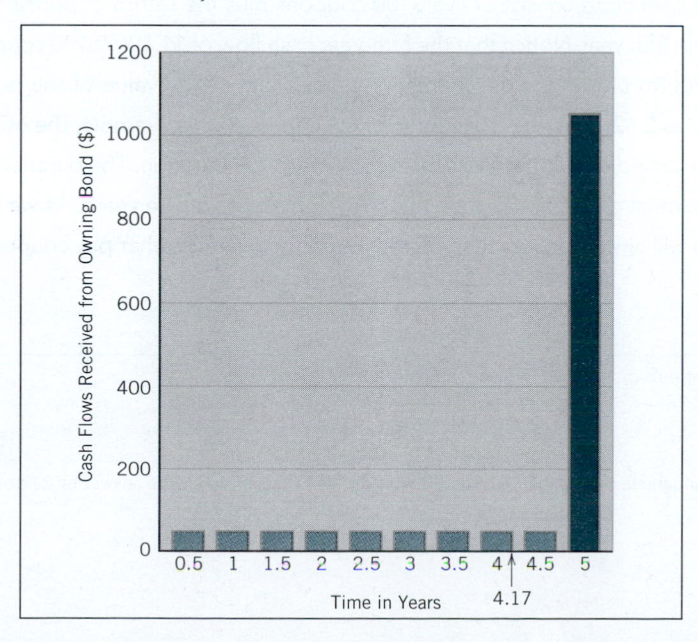

Figure 11-3
Illustration of the Cash Flow Pattern of a 10 Per Cent Coupon, Five-Year Maturity Bond Paying Interest Semi-Annually and Returning the Principal of $1,000 at Maturity

The present values of the cash flows serve as the weighting factors to apply to the time periods. Each weighting factor shows the relative importance of each cash flow to the bond's total present value, which is simply its current market price. The sum of the weighting factors will be 1.0, indicating that all cash flows have been accounted for. Putting this all together gives us the equation for duration:

$$\text{Macaulay Duration} = D = \sum_{t=1}^{n} \frac{PV(CF_t)}{\text{Market price}} \times t \qquad \textbf{(11-12)}$$

where

t = the year at which the cash flow is expected to be received
n = the number of years to maturity
$PV(CF_t)$ = value of the cash flow in period t discounted at the annual yield to maturity
Market price = the bond's current price (or the present value of all the cash flows)

As Equation 11-12 shows, duration is obtained by multiplying each year's weighted cash receipt (weighted by the price of the bond) by the number of years when each is to be received, and adding. Note that duration is measured in years and that for ease of exposition we state the equation on an annual basis although interest on bonds is often paid semi-annually.

EXAMPLE: CALCULATING DURATION

Table 11-3 provides an example of calculating the duration for a bond, using the same bond as shown in Figure 11-3 except now for ease of exposition, the calculation is done on an annual basis. This is a 10 per cent coupon bond with five years remaining to maturity. The bond is priced at $1,000 for simplicity, and the YTM is 10 per cent.[13]

The cash flows consist of five $100 coupons plus the return of principal at the end of the fifth year. Notice that the fifth-year cash flow of $1,100 ($100 coupon plus $1,000 return of principal) accounts for 64 per cent of the value of the bond and contributes 3.42 years to the duration of 4.17 years. In this example, the other cash flows combined contributed less than one year to the duration. The duration of 4.17 years is almost one year less than the term to maturity of five years. As we will see, duration will always be less than time to maturity for bonds that pay coupons.

[13] A shortcut formula can be used for coupon bonds selling at face value:

$$\text{Duration} = \frac{1 + YTM}{YTM}\left[1 - (1/(1 + YTM)^n)\right]$$

Using a semi-annual rate and doubling the number of periods, we must divide the answer by 2.0 to put it on an annual basis.

Table 11-3

An Example of Calculating the Duration of a Bond Using a 10 Per Cent Coupon, Five-Year Maturity Bond Priced at $1,000 and Paying Annual Interest

(1) Years	(2) Cash Flow	(3) PV Factor	(4) $ (2) × (3)	(5) (4) / Price	(6) (1) × (5)
1	$100	.909	90.90	.0909	.0909
2	100	.826	82.60	.0826	.1652
3	100	.751	75.10	.0751	.2253
4	100	.683	68.30	0.683	.2732
5	1100	.621	683.10	.6831	3.4155
					Duration = 4.1701

Understanding Duration

How is duration related to the key bond variables previously analyzed? An examination of Equation 11-12 shows that the calculation of duration depends on three factors:

1. The maturity date of the bond
2. Coupon payments
3. Yield to maturity.

1. *The maturity date of the bond.* Holding the size of coupon payments and the yield to maturity constant, duration expands with time to maturity but at a decreasing rate, particularly beyond 15 years to maturity. Even between five and 10 years time to maturity, duration is expanding at a significantly lower rate than was the case before the five year mark, where it expands rapidly.[14] Note that for all coupon-paying bonds, duration is always less than maturity. For a zero-coupon bond, duration is equal to time to maturity.
2. *Coupon payments.* Holding maturity and yield to maturity constant, coupon is inversely related to duration. This is logical because higher coupons lead to quicker recovery of the bond's value, resulting in a shorter duration, relative to lower coupons.
3. *Yield to maturity.* Holding coupon payments and maturity constant, yield to maturity is inversely related to duration.

Why is duration important in bond management and analysis? First, it tells us the difference between the effective lives of alternative bonds. Bonds A and B, with the same duration but different years to maturity, have more in common than bonds C and D with the same maturity but different durations. For any particular bond, as maturity increases the duration grows at a decreasing rate.[15]

[14] The duration of a perpetuity is (1 + YTM)/YTM. This indicates that maturity and duration can differ greatly since the maturity of a perpetuity is infinite, but duration is not. That is, perpetuities have an infinite maturity but a finite duration.

[15] Deep discount bonds are an exception to the general rule. Their duration first increases with time to maturity, up to some distant point, and then decreases in duration beyond this point. This is because deep discount bonds with very long maturities behave like perpetuities.

EXAMPLE: DURATION AND TERM TO MATURITY

Given the 10 per cent coupon bond discussed above with a yield to maturity of 10 per cent and a five-year life, we saw that the duration was 4.17 years. If the maturity of this bond was 10 years, it would have an effective life (duration) of 6.76 years, and with a 20-year maturity it would have an effective life of 9.36 years — quite a different perspective. Furthermore, under these conditions, a 50-year maturity for this bond would change the effective life to only 10.91 years. The reason for the sharp differences between the term to maturity and the duration is that cash flows received in the distant future have very small present values and therefore add little to a bond's value.

Second, the duration concept is used in certain bond management strategies, particularly immunization, as explained later in the chapter.

Third, duration is a measure of bond price sensitivity to interest rate movements, a very important part of any bond analysis. Malkiel's bond price theorems are inadequate to examine all aspects of bond price sensitivity. This issue is considered in some detail below because of its potential importance to bond investors.

Estimating Price Changes Using Duration

The real value of the duration measure to bond investors is that it combines coupon and maturity, the two key variables that investors must consider in response to expected changes in interest rates. As noted earlier, duration is related positively to maturity and negatively to coupon. However, bond price changes are directly related to duration; that is, the percentage change in a bond's price, given a change in interest rates, is proportional to its duration. The reason for this relationship is that Macaulay's duration can be derived by taking the first derivative of the bond pricing equation with respect to $(1 + r)$. This derivation is shown in Appendix 11-C at the end of the chapter. Most students who have studied calculus will recall that the first derivative of a function (in this case the bond pricing equation) is its slope. The slope, in turn, measures the responsiveness of the function value (or the bond price) with respect to changes in the chosen variable (in this case $(1 + r)$). Therefore, duration can be used to measure interest rate exposure.

Modified Duration
Duration divided by (1 + yield to maturity).

The term **modified duration** refers to Macaulay's duration in Equation 11-12 divided by $(1 + r)$, or

$$\text{Modified duration} = D^* = D / (1 + r) \tag{11-13}$$

where
D^* = modified duration
r = the bond's yield to maturity

EXAMPLE: CALCULATING MODIFIED DURATION

Using the duration of 4.17 years calculated earlier and the YTM of 10 per cent, the modified duration based on annual interest would be

$$D^* = 4.17 / (1 + 0.10) = 3.79$$

The modified duration can be used to calculate the percentage price change in a bond for a given change in r, which arises from the result demonstrated in Appendix 11-C. This is shown by Equation 11-14, which is an approximation:

$$\text{Percentage change in bond price} \approx \frac{-D}{(1 + r)} \times \text{Percentage point change in } r \tag{11-14}$$

or

$$\Delta P/P \approx -D^*\Delta r \tag{11-15}$$

where

ΔP = change in price
P = the price of the bond
$-D^*$ = modified duration with a negative sign
Δr = the instantaneous change in yield

EXAMPLE: MODIFIED DURATION AND CHANGES IN BOND PRICES

Using our same bond with a modified duration of 3.79, assume an instantaneous yield change of 20 basis points (+0.0020) in the YTM, from 10 to 10.20 per cent. The approximate change in price, based on Equation 11-15 would be

$$\Delta P/P = -(3.79)(+0.0020)(100) = -0.758\%$$

Given the original price of the bond of $1,000, this percentage price change would result in an estimated bond price of $992.42. This is very close to the price of $992.32 (0.768 per cent decline), that we would get if we determined the bond price based on a YTM of 10.20 per cent using the bond valuation equation. For very small changes in yield, Equations 11-14 or 11-15 provide good approximations. However, for larger changes, such as 100 or 200 basis points, the approximate percentage price change is less accurate. This is because the relationship is derived using the first derivative of the bond valuation equation. First derivatives measure the slope of a function (bond prices in this case) accurately over small intervals or for small changes in the variable that is being allowed to vary (interest rates in this case).

Convexity

Although Equation 11-14 is only an approximation, for very small changes in the required yield, the approximation is quite close. However, as the changes become larger, the approximation becomes poorer. The problem is that modified duration produces symmetric percentage price change estimates using Equation 11-12 (if r had decreased 0.20 per cent, the price change would have been +0.758 per cent) when, in actuality, the price-yield relationship is not linear. This relationship is, in fact, convex, and calculations of price changes should properly account for the convexity of the price-yield relationship. **Convexity** is the term used to refer to the degree to which duration changes as the yield to maturity changes.[16]

Convexity
A measure of the degree to which the relationship between a bond's price and yield departs from the straight line, that is, the degree to which duration changes as the yield to maturity changes.

To understand the convexity issue, Figure 11-4 repeats the analysis from Figure 11-2 that shows a 10 per cent coupon bond at different market yields and prices. We can think of modified duration graphically as the slope of a line that is tangent to the convex price-yield curve of Figure 11-4 at the current price and yield of the bond, which is assumed to be $1,000 and 10 per cent.[17]

Figure 11-4
Convex Relationship between Yields and Prices and Tangent Line Representing Modified Duration for a 10 Per Cent, 10-Year Bond

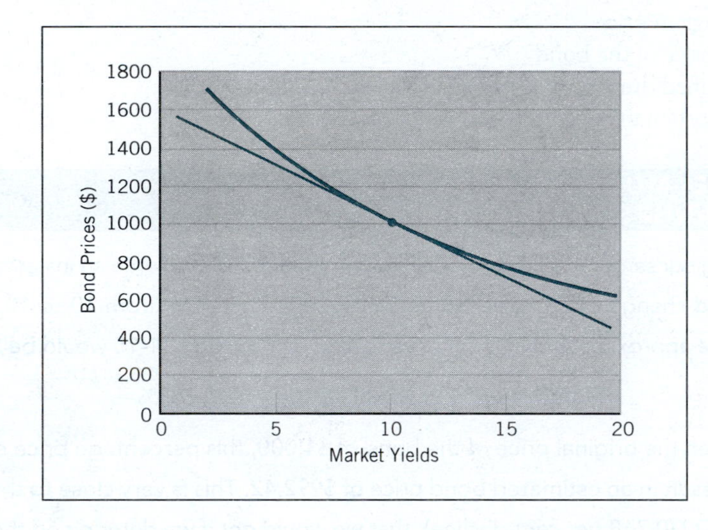

In effect, we are using a tangent line to measure the slope of the curve that depicts the inverse relationship between bond price and yield. For a very small change in yield, such as a few basis points, the slope of the line — the modified duration — provides a good

[16] An in-depth discussion of convexity is beyond the scope of this text, however, we would note that it is derived by taking the second derivative of the bond valuation equation with respect to interest rates. For a more detailed discussion, see F. J. Fabozzi and T. D. Fabozzi, *The Handbook of Fixed Income Securities*, Fifth Edition (Irwin Professional Publishing, 1997).

[17] Technically, the slope of the tangent line in Figure 11-4 is equal to the negative of modified duration multiplied by the bond's current market price.

approximation for the rate of change in price, given a change in yield. As the change in yield increases, the error that results from using a straight line to estimate a bond's price behaviour as given by a curve increases.[18]

As we move away from the point of tangency in Figure 11-4 in either direction, we underestimate the price of the bond using modified duration; that is, the price change is always more favourable than suggested by the modified duration. Notice that the shaded area in Figure 11-4 captures the convexity areas both above and below the starting point of 10 per cent and $1,000. If yields decrease, prices increase, and the duration tangent line fails to indicate the true higher price. Conversely, when yields increase, prices decrease, but the duration tangent line overstates the amount of the price decrease relative to the true convex relationship. This helps illustrate what is meant by the term positive convexity.

Convexity is largest for low coupon bonds, long-maturity bonds, and low yields to maturity. If convexity is large, extensive changes in duration are implied, with corresponding inaccuracies in forecasts of price changes. Convexity calculations can be made similar to those with modified duration discussed earlier. These calculations produce an approximate percentage price change due to convexity that can be added to the one based on duration discussed earlier. This total percentage price change is still an approximation, but it is considerably improved over that using only duration.

Some Conclusions on Duration

What does this analysis of price volatility mean to bond investors? The message is simple — to have the maximum (minimum) price volatility from a bond, investors should choose bonds with the longest (shortest) duration. If an investor already owns a portfolio of bonds, he or she can act to increase the duration of the portfolio if a decline in interest rates is expected and the investor is attempting to achieve the largest price appreciation possible. Fortunately, duration is additive, which means that a bond portfolio's duration is a weighted average of each individual bond's duration.

The duration concept has become so popular in today's investment world that it is widely known and discussed in the popular press. Investors can find duration numbers in a variety of sources, particularly with regard to bond funds. As the Real-World Returns box above suggests, investors should basically forget maturity and think in terms of duration.

Although duration is an important measure of bond risk, it is not necessarily always the most appropriate one. Duration measures volatility, which is important but is only one aspect of the risk in bonds. If an investor considers price volatility an acceptable proxy for risk, duration is the measure of risk to use along with the correction for convexity. Duration may not be a complete measure of bond risk, but it does reflect some of the impact of changes in interest rates.

[18] As the yield changes, the tangency line and slope also change; that is, modified duration changes as yield changes.

REAL-WORLD RETURNS

Using Duration to Estimate the Risk of a Bond

To predict how your bond fund will perform when the bond market gets walloped, look at its duration.

Duration is the single most important measure of how risky most bond funds are because it measures their sensitivity to interest-rate changes. Duration tells you how a bond or bond fund will react to a one-percentage-point change in interest rates. For example, if a bond has a duration of 8 years, it should lose 8% of its value if interest rates on similar bonds rise by one percentage point — and gain 8% in value if interest rates fall by one percentage point. A bond with a duration of 5 years should lose only 5% of its value if rates go up by one percentage point — and gain only 5% if rates drop one percentage point. (Although duration is expressed technically in years, think of it as a percentage change.)

Doubling a bond's duration can give you a good idea of how that bond will react if rates change by two percentage points rather than one. For instance, a bond with a duration of 8 years will lose roughly 16% of its value if rates climb two percentage points.

Because it's such a good measure, bond-fund managers almost always keep a tight grip on the duration of their holdings. "Every trade I make, I recalculate the duration of the portfolio," says Jerome Jacobs, manager of Vanguard Municipal Long Term. (Alas, when we called Vanguard's 800 number, we got a garbled definition of duration and a slightly different number from the one Jacobs quoted.)

Investors don't need to analyze their holds with pinpoint accuracy any more than they need to know the precise braking distance on a new car. But it's good to have at least a rough idea of the duration of the bonds and bond funds you own — as well as those that you're considering buying.

Duration is of far more value than the number that many inexperienced investors focus on: yield. "People who buy bond funds tend to do so on the basis of yield, but often the higher the yield the higher the duration," says Kurt Brouwer, a San Francisco investment adviser. A lot of investors who left the safety of certificates of deposit last fall for the higher yields of bond funds have found out the hard way that concentrating too much on yield can be costly.

While many investors don't understand duration, most are at least familiar with a less-precise measure of bond funds' interest-rate risk: maturity. Maturity is simply the number of years until a bond pays back its principal. Measure the maturities of the bonds in a fund and weight each bond according to how big a position it has in the portfolio, and you have the fund's weighted average maturity. The longer a fund's maturity, the more affected it tends to be by interest-rate swings.

But maturity is a flawed measure of interest-rate risk. "Duration is a much better guide for quantifying risk than is maturity," says Tom Poor, portfolio manager of Scudder Short-Term Bond fund. Why? Simply because duration takes into account both the amount paid on maturity *and* the value of the interest payments made along the way.

Consider two hypothetical 20-year bonds. One, a zero-coupon bond, doesn't pay a penny in interest until the day it matures. The other pays 7% interest annually. Common sense tells you that a bond that pays 7% annually is less volatile than one that pays nothing for 20 years.

But duration gives a more precise method of comparing the interest-rate sensitivity of the two bonds. Because the zero-coupon bond doesn't pay any interest until it matures, its duration is virtually the same as its maturity — 20 years. Meanwhile, the other bond, priced at $100 and yielding 7% annually, has a duration of 10.7 years. Other things being equal, the higher a bond's yield, the *shorter* its duration. Take a 20-year bond also priced at $100 but with a 10% yield. Its duration is 8.6 years, or more than two years shorter than the duration of the 7% bond.

Some of the equations used in determining duration are so complex that without today's computers, duration would be an impractical tool. Fortunately, investors don't have to bother with the math. Even many portfolio managers don't know exactly how durations are figured. "If you call a bond trader and ask him how he calculates a duration, he's going to say he punches up a computer screen and looks at it," says Vanguard's Jacobs.

If you could know only one number about a bond fund, it should be its duration. But there is a second important number to use in choosing a bond fund — total return. While duration measures interest-rate risk, total return shows an investor how much a bond fund has earned, both in yield and in capital gains.

A good general rule in investing is that the more risk you take the higher your potential rewards should be. But the best funds manage to produce top returns without undue risk.

Keeping Names Straight

As good a measure as it is, duration isn't perfect. One flaw is that it changes as as interest rates change. When interest rates climb, bond-fund durations shorten. When rates fall, durations lengthen. Unless rates shift dramatically, however, changes in duration should be fairly small, particularly for short- and intermediate-term bond funds. A bond fund's duration can also change when the fund trades the bonds in its portfolio. Check your fund's duration periodically to avoid unpleasant surprises.

There are a few other things to be aware of in using duration as an evaluation tool. It won't tell you anything about the credit quality of your bonds. A high-yield junk bond reacts as much to investor concerns about the stability of the economy and the issuing company as it does to interest rates. For that reason, duration is of less value in assessing junk bonds or funds. Similarly, foreign bonds change in value with currency swings, as well as with changes in interest rates. So duration isn't all that helpful in evaluating foreign bonds, either.

It also pays to keep in mind that duration is a theoretical measure of interest-rate risk. The ultimate test of a bond's worth is the marketplace. During times of extreme volatility — such as the first quarter of this year — liquidity can dry up and buyers may become scarce, regardless of what duration indicates the price should be. "In a rapidly moving market environment, bonds aren't necessarily going to behave the way bond math suggests," cautions Brad Tank, manager of Strong Short-Term Bond fund. This is particularly true of complex derivatives, used by some bond-fund managers to enhance returns.

Be aware that duration can be expressed in more than one way. The most accurate measure is *effective duration*, which takes into account the impact of bonds being called — that is, redeemed early by the issuer. In the municipal-bond market, bonds are often issued with maturities of 20 or 30 years but contain a provision that allows the issuer to pay them off earlier, typically after ten years. Effective duration also takes into account the prepayment risk in mortgage-backed bonds. If rates decline, many homeowners will refinance, lowering the duration of the bonds in mortgage-securities funds.

Although it's not as accurate, modified duration is the number that funds are most willing to make public. It does not take into account the probable effect of prepayments and calls. In municipal-bond and mortgage funds, especially, modified duration is likely to overstate slightly the interest-rate risk.

Source: Adapted and reprinted with permission from Kiplinger's Personal Finance Magazine, *June 1994.*

SUMMARY

This summary relates to the learning objectives provided on page 311.

1. **Calculate the price of a bond.**
   A bond's intrinsic value is its estimated value, or the present value of the expected cash flows from that asset. Bond prices are determined according to Equation (11-2).
2. **Explain the bond valuation process.**
   Bonds are valued using a present value process. The expected future cash flows for a bond — interest payments and principal repayments — are discounted at the bond's required yield. Bond prices change in response to changes in the level of market interest rates on similar instruments.
3. **Calculate major bond yield measures, including yield to maturity, yield to call, and horizon return.**
   The yield to maturity is defined as the promised compounded rate of return an investor will receive from a bond purchased at the current market price and held to maturity. The yield to call is the promised yield to the end of the period when a bond can first be called. The horizon return is the total rate of return earned on a bond over some time period given certain specified reinvestment rates of return.
4. **Account for changes in bond prices.**
   Bond prices move inversely with interest rates; prices increase as the required yield decreases and vice versa. Changes in bond prices are directly related to time to maturity and inversely related to bond coupons. Given a change in interest rates the two most important bond variables in assessing the change in a price of a bond are its coupon and its maturity.
5. **Explain and apply the concept of duration.**
   Duration is the weighted average time to recovery of all interest payments plus principal repayment. Duration expands with time to maturity but at a decreasing rate, and it is inversely related to coupon and yield to maturity. The modified duration can be used to calculate the percentage price change in a bond for a given change in the bond's yield to maturity. The bond price-yield relationship is not linear but convex, and precise calculations of price changes should properly account for this convexity.

KEY TERMS

Basis points
Conversion premium (Appendix 11-A)
Conversion price (Appendix 11-A)
Conversion ratio (Appendix 11-A)
Conversion value (Appendix 11-A)
Convertible securities (Appendix 11-A)
Convexity
Current yield
Duration
Horizon return
Interest on interest
Intrinsic value
Modified duration
Real risk-free rate of interest
Reinvestment rate risk
Yield to call
Yield to maturity (YTM)

ADDITIONAL RESOURCE

Sixty-two chapters of detailed information on fixed-income securities, written by well-known authorities on fixed-income securities, can be found in Fabozzi, Frank J., Editor. *The Handbook of Fixed Income Securities*. Fifth Edition. Burr Ridge, IL: Irwin Professional Publishing, 1997.

REVIEW QUESTIONS

1. What does it mean to say that YTM is a promised yield?
2. What is meant by interest on interest?
3. Distinguish between promised yield and realized yield. How does interest on interest affect realized return?
4. How is the intrinsic value of any asset determined? How are intrinsic value and present value related?
5. How is the price of a bond determined? Why is this process relatively straightforward for a bond?
6. What effect does the use of semi-annual discounting have on the value of a bond in relation to annual discounting?
7. When is a bond selling at a discount, based on coupon rate and current yield? When is it selling at a premium?
8. Define YTM. How is YTM determined?
9. Why is YTM important?
10. If YTM is merely a promised yield, why do investors not use some other measure of yield?
11. Which bond is more affected by interest-on-interest considerations?
    a. Bond A — 12 per cent coupon, 20 years to maturity
    b. Bond B — 6 per cent coupon, 25 years to maturity
12. How can bond investors eliminate the reinvestment rate risk inherent in bonds?
13. How does duration differ from time to maturity? What does duration tell you?
14. Assume that a bond investor wishes to maximize the potential price volatility from a portfolio of bonds about to be constructed. What should this investor seek in the way of coupon, maturity, and duration?
15. Is duration a complete measure of bond risk? Is it the best measure? Why?
16. What assumptions are involved in calculating the horizon return?
17. Differentiate between yield to call and yield to maturity. Will the yield be the same for both? Explain.
18. What are the implications of Malkiel's bond price theorems to bond investors? Which two bond variables are of major importance in assessing bond price changes?
19. How is duration related to time to maturity? to coupon payments? to the yield to maturity? Do the same relationships hold for a zero-coupon bond?
20. What is convexity? Why should bond investors consider it?
21. With the exception of zero-coupon bonds, a bond's duration will always be less than the bond's time to maturity. Why?

PREPARING FOR YOUR PROFESSIONAL EXAMS

Special Note to CSC Students

Ensure that you have read and understood the following topics:*

Bond prices, pp. 312–318
Bond yields, pp. 318–326
Bond price changes, pp. 326–331
Appendix 11-A: Convertible bonds, pp. 346–351
Appendix 11-B: Interest Rates, the Bank of Canada, and Canadian Monetary Policy, pp. 352–354
CSC Notes: Treasury bill yields and prices (Appendix 11-B), p. 354

**Reading these CSC-related topics should provide you with additional understanding of CSC material. However, it should not be seen as a substitute for reading the CSC textbook itself, which is the basis for the CSC exam.*

CSC REGISTRATION QUESTIONS

The Canadian Securities Institute issued the following sample questions in the 1997 CSC registration package as a means for students to self-assess their understanding of CSC-related material.

1. A 9.5 per cent bond has a yield of 9.75 per cent. The bond is selling at a price that is _______ par.

   a. higher than

   b. lower than

   c. the same as

2. (Refer to Appendix 11-A on convertible bonds for this question.)

   If a convertible bond is said to be "selling off the stock," its price is _________ its stated par value.

   a. higher than

   b. lower than

   c. the same as

3. (Refer to Appendix 11-B on interest rates, the Bank of Canada, and Canadian monetary policy for this question.)

   In a __________, the Bank of Canada moves federal government deposits from the direct clearer's account to its own.

4. The relationship between the yields of bonds of the same quality but different maturities is best demonstrated in graphic form by using a(n) _________.

5. Answer each of the following questions regarding the bond quote shown below. Do not consider accrued interest in formulating your answers.

XYZ Inc.	10.25%	15 Sept. 96/02	98.625	99.50

   Note: the bond was issued at par

a. If the bondholder does nothing to prevent it, what will happen to the bond on September 15, 1996?

b. At what price?

i. 98.625
ii. 99.50
iii. 100.00
iv. at some price below 100.00

c. This bond has a special feature. What is it called?

d. What effect would this feature have had on the interest rate of this bond?

e. Since the time the bond was issued, interest rates have _____________.

i. risen
ii. fallen
iii. not changed
iv. The above quote does not provide enough information to answer this question.

f. What is the spread on this bond?

i. 875 points
ii. 87.5 points
iii. 0.875 points
iv. 8.75 points

g. Investor X buys this bond on Monday, June 8. Assuming there are no holidays during the settlement period, what is the settlement date?

h. On what date(s) each year would interest payment(s) be made?

PAST CFA EXAM PROBLEMS

The following question was asked on the 1984 CFA Level I examination:

1. Assume a $10,000 par-value zero-coupon bond with a term-to-maturity at issue of 10 years and a market yield of 8 per cent.

a. Determine the duration of the bond.

b. Calculate the initial issue price of the bond at a market yield of 8 per cent, assuming semi-annual compounding.

c. Twelve months after issue, this bond is selling to yield 12 per cent. Calculate its then-current market price. Calculate your pre-tax rate of return assuming you owned this bond during the 12-month period.

Assume a 10 per cent coupon bond with a Macaulay duration of 8 years, semi-annual payments, and a market rate of 8 per cent.

a. Determine the modified duration of the bond.

b. Calculate the per cent change in price for the bond, assuming market rates decline by two percentage points (200 basis points).

The following question was asked on the 1988 CFA Level I examination:

2. You are asked to consider the following bond for possible inclusion in your company's fixed income portfolio:

Issuer	Coupon	Yield-to-Maturity	Maturity	Duration
Wiser Company	8%	8%	10 years	7.25 years

a. Explain why the Wiser bond's duration is less than its maturity.

b. Explain whether a bond's duration or its maturity is a better measure of the bond's sensitivity to changes in interest rates.

Briefly explain the impact on the duration of the Wiser Company bond under each of the following conditions:

a. The coupon is 4 per cent rather than 8 per cent.

b. The yield-to-maturity is 4 per cent rather than 8 per cent.

c. The maturity is seven years rather than ten years.

PROBLEMS

1. a. Consider a bond with a coupon rate of 10 per cent, a maturity value of $1,000, and with three years to maturity, while the appropriate discount rate is 8 per cent. Show that the price of the bond is $1,051.54 with annual discounting and $1,052.24 with semi-annual discounting. Use a calculator to determine the discount factors.

   b. What would be the price of this bond if both the coupon rate and the discount rate were 10 per cent?

2. With reference to Problem 1(a), what would be the price of the bond if the coupons were paid quarterly?

3. Calculate the price of a 10 per cent coupon bond with eight years to maturity, given an appropriate discount rate of 12 per cent, using both annual and semi-annual discounting.

4. Calculate the price of the bond in Problem 3 if the maturity is 20 years rather than eight years, using semi-annual discounting. Which of Malkiel's principles are illustrated when comparing the price of this bond to the price determined in Problem 3?

5. The YTM on a 10 per cent, 15-year bond is 12 per cent. Calculate the price of the bond if coupons are paid semi-annually.

6. Consider a junk bond with a 12 per cent coupon (paid annually) and 20 years to maturity. The current required rate of return for this bond is 15 per cent. What is its price? What would its price be if the required yield rose to 17 per cent? 20 per cent?

7. a. Calculate the YTM for a 10-year zero-coupon bond sold at $400. Recalculate the YTM if the bond had been priced at $300.

   b. Determine the price of a 15-year zero-coupon bond if the required rate of return is 12 per cent.

8. Calculate the realized compound yield for a 10 per cent bond paying semi-annual coupons with 20 years to maturity and an expected reinvestment rate of 8 per cent.
9. Consider a 12 per cent 10-year bond paying annual coupons purchased at face value. Based on Table 11-1 and assuming a reinvestment rate of 10 per cent, calculate:
   a. The interest on interest
   b. The total return
   c. The realized return given the 10 per cent reinvestment rate
10. Consider a 4 per cent coupon bond with 15 years to maturity that pays semi-annual coupons. Determine the YTM that would be necessary to drive the price of this bond to $300.
11. Calculate the YTM for the following bonds that all pay coupons semi-annually.
    a. A 12 per cent, 20-year bond with a current price of $975
    b. A 6 per cent, 10-year bond with a current price of $836
    c. A 9 per cent, eight-year bond with a current price of $714
12. Bank of Nova Scotia's bonds, with a coupon rate of 6.25 per cent are selling at 103.51 and pay annual coupons. Exactly eight years remain to maturity. Determine the
    a. Current yield
    b. Yield to maturity
13. Domtar Inc.'s bonds, with a coupon rate of 10.00 per cent, sell to yield 7.51 per cent. Exactly 13 years remain to maturity. What is the current market price of the bonds assuming semi-annual coupons. If the YTM had been 11.5 per cent, what would the price of the bonds be? Explain why this difference occurs.
14. A 12 per cent coupon bond has 20 years to maturity and pays annual coupons. It is currently selling for 20 per cent less than face value. Determine its YTM.
15. Given a 10 per cent, three-year bond with a price of $1,052.24 that pays semi-annual coupons. If the market yield is 8 per cent, calculate its duration using the format illustrated in Table 11-3.
16. A 12 per cent coupon bond with 10 years to maturity is currently selling for $913.50. Determine the modified duration for this bond.
17. Calculate the yield to first call for a 10 per cent, 10-year bond that pays annual coupons and is callable five years from now. The current market price is $970, and the call price is $1,050.
18. Using Problem 12, assume that 18 years remain to maturity. How would the yield to maturity change? Does the current yield change?
19. Using the duration from Problem 15, determine:
    a. The modified duration
    b. The percentage change in the price of the bond if r changes 0.50 per cent.
20. Calculate the duration of a 12 per cent coupon bond with 10 years remaining to maturity and selling at par.
21. Given the duration calculated in Problem 20, calculate the percentage change in bond price if the market discount rate for this bond changes by 0.75 per cent.

APPENDIX 11-A

CONVERTIBLE BONDS

Convertible Securities Bonds or preferred stock convertible into common stock.

The convertible bond is a form of equity-derivative securities (discussed in Chapter 19) that permits the owner to convert it into common stock under specified conditions. **Convertible securities** or "convertibles," which also encompass convertible preferred stock, carry a claim on the common stock of the issuer, which is exercisable at the owner's initiative. If the option is never exercised, the convertible bond remains in existence until its maturity date, whereas a convertible preferred could remain in existence forever, since preferred stock has no maturity date.[19]

Unlike puts and calls and warrants, convertible securities derive only part of their value from the option feature (i.e., the claim on the underlying common stock). These securities are valuable in their own right, as either bonds or preferred stock. Puts and calls and warrants, on the other hand, are only as valuable as the underlying common stock and have no value beyond their claim on the common stock. Convertibles have increased in popularity in recent years because they offer a unique combination of equity and bond characteristics.

Terminology for Convertible Securities

Conversion Ratio The number of shares of common stock that the owner of a convertible security receives upon conversion.

Conversion Price The par value of a convertible security divided by the conversion ratio.

Conversion Value A convertible security's value based on the current price of the common stock.

Conversion Premium The dollar difference between the market price of a convertible security and its conversion value.

Convertible securities, whether bonds or preferred stock, have a certain terminology.

1. The **conversion ratio** is the number of shares of common stock that a convertible holder receives on conversion, which is the process of tendering the convertible security to the corporation in exchange for common stock.[20]
2. The **conversion price** is the par value of the bond or preferred divided by the conversion ratio.[21]

(11-16) Conversion price = Par value/Conversion ratio

3. The **conversion value** is the convertible's value based on the current price of the common stock. It is defined as

(11-17) Conversion value = Conversion ratio × Current price of common

4. The **conversion premium** is the dollar difference between the market price of the security and its conversion value.

(11-18) Conversion premium = Market price of convertible − Conversion value

[19] Many convertible bonds cannot be converted for an initial period of six to 24 months.

[20] Forced conversion results when the issuer initiates conversion by calling the bonds.

[21] It is obvious that the conversion privilege attached to a convertible can be expressed in either conversion ratio or conversion price terms. Both the conversion price and the conversion ratio are almost always protected against stock splits and dividends.

Convertible securities are, by construction, hybrid securities. They have some characteristics of debt or preferred stock and some of the common stock on which they represent an option. Therefore, to value them one must consider them in both contexts.

EXAMPLE: CONVERSION PREMIUM FOR MACMILLAN BLOEDEL

Consider the convertible debentures of **MacMillan Bloedel** that have a maturity date of May 1, 2007 and a coupon rate of 5 per cent, with coupons paid semi-annually. Its conversion ratio on July 3, 1998 was $100 worth of par value for 3.49 common shares. The conversion price at that time was $28.63, or approximately $100/3.49.[22] MacMillan's common stock was selling at $16.05 on that date, while the debentures were selling at $87.00 per $100 par value. The conversion value of MacMillan's convertibles on this date was therefore 3.49 × $16.05 = $56.01. Thus, the conversion premium on that date was $87.00 − $56.01 = $30.99 (or 55.3 per cent of the conversion value of $56.01).

The Basics of Convertible Bonds

Convertible bonds are issued by corporations as part of their capital-raising activities. Similar to a warrant, a convertible feature can be attached to a bond as a sweetener to make the issue more attractive to investors. They allow the issuer to pay a lower interest rate by offering investors a chance for future gains from the common stock. Convertibles are sometimes sold as temporary financing instruments with the expectation that over a period of months (or years) the bonds will be converted into common stock. The bonds are a cheaper source of financing to the issuer than the common stock, and their gradual conversion places less price pressure on the common stock. Finally, convertibles offer a corporation the opportunity to sell common stock at a higher price than the current market price. If the issuer feels that the stock price is temporarily depressed, convertible bonds can be sold at a 15 to 20 per cent premium. The result of this premium is that the price of the stock must rise by that amount before conversion is warranted.

Most bonds, whether convertible or not, are callable by the issuer. This results in additional concerns for the convertible bondholder.

Convertible bonds are typically issued as debentures. They are often subordinated to straight (non-convertible) debentures, increasing their risk. According to bond rating agencies, most convertible bonds are one class below a straight debenture issue. Nevertheless, convertible bonds enjoy good marketability. Large issues are often more actively traded than many non-convertible issues of the same quality.

Analyzing Convertible Bonds

A convertible bond offers the purchaser a stream of interest payments and a return of principal at maturity. It also offers a promise of capital gains if the price of the stock rises sufficiently.

[22] Many convertible bonds have a conversion price that increases over time.

To value a convertible bond, it is necessary to account for all of these elements. The convertible bond model is illustrated graphically in Figure 11-5 to provide a framework for analysis. We shall then illustrate the components of value individually.

Graphic Analysis of Convertible Bonds

Figure 11-5 shows the components of the convertible bond model. This diagram depicts the expected relationships for a typical convertible bond. The horizontal line from PV (par value) on the left to the maturity value (MV) on the right provides a reference point; any bond sold at par value would start out at PV, and all bonds will mature at their maturity value. If such a bond is callable, the call price will be above the par value in the early years because of the call premium; by maturity this price would converge to the maturity value.

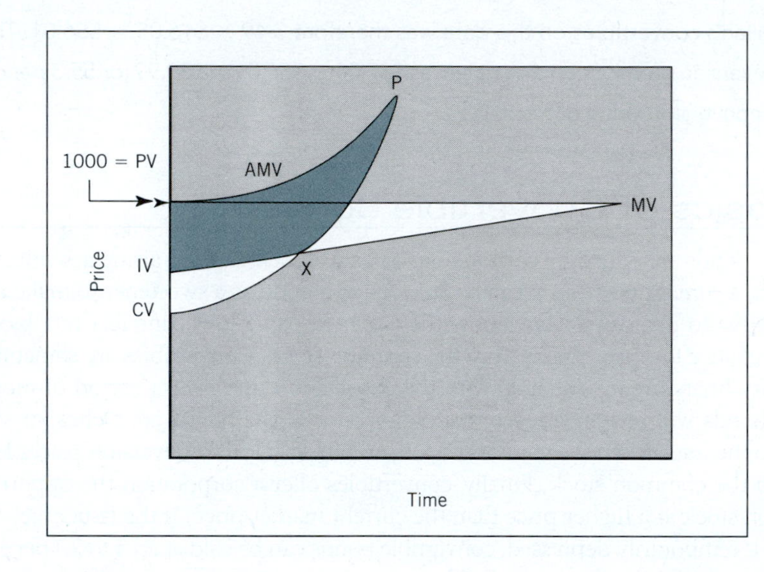

Figure 11-5
Conceptual Model for Understanding Convertible Bonds

Each convertible bond has an investment value (IV) or straight-debt value, which is the price at which a convertible would sell to equal the yield on a comparable non-convertible. In other words, the investment value is the convertible's estimated value as a straight bond. By evaluating the coupons and the maturity value of the convertible at the going required rate of return for a comparable straight bond, the beginning investment value can be determined. Remember that the straight (i.e., non-convertible) bond has a higher market yield because it does not offer a speculative play on the common stock. The investment value is represented in Figure 11-5 by the line from IV to MV, the maturity value.

Each convertible has a conversion value at any time. The original conversion value (point CV) is established by multiplying together the conversion ratio and the price of the common stock at the time the convertible is issued. The conversion value curve in Figure 11-5 is then drawn on the assumption that the price of the stock will grow at a constant rate, g; that is,

$$P_1 = P_0 (1 + g)$$

$$P_2 = P_1(1 + g)$$

and so forth. Obviously, this is an expected relationship and may not occur in this manner. Using this assumption, the conversion value rises above the par value as the price of the stock rises, tracing out the curve CV-P in Figure 11-5.

Finally, because the convertible often sells at a premium, it is necessary to draw an actual market value (AMV) curve, which is shown in Figure 11-5 as AMV-P. This curve eventually approaches the conversion value curve as the conversion value increases. This is primarily because the convertible may be called, forcing conversion. If this occurs, the convertible holder can receive only the conversion value. Therefore, investors are not likely to pay more than this for the convertible.

The shaded area in Figure 11-5 is the premium over conversion value, which declines as the market price of the convertible rises. This reflects the fact that the bond is callable.

Bond Value

Every convertible bond has a *straight bond value* or an investment value, which is the price at which the bond would sell with no conversion option. This price is given by the present value calculations for a bond, as explained in Chapter 11.

$$SBV = C \times (PVA_{r,n}) + MV \times (PV_{r,n}) \quad \textbf{(11-19)}$$

where
SBV = straight bond value (or investment value)
C = the interest payments (coupons)
MV = maturity value of the bonds
n = number of periods to maturity
r = appropriate required rate of return

EXAMPLE: STRAIGHT BOND VALUE OF MACMILLAN BLOEDEL

Let's consider again the convertible debentures of **MacMillan Bloedel** that were discussed in the previous example. Assuming an appropriate discount rate for similar non-callable bonds at that time of 7.5 per cent, and assuming a term to maturity of exactly nine years (which is relatively close to the exact term), we obtain the following estimate of the investment value or straight bond value of MacMillan's convertibles:

$$SBV = 2.50 \times (PVA_{3.75\%,18}) + 100 \times (PV_{3.75\%,18}) = 32.30 + 52.55 = \$83.85$$

Of course, the bond value fluctuates over time as market interest rates change.

Conversion Value

Every convertible bond has a conversion value that is the value of the common stock received upon conversion. At the time it is issued a convertible bond has a conversion value equal to the market price of the common stock multiplied by the number of shares of stock that can be received by converting. As noted, the conversion price is usually set 15 to 20 per cent above the current market price of the common, so that conversion would not be worthwhile. Over time, if the price of the common stock increases, the conversion value should also grow at the same rate.

Minimum (Floor) Value

Every convertible bond has a minimum or floor value. A convertible will always sell for no less than the greater of (1) its bond (straight) value or (2) its conversion value. In other words,

(11-20) Floor value of a convertible = Maximum (Straight bond value; conversion value)

Even if the value of the conversion feature is zero, with virtually no prospect of a change in this value, a convertible bond would have a minimum price of its investment or straight bond value (i.e., its value as a non-convertible debt instrument). If the price were to decline below this value, bond investors would buy it because its yield would be greater than alternative comparable bonds. The straight bond value for the MacMillan debentures on the valuation date was $83.85, the absolute minimum price for this bond as of that time.

Actual Bond Value (Price)

INVESTING tip

In a similar manner, a convertible bond cannot sell below its conversion value. If it did, arbitragers would buy the bond, convert it into common stock, and sell the shares, or simply establish a position in the underlying common stock at a cost lower than would otherwise be possible. Since the MacMillan conversion value of $56.01 was lower than its bond value, the bond value was its minimum, or floor value at the time of these calculations. In Figure 11-5, the line IV-X-P represents the minimum market value for the convertible bond. This minimum market value is made up of part of the investment value line (IV to X) and part of the conversion value curve (X to P). We can call this the effective market value floor.

Convertible bonds usually sell at prices above their minimum value, and, as we have seen, that is the higher of the bond value or the conversion value. For example, the MacMillan bond sold for $87.00, $4.15 above its bond value (and floor value), and was $30.99 above its conversion value.

Two of the reasons convertibles sell at premiums are:

1. The conversion option has a positive value because the right to convert any time during the life of the bond is valuable and investors are willing to pay for it. In effect, this is equivalent to owning a call option on the stock, and calls command positive premiums (as explained in Chapter 19).
2. A convertible bond offers investors downside protection, thereby decreasing their risk. If the price of the common stock declines sharply, resulting in a sharp decline in the conversion value, the convertible will still sell as a bond and will have a bond value determined by the present value of interest payments and principal. This dual minimum-price feature of convertibles reduces investors' risk and commands a premium in doing so.

In evaluating convertible bonds, certain details in addition to the preceding factors should be kept in mind. When a convertible bond is converted, the holder loses the accrued interest from the last interest payment date. Furthermore, if a holder converts after the ex dividend date, the common stock dividend on the newly received common shares could be lost. Since the issuer can call the bonds and force conversion, these factors can be important, and it is not unusual for issuers to choose a time favourable to themselves.

A bond is subject to call if the market price exceeds the call price. Investors who pay a premium over the conversion value in these circumstances run a risk of having the bond called as the company forces conversion.

Should Investors Buy Convertible Bonds?

Why should investors consider convertible bonds? As for advantages, convertible bonds offer investors a unique combination of an income stream from a fixed-income security and a chance to participate in the price appreciation of the common stock. Convertibles offer downside protection in relation to owning the common stock, because regardless of what happens to the price of the common stock, the convertible bond will not decline below its value as a straight bond. They offer upside potential, because a convertible bond must always be worth at least its conversion value as the price of the common stock rises. Furthermore, the yield on a convertible bond usually exceeds the dividend yield of the underlying common stock, and interest payments have first order of priority. Compared to common stock owners, convertible bond holders enjoy a yield advantage while awaiting appreciation in the stock price.

As for disadvantages, convertible bonds yield less than do straight bonds of similar risk and maturity. Investors must give up some yield to receive the conversion feature. Convertibles are callable, and in many cases the issuer can and will force conversion. When a convertible bond is called, the holder will choose the better alternative — accept the call price or convert into common stock. If a corporation calls a bond at, say, $1,100 (face value of $1,000 plus one year's interest of $100 for a call premium), and the conversion value is, say, $1,200, the bondholders in effect are forced to convert. They give up their fixed-income security and the chance for future capital gains from the common stock.

APPENDIX 11-B

INTEREST RATES, THE BANK OF CANADA, AND CANADIAN MONETARY POLICY

Interest Rates

Interest rates are probably the most important financial variables affecting securities markets, since they are essentially the price of credit, as determined by the forces of supply and demand. Interest rates vary according to duration of the borrowing, terms of the loan, and creditworthiness of the borrower. High interest rates tend to: (1) raise the cost of capital to firms thereby reducing business investment; (2) discourage consumer spending (particularly for durables); and (3) reduce disposable income available for net borrowers due to higher debt servicing charges.

Some key interest rate determinants include: (1) inflation — rates rise to compensate lenders for loss in purchasing power as inflation rises; (2) foreign developments and the exchange rate — foreign interest rates and domestic exchange rate affect the demand for Canadian debt instruments; (3) government deficits or increases in investment spending cause an increased demand for capital, which increases rates unless there is a corresponding increase in savings; (4) the greater the default risk of the borrower, the greater the rate that must be paid to borrow funds; and (5) the Bank of Canada can have an impact on short-term rates directly, and on long-term rates less directly through the credibility of its commitment to controlling inflation.

The bank rate is the rate at which the Bank of Canada lends money to financial institutions in Canada. Until recently, it was set at 25 basis points (one quarter of a percentage point) above the average yield on three-month Treasury bills. In 1996, a new policy was adopted whereby the bank rate will be set at the ceiling of its target range for overnight money rates (discussed below).

The Bank of Canada

The Bank of Canada was founded in 1935. It is governed by a board of directors composed of the governor, the senior deputy governor and 12 directors — by tradition, at least one member from each province. The directors are appointed by the minister of finance for three-year terms. The directors, with the approval of the Governor-in-Council, appoint the governor and senior deputy governor for seven-year terms. The governor is chairman of the board and chief executive officer and is responsible for formulation and execution of monetary policy. The deputy minister of finance also sits on the board but has no voting rights.

The major functions of the Bank of Canada are:

1. Acting for the government in issuing and removing bank notes.
2. Acting as the government's chief fiscal agent and financial advisor. As a fiscal agent, the bank: advises the government on financial matters; administers the deposit and fund accounts; manages international currency reserves and operates for the government in

foreign exchange markets; acts as a depository for gold; and acts as the government's debt manager in issuing new debt securities and paying interest on them and retiring them.

3. Acting as controller of the banks' clearing system.
4. Acting as a lender of last resort to chartered banks. The bank often makes these funds available using purchase and resale agreements (PRAs), where the bank buys eligible securities from the dealer and simultaneously resells them to the dealer for settlement at a later date. The bank may also provide assistance to a financial institution that is in serious financial difficulty (but only in cooperation with the superintendent of financial institutions).
5. Maintenance of orderly conditions in the financial marketplace. This responsibility is over and above any aims it may have as to target interest rate and exchange rate levels.
6. Conducting monetary policy is the bank's most important function. (It is discussed in the section below.)

The bank is responsible for maintaining stability in the general level of prices, employment, output and trade, and the external value of the Canadian dollar. In recent years, the bank has focused on price stability, which it sees as the best way monetary policy can contribute to stability in employment, output, and the exchange rate. Generally, the bank announces joint targets in cooperation with the federal government. Since 1961, in the event of a dispute, the finance minister may issue a directive instructing the bank to follow a certain policy, however, no such directive has ever been issued.

The bank attempts to control inflation primarily through raising and lowering interest rates, although its open market transactions do impact money supply as well. It recognizes that monetary conditions are the combined effect of interest rates and exchange rates, and it combines the two variables in a "monetary conditions index." Recently the bank has estimated that a 1 per cent rise in interest rates is equivalent to a 3 per cent increase in the trade-weighted exchange rate. This means that if rates rose 1 per cent, but the Canadian dollar fell 3 per cent (say, from $0.71 US to $0.6887 US), monetary conditions would be relatively unaffected.

Monetary Policy

Monetary policy refers to the use of interest rates, the exchange rate, and rate of money supply growth to influence demand and inflation. The bank's most important tool for influencing interest rates involves managing highly liquid reserves in the banking system through its "drawdown" and "redeposit" mechanism (cash management). All banks and other financial institutions that clear payments through the Canadian Payments Association (CPA) have accounts with the bank. Therefore, the bank can tighten or loosen the supply of cash in the banking system by increasing or decreasing the amount of money in these accounts.

Generally, the bank shifts federal funds between accounts at the Bank of Canada, and demand deposits at the clearing banks, in order to give institutions unexpected positive or negative settling balances. If the clearing banks find themselves with a positive balance, they will lend out the excess funds and buy securities, putting downward pressure on interest rates. The bank achieves this using a redeposit which moves deposits from its own account to those of the clearing banks. The reverse happens if the clearing banks find themselves with a negative balance that the bank induces using a drawdown (which is the reverse of a redeposit). Financial institutions often use this information to make judgements regarding the bank's short-term stance.

The bank can also influence rates by trading money market securities in the open market (open market operations). Generally, it targets three-month T-bill rates and/or the overnight rate. The bank affects T-bill rates by buying and selling T-bills from its own inventory, which represents the most aggressive signal on interest rates the bank can send. To lower interest rates through this mechanism, it buys T-bills by offering a price above the present market price. This lowers rates due to the inverse relationship between rates and prices. It also expands the bank's balance sheet and effectively increases the money supply, since the dealer which sells the T-bills will likely lend out the funds it receives from the bank. Since the bank is targeting interest rates and not money supply, it will often attempt to neutralize the effect on money supply through drawdowns. When the bank sells T-bills, the reverse effect occurs.

The bank affects overnight rates by: offering to lend overnight money through a special purchase and resale agreement (PRA), or repo, at stated rates (when it wants to reduce rates); and offering to borrow overnight at given rates from financial institutions through a reverse special PRA (when it wants to increase rates). Since 1994, the Bank of Canada has established 50-basis point operating bands for overnight money by conducting repos (or specials) at the ceiling rate and reverses 50 basis points below the ceiling. The target rate is the mid-point in this range.

The bank can also affect interest rates using "moral suasion," which involves simply asking financial institutions to tighten or loosen credit conditions in order to achieve its policy without action in the money market.

CSC NOTES

Treasury Bill Yields and Prices

Treasury bills are sold in Canada on a discount basis, based on their bond equivalent yield, which is determined using the following equation:

$$r_{\text{BEY}} = \frac{\text{Face} - \text{P}}{\text{P}} \times \frac{365}{n} \times 100$$

where

r_{BEY} = the bond equivalent yield
P = the T-bill price
Face = the T-bill face value
n = the number of days to maturity

For example, the yield on an 89-day Government of Canada Treasury bill that is presently selling at a price (P) of 98 per 100 of face value, can be determined in the following manner:

$$r_{\text{BEY}} = \frac{100 - 98}{98} \times \frac{365}{89} \times 100 = 8.3696\%$$

Rearranging this equation, we can see that T-bills are priced according to the following relationship:

$$\text{P} = \frac{\text{Face}}{(1 + r_{\text{BEY}} \times \frac{n}{365})}$$

Yields on US T-bills are quoted based on the bank discount yield, which is determined using a slightly different procedure than that used to calculate the bond equivalent yield in Canada. The differences arise from the use of face value instead of price in the denominator of the first term, and that 360 days instead of 365, is used to annualize the rate. The resulting equation is given by:

$$r_{\text{BDY}} = \frac{\text{Face} - \text{P}}{\text{Face}} \times \frac{360}{n} \times 100$$

where
r_{BDY} = the bank discount yield

APPENDIX 11-C

DURATION, BOND PRICES, AND INTEREST RATES

With the use of some relatively straightforward calculus it is easy to show that duration is a good measure of the sensitivity of bond prices with respect to changes in interest rates. We begin by expressing the bond valuation equation in the following manner

$$P = C \times \frac{1}{(1+r)^1} + C \times \frac{1}{(1+r)^2} C \times \frac{1}{(1+r)^3} + \ldots + C + \frac{1}{(1+r)^{n-1}} + (C + MV) \times \frac{1}{(1+r)^n}$$

or

$$P = C \times (1+r)^{-1} + C \times (1+r)^{-2} + C \times (1+r)^{-3} + \ldots + C \times (1+r)^{-(n-1)} + (C + MV) \times (1+r)^{-n}$$

Taking the first derivative of this equation with respect to $(1 + r)$, we have

$$\frac{\partial P}{\partial(1+r)} = -\begin{bmatrix} (1 \times C \times (1+r)^{-2}) + (2 \times C \times (1+r)^{-3}) + (3 \times C \times (1+r)^{-4}) \\ + \ldots + ((n-1) \times C \times (1+r)^{-n}) + (n \times (C + MV) \times (1+r)^{-(n+1)}) \end{bmatrix}$$

If we factor $(1 + r)^{-1}$ out of the bracketed term, we get

$$\frac{\partial P}{\partial(1+r)} = -(1+r)^{-1} \begin{bmatrix} (1 \times C \times (1+r)^{-1}) + (2 \times C \times (1+r)^{-2}) + (3 \times C \times (1+r)^{-3}) \\ + \ldots + ((n-1) \times C \times (1+r)^{-(n-1)}) + (n \times (C + MV) \times (1+r)^{-n}) \end{bmatrix}$$

If we divide both sides by the bond price (P), we get

$$\frac{\partial P}{P \times \partial(1+r)} = -(1+r)^{-1} \frac{\begin{bmatrix} (1 \times C \times (1+r)^{-1}) + (2 \times C \times (1+r)^{-2}) + (3 \times C \times (1+r)^{-3}) \\ + \ldots + ((n-1) \times C \times (1+r)^{-(n-1)}) + (n \times (C + MV) \times (1+r)^{-n}) \end{bmatrix}}{P}$$

The second term on the right hand side of this equation equals the Macaulay duration (D) measure, so we have

$$\frac{\partial P}{P \times \partial(1+r)} = -(1+r)^{-1} \times D$$

Rearranging this expression, we get

$$D = -\frac{\frac{\partial P}{P}}{\frac{\partial(1+r)}{(1+r)}}$$

This expression implies that duration equals minus one times the percentage change in bond prices $\left[\frac{\partial P}{P}\right]$ for a given percentage change in one plus the interest rate $\left[\frac{\partial(1+r)}{(1+r)}\right]$. In other words, duration measures the approximate percentage change in bond prices for a given change in interest rates. This is the reason that duration is such an effective measure of the interest rate sensitivity of bond prices. Unfortunately, as is the usual case for using derivatives to measure slopes, it only works well for small changes in the underlying variable (interest rates or $(1 + r)$ in this situation). In addition, it is based on the notion of a flat yield curve (discussed in Chapter 12), since the interest rate for each period is assumed equal to the YTM.

CHAPTER 12

BONDS: ANALYSIS AND STRATEGY

LEARNING OBJECTIVES

After reading this chapter, you will be able to

1. Explain why investors buy bonds.
2. Discuss major considerations in managing a bond portfolio.
3. Explain what is meant by the term structure of interest rates.
4. Differentiate between passive and active strategies for managing a bond portfolio.
5. Describe how both conservative and aggressive investors build a fixed-income portfolio.

CHAPTER PREVIEW

In Chapter 11, we learned how to calculate bond prices and yields and identified key factors such as interest rate changes that affect the bond market. In this chapter we conclude our discussion of bonds by examining some of the broader issues involved in the management of a bond portfolio. We consider why investors buy bonds and discuss important issues such as the term structure of interest rates and yield spreads. We differentiate between passive and active strategies of managing a bond portfolio. Finally, we look at the importance of the global bond market to investors.

WHY BUY BONDS?

As noted in Chapter 6, the total return on bonds can be separated into two components: income from the coupons, and the capital gains (or losses) due to changes in bond prices. This explains why bonds appeal to both conservative investors seeking steady income and aggressive investors seeking capital gains. A wide range of investors participate in the fixed-income securities marketplace, ranging from individuals who own a few government or corporate bonds to large institutional investors who own billions of dollars of bonds. Most of these investors are presumably seeking the basic return-risk characteristics that bonds offer; however, quite different overall objectives can be accomplished by purchasing bonds. Table 12-1 outlines some key investment considerations for many of the fixed-income investment alternatives available to Canadian investors.

As fixed-income securities, bonds are attractive for many investors because they offer a steady stream of interest income over the life of the obligation and a return of principal at maturity. Buyers know the promised yield on a bond held to maturity, and barring default by the issuer, they will have the bond principal returned to them at maturity. By holding to maturity, investors can escape the risk that interest rates will rise, thereby driving down the price of the bonds, although other risks may not be eliminated.

As an illustration of the return and risk situation for an investor who is seeking steady returns, consider Figure 12-1, which shows total return indexes and total returns for long-term Government of Canada bonds for the period 1924 to 1997. These bonds possess no practical risk of default. At the end of 1997, investors in these government bonds, with coupons reinvested, would end up with $74.79 per dollar invested. This is a compound growth rate of 6.1 per cent. As the bottom panel shows the total annual returns have generally been positive, and if held to maturity the nominal returns on these bonds would always be positive.

Some investors are interested in bonds precisely because bond prices will change with interest rates. change. If interest rates rise, bond prices will fall and vice versa. These investors are interested not in holding the bonds to maturity but rather in earning the capital gains that are possible if they correctly anticipate movements in interest rates. Because bonds can be purchased on margin, large potential gains are possible from speculating on interest rates. (Of course, large losses are also possible.)

To get some idea of the changes in returns that can result from fluctuations in interest rates, consider again Figure 12-1. Notice that some of the total annual returns were very large, far beyond the yield component alone. For example, the total return was 43 per cent in 1982, 25 per cent in 1985, and 26 per cent in 1995. Clearly, successful bond speculation in each of those years resulted in very large returns. Note, however, that returns were also negative in 17 out of 74 years.

Speculation has been heavy in the bond markets in recent years. In the past, bonds were viewed as very stable instruments whose prices fluctuated very little in the short run. This situation has changed drastically however, with bond markets becoming quite volatile. Interest rates in the early 1980s reached record levels, with long-term government bonds offering yields over 15 per cent in 1981. The high interest rate levels caused large changes in bond prices.

There are many kinds of bond speculators from financial institutions to individual investors, but they all have one thing in common. Each is trying to take advantage of an expected movement in interest rates. Thus, investors seeking income from bonds, as well as investors attempting to speculate with bonds, are keenly interested in the level of interest rates and any likely changes.

Buying Foreign Bonds

Why do Canadian investors have foreign bonds in their portfolios? One obvious reason is that approximately 98 per cent of the fixed income investment opportunities available in the world exist outside Canada. Canada's bond market is small relative to those in countries such as the US and Japan, as can be seen in Table 12-2. For example, in 1997, Canada's debt outstanding totaled $506 billion (US), which represented only 2 per cent of all outstanding debt on the world's largest bond markets. On the other hand, US and Japanese bond markets accounted for 48 per cent and 17 per cent of the world market respectively. In addition, Canada's private bond market is even smaller in relation to the global one. In 1997, there was approximately $75 billion (US) in Canadian private debt outstanding, representing only 0.8 per cent of the global market. This pales in comparison to the US, which had over $5 trillion (US) in 1997 (approximately 52 per cent of the world's private debt market).

Although the performance of bonds, like equities, changes continuously, foreign bonds may offer higher returns than alternative domestic bonds. Based on historical performance standards, Canada has not had one of the best performing international bond markets. For example, from 1978 to 1997 Canada had the best bond performance only once (in 1989), but was the worst international performer twice (in 1978 and 1990). Investing globally increases the likelihood that a portion of the investment will be placed in a high-performing country.

Another important reason for buying foreign bonds is the diversification, which is extremely important for both stock and bond portfolios. Given the relatively small size of the Canadian bond market, taking a global perspective greatly expands the number of available investment opportunities. This increases the likelihood of developing a well-diversified fixed-income portfolio. When Canadian bond prices are declining those in some foreign countries may be rising.

As we now know when considering investment opportunities, investors do not receive something for nothing. First of all, individual investors find it difficult to invest directly in foreign bonds. It is relatively costly and can be time consuming. Furthermore, some brokerage firms do not offer foreign bonds to individual investors, while others require a minimum investment of $10,000 and often much more. Selling foreign bonds that are directly owned also can be a problem, since many foreign secondary markets face liquidity problems. This means that individual investors selling small amounts of foreign bonds abroad generally will not be able to demand the top prices.

Table 12-1

The Fixed-Income Investment Guide

Instrument	Term & Availability	Quality	Backed By	Liquidity	Income Frequency
SHORT-TERM INSTRUMENTS					
Federal T-Bills	1 day to 1 year	Highest	Federal Gov't	Highest	Maturity
Provincial T-Bills	1 day to 1 year though availability is generally limited after 3 months	Good	Prov. Gov't	Good	Maturity
Crown Corporate Commercial Paper		Highest	Federal Gov't	Good	Maturity
Bankers Acceptances		Good	Canadian Banks	Good	Maturity
Commercial Paper		Varies	Cdn. Corps.	Good	Maturity
LONG-TERM INSTRUMENTS					
Strip Coupons and Residuals	1 month to 30 years	Varies by issuer	Fed., Prov., and Corp. Issuers	Good	No income is received before maturity.
Coupon Annuity Packages (CAPs)	5 to 20 years	Good	Fed. & Prov. Gov't	Good	Provides maturities on an ann. or semi-ann. basis.
Callable Residuals	3 months to 10 years, availability in some terms may be limited.	Varies by issuer	Prov. Gov't	Good	None
Discount Savings Bonds (DSBs)	5 to 20 years	Good	Prov. and Fed Gov't	Good	Pays no income until specified future date, then semi-annual
Guaranteed Income Certificates (GICs)	1-5 years	High	Fed. Gov't through the CDIC, up to $60,000	Limited	Monthly/Semi/ Ann/Comp
Canada Savings Bonds (CSBs)	Varies, 10-12 Years	Highest	Federal Gov't	Good	Ann/Comp
Provincial Savings Bonds	3-5 years, availability in secondary market may be limited.	Good	Prov. Gov't	Varies	Semi/ Ann/Comp
Federal Bonds	1-30 years	Highest	Federal Gov't	Highest	Semi-Annual
Provincial Bonds	1-30 years	Good	Prov. Gov't	Good	Semi-Annual
Municipal Bonds	1-30 years	Good	Municipal Gov't	Limited	Semi-Annual
Corporate Bonds	1-30 years	Varies	Corporations	Good	Semi-Annual
Monthly Pay Bonds	1-5 years	Varies by issuer	Fed./Prov./Corp.	Good	Monthly
Monthly Income Bond Packages (GEMs)	2-10 years. Laddered GEMs are also available.	Good	Fed. & Prov. Gov't	Good	Monthly
NHA Mortgage Backed Securities (NHA MBS)	1-5 years	Highest	Federal Gov't	Good	Monthly
Foreign Currency Bonds	1-30 years	Good	Foreign Gov't/Corps.	Limited	Annual
Canadian Dollar Euro Bonds	1-30 years	Good	Foreign Gov't/Corps.	Fair	Annual
Real Return Bonds	20-25 years	Highest	Federal Gov't	Good	Semi-Annual
Real Return Strip Coupons	5-25 years	Highest	Federal Gov't	Good	Semi-Annual
Step-Up Bonds / Issuer Extendible Notes	First maturity usually after 2 or 3 years, extendible by the issuer up to a specified term.	Varies	Fed./Prov./Corp.	Fair	Semi-Annual

The information contained in this report has been compiled by RBC Dominion Securities Inc. ("RBCDS-Canada") from sources believed by it to be reliable, but no representations or warranty, express or implied, is made by RBCDS-Canada or any other person as to its accuracy, completeness or correctness. All opinions and estimates contained in this report constitute RBCDS-Canada's judgement as of the date of this report, are subject ot change without notice and are provided in good faith but without legal responsibilitiy. This report is not an offer to sell or a solicitation of an offer to buy any securities. RBCDS-Canada and its affiliates may have an investment banking or other relationship with some or all of the issuers mentioned herein and may trade in any of the securities mentioned herein either for their own account or the accounts of their customers. RBCDS-Canada and its affiliates also may issue options on securities mentioned herein and may trade in options issued by others. Accordingly, RBCDS-Canada or its affiliates may at any time have a long or short position in any such security or option thereon. The securities discussed in this report may not be eligible for sale in some states or in some countries. Neither RBCDS-Canada or any of its affiliates, not any other person, accepts any liability whatsoever for any direct or consequential loss arising from any use of this report or the information

Trade Denominations	Taxation	Other Characteristics	Recommended For:
$1,000	Interest Income	These securities are priced at a discount to mature at par (100)	Investors who have cash that will be needed for future investment opportunities, or who have temporary cash balances to be put to work
$100,000	Interest Income		
$50,000	Interest Income		
$100,000	Interest Income		
Varies	Interest Income		
$1	Interest Income. As no income is received until maturity or a future date, these instruments are recommended for RSP accounts.	Eliminates reinvestment risk through compounding interest. Price movements more volatile than normal bonds.	RSP or RIF investors who do not need current income.
1 package		CAPs are a pre-packaged strip coupon portfolio.	Investors planning future cash flows and RIFs
$1,000		Similar to strip coupon. If not called, the residual turns into a regular semi-annual bond.	Investors willing to accept the risk of not being called to gain yield.
$1,000		Similar to strip coupon until semi-annual interst payments commence.	Investors planning future cash flows and RIFs.
$1	Interest Income	CDIC guarantee does not cover principal and income in excess of $60,000.	Highly conservative investors.
$100	Interest Income	Come in many forms, can be cashed in with no penalty.	Highly conservative investors.
$100	Interest Income	Come in many forms, often cashable.	Highly conservative, residents of the issuing province.
$1,000	Interest Income	Forms the benchmark for pricing all other bonds.	Highly conservative investors.
$1,000	Interest Incomes		
$1,000	Interest Income		Investors willing to give up some liquidity for yield.
$1,000	Interest Income	Often come with a call feature.	Investors willing to invest time investigating credit quality in order to pick up yield.
$1,000	Interest Income	Monthly income = coupon/12	Investors who require monthly income.
1 package	Interest Income	A package of government backed bonds.	Investors who require monthly income.
$5,000	Interest Income	Payments include interest and some principal.	Investors who require monthly income.
Varies by country	Interest Income	Investor assumes currency and interest rate risk.	Investors who are willing to accept currency risk, or who wish to diversify.
$1,000	Interest Income	Trades in the "Euro" market.	Investors who require regular, but not semi-annual income.
$1,000	Interest Income	Income and maturity value linked to inflation. Actual cash flows are unknown, while purchasing power is known	Investors who wish to diversify their portfolio with an inflation hedge.
$1	Interest Income		
$1,000	Interest Income	Extendable at issuer's option. Offers higher initial interest payments that increase over time.	Investors willing to give up a portion of potential capital gains and take the risk of being called in exchange for higher current income.

contained herein. Any U.S. recipient of this report that is not a registered broker-dealer or a bank acting in a broker or dealer capacity and that wish further information regarding, or to effect any transaction in, any of the securities discussed in this report, should contact and place orders with RBC Dominion Securities Corporation, a U.S. registered broker-dealer affiliate of RBCDS-Canada, at (212) 361-2619, which, without in any way limiting the foregoing, accepts responsibility (within the meaning, and for the purposes, of Rule 15a-6 under the U.S. Securities Exchange Act of 1934), for this report and its dissemination in the United States. This report may not be reproduced, distributed or published by any recipient hereof for any purpose.

Source: *The Fixed-Income Investment Guide* (Toronto: RBC Dominion Securities, Fall 1997), pp. 10-11. Reprinted with permission from RBC Dominion Securities.

Figure 12-1(a)
Long Canada Bonds Total Return Index (1924–97)

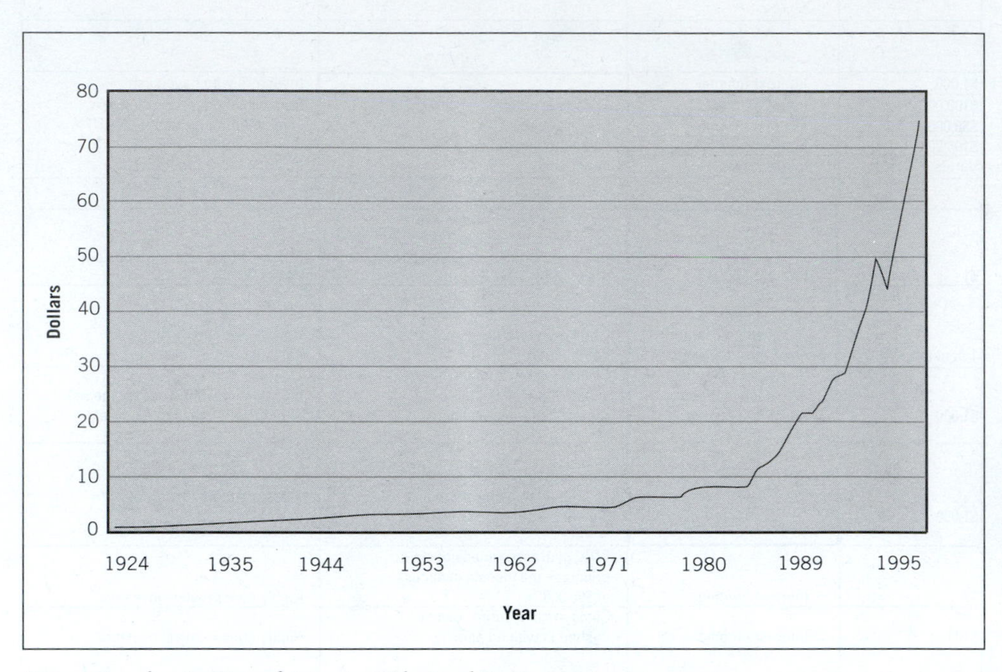

Source: Canadian Institute of Actuaries Web site: <http://www.actuaries.ca>.

Figure 12-1(b)
Long Canada Bonds Total Annual Returns (1924–97)

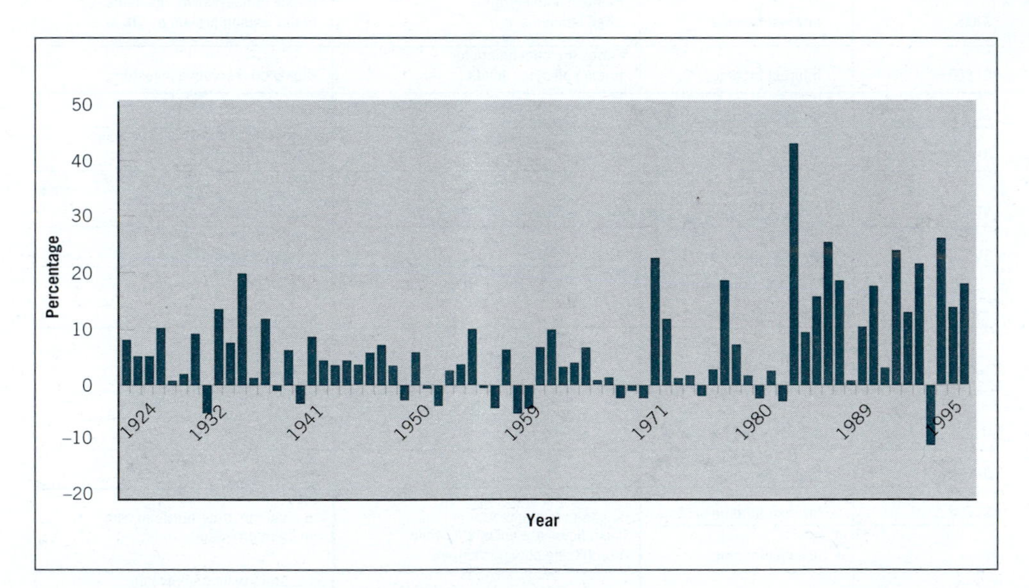

Source: Canadian Institute of Actuaries Web Site: <http://www.actuariesca>.

Investors who are considering direct investment in foreign bonds face the additional issue of transaction costs. Dollars must be converted into the foreign currency to make purchases and converted back into dollars when they are sold. On small transactions these costs can significantly eat into returns.

Finally, investors in foreign bonds must deal with exchange rate risk. An adverse movement in the dollar can result in a Canadian investor's return being lower than the actual return on the asset; in some case that return could even be negative.

Table 12-2

Global Bond Markets

	Outstanding Amounts ($US billions)			Percentages		
	1995	1996	1997	1995	1996	1997
Argentina	49.0	55.4	70.5	0.2	0.2	0.3
Australia	162.5	187.0	160.2	0.7	0.7	0.6
Austria	147.1	144.7	136.5	0.6	0.6	0.5
Belgium	426.9	407.3	349.9	1.7	1.6	1.4
Brazil	209.8	265.1	304.0	0.8	1.0	1.2
Canada	**502.7**	**516.2**	**506.7**	**2.0**	**2.0**	**2.0**
China	93.1	119.4	129.1	0.4	0.5	0.5
Czech Republic	12.1	12.3	12.4	0.0	0.0	0.0
Denmark	296.7	287.9	262.6	1.2	1.1	1.0
Finland	86.0	84.1	79.9	0.3	0.3	0.3
France	1278.1	1241.7	1113.2	5.1	4.8	4.3
Germany	1909.4	1877.0	1730.0	7.6	7.2	6.7
Greece	86.7	100.5	93.9	0.3	0.4	0.4
Hong Kong	21.9	21.5	29.5	0.1	0.1	0.1
Hungary	12	15.2	13.8	0.0	0.1	0.1
Iceland	3.8	4.3	4.7	0.0	0.0	0.0
India	97.5	110.8	111.4	0.4	0.4	0.4
Ireland	28.2	30.6	29.5	0.1	0.1	0.1
Italy	1526.0	1689.3	1471.7	6.1	6.5	5.7
Japan	4955.6	4747.6	4433.7	19.8	18.3	17.2
Korea South	227.3	239.0	125.2	0.9	0.9	0.5
Luxembourg	0.6	1.0	0.9	0.0	0.0	0.0
Malaysia	62.4	73.1	49.3	0.2	0.3	0.2
Mexico	22.2	26.1	35.5	0.1	0.1	0.1
Netherlands	268.9	258.2	227.8	1.1	1.0	0.9
New Zealand	20.3	21.7	17.1	0.1	0.1	0.1
Norway	65.2	66.8	65.3	0.3	0.3	0.3
Poland	24.9	25.7	25.0	0.1	0.1	0.1
Portugal	60.3	64.3	55.7	0.2	0.2	0.2
Russia	16.5	42.6	64.6	0.1	0.2	0.3
Singapore	48.8	55.3	46.2	0.2	0.2	0.2
Spain	327.6	340.8	315.7	1.3	1.3	1.2
Sweden	302.6	302.7	257.0	1.2	1.2	1.0
Switzerland	242.2	199.3	180.0	1.0	0.8	0.7
Turkey	21.4	26.5	41.4	0.1	0.1	0.2
United Kingdom	600.1	728.3	767.8	2.4	2.8	3.0
United States	10780.3	11620.4	12414.6	43.1	44.7	48.2
TOTAL	24996.3	26009.7	25732.2	100.0	100.0	100.0

Source: Used with permission from "International Banking and Financial Market Developments, "Bank for International Settlements (BIS) Web site: <http://www.bis.org>.

IMPORTANT CONSIDERATIONS IN MANAGING A BOND PORTFOLIO

Understanding the Bond Market

The first consideration for any investor is to understand the basic nature of the bond market. It has been commonplace to talk about the bond market benefiting from a weak economy. This refers to the fact that if the economy is growing slowly, interest rates may decline and bond prices rise. In effect, a decline in economic growth may lead to fewer investment opportunities, leading savers to increase their demand for bonds, pushing bond prices up and bond yields down. While this result benefits existing bondholders, it may make bond yields unattractive to potential new investors. Nonetheless, talk of a rapidly growing economy is thought to frighten bond investors, since it will increase inflationary and interest rate expectations, thus putting downward pressure on bond prices.

The relationship that really matters in this view is between bond yields and inflation, not between economic growth and bond yields. As we know from Chapter 11, interest rates reflect expected inflation. If investors expect a rise in inflation, they demand more from a bond to compensate for the expected decline in the purchasing power of the future cash flows. Therefore, an increase in expected inflation tends to depress bond prices and increase yields.

Figure 12-2 shows a plot of annual yields on long-term Government of Canada bonds, and annual growth rates in the Consumer Price Index (CPI), which is a measure of inflation, over the period 1957 to 1996. Notice that bond yields followed an upward trend until 1981 and a downward trend thereafter. The CPI growth rate behaved in similar fashion, and there was a high positive correlation coefficient of 0.60 between CPI and bond yields. This should not be surprising since CPI measures actual inflation levels, which we would expect to be highly correlated with expected inflation.

Figure 12-2
Changes in CPI and Long-Term Canada Bond Yields

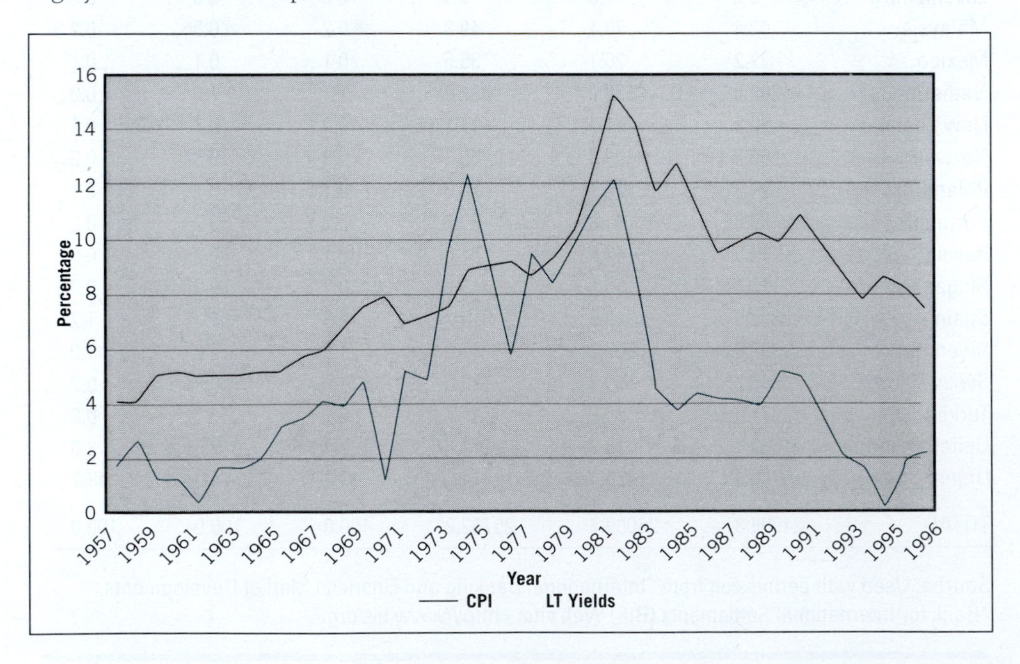

We can say that bond markets clearly dislike inflation because of its negative effect on fixed-income securities, and they favour Bank of Canada actions that temper economic growth and reduce inflation. Thus, bond investors may react quite favourably to a tightening of monetary policy because this helps to calm inflation fears, which is one reason why investors carefully monitor Bank of Canada actions, both realized and prospective. One such restrictive monetary policy, referred to as "tilting the yield curve," is discussed in the CSC Notes box below.

CSC NOTES

Tilting the Yield Curve

When short-term rates rise while long-term rates fall, it is referred to as a "tilting of the yield curve." This is significant for capital markets because it indicates a temporary reprieve from more short-term interest rate pressure and less competition for equities from bond yields. The general process by which a yield curve tilts in response to observed new economic growth is:

1. Initially, rising bond yields cause bond prices to fall.
2. Short-term rates escalate and the rate at which long-term bond yields increase slows.
3. As short rates continue to rise, the economy slows. Bond prices begin to stabilize and briefly fall less than equity prices. This is because slower economic growth is generally better for bonds than for stocks.
4. Suddenly, as short-term rates continue to increase, long-term rates actually begin to fall, causing bond prices to rise. This will occur when the bond market becomes satisfied with the slowing of economic growth.

A decline in long rates reduces the competition between equities and bonds and may also lead to eventual reductions in short rates. The reduced upward pressure on short rates relative to earnings growth is good for stocks. On the other hand, the high real rates offered by bonds increase the attractiveness of these instruments to investors, which, in turn, increases the competition between bonds and equities, to the detriment of equity prices.

On average, these tilts cause equity market rallies. Strong evidence suggests that US and Canadian equity markets rally when the yield curve tilts, and the gains increase as the degree of tilt increases. Table 12-3 demonstrates the three-month performance of the TSE 300 and the S&P 500, subsequent to tilts in the yield curve. The TSE 300 recorded an average three-month total return of 2.51 per cent during periods where there was no tilting of the yield curve. However, during periods where there was a tilt of any degree, we observe an average three-month return of 3.28 per cent. This number increases when we examine periods of more severe tilting. For example, the three-month TSE 300 return was 6.90 per cent during periods where the short rate rose more than 2 per cent, while the long rates fall more than 1 per cent. (The three-month return for such severe tilts occurring since 1982 was 9.76 per cent, although there were only seven such periods).

Table 12-3

Three Month Total Return Changes for Various Degrees of Tilting

	TSE 300		S&P 500	
Degree of Tilting*	**All Data**	**Post 1982**	**All Data**	**Post 1982**
Underlying Data (No Tilting)	2.51%	2.71%	3.05%	3.83%
Any Degree of Tilting	3.28	5.15	3.26	5.51
1%	4.74	6.88	4.17	7.53
1.5%	5.46	9.49	3.58	8.21
Short ↑ 2%, long ↑ 1.5%	6.90	9.76	4.53	8.30

*Short rate up, long rate down

Source: *Canadian Securities Course Textbook* (Toronto: Canadian Securities Institute, August 1998), p. 9-24. ©1998 Canadian Securities Institute. Reprinted with permission.

The bond market may also respond favourably to a strengthening of the dollar. A stronger dollar increases the value of dollar-denominated assets to foreign investors. The traditional relationships in the bond market may be changing because of the global nature of money management and the increasing use of derivatives. Leverage has become a big factor in the bond markets and has magnified the swings in bond prices. According to some sources, leveraged speculation resulted in the bond rally of 1993 and the major debacle in 1994. *Fortune* magazine estimated that as of mid-September 1994, the rise in rates on 30-year US Treasury bonds (about one and one-half percentage points) resulted in a $600 billion loss on US bonds and a possible $1.5 trillion loss worldwide.[1] Is it any wonder that *Fortune* titled this article "The Great Bond Market Massacre"?

The Term Structure of Interest Rates

Term Structure of Interest Rates
The relationship between time to maturity and yields for a particular category of bonds at a particular time.

The **term structure of interest rates** refers to the relationship between time to maturity and yields for a particular category of bonds at a particular time. Ideally, other factors are held constant, particularly the risk of default. The easiest way to do this is to examine Government of Canada securities, which have no practical risk of default, have no sinking fund, and are taxable. By eliminating those that are callable and those that may have some special feature, a quite homogeneous sample of bonds is obtained for analysis.

Yield Curves

Yield Curve
A graphical depiction of the relationship between yields and time to maturity for bonds that are identical except for maturity.

The term structure is usually plotted in the form of a **yield curve**, which is a graphical depiction of the relationship between yields and time for bonds that are identical except for maturity. The horizontal axis represents time to maturity, whereas the vertical axis represents yield to maturity.

Figure 12-3
Yield Curves

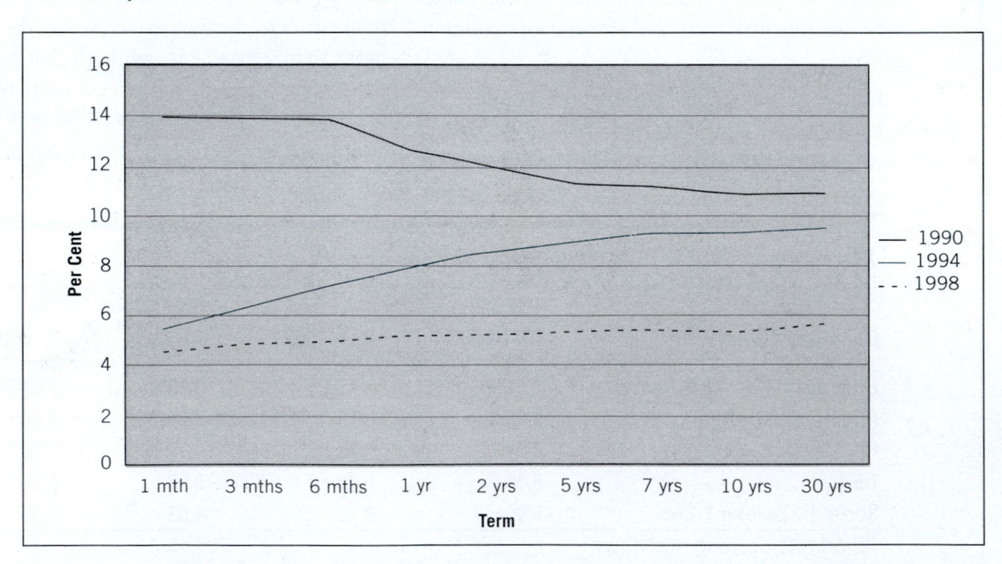

Yield curves are for Government of Canada securities as of the end of June for the respective years.

[1] Al Ehrbar, "The Great Bond Market Massacre," *Fortune*, October 17, 1994, pp. 77–92.

Figure 12-3 shows three yield curves for Government of Canada T-bills and bonds at the end of June in 1990, 1994, and 1998.[2] The upward-sloping curve in 1994 is considered typical; that is, interest rates that rise with maturity are considered the "normal" pattern. The downward-sloping curve for 1990 is less common, with short-term rates above long-term rates. These "inverted" yield curves are unusual, and some market participants believe they indicate that short-term rates will fall and, in fact they did decline in the 1991 to 1993 period. Another less common shape is the relatively flat yield curve existing in 1998, which indicates that long- and short-term rates are very similar.

Most observations about yield curves involve tendencies and not exact relationships. For example, there generally is a negative relationship between short rates and the yield spread. A higher short rate is usually associated with a flatter yield curve because long rates do not increase by quite as much. However, this relationship does not always hold, as was the case for 1998 when the yield curve was flat despite the existence of low short-term rates.

Implied Forward Rates

The following yields offered by Government of Canada securities were used to construct the yield curve depicted in Figure 12-3, for June 30, 1998:

Time to Maturity	Yield (%)
1-month T-bills	4.60
3-month T-bills	4.76
6-month T-bills	4.90
1-year T-bills	5.11
2- year Canada bonds	5.14
5-year Canada bonds	5.23
7-year Canada bonds	5.29
10-year Canada bonds	5.30
30-year Canada bonds	5.47

The rates above are referred to as "spot" rates, and we use them to compute implied forward rates. For example, the one-year spot rate is 5.11 per cent and the two-year spot rate is 5.14 per cent. The implied forward rate is the one that solves the following expression:

$$({}_tR_1 + 1)\,(1 + {}_1f_2) = (1 + {}_tR_2)^2$$

where,

${}_tR_1$ = the current known one-year spot rate prevailing at time t

${}_tR_2$ = the current known two-year spot rate prevailing at time t

${}_1f_2$ = the implied one-year forward rate, from the end of year 1 to the end of year two

In this example,

$$(1 + {}_1f_2) = (1 + {}_tR_2)^2 \,/\, ({}_tR_1 + 1) = (1.0514)^2 \,/\, (1.0511) = 1.0517,$$

$$\text{so } {}_1f_2 = 5.17\%$$

2 These are only three examples — there are numerous other shapes that yield curves can assume.

Similarly, if the three-year rate was 5.20 per cent, then the implied forward rate from year two to year three could be calculated as:

$$(1 + {}_2f_3) = (1 + {}_tR_3)^3 / ({}_tR_2 + 1)^2 = (1.0520)^3 / (1.0514)^2 = 1.0532,$$
$$\text{so } {}_2f_3 = 5.32\%$$

Term Structure Theories

A theory of the term structure of interest rates is needed to explain the shape and slope of the yield curve and why it shifts over time. Four theories traditionally advanced are the expectations theory, the liquidity premium theory, the preferred habitat theory, and the market segmentation theory.

Expectations Theory The hypothesis that the long-term rate of interest is equal to an average of the short-term rates that are expected to prevail over the long-term period.

The pure or "unbiased" **expectations theory** of the term structure of interest rates asserts that financial market participants determine security yields such that the return from holding an n-period security equals the average return expected from holding a series of one-year securities over the same n periods. In other words, the long-term rate of interest is equal to an average of the present yield on short-term securities plus the expected future yields on short-term securities that are expected to prevail over the long-term period. For each period, the total rate of return is expected to be the same on all securities regardless of time to maturity.

Forward Rates Unobservable rates that are expected to prevail in the future.

In effect, the term structure consists of a set of forward rates and a current known rate. **Forward rates** are those that are expected to prevail in the future; that is, they are unobservable but anticipated future rates. In essence, the pure expectations theory suggests that the implied forward rates calculated above, equal the expected future spot rates.

Under the expectations theory, long rates must be an average of the present and future short-term rates. For example, a three-year bond would carry an interest rate that is an average of the current rate for one year and the expected forward rates for the next two years. The same principle holds for any number of periods; therefore, the market rate for any period to maturity can be expressed as an average of the current rate and the applicable forward rates. Technically, the average involved is a geometric rather than an arithmetic average.

For expositional purposes:

${}_tR_n$ = the current known yield (at time t) on a security with n periods to maturity

${}_{t+1}r_n$ = the yield expected to prevail one year from today (at time $t + 1$) for n periods – these are forward rates

The rate for the three-year bond referred to above must be a geometric average of the current one-year rate (${}_tR_1$) and the expected forward rates for the subsequent two years. Therefore, in equation form

$$(1 + {}_tR_3) = [(1 + {}_tR_1)(1 + {}_{t+1}r_1)(1 + {}_{t+2}r_1)]^{1/3} - 1.0 \quad \textbf{(12-1)}$$

where

$(1 + {}_tR_3)$ = the rate on a three-year bond $(1 + {}_tR_1)$ = the current known rate on a one-year bond

$(1 + {}_{t+1}r_1)$ = the expected rate on a bond with one year to maturity beginning one year from now

$(1 + {}_{t+2}r_1)$ = the expected rate on a bond with one year to maturity beginning two years from now

EXAMPLE: USING FORWARD RATES

Assume the current one-year bond rate (${}_tR_1$) is 0.07, and the two forward rates are 0.075 (${}_{t+1}r_1$) and 0.082 (${}_{t+2}r_1$). The rate for a three-year bond, $(1 + {}_tR_3)$, would be

$$\begin{aligned}(1 + {}_tR_3) &= [(1.07)(1.075)(1.082)]^{1/3} - 1.0\\ &= 1.07566 - 1.0\\ &= 0.07566 \text{ or } 7.566\%\end{aligned}$$

The same principle applies for any number of periods. Any long-term rate is a geometric average of consecutive one-period rates.

Forward rates cannot be easily measured, but they can be inferred for any one-year future period. The expectations theory, however, does not say that these future expected rates will be correct; it simply says that there is a relationship between rates today and those expected in the future.

According to this hypothesis, investors can expect the same return regardless of the choice of investment, because any combination of securities for a specified period will have the same expected return. For example, a five-year bond will have the same expected return as a two-year bond held to maturity plus a three-year bond bought at the beginning of the third year. The assumption under this hypothesis is that expected future rates are equal to implied forward rates. Profit-seeking individuals will exploit any differences between forward rates and expected rates, ensuring that they level out.

The second theory, the **liquidity preference theory**, states that interest rates reflect the sum of current and expected short rates, as in the expectations theory, plus liquidity (risk) premiums. Because uncertainty increases with time, investors prefer to lend for the short run. Borrowers, however, prefer to borrow for the long run in order to be assured of funds. Investors receive a liquidity premium to induce them to lend long term, while paying a price premium (in the form of lower yields) for investing short term. The implication of this theory is that longer-term bonds should offer higher yields, which is consistent with the observation that yield curves are generally upward sloping.

Liquidity Preference Theory
The idea that interest rates reflect the sum of current and expected short rates, as in the expectations theory, plus liquidity (risk) premiums.

The difference between the liquidity preference theory and the expectations theory is the recognition that interest rate expectations are uncertain. Risk-averse investors seek to be compensated for this uncertainty. Forward rates and estimated future rates are not the same; they differ by the amount of the liquidity premiums. In other words, under the liquidity preference theory, the implied n-period forward rate for some future time period t, will equal the expected n-period spot rate at time t, plus a liquidity premium

$${}_tf_{t+n} = {}_tr_n + \text{liquidity premium} \qquad (12\text{-}2)$$

Preferred Habitat Theory
Investors have preferred maturity sectors or habits in which they seek to invest but are willing to shift to other maturities if they can expect to be adequately compensated.

Market Segmentation Theory
Investors confine their activities to specific maturity sectors and are unwilling to shift from one sector to another to take advantage of opportunities.

A third hypothesis for explaining the term structure of interest rates is the **preferred habitat theory**, which states that investors have preferred maturity sectors or habitats. For example, a financial institution with many five-year debentures to pay off will not want to take the reinvestment rate risk that would result from investing in one-year T-bills.

What if imbalances arise in a given maturity range between the demand and supply of funds? The preferred habitat theory states that borrowers and lenders can be induced to shift maturities if they are adequately compensated by an appropriate risk premium, which distinguishes this theory from the market segmentation theory explained below. The implication of this theory for the term structure is that both expectations concerning future interest rates and risk premiums play a role, and the yield curve can take any shape.

The preferred habitat theory is related to, but not identical with, the **market segmentation theory**. This theory states that the various investors, having different maturity needs dictated by the nature of their liabilities, confine themselves to specific maturity segments. Investors are not willing to shift from one maturity sector to another to take advantage of any opportunities that may arise. Under the market segmentation theory, the shape of the yield curve is determined by the supply and demand conditions for securities within each of the multiple maturity sectors.

Which of these theories is correct? The issue of the term structure has not been resolved; although many empirical studies have been done, the results are at least partially conflicting. Therefore, definitive statements cannot be made. The empirical evidence on the expectations hypothesis is equivocal at best. The evidence on the liquidity premium hypothesis is the most persuasive. Substantial evidence suggests that risk premiums exist, but their behaviour over time is subject to debate.

In actual practice, market observers and participants do not tend to be strict adherents to a particular theory. Rather, they accept the reasonable implications of all of them and try to use any available information in assessing the shape of the yield curve. For example, many market participants will focus on expectations but allow for liquidity premiums.

Generally, upward-sloping yield curves have been the norm, as would be predicted by the liquidity preference theory. This theory is more compatible than the others with the study of investments since it emphasizes the risk-return trade-off that exists. The liquidity preference theory stresses the idea that because of larger risks, longer maturity securities require larger returns or compensation.[3]

Regardless of which of the theories is correct, it seems reasonable to assert that investors demand a premium from long-term bonds because of their additional risk. After all, uncertainty increases with time, and as we have seen, long-term bonds are more sensitive to interest rate fluctuations than are short-term bonds. Furthermore, the typical shape of the yield curve is upward sloping, which indicates that investors are more averse to the risk of long bonds than to short-term securities.

On the other hand, the most reasonable explanation for downward-sloping yield curves is that investors expect short-term rates to decline in the near future. Otherwise, investors could earn higher returns from short-term assets, which have less risk than long-term assets. One could not expect this relationship to persist for long periods of time, since it runs counter to the risk-expected return trade-off we associate with financial assets.

Historical data can be used to provide some insights into bond horizon (maturity) premiums between 1934 and 1997. One simple approximation of the average bond horizon

[3] The expectations theory categorizes investors as return maximizers, whereas the preferred habitat theory categorizes investors as risk minimizers.

premium is the difference between the average annual returns on long-term government bonds and 91-day government T-bills. The data indicate that the annual arithmetic mean for T-bills was 5.1 per cent versus 6.5 per cent for long-term bonds, making the average horizon premium for this period 1.4 per cent.

The Risk Structure of Interest Rates — Yield Spreads

Assume that market interest rates on risk-free securities are determined as previously discussed. If the expected rate of inflation rises, the level of rates does also. Similarly, if the real rate of interest were to decline, market interest rates would decline; that is, the level of rates would decrease. Furthermore, as seen in the term structure analysis, yields vary over time for issues that are otherwise homogeneous. The question that remains is this: Why do rates differ between different bond issues or segments of the bond market?

The answer lies in what bond analysts call the risk structure of interest rates, or simply yield spreads. **Yield spreads** refer to the relationships between bond yields and the particular issuer and issue characteristics and constitute the risk premiums mentioned earlier. Yield spreads are often calculated among different bonds holding maturity constant. They are a result of the following factors:

Yield Spreads
The relationship between bond yields and the particular features on various bonds such as quality, callability, coupon rates, marketability, and taxes.

1. Differences in quality or risk of default. Clearly, other things being equal, a bond rated BAA will offer a higher yield than one rated AAA because of the difference in default risk.
2. Differences in call features. Bonds that are callable have higher yields to maturity (YTMs) than otherwise identical non-callable bonds. If the bond is called, bondholders must give it up, and they could replace it only with a bond carrying a lower YTM. Therefore, investors expect to be compensated for this risk.
3. Differences in coupon rates. Bonds with low coupons have a larger part of their YTM in the form of capital gains.
4. Differences in marketability. Some bonds are more marketable — have better liquidity — than others. They can be sold either more quickly, with less of a price concession, or both. The less marketable a bond, the higher the YTM.
5. Differences in tax treatments.
6. Differences between countries.

Other Factors Affecting Yield Spreads

Clearly, yield spreads are a function of the variables connected with a particular issue or issuer. Investors expect to be compensated for the risk of a particular issue, and this is reflected in the risk premium. However, investors are not the only determining factor in yield spreads. The actions of borrowers also affect them. Heavy government financing, for example, may cause the yield spreads between government and corporate bonds to narrow as the large increase in the supply of government securities pushes up the yields on government debt.

The level of interest rates also plays a role in explaining yield spreads. As a general proposition, risk premiums tend to be high when the level of interest rates is high.

Yield Spreads Over Time

Yield spreads among alternative bonds may be positive or negative at any time. Furthermore, the size of the yield spread changes over time. Whenever the differences in yield become smaller, the yield spread is said to narrow; as the differences increase, it widens.

One yield spread of interest to investors is the difference between the yields on corporate and government bonds. This spread is often referred to as the default risk premium, which can change for a number of reasons. The Real-World Returns box "Canadian Bonds" in Chapter 11 included many examples demonstrating the existence of default spreads. In other words, there were many cases where bonds from different issuers that had similar features with respect to maturity dates and coupon rates, were providing quite different yields to investors. For example, the Government of Canada 7.25 per cent bonds maturing on June 1, 2007 were providing a yield of 5.37 per cent. At the same time the GTC Trans and Trizec Hahn corporate bonds with the same maturity date, were providing yields of 6.01 per cent and 7.44 per cent respectively.

Figure 12-4 graphs the yield spread between long-term Canadian corporate bonds and long-term Government of Canada bonds between 1978 and 1994 based on monthly observations. Over this period, the average spread was 0.92 per cent, ranging from a maximum spread of 2.01 per cent in April 1982, to a minimum of 0.43 per cent in February 1980.

Figure 12-4
Yield Spreads

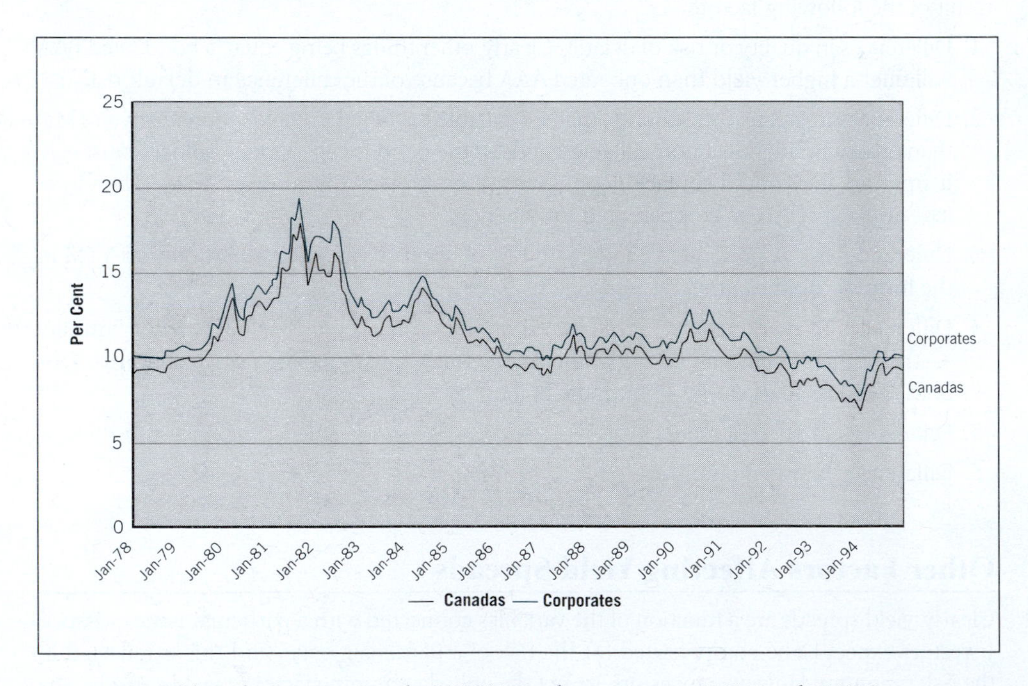

Source: Adapted from the Statistics Canada CANSIM Database series nos. B14013 and B14048.

Another yield spread that is very important for Canadian investors is the one between the yields on Canadian and US bonds and money market instruments. Generally, US debt instruments have offered lower yields than their Canadian counterparts, however, between 1995 and 1997 Canadian yields (both short-term and long-term) were below those of the US. Figure 12-5 depicts the yield spreads for the difference between Canadian and US government T-bills and long-term bonds during 1997 and up to August 1998.

Notice how Canadian T-bill rates were over 2 per cent below US T-bill rates (i.e., a spread of −2 per cent) at the beginning of 1997, however, that began to narrow during the fall of 1997, when turmoil in Asian financial markets caused global uncertainty. This trend continued throughout 1997 and 1998, and by August of 1998, Canadian T-bills offered yields approaching 1 per cent above US T-bills (i.e., a spread of +1 per cent). The movement in the Canada-US long-term bond yield spread was much less dramatic, however. It went from approximately zero, to approximately 1 per cent over this period. This is consistent with investors searching for the relatively safer US securities in response to global uncertainty, thus Canadian securities would need to offer higher yields.

Generally, yield spreads widen during recessions, when investors become more risk-averse, and narrow during times of economic prosperity. Since the probability of default is greater during a recession, investors demand more of a premium. Yield spreads were at their widest during the early 1930s when the Great Depression was at its worst. In contrast, yield spreads narrow during boom periods because even financially weak companies have a good chance of surviving and paying their debts. Historical evidence supports these trends; thus, we can state that the yield spread varies inversely to the business cycle.

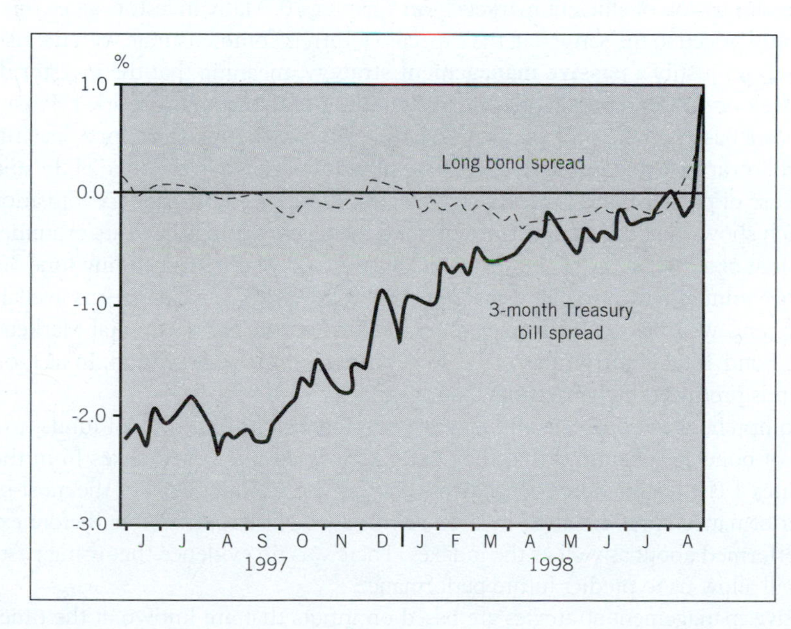

Figure 12-5
Canada-US Interest Rate Spreads

Source: "TD Weekly Digest of Economics and Financial Developments," August 28, 1998, TD Economics Section of TD Bank Financial Group Web site: http://www.tdbank.ca/tdeconomics/archives/082898wd/wd828.htm>.

BOND STRATEGIES

We now consider the basic approaches that investors can use in managing their bond portfolios, or the bond portion of their overall portfolio. An understanding of these strategies requires more than a comprehension of the basic factors affecting the valuation and analysis of bonds.

Bond investing has become increasingly popular, no doubt as a result of the high yields provided by bonds in recent years. Unfortunately, the theoretical framework for bond portfolio management has not developed to the same extent as that for common stocks. In some ways common stocks have been more "glamorous," and more attention has been devoted to them. Furthermore, there is generally more data available for common stocks.

Bond investors may adopt a variety of different strategies, depending on their risk preferences, knowledge of the bond market, and investment objectives. For organizational purposes, and because this scheme corresponds to the two broad strategies that any investor can follow with any type of portfolio, we will concentrate primarily on passive and active management of bond portfolios, as well as discussing a hybrid approach referred to as immunization. Active and passive approaches can be distinguished by the types of inputs needed. Active management relies heavily on expectations data, while passive strategies do not.

Passive Management Strategies

Passive Management Strategy
A strategy whereby investors do not actively seek out trading possibilities in an attempt to outperform the market.

Recall the discussion of efficient markets from Chapter 10. Many investors agree that securities are fairly priced in the sense that the expected return is commensurate with the risk taken. This belief can justify a **passive management strategy**, meaning that the investor does not actively seek out trading possibilities in an attempt to outperform the market. Passive bond strategies are based on the proposition that bond prices are fairly determined, leaving risk as the portfolio variable to control. In effect, the inputs are known at the time of the analysis.

The use of passive bond investment strategies is supported by evidence for various periods, which shows that the performance of bond managers during the years examined failed to equal that of a market index. For example, over the 10-year period ending June 30, 1998, the average annual return for 56 Canadian bond funds with 10-year returns available, was 9.67 per cent, well below the average annual return on the Scotia Capital Markets (SCM) Universe Bond Total Return Index of 11.36 per cent over the same period. In fact, only four of the funds produced higher returns than the index.

A comprehensive study examining the performance of bond mutual funds, using two samples of bond funds, found that they underperformed relevant indexes from the fixed-income area.[4] The results were robust across a wide choice of models. For the most part, this underperformance approximated the average management fees; therefore, before expenses, funds performed about as well as the indexes. There was no evidence that using past performance will allow us to predict future performance.

Passive management strategies are based on inputs that are known at the time, rather than expectations. These strategies have a lower expected return and risk than do active strategies. *A passive investment strategy does not mean that investors do nothing*. They must still

[4] C. Blake, E. Elton, and M. Gruber, "The Performance of Bond Mutual Funds," *The Journal of Business* 66 (July 1993), pp. 371–403.

monitor the status of their portfolios in order to match their holdings with their risk preferences and objectives. Conditions in the financial markets change quickly, and investors must also make fast changes when necessary. Passive management does not mean that investors accept changes in market conditions, securities, and so on, if these changes cause undesirable modifications in the securities they hold.

In following a passive management approach, bond investors must first determine whether the bonds to be held are suitable investment opportunities. They must assess default risk and diversify their holdings to protect themselves against changes in the probability of default. Similarly, call risk must be examined at the outset. Ideally, investors may be able to find bonds that are not callable over the period that they will be held. The higher the coupon on a bond, the more likely it is to be called. A third factor affecting investors is the marketability of a bond. Some bonds cannot be readily sold without a price concession, a lag in the time required to sell the bond, or both.

Other factors that the passive bond investor must consider at the outset of the program and monitor during the life of the investment include their current income requirement and taxes. Some bond investors need large current yields. This suggests large coupons, other things being equal. Taxes are also a factor, because the after-tax return is very important.

Strategies for investors following a passive bond management approach include buy and hold, and indexing.

Buy and Hold

An obvious strategy for any investor interested in non-active trading policies is simply to buy and hold. Having considered the factors just mentioned, this investor carefully chooses a portfolio of bonds and does not attempt to trade them in a search for higher returns. An important part of this strategy is to choose the most promising bonds that meet the investor's requirements. Making this selection requires some knowledge of bonds and markets. Simply because an investor is following a basic buy-and-hold strategy does not mean that the initial selection is unimportant. The investor must have knowledge of the yield advantage of corporate securities over government debt instruments, the yield advantage of utilities over industrials, and other factors.

One alternative for the buy-and-hold investor is to try to duplicate the overall bond market by purchasing a broad cross-section of bonds. Bond index funds, a relatively new and increasingly popular innovation, has now made it easy to accomplish this strategy. We consider this possibility separately under indexing.

Indexing

In Chapters 1 and 10 we learned that one factor affecting the investments environment is the efficiency of the markets. If capital markets are efficient — meaning that securities prices reflect information fully and quickly — investors may not be able to gain by actively searching for undervalued securities or by attempting to time market movements. The available research on this issue has led many investors to decide that they are unlikely to outperform a market index. Therefore, they are willing to build, or, more likely, buy a portfolio that will match the performance of a well-known bond index such as the SCM Universe Bond Total

Return Index in Canada. Two common US bond indexes are the Shearson Lehman Index and the Salomon Brothers Index. Mutual funds designed to match the performance of some index are known as **index funds**, and such funds are available for both bonds and stocks (stock index funds are discussed in Chapter 14).[5]

Index Funds
Mutual funds holding a bond or stock portfolio designed to match a particular market index.

One example of such an index fund is the CIBC Canadian Bond Index Fund, which is a diversified fund that seeks to match the performance of the SCM Universe Bond Index. Given the performance of bond managers discussed above, bond index funds may become a popular alternative for investors.

Active Management Strategies

Although bonds are often purchased with the intention of being held to maturity, frequently they are not. Henry Kaufman, a well-known forecaster of interest rates, commented some years ago that bonds are bought for their price appreciation potential and not for income protection. Many bond investors feel this way and use **active management strategies**. Such strategies have traditionally sought to profit from active management of bonds by either:

Active Management Strategy
A strategy designed to provide additional returns by pursuing active trading activities.

1. Forecasting changes in interest rates, because we know that bond prices will rise or fall as a result of these movements, or
2. Identifying relative mispricing between various fixed-income securities.

Notice that, unlike the passive strategy, the key inputs are not known at the time of the analysis. Instead, investors have expectations about interest rate changes and mispricings among securities.

We will consider each of these alternatives in turn. We will also examine briefly some of the newer techniques for actively managing a bond portfolio.

Forecasting Changes in Interest Rates

Changes in interest rates are the chief factor affecting bond prices because of the inverse relationship between bond prices and interest rates. When investors project interest rate declines, they should take action to invest in the right bonds for price appreciation opportunities. When interest rates are expected to rise, the objective is to minimize losses by holding bonds with shorter durations or by not holding bonds at all.

While it is difficult for the average investor to forecast interest rates very well on a consistent and accurate basis, it is not an entirely fruitless exercise. Reasonable forecasts can be made about the likely growth rate of the economy and the prospects for inflation, both of which affect interest rates and, therefore, bond investors. Assuming that an investor has a forecast of interest rates, what strategy can be used? The basic strategy is to change the duration of the portfolio. Specifically, an investor should lengthen the duration of a bond portfolio when interest rates are expected to decline, or shorten them whey they are expected to rise.

It is important to be aware of the trade-offs in strategies involving maturity.

1. Shorter durations sacrifice price appreciation opportunities but serve to protect the investor when rates are expected to rise.

[5] In practice, it is not feasible to replicate a broad bond index exactly. This is a result of the rebalancing problems that occur as bonds are dropped from the index because their maturities fall below one year and as new bonds are issued. Thus, the bonds used to compute an index change frequently.

2. Longer durations provide for greater price fluctuations; therefore, the chance for bigger gains (and losses) is magnified. However, longer maturity bonds may be less liquid than T-bills.

An important component in forecasting interest rates is the yield curve, discussed earlier in connection with the term structure of interest rates. The shape of the yield curve at any point in time contains potentially valuable information about the future course of interest rates. Bond market participants in particular, and investors in general, pay close attention to yield curves as an aid in forecasting interest rates and as part of deciding what segments of the bond market to invest in.

EXAMPLE: CHANGING YIELDS CURVES AND BOND RETURNS

Consider the situation at the end of June 1994. At that time, one-month T-bills offered a yield of 5.45 per cent, while 30-year bonds were almost 4 percentage points higher at 9.42 per cent. This difference in yields was high by historical standards, since the difference was usually less than 3 per cent, with an average difference of 1.4 per cent between 1934 and 1997. This caused many observers to predict a decrease in long-term rates in order to restore the yield curve to a more "normal" shape. Active bond investors sharing this belief would have moved to lengthen the duration of their bond portfolios, by increasing their holdings of longer term (duration) bonds, and selling shorter term (duration) securities. These beliefs turned out to be well founded, and within a year, long-term yields fell over 1 per cent. The result of this decline in long-term rates was that long-term bond investors produced some very impressive returns (in excess of 20 per cent) over this holding period.

One form of interest rate forecasting, horizon analysis, involves the projection of bond performance over a planned investment horizon. The investor evaluates bonds that are being considered for purchase over a selected holding period in order to determine which will perform the best. To do this, the investor must make assumptions about reinvestment rates and future market rates and calculate the horizon returns for the bonds being considered based on that set of assumptions. Note that this concept is different from yield-to-maturity, which does not require expectations to be integrated into the analysis. Horizon analysis requires users to make assumptions about reinvestment rates and future yields but allows them to consider how different scenarios will affect the performance of the bonds being considered. Horizon analysis was discussed in Chapter 11.

Identifying Mispricings Among Securities

Managers of bond portfolios attempt to adjust to the constantly changing environment for bonds (and all securities, for that matter) by engaging in what are called **bond swaps**. The term usually refers to the purchase and sale of bonds in an attempt to improve the rate of return on the bond portfolio by identifying relative mispricings among different types of bonds

Bond Swaps
An active bond management strategy involving the purchase and sale of bonds in an attempt to improve the rate of return on the bond portfolio.

in the market. There are several different types of bond swaps, the best known of which are discussed briefly below.[6]

1. The **substitution swap** involves bonds that are perfect (or very close) substitutes for each other with regard to characteristics such as maturity, quality rating, call provisions, marketability, and coupon payments. The only difference is that at a particular time, the two bonds sell at slightly different prices (and, therefore, a different yield to maturity). The swap is made into the higher yielding bond, which, if its yield declines to that of the other bond will provide capital gains as well as a higher current yield.
2. A **pure yield pickup swap** involves no expectations about market changes, as does the substitution swap (where the buyer expects the yield on the higher yeilding bond to drop). This swap simply involves selling a lower yielding bond and purchasing a higher yielding one of the same quality and maturity. The motivation is strictly to obtain higher yield.
3. The **rate anticipation swap** is based on a forecast of interest rates. When rates are expected to rise (fall), swaps are made into short (long) duration bonds (or cash).
4. The **intermarket spread (sector) swap** is designed to take advantage of expected changes in the yield spread relationships between various sectors of the bond market. For example, a bond investor may perceive a misalignment between government bonds and utility bonds. If the yield spread between the two sectors is too wide and is expected to narrow, a switch may be made into the higher yielding security.

Use of Newer Techniques

The bond markets have changed rapidly in recent years because of numerous structural alterations. These have been accompanied by new techniques for the active management of fixed-income portfolios.

The distinction between the bond market and the mortgage market is now blurred, with mortgage instruments competing in the capital markets in the same manner as bonds. The mortgage has been transformed into a security, and the mortgage market has become more uniform and standardized. These securities are alternatives to bonds, especially corporate bonds, and can be used in the portfolio as substitutes.

Financial futures are now a well-known part of the investor's alternatives. Their use has grown tremendously, in particular to hedge positions and to speculate on the future course of interest rates. Futures will be discussed in more detail in Chapter 20.

Interest Rate Swaps

Interest Rate Swaps A contract between two parties to exchange a series of cash flows based on fixed-income securities, but without actually exchanging the securities directly.

One of the new techniques in bond management that has generated considerable attention is **interest rate swaps**. This term refers to a contract between two parties to exchange a series of cash flows based on different securities, but without actually exchanging the securities directly. This contract involves trading between private parties, typically large institutions, on a global basis.

[6] For a complete discussion of these swaps, see S. Homer and M. Leibowitz, *Inside the Yield Book* (Englewood Cliffs, NJ: Prentice Hall, 1972).

In a simple interest rate swap, a large institution could commit to pay a fixed interest rate in exchange for receiving payments based on a short-term floating rate. In effect, the institution swaps the cash flow from the fixed interest rate amount of funds for a cash flow generated by the short-term floating rate applied to some amount of funds. No securities are actually traded. Instead, the institution pays interest on a "notational principal" and receives a cash flow based on the amount of that principal. In this example, the institution has effectively converted a bond portfolio with a fixed rate into a (synthetic) portfolio with a floating rate.

Interest rate swaps are used primarily to hedge interest rate risk, but they can also be used in other ways. For example, a bond manager could speculate on changing conditions in the bond market or a financial institution could convert its floating-rate liabilities to fixed-rate liabilities.

Swaps typically involve a dealer, such as a bank, which quotes swap prices on a regular basis. The spread between what the dealer pays and receives constitutes the dealer's revenue. Growth in the market for interest rate swaps has been rapid, as can be seen in Table 12-4. The first swaps occurred in 1982; however, by 1996, the notational principal of all outstanding swaps exceeded $19 trillion worldwide.

Table 12-4

National Amounts of Interest Rate Swaps Outstanding by Currency December 31 (Billions of $US)

	1991	1992	1993	1994	1995	1996
Australian dollar	72.3	103.9	131.1	148.5	167.7	258.8
Belgian franc	7.5	14.2	31.1	50.6	74.6	166.1
Canadian dollar	**61.3**	**98.6**	**126.3**	**224.5**	**219.7**	**331.5**
Danish kroner	0.9	5.1	9.1	18.8	45.7	94.6
Deutsche mark	263.4	344.4	629.7	911.7	1438.9	24686.2
Dutch guilder	18.7	31.2	52.1	57.0	101.8	157.2
ECU	72.8	93.1	133.1	163.5	223.1	302.5
French franc	115.6	139.1	456.4	461.7	1219.9	1560.9
Hong Kong dollar	3.4	1.3	6.2	5.5	6.1	22.6
Italian lira	34.3	58.2	162.0	259.5	405.4	807.2
Japanese yen	478.9	706.0	1247.4	1987.4	2895.9	4441.8
New Zealand dollar	3.4	1.3	6.2	5.5	6.1	22.6
Pound sterling	253.5	294.8	437.1	674.0	854.0	1367.1
Spanish peseta	0.0	15.2	42.1	99.3	163.7	316.7
Swedish krona	18.2	17.7	32.0	147.3	93.8	207.5
Swiss franc	137.6	140.4	182.2	201.7	331.7	453.6
US dollar	1506.0	1760.2	2457.0	3230.1	4371.7	5827.5
Other	17.6	22.2	32.7	153.2	157.2	286.7
TOTAL	3065.1	3850.8	6177.3	8815.6	12810.7	19170.9

Source: Used with permission from "International Banking and Financial Market Developments," Bank for International Settlements Web site: <http://www.bis.org>.

Immunization — A Hybrid Strategy

Immunization
The strategy of protecting or immunizing a portfolio against interest rate risk by cancelling out its two components: price risk and reinvestment rate risk.

Because interest rates change over time, investors face uncertainty about the realized returns from bonds. This, of course, is the nature of interest rate risk. The strategy of protecting a portfolio against interest rate risk (i.e., changes in the general level of interest rates) is called **immunization**.

To see how such a strategy works, think of interest rate risk as being composed of two parts:

1. The price risk, resulting from the inverse relationship between bond prices and required rates of return.
2. The reinvestment rate risk, resulting from the uncertainty about the rate at which future coupon income can be reinvested.

As discussed in Chapter 11, the YTM calculation assumes that future coupons from a given bond investment will be reinvested at the calculated yield to maturity. If interest rates change so that this assumption is no longer operable, the bond's realized YTM will differ from the calculated (expected) YTM.[7]

Notice that these two components of interest rate risk move in opposite directions:

- If interest rates rise, reinvestment rates (and therefore income) rise, whereas the price of the bond declines.
- If interest rates decline, reinvestment rates (and therefore income) decline, whereas the price of the bond rises.

In effect, the favourable results on one side can be used to offset the unfavourable results on the other. This is what immunization is all about, protecting a bond portfolio against interest rate risk by cancelling out the two components of interest rate risk, reinvestment rate risk, and price risk.

The duration concept discussed earlier is the basis for immunization theory. Specifically, a portfolio is said to be immunized (the effects of interest rate risk are neutralized) if the duration of the portfolio is made equal to a pre-selected investment horizon for the portfolio. Note carefully what this statement says. An investor with, say, a ten-year horizon does not choose bonds with ten years to maturity but bonds with a duration of ten years, which is something quite different. The duration strategy will usually require holding bonds with maturities in excess of the investment horizon, unless they are zeroes, whose duration exactly equals their maturity.

For an example of the immunization concept, consider Table 12-5, which illustrates for a portfolio of a single bond what ideally could happen with a portfolio of several bonds. Assume an investor has a five-year investment horizon after which she wishes to liquidate her bond portfolio and spend the proceeds. The current yield to maturity for AAA-rated bonds, the only investment grade our investor is willing to consider, is 7.9 per cent for both five-year and six-year bonds because of the flatness of the yield curve. In order to simplify the calculations, we will assume that interest is paid annually so that we can concentrate on the immunization principle.

[7] For additional information on reinvestment rate risk, see R. W. McEnally, "How to Neutralize Reinvestment Rate Risk," *The Journal of Portfolio Management* 6 (Spring 1980), pp. 59–63; and W. L. Nemerever, "Managing Bond Portfolios Through Immunization Strategies," In Donald L. Tuttle, *The Revolution in Techniques for Managing Bond Portfolios* (Charlottesville, VA: Institute of Chartered Financial Analysts, 1983), p. 140.

Because the YTM is 7.9 per cent, our investor, understanding the reinvestment rate implications of bonds, expects that after five years her investment should yield a ratio of $(1.079)^5$, or 1.46254. That is, if she invests $1,000 in a bond today and the intermediate coupons are reinvested at 7.9 per cent each, as the YTM calculation assumes, the ending wealth for this investment in a bond that can be purchased for face value should be $\$1{,}000\ (1.079)^5$, or $1,462.54.

Our investor can purchase bond A, with a 7.9 per cent coupon and a five-year maturity, or bond B, with a 7.9 per cent coupon, a six-year maturity, and a duration of five years. The top panel of Table 12-5 illustrates what happens if bond A is purchased, and market yields remain constant for the five-year investment horizon. Because the intermediate cash flows are reinvested at exactly 7.9 per cent each year, the amounts cumulate toward the final amount of $1,462.54, a wealth ratio of 1.46254. Notice in these examples that we separate year five from the other four because of the return of principal ($1,000) at the end of year five; obviously, no compound interest is earned on the return of this $1,000 at the end of the year. In a similar manner, no interest is earned on the first year's cash flow of $79, which is assumed to occur at the end of the year.

Now consider what would happen if our investor bought bond A and in the third year of its five-year life market yields for this and comparable bonds declined to 6 per cent and remained at that level for the remainder of the five-year period. As a result, the intermediate cash flows in the last three years of the bond's life would be reinvested at 6 per cent rather than at 7.9 per cent. Therefore, the reinvestment rate risk present in bond investments has a negative impact on this particular bond investment.

The results of a drop in the reinvestment rate are shown in the middle panel of Table 12-5, using the same format as before. As this panel shows, at the end of year five the ending amount of wealth for bond A now is only $1,447.13, representing a shortfall for the investor's objective. This result occurred because she did not immunize her bond portfolio against interest rate risk, but instead purchased a bond based on matching the maturity of the bond with her investment horizon. As explained above, to protect against this interest rate risk it is necessary to purchase a bond whose duration, not maturity, is equal to the investor's investment horizon.

Assume that a $1,000 bond with a coupon rate of 7.9 per cent and a six-year maturity could have been purchased at the same time. The duration of this bond, which we call bond B, is exactly five years, matching the investor's investment horizon. In this case, the bond would be immunized against interest rate risk because any shortfall arising from a declining reinvestment rate would be offset by a higher price for the bond at the end of the investment horizon (because the drop in interest rates produces an increase in the price of the bond). Note that at the end of five years, which is our investor's investment horizon, bond B has one year left to maturity and could be sold in the market.

The bottom panel of Table 12-5 illustrates the same process as before for bond B. Notice that the ending cash flows are the same for the first four years as they were for the previous situation with the five-year bond. At the end of year five, the bond still has one year to go to maturity, but its price has risen because of the drop in interest rates. As the analysis in Table 12-5 demonstrates, the ending wealth of $1,465.05 is more than enough to meet the investor's objective of $1,462.54 per $1,000 invested.

Thus, the example in Table 12-5 illustrates the basic concept of immunization. By choosing a bond or a portfolio of bonds with a duration equal to a predetermined investment horizon, it is possible, in principle, to immunize the portfolio against interest rate risk.

Table 12-5

Ending Wealth for a Bond Following a Change in Market Yields With and Without Immunization

Bond A: Purchased for $1,000, five-year maturity, 7.9 per cent coupon, 7.9 per cent yeld to maturity.

Bond B: Purchased for $1,000, six-year maturity, 7.9 per cent coupon, 7.9 per cent yield to maturity, duration = 5.00 years

Part A: Ending Wealth for Bond A if Market Yields Remain Constant at 7.9 Per Cent

Years	Cash Flow	Reinvestment Rate (%)	Ending Wealth
1	$ 79	—	$ 79.00
2	79	7.9	164.24
3	79	7.9	256.22
4	79	7.9	355.46
5	79	—	462.54
5	1000	—	1462.54

Part B: Ending Wealth for Bond A if Market Yields Decline to 6 Per Cent in Year 3

Years	Cash Flow	Reinvestment Rate (%)	Ending Wealth
1	$ 79	—	$ 79.00
2	79	7.9	164.24
3	79	6.0	253.10
4	79	6.0	347.29
5	79	—	477.13
5	1000	—	1447.13

Part C: Ending Wealth for Bond B if Market Yields Decline to 6 Per Cent in Year 3 (Bond B has a duration of five years.)

Years	Cash Flow	Reinvestment Rate (%)	Ending Wealth
1	$ 79	—	$ 79.00
2	79	7.9	164.24
3	79	6.0	253.10
4	79	6.0	347.29
5	79	—	477.13
5	1017.92[a]	—	1465.05

[a]The price of bond B with one year left to maturity and a market yield of 6 per cent is $1,017.92.

Notice that reinvestment rate risk could have been completely eliminated by purchasing a zero-coupon bond with a maturity (and duration) of five years. The usefulness of zeroes for immunization purposes is one reason they have grown in popularity in recent years.

EXAMPLE: IMMUNIZATION

Bond portfolios that will achieve target wealth despite changes in interest rates are said to be immunized. Immunization is possible if the duration of the bond or portfolio equals the investor's horizon. If an investor needed $2,580 at end of 10 years, he could achieve this by purchasing a 10-year zero-coupon bond with a maturity value of $2,580. If no suitable zero could be purchased, the investor could immunize himself in the short run using any traditional coupon bond, provided it had a duration of 10 years. For example, suppose the investor purchases a 20-year, 10 per cent coupon bond with a duration of 10 years. He would be protected against rate changes in the immediate future. Assuming interest rates are presently at 8 per cent, and remain at that level for the next 10 years, the bond would provide the owner with total income of $2,582.86 — $1,448.66 from the coupons reinvested at 8 per cent and $1,134.20 from the value the bond would have at that point.

If rates fall to 7.5 per cent (and remain at that level) during the first year after the investor buys the bond but before the first coupon payment, the total value after 10 years would be $2,586.31. This total is composed of $1,414.71 from reinvesting the coupons at 7.5 per cent and $1,171.60 from the value of the bond in 10 years. The difference in value is only $3.45, because what the investor lost on reinvesting the coupons at only 7.5 per cent, is made up in the increased bond value.

Immunization is in many respects a hybrid strategy between passive and active. Although the classical immunization discussed here could be thought of as a passive strategy, we must be aware of the real-world problems involved in implementing such a plan. In truth, this strategy is difficult to implement, and it is not a passive strategy in application. Immunization strategies based on duration matching only work well for small changes in interest rates, and for short periods of time. To achieve immunization as discussed here requires frequent rebalancing because duration should always be equal to the investment horizon. An investor simply cannot set duration equal to investment horizon at the beginning of the process and ignore the bond or portfolio thereafter (unless they hold zeroes). Finally, immunization based on duration matching is based on the assumption of a flat yield curve, and that changes in interest rates are parallel across the yield curve, which is generally not the case in practice.

There are several other variations of the basic immunization strategy. The most popular variation is called horizon-matching or combination matching. This involves a portfolio that is duration-matched and also cash-matched in the first few years. Another variation is contingent immunization, which involves active management plus a lower floor return that is ensured for the horizon period. The portfolio manager must act to earn the floor return by immunizing the portfolio if necessary. Otherwise, the manager can actively manage the portfolio or some portion thereof.

BUILDING A FIXED-INCOME PORTFOLIO

Having reviewed some active and passive strategies for managing a bond portfolio, we will now consider how to build a fixed-income portfolio. The first consideration, which is true throughout the range of investment decisions, is to decide on the risk-return trade-off that all investors face. If investors seek higher expected returns, they must be prepared to accept greater risk. In building a fixed-income portfolio, it is useful to think of the two broad approaches an investor can take — conservative and aggressive. We will use these two broad strategies below to organize the discussion.

Conservative Investors

Conservative investors view bonds as fixed-income securities that will pay them a steady stream of income. In order to maintain low levels of risk they will lean towards government issues that have practically no risk of default. These investors tend to use a buy-and-hold approach. This sort of investor seeks to maximize their current income subject to the risk (quality of issue) they are willing to assume: corporates should return more than government issues, BBB issues more than those rated A or AA, longer durations more than shorter durations, and so on.

Even conservative investors in bonds must consider a number of factors. Assume that an investor wishes to purchase only Government of Canada issues, thereby avoiding the possible risk of default. Careful consideration should be given to the duration of the issue, since the range is from T-bills of a month's duration to bonds maturing well into the twenty-first century. Reinvestment rate risk must be considered. For investors who may need their funds back before the bonds mature, interest rate risk is relevant.

The investor's choice will depend to a large extent on interest rate forecasts. Even conservative buy-and-hold investors should probably avoid long-term issues if interest rates are expected to rise over an extended period of time. Finally, investors may wish to consider the differences in coupons between issues. Previous discussion has shown that the lower the coupon on a bond, the higher the price volatility. Although many investors in this group may plan to hold to maturity, conditions can change, and they may need to sell some of these bonds before maturity.

EXAMPLE: CONSERVATIVE INVESTORS AND BOND PORTFOLIOS

As an example of what can happen to conservative investors when they are buying and holding a bond portfolio, consider the situation faced by municipal bond investors in the US in mid-1992. Most municipal bonds can be called after 10 years, and many investors had bought municipals in 1982 when interest rates were at record highs. On July 1, 1992, several billion dollars of municipals were redeemed, with more calls expected in the future on the typical call dates, January 1 and July 1. Investors were forced to give up high-yielding municipals at a time when interest rates were quite low. Moreover, in trying to replace the income stream, they had to consider alternatives with lower quality (and therefore greater risk) and/or longer maturity (and therefore subject to interest rate risk as rates rose), or simply resign themselves to a bond portfolio with a new, lower return.

Indirect investing through bond funds is another possibility. In addition to traditional bond funds that hold government securities, corporate bonds, or mixtures of these, with a wide range of maturities, investors can consider flexible-income funds. These invest in bonds of all types, convertible securities, and stocks. The emphasis on these funds tends to be on income, but their investment strategies vary greatly.

Aggressive Investors

Aggressive investors are more focused on the capital gains that arise from a change in interest rates. There exists a substantial range of aggressiveness, from the really short-term speculator to the somewhat less aggressive investor who is willing to realize capital gains over a longer period while possibly earning high yields.

The short-term speculator studies interest rates carefully and moves into and out of securities on the basis of interest rate expectations. If rates are expected to fall, this investor can buy long-term, low-coupon issues and achieve maximum capital gains if the interest rate forecast is correct. Government bonds can be bought on margin to further magnify gains (or losses). Alternatively, the aggressive investor can turn to interest rate options or futures contracts on interest rate instruments, which are discussed in Chapter 19 and Chapter 20, respectively.

Another form of aggressive behaviour involves seeking the highest total return, whether from interest income or capital gains. Investors who follow this strategy plan on a long horizon in terms of holding a portfolio of bonds but engage in active trading during certain periods when such actions seem particularly appropriate. One such period was 1982, when bonds were offering record yields to maturity and interest rates were widely expected to decline. Even mildly aggressive investors could purchase government bonds yielding high-coupon income and have a reasonable expectation of capital gains. The downside risk in this strategy at this time was small. These investors still needed to consider maturity and coupon questions, however, because no interest rate decline can be assumed with certainty.

The International Perspective

When investors build bond portfolios, they should consider the opportunities available in international markets. Investors can invest directly or indirectly in foreign bonds by making their own decisions and using their broker or by purchasing units in an investment fund holding foreign bonds.

As we know by now, larger returns are associated with larger risks. Speculative investors who purchase foreign bonds are implicitly betting on the future direction of interest rates in these countries, which, in turn, reflects bets on their economies. A slowdown would favour the odds of lower interest rates and higher bond prices. Furthermore, investors in foreign bonds face exchange rate or currency risk. Adverse currency fluctuations can significantly reduce the returns to a cash bond investor and wipe out an investor on margin. Therefore, investors must decide whether to hedge the position against adverse currency movements. Investors who are bearish on the foreign currency would probably choose to hedge their positions while investors who were bullish would not.

In Chapter 2 we noted that investors always have an alternative to direct investing. They can invest indirectly by purchasing units of investment funds that, in turn, invest in the securities in which they are interested. For example, a Canadian investor purchasing units in the **Templeton Global Bond Fund** would hold a diversified portfolio of North American,

European, and some Australian and New Zealand bonds. As of June 30, 1998, Templeton's Global Bond Fund had approximately 40 per cent of its holdings in European bonds. Other global bond funds focus on the debt securities of only one country or on particular geographic areas such as Europe.

How does the Canadian dollar affect the foreign bond investor? If the Canadian economy improves, the dollar will probably rise, and if it rises against the currencies involved in the foreign bonds, after converting back to dollars, the returns to Canadian investors are negatively impacted. Most global bond funds recognize the importance of fluctuations in exchange rates and adopt a foreign exchange hedging policy, which may involve fully hedged, partially hedged, or completely unhedged positions, relative to a given currency. For example, the Templeton Global Bond Fund mentioned above, used foreign currency contracts to hedge 53 per cent of the combined European currency risk and 82 per cent of the combined Australia/New Zealand position.

SUMMARY

This summary relates to the learning objectives provided on page 357.

1. **Explain why investors buy bonds.**
   A wide range of investors are interested in bonds, ranging from those who seek a steady stream of interest income and return of principal to those seeking capital gains by speculating on future interest rate movements.
2. **Discuss major considerations in managing a bond portfolio.**
   The future level of interest rates is the key factor affecting bond portfolio performance. Inflationary expectations play a key role in understanding what drives the bond market since they have a direct influence on interest rates. Yield spreads are the relationship between bond yields and particular bond features such as quality and callability. Differences in type, quality, and coupon account for most of the yield spreads.
3. **Explain what is meant by the term structure of interest rates.**
   The term structure of interest rates denotes the relationship between market yields and time to maturity. A yield curve depicts this relationship graphically with upward-sloping curves being the most common. None of the prevalent theories proposed to explain term structure — the expectations theory, the liquidity preference theory, the preferred habitat theory, or the market segmentation theory — is dominant.
4. **Differentiate between passive and active strategies for managing a bond portfolio.**
   Bond investment strategies can be divided into passive and active. Passive bond strategies, whereby the investor does not try to outperform the market by actively seeking out trading possibilities, include buy and hold, and indexing. Active management strategies can be broadly divided into forecasting changes in interest rates and identifying relative mispricing between various fixed-income securities. New techniques include the use of mortgage instruments and strategies with financial futures. Interest rate swaps are now a significant item in the management of bond portfolios by institutions. A "hybrid" strategy is immunization, which involves protecting (immunizing) a portfolio against interest rate risk by attempting to have the two components of interest rate risk — reinvestment rate risk and price risk — cancel each other out.

5. **Describe how both conservative and aggressive investors build a fixed-income portfolio.**
   In building a bond portfolio, investors must make a decision on the risk–return trade-off. Conservative investors tend to use a buy-and-hold approach, whereas aggressive investors seek higher returns by speculating on interest rates or trading actively during certain periods.

KEY TERMS

Active management strategy
Bond swaps
Expectations theory
Forward rates
Immunization
Index funds
Interest rate swaps
Liquidity preference theory
Market segmentation theory
Passive management strategy
Preferred habitat theory
Term structure of interest rates
Yield curve
Yield spreads

ADDITIONAL RESOURCES

Bond return strategies for investors are discussed in: Fong, H. Gifford, and Fabozzi, Frank J. "How to Enhance Bond Returns with Naive Strategies." *The Journal of Portfolio Management*. (Summer 1985), pp. 58–60.

A good discussion of duration and reinvestment rate risk can be found in: McEnally, Richard W. "Duration as a Practical Tool for Bond Management." *The Journal of Portfolio Management*. (Summer 1977), pp. 53–57.

McEnally, Richard W. "How to Neutralize Reinvestment Rate Risk." *The Journal of Portfolio Management*. (Spring 1980), pp. 59–63.

Interest rate risk and related concepts are discussed in: Maloney, Kevin J., and Yawitz, Jess B. "Interest Rate Risk, Immunization, and Duration." *The Journal of Portfolio Management*. (Spring 1986), pp. 41–48.

REVIEW QUESTIONS

1. Describe two different types of investors interested in bonds.
2. List some of the problems involved for Canadian investors in buying and selling foreign bonds.
3. Identify and explain at least two passive bond management strategies.
4. Why is the yield on Government of Canada bonds used as the benchmark for comparing yields on various types of bonds.
5. Explain the difference between the expectations theory and the liquidity preference theory of term structure.

6. What is the normal slope of the yield curve for bonds?
7. What is the difference between a spot rate and a forward rate?
8. How would proponents of the liquidity preference theory explain the existence of a downward-sloping yield curve?
9. What is the key factor in analyzing bonds? Why?
10. Identify and explain two specific active bond management strategies. Are the two related?
11. You have correctly forecast that interest rates will soon decline sharply. Assuming that you will invest only in fixed-income securities and that your time horizon is one year, how would you construct a portfolio?
12. When would investors find bonds with long maturities, selling at large discounts, particularly unattractive as investment opportunities?
13. How can horizon analysis be used to manage a bond portfolio?
14. You are interested in some British government bonds that are currently yielding three percentage points more than comparable Government of Canada securities. If you think the British economy will slow down, is this favourable or unfavourable for your decision to purchase British bonds? If you are bullish on the British pound, does this suggest a hedged or unhedged position when you buy the bonds?
15. If you have constructed a bond portfolio that is properly immunized, would you sell the bonds on their maturity dates or before? Why?
16. Explain the concept of immunization. What role, if any, does duration play in this concept?
17. Describe four types of bond swaps. Indicate the assumption(s) being made by an investor in undertaking these swaps.

PREPARING FOR YOUR PROFESSIONAL EXAMS

Special Note to CSC Students

Ensure that you have read and understood the following topics:*

Why buy bonds?, pp. 358–363
Important considerations in managing a bond portfolio, pp. 364–373
CSC Notes: Tilting the Yield Curve, p. 365
Bond strategies, pp. 374–383
Building a fixed-income portfolio, pp. 384–386

**Reading these CSC-related topics should provide you with additional understanding of CSC material. However, it should not be seen as a substitute for reading the CSC textbook itself, which is the basis for the CSC exam.*

CSC REGISTRATION QUESTION

The Canadian Securities Institute issued the following sample question in the 1997 CSC registration package as a means for students to self-assess their understanding of CSC-related material.

1. During the contraction phase of the business cycle, a good investment strategy would be to _______.

   a. sell growth stocks

   b. buy long term bonds

   c. buy short term bonds

   d. buy cyclical stocks

PAST CFA EXAM QUESTIONS AND PROBLEMS

The following question was asked on the 1990 CFA Level I examination:

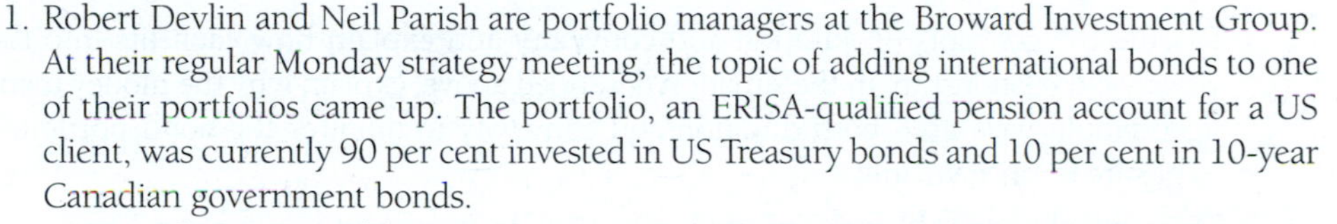

1. Robert Devlin and Neil Parish are portfolio managers at the Broward Investment Group. At their regular Monday strategy meeting, the topic of adding international bonds to one of their portfolios came up. The portfolio, an ERISA-qualified pension account for a US client, was currently 90 per cent invested in US Treasury bonds and 10 per cent in 10-year Canadian government bonds.

   Devlin suggested buying a position in 10-year West German government bonds, while Parish argued for 10-year Australian government bonds.

   a. Briefly discuss the three major issues that Devlin and Parish should address in their analysis of the return prospects for German and Australian bonds relative to those of US bonds.

      Having made no changes to the original portfolio, Devlin and Parish hold a subsequent strategy meeting and decide to add positions in the government bonds of Japan, United Kingdom, France, West Germany, and Australia.

   b. Identify and discuss two reasons for adding a broader mix of international bonds to the pension portfolio.

The following question was asked on the 1992 CFA Level I examination:

2. The table below shows selected data on a German government bond (payable in deutsche marks) and a US government bond. Identify the components of return and calculate the total return in US dollars for both of these bonds for the year 1991. Show the calculations for each component. (Ignore interest on interest in view of the short time period.)

	Coupon	Market Yield 1/1/91	Market Yield 1/1/92	Modified Duration	Exchange Rate (DM/$US) 1/1/91	Exchange Rate (DM/$US) 1/1/92
German government bond	8.50%	8.50%	8.00%	7.0	1.55	1.50
US government bond	8.00%	8.00%	6.75%	6.5	—	—

The following question was asked on the 1991 CFA Level I examination:

3. Bill Peters is the investment officer of a $60 million pension fund. He has become concerned about the big price swings that have occurred lately in the fund's fixed-income securities. Peters has been told that such price behaviour is only natural given the recent behaviour of market yields. To deal with the problem, the pension fund's fixed-income money manager keeps track of exposure to price volatility by closely monitoring bond duration. The money manager believes that price volatility can be kept to a reasonable level as long as portfolio duration is maintained at approximately seven to eight years.

   a. Discuss the concepts of duration and convexity and explain how each fits into the price/yield relationship. In the situation described above, explain why the money manager should have used both duration and convexity to monitor the bond portfolio's exposure to price volatility.

   b. One of the bonds held in the portfolio is a 15-year, 8 per cent US Treasury bond with a modified duration of 8.0 years and a convexity of 94.36. It has been suggested that the fund swap out of the 15-year bond and into a "barbell" position made up of the following two US Treasury issues:

Bond	Coupon	Maturity	Modified Duration	Convexity
1	8%	5 years	3.97 years	19.58
2	8%	30 years	9.73 years	167.56

   Construct a barbell position from these two bonds that results in a modified duration of 8.0 years. Compare the price volatility of the position to the bond currently held under each of the following interest rate environments:

   i. Market rates drop by 50 basis points (e.g., from 9 to 8.50 per cent), and

   ii. Market rates drop by 250 basis points (e.g., from 9 to 6.50 per cent).

The following question was asked on the 1989 CFA Level I examination:

4. On June 1, 1989, a bond portfolio manager is evaluating the following data concerning three bonds held in his portfolio.

Bond	Bond Rating	Coupon	Maturity	Call Price (Date)	Market Price ($)	Yield-to Maturity	Modified Duration	Change in Market Price*
X	AA	0%	8/14/94	Non-callable	59.44	10.25%	5.2 years	+5.1%
Y	AA	14.00%	3/30/98	Non-callable	116.60	11.00%	5.2 years	+5.5%
Z	AA	10.25%	7/15/97	100 6/1/90	98.63	10.50%	5.2 years	+2.4%

*Following a 100-basis-point decline in rates

It is noted that all three bonds have the same modified duration and thus are expected to rise in price by 5.20 per cent for a 100-basis-point decline in interest rates. However, the data show that a different change in price occurs for each bond.

Discuss three reasons for the discrepancy between the expectations and the actual change in market price for the bonds.

PROBLEMS

1. Assume the current one-year spot rate is 8 per cent, and the implied forward rates for one, two, and three years hence are as follows:

$$_1f_2 = 9\%$$
$$_2f_3 = 10\%$$
$$_3f_4 = 11\%$$

   a. What price should a $1,000 face-value zero-coupon bond sell for that has four years until maturity?

   b. Based on the expectations theory, what are the expected one-year interest rates for years 2, 3, and 4?

   c. Based on the liquidity preference theory, are the expected one-year interest rates for years 2, 3, and 4 the same as in part (b)? Why or why not?

2. If the yield on a one-year Government of Canada Treasury bill is 7.8 per cent, and the yield on a two-year Government of Canada Bond is 8.05 per cent, what is the implied one-year forward rate for the second year ($_1f_2$)?

CHAPTER 13

COMMON STOCK VALUATION

LEARNING OBJECTIVES

After reading this chapter, you will be able to

1. Name two approaches to the valuation of common stocks used in fundamental security analysis.
2. Explain the present value approach.
3. Use the dividend discount model to estimate stock prices.
4. Explain the P/E ratio approach.
5. Outline other relative valuation approaches.

CHAPTER PREVIEW

In the next few chapters we explore the approaches that investors use to value and select common stocks. In this chapter, we concentrate on two valuation methods used in fundamental security analysis, which seeks to estimate the intrinsic value of a stock: present value and P/E ratio or earnings multiplier. Under present value, we explain how to use the dividend discount model to estimate stock prices. We then consider the P/E ratio, the approach most widely used by practicing security analysts, as well as other valuation methods.

THE PRESENT VALUE APPROACH

The classic method of calculating intrinsic (estimated or formula) value involves the use of present value analysis, which is often referred to as the capitalization of income method. As explained in Chapter 11, a present value process involving the capitalization (discounting) of expected future cash flows can be used to estimate the value of any security. That is, the intrinsic value of a security can be estimated as the discounted (present) value of the future stream of cash flows that an investor expects to receive from the asset. Repeating from Chapter 11,

(13-1)

$$\text{Estimated value of security} = \sum_{t=1}^{n} \frac{\text{Cash Flows}}{(1 + k)^t}$$

where
k = the appropriate discount rate or required rate of return[1]

To use such a model, an investor must

1. Estimate an appropriate required rate of return.
2. Estimate the amount and timing of the future stream of cash flows.
3. Use these two components in a present value model to estimate the value of the security, which is then compared to the current market price of the security.

Figure 13-1 summarizes the present value process commonly used in fundamental analysis. It emphasizes the factors that go into valuing common stocks. The exact nature of the present value process used by investors in the marketplace depends upon assumptions made about the growth rate in the expected stream of cash flows, as explained later in this chapter.

The Required Rate of Return

An investor who is considering the purchase of a common stock must assess its risk and the associated minimum expected rate of return that will be required to induce the investor to make the purchase. This minimum expected return, or *required rate of return*, is an opportunity cost. It is the same concept as the required yield used in Chapter 11 to value bonds.

The *required rate of return*, *capitalization rate*, and *discount rate* are interchangeable terms in valuation analysis. Regardless of which term is used, it is challenging to determine the

[1] The concept of required rate of return is explained in more detail in Chapter 14.

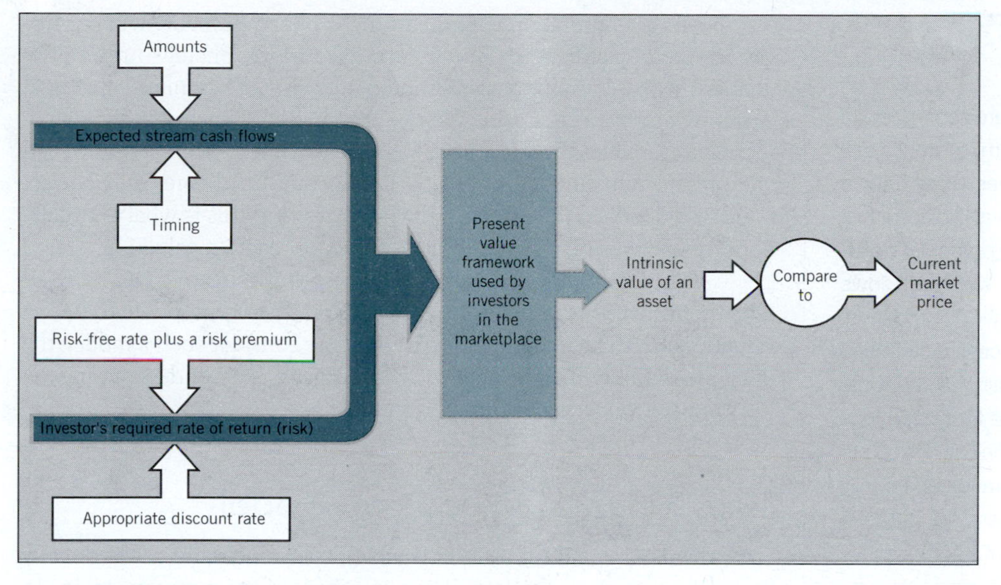

Figure 13-1
The Present Value Approach to Valuation

numerical value to use for a particular stock. While in theory we know what this variable is, in practice it is not easy to arrive at the precise number to use. Because of this complexity, we will generally assume that we know the capitalization rate and concentrate on the other issues involved in valuation, which are difficult enough. In the next chapter, we consider the required rate of return in more detail.

The Expected Cash Flows

The other component that goes into the present value framework is the expected stream of cash flows. Just as the value of a bond is the present value of all interest payments plus the present value of the bond's face value that will be received at maturity, the value of a common stock is the present value of all the cash flows to be received from the issuer (corporation). The questions that arise are:

1. What are the cash flows to use in valuing a stock?
2. What are the expected amounts of the cash flows?
3. When will the expected cash flows be received?

Shareholders may plan to sell their shares sometime in the future resulting in a cash flow from the sales price. As we will see later, however, even if investors think of the total cash flows from common stocks as a combination of dividends and a future price at which the stock can be sold, this is equivalent to using the stream of all dividends to be received on the stock.

What about earnings? Are they important? Can they be used in valuing a stock? The answer to both questions is yes. Dividends are paid out of earnings and are clearly important. An alternative approach to fundamental analysis, which is considered later, uses the earnings and a P/E ratio to determine intrinsic value. Therefore, earnings are an important part of fundamental analysis; in fact, earnings receive more attention from investors than any other single variable.

INVESTING tip

To find which cash flows are appropriate in the valuation of a common stock, ask yourself the following question: If I buy a particular common stock and place it in a special trust fund for the perpetual benefit of myself and my heirs, what cash flows will be received? The answer is dividends, because this is the only cash distribution that a corporation actually makes to its shareholders. Although a firm's earnings per share in any year technically belong to the shareholders, corporations generally do not pay out all their earnings but reinvest a portion into the firm.

If the corporation retains earnings, they presumably will be reinvested, thereby enhancing future earnings and, ultimately, future dividends. The present value analysis should not count the earnings reinvested currently and paid later as dividends. If properly defined and separated, these two variables produce the same results. This means that more than one present value model is possible.[2] However, it is theoretically correct to use dividends in the present value analysis, and this is what is usually done when investors use the present value approach to valuation.

Because dividends are the only cash flow stream to be received directly by investors under normal conditions, it is appropriate to have a valuation model based on dividends. We now consider such a model, the dividend discount model, which provides the basis for understanding the fundamental valuation of common stocks.

The Dividend Discount Model

Since dividends are the only cash payment a shareholder receives directly from a firm, they are the foundation of valuation for common stocks. In adapting Equation 13-1 specifically to value common stocks, the cash flows are the dividends expected to be paid in each future period. An investor or analyst using this approach carefully studies the future prospects for a company and estimates the likely dividends to be paid. In addition, the analyst estimates an appropriate required rate of return or discount rate based on the risk foreseen in the dividends and given the alternatives available. Finally, he or she would discount to the present, the entire stream of estimated future dividends (properly identified as to amount and timing).

Dividend Discount Model (DDM)
A model for determining the estimated price of a stock by discounting all expected future dividends by the appropriate required rate of return for the stock.

The present value approach to calculating the value of a common stock is conceptually no different from the approach used in Chapter 11 to value bonds or in Appendix 13-A at the end of the chapter to value preferred stock. Specifically, Equation 13-1 adapted for common stocks, where dividends are the expected future cash flows, results in Equation 13-2. This equation, known as the **dividend discount model (DDM)**, states that the value of a stock today is the discounted value of all future dividends:

$$\hat{P}_{CS} = \frac{D_1}{(1 + k_{CS})^1} + \frac{D_2}{(1 + k_{CS})^2} + \ldots + \frac{D_\infty}{(1 + k_{CS})^\infty} \tag{13-2}$$

$$= \sum_{t=1}^{\infty} \frac{D_t}{(1 + k_{CS})^t}$$

$$= \text{Dividend discount model (DDM)}$$

where

$\hat{P}_{CS}$ = intrinsic or estimated value of a common stock today based on the model user's estimates of the future dividends and the required rate of return

$D_1, D_2, \ldots$ = the dividends expected to be received in each future period

k_{cs} = the required rate of return for this stock, which is the discount rate applicable for an investment with this degree of riskiness (again, the opportunity cost of a comparable risk alternative)

[2] In addition to dividends and earnings, the variable referred to as "cash flow" (earnings after tax plus depreciation) has been suggested for these models.

There are two immediate problems with Equation 13-2:

1. The last term in Equation 13-2 indicates that investors are dealing with infinity. They must value a stream of dividends that may be paid forever, since common stock has no maturity date.
2. The dividend stream is uncertain:
   a. There are no specified number of dividends, if, in fact, any are paid at all. If dividends are to be paid, they must be declared periodically by the firm's board of directors. (Technically, they are declared quarterly but conventional valuation analysis uses annual dividends.)
   b. The dividends for most firms are expected to grow over time; therefore, investors usually cannot simplify Equation 13-2 to a **perpetuity** as in the case of a preferred stock.[3] Only if dividends are not expected to grow can such a simplification be made. Although such a possibility exists, and is covered below, it is unusual.

Perpetuity
An annuity with no maturity date.

How are these problems resolved? The first problem, that Equation 13-2 involves an infinite number of periods and dividends, will be resolved when we deal with the second problem, specifying the expected stream of dividends. However, from a practical standpoint this problem is not as troublesome as it first appears. At reasonably high discount rates, such as 12, 14, or 16 per cent, dividends received 40 or 50 years in the future are worth very little today, so that investors need not worry about them. For example, if the discount rate is 15 per cent, the present value of $1 to be received 50 years from now is $0.0009.

The conventional solution to the second problem, that the dollar amount of the dividend is expected to grow over time, is to make some assumptions about the expected growth rate of dividends. That is, the investor or analyst estimates or models the expected percentage rate of growth in the future stream of dividends. To do this, he or she classifies each stock to be valued into one of three categories based on the expected growth pattern in dividends. In summary: We operationalize the dividend discount model by estimating the expected growth rate(s) in the dividend stream.

A timeline will be used to represent the three alternative growth rate versions of the dividend discount model. All stocks that pay a dividend, or that are expected to in the future, can be modelled using this approach. It is critical to remember in using the DDM that an investor must account for all dividends from now to infinity by modelling the growth rate(s). As shown below, the mechanics of this process are such that we don't actually see all of these dividends because the formulas reduce to a simplified form, but nevertheless we are accounting for all future dividends when we use the DDM.

It is necessary in using the DDM to remember that the dividend currently being paid on a stock (or the most recent dividend paid) is designated as D_0 and is, of course, known. However, investors must estimate the future dividends to be paid, starting with D_1, the dividend expected to be paid in the next period.

The three growth rate models for dividends are:

1. A dividend stream with a zero-growth rate resulting from a fixed dollar dividend equal to the current dividend, D_0, being paid every year from now to infinity. This is typically referred to as the no-growth rate or zero-growth rate model:

D_0	D_0	D_0	D_0	+ ... +	D_0	Dividends
0	1	2	3	+ ... +	∞	Time period

[3] Refer to Appendix 13-A at the end of the chapter for details regarding the valuation of preferred stock.

2. A dividend stream that is growing at a constant rate, g, starting with D_0. This is typically referred to as the constant or normal growth version of the dividend discount model:

D_0	$D_0(1+g)^1$	$D_0(1+g)^2$	$+ \ldots +$	$D_0(1+g)^\infty$	Dividends
0	1	2	$+ \ldots +$	∞	Time period

3. A dividend stream that is growing at variable rates, for example, g_1 for the first two years and g_2 thereafter, is referred to as the multiple-growth version of the dividend discount model:

D_0	$D_1 = D_0(1+g_1)$	$D_2 = D_1(1+g_1)$	$D_3 = D_2(1+g_2)$	$+ \ldots +$	$D_\infty = D_{\infty-1}(1+g_2)$	Dividends
0	1	2	3	$+ \ldots +$	∞	Time period

The Zero-Growth Model

Under the non-growth case, the dividend model reduces to a perpetual annuity or perpetuity. Assuming a constant dollar dividend, Equation 13-2 simplifies to the no-growth model shown as Equation 13-3.

$$\hat{P}_0 = \frac{D_0}{k_{CS}} = \text{Zero} - \text{growth version of the DDM} \tag{13-3}$$

where D_0 is the constant dollar dividend expected for all future time periods and k_{cs} is the opportunity cost or required rate of return for this particular common stock.

The no-growth case is equivalent to the valuation process for a preferred stock discussed at the end of this chapter because, exactly like a preferred stock, the dividend (numerator of Equation 13-3) remains unchanged. Therefore, the dividends arising from a zero-growth rate common stock represent a perpetuity that can be easily valued once k_{cs} is determined.

It is extremely important in understanding the valuation of common stocks using the DDM to recognize that in all cases an investor is discounting the future stream of dividends from now to infinity. This fact tends to be overlooked when using the perpetuity formula involving the zero-growth rate case because the discounting process is greatly simplified. Nevertheless, in this case, as in all others, we are accounting for all dividends from now to infinity. It is simply a mathematical fact that dividing a constant dollar amount by the discount rate, k, produces a result equivalent to discounting each dividend from now to infinity separately and summing all of the present values.

The Constant Growth Model

The other two versions of the DDM indicate that to establish the cash flow stream of expected dividends, which is to be subsequently discounted, it is first necessary to compound some beginning dividend into the future. Obviously, the higher the growth rate used, the greater the future amount, and the longer the time period, the greater the future amount.

A well-known scenario in valuation is the case in which dividends are expected to grow at a constant rate over time. This constant- or normal-growth model[4] is shown as Equation 13-4.

$$\hat{P}_0 = \frac{D_0(1+g)}{(1+k_{CS})^1} + \frac{D_0(1+g)^2}{(1+k_{CS})^2} + \frac{D_0(1+g)^3}{(1+k_{CS})^3} + \ldots + \frac{D_0(1+g)^\infty}{(1+k_{CS})^\infty} \quad \textbf{(13-4)}$$

where D_0 is the current dividend being paid and growing at the constant rate g, and k_{cs} is the appropriate discount rate.

Equation 13-4 can be simplified to the following equation:[5]

$$\hat{P}_0 = \frac{D_1}{k_{CS} - g} \quad \textbf{(13-5)}$$

where D_1 is the dividend expected to be received at the end of Year 1. Notice that k must be greater than g, or else the results are uninformative.

Equation 13-5 is used whenever the growth rate of future dividends is estimated to be constant to infinity. It is used quite often in actual practice because of its simplicity and because in many circumstances, it is a reasonable description of the actual behaviour of a large number of companies, as well as the market as a whole.

EXAMPLE: ESTIMATING PRICE FOR SUMMA CORPORATION

Summa Corporation is currently paying $1 per share in dividends and investors expect those to grow at the rate of 7 per cent a year for the foreseeable future. For investments at this risk level, investors require a return of 15 per cent a year. The estimated price of Summa is:

$$\hat{P}_0 = \frac{D_1}{k_{CS} - g} = \frac{\$1.00(1.07)}{0.15 - 0.07} = \$13.38$$

Note that a current dividend (D_0) must be compounded for one period because the constant growth version of the DDM specifies the numerator as the dividend expected to be received one period from now, which is (D_1). This is consistent with the model's general approach of valuing stocks based on expected future cash flows. In valuation terminology, D_0 represents the dividend currently being paid, and D_1 represents the dividend expected to be paid in the next period. If D_0 is known, D_1 can always be estimated:

$$D_0 = \text{Current dividend}$$
$$D_1 = D_0(1 + g)$$

where g is the expected growth rate of dividends.[6]

---

[4] The constant-growth model is often referred to as the Gordon model named after Myron J. Gordon, who played a large part in its development and use.

[5] Equation 13-4 represents a geometric series that is being multiplied by $(1 + g)/(1 + k)$ every period. The sum of this series is represented by Equation 13-5 as the number of periods involved approaches infinity.

[6] Similarily, D_2 can be determined in the constant growth model as $D_0(1 + g)^2$ or $D_1(1 + g)$.

To completely understand the constant-growth model, which is widely used in valuation analysis, it is instructive to think about the process that occurs under constant growth. Table 13-1 illustrates the case of Summa's growth stock with a current dividend of $1 per share ($D_0$), an expected constant growth rate of 7 per cent, and a required rate of return, k, of 15 per cent.

Table 13-1

Present Value of 60 Years of Dividends
(current dividend = $1 g = 7% k = 15%)

Period	Dollar Dividend	PV Factor	PV of Dollar Dividend
1	1.07	0.8696	0.93
2	1.14	0.7561	0.87
3	1.23	0.6576	0.81
4	1.31	0.5718	0.75
5	1.40	0.4972	0.70
6	1.50	0.4323	0.65
7	1.61	0.3759	0.60
8	1.72	0.3269	0.56
9	1.84	0.2843	0.521
10	1.97	0.2472	0.49
11	2.10	0.2149	0.45
12	2.25	0.1869	0.42
13	2.41	0.1625	0.39
14	2.58	0.1413	0.36
15	2.76	0.1229	0.34
16	2.95	0.1069	0.32
17	3.16	0.0929	0.29
18	3.38	0.0808	0.27
19	3.62	0.0703	0.25
20	3.87	0.0611	0.24
21	4.14	0.0531	0.22
22	4.43	0.0462	0.20
23	4.74	0.0402	0.19
24	5.07	0.0349	0.18
25	5.43	0.0304	0.16
26	5.81	0.0264	0.15
27	6.21	0.0230	0.14
28	6.65	0.0200	0.13
29	7.11	0.0174	0.12
30	7.61	0.0151	0.11
31	8.15	0.0131	0.11
32	8.72	0.0114	0.10
33	9.33	0.0099	0.09
34	9.98	0.0086	0.09

35	10.68	0.0075	0.08
36	11.42	0.0065	0.07
37	12.22	0.0057	0.07
38	13.08	0.0049	0.06
39	13.99	0.0043	0.06
40	14.97	0.0037	0.06
41	16.02	0.0032	0.05
42	17.14	0.0028	0.05
43	18.34	0.0025	0.05
44	19.63	0.0021	0.04
45	21.00	0.0019	0.04
46	22.47	0.0016	0.04
47	24.05	0.0014	0.03
48	25.73	0.0012	0.03
49	27.53	0.0011	0.03
50	29.46	0.0009	0.03
51	31.52	0.0008	0.03
52	33.73	0.0007	0.02
53	36.09	0.0006	0.02
54	38.61	0.0005	0.02
55	41.32	0.0005	0.02
56	44.21	0.0004	0.02
57	47.30	0.0003	0.02
58	50.61	0.0003	0.02
59	54.16	0.0003	0.01
60	57.95	0.0002	0.01

Sum of dividends = $870.47

Sum of first 60 years of discounted dividends = $13.20

As Table 13-1 shows, the expected dollar dividend for each period in the future grows by 7 per cent. Therefore, D_1 = \$1.07, D_2 = \$1.14, D_{10} = \$1.97, and so forth. Only the first 60 years of growth are shown, at the end of which time the dollar dividend is $57.95. The last column of Table 13-1 shows the discounted value of each of the first 60 years of dividends. Thus, the present value of the dividend for Period 1, discounted at 15 per cent, is $0.93. While the actual dollar amount of the expected dividend in Year 60 is $57.95, its present value in today's dollars is only $0.01. Obviously, dividends received far in the future, assuming normal discount rates, are worth very little today.

Figure 13-2 depicts the growth in the dollar dividend for only the first 30 years in order to provide some scale to the process. Because k is greater than g, the present value of each future dividend is declining, since the dividends are growing at a rate (g) that is below the discount rate (k) being used in the denominator of the discount procedure. For example, the present value of D_1 = \$0.93, the present value of D_2 = \$0.87, and the present value of D_{10} = \$0.49. Therefore, the present-value-of-dividends curve at the bottom of Figure 13-2 is declining more rapidly than the estimated-dollar-dividend-over-time curve above it is increasing.

The estimated price of Summa, as illustrated in Table 13-1 and Figure 13-2, is the sum of the present values of each of the future dividends. Adding each of these present values together from now to infinity would produce the correct estimated value of the stock. Note from Table 13-1 that adding the present values of the first 60 years of dividends together produces an estimated value of $13.20. The correct answer, as obtained from adding all years from now to infinity, was calculated as $13.38 in the example above, for a difference of only $0.18. This implies that the dividends received from Years 61 to infinity add a total value of $0.18 to the stock price (i.e., the present value of all dividends received from Year 61 to infinity is only $0.18 in year 0). The reason for this is the extremely low values for the PV factors as the number of periods increases.

Figure 13-2
The Constant Growth Model

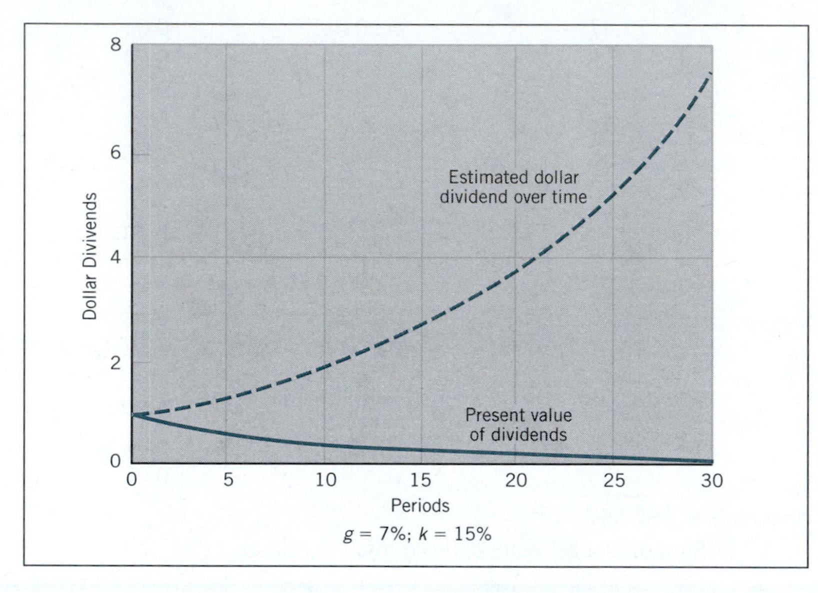

Table 13-1 illustrates the very important point about these valuation models that was explained earlier. The constant-growth version of the DDM given in Equation 13-5 takes account of all future cash flows from now to infinity, although this is not apparent from simply looking at the equation itself. Although Equation 13-5 has no summation or infinity sign, the results produced by this equation are equivalent to the sum that would be obtained by adding together the discounted value of all future dividends (as described in footnote 5). As was the case for the zero-growth model, the mathematics of the process involving a constant growth rate to infinity reduces to a very simple expression, masking the fact that all dividends from now to infinity are being accounted for.

The constant-growth DDM can also provide a useful assessment of the market's perception of growth opportunities available to a company. For example, let's assume that a firm with no profitable growth opportunities should not reinvest residual profits in the company, but rather pay out all its earnings in the form of dividends. This implies $g = 0$, and $D_1 = EPS_1$, where EPS_1 represents the expected earnings per common share in the upcoming year. Under these assumptions, the constant-growth DDM reduces to the following expression:

$$\hat{P}_0 = \frac{EPS_1}{k_{CS}} \tag{13-6}$$

Although we may not find many no-growth firms in practice, the result above can be applied to firms that do have growth opportunities available to them. Thus, at any given time we can view the share price of any common stock (that satisfies the assumptions of the DDM), as being comprised of two components: its no-growth component and the present value of growth opportunities (PVGO). This can be expressed as

$$\hat{P}_0 = \frac{EPS_1}{k_{CS}} + PVGO \tag{13-7}$$

EXAMPLE: ESTIMATING PVGO FOR SUMMA CORPORATION

Assume the expected year one earnings per share (EPS_1) for Summa is \$2.00. If their shares were trading at the intrinsic value of \$13.38 (estimated on the previous page) implies that only \$0.05 for the present value of growth opportunities (PVGO) is factored by market participants into Summa's share price:

$$PVGO = \hat{P}_0 - \frac{EPS_1}{k_{CS}} = 13.38 - \frac{2.00}{0.15} = 13.38 - 13.33 = \$0.05$$

This suggests that very little of Summa's share price is attributable to future growth opportunities.

To fully understand the constant growth rate version of the DDM, it is also important to realize that the model shows that the stock price for any one period is estimated to grow at the same rate as the dividends, which is g. This means that the expected growth rate in price, plus the expected percentage return received in the form of dividends, will equal the required rate of return (k). This is obvious if we rearrange the constant-growth DDM in the following manner, using the present market price in place of intrinsic value, to obtain an estimate of the return required by investors on a particular share:

$$k_{CS} = \frac{D_1}{P_0} + g \tag{13-8}$$

The first term in Equation 13-8 represents the expected dividend yield on the share, therefore, we may view the second term, g, as the expected capital gains yield, since the total return must equal the dividend yield plus capital gains yield. This provides an appropriate approximation for required return, only if the conditions of the constant-growth DDM are met (in particular the assumption regarding constant growth in dividends to infinity must be satisfied). It also assumes that markets are reasonably efficient, by assuming that the market price equals the intrinsic value.

EXAMPLE: ESTIMATING PRICE CHANGE FOR SUMMA CORPORATION

For Summa, the estimated price today is $13.38, while the estimated dividend at the end of this year (D_1) is $1.07, and the estimated long-term growth rate in dividends, *g*, is 7 per cent. This implies an expected rate of return of 15 per cent:

$$k_{CS} = \frac{D_1}{P_0} + g = \frac{1.07}{13.38} + 0.07 = 0.08 + 0.07 = 0.15$$

This suggests that the expected return on Summa is comprised of a dividend yield of 8 per cent and a capital gains yield of 7 per cent. In other words, we expect Summa's share price to increase by 7 per cent over this year. We can check this out by using Equation 13-5 to estimate the intrinsic value of Summa at the end of Period 1:

$$\hat{P}_1 = \frac{D_2}{k_{CS} - g} = \frac{\$1.07(1.07)}{0.15 - 0.07} = \$14.31$$

This estimated price at the end of Period 1 is 7 per cent higher than the estimated price today of $13.38 (rounding causes slight differences):

$$\text{Price change} = \frac{\text{Ending price} - \text{Beginning price}}{\text{Beginning price}}$$

$$= (\$14.31 - \$13.38) / \$13.38 = 7\%$$

This result is intuitive, since the equation used to determine is the same equation used to determine $\hat{P}_0$, multiplied by $(1 + g)$.

EXAMPLE: ESTIMATING IMPLIED RATE OF RETURN FOR SUMMA CORPORATION

Notice that in the previous example, our estimate of the expected return exactly equals the required return of 15 per cent that we used to determine the intrinsic value of Summa. This is because we assumed the share is trading at its intrinsic value. What if Summa was actually trading in the market at a price of $15? Under these circumstances, we estimate an expected return of 14.13 per cent:

$$k_{CS} = \frac{D_1}{P_0} + g = \frac{1.07}{15.00} + 0.07 = 0.0713 + 0.07 = 0.1413$$

At a price of $15, Summa's shares are not attractive investments, since they offer a rate of return of 14.13 per cent, which is below our required rate of return of 15 per cent. In other words, based on our analysis, they are overpriced at $15.

Similarly, if Summa's shares were trading below $13.38, they would be undervalued according to our analysis, and we would expect to earn above our required rate of return. For example, if they were trading at $12, the expected rate of return would be 15.92 per cent, well above 15 per cent:

$$k_{CS} = \frac{D_1}{P_0} + g = \frac{1.07}{12.00} + 0.07 = 0.0892 + 0.07 = 0.1592$$

An examination of Equation 13-5 quickly demonstrates the factors affecting the price of a common stock, assuming the constant-growth version of the dividend discount model to be the applicable valuation approach:

1. If the market lowers the required rate of return for a stock, price will rise (other things being equal).
2. If investors decide that the expected growth in dividends will be higher as the result of some favourable development for the firm, price will also rise (other things being equal).

Of course, the converse for these two situations also holds — a rise in the discount rate or a reduction in the expected growth rate of dividends will lower price.

The present value or intrinsic value calculated from Equation 13-5 is quite sensitive to the estimates used by the investor in the equation. Relatively small variations in the inputs can change the estimated price by large percentage amounts.

EXAMPLE: EFFECT OF THE DISCOUNT RATE ON PRICE FOR SUMMA CORPORATION

For Summa, assume the discount rate used, k, is 16 per cent instead of 15 per cent, with other variables held constant:

$$\hat{P}_0 = \frac{\$1.00(1.07)}{0.16 - 0.07} = \$11.89$$

In this example, a one-percentage-point rise in k results in an 11.14 per cent decrease in price, from \$13.38 to \$11.89.

EXAMPLE: EFFECT OF THE GROWTH RATE ON PRICE FOR SUMMA CORPORATION

Assume that for Summa the growth rate, g, is 6 instead of 7 per cent, with other variables held constant:

$$\hat{P}_0 = \frac{\$1.00(1.06)}{0.15 - 0.06} = \$11.78$$

In this example, a one-percentage-point decline in g results in an 11.96 per cent decrease in price, from \$13.38 to \$11.78.

EXAMPLE: EFFECT OF MULTIPLE VARIABLES ON PRICE FOR SUMMA CORPORATION

ssume that for Summa the discount rate rises to l6 per cent, and the growth rate declines to 4 per cent:

$$\hat{P}_0 = \frac{\$1.00(1.04)}{0.16 - 0.04} = \$8.67$$

In this example, the price declines from \$13.38 to \$8.67, a 35.20 per cent change.

These differences demonstrate why stock prices constantly fluctuate as investors make their buy and sell decisions. Even if all investors use the constant-growth version of the dividend discount model to value a particular common stock (which in practice they don't), many different estimates of value will be obtained because of the following:

1. Each investor has his or her own required rate of return based on their estimate of the risk associated with the stock and future market conditions, resulting in a relatively wide range of values of k.
2. Each investor has his or her own estimate of the expected growth rate in dividends. Although this range may be reasonably narrow in many valuation situations, small differences in g can produce significant differences in price, everything else held constant. In addition, there are several situations under which there will be large ranges of possible estimates for k and g, which suggests why investors can hold such varied opinions about the true value of common shares.

Thus, at any time, some investors are willing to buy, whereas others wish to sell a particular stock, depending on their evaluation of its prospects. This helps to make markets active and liquid.

The Multiple-Growth Case

Many firms grow at a rapid rate (or rates) for a number of years and then slow down to an "average" growth rate. Other companies pay no dividends for a period of years, often during their early growth period. The constant-growth model discussed earlier is not formulated to deal with these situations. A model that can incorporate such a variation of the DDM is the multiple-growth model.

In addition, short-term earnings and dividend estimates should be much more reliable than those covering a longer period of time, which are often calculated using some very general estimates of future economic, industry, and company conditions. In order to use the best information available at any time, it often makes sense to estimate growth as precisely as possible in the short-term before assuming some long-term rate of growth.

Multiple growth is defined as a situation in which the expected future growth in dividends must be described using two or more growth rates. Although any number of growth rates is possible, most stocks can be described using just two or three. It is important to remember that at least two different growth rates are involved; this is the distinguishing characteristic of multiple-growth situations.

A number of companies have experienced rapid growth that could not be sustained forever. During part of their lives their growth exceeded that of the average company in the economy, but later the growth rate slowed. This seems reasonable since we would expect that competitive pressures and/or business cycle influences will prevent firms from maintaining extremely high growth in earnings for long periods of time. Some well-known examples from the past include McDonald's, Disney, Polaroid, Xerox, and IBM.

To capture the expected growth in dividends under this scenario, it is necessary to model the dividend stream during each period of different growth. It is reasonable to assume that at some point the company's growth will slow down to some steady rate such as that of the economy as a whole. At this time, the company's growth in future dividends can be described by the constant-growth model (Equation 13-5). What remains, therefore, is to model the exact dividend stream up to the point at which dividends slow to a normal growth rate and to find the present value of all the components. This can be described in equation form as:

$$\hat{P}_0 = \frac{D_1}{(1 + k_{CS})^1} + \frac{D_2}{(1 + k_{CS})^2} + \ldots + \frac{D_n}{(1 + k_{CS})^n} + \frac{\hat{P}_n}{(1 + k_{CS})^n} \quad \textbf{(13-9)}$$

where $\hat{P}_n = \dfrac{D_{n+1}}{k_{CS} - g}$

n = the time at which constant growth in dividends to infinity is assumed to begin[7]

Essentially, we estimate dividends up to the beginning of the period where it is reasonable to assume constant growth to infinity. Then we can use the constant version of the DDM to estimate the intrinsic value or market price of the stock at that point in time ($\hat{P}_n$). Finally, we discount back to the beginning of the evaluation period (time 0): (1) all of the estimated dividends up to the beginning of constant growth period; and, (2) the estimated intrinsic value at that time. This provides us with today's estimate of the share's intrinsic value.

How does this approach provide us with the present value of all expected future dividends from Period 1 to infinity? Recall from the constant growth version of the DDM that the intrinsic value determined at time n ($\hat{P}_n$), represents the present value of all expected dividends (at time $t = n$), from $n+1$ to infinity. Because $\hat{P}_n$ is the expected price of the stock at the end of period n, it must be discounted back to the present. When we discount $\hat{P}_n$ back to time 0, and add it to the present value of all dividends from $t = 1$ to $t = n$, we end up with the present value (at time $t = 0$) of all expected future dividends from time $t = 1$ to infinity. This is the estimated value of the stock today, according to the DDM.

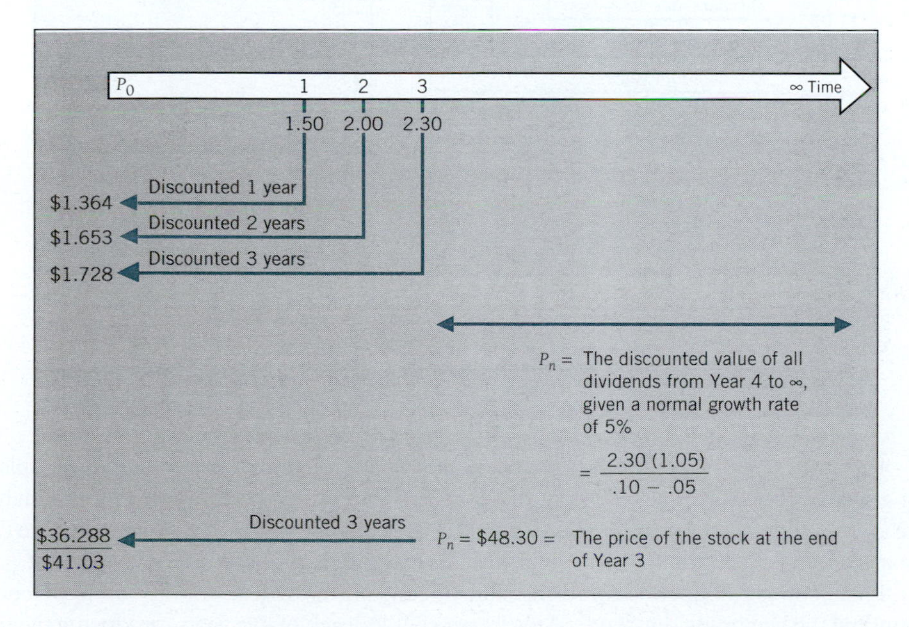

Figure 13-3
Valuing a Multiple-Growth Rate Company

[7] The dividend at period $n + 1$ is equal to the dividend paid in period n compounded up by the growth rate expected from period n to infinity. The designation $n + 1$ refers to the first period after the years of abnormal growth.

Figure 13-3 illustrates the concept of valuing a multiple-growth rate company that is expected to pay a dividend of \$1.50 at the end of this year, a \$2.00 dividend at the end of Year 2, and a \$2.30 dividend at the end of Year 3. It is estimated dividends will grow at a constant rate of 5 per cent per year thereafter. To determine the intrinsic value of this company's common shares if the required rate of is 10 per cent, the first step is to estimate dividends up to the start of constant growth to infinity — D_1 = \$1.50, D_2 = \$2.00, D_3 = \$2.30. Next, you must estimate the intrinsic value at the beginning of constant growth to infinity period —

$$\hat{P}_3 = \frac{D_4}{k_{CS} - g} = \frac{(2.30)(1.05)}{0.10 - 0.05} = \$48.30$$

Finally, discount back the relevant cash flows to time 0 and add:

$$\hat{P}_0 = \frac{1.50}{(1.10)^1} + \frac{2.00}{(1.10)^2} + \frac{2.30}{(1.10)^3} + \frac{48.30}{(1.10)^3} = 1.364 + 1.653 + 1.728 + 36.288 = \$41.03$$

A well-known multiple-growth model is the two-stage growth rate model. This model assumes near-term growth at a rapid rate for some period (typically, 2 to 10 years) followed by a steady long-term growth rate that is sustainable (i.e., a constant-growth rate as discussed earlier).

Figure 13-4
Valuing a Two-Stage Growth Rate Company

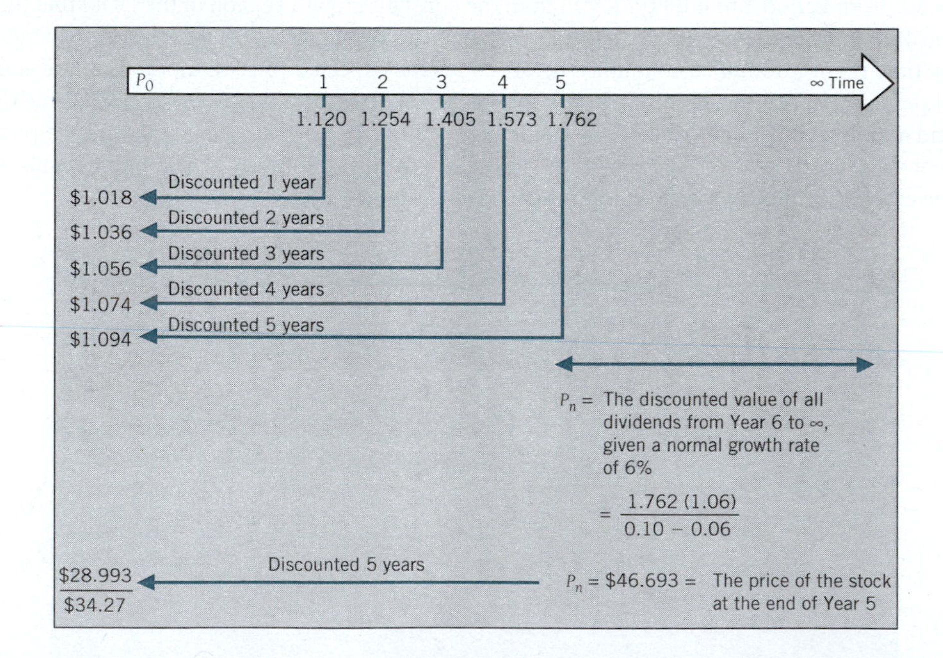

Figure 13-4 illustrates the concept of valuing a multiple-growth rate company displaying growth in two stages. The current dividend is \$1 and is expected to grow at the higher rate (g_1) of 12 per cent a year for five years, at the end of which time the new growth rate (g_c) is expected to be a constant 6 per cent a year. The required rate of return is 10 per cent.

First estimate dividends up to the start of constant growth to infinity done by compounding the beginning dividend, \$1, at 12 per cent for each of five years, producing the following: D_0 = \$1.00, D_1 = \$1.00(1.12) = \$1.120, D_2 = \$1.00(1.12)^2 = \$1.254, D_3 = \$1.00(1.12)^3 = \$1.405, D_4 = \$1.00(1.12)^4 = \$1.573, D_5 = \$1.00(1.12)^5 = \$1.762.

Then estimate the price at the beginning of constant growth to infinity period:

$$\hat{P}_5 = \frac{D_6}{k_{CS} - g} = \frac{(1.762)(1.06)}{0.10 - 0.06} = \$46.693$$

And finally discount back the relevant cash flows to time 0:

$$\hat{P}_0 = \frac{1.120}{(1.10)^1} + \frac{1.254}{(1.10)^2} + \frac{1.405}{(1.10)^3} + \frac{1.573}{(1.10)^4} + \frac{1.762}{(1.10)^5} + \frac{46.693}{(1.10)^5}$$

$$= 1.018 + 1.036 + 1.056 + 1.074 + 1.094 + 28.993 = \$34.27$$

Dividends, Dividends — What about Capital Gains?

In their initial study of valuation concepts, investors often are bothered by the fact that the dividend discount model contains only dividends and an infinite stream of dividends at that. Although this is true, many investors are sure that (1) they will not be here forever and (2) they really want capital gains. Dividends may be nice, but buying low and selling high is so much better! Since so many investors are interested in capital gains, which by definition involves the difference between the price paid for a security and the price at which it is later sold, a valuation model should seemingly contain a stock price somewhere. Thus, in computing present value for a stock, investors are interested in the present value of the expected price two years from now, or six months from now, or whatever the expected holding period is. How can price be incorporated into the valuation — or should it be?

According to the DDM, the only cash flows that an investor needs to be concerned with are dividends. Expected future price is built into the dividend discount model given by Equation 13-2, it is simply not visible. To see this, ask yourself at what price you can expect to sell a common stock that you have bought. Assume, for example, that you purchase today and plan to hold for three years. The price you receive three years from now will reflect the buyer's expectations of dividends from that point forward (at the end of Years 4, 5, etc.).[8] The estimated price today of the stock is equal to

$$\hat{P}_0 = \frac{D_1}{(1 + k_{CS})^1} + \frac{D_2}{(1 + k_{CS})^2} + \frac{D_3}{(1 + k_{CS})^3} + \frac{P_3}{(1 + k_{CS})^3} \qquad \textbf{(13-10)}$$

But $\hat{P}_3$ (the estimated price of the stock at the end of Year 3) is, in turn, equal to the discounted value of all future dividends from Year 4 to infinity. That is,

$$\hat{P}_3 = \frac{D_4}{(1 + k_{CS})^1} + \frac{D_5}{(1 + k_{CS})^2} + \frac{D_6}{(1 + k_{CS})^3} + \dots + \frac{\hat{P}_\infty}{(1 + k_{CS})^{\infty - 2}} \qquad \textbf{(13-11)}$$

Substituting Equation 13-11 into 13-10 produces Equation 13-2, the basic dividend discount model. Thus, the result is the same whether investors discount only a stream of dividends or a combination of dividends and price. Since price at any point in the future is a function of the dividends to be received after that time, the price today for a common stock is best thought of as the discounted value of all future dividends.

[8] This is the exact assumption we used to implement the multi-stage growth model. Not surprisingly, Equation 13-10 is identical to Equation 13-9 with $n = 3$.

Intrinsic Value

After making careful estimates of the expected stream of benefits and the required rate of return, the intrinsic value of the stock can be determined using present value analysis, via the dividend discount model. Determining the intrinsic value is the objective of fundamental analysis. What does intrinsic value imply? Traditionally, investors and analysts specify a relationship between the estimated intrinsic value (IV) of an asset and its current market price (CMP). Specifically:

If IV > CMP, the asset is undervalued and should be purchased or held if already owned.
If IV < CMP, the asset is overvalued and should be avoided, sold if held, or possibly sold short.
If IV = CMP, this implies an equilibrium in that the asset is correctly valued.

Does the problem of varying estimates of value render valuation models useless? No, because individual investors cannot make intelligent investment decisions without having an intelligent estimate of the value of an asset. If the common shares of Nova Scotia Power Corporation (NSPC) are currently priced at $20 a share, is it a good buy for you? It may or may not be, depending on your own required rate of return (discount rate), your estimate of the future benefit stream to be derived from owning NSPC, and certain other factors.[9]

INVESTING tip

Intrinsic value is generally derived from a present value process involving estimates of uncertain (future) benefits and the use of (varying) discount rates by different investors. Therefore, the same asset may have many estimated intrinsic values, depending on who is, and how many are doing the evaluation. This is why, for a particular asset on a particular day, some investors are willing to buy and some to sell. Because future benefits and the required rate of return are uncertain and must be estimated, investors will arrive at different inputs to be used in the valuation process. In addition, it is unlikely that investors will all use the same valuation models. All of these factors result in varying estimates of the intrinsic value of an asset. The market price of an asset at any point is, in this sense, the consensus intrinsic value of that asset for the market.

EXAMPLE: INTRINSIC VALUE OF NOVA SCOTIA POWER CORPORATION

Assume that you require 10 per cent return to invest in **Nova Scotia Power Corporation** (NSPC); that is, your best estimate of the opportunity cost for alternative investment opportunities of similar risk is 10 per cent. Also assume that the current dividend is $0.82 and you expect it to grow at the rate of 5 per cent a year for the indefinite future. Based on these figures and using the constant-growth dividend discount model, the intrinsic value (justified price) of NSPC to you would be estimated at $17.22 per share. Based on the intrinsic value principle, NSPC is overvalued at $20 and should not be purchased, should be sold if held, or sold short if not held.

[9] As we know from Part II, securities should be chosen on the basis of a portfolio concept — that is, how they fit together to form a unified whole.

Notice that this valuation process tells you that if you pay $17.22 per share for NSPC, you will earn your required rate of return of 10 per cent, if the assumed dividend growth rate is correct. You can, therefore, pay less, say $17 or $15 per share and earn more than the required rate of return.[10]

Other investors with different estimates for k and g may be at the margin valuing this security, with estimated values only slightly higher or lower than $20. They are potential traders if the price moves slightly or if a news event causes even slight variations in their *k* or their *g*.

The Dividend Discount Model in Practice

Many money managers and investment services firms use the DDM in various ways to estimate the intrinsic values of stocks. Regardless of who uses the model, and how it is used, estimates are always involved. Investors should always remember this in using or evaluating output from these models.

The DDM has a great deal of intuitive appeal because it links equity prices to two important fundamentals:

1. Corporate profitability (through their link with dividends)
2. The general level of interest rates (through their impact on the discount rate).

In particular, the model predicts that the intrinsic value of common shares will increase as a result of: increases in expected dividends (which are closely related to profitability); increases in the growth rate of these dividends; and/or decreases in the appropriate discount rate. From previous chapters, we know that the discount rate will be an increasing function of the general level of interest rates, as well as the riskiness of the underlying security.

For these reasons the DDM provides a great deal of insight into the factors affecting the general level of security prices in an economy. The CSC Notes box below discusses how changes in macroeconomic variables impact the values of *k* and g in the DDM through different phases of the equity cycle. The changes in these variables, in turn, impact the general level of equity prices in an economy.

INVESTING *tip*

The valuation process can establish justified prices for assets or indicate whether or not you can expect to earn your required rate of return on a prospective asset. Remember, however, that you are not assured of earning your required rate of return. Investment decisions always involve a forward-looking process. Estimates are based on the best information available, but there is always uncertainty. But even the best estimates may not be realized. As discussed in Chapter 1, uncertainty will always be the dominant feature of the environment in which investment decisions are made. Furthermore, other factors are at play, including the psychology of the market. On the Internet investors can interact with each other there, and information, sometimes false or misleading, can be spread quickly, and prices affected accordingly. See the Real-World Returns box below for a discussion of what can happen to a stock as a result of the rise of investors connected on the Internet.

[10] To determine the expected return for an investor who purchases the shares at $15, we can use Equation 13-8, along with an estimate for D_1 = ($0.82)(1.05) = $0.86 to obtain the following expected annual return: k_{CS} = (0.86)/(15) + 0.05 = 0.1073, or 10.73 percent (well above the required return of 10 percent).

REAL-WORLD RETURNS

Cyber Postings and Diana Corp. Stock Value

The stock symbol for **Diana Corp.** is DNA — the same as the building blocks of life itself. But lately, Diana stock has been death incarnate. In just four weeks, this Milwaukee-based company's stock has fallen from 103 on May 28 to 39¼ on June 26 — after climbing all the way up from 5 a year ago. Some of the gyrations were caused by ordinary market influences. But for much of Diana's wild ride, the stock was sent careening by a potent new force in the markets: the power of online services.

Diana's rise was fuelled by postings online — particularly America Online Inc.'s Motley Fool electronic bulletin boards. But so was its fall — and in a manner so troubling that it has apparently drawn the interest of regulators. The New York Stock Exchange, where Diana's stock is listed, is investigating trading in the stock, according to company officials. Diana executives maintain that the company's shares were driven down by disclosure of inside information that was posted on Motley Fool message boards. If so, the implications could be serious for the on-line world, which is getting increased scrutiny from regulators as a medium for market manipulation.

In Diana's case, the negative information posted on Motley Fool was accurate — but premature. On June 13, a person with the AOL handle Duke121 wrote in the Diana "folder" of the Motley Fool that the company would take an $850,000 writedown in its fourth quarter on the meat distribution business the company has been trying to sell. Without any other major news, Diana's stock slid 8¼ to close the day at 77¼. And then, lo and behold, 12 days later the company reported fourth-quarter financial results — and they included an $852,000 writedown. "That was clearly inside information," says Diana Chairman Richard Y. Fisher. "We are going to look into how that got on the bulletin board."

Purported Experts

At first glance, Diana is an unlikely company to find in the middle of an Internet controversy. Its primary business is distributing meat and seafood. What's driving interest in Diana is its 80% stake in **Sattel Communications Corp.**, which makes switches aimed at lowering the cost of providing access to the Internet. The Motley Fool forum is full of messages from purported experts who expound in detail on Diana's technology. Since Diana's stock is thinly traded — only 4.1 million shares are outstanding — the stock is more prone than most to online influence.

What has been added to that mixture in Motley Fool are alarmist comments, both positive and negative. In February, a Fool forum participant with the handle VALUSPEC posted a public message saying that a "very bullish" announcement would come in the "not-too-distant" future. In March, the same author wrote that "MCI might be interested in" Diana. The posters of these messages, who would not respond to e-mail queries from *Business Week*, are anonymous AOL subscribers. VALUSPEC describes him- or herself in a member profile as a 34-year-old owner of a landscaping business, while Duke121 will only disclose her gender and marital status.

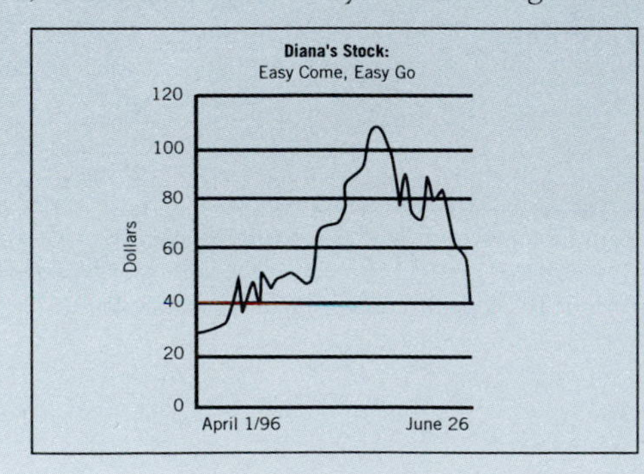

Sometimes the on-line leads are correct, sometimes not. Diana did announce a major deal to sell 21 switches in May, which helped its stock rise even further. But no MCI Communications Corp. interest has materialized. "I think the Motley Fool postings have definitely helped drive Diana through the stratosphere," says Richard Keim, whose Keim Wilson Associates has a short position in the stock.

Since late May, the bears have had their way in the Motley Fool forum and with Diana. On May 29, Aensio & Co., a New York research and trading firm, posted a sell recommendation on the motley Fool bulletin board. The stock dropped 2¾ to close at 101. The next day, "SsOprtr" posted a report that the Securities & Exchange Commission was looking into possible manipulation of Diana's Stock — and the stock slipped another 2¼. Fisher says he knows of no SEC investigation, and the SEC declined to comment.

The Diana saga shows that the Internet and on-line services are providing a new way to discuss securities: Anonymous people who may have hidden agendas can post any information they want, accurate or not, in a public forum. But perhaps less has changed than meets the eye. "The lesson is what it's always been: Investigate before you invest," says Merton Miller, a University of Chicago economist and Nobel prize-winner. "Even in the new world of cyberspace, the old lessons of investing apply."

Source: Peter Elstrom, "Now the Medium Is the Message," Business Week, *July 8, 1996. Reprinted by special permission, copyright © 1996 by The McGraw-Hill Companies, Inc.*

RELATIVE VALUATION APPROACHES

Relative valuation approaches determine the value of common shares by comparing the market prices of "similar" companies, relative to some common variable such as earnings, cash flow, book values, or sales. Although relatively simple to apply, using multiples based on comparable companies has the potential to build market errors into the value estimation process. This section discusses the application and appropriateness of some of these approaches, with particular emphasis on the P/E ratio, the most commonly cited one for common share valuation.

The P/E Ratio Approach

An alternative fundamental analysis method of valuation frequently used by practicing security analysts is the **P/E ratio** or **earnings multiplier** approach. The P/E ratio is the number of times investors value earnings as expressed in the stock price.

P/E Ratio (Earnings Multiplier) The price to earnings (P/E) ratio for a stock measures the stock price relative to the earnings per share.

Practicing security analysts probably use this method more often than dividend discount models. Although the P/E ratio model appears easier to use than the DDM, its very simplicity causes investors to forget that estimation of the uncertain future is also involved here. This is an important point to remember. Every valuation model and approach, properly done, requires estimates of the uncertain future.

The conceptual framework for the P/E model is not as solidly based on economic theory as the DDM. However, a P/E ratio model is consistent with the present value analysis because it concerns the intrinsic value of a stock or the aggregate market, exactly as before.

The P/E ratio as reported daily in such sources as *The Globe and Mail* and the *National Post* is simply an identity calculated by dividing the current market price of the stock by the latest 12-month earnings. As such, it tells investors the price being paid for each $1 of the company's most recent earnings. For example, in June 1998 investors were willing to pay 34

CSC NOTES

Equity Cycles and the Dividend Discount Model (DDM)

EQUITY CYCLES

Phases of the equity cycle (which traces movements in the stock market) can be described as expansionary (rising prices), peak (prices hit new maximum levels), contraction (prices declining), and trough (prices "bottom out"). It is important to note that there may be temporary setbacks or corrections within the overall phases, and that equity cycles are very similar to economic or business cycles.[11] However, equity cycles tend to lead business cycles, which is why the TSE 300 Composite Index is included in the Canadian Composite Leading Indicator that is used to forecast future economic conditions.

Many investors attempt to identify peaks and troughs in the equity cycle in order to employ asset class timing (or asset allocation) strategies. The rationale underlying these approaches is that improved returns can result when investors recognize when to shift from stocks to T-bills and/or bonds.

Some general asset class timing strategies in relation to the equity cycle include:

1. Lengthen terms of bond holdings and avoid stocks during contraction phase, since interest rates will begin to fall, which will have a favourable impact on long-term bond prices.
2. Sell long-term bonds that had rallied ahead of stocks in response to falling interest rates during the trough phase because stocks will now likely rally more dramatically.
3. Maintain or increase stock position during expansionary phase, since stocks tend to do well during sustained economic growth periods.
4. Stop buying stock and invest in short-term instruments as peak approaches, since interest rates are likely to increase.

The problems with these strategies are that variations occur within the cycles and it is difficult to anticipate the arrival and duration of these phases.

THE DDM AND EQUITY CYCLES

The dividend discount model (DDM) links equity prices to two important "fundamentals": corporate profitability (through their link with dividends); and, the general level of interest rates (through their impact on the discount rate). In particular, the model predicts that the intrinsic value of common shares will increase as a result of: increases in expected dividends (which are closely related to profitability); increases in the growth rate of these dividends; and/or decreases in the appropriate discount rate. From previous chapters, we know that the discount rate will be an increasing function of the general level of interest rates, as well as the riskiness of the underlying security. For these reasons the DDM provides a great deal of insight into the factors affecting the general level of security prices in an economy.

Table 13-2 shows how the DDM can be used to interpret changes in equity prices in relation to the equity cycle. In particular: (i) k is rising and g is falling during the contraction phase (one to two years), which causes prices to fall; (ii) k is falling faster than g during the trough period of the cycle, which often causes a medium-term interest rate driven rally in stock (five to 13 months); (iii) k briefly rises faster than g during the expansionary period, which causes a brief decline in stock prices (six to nine months); and, (iv) g rises faster than k from the expansionary to peak period, which increases stock prices (one to three years).

Despite its intuitive appeal, it is often difficult to put the DDM into practice, particularly for Canadian companies. This is because the model is based on several assumptions that are not met by a large number of firms in Canada. It is best suited for companies: (1) with a stable dividend payout history that they wish to maintain in the future; and (2) that are growing at a steady and sustainable rate. Hence, the DDM works reasonably well for large corporations in mature industries with stable profits and an established dividend policy. In Canada, the banks and utility companies fit this profile, while in the United States, there are numerous NYSE-listed companies of this nature.

Not surprisingly, it does not work well for a lot of resource-based companies that are cyclical in nature and often display erratic growth in earnings and dividends. In addition, many of these companies (especially the smaller ones) do not distribute a great deal of profits to shareholders in the form of dividends. Thus the DDM may not provide meaningful value estimates for a large number of Canadian corporations, since resource-based and cyclical companies comprise a large proportion of the TSE 300 Composite Index, and dominate other Canadian equity markets such as the VSE, the ASE, and the over-the-counter market.

The DDM will also not work well for firms in distress, firms that are in the process of restructuring, firms involved in acquisitions, and/or private firms. Finally, if a company enters into substantial share repurchase arrangements, the model will require adjustments, since share repurchases also represent a method of distributing wealth to shareholders.

[11] Business cycles are discussed at some length in Chapter 15.

Table 13-2

The Dividend Discount Model and the Equity Cycle

Point in Equity Cycle	Changes in Denominator	Cause of Changes in Denominator
A. Contraction Phase *End of equity cycle.* Examples: 1981, 1990. Recession-related decline in stock prices.	*r* is still rising, and *g* is beginning to fall. Therefore, prices are implied to fall. This period often lasts one to two years. $\downarrow P = \frac{Div}{\uparrow r - g \downarrow}$	Interest rates are rising because of central bank policy aimed at causing a slowdown and because of currently robust economic growth. Higher interest rates are designed to reverse the recently higher inflationary trend. The higher interest rate policy is beginning to take its toll. The economy is beginning to slow and corporate profits are beginning to fall.
B. Stock Market Trough *Interest rate driven rally in stock prices.* Examples: August 1982-July 1983 and October 1990-April 1991. The beginning of a new equity cycle. Short-term rally in stock prices.	*g* is still falling; however, *r* is falling at a faster rate. Therefore, prices are temporarily assumed to be bid up. This period has often lasted five to 13 months. $\uparrow P = \frac{Div}{\downarrow r - g \downarrow}$	The rapid decline in r reflects the recent decline in interest rates owing to the recession and an attempt by the central bank to direct a new economic expansion, in part, by using lower interest rates. Stock prices tend to rally rapidly owing to a more rapid fall in *r* than *g*. Investors also *anticipate* a recovery in corporate profit growth that should result from an economic recovery. As T-bill rates fall, the implied return in stocks begins to look relatively more attractive and a sudden flow of hot capital from T-bills to equities tends to produce a rapid but unsustainable rise in stock prices.
C. Expansion Phase of the Equity Cycle *Early cycle interest rate shock and brief decline in stock prices.* Examples: 1976, 1983–84.	*g* is beginning to rise with a new economic recovery; however, *r* briefly rises more rapidly. Therefore, prices are implied to fall during a sudden adjustment to higher interest rates. This period often lasts six to nine months. $\downarrow P = \frac{Div}{\uparrow r - g \uparrow}$	Interest rate policy tends to serve as a tool for directing economic expansions and contractions. Because interest rates tend to overshoot on the downside (as well as on the upside), there is a period at the beginning of a new economic cycle where rates are temporarily too low and must be raised or "normalized" in order to moderate the rate of new economic growth. This causes a rate shock.
D. The Profit-Driven Cycle in Stock Prices — Expansion Phase to Peak Examples: 1978–80, 1988–89.	*r* is stable or rising, but rising less quickly than *g*. *g* is expected to continue growing with the sustained and later cycle economic recovery. Therefore, prices are implied to rise. This period of the equity cycle often lasts one to three years. $\uparrow P = \frac{Div}{\uparrow r - g \uparrow}$	Generally stock prices appreciate *steadily*, though less rapidly than in period B. As long as the economic expansion leads to a rise in *g* which exceeds the rate of rise in *r*, prices should rise. However, the economic cycle is getting older and any unexpected upward inflation pressure can lead to sudden increases in *r*, possibly resulting in an interest rate shock as in (C) or leading to the end of that equity cycle as in (A).

Note: $K_{cs} = r$, and D_1 = Div.

Source: *Canadian Securities Course Textbook* (Toronto: Canadian Securities Institute, August 1998), p. 9-31.

times (the most recent 12-month) earnings for **Bombardier** but only 12 times earnings for **Laurentian Bank**, while **Dylex Corporation** was selling at only six times earnings. These P/E ratios, however, provide no basis for valuation other than showing the underlying identity on which the P/E valuation model is based: This identity is[12]

(13-12) $$P_0 = \text{Current market price} = E_0 \times P_0/E_0$$

To implement the earnings multiplier model and estimate the value of the stock today, we must estimate the values on the right-hand side of Equation 13-12. The typical P/E formulation uses estimated earnings for the next 12 months. The basic equation then becomes

(13-13) $$\begin{aligned} P_0 &= \text{Estimated earnings} \times \text{Justified P/E ratio} \\ &= E_1 \times P_0/E_1 \end{aligned}$$

EXAMPLE: EFFECT OF P/E RATIO ON PRICE

If investors are willing to pay 15 times expected earnings, a stock with estimated earnings of $3 per share for the next 12 months will sell for $45. This price will change as estimates of earnings or the justified P/E changes.

Determinants of the P/E Ratio

What determines a P/E ratio? The P/E ratio can be derived from the dividend discount model, which, as we have seen, is the foundation of valuation for common stocks. We will illustrate this process only for the case of constant growth. If a multiple-period growth model is applicable to the stock being considered, a more complicated formulation than the one presented here is required.

Start with Equation 13-5, the estimated price of a stock using the constant-growth version of the model. We use P_0 to represent estimated price from the model.

(13-14) $$P_0 = \frac{D_1}{k_{CS} - g}$$

Dividing both sides of Equation 13-14 by expected earnings, E_1,

(13-15) $$\frac{P_0}{E_1} = \frac{D_1/E_1}{k_{CS} - g}$$

Equation 13-15 indicates those factors that affect the estimated P/E ratio.

1. The expected dividend payout ratio (D_1/E_1)
2. The required rate of return (k_{CS})
3. The expected growth rate of dividends (g)

[12] E_0 here refers to the earnings used to calculate the P/E ratio as reported; for example, in the case of *The Globe and Mail / Report on Business*, it is the most recent 12-month earnings.

The following relationships should hold, other things being equal:

- The higher the expected payout ratio, the higher the P/E.
- The higher the expected growth rate, g, the higher the P/E.
- The higher the required rate of return, k, the lower the P/E.

It is important to remember the phrase "other things being equal," because usually other things are not equal and the preceding relationships do not hold by themselves. It is quite obvious, upon reflection, that if a firm could increase its estimated P/E ratio, and therefore its market price, by simply raising its payout ratio, it would be very tempted to do so. However, such an action would in all likelihood reduce future growth prospects, lowering g, and thereby defeating the increase in the payout. Similarly, trying to increase g by taking on particularly risky investment projects would cause investors to demand a higher required rate of return, thereby raising k. Again, this would work to offset the positive effects of the increasing.

Variables 2 and 3 are typically the most important factors in the preceding determination of the P/E ratio because a small change in either can have a large effect on its value.

EXAMPLE: EFFECT OF RATE OF RETURN AND GROWTH RATE ON THE P/E RATIO

Assume that the expected payout ratio is 53.5 per cent (i.e., $D_1/E_1 = 1.07/2.00 = 0.535$). By varying k and g, and therefore changing the difference between the two (the denominator in Equation 13-15), investors can assess the effect on the P/E ratio as follows:

Assume $k_{CS} = 0.15$ and $g = 0.07$

$$\frac{P_0}{E_1} = \frac{D_1/E_1}{k_{CS} - g} = \frac{0.535}{0.15 - 0.07} = 6.69$$

Now assume k increases to 0.16, while g falls to 0.06, the justified P/E ratio falls to 5.35.

$$\frac{P_0}{E_1} = \frac{D_1/E_1}{k_{CS} - g} = \frac{0.535}{0.16 - 0.06} = 5.35$$

This is not surprising since both of these events produce a negative impact on the justified P/E ratio.

Now assume that k falls to 14 per cent, while g increases to 8 per cent, which are both favourable events.

$$\frac{P_0}{E_1} = \frac{D_1/E_1}{k_{CS} - g} = \frac{0.535}{0.14 - 0.08} = 8.92$$

Think about each of these P/E ratios being used as a multiplier with an expected earnings for Summa for next year of $2. The possible prices for Summa would be $13.38, $10.70, and $17.84, respectively, which is quite a range, given the small changes in k and g that were made.

Understanding the P/E Ratio

Most investors intuitively realize that the P/E ratio should be higher for companies whose earnings are expected to grow rapidly. However, it is not easy to determine how much higher. The market will assess the degree of risk involved in the expected future growth of earnings — if the higher growth rate carries a high level of risk, the P/E ratio will be affected accordingly, by the corresponding increase in the required rate of return (k_{CS}). Furthermore, the high growth rate in earnings may be attributable to several different factors, some of which are more desirable than others. For example, rapid growth in unit sales owing to strong demand for a firm's products is preferable to favourable tax situations, which may change, or liberal accounting procedures, which may cause future reversals in the firm's situation.

P/E ratios reflect investors' expectations about the growth potential of a stock and the risk involved. However, evidence provided in Chapter 10 suggests that stocks with low P/E ratios tend to outperform those with higher P/E ratios, on a risk-adjusted basis. For example, Bourgeois and Lussier examined the 300 largest common stocks trading on the TSE every year from 1973 to 1988 (based on market capitalization).[13] They found that the quintile of stocks with the lowest P/E multiples produced an average annual return of 15.6 per cent over this period. This performance was well above the average TSE 300 return of 11.6 per cent, and the 6.1 per cent return provided by the quintile of stocks with the highest P/E ratios. Bauman and Miller and several other studies have also verified the superior performance of US stocks with low P/E ratios.[14]

Estimating the P/E Ratio

Estimates of the justified P/E ratio ultimately involve a great deal of subjectivity. While the valuation procedure itself is relatively easy, the estimation of an appropriate P/E ratio is difficult. As the discussion in the previous section suggests, determining an appropriate P/E ratio requires much analysis and judgement regarding the firm's growth opportunities, position within the industry, and the riskiness associated with the firm, its industry, and the economy as a whole.

Despite the intuitive appeal of estimating the justified P/E ratio based on Equation 13-15, it is only appropriate under certain conditions, since it is merely a reformulation of the constant-growth DDM. It will only work well for firms that exhibit stable and growing dividends, at a rate below the required return on their common shares (i.e., k_{CS} must be $> g$). An alternative approach is to find "comparable" companies, rate one company relative to the others, and estimate a target P/E ratio for the company being analyzed, based on this comparison, and based on the P/E ratios of the comparable companies. Often this approach involves scaling an industry average P/E ratio up or down, based on the analyst's opinion regarding how well the company stacks up against its peers.

A comparison of one company with its peers also involves a great deal of subjectivity regarding several company-specific characteristics including risk, potential for growth, and

[13] J. Bourgeois and J. Lussier, "P/Es and Performance in the Canadian Market," *Canadian Investment Review* 7 (Spring 1994), pp. 33–39.

[14] S. Bauman and R. Miller, "Investor Expectations and the Performance of Value versus Growth Stocks," *The Journal of Portfolio Management* 23 (Spring 1997), pp. 57–68.

overall financial health of the company. Some other approaches to estimating justified P/E multiples include using historical averages for the company or the company's industry. An alternative approach is to determine the ratio based on its historic relationship to P/E multiples in the market as a whole. For example, a company or industry may historically have traded at P/E ratios that average 90 per cent of the P/E ratio for the TSE 300, so you could estimate an appropriate P/E multiple based on 90 per cent of the TSE 300's current P/E ratio. The problem with any of these ways of estimating justified P/E ratios is that they may build market errors into the value estimation process. For example, we could overestimate the appropriate P/E multiple based on industry averages if the market has systematically overvalued the particular industry that the company is in. Similar results would occur if we scale the TSE 300 multiple by 90 per cent but find that the entire market is overvalued.

Aside from the difficulties in estimating an appropriate P/E ratio, there are several other practical concerns regarding the informativeness of the P/E ratios themselves. One important concern is that P/E ratios are uninformative when companies have negative (or very small) earnings. Finally, the volatile nature of earnings implies a great deal of volatility in P/E multiples. For example, the earnings of cyclical companies fluctuate much more dramatically throughout the business cycle than their stock prices. As a result, their P/E ratios tend to peak during recessionary periods (in response to low earnings) and hit low points during the peak of business cycles (in response to high earnings). In response to some of these concerns, there are a number of similar approaches described below, which are often used for valuation purposes.

Market-to-Book Ratio (M/B)

Book value, the accounting value of the firm as reflected in its financial statements, measures the actual values recorded under accounting conventions. As such, book values have the advantages and disadvantages of accounting numbers. The book value of equity is defined as the book value of assets minus the book value of liabilities. It represents an accounting measure of the amount of unencumbered assets to which equity holders are entitled. In Canada and the United States, the book value of assets equals their original cost minus allowable depreciation, while the liability values reflect their values when incurred.

Market-to-Book ratio (M/B) or Price-to-Book Value
The ratio of stock price to per share shareholders' equity.

The **market-to-book ratio (M/B)** or **price-to-book value** is determined using the following equation: $M/B = P_0/BV_0$, where P_0 is the market price per common share and BV_0 is the book value per common share (determined by dividing the net book value of the firm by the number of common shares outstanding). This variable is followed closely by investors and analysts. Stocks selling below the book value of equity represent good candidates for "value" portfolios, while stocks trading at high multiples, relative to book value, are often categorized as "growth" stocks.

Estimates of the intrinsic value of a share can be determined by multiplying the justified M/B ratio times the company's book value per share (which is easily determined from the balance sheet). We end up with the following valuation equation, similar to Equation 13-13, which was used for valuing shares based on their justified P/E ratio:

$$\begin{aligned} \hat{P}_0 &= \text{Book value per share} \times \text{Justified M/B ratio} \\ &= BV_0 \times M/B \end{aligned} \qquad \textbf{(13-16)}$$

There are several reasons why valuing stocks relative to their M/B is attractive. Book value provides a relatively stable, intuitive measure of value relative to market values which can be easily compared to those of other companies, provided accounting standards do not vary greatly across the comparison group. It eliminates the problems arising from the use of P/E multiples, since book values are rarely negative and do not exhibit the volatility associated with earnings levels. On the other hand, book values are sensitive to accounting standards and practices, which often vary from firm to firm. In addition, they may be uninformative for companies that do not have a large proportion of fixed assets (such as service firms or emerging high-technology firms).

Similar to P/E ratios, the justified M/B ratio can be estimated by comparing with industry ratios, aggregate market ratios, past trends, and by relating to the fundamentals used in the DDM. In order to relate M/B ratios to the constant-growth version of the DDM provided in Equation 13-5, we begin by noting that D_1 may be expressed as: $D_1 = EPS_1 \times$ Payout ratio. Next, we note that EPS_1 can be expressed as $EPS_0 \times (1+g)$, if we assume that earnings and dividends grow at the same rate. Thus we can say that $D_1 = EPS_0 \times (1+g) \times$ Payout ratio. Finally, it is an accounting identity that $EPS_0 = ROE_0 \times BV_0$, so we can say that $D_1 = ROE_0 \times BV_0 \times (1+g) \times$ Payout ratio.[15]

When we substitute this expression for D_1 into the numerator of the constant-growth DDM equation, we obtain the following relationship:

$$P_0 = \frac{ROE_0 \times BV_0 \times \text{Payout ratio} \times (1+g)}{k_{CS} - g}$$

Finally, dividing both sides by book value per share (BV_0), we are left with:

$$\frac{P_0}{BV_0} = \frac{ROE_0 \times \text{Payout ratio} \times (1+g)}{k_{CS} - g} \qquad \text{(13-17)}$$

This equation provides a method of estimating a justified M/B ratio based on underlying fundamentals. It implies that M/B is positively related to its profitability (as measured by ROE), and to its expected growth rate. Similar to the P/E ratio, it will increase as a result of decreases in the discount rate k_{CS}.

EXAMPLE: ESTIMATING MARKET-TO-BOOK RATIO FOR SUMMA CORPORATION

Suppose that in addition to the previous information, we are given that Summa's most recent return on equity (ROE_0) is 16 per cent, while its current book value per share (BV_0) is \$12.40. The justified M/B ratio is 1.145.

$$M/B = \frac{P_0}{BV_0} = \frac{ROE_0 \times \text{Payout ratio} \times (1+g)}{k_{CS} - g} = \frac{(0.16)(0.535)(1.07)}{0.15 - 0.07} = 1.145$$

Using Equation 13-16, we obtain an estimate a value of \$14.20 for Summa's shares:

$$\hat{P}_0 = M/B \times BV_0 = (1.145)(12.40) = \$14.20$$

[15] It is an accounting identity that $EPS_0 = ROE_0 \times BV_0$, because EPS = net income/number of common shares outstanding, ROE = net income/total common equity, while BV = total common equity/number of common shares outstanding.

Several analysts recommend choosing stocks with low price-to-book value ratios as a stock selection rule. The M/B ratio has received support in empirical tests, several of which were discussed in Chapter 10. The most notable evidence is provided by the 1992 study by Eugene Fama and Kenneth French. They found that two basic variables, size (as measured by the market value of equity) and book-to-market value of equity (which is the reciprocal of the M/B ratio), effectively combined to capture the cross-sectional variation in average stock returns during the period 1963–90. Furthermore, the book-to-market equity ratio had a consistently stronger role in average returns.[16]

Price/Sales Ratio (P/S)

A valuation technique that has received increased attention recently is the **price/sales (P/S) ratio** calculated by dividing a company's total market value (price times number of shares) by its sales. In effect, it indicates what the market is willing to pay for a dollar of the firm's revenues.

Price/Sales (P/S) Ratio A company's total common equity market value divided by its sales.

The P/S ratio has several properties that make it attractive for valuation purposes. Unlike earnings and book values, sales are relatively insensitive to accounting decisions and are never negative. Sales are not as volatile as earnings levels, hence, P/S ratios are generally less volatile than P/E multiples. In addition, sales figures provide useful information about corporate decisions such as the impact of pricing and credit policies. On the other hand, sales do not impart much information about cost control and profit margins, which are important determinants of company performance.

The expression for obtaining the share value estimate using this approach is similar to Equation 13-12 for using the P/E ratio and Equation 13-16 for using the M/B ratio:

$$\begin{aligned}\hat{P}_0 &= \text{Sales per share} \times \text{Justified price-to-sales ratio} \\ &= \text{Sales}_0 \times \text{P/S}\end{aligned} \qquad (13\text{-}18)$$

Similar to P/E multiples and M/B ratios, justified P/S ratios can be estimated by reference to industry peers, market ratios, and past trends. We can also alter the DDM to determine an estimate of an appropriate P/S ratio based on fundamentals. We focus on the constant-growth version of the DDM, and begin by noting as we did in the previous section, that D_1 can be expressed as $D_1 = EPS_0 \times (1+g) \times$ Payout ratio. We also note that EPS_0 = Net income margin (NI%) × Sales per share ($Sales_0$). By making the appropriate substitution for D_1 in the numerator of Equation 13-5, we can rewrite the constant-growth DDM as:

$$P_0 = \frac{\text{NI\%} \times \text{Sales}_0 \times \text{Payout ratio} \times (1+g)}{k_{CS} - g}$$

Finally, dividing both sides by $Sales_0$, we get:

$$\frac{P_0}{\text{Sales}_0} = \frac{\text{NI\%} \times \text{Payout ratio} \times (1+g)}{k_{CS} - g} \qquad (13\text{-}19)$$

This calculation shows that the P/S ratio will increase in response to growth in profit margins and the growth rate and decreases in k_{CS}.

[16] E. Fama and K. French, "The Cross-Section of Expected Stock Returns," *Journal of Finance* 47 (June 1992), pp. 427–465.

EXAMPLE: ESTIMATING THE PRICE/SALES RATIO FOR SUMMA CORPORATION

Suppose Summa has a net income margin (NI%) of 5 per cent, and sales per share ($Sales_0$) of $40. This implies Summa's shares are worth $14.32 each.

$$\frac{P_0}{Sales_0} = \frac{NI\% \times \text{Payout ratio} \times (1 + g)}{k_{CS} - g} = \frac{(0.05)(0.535)(1.07)}{0.15 - 0.07} = 0.358$$

$$= Sales_0 \times P/S = (40)(0.358) = \$14.32$$

A well-known 1996 book, *What Works on Wall Street*, by James O'Shaugnessy,[17] gives new emphasis to the price/sales ratio. Using Compustat data back to 1951, he analyzed all of the basic investment strategies used to select common stock, such as book value, cash flow, P/E, ROE, yield, and so forth. O'Shaugnessy found that the 50 stocks with the lowest P/S ratios, based on an annual rebalancing of the portfolio, performed at an annual rate of 15.42 per cent over the 40 years from 1954 through 1994, compared to 12.45 per cent annually for his universe of stocks. Stocks with the highest P/S ratios earned only 4.15 per cent annually. Furthermore, combining low P/S stocks (generally, a P/S of 1.0 or lower) with stocks showing momentum (the best 12-month price performance) produced results of 18.14 per cent annually over the full 40-year period.

Other Relative Valuation Approaches

Another commonly used ratio is the multiple of price-to-cash flow (P/CF). Generally cash flow (CF) is estimated as CF = net income + depreciation + deferred taxes.[18] This ratio alleviates some of the accounting concerns regarding accounting measures of earnings.

Finally, the price-to-earnings before interest and taxes (EBIT) ratio can also be used for valuation purposes. Using EBIT instead of net earnings eliminates a significant proportion of volatility caused in EPS figures by the use of debt. This is useful if we want to reduce the impact of capital structure on our valuation process.

OTHER VALUATION ISSUES

There is growing interest in two value-added performance measures: economic value added and market value added. These measures are used by a number of companies to evaluate the performance of managers in enhancing firm value. More recently, these measures are also being used by security analysts as possible indicators of future equity returns.

[17] James P. O'Shaugnessy, *What Works on Wall Street: A Guide to the Best-Performing Investment Strategies of All Time* (New York: McGraw-Hill, 1997).

[18] Some analysts focus on "free" cash flow available to equity holders, which is estimated as: net income + depreciation + deferred taxes − capital spending − the change in net working capital − principal repayments + new external finance.

Economic Value Added

Economic value added (EVA) is a variation of the cash flow valuation approach.[19] In particular, it considers economic profit, which is similar to the net present value (NPV) approach for making capital budgeting decisions. NPV determines asset values based upon the present value of the cash flows it generates during its useful life. However, EVA advocates suggest firm managers cannot be evaluated based on the determination of firm value in this manner. The reason is that it is hard to determine the value impact of cash flows, without due regard to their intended use. For example, negative cash flows in a particular period could be detracting from firm value (i.e., when its losing money), or adding to firm value (i.e., reinvesting in profitable long-term projects). The same can be said of positive cash flows, which could be enhancing value (i.e., increasing profits), or destroying value (i.e., disposing of valuable long-term assets).

Economic Value ADded (EVA)
A technique for focusing on a firm's return on capital in order to determine if shareholders are being rewarded.

EVA addresses these concerns by considering not only profitability, but also the amount of capital resources used to generate these profits. It may be calculated using two approaches: using residual income or refined earnings. The residual income approach determines EVA in the following manner:

$$\text{EVA} = (\text{ROC} - \text{WACC}) \times \text{Capital} \tag{13-20}$$

where ROC is the return on total capital, WACC is the firm's weighted average cost of capital, and Capital is the average total capital (or net assets) employed by the company during the period.

Notice from Equation 13-20 that this measure penalizes decreases in capital (which proxies for growth) as well as decreases in profitability. As a result, managers who are evaluated on this measure will be less likely to enter into short-term, high-return projects if they detract from overall long-term growth in capital assets. In essence, managers are penalized to some extent if they attempt to sacrifice either profitability or growth at the expense of the other.

EVA is also calculated using the refined earnings approach in the following manner:

$$\text{EVA} = \text{NOPAT} - (\text{WACC} \times \text{Capital}) \tag{13-21}$$

where NOPAT is the firm's net operating profit after taxes. This approach results in a comparison of the dollar cost of capital (i.e., WACC × Capital) with the operating profits generated by the employed capital. Any negative EVA is a bad signal because it means that value is being destroyed, however, even if it is negative, the goal should be to improve upon the value in the previous period.

EXAMPLE: ESTIMATING EVA FOR SUMMA CORPORATION

Suppose that Summa's ROC is 14 per cent, its WACC is 12 per cent, its NOPAT is $21 million, and it employs $150 million worth of capital. Equations 13-20 and 13-21 both result in EVA of $3 million.

$\text{EVA} = (\text{ROC} - \text{WACC}) \times \text{Capital} = (0.14 - 0.12) \times (\$150\text{m}) = \$3 \text{ million}$

$\text{EVA} = \text{NOPAT} - (\text{WACC} \times \text{Capital}) = \$21\text{m} - (0.12 \times \$150\text{m}) = \$3 \text{ million}$

[19] The term economic value added (EVA) has been trademarked by Stern Stewart, a consulting firm that pioneered the use of this concept.

Some studies have shown that stock price is more responsive to changes in EVA than to changes in earnings, the traditional variable of importance.[20] Some mutual funds are now using EVA analysis as the primary tool for selecting stocks for the fund to hold. One recommendation for investors interested in this approach is to search for companies with a return on capital in excess of 20 per cent because this will, in all likelihood, exceed the cost of capital, and, therefore, the company is adding value.

Market Value Added

Unlike EVA, which evaluates internal performance, market value added (MVA) is a measure of external performance. It determines how the market has evaluated the firm's performance as reflected in the market prices of its outstanding debt and equity, relative to the capital invested in the company. MVA can be estimated for any period as follows:

$$\text{MVA} = \text{Market value of the firm} - \text{Capital} \quad \text{(13-22)}$$

Similar to EVA, it is the changes in this measure that are important. MVA relies on market perceptions and is more forward looking than EVA (which measures the performance in one period only).

EXAMPLE: ESTIMATING MVA FOR SUMMA CORPORATION

We can determine the MVA for Summa for the most recent period, if we are given a year-end market value for their total equity and debt of $172 million.

$$\text{MVA} = \text{Market value} - \text{Capital} = \$172\text{m} - \$150\text{m} = \$22 \text{ million}$$

which is a very positive result.

The use of EVA and MVA to evaluate management performance has attracted a great deal of support from the corporate world in recent years. Proponents suggest there is an important relationship between EVA and firm market values. On the other hand, detractors criticize EVA for its reliance on accounting measures and for its short-term focus. Empirical evidence regarding the relationship between EVA and MVA is fairly limited at this time, and the conclusions offered by prospective researchers are mixed. For example, O'Byrne documents a strong relationship between market values and EVA, while Kramer and Pushner find evidence to the contrary.[21] The relative merit of these approaches will be evaluated in the years to come, but it seems likely they will to continue to grow in importance.

---

[20] This discussion is based on Maggie Topkis, "A New Way to Find Bargains," *Fortune*, December 6, 1996, pp. 265–266.

[21] S. O'Byrne, "EVA and the Shareholder," *Financial Practice and Education* 7 (Spring/Summer 1997), pp. 50–54; J. Kramer and G. Pushner, "An Empirical Analysis of Economic Value Added as a Proxy for Market Value Added," *Financial Practice and Education* 7 (Spring/Summer 1997), pp. 41–49.

WHICH VALUATION METHOD TO USE?

We have described several valuation procedures here, including the two most often used — the dividend discount model and the P/E ratio (multiplier) model. Which of these should be used?

In theory, the dividend discount model is a correct, logical, and sound position. The best estimate of the current value of a company's common stock is probably the present value of the (estimated) dividends to be paid by that company to its shareholders. However, some analysts and investors feel that this model is unrealistic. After all, they argue, no one can forecast dividends into the distant future with very much accuracy. Technically, the model calls for an estimate of all dividends from now to infinity, which is an impossible task. Finally, many investors want capital gains and not dividends, and some of these investors feel that focusing solely on dividends is not desirable. The discussion in previous sections has dealt with these objections that have been raised about the dividend discount model.

Possibly because of the objections to the dividend discount model cited here, or simply because it is easier to use, the earnings multiplier or P/E model remains the most popular approach to valuation. It is a less sophisticated and more intuitive model. In fact, understanding the P/E model can help investors comprehend the dividend discount model. Because dividends are paid out of earnings, investors must estimate the growth in earnings before they can figure out the growth in dividends or dividends themselves.

Rather than view these approaches as competing alternatives, it is better to view them as complements. Each is useful, and together they provide analysts with a better chance of valuing common stocks. There are several reasons for viewing them as complementary:

1. The P/E model can be derived from the constant growth version of the dividend discount model. They are, in fact, alternative methods of looking at value. In the dividend discount model, the future stream of benefits is discounted. In the P/E model, an estimate of expected earnings is multiplied by a P/E ratio or multiplier.
2. Dividends are paid out of earnings. To use the dividend discount model, it is necessary to estimate the future growth of earnings. The dividends used in the dividend discount model are a function of the earnings of the firm, an estimate of which is used in the earnings multiplier model.
3. Finally, investors must always keep in mind that valuation is no less an art than a science, and estimates of the future earnings and dividends are subject to error. In some cases it may be desirable to use one or the other method, and in other cases both methods can be used as a check on each other. The more procedures investors have to value common stocks, the more likely they are to obtain reasonable results.

In addition, certain techniques will be more appropriate for certain companies and industries.[22] Regardless of which method is used, it is important to remember that valuation employing fundamental analysis, or any other approach, is always subject to error. This is because we are dealing with the uncertain future. No matter who does the analysis, or how it is done, mistakes will be made.

---

[22] For an excellent review of the techniques most commonly employed for valuing firms in different industries in Canada, refer to Joe Kan, Editor, *Handbook of Canadian Security Analysis: A Guide to Evaluating the Industry Sectors of the Market from Bay Street's Top Analysts* (Toronto: John Wiley & Sons Canada, 1997).

In Chapters 15, 16, and 17, we utilize the overall logic of the fundamental valuation approach — namely, that the intrinsic value of a common stock, or the aggregate market, is a function of its expected returns and accompanying risk, as proxied by the required rate of return. The dividend discount model and the P/E ratio model are both used to illustrate the fundamental valuation process.

SUMMARY

This summary relates to the learning objectives provided on page 393.

1. **Name two approaches to the valuation of common stocks used in fundamental security analysis.**
One commonly employed approach for analyzing and selecting common stocks is fundamental analysis, which should take into account efficient market considerations. Fundamental analysis seeks to estimate the intrinsic value of a stock, which is a function of its expected returns and risk. Two fundamental approaches to determining value are present value and the earnings multiplier (P/E ratio).
2. **Explain the present value approach.**
The present value approach for common stocks is similar to that used with bonds. A required (minimum) expected rate of return must be determined, based on the risk-free rate and a risk premium. As for expected returns, since dividends are the only cash flows directly paid by a corporation, they are the usual choice for expected future cash flows to be discounted in a present value model.
3. **Use the dividend discount model to estimate stock prices.**
According to the dividend discount model, the value of a stock today is the discounted value of all future dividends. This model implicitly accounts for the terminal price of a stock. To account for an infinite stream of dividends, stocks to be valued are classified by their expected growth rate in dividends. If no growth is expected, the dividend discount model reduces perpetuity to a valuation problem. If two or more growth rates are expected, a multiple growth model must be used in which the future stream of dividends is identified before being discounted. The constant-growth version of the dividend discount model is used most frequently. It reduces to the ratio of the dividend expected next period to the difference between the required rate of return and the expected growth rate in dividends. The dividend discount model is sensitive to the estimates of the variables used in it; therefore, investors will calculate different prices for the same stock while using an identical model.
4. **Explain the P/E ratio approach.**
The P/E ratio or multiplier approach is based on the identity that a stock's current price is the product of its actual earnings per share and the P/E ratio. It follows that the P/E ratio can be calculated by dividing the current price by the actual earnings per share. To implement the P/E ratio to estimate the value of a stock, we must estimate the earnings and the P/E ratio for the next period. The P/E ratio itself may be expressed as a function of the dividend payout ratio, the required rate of return, and the expected growth rate of dividends (under uncertain conditions). P/E ratios are also inversely related to interest rates because interest rates are directly related to required rates of return.

5. **Outline other relative valuation approaches.**
   Other relative valuation approaches include the use of market-to-book ratios, price-to-sales ratios, price-to-cash flow ratios, and price-to-EBIT ratios.

KEY TERMS

Dividend discount model (DDM)
Economic Value Added (EVA)
Market-to-book ratio (M/B) or Price-to-book value
P/E ratio (Earnings multiplier)
Perpetuity
Price/sales ratio

ADDITIONAL RESOURCES

An excellent review of common stock valuation approaches can be found in: Damodaran, Aswath. *Damodaran on Valuation: Security Analysis for Investment and Corporate Finance*. New York: John Wiley & Sons, 1994.

For an excellent discussion of valuation approaches employed for analyzing firms in different industries in Canada, refer to: Kan, Joe. Editor. *Handbook of Canadian Security Analysis: A Guide to Evaluating the Industry Sectors of the Market from Bay Street's Top Analysts*. Toronto: John Wiley & Sons Canada, 1997.

A book that is popular among practitioners and examines 40 years of stock market data using various selection criteria: O'Shaughnessy, James. *What Works on Wall Street: A Guide to the Best-Performing Investment Strategies of All Time*. New York: McGraw-Hill, 1997.

REVIEW QUESTIONS

1. What is meant by intrinsic value? How is it determined?
2. Why can earnings not be used as readily as dividends in the present value approach?
3. What problems are encountered in using the dividend discount model?
4. Describe the three possibilities for dividend growth.
5. Since dividends are paid to infinity, how is this problem handled in the present value analysis?
6. Once an investor calculates intrinsic value for a particular stock, how does he or she decide whether or not to buy it?
7. Why is the required rate of return for a stock the discount rate to be used in valuation analysis?
8. What is the dividend discount model? Write this model in equation form.
9. Demonstrate how the dividend discount model is the same as a method that includes a specified number of dividends and a terminal price.

10. How valuable are the P/E ratios shown daily in *The Globe and Mail* and the *National Post*?
11. What factors affect the P/E ratio? How sensitive is it to these factors?
12. Assume that two investors are valuing a company and have both decided to use the constant-growth version of the dividend valuation model. Both use $3 a share as the expected dividend for the coming year. Are these two investors likely to derive different prices? Why or why not?
13. Some investors prefer the P/E ratio model to the present value analysis on the grounds that the latter is more difficult to use. State these alleged difficulties and respond to them.
14. Indicate the likely direction of change in a stock's P/E ratio, and the reason(s) why, if
    a. The dividend payout decreases.
    b. The required rate of return rises.
    c. The expected growth rate of dividends rises.
    d. The riskless rate of return decreases.
15. Indicate the likely direction of change in a stock's M/B ratio, and the reason(s) why, if
    a. The dividend payout decreases.
    b. The required rate of return rises.
    c. The expected growth rate of dividends rises.
    d. The riskless rate of return decreases.
    e. The firm's ROE increases.
16. Indicate the likely direction of change in a stock's P/S ratio, and the reason(s) why, if
    a. The dividend payout decreases.
    b. The required rate of return rises.
    c. The expected growth rate of dividends rises.
    d. The riskless rate of return decreases.
    e. The firm's net income margin decreases.

PREPARING FOR YOUR PROFESSIONAL EXAMS

Special Note to CSC Students

Ensure that you have read and understood the following topics:*

The present value approach, pp. 394–413
Relative valuation approaches, pp. 413–422
CSC Notes: Equity Cycles and the DDM, p. 414
Which valuation method to use?, pp. 425–426
Appendix 13-A: The analysis and valuation of preferred stock, pp. 436–437

**Reading these CSC-related topics should provide you with additional understanding of CSC material. However, it should not be seen as a substitute for reading the CSC textbook itself, which is the basis for the CSC exam.*

CSC REGISTRATION QUESTIONS

The Canadian Securities Institute issued the following sample questions in the 1997 CSC registration package as a means for students to self-assess their understanding of CSC-related material.

1. In a prolonged bull market, most price-earnings ratios are _______ those during bear markets.
   a. higher than
   b. lower than
   c. the same as
2. The dividend ____________ model is used to evaluate common shares.

PAST CFA EXAM PROBLEMS

The following question was given on the 1991 CFA Level I Examination.

1. As a firm operating in a mature industry, Arbot Industries is expected to maintain a constant dividend payout ratio and constant growth rate of earnings for the foreseeable future. Earnings were $4.50 per share in the recently completed fiscal year. The dividend payout ratio has been a constant 55 per cent in recent years and is expected to remain so. Arbot's return on equity (ROE) is expected to remain at 10 per cent in the future, and you require an 11 per cent return on the stock.
   a. Using the constant-growth dividend discount model, calculate the current value of Arbot common stock. Show your calculations.

   After an aggressive acquisition and marketing program, it now appears that Arbot's earnings per share and ROE will grow rapidly over the next two years. You are aware that the dividend discount model can be useful in estimating the value of common stock even when the assumption of constant growth does not apply.

   b. Calculate the current value of Arbot's common stock using the dividend discount model, assuming Arbot's dividend will grow at a 15 per cent rate for the next two years, return in the third year to the historical growth rate, and continue to grow at the historical rate for the foreseeable future. Show your calculations.

The following question was given on the 1990 CFA Level I Examination.

2. The constant-growth dividend discount model can be used both for the valuation of companies and for the estimation of the long-term total return of a stock.

   Assume: $20 = the price of a stock today
   8% = the expected growth rate of dividends
   $0.60 = the annual dividend one year forward

   a. Using only the above data, compute the expected long-term total return on the stock using the constant-growth dividend discount model. Show calculations.
   b. Briefly discuss three disadvantages of the constant-growth dividend discount model in its application to investment analysis.
   c. Identify three alternative methods to the dividend discount model for the valuation of companies.

DEMONSTRATION PROBLEMS

1. Puglisi Pharmaceuticals is currently paying a dividend of $2 per share, which is not expected to change. Investors require a rate of return of 20 per cent to invest in a stock with the riskiness of Puglisi. Calculate the intrinsic value of the stock.

Solution:

The first step to solving a common stock valuation problem is to identify the type of growth involved in the dividend stream. The second step is to determine whether the dividend given in the problem is D_0 or D_1.

In this problem it is clear that the growth rate is zero and that we must solve a zero-growth valuation problem (Equation 13-3). The second step is not relevant here because all of the dividends are the same.

$$\hat{P}_0 = \frac{D_0}{k_{CS}} = \frac{2.00}{0.20} = \$10.00$$

2. Richter Construction Company is currently paying a dividend of $2 per share, which is expected to grow at a constant rate of 7 per cent per year. Investors require a rate of return of 16 per cent to invest in stocks with this degree of riskiness. Calculate the implied price of Richter.

Solution:

Since dividends are expected to grow at a constant rate, we use the constant-growth version of the dividend discount model (Equation 13-5). Note carefully that this equation calls for D_1 in the numerator and that the dividend given in this problem is the current dividend being paid, D_0. Therefore, we must compound this dividend up one period to obtain D_1 before solving the problem.

$$D_1 = D_0 (1 + g) = \$2.00 (1.07) = \$2.14$$

and

$$\hat{P}_0 = \frac{D_1}{k_{CS} - g} = \frac{2.14}{0.16 - 0.07} = \$23.78$$

3. Baddour Legal Services is currently selling for $60 per share and is expected to pay a dividend of $3. The expected growth rate in dividends is 8 per cent for the foreseeable future. Calculate the required rate of return for this stock.

Solution:

To solve this problem, note first that this is a constant-growth model problem. Second, note that the dividend given in the problem is D_1 because it is stated as the dividend to be paid in the next period. To solve this problem for k, the required rate of return, we simply rearrange Equation 13-5:

$$k_{CS} = \frac{D_1}{P_0} + g = \frac{3.00}{60} + 0.08 = 0.13$$

4. Wrenn Restaurants has been undergoing rapid growth for the last few years. The current dividend of $2 per share is expected to continue to grow at the rapid rate of 20 per cent a year for the next three years. After that time Wrenn is expected to slow down, with the dividend growing at a more normal rate of 7 per cent a year for the indefinite future. Because of the risk involved in such rapid growth, the required rate of return on this stock is 22 per cent. Calculate the implied price for this stock.

Solution:

We can recognize at once that this is a multiple-growth case of valuation because more than one growth rate is given. To solve for the value of this stock, it is necessary to identify the entire stream of future dividends from Year 1 to infinity, and discount the entire stream back to time period zero. After the third year a constant growth model can be used which accounts for all dividends from the beginning of Year 4 to infinity.

First, estimate dividends up to the start of constant growth to infinity by compounding the beginning dividend, $2, at 20 per cent for each of three years, which produces the following:

$$D_1 = \$2.00\,(1 + 0.20) = \$2.40$$
$$D_2 = \$2.00\,(1 + 0.20)^2 = \$2.88$$
$$D_3 = \$2.00\,(1 + 0.20)^3 = \$3.456$$

Second, estimate the price at the beginning of constant growth to infinity period

$$\hat{P}_3 = \frac{D_5}{k_{CS} - g} = \frac{(3.456)(1.07)}{0.22 - 0.07} = \$24.653$$

Third, discount back the relevant cash flows to time 0 and sum

$$\hat{P}_0 = \frac{2.40}{(1.22)^1} + \frac{2.88}{(1.22)^2} + \frac{3.456}{(1.22)^3} + \frac{24.653}{(1.22)^3}$$

$$= 1.967 + 1.935 + 1.903 + 13.577 = \$19.38$$

5. Company BDC has an expected dividend payout ratio of 0.43 next year, and their dividends are expected to grow at an annual rate of 8 per cent to infinity. The required rate of return on their shares is 11.81 per cent, and the expected EPS is $3.45.
   a. Using the information above, determine an appropriate P/E multiple based on company fundamentals, and estimate an appropriate share price for BDC.
   b. Re-estimate the value of BDC's shares based on their five-year average P/E ratio of 8.62.
   c. Repeat using the average industry P/E ratio of 8.83.

Solution:

$$P/E = \frac{D_1/E_1}{k_{CS} - g} = \frac{0.43}{0.1181 - 0.08} = 11.29$$

a. Based on this multiple, BDC's shares are worth

$$\hat{P}_0 = (P/E) \times (EPS_1) = (11.29)(\$3.45) = \$38.95$$

b. Based on BDC's historical P/E multiple of 8.62, BDC's shares are worth

$$\hat{P}_0 = (P/E) \times (EPS_1) = (8.62)(\$3.45) = \$29.74$$

c. Based on the industry average P/E multiple, BDC's shares are worth

$$\hat{P}_0 = (P/E) \times (EPS_1) = (8.83)(\$3.45) = \$30.46$$

PROBLEMS

1. Billingsley Products is currently selling for $45 a share with an expected dividend in the coming year of $2 per share. If the growth rate in dividends expected by investors is 9 per cent to infinity, what is the implied required rate of return for this stock?

2. Assume that Chance Industries is expected by investors to have a dividend growth rate over the foreseeable future of 8 per cent a year and that the required rate of return for this stock is 13 per cent. The current dividend being paid (D_0) is $2.25. What is the price of the stock?

3. Mittra Motors is currently selling for $50 per share and pays $3 in dividends ($D_0$). Investors require 15 per cent return on this stock. What is the expected perpetual growth rate of dividends?

4. Howe Poultry pays $1.50 a year in dividends, which is expected to remain unchanged. Investors require a 15 per cent rate of return on this stock. What is its price?

5. Refer to Appendix 13-A for this question.)

   a. Given a preferred stock with an annual dividend of $3 per share and a price of $40, what is the required rate of return?

   b. Assume now that interest rates rise, leading investors to demand a required rate of return of 9 per cent. What will be the new price of this preferred stock?

6. The required rate of return for Peterson Industries is 15.75 per cent. The stock pays a current dividend of $1.30, and the expected annual growth rate is 11 per cent to infinity. Calculate the intrinsic value.

7. In Problem 6, assume that the expected annual growth rate is 16 per cent to infinity. Calculate the intrinsic value for this stock.

8. Brockbank Computer Suppliers is currently paying a dividend of $1.60 per year, and this dividend is expected to grow at a constant rate of 8 per cent a year forever. Investors require a 16 per cent rate of return on Brockbank. What is its estimated price?

9. Wilson Industries is currently paying a dividend of $1 per share, which is not expected to change in the future. The current price of this stock is $12. What is the implied required rate of return on this stock?

10. Cascade Gas is currently selling for $40. Its current dividend is $2, and this dividend is expected to grow at a rate of 7 per cent a year forever. What is the expected rate of return for this stock?

11. General Foods is currently selling for $50. It is expected to pay a dividend of $2 next period. If the required rate of return is 10 per cent, what is the expected perpetual growth rate?

12. An investor purchases the common stock of a well-known house builder, DeMong Construction Company, for $25 per share. The expected dividend for the next year is $3 per share, and the investor is confident that the stock can be sold one year from now for $30. What is the implied required rate of return?

13. a. The current risk-free rate (RF) is 10 per cent, and the expected return on the market for the coming year is 15 per cent. Calculate the required rate of return for

    i. stock A, with a beta of 1.0

    ii. stock B, with a beta of 1.7

    iii. stock C, with a beta of 0.8.

    b. How would your answers change if RF in part (a) were to increase to 12 per cent, with the other variables unchanged?

    c. How would your answers change if the expected return on the market changed to 17 per cent with the other variables unchanged?

14. Wingler Company is currently selling for $36, paying $1.80 in dividends, and investors expect dividends to grow at a constant rate of 8 per cent a year forever. CEO Tony Wingler believes the stock is undervalued.

    a. If an investor requires a rate of return of 14 per cent for a stock with the riskiness of Wingler Company, is it a good buy for this investor?

    b. What is the maximum an investor with a 14 per cent required return should pay for Wingler Company? What is the maximum if the required return is 15 per cent?

15. The Hall Dental Supply Company sells at $32 per share, and CEO Randy Hall estimates the latest 12-month earnings are $4 per share with a dividend payout of 50 per cent.

    a. What is Hall's current P/E ratio?

    b. If an investor expects earnings to grow by 10 per cent a year forever, what is the projected price for next year if the P/E ratio remains unchanged?

    c. Ray Parker, president of Hall Dental Supply, analyzes the data and estimates that the payout ratio will remain the same. Assume the expected growth rate of dividends is 10 per cent per year forever, and an investor has a required rate of return of 16 per cent. Would this stock be a good buy? Why or why not?

    d. If interest rates are expected to decline, what is the likely effect on Hall's P/E ratio?

16. McEnally Motorcycles is a rapidly growing firm. Dividends are expected to grow at the rate of 18 per cent annually for the next 10 years. The growth rate after the first 10 years is expected to be 7 per cent annually to infinity. The current dividend is $1.82. Investors require a rate of return of 19 per cent on this stock. Calculate the intrinsic value of this stock.

17. BSC Ltd. is expected to earn $2 per share next year. BSC has a payout ratio of 40 per cent. Earnings and dividends have been growing at a constant rate of 10 per cent per year, but analysts are estimating that the growth rate will be 7 per cent a year for the indefinite future. Investors require a 15 per cent rate of return on BSC. What is its estimated price?

18. General Foundries is expected to pay a dividend of $0.60 next year, $1.10 the following year, and $1.25 each year thereafter. The required rate of return on this stock is 18 per cent. How much should investors be willing to pay for this stock?

19. Griggs Company is not expected to pay a dividend until five years have elapsed. At the beginning of Year 6, investors expect the dividend to be $3 per share and to remain at that amount forever. If an investor has a 25 per cent required rate of return for this stock, what should he or she be willing to pay for Griggs?

20. Poindexter Industries is expected to pay a dividend of $10 per year for 10 years and then increase the dividend to $15 per share for every year thereafter. The required rate of return on this stock is 20 per cent. What is the estimated stock price for Poindexter?

21. Roenfeldt Components recently paid a dividend of $1 per share. This dividend is expected to grow at a rate of 25 per cent a year for the next five years, after which it is expected to grow at a rate of 7 per cent a year forever. The required rate of return for this stock is 18 per cent. What is the estimated price of the stock?

22. Agrawa Corporation makes advanced computer components. It pays no dividends currently, but it expects to begin paying $1 per share four years from now. The expected dividends in subsequent years are also $1 per share. The required rate of return is 14 per cent. What is the estimated price for Agrawa?

23. Rader Chocolate Company is currently selling for $60 and is paying a $3 dividend.

    a. If investors expect dividends to double in 12 years, what is the required rate of return for this stock?

    b. If investors had expected dividends to approximately triple in six years, what would be the required rate of return?

24. Avera Free Range Poultry is currently paying a dividend of $1.20. This dividend is expected to grow at the rate of 30 per cent a year for the next five years, followed by a growth rate of 20 per cent a year for the following five years. After 10 years the dividend is expected to grow at the rate of 6 per cent a year forever. CEO Bill Avera estimates that the required rate of return for this stock is 21 per cent. What is its intrinsic value?

25. In Problem 24, assume that the growth rate for the first five years is 25 per cent rather than 30 per cent. How would you expect the value calculated in Problem 24 to change? Confirm your answer by calculating the new intrinsic value.

26. Rocky Mountain Power and Gas is currently paying a dividend of $1.80. This dividend is expected to grow at a rate of 6 per cent in the foreseeable future. Rocky Mountain Power is 10 per cent less risky than the market as a whole. The market risk premium is 7 per cent, and the risk-free rate is 5 per cent. What is the estimated price of this stock?

27. Rendleman Software is expected to enjoy a very rapid growth rate in dividends of 30 per cent a year for the next three years. This growth rate is then expected to slow to 20 per cent a year for the next five years. After that time, the growth rate is expected to level out at 6 per cent a year forever. D_0 is $2. The required rate of return is 20 per cent. What is the estimated price of the stock?

28. SLC Ltd. has an expected Year 1 EPS of $3.45, an expected Year 1 payout ratio of 0.456, and an expected annual growth rate in dividends to infinity of 8 per cent. Shareholders require a 9.68 per cent return on these shares. SLC's five-year average P/E ratio is 26.68, and the present industry average P/E ratio is 27.93. Determine three estimates of SLC's value.

29. Using the information for SLC Ltd. provided in Problem 28, and assuming the companies most recent ROE was 17.92 per cent, and that their current book value per share (BV_0) is $17.86, determine the value of SLC based on the M/B ratio approach.

30. Using the information for SLC Ltd. provided in Problem 28, and assuming the companies most recent net income margin (NI%) was 3.31 per cent, and that their most recent sales per share ($Sales_0$) is $85.71, determine the value of SLC based on the P/S ratio approach.

31. Bilco Limited has a policy of paying out 60 per cent of its earnings as cash dividends to its shareholders. Bilco recently paid out a $3 per share annual dividend. The required rate of return on stocks with similar risk is 13 per cent. Bilco's earnings and dividends are expected to grow at an annual rate of 8 per cent forever.

    a. What is Bilco's implied P/E ratio?

    b. If Bilco changed its policy to one where it paid out 80% of their earnings as dividends, what would Bilco's implied P/E ratio be?

32. Ladslow Incorporated has a required rate of return of 14 per cent, and expects that its earnings and dividends will grow at an annual rate of 6 per cent forever. Its dividend payout ratio is 40 per cent. Ladslow's most recent return-on-equity (ROE) was 20 per cent.

    a. What is the implied market-to-book (M/B) ratio?

    b. If the company has assets of $1,000,000 (book value), has 100,000 shares outstanding, and has no debt, what should the price per share be?

33. Using the Price/Sales (P/S) ratio approach, what should a company's stock price be based on the following information: required rate of return of 16 per cent; perpetual annual growth rate of earnings and dividends of 6 per cent; assets of $100,000,000 (book value); no debt; 20,000,000 shares outstanding; most recent annual sales of $50,000,000; most recent net income of $5,000,000; 50 per cent dividend payout ratio.

APPENDIX 13-A

THE ANALYSIS AND VALUATION OF PREFERRED STOCK

In Chapter 2, preferred stock was classified for investment analysis purposes as a fixed-income security, although technically it is an equity security. It is best described as a hybrid security, having some characteristics similar to fixed-income securities (i.e., bonds) and some similar to common stocks.

Analysis

Preferred stock can be described as a perpetuity, or perpetual security, since it has no maturity date, and it will pay the indicated dividend forever. Although perpetual, many preferred stock issues carry a sinking fund, which provides for early retirement of the issue, usually over a period of many years. Furthermore, many preferred stocks are callable by the issuer, which also potentially limits the life of preferreds. Finally, roughly half of all preferred stocks issued in recent years are convertible into common stock. Therefore, although preferred stock is perpetual by definition, in reality many of the issues will not remain in existence forever.

Dividends from preferred stock, unlike those from common stock, are fixed when the stock is issued and do not change. These dividends are specified as an annual dollar amount (although paid quarterly) or as a percentage of par value, which is often either $25 or $100. The issuer can forgo paying the preferred dividend if earnings are insufficient. Although this dividend is specified, failure to pay it does not result in default of the obligation, as is the case with bonds. However, most preferred issues have a cumulative feature, which requires that all unpaid preferred dividends, both current and arrears, must be paid before those for common stocks.

Investors regard preferred stock as less risky than common stock because the dividend is specified and must be paid before a common stock dividend can be paid. They regard preferreds as more risky than bonds, however, because bondholders have priority in being paid and in case of liquidation. That is why investors require higher rates of return on preferred stock than on bonds but a smaller required return than on common stocks. However, since most dividends received by individuals qualify for the dividend tax credit, they are taxed at a lower rate than interest income. As a result of this tax advantage, preferred stocks often carry slightly lower yields than bonds of comparable quality.

Valuation

The value of any perpetuity can be calculated as follows:

$$V_p = \frac{C}{(1 + k_p)^1} + \frac{C}{(1 + k_p)^2} + \dots + \frac{C}{(1 + k_p)^\infty} \tag{13-23}$$

$$= \frac{C}{k_p}$$

where
V_p = the value of a perpetuity today
C = the constant annual payment to be received
k_p = the required rate of return appropriate for this perpetuity

Because the dividends provided by a straight preferred share represent a perpetuity, Equation 13-23 is applicable in its valuation. We simply substitute the preferred dividend (D) for C and the appropriate required return (k_{ps}) for k_p, resulting in Equation 13-24.[23]

$$V_{ps} = \frac{D}{k_{ps}} \tag{13-24}$$

A preferred stock, or any perpetuity, is easy to value because the numerator of Equation 13-24 is known and fixed forever. No complex present value calculations are needed for a perpetuity, which simplifies the valuation process considerably. If any two of the values in 13-24 are known, the third can easily be found.

As an example of the valuation analysis, consider preferred shares with a fixed annual dividend of \$1.93. To value this preferred, investors need to estimate the required rate of return appropriate for its degree of riskiness. Suppose the required rate of return (k_{ps}), is 10 per cent. The value of this preferred would be

$$V_{ps} = \frac{D}{k_{ps}} = \frac{1.93}{0.10} = \$19.30$$

On the other hand, a required rate of return of 11 per cent would result in a value of \$17.54.

If the current price for this preferred, as observed in the marketplace (P_{ps}), is substituted into Equation 13-24 for V_{ps}, the yield can be solved by using Equation 13-25.

$$k_{ps} = \frac{D}{P_{ps}} \tag{13-25}$$

In the case of the company above, if we observed a price of \$27, this implies the yield, or required rate of return, is 7.15 per cent.

$$k_{ps} = \frac{D}{P_{ps}} = \frac{1.93}{27.00} = 0.0715$$

Notice from Equation 13-24 that as the required rate of return rises, the price of the preferred stock declines; obviously, the converse is also true. Because the numerator is fixed, the value (price) of a preferred stock changes as the required rate of return changes. Clearly, investors' required rates of return fluctuate across time as interest rates and other factors change. As rates fluctuate, so do preferred stock prices. In fact, because they are fixed income securities with no maturity date, we observe that their prices will be extremely sensitive to changes in the level of interest rates, similar to long-term bonds.

[23] Notice that this equation is identical to the no-growth version of the DDM expressed in Equation 13-3, with $D = D_0$ and $k_{ps} = k_{CS}$. This is because the dividend paid on a preferred share is a constant, or given amount.

CHAPTER 14

COMMON STOCKS: ANALYSIS AND STRATEGY

LEARNING OBJECTIVES

After reading this chapter, you will be able to

1. Discuss the impact of the overall market on common stock investors.
2. Explain the importance of the required rate of return.
3. Distinguish between passive and active investment strategies.
4. Differentiate between technical and fundamental analysis.
5. Describe the bottom-up and top-down approaches in fundamental analysis.

CHAPTER PREVIEW

This chapter covers the analysis and strategy for selecting and holding common stocks. Similar to the passive approach to bond investing, common stock investors can follow a buy-and-hold strategy or buy index funds that mimic some market index. Under the active approach, we analyze the primary alternatives of stock selection, sector rotation, and market timing and consider the implications of the Efficient Market Hypothesis (which was discussed in Chapter 10). We conclude by considering the two basic methods used in security analysis: technical and fundamental analysis.

SOME IMPORTANT ISSUES INVOLVING COMMON STOCKS

In Chapter 11 we analyzed bonds in terms of interest rates because of the fundamental relationship between interest rates and bond prices. In similar fashion, we now consider the impact of market risk on common stock investors. The impact of the market on every investor in common stocks is pervasive and dominant and must be fully appreciated by investors if they are to be successful.

We also consider the required rate of return in detail. This variable is important in any analysis of common stocks. As we saw in Chapter 13, the required rate of return is a very important component of the valuation process using the dividend discount model, as well as in other valuation approaches.

The Impact of the Overall Market on Individual Stocks

Overall, market risk is the single most important risk affecting the price movements of common stocks. The aggregate market remains the largest single factor explaining fluctuations in both individual stock prices and portfolios of stocks. This is particularly true for a diversified portfolio of stocks, and as we know, the basic tenet of portfolio theory is to diversify into a number of properly chosen securities. For adequately diversified portfolios, market effects often account for 90 per cent and more of the variability in the portfolio's return. In other words, for a well-diversified portfolio, the market is the dominant factor affecting the variability of its return. Although any given portfolio may clearly outperform the market, it will usually be significantly influenced by what happens on an overall basis.

EXAMPLE: MARKET RISK AND AIC ADVANTAGE EQUITY FUND

Consider the performance of **AIC Advantage Equity Fund** over a recent five-year period, as shown in Figure 14-1. This fund, part of the well-known AIC family of funds, invests primarily in Canadian common shares. Notice that although this fund outperformed the aggregate market (as measured by the TSE 300 Total Return Index) by over 18 per cent on an annual basis, its movements roughly paralleled those of the market.

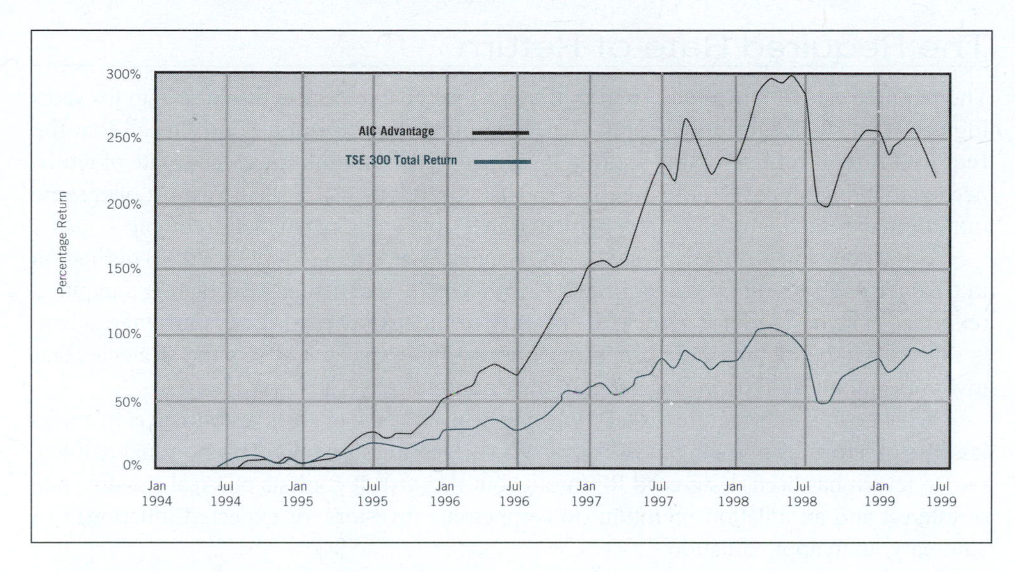

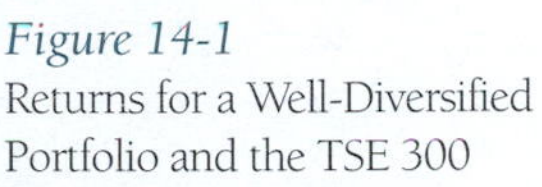

Figure 14-1
Returns for a Well-Diversified Portfolio and the TSE 300

Source: Globefund Web site: <http://www.globefund.com>. Reprinted with permission from The Globe and Mail.

The International Perspective

Canadian investors buying foreign stocks face the same issues as they do at home when it comes to market risk. Some of these markets have performed very well, and some have performed poorly over specified periods of time. The investor fortunate enough to have invested in the Mexican stock market in 1997 experienced an average gain of 55 per cent, whereas in the Thailand market he or she would have lost about 55 per cent during the same period.

Perhaps the best foreign example of the impact of the overall market on investors is Japan, clearly an economic superpower in recent years. In the 1980s Japan seemed invincible in its economic performance, and its stock market, as measured by the Nikkei stock index, reflected Japan's success with seemingly unending rises in stock prices. By the 1990s, however, this situation had changed dramatically, with assets in Japan down sharply from the previous record levels.

EXAMPLE: IMPACT OF FOREIGN MARKETS — THE NIKKEI

The Nikkei stock index described in Chapter 4 peaked at the end of 1989 at a level of almost 39,000. By mid-1992, the index had declined below the 15,000 level, representing a staggering decline of some 60 per cent. As one well-known magazine put it, this was the "biggest erasure of wealth in history." As of mid-1997, the Japanese stock market, suffering a six-year slump, was 50 per cent below its peak. Such is the impact of the overall market on investor wealth.

The Required Rate of Return

Required Rate of Return
The minimum expected rate of return necessary to induce an investor to purchase a security.

The required rate of return was used in the previous chapter as the discount rate for valuing common stocks and in Chapter 11 to determine the price of a bond. Recall that the **required rate of return** for any security is defined as the minimum expected rate of return needed to induce an investor to purchase it. That is, given its risk, a security must offer some minimum expected return before a particular investor can be persuaded to buy it.

This discussion is directly related to the Capital Asset Pricing Model (CAPM) discussion in Chapter 9. The CAPM provides investors with a method of actually calculating a required (expected) rate of return for a stock, an industry, or the market as a whole. Our interest here is to think of the required rate of return on an overall basis as it affects the strategies that investors employ and the management of their portfolios.

What do investors require (expect) when they invest? First of all, investors can earn a riskless rate of return by investing in riskless assets such as Treasury bills. This nominal risk-free rate of return has been designated RF throughout this text. It consists of a real risk-free rate of interest and an inflation premium (to compensate investors for expected inflation).[1] In summary, as an approximation:[2]

$$\text{Risk-free rate of return} = \text{Real rate of return} + \text{Inflation premium} \quad (14\text{-}1)$$

Risk Premium
That part of a security's return above the risk-free rate of return. The greater the risk of the asset, the greater the associated risk premium.

In addition to the risk-free rate of return available from riskless assets, rational risk-averse investors purchasing a risky asset expect to be compensated for this additional risk. Therefore, a risky asset must offer a **risk premium** above and beyond the riskless rate of return, and the greater the risk of the asset, the greater the promised risk premium must be.

The risk premium must reflect the uncertainty involved in investing in the asset. Thinking of risk in terms of its traditional sources, such components as the business risk and the financial risk of a corporation would certainly contribute to the risk premium demanded by investors for purchasing the common stock of the corporation. After all, the risk to the investor is that the expected income (return) will not be realized because of unforeseen events.

The particular line of business in which a company operates will significantly affect the risk to the investor. One has only to look at the performance of companies in commodity-based industries to see the importance of business risk. As one would expect, the performance of stocks in these industries is very sensitive to world commodity prices, since these prices have a pervasive influence on their profits. For example, during 1997 and 1998 world commodity prices were generally declining, which had a negative impact on the share prices of companies in related industries. After experiencing average gains of around 10 per cent in 1996, the TSE indexes for metals and minerals and for gold and precious metals declined 27.6 per cent and 43.6 per cent respectively in 1997, followed by declines of 19.3 per cent and 7.2 per cent in 1998. Similarly, the TSE Oil and Gas Index returned a mere 2.8 per cent in 1997, followed by a 30.4 per cent decline in 1998.

In addition to business risk, the financial decisions that a firm makes (or fails to make) will also affect the riskiness of the stock.

---

[1] The real risk-free rate of interest (i.e., the real time value of money) is the basic exchange rate in the economy or the price necessary to induce someone to forego consumption and save in order to consume more in the next period. It is defined within a context of no uncertainty and no inflation.

[2] The more precise calculation involves adding 1.0 to both the real rate and the inflation premium, multiplying the two together, and subtracting the 1.0 from the product. For example, assuming a real rate of 2 per cent and an inflation rate of 5 per cent:

$$(1 + \text{RF}) = (1 + \text{Real rate})(1 + \text{Inflation premium}) = (1 + 0.02)(1 + 0.05) = (1.071).$$

This implies RF = 0.071, or 7.1%.

Understanding the Required Rate of Return

The required rate of return for any investment opportunity can be expressed as Equation 14-2. One commonly used version of this equation is the CAPM, and another variation is the Fama and French three-factor model, both discussed in Chapter 9.

$$\text{Required rate of return} = \text{Risk-free rate} + \text{Risk premium} \tag{14-2}$$

It is important to note that there are many financial assets and therefore many different required rates of return. The average required rate of return on bonds is different from that on preferred stocks, and both are different from what is generally required from common stocks, warrants, or puts and calls. Furthermore, within a particular asset category such as common stocks, there are many required rates of return. Common stocks cover a relatively wide range of risk, from conservative utility stocks to small, risky high-technology stocks.

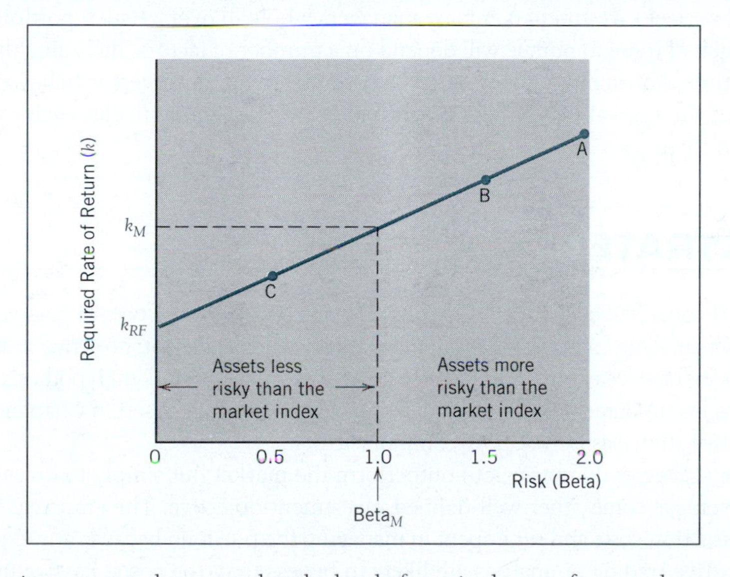

Figure 14-2
Required Rate of Return Versus Risk for Common Stocks

It is also important to be aware that the level of required rates of return changes over time. For example, required rates of return change with inflationary expectations, because the inflation premium is a component of the risk-free rate of return, which, in turn, is a component of the required rate of return. The level also changes as the risk premiums change. Investor pessimism will increase the risk premium and the required rate; investor optimism lowers both.

Risk and Required Rate of Return

We know from Chapter 9 that the CAPM suggests the trade-off between the required rate of return and risk is linear and upward sloping, as shown in Figure 14-2. In other words, the required rate of return increases as the risk, measured by beta, increases. Taken as a whole the stock market has a beta of 1.0, indicated by Point M in the diagram. The required rate of return for all stocks is therefore k_m. Stock C, with a beta lower than 1.0, has a required rate of return below k_m because its risk (beta) is less than that of the market. On the other hand, a stock with a beta greater than 1.0 has a required rate of return greater than that of the market. Stock A has a beta of 2.0 and Stock B a beta of 1.5.

BUILDING STOCK PORTFOLIOS

We now consider how investors go about selecting stocks to be held in portfolios. As noted in Chapter 8, individual investors often consider the investment decision as consisting of two steps:

1. Asset allocation
2. Security selection.

We will assume that the asset allocation decision has been made so that our focus is only on common stocks. The common stock portion could constitute 100 per cent of the total portfolio or some other percentage an investor chooses. For example, the **AIC Advantage Equity Fund** discussed in the example above, consisted of 89.5 per cent equity and 10.5 per cent cash and short-term securities as of June 30, 1998.

Recall that in our discussion of bond strategies we considered the passive and active approaches. These are also applicable to investors as they select and manage common stock portfolios or select investment company managers who will oversee such portfolios on their behalf. Which of these to pursue will depend on a number of factors, including the investor's expertise, time, and temperament, and, importantly, what an investor believes about the efficiency of the market, as discussed in Chapter 10. We will consider each of these two strategies in turn.

THE PASSIVE STRATEGY

A natural outcome of a belief in efficient markets is to employ some type of passive strategy in owning and managing common stocks. If the market is totally efficient, no active strategy should be able to beat the market on a risk-adjusted basis. The Efficient Market Hypothesis (EMH) has implications for fundamental analysis and technical analysis (discussed in Chapter 18), which are both active strategies for selecting common stocks.

Passive strategies do not seek to outperform the market but simply to do as well as the market or achieve some other well-defined investment objective. The emphasis is on minimizing transaction costs and time spent in managing the portfolio because any expected benefits from active trading or analysis are likely to be less than the costs. Passive investors act as if the market is efficient and accept the consensus estimates of return and risk, accepting current market price as the best estimate of a security's value.

Paralleling our discussion of passive approaches to bond management, an investor can simply follow a buy-and-hold strategy for whatever portfolio of stocks is owned. Alternatively, a very effective way to employ a passive strategy with common stocks is to invest in an indexed portfolio. We will consider each of these strategies in turn.

Buy-and-Hold Strategy

A buy-and-hold strategy means exactly that — an investor buys stocks and basically holds them until some future time in order to meet a particular objective. The emphasis is on avoiding transaction costs, additional search costs, and so forth. The investor believes that such a strategy will produce results that are as good as alternatives requiring more active management. These alternatives will invariably result in greater transaction costs and increase the likelihood of making errors in the stock selection process.

Notice that a buy-and-hold strategy is applicable to the investor's portfolio, whatever its composition. It may be large or small, and it may emphasize various types of stocks. Also note the critical importance of the initial selection decisions that must be made to implement the strategy. The investor must decide to buy stocks A, B, and C and not X, Y, and Z. Once the initial selections have been made, the investor will have to perform certain functions while the buy-and-hold strategy is in existence. For example, any income generated by the portfolio may be reinvested in the same or in other securities. Alternatively, a few stocks may do so well that they dominate the total market value of the portfolio and reduce its diversification. If the portfolio changes in such a way that it is no longer compatible with the investor's risk tolerance, adjustments may be required. The point is simply that even under such a strategy investors must still be ready to take certain actions.

Index Funds

As discussed in Chapter 10, an increasing number of mutual fund and pension fund assets can be described as passive equity investments. Using **index funds**, these asset pools are designed to duplicate as precisely as possible the performance of some market index, similar to bond index funds discussed in Chapter 12.

Index Funds
Mutual funds holding a bond or stock portfolio designed to mimic the performance of a particular market index.

A stock-index fund may consist of all the stocks in a well-known market average such as the TSE 300 Index. No attempt is made to forecast market movements and act accordingly or to select under- or overvalued securities. Expenses are kept to a minimum, including research costs (security analysis), portfolio managers' fees, and brokerage commissions. Index funds can be run efficiently by a small staff.

EXAMPLE: CIBC SECURITIES NO-LOAD INDEX PORTFOLIOS

The **CIBC Securities** group of funds offers a variety of no-load Index portfolios, each with a management expense ratio of 0.90 per cent. These funds allow investors to duplicate several domestic and international capital market indices, including the following:

1. The **Canadian Bond Index Fund** is managed to mirror the return performance of the Scotia Capital Markets Universe Bond Index (SCM Index).
2. The **Global Bond Index Fund** is managed to mirror the return performance of the J.P Morgan Global Government Bond Index (excluding Canada).
3. The **Canadian Index Fund** is managed to mirror the return performance of the TSE 300 Total Return Index. In order to accomplish this objective, the fund invests primarily in securities of companies comprising the TSE 300, as well as by investing a portion in index participation units such as Toronto 35 Index Participation Units (TIPs) or TSE 100 Index Participation Units (HIPs).

4. The **US Index RRSP Fund** is managed to mirror the return performance of the S&P 500 Total Return Stock Price Index. In order to accomplish this objective, the fund invests primarily in options, futures, and forward contracts based on the S&P 500 Index, futures and forward contracts based on the US exchange rate, as well as Government of Canada T-bills and other high-quality short-term money market instruments. The fund may also invest directly in securities of companies comprising the S&P 500 Index, Standard and Poor's Depository Receipts (SPDRs), and other similar instruments.

While it is relatively straightforward for professional money managers to construct index portfolios, this may pose a problem to the average individual investor who may lack the necessary financial resources and/or investment knowledge. Two readily available alternatives for Canadian investors are TSE 35 Index Participation Units (TIPs) and TSE 100 Index Participation Units (HIPs), both of which are discussed in the CSC Notes box in Chapter 8.

THE ACTIVE STRATEGY

> **INVESTING tip**
>
> Index funds have become increasingly popular in response to the large body of evidence concerning the efficiency of the market that has demonstrated the inability of mutual funds to consistently outperform the market on a risk-adjusted basis. If the market is efficient, many of the activities normally engaged in by funds are suspect; that is, the benefits are not likely to exceed the costs. The available evidence indicates that many investment companies have failed to match the performance of broad market indexes. For example, over the ten-year period ending July 30, 1998, the average return for all Canadian equity funds was 8.9 per cent, well below the TSE 300 annual performance of 10.5 per cent.

Most of the techniques discussed in this text involve an active approach to investing. In the area of common stocks the use of valuation models to value and select stocks indicates that investors are analyzing and valuing stocks in an attempt to improve their performance relative to some benchmark such as a market index. They assume or expect the benefits to be greater than the costs.

Pursuit of an active strategy suggests that investors believe they possess some advantage relative to other market participants. Such advantages could include superior analytical or judgement skills, superior information, or the ability or willingness to do what other investors, particularly institutions, are unable to do. For example, many large institutional investors cannot take positions in very small companies, leaving this field for individual investors. Furthermore, individuals are not required to own diversified portfolios and are not prohibited from short sales or margin trading as are some institutions.

Many investors still favour an active approach to common stock selection and management, despite the evidence from efficient market studies and the published performance results of institutional investors. The reason for this is obvious — the potential rewards are very large, and many investors feel confident that they can achieve such awards even if other investors cannot.

There are numerous active strategies involving common stocks. We consider the most prominent ones below. Because of its importance, we then consider the implications of market efficiency for these strategies.

Security Selection

The most traditional and popular form of active stock strategies is the selection of individual stocks identified as offering superior return-risk characteristics. Such stocks are selected using fundamental security analysis or technical analysis or some combination of the two. Many investors have always believed, and continue to believe despite evidence to the contrary from the EMH, that they possess the requisite skill, patience, and ability to identify undervalued stocks.

We know from Chapter 1 that a key feature of the investments environment is the uncertainty that always surrounds investing decisions. Most stock pickers recognize the pervasiveness of this uncertainty and protect themselves accordingly by diversifying. Therefore, the standard assumption of rational, intelligent investors who select stocks to buy and sell is that such selections will be part of a diversified portfolio.

The Importance of Stock Selection

Evidence suggests that 80 to 90 per cent of the total return on a portfolio is attributable to asset allocation decisions, among various financial asset classes. If this is the case, then how important is stock selection in the overall investment process? Most active investors, individuals or institutions, are, to various degrees, stock selectors. The majority of investment advice and investment advisory services is geared to the selection of stocks thought to be attractive candidates at the time. *The Value Line Investment Survey*, the world's largest investment advisory service in terms of number of subscribers, is a good example of stock selection advice offered to the investing public.

To gain some appreciation of the importance of stock selection, consider the wide variation observed in the returns across common stocks, referred to as cross-sectional variation in returns. Latané, Tuttle, and Jones were the first to point out the widely differing performances of stocks in a given year using the interquartile range.[3] Examining data through 1972, they found a remarkable constancy from year to year in the spread between the performance of stocks in the upper quartile and the performance of stocks in the lower quartile.[4]

A subsequent study by McEnally and Todd for the period 1946 to 1989 found that investors who successfully confined stock selection to the stocks in the highest quartile would have largely avoided losing years and even the bad years showed only modest losses.[5] Conversely, for the bottom quarter, results were negative about 55 per cent of the time, and about 25 per cent of the time even the best stocks would have lost money despite generally favourable market conditions. The implication of these results is that "For those who do attempt to pick stocks, the rewards can be very high, but the risk and negative consequences of poor selection are substantial."[6] An additional finding of this study is that cross-sectional variation of returns has been increasing steadily over the decades, making stock selection even more important in recent years.

---

[3] In an ordered set of numbers, the interquartile range is the difference between the value that cuts off the top quarter and the bottom quarter of these numbers. The interquartile range is an alternative measure of dispersion.

[4] H. Latané, D. Tuttle, and C. Jones, *Security Analysis and Portfolio Management*, Second Edition (New York: Ronald Press, 1975), pp. 192–193.

[5] R. McEnally and R. Todd, "Cross-Sectional Variation in Common Stock Returns," *Financial Analysts Journal* 48 (May/June 1992), pp. 59–63.

[6] McEnally and Todd, p. 61.

The importance of stock selection cannot be overemphasized. Although we outline an approach to security analysis below that logically places company analysis last, its importance is obvious. As Peter Lynch, one of the most celebrated portfolio managers of recent years as former head of **Fidelity's Magellan Fund**, states: "If it's a choice between investing in a good company in a great industry, or a great company in a lousy industry, I'll take the great company in the lousy industry any day." Lynch goes on to discuss what we can learn from the top 100 winners over the past decade. The basic lesson is that small stocks make big moves — the trick is identifying them. But as Lynch notes, "What do the great successes of the past 20 years tell us? It's the company, stupid."[7]

The Role of the Security Analyst

Two types of investors buy stocks: individuals and institutions. Institutional investors generally have their own analysts, and individual investors may choose to rely on the recommendations of professionals rather than attempt their own security analysis. An important part of the institutional side of stock selection and recommendation is the role of the security analyst (also called investment analyst or simply analyst) in the investment process.

The security analyst typically works for an institution concerned with stocks and other financial assets, but the analysts' product is often available to the individual investor in the form of brokerage reports and newsletters, reports from investment advisory services, and so forth. Therefore, when considering stock selection it is important to analyze the role of the analyst.

The central focus of the analysts' job is to attempt to forecast stock returns. This task usually involves a direct forecast of a specific company's return. Alternatively, it can involve the inputs to a valuation model such as those we considered in the previous chapter. Investors interested in stock selection use valuation models, and for inputs they can utilize their own estimates or use those provided by analysts.[8]

What sources of information do analysts use in evaluating common stocks for possible selection or selling?[9] The major sources are presentations from the top management of the companies being considered, annual reports, as well as annual information reports that must be filed by companies with the appropriate regulatory body (such as the Ontario Securities Commission [OSC] for companies listed on the TSE). According to surveys of analysts, they consistently emphasize the long term over the short term. Variables of major importance in their analysis include expected changes in earnings per share, expected return on equity (ROE), and industry outlook. The important point to note here is that the security analysis process used by financial analysts is the same one that we will examine in Part V.

One of the most important responsibilities of an analyst is to forecast earnings per share for particular companies because of the widely perceived linkage between expected earnings and stock returns. Earnings are critical in determining stock prices, and what matters is expected earnings (what is referred to on Bay Street or Wall Street as earnings estimates). Therefore,

---

[7] Peter Lynch, "The Stock Market Hit Parade," *Worth* (July/August 1994), p. 32.

[8] In Chapter 17 we will consider company analysis in detail, and this discussion will be organized around the two valuation models we studied in the previous chapter — the dividend discount model and the P/E ratio model.

[9] This discussion is based on T. D. Coggin, "The Analyst and the Investment Process: An Overview," reprinted in *The CFA Candidate Readings, Level I*, Institute of Chartered Financial Analysts, Charlottesville, VA, 1992. The Candidate Readings and other publications issued by the institute are a valuable source of information for any serious investor as well as investment professionals.

the primary emphasis in fundamental security analysis is on expected earnings, and analysts spend much of their time forecasting earnings. Security analyst earnings forecasts are publicly available through a variety of sources including securities firms' research reports, *The Value Line Investment Survey*, Institutional Brokers Estimate System (IBES) International, and Zack's Investment Research.

The information value of analyst reports depends upon a variety of factors and is generally enhanced by:

- The amount of recent company information that is used
- The number of analysts following the stock
- The degree of consensus among analysts
- The quality of analysts following the stock.

Empirical studies indicate that current expectations of earnings, as represented by the average of the analysts' forecasts, are incorporated into current stock prices. Perhaps more importantly, revisions in the average forecast for year-ahead earnings have predictive ability concerning future stock returns.[10]

Intuitively, one would expect analyst earnings predictions to be superior to those obtained using historical data and trends in earnings, since they use more information. However, there is a great deal of evidence that analysts tend to be overly optimistic on average. Supporting US studies include O'Brien, and DeBondt and Thaler, while Canadian evidence is documented by Hennessey, and Ackert and Athanassakos.[11]

The optimism of analysts is not surprising since they have greater incentive to issue buy rather than sell recommendations. They are under pressure by the companies they follow to avoid issuing sell recommendations. In fact, sell recommendations are rare, as can be seen in the Real-World Returns box "Bay Street's Ratings Game" in Chapter 17. This pressure will be greater if the brokerage firm they work for is trying to the sell shares of the company being analyzed or if there exists an investment banking relationship with the company. In addition, analysts may prefer to make estimates that do not stand out from the crowd. These notions are supported by the results of Ackert and Athanassakos who find that analysts are "more optimistic when there is greater dispersion in earnings forecasts."[12]

Several empirical studies, including the 1993 Canadian study by Hennessey, suggest that investors can benefit from earnings estimate revisions. In particular, portfolios of stocks that have experienced positive earnings forecast revisions, produce excess positive returns subsequent to the revision. The larger the revisions, the greater the excess returns. This implies that investors can earn abnormal returns using publicly available information, which contradicts the semi-strong form of the EMH. In a subsequent study, Hennessey demonstrates that this effect is greater for small capitalization firms, which is consistent with less information being publicly available for these stocks.[13]

---

[10] E. Elton, N. Gruber and M. Gultekin, "Expectations and Share Prices," *Management Science* 27 (September 1981), pp. 975–987; E. Hawkins, S. Chamberlin, and W. Daniel, "Earnings Expectations and Security Prices," *Financial Analysts Journal* 40 (September-October 1984), pp. 24–38.

[11] P. O'Brien, "Analyst's Forecasts as Earnings Expectation," *Journal of Accounting and Economics* 10 (January 1988), pp. 53–83; W. DeBondt and R. Thaler, "Do Security Analysts Overreact?" *American Economic Review* 80 (May 1990), pp. 52–57 ; S. Hennessey, "Can Active Managers Profit from Earnings Forecast Revisions?" *Canadian Investment Review* 6 (Spring 1993), pp. 39–45; L. Ackert and G. Athanassakos, "Expectations of the Herd," *Canadian Investment Review* 9 (Winter 1996/97), pp.7–11.

[12] L. Ackert and G. Athanassakos, "Expectations of the Herd," *Canadian Investment Review* 9 (Winter 1996/97), pp. 7–11.

[13] S. Hennessey, "Get the Drift," *Canadian Investment Review* 8 (Winter 1995/96), pp. 23–28.

The profitability of a trading strategy based on earnings revisions, supports the notion that stock prices are affected not only by the level of and growth in earnings but also by the market's expectations of earnings. Latané and Jones point out that "earnings surprises" (i.e., when actual EPS is different than expected) represent unexpected new information that will affect share prices.[14] Positive surprises cause price increases, while negative surprises cause price decreases. The magnitude of the resulting price changes is directly proportional to the size of the surprise.

Sector Rotation

An active strategy that is similar to stock selection is group or sector rotation. This strategy involves shifting sector weights in the portfolio in order to take advantage of those sectors that are expected to do better and avoiding or reducing emphasis on those that are expected to do worse. Investors employing this strategy are betting that particular sectors will repeat their price performance relative to the current phase of the business and credit cycle.

An investor could think of larger groups as the relevant sectors, shifting between cyclicals, growth stocks, and value stocks. It is quite standard in sector analysis to divide common stocks into four broad sectors: interest-sensitive stocks, consumer durable stocks, capital goods stocks, and defensive stocks. Each of these sectors is expected to perform differently during the various phases of the business and credit cycles. For example, interest-sensitive stocks would be expected to be hurt during periods of high interest rates, and such periods tend to occur at the latter stages of the business cycle. As interest rates decline, the earnings of the companies in this sector — banks and other financial institutions, utilities, and residential construction firms — should improve.

INVESTING tip

Perhaps because of their rarity, sell recommendations have a pronounced effect. According to one study, sell recommendations result in an average two-day decline of almost 5 per cent and an additional 9 per cent decline in the next six months. Another study confirmed the six-month decline but found that such stocks had a turnaround and subsequently beat the market.

The term "defensive stocks" needs some explanation. Included here are companies in such businesses as food production, soft drinks, beer, pharmaceuticals, and so forth that often are not hurt as badly as other companies during the downside of the business cycle because people will still purchase bread, milk, soft drinks, and the like. As the economy worsens and more problems are foreseen, investors may move into these stocks for investment protection. These stocks often do well during the late phases of a business cycle.

Investors may view industries as they do sectors, and act accordingly. For example, if interest rates are expected to drop significantly, increased emphasis could be placed on the interest-sensitive industries such as housing, banking, and utilities. Effective strategies involving sector rotation depend heavily on an accurate assessment of current economic conditions. A knowledge and understanding of the phases of the business cycle are important, as is an understanding of political environments, international linkages among economies, and domestic and international credit conditions.

Peter Gibson shows that while industry moves are generally in the same direction, relative differences in changes are often dramatic.[15] He suggests the key to industry timing is to identify the best industry leadership at each stage of the market cycle. In this regard, for

[14] H. Latané and C. Jones, "Standardized Unexpected Earnings — A Progress Report," *Journal of Finance* 32 (December 1977), pp.1457–1465.

[15] P. Gibson, "Strategy," in Joe Kan, Editor, *Handbook of Canadian Security Analysis: A Guide to Evaluating the Industry Sectors of the Market from Bay Street's Top Analysts* (Toronto: John Wiley & Sons Canada, 1997), pp. 537–644.

purposes of industry analysis, industry groups should be formed on the basis of factors such as type of business, degree of economic sensitivity, and exposure to international markets.

Chapter 16 provides a detailed discussion of industry analysis; however, at this point we provide some general principles that must be kept in mind. First, prices for industries with similar economic sensitivity tend to move together (and hence display positive correlations among returns), which reduces the potential benefits of rotation gains. Second, it is important to focus on industry activity and not size. Third, be aware that diversification within and across industries is not a straightforward task in Canada. In particular, 11 of the 39 industries identified within the TSE 300 make up over 70 per cent of the total TSE 300 market capitalization. In addition, most TSE 300 industries are dominated by one or two companies, with the notable exceptions of the banks, the paper and forest producers, and the oil and gas producers.

The success of sector rotation strategies depends heavily on forecasting overall market activity, as well as activity within several industry categories. There are great potential benefits to this approach. However, as always, it is easy to say what should have been done after the fact, but it is a very difficult thing to predict which sectors will excel, ahead of time. The bottom line is that forecasting economic and market activity is a daunting task, and there is little evidence that it can produce superior results on a consistent basis.

Indirect Investing in Sectors

Investors can invest in sectors using mutual funds. This indirect sector investing offers the potential of large returns, but the risks are also large. For example, over the six-month period ending June 30, 1998, the financial company sector performed extremely well and the resource sector performed poorly. Over this period, the **CIBC Financial Companies Fund** produced a 16.1 per cent return, well above the TSE 300 return of 4.2 per cent over the same period, and 37 per cent above the **Canadian Resource Equity Funds** average of −20.9 per cent.

Market Timing

Market timers attempt to earn excess returns by varying the percentage of portfolio assets in equity securities. When equities are expected to do well, timers shift from cash equivalents such as money market funds to common stocks. When equities are expected to do poorly, the opposite occurs. Alternatively, market timers could increase the betas of their portfolios when the market is expected to rise and carry most stock prices up, or decrease them when the market is expected to go down. One important factor affecting the success of a market timing strategy is the amount of brokerage commissions and taxes paid with such a strategy as opposed to a buy-and-hold strategy. The CSC Notes box at the end of this section discusses some of the more common asset allocation strategies based on the ability to time changes in the market.

Market timing means that managers invest more aggressively in anticipation of strong markets and more conservatively in anticipation of slow markets. Robert Merton illustrated the astonishing profit potential associated with perfect market timing ability.[16] He showed that an investor with $1,000 to invest in 1927, could have accumulated $5.36 billion after 52 years (at the end of 1978), by correctly investing in either T-bills or the NYSE index (whichever

[16] R. Merton, "On Market Timing and Investment Performance: An Equilibrium Theory of Market Forecasts," *Journal of Business* 54 (July 1981), pp. 363–406.

produced a higher return during a given month). This amount dwarfs the $3,600 that would have been accumulated had the investor remained in T-bills the entire period, as well as the $67,500 had the investor held the market index the entire period.

The example above illustrates the importance of market timing ability for investors. However, like many issues in the investing arena, the subject of market timing is controversial. Can some investors regularly time the market effectively enough to provide excess returns on a risk-adjusted basis? The available evidence on the subject is mixed, and it is important to keep in mind that market timing is a broad topic and that it is difficult to summarize all viewpoints.

Much of the empirical evidence on market timing comes from studies of mutual funds. A basic issue is whether fund managers increase the beta of their portfolios when they anticipate a rising market and reduce it when they anticipate a declining market. Several studies found no evidence that funds were able to time market changes and change their risk levels in response. Veit and Cheney, for example, found in a study of 74 mutual funds that they were not able to successfully change their risk levels based on their timing strategies.[17]

Chang and Lewellen examined the performance of mutual funds and found little evidence of any market timing ability; furthermore, the average estimated downmarket beta turned out to be slightly higher than the average estimated up-market beta.[18] Overall, this study supported the conclusion that mutual funds do not outperform a passive investment strategy. This conclusion was also supported by Henriksson in a study of 116 mutual funds using monthly data.[19] He found that mutual fund managers are not able to successfully employ strategies involving market timing, and they were not even successful with market timing involving large changes in the market.

On the other hand, Weigel examined the market timing performance of 17 US managers who used a tactical asset allocation approach (described in the CSC Notes box below) and found they had reliable market timing skills.[20] Studies by both Foerster and Turnbull, and Beveridge and Bauer have demonstrated the potential benefits of using market timing approaches in Canada.[21] There is also a great deal of evidence that international portfolio managers using dynamic asset allocation strategies can add considerable value to international portfolios.[22]

Mark Hulbert, publisher of a service that monitors the performance of investment advisory letters called the *Hulbert Financial Digest*, believes that the popularity of market timing follows a cycle of its own.[23] If the market is strongly up, market timing falls into disrepute, and buying and holding is the popular strategy. Following a market decline, however, market timing comes into vogue and the buy-and-hold strategy is not popular. According to Hulbert, on a pure timing basis only 3 per cent of the stock timing strategies tracked over the most recent five- and eight-year periods outperformed a buy-and-hold approach.[24]

---

[17] E. T. Veit and J. M. Cheney, "Are Mutual Funds Market Timers?" *Journal of Portfolio Management* 8 (Winter 1982), pp. 35–42.

[18] E. Chang and W. Lewellen, "Market Timing and Mutual Fund Investment Performance," *Journal of Business* 57, Part 1 (January 1984), pp. 57–72.

[19] R. D. Henriksson, "Market Timing and Mutual Fund Performance: An Empirical Investigation," *Journal of Business* 57, Part 1 (January 1984), pp. 73–96.

[20] E. Weigel, "The Performance of Tactical Asset Allocation," *Financial Analysts Journal* 47 (Sept/Oct 1991), pp. 63–70.

[21] S. Foerster and A. Turnbull, "The Key to Effective Tactical Asset Allocation," *Canadian Investment Review* 6 (Spring 1993), pp. 13–19; S. Beveridge and L. Bauer, "How to Market Time Using Interest Rate Signals," *Canadian Investment Review* 7 (Summer 1994), pp.13–16.

[22] For example, refer to R. Arnott and R. Henriksson, "A Disciplined Approach to Global Asset Allocation," *Financial Analysts Journal* 45 (Mar/Apr 1989), pp.17–28; M. Keppler, "The Importance of Dividend Yield in Country Selection," *Journal of Portfolio Management* 17 (Winter 1991), pp. 24–29; and, W. Fouse, "Allocating Assets Across Country Markets," *Journal of Portfolio Management* 18 (Winter 1992), pp. 20–27.

[23] M. Hulbert, "New Tool for Contrarians," *Forbes*, November 18, 1996, p. 298.

[24] Ibid.

Many successful portfolio managers such as Warren Buffet and Peter Lynch suggest that market timing is one of the most difficult things for an investor to accomplish. Based on this belief, they establish their investment policies with long-term objectives in mind, in order to avoid having to continually make market timing decisions. On the other hand, there are several studies that indicate the potential benefits of market timing strategies. In fact, most funds employ market timing strategies to a certain degree, which is reflected in the varying cash ratios exhibited by their portfolios.

Considerable research suggests that the biggest risk of market timing is that investors will not be in the market at critical times, thereby significantly reducing their overall returns. Investors who miss only a few key months may suffer significantly. For example, over a recent 40-year period, investors who missed the 34 best months for stocks would have seen an initial $1,000 investment grow to only $4,492 instead of $86,650. Even T- bills would have been a better alternative in this situation.[25]

If you are still considering market timing as a strategy suitable for the average individual investor, consider the following US evidence. For the 10-year period 1986 to 1995, inclusive, returns on the S&P 500 Composite Index were:

Fully invested annualized rate of return = 14.8 per cent
Take out the 10 best days = 10.2 per cent
Take out the 20 best days = 7.3 per cent
Take out the 30 best days = 4.8 per cent
Take out the 40 best days = 2.5 per cent

CSC NOTES

Asset Allocation Strategies

Asset allocation strategies are based on the ability to time the performance of the major financial asset categories, which include short-term money market instruments (such as T-bills and commercial paper), long-term bonds, and equity securities. The most commonly referred to strategy is tactical asset allocation (TAA), a moderately active asset allocation approach that allows managers short-term deviations from longer-term asset mixes to take advantage of market timing skills. Evidence was presented above regarding the relative success of such strategies.

Several other asset allocation techniques may be employed. Strategic asset allocation involves adhering to a long-term mix by monitoring and rebalancing the portfolio as necessary. In order to achieve a desired asset mix of, say, 60 per cent equity and 40 per cent bonds, rebalancing is necessary as equity and bond prices change through time, which alters the portfolio asset mix. The asset mix can be returned to the strategic long-term position by buying bonds (or stocks) when they become cheap and selling them when they increase in value. For example, suppose stock prices fell and bond prices rose, so that the actual asset mix changed to 55 per cent equity and 45 per cent bonds. This would require the manager to sell bonds, which had risen in price, and buy equities, whose prices had fallen. This buy low and sell high strategy is consistent with the notion underlying contrarian or value investment strategies.

Insured asset allocation allows managers discretion in deciding asset amounts only if they exceed a base portfolio value that must be guaranteed by formula. This involves maintaining a predetermined amount in riskless securities or by using put options or futures contracts to "immunize" the portfolio value (i.e., portfolio insurance). Dynamic asset allocation is an active management technique that adjusts the mix between risk-free and risky assets as market conditions change by selling equities when markets fall and buying them when they rise. This strategy is consistent with the rationale underlying growth investment strategies.

Finally, integrated asset allocation represents an all-encompassing strategy including several of the approaches above. It examines market conditions and investor objectives and constraints separately, and based on this analysis, the optimal asset mix is determined. That asset mix is adjusted at regular intervals to reflect the fact that both market conditions and investor needs change through time.

The Real-World Returns box below provides investors with a glimpse of the benefits that can be derived from effective asset allocation. Before running out with this new formula for investing success, keep in mind that the potential benefits are demonstrated only after the fact, based on the assumption that investors had perfect foresight.

[25] See J. D. Pond, "The Harsh Reality of Market Timing," *Worth* (May 1994), pp. 117–118.

REAL-WORLD RETURNS

Optimal Returns Require a Rejuggling of Asset Mix

As this RRSP season counts down, investors everywhere are hunting for well-managed funds that will enhance their overall investment performance without taking on unseemly risk.

But before making any selections, they should consider this: Average Canadian investors could do a much better job of managing their risk-reward equation by rejigging their asset mixes.

In fact, a study of Canadian mutual-fund investors' portfolios over the past 15 years shows that, on average, fund holders could have gotten better returns for the same level of risk they took. Or, alternatively, they could have achieved the returns they got but with a lower level of risk.

It's all a matter of the makeup of their holdings, and finding the right asset mix to achieve what is called optimal returns — the highest return for the level of risk incurred.

For the 15 years between 1984 and 1998, Canadian mutual-fund investors, on average, earned an annual return of 10.6 per cent. The risk associated with the portfolio, as measured by standard deviation (a statistic of the variation in a fund's annual return over the 15-year period) was 8.4 per cent, which is a moderate level of risk.

By shifting out of Canadian balanced funds, cutting back on their Canadian and international equities and focusing much more on fixed income as well as dividend funds, the average fund investor would have ended up with an equally rewarding but more conservative portfolio.

In short, the average Canadian fund investor has suffered from suboptimal results. The culprit behind this sad reality has been the high portfolio concentration in dismal performing Canadian equity funds.

Over the past 15 years, Canadian equity funds have eked out a tepid 9.2-per-cent average annual return, compared with 14.5 per cent for US and 12.9 per cent for international equity funds.

Yet, the risk level of Canadian equity funds has been approximately the same as for US and international funds. In fact, even Canadian bonds outperformed Canadian equities by earning 10.2 per cent over the past 15 years — at a risk level nearly half that of Canadian equities.

Hindsight, of course, is always 20-20. The next 15 years undoubtedly will be different. For example, the depreciation of our dollar has been a real factor in the historically superior US and international equity performance. At today's low levels, a rebound in the loonie could dramatically close this performance gap. Inflation could also lift commodity prices down the road, boosting Canadian returns.

Nevertheless, there are some important lessons to be learned from history that do have application to planning today. Among them:

- **Start with a diversified asset mix strategy** that diversifies across numerous asset classes.
- **Diversify internationally** — ensure 25 per cent of your fixed-income holdings are in global bonds and 50 per cent of your equity mix is US and international. If the foreign-content limits for your RRSP are a problem, use Canadian equity funds that invest a portion of their holdings internationally or consider the use of RRSP-eligible international equity funds.
- **Don't run from Asia and emerging markets.** Unlike 10 years ago, Japan, Asia, and the emerging markets represent the cheapest markets globally, while the United States is the most expensive.
- **Invest in real-estate investment trusts.** American REITs, in particular, offer diversity of choice in property type, geography, and size and can improve overall portfolio performance because their returns don't move in tandem with equities.
- **Don't overlook Canadian dividend funds** that can give you exposure to larger, blue-chip Canadian companies in the financial services, industrial, and other sectors without excessive exposure to small- and medium-sized companies or the natural-resources sector.

If you follow these tips and get the right asset mix in hand, you can get down to the next step — picking the top funds in each asset class.

Aiming for the Optimal Results

	Average Portfolio Mix	**Mix for Same Return/ Lower Risk**	**Mix for Higher Return/ Same Risk**
	Return: 10.6%	Return: 10.6%	Return: 12.4%
Asset type	Risk: 8.4%	Risk: 6.4%	Risk: 8.4%
Canadian bond	8.0%	40.0%	15.0%
Mortgage	3.0	10.0	0.0
International bond	2.0	10.0	10.0
Canadian balanced	21.0	0.0	0.0
Canadian equity	26.0	10.0	5.0
Dividend	6.0	15.0	10.0
US equity	8.0	10.0	35.0
International equity	17.0	5.0	25.0
Regional equity*	5.0	0.0	0.0
Other†	4.0	0.0	0.0
Total	100.0%	100.0%	100.0%

Data Source: Assante Wealth Management.

Return is the average annual return over 15 years. Risk is measured by standard deviation.

*Regional equity includes European equity, Asian and Pacific, Latin America and emerging markets.

†Others include precious metals, sector equity, labour-sponsored, and international balanced funds.

Source: Excerpted from Michael Nairne, "Optimal Returns Require a Rejuggling of Asset Mix," The Globe and Mail / Report on Mutual Funds, *Thursday, February 18, 1999, p. C4. Reprinted with permission.*

Efficient Markets and Active Strategies

One of the most significant developments in recent years is the proposition that securities markets are efficient. This idea has generated considerable controversy concerning the analysis and valuation of securities because of its significant implications for investors. Regardless of how much (or how little) an investor learns about investments, and regardless of whether an investor ends up being convinced by the efficient markets literature, it is essential to be aware of the implications of market efficiency early in one's study of investments.

Much evidence exists to support the basic concepts of the Efficient Market Hypothesis (EMH), and it cannot be ignored simply because one is uncomfortable with the idea or because it sounds too improbable. It is appropriate to consider this concept with any discussion of active strategies designed to produce excess returns — that is, returns in excess of those commensurate with the risk being taken. After all, if the evidence suggests that active strategies are unlikely to be successful over time after all costs have been assessed, the case for a passive strategy becomes much more persuasive.

As we learned in Chapter 10, the EMH is concerned with the assessment of information by investors. Security prices are determined by expectations about the future. Investors use the information available to them in forming their expectations. If security prices fully reflect all the relevant information that is available and usable, a securities market is said to be efficient.

If the stock market is efficient, prices reflect their fair economic value as estimated by investors. Even if this is not strictly true, prices may reflect their approximate fair value after transaction costs are taken into account, a condition known as economic efficiency. In such a market, where prices of stocks depart only slightly from their fair economic value, investors should not try to employ trading strategies designed to beat the market by identifying undervalued stocks. Nor should they attempt to time the market in the belief that an advantage can be gained. Sector rotation also will be unsuccessful in a highly efficient market.

The implications of an efficient market are extremely important for investors. They include one's beliefs about how to value securities in terms of the two approaches to selecting common stocks discussed below — the fundamental and the technical — which, in turn, encompasses questions about the time and effort to be devoted. Other implications include the management of a portfolio of securities. Again, in terms of the above discussion, should management be active or passive? Efficient market proponents often argue that less time should be spent on deciding which securities to include in a portfolio and more on considerations such as reducing taxes and transaction costs and maintaining the chosen risk level of a portfolio over time.

Suffice it to say that an intelligent investor must be aware of this issue and form some judgement about its implications if he or she is to formulate a reasonable investment strategy. An investor's beliefs about market efficiency will have a significant impact on the type of stock strategy implemented. The efficiency of the market, and how investors should act in selecting portfolios of stocks, remains controversial.

Investors are constantly being bombarded with reports of techniques and procedures that appear to offer above-average returns, thereby contradicting the idea that the market is so efficient that they should not attempt to outperform it. Intelligent investors examine such claims and strategies carefully before using them.

WAYS OF ANALYZING AND SELECTING STOCKS

The two traditional and well-known ways of analyzing and selecting common stocks are fundamental analysis and technical analysis. Both of these are given careful consideration in Part V, which is devoted to security analysis. Technical analysis is also discussed in Part V, but greater emphasis is placed on fundamental analysis.

These two basic approaches are described briefly here, followed by a consideration of the concept of efficient market and its implications. The fundamental approach is then developed in some detail in the remainder of this chapter, setting the stage for the next three chapters, which analyze the fundamental approach in a specific, recommended order.

Technical Analysis

Technical Analysis
The use of specific market data for the analysis of both individual and aggregate security prices for the purpose of identifying recurring price patterns.

One of the two traditional strategies long available to investors is technical analysis, which is examined in detail in Chapter 18. In fact, technical analysis is the oldest strategy and can be traced back to at least the late nineteenth century.

The term **technical analysis** refers to the methodology of forecasting fluctuations in securities prices. This methodology can be applied either to individual securities or to the market as a whole (i.e., forecasting a market index such as the TSE 300 Composite Index).

The rationale behind technical analysis is that the value of a stock is primarily a function of supply and demand conditions. These conditions, in turn, are determined by a range of factors, from scientific analyses to opinions and guesses, all of which play a part in determining the changes in prices. The price trends persist, or they may change with supply and demand conditions. Technicians seek to detect, and act upon, changes in the direction of stock prices.

In its purest sense, technical analysis is not concerned with the underlying economic variables that affect a company or the market; therefore, the causes of supply and demand shifts are not important. The basic question to be asked is: Does excess supply or demand exist for a stock, and can such a condition be detected by studying either the patterns of past price fluctuations or the movements of certain technical indicators or rules? Technicians study the market using graphical charting of price changes, volume of trading over time, and a number of technical indicators.

Momentum Strategies

One of the most popular technical analysis techniques is that of **momentum investing**, which is basically a relative strength approach (relative strength is examined in Chapter 18). The basic premise of momentum investing is that if a stock has outperformed the market over some recent period, it is likely to continue to do so. In other words, this approach is one of following the trend.

Momentum investing is a short-run approach. For example, stocks that are strong for the prior six months tend to outperform the market only over the next six to 12 months. Evidence of the success of momentum investment strategies was discussed in Chapter 10.

Momentum Investing Investing on the basis of recent movements in the price of a stock, which generally means buying stocks that have outperformed the market recently. In other words, it is following the trend.

Fundamental Analysis

Fundamental analysis is based on the premise that any security (and the market as a whole) has an **intrinsic value**, which is the true value as estimated by an investor. This value is a function of the firm's underlying variables, which combine to produce an expected return and an accompanying risk. By assessing these fundamental determinants of the value of a security, an estimate of its intrinsic value can be determined. This estimated intrinsic value can then be compared to the current market price of the security, as discussed in Chapter 11 with regard to bonds, and in Chapter 13 with regard to common stocks.

In equilibrium, the current market price of a security reflects the average of the intrinsic value estimates made by investors. An investor whose intrinsic value estimate differs from the market price is, in effect, disagreeing with the market consensus of the estimate of either expected return or risk or both. Investors who can perform good fundamental analysis and spot discrepancies should be able to profit by acting before the market consensus reflects the correct information.

Fundamental Analysis The estimation of a stock's value using basic data such as its earnings, sales, risk, and so forth.

Intrinsic Value The estimated or true value of a security as determined by an investor after examining a firm's underlying variables.

Efficient Market Implications

The rise, and increasing acceptance, of the efficient market concept has had an impact on traditional investing practices. Hardest hit has been technical analysis. If prices fluctuate in accordance with the efficient markets model, there is little chance that pure technical analysis is valid.

The EMH also has implications for fundamental analysis. If the market is efficient, prices will react quickly to new information, and with many active investors buying and selling, prices should be close to their fair economic values. However, fundamental analysis is still needed in an efficient market, because without it, the market would be less efficient. One can argue that what makes the market efficient is the very fact that investors do fundamental analysis, based on the belief that the market is not efficient.

Given the widespread discussion of market efficiency, investors sometimes overlook the issue of psychology in financial markets — that is, the role that emotions play. Particularly in the short run, investors' emotions affect stock prices and markets, and those making investment decisions need to be aware of this.

A FRAMEWORK FOR FUNDAMENTAL ANALYSIS

With any fundamental analysis, an investor will obviously have to work with individual company data. Does this mean that the investor should plunge into a study of company data first and then consider other factors such as the industry within which a particular company operates or the state of the economy, or should the reverse procedure be followed? In fact, when doing fundamental analysis investors and security analysts may use each of these approaches, which are referred to as the "bottom-up" and the "top-down" approaches.

Bottom-Up Fundamental Analysis

With the bottom-up approach, investors focus directly on a company's basics or fundamentals. Analysis of such information as the company's products, its competitive position, and its financial status leads to an estimate of the company's earnings potential and, ultimately, its value in the market.

Considerable time and effort are required to produce the type of detailed financial analysis needed to understand even relatively small companies. The emphasis in this approach is on finding companies with good long-term growth prospects and on making accurate earnings estimates. To organize this effort, bottom-up fundamental research is often broken into two areas, growth investing and value investing.

Value Versus Growth

Growth stocks carry investor expectations of above-average future growth in earnings and valuations as a result of high price/earnings ratios. Investors expect these stocks to perform well in the future, and they are willing to pay high multiples for this. Recent examples include Microsoft and Intel, as well as the stocks of many Internet-related companies.

Value stocks, on the other hand, feature cheap assets and strong balance sheets. Value investing can be traced back to the value-investing principles laid out by the well-known Benjamin Graham, who wrote a classic book on security analysis that has been the foundation for many subsequent security analysts.[26]

Growth stocks and value stocks tend to be in vogue at different times, and the advocates of each camp prosper and suffer accordingly. For example, the Real-World Returns box below demonstrates that value investing outperformed growth stock investing in 1993, 1994, 1996, and 1997, while growth stock investing outperformed value investing in 1991, 1992, and 1995.

[26] Benjamin Graham and David Dodd, *Security Analysis: Principles and Technique* (New York: McGraw-Hill, 1934). This topic is discussed at some length in Chapter 10.

REAL-WORLD RETURNS

Value the Style to Beat this Year

Mutual fund portfolio managers are in a constant battle over the right styles for markets. And style watchers say that 1998 looks like a year in which managers of value funds will outshine those who run growth funds.

Value stocks, often disdained by investors as bargain-priced mutts of the market, have already had two years of beating growth stocks, the closely watched darlings of the day that report rapidly rising earnings, according to data from portfolio analysis company **Frank Russell Canada Ltd**.

Last year, Canadian equity funds run on value principles had an average total return of 19.1 per cent, versus 7 per cent for growth funds, according to Frank Russell. The year before, funds run on value principles earned an average 31.5 per cent versus 25.3 per cent for growth funds. In 1995, however, growth funds were the winners, earning an average 18.1 per cent versus 11.3 per cent, Frank Russell says.

Key to classifying funds as value or growth are market benchmarks. Funds that have ratios of such indicators as price-to-earnings and price-to-book value above their benchmarks — usually the Toronto Stock Exchange 300 Composite Index — are considered growth stocks. Those below the benchmarks are value stocks, says Harry Marmer, Frank Russell's director of investment management services.

For the 12 months ended Dec. 31, 1997, the TSE 300 index average P/E ratio was 19.8, its average price to book ratio 2.2, according to Portfolio Analytics Ltd., a mutual fund data service.

There's no doubt that style plays a crucial role in returns, Mr. Marmer says. "An analysis of the returns of active Canadian equity managers found that about 84 per cent of the variation of return can be explained by style," he says.

So what portends value's superiority over growth this year? The fact that the market is trading near peak historical price-to-earnings and other ratios, for one.

"I would not be surprised that value stocks will outperform. Multiples on growth stocks have skyrocketed so much that there is a risk that they will correct, bringing down the prices of growth stocks," says Sebastian van Berkom, manager of the $204-million small- to mid-cap **Talvest/Hyperion Small Cap Canadian Equity Fund**. "Value stocks, which are already cheap, are a safe haven."

Bonnie Bloomberg, manager of the $497-million **Green Line Value Fund**, agrees: "This year, the rate of economic growth could slow. That will mean that stocks with a large growth premium will fall in price as investors correct their former optimism. In this market, a fund with constraints on valuation will be able to perform well if earnings reports exceed expectations and to survive with only moderate losses if earnings don't match forecasts."

Even growth managers concede that their style may go out of favour if corporate earnings don't meet expectations. Lewis Jackson, who manages the $331-million **McLean Budden Pooled Canadian Growth Equity Fund** on growth principles, says that if 1998 is a lousy year for markets, aggressive growth portfolios will be beaten by more timid value portfolios.

"If the market goes down, fully invested growth managers will have nowhere to hide," Mr. Jackson says. "The consequence of slower growth of corporate earnings would be contraction of price/earnings multiples. That would have a larger impact on growth stocks, which could be said to magnify volatility in comparison to value funds that have lower multiples. Growth stocks would also tend to lack support from dividend yields, which are usually higher in value stocks."

Mr. Jackson has seen the anxiety of growth fund unit holders. They phone when markets sag, he says. But he says he is not worried. "For short periods, if an investor is very worried about a huge collapse, he should be in cash. If he is just concerned, he should be in value funds."

Ms. Bloomberg's value principles have produced results consistent with market results. In 1996, when value managers clobbered markets, the Green Line fund had a total return of 48.3 per cent, well ahead of corresponding growth fund average returns of 25.3 per cent.

But when value management was out of favour in 1995, Green Line Value Fund had a total return of 11.3 per cent, less than the growth fund average return of 18.1 per cent.

Finding genuine value funds requires some research. According to Patrick McKeough, publisher of *The Successful Investor*, a Toronto-based advisory newsletter, it is getting harder to find pure value managers because as stocks rise in price, to-die-for bargains tend to be priced above value criteria.

"You won't find many good companies priced below book value, the traditional test of a real value stock," he says. "Today, value managers have to seek relative value, and that tends to mean out-of-favour stocks that have merit but that are priced cheap."

Ms. Bloomberg suggests that an investor in search of a value fund should examine its record to ensure that average price earnings and book value ratios are below market benchmarks.

An investor should also take a look at the companies in a fund's portfolio, she says. Research the companies if necessary to see if they fit value criteria. If they do, then the fund could be a candidate for purchase, she says.

Experts think it pays to seek the appropriate style for a market. "Make the right choice," Mr. Marmer says. "If you pick an out-of-favour style, you could be dead wrong."

Source: Excerpted from Andrew Allentuck, "Value the Style to Beat this Year," The Globe and Mail / Report on Mutual Funds, *Thursday, February 5, 1998, p. C20. Reprinted with permission of the author.*

In many cases bottom-up investing does not attempt to make a clear distinction between growth and value. Many companies feature strong earning prospects and a strong financial base or asset value and therefore have characteristics associated with both categories.

Top-Down Fundamental Analysis

The top-down approach is the opposite of the bottom-up one. Investors begin with the economy and the overall market, considering such important factors as interest rates and inflation. They next consider industries or sectors of the economy that are likely to do particularly well. Finally, having assessed the effect of macro factors on equity investing, and having determined which parts of the overall economy are likely to perform well, individual companies are analyzed.

There is no "right" answer to which of these two approaches to follow. However, fundamental analysis can be overwhelming in its detail, and a structure is needed. This text takes the position that the better way to proceed is top-down in fundamental analysis:

1. First, analyze the overall economy and securities markets to determine if now is a good time to commit additional funds to equities.
2. Second, analyze industries and sectors to determine which have the best prospects for the future.
3. Finally, analyze individual companies.

This is consistent with the observation that between 80 and 90 per cent of the return on a portfolio is determined by the asset allocation decision. Using this structure, the valuation models presented in Chapter 13 can be applied successively at each of the three levels.

Thus, the preferred order for fundamental security analysis used here is (1) the economy and market, (2) the industry, and (3) the company. Part V explains fundamental security analysis in detail and we consider here only the justification for this approach.

Economy/Market Analysis

It is very important to assess the state of the economy and the outlook for primary variables such as corporate profits and interest rates. Investors are heavily influenced by these variables in making their everyday investment decisions. If a recession is likely, or under way, stock prices will be heavily affected at certain times during the contraction. Conversely, if a strong economic expansion is under way, stock prices will be heavily affected, again at particular times during the expansion. Thus, the status of economic activity has a major impact on overall stock prices. It is, therefore, very important for investors to assess the state of the economy and its implications for the stock market.

In turn, the stock market impacts each individual investor. Investors cannot compete very well against market trends. If the market goes up (or down) strongly, most stocks are carried along. Company analysis is unlikely to produce high returns in a year such as 1990, when the stock market was down approximately 15 per cent. On the other hand, most equity investors did well in 1993 regardless of their specific company analysis, because the market was up over 32 per cent as measured by the TSE 300.

Another indication of the importance of the economy/market on common stocks is the impact on the earnings for a particular company. Available evidence suggests that from a quarter to a half of the variability in a company's annual earnings is attributable to the overall economy (plus some industry effect).[27]

The economy also significantly affects what happens to various industries. One has only to think of the effects of import quotas, record high interest rates, and so forth, to see why this is so. Therefore, economy analysis must precede industry analysis.

Industry Analysis

After completing an analysis of the economy and the overall market, an investor can decide if it is a favourable time to increase or decrease the amount invested in common stocks. The next step should be industry analysis, since industry factors are the second most important component (after overall market movements) affecting the variability in stock returns.

Individual companies and industries tend to respond to general market movements, but the degree of response can vary significantly. Industries undergo significant movements over both relatively short and relatively long periods. Industries will be affected to various degrees by recessions and expansions. For example, the heavy goods industries will be severely affected in a recession. (Examples include the auto and steel industries in the 1981–82 recession.) Consumer goods will probably be much less affected during such a contractionary period. During a severe inflationary period such as the late 1970s and early 1980s, regulated industries such as utilities were severely hurt by their inability to pass along all price increases. Finally, new "hot" industries emerge from time to time and enjoy spectacular (if short-lived) growth. Refer to Chapter 16 for related examples as well as a more detailed discussion of various industry categories.

---

[27] E. J. Elton and M. J. Gruber, *Modern Portfolio Theory and Investment Analysis*, Fifth Edition (New York: John Wiley, 1995).

Company Analysis

Although the first two steps are important and must be done in the indicated order, great attention and emphasis should also be placed on company analysis. Security analysts are generally organized along industry lines, but the reports that they issue usually deal with one specific company (sometimes more).

The bottom line for companies, as far as most investors are concerned, is earnings per share. There is a very close relationship between earnings and stock prices, and for this reason most attention is paid to earnings. After all, dividends are closely tied to past, present, and future earnings.

A number of factors are important in analyzing a company, but because investors tend to focus on earnings and dividends, we need to understand the relationship between these two variables and between them and other variables. We also need to consider the possibilities of forecasting earnings and dividends.

Because dividends are paid out of earnings, we will concentrate on the latter in our discussion of company analysis in Chapter 17. Earnings and interest rates are the real key to the fundamental analysis of a common stock. A good understanding of these concepts is vital if an investor is to understand, and perform, fundamental analysis.

The Framework for Fundamental Analysis in Perspective

It is useful to summarize the framework for fundamental analysis we are using because the following three chapters are based on it. Figure 14-3 depicts the fundamental valuation process. We should examine the economy and market first, then industries, and finally individual companies. Fundamental valuation is usually done within the context of a present value model (such as the dividend discount model) or a relative valuation model (such as the P/E ratio model). In either case, the two components of the value of any security being examined are (1) the expected stream of benefits, either earnings or dividends, and (2) the required rate of return or discount rate and/or the multiplier or P/E ratio. Investors should concentrate on these two factors as they systematically proceed through the three levels of analysis: economy/market, industry, and company.

SUMMARY

This summary relates to the learning objectives provided on page 439.

1. **Discuss the impact of the overall market on common stock investors.**
   Market risk is the single most important risk affecting the price movements of common stocks. For well-diversified portfolios, market effects account for 90 per cent and more of the variability in the portfolio's return.

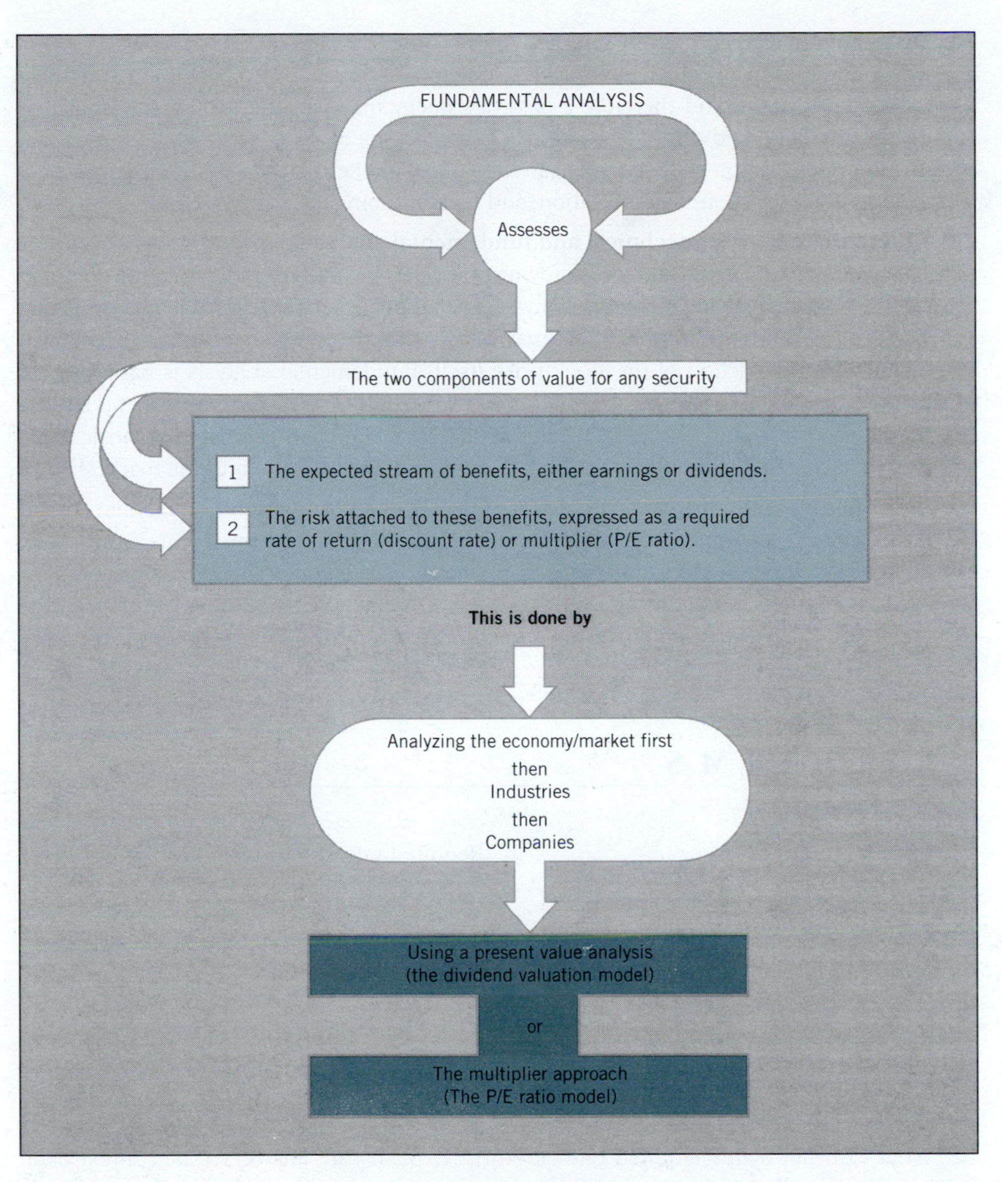

Figure 14-3
A Framework for Fundamental Security Analysis

2. **Explain the importance of the required rate of return.**
The required rate of return for a common stock, or any security, is defined as the minimum expected rate of return needed to induce an investor to purchase the stock. The required rate of return for any investment opportunity can be expressed as the sum of the risk-free rate of return and a risk premium. The trade-off between the required rate of return and risk is linear and upward sloping, which means that the required rate of return increases as the risk increases. The relevant risk, according to the Capital Asset Pricing Model (CAPM), is measured by beta.

3. **Distinguish between passive and active investment strategies.**
If the market is totally efficient, no active strategy should be able to beat the market on a risk-adjusted basis, and therefore a passive strategy may be superior. Passive strategies include buy-and-hold and the use of index funds. Pursuit of an active strategy assumes that investors possess some advantage relative to other market participants. Active strategies include stock selection, sector rotation, and market timing.

4. **Differentiate between technical and fundamental analysis.**
There are two traditional and well-known approaches to analyzing and selecting common stocks: fundamental and technical analysis. The rationale behind technical analysis is that stock prices will move in trends that may persist and that these changes can be detected by analyzing the action of the stock price itself. Fundamental analysis is based on the premise that any security (and the market as a whole) has an intrinsic value that is a function of the firm's (and the market's) underlying variables. This estimated intrinsic value may then be compared to the current market price of the security (and the market).

5. **Describe the bottom-up and top-down approaches in fundamental analysis.**
Fundamental security analysis can be done following a bottom-up or a top-down approach. With the bottom-up approach, investors focus on information about a company such as products, competitive position, and financial status. The top-down approach used in Part V of this textbook considers, in order: (1) the economy/market, (2) the industry, and (3) the company.

KEY TERMS

Fundamental analysis
Index funds
Intrinsic value
Momentum investing
Required rate of return
Risk premium
Technical analysis

REVIEW QUESTIONS

1. What impact does the market have on well-diversified portfolios? What does this suggest about the performance of mutual funds?
2. What is meant by the required rate of return? Explain your answer in the context of an investor considering the purchase of Bombardier's common shares.
3. What are the two components of the required rate of return?
4. What is the shape of the trade-off between the required rate of return for a stock and its risk? Must this shape always prevail?
5. What is the rationale for passive investment strategies.
6. What does the evidence cited on market timing suggest about the likelihood of success in this area?
7. Identify and differentiate the two traditional approaches to analyzing and selecting common stocks.

8. What is the recommended framework for fundamental analysis? Is this a top-down or bottom-up approach? Explain the difference.
9. How does this recommended framework relate to the discussion about the impact of the market on investors?
10. What is the relationship between fundamental analysis and intrinsic value?
11. Explain how technical analysis is primarily based on supply and demand conditions.
12. Why is technical analysis inconsistent with the Efficient Market Hypothesis?
13. How does an investor in common stocks reconcile the large variability in stock returns, and the big drops that have occurred, with taking a prudent position in owning a portfolio of financial assets?
14. Given the drastic — some would say unprecedented — drop in the prices of Japanese stocks, how can Canadian investors justify owning foreign stocks?
15. Is there one required rate of return? If not, how many are there?
16. What is the required rate of return on the overall market?
17. Describe three active strategies that involve the use of common stocks.
18. What are the major sources of information used by security analysts in evaluating common stocks?
19. How does the cross-sectional variation in common stock returns relate to the issue of stock selection?
20. What is meant by sector rotation? What is the key input in implementing effective strategies in sector rotation?
21. What is the basic idea behind the Efficient Market Hypothesis?
22. What are the implications of the Efficient Market Hypothesis to both stock selectors and market timers?
23. What are the advantages and disadvantages to the top-down approach?
24. What are the advantages and disadvantages to the bottom-up approach?

PREPARING FOR YOUR PROFESSIONAL EXAMS

Special Note to CSC Students

Ensure that you have read and understood the following topics:*

Building stock portfolios, p. 444
The passive strategy, pp. 444–446
The active strategy, pp. 446–456
CSC Notes: Asset allocation strategies, p. 453
Ways of analyzing and selecting stocks, pp. 456–458
A framework for fundamental analysis, pp. 458–463

**Reading these CSC-related topics should provide you with additional understanding of CSC material. However, it should not be seen as a substitute for reading the CSC textbook itself, which is the basis for the CSC exam.*

CSC REGISTRATION QUESTIONS

CANADIAN SECURITIES INSTITUTE

The Canadian Securities Institute issued the following sample questions in the 1997 CSC registration package as a means for students to self-assess their understanding of CSC-related material.

1. The __________ approach to asset allocation involves rebalancing to return the mix to its strategic long-run position.
2. During the contraction phase of the business cycle, a good investment strategy would be to __________.

   a. sell growth stocks

   b. buy long term bonds

   c. buy short term bonds

   d. buy cyclical stocks

CHAPTER 15

ANALYSIS OF THE ECONOMY AND THE STOCK MARKET

LEARNING OBJECTIVES

After reading this chapter, you will be able to

1. Describe the relationship between the stock market and the economy.
2. Analyze the determinants of stock market values.
3. Make basic forecasts of market changes.

CHAPTER PREVIEW

In this chapter we consider the first step of the top-down approach in fundamental security analysis that was described in Chapter 14—economy/market analysis. Based on our understanding of the relationship between the stock market and the economy, we apply the valuation concepts presented in earlier chapters to the market. We also consider how to make forecasts of changes in the stock market.

THE ECONOMY AND THE STOCK MARKET

Ultimately, investors must make intelligent judgements about the current state of financial markets as well as changes that have a high probability of occurring in the future. Is the stock market at unusually high or low levels, and what is it likely to do in the next three months or year or five years?

A logical starting point in assessing the stock market is to analyze the economic factors that affect stock prices. Understanding the current and future state of the economy is the first step in understanding what is happening and what is likely to happen to the market.

The stock market is, of course, a significant and vital part of the overall economy. Clearly, a strong relationship exists between the two. If the economy is doing poorly, most companies will also be displaying poor performance, which will have an adverse effect on the stock market. Conversely, if the economy is prospering, most companies will also be doing well, and the stock market will reflect this economic strength.

Measures of Economic Activity

Gross Domestic Product (GDP) is the value of all goods and services produced in a country in a given year. It must equal gross domestic income, which will be the same as gross domestic expenditures. Income includes income earned by: labour (wages and salaries); business (corporate profits); lenders (interest); and government (taxes). Total expenditures is comprised of: consumer spending (C); investment in household residences, business investment in inventories and capital equipment (I); government spending (G); and foreigners' spending on Canadian exports (X) minus Canadians' spending on foreign imports (M). The following equation depicts GDP level:

$$GDP = G + C + I + (X - M)$$

Another measure of aggregate economic activity, Gross National Product (GNP), differs slightly from GDP. It is defined as the value of all goods and services produced by Canadian nationals, whether at home or abroad, and it is the preferred measure of economic activity in some countries.

For discussion purposes, we often think of the economy in terms of the **business cycle**. Investors are very concerned about whether the economy is experiencing an expansion or a contraction because stock prices will clearly be affected. This recurring pattern of expansion and contraction, referred to as the business cycle, is described in the section below.

Business Cycle
The recurring patterns of expansion, boom, contraction, and recession in the economy.

The Business Cycle

While the economy has grown over the long run, it typically fluctuates in a series of patterns referred to as business cycles. The business cycle reflects movements in economic activity as a whole, which is comprised of many diverse parts. The diversity of the parts ensures that business cycles are virtually unique, with no two parts identical. However, cycles do have a common framework, with a beginning (a trough), a peak, and an ending (another trough). Thus, economic activity starts in depressed conditions, builds up in the expansionary phase, and ends in a downturn, only to start again.

The five major phases of these cycles are:

1. **Expansion:** Normal growth stages are characterized by: stable inflation; rises in corporate profits; increased job start-ups and reduced bankruptcies; increasing inventories and investment by business to deal with increased demand; strong stock market activity; and, job creation and falling unemployment.
2. **Peak:** Demand has begun to outstrip economic capacity, causing inflationary pressures that lead to rising interest rates and falling bond prices. Investment and sales of durable goods falls, and eventually stock market activity and stock prices decline.
3. **Recession:** Often defined as two consecutive quarters of negative growth (although this definition is not used by Statistics Canada [StatsCan] or the US National Bureau of Economic Research [NBER]). StatsCan judges a recession by the depth, duration, and diffusion of the decline in business activity (i.e., the decline must be of significant magnitude, last longer than two months, and be spread throughout the entire economy). Table 15-1 demonstrates the length and severity of historical economic recessions in Canada since World War II.
4. **Trough:** Near the end of a recessionary period, falling demand and excess capacity lead to drops in prices and wages. The resulting decline in inflation leads to falling interest rates, which will begin to rally the economy.
5. **Recovery:** During this period GDP returns to its previous peak. It typically begins with a revival of purchases of interest rate sensitive items such as houses and cars, and then spreads throughout the entire economy. When GDP passes its previous peak, another expansion has begun.

The term "soft landing" refers to a business cycle phase that occurs when economic growth slows sharply but does not turn negative, while inflation falls or remains low. Regulatory authorities attempt to use policies at their disposal to prevent recessions and promote so-called soft landings, although these policies have not always met with a great deal of success.

Table 15-1

Post-War Periods of Economic Slowdown and Recession in Canada

Dates	Duration	Highest Unemployment Rate	Peak-to-Trough Decline in:		
			Real GNP	IPI	Employment
*June '51 – Dec. '51	7 months	3.6%	0.7%	3.6%	2.0%
*June '53 – June '54	13 months	5.2	3.1	3.2	1.8
*Feb. '57 – Jan. '58	12 months	6.5	0.5	5.0	2.0
*Apr. '60 – Jan. '61	10 months	7.7	1.7	4.4	1.0
†Feb. '70 – Sept. '70	8 months	6.7	0.5	2.4	0.3
*June '74 – Mar. '75	10 months	7.2	0.6	9.6	0.6
*Nov. '79 – June '80	8 months	7.8	1.9	5.5	0.6
*July '81 – Dec. '82	18 months	12.7	6.5	17.5	5.1
Apr. '90 – Mar. '92	23 months	11.5	3.6	7.3	3.5

*Recession as determined by Statistics Canada

IPI = Industrial Production Index

†Some economists feel that the February – September 1970 period should be regarded as a recession, breaking the expansion period from January 1961 to June 1974 into two segments.

Source: *Canadian Securities Course Textbook* (Toronto: Canadian Securities Institute, August 1998), p. 4-4. © 1998 Canadian Securities Institute. Reprinted with permission.

The business cycle in Canada has historically consisted of an expansion lasting between three and five years. Contractions generally last between six months and two years. However, these are only historical observations, and we cannot rely on them exclusively to interpret current or future situations. Business cycles cannot be neatly categorized as to length and turning points at the time they are occurring; such distinctions can be made only in hindsight.

To make good use of business cycle data, an investor needs to monitor indicators of the economy. A good source of help in this regard is StatsCan in Canada, and the National Bureau of Economic Research (NBER) in the US. StatsCan and the NBER attempt to identify those components of economic activity that move at different times from each other. Such variables can serve as indicators of the economy in general. Current practice involves the identification and monitoring of leading, coincident, and lagging composite indexes of general economic activity.

Leading indicators tend to peak and trough before the overall economy and provide useful tools for predicting the future direction of the economy. Some of the more important leading indicators include: housing starts (which precede construction); manufacturers new orders, especially for durables (which indicate expected consumer purchases); changes in profits (which generate a general mood of confidence or caution); spot commodity prices (which reflect demand for raw materials); average hours worked per week (which reflect demand for labour); stock prices (which reflect changing levels of profits); and money flows (which represent liquidity).

Statistics Canada's Composite Leading Indicator is an index that combines ten leading indicators, in order to predict future economic conditions. It is composed of:

1. The TSE 300 Composite Index
2. Real Money Supply (M1)
3. The United States Composite Leading Index
4. New Orders for Durable Goods
5. Shipments to Inventory Ratio — Finished Goods
6. Average Work Week
7. Employment in Business and Services
8. Furniture and Appliance Sales
9. Sales of Other Retail Durable Goods
10. Housing Spending Index.

Composite Leading Indicator
An index constructed by Statistics Canada that combines ten leading indicators, in order to predict future economic conditions.

Coincident indicators change at approximately the same time as the economy and are useful for identifying peaks and troughs after the fact. These include GDP, industrial production, personal income, and retail sales.

Lagging indicators change after the economy as a whole has changed. The most notable item is business investment spending. The unemployment rate, labour costs, inventory levels, and inflation levels are also classified as lagging indicators.

An increase in the composite leading indicator generally suggests that our economy will expand over the following three to 12 months, while a decrease indicates the likelihood of an immediate downturn. The coincident and lagging indicators serve to confirm (or negate) the indications of the leading series. If the leading index signal is not confirmed first by the coincident index and then by the lagging index, investors should reconsider the signal.

INVESTING *tip*

Why is the market a leading indicator of the economy? Basically, investors are discounting future earnings, because, as the valuation analysis in Chapter 13 (and the CSC Notes box in that chapter) showed, the value of stocks today is the discounted value of all future cash flows. Current stock prices reflect investor expectations of the future. Stock prices adjust quickly if investor expectations of corporate profits change. Of course, the market can misjudge corporate profits, resulting in a false signal about future movements in the economy. In other words, when an economic cycle peak or trough has occurred, we generally observe that the stock market had a major move up or down prior to the cycle turn. However, a major stock movement does not always mean a forthcoming business cycle turn.

An alternative explanation for stock prices leading the economy involves an investor change in the required rate of return, which again would result in an immediate change in stock prices. Note that the valuation model allows for a change in confidence (psychological elements) because that alters the required rate of return (in the opposite direction). These psychological elements are often useful in accounting for market movements.

The Stock Market and the Business Cycle

The relationship between the economy and the stock market is interesting — stock prices lead the economy. Historically, it is the most sensitive indicator of the business cycle. Therefore, we must deal with a complex relationship. The market and the economy are closely related, but stock prices tend to consistently turn before the economy. In other words, equity cycles (which were discussed in the CSC Notes box in Chapter 13) tend to lead business cycles. This is why the TSE 300 Composite Index is included in the composite leading index.

As with any indicator of the future, the stock market is not a perfect forecaster of future economic activity. While it remains an informative measure, it has also been known to provide false signals, and must be used with caution.

Has the Business Cycle Been Tamed?

As of April 1998, the Canadian and US economies had been expanding for more than six years. Both stock markets were hitting new highs day after day, with the TSE 300 reaching an all time high of 7822 and the Dow Jones Industrial Average (DJIA) having surpassed 9000. The Dow proceeded to set a record high of 9337 in July 1998. Some observers were asking if the business cycle was dead, based in part on the belief that slumps are not inevitable but rather are caused by accidents that happen. Also, as one CEO noted, "We are in a global economy ... that has changed the paradigm.... We don't see the cyclical events that characterized the past."[1]

The other side of the coin is that as the expansion continues people tend to forget the lessons learned from previous recessions. As one researcher on business cycles noted, "Who can eliminate herding?" referring to the tendency of people to get collectively carried away. In fact, by August 31, 1998 the TSE 300 had dropped to around 5530 (a decline of over 29 per cent from its high in April), while the DJIA had fallen to 7539 (a decline of over 19 per cent from its high in July). Ironically, most of these declines were attributed to turmoil in global markets, the very factor the CEO above saw as a stabilizing factor. At that time, analysts were still estimating positive economic growth for both economies, however, the growth estimates were revised downward. These forecasts turned out to be reasonably accurate, and both the US and Canadian economies grew at a reasonable pace through the later part of 1998 and the early part of 1999. By May 14, 1999 the DIJA had reached 10,913; however, the TSE 300 remained well below its previous record levels at 6,886. Only time will tell who is right in this debate.

Other Factors Affecting the Aggregate Economy

The Real-World Returns box below provides an interesting synopsis of some of the events affecting the Canadian economy and financial markets during the week of August 28, 1998. Global turmoil in Russia and several Asian countries contributed to instability in world currency and equity markets. Canada was hard hit as the Canadian dollar continued to set records for all time lows in terms of conversion into US dollars (at $0.6356 US).

The large decline in the Canadian dollar was partly attributed to nervous investors rushing to purchase US dollars, which were viewed as safer. This phenomenon is generally referred to as a "flight to quality." The other part of the decline in the dollar, and in Canadian equity markets, was attributable to the belief that world commodity prices were likely to fall even further, producing an adverse affect on the Canadian dollar. In response to this downward pressure on the dollar, the Bank of Canada increased the bank rate a full 100 basis points in an attempt to increase the attractiveness of the dollar to foreign and domestic investors. This interest rate increase met with little immediate success as the dollar slid even further. All of these items, taken together spelled bad news for the Canadian economy, which is reflected in the revised economic growth projections provided by the report.

Global Economic Factors

As the discussion above demonstrates, global factors play a major role in the Canadian economic environment. The state of the US economy is a very critical factor, since roughly 80 per cent of our exports go there, and around 75 per cent of our imports come from the US.

[1] This quotation and part of the discussion is based on J. M. Schlesinger, "The Business Cycle Is Tamed, Many Say, Alarming Some Others," *The Wall Street Journal*, November 15, 1996, pp. A1, A16.

REAL-WORLD RETURNS

TD Weekly Digest of Economic and Financial Developments Toronto, August 28, 1998

This week — which was characterized by continued volatility in global financial markets — culminated with a 100 basis-point-increase by the Bank of Canada on Thursday in an attempt to stem the headlong downward slide of the Canadian currency. The Canadian dollar had become increasingly immune to the Bank of Canada's policy — which had been in place for the past three weeks — of providing support to the currency through direct market intervention. The unexpected move by the central bank, which increased its target range for overnight funds by a full percentage point, to 5.5 – 6.0 per cent, was prompted by another round of heavy selling of the Canadian dollar that had sent the currency plummeting to 63.88 cents on Wednesday. Although the central bank's primary concern was to arrest the dollar's decline, signs of instability in domestic financial markets are also likely to have weighed heavily in the Bank of Canada's decision. Long-term bond yields had been climbing throughout this week, jumping by ten basis points on Wednesday alone, reflecting concerns that the dollar would continue to fall. This lifted Canadian long-term bond yields 40 basis points above their US counterparts — a far cry from the negative spread of −20 basis points recorded just over a month ago.

Dollar Roiled by Global Turmoil

The culprit behind the Canadian dollar's precipitous decline this week was once again to be found in the international arena, as political and economic problems in Russia added to the problems in Asia. President Boris Yeltsin sent shockwaves through world financial markets this week when he dismissed the entire Russian cabinet, creating a political vacuum in a country already in the midst of a financial crisis. Investor jitters were compounded when details of the restructuring of Russia's government debt were announced, indicating that international investors stood to lose as much as $33 billion US on the deal. At the same time, signs of deepening recessions in Asia continued to accumulate. The economies of Hong Kong, South Korea, and Malaysia each contracted by more than 5 per cent (annualized) in the second quarter, while the banking crisis in Japan apparently worsened, with current estimates of total bad loans outstanding now exceeding $1 trillion US. The combination of bleak economic prospects in Asia, and fears — albeit largely overblown — that Russia is poised to flood world commodity markets to raise funds, sent commodity prices (as measured by the CRB index) plunging to a 21-year low on Thursday.

What's Ahead for the Canadian Economy?

With the volatility in world financial markets likely to continue — and possibly intensify — in the weeks ahead, and commodity prices still declining, this week's increase in short-term interest rates is not likely to have permanently halted the Canadian dollar's slide. There are few indications that the increase in rates has accomplished the Bank of Canada's objectives. The Canadian dollar fell to a new low of 63.31 US cents after the Bank of Canada's move at Thursday's close, rebounding somewhat in Friday morning trading, while the Canada-US long-term bond spread remains above 40 basis points.

This week's rate hike has increased the risk of a significant slowdown in economic activity in Canada in the months ahead, especially in light of recent evidence that growth is already moderating substantially. Higher interest rates will serve to slow the economy further, by putting a damper on already-shaky consumer and business confidence. In addition, on Thursday, already-weak Canadian equity markets fell sharply following the central bank's move, as the TSE300 Index dropped by 6 per cent, and continued to fall on Friday morning. A further weakening of equity markets will also serve to increase unease among Canadian consumers and businesses.

ECONOMIC DEVELOPMENTS

Canada's Near-Term Economic Prospects Darken

In recent months, economic indicators have pointed to a notable slowdown in Canadian economic growth from the heady 4-per cent pace of 1997 and early 1998. Job growth has moderated sharply, retail sales growth has slackened, and manufacturing activity has been hit by the impact of low world commodity prices and strikes in the automotive and forestry sectors. The report on gross domestic product (GDP) for the second quarter — to be released on Monday — should confirm the softer pace of activity, with GDP growth unlikely to have exceeded 2.0 per cent (annualized). This week's rate hike by the Bank of Canada, combined with the ongoing turmoil in equity markets, will likely keep GDP on a slower growth path over the remainder of 1998 and in 1999.

Canadian Consumers Vulnerable

Although the Canadian economy is expected to continue to expand over the next few years, the risks of an economic downturn have increased. The greatest risk to the outlook lies with the consumer. Over the past few years, strong consumer spending has resulted in climbing personal debt burdens and shrinking personal savings rates, with individuals relying on rising equity prices to boost personal net worth. A combination of continued softness in job creation, weakness in stock markets, and the possibility of further rate hikes by the Bank of Canada would result in a major pullback in consumer spending.

The US Economy Remains Healthy

Amid all of the global economic uncertainty, investors were treated to some good news this week, as recent reports provided evidence that US domestic demand has remained strong in the third quarter of 1998. New orders for durable goods rose by 2.4 per cent in July, in spite of the negative effects of the GM strike, while existing home sales jumped by 4.0 per cent in the same month. These reports indicate that the US consumer, at least until now, has been largely immune to the Asian contagion. However, the second consecutive decline in the Conference Board's index of consumer confidence in August suggests that the recent turbulence in US stock markets — in part reflecting the deteriorating outlook for US corporate profits — is beginning to dampen the buoyant mood of consumers in the United States.

Source: "TD Weekly Digest of Economic and Financial Developments, August 28, 1998," TD Economics Section of TD Bank Financial Group Web site: <http://www.tdbank.ca/tdeconomics/archives/082898wd/wd828.htm>. © The Toronto-Dominion Bank. Reprinted with permission.

In addition to the US economy, Canada is particularly sensitive to world economic conditions because of the importance of commodity-based industries to our economy. According to StatsCan, these industries accounted for roughly half of all of Canada's merchandise exports in 1997, down from approximately 60 per cent in 1972. In particular, Canada's 1997 merchandise exports consisted of the following components: 28 per cent from raw materials, including farm goods, energy, and wood products (down from 38 per cent in 1972); 19 per cent from industrial goods, such as metals and chemicals which are made from natural resources (down from 22 per cent in 1972); 50 per cent from manufactured goods such as automobiles, auto parts, machinery, and consumer goods (up from 35 per cent in 1972); and 3 per cent from other sources.

Despite the trend toward reduced reliance on commodity-based industries, these industries continue to play a major role in Canada's economic performance. Many analysts suggest that the downward pressure exerted on the Canadian dollar was due to declining commodity prices, while its corresponding rebound in 1999 above $0.68 could be attributed to increasing commodity prices. The rationale is that global investors view the Canadian dollar as a "commodity currency," and its price will fall in response to falling commodity prices.[2] The fact that cyclical companies comprise a large proportion of the total market capitalization of the TSE 300 and the ME, while the VSE, ASE, and WSE are almost completely dominated by resource-based oil and mining companies, further highlights the importance of world commodity prices to the Canadian economy.

Interest Rates

The Real-World Returns box above focuses a great deal of discussion on the impact of interest rates on the economy. In fact, interest rates are probably the most important financial variables affecting securities markets, since they are essentially the price of credit, as determined by the forces of supply and demand.

High interest rates tend to:

1. Raise the cost of capital to firms, which reduces business investment.
2. Discourage consumer spending, particularly for durables.
3. Reduce disposable income available for net borrowers due to higher debt servicing charges.

Some key interest rate determinants include:

1. Inflation — rates rise to compensate lenders for loss in purchasing power as inflation rises.
2. Foreign developments and the exchange rate — foreign interest rates and the domestic exchange rate affect the demand for Canadian debt instruments.
3. Government deficits or increases in investment spending cause an increased demand for capital, which increases rates unless there is a corresponding increase in savings.
4. The greater the default risk of the borrower, the greater the rate that must be paid to borrow funds.
5. The Bank of Canada can influence short-term rates directly and may affect long-term rates less directly through its credibility of commitment to controlling inflation.

The Exchange Rate

The rapidly declining Canadian dollar was the primary cause of the bank rate increase discussed in the report above. The exchange rate affects the economy in several ways, most importantly through trade. All else being equal, a higher exchange rate tends to reduce Canada's trade balance. However, there are several other factors at work in determining the impact of a change in the exchange rate on trade. For example, if Canada has a lower inflation rate than the US, the affect of a higher exchange rate would be somewhat offset by Canada's lower costs.

[2] B. Little, "Commodities spur dollar woes," *The Globe and Mail*, December 15, 1997, pp. B1, B3.

The trade-weighted exchange rate measures the Canadian dollar's moves against ten major currencies (with about 80 per cent of the weight accounted for by the value of the US dollar). The following seven factors affect the exchange rate to varying degrees:

1. Inflation differentials — countries with lower inflation tend to appreciate through time to reflect their increased purchasing power relative to other countries.
2. Interest rate differentials — higher interest rates tend to attract more capital and make a currency value increase, provided the difference is not merely a reflection of higher inflation.
3. Current account — countries that continually run deficits will have excess demand for foreign currencies, which puts downward pressure on the domestic currency.
4. Economic performance — a strong economy attracts investment capital by offering higher returns and thus leads to more favourable exchange rates.
5. Public debt and deficits — countries with large debts are less attractive to foreign investors because: (i) they have higher incentive to allow inflation to grow (and repay in cheaper dollars); (ii) they rely more on foreign investment; and, (iii) debt accumulation affects the country's ability to repay.
6. Terms of trade — is the ratio of export prices to import prices, an increase in which suggests increased demand for the local currency.
7. Political stability — capital tends to exhibit a flight to quality, particularly in times of increased uncertainty, and instability exerts downward pressure on exchange rates. We saw evidence of this in the insert above, where the US dollar was appreciating against most world currencies, including Canada's.

Canada, like most countries, maintains a foreign exchange reserve, called the Exchange Fund Account, which belongs to the federal government and is managed by the Bank of Canada. It is comprised of foreign currencies (mainly US dollars), gold, and reserves in the IMF. For example, the value of these reserves as of July 31, 1998 was $22.5 billion US. This total amount consisted of $16.5 billion in US dollars (73 per cent of total), $2.9 billion in other currencies, $1 billion in special drawing rights, a $1.9 billion reserve position in the IMF, and $136 million in gold. This reserve is used to defend the value of the Canadian dollar in world currency markets. In recent years, Canada and most other countries whose currencies have been under downward pressure, have been relatively unsuccessful in preventing the downward trend in the value of their currency.

Inflation

Inflation is an important indicator for securities markets because it determines the speed at which the real value of investments are eroded. Inflation imposes several costs on an economy:

1. It erodes the standard of living for those on fixed income, which may aggravate social inequities.
2. It reduces the real value of investments such as loans, since they are paid back in dollars that are worth less.
3. It distorts signals to economy participants that are normally given through asset prices (since "relative" prices may be harder to establish).
4. Accelerating inflation may cause rising interest rates which may lead to recessionary periods.

The generally accepted measure of inflation is the Consumer Price Index (CPI), which tracks the price of a given typical basket of goods and services. It may overstate the true level of inflation by failing to capture improved quality of the basket and consumers' tendencies to switch to less expensive items in response to price increases for goods or services included in the basket. Inflation results from too much money chasing too few products. The output gap refers to the difference between the potential full capacity level of output and actual output. When actual output is near full capacity, increased demand will lead to inflation. A number of indicators are monitored for signs of changes in inflation including: commodity and wholesale prices; wage settlements; bank credit; and exchange rate movements.

Monetary economists argue that monetary supply is the main determinant of inflation, while non-monetarists argue that money supply increases in response to changes in demand and not vice versa. Standard measures of money supply used by the Bank of Canada include: (1) M1 — currency held outside the bank plus demand deposits less private sector float; (2) M2 — M1 plus personal savings deposits plus non-personal notice deposits; (3) M2+ — M2 plus deposits at trust companies and mortgage loan companies, credit unions, caisses populaires, plus money market mutual funds plus insurance annuities; and (4) M3 — M2 plus non-personal fixed term deposits plus foreign currency deposits of residents booked in Canada.

Unemployment

The unemployment rate represents the share of the workforce that is looking for, but hasn't found, employment. It may rise due to decreases in the number of people employed, to increases in the workforce, or both. There are two general types of unemployment: (1) cyclical —which arises due to temporary hirings or layoffs that may be attributable to business cycle influences; and (2) structural — which is caused by a variety of factors. Normal unemployment caused by people in transition between jobs is referred to as frictional unemployment. Other factors such as regulation and general economic health will contribute to the level of structural unemployment that will exist in an economy even if it is healthy. This level of unemployment is sometimes referred to as the natural or full employment unemployment rate.

The unemployment rate is an important factor in assessing economic performance because it affects consumer spending and overall investor confidence. Consumers will spend less, particularly for durable items, when unemployment levels are rising. On the other hand, as unemployment rates approach the full employment rate, upward pressure on wages creates inflationary strains for the economy.

Government Policies

The government of Canada has two general ways of attempting to influence general economic conditions — monetary policy and fiscal policy. Monetary policy refers to the use of interest rates, the exchange rate, and the rate of money supply growth to influence aggregate demand and the level of inflation. This function is performed by the Bank of Canada, as discussed in Appendix 11-B at the end of Chapter 11. Fiscal policy refers to the use of government taxation, spending, and deficits to affect growth. One of their generally accepted duties is to attempt to "smooth out" the business cycle by spending more and taxing less when the economy is weak. Fiscal policy is discussed in the CSC Notes box on the following page.

CSC NOTES

Fiscal Policy

Every year (usually in February), the finance minister presents the federal budget to the House of Commons for the coming fiscal year, which runs from April 1 to March 31. The budget contains projected revenues, spending, debt levels, and deficit levels for the coming year (and usually at least one additional year). An important part of the budget is the underlying economic assumptions on which the projections are based.

Fiscal policy affects the economy in four main ways:

1. **Spending:** Governments may purchase goods and services directly as they do when they construct new highways. Alternatively, they can provide direct transfers to citizens, as in the case with social security payments. Both methods increase the amount of spending in the economy, however, only the first kind of spending is included in GDP calculations.

2. **Taxes:** Taxes are levied in a variety of ways including: (i) direct taxes on the income of individuals and corporations; (ii) sales taxes, such as the GST; (iii) payroll taxes, which are levied as a share of wages; (iv) capital taxes, which are levied based on the size of a company's assets; and, (v) property taxes, levied on commercial and residential property. All taxes tend to discourage the type of activity being taxed. For example, income taxes reduce the incentive to work, capital taxes discourage capital investment by businesses, and sales taxes discourage consumer spending.

3. **Deficits or Surpluses:** A deficit occurs when spending exceeds revenues, and a surplus means spending is less than revenues. Generally, increasing deficits tend to stimulate the economy in the short run, while falling deficits generally do the opposite. This is because a rising deficit implies greater spending and/or lower taxes, and both of these actions tend to stimulate the economy. However, continually running a deficit over long periods of time can produce negative long-run consequences for an economy, as discussed below.

4. **Automatic Stabilizers:** These stabilizers automatically move counter to the business cycle. For example, the amount of unemployment insurance paid out rises with unemployment, while unemployment insurance premiums paid by individuals falls. As a result, the reduction in disposable income felt by the economy is not as great as it would be otherwise. Income taxes work similarly, falling as economic growth declines, thus lessening the tax burden for spenders in the economy. When the economy is growing, income taxes increase, which can reduce inflationary pressures to a certain extent.

Canada's failure to address deficits from the late 1970s through to the mid-1990s produced several negative consequences. The cost of interest payments grew to be the largest single expenditure of the federal government (26 per cent of GDP in 1994–95 versus 10 per cent in 1974–75). The combined debt of federal and provincial governments increased to 97 per cent of GDP in 1995 from 22 per cent in 1977.

In addition, during many periods in the past, fiscal policy has not been synchronized with monetary policy, which has increased the cost to the economy. For example, in the late 1980s, when there was strong economic growth, governments continued to run deficits, which fuelled inflation and lead to higher interest rates on borrowed funds. In the end, large debts restrict government's ability to run countercyclical policies, since it becomes costly (if not impossible) to continue to run large deficits to generate spending.

In recent years, Canada's federal and provincial governments have devoted a great deal of attention to eliminating fiscal deficits and paying down government debt. The 1997–98 federal budget was balanced for the first time since 1969–70, the 1998–99 budget was also balanced, and the 1999 federal budget predicted balanced budgets for 1999–2000 and 2000–01. This would mark the first time in almost 50 years that the federal government will have balanced its books for three or more consecutive years. Using comparable measures, Canada had the best fiscal balance among the Group of Seven (G7) countries in 1998.

The 1998 federal budget identified debt reduction as the government's major remaining fiscal challenge. The debt-to-GDP ratio began falling in 1997, and during the 1997–98 fiscal year it recorded its single largest decline since 1956–57, from 70.3 per cent in 1996–97, to 66.9 per cent. Declines in this ratio mean that economic growth began to outpace the growth of the debt, thereby reducing the burden of the debt on the economy. The debt-to-GDP ratio was projected to decline to 65.3 per cent in 1999–2000 and to just under 62 per cent in 2000–01. The 1998 and 1999 budgets proposed to put the debt-to-GDP ratio on a permanent downward track by using a two-track strategy: continued investments to support strong economic growth, and a debt repayment plan that will bring down the absolute level of the debt.

The Relationship between the Bond Market and the Stock Market

Investors today hear much talk about the relationship between bond and stock prices. What is the relationship, if any, and how does it affect stock investors?[3] Despite some claims to the contrary, historically bond and stock investors paid little attention to each other. However, the nature of the bond market has changed dramatically over time with the introduction of mortgage-backed and derivative securities of various types, the explosion of the federal debt in the 1980s, and the sharp swings in the inflation rate since the 1970s. Volatility has become pronounced in today's bond market.

Investors pay attention to the bond market because interest rates are available as a daily indicator of what is happening in the economy. The bond market provides signals of what bond traders and investors think about the economy. Bond traders react to news of unemployment, rising sales, or changes in the money supply, which affect interest rates and bond prices on a daily basis. Thus, in today's investment climate bond investors react to daily information about the economy, and the stock market, in turn, is affected.

Macroeconomic Forecasts of the Economy

Good economic forecasts are of significant value to investors. Since the economy and the market are closely related, good forecasts of macroeconomic variables can be very useful. A variety of economic indicators are released on a periodic basis, and are tracked closely by economists, market analysts and investors. Some are published daily in the financial newspapers, as in Figure 15-1 below, while others are released at periodic intervals, such as those included in Figure 15-2. Notice that these indicators represent a variety of measures of the items we have discussed above, including interest rates, foreign exchange rates, economic growth, inflation, unemployment, and US economic conditions.

Evidence regarding the success of economic forecasts is mixed. Although well-known forecasters tend to outperform statistical rules of thumb for macro variables, the margin of superiority is small. A major problem facing economic forecasters is the multitude of factors that must be monitored simultaneously. In addition, one of the most important factors influencing the economy in today's environment is the world financial and economic climate, which is difficult to monitor with accuracy. It is even more difficult to predict what will happen in tomorrow's global marketplace, which is facing constant political and economic uncertainty from a number of directions.

UNDERSTANDING THE STOCK MARKET

What Do We Mean by the Market?

How often have you heard someone ask, "How did the market do today?" or "How did the market react to that announcement?" Virtually everyone investing in stocks wants a general idea of how the overall market for equity securities is performing, both to guide their

[3] This discussion is indebted to L. Birinyi Jr., "Coping with volatility," *Forbes*, August 12, 1996, p. 164.

Figure 15-1
Statistical Trends

Market Economy	Period	Latest	% Change from	
			Prev.	Yr Ago
Gross domestic prod./seasn. adj., annual rate, 1992 $bln	May	710.0	−0.2	3.0
Merch. exports/seasonally adjusted, bal. of payments basis, $bln	June	26.0	0.1	5.7
Merch. imports/seasonally adjusted, bal. of payments basis, $bln	June	24.5	−0.8	10.6
Retail trade/seasonally adjusted, $bln	June	20.4	−1.7	4.0
	Period	**Latest**	**Prev.**	**Yr Ago**
Merch. trade balance/seasn.adj., bal. of paymnts basis, $mln	June	1,541.0	1,328.5	2,482.9
New car sales/seasonally adjusted, units, 000s	June	63.2	63.9	61.3
Housing starts/seasonally adjusted, annual rate, 000s	July	123	133	145
Unemployment rate/seasonally adjusted, %	July	8.4	8.4	9.0
Service employment/seasonally adjusted, mln	July	10.5	10.5	10.4
Goods-producing employment/seasonally adjusted, mln	July	3.7	3.8	3.6
Financial Economy	**Period**	**Latest**	**Prev.**	**Yr Ago**
Dollar/weekly average, Toronto noon, US cents	Last wk	64.07	65.26	72.07
Gold/weekly average, London afternoon fix, $US	Last wk	280.69	284.54	321.80
Money supply, narrow/M1, $bln, seasonally adjusted	July	85.2	83.8	76.3
Money supply, narrow/M-2, $bln, seasonally adjusted	July	405.3	403.7	405.5
Money supply, broad/M-3, $bln, seasonally adjusted	July	555.0	554.9	529.3
Business credit/seasonally adjusted, $bln	July	693.3	684.5	621.7
Household credit/seasonally adjusted, $bln	June	540.2	536.9	506.8
Treasury bills/Bank of Canada holdings, $bln	Last wk	13.1	12.9	15.4
Bonds/Bank of Canada holdings, $bln	Last wk	15.4	15.4	11.0
Cda Savgs bnds/othr retail instrmts/outstndg., $bln	Last wk	29.0	29.0	32.0
Government of Canada cash balances/$bln	Last wk	14.2	10.9	4.7
Bank of Canada rate/%	Aug. 27	6.00	5.00	3.50
Treasury bill yield/91-day, %	Aug. 18	4.88	5.07	2.99
Chartered bank prime rate/%	Aug. 26	6.50	6.50	4.75
Canada bond yield/weighted long-term average, %	Aug. 28	5.80	5.64	6.49
Corporate bond yield/weighted long-term average, %	Aug. 26	6.50	6.34	6.85
Prices	**Period**	**Latest**	**% Change from**	
			Prev.	**Yr Ago**
Consumer price index/1992 = 100	July	108.8	0.0	1.0
Industrial production price index/1992 = 100	July	119.5	0.3	0.3
Raw materials price index/1992 = 100	July	107.3	0.3	−15.4
US Economy	**Period**	**Latest**	**% Change from**	
			Prev.	**Yr Ago**
GDP/seasonally adjusted, annual rate, 1992 $bln (Revised)	2Q	7,494.9	0.4	3.6
Merch. exports/seasonally adjusted, f.a.s. basis, $bln	June	55.5	0.1	−3.7
Merch. imports/seasonally adjusted, c.v. basis, $bln	June	75.2	−2.4	5.1
Consumer price index/1982-1984 = 100/seasonally adjusted	July	163.3	0.2	1.7
	Period	**Latest**	**Prev.**	**Yr Ago**
Merch. trade balance/seasonally adjusted c.v. basis, $bln	June	−19.7	−21.5	−13.9
Unemployment rate/seasonally adjusted, %	July	4.5	4.5	4.9
Federal reserve discount rate/%	Last wk	5.00	5.00	5.00
Bank prime rate/%	Last wk	8.50	8.50	8.50
Money supply, narrow/M-1, $bln, seasonally adjusted	Last wk	N/A	1,062.6	1,072.0
Money supply, narrow/M-2, $bln, seasonally adjusted	Last wk	N/A	4,233.3	3,958.9
Money supply, broad/M-3, $bln, seasonally adjusted	Last wk	N/A	5,676.4	5,213.4

Data Sources — Bank of Canada: bank and Treasury bill rates, business and household credit, and money supply. Canada Mortgage and Housing Corp.: housing starts. ScotiaMcLeod Ltd.: Canada and corporate bond yields. Statistics Canada: employment, exports, imports, gross domestic product, new car sales, price indexes, retail trade, trade balance, and unemployment rate. US statistics supplied by Dow Jones Telerate Canada and Datastream.

Source: "Statistical Trends," *The Globe and Mail / Report on Business*, August 31, 1993, p. B7. Reprinted with permission from *The Globe and Mail.*

Figure 15-2
The Numbers

Coming this week

Indicator	Day	Period	Previous	Forecast*
Canadian economy:				
GDP at market cost	Mon	Q2	+0.8%	+0.4%
-balance of payments			($3.85-bn)	($4.38-bn)
-implicit price deflator			−0.1%	−0.2%
GDP at factor cost	Mon	June	−0.2%	−0.3%
Help-wanted index	Wed	Aug	144	145
Int'l reserves	Thu	Aug	$22.52-bn	$17.86-bn
Building permits	Fri	July	+1.4%	+1.2%
Unemployment rate	Fri	Aug	8.4%	8.4%
-employment growth			+27,000	+35,000
US economy:				
New home sales	Mon	July	935,000	916,000
Purchasing managers survey	Tue	Aug	49.1	50.5
Construction spending	Tue	July	+1.7%	+0.3%
Leading indicators	Tue	July	−0.2%	+0.3%
Factory orders	Wed	July	+0.1%	+1.5%
Productivity (revision)	Wed	Q2	−0.2%	unch
Unemployment rate	Fri	Aug	4.5%	4.5%
-non-farm payrolls			+66,000	+350,000

Reported last week

Indicator	Period	Actual	Change
Canadian economy:			
Net foreign investment	June	+$414-mn	
Industrial price index	July	119.5	+0.3%
-raw materials index		107.3	+0.3%
Average weekly earnings (yr/yr)	June	$603.18	+0.8%
-number of employees (mth/mth)		11.56-mn	−0.2%
US economy:			
Consumer confidence	Aug	133.1	−4.1
Existing home sales (annual rate)	July	4.93-mn	+4.0%
Durable goods orders	July	$187.51-bn	+2.4%
GDP (preliminary)	Q2	$7.495-tn	+1.6%
-price index		112.55	+0.8%
Personal income	July	$7.14-tn	+0.5%
-consumption		$5.80-tn	−0.2%

*Thomson Global Markets consensus forecast

Source: "The Numbers," *The Globe and Mail / Report on Business*, August 31, 1998, p. B2. Statistics Canada, *Canadian Economic Observer*, Catalogue No. 11-010.

actions and to act as a benchmark against which to judge the performance of their securities. Furthermore, several specific uses of market measures can be identified, as discussed in the next section.

When most investors refer to the "market," they mean the stock market in general as proxied by some market index or indicator. Because the market is simply the aggregate of all security prices, it is most conveniently measured by some index or average of stock prices.

As we know from Chapter 4, the most frequently referred to market index in Canada is the TSE 300 Composite Index, which tracks the 300 largest stocks trading on the Toronto Stock Exchange. This index tracks the movement of the TSE as a whole, which in turn accounts for close to 90 per cent of the dollar volume traded on Canadian stock exchanges. When we refer to the market in Canada, we are usually referring to the TSE 300 Index. Other Canadian indexes include the Canadian Market Portfolio Index (XXM), which mirrors the performance of the Montreal Exchange, and the VSE Composite Index, which tracks the performance of the Vancouver Stock Exchange.

In the US, the two most frequently used indicators of market activity are the Dow Jones Industrial Average and the S&P 500 Composite Index (which is favoured by most institutional investors and money managers). A commonly used index of world equity market activity is the Morgan Stanley World Index, which consists of 2,700 stocks from 22 developed countries, with the stocks comprising over 60 per cent of the market capitalization of each country.

Uses of Market Measures

Market measures tell investors how all stocks in general are doing at any time or give them a feel for the market. Many investors are encouraged to invest if stocks are moving upward, whereas downward trends may induce some to liquidate their holdings and invest in money market assets or funds.

The historical records of market measures are useful for gauging where the market is in a particular cycle and may also provide insight into what will happen in the future. Assume, for example, that the market has never fallen more than X per cent, as measured by some index, in a six-month period. Although this information is no guarantee that such a decline will not occur, this type of knowledge aids investors in evaluating their potential downside risk over some period of time.

Market measures are useful to investors in quickly judging their overall portfolio performance. Because stocks tend to move up or down together, the rising or falling of the market will generally indicate to the investor how he or she is likely to do. Of course, to determine the exact performance, each investor's portfolio must be measured individually, a topic to be discussed in Chapter 22.

Technical analysts need to know the historical record of the market when they are seeking out patterns from the past that may repeat in the future. Detection of such patterns is the basis for forecasting the future direction of the market using technical analysis, which is discussed in Chapter 18.

Market indexes are also used to calculate betas, an important measure of risk discussed in earlier chapters. An individual security's returns are regressed on the market's returns in order to estimate the security's beta or relative measure of systematic risk.

The Determinants of Stock Prices

How are stock prices determined? In Chapter 13, we established the determinants of stock prices using the Dividend Discount Model (DDM) — dividends and the required rate of return — and, using the P/E ratio model — earnings and the P/E ratio. Although these are the ultimate determinants of stock prices, a more complete model of economic variables is desirable when we are attempting to understand the stock market. Such a model is shown in Figure 15-3, which is a flow diagram of stock-price determination described by US Federal Reserve economist, Michael Keran in 1971. It indicates the variables that interact to determine stock prices. Although nearly three decades old, this model remains a useful description of the conceptual nature of stock-price determination then, now, and for the future.

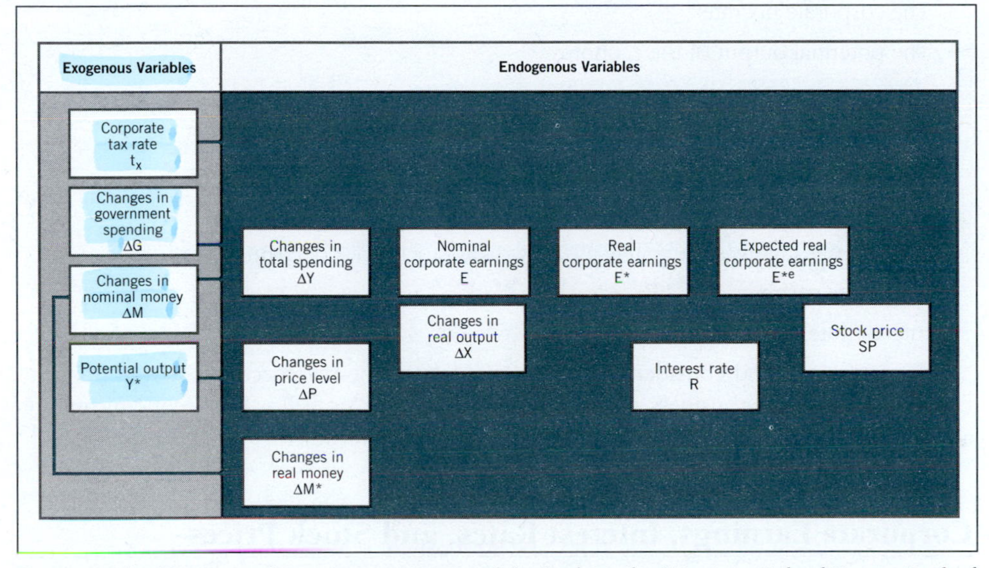

Figure 15-3
A Flow Diagram of Stock Price Determination

Source: Michael W. Keran, "Expectations, Money and the Stock Market," Review, *Federal Reserve Bank of St. Louis, January 1971, p. 27. Reprinted with permission.*

Figure 15-3 shows four exogenous (independent) variables that ultimately affect stock prices: the potential output of the economy (Y^*), which is a non-policy variable, and three policy variables (i.e., variables subject to government policy decisions) — the corporate tax rate (t_x), changes in government spending (G), and changes in nominal money supply (M). All variables to the right of the gray area are determined within the economy and are called endogenous (dependent) variables.

The two primary exogenous policy variables, G and M, affect stock prices through two channels:

1. They affect total spending (Y), which, together with the tax rate (t_x), affects corporate earnings.[4] Expected changes in (real) corporate earnings (E^*) are positively related to changes in stock prices (SP).

[4] Technically, both the current level and lagged changes in Y affect corporate earnings.

2. They affect total spending, which, together with the economy's potential output (Y^*) and past changes in prices, determine current changes in prices (P). Y and P determine current changes in real output (X). Changes in X and P generate expectations about inflation and real growth, which in turn influence the current interest rate (R). Interest rates, a proxy for the discount rate in a valuation model, have a negative influence on stock prices (SP).

The Keran model remains a classic description of stock-price determination because it indicates the major factors that determine stock prices. In this model, the active policy variables below affect three changes in the economy:

1. Fiscal policy (government spending)
2. Monetary policy (money supply)
3. The corporate tax rate
4. The potential output of the economy.

The corresponding changes in the economy are:

1. Total spending
2. Price level
3. Real money.

These three changes ultimately affect two key stock price determinants:

1. Corporate earnings
2. Interest rates.

Investors can find considerable information about the macroeconomy from financial newspapers, and other business and economics publications, as well as from economic reports and forecasts prepared by financial institutions and the government.

Corporate Earnings, Interest Rates, and Stock Prices

As the Keran model in Figure 15-3 shows, the ultimate determinants of stock prices are expected corporate earnings and interest rates (which serve as a proxy for investors' required rate of return). Empirical evidence supports this assertion. For example, Fama found that almost 60 per cent of the variance in annual US market returns for the period 1953 to 1987 was explained by changes in industrial production and interest rate factors.[5] Chen, Roll, and Ross identified the following economic factors that are likely to influence stock returns: expected and unexpected inflation; the term structure of interest rates; industrial production; returns on stock market indexes; the risk premium on bonds; consumption prices; and oil prices.[6] Their study found that unexpected inflation, the slope of the term structure, industrial production, and the risk premium on bonds are significant predictors of stock returns. Otuteye obtained similar results for 100 Canadian stocks over the 1970–84 period.[7] In particular, he finds that these four variables have predictive power, in addition to the market index.

While the Keran diagram and the DDM were formulated many years ago, the modern explanation of stock prices remains the same. Stocks rise strongly as expected earnings (and

[5] E. Fama, "Stock Returns, Expected Returns, and Real Activity," *Journal of Finance* 45 (September 1990), pp. 1098–1108.

[6] N. Chen, R. Roll and S. Ross, "Economic Forces and the Stock Market," *Journal of Business* 59 (July 1986), pp. 383–403.

[7] E. Otuteye, "How Economic Forces Explain Canadian Stock Returns," *Canadian Investment Review* 4 (Spring 1991), pp. 93–99.

dividends) climb and interest rates stay low. In other words, investors must be concerned with expected earnings, growth in earnings (and dividends), and interest rates as they assess the outlook for stocks.

It is logical to expect a close positive relationship between corporate profits and stock prices. The valuation discussion in Chapter 13 and the CSC Notes box in that chapter showed that the estimated value for one stock or the market as a whole should be a function of the expected stream of benefits to be received (cash flows) and the required rate of return demanded by investors. Therefore, if the economy is prospering, investors will expect corporate earnings and dividends to rise and, other things being equal, stock prices to follow. Historical evidence suggests this relationship holds — strong earnings performance is generally positively related to strong stock market performance.

Recall that two factors determine the price or value of the market (or a single stock) — earnings and a P/E ratio (multiplier). Other things often are not equal — earnings may rise, but the discount rate may also rise, leading to a decline in the multiplier, which, if strong enough, can cause a decline in stock prices. In some years, stock prices may rise sharply while corporate profits decline significantly. The reason is that the discount rate declines, resulting in an increase in the multiplier.

INVESTING tip

If interest rates rise, the riskless rate of return, RF, rises, because it is tied to interest rates, and other things being equal, the required rate of return (discount rate) rises because the riskless rate is one of its two components.

Interest rates represent the other key variable determining stock prices. This is because they are a basic component of discount rates, as shown in Figure 15-3, with the two usually moving together. There is clearly a relationship between interest rate movements and stock prices just as there is with GDP and corporate profits. In this case, however, the relationship is inverse; that is, as interest rates rise, stock prices fall (or vice versa), other things being equal. This is why analyst recommendations go to such great lengths to incorporate interest rate forecasts into their stock or portfolio recommendations.

Why is there an inverse relationship? Remember from Chapter 13 that the basic fundamental valuation model is given by the following equation (assuming the constant-growth version of the dividend valuation model):

$$P_0 = \frac{D_1}{k - g} \tag{15-1}$$

The k in Equation 15-1 is the required rate of return (discount rate) that investors use in discounting future cash flows. It is the rate of return that investors demand in order to invest in common stocks. This rate can be thought of as the sum of a riskless rate of interest plus a risk premium determined by the riskiness of the stock being valued. Most observers use the rate on government T-bills as a proxy for the riskless rate of return, because they have no practical risk of default and very little maturity risk. Therefore, the discount rate k is intimately tied to interest rates. That is why the Keran model (and others) refer to interest rates in discussing stock-price determination.

Like most relationships involving investing, the relationship between interest rates and stock prices is not exact. It is difficult to estimate the exact impact on stock prices because so many other things are happening simultaneously. This is illustrated in the newspaper article entitled "Rates rise, stocks plunge," included in the Real-World Returns box below. In the article, a chief bank strategist, David Marshall, attributes about half of a recent stock market plunge to increased interest rates and the remainder to "global pessimism in financial markets."

REAL-WORLD RETURNS

Rates Rise, Stocks Plunge

The widening global financial turmoil drove interest rates sharply higher and bloodied investors yesterday, while moves by the central bank failed to halt the Canadian dollar's free fall.

The Bank of Canada moved aggressively to shore up the beleaguered dollar with a hike in the bank rate of a full percentage point to 6 per cent, but the positive effect was short-lived.

Although the Bank of Canada's intervention at first caused the dollar to surge almost one-third of a cent, the gain didn't last, prompting heavy buying of the currency at several levels in foreign-exchange markets to try to halt the slide.

By the end of trading, the dollar had dipped to the fifth record low in as many days. The currency has lost almost two US cents in the past five days.

"It's utter bedlam," David Marshall, chief strategist at ABN-Amro Bank, said of Canadian stocks, bonds, and the currency. "It's kind of a disaster right across the board."

Worst Days on the Stock Markets

Dow Jones Industrial Average			
Date	**The Drop**		**The Next Day**
Oct. 27, 1997	554.26 pts.	7.2%	Up 337.17
Oct. 19, 1987	508.00	22.6	Up 102.27
Yesterday	357.36	4.2	—
Aug. 4, 1998	299.43	3.4	Up 59.47
Aug. 15, 1997	247.37	3.1	Up 108.70

TSE 300 Composite			
Date	**The Drop**		**The Next Day**
Oct. 27, 1997	434.25 pts.	6.2%	Up 137.07
Oct. 19, 1987	407.20	11.3	Down 214.10
Yesterday	372.84	6.0	—
Oct. 26, 1987	232.90	7.6	Up 29.60
Aug. 4, 1998	227.10	3.3	Up 26.65

Source: Datastream and Globe and Mail calculations. Douglas Coull/ The Globe and Mail

About half of the selling in Canadian markets was triggered by the bank-rate increase, the rest by the global pessimism in financial markets, Mr. Marshall said.

Commodity prices also collapsed, hitting 21-year lows, especially for grains, metals, and energy futures. The spot price of gold fell $5.50 to a 19-year low of $276.70.

"Predictably, the Bank of Canada's 100-basis-point hike today has been an abject failure in the face of an onslaught of selling pressures from crumbling commodity prices," said Jeff Rubin, chief economist at CIBC Wood Gundy. "The bank has gambled and the economy has lost." A basis point is one one-hundredth of a percentage point.

The interest-rate increase is expected to shave more than half a percentage point from economic growth in the next four quarters, and caused Wood Gundy to lower its forecast for economic growth over the next four quarters to 2.3 per cent from 2.9 per cent.

In its statement, the central bank said the increase was aimed at "providing support for the Canadian dollar in order to bolster confidence," and to sustain the present non-inflationary expansion of the economy.

Economists have become increasingly worried that the falling dollar would result in higher prices for imported food and manufactured goods.

Although the increase in the bank rate was hefty, it paled beside the 193-point increase in the fall of 1992 during the federal referendum on constitutional reform.

Bob White, president of the Canadian Labour Congress, slammed the interest-rate rise as "a false solution that is worse than the problem of a falling dollar.

"...Given that job creation has been virtually at a halt in recent months, despite the stimulus of a lower dollar, this increase in rates is highly likely to tip us into a recession," he said. "And it may well not even work to put an end to destructive speculation against the currency."

Allowing the dollar to fall gradually in recent weeks was the right policy, Mr. White said, since a lower dollar has helped cushion Canadian jobs against the impacts of a growing global crisis and has not sparked higher inflation.

Other critics of the central bank's move pointed to the failure of Norway to halt the slide in the krone, even with two interest-rate increases that lifted borrowing costs a total of 250 basis points since August 21. The krone has fallen 9 per cent against the US dollar despite the rate hikes.

Speaking to reporters in Montreal, Finance Minister Paul Martin said Canada is being hurt by a nervous and uncertain international scene.

"I very much share the concerns of Canadians about the decline of our Canadian dollar. But it is by managing our affairs prudently that we provide the best encouragement for a recovery in our currency once the international situation calms down."

"For some time now, commodity prices have been declining because of the Asian and Russian problems," Mr. Martin said. "Obviously, our currency isn't immune to this because 35 per cent of our exports are commodity-based, down from 60 per cent in the early 1980s."

"While these are turbulent times — and we have no choice but to deal with them — we must not lose sight of the fact that Canada is strongly positioned to weather the storm."

Mr. Martin defended the Bank of Canada, saying that the dollar still performed better than the currencies of other countries whose economies rely heavily on commodities, such as Australia and Norway.

"What the Bank of Canada must do — and I support this completely — is to act to maintain order and calm to the best extent possible on currency markets." Mr. Martin said.

Although many business analysts were highly critical of the Bank of Canada's rate increase, some economists supported the move.

"The bank did the right thing; they had no choice," said Sherry Cooper, chief economist at Nesbitt Burns Inc., one of the harshest critics of the Bank of Canada for staying on the sidelines watching the currency slide all summer.

"Where would the currency be if they hadn't raised rates?"

But with much uncertainty around the world, she added, the slide is far from over. "I'm afraid to wake up in the morning because there's a new calamity night after night."

Warren Jestin, chief economist at Bank of Nova Scotia, also supported the central bank's rate increase as a damage-control measure to bolster the dollar.

But the move was "totally swamped" by international forces, he said. "the best time for central banks to intervene is when there is relative tranquillity" in the market.

At one point yesterday, the dollar dipped as low as 63.13 cents.

Mr. Jestin said he expects the US Federal Reserve to cut interest rates within days, in the face of slower consumer spending and falling corporate profits.

Source: Excerpted from Marian Stinson, "Rates Rise, Stocks Plunge," The Globe and Mail, *August 28, 1998, pp. A1, A8. Reprinted with permission from* The Globe and Mail.

Investors need to understand the role of changes in interest rates in affecting investor expectations. Investors pay close attention to announcements by the Bank of Canada and the US Federal Reserve that could possibly affect interest rates, as well as to any other factors that may play a role. In turn, the popular press reports possible changes in interest rates as they might affect the stock market.

VALUING THE MARKET

To value the market using the approaches described in Chapter 13, we must refer to the primary variables used in fundamental analysis. Specifically, we focus our analysis on the expected cash flows (dividends) and the rate of return required by investors (or, alternatively, a multiplier or P/E ratio). The following estimates are needed:

1. Dividends or earnings
2. The required rate of return or the earnings multiplier.

These estimates are used in Equations 15-1, 15-2, and 15-3 and were explained in Chapter 13:

$$P_0 = \frac{D_1}{k - g} \tag{15-1}$$

$$P_0 / E_1 = \frac{D_1 / E_1}{k - g} \tag{15-2}$$

$$P_0 = P_0 / E_1 \times E_1 \tag{15-3}$$

where
P_0 = present market value
D_1 = expected dividends
E_1 = expected earnings
k = discount rate or required rate of return
g = expected growth rate in dividends or earnings

These equations apply equally to the aggregate market or individual stocks or portfolios. Here we are concerned with an aggregate market index such as the TSE 300 Composite Index. Conceptually, the value of this index is the discounted value of all future cash flows to be paid (i.e., the index value of dividends). Alternatively, it is the estimated earnings on the TSE 300 Index multiplied by the estimated forward P/E ratio, or multiplier.[8] In summary,

$$\text{Value of TSE 300 today} = \frac{\text{Dividends to be paid on index next period}}{\text{Required rate of return} - \text{Expected growth rate in dividends}}$$

or

$$\text{Value of TSE 300} = \text{Estimated earnings on the index} \times \text{Estimated forward P/E ratio}$$

We focus our discussion below on the multiplier approach.

The Earnings Stream

Estimating earnings for a market index for a future period is not an easy task. Several steps are involved. The item of interest is the earnings per share for a market index or, in general, corporate profits after taxes. The latter variable is related to GDP, since corporate earnings after taxes are derived from corporate sales, which in turn are related to GDP.

[8] Notice that Equation 15-3 uses the "forward" P/E ratio (P_0 / E_1) and an estimate of future earnings (E_1) to estimate today's price. This differs from the "trailing" P/E ratio (P_0 / E_0), which is the one usually reported in financial newspapers, analyst reports, and other stock-related reports.

A detailed fundamental analysis would involve estimating each of these variables, starting with GDP, then corporate sales, working down to corporate earnings before taxes, and finally to corporate earnings after taxes. Each of these steps can involve various levels of difficulty, as the following points suggest.

- To move from GDP to corporate sales, it may be possible to use a regression equation with percentage change in GDP as the independent variable and percentage change in corporate sales as the dependent variable. Based on this regression equation, a prediction could be made of sales given a forecast of change in GDP.
- To obtain corporate earnings after tax, it is necessary to estimate a net profit margin, which is a volatile series. After estimating the gross profit margin, multiplying by the sales (per share) would provide an estimate of earnings before depreciation and taxes. Both factors would have to be computed and deducted to obtain an estimate of expected earnings (per share) for the coming year.[9]

For a per share perspective of earnings for the market, consider Table 15-2, which shows prices, earnings, and other selected variables for the TSE 300 Index for the 1986–97 period. The table reports trailing P/E ratios (P_0 / E_0) for the TSE 300, which are determined by dividing the year-end index value by the most recent 12-month earnings (adjusted to the index). Notice that while earnings for the TSE 300 increased over the entire period, the amounts varied, and the percentage changes from year to year can be quite sharp.

Table 15-2

Prices, Earnings, Dividends, and Market Ratios (in Index Form) for the TSE 300 Composite Index, 1986–97

					Based on Year-End Prices		
Year	End-of-Year Index Value (Prices)	Earnings	Dividends	TR (%)[a]	P/E[b]	Dividend Yield (D/P) %	Dividend Payout
1986	3066.18	176.31	91.67	—	17.39	2.99	0.5199
1987	3160.05	220.67	97.32	6.23	14.32	3.08	0.4410
1988	3381.75	312.83	113.96	10.62	10.81	3.37	0.3643
1989	3969.79	268.41	129.01	21.28	14.79	3.25	0.4806
1990	3256.75	202.37	124.90	−14.81	16.09	3.83	0.6172
1991	3512.36	76.63	111.93	11.29	45.83	3.19	1.4606
1992	3350.44	21.40	102.34	−1.69	156.56	3.05	4.7822
1993	4321.43	34.68	97.81	31.90	124.61	2.26	2.8204
1994	4213.61	194.62	100.76	−0.16	21.65	2.39	0.5177
1995	4713.54	342.27	107.44	14.41	13.77	2.28	0.3139
1996	5927.03	245.04	108.63	28.05	24.19	1.83	0.4433
1997	6699.44	293.05	110.27	14.89	22.86	1.65	0.3763

[a] $TR (\%) = \frac{(P_t - P_{t-1} + D_t)}{P_{t-1}} \times 100$

[b] P/E is end-of-year price dividend by earnings during the most recent calendar year, which is referred to as the trailing P/E ratio (P_0 / E_0). The reported dividend yield is calculated similarly.

Source: *TSE Annual Review* for the years 1986 to 1997.

[9] An alternative is to estimate a gross profit margin by considering those factors that affect the gross margin, including unit labour costs, the utilization rate of plant and equipment, and the inflation rate.

The Multiplier

The multiplier to be applied to the earnings estimate is as important as the earnings estimate. Investors sometimes mistakenly ignore the multiplier and concentrate only on the earnings estimate.

Table 15-2 shows that the multiplier is even more volatile than the earnings component and is therefore even more difficult to predict. For example, the trailing P/E ratios in Table 15-2 vary from a low of 10.81 in 1988, to a high of 156.56 in 1992. The volatility in P/E ratios is likely to be even greater for individual stocks. The average trailing P/E multiple for the TSE 300 over the 12-year period reported in Table 15-2 is 40.24, however this is a misleading summary statistic due to the impact of the 1992 and 1993 multipliers, which exceed 100. These extreme multipliers are relatively uninformative since they exceed 100 as a result of extremely low corporate profits in those years. Two more meaningful summary statistics for the TSE 300 P/E ratio over this period are the 12-year median of 19.52 and the ten-year average excluding the two extreme multiples exceeding 100 of 20.17.

The lesson from this evidence is that investors cannot simply extrapolate P/E ratios, because dramatic changes occur over time. P/E ratios tend to be high when inflation and interest rates are low, such as 1996 and 1997. When earnings are growing and the upward profit trend appears sustainable, investors are willing to pay more for today's earnings. In addition, investors must be careful when using P/E ratios to place them in the proper context. This is because P/E ratios can refer to historical data (such as the trailing ratios included in Table 15-2), to an average for a given period, or to a future period such as the year ahead.

Putting the Two Together

Obviously, valuing the aggregate market is not easy, nor will it ever be, because it involves estimates of the uncertain future. If valuing the aggregate market were relatively easy, many investors would become wealthy by knowing when to buy and sell stocks.

As noted, it is difficult to analyze all the complicated details required to perform fundamental market analysis. It involves studying utilization rates, tax rates, depreciation, GDP, and other factors, as well as applying some sophisticated statistical techniques. It is instructive, however, to analyze some general results of our basic valuation techniques. Regardless of the difficulty in doing market analysis and the extent to which an analyst or investor goes, the methodology outlined above is the basis on which to proceed.

As an example of conceptually explaining the market, consider the information in Table 15-2, keeping in mind that these are end-of-year values for the TSE 300 Composite Index. Be very careful to understand what will be done here. We are going to "explain" the market in hindsight, based on year-end values. We will interpret what *did* happen, which is always much easier than predicting what *will* happen in the future. To value the market in actuality, an investor must forecast the two components of value — earnings and P/E ratios. Nevertheless, the reasoning process we will use is helpful in understanding how to value the market.

First, consider what happened to the market in 1988. Earnings on the TSE 300 Composite Index increased substantially to 312.83 from 220.67 in 1987 (an increase of approximately 42 per cent). As one would expect, market prices increased to 3381.75 in 1988 from 3160.05 in the previous year. This occurred despite increases in interest rates across the entire yield curve, which contributed to a decline in the trailing P/E ratio from 14.32 to

10.81. Thus, for 1988, the positive impact of the increase in profits outweighed the negative impact of an increase in interest rates and a decline in the P/E multiple.

Now let's consider the market performance in 1994. Earnings increased substantially from the abnormally low 1993 level of 34.68 to 194.62. However, interest rates rose across the entire yield curve, and investors became increasingly concerned about future profitability. As a result, the required rate of return demanded by investors rose, which had a negative impact on the P/E ratio. Thus, despite a 461 per cent increase in earnings, stock prices actually declined slightly, from 4321.43 to 4213.54, because the steep decline in the multiplier more than offset the increase in earnings for the year. The important point of this analysis is that at the beginning of 1994, an investor trying to value the market for the year ahead had to estimate what was likely to happen to the earnings stream for the market and to the P/E ratio (or discount rate). Estimating the earnings is only half the story and the less important half in many cases.

The conclusion of this analysis is that to value the market, an investor must analyze both factors that determine value: earnings (or dividends) and multipliers (or required rates of return). More important, the investor must make some type of prediction of these variables in order to forecast the market. We turn to this issue now.

FORECASTING CHANGES IN THE MARKET

Most investors want to forecast changes in financial markets. Not only do they want to know what these markets are doing currently and why, but also where they are likely to go in the future. Part of this process requires an analysis of the overall economy, as discussed earlier.

Accurate forecasts of the stock market, particularly short-term forecasts, are impossible for anyone to do consistently. Chapter 10 provided substantial evidence that the market is efficient, which means that future changes in the market cannot be predicted on the basis of past information. The available evidence on the performance success of professional investors supports the proposition that even professional money managers cannot consistently forecast the market using available information. Such implications are supported by a wealth of anecdotal data.

What investors should search for are clues as to the economy and the market's general direction and the duration of a likely change. For example, to say that we are confident the market will go to 5000 or 7000 (as measured by the TSE 300 Composite Index) one year from now is foolish. Similarly, a strong prediction that corporate earnings will rise or fall next year by 10 per cent is a prescription for embarrassment.

In truth, most individual investors — indeed, most professional investors — cannot time the market consistently, as discussed in Chapter 10 and Chapter 14. What, then, should they do? The best approach for most investors is to accept that fact but also to recognize that periodically situations will develop that may warrant portfolio adjustments.

Some evidence suggests that investors lose more by missing a bull market than they gain by dodging a bear market. This point was raised in Chapter 14, which showed that investors who were fully invested in the S&P 500 over the 1986–95 period would have received a 14.8 per cent annual return. However, had they missed the best 10 days, the return would have fallen to 10.2 per cent, and if they had missed the best 40 days, the return would have fallen to a mere 2.5 per cent. The most important point of this discussion is the same as before — the impact of the overall market on an investor's portfolio is enormous.

Using the Business Cycle to Make Market Forecasts

In his 1990 study of US stock returns between 1953 and 1987, Fama found that expected security returns exhibit a clear business cycle pattern.[10] They are high when times have been poor and improvement is anticipated and are lower when economic conditions are strong. Earlier we established the idea that certain composite indexes can be helpful in forecasting or ascertaining the position of the business cycle. However, stock prices are one of the leading indicators, tending to lead the economy's turning points, both peaks and troughs.

What is the investor who is trying to forecast the market to do? This leading relationship between stock prices and the economy must be taken into account in forecasting likely changes in stock prices. Stock prices generally decline in recessions, and the steeper the recession, the steeper the decline. However, investors need to think about the business cycle's turning points months before they occur in order to have a handle on the turning points in the stock market. If a business cycle downturn appears likely in the future, the market will also turn down some months ahead of the economic downturn.

As discussed in the CSC Notes box in Chapter 13, we can be somewhat more precise about the leading role of stock prices. Because of their tendency to lead the economy, total returns on stocks (on an annual basis) are often negative in years in which the business cycle peaks, due to increasing inflationary pressures, and the corresponding upward pressure on interest rates and downward pressure on future profits. Similarly, stock prices have almost always risen as the business cycle is approaching a trough, as inflation and interest rates decline, and expectations of future profits rise. These increases have been large, so that investors do well during these periods. Furthermore, stock prices often remain steady or even decline suddenly as the business cycle enters into the initial phase of recovery. After a previous sharp rise or as the peak is approached, a period of steady prices or even a decline typically occurs. The economy, of course, is still moving ahead.

Based on the above analysis an investor can do the following:

1. If the investor can recognize the bottoming out of the economy before it occurs, a market rise can be predicted, at least based on past experience, before the bottom is hit.
2. As the economy recovers, stock prices may level off or even decline. Therefore, a second significant movement in the market may be predictable, again based on past experience.
3. Based on previous economic slumps, the market P/E usually rises just before the end of the slump and remains relatively stable over the next year.

The analysis of business cycle turning points as an aid to market timing is important. Based on historical observations, investors would have increased their returns by switching into liquid assets such as T-bills before the business cycle peaks and into stocks before the cycle reaches its trough.

Using Key Variables to Make Market Forecasts

A number of key market indicators and macro variables have been touted by both individuals and organizations as potential predictors of future movements in the economy and/or the market. Perhaps the best known market indicator is the price/earnings ratio. Table 15-2

[10] E. Fama, "Stock Returns, Expected Returns, and Real Returns," *Journal of Finance* 45 (September 1990), pp. 1098–1108.

showed that the trailing P/E ratio for the TSE 300 Index has displayed significant volatility, raising above 100 in 1992 and 1993 in response to extremely low corporate earnings. The median of 19.52 over the 1986–97 period could be thought of as a "normal" P/E multiple. Some analysts may view the market as overvalued if the P/E ratio exceeds 20, although we know there are several other factors to consider.

Another widely watched indicator of likely market movements is the dividend yield, which averaged 2.76 per cent for the TSE 300 between 1986 and 1997, with a median of 3.02 per cent. Many market participants believe that when the dividend yield declines below historical levels, the market is in for a downward correction. The logic is that with stock prices high enough to make the dividend yield so low (say below 2 per cent), investors will abandon equities in favour of higher returns on safe fixed-income securities. The resulting sale of equities will drive down their prices and drive up the dividend yield, restoring a balance.

Empirical evidence supports the use of dividend yields for predicting future stock returns. For example, dividend yield supposedly has a higher correlation with future S&P 500 changes than any other indicator over the long run.[11] In addition, several studies have shown that lagged aggregate dividend yield is negatively related to equity returns. These results are intuitive if we view dividend yields as measures of general economic conditions. The existence of high dividend yields suggests equity prices have been bid down relative to current dividends reflecting a decline in recent economic growth. Conversely, low dividend yields generally occur when the economy is booming and equity prices have been bid up relative to current dividends. This suggests that dividend yields will be negatively correlated with recent GDP growth, which in turn is negatively correlated with future stock returns. Combining these two factors, we would expect a positive relationship between dividend yields and stock returns. Empirical evidence supports both of the claims above: dividend yields are negatively related to recent economic growth and are positively related to future stock returns.[12]

The problem with key market indicators is deciding when they are signalling a change and how reliable the signal is, especially given the high volatility in measures such as the P/E ratio, which was discussed above. In addition, we can reasonably assume that the "normal" value of some of these indicators changes over time so that what is regarded as a low or high signal at one point does not have the same meaning at some other time. Still another problem is how quickly any change signalled by key market indicators and macro variables might occur. In the final analysis, this is an inexact process, subject to considerable interpretations as well as errors.

EXAMPLE: COMPARING DIVIDEND YIELDS

Consider some of the key indicators and macro variables in recent years. On October 1, 1987, a few days prior to the great one-day crash of October 19, 1987 when the TSE 300 declined over 11 per cent, the trailing P/E ratio was 19.50. While this was high by historical standards at the time, so was the ending 1996 P/E ratio of 24.19, which was followed by an above average TSE 300 return of 14.89 per cent in 1997.

[11] "Will Overvaluation Overwhelm Stocks?" *Mutual Funds*, March 1995, pp. 17–19. This discussion is indebted to information in this article.

[12] N. Chen "Financial Investment Opportunities and the Macroeconomy," *Journal of Finance* 46 (June 1991), pp. 529–554; Fama in footnote 5.

A comparison of dividend yields shows that the dividend yield on October 1, 1987 stood at a relatively low level of 2.40 per cent prior to the market crash on October 19. However, the ending dividend yield of 1.83 per cent at the end of 1996 was extremely low by historical standards, yet the market performed admirably in 1997. In fact, by the end of 1997 the dividend yield had fallen even further to 1.65 per cent.

Investors attempting to forecast the economy should pay attention to certain important variables. Interest rates are an obvious variable to watch. In fact, one of the most commonly used variables in return predictability studies is the lagged domestic short-term interest rate, which generally mirrors expected future inflation. The short-term interest rate has been shown to be significant in predicting stock returns in many empirical studies.

Two other interest rate variables have also been shown to have predictive power regarding future stock returns. One of these is the term structure variable, which is defined as the lagged long-term domestic government bond yield minus the lagged government short-term interest rate. The other is the default spread, which is defined as the difference between the yield on long-term corporate bonds versus the yield on long-term government bonds. This variable is chosen to predict returns based on the fact that default spreads tend to widen during recessionary periods, as investors require additional compensation to hold riskier corporate bonds (i.e., there is a flight to quality during periods of uncertainty).

The direction and levels of commodity prices are also very important, especially for Canada. In addition, unit labour costs are considered by many to be an important economic indicator, with increases exceeding 3 per cent signalling a potential problem.

Finally, as you consider the state of the market and whether you should invest now, you might ask if any particular month is riskier than others. Some believe that October is, and the historical evidence seems to support this idea: Many of the largest daily market declines have occurred in October, including the market crashes of 1929 and 1987.

Using Valuation Models to Make Market Forecasts

Based on the valuation models developed earlier, we could use one of two approaches to make market forecasts:

1. Use D_1, k, and g, based on Equation 15-1, $P_0 = D_1/(k - g)$.
2. Use E_1 and P/E, based on Equation 15-3, $P_0 = E_1 \times P_0 / E_1$.

Notice that using Equation 15-3 requires estimates of future earnings (E_1) and the forward P/E ratio (P_0 / E_1), not the trailing P/E ratio (P_0 / E_0) referred to in Table 15-2. The reason forward P/E ratios are seldom reported in public sources such as the newspaper is because of the subjectivity involved in their estimation. In particular, they require estimates of the expected future earnings (E_1), and these will vary from analyst to analyst. For comparison purposes, we have included Table15-3, which includes forward P/E ratios (P_0 / E_1) for the TSE 300 Index from 1986 to 1997 based on the actual earnings that resulted in the following year. In other words, the P_0 / E_1 ratios reported in Table 15-3 represent the forward P/E ratios that would have been determined with perfect forecasting ability regarding future earnings at the beginning of each year. The ability to forecast future earnings perfectly is, of course, impossible in the real world, which is why we do not see these ratios reported regularly in the media. The average of these ratios is 39.40, while the median is 19.62. Notice that these summary statistics are very close to those observed for the trailing P/E ratios in Table 15-2 and similar to our experience with the trailing ratios: the average is uninformative due to two extreme values (164.13 for 1991 and 96.61 for 1992).

Table 15-3

Forward Price-Earnings ratios (P_0/E_1) for the TSE 300 Composite Index, 1986–97

Year	End-of-year Index Value (Prices)	Earnings	Forward P_0 / E_1 Ratio[a]
1986	3066.18	176.31	13.89
1987	3160.05	220.67	10.10
1988	3381.75	312.83	12.60
1989	3969.79	268.41	19.62
1990	3256.75	202.37	42.50
1991	3512.36	76.63	164.13
1992	3350.44	21.40	96.61
1993	4321.43	34.68	22.20
1994	4213.61	194.62	12.31
1995	4713.54	342.27	19.24
1996	5927.03	245.04	20.22
1997	6699.44	293.05	—

[a] P_0 / E_1 is current end-of-year price divided by earnings during the **next** calendar year.

Source: *TSE Annual Review* for the years 1986 to 1997.

If we are to attempt some forecasts of the stock market, we must form some judgements about likely changes in these variables. Let's consider two examples, one that attempts to determine the future value of the S&P 500 Composite Index in the US, and another that attempts to forecast the future level of the TSE 300 Composite Index in Canada.

We begin our discussion by considering a forecast for the TSE 300 for the 12-month period ending in September 1998, that was made in September 1997. Based on extensive analysis, real GDP was expected to grow at an annual rate of 4 per cent, inflation was expected to be about 2.4 per cent, and the Canadian dollar was expected to trade at about $0.74 US by September 1998. These projections were based upon several assumptions including a drop in long-term bond yields from 6.6 per cent to 6 per cent, an increase in three-month T-bill yields from 2.9 per cent to 4.4 per cent, and increased profits from non-oil resource sectors.

Based on this analysis of economic conditions, as well as a detailed analysis of the industries comprising the TSE 300, earnings for the year up to September 1998 were projected to be $337, representing a 5.64 per cent increase from the September 1997 earnings of $319. This seemed to be relatively conservative in comparison to the 1994–96 geometric average growth rate in earnings of 12.2 per cent, although it is above the 1986–96 geometric average growth rate of 3.3 per cent. Combining the 1998 earnings estimate with the observed market value of 6766 in September 1997, the implied P_0 / E_1 ratio was 20.1, which was consistent with the most recent market P_0 / E_1 multiples (shown in Table 15-3). The September 1997 dividend yield, based on September 1997 dividends of $108 was 1.6 per cent, which was below historical levels, but close to the 1996 yield of 1.83 per cent.

The forecast went on to project 1999 earnings of $357 (a 6 per cent increase from the projected 1998 estimate), and a September 1998 TSE 300 value of 7200. This implied a 1998 P_0 / E_1 ratio of 20.2, which is again consistent with the most recent multiples. The expected dividend yield for 1998 based on predicted dividends of $116, was 1.6 per cent, identical to the 1997 value.

This analysis was in line with other forecasts for the TSE 300 at the time, yet by September of 1998, the TSE 300 was trading at a level of 5682, well below the projected 7200, and 19 per cent below the September 1997 level. What happened? As is always the case with predictions, several things did not turn out as expected. On the positive side, inflation turned out to be only 1.6 per cent, while long-term bond yields fell to 5.7 per cent. On the negative side, three-month T-bill yields rose to 5.55 per cent, and real GDP growth fell to approximately 3 per cent. More importantly, world commodity prices plummeted, and the dollar fell to around $0.65 US. As a result of declining commodity prices, profits in the resource sector deteriorated contrary to the forecast. The end result was a decline in TSE 300 earnings to a level of $233, well below the forecast of $337.

What if we had used the DDM instead of the P/E approach? Would things have worked out any better? Probably not, because the TSE 300 is comprised of a large proportion of cyclical companies, and the DDM does not work well for such companies due to their volatile earnings and the inability of many to maintain a stable dividend record. Let's examine this possibility by using the constant-growth dividend discount model for the market, and assuming indefinite growth in dividends at the geometric average annual growth rate in earnings for the TSE 300 over the 1986–96 period of 3.30 per cent. Based on this approach we get the following estimate of the required rate of return for 1998, (assuming 1998 dividends of $116):

$$\begin{aligned} k &= D_1/P_0 + g \\ &= \$116/\$6766 + 0.033 \\ &= 5.01\% \end{aligned}$$

This is obviously not a realistic required return by stockholders, given that bonds (which are of lower risk) offered a return of 6.6 per cent at the time. The implied P/E multiple based on the estimated payout ratio of 34.4 per cent (i.e., $116/$337), and using a required rate of return on the market of 12 per cent (the long-term historical average return) would be too low to be considered reasonable:

$$P_0 / E_1 = \frac{D_1 / E_1}{k - g} = \frac{0.344}{0.12 - 0.033} = 3.95$$

The DDM would produce even worse results if we had used the 1986–96 geometric average growth rate in dividends of 1.8 per cent in the equation above.

Let's consider a similar US example, which attempts to value the S&P 500 Composite Index for the end of 1997. This forecast was based on an extensive economic and industry analysis in early 1997. Earnings and dividends for 1997 for the S&P 500 Index were estimated to be 42.22 and 16.24, both of which represented a 9 per cent increase from their 1996 levels. Based on this analysis and projected 1998 earnings of $46.02, the estimated value of the S&P 500 was figured to be 807, which implied a P_0 / E_1 multiple of 17.5. This indicated a 1997 dividend yield of 2 per cent (i.e., 16.24/807), identical to the 1996 yield.

Based on the 1996 ending value of the S&P 500 of 740.74, and assuming constant growth in earnings and dividends at a rate of 9 per cent indefinitely, the constant-growth DDM implies an 11.2 per cent required rate of return by US common stock investors, which seemed reasonable at the time:

$$k = D_1 / P_0 + g = (16.24/740.74) + 0.09 = 0.112 \text{ or } 11.2\ \%$$

Let's examine what would happen if we use the data above to estimate a justified P_0 / E_1 multiple based on fundamentals:

$$P_0 / E_1 = \frac{D_1 / E_1}{k - g} = \frac{(16.24/42.20)}{0.115 - 0.09} = \frac{0.385}{0.025} = 15.4$$

Using this multiple, we would estimate the value of the S&P 500 to be 15.4 (46.02 = 708.7, well below the forecast. This suggests that the estimate above is not particularly conservative, based on long-term fundamentals.

What happened? Well, at the end of 1997 the S&P 500 was around the 970 level, well above the forecast, and even further above the forecast based on fundamentals. Thus, even though this forecast did not seem to be particularly conservative at the time, it turned out to be in hindsight.

Both of these examples highlight the point made earlier — it is very difficult to predict what will happen in the market over short periods of time. Does this mean there is no point trying or that our models are useless? The answer to both of these questions is no. Attempting to value the market offers investors a prescription for making rational investment decisions. Using either of these models allows investors to focus their analysis on the key variables that will affect stock prices — future earnings, dividends and anticipated growth in these variables (which are affected by economic and industry conditions), and discount rates (which are affected by interest rates, inflation, and risk).

These examples illustrate the fundamental analysis approach to making some forecasts of the market using data readily available to investors. Such forecasts are not straightforward and are clearly subject to errors, some of which may be substantial. Investors should count on the unexpected occurring. Nevertheless, the average investor can make some intelligent and useful forecasts of the market at certain times, at least as to direction. By the end of 1974, for example, it was not too difficult to believe that the market could rise in the future, given the low point it had reached. If the economy could be expected to improve after the shock of the energy crunch, earnings could be expected to hold steady or improve. More important, if investor pessimism could be expected to decrease to any extent, the P/E ratio should increase, and therefore stock prices would increase. And this is exactly what happened!

Another example is 1981–82, when interest rates had reached record levels in both Canada and the United States and the North American economy was in a recession. Investors had only to convince themselves that some recovery would occur, thereby increasing earnings, or more important, that interest rates would decline, thereby lowering the required rate of return (i.e., raising the P/E ratio). This is exactly what happened, of course, launching a great bull market from mid-1982 to mid-1983.

Investors should consider the foregoing type of analysis when making forecasts for the stock market. Although it is not a perfect process by any means, forecasts of likely major market trends can be useful to all investors.

SUMMARY

This summary relates to the learning objectives provided on page 467.

1. **Describe the relationship between the stock market and the economy.**
   Macroeconomic forecasts require analysis of several domestic and global factors simultaneously. The recurring pattern of expansion and contraction in the economy is referred to as the business cycle, and stock prices are related to the phases of that business cycle. Leading, lagging, and coincident indicators are used to monitor the economy in terms of business cycle turning dates. It is important to remember that stock prices are leading indicators and generally lead the economy. Therefore, while the market and the economy are clearly related, stock prices usually turn before the economy does.
2. **Analyze the determinants of stock market values.**
   The market is the aggregate of all security prices and is conveniently measured by some average or index of stock prices. To understand the market (i.e., what determines stock prices), it is useful to think in terms of a valuation model. The two determinants of aggregate stock prices are the expected benefits stream (earnings or dividends) and the required rate of return (alternatively, the P/E ratio). Keran's model is useful for visualizing the economic factors that combine to determine stock prices. In trying to understand the market in conceptual terms, it is appropriate to think of corporate earnings and interest rates as the determinants of stock prices. Corporate earnings are directly related to stock prices, whereas interest rates are inversely related to stock prices. To value the market, investors should think in terms of corporate earnings and the P/E ratio, or, dividends and the discount rate.
3. **Make basic forecasts of market changes.**
   Forecasting market changes is difficult. The business cycle can be of help in understanding the status of the economy, which investors must then relate to the market (which usually leads the economy). Some intelligent estimates of possible changes in the market can be made by considering what is likely to happen to corporate profits and P/E ratios (or interest rates) over some future period, such as a year.

KEY TERMS

Business cycle

Composite leading indicator

REVIEW QUESTIONS

1. In terms of the Keran model, how can the Bank of Canada affect stock prices?
2. List and describe the five phases of the business cycle.
3. Differentiate between a leading indicator, a coincident indicator, and a lagging indicator.
4. List five key determinants of interest rates.

5. Why is market analysis so important?
6. What are the two major determinants of stock prices? How are these two determinants related to a valuation model?
7. What is the historical relationship between stock prices, corporate profits, and interest rates?
8. What was the primary cause of the rise in stock prices in 1988?
9. What is the "typical" business cycle-stock price relationship?
10. If an investor can determine when the economy will bottom out, when should stocks be purchased — before, during, or after such a bottom? Would stock prices be expected to continue to rise as the economy recovers (based on historical experience)?
11. Suppose that you know with certainty that corporate earnings next year will rise 15 per cent above this year's level of corporate earnings. Based on this information, should you buy stocks?
12. How can the Keran model use interest rates as one of the two determinants of stock prices when the interest rate does not appear in either the dividend valuation model or the earnings multiplier model?
13. How can investors go about valuing the market?

PREPARING FOR YOUR PROFESSIONAL EXAMS

Special Note to CSC Students

Ensure that you have read and understood the following topics:*

The economy and the stock market, pp. 468–479
CSC Notes: Fiscal Policy, p. 478
Understanding the stock market, pp. 479–487

**Reading these CSC-related topics should provide you with additional understanding of CSC material. However, it should not be seen as a substitute for reading the CSC textbook itself, which is the basis for the CSC exam.*

CSC REGISTRATION QUESTIONS

The Canadian Securities Institute issued the following sample questions in the 1997 CSC registration package as a means for students to self-assess their understanding of CSC-related material.

1. __________ constitute(s) a leading indicator.
   a. Business loans outstanding
   b. Housing starts
   c. GNP
   d. The unemployment rate
2. __________ indicators change at approximately the same time and in the same direction as the whole economy.

PAST CFA EXAM QUESTION

The following question was asked on the 1993 CFA Level II examination:

1. Universal Auto is a large multinational corporation headquartered in the United States. For segment reporting purposes, the company is engaged in two businesses: production of motor vehicles and information processing services. The motor vehicle business is by far the larger of Universal's two segments. It consists mainly of domestic US passenger car production, but also includes small truck manufacturing operations in the US and passenger car production in other countries. This segment of Universal has had weak operating results for the past several years, including a large loss in 1992. While the company does not break out the operating results of its domestic passenger car business, that part of Universal's business is generally believed to be primarily responsible for the weak performance of its motor vehicle segment. Idata, the information processing services segment of Universal, was started by Universal about 15 years ago. This business has shown strong, steady growth which has been entirely internal; no acquisitions have been made. The research report continued as follows: "... With a business recovery already underway, the expected profit surge should lead to a much higher price for Universal Auto stock. We strongly recommend purchase."

   a. Discuss the business cycle approach to investment timing. (Your answer should describe actions to be taken on both stocks and bonds at different points over a typical business cycle.)

   b. Assuming that a business recovery is already underway, evaluate the timeliness of his recommendation to purchase Universal Auto, a cyclical stock, based on the business cycle approach to investment timing.

Reprinted, with permission, from the Level II 1994 CFA Study Guide. *Copyright 1994, Association for Investment Management and Research, Charlottesville, VA. All rights reserved.*

PROBLEM

Use the following annual data for a common stock index provided for the years 19X1 through 19X6. The 19X6 values in italics are projected.

Year	End-of-Year Price (P_0)	Earnings (E_0)	Dividends (D_0)	P_0/E_0	Payout (D_0 / E_0)	Div. Yield (D_0 / P_0)
19X1	107.21	13.12	5.35	8.17	40.78	4.99
19X2	121.02	16.08	6.04	7.53	37.56	4.99
19X3	154.45	16.13	6.55	9.58	40.61	4.24
19X4	137.12	16.70	7.00	8.21	41.92	5.11
19X5	157.62	13.21	7.18	11.93	54.35	4.56
19X6	*186.24*	*15.24*	*6.97*			

a. Calculate the 19X6 values for those columns left blank.

b. Assuming a projection that 19X7 earnings will be 25 per cent greater than the 19X6 value and assuming that the 19X7 dividend-payout ratio will be 0.40, determine the P_0 / E_1 ratio for 19X6, using the 19X6 price in the table above.

c. Using the projected earnings and dividends for 19X7, and $k = 13.2$ per cent and $g = 9.5$ per cent, use Equation 16-2 in Chapter 16 to determine the implied P_0 / E_1 ratio for 19X6.

d. Recalculate the values for 19X6 P_0 / E_1 and P_0, using the same $g = 0.095$, but with (1) $k = 0.14$; and (2) $k = 0.12$.

CHAPTER 16

INDUSTRY ANALYSIS

LEARNING OBJECTIVES

After reading this chapter, you will be able to

1. State the importance of industry analysis.
2. Explain how industries are classified.
3. Analyze the life cycle and qualitative factors that affect industries.
4. Evaluate future industry prospects by analyzing the business cycle.

CHAPTER PREVIEW

In this chapter we examine industry analysis — the second step in the top-down approach in fundamental security analysis. After explaining the importance of industry factors to company performance, we describe how industries are defined and classified. We look at the concept of a life cycle and at qualitative factors that are useful in industry analysis. Finally, we evaluate future industry prospects by analyzing the business cycle.

THE IMPORTANCE OF INDUSTRY ANALYSIS

The second step in the fundamental analysis of common stocks is industry analysis. An investor who is convinced that the economy and the market offer favourable conditions for investing should proceed to consider those industries that promise the best opportunities in the coming years. In the first decade of the 2000s, for example, investors will not view some Canadian industries with the same enthusiasm they would have even ten years earlier. On the other hand, it is obvious that the telecommunications and computer-related industries such as Internet companies are changing the way most Canadians live.

The actual analysis of industries done by professional security analysts is often a detailed and lengthy process. Numerous factors must be considered, including multiple demand and supply factors, a detailed analysis of price factors, labour issues, government regulation, and so forth.

In this chapter, we concentrate on the conceptual issues involved in industry analysis. The basic concepts of industry analysis are closely related to our previous discussion of valuation principles. Investors can apply these concepts in several ways, depending on the degree of rigor sought, the amount of information available, and the specific models used. What we seek to accomplish here is to learn to think analytically about industries.

The significance of industry analysis can be established by considering the performance of various industries over several periods. This analysis will indicate the value to investors of selecting certain industries while avoiding others at certain times. We will also establish the need for investors to analyze industries on a continuous basis, by showing the inconsistency of industry performance over consecutive periods.

Performance of Industries Over Time

The importance of industry factors for investment managers is irrefutable. For example, while the 1997 return for the TSE 300 Composite Index was 13.0 per cent, the returns for the 14 industry groups varied from 51.5 per cent for the Financial Services Index to −43.6 per cent for the Gold and Precious Metals Index. Obviously portfolios that were weighted heavily in financial services companies and light in gold companies would have performed well during this year. In 1998 the TSE 300 fell 3.2 per cent, while industry returns ranged from a high of 19.1 per cent for consumer products to a low of −30.4 per cent for oil and gas companies.

Peter Gibson highlights the potential benefits to predicting future industry performance (based on the ten largest industries in the TSE 300 in 1996).[1] He shows that an investor using

[1] Peter Gibson, "Chapter 14: Strategy," in Joe Kan, ed., *Handbook of Canadian Security Analysis: A Guide to Evaluating the Industry Sectors of the Market, from Bay Street's Top Analysts* (Toronto: John Wiley and Sons Canada, 1997), pp. 537–644.

an industry rotation strategy (discussed in the CSC Notes box at the end of this chapter) with perfect foresight could have earned 205 per cent per year over the 1973–96 period, by allocating his or her portfolio correctly to the best performing industry sector on a monthly basis. Although, perfect foresight is not possible, this example serves to highlight the importance of examining industry factors, as well as the potential benefits of diversifying across industry categories.

Before embarking on industry analysis, we should consider its potential value. To establish the value of industry analysis, we can assess the performance of industry groups over long periods of time. The Toronto Stock Exchange calculates stock price indexes for 14 industry groups, which are available on a continuous basis. Since the data are reported as index numbers, long-term comparisons of price performance can be made for any industry covered.

Table 16-1 shows the price performance of all the 14 industry groups for the years 1977, 1982, 1987, 1992, and 1997.[2] The TSE 300 Composite Index increased almost sevenfold during the 20-year period, which translates into an average annual increase of 10.2 per cent, as can be seen in the last column of Table 16-1.[3] During this same 20-year period, performance of the industry groups varied substantially, from the 14.0 per cent growth in communications and media, to 3.6 per cent for real estate.

Table 16-1

Year-End Industry Index Prices for the TSE 300 Composite Index, 1977, 1982, 1987, 1992, and 1997

Industry Group	1977	1982	1987	1992	1997	Average Annual Change* 1977–87	Average Annual Change 1987–97	Average Annual Change 1977–97
Metals & Minerals	894	1857	2688	2815	3802	13.0%	3.9%	7.9%
Gold & Precious Metals	1284	4218	7530	5250	6379	21.7%	−1.8%	8.8%
Oil & Gas	1489	2683	3280	3327	6670	9.2%	8.2%	8.2%
Paper/ Forest Products	890	1496	4371	3130	4039	19.3%	−1.1%	8.3%
Consumer products	940	2156	3975	6110	10176	17.4%	11.0%	13.4%
Industrial products	876	1417	1835	2010	4758	8.6%	11.2%	9.3%
Real Estate	1426	3727	11675	3181	2787	26.3%	−14.7%	3.6%
Transportation/ Environmental Services	1161	2457	7622	4371	8223	23.2%	1.2%	10.8%
Pipelines	1355	2163	2798	3410	6937	8.4%	10.6%	9.0%
Utilities	1265	1802	2622	3028	6248	8.4%	10.1%	8.77%
Communications & Media	1086	2126	5856	7158	13093	20.6%	9.3%	14.0%
Merchandising	870	1695	3008	3774	5876	14.8%	7.7%	10.6%
Financial Services	967	1527	2010	2612	8314	8.5%	17.1%	12.0%
Conglomerates	1217	1828	4713	3663	9238	16.2%	9.6%	11.3%
TSE 300 Index	1060	1958	3160	3350	6699	12.9%	8.7%	10.2%

*All average annual changes are geometric averages for the indicated periods.
Source: *TSE Annual Review* for the years 1986 to 1997.

[2] All data are based on December closing index values.

[3] All reported average annual changes are geometric averages for the indicated periods.

The ten-year average growth rates for the index values for the periods 1977–87 and 1987–97 are also presented in the second and third last column of Table 16-1. While there was a decline in the performance of the TSE 300 Index from 12.9 per cent during the 1977–87, to 8.7 per cent in 1987-97, the change was much more drastic for the industry groups. Consider the increases in the indexes for the following industries during the 1977–87 period: real estate (26.3 per cent), gold and precious metals (21.7 per cent), transportation and environmental services (23.2 per cent), and paper/forest products (19.3 per cent). Investors who had the foresight to be heavily weighted in these industries over this period would likely have been very successful.

However, if we look at the performance of the same four industries between 1987 and 1997, we would have observed the following sub-par performances of these industries: real estate (−14.7 per cent), gold and precious metals (−1.8 per cent), transportation and environmental services (1.2 per cent), and paper/forest products (−1.1 per cent). In all likelihood, investors who were heavily weighted in these four industries during this period would have been disappointed by their performance. Over five-year intervals, performance varies even more substantially across industries and within the same industry. This is obvious if we look at changes in the index levels over five-year intervals as depicted in Table 16-1. Obviously, there is no assurance that strong industry performance in the past will continue in the future.

What about industry performance over shorter periods of time? Should investors screen industries to find those that are currently performing well and are, therefore, likely to be the source of the most promising opportunities, from which company analysis will be done? Such a procedure may produce some good results but with wide variance. There are many examples of industries performing at opposite ends of the scale from one period to the next, while others continue to perform well for two or three years in a row. For example, after increasing 54.6 per cent during 1996 and 51.5 per cent in 1997, the Financial Services Index continued to rise during the first few weeks of 1998 in response to proposed mergers among four of the major banks. However, by September 4, 1998 the index had declined almost 20 per cent from its 1997 year-end value, before recovering in the fourth quarter to end with a 1.4 per cent gain for 1998.

Table 16-2 shows the average annual returns and standard deviations for the ten largest industries in the TSE 300 as of 1996, over the 1973–96 period. This table demonstrates some expected results. For example, we notice that the standard deviation for golds is higher than for the other industries, while other resource-based industries such as oil and gas, integrated oils, paper and forest, and mines also display high volatility in returns. On the other hand, returns to banks have been less volatile, while telephone utilities, as one would expect, display very low return volatility, relative to the other industries.

The lesson to be learned from this discussion is simple. Industry analysis pays because industries perform very differently over time, and investor performance will be significantly affected by the particular industries in which investors select stocks. Investors seek to identify the growing industries of the future, and avoid those industries that are in decline. Industry rankings on some periodic basis (e.g., yearly or quarterly) are not consistent. Investors cannot simply choose those industries that have performed well recently and reliably expect them to continue to do so for the next several periods. While some continuation in performance occurs, so do surprises.

Perhaps just as important, investors should not ignore industries simply because their recent performance has been poor. Their subsequent performance over relatively short periods of time may be, and often is, at the opposite extreme! It is necessary, therefore, to learn the basic concepts of industry analysis. Before we consider these concepts, let us first define exactly what an industry is.

Table 16-2

TSE Industry Average Annual Returns and Standard Deviations (1973–96)

Industry	Average Return (%)	Standard Deviation (%)
Banks	12.47	20.76
Golds	14.46	48.81
Oil & Gas	6.25	35.59
Mines	10.07	26.85
Telephone Utilities	13.51	14.57
Paper & Forest	9.91	28.82
Chemicals	11.00	25.28
Technology	12.34	28.90
Conglomerates	11.06	25.11
Integrated Oils	8.78	31.17

Source: Peter Gibson, "Chapter 14: Strategy," in Joe Kan, editor, *Handbook of Canadian Security Analysis* (Toronto: John Wiley & Sons Canada, 1997), pp. 537–644.

WHAT IS AN INDUSTRY?

At first glance, the term industry may seem self-explanatory. After all, everyone is familiar with the auto industry, the drug industry, and the electric utility industry. But are these classifications as clear-cut as they seem? For example, a consumer can drink beer out of glass containers, aluminum cans, or steel cans. Does this involve one industry, containers, or three — the glass, aluminum, and steel industries (or perhaps two: glass and metals). The problem becomes even messier because many companies are diversified along several lines of business.

EXAMPLE: INDUSTRY DIVERSIFICATION

Imasco Limited is commonly classified as a consumer products and services company in the tobacco industry, which seems reasonable, since they held over 60 per cent of the 1997 market share in this industry in Canada, through their ownership of Imperial Tobacco. However, over 30 per cent of Imasco's 1997 operating profits came from the financial services industry, as a result of its ownership stake in Canada Trust, while another 10 per cent of their 1997 operating profits came from their holdings in Shoppers Drug Mart.

The message is clear. In many cases industries cannot be casually identified and classified. It seems safe to assert that industries have been, and will continue to become, more mixed in their activities and less identifiable with one product or service. This implies that we must be cautious in our comparisons of companies within a particular industry, since they will often be very different in their underlying nature. Making comparisons across industry groups is also often very difficult, particularly in Canada. This is because many industries are dominated by one or two companies. For example, Imasco and Rothmans Inc. dominate the Canadian tobacco industry, and are the only two companies included in the Tobacco Index in the TSE 300.

Classifying Industries

Regardless of the problems, it is important for analysts and investors to classify industries, since company profitability is a function of industry structure and the product that the industry sells. Industry structure results from strategies that companies pursue relative to their competition. The TSE Composite Index classifies stocks into 14 major groups and 40 subgroups based on business activity. This breakdown is depicted in the Real-World Returns box below, which shows the December 31, 1998 composition of the TSE 300 Index by industry group and subgroup. Several of the industry groups and subgroups are dominated by a few companies.

Similar to the TSE industry groups, US companies such as Standard & Poor's Corporation, and *The Value Line Investment Survey* break down US companies into several industry categories and maintain indexes of their performance.

Standard Industrial Classification (SIC) System
A classification of firms on the basis of what they produce, according to standardized five-digit codes.

One well-known and widely used system for classifying industries is the **Standard Industrial Classification (SIC) system**, which was developed to classify firms on the basis of what they produce. SIC codes have 11 divisions, designated A through K. For example, agriculture-forestry-fishing is industry division A, mining is B, retail trade is G, and K, the last group, is non-classifiable establishments. Within each of these divisions are several major industry groups, designated by a two-digit code. The primary metal industries, for example, are a part of division D, manufacturing, and are assigned the two-digit code 33.

The major industry groups within each division are further subdivided into three-, four-, and five-digit SIC codes to provide more detailed classifications. A specific industry is assigned a three-digit code, as are entire companies.[4] Plants carrying out specific functions (such as producing steel) are assigned four-digit SIC codes. A five-digit code indicates a specific product. Thus, the larger the number of digits in the SIC system, the more specific the breakdown.

SIC codes provide a consistent basis for describing industries and companies. Analysts can use SIC codes to focus on economic activity in as broad, or as specific, a manner as desired.

Other sources of information use different numbers of industries in presenting data. The important point to remember is that no one industry classification system is widely used in the standard investment publications.

ANALYZING INDUSTRIES

Similar to markets and companies, industries can be analyzed through the study of a wide range of data, including sales, earnings, dividends, capital structure, product lines, regulations, innovations, and so on. Such analysis requires considerable expertise and is usually performed by industry analysts employed by brokerage firms and other institutional investors.

A useful first step is to analyze industries in terms of their stage in the life cycle. The idea is to assess the general health and current position of the industry. A second step involves a qualitative analysis of industry characteristics designed to assist investors in assessing the future prospects for an industry. Each of these steps is examined in turn.

[4] Companies involved in several lines of activity are assigned multiple SIC codes.

REAL-WORLD RETURNS

TSE 300 Composite Index

1.00 METALS & MINERALS
1.01 Integrated Mines
1.02 Mining

2.00 GOLD & PRECIOUS MINERALS
2.03 Gold & Precious Minerals

3.00 OIL & GAS
3.01 Integrated Oils
3.02 Oil & Gas Producers
3.03 Oil & Gas Services

4.00 PAPER & FOREST PRODUCTS
4.01 Paper & Forest Products

5.00 CONSUMER PRODUCTS
5.01 Food Processing
5.02 Tobacco
5.03 Distilleries
5.04 Breweries & Beverages
5.05 Household Goods
5.08 Biotechnology/Pharmaceuticals

6.00 INDUSTRAIL PRODUCTS
6.01 Steel
6.02 Fabricating & Engineering
6.04 Transportation Equipment
6.05 Technology - Hardware
6.06 Building Materials
6.07 Chemicals and Fertilizers
6.10 Technology - Software
6.11 Autos & Parts

7.00 REAL ESTATE
7.03 Real Estate

8.00 TRANSPORTATION & ENVIRONMENTAL SERVICES
8.01 Transportation & Environmental Services

9.00 PIPELINES
9.03 Pipelines

10.00 UTILITIES
10.03 Telephone Utilities
10.04 Gas/Electric Utilities

11.00 COMMUNICATIONS & MEDIA
11.01 Broadcasting
11.02 Cable & Entertainment
11.03 Publishing & Printing

12.00 MERCHANDISING
12.01 Wholesale Distributors
12.02 Food Stores
12.03 Department Stores
12.05 Specialty Stores
12.06 Hospitality

13.00 FINANCIAL SERVICES
13.01 Banks and Trusts
13.03 Investment Cos. & Funds
13.05 Insurance
13.06 Financial Management Cos.

14.00 CONGLOMERATES
14.01 Conglomerates

Source: TSE Review, *December 1998.*

The Industry Life Cycle

Industry Life Cycle
The stages of an industry's evolution from pioneering to growth, stabilization, and decline.

Many observers believe that industries evolve through at least three stages: the pioneering stage, the expansion stage, and the stabilization stage. There is an obvious parallel in this idea to human development. The concept of an **industry life cycle** could apply to industries or product lines within industries. The industry life cycle concept is depicted in Figure 16-1, and each stage is discussed in the following section.

Figure 16-1
The Industry Life Cycle

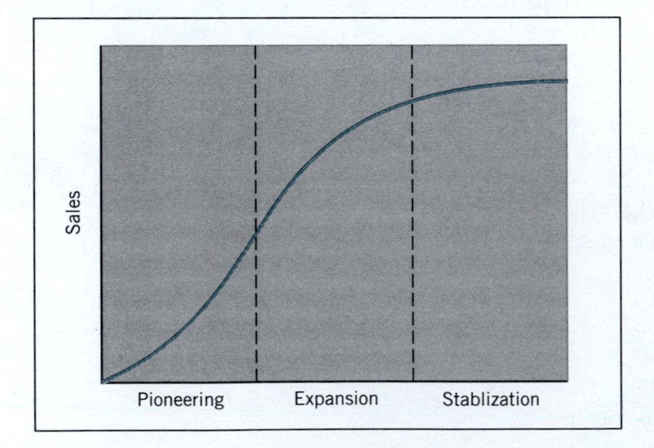

Pioneering Stage

In the pioneering stage, rapid growth in demand occurs. Although a number of companies within a growing industry will fail at this stage because they will not survive the competitive pressures, many will experience rapid growth in sales and earnings, possibly at an increasing rate. The opportunities available may attract a number of companies, as well as venture capital. Considerable jockeying for position occurs as the companies battle each other for survival, with the weaker firms failing and dropping out. Investor risk in an unproven company is high, but so are expected returns if the company succeeds. At the pioneering stage of an industry, it can be difficult for security analysts to identify the likely survivors, never mind future strong performers. By the time the real winners become apparent, the price of their stock will probably have been bid up considerably beyond what they were in the earlier stages of development.

Expansion Stage

In the second period of an industry's life cycle, the expansion stage, the survivors from the pioneering stage are identifiable. They continue to grow and prosper, but at a more moderate rate. At the expansion stage of the cycle, industries are improving their products and perhaps lowering their prices. They are more stable and solid, and at this stage they often attract considerable investment capital. Investors are more willing to invest in these industries now that their potential has been demonstrated and the risk of failure has decreased.

Financial policies become firmly established at this stage. The capital base is widened and strengthened. Companies are often able to pay dividends, further enhancing their attractiveness to a number of investors.

Stabilization Stage

Finally, industries evolve into the stabilization (or maturity) stage, at which point the growth begins to moderate. Sales may still be increasing but at a much slower rate than before. Products become more standardized and less innovative, the market place is full of competitors, and costs are stable rather than decreasing through efficiency, for example. Industries at this stage continue to move along but without significant growth. Stagnation may occur for considerable periods of time or intermittently.

Assessing the Industry Life Cycle

This three-part classification of industry evolvement helps investors to assess the growth potential of different companies in an industry. Based on the stage of the industry, they can better assess the potential of different companies within it. However, there are limitations to this type of analysis. First, it is only a generalization, and investors must be careful not to attempt to categorize every industry, or all companies within a particular industry, into neat categories that may not apply. Second, even the general framework may not apply to some industries that are not categorized by many small companies struggling for survival. Finally, the bottom line in security analysis is stock prices, a function of the expected stream of benefits and the risk involved.

The industrial life cycle tends to focus on sales and share of the market and investment in the industry. Although these factors are important to investors, they are not the final items of interest. Given these qualifications to industry life cycle analysis, what are the implications for investors?

The pioneering stage may offer the highest potential returns, but it also poses the greatest risk because many companies in a particular industry will fail or do poorly. Such risk may be appropriate for some investors, but many will wish to avoid it.

Investors interested primarily in capital gains should avoid the maturity stage. Companies at this stage may have relatively high dividend payouts because they have fewer growth prospects. On the other hand, these companies often offer stability in earnings and dividend growth.

It is the second stage, expansion, that is probably of most interest to investors. Industries that have survived the pioneering stage often offer good opportunities, since the demand for their products and services is growing more rapidly than the economy as a whole. Growth is rapid but orderly, an appealing characteristic to investors.

Perhaps a fourth stage could be added to the analysis of the industrial life cycle — decline. Whether decline is seen in relative or absolute terms, clearly, investors should seek to spot and avoid industries in this stage. In the years to come, with the rapid growth of technology, certain industrial sectors will decline. (In some cases, this decline has already started.)

Qualitative Aspects of Industry Analysis

The analyst or investor must consider several important qualitative factors that can help investors to analyze a particular industry and aid in assessing its future prospects. The four crucial factors examined below are: 1) historical performance, 2) competition, 3) government effects, and 4) structural changes.

1. *Historical Performance.* As we have seen, some industries perform well and others poorly over both long and short periods of time. Although performance is not always consistent and predictable on the basis of the past, an industry's track record cannot be ignored. In Table 16-1 we saw that the real estate industry performed extremely well between 1977 and 1987 but very poorly in the 1987–97 period. The communications and media industry, on the other hand, outperformed the TSE 300 Index in both periods.

   Investors should consider the historical record of sales and earnings growth and price performance. Although the past cannot simply be extrapolated into the future, it does provide some useful information.

2. *Competition.* The nature of the competitive conditions existing in an industry can provide useful information in assessing its future. Is the industry protected from the entrance of new competitors as a result of control of raw materials, prohibitive cost of building plants, the level of production needed to operate profitably, and so forth?

   Michael Porter has written extensively on the issue of competitive strategy, which involves the search for a competitive position in an industry. The intensity of competition in an industry determines that industry's ability to sustain above-average returns.[5] This

[5] M. Porter, "Industry Structure and Competitive Strategy: Keys to Profitability," *Financial Analysts Journal* 36 (July–August 1980), pp. 30–41. See also M. Porter, *Competitive Advantage: Creating and Sustaining Superior Performance* (New York: Free Press, 1985).

intensity is not a matter of luck but rather a reflection of underlying factors that determine the strength of five basic competitive factors:

i. Threat of new entrants

ii. Bargaining power of buyers

iii. Rivalry among existing firms

iv. Threat of substitute products or services

v. Bargaining power of suppliers.

These five competitive forces are shown as a diagram in Figure 16-2. Because the strength of these five factors varies across industries (and can change over time), industries vary from the standpoint of inherent profitability.

These five competitive forces determine industry profitability because they influence the components of return on investment. The strength of each of these factors is a function of industry structure. The important elements of industry structure are shown in Figure 16-2. This figure shows all the elements of industry structure that affect competition within an industry.

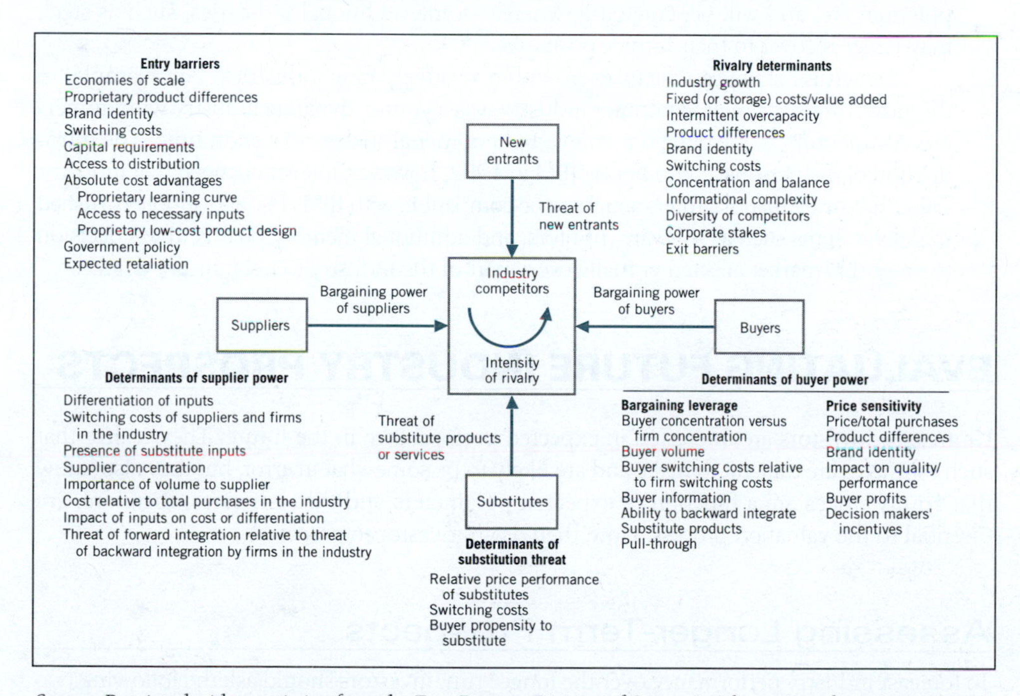

Figure 16-2
Competitive Forces and Industry Profitability

Source: Reprinted with permission from the Free Press, a Division of Simon & Schuster Inc. from Competitive Advantage: Creating and Sustaining Superior Performance *by Michael E. Porter. Copyright © 1985, 1998 by Michael E. Porter.*

The central point of the Porter analysis is that industry profitability is a function of industry structure. Investors must analyze industry structure to assess the strength of the five competitive forces, which, in turn, determine industry profitability.

3. *Government Effects.* Government regulations and actions can have significant effects on industries. The investor must attempt to assess the results of these effects or, at the very least, be well aware that they exist and may continue.

   Consider the deregulation of the long distance telephone service industry in Canada. This action has changed the Canadian telecommunications industry permanently and perhaps others as well. As a second example, consider the deregulating of the financial services industries, which allowed banks to own subsidiaries in the securities industry. This has resulted in most of the major securities firms now being wholly owned subsidiaries of the major banks. In December of 1998, the government made a major decision by rejecting the proposed mergers between the Royal Bank of Canada and the Bank of Montreal, and between the Canadian Imperial Bank of Commerce and the Toronto Dominion Bank. Had these mergers been approved it would have changed the face of the banking industry in Canada as we have come to know it over the past few decades.

4. *Structural Changes.* A fourth factor to consider is the structural changes that occur in the economy. As Canada continues to move from an industrial society to an information-communications one, major industries will be affected. New enterprises with tremendous potential are, and will be, emerging, whereas some traditional industries, such as steel, may never recover to their former positions.

   Structural shifts can occur even within relatively new industries. For example, in the early 1980s the microcomputer industry was a young, dynamic industry with numerous competitors, some of whom enjoyed phenomenal success in a short time. The introduction of the personal computer by IBM in 1982, however, forever changed that industry. Other hardware manufacturers sought to be compatible with IBM's PC, and suppliers rushed to deliver items such as software, printers, and additional memory boards. IBM's decision to enter this market affected virtually every part of the industry to a significant degree.

EVALUATING FUTURE INDUSTRY PROSPECTS

Ultimately, investors are interested in expected performance in the future. They realize that such estimates are difficult to make and are likely to be somewhat in error, but they also know that equity prices are a function of expected parameters and that estimates, therefore, are essential to the valuation process. How, then, is an investor to proceed?

Assessing Longer-Term Prospects

To forecast industry performance over the longer run, investors should ask the following two questions:

1. Which industries are obvious candidates for growth and prosperity over, say, the next decade? (In the early 1980s, such industries as microcomputers, software, telecommunications, and cellular telephones could have been identified; in the early 1990s, it was software and technology firms; in the late 1990s, investors focused a great deal of attention on Internet companies and high technology firms.)
2. Which industries appear likely to have difficulties as Canada changes from an industrial to an information-collecting and -processing economy?

Picking Industries for Next Year

On a shorter-run basis, investors would like to value industries along the lines discussed in Chapter 15 for the market. They would like to be able to estimate the expected earnings for an industry and the expected multiplier and combine them to produce an estimate of value. However, this is not easy to do. It requires an understanding of several relationships and estimates of several variables. Fortunately, considerable information is readily available to help investors in their analysis of industries.

To determine industry performance for shorter periods of time (e.g., one year), investors should ask themselves the following question: Given the current and prospective economic situation, which industries are likely to show improving earnings? In many respects, this is the key question for industry security analysis. The investment advisory services provided by Canadian securities firms and banks provide such information on a timely basis. Alternatively, investors can turn to the Institutional Brokers Estimate System (IBES) International and Zack's Investment Research. Both of these entities compile institutional brokerage earnings estimates as well as revisions that occur throughout the year.

Given the importance of earnings, and the availability of earnings estimates for industries and companies, are investors able to make relatively easy investment choices? The answer is no, because earnings estimates are notoriously inaccurate. For example, there is a great deal of evidence that analysts tend to be overly optimistic on average. Supporting studies include those by O'Brien and by DeBondt and Thaler in the US, as well as Canadian evidence documented by Hennessey and by Ackert and Athanassakos.[6]

Dreman reports on a study of 61 industries for a 17-year period. Three-quarters of all estimates within industries missed reported earnings by 30 per cent or more, and 15 per cent showed errors of 80 per cent or more. The average forecast error grouped by industries was 50 per cent (median error of 43 per cent). Only 16 of the 61 industries over the 17 years showed forecast errors of 29 per cent or less.[7] These results highlight the point made earlier — even for well-informed and knowledgeable individuals, it is difficult to predict the future performance of industries.

Of course, investors must also consider the likely P/E ratios for industries. Which industries are likely to show improving P/E ratios? Dreman has also tackled the question of whether investors pay too much for favoured companies in an industry. Buying the lowest 20 per cent of P/Es in each of 44 industry groups over 25 years (based on the 1,500 largest companies rated by market capitalization in the Compustat database, which contains comprehensive financial data for several thousand US and several hundred Canadian companies) produced an average annual return of 18 per cent compared to 12.4 per cent for the highest 20 per cent P/E group. Dreman also found that buying the lowest P/E stocks across industries produced smaller losses when the market is down relative to the market as a whole and to the highest P/E group.[8]

---

[6] P. O'Brien, "Analyst's Forecasts as Earnings Expectation," *Journal of Accounting and Economics* 10 (January 1988), pp. 53–83; W. DeBondt and R. Thaler, "Do Security Analysts Overreact?" *American Economic Review* 80 (May 1990), pp. 52–57; S. Hennessey, "Can Active Managers Profit from Earnings Forecast Revisions?" *Canadian Investment Review* 6 (Spring 1993), pp. 39–45; L. Ackert and G. Athanassakos, "Expectations of the Herd," *Canadian Investment Review* 9 (Winter 1996/97), pp. 7–11.

[7] D. Dreman, "Cloudy Crystal Balls," *Forbes*, October 10, 1994, p. 154.

[8] D. Dreman, "A New Approach to Low-P/E Investing," *Forbes*, September 23, 1996, p. 241.

Other questions to consider are the likely direction of interest rates and which industries would be most affected by a significant change in them. A change in interest rates, other things being equal, leads to a change in the discount rate (and a change in the multiplier). Which industries are likely to be most affected by possible future political events, such as a new federal or provincial government, tax cuts, a vote by Quebec to separate from Canada, and so on?

As with all security analysis, we can use several procedures in analyzing industries. Much of this process is common sense. For example, if you can reasonably forecast a declining number of competitors in an industry, it stands to reason that the remaining firms will be more profitable, other things being equal.

Business Cycle Analysis

A useful procedure for investors to assess industry prospects is to analyze industries by their operating ability in relation to the economy as a whole. That is, some industries perform poorly during a recession, whereas others are able to weather it reasonably well. Some industries move closely with the business cycle, performing better than average in good times and underperforming in bad times. Investors, in analyzing industries, should be aware of these relationships.

Growth Industries
Industries with expected earnings growth significantly above average.

Most investors know about, and are usually looking for, growth companies. In **growth industries**, earnings are expected to grow significantly faster than the average of all industries, and such growth may occur regardless of setbacks in the economy. Growth industries in the 1980s included genetic engineering, microcomputers, and new medical devices. Current growth industries include cellular telephones and Internet companies. Clearly, one of the primary goals of fundamental security analysis is to identify the growth industries of the near and far future.

Growth stocks suffer much less during a recession, such as in 1990, than do the cyclical stocks (explained below). For example, US growth stocks gained 2.5 per cent in 1990 while cyclicals lost about 20 per cent.

Defensive Industries
Industries least affected by recessions and economic adversity.

At the opposite end of the scale are the **defensive industries** — those that are least affected by recessions and economic adversity. Food has long been considered such an industry. People must eat regardless of the economy. Public utilities would also be considered a defensive industry since they are necessities, and their profits remain relatively stable throughout the business cycle.

Cyclical Industries
Industries most affected, both up and down, by the business cycle.

Cyclical industries are the most volatile — they do unusually well when the economy prospers but are likely to be hurt more when the economy falters. Durable goods are a good example of the products involved in cyclical industries. Automobiles, refrigerators, and stereos, for example, may be avidly sought when times are good, but such purchases may be postponed during a recession, because consumers can often make do with the old units.

Cyclicals are said to be "bought to be sold" — that is, investors dump them when the economy turns down. Many professionals advise investors to pursue cyclical industries when the prices of companies in the industry are low, relative to the historical record, and P/Es are high. This seems counterintuitive to many investors, but the rationale is that earnings are severely depressed in a recession and therefore the P/E is high, and this may occur shortly before earnings turn around.

Most TSE 300 cyclical companies are large international exporters of commodities such as lumber, nickel, copper, and oil. Commodity-based cyclicals include industries such as forestry products, mining, and chemicals. Industrial cyclicals include transportation, capital goods, and basic industries (steel, building materials), while consumer cyclicals include merchandising companies and automobiles.

Countercyclical industries also exist, actually moving opposite to the prevailing economic trend. The gold mining industry has followed this pattern during several periods in the past — rising in price during economic recessions and declining during boom time.

As a rule, the return on equity (ROE) of cyclical industries would vary by at least 100 per cent over a complete business cycle, compared to one third for defensive industries, and 55 per cent for the TSE 300 as a whole. The TSE 300 has about 80 deeply cyclical companies and about 220 stable ones; however, the cyclical ones are larger, so the resulting percentages of market capitalization of the index are close to fifty-fifty.

These classifications of industries according to economic conditions do not constitute an exhaustive set. For example, people often refer to blue chip stocks, such as IBM or Xerox, which are top investment quality companies that maintain earnings in good times and bad. Their record usually reflects a dominant market position, strong internal financing, and effective management. Another categorization refers to speculative industries, which are so called because there is a great deal of risk and uncertainty associated with them due to the absence of definitive information.

Another important industry classification is the identification of **interest-sensitive industries**, which are particularly sensitive to changes in interest rates. The financial services, banking, and real estate industries are obvious examples of interest-sensitive industries. Another is the construction industry.

Interest-Sensitive Industries
Industries particularly sensitive to changes in interest rates, such as financial services, real estate, and the construction industries.

The *Handbook of Canadian Security Analysis* classifies the TSE 300 industries into three categories based on their sensitivity to interest rates and the cyclicality of profitability as measured by ROE, which are two of the key factors affecting equity performance. The categories include:

1. High Economic Sensitivity (HES) industries
2. Low Economic Sensitivity (LES) industries
3. Emerging Economy (EE) industries.

In Chapter 14 of the *Handbook*, Gibson examines industry returns for each TSE 300 industry between 1962 and 1996 and finds that no other fundamental factor contributed more to higher industry returns than falling interest rates. Every industry, regardless of their categorization, displayed higher returns during periods of falling interest rates.

Gibson's results are summarized above in Table 16-3, which is taken from his discussion. He finds that on average, interest rates produce a greater affect on industry share prices than increases in profitability as measured by ROE. This is true for all 20 HES industries and for 11 of the 12 LES industries. On average, the LES industries produced a 3.97 per cent higher return during periods of falling rates than during periods of rising ROE, while the comparable number for HES industries was 3.70 per cent. What does all of this mean to investors? Obviously, it is desirable to purchase shares in an industry entering into an environment where ROE is increasing, or interest rates are falling. It would be even more desirable to purchase shares

Table 16-3

TSE 300 Performance

Sector	Interest Rates		ROE		Relative ROE		Combinations			
	↓Rates	↑Rates	↓ROE	↑ROE	↓Rel. ROE	↑Rel. ROE	↑ROE ↓RATES	↓ROE ↓RATES	↑ROE ↑RATES	↓ROE ↑RATES
LOW ECONOMIC SENSITIVITY										
Defensive & Interest Sensitive Utilities	%	%	%	%	%	%	%	%	%	%
Gas/Electrical Utilities	–	–	–	–	–	–	–	–	–	–
Pipelines	13.3	7.7	11.9	10.2	12.4	9.2	10.8	12.7	8.8	9.1
Financials										
Banks & Trusts	17.3	9.8	14.6	12.3	11.3	14.9	13.7	15.8	10.9	11.1
Investment Cos. & Funds	18.2	8.6	18.9	8.7	17.8	9.0	14.9	15.6	7.1	13.8
Insurance	–	–	–	–	–	–	–	–	–	–
Financial Management	12.4	2.6	7.8	6.2	6.9	6.9	9.7	9.0	4.4	4.5
Consumer Staples										
Broadcasting	20.9	10.4	16.5	18.4	16.8	16.5	19.0	17.4	12.6	13.3
Cable & Entertainment	24.0	8.9	12.7	20.5	17.6	14.7	17.4	21.2	14.9	8.8
Food Processing	13.8	8.5	11.3	11.2	10.5	11.9	12.0	12.3	9.4	9.5
Food Stores	13.3	5.6	9.4	10.6	8.9	11.4	11.1	11.6	9.7	5.3
Tobacco	21.5	14.6	16.9	17.3	16.2	17.2	18.4	17.9	14.2	15.4
Distilleries	17.5	10.7	9.3	18.6	10.4	16.8	13.3	16.9	16.9	6.6
Breweries & Beverages	15.0	3.9	8.2	10.0	7.0	11.3	10.1	13.3	7.4	5.0
Communication Services										
Telephone Utilities	13.3	7.2	12.6	8.8	8.7	112.2	12.2	11.1	6.8	10.5
HIGH ECONOMIC SENSITIVITY										
Cyclicals & Profit Growth Sensitive										
Consumer Cyclicals	%	%	%	%	%	%	%	%	%	%
Department Stores	7.9	4.1	4.8	6.9	8.1	5.0	6.6	6.8	4.0	5.7
Specialty Stores	14.3	7.9	10.7	13.1	7.4	17.0	12.8	12.3	8.5	10.2
Household Goods	11.0	4.9	8.3	4.4	4.3	6.8	6.2	11.1	5.7	5.4
Publishing & Printing	21.3	10.2	18.5	14.0	15.5	16.3	17.4	18.3	11.0	13.7
Autos & Parts	26.2	5.6	15.1	18.7	14.5	18.9	18.8	18.6	13.2	11.8
Building Materials	17.4	6.6	9.2	13.6	11.9	10.3	14.0	13.8	9.4	7.6
Industrial Basic										
Transportation	14.6	11.9	9.5	13.5	11.0	11.8	12.8	9.4	12.8	12.0
Conglomerates	18.4	7.6	15.0	12.3	15.9	11.0	15.1	15.8	9.6	10.5
Industrial Capital Goods										
Wholesale Distributors	18.8	7.7	11.0	15.7	9.4	16.9	15.0	15.9	12.5	7.5
Hospitality	–	–	–	–	–	–	–	–	–	–
Transportation Equipment	15.4	5.1	6.4	14.8	6.0	8.8	12.3	12.2	12.8	2.4
Fabricating & Engineering	17.2	8.4	8.6	15.6	9.7	14.5	15.6	12.6	11.7	7.8
Real Estate	4.3	2.9	7.1	0.9	1.7	4.9	4.8	3.6	-0.5	7.7
Commodity Basic										
Integrated Mines	10.6	6.2	8.0	9.9	8.5	6.8	8.6	10.4	8.1	6.5
Mining	11.6	5.6	10.1	5.8	12.0	4.2	8.6	10.4	5.2	7.9
Paper & Forest Products	12.9	7.0	6.1	11.7	6.6	11.1	12.6	8.8	7.6	7.9
Steel	8.2	3.9	6.2	5.3	6.7	4.8	5.7	7.9	4.7	4.6
Chemicals & Fertilizers	14.0	6.8	10.1	7.8	11.0	6.8	10.0	12.5	8.1	7.3
Gold & Precious Minerals	20.8	10.8	12.8	15.1	16.2	11.9	15.1	18.4	12.0	11.6
Energy										
Integrated Oils	15.4	8.8	11.6	10.8	11.5	10.7	13.3	12.5	9.8	9.5
Oil & Gas Producers	13.6	6.5	9.9	9.9	12.9	5.7	9.6	13.2	10.3	5.4
EMERGING ECONOMY										
Technology — Hardware	21.0	9.5	18.4	10.2	14.3	13.6	16.3	17.4	8.3	14.1
Technology — Software	–	–	–	–	–	–	–	–	–	–
Biotechnology/Pharmaceuticals	–	–	–	–	–	–	–	–	–	–

Source: Peter Gibson, "Chapter 14: Strategy," in Joe Kan, editor, *Handbook of Canadian Security Analysis* (Toronto: John Wiley & Sons Canada, 1997), pp. 547–548.

when both of these events are occurring, however, such forecasting ability is extremely difficult, and rare according to empirical evidence discussed in Chapter 10.

What are the implications of these classifications for investors? To predict the performance of an industry over shorter periods of time, investors should carefully analyze the stage of the business cycle and the likely movements in interest rates. If the economy is heading into a recession, cyclical industries are likely to be affected more than others, whereas defensive industries are the least likely to be affected. With such guidelines investors may make better buy or sell decisions. Similarly, an expected rise in interest rates will have negative implications for the financial services industry and the home building industry, whereas an expected drop in interest rates will have the opposite effect.

INVESTING tip

Clearly, business cycle analysis for industries is a logical and worthwhile part of fundamental security analysis. Industries have varying sensitivities to the business conditions and interest rate expectations at any given time, and the smart investor will think carefully about these factors. The CSC Notes box below discusses industry rotation strategies and their relationship with the macroeconomic factors discussed above.

These statements reinforce the importance of market analysis. Not only do investors need to know the state of the economy and market before deciding to invest, but such knowledge is valuable in selecting (or avoiding) particular industries. Furthermore, investors need to consider the possibility of overcapacity as well as global competition.

We end this chapter by referring to Table 16-4, which is also taken from Chapter 14 of the *Handbook of Canadian Security Analysis*. It provides a brief overview of some of the key factors (most of which have been discussed here or in Chapter 15) affecting the profitability and common share performance of a variety of Canadian industries.

CSC NOTES

Industry Rotation

Industry rotation is an investment strategy that shifts portfolio weights in various industries in order to achieve improved results. The strategy can be profitable if one can successfully predict turning points in economic cycles and their impact on the security prices of various industries.

Industry rotation is concerned with trying to outperform market averages such as the TSE 300 Index. For example, during the late stages of a recessionary period, bank stocks may recover first, in response to declining interest rates. Consumer stocks would improve shortly thereafter, while other industries such as durable goods producers would benefit in the later stages of economic recovery. Successfully shifting between these groups can produce above average results, although it is not as easy as it sounds (as the discussion in this chapter makes clear).

The most basic industry rotation strategy involves shifting back and forth between cyclical and defensive industries. During periods of declining prices, cyclical stocks tend to fall faster, and during times of rising prices, they tend to increase at a more rapid pace. Another strategy is to move in and out of interest rate sensitive industries in response to interest rate forecasts.

Variations in the economic cycle often have a dramatic affect on the timing of industry rotation. Generally, two-thirds of a new economic recovery is driven by increased consumer spending, which tends to precede increases in business spending. During such a period in a normal economic cycle, investors may focus on consumer growth, transportation, consumer cyclical, energy, and capital goods industries in that order.

Table 16-4

Key Macroeconomic and Microeconomic Factors Behind the Timing of Profit Cycles

LOW ECONOMIC SENSITIVITY		
Utilities	Pipelines Gas/Electric	1. Interest Rates 2. GDP growth and capital investment 3. Deregulation trends and regulatory environment 4. Franchise and non-franchise growth opportunities 5. Management quality
Financials	Banks	1. Long bond rates — relative valuation 2. Yield curve — borrow short, invest long 3. Competition — margins, consolidation 4. Earnings momentum and dividend growth 5. Growth in book value
	Insurance	1. GDP and wealth growth 2. Population growth 3. Savings rates 4. Disease/epidemics/natural disasters 5. Competitive environment
Consumer Staples	Broadcasting	1. Consumer confidence/spending 2. GDP and economic growth 3. Income growth — especially real wages 4. Advertising volumes 5. Digital technology evolution
	Food Stores	1. Food inflation 2. Demographics (geography) 3. Personal disposable income 4. New product development 5. Consumer confidence
Communication Services	Telephone/Utilities Communications	1. GDP growth 2. Household growth 3. Regulation, marketing effectiveness 4. Ten-year Canada bond yield 5. Technological developments
HIGH ECONOMIC SENSITIVITY		
Consumer Cyclical	Publishing/Printing	1. Consumer confidence/spending 2. GDP and employment growth 3. Income growth — especially real wages 4. Advertising volumes, expenses, paper, and labour 5. Digital technology evolution
	Auto & Retailing	1. Consumer confidence/spending 2. Personal disposable income 3. GDP and employment growth 4. Interest rates 5. Technology and auto outsourcing
Industrial Transportation	Airlines	1. Interest rates 2. Fuel costs 3. Consumer spending/confidence 4. Aircraft purchases 5. Load factors and price wars
	Trucking and Railroads	1. GDP growth 2. Fuel costs 3. Retail shipments

		4. Industrial production 5. Commodity mix — grain
Industrial Basic & Capital Goods	Fabricating	1. Canadian capital investment 2. Secular growth of emerging markets 3. Size of firms 4. Private sector financing vehicles 5. Access to multiple sources of credit
	Real Estate	1. Inflation expectations 2. Interest rates and GDP growth 3. Vacancy rates 4. Building regulations 5. Availability of funds
Commodity Basic (Specific Commodity Prices Important)	Metals & Minerals	1. OECD industrial production 2. US dollar 3. Inventories 4. Capacity utilization 5. Consumption
	Golds	1. Reserve growth 2. Real interest rates 3. International mining regulations 4. New technology 5. Personnel available
	Paper & Forest	1. Global GDP 2. Real exchange rates 3. Economic development and trade 4. Inventory cycle 5. Capacity additions, input costs
	Chemicals	1. GDP growth 2. Technological breakthroughs 3. Harvest quality/quantity 4. Strategic advantages/disadvantages 5. Product supply/demand
	Steel	1. GDP growth 2. Auto sales 3. Capacity utilization 4. New capacity 5. Changes in international cost position of steel markets
Energy	Oil & Gas	1. Exploration success 2. Technological innovation 3. Success/failure in production targets 4. US dollar 5. Marketing and refining margins
EMERGING ECONOMY		
Biotechnology Technology		1. Machine and equipment spending 2. International GDP growth 3. R&D investment and tax credits 4. Component pricing 5. Computer sales and consumer confidence

Source: Peter Gibson, "Chapter 14: Strategy," in Joe Kan, editor, *Handbook of Canadian Security Analysis* (Toronto: John Wiley & Sons Canada, 1997), pp. 605–606.

SUMMARY

This summary relates to the learning objectives provided on page 503.

1. **State the importance of industry analysis.**
   Industry analysis is the second of three steps in a top-down framework of fundamental security analysis, between economy/market analysis and individual company analysis. The objective is to identify those industries that will perform best in the future in terms of returns to stockholders. Industry analysis is valuable because over the long term some industries perform better than others. Industry performance is not consistent because past price performance does not always predict future price performance. Particularly over shorter periods such as one or two years, industry performance rankings often completely reverse themselves.
2. **Explain how industries are classified.**
   Although the term industry at first seems self-explanatory, definitions and classifications of it are not straightforward, and the trend toward diversification of activities over the years has blurred the lines even more. The TSE 300 Composite Index classifies stocks into 14 major groups and 40 subgroups based on business activity. The Standard Industrial Classification (SIC) system, is a comprehensive scheme for classifying major industry groups, specific industries, specific functions, and specific products.
3. **Analyze the life cycle and qualitative factors that affect industries.**
   To analyze industries, a useful first step is to examine their stage in the life cycle, which in its simplest form consists of the pioneering, expansion, and maturity stages. Most investors will usually be interested in the expansion stage, in which growth is rapid and risk is tolerable. Investors also need to consider qualitative aspects such as historical performance, competition, government effects, and structural changes.
4. **Evaluate future industry prospects by analyzing the business cycle.**
   A second industry analysis approach involves business cycle analysis since the performance of different industries varies substantially throughout the stages of the business cycle. Investors interested in evaluating future industry prospects have a wide range of data available for their use. These data can be used for a detailed, in-depth analysis of industries using standard security analysis techniques for examining recent ratings of industry performance or for ranking likely industry performance.

KEY TERMS

Cyclical industries
Defensive industries
Growth industries
Industry life cycle
Interest-sensitive industries
Standard Industrial Classification (SIC) System

ADDITIONAL RESOURCES

An excellent discussion of industry analysis in Canada can be found in:

Kan, Joe, ed. *Handbook of Canadian Security Analysis: A Guide to Evaluating the Industry Sectors of the Market, from Bay Street's Top Analysts*. Toronto: John Wiley and Sons Canada, 1997.

One of the most detailed and well-known analyses of industries can be found in Michael Porter's work. See, as examples:

Porter, Michael E. "Industry Structure and Competitive Strategy: Keys to Profitability." *Financial Analysts Journal* 36 (July–August 1980), pp. 30–41.

Porter, Michael E. *Competitive Advantage: Creating and Sustaining Superior Performance*. New York: Free Press, 1998.

REVIEW QUESTIONS

1. Why is it difficult to classify industries?
2. How consistent is year-to-year industry performance?
3. What are the stages in the life cycle of an industry? Can you think of other stages to add?
4. Name one industry in each of the three life cycle stages today.
5. During which stage of the industry life cycle do investors face the highest risk of losing a substantial part of the investment?
6. Name the 14 industry groups that are distinguished within the TSE 300 Composite Index.
7. Why is industry analysis valuable?
8. Name some industries that you would expect to perform well in the next five years and in the next ten to 15 years.
9. Which industries are the most sensitive to the business cycle? the least sensitive?
10. Explain how aggregate market analysis can be important in analyzing industries in relation to the business cycle.
11. Explain the concept used in valuing industries.
12. Explain how Figure 16-1 might be useful to an investor doing industry analysis.

PREPARING FOR YOUR PROFESSIONAL EXAMS

Special Note to CSC Students

Ensure that you have read and understood the following topics:*

What is an industry, pp. 507–508
Analyzing industries, pp. 508–514
Business cycle analysis, pp. 516–519
CSC Notes: Industry Rotation, p. 519

**Reading these CSC-related topics should provide you with additional understanding of CSC material. However, it should not be seen as a substitute for reading the CSC textbook itself, which is the basis for the CSC exam.*

CSC REGISTRATION QUESTIONS

The Canadian Securities Institute issued the following sample questions in the 1997 CSC registration package as a means for students to self-assess their understanding of CSC-related material.

1. Yields on growth stocks are usually __________ yields on blue chip stocks.
   a. higher than
   b. lower than
   c. the same as
2. A company that operates in a variety of unrelated industries is called a(n) __________.

PAST CFA EXAM QUESTIONS

AIMR℠

The following question was asked on the 1991 CFA Level II examination:

1. INTRODUCTION

   The KCR Fund, a tax-exempt retirement plan, has owned shares of Merck & Co., Inc., a major international drug company, for many years. The investment in Merck has performed well due to rapid growth in sales and earnings.

   Peter Higgens, CFA, an analyst employed by the investment manager of the KCR Fund, has been asked to recommend whether the investment in Merck should be replaced by one in Ford Motor Company.

   Ford is an international manufacturer of motor vehicles, parts, and accessories, and derives 70 per cent of its revenues from sales of these products in North America. Automotive and financial services operations have generated substantially all of Ford's earnings in the past five years. While Ford is the second largest North American auto manufacturer, it is the largest US automaker overseas. The mature auto industry is sensitive to business cycles, and Japanese and European products have eroded the position of the three largest auto producers in North America.

   Merck is one of the largest and "purest" of the major US drug companies. It is a long-term leader in patent-protected drugs for two chronic diseases — hypertension and arthritis — and has recently captured a major position in intravenous antibiotics and anti-ulcer drugs. Merck's research and development effort is the largest in the industry. Imported drugs account for less than 5 per cent of total industry sales in the United States.

   The competitive environment faced by Ford is significantly different than that faced by Merck. Higgens suspects this is the major reason Merck has been more profitable than Ford, and that Merck would likely remain so in the future.

   Higgens is aware of three general strategies that companies may follow in seeking to create a strong competitive position: 1) cost leadership, 2) product differentiation, and 3) focus on market segments. Generally, Ford has not been able to exploit these strategies. Merck, however, appears to have successfully implemented one or more of them.

   Higgens is also aware of five competitive forces faced by companies. Explain how three of these competitive forces faced by Ford and Merck may have affected the relative ability of the two companies to utilize one or more of the general strategies listed above.

The following question was asked on the 1993 CFA Level II examination:

2. Universal Auto is a large multinational corporation headquartered in the United States. For segment reporting purposes, the company is engaged in two businesses: production of motor vehicles and information processing services.

   The motor vehicle business is by far the larger of Universal's two divisions. It consists mainly of domestic US passenger car production, but also includes small truck manufacturing operations in the United States and passenger car production in other countries. Universal's production of motor vehicles has had weak operating results for the past several years, including a large loss in 1992. While the company does not break out the operating results of its domestic passenger car business, that part of Universal's business is generally believed to be primarily responsible for the weak performance of its motor vehicle segment.

   The information processing services segment of Universal started about 15 years ago and has shown strong, steady growth that has been entirely internal; no acquisitions have been made.

   A research report states:

   "Based on our assumption that Universal will be able to increase prices significantly on US passenger cars in 1993, we project a multi-billion dollar profit improvement..."

   a. Discuss the concept of an industrial life cycle by describing each of its four phases.

   b. Identify where each of Universal's two primary businesses, passenger cars and information processing, is in such a cycle.

   c. Discuss how product pricing should differ between Universal's two businesses, based on the location of each in the industrial life cycle.

CHAPTER 17

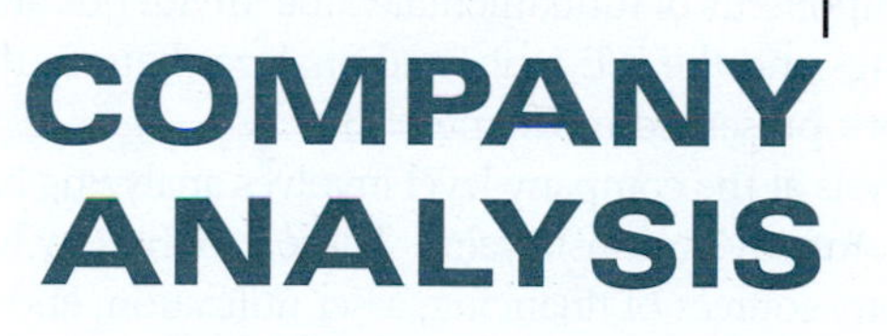

COMPANY ANALYSIS

LEARNING OBJECTIVES

After reading this chapter, you will be able to

1. Define fundamental analysis at the company level.
2. Explain the accounting aspects of a company's earnings.
3. Describe the importance of EPS forecasts.
4. Estimate the P/E ratio of a company.
5. Use the beta coefficient to estimate the risk of a stock.

CHAPTER PREVIEW

In this chapter we consider the third and final step in top-down fundamental analysis: company analysis. Using the valuation framework outlined in Chapter 13, we use earnings per share (EPS) and the price-earnings (P/E) ratio to determine if the stock price for a company is undervalued or overvalued. We touch on the accounting aspects of EPS, examine the impact of earnings announcements and surprises on stock prices, and consider how practicing analysts carry out fundamental security analysis. At the end of the chapter, we bring all the pieces together in an analysis of **Bombardier Inc.**

FUNDAMENTAL ANALYSIS

Once analysis of the economy and the market has indicated a favourable time to invest in common stocks and industry analysis has been performed to find those industries that are expected to perform well in the future, it remains for the investor to choose promising companies within those industries. The last step in top-down fundamental analysis, therefore, is to analyze individual companies. As with the previous two steps, an investor should think in terms of the two components of fundamental value: dividends and required rate of return or, alternatively, earnings and the P/E ratio, and analyze them to the extent practical using the valuation framework presented in Chapter 13.

Fundamental analysis at the company level involves analyzing basic financial variables in order to estimate the company's intrinsic value. These variables include sales, profit margins, depreciation, the tax rate, sources of financing, asset utilization, and other factors. Additional analysis could involve the firm's competitive position in its industry, labour relations, technological changes, management, foreign competition, and so on. The end result of fundamental analysis at the company level is the data needed to calculate the estimated or intrinsic value of a stock using one or more valuation models.

As discussed in Chapter 13, investors can use the dividend discount model (DDM) to value common stocks for companies that maintain relatively stable dividend payments. In some circumstances it is reasonable to assume that the dividend growth rate for a particular company will be approximately constant over the future, which allows us to use the constant-growth version of the DDM shown as Equation 17-1 (Equation 13-5 from Chapter 13):

(17-1)

$$\text{Intrinsic value} = \hat{P}_0 = \frac{D_1}{k - g}$$

where

$\hat{P}_0$ = the estimated value of the common stock today
D_1 = the expected dollar dividend to be paid next period
k = the required rate of return
g = the estimated future growth rate of dividends expected to continue indefinitely

In fundamental analysis, the intrinsic or estimated value of a stock is its justified price, the price justified by a company's fundamental financial variables.

Alternatively, the earnings multiplier model could be used. Intrinsic value is the product of the estimated earnings per share (EPS) for next year and the multiplier or forward P/E ratio (P_0 / E_1), as shown in Equation 17-2.[1]

$$\text{Intrinsic value} = \hat{P}_0 = \text{Estimated EPS} \times P_0 / E_1 \text{ ratio} \qquad (17\text{-}2)$$
$$= E_1 \times P/E$$

Using either Equation 17-1 or Equation 17-2, we can compare a stock's calculated intrinsic value to its current market price. If the intrinsic value is larger than the current market price, the stock can be considered undervalued — a buy. If intrinsic value is less than the market price, the stock is considered overvalued and should be sold if owned, and avoided or sold short if not owned.

For purposes of discussion, we concentrate on earnings and P/E ratios for several reasons. First, dividends are paid from earnings. Although the two series are not perfectly correlated, future dividend growth typically must come from future earnings growth. Second, the close correlation between earnings changes and stock-price changes is well documented. For example, Elton, Gruber, and Gultekin examined the risk-adjusted excess returns available from buying stocks on the basis of next year's growth in earnings and found that those stocks with the highest future growth in earnings per share (EPS) showed the highest risk-adjusted returns.[2] For the 30 per cent of the companies with the highest growth in EPS, the risk-adjusted excess return was 7.48 per cent; for the 30 per cent with the lowest growth, the risk-adjusted excess return was −4.93 per cent. This study demonstrates that growth in reported earnings affects stock prices in a significant manner.

THE ACCOUNTING ASPECTS OF EARNINGS

If investors are to focus on a company's earnings per share, a critical variable in security analysis, they should understand how EPS is derived, and what it represents. For investors, an EPS figure is often the bottom line — the item of major interest — in a company's financial statements. Furthermore, they must understand the components of EPS before they can attempt to forecast it.

The Financial Statements

Investors rely heavily on the **financial statements** of a corporation, which provide the major financial data about companies. Before proceeding with our discussion of how this information can be used by analysts, we note that the information contained in financial statements

Financial Statements The principal published financial data about a company, primarily the balance sheet and income statement.

[1] Technically, to calculate the intrinsic value of a stock using the multiplier method, analysts often determine what is called the normalized EPS, defined as the normal earnings for a company under typical operating conditions. This adjusts for unusual impacts on earnings such as non-recurring or extraordinary earnings.

[2] This study is discussed in E. Elton and M. Gruber, *Modern Portfolio Theory and Investment Analysis*, 4th ed. (New York: John Wiley & Sons, 1991), pp. 487–488.

is generally somewhat dated. This is because of the time involved in compiling financial statements, which implies they will not be available to the public for several days after the end of the reporting period. For annual financial statements, for example, the lag between the fiscal year-end and the public availability of financial statements often exceeds two months, with ninety days being the norm, while the release of quarterly statements is somewhat more timely. In the interim period, companies generally release some highlights (such as earnings per share and sales figures) well before the comprehensive statements are made public.

To illustrate the use of financial statements in doing company analysis, we examine the 1997 and 1998 consolidated financial statements for **Bombardier Inc.**, a well-known Canadian transportation equipment company that competes in the aerospace, mass transit, and motorized consumer product markets. Bombardier has extensive multinational operations, generating revenues in many different currencies. As of March 1999, it was included in the TSE300, TSE100, S&P/TSE60, and TSE35 indexes, which contain the largest and most actively traded stock issues in Canada.

The Balance Sheet

The balance sheet shows the portfolio of assets for a corporation, as well as its liabilities and shareholders' equity, at a given time. The amounts at which items are carried on the balance sheet are dictated by accounting conventions. Cash is the actual dollar amount, whereas marketable securities could be at cost or market value. Shareholders' equity and fixed assets are on a book value basis.

The balance sheet for Bombardier, shown in Table 17-1, shows the company's consolidated financial position for 1997 and 1998, as of January 31, which is the company's fiscal year-end. Two items account for almost two-thirds of Bombardier's 1998 total assets of $10.575 billion. The first item is inventory, which totals $3.791 billion, or 35.8 per cent of total assets. Given the nature of the company's products, it is not surprising to observe high inventory levels. The other asset that comprises a substantial percentage of the company's total assets is finance receivables and other, which totals $2.989 billion, or 28.3 per cent of total assets. This might seem surprising at first glance, however, remember we are looking at consolidated financial statements. In particular, almost all of these finance receivables come from the balance sheet of Bombardier Capital, which is the wholly owned financial subsidiary of Bombardier.

The liability and equity side of the balance sheet is comprised of $2.175 billion in bank loans and equivalent, $2.663 billion in accounts payable and accrued liabilities, $0.091 billion in the current portion of long-term debt, $0.852 billion in advances and progress billings in excess of related costs, $1.549 billion in long-term debt, $0.357 billion in other liabilities, and $2.889 billion in shareholders' equity. The shareholders' equity consists of several components including $1.491 billion in retained earnings. It is important to recognize that the retained earnings item does not represent "spendable" funds for a company; rather, it designates that part of previous earnings not paid out as dividends.

Several financial ratios that can be calculated from balance sheet data are useful in assessing the company's financial strength (e.g., the current ratio, a measure of liquidity, or the debt-to-total-assets ratio, a measure of leverage). These ratios are part of the standard ratio analysis, which is often performed by managers, creditors, stockholders, and other interested groups, and are covered in most financial management texts and courses. Some of these ratios are demonstrated later in the analysis, and a detailed description of many other financial ratios is included in Appendix 17-A at the end of this chapter.

Table 17-1

Consolidated Balance Sheets for Bombardier Inc.

January 31	**1998**	**1997**
(In millions of Canadian dollars)		
Assets:		
Cash and term deposits	$1227.7	$895.7
Accounts receivable	693.2	358.4
Inventory	3790.9	3455.2
Finance receivables and other	2989.4	1811.4
Fixed assets (net)	1646.7	1200.0
Other assets	227.3	229.6
Total assets	**$10575.2**	**$7950.3**
Liabilities and Shareholders' Equity:		
Bank loans and equivalent	$2174.7	$1233.1
Accounts payable and accrued liabilities	2663.0	2124.6
Current portion of long-term debt	90.9	169.3
Advances and progress billings in excess of related costs	851.6	591.4
Long-term debt	1548.7	1354.9
Other liabilities	357.0	264.4
Total Liabilities	7685.9	5737.7
Convertible notes — equity component	165.8	152.3
Preferred stock	300.0	30.9
Common stock	796.2	763.2
Retained earnings	1491.0	1201.1
Other equity component	136.3	65.1
Total shareholders' equity	2889.3	2212.6
Total liabilities and shareholders' equity	**$10575.2**	**$7950.3**

The consolidated balance sheets are presented in an unclassified format because the activities of Bombardier Inc. and its subsidiaries are concentrated in five main segments, each having its own operating cycle.

Source: Bombardier Inc., *Annual Report*, 1998. Reprinted with permission from Bombardier Inc.

The Income Statement

This statement is used more frequently by investors, not only to assess current management performance but also as a guide to the company's future profitability. The income statement represents flows for a particular period, usually one year. Table 17-2 shows the Consolidated Income Statements for Bombardier for the years 1997 and 1998.

Table 17-2

Consolidated Income Statements for Bombardier Inc.

Year Ended January 31	**1998**	**1997**
(In millions of dollars except per share data)		
Total Revenue	$8508.9	$7975.7
Cost of sales	7614.9	7137.3
Depreciation/amortization	180.1	165.8
Operating Income	713.9	672.6
Interest income	28.4	23.6
Interest expense	115.1	89.9
Income Before Tax	627.2	606.3
Income taxes	207.0	200.1
Net Income	420.2	406.2
Earnings Per Common Share	$1.18	$1.18

Source: Bombardier Inc., *Annual Report*, 1998. Reprinted with permission from Bombardier Inc.

The key item for investors on the income statement is the after-tax net income, which, divided by the average number of common shares outstanding, produces earnings per share. Earnings from continuing operations typically are used to judge the company's success and are almost always the earnings reported in the financial press. Non-recurring earnings, such as net extraordinary items that arise from unusual and infrequently occurring transactions, are separated from income from continuing operations.[3]

Table 17-2 clearly illustrates the "flow" in an income statement. The cost of sales (which includes the cost of goods sold, as well as selling, administrative, and general expenses) is subtracted from total revenue (or total net sales), resulting in operating income, which was $713.9 million for Bombardier in 1998. Operating income is often referred to as earnings before interest and taxes, or EBIT for short.

Operating income is then adjusted by adding interest income and subtracting the interest expense, which represents an important item for companies because interest is tax-deductible. Netting these items with operating income produces Bombardier's 1998 income before tax figure of $627.2 million. Finally, subtracting out income taxes results in net income, which was $420.2 million for Bombardier in 1998. In many instances, it may be necessary to account for extraordinary items. Under these circumstances, the procedure above would produce an item referred to as net income before extraordinary items, which would then be adjusted by the extraordinary item (net of taxes), to produce net income.

Finally, dividing by the average number of shares outstanding produces EPS of $1.18. Investors trying to understand the financial statements with regard to items such as EPS may need to consult the company's annual report in order to determine the average common shares

[3] An extraordinary item is one that is not likely to reoccur, such as a loss due to a disposal of an operating division.

outstanding, which is not always a straightforward process. For example, Bombardier reports 1998 net income of $420.2 million, and also states that the average number of common shares outstanding during 1998 was 338.3 million. This implies an EPS of ($420.2 million/338.3 million shares) = $1.24. They go on to note however, that the reported basic EPS figure of $1.18 "gives effect to the increase in the carrying amount of the equity component of the convertible notes." Obviously, ratio calculations for actual companies are not as straightforward as they are made out to be in introductory finance and accounting textbooks.

The charge to earnings because of an accounting change or due to extraordinary items are important to investors in trying to understand earnings. What investors seek to determine is the "true" earning power of a company because ultimately they will be attempting to forecast future earnings. Although no such items are reported for Bombardier in 1997 or 1998, these items can have large impacts on the reported earnings of companies at various times.

Certifying the Statements

The earnings shown on an income statement are derived on the basis of **generally accepted accounting principles (GAAP)**. The company adheres to a standard set of rules developed by the accounting profession on the basis of historical costs and accrual-based income, which can be measured objectively. An auditor from an independent accounting firm certifies that the earnings have been derived according to accounting standards in a statement labelled the "auditor's report."

Generally Accepted Accounting Principles (GAAP)
Financial reporting requirements establishing the rules for producing financial statements developed by the accounting profession on the basis of historical costs and accrual-based income.

The auditor's report is required by Canadian corporate law and generally consists of just two or three paragraphs. The first paragraph (or two) describe the scope of the examination, and usually indicates that the examination was made in accordance with GAAP. The final paragraph (or so) of the report gives the auditor's opinion on whether the statements fairly present the firm's financial position. If the auditor finds discrepancies from GAAP, they may be unable to give an opinion, or may offer a "qualified" opinion that refers to the dubious points. A qualified report can be viewed as a signal that the statements may not fairly represent the company's financial condition and is not allowed in some provinces. Figure 17-1 includes the auditor's report for Bombardier's 1998 consolidated financial statements.

Note that the auditor's report does not guarantee the accuracy or the quality of the earnings in an absolute sense; rather, it only attests that the statements are a fair presentation of the company's financial position for a particular period. The auditors are in effect certifying that generally accepted accounting principles were applied on a consistent basis. In Canada, the Canadian Institute of Chartered Accountants (CICA) formulates accounting standards, while in the US the Financial Accounting Standards Board (FASB) performs this function.

The Problem with Reported Earnings

Although earnings in particular, and financial statements in general, are derived on the basis of GAAP and are certified in an auditor's report, a problem exists with earnings. The problem, simply stated, is that reported EPS for a company (i.e., accounting EPS) is not a precise figure that is readily comparable over time, and the EPS figures for different companies often are not comparable to each other.

Figure 17-1
Auditor's Report for Bombardier Inc.'s 1998 Consolidated Financial Statements

To the Shareholders of **Bombardier Inc.**

We have audited the consolidated balance sheets of **Bombardier Inc.** (a Canadian corporation) as at January 31, 1998 and 1997 and the consolidated statements of shareholders' equity, income, and changes in financial position for the years then ended. These financial statements are the responsibility of the corporation's management. Our responsibility is to express an opinion on these financial statements based on our audits.

We conducted our audits in accordance with generally accepted auditing standards. Those standards require that we plan and perform an audit to obtain reasonable assurance whether the financial statements are free of material misstatement. An audit includes examining, on a test basis, evidence supporting the amounts and disclosures in the financial statements. An audit also includes assessing the accounting principles used and significant estimates made by management, as well as evaluating the overall financial statement presentation.

In our opinion, these consolidated financial statements present fairly, in all material respects, the financial position of the corporation as at January 31, 1998 and 1997 and the results of its operations and the changes in its financial position for the years then ended in accordance with generally accepted accounting principles.

Caron Bélanger, Ernst & Young
Chartered Accountants
Montréal, Canada
February 27, 1998

Source: Bombardier Inc., Annual Report, *1998. Reprinted with permission from Bombardier Inc.*

The problem with earnings is that alternative accounting principles can be, and are, used to prepare the financial statements. Many of the items in the balance sheet and income statement can be accounted for in more than one manner, resulting in what one might call a conservative or a liberal treatment of EPS. Given the number of items that constitutes the financial statements, the possible number of acceptable (i.e., that conform to GAAP) combinations that could be used is large. Holding everything else constant, such as sales, products, and operating ability, a company could produce several legal and permissible EPS figures, depending solely on the accounting principles used. The question that investors must try to answer is, "Which EPS best represents the *true* position of a company?"

Because reported EPS is a function of the many alternative GAAPs in use, it is extremely difficult, if not impossible, for the "true" performance of a company to be reflected consistently in one figure. Since each company is different, is it reasonable to expect one accounting system to capture the true performance of all companies? With the business world so complex, one can make a case for the necessity of alternative treatments of the same item or process, such as inventories or depreciation.

Some EPS figures are better than others in the sense that they have been derived using more conservative principles. In other words, they are of higher quality. In an article on the quality of earnings, Bernstein and Seigel stated:

> a company's reported earnings figure is often taken by the unsophisticated user of financial statements as the quantitative measure of the firm's well-being. Of course, any professional knows that earnings numbers are in large part the product of conscious and often subjective choices between various accounting treatments and business options, as well as of various external economic factors. If he wants to assess the true earning power of each company, the financial statement user must make some determination of the *quality of its earnings* [emphasis added].[4]

[4] L. Bernstein and J. Seigel, "The Concept of Earnings Quality," *Financial Analysts Journal* 35 (July–August 1979), p. 72.

Quality assessments are usually difficult to make and require considerable expertise in accounting and financial analysis. The best advice for the investor is to go ahead and use the reported EPS because it is all that is normally available, and the majority of investors will also have to rely on this figure. Investors should, however, be aware of the potential problems involved in EPS and should constantly keep in mind its nature and derivation.

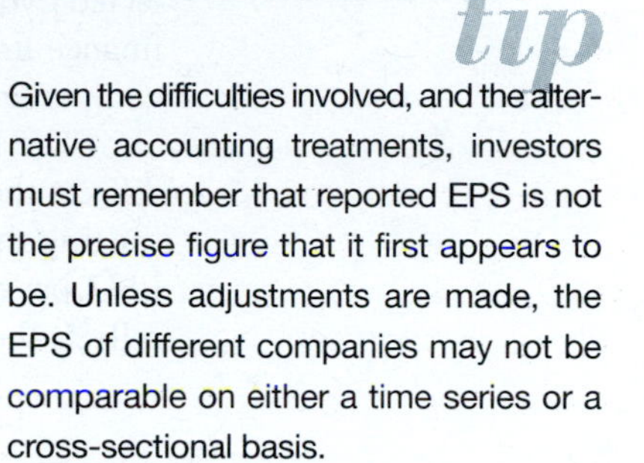
INVESTING tip

Given the difficulties involved, and the alternative accounting treatments, investors must remember that reported EPS is not the precise figure that it first appears to be. Unless adjustments are made, the EPS of different companies may not be comparable on either a time series or a cross-sectional basis.

ANALYZING A COMPANY'S PROFITABILITY

At the company level, EPS is the culmination of several important factors. Accounting variables can be used to examine these determining factors by analyzing key financial ratios. Analysts examine the components of profitability in order to try to determine whether a company's profitability is increasing or decreasing and why. Primary emphasis is on the **return on equity (ROE)** — the accounting net income available to the common stockholders — because it is a key component in determining earnings and dividend growth.

Return on Equity (ROE) The accounting rate of return on stockholders equity.

We begin our discussion by noting that EPS = ROE × Book value per share (which is the accounting value of shareholders' equity on a per share basis), which demonstrates the relationship between EPS and ROE. Since book value typically changes rather slowly, ROE is the primary variable on which to concentrate.

ROE can be determined using the following equation:

$$\text{ROE} = \text{Net income/Shareholders' equity} \quad \textbf{(17-3)}$$

Using Bombardier's data from Tables 17-1 and 17-2, we would calculate the ROE for 1998 as follows:

$$\text{ROE} = \text{Net income/Shareholders' equity} = (\$420.2)/(\$2889.3) = 0.145 = 14.5\%$$

The ROE is the accounting rate of return that stockholders earn on their portion of the total capital used to finance the company; in other words, it is the return on equity.

Analyzing Return on Equity (ROE)

The ROE is the end result of several important variables that are often analyzed by what is referred to as the DuPont system of analysis because it originated at the DuPont Corporation. The idea is to decompose the ROE into its critical components in order both to identify adverse impacts on ROE and to help analysts predict future trends in ROE.

Different combinations of financial ratios can be used to decompose ROE. One approach is to use a multiplicative relationship that consists of five financial ratios, all multiplied together to produce ROE. The first four can be multiplied together to determine **return on assets (ROA)**, an important measure of a company's profitability. ROA measures the only return on assets, while ROE measures the return to the stockholders, who finance only part of the assets (the creditors finance the other part). The five financial ratios are: (1) EBIT efficiency, (2) asset turnover, (3) interest burden, (4) tax burden, and (5) leverage.

Return on Assets (ROA) The accounting rate of return on a firm's assets.

1. A key component of a company's profitability is its operating efficiency, which is unaffected by interest charges, taxes, or the amount of debt financing used by a company to finance its assets (that is, the leverage). To determine operating efficiency, analyze its components — operating income or EBIT — and asset turnover.

   The EBIT/sales ratio is a measure of the firm's ability to operate efficiently. EBIT reflects the earnings before the financing decision is accounted for as a result of subtracting the interest expense and before the provision for income taxes. The larger the EBIT per dollar of sales, the better in terms of operational efficiency. In effect, the EBIT reflects the operating margin on sales:

   EBIT/Sales = Pre-tax, pre-interest profit margin = EBIT efficiency

2. Asset turnover is a measure of efficiency. Given some amount of total assets, how much can be generated in sales? The more sales per dollar of assets the better it is for a firm, since each dollar of assets has to be financed with a source of funds bearing a cost. The firm may have some assets that are unproductive, thereby adversely affecting its efficiency:

   Sales/Total assets = Asset turnover

3. Next, consider the impact of interest charges. Interest expense for most companies is an important tax-deductible item. The "interest burden" can be calculated as the ratio of pre-tax income to EBIT:

   Pre-tax income/EBIT = Interest burden

4. The last variable that must be considered as part of the analysis of a company's return on assets is the tax burden. To calculate this amount, divide net income by pre-tax income:

   Net income/Pre-tax income = Tax burden

   Return on assets (ROA) can now be calculated from these four variables that have important impacts on a company's return on assets:

(17-4) ROA =
[EBIT/Sales × Sales/Total assets × Pre-tax income/EBIT × Net income/Pre-tax income]

EXAMPLE: CALCULATING ROA FOR BOMBARDIER INC.

Using the data for **Bombardier** for 1998 from Tables 17-1 and 17-2:

EBIT/Sales = $713.9/$8508.9 = 0.0839

Sales/Total Assets = $8508.9/$10575.2 = 0.8046

Pre-tax Income/EBIT = $627.2/$713.9 = 0.8785

Net Income/Pre-tax Income =$420.2/$627.2 = 0.6700

ROA = 0.0839 × 0.8046 × 0.8785 × 0.6700 = 0.0397 = 3.97%

Return on assets (ROA) is a fundamental measure of firm profitability, reflecting how effectively and efficiently the firm's assets are used. Obviously, the higher the net income for a given amount of assets, the better the return. For Bombardier, the 1998 return on assets is 3.97 per cent. The ROA can be improved by increasing the net income more than the assets (in percentage terms) or by using the existing assets even more efficiently.

5. Finally, the effects of leverage must be considered. The leverage ratio measures how the firm finances its assets.[5] Basically, firms can finance with either debt or equity. Debt, though a cheaper source of financing, is a riskier method, because of the fixed interest payments that must be systematically repaid on time to avoid bankruptcy. Leverage can magnify the returns to the stockholders (favourable leverage) or diminish them (unfavourable leverage).

   To capture the effects of leverage, use a multiplier rather than a debt percentage.

$$\text{Leverage} = \text{Total assets/Shareholders' equity}$$

INVESTING *tip*

What this analysis does not show is the impact of leverage on the risk of the firm. Remember that in this analysis we are examining only the determinants of EPS. However, as we know from our discussion of valuation, two factors, EPS and a multiplier, are required to determine value. An increase in leverage may increase the riskiness of the company more than enough to offset the increased EPS, thereby lowering the company's value. Investors must always consider both dimensions of the value of a stock, the return side and the risk side.

EXAMPLE: CALCULATING LEVERAGE FOR BOMBARDIER INC.

In 1998 **Bombardier**'s ratio of total debt (all sources) to total assets was 72.68 per cent. Thus, the creditors were financing close to three-quarters of the assets, and the equity holders were underwriting the remainder. Dividing total assets by equity (10575.2/2889.3) produces an equity multiplier of 3.6601, which is used as the measure of leverage.

Finally, the last step in the ROE analysis is to relate ROA and leverage:

$$\text{ROE} = \text{ROA} \times \text{Leverage} \tag{17-5}$$

EXAMPLE: RELATING ROA AND LEVERAGE

Combining these two factors, ROA and leverage, for Bombardier for 1998 produces the following ROE:

$$\text{ROE} = 0.0397 \times 3.6601 = 0.145 = 14.5\%$$

A standard formulation of the ROE analysis often used in the CFA curriculum combines all factors considered above into one long multiplication equation based on these ratios or variations to accommodate the multiplication:

$$\text{ROE} = \text{EBIT efficiency} \times \text{Asset turnover} \times \text{Interest burden} \times \text{Tax burden} \times \text{Leverage} \tag{17-6}$$

$$\text{ROE} = \text{EBIT/Sales} \times \text{Sales/Assets} \times \text{Pre-tax income/EBIT} \times \text{Net income/Pre-tax income} \times \text{Assets/Equity}$$

[5] Leverage can be measured in several other ways, such as the ratio of total debt to total assets or the ratio of debt to equity.

EXAMPLE: CALCULATING ROE FOR BOMBARDIER INC.

For **Bombardier**, using 1998 data:

$$ROE = 0.0839 \times 0.8046 \times 0.8785 \times 0.6700 \times 3.6601 = 0.145 = 14.5\%$$

Estimating the Internal (Sustainable) Growth Rate

Internal (Sustainable) Growth Rate The estimated earnings growth rate, calculated as the product of ROE and the retention rate.

An important part of company analysis is the determination of a sustainable growth rate in earnings and dividends. Such a growth rate estimate can be used in the dividend discount model or to estimate an appropriate P/E multiple.

What determines the sustainable growth rate? The **internal (sustainable) growth rate** of earnings or dividends, g, can be determined as the product of the ROE and the retention ratio — which is calculated as 1.0 minus the dividend payout ratio — as shown in Equation 17-7.[6]

$$g = ROE \times (1 - \text{Payout ratio}) \quad (17\text{-}7)$$

Equation 17-7 is one of the principal calculations in fundamental security analysis and is often used by security analysts. We can calculate g by using data for a particular year, using long-term averages, or using "normalized" figures for ROE and payout ratio. The intuition behind this measure is that growth in earnings (and dividends) will be positively related to the amount of each dollar of earnings reinvested in the company (as measured by the retention ratio), times the return earned on reinvested funds (ROE). For example, a firm that retains all its earnings and earns 15 per cent on its equity would see its equity base grow by 15 per cent per year. If the same firm paid out all of its earnings, then it would not grow. Similarly, a firm that retained a proportion (b), would earn 15 per cent on that proportion, resulting in $g = b \times ROE$. A weakness of this approach is its reliance on accounting figures that are based on book values and the accrual method of accounting. As a result, they may not always serve as reliable proxies for market values and cash flows.

EXAMPLE: INTERNAL GROWTH RATE ESTIMATE FOR BOMBARDIER INC.

For 1998 **Bombardier**'s ROE was 0.145 and their dividend payout ratio was 0.2595. The internal growth rate estimate based on 1998 data is 10.76 per cent:

$$g = ROE \times (1 - \text{Payout ratio}) = (0.145) \times (1 - 0.2595) = 0.1076 = 10.76\%$$

The earnings growth rate, or persistence in the earnings trend, is seldom easy to predict. Investors cannot blindly use the current or past internal growth rate for EPS to predict the future rate of growth.

The internal growth rate estimate produced by Equation 17-7 is reliable only if a company's profitability as measured by ROE remains in balance and if the company maintains a stable payout ratio. If, for example, the ROE or payout ratio for a company grow significantly in the future or decline significantly, the actual EPS growth rate will turn out to be quite different than the internal growth rate estimate produced by Equation 17-7.

[6] Technically, g is defined as the expected growth rate in dividends. However, the dividend growth rate is clearly influenced by the earnings growth rate. Although dividend and earnings growth rates can diverge in the short run, such differences would not be expected to continue for long periods of time. The standard assumption in security analysis is that g represents the growth rate for both dividends and earnings.

A problem associated with using a particular year to estimate the internal growth rate is that the year used may not be a "normal" one. Basing a projection on one year's results can result in a faulty estimate; this is particularly true for companies in cyclical industries.

Payout ratios for most companies vary over time, but reasonable estimates can often be obtained for a particular company using an average of recent years. Estimating future ROE is more challenging. The previous analysis is useful in analyzing the factors that affect ROE. The challenge for analysts and investors is trying to determine how these factors will change in the future.

What matters is the future expected growth rate, not the actual historical growth rate. If investors expect the growth rate to be different in the future, they should use the expected growth rate and not simply the calculation based on current data.

There are alternative approaches that can be used to determine expected future growth rates. One approach is to examine historic rates of growth in dividends and earnings levels, including long-term trends in these growth rates for the company, the industry, and the economy as a whole. Predictions regarding future growth rates can be determined based on these past trends using arithmetic or geometric averages or using more involved statistical techniques such as regression analysis.

Another important source of information regarding company growth, particularly for the near term, can be found in analyst estimates, which is discussed at length in the following section. Investors may be especially interested in consensus estimates, because it is quite likely that market values are based to a large extent on these estimates. Deviations from these estimates could signal that a security is mispriced in the market, which may represent an exploitable investment opportunity.

EARNINGS ESTIMATES

The EPS that investors use to value stocks is the future (expected) EPS. Current stock price is a function of future earnings estimates and the appropriate P_0 / E_1 ratio, not the past. If investors knew what the EPS for a particular company would be next year, they could achieve good results in the market.

When performing fundamental security analysis using EPS, an investor needs to (1) know how to obtain an earnings estimate, (2) consider the accuracy of any earnings estimate obtained, and (3) understand the role of earnings surprises in impacting stock prices. We consider each of these topics in turn.

A Forecast of EPS

Security Analysts' Estimates of Earnings

Among the most obvious sources of earnings estimates are security analysts, who make such forecasts as part of their job. This type of earnings information is widely available. All of the major investment dealers in Canada provide such estimates in their research reports. *The Value Line Investment Survey* is the largest and probably most well-known investment advisory service in the United States. It provides subscribers with quarterly earnings forecasts for several quarters ahead for the more than 1,700 companies that it monitors. I/B/E/S/ International <http://www.ibes.com> is the best-known New York firm that tracks earnings estimates by analysts and makes them available. Earnings estimates are also available from other companies such as Zacks Investment Research <http://www.zacks.com>, and First Call Corporation <http://www.firstcall.com>.

Several studies suggest that individual analysts are by and large undistinguishable in their ability to predict EPS. The practical implication of these findings is that the consensus forecast is likely to be superior to the forecasts of individual analysts.

Mechanical Estimates of Earnings

An alternative method of obtaining earnings forecasts is the use of mechanical procedures such as time series models. In deciding what type of model to use, some of the evidence on the behaviour of earnings over time should be considered.

Time series analysis involves the use of historical data to make earnings forecasts. The model assumes that the future will be similar to the past. The series being forecast, EPS, is assumed to have trend elements, an average value, seasonal factors, and error. The moving average technique is a simple example of the time series model for forecasting EPS. Exponential smoothing, which assigns differing weights to past values, is an example of a more sophisticated technique. A regression equation would represent another technique for making forecasts; the regression equation could handle several variables, such as trend and seasonal factors. More sophisticated models can also be used.

Studies of the behaviour of the time path of earnings have produced mixed results. Most of the early studies indicated randomness in the growth rates of annual earnings. Other studies found some evidence of patterns. More recent studies, particularly those of quarterly earnings, have indicated that the time series behaviour of earnings is not random.

The Accuracy of Earnings Forecasts

Intuitively, one would expect analyst earnings predictions to be superior to those obtained using historical data and trends in earnings, since they use more information. Several studies including Brown and Rozeff as well as O'Brien, suggest that analysts provide superior short-term earnings forecasts (one to three quarters ahead) than mechanical methods.[7] The evidence is mixed regarding the superiority of analyst reports for long-term earnings projections.

Even if investors accept the relative superiority of analysts' estimates to mechanical methods, the fact remains that analysts often over- or underestimate the earnings that are actually realized. Analysts are typically far off target on their estimates. According to one study of almost 400 companies, analysts' estimates averaged 57 per cent too high in the first month of a fiscal year, and the error was still up by an average 12 per cent by year-end.

Another study by Dreman and Berry covered 66,100 analysts' consensus forecasts for the period 1974–90. Analysts were given every advantage in the study — for example, forecasts could be made in the same quarter as earnings were reported, and the forecasts could be changed up to two weeks before the end of the quarter. Nevertheless, the average annual error was 44 per cent, and only 25 per cent of consensus estimates came within plus or minus 5 per cent of reported earnings. Looking at the estimates on the basis of the 61 industries involved, only one industry had forecast errors averaging under 10 per cent for the entire time period and, overall, the average forecast error grouped by industries was 50 per cent (the median error was 43 per cent).[8]

The information value of analyst reports depends upon a variety of factors and is generally enhanced by: the amount of recent company information that is used; the number of analysts

[7] L. Brown and M. Rozeff, "Analysts Can Forecast Accurately!" *Journal of Portfolio Management* 6 (Spring 1980), pp. 31–34; P. O'Brien, "Analyst's Forecasts as Earnings Expectation," *Journal of Accounting and Economics* 10 (January 1988), pp. 53–83.

[8] D. Dreman, "Cloudy Crystal Balls," *Forbes*, October 10, 1994, p. 154.

following the stock; the degree of consensus among analysts; and the quality of analysts following the stock. However, there is a great deal of evidence that analysts tend to be overly optimistic on average. Supporting studies include the O'Brien study mentioned above, as well as Canadian evidence documented by Hennessey as well as Ackert and Athanassakos.[9]

These results may not be that surprising since analysts have greater incentive to issue buy rather than sell recommendations. They are under pressure by the companies they follow to avoid issuing sell recommendations. In fact, sell recommendations are rare, which is discussed in the Real-World Returns box below. This pressure will be greater if the brokerage firm they work for is trying to the sell shares of the company being analyzed or if there exists an investment banking relationship with the company. In addition, analysts may prefer to make estimates that do not stand out from the crowd. These notions are supported by the results of Ackert and Athanassakos who find that analysts are "more optimistic when there is greater dispersion in earnings forecasts."[10]

Inaccurate earnings estimates can provide opportunities for investors. Analysts are frequently wrong, and if investors can make better estimates of earnings, they can expect to profit from their astuteness. In addition, several empirical studies, such as Hawkins, Chamberlin and Daniel, and Hennessey suggest that investors can benefit from earnings estimate revisions.[11] In particular, portfolios of stocks that have experienced positive earnings forecast revisions, produce excess positive returns subsequent to the revision. The larger the revisions, the greater the excess returns.

Earnings Surprises

We have established that changes in earnings and stock prices are highly correlated. We have also discussed the necessity of estimating EPS and how such estimates can be obtained. What remains is to examine the role of expectations about earnings in selecting common stocks.

The association between earnings and stock prices is more complicated than simply demonstrating a correlation between earnings growth and stock-price changes. Elton, Gruber, and Gultekin found that investors could not earn excess returns by buying and selling stocks on the basis of the consensus estimate of earnings growth. (The consensus estimate was defined as the average estimate of security analysts at major brokerage houses.) They also found that analysts tended to overestimate earnings for companies they expected would perform well and to underestimate for companies they expected would perform poorly.[12]

Investors must form expectations about EPS, and these will be incorporated into stock prices if markets are efficient. Although these expectations are often inaccurate, they play an important role in affecting stock prices. Malkiel and Cragg concluded that in making accurate one-year predictions, "It is far more important to know what the market will think the growth rate of earnings will be next year rather than to know the (actual) realized long-term growth rate.[13]

[9] S. Hennessey, "Can Active Managers Profit from Earnings Forecast Revisions?" *Canadian Investment Review* 6 (Spring 1993), pp. 39–45; L. Ackert and G. Athanassakos, "Expectations of the Herd," *Canadian Investment Review* 9 (Winter 1996/97), pp. 7–11.

[10] L. Ackert and G. Athanassakos, "Expectations of the Herd," p. 7.

[11] E. Hawkins, S. Chamberlin and W. Daniel, "Earnings Expectations and Security Prices," *Financial Analysts Journal* 40 (Sept/Oct 1984), pp. 24–37; S. Hennessey, "Can Active Managers Profit from Earnings Forecast Revisions?" *Canadian Investment Review* 6 (Spring 1993), pp. 39–45.

[12] E. Elton, N. Gruber, and M. Gultekin, "Expectations and Share Prices," *Management Science* 27 (September 1981), pp. 975–987.

[13] B. Malkiel and J. Cragg, "Expectations and the Structure of Share Prices," *American Economic Review* 60 (September 1970), p. 616.

REAL-WORLD RETURNS

Bay Street's Ratings Game

Stock analysts had some explaining to do when **Loewen Group Inc.** announced an $80-million (US) writedown and third-quarter loss in September 1997.

During a year of promoting Loewen as a "strong buy" or "buy," half a dozen stock watchers missed danger signs at North America's second-largest funeral home and cemetery operator. Most alerted investors to bail after the news broke, but it was too late. More than $340-million of Loewen's market value went into the grave within two days of the announcement, when the company's stock price fell 16 per cent to $35.20 on the New York Stock Exchange.

Investors would have been better advised to listen to a pair of persistent Loewen bears, Susan Little, with Raymond James & Associates Inc. in Florida, and Steven Saltzman, with ABN Amro Chicago Corp., who began downgrading the company in late 1995.

By the spring of 1997, the two analysts were warning investors that the rapid pace of Loewen's acquisition program would erode profit growth and pose operating risks. Their prophecy came true in September when Loewen revealed the huge writedown to reduce excess overhead, staff, and borrowing costs.

How come most other analysts didn't speak up? The answer to that strikes at the heart of a growing controversy in the investment community. Many investors believe the tardy warning calls on Loewen are symptomatic of a broader deterioration in Bay Street research.

Today, the Street is a world where a "buy" recommendation can sometimes mean "sell"; investors must navigate a bewildering array of euphemistic recommendations such as "underweight" and "neutral" to shape investment decisions; and a positive research report can sometimes mean the difference between winning and losing a lucrative underwriting contract.

Many pension funds and mutual funds, which account for 60 per cent of Canada's stock trades, are becoming so reluctant to rely on brokerage research that they're spending millions to beef up in-house research teams and hire independent analysts.

Some investors blame research lapses on the fevered atmosphere of the bull market, the longest in history. With market momentum pushing so many stocks into the stratosphere, analysts can become complacent about the fundamentals of companies they follow.

There are other, more cynical opinions. Investors complain of a growing tendency for analysts to serve as cheerleaders, rather than critics of the companies they follow. In a number of cases, analysts recommend companies that also happen to be clients of their firm's corporate finance division, which generates the bulk of brokerage profits from underwriting and advisory commissions.

No matter which argument you believe, many investors seem unified about one thing — Bay Street research is not as reliable as it used to be.

The Analyst Decoder

Imagine an investment world where there are only "buys" and "sells."

Not sort of buys, or kind of sells, or sell soons, or think about buyings, or lighten up because trouble is brewing, or get on board before this thing lifts off the launch pads — just plain, old, garden-variety buy and sell recommendations for stocks.

It'll never happen. Not in a world of accumulate, underperform, swaps and trading buys, a morass of fuzzy categories that take a steady compass for investors to navigate successfully. The rating system is a secret language that investment professionals usually understand but can be Greek to the guy in the street.

Here's a quick guide to some of the typical rankings:

Strong buy: Love it, buy it, strap on your seat belt, this rocket's going to the moon. Unless we're wrong, in which case the next stop may be a hold.

Buy: We like it, you might want to buy it, but it's not a real crank turner. Think of it as a strong buy light. It may have been a strong buy once, but the stock has rallied so there's less upside.

Accumulate: Better than a hold, but not a buy. So rather than simply going out and buying it, you might want to accumulate the stock. Clear? Accumulate's evil twin is the reduce rating, which isn't an outright sell but rather a suggestion that investors who own the stock reduce their holdings. Got it?

Hold: The hold or neutral category is the market's version of purgatory, a nether world between buy and sell. It's a place where turnaround stories on the road to accumulate or buy mingle briefly with the falling angels that are booked on the next train to underperform or, God forbid, sell.

An investor needs to know where the stock has been to define the true significance of a hold. It may just mean that a really good stock has gotten ahead of itself, or a mediocre stock has been beaten down to a level where there's little danger of more downside. Or if a stock is bouncing around all over the place, it's a place for analysts to park the stock so they don't look like dorks by flip-flopping between ratings every couple of weeks. Or a hold rating could simply be a polite pause on the way to something worse — or better. All of this raises the question: If a brokerage has a hold on one stock and a buy on another, why wouldn't you just sell the hold and buy the buy, in which case, isn't a hold really a sell? Just wondering.

Reduce: See evil twin accumulate above.

Sell: Means sell. Really. Given the incredible reluctance of analysts to utter the dreaded s-word, this is a rating that should be taken fairly seriously. It rarely means just that stock has gotten overpriced. More often it's an indication of fundamental problems.

Source: Excerpted from Jacquie McNish, Stephen Northfield, and Eric Reguly, "Bay Street's Ratings Game," The Globe and Mail / Report on Business, *Saturday, March 14, 1998, pp. B1, B4. Reprinted with permission from* The Globe and Mail.

As Latané and Jones have pointed out, new information about a stock is unexpected information.[14] The important point about EPS in terms of stock prices is the difference between what investors in general are expecting the EPS to be and what the company actually reports. Unexpected information about earnings calls for investors to revise their expectations about the future and therefore an adjustment in the price of the stock. A favourable **earnings surprise**, in which the actual earnings exceed the market's expectation, should bring about an adjustment to the price of the stock as investors alter their beliefs about the company's earnings. Conversely, an unfavourable earnings surprise should lead to a downward adjustment in price; in effect, the market has been disappointed in its expectations.

Earnings Surprise
The difference between a firm's actual earnings and the consensus earnings estimate.

In conclusion, stock prices are affected not only by the level of earnings and their growth, but also by the market's expectations of earnings. Investors should be concerned with both the forecast for earnings and the difference between the actual earnings and the forecast — that is, the surprise. Therefore, fundamental analysis of earnings should involve more than a forecast, which is difficult enough: It should involve the role of the market's expectations about earnings.

[14] H. Latané and C. Jones, "Standardized Unexpected Earnings — A Progress Report," *Journal of Finance* 32 (December 1977), pp. 1457–1465.

What happens when the quarterly earnings are reported and the figures are below analysts' estimates? Obviously, the stock price is likely to drop quickly, and in some cases sharply. In a number of cases, the stock market is very unforgiving about disappointments in the form of negative earnings surprises. Such disappointments, and the accompanying sharp drops in stock price, are a common occurrence on Bay and Wall streets. Similarly, it is not uncommon to see a stock price increase on news of a negative EPS, if the actual loss is not as great as had been expected.

If the price does drop sharply following the announcement of earnings below expectations, should an investor interested in owning the stock react quickly to take advantage of the price drop? According to one study of 2,000 large companies that experienced single-day price drops of over 10 per cent in one particular year, the average decline was 17 per cent the first day the stock traded after the bad news.[15] On average these stocks were 25 per cent cheaper 30 days after the report of bad news, and 90 per cent of the stocks were lower at that time. Sixty days after the bad news these stocks were still down an average of 23 per cent, and after 90 days almost 20 per cent. Why? The initial shock is often followed by additional shocks.

Useful Information for Investors about Earnings Estimates

Summarizing our discussion about earnings forecasts, we can note the following useful information about the role of earnings forecasts in selecting common stocks:

1. Earnings reports are a key factor affecting stock prices. However, it is the surprise element in the reports that really matters — the difference between the actual results reported and the results expected by the market.
2. Surprises occur because analyst estimates are often considerably off target.
3. There appears to be a lag in the adjustment of stock prices to earnings surprises.
4. One earnings surprise tends to lead to another; there is a 45 per cent chance of repeating an earnings surprise.
5. The best guidelines to surprises are revisions in analyst estimates. If estimates are steadily being adjusted upward, a buy signal is indicated; downward adjustments indicate a sell signal.
6. Stocks with significant revisions of 5 per cent or more — up or down — often show above or below average performance.
7. Investors interested in buying stocks that report bad news and suffer a sharp decline should wait awhile. Chances are the stock will be cheaper 30 and 60 days after the initial sharp decline.

THE P/E RATIO

Price/Earnings (P/E) Ratio The ratio of stock price to earnings, using historical, current, or estimated data. Also known as the earnings multiplier.

The other half of the valuation framework in fundamental analysis is the **price/earnings (P/E) ratio**, or the earnings multiplier. The P/E ratio (reported in *The Globe and Mail*, the *National Post*, and other financial newspapers) indicates how much per dollar of earnings investors currently are willing to pay for a stock, that is, the price for each dollar of earnings. In a sense, it represents the market's summary evaluation of a company's prospects.

[15] D. Dreman, "Let the Dust Clear," *Forbes*, October 12, 1992, p. 166.

In effect, the P/E ratio is a measure of the relative price of a stock. In September of 1998, for example, investors were willing to pay about 60 times earnings for **Baton Broadcasting**, but only one times earnings for **Repap Enterprises**. What are the reasons for such a large difference? To answer this question, it is necessary to consider the determinants of the P/E ratio.

Determinants of the P/E Ratio

Reviewing our earlier discussion in Chapter 13, we recall that the appropriate forward P/E ratio (P_0 / E_1) is conceptually a function of three factors, as expressed in the equation below:[16]

$$P_0 / E_1 = \frac{D_1 / E_1}{k - g} \tag{17-8}$$

where

D_1 / E_1 = the expected dividend payout ratio

k = the required rate of return for the stock

g = expected growth rate in dividends

Investors attempting to determine the P/E ratio that will prevail for a particular stock should think in terms of these three factors and their likely changes. Each of these is considered below.

The Dividend Payout Ratio

Dividends are clearly a function of earnings (although accounting earnings are an imprecise measure for cash flow, out of which dividends are paid). The relationship between these two variables, however, is more complex than current dividends being a function of current earnings. Dividends paid by corporations reflect established practices (i.e., previous earnings level) as well as prospects for the future (i.e., expected future earnings).

Many corporations whose stocks trade in Canadian equity markets pay dividends. For example, about half of the more than 1,700 TSE-listed companies paid dividends in 1997. Most companies behave as if dividends matter significantly to investors, and once dividend payments are established at a certain level, companies strive to maintain them at that level and increase them, if at all possible. Dividends are usually not reduced until and unless there is no alternative. In addition, they are generally not increased until it is clear that the new, higher level of dividends can be supported. In 1997, for example, 90 TSE-listed companies paid special dividends, instead of increasing their regular dividends. During the same year 121 companies increased their regular dividends, while only eight stocks reduced their dividends, and 11 others completely omitted them. As a result of this reluctance to decrease dividends, or to increase them unless they can be maintained, dividends adjust with a lag to earnings.

The P/E ratio can be expected to change as the expected dividend payout ratio changes. The higher the expected payout ratio, other things being equal, the higher the P/E ratio. However, "other things" are seldom equal. If the payout rises, the expected growth rate in earnings and dividends, g, will probably decline, thereby adversely affecting the P/E ratio. This decline occurs because less funds will be reinvested in the business, thereby leading to a decline in the expected growth rate, g.

[16] Strictly speaking, this relationship is only appropriate when it is reasonable to assume constant growth in dividends to infinity since this estimate for P_0 / E_1 is derived from the constant-growth version of the DDM.

The Required Rate of Return

As we know, the required rate of return, k, is a function of the riskless rate of return and a risk premium.

$$k = \text{RF} + \text{RP} \tag{17-9}$$

The riskless rate of return is usually proxied by the short-term government T-bill rate. The risk premium is the additional compensation demanded by risk-averse investors before purchasing a risky asset such as a common stock. In Chapter 9, we saw that the CAPM provides a method for estimating the size of the risk premium, based on a stock's (or portfolio's) market risk as measured by beta (refer to Equation 9-9).

Based on Equation 17-9, the following two statements can be made about a company's required rate of return:

1. Other things being equal, if the risk-free rate, RF, rises, the required rate of return, k, will rise. Thus, in periods of high interest rates such as 1980–81, k will be higher than in periods such as 1982–83, when interest rates had declined.
2. Other things being equal, if the risk premium rises as a result of an increase in risk (which could be caused by an increase in business risk, financial risk, or other risks), k will rise. Conversely, if the risk premium falls as a result of a decrease in risk, k will fall.

As we learned in Chapter 13, the relationship between k and the P/E ratio is inverse: Other things being equal, as k rises, the P/E ratio declines; as k declines, the P/E ratio rises. Because the required rate of return is a discount rate, P/E ratios and discount rates move inversely to each other.

The Expected Growth Rate

The third variable affecting the P/E ratio is the expected growth rate of dividends, g. We know that g = retention ratio × ROE, making the expected growth rate a function of the return on equity and the retention rate. The higher either of these variables is, the higher g will be, all other things being equal. What about the relationship between g and P/E? P/E and g are directly related: The higher the g, the higher the P/E ratio, other things being equal.

Investors are generally willing to pay more for a company with expected rapid growth in earnings than for one with expected slower growth in earnings. A basic problem in fundamental analysis, however, is determining how much more investors should be willing to pay for growth. In other words, how high should the P/E ratio be? There is no precise answer to this question. It depends on such factors as the following:

- The confidence that investors have in the expected growth. For some companies investors may be well justified in expecting a rapid rate of growth for the next few years because of previous performance, management's ability, and the high estimates of growth described in investment advisory services. This may not be the case for another company, where, because of competitive inroads and other factors, the high growth prospects are at great risk.
- The reasons for the earnings growth can be important. Is it a result of great demand in the marketplace or of astute financing policies that could backfire if interest rates rise sharply or the economy enters a severe recession? Is growth the result of sales expansion or cost cutting (which will be exhausted at some point)? DuPont analysis is designed to provide insight into these issues.

Analyzing the P/E Ratio

In analyzing a particular P/E ratio, we first ask what model describes the expected growth rate for that company. Recent rapid growth and published estimates of strong expected future growth would lead investors not to use the constant-growth version of the dividend valuation model. Instead, we should evaluate the company by using a multiple-growth model. At some point, however, this growth can be expected to slow down to a more normal rate. In such cases it would be more appropriate to use the multi-stage growth version of the DDM, described in Chapter 13.

Why P/E Ratios Vary among Companies

Stock prices reflect market expectations about earnings. Companies that the market believes will achieve higher earnings growth rates will tend to be priced higher than those that are expected to show low earnings growth rates. Thus, a primary factor in explaining P/E ratio differences among companies is investor expectations about the future growth of earnings.

FUNDAMENTAL SECURITY ANALYSIS IN PRACTICE

We have examined several important aspects of fundamental analysis as it is applied to individual companies. Obviously, such a process can be quite detailed, involving an analysis of a company's sales potential, competition, tax situation, cost projections, accounting practices, and so on. Regardless of detail and complexity, the underlying process is as described. Analysts and investors are seeking to estimate a company's earnings and P/E ratio and to determine whether the stock is undervalued (a buy) or overvalued (a sell).

In doing fundamental security analysis, investors need to use published and computerized data sources both to gather information and to provide calculations and estimates of future variables such as EPS. There are several sources of information including financial newspapers such as *The Globe and Mail* and the *National Post* in Canada, and international publications such as *The Wall Street Journal* and the *Financial Times*. In addition, there exist a large number of financial magazines including *Forbes*, *BusinessWeek*, *Fortune*, and *Money*.

Corporate annual and quarterly reports also provide extensive information about companies. The SEDAR (System for Electronic Document Analysis and Retrieval) Web site <www.sedar.com> provides on-line access to annual reports and various other information statements that are filed by companies with the appropriate regulatory authority.

Reports from investment dealers provide a current assessment of a number of companies, as does *The Financial Post Survey of Industrials*. In the US there are several large investment advisory services including *The Value Line Investment Survey*, Moody's *Industrial Manual*, and Standard & Poor's *Corporation Records and Industry Surveys*. In addition, there are numerous Web sites that provide up-to-date information regarding companies. Several Canadian Web sites are provided in the Investments on the Web section at the end of this chapter.

In modern investment analysis, the risk for a stock is often measured by its beta coefficient, as explained in Chapter 9. Beta reflects the relative systematic risk for a stock, or the risk that cannot be diversified away. The higher the beta coefficient, the higher the risk for an individual stock, and the higher the required rate of return. Beta measures the volatility of a stock's returns relative to fluctuations in market returns.

EXAMPLE: MEASURING RISK FOR BOMBARDIER INC.

According to a recent investment newsletter, the beta for **Bombardier Inc.** was 0.97 at the end of 1997. Therefore, we know that Bombardier had approximately the same systematic risk as the market as a whole (which has a beta of 1.0 by definition). That is, on average, its price fluctuates closely with market fluctuations. If, for example, the market is expected to rise 10 per cent over the next year, investors could, on average, expect Bombardier to rise approximately 9.7 per cent based on its beta of 0.97. In a market decline, Bombardier would be expected to decline approximately the same amount as the market.

INVESTING *tip*

It is extremely important in analyses such as these to remember that beta is a measure of volatility, indicating what can be expected to happen, on average, to a stock when the overall market rises or falls. In fact, Bombardier, or any other stock, will not perform in the predicted way every time. If it did, the risk would disappear. Investors can always find examples of stocks that, over some specific period of time, did not move as their beta indicated they would. This is not an indictment of the usefulness of beta as a measure of volatility; rather, it suggests that the beta relationship can only be expected to hold on the average.

In trying to understand and predict a company's return and risk, we need to remember that both are a function of two components. The systematic component is related to the return on the overall market. The other component is the unique part attributable to the company itself and not to the overall market. It is a function of the specific positive or negative factors that affect a company independent of the market.

It should come as no surprise that because security analysis always involves the uncertain future, mistakes will be made, and analysts will differ in their outlooks for a particular company. As we might expect, security analysis in today's world is often done differently than it was in the past. The reason for this change is not so much that we have a better understanding of the basis of security analysis, because the models we have discussed earlier — value as a function of expected return and risk — remain the basis of security analysis today. Rather, the differences now have to do with the increasingly sophisticated use of personal computers to perform many calculations quickly and objectively, as well as the timeliness and quantity of relevant information now available to investors and analysts.

PUTTING ALL THE PIECES TOGETHER

We conclude our discussion by illustrating how we could have used the information above to estimate the value of **Bombardier**'s common shares on January 31, 1998 at which time their closing price was $28.10.

We will use the following estimates obtained from the information provided above:

Sustainable growth rate (g) = 10.76%
Dividend payout ratio = 0.2595
Most recent dividend per share (D_0) = $0.306
Most recent earnings per share (EPS_0) = $1.18
Beta = 0.97

We will use the three-month T-bill rate at the end of January 1998 (4.5 per cent) as the measure of the risk free rate of return. Using 12 per cent as an estimate for the expected return on the market for the following year, we can determine the required return on Bombardier's shares using CAPM:

$$\text{Required return } k = 4.5 + (12 - 4.5)(0.97) = 11.78\%$$

We begin our analysis based on the assumption that the estimated 10.76 per cent growth rate is sustainable indefinitely. This implies we can use the constant-growth version of the DDM given in Equation 17-1. Based on this model, we get the following estimate for the value of Bombardier's shares at January 31, 1998:

$$\hat{P}_0 = \frac{D_1}{k - g} = \frac{(\$0.306) \times (1.1076)}{0.1178 - .1076} = \frac{\$0.339}{0.0102} = \$33.23$$

Alternatively, we could have used the P/E ratio approach to estimate the value of Bombardier's shares. If we again assume constant growth to infinity, we can determine the appropriate forward P/E ratio (P_0 / E_1) using Equation 17-8:

$$P/E = \frac{D_1 / E_1}{k - g} = \frac{0.2595}{0.1178 - 0.1076} = 25.44$$

We can estimate next year's EPS using the growth rate of 10.76 per cent to be:

$$EPS_1 = EPS_0 \times (1 + g) = (\$1.18) \times (1.1076) = \$1.31$$

Combining these results and using Equation 17-2, we get the following estimate for the value of Bombardier:

$$\hat{P}_0 = \text{Estimated EPS} \times P_0 / E_1 \text{ ratio} = \$1.31 \times 25.44 = \$33.33$$

These estimates are very close, which is attributable to the fact that they both use the same inputs and both assume constant growth in dividends at a rate of 10.76 per cent to infinity. This may or may not have been a reasonable assumption, and there are many alternative methods and assumptions available for valuing Bombardier, many of which were discussed at length in Chapter 13.

For ease of exposition, let's assume these estimates were considered reasonable at the time, and consider their implications. Both of these estimates suggested that Bombardier was undervalued at $28.10. Based on this analysis, an investor would have been inclined to hold Bombardier shares if already held, or purchase them if not held.

The analysis above uses the 1998 accounting figures to estimate future growth in earnings and dividends. One concern with this approach is that the use of a single year's earnings and dividend measures could provide a misleading estimate of future growth if the chosen year was not a typical one. One way to address this concern is to use averages over some longer period of time. For example, we could use five-year averages — say, 1993–97 — to estimate the sustainable growth rate in dividends (and earnings) for Bombardier. Over this period, the average ROE was 14.3 per cent, while the average dividend payout ratio was 0.2570, both of which are very close to the 1998 figures. Based on these figures the sustainable growth rate is estimated as:

$$g = (1 - 0.2579) \times (0.143) = 10.62\%$$

Notice that this estimate is also very close to the estimate obtained using the 1998 data, so obviously 1998 was a typical year for Bombardier.

Let's redo our analysis using this estimate of growth for Bombardier's earnings and dividends. Based on the constant-growth version of the DDM, we obtain the following estimate for Bombardier's share value:

$$\hat{P}_0 = \frac{(\$0.306) \times (1.1062)}{0.1178 - .1062} = \frac{\$0.338}{0.0116} = \$29.14$$

Using the P/E ratio approach, again assuming constant growth to infinity, we determine the appropriate forward P/E ratio to be:

$$P/E = \frac{0.2570}{0.1178 - 0.1062} = 22.16$$

We estimate next year's EPS using the growth rate of 10.62 per cent to be:

$$EPS_1 = (\$1.18) \times (1.1062) = \$1.30$$

Combining these results, we would estimate the value of Bombardier's shares to be:

$$\hat{P}_0 = \$1.30 \times 22.16 = \$28.80$$

These estimates are also very close to each other, and suggest that Bombardier is properly valued or very slightly undervalued at $28.10. Notice the substantial difference in estimates caused by such a slight variation in our growth estimate. This is because the estimated growth rate of 10.76 per cent is so close to the required rate of return of 11.78 per cent. This alludes to a matter discussed in Chapter 13 — the constant-growth version of the DDM does not always work that well for fast growing firms. This suggests we may want to employ some of the other valuation techniques discussed in Chapter 13 to value such firms, although we will not do so here in the interest of brevity.

A potentially greater problem with our approach is that there is never any guarantee that past performance will repeat itself, so there are always problems associated with using historical data to predict future performance (this is an issue we have been forced to deal with at various points throughout the text). In order to avoid these problems, we must obtain future estimates of growth based on other sources of information and analysis.

As it turned out, by January 31, 1999 Bombardier shares had fallen to $22.50. What went wrong? Several things did not unfold as expected over the next year. First, the market earned a return of just 0.4 per cent over the year, well below the expected return of 12 per cent. Second, Bombardier's earnings per share figure for 1999 turned out to be only $0.72, again well below our estimates of $1.31 and $1.30. Similarly, Bombardier's 1999 dividend per share was $0.17, not the estimated $0.339 or $0.338. This does not mean that fundamental analysis is a waste of time, but merely highlights a fact that we have been stressing throughout the text — it is difficult to predict the future, especially for relatively short periods of time. This is the unavoidable risk associated with investing in common stocks.

SUMMARY

This summary relates to the learning objectives provided on page 527.

1. **Define fundamental analysis at the company level.**
The analysis of individual companies, the last of the three steps in fundamental security analysis, examines the basic financial variables of the company, such as sales, management, and competition. It involves the application of the valuation procedures described in earlier chapters. Intrinsic value (a stock's justified price) can be estimated using a dividend valuation model, an earnings multiplier model, or many other approaches, several of which are discussed in Chapter 13. It is then compared to the current market price in order to determine whether the stock is undervalued or overvalued. An important first step in fundamental analysis is to understand the earnings per share (EPS) of companies. The financial statements can be used to understand the accounting basis of EPS.

2. **Explain the accounting aspects of a company's earnings.**
The balance sheet shows the assets and liabilities at a specific date, whereas the income statement shows the flows during a period for the items that determine net income. Although these statements must be prepared in accordance with a set of guidelines determined by the accounting profession — generally accepted accounting principles (GAAP) — the use of alternative permissible accounting practices can result in EPS figures that are not always precise, readily comparable figures. EPS is the result of the interaction of several variables. Changes in earnings are directly related to changes in stock prices. To assess expected earnings, investors often consider the earnings growth rate, which is often measured as the product of ROE and the earnings retention rate.

3. **Describe the importance of EPS forecasts.**
The lack of persistence in growth rates may lead investors to consider EPS forecasts, which are available mechanically or from analysts. All forecast methods are subject to error and the evidence is mixed on which method is better, although recent studies favour analysts' forecasts. The difference between actual and forecast EPS is important because of the role of the market's expectations about earnings.

4. **Estimate the P/E ratio of a company.**
The price/earnings (P/E) ratio is the other half of the earnings multiplier model, indicating the amount per dollar of earnings investors are willing to pay for a stock. It represents the relative price of a stock per dollar of earnings, with some companies carrying high P/E ratios and others having low ones at particular times. The P/E ratio is influenced directly by investors' expectations of the future growth of earnings and the payout ratio, and inversely by the required rate of return. P/E ratios vary among companies and for the

same company through time, primarily because of investors' expectations about the future growth of earnings. If investors lower their expectations, the price of the stock may drop while actual earnings remain constant or even rise.

5. **Use the beta coefficient to estimate the risk of a stock.**
The beta coefficient measures the volatility for a stock with respect to fluctuations in market returns. It indicates the average responsiveness of the stock's price to the overall market, with high beta stocks exhibiting larger changes than the overall market; low beta stocks show smaller changes.

KEY TERMS

Earnings surprise
Financial statements
Generally accepted accounting principles (GAAP)
Internal (sustainable) growth rate
Price/earnings (P/E) ratio
Return on assets (ROA)
Return on equity (ROE)

ADDITIONAL RESOURCES

INVESTMENTS ON THE WEB

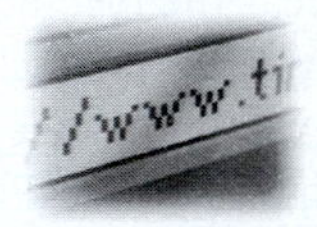

Some Canadian Web sites that provide up-to-date information regarding companies and investments-related issues are:

Canadian Stock Watch: <http://www.canada-stockwatch.com>
Carlson On-Line Services Inc.: <http://www.fin-info.com>
Quicken Financial Network: <http://www.quicken.ca>
imoney: <http://www.imoney.com>
Financial Post: <http://www.canoe.ca/fp/home.html>
GLOBE fund: <http://www.globefund.com>
The Investment Funds Institute of Canada: <http://www.mutfunds.com/ific>
The Canadian Institute of Financial Planning: <http://www.mutfunds.com/cifp>
Canadian Bankers Association: <http://www.cba.ca>
Canadian WealthNet: <http://www.nucleus.com/wealthnet>
Canadian Derivatives Clearing Corporation: <http://www.cdcc.ca>
Canadian Stock Market Reporter Inc.: <http://www.canstock.com>
SEDAR: <http://www.sedar.com>
Canadian News Wire: <http://www.newsire.ca>

REVIEW QUESTIONS

1. What is the intrinsic value of a stock?
2. How can a stock's intrinsic value be determined?

3. What are the limitations of using Equation 17-1 to determine intrinsic value?
4. What is meant by GAAP?
5. What does the auditor's report signify about the financial statements?
6. How can investors obtain EPS forecasts? Which source is better?
7. What problems do estimating accounting earnings present?
8. What is the concept of earnings quality?
9. Outline, in words, the determination process for EPS.
10. Assuming that a firm's return on assets exceeds its interest costs, why would it not boost ROE to the maximum through the use of debt financing since higher ROE leads to higher EPS?
11. How can the earnings growth rate be determined?
12. How well do earnings growth rates for individual companies persist across time?
13. What role do earnings expectations play in selecting stocks?
14. How can the unexpected component of EPS be used to select stocks?
15. Fred West, an investor, wants to know the beta coefficient for a particular company? How could Fred use this information when investing?
16. Is beta the only determinant of a company's return?
17. Explain the role of financing in a company's EPS.
18. What are the variables that affect the P/E ratio? Is the effect direct or inverse for each component?
19. Holding everything else constant, what effect would the following have on a company's P/E ratio?
    a. An increase in the expected growth rate of earnings
    b. A decrease in the expected dividend payout
    c. An increase in the risk-free rate of return
    d. An increase in the risk premium
    e. A decrease in the required rate of return.

PREPARING FOR YOUR PROFESSIONAL EXAMS

Special Note to CSC Students

Ensure that you have read and understood the following topics:*

Fundamental analysis, pp. 528–529
The accounting aspects of earnings, pp. 529–535
Analyzing a company's profitability, pp. 535–539
The P/E ratio, pp. 544–547
Fundamental security analysis in practice, pp. 547–548
Appendix 17-A: Financial Ratio Analysis: An Overview, pp. 563–567

**Reading these CSC-related topics should provide you with additional understanding of CSC material. However, it should not be seen as a substitute for reading the CSC textbook itself, which is the basis for the CSC exam.*

CSC REGISTRATION QUESTIONS

The Canadian Securities Institute issued the following sample questions in the 1997 CSC registration package as a means for students to self-assess their understanding of CSC-related material.

1. A balance sheet reflects a company's financial position ___________.
   a. over one fiscal year
   b. between two years
   c. after a new financing has occurred
   d. at one point in time
2. The largest item on an earnings statement is ___________.
   a. net earnings before extraordinary items
   b. earnings before interest charges
   c. earnings before taxes
   d. net earnings
3. The inventory turnover rate of a bakery would be _____ that of a steel manufacturer.
   a. higher than
   b. lower than
   c. the same as
4. If common shares are issued as payment for fixed assets, the company's working capital will be ______ it was before the share issue.
   a. higher than
   b. lower than
   c. the same as
5. Earnings per share calculated on a fully diluted basis are _______ earnings per share that do not take dilution into account.
   a. higher than
   b. lower than
   c. the same as
6. Briefly describe the chief difference between a *fixed asset* and a *current asset*.
7.

	Company F	**Company G**	**Company H**
Total debt	$6,000,000	$8,000,000	$7,000,000
Current assets	$15,000,000	$17,000,000	$16,000,000
Current liabilities	$5,000,000	$8,500,000	$4,000,000
Total assets	$33,000,000	$28,000,000	$22,000,000
Shareholders' equity	$16,750,000	$14,500,000	$11,250,000
Earnings per common share	$2.00	$1.50	$2.50
Common share price	$18.00	$15.00	$20.00
Dividend per common share	1.00	$0.60	$0.75
Debt / equity ratio	0.36:1	0.55:1	0.62:1
Interest coverage	1.5x	2.5x	2.0x
Inventory turnover	4.2x	3.0x	2.5x

Cash flow/total debt ratio	30.2%	20.0%	15.0%
Net profit margin	8.8%	8.0%	7.9%
Gross profit margin	9.5%	11.6%	10.2%
Net return on invested capital	7.2%	6.9%	8.4%
Net tangible assets per $1,000 of debt	$950	$2,000	$1,000

Using the above financial information for the same fiscal period for three industrial companies, answer the following questions. Calculate final answers to two decimal places.

a. Calculate total liabilities for all three companies. Show your calculations.

b. List four tests used to measure the investment quality of a company's debt. In each case indicate which one of the three companies has the superior rating.

c. Investors are paying the most for the earnings of which company? Show your calculations for each company and name the measure or test applied.

d. Which company is most generous in sharing its profit with its shareholders? Show your calculations for each company and name the measure or test applied.

e. Which company's management produced the best after-tax profit from funds provided by the company's creditors and shareholders? Specify why you think so.

f. Which company's management was the most efficient in turning over the company's goods and/or services at a before-tax profit? Specify why you think so.

g. Which company had the best inventory turnover performance? Specify why you think so.

PAST CFA EXAM PROBLEMS

The following question was asked on the 1991 CFA Level I examination:

1. The value of the components affecting the ROE of Merck & Co., Inc. for 1985 are indicated in Table 17-3 below. Selected 1990 income statement and balance sheet information for Merck can be found in Table 17-4 below.

   a. Calculate each of the five ROE components for Merck in 1990. Using the five components, calculate ROE for Merck in 1990. Show all calculations.

   b. Based on your calculations, describe how each ROE component contributed to the change in Merck's ROE between 1985 and 1990. Identify the major underlying reasons for the change in Merck's ROE.

Table 17-3

Merck & Co., Inc. 1985 ROE Components

Tax burden (net income / pretax income)	.628
Interest burden (pretax income / EBIT)	.989
Operating (or profit) margin	.245
Asset turnover	.724
Financial leverage	1.877

Table 17-4

Merck & Co., Inc. 1990 Selected Financial Data ($ millions)

Income Statement Data	
Sales revenue	$7,120
Amortization	230
Interest expense	10
Pretax income	2,550
Income taxes	900
Net income	1,650
Balance Sheet Data	
Current assets	$4,850
Net fixed assets	2,400
Total assets	7,250
Current liabilities	3,290
Long-term debt	100
Shareholders' equity	3,860
Total liabilities & shareholders' equity	7,250

The following information applies to Problems 2 through 5:
The following questions were asked on the 1992 CFA Level I examination:

Introduction

Eastover Company (EO) is a large, diversified forest products company. Approximately 75 per cent of its sales are from paper and forest products, with the remainder from financial services and real estate. The company owns 5.6 million acres of timberland, which is carried at very low historical cost on the balance sheet.

Peggy Mulroney, CFA, is an analyst at the investment counselling firm of Centurion Investments. She is assigned the task of assessing the outlook for Eastover, which is being considered for purchase and comparing it to another forest products company in Centurion's portfolios, Southampton Corporation (SHC). SHC is a major producer of lumber products in the United States. Building products, primarily lumber and plywood, account for 89 per cent of SHC's sales, with pulp accounting for the remainder. SHC owns 1.4 million acres of timberland, which is also carried at historical cost on the balance sheet. In SHC's case, however, that cost is not as far below current market as Eastover's.

Table 17-5

Eastover Company (EO) ($ millions, except shares outstanding)

Income Statement Summary

	1986	1987	1988	1989	1990
Sales	$5,652	$6,990	$7,863	$8,281	$7,406
Earnings before interest & taxes (EBIT)	$ 568	$ 901	$1,037	$ 708	$ 795
Interest expense (net)	(147)	(188)	(186)	(194)	(195)
Income before taxes	$ 421	$ 713	$ 851	$ 514	$ 600
Income taxes	(144)	(266)	(286)	(173)	(206)
Tax rate	34%	37%	33%	34%	34%
Net income	$ 277	$ 447	$ 565	$ 341	$ 394
Preferred dividends	(28)	(17)	(17)	(17)	(0)
Net income to common	$ 249	$ 430	$ 548	$ 324	$ 394
Common shares outstanding (millions)	196	204	204	205	201

Balance Sheet Summary

	1986	1987	1988	1989	1990
Current assets	$1,235	$1,491	$1,702	$1,585	$1,367
Timberland assets	649	625	621	612	615
Property, plant & equipment	4,370	4,571	5,056	5,430	5,854
Other assets	360	555	473	472	429
Total assets	$6,614	$7,242	$7,852	$8,099	$8,265
Current liabilities	$1,226	$1,186	$1,206	$1,606	$1,816
Long-term debt	1,120	1,340	1,585	1,346	1,585
Deferred taxes & other	1,000	1,000	1,016	1,000	1,000
Equity-preferred	364	350	350	400	0
Equity-common	2,904	3,366	3,695	3,747	3,864
Total liabilities & equity	$6,614	$7,242	$7,852	$8,099	$8,265

Table 17-6

Southampton Corporation (SHC) ($ millions, except shares outstanding)

Income Statement Summary

	1986	1987	1988	1989	1990
Sales	$1,306	$1,654	$1,799	$2,010	$1,793
Earnings before interest & taxes (EBIT)	$ 120	$ 230	$ 221	$ 304	$ 145
Interest expense (net)	(13)	(36)	(7)	(12)	(8)
Income before taxes	$ 107	$ 194	$ 214	$ 292	$ 137
Income taxes	(44)	(75)	(79)	(99)	(46)
Tax rate	41%	39%	37%	34%	34%
Net income	$ 63	$ 119	$ 135	$ 193	$ 91
Common shares outstanding (millions)	38	38	38	38	38

Table 17-6 (continued)

Balance Sheet Summary

	1986	1987	1988	1989	1990
Current assets	$ 487	$ 504	$ 536	$ 654	$ 509
Timberland assets	512	513	508	513	518
Property, plant & equipment	648	681	718	827	1,037
Other assets	141	151	34	38	40
Total assets	$1,788	$1,849	$1,796	$2,032	$2,104
Current liabilities	$ 185	$ 176	$ 162	$ 180	$ 195
Long-term debt	536	493	370	530	589
Deferred taxes & other	123	136	127	146	153
Equity	944	1,044	1,137	1,176	1,167
Total liabilities & equity	$1,788	$1,849	$1,796	$2,032	$2,104

Table 17-7

Current Information

	Current Share Price	Current Dividends	1992 EPS Estimate	Current Book Value Per Share
Eastover	$28	$1.20	$1.60	$17.32
Southampton	48	1.08	3.00	32.21
S&P 500	415	12.00	20.54	159.83

Table 17-8

Projected Growth Rates

	Next 3 Years (1992, 1993, 1994)	Growth Beyond 1994
Eastover	12%	8%
Southampton	13%	7%

2. Mulroney's supervisor asks her to first explore the relationship between industry lumber production and lumber production at EO and SHC. As part of this analysis, Mulroney runs two regressions, using industry lumber production as the independent variable and each company's lumber production as the dependent variable. The results are indicated below:

	Intercept (t-ratio)	Slope Coefficient (t-slope)	R^2
Eastover	2.79	−0.03	0.63
	(6.08)	(−0.25)	
Southampton	1.28	0.10	0.90
	(5.25)	(13.07)	

The t-ratio critical value at the 5 per cent level is 1.83.

a. The regressions produce the two intercepts and two slope coefficients shown above. Define the terms intercept and slope coefficient. State whether each of the two intercepts and each of the two slope coefficients are statistically significant.

b. Based on these regressions, identify the statistic that expresses the percentage of Eastover's and Southampton's lumber production that is explained by the independent variable (industry lumber production). State the percentage explained by the regression.

c. Based on your answer to (a) and (b), discuss the reliability of forecasts from each of the two regressions.

3. Mulroney continued her examination of Eastover and Southampton by looking at the five components of return on equity (ROE) for each company. For her analysis, Mulroney elected to define equity as total shareholders' equity, including preferred stock. She also elected to use year-end data rather than averages for the balance sheet items.

   a. Based on the data shown in Tables 17-5 and 17-6, calculate each of the five ROE components for Eastover and Southampton in 1990. Using the five components, calculate ROE for both companies in 1990. Show all calculations.

   b. Referring to the components calculated in (a), explain the difference in ROE for Eastover and Southampton in 1990.

   c. Using 1990 data, calculate an internal (i.e., sustainable) growth rate for both Eastover and Southampton. Discuss the appropriateness of using these calculations as a basis for estimating future growth.

4. Mulroney recalled from her CFA studies that the constant-growth discounted dividend model (DDM) was one way to arrive at a valuation for a company's common stock. She collected current dividend and stock price data for Eastover and Southampton, shown in Table 17-7.

   a. Using 11 per cent as the required rate of return (i.e., discount rate) and a projected growth rate of 8 per cent, compute a constant-growth DDM value for Eastover's stock and compare the computed value for Eastover to its stock price indicated in Table 17-7. Show calculations.

   Mulroney's supervisor commented that a two-stage DDM may be more appropriate for companies such as Eastover and Southampton. Mulroney believes that Eastover and Southampton could grow more rapidly over the next three years and then settle in at a lower but sustainable rate of growth beyond 1994. Her estimates are indicated in Table 17-8.

b. Using 11 per cent as the required rate of return, compute the two-stage DDM value of Eastover's stock and compare that value to its stock price indicated in Table 17-7. Show calculations.

c. Discuss two advantages and three disadvantages of using a constant-growth DDM. Briefly discuss how the two-stage DDM improves upon the constant-growth DDM.

5. Mulroney previously calculated a valuation for Southampton for both the constant growth and two-stage DDM as shown below:

	Discounted Dividend Model Using	
	Constant Growth Approach	Two-Stage Approach
Southampton	$29	$35.50

Using only the information provided and your answers to Questions 2, 3, and 4 select the stock (EO or SHC) that Mulroney should recommend as the better value, and justify your selection.

PROBLEMS

1. GF is a large producer of food products. In 19X5, the percentage breakdown of revenues and profits was as follows:

	Revenues (%)	Profits (%)
Packaged foods	41	62
Coffee	28	19
Processed meat	19	13
Food service — other	12	6
	100	100

International operations account for about 22 per cent of sales and 17 per cent of operating profit.

For the 19X1–19X5 fiscal years, ending March 31, the number of shares outstanding (in millions) and selected income statement data (in millions of dollars) were as follows:

Shares Outst.	Year	Revenues	Oper. Inc.	Cap. Exp.	Amort.	Int. Exp.	Net Income Before Tax	Net Income After Tax
49.93	19X1	$5472	$524	$121	$ 77	$ 31	$452	$232
49.97	19X2	5960	534	262	78	39	470	256
49.43	19X3	6601	565	187	89	50	473	255
49.45	19X4	8351	694	283	131	152	418	221
51.92	19X5	8256	721	266	133	139	535	289

For each year calculate:

a. Operating income as a percentage of revenues.

b. Net profits after tax as a percentage of revenues.

c. After-tax profits per share outstanding (EPS).

The balance sheet data for the same fiscal years (in millions of dollars) were as follows:

Year	Cash	Current Assets	Current Liabilities	Total Assets	Long-Term Debt	Common Equity
19X1	$291	$1736	$ 845	$2565	$251	$1321
19X2	178	1951	1047	2978	255	1480
19X3	309	2019	929	3103	391	1610
19X4	163	2254	1215	3861	731	1626
19X5	285	2315	1342	4310	736	1872

d. Calculate the ratio of current assets to current liabilities for each year.

e. Calculate the long-term debt as a percentage of common equity.

f. For each year calculate the book value per share as the common equity divided by the number of shares outstanding.

g. Calculate ROE.

h. Calculate ROA.

i. Calculate leverage.

j. Calculate the net income margin.

k. Calculate turnover.

l. Calculate the EBIT.

m. Calculate the income ratio.

n. Calculate operating efficiency.

o. On the basis of these calculations evaluate the current status of the health of GF and the changes over the period.

2. Combining information from an analyst's report on GF and some estimated data for 19X7, the following calendar-year data, on a per-share basis, are provided:

Year	Price Range Low	Price Range High	Earnings	Dividends	Book Value	(D/E) (%)	Annual Avg. P/E	ROE = E/Book (%)
19X1	$26.5	$35.3	$4.56	$1.72	$25.98	37.7	7.0	17.6%
19X2	28.3	37.0	5.02	1.95	29.15	38.8	6.2	17.2
19X3	23.5	34.3	5.14	2.20	32.11	42.8	5.8	16.0
19X4	27.8	35.0	4.47	2.20	30.86		7.7	
19X5	29.0	47.8	5.73	2.30	30.30		6.8	
19X6	36.6	53.5	6.75	2.40	39.85			
19X7			6.75	2.60	44.00			

a. Calculate the D/E, ROE, and TR for 19X4, 19X5, and 19X6. (Use the average of the low and high prices to calculate TRs.)

b. Show that from 19X2 through 19X6 the per annum growth rate in dividends was 6.9 per cent and for earnings was 8.2 per cent.

c. Using the current price of $47, with estimated earnings for 19X7 of $6.75, show that the P/E would be evaluated as 6.96.

d. On the basis of the annual average P/E ratios shown above and your estimate in (c), assume an expected P/E of 7. If an investor expected the earnings of GF for 19X7 to be $7.50, show that the intrinsic value would be $52.50.

e. What factors are important in explaining the difference in the P/E ratios of Bombardier and GF?

f. From your calculation of the growth rate of dividends in (b), assume that the annual rate is 7 per cent. If the required rate of return for the stock is 12 per cent and the expected dividend payout ratio is 0.4, show that P/E = 8.

g. If the dividend payout ratio is 0.4 and the return on equity is 15 per cent, show that $g = 0.09$.

h. Using $k = 0.14$ and $g = 0.09$, with expected 19X7 dividends of $2.60, show that the intrinsic value is $52.

i. Assume the beta for GF is 0.8 relative to Bombardier's beta of 0.97. Is this information of any help in explaining the different P/E ratios of these two companies?

APPENDIX 17-A

FINANCIAL RATIO ANALYSIS: AN OVERVIEW

Interpreting Financial Statements

Analyzing a company's historical financial statements and financial ratios can provide end users with useful information for estimating the magnitude of future cash flows (earnings and dividends) and the riskiness inherent in these estimates. Ratios are commonly used to analyze a company's financial performance. Although a single ratio has limited value, it does provide relative measures of performance/risk characteristics of firms when compared with other ratios.

Trend analysis compares ratios at a particular time with those of a previous period. It provides information regarding how the firm is evolving through time and enables comparison of the firm's most recent performance with that in earlier periods. One approach involves constructing internal trend lines by selecting a base period, and treating the ratio for that period as 100, and then dividing it successively into comparable ratios for subsequent periods. For example, if the earnings per share (EPS) figures for five successive years are $1.00, $1.20, $1.30, $1.10, and $0.90 and we set the base of 100 equal to the first year's EPS figure, the trend line values will be 100, 120, 130, 110, and 90. The advantages of this approach are that it simplifies the arithmetic and makes it easy to interpret changes through the years. The disadvantages are that the trend line may be misleading if the base year is not representative, and that it is impossible to apply this method if the base period figure is negative (e.g., if a loss occurred).

External comparisons of company ratios with those of similar companies or industry averages is used as a method of determining how well a company is performing in relation to its competitors. It is important to ensure that the comparison group consists of "similar" firms, whose ratios have been calculated according to the same basis. For example, it may be misleading to compare ratios of two firms in the same industry if they have different fiscal year ends, particularly if sales are seasonal. In Canada, Dun and Bradstreet, the Canadian Manufacturers Association, and some banks provide industry ratios for comparison purposes.

There are several limitations of financial statement analysis. A key concern is that it is hard to determine what is "good" performance. Trend analysis may provide uninformative results if the nature of a company changes substantially due to the acquisition of new companies and/or the divestiture of certain operating divisions. It is often difficult to determine comparable companies when examining multinational and/or conglomerate firms. Finding comparable companies is a significant problem for Canadian firms, because in certain industries there may be only one or two large companies. For example, within the transportation equipment industry sector in Canada, **Bombardier** and **Western Star Truck Holdings** were the largest two companies, and the only two included in the TSE300 Composite Index. However, Bombardier had 1996 revenues totaling $7.123 billion versus only $783 million for Western. Given the size discrepancy between the two companies, Western may not provide a useful benchmark against which to judge the financial performance of Bombardier (and vice versa). Using industry averages would likely provide even worse benchmarks since the remaining firms in the industry are much smaller than Western.

Another comparability issue arises because Bombardier and Western do not have the same fiscal year ends (January for Bombardier and June for Western). This can also bias industry averages, however, companies in a given industry often choose the same fiscal year ends. For example, in Canada all of the large chartered banks have fiscal years ending on October 31. An alternative is to compare Bombardier with similar US companies, however, one must be aware of potential biases that may arise due to the use of different accounting standards (even though, the standards are very similar across the two countries). In addition, inflation can distort results in certain situations, such as when trying to compare younger firms to older ones.

Despite some of the limitations of financial statement analysis, it is an excellent tool for analyzing company performance that provides analysts with information that is central to the company valuation process. Ratios provide insight into the performance of a variety of areas of the company's operations.

Four areas of operation that are often analyzed by reference to ratios are:

1. Liquidity — the firm's ability to generate required cash in a hurry to meet its short term obligations
2. Debt Management — how well the company is able to deal with its debt obligations with regard to its ability to repay and its ability to assume more debt
3. Profitability — how well the company has made use of its resources
4. Value — shows the worth of the company's shares or the returns for owning them.

We present some of the commonly used ratios below, based on the *CSC Textbook* definition of these ratios. We would note that the some of the CSC definitions differ from those that students have seen in introductory finance, investments, or accounting textbooks. This is not uncommon. In fact, if you pick up three or four different textbooks or analyst reports, it would be rare to see them all have the exact same definitions for all reported ratios. Despite the variations in the definitions, the ratios generally measure the same type of thing. The important point of this discussion is to make sure that all ratios that are to be compared with others are determined on the same basis. Otherwise, one runs the risk of arriving at erroneous conclusions by comparing apples with oranges.

Analyzing Liquidity

Commonly used liquidity indicators include the following:

$$\text{Working capital (or net current assets)} = \text{Current assets} - \text{Current liabilities}$$

$$\text{Current ratio} = \text{Current assets} \div \text{Current liabilities}$$

$$\text{Quick (or acid test) ratio} = (\text{Current assets} - \text{Inventory}) \div \text{Current liabilities}$$

The current ratio measures a firm's ability to repay current obligations from current assets, while the quick ratio is a more conservative estimate of liquidity that reflects the fact that inventories are generally not as liquid as other current assets. As with most ratios there is no absolute standard for these ratios, but higher values suggest greater firm liquidity. The Canadian Securities Course (CSC) provides some general rules of thumb for most of the ratios discussed here. For the current and quick ratios, the CSC suggests the values should be greater than 2.0 and 1.0 respectively. Cash forecasts can provide additional insight into the firm's liquidity situation.

Analyzing Debt

These are six commonly used indicators of a firm's debt situation.

1. *Asset coverage = (Total assets − Deferred charges − Intangible assets − Current liabilities less short-term debt such as bank advances and the current portion of long-term debt) ÷ (Total debt outstanding/1000)*

   This measures the protection provided by the firm's tangible assets, after all prior liabilities have been met. Assets well in excess of company debt are required to generate sufficient earnings to meet interest obligations and repay indebtedness. Also, asset coverage shows the book value amount of assets backing the debt securities. As a rule of thumb, the CSC suggests utilities should maintain at least $1,500 of net tangible assets per $1,000 of debt outstanding, while industrial companies should maintain at least $2,000.

2. *Debt percentage of total capital = Total debt ÷ Invested capital, where, Invested capital = Short-term debt + Current portion of long-term debt + Long-term debt + Preferred stock + Common equity (Note: some analysts also include deferred taxes as a source of capital)*

   This shows what percentage of total invested capital debt holders are entitled to. CSC rules of thumb are that total debt outstanding for utilities should not exceed 60 per cent of total capital, and for industrial companies it should not be more than 33 per cent.

3. *Debt/equity ratio = Total debt outstanding ÷ Book value of shareholders' equity*

   This ratio pinpoints the relationship of debt to equity and is a direct measure of financial risk. CSC rules of thumb suggest that utilities and industrials maintain debt/equity ratios below 1.5 and 0.5 respectively.

4. *Interest coverage = (Net earnings before extraordinary items [BEI] − Equity income + Minority interest in earnings of subsidiary companies + All income taxes + Total interest charges) ÷ Total interest charges*

   This ratio is generally considered to be the most important quantitative test, since it measures a firm's ability to meet debt obligations, and a stable trend is important. CSC rules of thumb are that utilities and industrials exhibit coverage ratios of at least 2.0 and 3.0 respectively.

5. *Cash flow/total debt = Cash flow ÷ Total debt, where, Cash flow = Net earnings BEI − Equity income + Minority interest in earnings of subsidiary companies + Deferred income taxes + Depreciation + Any other deductions not paid out in cash (e.g., depletion, amortization, etc.)*

   Cash flow provides a better indicator of a firm's ability to cover interest payments, pay dividends, and finance expansion because of the substantial size of non-cash items on earnings statements. CSC rules of thumb suggest that utilities and industrials maintain debt repayment capacity of at least 0.20 and 0.30 respectively.

6. *Preferred dividend coverage = (Net earnings BEI − Equity income + Minority interest in earnings of subsidiary companies + All income taxes + Total interest charges) ÷ (Total interest charges + Before-tax preferred dividend payments)*

   This is similar to interest coverage, except that before-tax preferred dividend payments are added to interest payments, as the fixed obligation to be covered. CSC rules of thumb are the same as for interest coverage ratios. Before-tax dividend payments may be calculated by multiplying actual payments (which come from after-tax earnings) by 100 ÷ (100 − tax rate).

Since it is not always possible to determine a company's actual tax rate, it is often useful to determine its apparent tax rate which may be calculated as follows:

Apparent tax rate = Current and deferred income taxes ÷ (Net earnings BEI − Equity income + Minority interest in earnings of subsidiary companies + Current and deferred taxes)

Analyzing Profitability

Some commonly used measures of profitability are discussed below:

1. *Gross profit margin = (Net sales − Cost of goods sold) ÷ Net sales*

   This ratio indicates the efficiency of management in turning over the company's goods at a profit.

2. *Operating profit margin = (Net sales − Cost of goods sold − Selling, general and administrative expenses) ÷ Net sales*

   This is similar to the gross margin, however, it is more stringent and also takes into account selling, general, and administrative expenses incurred in producing earnings.

3. *Net profit margin = (Net earnings BEI − Equity income + Minority interest in earnings of subsidiary companies) ÷ Net sales*

   This measure accounts for expenses and taxes and effectively sums up in one figure management's ability to run the business. To be comparable across firms and through time it is necessary to show net profit before minority interest has been deducted and equity income added in, since not all companies have these items.[17]

4. *Pre-tax return on capital = (Net earnings BEI + Income taxes + Total interest charges) ÷ Invested capital*

   This ratio is calculated without reference to who supplied the capital, and demonstrates how well management has employed the assets at its disposal.

5. *Net or after-tax return on capital = (Net earnings BEI + Total after-tax interest charges) ÷ (Invested capital, where Total after-tax interest charges = Total interest charges × (1 − tax rate))*

   This is the same as measure (4), except that taxes are also considered.

6. *Net (after-tax) return on common equity = (Net earnings BEI − Preferred dividend) ÷ Common equity*

   This ratio is of prime importance to common shareholders since it reflects the profitability of their capital in the business. Some analysts suggest that taxes are an expense of doing business, and note that the proportion of equity to capitalization changes from period to period, and therefore prefer measure (5) to measures (4) and (6).

7. *Inventory turnover ratio = Cost of goods sold ÷ Inventory*

   Sometimes net sales is used to replace cost of goods sold, if this information is unavailable. This ratio varies significantly across industries. If a company maintains a ratio above its industry average it signifies that the firm is maintaining a better balance between sales volume and inventory. As a result it faces less risk of being caught with too much inventory in the event of price declines or maintaining obsolete or damaged inventory. Low

[17] For an in-depth discussion of this point, and description of minority interest and equity income, refer to Chapter 2 of the *Canadian Securities Course Textbook*, August 1998.

inventory turnover can cause a significant increase in financing charges if inventory accumulates, since it represents a large part of a company's working capital. Possible causes of low turnover could be:

i. Inventory contains a large portion of unsaleable goods

ii. The firm has an *overbought* position

iii. The inventory value is overstated.

Analyzing Value

Some commonly used value ratios are provided below. These provide a way of relating market value to dividends and earnings.

1a. *Dividend payout (including preferred) = Total dividends ÷ Net earnings BEI*

b. *Dividend payout (common) = Common dividends ÷ (Net earnings BEI − Preferred dividends)*
These ratios indicate the percentage of earnings being paid out as dividends and the amount being reinvested for future growth. Since management generally tries to maintain steady dividend payments, an unstable payout ratio is usually associated with unstable earnings.

2a. *Earnings per share (EPS) = (Net earnings BEI − Preferred dividends) ÷ Number of common shares outstanding*

It is one of the most widely used and understood of all ratios, and provides common shareholders with a measure of earnings available to them after all other obligations have been met; it offers a clue as to the company's ability to maintain or increase dividend payments.

b. *Fully diluted EPS = Adjusted net earnings BEI ÷ Adjusted common shares outstanding*

This figure reflects the EPS available to common shareholders if all securities such as convertible preferred stock or debentures, stock options, and warrants were converted into common shares. The adjusted earnings figure would reflect the fact that interest would no longer be payable on convertible debt, and it would not be necessary to subtract the preferred dividends on the convertible preferred shares. The adjusted common shares figure would be increased to reflect the new number of shares outstanding if all securities were converted.

3. *Dividend yield = Annual dividend per share ÷ Current market share price*

This ratio offers a superficial comparison of the yield offered by different common shares.

4. Price-earnings (P/E) ratio = Current market share price ÷ EPS

This is probably the most useful and widely used ratio, because it is, in fact, all the other ratios combined into one figure. It represents the ultimate evaluation of a company and its shares by the investing public, with due consideration for tangible and intangible factors such as quality of management, future growth opportunities, and risks faced by the company. In fact, a major reason for calculating EPS is to enable a comparison with the share's market price. It enables comparisons across firms, provided they are in the same industry. The calculation above uses the most recent 12-month EPS figure, however, P/E ratios may also be calculated based on projected earnings.

CHAPTER 18

TECHNICAL ANALYSIS

LEARNING OBJECTIVES

After reading this chapter, you will be able to

1. Define technical analysis and explain why it is used.
2. Describe the major techniques used in technical analysis.
3. Discuss the limitations of technical analysis.

CHAPTER PREVIEW

In this chapter we explore an alternative approach to security analysis — technical analysis — which differs substantially from fundamental analysis. After a brief explanation of the differences between these two types of analysis, we describe the major techniques used by technical analysts. We conclude the chapter with an assessment of the limitations of technical analysis.

INTRODUCTION

As discussed in Chapter 14, technical analysis is the other traditional approach for selecting stocks. It differs from the fundamental approach to security analysis discussed in the last three chapters. Although the technical approach to common stock selection is the oldest used by analysts (dating back to the late 1800s), it remains controversial.[1] It has come under constant criticism from those espousing the merits of the efficient market hypothesis (EMH), since the use of technical analysis flies in the face of the notion that markets are efficient in the weak-form sense of the EMH.[2] However, it is important to recognize that analysis of any type, fundamental or technical, is essentially a waste of time if we accept the assumptions of the EMH. Thus, just as fundamental analysis was examined under the premise that it can help improve investment results if done properly, the same argument can be made for technical analysis. Indeed there are numerous examples of technicians earning superior returns, just as there are numerous examples of disappointing results obtained by following similar strategies. The primary objective of this chapter is to make students aware of the various technical strategies and available tools so that they can make informed decisions regarding how to integrate technical analysis into their investment program, if at all.

Anyone learning about investments will be exposed to technical analysis, because numerous investors, investment advisory firms, and the popular press talk about it and use it. As noted, it has been around for a long time and is widely known. Furthermore, it may produce some insights into the psychological dimension of the market. While it is likely that the debate regarding its usefulness will continue, many investors use technical information when making their investment decisions. Therefore, the prudent course of action is to study this topic, or indeed any other recommended approach to making investing decisions, and try to make an objective evaluation of its validity and usefulness.

Although technical analysis can be applied to bonds, currencies, and commodities as well as to common stocks, technical analysis typically involves the aggregate stock market, industry sectors, and/or individual common stocks. Therefore, we restrict our discussion in this chapter to common stocks.

WHAT IS TECHNICAL ANALYSIS?

Technical Analysis
The use of specific market data for the analysis of both individual and aggregate stock prices for the purpose of identifying recurring price patterns.

Technical analysis can be defined as the use of specific market-generated data for the analysis of both aggregate stock prices (market indexes or industry averages) and individual stocks. Martin J. Pring, in his book *Technical Analysis Explained*, states:

---

[1] Technical analysis itself can be traced back to the rice markets in seventeenth century Japan.

[2] Recall from Chapter 10 that the weak-form version of the EMH states that in efficient security markets, prices will accurately reflect all historical price and trading volume information.

> The technical approach to investing is essentially a reflection of the idea that prices move in trends which are determined by the changing attitudes of investors toward a variety of economic, monetary, political and psychological forces. The art of technical analysis — *for it is an art* — is to identify trend changes at an early stage and to maintain an investment posture until the weight of the evidence indicates that the trend is reversed.[3]

Technical analysis is sometimes called market or internal analysis, because it utilizes the record of the market itself to attempt to assess the demand for, and supply of, shares of a stock or the entire market. Thus, technical analysts believe that the market itself is its own best source of data — as they say, "let the market tell its own story."

Economics teaches us that prices are determined by the interaction of demand and supply. Technicians do not disagree, but argue that it is extremely difficult to assess all the factors that influence demand and supply. Since not all investors are in agreement on price, the determining factor at any time is the net demand (or lack thereof) for a stock based on how many investors are optimistic or pessimistic. Furthermore, once the balance of investors become optimistic — or pessimistic — this mood is likely to continue for the near term and can be detected by various technical indicators. As the chief market technician of one investment firm says, "All I care about is how people feel about those particular stocks as shown by their putting money in and taking their money out."[4]

Technical analysis is based on published **market data** as opposed to fundamental data, such as earnings, sales, growth rates, or government regulations. Market data includes the price of a stock or the level of a market index, volume (number of shares traded), and technical indicators (explained later), such as the short interest ratio. Many technical analysts believe that only such market data, as opposed to fundamental data, are relevant.

Market Data
Price and volume information for stocks or indexes.

Recall that in fundamental analysis, the dividend discount model, the earnings multiplier model, or some other valuation model uses fundamental company data regarding future earnings, dividends, and company risk to determine an estimate of a stock's intrinsic value, which is then compared to the market price. Fundamentalists believe that their data, properly evaluated, indicate the worth or intrinsic value of a stock. Technicians, on the other hand, believe that it is extremely difficult to estimate intrinsic value and virtually impossible to obtain and analyze good information consistently. In particular, they are dubious about the value to be derived from an analysis of published financial statements. Instead, they focus on market data as an indication of the forces of supply and demand for a stock or the market.

Technicians believe that the process by which prices adjust to new information is one of a gradual adjustment toward a new (equilibrium) price. As the stock adjusts from its old level to its new one, the price tends to move in a trend. The central concern is not why the change is taking place, but rather the very fact that it is taking place at all. Technical analysts believe that stock prices show identifiable trends that can be exploited by investors. They seek to identify changes in the direction of a stock and take a position in the stock to take advantage of the trend.

The following three points summarize technical analysis:

1. Technical analysis is based on published market data and focuses on internal factors by analyzing movements in the aggregate market, industry average, or stock. In contrast, fundamental analysis focuses on economic and political factors that are external to the market itself.

[3] Martin J. Pring, *Technical Analysis Explained* (New York: McGraw-Hill Publishers), 1991.

[4] Jonathan Butler, "Technical Analysis: A Primer," *Worth*, October 1995, p. 128.

2. The focus of technical analysis is identifying changes in the direction of stock prices, which tend to move in trends as the stock price adjusts to a new equilibrium level. These trends can be analyzed, and changes in trends detected, by studying the action of price movements and trading volume across time. The emphasis is on likely price changes.
3. Technicians attempt to assess the overall situation concerning stocks by analyzing breadth indicators, market sentiment, and momentum.

A Framework for Technical Analysis

Technical analysis can be applied to both an aggregate of prices (the market as a whole or industry averages) and individual stocks. It includes the use of graphs or charts, and technical trading rules and indicators. Figure 18-1 depicts the technical analysis approach to investing.

Figure 18-1
The Technical Analysis Approach to Common Stock Selection

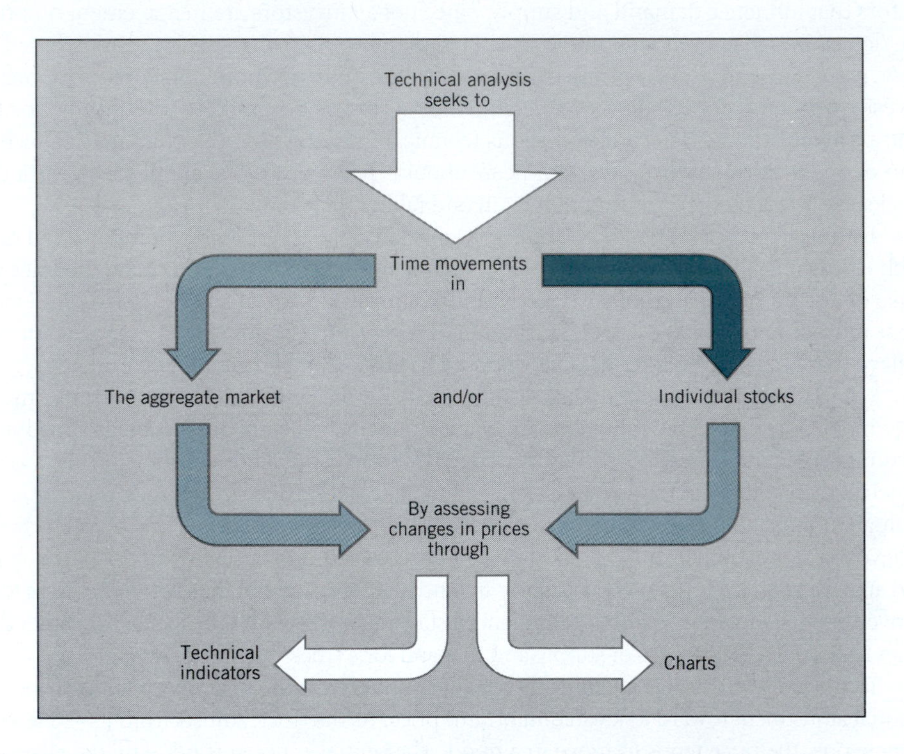

Price and volume are the primary tools of the pure technical analyst, and the chart is the most important mechanism for displaying this information. Technicians believe that the forces of supply and demand result in particular patterns of price behaviour, the most important of which is the trend or overall direction in price. Using a chart, the technician hopes to identify trends and patterns in stock prices that provide trading signals.

Volume data are used to gauge the general condition in the market and to help assess its trend. The evidence seems to suggest that rising stock prices are usually associated with rising volume and falling prices with falling volume. If stock prices rose but volume activity did not keep pace, technicians would be sceptical about the upward trend. An upward surge on contracting volume would be particularly suspect. A downside movement from some pattern or holding point, accompanied by low volume, would be taken as a bearish sign.

We first consider stock price and volume techniques, often referred to as charting. However, technical analysis has evolved over time, so that today it is much more than the charting of individual stocks or the market as a whole. In particular, technical analysts use indicators to assess market conditions and investor sentiment. They also engage in contrary analysis, which suggests investors should go against the crowd.

STOCK PRICE AND VOLUME TECHNIQUES

The Dow Theory

The oldest and best-known theory of technical analysis is the **Dow theory**. It was originally developed in the late 1800s by the editor of *The Wall Street Journal*, Charles H. Dow, who many regard as the father of technical analysis. Although Dow developed the theory to describe past price movements, William Hamilton followed up by using it to predict movements in the aggregate market. The Dow theory was very popular in the 1920s and 1930s. Articles offering support for it still appear periodically in the literature and several investment advisory services are based on the Dow theory.

Dow Theory
A technique for detecting long-term trends in the aggregate stock market.

The theory is based on the existence of three types of price movements:

1. Primary moves, a broad market movement that lasts several years
2. Secondary (intermediate) moves, occurring within the primary moves, which represent interruptions lasting several weeks or months
3. Day-to-day moves, occurring randomly around the primary and secondary moves.

The term **bull market** refers to an upward primary move, whereas **bear market** refers to a downward primary move. A major upward move is said to occur when successive rallies penetrate previous highs, whereas declines remain above previous lows. A major downward move is expected when successive rallies fail to penetrate previous highs, whereas declines penetrate previous lows.

Bull Market
An upward trend in the stock market.

Bear Market
A downward trend in the stock market.

The secondary or intermediate moves give rise to the so-called technical corrections, which are often mentioned in the popular press. These corrections supposedly adjust for excesses that have occurred. These movements are of considerable importance in applying the Dow theory.

Finally, the day-to-day ripples occur often and are of minor importance. Even ardent technical analysts do not usually try to predict day-to-day movements in the market.

Figure 18-2 illustrates the basic concept of the Dow theory, although numerous variations exist. The primary trend, represented by the dotted line, is up through time Period 1. Although several downward (secondary) reactions occur, these corrections do not reach the previous low. Each of these reactions is followed by an upward movement that exceeds the previously obtained high. Trading volume continues to build over this period.

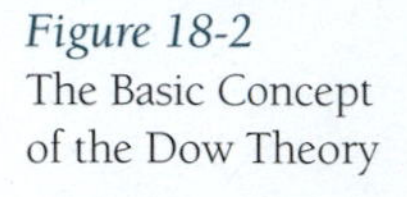

Figure 18-2
The Basic Concept of the Dow Theory

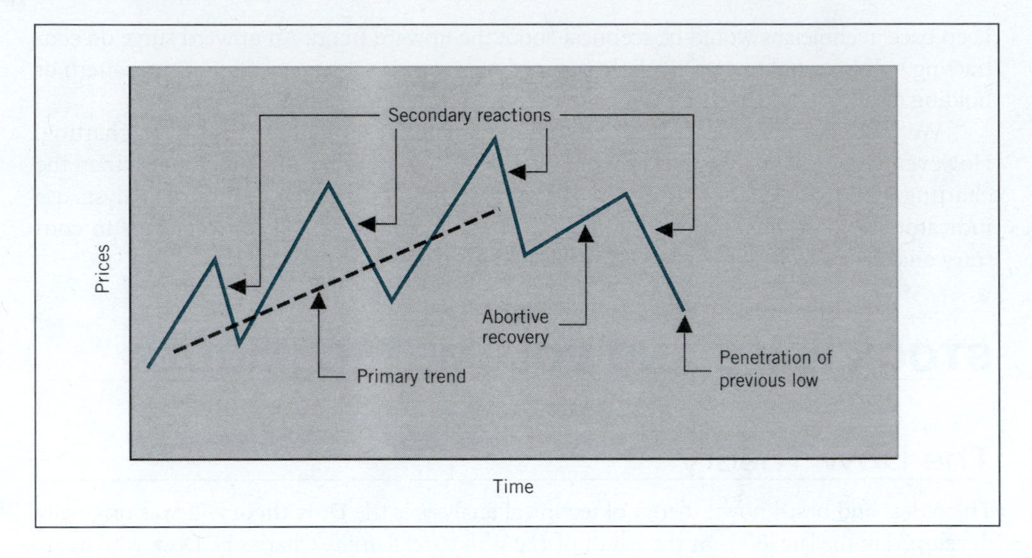

Although prices again decline after time Period 1 as another correction occurs, the price recovery fails to surpass the last peak reached. (This process is referred to as an abortive recovery.) When the next downward reaction occurs, it penetrates the previous low. This movement could suggest that a primary downturn or new bear market has begun, although it is subject to confirmation. As originally conceived, the Dow Jones Industrial and Rail Averages (which was later replaced by the Transportation Average) must confirm each other for the movement to be validated.

The Dow theory is intended to forecast the start of a primary movement, but it does not tell us how long the movement will last. The trend will continue as long as the averages confirm each other. Only these averages matter, and extensive records are not required, nor are chart patterns examined.

It is obvious that today's economy is vastly different from the one that existed when the Dow theory was developed. Many studies of its success rate have been disappointing; for example, over periods of as much as 25 years, investors would have been more successful with a buy-and-hold policy in the same stocks. In addition, confirmations are slow to arrive and are often unclear when they do, while the amount of price movement needed for a confirmation is ambiguous. Its users interpret the theory in various ways, and so it may predict different (and conflicting) movements at the same time. On the other hand, several investment letters have achieved various degrees of success based upon the Dow theory and it is still widely used by practitioners. In short, investors today are still debating its merits.

Charts of Price Patterns

To assess individual stock-price movements, technicians often rely on charts or graphs of price movements and on relative strength analysis. The charting of price patterns is one of the classic technical analysis techniques. Technicians believe that stock prices move in trends, with price changes forming patterns that can be recognized and categorized. By visually assessing the forces of supply and demand, technicians hope to be able to predict the likely direction of future movements.

Technicians seek to identify certain signals in a chart of stock prices and use certain terminology to describe the events. A **support level** is the level of price (or, more correctly, a price range) at which a technician expects a significant increase in the demand for a stock — in other words, a lower boundary on price where it is expected that buyers will act, supporting the price and preventing additional price declines. A **resistance level**, on the other hand, is the price level at which a technician expects a significant increase in the supply of a stock — in other words, an upper boundary on price where sellers are expected to act, providing a resistance to any further rise in price.

Support Level
A price range at which a technician expects a significant increase in the demand for a stock.

Resistance Level
A price range at which a technician expects a significant increase in the supply of a stock.

A trend line is a line drawn on a chart to identify a trend. If a trend exhibits support and resistance levels simultaneously that appear to be well defined, the trend lines are referred to as channel lines, and price is said to move between the upper channel line and the lower channel line. Momentum is used to indicate the speed with which prices are changing, and a number of measures of momentum exist, referred to as momentum indicators. When a change in direction occurs in a short-term trend, technicians say that a reversal has occurred. A correction occurs when the reversal involves only a partial retracing of the prior movement. Corrections may be followed by periods of consolidation, with the initial trend resuming following the consolidation.

Technical analysts rely heavily on bar charts and point-and-figure charts, although other types are also used.[5]

Bar Charts

Bar charts are probably the most popular chart in technical analysis and are clearly the simplest. These charts plot price on the vertical axis and time on the horizontal axis. Each day's price movement is represented by a vertical bar, top of which represents the high price for the day, and the bottom is the low price. (A small, horizontal tick is often used to designate the closing price for the day.) The bottom of a bar chart usually shows the trading volume for each day, permitting the simultaneous observation of both price and volume activity.[6] *The Globe and Mail / Report on Business* carries graphs of bar charts for the TSE 300 Composite Index and the Dow Jones Industrial Average each day, with trading volume shown on the bottom — refer to Figure 18-3. Figure 18-4 includes a more detailed chart for the TSE 300 that includes daily data for the one-year period ended December 16, 1998.

Bar charts
Graphs of daily stock price plotted against time.

Figure 18-5 shows a daily bar chart for Unfloppy Disks, Inc. The technician using charts will search for patterns in the chart that can be used to predict future price moves. Note in Figure 18-5 the strong uptrend occurring over a period of months. This trend ended with a rally on high volume (at Point 1 in the figure) that forms part of the left shoulder of a famous chart pattern called a top head-and-shoulders pattern. (The bottom head-and-shoulders pattern is the mirror image of the top pattern, with the logic being reversed for the interpretation of the movements).

[5] Technicians also use a basic line chart, which uses only one number — usually the closing price for the day — to reflect the price movement. Another type of chart gaining some popularity is the candlestick. Developed in Japan, the candlestick is similar to the bar chart, although it shows the opening price as well as the high, low, and closing prices.

[6] The time intervals do not have to be days but could be weeks, months, or anything else a particular analyst might choose.

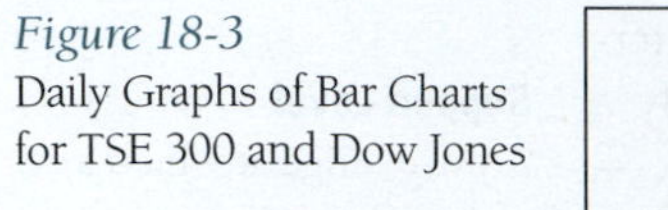
Figure 18-3
Daily Graphs of Bar Charts for TSE 300 and Dow Jones

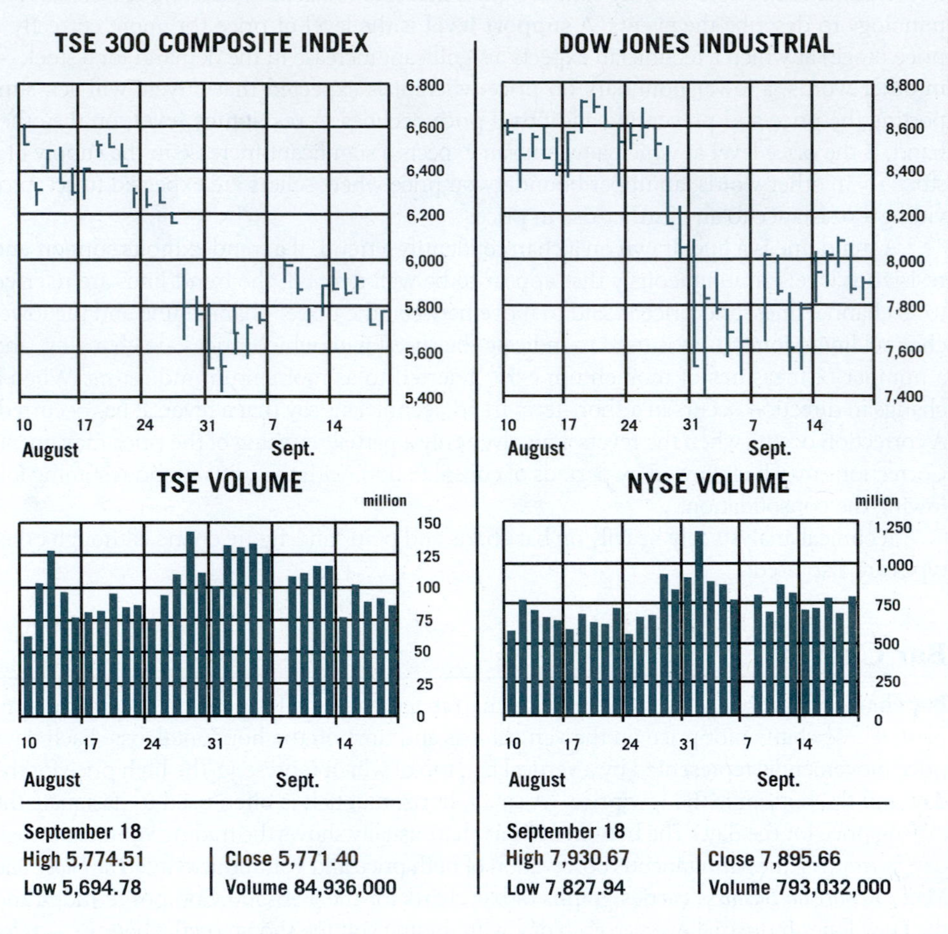

Source: The Globe and Mail / Report on Business, *September 19, 1998, p. B13. Reprinted with permission from* The Globe and Mail.

The left shoulder shows initially strong demand followed by a reaction on lower volume (Point 2), and then a second rally, with strong volume, carrying prices still higher (Point 3). Profit taking again causes prices to fall to the so-called neckline (Point 4), thus completing the left shoulder. (The neckline is formed by connecting previous low points.) A rally occurs, but this time on low volume, and again prices sink back to the neckline. This is the head (Point 5). The last step is the formation of the right shoulder, which occurs with light volume (Point 6). Growing weakness can be identified as the price approaches the neckline. As can be seen in Figure 18-5, a downside breakout occurs on heavy volume, which technicians consider to be a sell signal.

Figure 18-4 Daily Chart for TSE 300 for Year Ended December 16, 1998

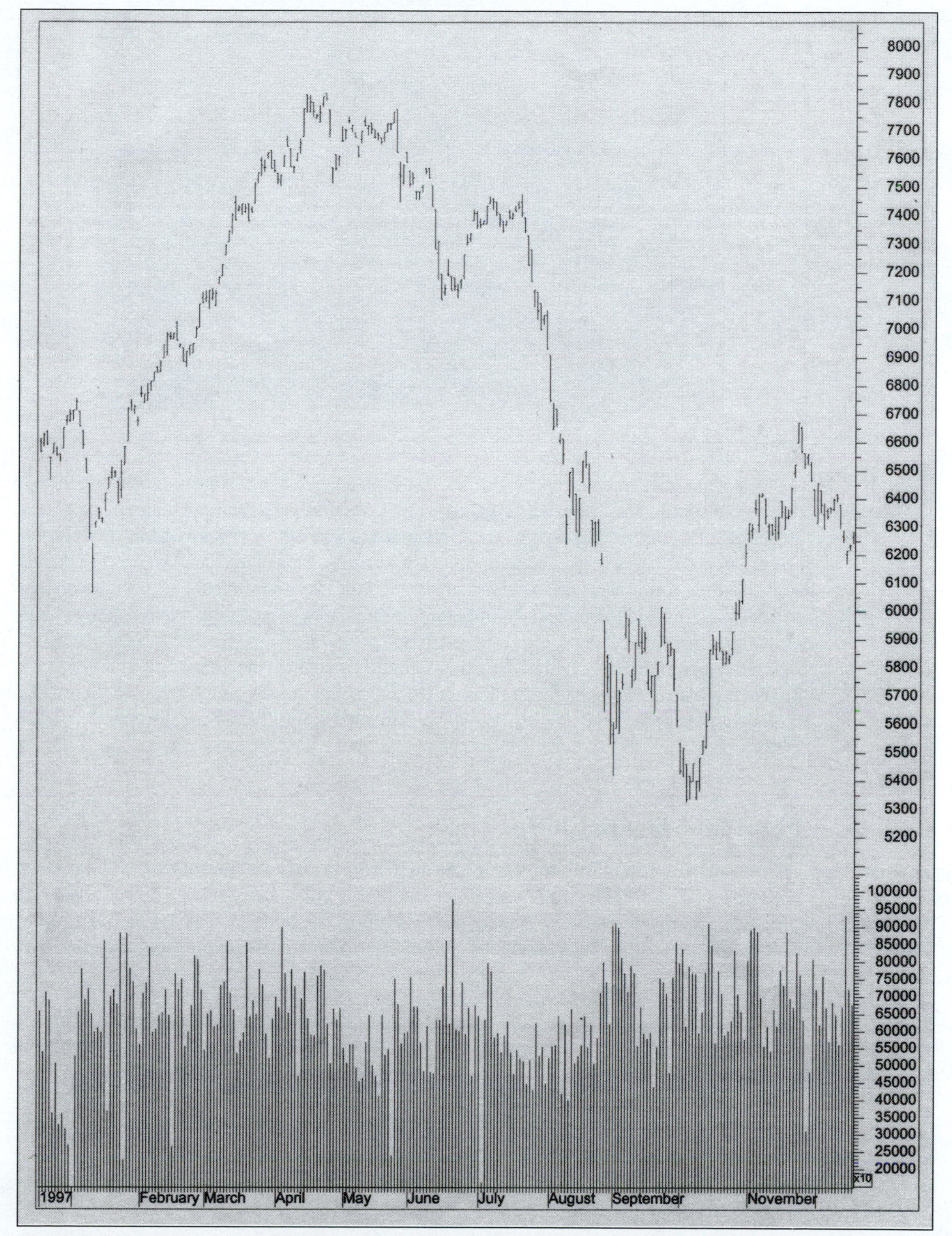

Source: Traders Access. Chart courtesy of Patrick A. Latham, Northern Alberta Institute of Technology.

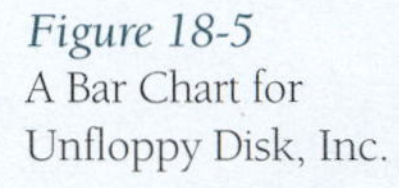

Figure 18-5
A Bar Chart for Unfloppy Disk, Inc.

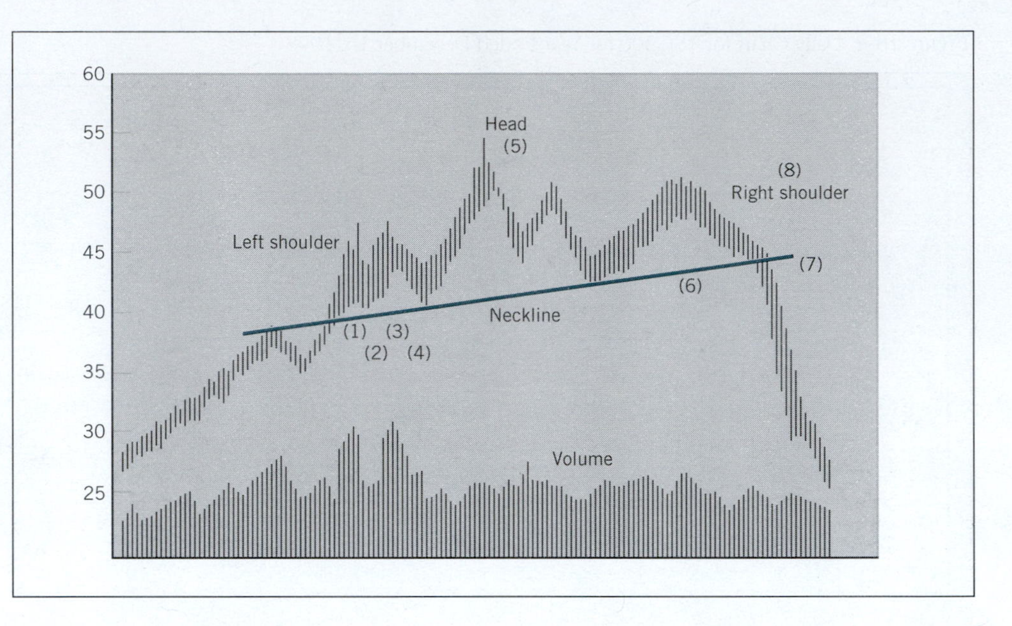

What about other patterns? Technicians have considered a very large number of such patterns. Some of the possible patterns include flags, pennants, gaps (of more than one type), triangles of various types (e.g., symmetrical, ascending, descending, and inverted), the inverted saucer or dome, the triple top, the compound fulcrum, the rising (and falling) wedge, the broadening bottom, the duplex horizontal, rectangles, and the inverted V. Figure 18-6 shows one set of price patterns said to be the most important for investors to recognize when reading charts of stock prices.

Obviously, numerous patterns are possible and can usually be found on a chart of stock prices. It is also obvious that most, if not all, of these patterns are much easier to identify in hindsight than at the time they are actually occurring. Such is the nature of trying to predict the future.

Point-and-Figure Charts

Point-and-Figure Charts
Graphs of stock prices showing only significant price changes.

Technicians also use **point-and-figure charts** that show only significant price changes and not volume. The user determines what is a significant price change ($1, $2, etc.) and what constitutes a price reversal ($2, $3, $4, etc.). Although the horizontal axis still depicts time, specific calendar time is not particularly important. (Some chartists do show the month in which changes occur.)

An X is used to show upward movements and an O for downward ones. Each X or O on a particular chart may represent $1 movements, $2 movements, $5 movements, and so on, depending on how much movement is considered significant for that stock. An X or O is recorded only when the price moves by the specified amount. Figure 18-7 illustrates a point-and-figure chart for the TSE 300 over the 1995–98 period.

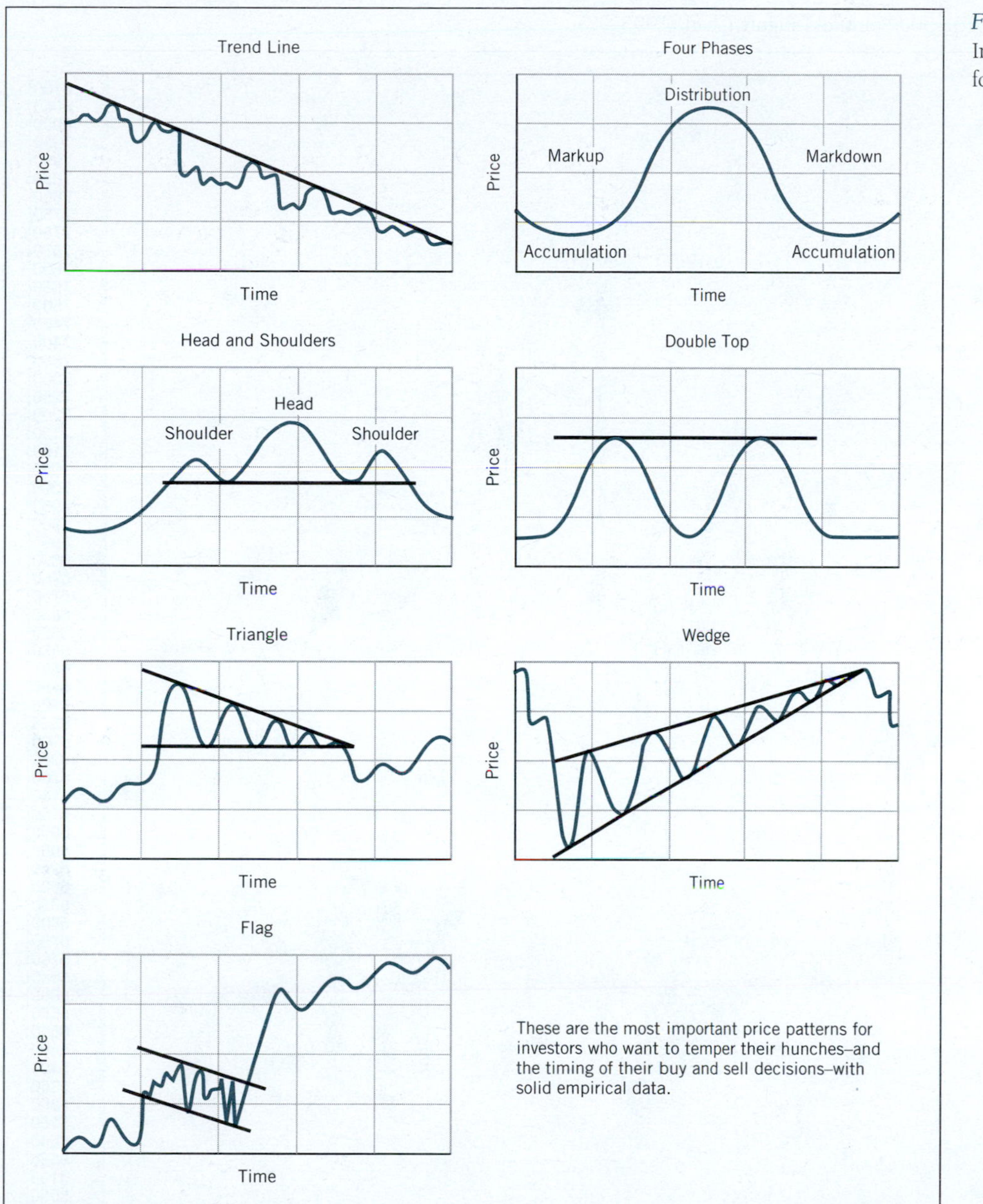

Figure 18-6
Important Price Patterns for Investors Using Charts

Source: Jonathan Butler, "Technical Analysis: A Primer," Worth*, October 1995, p. 133. Reprinted by permission of* Worth *magazine.*

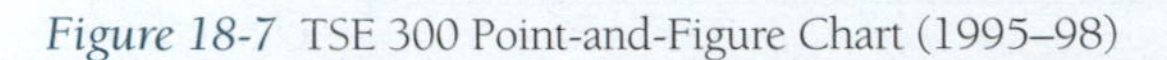

Figure 18-7 TSE 300 Point-and-Figure Chart (1995–98)

Source: Traders Access. Chart courtesy of Patrick A. Latham, Northern Alberta Institute of Technology.

A point-and-figure chart is designed to compress many price changes into a small space. By doing so, areas of "congestion" can be identified. A congestion area is a compacted region of price fluctuations (a closely compacted horizontal band of Xs and Os). The technician studies a congestion area in search of a breakout that will indicate an expected upward or downward movement in stock price.

Point-and-figure charts may be used for a variety of technical strategies such as the application of filter rules or the Dow theory. For example, a "three rule" filter strategy recommends that an investor does not buy or sell until there are three Xs or three Os in a column.

There are many chart patterns, some of which were mentioned earlier, and numerous technicians analyze and interpret these patterns. Due to the seemingly limitless number of patterns that can be identified in stock price movements, it is impossible to demonstrate conclusively the predictive significance of charting. In fact, very few scientific studies of the ability of chart patterns to predict the future direction of price movements have been conducted, and the conclusions of these studies have varied regarding their effectiveness. As a result, opinions about charting vary widely. Since the evidence is not conclusive, the controversy will continue.

Moving Averages

A moving average of prices is a popular technique for analyzing both the overall market and individual stocks. They are used to detect both the direction and the rate of change. Some number of days of closing prices is chosen to calculate a moving average. A well-known average for identifying major trends is the 200-day moving average (alternatively, a 10-week [50-day] average is used to identify intermediate trends). After initially calculating the average price, the new value for the moving average is calculated by dropping the earliest observation and adding the latest one. This process is repeated daily (or weekly). The resulting moving average line supposedly represents the basic trend of stock prices.

EXAMPLE: CALCULATING MOVING AVERAGE

Assume you are provided with the following week-end prices:

Week 1 — \$20; Week 2 — \$22; Week 3 — \$21; Week 4 — \$24; and Week 5 — \$25.

A five-week moving average could be determined in the following manner:

Moving average (five-week) = (20 + 22 + 21 + 24 + 25)/5 = \$22.40

If the next week-end price is \$23, the five-week moving average would then be:

Moving average (five-week) = (22 + 21 + 24 + 25 + 23)/5 = \$23.00.

Figure 18-8 shows the value of the TSE 300 Composite Index plotted for one year, with both a 200-day and a 50-day moving average included. Various publications offer plots of moving averages for some index plotted against the index itself. Figure 18-8 is but one example taken from the Yahoo Finance Web site <http://quote.yahoo.com> — numerous other Web sites also offer free charts for personal use.

Figure 18-8 TSE 300 — Moving Averages

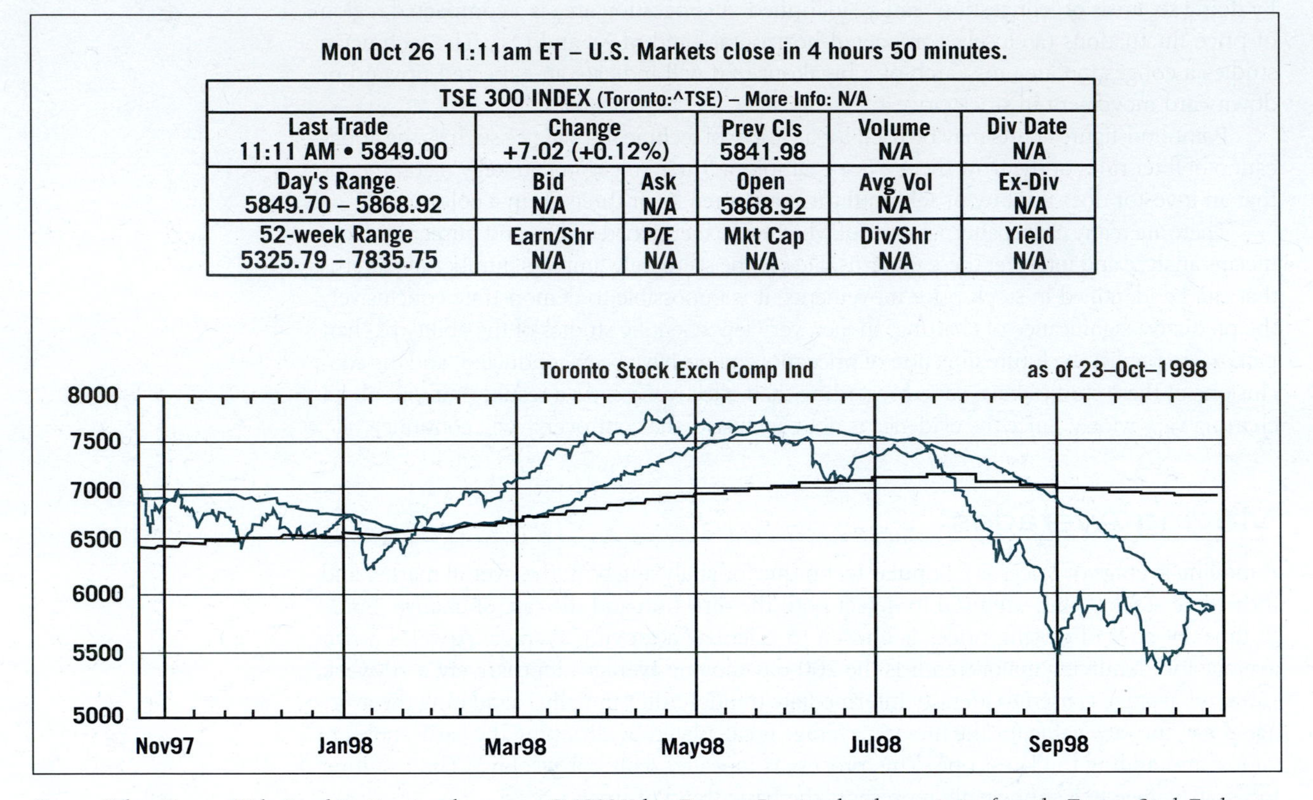

Mon Oct 26 11:11am ET – U.S. Markets close in 4 hours 50 minutes.

TSE 300 INDEX (Toronto:^TSE) – More Info: N/A					
Last Trade 11:11 AM • 5849.00	Change +7.02 (+0.12%)		Prev Cls 5841.98	Volume N/A	Div Date N/A
Day's Range 5849.70 – 5868.92	Bid N/A	Ask N/A	Open 5868.92	Avg Vol N/A	Ex-Div N/A
52-week Range 5325.79 – 7835.75	Earn/Shr N/A	P/E N/A	Mkt Cap N/A	Div/Shr N/A	Yield N/A

Source: Yahoo Finance Web site: <http://quote.yahoo.com>. © 1998 Yahoo Finance. Reprinted with permission from the Toronto Stock Exchange.

A comparison of the current market price to the moving average produces a buy or sell signal. The general buy signal is generated when actual prices rise through the moving average on high volume, with the opposite applying to a sell signal. Some specific buy and sell signals are described below, along with examples of where some of these signals would be generated for the TSE 300 Composite Index during the November 1997 to October 1988 period depicted in Figure 18-8.

Specific signals of a turning point generating a sell signal are the following:

1. Actual price is below the moving average, advances toward it, does not penetrate the average, and starts to turn down again. This occurs in Figure 18-8 in early July 1998, when the TSE 300 approaches the 50-day moving average but does not exceed it. As predicted, the TSE 300 price subsequently declined.
2. Following a rise, the moving average flattens out or declines, and the price of the stock or index penetrates it from the top. A glimpse of this pattern emerges in Figure 18-8 in late May 1998 with respect to the 50-day moving average, although the moving average was not completely flat, and it started to decline within a short period of time.
3. The stock price rises above the moving average line while the line is still falling. This pattern does not show up in a distinct manner anywhere in Figure 18-8.

Buy signals would be generated if these situations were reversed:

1. Actual price is above the moving average, declines toward it, does not penetrate the average, and starts to turn up again. This pattern emerges with respect to the 200-day moving average in June, however the resulting price increase (which is as predicted) is small, and of limited duration, and is subsequently followed by a severe downturn in prices.
2. Following a decline, the moving average flattens out or increases, and the price of the stock or index penetrates it from the bottom. This pattern emerges in Figure 18-8 in January with respect to both moving averages. This occurrence is followed by an increase in prices, as predicted.
3. The stock price falls below the moving average line while the line is still increasing. This occurs in late May with respect to the 50-day moving average, however, contrary to the prediction, prices continued to fall in the subsequent period.

The examples above are offered in hindsight, however, they demonstrate that the signals generated by following moving averages have predictive power in some circumstances, but fail in others. In other words, the results are inconclusive as to how much we could have profited from this information. Perhaps more experienced technicians would possess better differentiating power regarding which signals are strong enough to dictate action be taken and which signals are inconclusive, but perhaps not. In addition, even if we did profit from this analysis in one period, there is no guarantee that we would experience similar profits in the following period. Once again, this is the risky nature of investing in common stocks — we cannot be sure what will unfold in the future.

Relative Strength

A well-known technique used for individual stocks (or industries) is relative strength analysis. The **relative strength** for a given stock is calculated as the ratio of the stock's price to a market index, or an industry index, or the average price of the stock itself over some previous period. These ratios can be plotted to form a graph of relative price across time. In effect, the graph shows the strength of the stock relative to its industry, the market, or whatever. According to the chief market analyst at Merrill Lynch, "Very often changes in trend, from good to bad or from bad to good, will be preceded by a change in the stock's relative performance."[7]

Relative Strength
The ratio of a stock's price to some market or industry index, usually plotted as a graph.

The relative strength of a stock over time may be of use in forecasting. Because trends are assumed to continue for some time, a rising ratio (an upward-sloping line when relative strength is plotted) indicates relative strength. That is, it indicates a stock that is outperforming the market and that may continue to do so. A declining ratio would have the same implications for the downside. One rule of thumb is that a stock is attractive when the relative strength has improved for at least four months, but as with most technical indicators, technicians interpret some of these signals in different ways.

Relative strength is often used by technicians to identify industry sectors that look attractive, prior to selecting individual stocks. This is in line with our analysis in Part V that supports a top-down approach to security analysis, with industry analysis preceding company analysis. By focusing on the selection of promising industries, investors narrow the number of possibilities to be considered.

[7] Butler, "Technical Analysis: A Primer," p. 133.

This group selection approach may be helpful in supporting the proposition that an individual stock showing relative strength is not an anomaly, but the technique does not protect an investor against the chance that the overall market is weak, and that one or more groups which currently appear strong are next in line to show weakness. Such a possibility once again supports the case for a top-down approach that begins with market analysis in order to assess the likelihood that now is a good time to be investing in stocks. One of the problems with relative strength is that a stock or group could show increasing relative strength because it is declining less quickly than the market, not because it is, in fact, increasing. This suggests that relative strength is not a technique to be used in isolation.

Many sources publish a variety of relative strength indicators. For example, *The Globe and Mail / Report on Business* publishes weekly relative strength indicators for all of the TSE indexes and subindexes, as well as a table reporting the large-cap stocks that experienced the best return performance over the most recent 13-week period. Numerous investment information services also provide information on relative strength such as *The Value Line Investment Survey*, which divides a stock's price by the Value Line Composite Average and plots this relative strength ratio for each company it covers at the top of the page. Relative strength analysis lends itself well to computerized stock analysis, which contributes to its popularity among institutional investors who own highly automated and sophisticated data analysis systems. The extent to which a number of institutional investors use relative strength techniques and have the means to observe changes at about the same time can affect the volatility of a stock.

Obtaining Charts to Use in Technical Analysis

In today's computerized world, and with the proliferation of Internet sources of information, investors have many choices for obtaining charts and related information. Many financial magazines and Web sites offer charts of various degrees of complexity for thousands of companies, updatable in a variety of ways and time frequencies. Some of these publications and Web sites are included in the references at the end of the chapter.

TECHNICAL INDICATORS

The chart remains the technician's most important tool for making buy and sell decisions. However, in addition to looking at the plot of stock prices, technicians also like to examine the overall situation by analyzing such factors as breadth and market sentiment indicators.

Breadth Indicators

Breadth of the Market and the Advance-Decline Line

There are a number of indicators of stock market breadth. For example, *The Globe and Mail / Report on Business* reports several of these measures on a daily basis, as depicted in Figure 18-9.

Figure 18-9
Market Breadth

	Volume (thousands)									
	Trading	Adv.	Decl.	Trans.	Issues	Adv.	Decl.	Unch.	New High	New Low
Toronto	84936	49869	26339	38069	1178	445	462	271	5	47
Industrials	57401	32335	18838	31142	848	311	343	194	4	37
Mines	14674	10411	2745	3762	190	70	70	50	0	4
Oils	12856	7123	4752	3163	139	64	48	27	1	6
Montreal	11505	4491	4633	4924	416	166	168	82	5	10
Vancouver	16174	5737	4515	2422	486	166	174	146	4	25
Alberta	6967	2738	2382	1382	325	110	112	103	4	10
New York	793032	389663	370676	289046	3511	1928	1107	476	26	157
American	25289	14573	6495	10126	695	323	243	129	1	28
Nasdaq	647160	365922	236253	476580	5515	2305	1614	1596	13	151

Toronto Trading for the Week

	Industrials	Mines	Oils	Total
Volume (thousands)	289175	76759	75445	441379
Transactions	182494	19946	18503	220943
Issues traded	1123	259	167	1552
Advances	420	77	87	585
Unchanged	172	39	18	230
Declines	531	143	62	737
Highs	12	3	2	17
Lows	127	18	21	166

Source: The Globe and Mail / Report on Business, *September 19, 1998, p. B13. Reprinted with permission from* The Globe and Mail.

A common measure of market breadth is the advance-decline line. This line measures, on a cumulative daily basis, the net difference between the number of stocks advancing in price and those declining in price for a group of stocks such as those on the TSE or NYSE. Subtracting the number of declines from the number of advances produces the net advance for a given day (which, of course, can be negative). This measure may include hundreds or thousands of stocks.

The advance-decline line, often referred to as the breadth of the market, results from plotting a running total of these numbers across time. The line can be based on daily or weekly figures, which are readily available from daily newspapers.

The advance-decline line is compared to a stock index such as the TSE 300 in order to analyze any divergence — that is, to determine whether movements in the market indicator have also occurred in the market as a whole. Technicians believe that divergences signal that the trend is about to change.

The advance-decline line and the market averages normally move together. If both are rising, the overall market is said to be technically strong. If both are falling, the market is weak. If the advance-decline line is rising while the average is declining, the decline in the average should reverse itself. Particular attention is paid to a divergence between the two during a bull market. If the average rises while the line weakens or declines, this indicates a weakening in the market; the average would therefore be expected to reverse itself and start declining.

New Highs and Lows

Part of the information reported for the TSE and other stock exchanges is the 52-week high and low prices for each stock. Technicians regard the market as bullish when a significant number of stocks each day hit 52-week highs. On the other hand, technicians see rising market indexes and few stocks hitting new highs as a troublesome sign. (Figure 18-9 includes new highs and lows for a number of North American exchanges.)

Volume

Volume is an accepted part of technical analysis. High trading volume on exchanges, other things being equal, is generally regarded as a bullish sign. Heavy volume combined with rising prices is even more bullish.

Sentiment Indicators

Short-Interest Ratio
The ratio of total shares sold short to average daily trading volume.

Short-Interest Ratio

The short interest for a security is the number of shares that have been sold short but not yet bought back.

The **short-interest ratio** is defined as

$$\text{Short-interest ratio} = \text{Total shares sold short} \div \text{Average daily trading volume} \quad (18\text{-}1)$$

In effect, this ratio indicates the number of days necessary to "work off" the current short interest.[8] It is considered to be a measure of investor sentiment, and many investors continually refer to it.

Investors sell short when they expect prices to decline; therefore, it would appear, the higher the short interest, the more investors are expecting a decline. A large short-interest position for an individual stock should indicate heavy speculation by investors that the price will drop. However, many technical analysts interpret this ratio in the opposite way: A high short-interest ratio is taken as a bullish sign because the large number of shares sold short represents a large number of shares that must be repurchased in order to close out the short sales. If the ratio is low, the required future purchases are lower. In effect, the short seller must repurchase, regardless of whether or not his or her expectations were correct. The larger the short-interest ratio, the larger the potential demand that is indicated. Therefore, an increase in the ratio indicates more pent-up demand for the shares that have been shorted.

The short-interest ratio for a given month should be interpreted in relation to historical boundaries. However, one problem is that the boundaries keep changing. Short-interest figures have been distorted by hedging and arbitrage techniques that have become more popular. For example, if a fund buys Air Canada and shorts Canadian Airlines, how does this affect the interpretation of the short interest? Hedged short sellers are not likely to panic if their short position moves adversely, which otherwise might lead them to buy and push the price up.

Mutual Fund Liquidity

Several indicators are based on the theory of **contrary opinion**. The idea is to trade contrary to most investors, who supposedly almost always lose — in other words, to go against the crowd. This is an old idea and over the years technicians have developed several measures designed to capitalize on this concept.

Contrary Opinion
The theory that it pays to trade contrary to most investors.

Mutual fund liquidity can be used as a contrary opinion technique. Under this scenario, mutual funds are presumed to act incorrectly before a market turning point. Therefore, when mutual fund liquidity is low because the funds are fully invested, contrarians believe that the market is at, or near, a peak. The funds should be building up cash (liquidity); instead, they are extremely bullish and are fully invested. Conversely, when funds hold large liquid reserves, it suggests that they are bearish. Contrarians would consider this a good time to buy because the market may be at, or near, its low point.

Put/Call Ratio

Some technical analysts believe that people who play the options market are, as a group, consistent losers. Speculators buy calls when they expect stock prices to rise, and they buy puts when they expect prices to fall. Because they are generally more optimistic than pessimistic, the put to call ratio is usually well below 1.0. For example, a ratio of 0.60 indicates that only six puts are purchased for every ten calls. The rise of this ratio indicates increased pessimism on the part of speculators in options, but this is a buy signal to a contrarian. A low ratio would be a sell signal to a contrarian because of the rampant optimism such a ratio indicates.

[8] For example, a ratio of 1.0 means that the outstanding short interest approximates a day's trading volume.

CSC NOTES

Additional Techinical Indicators

The Odd-Lot Theory

An odd-lot transaction involves the purchase or sale of shares in less than a round lot, which varies according to stock price but is usually less than 100 shares. According to the odd-lot theory, small investors are more likely to buy or sell odd lots, and they are usually wrong in their actions at market peaks and troughs. (This is a classic example of a theory based on contrary opinion). Supposedly, such investors typically buy when the market is at or close to a peak and sell when it is near the bottom. In addition, it is assumed that small investors do not get involved with short sales unless they are particularly bearish.

Odd-lot ratios measure the total purchases and sales involving less than a round lot. An increase in odd-lot purchases is bearish, while an increase in odd-lot sales is bullish.

Credit-Debit Balance Ratio

The New York Exchange monthly credit balance is representative of the cash customer, while the debit balance represents the investors purchasing on margin (assumed to be speculators). Increases in the credit balance implies the cash customer is selling and building up reserves, which is bullish since it signals latent purchasing power. Increases in the debit balance indicates the margin purchasers (speculators) are continuing to buy, which is also technically bullish.

Barron's Confidence Index

This index measures the ratio of the yield on Barron's ten high grade corporate bonds relative to the average yield on the 40 bonds in the Dow Jones Bond Averages, which consists of ten high grade, ten second grade, ten industrial, and ten utilities bonds.

The indicator is based on the premise that institutional bond buyers are better informed than the average bond investor. Sophisticated bond investors will tilt their bond portfolios toward high quality bonds (the Barron's bonds) when they are bearish, and will lean toward lower quality, higher yielding bonds (the Dow bonds) when they become more bullish (or less nervous). In other words, there will be a flight to quality when these investors lose confidence in market conditions. Accordingly, a decrease in the index represents an increase the yield on the Dow bonds relative to the Barron's bonds. This implies an increase in the spread required by investors to hold lower quality bonds, which may signal an impending market decline.

The Bank-Credit Analyst

The bank-credit analyst examines ten money and bank credit figures throughout the US banking system to determine monetary conditions. The indicators are put into an overall index, the value of which suggests whether inflationary and business conditions provide a bullish or bearish environment for stock prices.

Elliot Wave Theory

This is a complicated theory, which suggests that the market moves in a series of huge waves and cycles, which are superimposed on smaller waves, and so on. The main contention is that the market moves up in a series of five waves and down in a series of three, all of which have smaller waves superimposed upon them. In addition, there are various refinements that restrict the information provided by these waves. Due to some of the restrictive assumptions, it is often difficult to determine which leg of the cycle we are at in any given time period. However, at other times this approach has provided experienced users with a clear-cut indication of the direction of future market movements.

While small changes are considered unimportant, extreme readings are said to convey information. According to one well-known analyst, this would correspond to a CBOE put/call ratio below 0.7 or above 0.9.[9]

[9] Butler, "Technical Analysis: A Primer," p. 129.

TESTING TECHNICAL ANALYSIS STRATEGIES

What constitutes a fair test of a technical trading rule? The adjustments that should be made include at least the following:

1. *Risk*. If the risk involved in two strategies is not comparable, a fair comparison cannot be made. As we know, other things being equal, a more risky strategy would be expected to outperform a less risky one.
2. *Transaction and other costs (e.g., taxes)*. Several technical trading rules may produce excess returns before transaction costs are deducted. However, after such costs are deducted, they may be inferior to a buy-and-hold strategy, which generates much lower trading costs.
3. *Consistency*. Can the rule outperform the alternative over a reasonable period of time, such as five or ten years? Any rule may outperform an alternative for a short period, but it will not be too useful unless it holds up over some longer term.
4. *Out-of-sample validity*. Has the rule been tried on data other than that used to produce the rule? It is always possible to find a rule that works on a particular sample if enough rules are tried; that is, it is possible to torture the data until it confesses.

If we conduct enough tests, we can find a rule that produces favourable results on a particular sample. Therefore, before we conclude that a trading rule is successful, we should conduct a fair test as outlined above. Risks must be comparable, and appropriate costs must be deducted. Finally, the rule should be tried on different samples of stocks over a sufficiently long-term period.

SOME CONCLUSIONS ABOUT TECHNICAL ANALYSIS

Technical analysis often appeals to those who are beginning a study of investments because it is easy to believe that stock prices form repeatable patterns over time or that certain indicators should be related to future market (or individual stock) price movements. It is easy to look at a chart of a particular stock and immediately see what we believe to be patterns in the price changes and clear evidence of trends that should be obvious to anyone studying it. How should we view this situation?

On the one hand, most academics, numerous practitioners, and anyone believing in the weak-form version of the EMH are highly sceptical of technical analysis, to say the least. On the other hand, many practitioners, both professional and amateur, use technical information to assist them in their investment decisions. Indeed, it is rare to see any type of analytical report on a stock that does not include some sort of historical price information or a price chart.

One of the contributing factors to this debate is that it is impossible to test all the techniques of technical analysis and their variations and interpretations. The techniques of this approach are simply too numerous, and technical analysis is broader than the use of only price information. As a result, technical analysis has not been tested thoroughly and definitive statements about this subject cannot be made. A good example of the omissions in this area is the use of volume in technical strategies. Although volume is a recognized part of technical analysis, few tests have been conducted on its use in conjunction with the rest of technical analysis.[10]

[10] O. Joy and C. Jones, "Should We Believe the Tests of Market Efficiency?" *Journal of Portfolio Management* 12 (Summer 1986), pp. 49–54.

INVESTING *tip*

No inherent reason exists for stock price movements to repeat themselves. For example, flipping a coin 100 times should, on average, result in about 50 heads and 50 tails. While it is possible that the first 10 tosses could produce 10 heads, the chance of that pattern repeating itself is extremely small.

In addition to the lack of abundance of empirical evidence, the evidence that has been produced has not led to unilateral conclusions on the subject. While a large number of thorough tests of technical analysis techniques have failed to confirm the value of technical trading strategies, several recent studies have found conflicting evidence. For example, a recent article by Brock, Lakonishik, and LeBaron demonstrated the profitability associated with the use of some standard technical trading strategies.[11] They used 90 years of daily data over the period 1897 to 1986 to demonstrate the superior returns produced by moving average and trading range breakout strategies.

Jegadeesh found predictable patterns in stock prices based on monthly returns for the period, 1934–1987.[12] His study showed that stocks with large losses in one month are likely to show a significant reversal in the following month and that stocks with large gains in one month are likely to show a significant loss in the next month. Interestingly, in a subsequent study of US stock returns, Jegadeesh and Titman documented the success associated with "momentum" trading strategies, which involves purchasing stocks that have performed well in the recent time period, and selling those that have performed poorly.[13] These results have been confirmed in Canada by Foerster, Prihar and Schmitz, and by Cleary and Inglis.[14]

There are several other troubling features of technical analysis for non-believers. First, several interpretations of each technical tool and chart pattern are not only possible but usual. One or more of the interpreters will be correct (more or less), but it is virtually impossible to know beforehand who these will be. After the fact we will know which indicator or chart, or whose interpretation was correct, but only those investors who used that particular information will benefit. Tools such as the Dow theory are well known for their multiple interpretations by various observers who disagree over how the theory is to be interpreted.

Furthermore, consider a technical trading rule (or chart pattern) that is, in fact, successful. When it gives its signal on the basis of reaching some specified value (or forms a clear picture on a chart), it correctly predicts movements in the market or some particular stock. Such a rule or pattern, if observed by several market participants, will be self-destructive as more and more investors use it. Price will reach its equilibrium value quickly, taking away profit opportunities from all but the quickest. Some observers will start trying to act before the rest on the basis of what they expect to happen. (For example, they may act before a complete head and shoulders pattern forms.) Price will then reach an equilibrium even more quickly, so that only those who act earliest will benefit. Eventually, the value of any such rule will be negated entirely (i.e., the pattern will disappear).[15]

---

[11] W. Brock, J. Lakonishok, and B. LeBaron, "Simple Technical Trading Rules and the Stochastic Properties of Stock Returns," *Journal of Finance* 47 (December 1992), pp. 1731–1764.

[12] Narasimhan Jegadeesh, "Evidence of Predictable Behavior of Security Returns," *Journal of Finance* 45 (July 1990), pp. 881–898.

[13] N. Jegadeesh and S. Titman, "Returns to Buying Winners and Selling Losers: Implications for Stock Market Efficiency," *Journal of Finance* 48 (March 1993), pp. 65–91.

[14] S. Foerster, A. Prihar, and J. Schmitz, "Back to the Future: Price Momentum Models and How They Beat the Canadian Equity Markets," *Canadian Investment Review* 7 (Winter 1994/95), pp. 9–13; S. Cleary and M. Inglis, "Momentum in Canadian Stock Returns," *Canadian Journal of Administrative Sciences* 15 (September 1998), pp. 279–291.

[15] Readers should recognize that having technicians identify and exploit these opportunities will contribute to market efficiency, since the patterns should eventually disappear.

What can we conclude about technical analysis? While technical analysis attempts to measure the psychology behind the forces of supply and demand, it is as much an art as it is a science. While it does not meet several criteria for academic acceptance, it remains popular among many investors. It is important to recognize that no investment system — technical, fundamental, or one based on the use of modern portfolio theory — will work in all markets all the time, since we are dealing with the uncertain future. The important matter is that investors should attempt to gain value added wherever possible, and along these lines, a basic knowledge of the tenets of technical analysis may prove useful.

SUMMARY

This summary relates to the learning objectives provided on page 569.

1. **Define technical analysis and explain why it is used.**
Technical analysis, an alternative to fundamental analysis, is the oldest approach used by investors. Technical analysis relies on published market, and primarily price and volume data, to predict the short-term direction of individual stocks or the market as a whole. The emphasis is on internal factors that help to detect demand-supply conditions in the market. The rationale for technical analysis is that the net demand (or lack thereof) for stocks can be detected by various technical indicators and that trends in stock prices occur and continue for considerable periods of time. Stock prices require time to adjust to the change in supply and demand.

2. **Describe the major techniques used in technical analysis.**
Price and volume are primary tools of the technical analyst, as are various technical indicators. Technical analysis can be applied to both the aggregate market and individual stocks. Aggregate market analysis originated with the Dow theory, the best-known technical theory. It is designed to detect the start of major movements. Other technical indicators of the aggregate market include, but are not limited to, the following:

   a. Moving averages, which are used to detect both the direction and the rate of change in prices.

   b. The advance-decline line (breadth of market), which is used to assess the condition of the overall market.

   c. Mutual fund liquidity, which uses the potential buying power (liquidity) of mutual funds as a bullish or bearish indicator.

   d. Short-interest ratio, which assesses potential demand from investors who have sold shares short.

   e. Contrary opinion, which is designed to go against the crowd. Included here are mutual fund liquidity and the put/call ratio, as well as the odd-lot theory.

   Technical analysis also involves the use of charts of price patterns to detect trends that are believed to persist over time. The most frequently used charts are bar charts, which show each day's price movement as well as volume, and point-and-figure charts, which show only significant price changes as they occur. Numerous chart patterns are recognizable to a technician. However, all patterns are subject to multiple interpretations because different technicians will read the same chart differently.

Another well-known technique for individual stocks is relative strength, which shows the strength of a particular stock in relation to its average price, its industry, or the market.

3. **Discuss the limitations of technical analysis.**
Technical analysis is popular among investors but is not generally accepted by academics who see it as more an art than a science. The techniques of technical analysis are too numerous to test empirically, and the evidence that does exist is inconclusive. Critics point out that the same technical information can lead analysts to several different interpretations.

KEY TERMS

Bar charts
Bear market
Bull market
Contrary opinion
Dow theory
Market data
Point-and-figure charts
Relative strength
Resistance level
Short-interest ratio
Support level
Technical analysis

ADDITIONAL RESOURCES

Basics on technical analysis are available in the popular press, such as:
Butler, Jonathan. "Technical Analysis: A Primer," *Worth*, October 1995, pp. 128–134.

One of the classic commentaries on this and related subjects such as the Efficient Market Hypothesis is:
Malkiel, Burton G. *A Random Walk Down Wall Street*. Sixth Edition. New York: W. W. Norton, 1995.

A well-known primer on technical analysis is:
Pring, Martin J. *Technical Analysis Explained*. Third Edition. New York: McGraw-Hill, 1991.
Pring also has a CD-ROM seminar and workbook:
Pring, Martin J. *Introduction to Technical Analysis*. New York: McGraw-Hill, 1997.

INVESTMENTS ON THE WEB

Useful Web sites regarding technical analysis include:
<http://www.clearstation.com>
<http://www.stocksignals.com>
<http://www.traders.com>

REVIEW QUESTIONS

1. Describe the rationale for technical analysis.
2. What do technicians assume about the adjustment of stock prices from one equilibrium position to another?
3. What role does volume play in technical analysis?
4. How does the Dow theory forecast how long a market movement will last?
5. Differentiate between support levels and resistance levels.
6. What is relative strength analysis?
7. Why is the advance-decline line called an indicator of breadth of the market?
8. Why is a rising short-interest ratio considered to be a bullish indicator?
9. What is the rationale for the theory of contrary opinion?
10. Why do stock-price movements repeat themselves?
11. Differentiate between fundamental analysis and technical analysis.
12. What is the Dow theory? What is the significance of the confirmation signal in this theory?
13. Using a moving average, how is a sell signal generated?
14. Distinguish between a bar chart and a point-and-figure chart.
15. What new financial instruments have caused the short-interest ratio to be less reliable? Why?
16. Describe a bullish sign when using a moving average; a bearish sign. Do the same for the advance-decline line.
17. Assume that you know a technical analyst who claims success on the basis of his or her chart patterns. How might you go about scientifically testing this claim?
18. Is it possible to prove or disprove categorically the validity of technical analysis?
19. On a rational economic basis, why is the study of chart patterns likely to be an unrewarding activity?
20. Consider the plot of stock X in Figure 18-9. The plot shows weekly prices for one year, based on a beginning price of $30.
    a. Do you see any chart patterns in this figure?
    b. Do any patterns you see in this chart help you to predict the future price of this stock?
    c. What is your forecast of this stock's price over the next three months?

PREPARING FOR YOUR PROFESSIONAL EXAMS

Special Note to CSC Students

Ensure that you have read and understood the following topics:*

What is technical analysis?, pp. 570–573
Stock price and volume techniques, pp. 573–584

Figure 18-9
Stock X

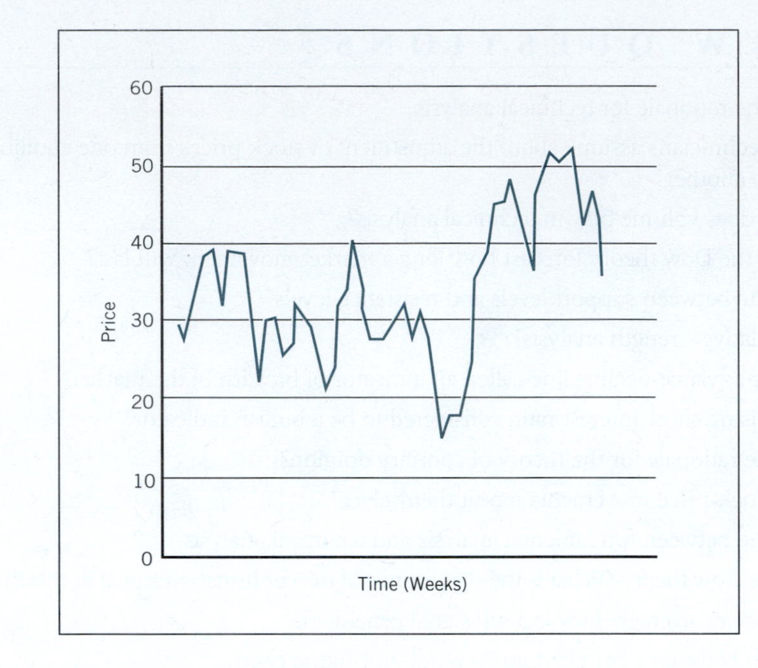

Technical indicators, pp. 585–588
CSC Notes: Additional Technical Indicators, p. 588

Reading these CSC-related topics should provide you with additional understanding of CSC material. However, it should not be seen as a substitute for reading the CSC textbook itself, which is the basis for the CSC exam.

CSC REGISTRATION QUESTIONS

The Canadian Securities Institute issued the following sample questions in the 1997 CSC registration package as a means for students to self-assess their understanding of CSC-related material.

1. Each of the following is associated with technical analysis except the ____________.
   a. random walk theory
   b. odd-lot theory
   c. Elliot Wave theory
   d. Dow theory
2. At stock market peaks, odd lot selling is ______ it is at stock market bottoms.
   a. higher than
   b. lower than
   c. the same as

CHAPTER 19

OPTIONS

LEARNING OBJECTIVES

After reading this chapter, you will be able to

1. Define options and discuss why they are used.
2. Describe how options work and give some basic strategies.
3. Explain the valuation of options.
4. Identify types of options other than puts and calls.

CHAPTER PREVIEW

This chapter analyzes options, which are important derivative securities that provide flexibility for investors in managing investment risk and the opportunity to speculate in security markets. We explain the advantages of options and provide some basic strategies. We also discuss how options are valued using the Black-Scholes model. Although our focus is on put and call options, we take a look at interest rate, currency, and stock-index options at the end of the chapter.

INTRODUCTION

Rather than trade directly in common stocks, investors can purchase securities representing a claim — an option — on a particular stock or group of stocks. This option gives the holder the right to receive or deliver shares of stock under specified conditions. The option need not be exercised (and often will not be worth exercising). Instead, an investor can simply buy and sell these **equity-derivative securities** that derive their value from the equity prices of the same corporation. Gains or losses will depend on the difference between the purchase price and the sales price.

Equity-Derivative Securities Securities that derive their value in whole or in part by having a claim on the underlying common stock.

This chapter looks at put and call options. Appendix 11-A discussed convertible securities, and Appendix 19-B at the end of this chapter examines warrants and rights. All are equity-derivative securities.[1] We concentrate primarily on options on individual stocks and stock indexes, and to a much lesser extent on interest rate options. In Chapter 20, we consider futures contracts, which together with options constitute the most commonplace equity-derivative securities used by the average investor. Since we are focusing on investing instruments, we limit our discussion to financial derivatives.

Our emphasis is on how puts and calls work and on their importance to portfolio managers. As derivative securities, options are innovations in risk management, not in risk itself, and as such they should be both welcomed and used by investors and portfolio managers. Since our emphasis is on equity securities, our examples revolve around common stocks.

Options

Options Rights to buy or sell a stated number of shares of stock within a specified period at a specified price.

Options, which typically represent claims on an underlying common stock, are created by investors and sold to other investors. The corporation whose common stock underlies these claims has no direct interest in the transaction, being in no way responsible for creating, terminating, or executing put and call contracts.

Call An option to buy a specified number of shares of stock at a stated price within a specified period.

A **call** option contract gives the holder the right to buy (or "call away") 100 shares of a particular common stock at a specified price any time prior to a specified expiration date.[2] Investors purchase calls if they expect the stock price to rise because the price of the call and

[1] Interest rate derivative securities such as bond options and futures contracts on banker's acceptances are also commonly used derivatives, as discussed in Chapters 2 and 4. Interest rate swaps (which are discussed in Chapter 12) are used primarily by financial institutions and large corporations.

[2] It is important to remember throughout this discussion that the standard option contract on the organized exchanges is for 100 shares of the underlying common stock.

the common stock will move together. Therefore, calls permit investors to speculate on a rise in the price of the underlying common stock without buying the stock itself. For example, a **BCE Inc.** six-month call option at $50 per share gives the buyer the right (an option) to purchase 100 shares of BCE at $50 per share from a writer (seller) of the option anytime during the six months before the specified expiration date.

A **put** option contract gives the buyer the right to sell (or "put away") 100 shares of a particular common stock at a specified price prior to a specified expiration date. If exercised, the shares are sold by the owner (buyer) of the put contract to a writer (seller) of this contract who has been designated to take delivery of the shares and pay the specified price. Investors purchase puts if they expect the stock price to fall, because the value of the put will rise as the stock price declines. Therefore, puts allow investors to speculate on a decline in the stock price without selling the common stock short. For example, the writer (seller) of a BCE Inc. six-month put at $50 per share is obligated, under certain circumstances, to receive from the holder of this put 100 shares of BCE for which the writer will pay $50 per share.

Put
An option to sell a specified number of shares of stock at a stated price within a specified period.

Why Options Markets?

An investor can always purchase shares of common stock if he or she is bullish about the company's prospects rather than buy a call (or sell a put). Similarly, one can sell a company's shares short if bearish about the stock rather than buy a put (or sell a call). Why, then, should we create these indirect claims on a stock as an alternative way to invest? Several reasons have been advanced, including the following:

1. Puts and calls expand the opportunity set available to investors, making available risk-return combinations that otherwise would be impossible or that improve the risk-return characteristics of a portfolio. For example, an investor can sell a stock short and buy a call. This decreases the risk on the short sale for the life of the call since the investor has a guaranteed maximum purchase price until the call option expires.[3]
2. In the case of calls, an investor can control (for a short period) a claim on the underlying common stock for a much smaller investment than required to buy the stock itself. In the case of puts, an investor can duplicate a short sale without a margin account and at a modest cost in relation to the value of the stock. In addition, the option buyer's maximum loss is known in advance. If an option expires worthless, the most the buyer can lose is the cost (price) of the option.
3. Options provide leverage by magnifying the percentage gains in relation to buying or short selling the underlying stock. In fact, options can provide greater leverage potential than fully margined stock transactions.
4. Using options on a market index such as the TSE 35 Index, an investor can participate in market movements with a single trading decision.

[3] Many stocks do not have puts and calls available in the organized options market exchanges. For example, the active options trading on the Canadian Equity Options Market consists of less than a hundred stocks, while a few hundred stocks dominate the listings and trading activity on large US options markets such as the Chicago Board Options Exchange (CBOE). There are also a large number of stock options that trade in the over-the-counter market through brokers.

UNDERSTANDING OPTIONS

Options Terminology

To understand puts and calls, one must understand the terminology used in connection with them. Our discussion here applies specifically to options on the organized exchanges as reported daily in such sources as *The Globe and Mail* and the *National Post*.[4] Important options terms include the following:

Exercise (Strike) Price
The per-share price at which the common stock may be purchased from (in the case of a call) or sold to (in the case of a put) a writer.

Expiration Date
The date on which an option expires.

Option Premium
The price paid by the option buyer to the seller (writer) of the option.

1. The **exercise (strike) price** is the per-share price at which the common stock may be purchased (in the case of a call) or sold (in the case of a put). Most options are available at several different exercise prices, thereby giving investors a choice. As the stock price changes, options with new exercise prices are added.[5]
2. The **expiration date** is the last date at which an option can be exercised. All puts and calls are designated by the month of expiration, with equity options expiring on the Saturday following the third Friday of the month. This forces clients to make their exercise decisions on the Friday. The expiration dates for options contracts vary from stock to stock.
3. The **option premium** is the price paid by the option buyer to the writer (seller) of the option, whether put or call. The premium is stated on a per share basis for options on organized exchanges, and since the standard contract is for 100 shares, a $3 premium represents a cost per contract of $300, a $15 premium represents a cost of $1,500, and so forth.

Options exchanges have introduced combinations of standardized expiration dates (known as trading cycles) and standardized exercise prices. For example, there would be 18 different option series for a stock trading at $45: puts and calls with strike prices of $40, $45, and $50, with maturities of three, six, and nine months. Additional series are started as time passes and if the price changes. For example, if the stock price increased to $51, a $55 series would begin in addition to those already established.

Figure 19-1 is an excerpt from *The Globe and Mail / Report on Business*, which shows market activity on the Canadian Equity Options Market. It shows that the most active contracts for the day are reported along with the individual equity options. In addition to reporting bid and ask prices, as well as the last trading price for the option, we observe volume and open interest information. The volume shows the number of options contracts that were traded the previous day, while the open interest represents the number of options of a particular series that are presently outstanding. It is usually used as a measure of liquidity, along with the volume of trading.

Consider the top row referring to the **BCE Inc.** options, reported as:

Stock	Close	Total Vol	Total Op Int
BCE Inc.	$52.30	3180	25263

[4] Puts and calls existed for many years before the existence of organized exchanges. They could be bought or sold in the over-the-counter (OTC) market. The terms of each individual contract (price, exercise date, etc.) had to be negotiated between buyer and seller. This was clearly a cumbersome, inefficient process. The OTC market for options is unregulated, and transactions are not reported. Although specific information is not available, a very large OTC market for options does exist and is widely used by corporations and portfolio managers for hedging purposes.

[5] Options sold on these exchanges are protected against stock dividends and stock splits; both the exercise price and the number of shares in the contract are adjusted for dividends or splits, as necessary.

Figure 19-1
Canadian Equity Options

Trading in Canadian equity options on the Toronto and Montreal exchanges by the Canadian Derivatives Corp. P is a Put.

Five Most Recent Active Option Classes

	Volume	Op Int
ATI Techs	3674	28377
BCE Inc	3180	25263
Nortel	2838	28424
Royal Bank	2047	10582
Biochem	2029	14457

		Close	Total Vol		Tot Op Int	
Stock	**Series**	**Bid**	**Ask**	**Last**	**Vol**	**Op Int**
Air Canada		**$5.90**			**330**	**15534**
Nov98	$6 p	0.25	0.35	0.30	73	1087
	$7	0.06	0.10	0.10	20	1370
Jan99	$5	1.30	1.40	1.40	2	49
	$6	0.60	0.75	0.65	16	318
	$7	0.25	0.35	0.40	20	930
Apr99	$5	1.70	1.75	1.70	60	272
	$5 p	0.30	0.45	0.45	13	740
	$6	1.00	1.10	1.00	50	804
	$6 p	0.75	0.90	0.75	25	411
	$7	0.65	0.75	0.75	50	614
	$7 p	1.35	1.50	1.35	10	228
BCE Inc		**$52.30**			**3180**	**25263**
Nov98	$45	7.50	7.80	7.70	8	183
	$471/2	5.20	5.50	5.10	62	679
	$50	3.20	3.45	3.20	37	2793
	$50 p	0.75	0.90	0.90	50	563
	$521/2	1.70	1.90	1.70	1.55	542
	$55	0.70	0.80	0.65	40	367
	$621/2	0.05	0.10	0.10	250	884
Dec98	$471/2	5.70	6.00	5.90	540	785
	$50	3.90	4.14	4.20	25	135
	$50 p	1.55	1.75	1.55	1000	1010
	$521/2	2.55	2.75	2.75	556	556
Feb99	$40 p	0.40	0.60	0.50	30	151
	$45	8.80	9.05	8.80	5	87
	$45 p	1.15	1.40	1.45	2	139
	$471/2	7.00	7.25	7.30	63	122
	$471/2 p	1.80	2.05	1.85	5	39
	$50	5.45	5.75	5.75	42	344
	$521/2	4.15	4.40	4.45	18	230
	$55	3.05	3.30	3.05	114	746
	$571/2	2.25	2.45	2.25	96	189
	$60	1.60	1.80	1.70	41	438
	$65	0.75	0.95	0.95	6	145
	$65 p	12.65	12.90	13.80	10	10
May99	$50	6.80	7.05	6.90	10	375
	$50 p	3.70	3.95	3.70	10	44
	$521/2	5.35	5.60	5.35	5	5
BmbrB		**$18.30**			**273**	**20536**
Nov98	$19	0.30	0.55	0.40	21	803
	$19 p	1.00	1.25	0.80	20	30
Jan99	$15	3.45	3.70	3.90	4	492
	$16	2.65	2.90	3.10	5	514
	$17	1.70	1.95	2.25	16	1114
	$18	1.20	1.30	1.55	10	1079
	$19	1.00	1.05	1.25	30	1273
Apr99	$15	3.85	4.10	4.10	50	55
	$19	1.30	1.45	1.80	5	204
	$20	0.85	1.10	1.25	7	2.00
	$20 p	2.55	2.80	2.40	10	12
Jul99	$19 p	2.25	2.50	2.10	10	10
	$20	1.40	1.65	1.70	20	20
Jan00	$15	5.15	5.65	5.25	14	615
	$16	4.60	5.10	4.75	24	443
	$18	3.60	4.10	4.15	2	275
	$19	3.15	3.65	3.20	5	141
Jan01	$17	6.15	6.65	6.50	10	464
	$20	4.50	5.00	4.60	10	560
TSE 35		**$343.07**			**1051**	**24713**
Nov98	$290 p	0.25	0.40	0.40	10	397
	$300	43.45	43.95	45.65	1	10
	$300 p	0.45	0.65	0.70	20	217
	$305 p	0.55	0.75	0.80	10	64
	$310 p	0.70	0.90	0.70	5	306
	$315 p	0.85	1.05	0.95	5	31
	$320 p	1.10	1.30	1.05	29	56
	$325	19.60	20.10	20.50	6	99
	$325 p	1.55	1.75	1.75	32	174
	$330	15.25	15.75	18.30	5	43
	$330 p	2.25	2.45	2.40	30	115
	$335	11.30	11.80	11.70	9	44
	$340	8.05	8.55	10.10	27	70
	$340 p	4.85	5.25	4.90	50	34
	$345	5.50	6.00	6.30	39	25
	$345 p	7.10	7.50	7.80	20	20
	$350	3.55	3.85	4.35	93	213
	$350 p	9.70	10.20	8.90	19	22
Dec98	$295 p	2.65	2.85	2.65	20	66
	$300 p	2.95	3.15	2.60	20	164
	$310 p	3.65	3.95	4.50	5	43
	$330	21.40	21.90	24.00	7	282
	$330 p	7.60	8.10	9.90	4	1402
	$335	17.65	18.15	17.40	1	114
	$335 p	8.85	9.35	9.90	5	51
	$340 p	10.10	10.60	10.55	5	1903
	$345 p	12.35	12.85	12.30	31	41
	$370	3.55	3.85	4.50	17	158
	$375	2.65	2.85	2.85	5	244
	$380	2.00	2.20	3.15	20	293
	$385	1.50	1.70	1.90	5	39
	$390	1.10	1.30	1.50	6	226
	$395	0.75	0.95	1.40	13	285
	$395 p	51.85	52.35	55.05	2	16
Mar99	$290 p	6.00	6.50	6.60	1	11
	$305 p	8.50	9.00	8.80	12	44
	$310 p	9.65	10.15	9.30	23	50
	$330	31.55	32.05	30.50	2	11
	$350 p	24.20	24.70	24.00	420	413
	$370	11.95	12.45	12.15	6	5
	$395	595	6.45	6.75	1	1
Jun99	$345 p	28.65	29.65	29.40	10	10
TIPS 35		**$34.45**			**741**	**14563**
Nov98	$32	2.60	2.75	2.55	10	40
	$33 p	0.35	0.50	0.40	20	68
	$34	1.10	1.25	1.05	10	72
	$34 p	0.70	0.75	1.00	5	59
	$35	0.55	0.65	0.55	20	214
	$35 p	1.05	1.20	1.25	50	52
Dec98	$30 p0.350.45		0.45	0.40	50	1476
	$31	3.90	4.05	3.85	2	11
	$33	2.30	2.45	2.15	50	275
	$34	1.65	1.80	1.85	50	147
	$34 p	1.05	1.20	1.20	10	133
	$35	1.10	1.25	1.10	100	589
	$35 p	1.45	1.60	1.55	26	98
	$36	0.75	0.85	0.30	5	94
	$400	0.60	0.80	1.40	9	565
	$410	0.35	0.55	0.65	1	6
	$415	0.20	0.40	0.80	20	13
	$420	0.10	0.30	0.50	22	48
Mar99	$29 p	0.55	0.65	0.65	60	264
	$30	5.25	5.40	5.60	10	517
	$30 p	0.70	0.85	0.70	40	302
	$31	4.50	4.65	4.30	19	70
	$31 p	0.85	1.00	0.95	10	319
	$32	3.80	3.95	4.05	15	57
	$32 p	1.10	1.25	1.25	30	207
	$33	3.20	3.35	3.35	25	42
	$33 p	1.40	1.55	1.55	5	231
	$34	2.60	2.75	2.85	15	62
	$35	2.05	2.20	2.00	20	91
	$35 p	2.25	2.40	2.40	4	174
	$37	1.25	1.40	1.25	10	137
	$38	0.90	1.05	0.85	10	276
	$39	0.70	0.85	0.80	4	14
Jun99	$35	3.00	3.05	2.75	4	14
TIPS 100		**$38.60**			**4**	**251**
Dec98	$40	1.00	1.15	1.00	4	4

Source: Excerpted from *The Globe and Mail/Report on Business*, October 31, 1998, p. B22. Reprinted with permission from *The Globe and Mail.*

We can see (in bold beside the company name) that the common shares of BCE Inc. closed trading on October 30, 1998 at $52.30 per share. The other numbers in bold along the top row represent total trading volume and open interest statistics for all series of BCE options. At that time, there were several puts (denoted by "p" beside the exercise price) and calls available with strike prices ranging from $40 to $65, and four expiration dates ranging from November 1998 to May 1999.

Now consider the first row below the company name, presented as:

Series		Bid	Ask	Last	Vol	Op Int
Nov98	$45	7.50	7.80	7.70	8	183

This refers to call options with a strike price of $45 that expire in November 1998. The closing bid price for these options was $7.50 per option (or $7.50 × 100 = $750 per option contract), while the closing ask price was $7.80 per option. The last sale price (or last premium traded) was $7.70 per option, the traded volume in this option series that day was eight contracts, and the open interest was 183 contracts.

Long-Term Options (LEAPs) Options on individual stocks with maturities greater than one year.

Figure 19-1 also includes information for **long-term options or LEAPS** (short for Long-Term Equity AnticiPation Securities).[6] These are long-term options with maturities greater than one year and ranging to two years and beyond. They are available on a relatively few well-known stocks, with more being traded all the time. For example, in October 1998 an investor could purchase a long-term call option on **Bombardier**, with a choice of two maturity dates, January 2000 or January 2001.

How Options Work

As noted, a standard call (put) contract gives the buyer the right to purchase (sell) 100 shares of a particular stock at a specified exercise price before the expiration date. Both puts and calls are created by sellers who write a particular contract. Sellers (writers) are investors, either individuals or institutions, who seek to profit from their beliefs about the underlying stock's likely price performance, just as the buyer does.

The buyer and the seller have opposite expectations about the likely performance of the underlying stock and therefore the performance of the option.

- The call writer expects the price of the stock to remain roughly steady or perhaps move down.
- The call buyer expects the price of the stock to move upward and relatively soon.
- The put writer expects the price of the stock to remain roughly steady or perhaps move up.
- The put buyer expects the price of the stock to move down and relatively soon.

EXAMPLE: BUYING A CALL OPTION ON BCE INC.

Consider an individual named Carl who is optimistic about **BCE**'s prospects. Carl instructs his broker to buy a February 1999 call option on BCE at a strike price of $55. Assume that the negotiated premium is $3.05 (i.e. the value reported in Figure 19-1). This implies the cost of one option contract is $305 plus brokerage commissions.

[6] LEAPs is a registered trademark of the Chicago Board Options Exchange.

Three courses of action are possible with any option:

1. *The option may expire worthless*. Assume the price of BCE fluctuates up and down but is at $50 on the expiration date. The call gives the buyer (owner) the right to purchase BCE at $55, but this would make no sense when BCE can be purchased on the open market at $50. Therefore, the option will expire worthless.
2. *The option may be exercised*. If BCE appreciates above $55, Carl could exercise the option by paying $5,500 (the $55 exercise price multiplied by 100 shares) and receiving 100 shares of BCE. For example, if the shares appreciated to $60 before expiration, Carl could purchase 100 shares for $5,500 plus commission fees, and resell them in the market for $6,000 less commission fees. His resulting profit would be $6,000 − $5,500 − $305 (the original cost of the option contract) − total commission fees.
3. *The option can be sold in the secondary market*. If BCE appreciates, the value (price) of the call will also. Carl can easily sell the call in the secondary market to another investor who wishes to speculate on BCE because listed options are traded continuously. Most investors trading puts and calls do not exercise those that are valuable; instead, they simply sell them on the open market, exactly as they would the common stock.[7]

Puts work the same way as calls, except in reverse. A writer creates a particular put contract and sells it for the premium that the buyer pays. The writer believes that the underlying common stock is likely to remain flat or appreciate, while the buyer believes that the stock price is likely to decline. Unlike a buyer, a writer may have to take action in the form of taking delivery of the stock.

EXAMPLE: SELLING A PUT OPTION ON BCE INC.

Assume a writer sells a December **BCE** put option contract with an exercise price of $50 when the stock price is $52.30. A premium of $1.55 (the closing price in Figure 19-1) means a total of $155 per option contract, which the buyer of the put pays and the writer receives (brokerage costs would be involved in both cases).

Suppose the price of BCE declines to $45 near the expiration date. The put owner (buyer), who did not own BCE previously, could instruct the broker to purchase 100 shares of BCE in the open market for $4,500. The buyer could then exercise the put, which means that a chosen writer must accept the 100 shares of BCE and pay the put owner $50 per share, or $5,000 total (although the current market price has fallen to only $45). The put buyer earns $345 before commission fees ($5,000 received less $4,500 cost of 100 shares less the $155 paid for the put contract). The put writer suffers an immediate paper loss because the 100 shares of BCE are worth $45 per share but have a cost of $50 per share, although the premium received by the writer reduces this loss by $155. (Brokerage costs have once again been omitted in the example.)

[7] One of the implications of the option pricing model to be considered later is that American calls on stocks that do not pay a cash dividend should never be exercised before the expiration date, but those with dividends might be exercised.

As in the case of a call, two other courses of action are possible in addition to the exercise of the put. If the market price of the shares were below $50 (the exercise price), it is far more likely that the put owner would sell the put in the secondary market for a profit (or a loss), rather than exercising the option. As in the case of calls, most put investors simply buy and sell their options in the open market. Alternatively, if the price of BCE is at or above $50, the put would expire worthless because the price of the common stock did not decline enough to justify exercising the put.

The Mechanics of Trading

The Options Exchanges

Most exchange listed equity options are American style, which can be exercised at any time up to and including the expiration date. Index options and over-the-counter (OTC) options are typically European, which means they can only be exercised on the expiration date. Options can be bought or sold through an exchange facility or privately arranged (OTC options).

In 1973, the Chicago Board of Options Exchange (CBOE) was formed to begin trading in options. Liquidity problems, which had plagued the OTC options markets were overcome by:

1. Standardizing option contracts
2. Introducing a clearing corporation that would guarantee the performance of the seller of an options contract (i.e., effectively it becomes the buyer and seller for each option contract).

The secondary markets for puts and calls have worked well in the years since CBOE started operations. Trading volume has been large and has been growing in recent years, and the number of puts and calls available has expanded.

The options markets provide liquidity to investors, which is a very important requirement for successful trading. Investors know that they can instruct their broker to buy or sell whenever they desire, at a price set by the forces of supply and demand. These exchanges have made puts and calls a success by standardizing the exercise date and exercise price of contracts. For example, one BCE February 55 call option is identical to every other BCE February 55 call option.

The same types of orders discussed in Chapter 5, in particular, market, limit, and stop orders, are used in trading puts and calls.[8] Certificates representing ownership are not used for puts and calls; instead, transactions are handled as bookkeeping entries. Option trades settle on the next business day after the trade. The exercise of an equity option settles in three business days, the same as with a stock transaction. An investor must receive a risk disclosure statement issued by the clearing corporation (discussed in the following section) before the initial order is executed.

In 1997, the Vancouver Stock Exchange ceased trading of options, with the result being that all exchange-traded options in Canada are presently traded on the TSE or the Montreal Exchange (ME). This may change in the near future, if the recently proposed changes to Canadian security markets are accepted. As discussed in Chapter 4, one of the recommended reforms is that the ME will become our national derivatives market and handle all exchange

[8] While these orders are available, the manner in which some types of orders are executed on some of the options exchanges varies from that used on the stock exchanges.

trading in derivatives. Table 19-1 shows the equity option volume on the Canadian exchanges for 1994 to 1997. The ME is the only market for bond options, while the TSE is presently the only market for index options.

Table 19-1

CDCC Option Volumes

Options Product Group	1994 Contracts		1995 Contracts		1996 Contracts		1997 Contracts	
	Millions	%	Millions	%	Millions	%	Millions	%
Equity	1.791	79.10	2.300	78.87	3.263	85.64	4.061	83.32
Index	0.265	11.72	0.354	12.13	0.305	8.01	0.495	10.16
Govt. Bonds	0.051	2.26	0.040	1.38	0.030	0.79	0.023	0.48
Leaps	0.111	4.92	0.167	5.73	0.135	3.54	0.138	2.83
Metals	0.010	0.42	0.001	0.04	0.001	0.03	0.000	0.01
Options on Futures	0.036	1.58	0.054	1.85	0.076	1.99	0.156	3.20
Totals	2.264	100.00	2.916	100.00	3.810	100.00	4.873	100.00

Source: CDCC, *Annual Report*, 1997.

A significant problem with the Canadian options markets is thin trading. As a result, many investors take their option trades to US markets, which deal with much larger trading volumes. For example, the largest options exchange in the world is the Chicago Board Options Exchange (CBOE). The volume of trading in all options on this exchange for their fiscal year ending June 30, 1998 was over 196 million contracts — more than 43 times the volume of all Canadian Derivatives Clearinghouse Corporation trades during 1997.

The other major US option exchanges include: the American, the Philadelphia, the Pacific, and the New York. All five exchanges are continuous markets, similar to stock exchanges. Currently, the CBOE and the American Exchange are the most important US markets and control roughly 75 per cent of all trading in US options. For the year ended June 30, 1998, the CBOE accounted for 51.8 per cent of total option trading, 42.7 per cent of equity option trading, and 91.1 per cent of equity index option trading. Over the same period the American Exchange accounted for 24.5 per cent of all option trading, 29.7 per cent of equity option trading, and only 4.7 per cent of equity index option trading.[9]

In addition to the equity options that are available on the TSE, ME, and the OTC markets in Canada, and through the US markets, there are a variety of alternative option products available to Canadian investors. Stock-index options on the TSE 35 Index are available in Canada on the TSE, although they are scheduled to be replaced by S&P/TSE 60 Index options in the near future, as discussed in Chapter 4. Options also trade on TIPs 35 and TIPs

[9] Source: Chicago Board Options Exchange 1998 annual report at the following Web site: <http://www.cboe.com/exchange/annrpt4.htm>.

100 (or HIPs), whose values are determined by the levels of the TSE 35 and TSE 100 Indexes respectively. These options are also scheduled to be replaced by S&P/TSE 60 Index products.

Index options on the Standard & Poor's 100 Index plus others in US are also available. Stock-index options are "cash-settled" based on 100 times the value of the index at expiration date. Bond options trade on the ME on Government of Canada bonds covering $25,000 face value at maturity (since 1982). In addition currency options are available on the Philadelphia Stock Exchange.

The Clearing Corporation

Canadian Derivatives Clearing Corporation (CDCC)
The clearing corporation that issues and guarantees all equity, bond, and stock index positions on options exchanges in Canada.

In Canada, all equity, bond, and stock index positions are issued and guaranteed by a single clearing corporation, the **Canadian Derivatives Clearing Corporation (CDCC)**, formerly Trans Canada Options Inc. (TCO), which is owned equally by the TSE and the ME. In the US all listed options are cleared through the Options Clearing Corporation (OCC). Exercise on options trading on exchanges is accomplished by submitting an exercise notice to the clearing corporation. The clearing corporation then assigns the exercise notice to a member firm, which then assigns it to one of its accounts.

These clearing corporations perform a number of important functions that contribute to the success of the secondary market for options. They function as intermediaries between the brokers representing the buyers and the writers. That is, once the brokers representing the buyer and the seller negotiate the price on the floor of the exchange, they no longer deal with each other but with the CDCC (or the OCC in the US). Through their brokers, call writers contract with the CDCC itself to deliver shares of the particular stock, and buyers of calls actually receive the right to purchase the shares from the CDCC. Thus, the CDCC becomes the buyer for every seller and the seller for every buyer, guaranteeing that all contract obligations will be met. This prevents the risk and problems that could occur as buyers attempted to force writers to honour their obligations. The net position of the CDCC is zero, because the number of contracts purchased must equal the number sold.

Investors wishing to exercise their options inform their brokers, who in turn inform the CDCC of the exercise notice. Once the option holder submits the exercise note, the process is irrevocable. The CDCC randomly selects a broker on whom it holds the same written contract, and the broker randomly selects a customer who has written these options to honour the contract. Writers chosen in this manner are said to be assigned an obligation or to have received an assignment notice.[10] Once assigned, the writer cannot execute an offsetting transaction to eliminate the obligation; that is, a call writer who receives an assignment must sell the underlying securities, and a put writer must purchase them.

One of the great advantages of a clearing house is that transactors in this market can easily cancel their positions prior to assignment. Since the CDCC maintains all the positions for both buyers and sellers, it can cancel out the obligations of both call and put writers wishing to terminate their position. For example, a call writer can terminate the obligation to deliver the stock any time before the expiration date (or assignment) by making a "closing purchase transaction" at the current market price of the option. The CDCC offsets the outstanding call

[10] Assignment is virtually certain when an option expires in the money.

written with the call purchased in the closing transaction. A put writer can also close out a position at any time by making an offsetting transaction.

Options cannot be purchased on margin, and buyers must pay 100 per cent of the purchase price. With regard to puts and calls, *margin* refers to the collateral that option writers provide their brokers to ensure fulfillment of the contract in case of exercise. This collateral is required by the CDCC of its member firms whose clients have written options, in order to protect the CDCC against default by option writers. The member firms, in turn, require its customers who have written options to provide collateral for their written positions. This collateral can be in the form of cash or marketable securities (including shares in the underlying security).

SOME BASIC OPTIONS CHARACTERISTICS

In the Money, At the Money, and Out of the Money

Special terminology is used to describe the relationship between the exercise price of the option and the current stock price. If the price of the common stock, S, exceeds the exercise price of a call, E, the call is said to be *in the money* and has an immediate exercisable value. On the other hand, if the price of the common is less than the exercise price of a call, it is said to be out *of the money*. Finally, calls that are near the money are those with exercise prices slightly greater than current market price, whereas calls that are *at the money* are those with exercise prices equal to the stock price.

These same definitions also apply to puts, but in reverse.

In summary,

If $S > E$, a call is in the money and a put is out of the money.

If $S < E$, a call is out of the money and a put is in the money.

If $S = E$, an option is at the money.

Intrinsic Values

Intrinsic Value (Option) The value of an option if today was the expiration date.

If a call is in the money (the market price of the stock exceeds the exercise price for the call option), it has an *immediate* value equal to the difference in the two prices. This value will be designated as the **intrinsic value** of the call; it could also be referred to as the option's minimum value, which in this case is positive. If the call is at or out of the money, the intrinsic value is zero and the price of the option is based entirely on its speculative appeal. The intrinsic value can never fall below $0, since exercise is optional. Summarizing, where S_0 = current stock price:

$$\text{Intrinsic value of a call} = \text{Maximum } \{(S_0 - E), 0\} \quad \textbf{(19-1)}$$

EXAMPLE: CALCULATING INTRINSIC VALUE OF AN AIR CANADA CALL

We observe a closing price of $5.90 for the common shares of **Air Canada** on October 30, 1998 (as shown in Figure 19-1). A January 1999 call option on Air Canada with a $5 strike price is available and last traded at a premium of $1.40. This option is in the money because the stock price is greater than the exercise price. The intrinsic value of the January 5 call is

Intrinsic value of Air Canada January 5 call
$$= \text{Maximum } \{(\$5.90 - \$5.00), 0\} = \$0.90$$

Puts work in reverse. If the market price of the stock is less than the exercise price of the put, the put is in the money and has an intrinsic value. Otherwise, it is at or out of the money and has a zero intrinsic value. Thus:

$$\text{Intrinsic value of a put} = \text{Maximum } \{(E - S_0), 0\} \quad (19\text{-}2)$$

EXAMPLE: CALCULATING INTRINSIC VALUE OF AN AIR CANADA PUT

There was an April 1999 put on **Air Canada** stock available on October 30, 1998 with an exercise price of $7.00 (it last traded at a price of $1.35). Given the market price for Air Canada shares of $5.90 at that time, the intrinsic value for this put can be determined in the following manner:

Intrinsic value of Air Canada April 7 put
$$= \text{Maximum } \{(\$7.00 - \$5.90), 0\} = \$1.10$$

PAYOFFS AND PROFITS FROM BASIC OPTION POSITIONS

We can better understand the characteristics of options by examining their potential payoffs and profits. The simplest way to do this is to examine their value at expiration. At the expiration date, an option has an investment value, or payoff, which equals the option's intrinsic value at that time. In addition, we can also examine the net profit, which takes into account the price of the stock, the exercise price of the option, and the cost of the option. We consider both variables because option traders are interested in their net profits, but option valuation is perhaps better understood by focusing on payoffs.

As part of this analysis, we use letters to designate the key variables:

S_T = the value of the stock at expiration date T
E = the exercise price of the option

Calls

Buying a Call

Consider first the buyer of a call option. At expiration, the investment value or payoff to the call holder is:

Payoff to call buyer at expiration:
$= S_T - E$ if $S_T > E$
$= 0$ if $S_T \leq E$

Notice that this payoff is the intrinsic value for a call option at time T, as presented in Equation 19-1. This payoff to a call buyer is illustrated in Figure 19-2. The payoff is $0 until the exercise price is reached, at which point the payoff rises as the stock price rises.

EXAMPLE: DETERMINING PAYOFF ON A BCE CALL

Assume an investor buys a **BCE** December call option with an exercise price of $50. The payoff for the call at expiration is a function of the stock price at that time. For example, at expiration the value of the call relative to various possible stock prices would be calculated as in the following partial set of prices:

BCE stock price at expiration	$40	45	50	55	60
BCE call value (payoff) at expiration	$ 0	0	0	5	10

Notice that the payoff is not the same as the net profit to the option holder or writer. For example, if BCE is at $60 per share, the payoff to the option buyer is $10, but the net profit must reflect the cost of the call. In general, the profit to an option holder is the value of the option less the price paid for it. For the example above, if the cost of the BCE December 50 call option was originally $4.20, the net profit to the option holder (ignoring transactions costs) would be:

Net profit (option holder) = Option payoff − Option cost
Net profit (option holder) = $10 − $4.20 = $5.80

EXAMPLE: DETERMINING NET PROFIT ON CALL AND PUT OPTIONS

Figure 19-3 illustrates the profit situation for a call buyer. The price of the stock is assumed to be $48, and a six-month call is available with an exercise price of $50 for a premium of $4 per option, or $400 per option contract. If this call expires worthless, the maximum loss is the $400 premium. Up to the exercise price of $50, the loss is $4 per option. The break-even point for the investor is the sum of the exercise price and the premium, or $50 + $4 = $54. Therefore, the profit-loss line for the call buyer crosses the break-even line at $54. If the price of the stock rises above $54, the value of the call will increase with it, at least point for point, as shown by the two parallel lines above the $0 profit-loss line.

Figure 19-2
Payoff Profiles for Call and Put Options at Expiration

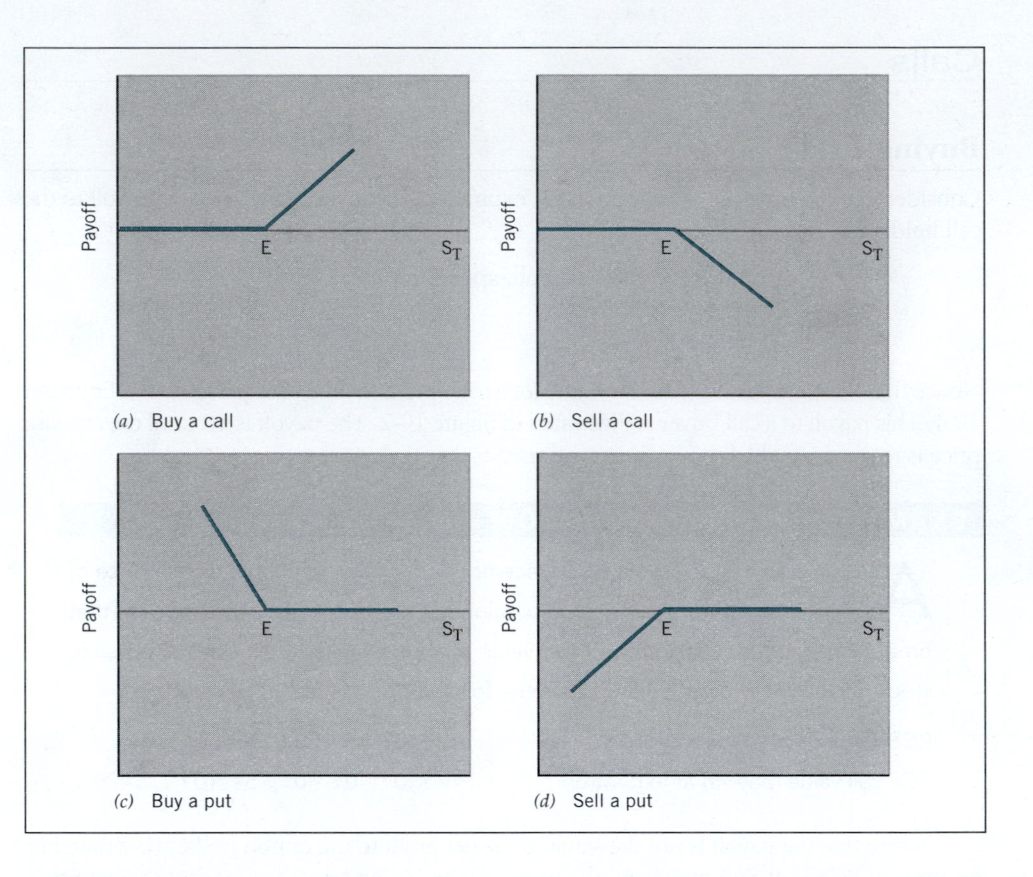

Selling (Writing) a Call

A "naked" or uncovered option writer is one who does not have their position "covered" in the underlying stock — in other words, does not own shares in the underlying stock to make available if the call option is exercised. Naked call option writers (or sellers) incur losses if the stock's price increases, as shown by the payoff profile in part (b) of Figure 19-2. The payoff is flat at the amount of the premium until the exercise price is reached, at which point it declines as the stock price rises. The call writer loses and the call buyer gains if the stock price rises.

Payoff to naked call writer at expiration:

$$= -(S_T - E) \text{ if } S_T > E$$
$$= 0 \qquad \text{if } S_T < E$$

The net profit line in Figure 19-4 is the mirror image of that for the call buyer, with positive profit levels up to the exercise price because the call writer is receiving the premium. The horizontal axis intercept in Figure 19-4 occurs at the break-even point for the option writer — the sum of the exercise price and the option premium received (note that the break-even point is identical to that of the call buyer). As the stock price exceeds the break-even point, the call writer loses. In fact, there is no conceptual limit to the call option writer's losses, since there is no upward limit on the price of the underlying share.

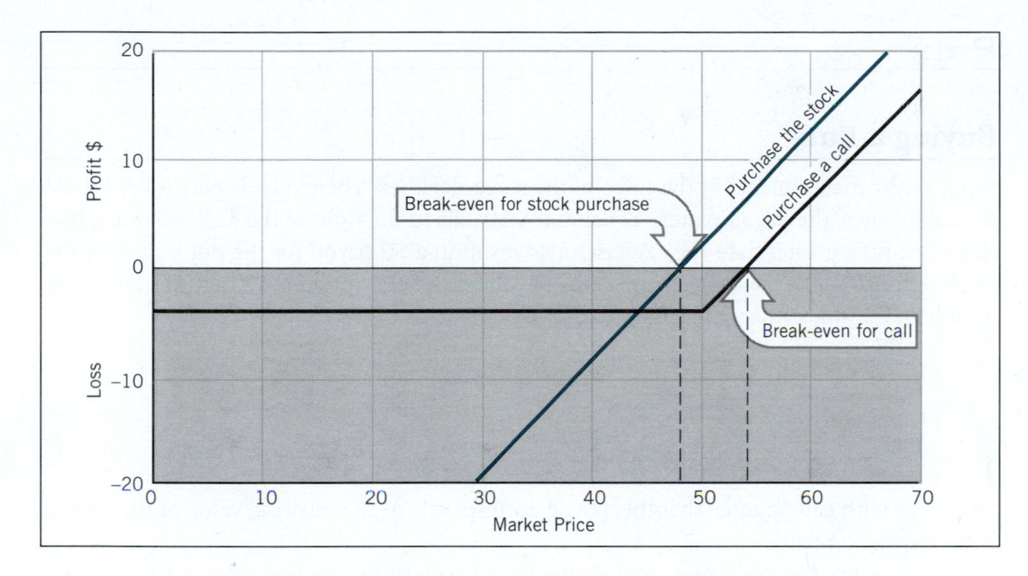

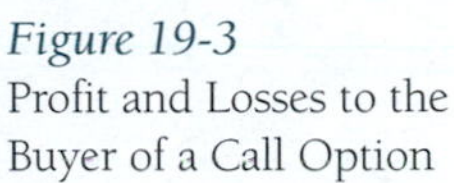
Figure 19-3
Profit and Losses to the Buyer of a Call Option

The mirror images of the payoff and net profit profiles for the call buyer (Figure 19-2(a) and Figure 19-3) and the call writer (Figure 19-2(b) and Figure 19-4) illustrate an important point. Option trading is often referred to as a zero-sum game, because whatever the option buyer gains, the option writer loses and vice versa. With commissions, options trading could be unprofitable for both buyers and sellers and must be unprofitable for both taken together since it is a zero-sum game. However, even though no actual wealth is created, both parties may achieve their investment objectives.

To illustrate this zero-sum game notion, consider the BCE December 50 call option discussed above that had a payoff of $10 to the option holder, when the ending share price was $60. Under the same circumstances, the payoff to the option writer would be −$10. Assuming this option writer had received $4.20 per option (the price paid by the option holder), the option writer's net profit would be the exact opposite of the net profit to the option holder, or:

$$\text{Net profit (option writer)} = \text{Option premium} - \text{Option payoff}$$
$$\text{Net profit (option writer)} = \$4.20 - \$10.00 = -\$5.80$$

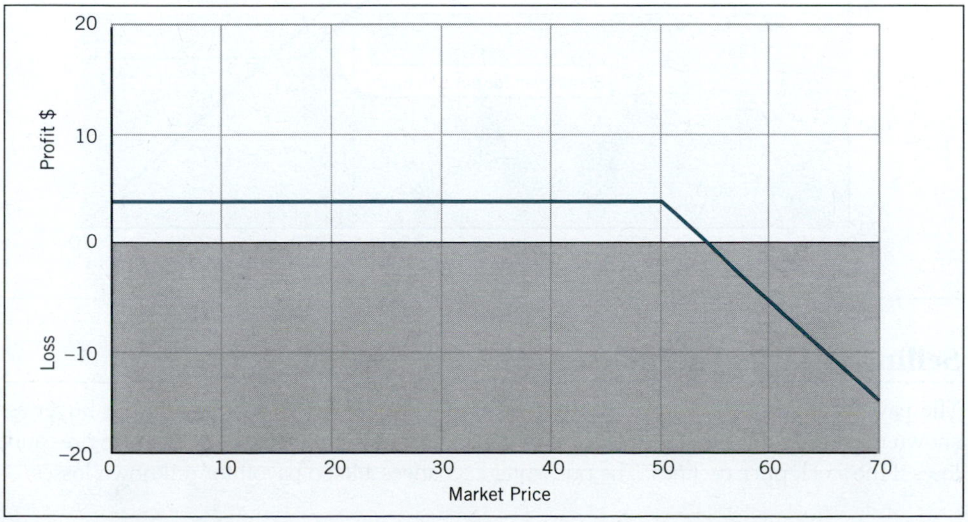

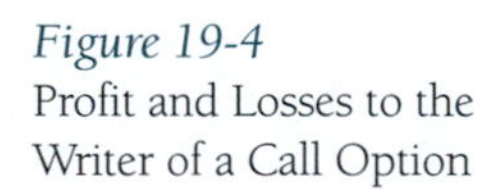
Figure 19-4
Profit and Losses to the Writer of a Call Option

Puts

Buying a Put

A put buyer makes money if the price of the stock declines. Therefore, as part (c) of Figure 19-2 illustrates, the payoff pattern is flat at the $0 axis to the right of the exercise price; that is, stock prices greater than the exercise price result in a $0 payoff for the put buyer. As the stock declines below the exercise price, the payoff for the put option increases. The larger the decline in the stock price, the larger the payoff.

Payoff to put buyer at expiration:

$= 0 \quad \text{if } S_T > E$

$= E - S_T \text{ if } S_T \leq E$

Notice, as with call options, that this payoff corresponds to the intrinsic value of the option at the expiration date.

Once again, the profit line parallels the payoff pattern for the put option at expiration. As Figure 19-5 illustrates, the investor breaks even (no net profit) at the point where the stock price is equal to the exercise price minus the premium paid for the put. Beyond that point, the net profit line parallels the payoff line representing the investment value of the put.

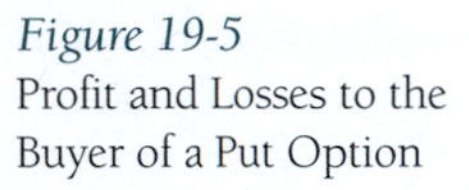
Figure 19-5
Profit and Losses to the Buyer of a Put Option

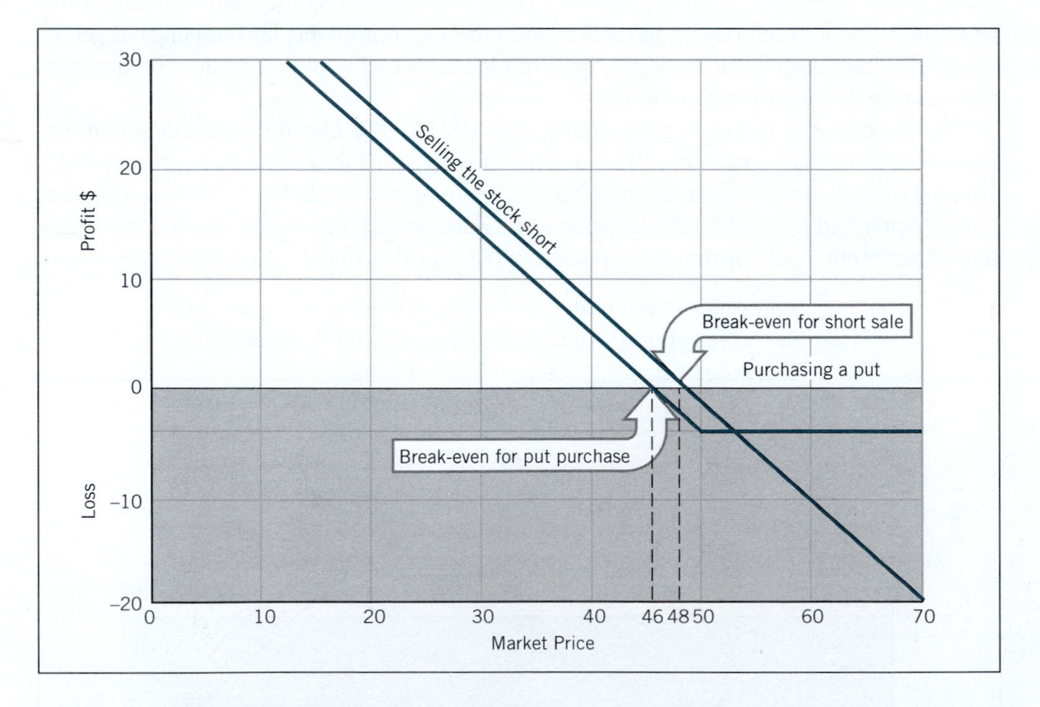

Selling (Writing) a Put

The payoff pattern for the naked put writer is the mirror image of that for the put buyer as shown in part (d) of Figure 19-2. The put writer retains the premium if the stock price rises and loses if the stock price declines. The put writer exchanges a fixed payoff for unknown losses.

Payoff to naked put writer at expiration:
$= 0 \quad \text{if } S_T \geq E$
$= -(E - S_T) \text{ if } S_T < E$

Writers (sellers) of puts are seeking the premium income exactly as are call writers. The writer obligates himself or herself to purchase a stock at the specified exercise price during the life of the put contract. If stock prices decline, the put buyer may purchase the stock and exercise the put by delivering the stock to the writer, who must pay the specified price.

Note that the put writer may be obligated to purchase a stock for, say, $50 a share when it is selling in the market for $40 a share. This represents an immediate paper loss (less the premium received for selling the put). Also note that the put writer can cancel the obligation by purchasing an identical contract in the market.[11]

EXAMPLE: DETERMINING PROFITS AND LOSSES

Figure 19-6 illustrates the profit-loss position for the seller of a put. Using the previous figures, we see that a six-month put is sold at an exercise price of $50 for a premium of $4. The seller of a naked put receives the premium and hopes that the stock price remains at or above the exercise price. As the price of the stock falls, the seller's position declines. The seller begins to lose money below the break-even point, which in this case is $50 − $4 = $46. Losses could be substantial if the price of the stock declined sharply. The price of the put will increase point for point as the stock price declines. The maximum loss for the put writer is bounded, unlike that for the call writer, since the price for the underlying share cannot fall below zero. In this example, the most the put writer could lose is $4 − $50 = −$46 (where −$50 is the payoff if the shares became worthless).

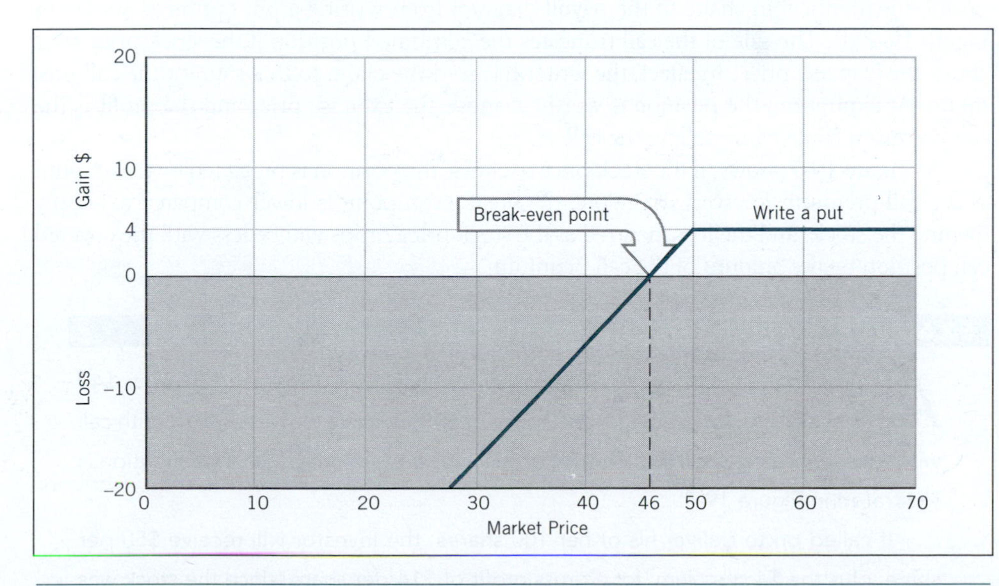

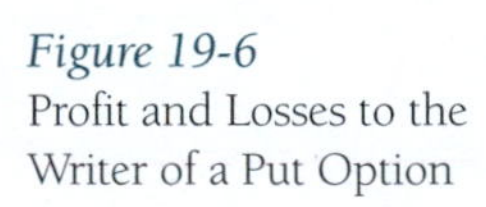
Figure 19-6
Profit and Losses to the Writer of a Put Option

[11] Of course, if the price of the stock has declined since the put was written, the price of the put will have increased and the writer will have to repurchase at a price higher than the premium received when the put was written.

SOME BASIC OPTIONS STRATEGIES

Hedge
A strategy using derivatives to offset or reduce the risk resulting from exposure to an underlying asset.

In the previous section, we examined the payoffs, and profit/losses, for basic uncovered (or naked) positions involving options. These four basic uncovered option positions are: buy call, write call, buy put, and write put. In this section we analyze covered positions involving hedges. Spreads and combinations, which are also covered positions, are discussed in Appendix 19-A.

A **hedge** is a combination of an option and its underlying stock designed such that the option protects the stock against loss or the stock protects the option against loss. In the next section, we consider some of the more popular hedges.

Covered Calls

Covered Call
A strategy involving the sale of a call option to supplement a long position in an underlying asset.

A **covered call** involves the purchase of stock and the simultaneous sale (or writing) of a call on that stock; that is, it is a long position in the stock and a short position in a call. The position is covered because the writer owns the stock and could deliver it if called to do so as a result of the exercise of the call option by the holder. In effect, the investor is willing to sell the stock at a fixed price (the exercise price), limiting the gains if the stock price rises, in exchange for cushioning the loss by the amount of the call premium, if the stock price declines.

Using our previous notation, the payoff profile at expiration is:

	$S_T \leq E$	$S_T > E$
Payoff of stock	S_T	S_T
− Payoff of call	-0	$-(S_T - E)$
Total payoff	S_T	E

Figure 19-7 illustrates the payoffs on the covered call hedge by showing all three situations: purchase of the stock, writing a call, and the combined position. Notice that the combined position is identical in shape to the payoff diagram from writing a put option as shown in Figure 19-2(d). The sale of the call truncates the combined position if the stock price rises above the exercise price. In effect, the writer has sold the claim to this gain for the call premium. At expiration, the position is worth, at most, the exercise price and the profit is the call premium received by selling the call.

As Figure 19-7 shows, if the stock price declines, the position is protected by the amount of the call premium received. Therefore, the break-even point is lower compared to simply owning the stock, and the loss incurred as the stock price drops will be less with the covered call position by the amount of the call premium.

EXAMPLE: CALL PREMIUM ON BCE INC.

Assume that an investor had previously purchased 100 shares of **BCE** for $40 per share and now with the stock price at $48, writes a (covered) six-month call with an exercise price of $50. The writer receives a premium of $4. This situation is illustrated in Figure 19-8.

If called on to deliver his or her 100 shares, the investor will receive $50 per share, plus the $4 premium, for a gross profit of $14 per share (since the stock was

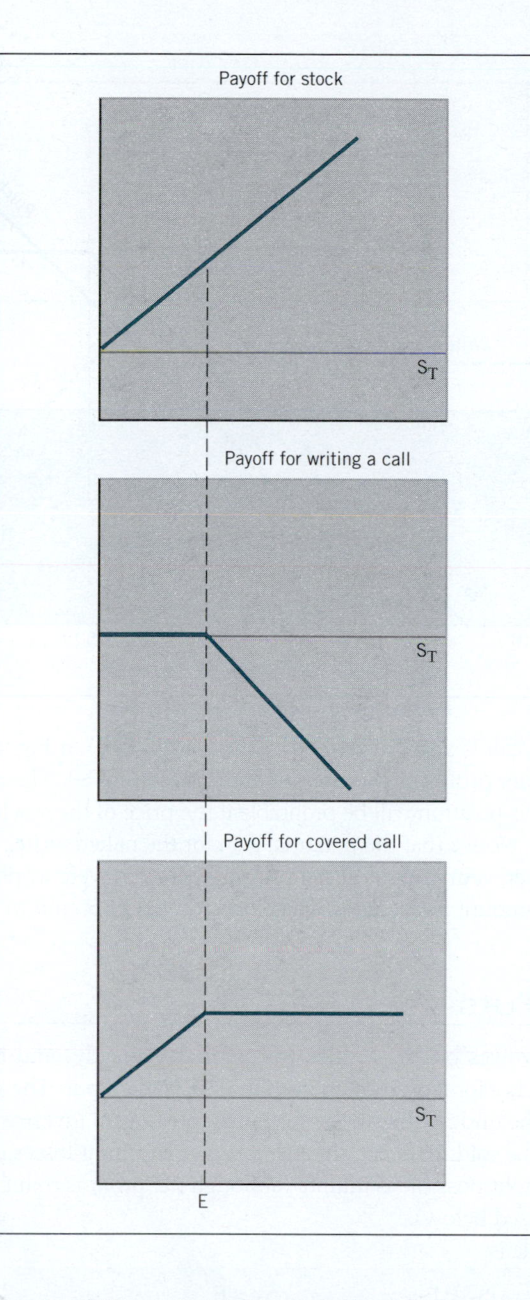

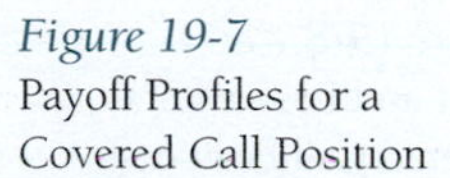
Figure 19-7
Payoff Profiles for a Covered Call Position

originally purchased at $40 per share). However, the investor gives up the additional potential gain if the price of this stock rises above $50 as illustrated by the flat line to the right of $50 for the covered call position in Figure 19-8. If the price rises to $60 after the call is sold, for example, the investor will gross $14 per share but could have grossed $20 per share if no call had been written. However, should the price fall to $30, the investor would offset the loss of $10 per share held by the amount of the option premium ($4 per option) that was originally received, resulting in a net loss of only $6 per share.

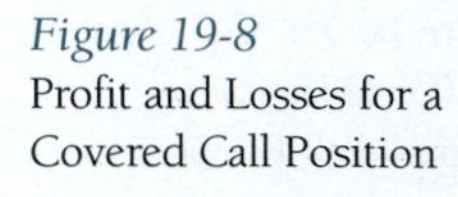
Figure 19-8
Profit and Losses for a Covered Call Position

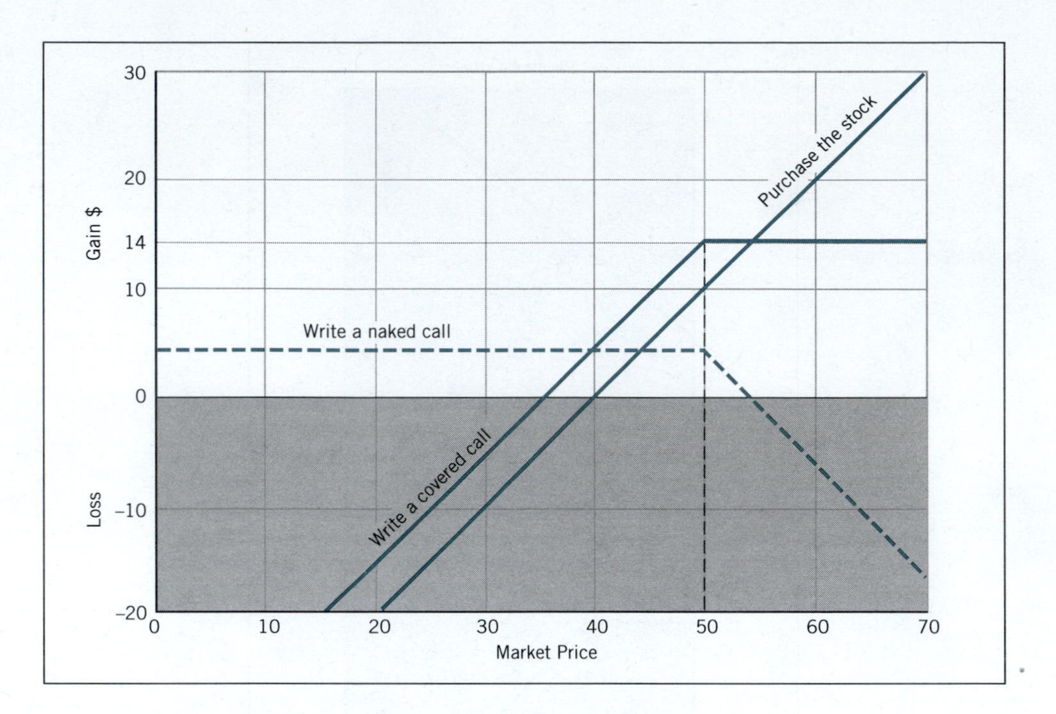

Writing a naked call is also illustrated (by the broken line) in Figure 19-8. If the call is not exercised, the writer profits by the amount of the premium, \$4. The naked writer's break-even point is \$54. This position will be profitable if the price of the stock does not rise above the break-even point. Notice that the potential gain for the naked writer is limited to \$4. The potential loss, however, is unlimited. If the price of the stock were to rise sharply, the writer could easily lose an amount in excess of what was received in premium income.

Protective Puts

Protective Put
A strategy involving the purchase of a put option as a supplement to a long position in an underlying asset.

A **protective put** involves buying a stock (or owning it already) and buying a put for the same stock; that is, it is a long position in both the stock and a put. The put acts as insurance against a decline in the underlying stock price, guaranteeing an investor a minimum price at which the stock can be sold. In effect, the insurance acts to limit losses or unfavourable outcomes. The largest profit possible is infinite (although the profit is reduced by the cost of the put option, as discussed below).

The payoff profile is:

	$S_T < E$	$S_T \geq E$
Payoff of stock	S_T	S_T
+ Payoff of put	$E - S_T$	0
Total payoff	E	S_T

For stock prices at or above the exercise price, the payoff reflects the increase in the stock price. Below the exercise price, the payoff is worth the exercise price at expiration.

Figure 19-9 shows the protective put versus an investment in the underlying stock. As always, the payoff for the stock is a straight line, and the payoff for the option strategy is an asymmetrical line consisting of two segments. The payoff for the protective put clearly illustrates what is meant by the term *truncating* the distribution of returns. Below a certain stock price (the exercise price), the payoff line is flat or horizontal. Therefore, the loss is limited to the cost of the put. Above the break-even point, the protective put strategy shares in the gains as the stock price rises. This is one of the true benefits of derivative securities and the reason for their phenomenal growth — derivatives provide a quick and inexpensive way to alter the risk of a portfolio.

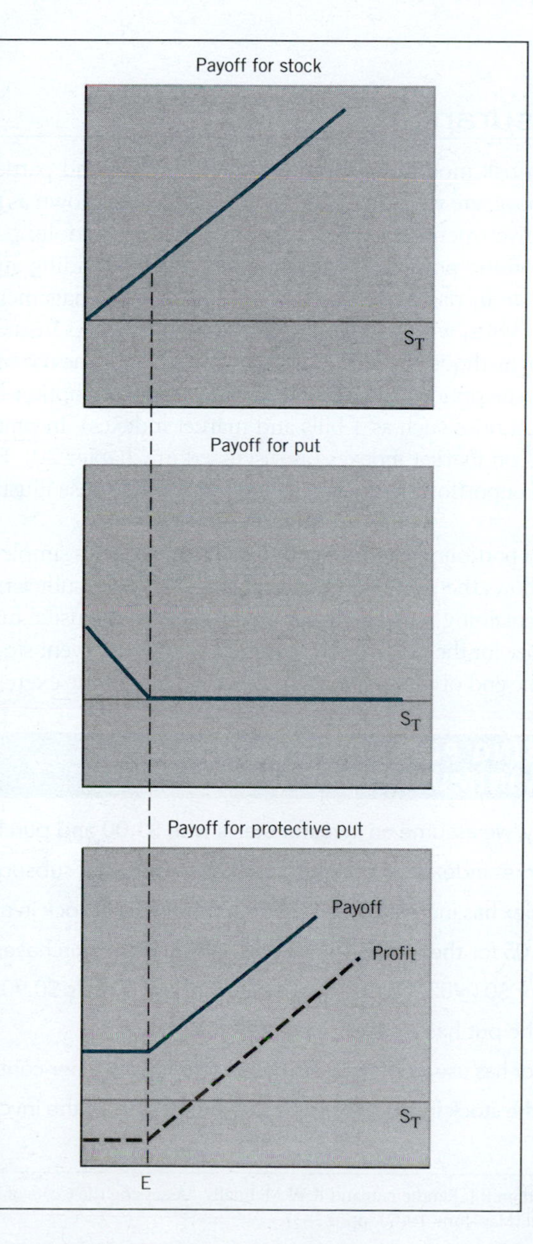

Figure 19-9
Payoff Profile and Profit/Losses for a Protective Put Position

Figure 19-9 illustrates how a protective put offers some insurance against a decline in the stock price. This insurance feature limits losses but at a cost if the insurance turns out not to be needed — the cost of the put. Above the exercise price, the profit is less than the payoff profile for the investment because of the cost of the put. Below the exercise price, losses in the stock price are partially offset by gains from the put, resulting in a constant loss equal to the cost of the put.

This position is identical to purchasing a call except for a different intercept on the vertical axis.

The protective put illustrates a well-known concept called portfolio insurance, which is explained below.

Portfolio Insurance

Portfolio Insurance
An asset management technique designed to provide a portfolio with a lower limit on value while permitting it to benefit from rising security prices.

The potential return-risk modification properties of options, and particularly the insurance aspects discussed above, are well illustrated by the technique known as **portfolio insurance**. This term refers to investment strategies designed to hedge portfolio positions by providing a minimum return on the portfolio while simultaneously providing an opportunity for the portfolio to participate in rising security prices. This asset management technique became very popular in the 1980s, with many billions of dollars of assets insured.

There are several methods of insuring a portfolio, including the use of options, futures, and the creation of synthetic options (which refer to the creation of option-like payoffs by taking positions in other securities such as T-bills and market indexes). In practice it is common to use futures contracts on market indexes (as discussed in Chapter 20). However, in principal options can be used in portfolio insurance strategies, and their use illustrates the basic nature of a hedge.

The idea behind portfolio insurance with regard to options is simple. A protective put can be purchased that allows the portfolio to be sold for an amount sufficient to provide the minimum return. The remaining portfolio funds are invested in the usual manner. The protective put provides insurance for the portfolio by limiting losses in the event stock prices decline. The portfolio's value at the end of the period must equal or exceed the exercise price of the put.

EXAMPLE: USING PORTFOLIO INSURANCE TO ENSURE MINIMUM RETURN

For simplicity, we assume an investor starts with \$1.00 and purchases one unit of a stock market index that sells for \$0.9097.[12] During a subsequent period, the value of the index has increased and the investor wants to lock in a guaranteed selling price of \$1.05 for the index. To this end, the investor purchases a European put on this index for \$0.0903. Notice the net investment equals \$0.9097 + \$0.0903 = \$1.0000, and the put has a strike price of \$1.05.

The investor has used portfolio insurance to ensure a 5 per cent minimum return. If the value of the stock index exceeds \$1.05 by the end of the investing period, the

---

[12] This example is based on R.J. Rendleman and R.W. McEnally, "Assessing the Costs of Portfolio Insurance," *Financial Analysts Journal* (May–June 1987), pp. 27–37.

investor is ahead that much and allows the put to expire worthless. If the value of the index is less than $1.05 by the end of the period, the investor can exercise the option and sell the stock index for $1.05, thereby earning the required 5 per cent minimum return on the initial investment of $1.00. Portfolio insurance has provided protection against the downside while allowing the investor to participate in stock price advances.

This example illustrates the conceptual use of puts in portfolio insurance strategies. In practice, however, puts and calls are not used to insure portfolios because those typically available to investors are American and not European. The exercise-at-any-time feature of American options makes them not only more valuable than corresponding European options but also much more costly for portfolio insurance purposes. Furthermore, it generally is not possible to find puts and calls with the exact time to expiration, exercise price, and so on that matches a particular portfolio.

It should also be noted that portfolio insurance is not without cost. The costs include:

- The *cost of the option itself* — in our example, the put cost $0.0903. Obviously, if stocks advance and the put expires worthless, the cost of the put has been lost relative to an uninsured strategy. This can be thought of as the insurance premium.
- An *opportunity cost*. An investor who places 100 per cent of investment funds in the stock index would participate fully in any market rise. In our example, the insured investor would participate in only 90.97 per cent of any market rise.

OPTION VALUATION

A General Framework

In this section, we examine the determinants of the value of a put or call. An option's premium almost never declines below its intrinsic value. The reason is that market arbitrageurs, who constantly monitor option prices for discrepancies, would purchase the options and exercise them, thus earning riskless returns. **Arbitrageurs** are speculators who seek to earn a return without assuming risk by constructing riskless hedges. Short-lived deviations are possible, but they will quickly be exploited.

Arbitrageurs
Investors who seek discrepancies in security prices in an attempt to earn riskless returns.

Suppose a call option with an exercise price of $20 is selling for $2, when the price of the underlying share is $23. Notice that the intrinsic value of this option is $3, since the call enables you to purchase a share that is worth $23, for only $20. An arbitrageur (or anyone else recognizing that the option price is below its intrinsic value) could purchase an option contract for $200 ($2 × 100). The investor could then immediately exercise the option, purchasing 100 shares at a cost of $2,000 ($20 × 100). These shares could be sold in the market at a price of $23 per share, for a total of $2,300. The net result (ignoring transactions costs) would be a profit of $100: $2,300 − $2,000 (cost of exercising the options) − $200 (cost of the options). This profit is earned without assuming any risks and is referred to as arbitrage profit, hence the name arbitrageurs. Clearly, these opportunities should not exist in efficient markets, since rational investors will recognize them, exploit them, and hence eliminate them.

Time Values

Time Value
The difference between the intrinsic value of an option and its market price.

Option prices almost always exceed intrinsic values, with the difference reflecting the option's potential appreciation, referred to as the **time value**. This is somewhat of a misnomer because the actual source of value is volatility in price. However, price volatility decreases with a shortening of the time to expiration hence the term time value.

Because buyers are willing to pay a price for potential future stock-price movements, time has a positive value — the longer the time to expiration for the option, the more chance it has to appreciate in value. However, when the stock price is held constant, options are seen as a wasting asset whose value approaches intrinsic value as expiration approaches. In other words, as expiration approaches, the time value of the option declines to zero.

The time value can be calculated as the difference between the option price and the intrinsic value:

(19-3) $$\text{Time value} = \text{Option price} - \text{Intrinsic value}$$

EXAMPLE: CALCULATING TIME VALUE ON AIR CANADA OPTIONS

For the **Air Canada** options referred to in the examples of intrinsic value on page 606:

Time value of January 5 call = \$1.40 − \$0.90 = \$0.50

Time value of April 7 put = \$1.35 − \$1.10 = \$0.25

We can now understand the premium for an option as the sum of its intrinsic value and its time value, or

(19-4) $$\text{Premium or option price} = \text{Intrinsic value} + \text{Time value}$$

EXAMPLE: CALCULATING PREMIUM FOR AIR CANADA OPTIONS

For the **Air Canada** options:

Premium for January 5 call = \$0.90 + \$0.50 = \$1.40

Premium for April 7 put = \$1.10 + \$0.25 = \$1.35

Notice an important point about options based on the preceding discussion. An investor who owns a call option and wishes to acquire the underlying common stock will always find it preferable to sell the option and purchase the stock in the open market rather than exercise the option (at least if the stock pays no dividends). Why? Because otherwise, he or she will lose the speculative premium on the option.

Consider the Air Canada January 5 call option, with a market price of the common share of \$5.90. An investor who owned the call and wanted to own the common share would be better off to sell the option at \$1.40 and purchase the common stock for \$5.90, for a net investment of \$4.50 per share. Exercising the call option, the investor would have to pay \$5.00 per share for shares of stock worth \$5.90 in the market, for a net investment of \$5.00 per share. Thus selling the options reduces the required investment to own a share of Air Canada by \$0.50 — the amount of the time value. (Brokerage commissions are ignored in this example.)

On the other hand, under some circumstances, it may be optimal to exercise an American put early (on a non-dividend paying stock). A put sufficiently deep in the money should be exercised early because the payment received at exercise can be invested to earn a return. Under certain circumstances it may also be desirable to exercise an American call option on a dividend-paying stock before the expiration date. (This is because dividends reduce the stock price on the ex dividend date, which in turn reduces the value of the call option).

Boundaries on Option Prices

In the previous section we learned what the premium, or price, of a put or call consists of, but we have not considered why options trade at the prices they do and the range of values they can assume. In this section we learn about the boundaries for option prices, and in the next section we discuss the exact determinants of options prices.

The value of an option must be related to the value of the underlying security. The basic relationship is most easy to understand by considering an option immediately prior to expiration, when there is no time premium. If the option is not exercised, it will expire immediately, leaving the option with no value. Obviously, investors will exercise it only if it is worth exercising (if it is in the money).

Figure 19-10(a) shows the values of call options at expiration, assuming a strike price of \$50. At expiration, a call must have a value equal to its intrinsic value. Therefore, the line representing the value of a call option must be horizontal at \$0 up to the exercise price and then rise as the stock price exceeds the exercise price. Above \$50 the call price must equal the difference between the stock price and the exercise price.

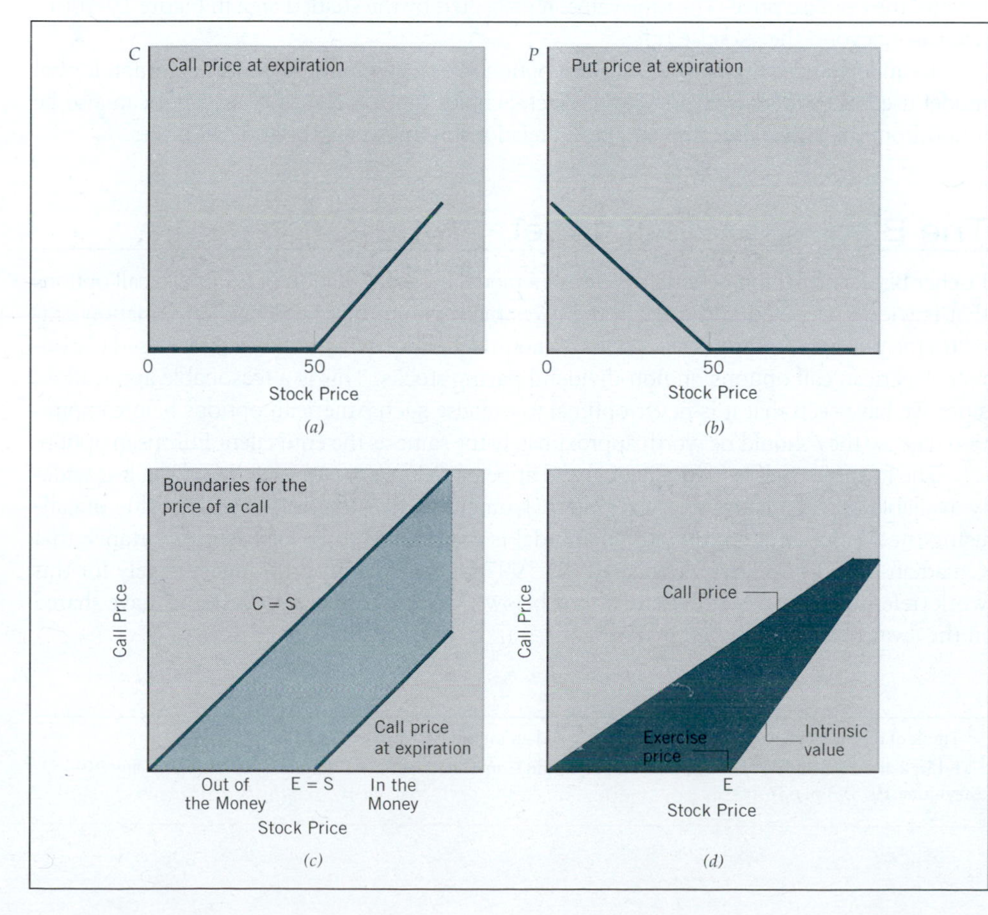

Figure 19-10
Determining the Boundaries on Option Prices

For puts the situation is reversed. At expiration, a put must have a value equal to its intrinsic value. Therefore, the line in Figure 19-10(b) representing the value of a put option must be horizontal at $0 beyond the exercise price. Below $50 the put price must equal the difference between the exercise price and the stock price. Note that a put option has a strict upper limit on intrinsic value, whereas the call has no upper limit. A put's strike price is its maximum intrinsic value.

What is the maximum price an option can assume? To see this, think of a call. Since the call's value is derived from its ability to be converted into the underlying stock, it can never sell for more than the stock itself. It would not make sense to pay more for a call on one share of stock than the price of the stock itself. Therefore, the maximum price for a call is the price of the underlying stock.

Based on the preceding, we can establish the absolute upper and lower boundaries for the price of a call option, as shown in Figure 19-10(c). The upper boundary is a 45 degree line from the origin representing a call price equal to the stock price.[13] The lower boundary is the price of the option at expiration, which must be either zero or its in-the-money value. This is represented by the 45 degree line starting at the exercise price. Once again, the lower boundary can be interpreted as the value of the call at the moment the call is exercised, or its intrinsic value.

Finally, Figure 19-10(d) illustrates more precisely and realistically the variation in price for a call option by illustrating how the price of a call varies with the stock price and the exercise price. The call price is always above intrinsic value and rises as the stock price increases beyond the exercise price. The time value, represented by the shaded area in Figure 19-10(d), decreases beyond the exercise price.

To understand fully the price of a call option, we will examine the most common formal model used to estimate call prices, the Black-Scholes model. The price of a put can also be found from this model because of a parity relationship between put and call prices.

The Black-Scholes Model

Fischer Black and Myron Scholes developed a model for the valuation of European call options that is widely accepted and used in the investment community.[14] While the equation estimates the price of European call options on non-dividend paying stocks, it is also used to evaluate American call options on non-dividend paying stocks. This is a reasonable application, since we have seen that it is never optimal to exercise such American options before expiration date, so they should be worth approximately the same as the equivalent European option.

Black-Scholes Model
A widely used model for the valuation of call options.

The formula itself is mathematical and appears to be very complex; however, it is widely available on calculators and computers. Numerous investors estimate the value of calls using the **Black-Scholes model**. The model is considered to be of such importance that Canadian-born Myron Scholes shared the 1997 Nobel Prize in economics, largely for this work (refer to the Real-World Returns box below). Black would almost certainly have shared in the award had he not died in 1995.

[13] Think of this as a call with a zero exercise price and an infinite maturity.

[14] F. Black and M. Scholes, "The Pricing of Options and Corporate Liabilities," *Journal of Political Economy* 81 (May–June 1973), pp. 637–654.

REAL-WORLD RETURNS

Black-Scholes Model Founders

Carrying on a University of Chicago tradition, Myron S. Scholes, MBA'64, PhD'70, took home the 1997 Nobel Prize in economic sciences in October-making him the University's 69th Nobelist, and the 19th to win the economics prize since it was first awarded in 1969. Scholes, who taught in the Graduate School of Business (GSB) for ten years before joining the Stanford faculty in 1983, and who studied under 1990 Nobel laureate Merton Miller, was honored along with Harvard professor Robert C. Merton, LL.D.(Hon)'91, for developing a method to determine the value of derivatives. Collaborator Fischer Black, also a former U of C faculty member, died in 1995 but would likely have shared the prize had he lived.

Black and Scholes made their names with the Black-Scholes formula, a method of pricing options that was first published in 1973 in the U of C's *Journal of Political Economy*. Just one month before the formula's publication, the Chicago Board Options Exchange had opened, providing the first formal market for options trading.

Options give investors the opportunity, but not the obligation, to buy or sell assets at a prespecified price. Until the Black-Scholes formula, investors in share options, futures, and other derivative securities — called derivatives because their worth is affected by, or derived from, fluctuations in the value of other assets — could not be sure of the value of their securities. Many researchers tried to determine the values with formulas that required assigning risk premiums. Black and Scholes realized that a stock's price already reflected the option's risk and devised their famous formula accordingly.

In the past quarter century, the options market has exploded, with the Black-Scholes formula awarded much of the credit. In the first nine months of 1997, *The Wall Street Journal* reported the value of US exchange-traded options reached $155 billion.

"Nowadays, thousands of traders and investors use the formula everyday to value stock options in markets throughout the world," wrote the Nobel committee. "Such rapid and widespread application of a theoretical result was new to economics."

Merton, who influenced the work of the other two and published his own article on option valuation in 1973, generalized the formula, taking it beyond options on shares and applying it to other derivatives. The Black-Merton-Scholes methodology has been used, for example, to design optimal financial contracts and to determine values of insurance contracts and guarantees.

Though best known for his work in options, Scholes has also studied the effect of dividends on share prices and researched the effects of global tax policies on decision making.

While an MBA student at the U of C, Scholes began working for GSB professor Merton Miller, who needed "a computer whiz" to help with some research. Scholes worked on several more projects with Miller, who later served as Scholes' thesis adviser, also chairing his PhD examining committee.

"I feel about Myron's award the same as I would if it had been won by one of my children," says Miller. "This is well-deserved."

After earning his PhD, Scholes joined MIT's Sloan School of Management as an assistant professor. He returned to Chicago in 1973, and in 1983 accepted an offer from Stanford, where he is the Frank E. Buck professor of finance emeritus and was a senior research fellow at the Hoover Institution.

These days, Scholes keeps busy as a principal and partner in Long-Term Capital Management, a Greenwich, Connecticut, investment-management firm that he helped found with Robert Merton. No doubt he'll be in great demand as a speaker, too: In fact, Scholes is already planning a May visit to Chicago, where he'll give the keynote address at the GSB's 1998 Management Conference.

Source: "Value-Driven: GSB Alumnus and Former Faculty Member Scholes Wins Nobel," University of Chicago Magazine, *December 1997, pp. 38a, 38b. Reprinted with permission.*

The Black-Scholes model uses five variables to value the call option of a non-dividend-paying stock.[15] These five variables, all but the last of which are directly observable in the market, are as follows:

1. The price of the underlying stock
2. The exercise price of the option
3. The time remaining to the expiration of the option
4. The interest rate
5. The volatility of the continuously compounded rate of return on the underlying stock.

The first two variables are of obvious importance in valuing an option, because, as noted before, they determine the option's intrinsic value whether it is in the money or not. If it is out of the money, it has only a time value based on the speculative interest in the stock.

Time to expiration (measured as a fraction of a year) is also an important factor in the value of an option because value generally increases with maturity. This is logical because the longer to the expiration date, the more time is available to profit from price changes. The relationship between time and value is not proportional, however. The time value of an option is greatest when the market price and the exercise price are equal.

The interest rate affects option values because of the opportunity cost involved. Buying an option is a substitute to some degree for buying on margin, on which interest must be paid. The higher interest rates are, therefore, the more interest cost is saved by the use of options. This adds to the value of the option and results in a direct relationship between the value of a call option and interest rates in the market.

The last factor, and the only one not directly observable in the marketplace, is the stock's volatility. The greater the volatility, the higher the price of a call option because of the increased potential for the stock to move up. Therefore, a positive relation exists between the volatility of the stock and the value of the call option.[16]

The Black-Scholes option pricing formula can be expressed as[17]

(19-5)
$$C = S[N(d_1)] - E\,[N(d_2)] \times \frac{1}{e^{rt}}$$

where

C = the price of the call option
S = current market price of the underlying common stock
$N(d_1)$ = the cumulative density function of d_1 (assuming this variable is normally distributed)
E = the exercise price of the option
e = the base of natural logarithms (approximately 2.71828)
r = the continuously compounded riskless rate of interest quoted on an annual basis
t = the time remaining before the expiration date of the option, expressed as a fraction of a year
$N(d_2)$ = the cumulative density function of d_2 (assuming this variable is normally distributed)[18]

---

[15] Options traded on organized exchanges are not protected against cash dividends, and this can have significant effects on option values. When a cash dividend is paid, the stock price should decline to reflect this payment. Any event that reduces the stock price reduces the value of a call and increases the value of a put.

[16] Volatility as used in the options model is not the same concept as a stock's beta as used in Chapter 9. Volatility is used here as a measure of the variability in the stock return (as measured by standard deviation) as opposed to sensitivity to market movements.

[17] This version of the model applies to non-dividend-paying stocks. Adjustments can be made for stocks that pay dividends.

[18] This assumption does not mean that stock returns themselves are normally distributed, but that the variables d_1 and d_2 are normally distributed. In fact, one of the technical assumptions of the model is that stock prices are log-normally distributed.

To find d_1 and d_2, it is necessary to solve these equations:

$$d_1 = \frac{\ln (S/E) + (r + 0.5\sigma^2)t}{(\sigma[(t)^{1/2}])} \tag{19-6}$$

$$d_2 = d_1 - (\sigma[(t)^{1/2}]) \tag{19-7}$$

where
ln (S/E) = the natural logarithm of (S/E)
σ = the standard deviation of the annual rate of return on the underlying common stock

The five variables previously listed are needed as inputs. Variables 1 to 4 are immediately available. Variable 5 is not, however, because what is needed is the variability expected to occur in the stock's rate of return. Although historical data on stock returns are generally used to estimate this standard deviation, variability does change over time. A formula user should try to incorporate expected changes in the variability when using historical data. To do so, the user should examine any likely changes in either the market's or the individual stock's variability.

Variables 1 to 3 should be identical for a given stock for everyone using the Black-Scholes model. Variable 4 should be identical or very close among formula users, depending on the exact proxy used for the riskless rate of interest. Variable 5 will vary among users, providing different option values. Empirical studies have shown that estimates of the variance obtained from other than historical data are more valuable than the estimates based on historical data. Because the price of an option can be observed at any time, it is possible to solve the Black-Scholes formula for the implied standard deviation of the stock's return. This is an important application of the Black-Scholes equation that is frequently used by practitioners. Henry Latané and Richard Rendleman found that better forecasts of the actual standard deviation could be obtained by preparing forecasts from the model itself.[19]

EXAMPLE: USING BLACK-SCHOLES TO CALCULATE OPTION PRICE

The following is an example of the use of the Black-Scholes option pricing formula:

Assume
S = \$40
E = \$45
$r = 0.10$
$t = 0.5$ (6 months)
$\sigma = 0.45$

Step 1: Solve for d_1.

$$d_1 = \frac{\ln (40/45) + [0.10 + 0.5(0.45)^2]\, 0.5}{0.45\, [(0.5)^{1/2}]}$$

$$= \frac{-0.1178 + 0.1006}{0.3182}$$

$$= -0.054$$

[19] H. Latané and R. Rendleman, Jr., "Standard Deviations of Stock Price Ratios Implied in Option Prices," *Journal of Finance* 31 (May 1976), pp. 369–382.

Step 2: Use a cumulative probability distribution table (such as the one provided in Table A-5 at the end of the book) to find the value of $N(d_1)$.

$$N(d_1) \approx 0.4801$$

where $d_1 = -0.054$

Step 3: Find d_2.

$$d_2 = -0.054 - [0.45((0.5)^{1/2})]$$
$$= -0.372$$

Step 4: Find $N(d_2)$.

$$N(d_2) \approx 0.3557$$

Step 5: Solve for C.

$$C = S[0.4801] - E[0.3557] \times \frac{1}{e^{(.10)(0.5)}}$$
$$= (40)(0.4801) - (45)(0.3557)(0.9512)$$
$$= 19.20 - 15.23$$
$$= \$3.97$$

The theoretical (fair) value of the option, according to the Black-Scholes formula, is $3.97. If the current market price of the option is greater than the theoretical value, it is overpriced; if less, it is underpriced — according to the Black-Scholes model.

Put Option Valuation

Put-Call Parity The formal relationship between a European call and put on the same item which must hold if no arbitrage is to occur.

To establish put prices, we can take advantage of the principle of put-call parity.

The **put-call parity** principle expresses the relationship between the prices of European puts and calls on the same stock with the same exercise price that must hold if arbitrage is to be ruled out. In other words, unless the price of the put and the call bear a certain relationship to each other, there will be opportunities for earning riskless profits (arbitrage). The put-call parity can be expressed as

$$\text{Price of put} = E/(e^{rt}) - S + C \tag{19-8}$$

where all terms are as defined before.[20]

EXAMPLE: CALCULATING PUT-CALL PARITY

Use the information for the call given in the previous example. Since the Black-Scholes model uses continuous interest, the discount factor is expressed in continuous form.[21] It is equal to e^{rt} or $e^{10(.5)}$. Using a calculator, this value is 1.051. Therefore,

$$\text{Price of put} = 45/1.051 - 40 + 3.97 = \$6.79$$

[20] This can be easily proven using the following no-arbitrage argument, which ignores transactions costs. Refer to Appendix 19-C for a more detailed discussion of the no-arbitrage argument.

[21] The value e^k is the equivalent of $(1 + r)$ in continuous compounding. If r is 5 percent, the value of e^k is $e^{0.05}$, or 1.051.

Summarizing the Factors Affecting Options Prices

If we allow for stocks that pay dividends, we can summarize the factors affecting options prices into a table with six elements, as shown in Table 19-2. The plus sign indicates a direct relation, and a negative sign a negative relation. The assumption behind Table 19-2 is that all other variables remain fixed as we consider any of the six variables.

Table 19-2

Effects of Various Variables on Options Prices

Variable	Calls	Puts
Stock price	+	−
Exercise price	−	+
Time to expiration	+	+
Stock volatility	+	+
Interest rates	+	−
Cash dividends	−	+

The following discussion provides a basis for the intuition regarding how these six factors affect option prices (holding all other factors unchanged). Recall that the Option price = Intrinsic value + Time value (or speculative premium). Based on this framework, we note the following:

1. As share prices increase, the intrinsic value (IV) of calls increase and the IV of puts decrease.
2. As exercise prices increase, the IV of calls decrease and the IV of puts increase.
3. The greater the time to expiration, the greater the chance the option will be in the money, hence the greater the time value (or speculative premium).
4. As share price volatility increases, there is a greater chance that shares will end up in the money, so the time value, or speculative premium, increases.
5. As the riskless rate increases, the advantage of delayed ownership increases for call options. Conversely, the delay of exercising put options, which involves selling assets for cash today, becomes more costly.
6. Share prices fall by roughly the amount of a dividend that is paid. Hence, dividend increases tend to reduce share prices, which reduces the IV of calls and increases the IV of puts.

Hedge Ratios

A key concept with options is their use as a hedging device. Although risky assets themselves, options can be used to control risk. In particular, options can be used to control the riskiness inherent in common stocks.

To hedge a long stock position with options, an investor would write one call option while simultaneously buying a certain number of common shares. The required number of shares is given by the **hedge ratio**, which is $N(d_1)$ from the Black-Scholes model for call options.[22] The

Hedge Ratio The ratio of options written to shares of stock held long in a riskless portfolio.

[22] Technically, the hedge ratio is the slope of the functional relationship between the value of the option (vertical axis) and the value of the stock (horizontal axis), evaluated at the current stock price. It is determined by taking the partial first derivative of the option price with respect to the underlying stock price.

hedge ratio for an option, commonly referred to as the option's delta, indicates the change in the price of the option for a \$1 change in the price of the underlying common share. Since the hedge ratio with a call option is $N(d_1)$, for a put option it is $N(d_1) - 1$.

EXAMPLE: DETERMINING THE HEDGE RATIO FOR OPTIONS

In the example on page 624, $N(d_1)$ was 0.48; therefore, for every call option written, 0.48 share of the common stock would be required to hedge the position. For a standard 100-share option contract, 48 shares of stock would be required. A \$1 increase in the price of the stock should produce a \$0.48 change in the price of the option. The loss on the call options written is 100 × \$0.48, or \$48, which is offset by the gain on the 48 shares of stock of \$48. A perfectly hedged position leaves total wealth unchanged.

Since the maximum value for $N(d_1)$ is 1.0, hedge ratios are usually less than 1.0, except for the case of deep in the money options where the ratio tends to one. This indicates that option values change with stock prices on less than a one-for-one basis. That is, dollar movements in options prices are smaller than dollar movements in the underlying stock. However, percentage price changes on the option generally will be greater than percentage price changes on the stock; this is referred to as the leverage effect.

Using the Black-Scholes Model

What does it mean if we calculate an intrinsic value for an option that is significantly different from the market price? Although this may represent an investment opportunity, we must remember that the original Black-Scholes model is based on some simplifying assumptions, such as the non-payment of dividends, constant volatility, and continuous lognormally distributed stock prices. The standard deviation cannot be observed and must be estimated. Therefore, any observed discrepancies could reflect errors in the estimation of the stock's volatility.

Development of the Black-Scholes model was a significant event and has had a major impact on all options investors, both directly and indirectly. This model has been the basis of extensive empirical investigations into how options are priced. How well does this model work?

The numerous studies that have been conducted offer general support for the Black-Scholes model and the proposition that options are efficiently priced by the market. Some deficiencies have been noted.[23] The deviations and biases that appear to remain in option pricing models may derive from several sources. For example, the true stock-price volatility is unobservable. Despite any statistically significant biases that may exist in the prices generated by the option pricing models, however, the validity of these models remains intact.

AN INVESTOR'S PERSPECTIVE ON PUTS AND CALLS

What Puts and Calls Mean to Investors

Earlier we examined some simple strategies using puts and calls and briefly considered some more sophisticated strategies. It is important for investors to have an overall perspective on puts and calls and consider what they really add to the investment process.

[23] Dan Galai, "A Survey of Empirical Tests of Option-Pricing Models," in Menachem Brenner, Editor, *Option Pricing: Theory and Applications* (Lexington, MA: Lexington Books, 1983), pp. 45–80.

Option contracts are important to investors in terms of the two dimensions of every investment decision that we have emphasized throughout this book — the return and risk from an asset or portfolio. Options can be used for various types of hedging, which involves the management of risk. Options also offer speculators a way to leverage their investment with a strict limit on downside risk.

The return-risk modification properties of puts and calls vary significantly from other derivative instruments such as futures contracts, which we consider in Chapter 20. The important point about options and portfolio return and risk is that the impact of options is not symmetrical. As discussed earlier, the distribution of payoffs is truncated, because in the case of buying a call the most the investor can lose is the premium, regardless of what happens to the stock price. The same is true when purchasing a put — relative to the profit-loss line when selling short, the distribution of possible profits and losses from purchasing a put is truncated. If the stock price continues to rise, adversely affecting the investor, the most that can be lost from the put purchase is the premium.

The Evolutionary Use of Options

Puts and calls on organized options exchanges have been available to investors since 1973, although financial derivatives were being used long before then. Puts and calls have been popular with individual investors since the beginning of CBOE trading, although the manner in which they are viewed has changed somewhat. At first, options were viewed more or less as speculative instruments and were often purchased for their leverage possibilities. Covered option writing was used to enhance portfolio yields. During the 1980s many investors were selling puts in order to capitalize on the rising trend in stock prices. This strategy worked well until the famous market crash in October 1987. As a result of the losses, many investors once again viewed options as speculative instruments and options volume did not return to the level reached in 1987 for several years.

The current emphasis by the brokerage industry is on educating investors as to how options can be used efficiently as part of their portfolio. Investors' desire to hedge their portfolios against a market decline as well as the introduction of new products such as options on new indexes, country funds, and LEAPs has drawn the public back into the market.

Today, options are increasingly valued for their use in strategic portfolio management. Options allow investors to create strategies that expand the set of outcomes beyond what could be achieved in the absence of options. In other words, investors and investment managers sometimes need the non-symmetric distributions of returns that options can provide. Options strategies increase the set of contingencies that can be provided for.[24]

OTHER TYPES OF OPTIONS

Newer innovations in the options market include **stock-index options**, **interest rate options** and **currency options**. We briefly discuss interest rate and currency options, before confining our discussion to stock-index options, in keeping with the general theme of the chapter, which is to focus on equity options.

Stock-Index Options
Option contracts on a stock market index such as the TSE 35 Index.

Interest Rate Options
Option contracts on fixed-income securities such as Government of Canada bonds.

Currency Options
Option contracts whose value is based on the value of an underlying currency, such as the Canadian dollar.

[24] This discussion is based on Richard Bookstaber, "The Use of Options in Performance Structuring," *Journal of Portfolio Management* 11 (Summer 1985), pp. 35–50.

Primary US interest rate options traded on the CBOE include 5-year, 10-year and 30-year Treasury yield options. Interest rate options trade in Canada in the form of options on Government of Canada bonds, which have traded on the ME since 1982. The volume of bond contracts outstanding represents a small proportion of the total options contracts that are traded in Canada. For example, Table 19-1 shows that these bond options accounted for a mere 0.48 per cent of CDCC option trading in Canada in 1997. Index options, on the other hand, accounted for over 10 per cent of the 1997 CDCC option trading, while standard equity options on common shares accounted for over 83 per cent of CDCC trading.

Currency options do not trade on organized exchanges in Canada, however they do trade on the Philadelphia Stock Exchange. Options trade on this exchange on several currencies including the Canadian dollar, US dollar, Australian dollar, Japanese yen, German mark, Swiss franc, British pound, French franc, and the European Currency Unit (ECU), which is a unit basket derived of European currencies.

The Basics of Stock-Index Options

Stock-index options presently trade in Canada on the TSE and are available on the TSE 35 Index, and on TIPs 35 and TIPs 100 (or HIPs), which derive their value from the appropriate stock indexes. As mentioned above, the trading of index options will likely be changed to S&P/TSE 60 Index products and may move to the ME. There are also a variety of US stock-index options on market indexes, including (but not limited to) the S&P 100 Index (OEX), the S&P 500 Index, the NYSE Index, the Russell 2000 Index, the Major Market Index, the Value Line Index, the S&P Midcap Index, the Japan Index, and the OTC Index. Index options are also available on some US industry subindexes, including Pharmaceuticals, Computer Technology, and Semiconductors. In addition, long-term index options (LEAPS) are available for the S&P 100 and 500 indexes and for the Major Market Index.

Stock-index options enable investors to trade on general stock market movements or industries in the same way that they can trade on individual stocks. Thus, an investor who is bullish on the market can buy a call on a market index, and an investor who is bearish on the overall market can buy a put. The investor need only make a decision about the market as a whole, not on an industry or an individual stock.

Most index options are European style (including the TSE 35 Index options), with a notable exception being the S&P 100 Index option that trades on the CBOE. Overall, stock-index options are similar to the options listed on the options exchanges. As usual, the exercise price and the expiration date are uniformly established. Investors buy and sell them through their broker in the normal manner. Index option information is read in the same manner as that for stock options. Unlike stock options that require the actual delivery of the stock upon exercise, buyers of index options receive cash from the seller upon exercise of the contract. The amount of cash settlement is equal to the difference between the closing price of the index and the strike price of the option multiplied by a specified dollar amount.

EXAMPLE: TSE 35 INDEX OPTION

Assume an investor holds a TSE 35 Index call option with a strike price of 300 and decides to exercise the option on a day that the TSE 35 Index closes at 343.07. The investor will receive a cash payment from the assigned writer equal to

$100 multiplied by the difference between the option's strike price and the closing value of the index, or

TSE 35 Index close	= 343.07
TSE 35 Index option strike price	= 300.00
	43.07 × $100 = $4,307

Note the use of the $100 multiplier for the TSE 35 Index option. The multiplier performs a function similar to the unit of trading (100 shares) for a stock option contract in that it determines the total dollar value of the cash settlement. Since options on different indexes may have different multipliers, it is important to know the multiplier for the stock index being used.

Strategies with Stock-Index Options

The strategies available for use with index options are similar to those for individual stock options. Investors expecting a market rise buy calls, and investors expecting a market decline buy puts. The maximum losses from these two strategies — the option premiums — are known at the outset of the transaction. The potential gains can be large because of the leverage involved with options.

EXAMPLE: LEVERAGE AND TSE 35 INDEX OPTIONS

In October, an investor expects the stock market to rise strongly over the next two to three months. This investor decides to purchase a TSE 35 Index November 350 call, that was selling for $4.35, on a day when the TSE 35 Index closed at 343.07. The total cost to the investor would be $435 (i.e. $4.35 × 100).

Assume that the market rises, as the investor expected, to a level of 370.52 (an 8 per cent increase) on the expiration date. The investor could exercise the option and receive a cash settlement equal to the difference between the index close (370.52) and the exercise price of 350, multiplied by $100, or

TSE 35 Index close	= 370.52
Call exercise price	= −350.00
	20.52 × $100 = $2,052

The investor's profit for this transaction (excluding commission fees) is:

$$\text{Profit} = \text{Payoff} - \text{Cost of option}$$
$$= \$2{,}052 - \$435 = \$1{,}617$$

The leverage offered by index options is illustrated in this example by the fact that an 8 per cent rise in the index leads to a 371.7 per cent profit on the option position (i.e., $1,617/$435 = 371.7 per cent). In this example, the investor would have benefited from the use of leverage. However, leverage can, and often does, work against an investor. If the market declined or remained flat, the entire option premium of $435 could be lost, for a 100 per cent loss on the investment. As with any option, however, the investor has a limited loss of a known amount — the premium paid.

Investors can use stock-index options to hedge their positions. For example, an investor who owns a diversified portfolio of stocks may be unwilling to liquidate his or her portfolio but is concerned about a near-term market decline. Buying a put on a market index will provide some protection to the investor in the event of a market decline. In effect, the investor is purchasing a form of market insurance. The losses on the portfolio holdings will be partially offset by the gains on the put. If the market rises, the investor loses the premium paid but gains with the portfolio holdings. A problem arises, however, in that the portfolio holdings and the market index are unlikely to be a perfect match. The effectiveness of this hedge will depend on the similarity between the two.

EXAMPLE: HEDGING WITH TSE 35 INDEX OPTIONS

Assume an investor has a portfolio of TSE common stocks currently worth $103,500. It is October, and this investor is concerned about a market decline over the next couple of months. The TSE 35 Index is currently at 345, and a TSE 35 Index December 345 put is available for $10. In an attempt to protect the portfolio's profits against a market decline, the investor purchases three of these puts (total cost = 3 × 100 × $10 = $3,000), which represents an aggregate exercise price of $103,500 (345 × 100 × 3 = $103,500).[25]

Assume that the market declines 10 per cent by the December expiration date, so that the TSE 35 Index is 310.50 at that point,

Put exercise price	= 345.00
TSE 35 Index price	= 310.50
	34.50 × $100 × 3 (puts) = $10,350

If the value of the investor's portfolio declines exactly 10 per cent, the loss on the portfolio of $10,350 will be exactly offset by the total gain on the three put contracts of $10,350. It is important to note, however, that a particular portfolio's value may decline more or less than the overall market as represented by one of the market indexes such as the TSE 35 Index.

As before, if the option is held to expiration and a market decline (of a significant amount) does not occur, the investor will lose the entire premium paid for the put(s). In our example, the investor could lose the entire $3,000 paid for the three puts. This could be viewed as the cost of obtaining "market insurance."

---

[25] The exercise value of an index option, like any stock option, is equal to 100 (shares) multiplied by the exercise price.

Stock-index options can also be useful to institutional investors (or individuals) who do not have funds available immediately for investment but anticipate a market rise. Buying calls will allow such investors to take advantage of the rise in prices if it does occur. Of course, the premium could be lost if the anticipations are incorrect.

Investors can sell (write) index options, either to speculate or to hedge their positions. As we saw in the case of individual options, however, the risk can be large. If the seller is correct in his or her beliefs, the profit is limited to the amount of the premium; if incorrect, the seller faces potential losses far in excess of the premiums received from selling the options. Although the writer of an individual stock call option can deliver the stock if the option is exercised, the writer of a stock-index call option that is exercised must settle in cash and cannot be certain that gains in the stock portfolio will *fully* offset losses on the index option.[26] It would be impractical (or impossible) to write a completely covered stock-index option if one had to buy the appropriate amounts of the individual shares comprising the stock index at all points in time. However, Canadian investors do have this luxury available to them due to the availability of TIPs 35. As discussed in the CSC Notes box in Chapter 8, these units can be purchased through a broker, and their value is determined by the value of the TSE 35 Index.

The Popularity of Stock-Index Options

Stock-index options appeal to speculators because of the leverage they offer. A change in the underlying index of less than 1 per cent can result in a change in the value of the contract of 15 per cent or more. Given the increased volatility in financial markets in recent years, investors can experience rapid changes in the value of their positions. Since introduced in 1983, stock-index options have grown in popularity and now account for more than 10 per cent of options traded through the CDCC, and more than 25 per cent of CBOE trading. Much of the initial volume was accounted for by professional speculators and trading firms. However, as familiarity with index options has increased, individual investors are assuming a larger role in this market.

SUMMARY

This summary relates to the learning objectives provided on page 595.

1. **Define options and discuss why they are used.**
Equity-derivative securities derive their value from the equity price of a corporation. They consist of puts and calls, created by investors, and warrants, rights, and convertible securities, created by corporations. A call is an option to buy a share of a particular stock at a stated price any time before a specified expiration date. Similarly, a put is an option to sell the stock. The seller receives a premium for selling either of these options, and the buyer pays the premium. Advantages of options include a smaller investment than transacting in the stock itself, knowing the maximum loss in advance, leverage, and an expansion of the opportunity set available to investors.

[26] Writers of index options are notified of their obligation to make a cash settlement on the business day following the day of exercise.

2. **Describe how options work and give some basic strategies.**
   Buyers of calls expect the underlying stock to perform in the opposite direction from the expectations of put buyers. Writers of each instrument have opposite expectations from the buyers. The basic strategies for options involve a call writer and a put buyer expecting the underlying stock price to decline, whereas the call buyer and the put writer expect it to rise. Options may also be used to hedge against a portfolio position by establishing an opposite position in options on that stock. More sophisticated options strategies include combinations of options, such as strips, straps, straddles and spreads (which include money spreads and time spreads). These strategies are discussed in Appendix 19-A.
3. **Explain the valuation of options.**
   Options have an intrinsic value ranging from $0 to the "in the money" value. Most sell for more than this, representing a speculative premium, referred to as the time value. According to the Black-Scholes option valuation model, value is a function of the price of the stock, the exercise price of the option, time to maturity, the interest rate, and the volatility of the underlying stock. The available empirical evidence seems to suggest that the options market is efficient, with trading rules unable to exploit any biases that exist in the Black-Scholes or other options pricing models.
4. **Identify types of options other than puts and calls.**
   Interest rate, currency, and stock-index options are also available to investors. Stock-index options are a popular innovation in the options area that allow investors to buy puts and calls on broad stock market indexes. A distinguishing feature of these option contracts is that settlement is in cash. In effect, stock-index options allow investors to make only a market decision and to purchase a form of market insurance. The strategies with index options are similar to those for individual stock options. Investors can both hedge and speculate.

KEY TERMS

Arbitrageurs
Black-Scholes model
Call
Canadian Derivatives Clearing Corporation (CDCC)
Covered call
Currency options
Equity-derivative securities
Exercise (strike) price
Expiration date
Hedge
Hedge ratio
Interest rate options
Intrinsic value
Long-term options (LEAPS)
Option premium
Options
Portfolio insurance
Protective put
Put
Put-call parity
Right (Appendix 19-B)
Spread (Appendix 19-A)
Stock-index options
Straddle (Appendix 19-A)
Time value
Warrant (Appendix 19-B)

ADDITIONAL RESOURCES

The Canadian Securities Institute offers the Derivatives Fundamental Course and the Options Licensing Course. These two courses must be completed in sequence (in addition to the Canadian Securities Course and the Conduct and Practices Handbook Course) before an individual can serve as an investment advisor involved in trading options. These courses contain useful reference materials for the student who is interested in options.

A good tutorial on options and financial futures is available through the Association for Investment Management and Research (AIMR) as part of the CFA curriculum by contacting PBD, Inc., P. O. Box 6996, Alpharetta, GA, 30239-6996 (800/789-AIMR):
Clarke, Roger G. *Options and Futures: A Tutorial*, The Research Foundation of the Institute of Chartered Financial Analysts, P. O. Box 3668, Charlottesville, VA, 1992.

An excellent discussion of options, as well as futures, can be found in:
Hull, John. *Introduction to Futures and Options Markets*. Third Edition. Englewood Cliffs, NJ: Prentice Hall, 1998.

Chance, Don M. *An Introduction to Derivatives*. Third Edition. Orlando, FL: The Dryden Press, 1995.

Some empirical results from the option pricing model can be found in:
Gultekin, N., et al. "Option Pricing Model Estimates: Some Empirical Results." *Financial Management* (Spring 1982), pp. 58–69.

REVIEW QUESTIONS

1. Distinguish between call options, warrants, and rights. (Refer to Appendix 19-B for this question.)
2. Explain the following terms used with puts and calls:
   a. Strike price
   b. Naked option
   c. Premium
   d. Out-of-the-money option
3. Who writes puts and calls? Why?
4. What role do clearing corporations play in options markets?
5. What is the relationship between option prices and their intrinsic values? Why?
6. What is meant by the time value of an option?
7. Why do investors write calls? What are their obligations?
8. What is an index option? What index options are available in Canada?
9. What are the major differences between a stock option and an index option?

10. How does writing a covered call differ from writing a naked call?
11. What does it mean to say that an option is worth more alive than dead?
12. What are the potential advantages of puts and calls?
13. Explain the factors used in the Black-Scholes option valuation model. What is the relationship between each factor and the value of the option?
14. Give three reasons why an investor might purchase a call.
15. What is a straddle? When would an investor buy one? Write one? (Refer to Appendix 19-A for this question.)
16. What is a spread? What is its purpose? (Refer to Appendix 19-A for this question.)
17. Explain two types of spreads. (Refer to Appendix 19-A for this question.)
18. Why is the call or put writer's position considerably different from the buyer's position?
19. How can a put be used to protect a particular position? a call?
20. Which is greater for an option relative to the underlying common share, dollar movements or return volatility? Why?
21. Assume that you own a diversified portfolio of 50 stocks and fear a market decline over the next six months.
    a. How could you protect your portfolio during this period using stock-index options?
    b. How effective would this hedge be?
    c. Other things being equal, if your portfolio consisted of 150 stocks, would the protection be more effective?
22. Assume that you expect interest rates to rise and that you wish to speculate on this expectation. How could interest rate options be used to do this?

PREPARING FOR YOUR PROFESSIONAL EXAMS

Special Note to CSC Students

Ensure that you have read and understood the following topics:*

Introduction, pp. 596–597
Understanding options, pp. 598–605
Some basic options characteristics, pp. 605–606
Payoffs and profits from basic option positions, pp. 606–611
Option valuation, pp. 617–626
Other types of options — stock-index options, pp. 627–631
Appendix 19-B: Rights and Warrants, pp. 641–644

Reading these CSC-related topics should provide you with additional understanding of CSC material. However, it should not be seen as a substitute for reading the CSC textbook itself, which is the basis for the CSC exam.

CSC REGISTRATION QUESTIONS

The Canadian Securities Institute issued the following sample questions in the 1997 CSC registration package as a means for students to self-assess their understanding of CSC-related material.

1. Describe the chief difference between a call option and a put option.
2. (Refer to Appendix 19-B.) The life span of a warrant is usually ________ the life span of a right.
   a. higher than
   b. lower than
   c. the same as
3. The life span of LEAPS is usually ______ the life span of regular options contracts.
   a. higher than
   b. lower than
   c. the same as
4. (Refer to Appendix 19-B.) The following pertains to a rights issue by BRU Co. Ltd.:

Terms:	one right issued for each common share held one new common share for every four rights held
Subscription price:	$20.00
Record date:	Tuesday, October 23
Expiry date:	Monday, November 19
Common shares outstanding on Tuesday, October 23:	8,800,000

Market Prices for BRU Common

Monday, October 15	$23.75	Monday, October 22	$22.50
Tuesday, October 16	$23.50	Tuesday, October 23	$22.25
Wednesday, October 17	$23.00	Thursday, October 25	$22.00
Thursday, October 18	$23.25	Friday, November 16	$21.75
Friday, October 19	$22.75	Monday, November 19	$21.00

   Assume there are no holidays (other than Saturdays and Sundays) during the period. Calculate the final answers to two decimal places. Show your calculations.
   a. What is the theoretical intrinsic value of 1 BRU right on the last day it trades "cum rights"?
   b. What is the theoretical intrinsic value of 1 BRU right on the first day it trades "ex rights"?
   c. Trades in the rights on November 19 would be settled on what basis?
   d. List two differences between rights and warrants.
   e. The rights offering is fully subscribed. How much money did BRU raise as a result of the rights issue?
5. (Refer to Appendix 19-B.) The following pertains to warrants of WCB Co.:

Terms:	1 warrant is required to purchase 1 common share
Exercise price of warrants:	$7.50
Market price of one warrant:	$2.25
Market price of one common share:	$9.00
Number of warrants issued:	3,000,000
Number of common shares outstanding prior to the exercise of any warrants:	60,000,000

Calculate final answers to two decimal places. Show your calculations.

a. What is the intrinsic value of one WCB warrant?

b. What is the time value of one WCB warrant?

c. What is the percentage overvaluation of the warrants?

d. List two factors contributing to warrants' overvaluation.

e. After all warrants have been exercised, the company's directors decide to declare a 3-for-1 stock split. How many common shares will there be as a result?

PROBLEMS

Assume the common stock of ABC Company trades on the TSE. ABC has never paid a cash dividend. The stock is relatively risky. Assume that the beta for ABC is 1.3 and that ABC closed at a price of $162. Hypothetical option quotes on ABC are as follows:

Strike		**Call**			**Put**	
Price	**Apr**	**Jul**	**Oct**	**Apr**	**Jul**	**Oct**
140	23.50	s	s	s	s	s
150	16	21	25	1	3.75	r
160	8.88	14	20	3	7	9
170	3	9	13.25	9	10	11
180	1.25	5.25	9	r	20	r

r = not traded; s = no option offered.

1. Based on the ABC data, answer the following questions:

   a. Which calls are in the money?

   b. Which puts are in the money?

   c. Why are investors willing to pay 1.25 for the 180 April call but only 1.00 for the 150 April put, which has an exercise price that is closer to the current market price?

2. Based on the ABC data answer the following:

   a. Calculate the intrinsic value of the April 150 and the October 170 calls.

   b. Calculate the intrinsic value of the April 150 and the October 170 puts.

   c. Explain the reasons for the differences in intrinsic values in parts (a) and (b).

3. Using the ABC data, answer the following:

   a. What is the cost of 10 October 150 call contracts in total dollars (excluding commission fees)?

   b. What is the cost of 20 October 160 put contracts in total dollars (excluding commission fees)?

c. On the following day, assume ABC closed at \$164. Which of the options would you have expected to increase? decrease?

d. If the new quote on the October 150 call was 26, what would have been your one-day profit on the 10 contracts? What would have been your percentage return?

e. If the new quote on the October 160 put was 7.50, what would have been your one-day profit on the 20 contracts? What would have been your percentage return?

f. What is the most you could lose on these 20 contracts?

4. You are considering some put and call options and have available the following data (assume no dividends are paid by ABC or DEF):

	Call ABC	Call DEF	Put ABC
Time to expiration (months)	3	6	3
Annual risk-free rate	8%	8%	8%
Exercise price	\$50	\$50	\$50
Option price	\$3		\$4
Stock price	\$45	\$45	\$45

a. Comparing the two calls, should DEF sell for more or less than ABC if their shares have the same volatility? Why?

b. What is the call option time value for call option ABC?

c. Based on the information for the call and the put for ABC, determine if put-call parity is working.

5. Assume that the value of a call option using the Black-Scholes model is \$8.94. The interest rate is 8 per cent, and the time to maturity is 90 days. The price of the underlying stock is \$47.38, and the exercise price is \$45. Calculate the price of a put using the put-call parity relationship.

6. Using the Black-Scholes formula, calculate the value of a call option given the following information:

   Stock price = \$50
   Exercise price = \$45
   Interest rate = 7%
   Time to expiration = 90 days
   Standard deviation = 0.4

   What is the price of the put using the same information?

7. Using the information in Problem 6, determine the sensitivity of the call value to a change in inputs by recalculating the call value if

a. the interest rate doubles to 14 per cent but all other values remain the same.

b. the standard deviation doubles to 0.8 but all other values remain the same.

c. Which change causes the greatest fluctuation in the value of the call? What can you infer from this?

8. Given the following information, determine the number of shares of stock that must be purchased to form a hedged position if one option contract (covering 100 shares of stock)

is to be written.

Stock price = \$100
Exercise price = \$95
Interest rate = 8%
Time to expiration = 180 days
Standard deviation = 0.6

9. Given the information in Problem 8, determine how the value of the call would change if
   a. the exercise price is \$100
   b. the time to expiration is 80 days (use the original exercise price of \$95)
   c. the time to expiration is 8 days
10. Determine the value of Ribex call options if the exercise price is \$40, and the option is currently \$2 out of the money, the time to expiration is 90 days, the interest rate is 0.10, and the variance of return on the stock for the past few months has been 0.81.
11. Using the information in Problem 10, decide intuitively whether the put or the call will sell at a higher price and verify your answer.

APPENDIX 19-A

SPREADS AND COMBINATIONS

Puts and calls offer investors a number of opportunities beyond the simple strategies discussed in Chapter 19. We briefly describe here some combinations of options that can be written or purchased. We also consider the use of spreads.

Combinations of Options

Options can be mixed together in numerous ways. Some typical combinations include a straddle, a strip, and a strap. A **straddle** is a combination of a put and a call on the same stock with the same exercise date and exercise price. A purchaser of a straddle believes that the underlying stock price is highly volatile and may go either up or down. Buying the straddle eliminates the need to predict the direction of the market correctly. The buyer of the straddle can exercise each part separately, and therefore can profit from a large enough move either way. However, the price of the stock must rise or fall enough to equal the premium on both a put and a call; therefore, the straddle buyer must be confident that the underlying stock has a good chance of moving sharply in at least one direction.

Straddle
A combination of a put and a call on the same stock with the same exercise date and exercise price.

Straddles can also be sold (written). The seller believes that the underlying stock price will exhibit small volatility but could go up or down. Unlike the buyer, the writer does not forecast that a substantial movement in one direction or the other is likely.

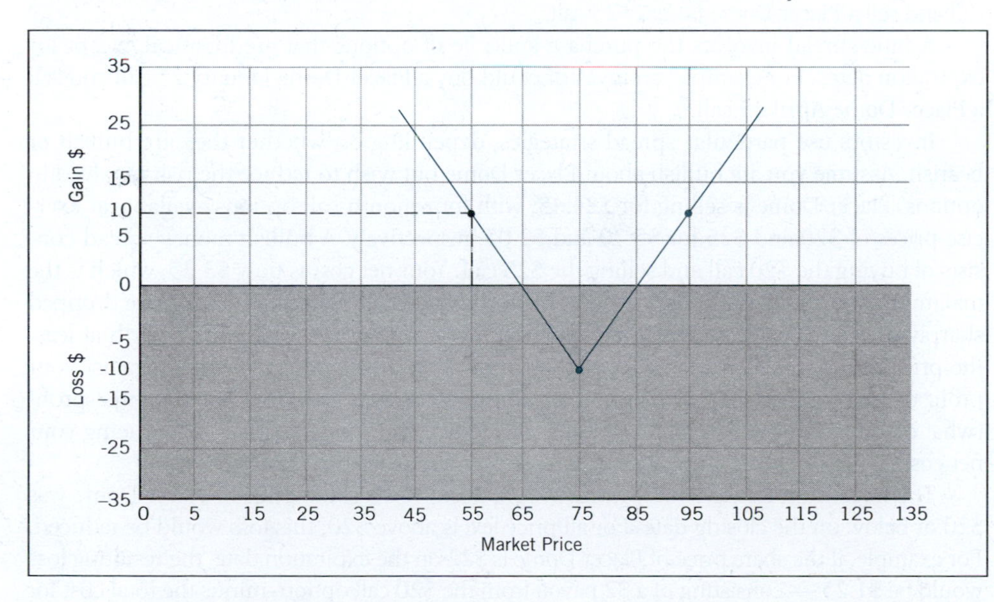

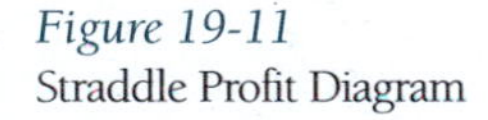
Figure 19-11
Straddle Profit Diagram

Consider a stock selling at $75 with a six-month straddle available with an exercise price of $75 and, for simplicity, call and put prices of $5 each. The seller of such a straddle is protected (i.e. makes a profit) in the range of $65–85 (ignoring commissions). They earn the maximum return of $10, if the price remains at $75, since neither option would be exercised at this price. The buyers hope that the price exceeds one of these boundaries (i.e. $65 or $85) before expiration. In any event, if the price is above or below $75, one of the options would be in the money, and hence be exercised. However, in order for the buyer to achieve a positive profit by exercising the option, the price would have to move up or down by more than $10 (i.e., in order to cover the original cost of $10).[27] The profit diagram for this straddle is shown in Figure 19-11 above.

A *strip* is a combination of two puts and a call on the same security, again with the same expiration date and exercise price. In this case, the purchaser believes that the price will probably decline rather than rise and therefore wants two puts (but also wants some protection in the opposite direction). The seller obviously believes the opposite.

A *strap* is similar to a strip but combines two calls with a put. Here, of course, the purchaser believes the probability of a price increase exceeds that for a price decrease, and again, the writer expects the opposite.

Spreads

Spread
The purchase and sale of an equivalent option varying in only one respect.

Rather than being only the buyer or the seller of various combinations of puts and calls, an investor can be both simultaneously by means of a spread. A **spread** is defined as the purchase and sale of an equivalent option varying in only one respect. Its purpose is to reduce risk in an option position, and it is a popular practice.

The two basic spreads are the *money spread* and the *time spread*. A money spread involves the purchase of a call option at one exercise price and the sale of the same-maturity option, but with a different exercise price. For example, an investor could buy a **Placer Dome** January 20 call and sell a Placer Dome January 25 call.

A time spread involves the purchase and sale of options that are identical except for expiration dates. For example, an investor could buy a Placer Dome January 25 call and sell a Placer Dome April 25 call.

Investors use particular spread strategies, depending on whether they are bullish or bearish. Assume you are bullish about Placer Dome but wish to reduce the risk involved in options. Placer Dome is selling for $24.45, with four-month call options available at exercise prices of $20 and $25 for $5.30 and $2.05, respectively. A bullish money spread consists of buying the $20 call and selling the $25 call. Your net cost is now $3.25, which is the maximum you could lose if the calls expire worthless because Placer Dome's price dropped sharply. Should Placer Dome rise above $20, however, your $20 call will be worth at least the price of the stock minus the exercise price of $20. This amount is netted against your profit or loss on the $25 call that you wrote. In effect, you give up some potential profit (what could have been earned on the $20 call alone) to reduce your risk (by reducing your net cost) if the stock price declines.

The maximum loss is $3.25, which would occur if the share price of Placer Dome was $20 or below on the closing date. For all price levels above $20, this loss would be reduced. For example, if the share price of Placer Dome is $22 on the expiration date, the resulting loss would be $1.25 — consisting of a $2 payoff from the $20 call option, minus the total cost for

[27] Of course, we know that early exercise is generally less profitable than selling the option in the market, since the seller would receive a time value premium in addition to the intrinsic value (which is the value obtained if the option is exercised).

the strategy of $3.25. If the share price was $25 on the expiration date, the resulting profit would be $1.75 ($5 − $3.25). For share prices beyond $25, for each $1 you gain on the $20 call you bought, you lose $1 on the $25 call you wrote, so the effects cancel out. As a result, the maximum profit from this bullish spread is $1.75. For example, if the share price is $30, the profit from the $20 call is $4.70 ($10 − $ 5.30), while the loss from the $25 call is −$2.95 ($2.05 − $5.00). This results in a net profit of $1.75 ($4.70 − $2.95). The profit diagram for this bullish money spread is shown in Figure 19-12 below. (This example ignores commission fees).

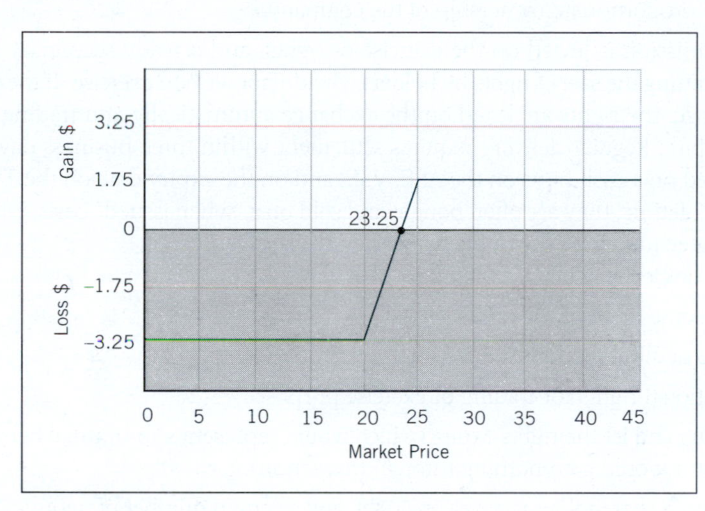

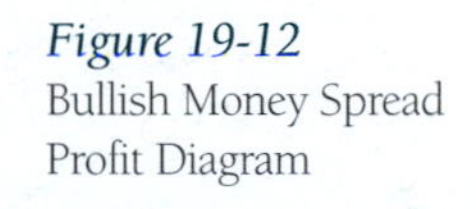
Figure 19-12
Bullish Money Spread Profit Diagram

APPENDIX 19-B

RIGHTS AND WARRANTS

Rights and warrants are similar to call options because they both give the holder the right to purchase shares at specified prices until the expiration date. Rights are generally short-term in nature, while warrants tend to be issued with maturities of three to five years. Unlike options, they are issued by the corporation itself, and result in dilution of the common equity capital base.

Rights

A **right** is the term applied to a privilege granted to a shareholder to acquire additional shares at a predetermined (subscription) price which is generally lower than the current market price. This creates value for the shareholder and induces them to exercise this option. Rights generally have short maturities consisting of a few weeks to three months. They are usually transferable, and certificates are mailed to shareholders on the record date. Shares trade ex rights two business days prior to a record date, which means they trade without the right privilege attached. Prior to the ex rights date, the stock is said to trade cum rights, since it

Right
A corporate-created option to purchase a stated number of common shares at a specified price within a specified time (typically a few months).

trades with the right privilege attached. Typically the share price will drop by the theoretical intrinsic value of the right on the ex rights date.

Rights may be offered because:

1. Current market conditions are not conducive to traditional common share issues
2. Management wants to give existing shareholders the opportunity to acquire shares, possibly at a discount to present market price
3. It enables new funds to be raised while providing existing shareholders the right to maintain their proportionate ownership of the company.

No commission is levied on the exercise of rights, and a ready secondary market can develop permitting the sale of rights by holders who do not wish to exercise. If the shares trade on an exchange, the rights are listed on the exchange automatically and trading takes place until they expire. Regular delivery requires settlement within three business days, however, they are traded on a cash basis on the ASE, VSE, and on the expiry date on the TSE. Because of their short lifetime, they are often bought and sold on a "when issued" basis, which implies that sellers agree to deliver the rights when they are received.

A rights holder may take four courses of action:

1. Exercise some or all of the rights
2. Sell some or all of the rights
3. Buy additional rights for trading or exercise purposes
4. Do nothing and let the rights expire (which would represent sub-optimal behaviour since the investor would gain nothing through this action).

Usually each shareholder receives one right, and a certain number of rights (N) is required to purchase one share (purchase of fractional shares may or may not be permitted, depending on the details of the issue). The theoretical intrinsic value (IV) of a right, by necessity, is calculated using two methods described below.

During the cum rights period:

$$\text{IV} = \frac{(\text{Market price of the stock} - \text{Subscription price})}{\text{N} + 1} \tag{19-9}$$

The addition of 1 to N reflects the fact that the market price of the share includes the value of one right.

During the ex rights period:

$$\text{IV} = \frac{(\text{Market price of stock} - \text{Subscription price})}{\text{N}} \tag{19-10}$$

EXAMPLE: CALCULATING INTRINSIC VALUE CUM AND EX RIGHTS

A share is trading for $40 cum rights. Four rights are required to purchase a share at the subscription price of $35.

$$\text{IV} = (40 - 35) / (4 + 1) = \$1.00$$

Two days after the ex rights date the share price above has fallen to $39.20.

$$\text{IV} = (39.20 - 35) / 4 = \$1.05$$

Warrants

Warrants are corporate issued securities with an option to buy shares from the issuer at a set price for a set period of time. Warrants are generally long-term in nature, and tend to be issued with three to five years to maturity, although some have longer lives. They are often attached to debt or preferred share issues as a sweetener (to make the issue more attractive to investors). They are usually detachable either immediately or after a certain holding period, and then trade separately.

Warrant
An option created by a corporation to purchase a stated number of common shares at a specified price within a specified time (often several years).

Investors may be attracted to warrants because they provide "leverage" which is attractive to speculators. In other words, the market price of a warrant is generally much lower than the price of the underlying security, yet its price moves together with the underlying asset price. The result is greater percentage swings in warrant prices than for the underlying asset, which magnifies gains (or losses) in percentage terms. A ratio that may be used to measure this leverage potential is:

$$\text{Leverage potential} = \frac{\text{Market price of the underlying share}}{\text{Market price of the warrant}} \quad \textbf{(19-11)}$$

Generally speaking, the larger this ratio, the greater the leverage effect, however, other factors such as the amount of overvaluation must also be considered. Other factors to be considered by investors when selecting warrants include marketability and protection against stock splits and/or stock dividends (which is usually provided).

Warrants have an intrinsic value and a time value. The intrinsic value refers to the amount by which the market price of the underlying stock exceeds the exercise price of the warrant. It can never go below zero, since exercise is at the option of the warrant holder. Time value refers to the amount by which the market price exceeds the intrinsic value.

There is also usually an overvaluation associated with warrants, which is calculated as follows:

$$\begin{aligned}\text{Overvaluation} = {} & \text{Market price of warrant} + \text{Exercise price of warrant} \\ & - \text{Market value of underlying asset}\end{aligned} \quad \textbf{(19-12)}$$

This will equal the time value whenever there is a positive intrinsic value but may exceed the time value when the intrinsic value is nil.

EXAMPLE: DETERMINING INTRINSIC VALUE, TIME VALUE, OVERVALUATION, AND LEVERAGE

Determine the intrinsic value, time value, percentage overvaluation, and leverage potential of the following warrants:

a. Share price is $50, warrant price is $8 and exercise price of warrants is $52

b. Share price is $40, warrant price is $15 and exercise price of warrants is $30.

Solution:

a. IV = Max (50 − 52, 0) = 0

Time Value = 8 − 0 = $8

Overvaluation = 8 + 52 − 50 = 10

Percentage overvaluation = 10/50 = 0.20 or 20%

Leverage potential = 50/8 = 6.25

b. IV = Max (40 − 30, 0) = 10

Time Value = 15 − 10 = $5

Overvaluation = 15 + 30 − 40 = 5

Percentage overvaluation = 5/40 = 0.125 or 12.5%

Leverage potential = 40/15 = 2.67

Factors to be examined by investors in order to determine the appropriateness of warrant overvaluation include:

1. The prospects for the underlying assets
2. Time to expiration
3. Volatility of underlying asset price
4. Higher premiums may be associated with higher price-earnings ratios of underlying shares
5. Lower over-valuations should result for warrants on assets paying higher dividends to compensate the warrant holder for not receiving the dividend.

Some special types of warrants include:

1. Piggyback warrants — which may be received as part of the exercise of original warrants (and typically have higher exercise prices)
2. Put warrants — on stock indices, etc. which result in cash settlement if the price of the underlying is below a specified price
3. Commodity-indexed warrants — where the exercise price is linked to market prices of a specified commodity.

APPENDIX 19-C

PUT-CALL PARITY: THE NO-ARBITRAGE ARGUMENT

Unless the price of a European put and call on the same non-dividend paying stock with the same exercise price bear a certain relationship to each other, there will be opportunities for earning riskless profits (arbitrage). We can prove this by using the following no-arbitrage argument, which ignores transactions costs. Consider the following investment portfolios: Portfolio A involves the purchase of a European call option for an underlying share that does not pay dividends (at a cost of C), and investing the present value of the exercise price on this option (PV(E) dollars) in a riskless investment (government T-bills) that will pay off E dollars at the maturity date; portfolio B involves the purchase of one share of the underlying stock (at a cost of S), and also buying one European put on the underlying share (at a cost of P). These actions and their payoffs at expiration date T are depicted below.

Portfolio	**Action**	**Payoff at T**	
		S(T) < E	**S(T) > E**
A	Buy 1 call	0	S(T) − E
	Invest PV(E) in T-bills	E	E
	Total Payoff	**E**	**S(T)**
B	Buy 1 share	S(T)	S(T)
	Buy 1 put	E − S(T)	0
	Total Payoff	**E**	**S(T)**

Notice that portfolios A and B always have the same payoff at T because they will both pay off S(T) at T when S(T) > E, and will both pay off E at T when S(T) < E. Since both the call and the put are European options, we also know that early exercise of either option is impossible. Therefore, since the two strategies must have identical payoffs at the expiration date, and since the options cannot be exercised early, they must have identical costs for constructing the portfolios. If they did not, investors could make riskless (or arbitrage) profits by taking a long position in the undervalued portfolio and taking a short position in the overvalued portfolio. For example, if the cost of constructing A was $10, while the cost of constructing B was $8, one could take a long position in B and a short position in A, and receive $2 today. Since both portfolios have the same payoff at T, the returns from B can always be used to pay off the short position in A, so there is no risk associated with this strategy, yet the payoff is positive. This condition could never exist in efficient markets and would quickly disappear as traders recognized the discrepancy and exploited it. So:

Total cost to construct portfolio A = Total cost to construct portfolio B, or

$$C + PV(E) = P + S$$

This can be rearranged to solve for the price of the put as follows:

$$P = PV(E) - S + C$$

Finally, we note that the present value of E using a continuous discount rate r, and with a time to maturity (in years) equal to t, can be expressed as $PV(E) = E/e^{rt}$, so we are left with Equation 19-8: $P = E/e^{rt} - S + C$.

CHAPTER

FUTURES

LEARNING OBJECTIVES

After reading this chapter, you will be able to

1. Describe the structure of futures markets.
2. Outline how futures work and what types of investors participate in futures markets.
3. Explain how financial futures are used.

CHAPTER PREVIEW

This chapter discusses financial futures, the other derivative security of primary importance to investors. As with options, futures allow investors to manage investment risk and to speculate in the equity, fixed-income, and currency markets. Here we discuss the structure of futures markets, explain the procedures of using futures, and give some basic strategies. We also consider interest rate and stock-index futures.

INTRODUCTION

Futures markets play an important role in today's investments world. New instruments in this area have proliferated, and techniques involving the use of futures, such as program trading, have captured wide media attention. Of particular importance to many investors is the array of financial futures now available. Anyone studying investments should understand what futures contracts are, the wide variety of choices now available, and how financial futures can be used both to hedge portfolio positions and to speculate in fixed-income and equity areas. Futures contracts are an important component of derivative securities and, like options, they represent a major innovation in risk management.

UNDERSTANDING FUTURES MARKETS

Why Futures Markets?

Physical commodities and financial instruments typically are traded in cash markets. A *cash contract* calls for immediate delivery and is used by those who need a commodity now (e.g., food processors). Cash contracts cannot be cancelled unless both parties agree. The current cash prices of commodities and financial instruments can be found daily in such sources as *The Globe and Mail*, the *National Post*, and *The Wall Street Journal*.

There are two types of cash markets: spot markets and forward markets. Spot markets are for immediate delivery.[1] The spot price refers to the current market price of an item available for immediate delivery. Forward markets are for deferred delivery. The forward price is the price of an item that is to be delivered at some specified time in the future.

Suppose that a manufacturer of high school and college class rings is gathering orders to fill for this school year and wishes to ensure an established price today for gold to be delivered six months from now, when the rings will actually be manufactured. The spot price of gold is not the manufacturer's primary concern, because the gold will not be purchased until it is needed for the manufacturing process. However, to reduce its risk the manufacturer is interested in contracting for gold to be delivered in six months at a price established today. This will allow the manufacturer to price its rings more accurately.

Our manufacturer could find a gold supplier who was willing to enter into a *forward contract*, which is simply a commitment today to transact in the future. The other party to the contract, such as a mining company, agrees to deliver the gold six months from now at

[1] "Immediate" means in the normal course of business. For example, it may normally take two days for an item to be delivered after being ordered.

a price negotiated today. Both parties have agreed to a deferred delivery at a sales price that is currently determined. No funds have been exchanged. Both parties have reduced their risk in the sense that the mining company knows what it will receive for the gold when it is sold six months from now and the ring manufacturer knows what it will pay for the gold when it actually needs to take delivery six months from now.

Obviously, one of the parties may be disappointed six months later when the price of gold has changed, but that is the advantage of hindsight. If investors could foresee the future, they would know what to do to start with and would not have to worry about risk. The forward and futures markets were developed to allow individuals to deal with the risks they face.

Forward contracts are centuries old, traceable to at least the ancient Romans and Greeks. Organized futures markets, on the other hand, only go back to the mid-nineteenth century in Chicago. Futures markets are, in effect, organized and standardized forward markets. An organized futures exchange standardizes the non-standard forward contracts, establishing such features as contract size, delivery dates, and condition of the items that can be delivered. Only the price and number of contracts are left for futures traders to negotiate. Individuals can trade without personal contact with each other because of the centralized marketplace. Performance is guaranteed by a clearing house, relieving one party to the transaction from worry that the other party will fail to honour its commitment.

The futures markets serve a valuable economic purpose by allowing hedgers to shift price risk to speculators. The risk of price fluctuations is shifted from participants unwilling to assume such risk to those who are. Another economic function performed by futures markets is price discovery. Because the price of a futures contract reflects current expectations about values at some future date, transactors can establish current prices against later transactions.

Current Futures Markets

To most people, futures trading traditionally has meant trading in commodities such as gold, wheat, and oil. However, money can be thought of simply as another commodity, and *financial futures* have become a particularly viable investment alternative for numerous investors. Therefore, futures contracts currently traded on futures exchanges can be divided into two broad categories:

1. Commodities — agricultural, metals, and energy-related
2. Financials — foreign currencies as well as debt and equity instruments.

Each category can be further subdivided as shown in Table 20-1, which shows the futures contracts traded in the United States. As we can see, the futures markets involve trading in a variety of both commodities and financials.

For each type of contract, such as corn or silver, different delivery dates are available. Each contract will specify the trading unit involved and, where applicable, the deliverable grade necessary to satisfy the contract. Investors can also purchase options on futures contracts. Appendix 20-A explains futures options.

One of the striking features of Table 20-1 is the proliferation of foreign-based futures contracts on US futures exchanges. This is true for interest rate futures and stock-index futures and is good evidence of the move toward globalization that is occurring throughout the investing world.

Table 20-1

Futures Contracts Traded in the United States, by Category

The major commodities traded in the United States can be classified into the following categories (as shown in *The Wall Street Journal*):

	I. Commodities
Grains and oilseeds	Wheat, corn, oats, soybeans, soybean oils, soybean meal, flaxseed, rapeseed, rye, and canola
Livestock and meats	Cattle (both live and feeders), pork bellies, and hogs
Foods	Cocoa, coffee, orange juice, and sugar
Fibers	Cotton
Metals	Copper, gold, platinum, silver, and palladium
Oil	Gasoline, heating oil, crude oil, gas oil, and propage
Wood	Lumber
	II. Financials
Interest rates	Canadian government bond, Treasury bills, Treasury notes, Treasury bonds, municipal bond index, 30-day federal funds, Eurodollar, 1-month LIBOR, Sterling Long Gilt, Euromark, EuroSwiss, EuroLira, German government bond, Italian government bond
Stock indexes	Toronto 35 Index, S&P 500 Index, S&P MidCap 400, NYSE Composite Index, Major Market Index, KR-CRB Index, KC Value Line Index, Russell 2000, CAC 40, Nikkei 225 Index, GSCI, FT-SE 100 Index
Foreign currencies	US dollar, Japanese yen, German mark, British Pound, Swiss franc, Australian dollar

The only commodity exchange in Canada is the Winnipeg Commodity Exchange where trading has taken place in wheat, canola, flaxseed, oats, barley, and rye for several years. Futures on canola are by far the most active commodity futures that are traded in Canada, as shown in Table 20-2.

Table 20-2

Listed Futures Products on the Winnipeg Commodity Exchange

(figures are for August 1995–July 1996 and reflect the crop year)

Commodity Futures	**Volume**
Wheat	181,383
Oats	7,988
Barley	256,480
Canola	1,271,190
Flaxseed	112,553
Options on Commodity Futures	**Calls & Puts Volume**
Wheat	394
Barley	2,748
Canola	74,072
Flaxseed	821

Source: *Canadian Securities Course Textbook* (Toronto: Canadian Securities Institute, August 1998), p. 8–25. © 1998 Canadian Securities Institute. Reprinted with permission.

Financial futures contracts presently trade in Canada on the ME and the Toronto Futures Exchange (TFE), a subsidiary of the TSE. The ME trades contracts on three-month and one-month bankers' acceptances (which call for cash delivery), as well as on Government of Canada bonds. Table 20-3 shows the 1997 volume for Canadian bankers' acceptances was 4.14 million contracts, while the volume for Government of Canada bonds was 1.32 million contracts. The TFE presently trades several futures contracts including those based on 500 times the TSE 35 Index and 500 times the TSE 100 Index, which both call for cash delivery. These products are scheduled to be replaced by S&P/TSE 60 futures contracts in the near future. The 1997 volumes for TSE 100 Index Futures and TSE 35 Index Futures was 19,317 and 317,372 contracts traded. As mentioned in previous chapters, the TFE may become obsolete in the future if the ME becomes our national derivatives market, as has been recently proposed by the Canadian exchanges.

Table 20-3

Financial Futures Volumes on the ME and TFE (1994–97)

Futures Product Group	1994 Contracts		1995 Contracts		1996 Contracts		1997 Contracts	
	Millions	%	Millions	%	Millions	%	Millions	%
Canadian Bankers' Acceptances (ME)	1.931	54.51	2.334	65.98	2.416	65.50	4.140	71.37
Canada Goverment Bonds (ME)	1.496	42.24	1.091	30.83	1.108	30.04	1.324	22.83
TSE 100 Index Future (TFE)	0.011	0.31	0.003	0.08	0.008	0.24	0.019	0.33
TSE 35 Index Futures (TFE)	0.104	2.94	0.110	3.11	0.156	4.22	0.317	5.47
Totals	3.542	100.00	3.538	100.00	3.688	100.00	5.800	100.00

Source: CDCC, *Annual Report*, 1997.

The centre of commodity futures trading in North America is the Chicago Board of Trade and the Chicago Mercantile Exchange (CME), however, there are several other important exchanges in New York including the Commodity Exchange, the New York Mercantile Exchange, the New York Coffee, Sugar and Cocoa Exchange, the New York Cotton Exchange, and the New York Futures Exchange. Futures markets in Canada are very small and much less developed than those in the US, both in terms of the variety of available products and trading volume. For example, the CME alone traded over 200 million contracts in 1997, more than 100 times the number of contracts traded on the WSE for the year ended July 1996, and about 35 times the volume of financial futures traded on the ME and TFE in 1997.

International Futures Markets

European futures exchanges are quite competitive, with the German and French exchanges now striving to compete with contracts offered by the London International Financial Futures Exchange.[2] Most of these systems are fully automated order-matching systems.

Japan, which banned financial futures until 1985, is now very active in developing futures exchanges. The 10- and 20-year yen bond futures contracts introduced on the Tokyo Stock Exchange in 1985 are among the most heavily traded futures in the world. With regard to stock-index futures, the Nikkei 225 contract, the most active Japanese index futures contract, trades on the Osaka Securities Exchange.

Futures Contracts

Futures Contract
Agreement providing for the future exchange of a particular asset between buyer and seller at a specified date for a specified amount.

A **futures contract** is a standardized, transferable agreement providing for the deferred delivery of either a specified grade and quantity of a designated commodity within a specified geographical area or of a financial instrument (or its cash value). The futures price at which this exchange will occur at contract maturity is determined today. The trading of futures contracts means only that commitments have been made by buyers and sellers; therefore, "buying" and "selling" does not have the same meaning in futures transactions as it does in stock and bond transactions. Although these commitments are binding because futures contracts are legal contracts, a buyer or seller can eliminate the commitment simply by taking an opposite position in the same commodity or financial instrument for the same futures month.

Futures contracts trading on the TFE and ME is regulated by provincial securities administrators. Futures trading on the Winnipeg Commodity Exchange is regulated by the Canadian Grain Commission, which oversees trading on this market under provisions in the Federal Grain Futures Act. Futures trading in the US is regulated by the Commodity Futures Trading Commission (CFTC), a federal regulatory agency that is responsible for regulating trading in all domestic futures markets. In practice, much of the supervisory functions are performed by the self-regulatory organizations, which include the Investment Dealers Association (IDA) and the exchanges in Canada, and the National Futures Association in the US. In addition, each futures exchange has a supervisory body to oversee its members. In Canada, investment advisors must pass the Derivatives Fundamental Course and the Futures Licensing Course before dealing in futures or options on futures.

THE STRUCTURE OF FUTURES MARKETS

Futures Exchanges

As noted, futures contracts are traded on designated futures exchanges, which are voluntary, non-profit associations, typically unincorporated. The exchange provides an organized marketplace where established rules govern the conduct of the members. It is financed by both membership dues and fees charged for services rendered.

[2] This discussion is indebted to Peter A. Abken, "Globalization of Stock, Futures, and Options Markets," in *Financial Derivatives* (Atlanta: Federal Reserve Bank of Atlanta, 1993), pp. 3–24.

There are a limited number of memberships for futures exchanges, which like stock exchange seats, can be traded at market-determined prices. Members can trade for their own accounts or as agents for others. For example, floor traders trade for their own accounts, whereas floor brokers (or commission brokers) often act as agents for others. Futures commission merchants (FCMs) act as agents for the general public, for which they receive commissions. Thus, a customer can establish an account with an FCM, who, in turn may work through a floor broker at the exchange.

A risk disclosure statement must be signed by clients before any trading can take place. This document serves as evidence that the investor understands the risks involved in futures trading. A copy of part I of this form is included in the figure below.

Figure 20-1
Risk Disclosure and Information Statement

Risk Disclosure and Information Statement

PART I

TO: PROSPECTIVE FUTURES CUSTOMERS

For the speculator, futures trading is a high risk activity in which it may not be possible to limit the extent of potential liability. Before you buy or sell a contract you should be certain you can afford to lose not only the money you put up initially but additional money as well.

Attached is an information statement on certain aspects of futures trading. The following are among the points that you should consider in studying this statement:

1. **Financial exposure.** You should fully understand the description of margin arrangements and of how you can be required to put up additional money even after your initial trade. See the section headed "Risk."
2. **Settlement procedures.** Once you have made a trade, you cannot sit back and treat it as a long-term investment. You must arrange to meet margin calls. Before the end of the contract term you must arrange to meet margin calls. Before the end of the contract term you must arrange an offsetting transaction, if you want to avoid having to settle by making or taking physical delivery. See the section headed "Settlement of Contracts."
3. **Use of funds.** Money you deposit with a dealer as margin may earn interest or be used by the firm in its business and you should be aware of the firm's policy as to whether it will pay you interest on this money. Also, if the value of the contract moves in your favour, money will be credited by the clearing house and you should be aware of your dealer's policy as to whether it will permit you to withdraw any amounts credited to it when the contract moves in your favour. These policies, discussed under "Interest on Customer's Balance" and "Disbursement of Funds during Life of Contract" can have a significant impact on the economic results of your trading.

These are not the only parts of the attached material that are important. You should study the material carefully, and ask any questions about it that may occur to you, before you enter your first transaction.

NAME OF FIRM

Source: "Part I: Risk Disclosure and Information Statement," Part II Study Material, Canadian Futures Exam, 1997, p. 10. © 1997 Canadian Securities Institute. Reprinted with permission.

The Clearing Corporation

Similar to options markets, futures markets use a clearing corporation to reduce default risk and to arrange deliveries as required. The clearing corporations also ensure that participants maintain margin deposits or earnest money, to ensure fulfillment of the contract. In Canada, the Canadian Derivatives Clearing Corporation (CDCC) currently issues and clears futures and futures options contracts, in addition to options contracts (discussed in Chapter 19). Futures contracts presently include those on 91-day Canadian Treasury bills, the US dollar, 5-year and 10-year Government of Canada bonds, 1-month and 3-month bankers' acceptances, the TSE 35 Index, and the TSE 100 Index. Futures options contracts include options on the 10-year Government of Canada bond futures and the 3-month bankers' acceptance futures.

Essentially, the clearing house for futures markets operates in the same way as the one for options, which was discussed in some detail in Chapter 19. Buyers and sellers settle with the clearing house, not each other, and it is actually on the other side of every transaction and ensures that all payments are made as specified. It stands ready to fulfill a contract if either buyer or seller defaults, thereby helping to facilitate an orderly market in futures. The clearing house makes the futures market impersonal, which is the key to its success because any buyer or seller can always close out a position and be assured of payment. The first failure of a clearing member in modern times occurred in the 1980s, and the system worked perfectly in preventing any customer from losing money. Finally, as explained below, the clearing house allows participants to easily reverse a position before maturity because it keeps track of each participant's obligations.

THE MECHANICS OF TRADING

Basic Procedures

Because the futures contract is a commitment to buy or sell at a specified future settlement date, a contract is not really being sold or bought, as in the case of T-bills, bonds, or stocks, because no money is exchanged at the time the contract is negotiated. Instead, the seller and the buyer simply are agreeing to make and take delivery, respectively, at some future time for a price agreed upon today. As noted above, the terms buy and sell do not have the same meanings here. It is more accurate to think in terms of a

Short Position
An agreement to sell an asset at a specified future date at a specified price.

Long Position
An agreement to purchase an asset at a specified future date at a specified price.

- **Short position** (seller), which commits a trader to deliver an item at contract maturity.
- **Long position** (buyer), which commits a trader to purchase an item at contract maturity.

Selling short in futures trading means only that a contract not previously purchased is sold. For every futures contract, someone sells it short and someone else holds it long. Like options, futures trading is a zero-sum game, because the amount that is gained by one party, is lost by the one on the other side of the contract.

Unlike an options contract, which involves the *right* to make or take delivery, a futures contract involves an *obligation* to take or make delivery. However, futures contracts can be settled by delivery or by offset. Delivery, or settlement of the contract, occurs in months that are designated by the various exchanges for each of the items traded. Delivery occurs in less than 1 per cent of all transactions.[3]

[3] Instruments that can be used in a delivery are explicitly identified in delivery manuals issued by the appropriate exchange.

Offset is the typical method of settling a contract. Holders liquidate a position by arranging an offsetting transaction. This means that buyers sell their positions and sellers buy their positions sometime prior to delivery. Thus, to eliminate a futures market position, the investor simply does the reverse of what was done originally. As explained above, the clearing house makes this easy to accomplish. It is essential to remember that if a futures contract is not offset, it must be closed out by delivery.

Offset
Liquidation of a futures position by an offsetting transaction — buyers sell their positions and sellers buy their positions prior to the settlement of the contract (delivery).

Each exchange establishes price fluctuation limits on the various types of contracts. Typically, a minimum price change is specified. In the case of TSE 35 Index Futures, for example, it is 0.02 of an index point or $10 per contract. Maximum daily price limits are also in effect for futures contracts. For the TSE 35 Index Futures the expanded price limit is 20.25 points (or $10,125 per contract) above or below the previous day's settlement price.

With stocks, short-selling can be done only on an uptick, but futures have no such restriction. Stock positions, short or long, can literally be held forever. However, futures positions must be closed out within a specified time, either by offsetting the position or by making or taking delivery.

There are no specialists on futures exchanges and each futures contract is traded in a specific pit, which is a ring with steps descending to the centre. Trading follows an auction market process in which every bid and offer competes without priority as to time or size. A system of open outcry is used, whereby any offer to buy or sell is communicated verbally and/or through the use of hand signals, and must be made to all traders in the pit.

Brokerage commissions on commodities contracts are paid on the basis of a completed contract (both a purchase and sale), rather than being charged for each purchase and each sale, as in the case of stocks. As with options, no certificates exist for futures contracts.

The open interest indicates contracts that are not offset by opposite transactions or delivery. That is, it measures the number of unliquidated contracts at any time, on a cumulative basis.[4] The open interest increases when an investor goes long on a contract and is reduced when the contract is liquidated.

Margin

Recall that in the case of stock transactions the term *margin* refers to the down payment in a transaction in which money is borrowed from the broker to finance the total cost. A **futures margin**, on the other hand, is not a down payment because ownership of the underlying item is not being transferred at the time of the transaction. Instead, it refers to the "good faith" (or earnest money) deposit made by both buyer and seller to ensure the completion of the contract. In effect, margin is a performance bond. In futures trading, unlike stock trading, margin is the norm.[5]

Futures Margin
The good faith (earnest money) deposit made by the buyer or seller to ensure the completion of a contract.

Each clearing house sets its own minimum initial margin requirements (in dollars), which are identical for both buyers and sellers of futures contracts. Furthermore, brokerage firms can require a higher margin and typically do so. The margin required for futures contracts, which is small in relation to the value of the contract itself, represents the equity of the transactor (either buyer or seller). It is not unusual for the initial margin to be in the range of $1,500 to

[4] The open interest can be measured using either the open long positions or the open short positions but not both.

[5] Because no credit is being extended, no interest expense is incurred on that part of the contract not covered by the margin, as is the case when stocks are purchased on margin. With futures, customers often receive interest on margin money deposited. A customer with a large enough requirement (roughly, $10,000 and over) can use T-bills as part of the margin.

$2,500 per contract, representing some 2 to 10 per cent of the value of the contract. Since the equity is small, the risk is magnified.

Assume the initial margin is equal to 5 per cent of the total value and an investor holds one contract in an account. If the price of the contract changes by 5 per cent because the price of the underlying commodity changes by 5 per cent, this is equivalent to a 100 per cent change in the investor's equity. This example shows why futures trading can be so risky!

In addition to the initial margin requirement, each contract requires a maintenance margin or variation margin, below which the investor's net equity cannot drop.[6] The net equity is defined as the value of deposited funds (or the marginable value of marketable securities) plus the open profit or minus the open loss. If the market price of a futures contract moves adversely to the owner's position, the equity declines. Margin calls occur when the price goes against the investor causing the investor's equity to fall below the maintenance margin level, requiring the transactor to deposit additional cash or to close out the account. Conversely, withdrawal of funds from a futures account can only occur if net equity rises above the initial margin requirement. To understand precisely how this works, we must first understand how profits and losses from futures contracts are debited and credited daily to an investor's account.

Marked to the Market
All profits and losses on a contract are credited and debited to each investor's account every trading day.

All futures contracts are **marked to the market** daily, which means that all profits and losses on a contract are credited and debited to each investor's account every trading day.[7] Those contract holders with a profit can withdraw the gains, whereas those with a loss will receive a margin call when the equity falls below the specified variation margin. This process is referred to as daily resettlement, and the price used is the contract's settlement price.[8]

Table 20-4
An Example of Investor Accounts, Using Stock-Index Futures, Marked to the Market

	Buyer (Long)	Seller (Short)
Account after one day		
Original equity (initial margin)	$3,500	$3,500
Day 1 mark to the market	(250)	250
Current equity	$3,250	$3,750
Account after two weeks		
Original equity (initial margin)	$3,500	$3,500
Cumulative mark to the market	2,500	(2,500)
Current equity	6,000	1,000
Withdrawable excess equity	$2,500	
Margin call		$2,500

6 Maintenance margins are usually set at 75 per cent of the initial margin requirements.
7 This is not true of forward contracts, where no funds are transferred until the maturity date.
8 The settlement price does not always reflect the final trade of the day. The clearing house establishes the settlement price at the close of trading.

Table 20-4 illustrates how accounts are marked to the market daily and how a margin call can occur. Consider an investor who buys a stock-index futures contract for 350 and a second investor who sells (shorts) the same contract at the same price. Assume these contracts are on the TSE 35 Index, where the contract is for $500 times the index value. For example, a price advance from 350 to 351, or one point, represents an advance of $500 on the contract value. Each investor puts up an initial margin of $3,500, representing 2 per cent of the contract value of $175,000 ($500 × 350). For purposes of this example, we will assume the maintenance margin is $2,800, or 80 per cent of the initial margin requirement.

Table 20-4 traces each investor's account as it is marked to the market daily.[9] At the end of Day 1, the price of the contract has dropped to a settlement price of 349.5, a decrease of one half an index point, causing a change in the futures contracts values of $250. This amount is credited to the seller's account because the seller is short and the price has dropped. Conversely, $250 is debited to the buyer's account because the buyer is long, and the price moved adversely to this position. Table 20-4 shows that the current equity at the end of Day 1 is $3,250 for the buyer and $3,750 for the seller.

Two weeks have passed, during which time each account has been marked to the market daily. The settlement price on this contract has reached 355.00. The aggregate change in market value for each investor is the difference between the current price and the initial price multiplied by $500, the value of one point in price, which in this example is 355 − 350 = 5.00 × $500 = $2,500.

As shown in Table 20-4, this amount is currently credited to the buyer because the price moved in the direction the buyer expected. Conversely, this same amount is currently debited to the seller, who is now on the wrong side of the price movement. Therefore, starting with an initial equity of $3,500, after two weeks the cumulative mark to the market is $2,500. This results in a current equity of $6,000 for the buyer and $1,000 for the seller. The buyer has a withdrawable excess equity of $2,500, because of the favourable price movement, whereas the seller has a margin call of $2,500, assuming a $2,800 maintenance margin. In other words, the investor would have received a margin call since his or her equity value fell below the required margin of $2,800. The seller would be required to add $2,500 ($3,500 − $1,000) to restore the account to the initial margin level of $3,500.

This example illustrates what is meant by the expression that futures trading, like options trading, is a zero-sum game. The aggregate gains and losses net to zero. The aggregate profits enjoyed by the winners must be equal to the aggregate losses suffered by the losers. This also means that the net exposure to changes in the commodity's price must be zero.

USING FUTURES CONTRACTS

Who uses futures and for what purpose? Traditionally, participants in the futures market have been classified as either hedgers or speculators. Because both groups are important in understanding the role and functioning of futures markets, we will consider each in turn. The distinctions between these two groups apply to financial futures as well as to the more traditional commodity futures.

[9] This example is similar to an illustration in *Introducing New York Stock Exchange Index Futures* (New York: New York Futures Exchange), p. 8. The level of the index used here is for illustrative purposes only.

Hedgers

Hedgers are parties at risk with a commodity or an asset, which means they are exposed to price changes. They buy or sell futures contracts in order to offset their risk. In other words, hedgers actually deal in the commodity or financial instrument specified in the futures contract. By taking a position opposite to that of one already held, at a price set today, hedgers plan to reduce the risk of adverse price fluctuations — that is, to hedge the risk of unexpected price changes. In effect, this is a form of insurance. The benefits of **Barrick's** hedging program during the recent period of low gold prices are illustrated in the Real-World Returns box below.

In a sense, the real motivation for all futures trading is to reduce price risk. With futures, risk is reduced by having the gain in the futures position offset the loss on the cash position and vice versa. A hedger is willing to forego some profit potential in exchange for having someone else assume part of the risk. Figure 20-2 illustrates the hedging process as it affects the return-risk distribution. Notice that the unhedged position not only has a greater chance of a larger loss but also a greater chance of a larger gain. The hedged position has a smaller chance of a low return but also a smaller chance of a high return.

Figure 20-2
Return Distributions for Hedged and Unhedged Positions

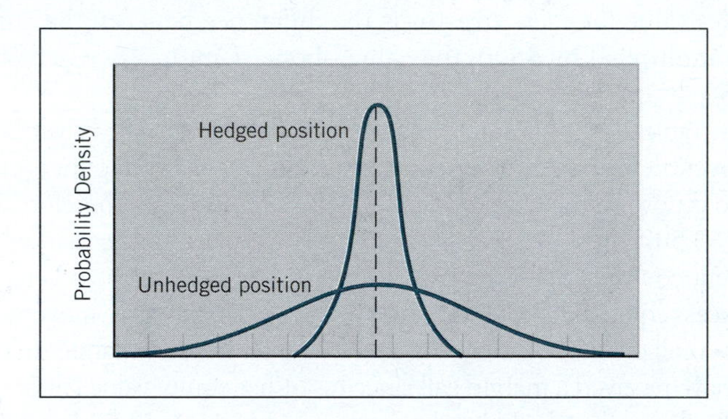

The use of hedging techniques illustrates the trade-off that underlies all investing decisions: Hedging reduces the risk of loss, but it also reduces the return possibilities relative to the unhedged position. Thus, hedging is used by investors who are uncertain of future price movements and who are willing to protect themselves against adverse price movements at the expense of possible gains. There is no free lunch!

How to Hedge with Futures

The key to any hedge is that a futures position is taken opposite to the position in the cash market. That is, the nature of the cash market position determines the hedge in the futures market.[10] A commodity or financial instrument held (in effect, in inventory) represents a long position because these items could be sold in the cash market. On the other hand, an investor who sells a futures contract has created a short position. Since investors can assume two basic positions with futures contracts, long and short, there are two basic hedge positions.

[10] The cash position may currently exist (a cash hedge) or may be expected to exist in the future (an anticipatory hedge).

REAL-WORLD RETURNS

Barrick Beats Market Turmoil

No one seems to have told **Barrick Gold Corp.** about the constant turmoil in gold markets.

The Toronto-based mining company reported a 25-per cent increase in its second-quarter profit yesterday, continuing its trend of growing profitability despite a long-term drop in the price of gold to 20-year lows.

"We are making more money today than ever before, selling our gold for three times the cost of production," chief executive officer Randall Oliphant said.

The company also disclosed more positive news about exploration at its new Pascua project on the border of Chile and Argentina, saying it has committed $20-million more for exploration at the site this year.

Barrick said it drilled a surface hole during the second quarter that has the best results of any the company has created since its Meikle discovery hole in 1989 at its Goldstrike property in Nevada, possibly making Pascua the biggest gold and silver deposit in South America.

The positive news comes as many gold companies are in a prolonged slump — continuing to make Barrick a favourite with analysts.

"Barrick was expected to be the most profitable gold mining company in North America this year, and is doing just that," said Larry Strauss, a gold analyst at Canaccord Capital Corp. in Toronto. "The company grew by acquisition and acquired low-cost mines. Coupled with its hedging program, it has met with a lot of success."

Barrick's share price climbed 55 cents to $27.20 yesterday on the Toronto Stock Exchange.

Barrick said yesterday that it earned a profit of $84-million (US) or 20 cents a share in the second quarter, up from $67-million or 18 cents last year. Revenue climbed to $373-million from $293-million.

The company said its gold production was up 29 per cent to 969,324 ounces in the second quarter, compared with 754,459 million last year. And the cash cost of producing an ounce of gold fell to $128, compared with $161. Barrick said it is on track to meet its target of lowering cash production costs to $125 an ounce this year from $160 last year.

One of Barrick's biggest advantages over other mining companies is its extensive hedging program, which allows it to sell forward its gold production and earn even more by investing the money for the term of the contract. Although gold has fallen to 20-year lows this year, closing at $256.40 an ounce yesterday, Barrick still is reaping the gains of sales it booked three years ago.

The company said its hedging program added $208-million to revenue in the first half of 1999, allowing it to realize an average sales price of $385 an ounce, a premium of $105 above the average $280-an-ounce spot price of gold in the first six months this year.

Barrick currently has 13.3 million ounces of gold sold forward at an average price of $385 an ounce, providing a huge cushion for a company that expects to produce 3.6 million ounces this year.

Mr. Strauss said the continuing excellent news about exploration at the Pascua site is exciting, but the big question is whether Barrick will commit the money to develop a mine at the site while gold prices are still so low.

"It's a contentious point in a $250 gold market whether to spend nearly $1-billion developing anything," he said.

The company still has made no decision about developing a mine at Pascua.

However, Barrick plans to add another $20-million to its planned exploration spending of $10-million at Pascua in the second half of the year. It said it has confirmed that mineralization at the site extends from Chile into Argentina, and that a drill hole had nearly 300 metres with a grade of 4.86 grams of gold a tonne, the best hole since Meikle. The company plans to extend its Pascua pit at least one kilometre into Argentina.

Another positive sign is at the company's new Pierina Mine in Peru, which opened last November. It contributed 554,469 ounces, or about one-quarter of the company's total output for the first six months this year, at a cash cost of only $38 an ounce.

However, Barrick spokesman Vincent Borg said the mine is expected to yield a lower grade of ore in the second half of the year, and that it is not realistic to expect full-year production will be double that in the first half.

He said Barrick has not yet changed its forecast that Pierina will produce 835,000 ounces this year at an average cash cost of $45 an ounce.

Source: Excerpted from Janet Mcfarland, "Barrick Beats Market Turmoil with 25-Per-Cent Rise in Profit," The Globe and Mail / Report on Business, *July 23, 1999, pp. B1, B6. Reprinted with permission from* The Globe and Mail.

1. *The short (sell) hedge*. A cash market inventory holder must sell (short) the futures. Investors should think of short hedges as a means of protecting the value of their portfolios. Since they are holding securities, they are long in the cash position and need to protect themselves against a decline in prices. A **short hedge** reduces, or possibly eliminates, the risk taken in a long position.

Short Hedge
A transaction involving the sale of futures (a short position) while holding the asset (a long position).

2. *The long (buy) hedge*. An investor who currently holds no cash inventory (holds no commodities or financial instruments) is, in effect, short in the cash market; therefore, to hedge with futures requires a long position. Someone who is not currently in the cash market but who plans to be in the future and wants to lock in current prices and yields until cash is available to make the investment can use a **long hedge**, which reduces the risk of a short position.

Long Hedge
A transaction where the asset is currently not held but futures are purchased to lock in current prices.

Hedging is not an automatic process. It requires more than simply taking a position. Hedgers must make timing decisions as to when to initiate and end the process. As conditions change, hedgers must adjust their hedge strategy.

One aspect of hedging that must be considered is "basis" risk. The basis for financial futures often is defined as the difference between the cash price and the futures price of the item being hedged:[11]

$$\text{Basis} = \text{Cash price} - \text{Futures price}$$

The basis must be zero on the maturity date of the contract. In the interim, the basis fluctuates in an unpredictable manner and is not constant during a hedge period. Basis risk, therefore, is the risk that hedgers face as a result of unexpected changes in basis. Although changes in the basis will affect the hedge position during its life, a hedge will reduce risk as long as the variability in the basis is less than the variability in the price of the asset being hedged. At maturity, the futures price and the cash price must be equal, resulting in a zero basis. (Transaction costs can cause discrepancies.)

The significance of basis risk to investors is that risk cannot be entirely eliminated. Hedging a cash position will involve basis risk.

[11] The typical definition for basis is the cash price minus the futures price. For financial futures, the definition is often reversed.

Speculators

In contrast to hedgers, speculators buy or sell futures contracts in an attempt to earn a return. They are willing to assume the risk of price fluctuations, hoping to profit from them. Unlike hedgers, speculators typically do not transact in the physical commodity or financial instrument underlying the futures contract. In other words, they have no prior market position. Some speculators are professionals who do this for a living; others are amateurs, ranging from the very sophisticated to the novice. Although most speculators are not actually present at the futures markets, floor traders (or locals) trade for their own accounts as well as others and often take very short-term (minutes or hours) positions in an attempt to exploit any short-lived market anomalies.

Speculators are essential to the proper functioning of the futures market, absorbing the excess demand or supply generated by hedgers and assuming the risk of price fluctuations that hedgers wish to avoid. Speculators contribute to the liquidity of the market and reduce the variability in prices over time.

Why speculate in futures markets? After all, one could speculate in the underlying instruments. For example, an investor who believed interest rates were going to decline could buy Government of Canada bonds directly and avoid the bond futures market. The potential advantages of speculating in futures markets include:

1. *Leverage*. The magnification of gains (and losses) can easily be 10 to 1.
2. *Ease of transacting*. An investor who thinks interest rates will rise will have difficulty selling bonds short, but it is very easy to take a short position in a bond futures contract.
3. *Transaction costs*. These are often significantly smaller in futures markets.

By all accounts, an investor's likelihood of success when speculating in futures is not very good, and the small investor is up against stiff odds.

FINANCIAL FUTURES

Financial futures are futures contracts on equity indexes, fixed-income securities, and currencies. They give investors a greater opportunity to fine-tune the risk-return characteristics of their portfolios. In recent years, this flexibility has become increasingly important as interest rates have become much more volatile and as investors have sought new techniques to reduce the risk of equity positions. The drastic changes that have occurred in the financial markets in the last 15 to 20 years could be said to have generated a genuine need for new financial instruments that allow market participants to deal with these changes.

Financial Futures Futures contracts on financial assets such as equity indexes, fixed-income securities, and currencies.

The procedures for trading financial futures are the same as those for any other commodity, with a few exceptions. At maturity, stock-index futures settle in cash because it would be impossible or impractical to deliver all the stocks in a particular index.[12] The expanded limit for maximum daily price fluctuations on TSE 35 Index futures is 20.25 index points (or $10,125 per contract), while for TSE 100 Index futures the limit is 24.75 index points (or $12,375 per contract). US stock-index futures typically have no daily price limits (although they can be imposed).

[12] Gains and losses on the last day of trading are credited and debited to the long and short positions in the same way — marked to the market — as was done for every other trading day of the contract. Therefore, not only is there no physical delivery of securities, but also the buyer does not pay the full value of the contract at settlement.

We will divide the subsequent discussion of financial futures into the two major categories of contracts: interest rate futures and stock-index futures. Hedging and speculative activities within each category are discussed separately.

Interest Rate Futures

Bond prices are highly volatile, and investors are exposed to adverse price movements. Financial futures allow bondholders and others who are affected by volatile interest rates to transfer the risk. One of the primary reasons for the growth in financial futures is that portfolio managers and investors are trying to protect themselves against adverse movements in interest rates. An investor concerned with protecting the value of fixed-income securities must consider the possible impact of interest rates on the value of these securities.

Today's investors have the opportunity to consider several different interest rate futures contracts that are traded on various exchanges.[13] Available short-term interest rate futures contracts include Three-Month Canadian Bankers' Acceptance (BA) Futures (BAX), which have traded on the ME since April 1988, and One-Month BA Futures (BAR), available since 1992. The contract unit for the BAX is $1 million principal of BAs, while the unit for the BAR is $3 million of principal. The minimum price fluctuation for both contracts is 1 basis point (i.e. 0.01) or $25 per contract and prices are quoted on a basis of 100 minus the yield on the underlying BA (based on an index of 100 points). There is no maximum daily price fluctuation for either contract.

Available long-term interest rate futures contracts include ten-year Government of Canada bond futures (CGB), which have traded on the ME since September of 1989, and five-year Government of Canada bond futures (CGF) since 1995. The contract unit for both of these futures contracts is $100,000 nominal value of Government of Canada bonds, however, the five-year bond futures are for government bonds with a 6 per cent coupon rate, while the ten-year bond futures are for government bonds with a 9 per cent coupon rate. Prices for both contract types are quoted per $100 nominal value (e.g., 97.58), just like bonds. The minimum price fluctuation is one basis point or $10 per contract, and the maximum daily price fluctuation is three points (or $3,000 per contract) above or below the previous day's settlement price.

In the United States, the Chicago Mercantile Exchange trades contracts on US Treasury bills and the one-month London Interbank Offered Rate (LIBOR) as well as Eurodollars. The Chicago Board of Trade (CBT) specializes in longer-maturity instruments, including Treasury notes (of various maturities, such as two-year and five-year) and Treasury bonds (of different contract sizes). Contracts are available on various maturities of US Treasury notes in trading units of $100,000 and $200,000, on Treasury bonds in units of both $50,000 and $100,000, and on Treasury bills in trading units of $1 million. The contracts for US Treasury bonds are by far the most important.[14]

---

[13] The Chicago Board of Trade launched financial futures trading in 1975 by opening trading in Government National Mortgage Association (GNMA or Ginnie Mae) bonds. The concept accelerated in 1976, when the International Monetary Market started trading in Treasury bills. Treasury bond futures appeared in 1977.

[14] Futures prices on Treasury bonds are quoted with reference to an 8 per cent, 20-year bond. Settlement prices are translated into a settlement yield to provide a reference point for interest rates.

Hedging with Interest Rate Futures

We now consider an example of using interest rate futures to hedge an investment position. Our objective here is to illustrate the basic concepts involved in such a hedge. In this example, we concentrate on the short hedge since it is by far the more common and discuss the concept of the long hedge later in the chapter.

Short Hedge

Suppose an investor has a bond portfolio and wishes to protect the value of his or her position.[15] This type of hedge is sometimes referred to as the inventory hedge.

EXAMPLE: SHORT HEDGING ON GOVERNMENT OF CANADA BONDS

On November 1, 1999, a pension fund manager holds $1 million principal (or face) value of 10 per cent Government of Canada bonds due June 1, 2009. The manager plans to sell the bonds four months in the future but wishes to protect their value against a rise in interest rates. Since assets are owned (a long position), a short hedge is used.

To protect the position, the manager hedges by going short (selling) in the futures market. As illustrated in Table 20-5, the manager sells 10 March 2000 ten-year Government of Canada bond contracts (since each contract is worth $100,000) at a current price of $126.55. In this example, we assume interest rates have risen by March 1, 2000. This produces a loss on the cash side (i.e., in the prices of the bonds held in the cash market) and a gain on the futures side (i.e., the manager can cover the short position at a lower price, which produces a profit). The futures position in this example more than offsets the cash market loss resulting in a net profit $10,500.[16]

The manager in this example was able to offset more than 100 per cent of the cash market loss because the Government of Canada bond contract is based on 9 per cent coupon bonds, whereas the manager was holding 10 per cent bonds. In this example, the dollar value of lower coupon bonds changes by a larger amount than the dollar value of higher coupon bonds, for the given change in yields. However, if interest rates had fallen, the loss on the futures contract would have exceeded the profit on the long bond position, resulting in a loss. One way

---

[15] This example is similar to one used by *US Treasury Bond Futures* (Chicago: Chicago Board of Trade), p. 10.

[16] The $96,900 gain on the futures contract in Table 20-5 is calculated as follows: The gain per contract is $9,690 = [(126.55 − 116.86) × 1,000]. Since each contract is based on par value of $100,000, the gain is: $96,900 = ($9,690 × 10 contracts).

to overcome this difference is to execute a "weighted" short hedge, adjusting the number of futures contracts used to hedge the cash position. For example, using the data in Table 20-5, selling 9 March contracts would result in a profit on the futures position of $87,390, which is very close to the $86,400 cash market loss.[17]

Table 20-5

Illustration of Hedges Using Interest Rate Futures: A Short Hedge

Cash Market	Futures Market
Short Hedge	
November 1, 1999	November 1, 1999
Hold $1 million principal value of 10% Government of Canada bonds maturing June 1, 2008	Sells 10 ten-year Government of Canada bond futures contracts at a price of $126.55
Current market price: $136.25 (yielding 5.15%)	
March 1, 2000	March 1, 2000
Sells $1 million principal value of 10% bonds at $127.61	Buys 10 bond futures contracts at $116.86 (to close out position)
Loss: $86,400 (i.e., $1,276,100 − $1,362,500)	Gain: $96,900 (i.e., $1,265,500 − $1,168,600)

Other Hedges

An alternative hedge is the anticipatory hedge, whereby an investor purchases a futures contract as an alternative to buying the underlying security. At some designated time in the future, the investor will purchase the security and sell the futures contract. This results in a net price for the security position at the future point in time which is equal to the price paid for the security minus the gain or loss on the futures position.

Consider an investor who would like to purchase an interest rate asset now but will not have the cash for three months. If rates drop, the asset will cost more at that point in time. By purchasing a futures contract on the asset now, as a hedge, the investor can lock in the interest rate implied by the interest rate futures contract. This may be a good substitute for not being able to lock in the current interest rate because of the lack of funds now to do so. At the conclusion of this transaction, the investor will pay a net price which reflects the ending cash price minus the gain on the futures contract. In effect, the gain on the futures increases the rate of return earned on the interest rate asset.

[17] The market value of the nine futures contracts changes from an initial value of $1,138,950 to $1,051,560. Different bonds are related to the nominal 9 per cent coupon, 10-year Government of Canada bond used in the futures contract by means of a set of conversion factors that represent the relative values of the various deliverable bonds. The conversion factor for the 10 per cent coupon bond used in this example, rounded off, is 0.90.

Speculating with Interest Rate Futures

Investors may wish to speculate with interest rate futures as well as to hedge with them. To do so, investors make assessments of likely movements in interest rates and assume a futures position that corresponds with this assessment. If the investor anticipates a rise in interest rates, he or she will sell one (or more) interest rate futures, because a rise in interest rates will drive down the prices of bonds and therefore the price of the futures contract. The investor sells a contract with the expectation of buying it back later at a lower price. Of course, a decline in interest rates will result in a loss for this investor, since the price will rise.

EXAMPLE: SPECULATING ON GOVERNMENT OF CANADA BONDS

Assume that in November a speculator thinks interest rates will rise over the next month and wishes to profit from this expectation. The investor can sell one December ten-year Government of Canada bond futures contract at a price of 126.55. One month later the price of this contract has declined to 120 because of rising interest rates. This investor would have a gain of 6.55, or $6,550, and could close out this position by buying an identical contract.

The usefulness of interest rate futures for pursuing such a strategy is significant. A speculator who wishes to assume a short position in bonds cannot do so readily in the cash market (either financially or mechanically). Interest rate futures provide the means to short bonds easily.

In a similar manner, investors can speculate on a decline in interest rates by purchasing interest rate futures. If the decline materializes, bond prices and the value of the futures contract will rise. Because of the leverage involved, the gains can be large; however, the losses can also be large if interest rates move in the wrong direction.

Stock-Index Futures

Stock-index futures trading was initiated in 1982 with several contracts quickly being created. Although stock-index futures are unavailable on individual stocks as in the case of options, investors can trade futures contracts on major market indexes such as the TSE 35 Index and the TSE 100 Index, which will eventually be replaced by contracts on the S&P/TSE 60 Index. The contract size for each of these indexes is $500 times the index level. Several other futures contracts are available on other stock indexes around the world.

Delivery is not permitted in stock-index futures because of its impracticality. Instead, each remaining contract is settled by cash on the settlement day by taking an offsetting position using the price of the underlying index. For example, the cash settlement price for the TSE indexes is $500 times the closing index value to the nearest two decimal places.

Stock-index futures offer investors the opportunity to act on their investment opinions concerning the future direction of the market. They need not select individual stocks, and it is easy to short the market. Furthermore, investors who are concerned about unfavourable short-term market prospects but remain bullish for the longer run can protect themselves in the interim by selling stock-index futures.

Hedging With Stock-Index Futures

Common stock investors hedge with financial futures for the same reasons that fixed-income investors use them. Investors, whether individuals or institutions, may hold a substantial stock portfolio that is subject to the risk of the overall market, that is, systematic risk. A futures contract enables the investor to transfer part or all of the risk to those willing to assume it. Stock-index futures have opened up new, and relatively inexpensive, opportunities for investors to manage market risk through hedging.

Chapter 8 pointed out the two types of risk inherent in common stocks: systematic risk and non-systematic risk. Diversification will eliminate most or all of the non-systematic risk in a portfolio but not the systematic risk. Although an investor could adjust the beta of the portfolio in anticipation of a market rise or fall, this is not an ideal solution because of the changes in portfolio composition that might be required.

Investors can use financial futures on stock market indexes to hedge against an overall market decline. That is, investors can hedge against systematic or market risk by selling the appropriate number of contracts against a stock portfolio. In effect, stock-index futures contracts give an investor the opportunity to protect his or her portfolio against market fluctuations.

To hedge market risk, investors must be able to take a position in the hedging asset (in this case, stock-index futures), such that profits or losses on the hedging asset offset changes in the value of the stock portfolio. Stock-index futures permit this action because changes in the futures prices themselves generally are highly correlated with changes in the value of the stock portfolios that are caused by marketwide events. The more diversified the portfolio, and therefore the lower the non-systematic risk, the greater the correlation between the futures contract and the stock positions.

Figure 20-3 shows the price of the S&P 500 Index futures plotted against the value of a portfolio that is 99 per cent diversified. That is, market risk accounts for 99 per cent of its total risk.[18] The two track each other very closely, which demonstrates that stock-index futures can be very effective in hedging the market risk of a portfolio.

Figure 20-3
The Value of a Well-Diversified Stock Portfolio Versus the Price of the S&P 500 Index Futures

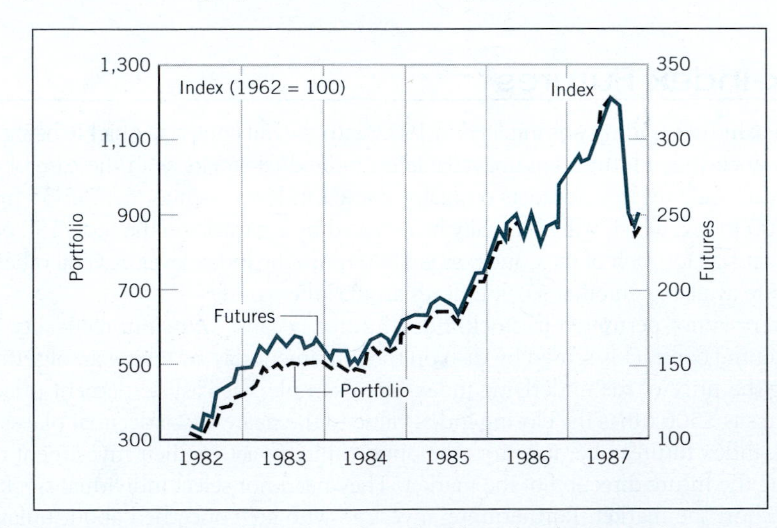

Source: Charles S. Morris, "Managing Stock Market Risk with Stock Index Futures," Economic Review 74 *(June 1989), p. 9. Reprinted with permission from the Federal Reserve Bank of Dallas.*

[18] This example is taken from C.S. Morris, "Managing Stock Market Risk with Stock Index Futures," *Economic Review* 74 (June 1989), pp. 3–16.

Short Hedges

Since so much common stock is held by investors, the short hedge represents a natural type of contract for most investors. Investors who hold stock portfolios hedge market risk by selling stock-index futures, which means they assume a short position.

A short hedge can be implemented by selling a forward maturity of the contract. The purpose of this hedge is to offset (in total or in part) any losses on the stock portfolio with gains on the futures position. To implement this defensive strategy, an investor would sell one or more index futures contracts. Ideally, the value of these contracts would equal the value of the stock portfolio. If the market falls, leading to a loss on the cash (the stock portfolio) position, stock-index futures prices will also fall, leading to a profit for sellers of futures.

The reduction in price volatility that can be accomplished by hedging is shown in Figure 20-4, which compares the performance of a well-diversified portfolio (the unhedged one) with the same portfolio hedged by sales of the S&P 500 Index futures. Clearly, there is much less variability in the value of the hedged portfolio as compared to the value of the unhedged one. In fact, the volatility of the returns is 91 per cent lower.[19] Notice in particular what happened in the great market crash of October 1987. The value of the unhedged portfolio fell some 19 per cent, whereas the value of the hedged one fell only 6 per cent.

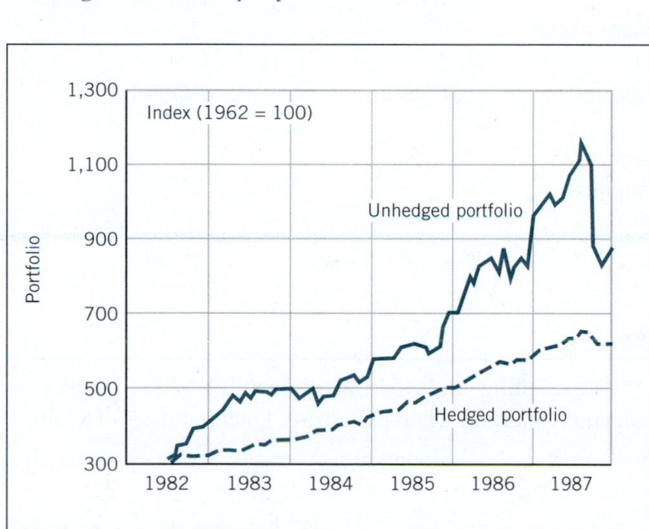

Figure 20-4
The Value of a Well-Diversified Portfolio Versus the Value of the Same Portfolio Hedged by Sales of S&P 500 Index Futures

Source: Charles S. Morris, "Managing Stock Market Risk with Stock Index Futures," Economic Review *74 (June 1989), p. 10. Reprinted with permission from the Federal Reserve Bank of Dallas.*

Table 20-6 (top) illustrates the concept of a short hedge using the TSE 35 Index futures contract when it is at 343.80. Assume that an investor has a portfolio of stocks valued at $175,000 that he or she would like to protect against an anticipated market decline. By selling one TSE 35 stock index future at 343.80, the investor has a short position of $171,900, because the value of the contract is $500 times the index quote. As the table illustrates, a decline in the stock market of 10 per cent results in a loss on the stock portfolio of $17,500 and a gain on the futures position of $17,190 (ignoring commissions). Thus, the investor almost makes up on the short side what is lost on the long side.

[19] Ibid.

Table 20-6

Examples of Short and Long Hedges Using Stock-Index Futures

Short Hedge	Current Position	Position after a 10% Market Drop	Change in Position
(Long position) Dollar value of portfolio	$175,000	$157,500	($17,500)
(Short position) Sell one TSE 35 Index futures contract at 343.80	$171,900	$154,710	$17,190
Net gain or loss after hedging			($310)

Long Hedge	Current Position	Position after a 10% Market Increase	Change in Position
(Long position) Buy one TSE 35 Index futures contract at 343.80	$171,900	$189,090	$17,190
Amount of money to be invested in stocks (i.e., cost of stock position)	$175,000	$192,500	($17,500)
Net gain or loss after hedging			($310)

Long Hedges

The long hedger, while awaiting funds to invest, generally wishes to reduce the risk of having to pay more for an equity position when prices rise. Potential users of a long hedge include:

- Institutions with a regular cash flow that use long hedges to improve the timing of their positions.
- Institutions switching large positions who wish to hedge during the time it takes to complete the process. (This could also be a short hedge.)

Assume an investor with $175,000 to invest believes that the stock market will advance but has been unable to select the stocks he or she wishes to hold. By purchasing one TSE 35 Index future, the investor will gain if the market advances. As shown in Table 20-6, a 10 per cent market advance will increase the value of the futures contract $17,190. Although in this example, the investor has to pay 10 per cent more (on average) for stocks purchased after the advance, he or she only pays $310 more than $175,000 because of the gain on the futures position.

Limitations of Hedging with Stock-Index Futures

Although hedging with stock-index futures can reduce an investor's risk, generally risk cannot be eliminated completely. As with interest rate futures, basis risk is present with stock-index futures. It represents the difference between the price of the stock-index futures contract and the value of the underlying stock index. A daily examination of the "Futures Prices" section of *The Globe and Mail*, the *National Post*, or *The Wall Street Journal* will show that each of the indexes quoted under the respective futures contracts differs from the closing price of the contracts.[20]

Basis risk as it applies to common stock portfolios can be defined as the risk that remains after a stock portfolio has been hedged.[21] Note here that stock-index futures hedge only systematic (market) risk. That is, when we consider a stock portfolio hedged with stock-index futures, the basis risk is attributable to nonsystematic (nonmarket or firm-specific) risk.

Figure 20-5a illustrates the effects of basis risk by comparing the value of a relatively undiversified portfolio with the price of the S&P 500 futures contract. In contrast to the 99 per cent diversified portfolio in Figure 20-3, this one is only 66 per cent diversified. Although the two series are related, the relationship is in no way as close as that illustrated in Figure 20-3. Therefore, stock-index futures will be less effective at hedging the total risk of the portfolio, as shown in Figure 20-5b. In this situation, the variance of returns on the hedged portfolio is only 27 per cent lower than the unhedged position. Note that in the crash of October 1987 both portfolios fell sharply, demonstrating that the hedge was relatively ineffective. (It did better than the unhedged position but not by much.)

From this analysis we can see that stock-index futures generally do not provide a good hedge for relatively undiversified portfolios.

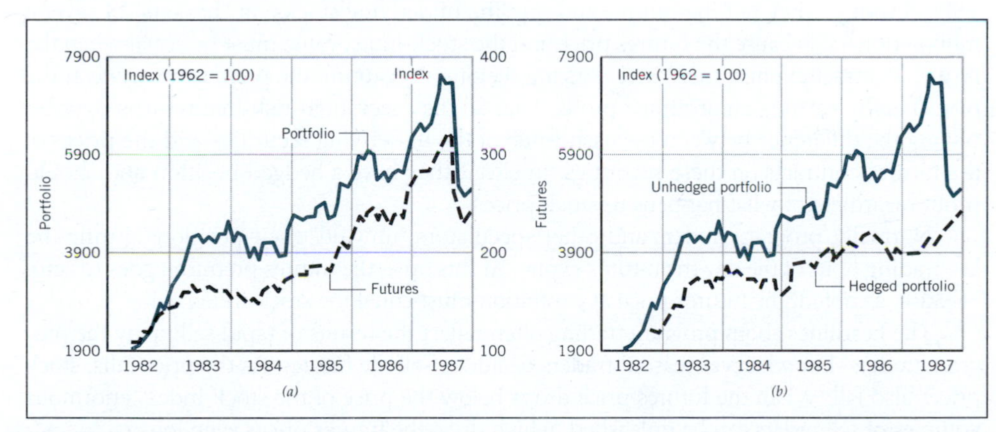

Figure 20-5
(*a*) The Value of a Relatively Undiversified Stock Portfolio and the Price of the S&P 500 Index Futures Contracts
(*b*) The Value of the Unhedged Portfolio and the Same Portfolio Hedged by Sales of S&P 500 Futures Contracts

Source: Charles S. Morris, "Managing Stock Market Risk with Stock Index Futures," Economic Review 74 *(June 1989), pp. 12–13. Reprinted with permission from the Federal Reserve Bank of Dallas.*

[20] Futures prices are generally more volatile than the underlying indexes and therefore diverge from them. The index futures tend to lead the actual market indexes. If investors are bullish, the futures are priced at a premium, with greater maturities usually associated with greater premiums. If investors are bearish, the futures are normally priced at a discount, which may widen as maturity increases.

[21] This discussion is based heavily on C.S. Morris, "Managing Stock Market Risk with Stock Index Futures," *Economic Review* 74 (June 1989), pp. 11–13.

Index Arbitrage and Program Trading

Program trading (see Chapter 4) hit Bay and Wall Streets in the 1980s, and it has captured much attention and generated considerable controversy. It leads to headlines attributing market plunges at least in part to program trading, as happened on October 19, 1987, when North American and world stock markets plummeted. Because program trading typically involves positions in both stocks and stock-index futures contracts, the topic is within the general discussion of hedging.

Index Arbitrage
Exploitation of price differences between stock-index futures and the index of stocks underlying the futures contract.

Program trading is commonly used for portfolio insurance applications, which were discussed in Chapter 19. It is also used for **index arbitrage**, which refers to attempts to exploit the differences between the prices of the stock-index futures and the prices of the index of stocks underlying the futures contract. For example, if the TSE 35 Index futures price is too high relative to the TSE 35 Index, investors could short the futures contract and buy the stocks in the index. In theory, arbitrageurs should be able to build a hedged portfolio that earns arbitrage profits equaling the difference between the two positions. If the price of the TSE 35 Index futures is deemed too low, investors could purchase the futures and short the stocks, again exploiting the differences between the two prices.

If investors are to be able to take advantage of discrepancies between the futures price and the underlying stock-index price, they must be able to act quickly. Program trading involves the use of computer-generated orders to coordinate buy and sell orders for entire portfolios based on arbitrage opportunities. The arbitrage occurs between portfolios of common stocks, on the one hand, and index futures and options, on the other. Large institutional investors seek to exploit differences between the two sides. Specifically, when stock-index futures prices rise substantially above the current value of the stock-index itself (e.g., the TSE 35 Index), they sell the futures and buy the underlying stocks, in "baskets" of several million dollars. Because the futures price and the stock-index value must be equal when the futures contract expires, these investors are seeking to "capture the premium" between the two, thereby earning an arbitrage profit. That is, they seek high risk-free returns by arbitraging the difference between the cash value of the underlying securities and the prices of the futures contracts on these securities. In effect, they have a hedged position and should profit regardless of what happens to stock prices.

Normally, program traders and other speculators "unwind" their positions during the last trading hour of the day the futures expire. At this time, the futures premium goes to zero, because, as noted, the futures price at expiration must equal the stock-index value.

The headlines about program trading often reflect the results of rapid selling by the program traders. For whatever reason, traders decide to sell the futures. As the price falls, stock prices also fall. When the futures price drops below the price of the stock index, enormous volumes of sell orders can be unleashed, which drive the futures prices even lower.

Speculating with Stock-Index Futures

In addition to the previous hedging strategies (and others not described), investors can speculate with stock-index futures if they wish to profit from stock market volatility by judging and acting on the likely market trends. Stock-index futures are effective instruments for speculating on movements in the stock market because minimal costs are involved in establishing a futures position, and stock-index futures mirror the market, offering just as much risk.

We can refer to one group of speculators as "active traders." These individuals are willing to risk their capital on price changes they expect to occur in the futures contracts. Such individuals are often sophisticated investors who are seeking the opportunity for large gains and who understand the risk they are assuming.

The strategies of active traders basically include long and short positions. Traders who expect the market to rise buy index futures. Because of the high leverage, the profit opportunities are great; however, the loss opportunities are equally great. The same is true for traders expecting a market decline who assume a short position by selling a stock-index futures contract. Selling a contract is a convenient way to go short on the entire market. It can be done at any time. (No wait for an uptick is required, as with stock short sales.)

Another form of speculation involves spreaders, who establish both long and short positions at the same time. Their objective is to profit from changes in price relationships between two futures contracts. There are two major types of spreads:

1. The intra-market spread, also known as a calendar or time spread. This spread involves contracts for two different settlement months, such as buying a March contract and selling a June contract.
2. The inter-market spread, also known as a quality spread. This spread involves two different markets, such as buying a S&P 500 Index contract and selling a TSE 35 Index contract (both for the same month).

Spreaders are interested in relative price as opposed to absolute price changes. If two different contracts appear to be out of line, the spreader hopes to profit by buying one and selling the other and waiting for the price difference to adjust. This adjustment may require the spread between the two contracts to widen in some cases and narrow in others.

SUMMARY

This summary relates to the learning objectives provided on page 647.

1. **Describe the structure of futures markets.**
   Futures markets play an important role in risk management. Spot markets are for immediate delivery, while forward markets are markets for deferred delivery. An organized futures exchange standardizes the non-standard forward contracts, with only the price and number of contracts left for futures traders to negotiate.
2. **Outline how futures work and what types of investors participate in futures markets.**
   A futures contract designates a specific amount of a particular item to be delivered at a specified date in the future at a currently determined market price. Buyers assume long positions and sellers assume short ones. A short position indicates only that a contract not previously purchased is sold. Most contracts are settled by offset, whereby a position is liquidated by an offsetting transaction. The clearing house is on the other side of every transaction and ensures that all payments are made as specified. Contracts are traded on designated futures exchanges, which set minimum price changes and may establish daily price limits. Futures positions must be closed out within a specified time. There are no

certificates and no specialists to handle the trading, so that each futures contract is traded in an auction market process by a system of open outcry. Margin, the norm in futures trading, is the good faith deposit made to ensure completion of the contract. All futures contracts are marked to the market daily; that is, all profits and losses are credited and debited to each investor's account daily. Hedgers buy or sell futures contracts to offset the risk in some other position. Speculators buy or sell futures contracts in an attempt to earn a return, and their role is valuable to the proper functioning of the market.

3. **Explain how financial futures are used.**
   Interest rate futures, one of the two principal types of financial futures, allow investors to hedge against, and speculate on, interest rate movements. Numerous contracts are available on both domestic and foreign instruments. Investors can, among other transactions, execute short hedges to protect their long positions in bonds. Stock-index futures are presently available on the TSE 35 and the TSE 100 Indexes in Canada and on numerous international indexes. Investors can use stock-index futures to hedge the systematic risk of common stocks, that is, the risk of broad market movements. Short hedges protect a stock position against a market decline, and long hedges protect against having to pay more for an equity position because prices rise before the investment can be made. Index arbitrage refers to attempts to exploit the differences between the prices of the stock-index futures and the prices of the index of stocks underlying the futures contract.

KEY TERMS

Financial futures
Futures contract
Futures margin
Index arbitrage
Long hedge
Long position
Marked to the market
Offset
Short hedge
Short position
Swap (Appendix 20-B)

ADDITIONAL RESOURCES

The Canadian Securities Institute offers the Derivatives Fundamental Course and the Futures Licensing Course. These two courses must be completed in sequence (in addition to the Canadian Securities Course and the Conduct and Practices Handbook Course) before an individual can serve as an investment advisor involved in trading futures. These courses contain useful reference materials for the student who is interested in futures.

An excellent discussion of futures, as well as options, can be found in:
Hull, John. *Introduction to Futures and Options Markets*. Third Edition. Englewood Cliffs, NJ: Prentice Hall, 1998.

Chance, Don M. *An Introduction to Derivatives*. Third Edition. Orlando, FL: The Dryden Press, 1995.

A good tutorial on financial futures is available through the Association for Investment Management and Research (AIMR) as part of the CFA curriculum by contacting PBD, Inc., P. O. Box 6996, Alpharetta, GA, 30239-6996 (800/789-AIMR):

Clarke, Roger G. *Options and Futures: A Tutorial*. The Research Foundation of the Institute of Chartered Financial Analysts, P. O. Box 3668, Charlottesville, VA, 1992.

REVIEW QUESTIONS

1. Carefully describe a futures contract.
2. Explain how futures contracts are valued daily and how most contracts are settled.
3. Describe the role of the clearing house in futures trading.
4. What determines whether an investor receives a margin call?
5. Explain the differences between a hedger and a speculator.
6. Given a futures contract on Government of Canada bonds, determine the dollar price of a contract quoted at 98.50.
7. Describe the differences between trading in stocks and trading in futures contracts.
8. How do financial futures differ from other futures contracts?
9. What is meant by basis? When is the basis positive?
10. When might a portfolio manager with a bond position use a short hedge involving interest rate futures?
11. Is it possible to construct a perfect hedge? Why or why not?
12. What is the difference between a short hedge and a weighted short hedge using interest rate futures?
13. Why would an investor have preferences among the different stock-index futures?
14. What type of risk does stock-index futures allow investors to hedge? Why would this be desirable?
15. Explain how a pension fund might use a long hedge with stock-index futures.
16. When would an investor likely do the following?
    a. Buy a call on a stock index future.
    b. Buy a put on interest rate futures.
17. What is program trading? How does it work?
18. (Refer to Appendix 20-A for this question.) With regard to futures options, fill in the following blanks with either "less than" or "greater than." The current futures price is 75.
    a. Put options with strike prices _________ 75 are in the money.
    b. Call options with strike prices _________ 75 are out of the money.
    c. Put options with strike prices _________ 75 are out of the money.
    d. Call options with strike prices _________ 75 are in the money.

PREPARING FOR YOUR PROFESSIONAL EXAMS

Special Note to CSC Students

Ensure that you have read and understood the following topics:*

Why futures markets?, pp. 648–649
The structure of futures markets, pp. 652–654
The mechanics of trading, pp. 654–657
Using futures contracts, pp. 657–661
Financial futures, pp. 661–662
Stock-index futures, p. 665
Index arbitrage and program trading, p. 670
Appendix 20-A: Futures Options, pp. 677–678
Appendix 20-B: Other Derivative Securities, pp. 678–680

**Reading these CSC-related topics should provide you with additional understanding of CSC material. However, it should not be seen as a substitute for reading the CSC textbook itself, which is the basis for the CSC exam.*

CSC REGISTRATION QUESTIONS

The Canadian Securities Institute issued the following sample questions in the 1997 CSC registration package as a means for students to self-assess their understanding of CSC-related material.

1. A computerized trading strategy designed to profit from price discrepancies between equity and futures markets is called ___________.
   a. formula investing
   b. program trading
   c. market surveillance
   d. efficient market trading
2. Two major types of participants in the futures markets are hedgers and _________.

PAST CFA EXAM QUESTIONS AND PROBLEM

The following question was asked on the 1993 CFA Level II Examination:

1. Michelle Industries issued a Swiss franc-denominated five-year discount note for SFr 200 million. The proceeds were converted to US dollars to purchase capital equipment in the United States. The company wants to hedge this currency exposure and is considering the following alternatives:
   a. At-the-money Swiss franc call options
   b. Swiss franc forwards
   c. Swiss franc futures

Contrast the essential characteristics of each of these three derivative instruments. Evaluate the suitability of each in relation to Michelle's hedging objective, including both advantages and disadvantages.

The following questions were asked on the 1996 CFA Level I Sample Examinations:

2. An investor in the common stock of companies in a foreign country may wish to hedge against the ______________ of the investor's home currency and can do so by ______________ the foreign currency in the forward market.
   a. depreciation; selling
   b. appreciation; purchasing
   c. appreciation; selling
   d. depreciation; purchasing
3. Which of the following best describes a stock-index arbitrage strategy?
   a. taking a long or short position in the cash (spot) market represented by a market basket of stocks
   b. trading in stock-index futures contracts and in individual stocks when a divergence occurs between the cash (stock) price of the market and the futures price
   c. trading call and put stock options in each stock represented in a market index
   d. selling stock-index futures contracts when the stock market falls

The following problem was asked on the 1993 CFA Level I Examination:

4. Chris Smith of XYZ Pension Plan has historically invested in the stocks of only US domiciled companies. Recently, he has decided to add international exposure to the plan portfolio.
   a. Identify and briefly discuss three potential problems that Smith may confront in selecting international stocks that he did not face in choosing US stocks.

   Rather than select individual stocks, Smith decides to use Nikkei futures to obtain his Japanese portfolio exposure. The Nikkei index is now at 15,000 with a 2 per cent dividend yield and the Japanese risk-free interest rate is 5 per cent.

   b. Calculate the price at which Smith can expect a six-month Nikkei futures contract to trade. Show all work.

PROBLEMS

1. An investor buys one March TSE 35 Index futures contract on February 1 at 340.00. The position is closed out after five days. The prices on the four days after purchase were 338.60, 339.80, 342.20, and 345.00. The initial margin is $7,000.
   a. Calculate the current equity on each of the next four days.
   b. Calculate the excess equity for these four days.
   c. Calculate the final gain or loss for the week.
   d. Recalculate (a), (b), and (c) assuming that the investor had been short over this same period.
2. Given the information in Problem 1, assume that the investor holds until the contract expires. Ignore the four days after purchase and assume that on the next to last day of trading in March the investor was long and the final settlement price on that date was 346. Calculate the cumulative profit.
3. Calculate the dollar gain or loss on Government of Canada bond futures contracts for the following transactions. In each case the position is held six months before closing it out.
   a. Sell 10 bond contracts at a price of 102.80 and buy 10 at 101.50.
   b. Sell 10 bond contracts at a price of 98.60 and buy 10 at 100.
   c. Buy 15 bond contracts at 110.20 and sell 15 at 112.30.
   d. Sell one bond contract at 98.50 and buy one at 105.
4. Assume a portfolio manager holds $1 million of 7.5 per cent Government of Canada bonds due in five years. The current market price is 111.62, for a yield of 4.88 per cent. The manager fears a rise in interest rates in the next three months and wishes to protect this position against such a rise by hedging in futures.
   a. Ignoring weighted hedges, what should the manager do?
   b. Assume five-year Government of Canada bond futures contracts are available at 104.21, and the price three months later is 99.20. If the manager constructs the correct hedge, what is the gain or loss on this position?
   c. The price of the Government of Canada bonds three months later is 105.50. What is the gain or loss on this cash position?
   d. What is the net effect of this hedge?

APPENDIX 20-A

FUTURES OPTIONS

In Chapter 19 we discussed options (puts and calls) on common stocks. In this chapter we discussed interest rate futures and stock-index futures. A more recent innovation in financial instruments is a combination of the two, futures options. The development of this new instrument is a good example of the ever-changing nature of financial markets, where new instruments are developed to provide investors with opportunities that did not previously exist.

Put and call options are offered on both interest rate futures and stock-index futures. In Canada in 1997, 156,000 option contracts on futures were traded, accounting for 3.20 per cent of the total CDCC exchange-traded options. Available financial futures options in Canada include options on ten-year Government of Canada bond futures, and on three-month BA futures, which trade on the ME. In addition, options trade on the Winnipeg Commodity Exchange on canola futures, flaxseed futures, domestic feed wheat futures and western domestic feed barley futures.

There are several options on futures contracts available in the United States, including (but not limited to):

- Options on foreign exchange: Pound, mark, Swiss franc, yen, Canadian dollar, and a US dollar index
- Options on interest rate futures: US Treasury bills, notes, and bonds and municipal bonds
- Options on stock-index futures: The S&P 500 Index (traded on the Chicago Mercantile Exchange (CME)), the NYSE Composite Index (traded on the New York Futures Exchange), and the Nikkei 225 Stock Average (CME)
- Options on commodities: Agricultural, oil, livestock, metals, and lumber.

Recall from Chapter 19 that an option provides the purchaser with the right, but not the obligation, to exercise the claim provided by the contract. An option on a futures contract gives its owner the right to assume a long or short position in the respective futures contract. If this right is exercised, the holder's position will be at the exercise (strike) price of the option that was purchased. For example, the exerciser of a call option buys the futures contract at the exercise price stated in the call option.

The key elements of an option contract on a particular futures contract are the exercise price and the premium. As in the case of stock options, premiums are determined in competitive markets. Each put and call option is either in the money or out of the money. With an in-the-money call option, the exercise price is less than the current price of the underlying futures contract. (If the exercise price is greater than the current price, it is out of the money.) For put options, the reverse is true.

Options on futures contracts can serve some of the same purposes as the futures contracts themselves. Specifically, both futures contracts and options can be used to transfer the risk of adverse price movements from hedgers to speculators. For example, a portfolio manager with bond holdings (a long position) who expects a rise in interest rates can hedge against the risk of the capital losses resulting from such a rise by selling futures contracts on government bonds. Alternatively, futures options on government bonds can be used to hedge against this risk because the option's price will change in response to a change in the price of the underlying commodity.

A rise in interest rates is bearish (bond prices will fall), therefore, the portfolio manager would either buy a put or sell a call. The value of these options would rise as the price of the futures contract declined. On the other hand, an investor bullish on bond prices (i.e., one who expects interest rates to decline) would either buy a call or sell a put. In addition to these simple strategies, a number of spreading techniques can be used with options on bond futures.

The general appeal of options on futures contracts is the limited liability assumed by the purchaser. Unlike a futures contract, which has to be settled by some means (say, by offset), once the contract is bought the purchaser has no additional obligation. Moreover, unlike futures, the purchaser is not subject to margin calls. Even if a speculator in futures is ultimately correct in his or her expectations, margin calls in the interim can wipe out all the equity. A writer (seller) of an option on a futures contract, however, does have an obligation to assume a position (long or short) in the futures market at the strike price if the option is exercised.[22] Sellers must deposit margin when opening a position.

APPENDIX 20-B

OTHER DERIVATIVE SECURITIES

Swaps

Swap
A cash settled forward agreement with a series of predetermined payments.

A **swap** is a type of cash settled forward agreement, however, unlike traditional forward agreements, there is a *series* of predetermined payments. In other words, one could view swaps as a series of forward agreements. The swap market is used extensively by banks for short-term (and to a much lesser extent for long-term) financing. Three types are discussed below: 1) interest rate swaps, 2) foreign exchange or currency swaps, and 3) swaptions.

1. *Interest rate swaps* represent agreements to exchange cash flows on an agreed upon formula. It is important to note that the notional or principal amount is not exchanged, either at initiation or maturity of the contract. The most common formula involves the exchange of payments based on a fixed interest rate, for floating rate payments of interest, based on some notional amount of principal. This is often referred to as a "plain vanilla" interest rate swap. Margins are required by both parties (unless one counter-party is a large chartered bank), and the floating rates are reviewed periodically. Floating rates are typically tied to Canadian bankers' acceptance rates or the six-month LIBOR (London Interbank Offered Rate).

EXAMPLE: "PLAIN VANILLA" INTEREST RATE SWAP

The notional value for a swap is $10 million, and the term is three years. Party A agrees to make fixed annual payments to Party B, based on a fixed interest rate of 8 per cent (i.e., A agrees to pay B $800,000 per year). Party B agrees to make payments to Party A based on the prevailing bankers' acceptance rate plus 50 basis points (or 0.50 per cent).

[22] This discussion is based on Stanley W. Angrist, "It's Your Option," *Forbes*, February 28, 1983, p. 138.

On the day the swap was arranged the BA rate was 7.75 per cent, so the floating rate to be paid by Party B would be 8.25 per cent (or $10 million × 0.0825 = $825,000). As a result, the net payment would have B pay A $25,000 ($825,000 – $800,000). However, this is subject to change because the BA rate is a floating rate and its level changes on a daily basis. For example, the floating rate paid by Party B could fall to 7 per cent (if the BA rate fell to 6.5 per cent), or rise to 9 per cent (if the BA rate rose to 8.5 per cent). Obviously, B feels the floating rate will fall, while A feels it will rise, unless one of the parties has entered into the agreement for hedging purposes.

2. *Foreign exchange swaps or currency swaps* are similar to interest rate swaps, however, there are two important differences:
   i. The cash flows are denominated in two different currencies, and hence the notional amount *is* actually exchanged at the beginning and end of the contract.
   ii. These swaps do not necessarily have to be fixed for floating, but can be fixed for fixed.

   Currency swaps involve two market transactions — for example, the sale of US dollars to buy Canadian dollars today (the near date), and the sale of Canadian dollars and purchase of US dollars at a specified future date (the far date) and price. The difference between the spot price and forward price is referred to as a premium if the forward is greater than the spot. If it is less, it is called a discount. The size of the premium or discount depends on the interest rate differential between the two currencies.

EXAMPLE: CURRENCY SWAP

Spot rate is $1.3873 Canadian per US$, term is 30 days, discount is 0.0004, so the forward price is (spot – discount) $1.3869 per US$. Suppose the US funds can be borrowed at a 3.50 per cent interest rate.

This implies the equivalent cost of borrowing funds in Canada is:

$$3.50\% - [(\text{discount/spot}) \times (365/30) \times 100] = 3.50\% - 0.35\% = 3.15\%.$$

3. *Swaptions* are options that give the holder the right, but not the obligation, to enter into a swap agreement. The advantage of swaptions over straight swaps is the limited risk characteristics, as well as the non-obligation by the buyer of the swaption contract. In other words, a swap obligates a party to a future transaction, while a swaption provides the right, but not the obligation, to enter into such future transactions.

Embedded Options

Embedded options include features such as convertible, callable, retractable, and extendible features associated with some debt or preferred share issues. Convertibles enable the holder to convert the bond (or preferred shares) into common shares at a predetermined conversion price — hence they have an embedded call option. The price of this option can be inferred by the difference between the price of a convertible bond, and the price of a similar non-convertible bond (which should sell for less since it has no conversion feature attached).

Callable bonds enable the corporation to buy back the bonds at a predetermined call price, which implies the buyer of a callable bond is selling the bond issuer a call option. The cost of this option would be the difference between the price of a callable and a similar non-callable bond. The non-callable bonds would sell for a greater price because they do not provide the bond issuers with the call privilege (the risk of which is borne by the bondholder).

Retractable bonds enable the bondholder to sell the bond back to the corporation at a predetermined price. This is analogous to the bond issuer writing a put option on the bond, which is held by the bond owner. Once again, the option price can be viewed as the difference in the prices of similar retractable versus non-retractable bonds (which will sell for less because they do not contain the retraction privilege).

An extendible bond allows the bondholder to extend the maturity date of the bonds beyond some more recent maturity date. This can be thought of as a short-term bond, with an option to purchase an additional bond at a predetermined price. Hence they include an embedded call option that is held by the bond owner, and was written by the bond issuer. As a result of this privilege, extendible bonds sell for a greater price than similar non-extendible bonds, the difference representing the cost of the embedded call option.

CHAPTER 21

PORTFOLIO MANAGEMENT

LEARNING OBJECTIVES

After reading this chapter, you will be able to

1. Discuss why portfolio management should be considered a process.
2. Describe the steps involved in the portfolio management process.
3. Assess related issues such as asset allocation.

CHAPTER PREVIEW

In this chapter we discuss how and why portfolio management should be thought of as a process. An understanding of the process allows any portfolio manager to apply a consistent framework to the management of a portfolio for any investor, whether individual or institutional. We walk through the steps of the process, from developing an investment policy to measuring and evaluating portfolio performance. We also consider related topics such as taxes, protection against inflation, how expectations about future market returns are formed, and the life cycle of investors.

PORTFOLIO MANAGEMENT AS A PROCESS

Portfolio management involves a series of decisions and actions that must be made by every investor, individual or institutional. Portfolios must be managed whether investors follow a passive or an active approach to selecting and holding their financial assets such as stocks and bonds. As we saw when we examined portfolio theory, the relationships among the various investment alternatives which are held as a portfolio must be considered if an investor is to hold an optimal portfolio and achieve his or her investment objectives.

Portfolio management can be thought of as a process. Having the process clearly in mind is very important and allows investors to proceed in an orderly manner. In this chapter we outline the investment management process, making it clear that a logical and orderly flow does exist. This process can be applied to each investor and investment manager. Details may vary from client to client, but the process remains the same.

The portfolio management process has been described by Maginn and Tuttle in their book that forms the basis for portfolio management as envisioned by the Association for Investment Management and Research (AIMR) and advocated in its curriculum for the CFA designation.[1] This is also the approach advocated by the Canadian Securities Course. It is important to develop a standardized framework rather than treating portfolio management on an ad hoc basis, matching investors with portfolios on an individual basis, one by one. Portfolio management should be structured so that any investment organization can carry it out in an effective and timely manner without serious omissions.

Maginn and Tuttle emphasize that portfolio management is a process, integrating a set of activities in a logical and orderly manner. Given the feedback loops and monitoring that are included, the process is both continuous and systematic. It is a dynamic and flexible concept that encompasses all portfolio investments, including real estate, precious metals, and other real assets.

The portfolio management process extends to all types of investment organizations and styles. In fact, Maginn and Tuttle specifically avoid advocating how the process should be organized, who should make the decisions, and so forth. Each investment management organization must decide for itself how best to carry out its activities, consistent with viewing portfolio management as a process.

Having structured portfolio management as a process, any portfolio manager can execute the necessary decisions for an investor. The process provides a framework and a control over

[1] John L. Maginn and Donald L. Tuttle, editors, *Managing Investment Portfolios*, Second Edition (Charlottesville, VA: Association for Investment Management and Research, 1990). This chapter follows the format advocated in this book and is indebted to it for much of the discussion.

the diverse activities involved and allows every investor, individual or institution, to be accommodated in a systematic, orderly manner.

As outlined by Maginn and Tuttle, portfolio management is an ongoing process by which:

1. Objectives, constraints, and preferences are identified for each investor. This leads to the development of explicit investment policies.
2. Strategies are developed and implemented through the choice of optimal combinations of assets. (This step relates to our discussion of portfolio theory in Part II.)
3. Market conditions, relative asset mix, and the investor's circumstances are monitored.
4. Portfolio adjustments are made as necessary to reflect significant changes that have occurred.

Figure 21-1 explains the portfolio construction, monitoring, and revision process in more detail. Notice that we begin with the specification of investor objectives, constraints, and preferences. This specification leads to a statement of portfolio policies and strategies. Next, capital market expectations for the economy as well as individual assets are determined and quantified.

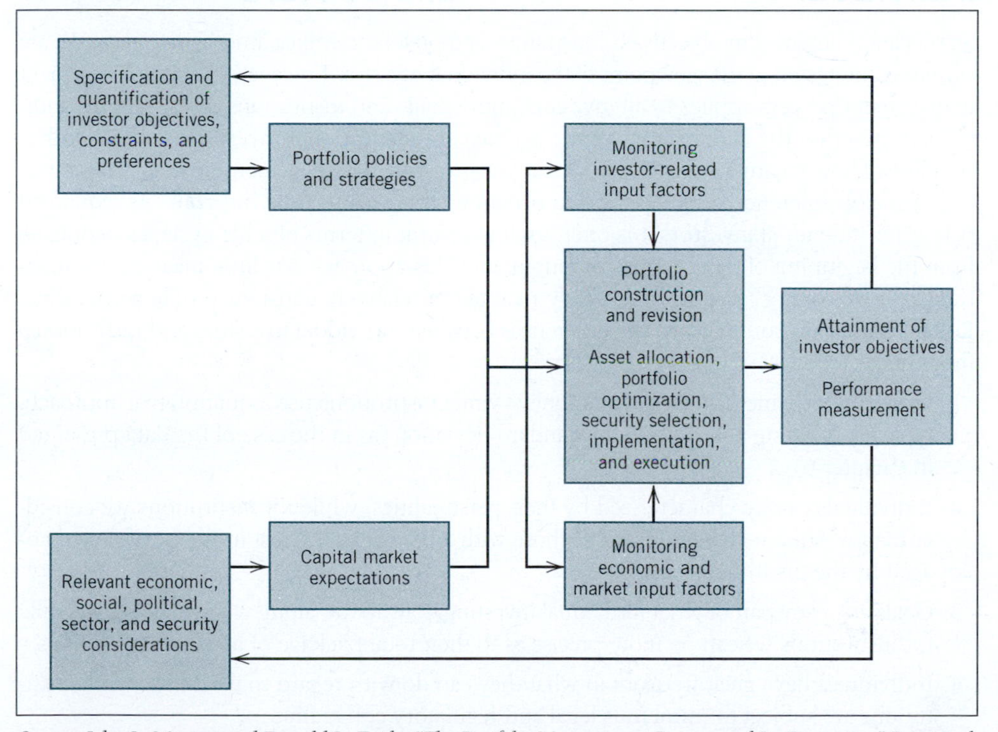

Figure 21-1
The Portfolio Construction, Monitoring, and Revision Process

Source: John L. Maginn and Donald L. Tuttle, "The Portfolio Management Process and Its Dynamics," Reprinted with permission from Managing Investment Portfolios, *Second Edition. Copyright 1990, Association for Investment Management and Research, Charlottesville, VA. All rights reserved.*

The combination of portfolio policies/strategies and capital market expectations provides the investment manager with the basis for portfolio construction and revision. This includes the asset allocation decision (discussed in Chapter 8), a very important determinant of the success of the investment program. Also included here are the portfolio optimization and security selection stages of portfolio management; that is, we must determine appropriate portfolio strategies and techniques for each asset class and the selection of individual securities.

Monitoring is an important part of the process. As indicated in Figure 21-1, the portfolio manager should monitor both investor-related input factors as well as economic and market input factors and rebalance as necessary. For example, the manager may need to respond to any changes in investor objectives and constraints and/or capital market expectations. Finally, the process concludes with the attainment of investor objectives. In order to assess success, we must measure and evaluate portfolio performance, which is discussed in Chapter 22.

We will discuss these steps in more detail below, but first we consider the differences between individual and institutional investors. As we noted in Chapter 2, investors can invest directly and indirectly through institutional investors, and an understanding of both types of investment decision making is important.

Individual Versus Institutional Investors

Significant differences in objectives, constraints, and preferences exist among investors. We are primarily interested in the viewpoint of the individual investor; however, the basic investment management process applies to all investors, individuals and institutions. Furthermore, individuals are often the beneficiaries of the activities of institutional investors, and an understanding of how institutional investors fit into the investment management process is desirable.

A major difference between the two occurs with regard to time horizons. As explained below, for individual investors it is often useful to think in terms of a life cycle, as people go from the beginning of their careers to retirement. This approach has little meaning for institutional investors because they generally maintain a relatively constant profile across time. Ronald Kaiser has summarized the differences between individual investors and institutional investors as follows:[2]

1. Individuals define risk as "losing money," while institutions use a quantitative approach, typically defining risk in terms of standard deviation (as in the case of the data presented in Chapter 6).
2. Individuals can be characterized by their personalities, while for institutions we consider the investment characteristics of those with a beneficial interest in the portfolios managed by the institutions.
3. Goals are a key part of what individual investing is all about, along with their assets, while for institutions we can be more precise as to their total package of assets and liabilities.
4. Individuals have great freedom in what they can do with regard to investing, while institutions are subject to numerous legal and regulatory constraints.
5. Taxes often are a very important consideration for individual investors, whereas many institutions, such as pension funds, are free of such considerations.

[2] Ronald W. Kaiser, "Individual Investors," in John L. Maginn and Donald L. Tuttle, editors, *Managing Investment Portfolios*, Second Edition (Charlottesville, VA: Association for Investment Management and Research, 1990).

The implications of all of this for the investment management process are as follows:

- For individual investors: Because each individual's financial profile is different, an investment policy for an individual investor must incorporate that investor's unique factors. In effect, preferences are self-imposed constraints. To investor A, after-tax income may be the most important factor, while for investor B safety of principal may be the paramount consideration.
- For institutional investors: Given the increased complexity in managing institutional portfolios, it is critical to establish a well-defined and effective policy. Such a policy must clearly delineate the objectives being sought, the institutional investor's risk tolerance, and the investment constraints and preferences under which it must operate.

The primary reason for establishing a long-term investment policy for institutional investors is twofold:

1. It prevents arbitrary revisions of a soundly designed investment policy
2. It helps the portfolio manager to plan and execute on a long-term basis and resist short-term pressures that could derail the plan.[3]

FORMULATE AN APPROPRIATE INVESTMENT POLICY

The determination of portfolio policies — referred to as the investment policy — is the first step in the investment process. It summarizes 1) the objectives and 2) constraints and preferences for the investor. A recommended approach in formulating an **investment policy** is simply to provide information, in the following order, for any investor, individual or institutional:

Investment Policy The first step in the portfolio management process, involving investor objectives, constraints, and preferences.

1. Objectives:

- return requirements
- risk tolerance

2. Constraints and preferences:

- liquidity
- time horizon
- laws and regulations
- taxes
- unique preferences and circumstances

A useful starting point for investment advisors working with individual investors is to have clients fill out the New Client Application Form (see Figure 21-2), and review this with the client. This provides an opportunity for both the advisor and the investor to formalize objectives and identify the relevant constraints and preferences associated with achieving these objectives. Each of these items is discussed in turn below.

[3] "Portfolio Management: The Portfolio Construction Process," in *1997 CFA Level I Candidate Readings* (Charlottesville, VA: Association for Investment Management and Research 1997), p. 177.

Figure 21-2
New Client Application Form

TABLE 1
New Client Application Form
(to be completed by Investment Advisor)

Account Supervision			
Office	Account		I.A.

(1) (a) Name Mr / Mrs / Miss (Please Print)

Home (Street)
Address (City) (Province) (Postal Code)

Phones: Home / Business / Other / Fax

Date of Birth . Client's Social Insurance Number . Client's Citizenship

(b) Is I.A. registered in the Province or Country in which the client resides? Yes / No

Type of Account Requested: Cash / Margin / D.A.P / RRSP/RRIF / Other / Pro / U.S. Funds / CDN Funds

(2) Special Instructions: Hold in Account / Duplicate Confirmation / And/Or Statement
Name:
Address:
Postal Code:

Register And Deliver . DAP
Name:
Address:
Postal Code:

(3) Client's Employer: Name / Address
Type of Business
Client's Occupation

(4) Family Information:
Spouse' Name
Occupation
No. of Dependents
Employer
Type of Business

(5) How long have you know client? Advertising Lead / Personal Contact / Phone In / Walk In
Have you met the client face to face? Yes / No
Referral by: (name) (if customer, give account no,)

(6) If yes for Questions 1, 2, or 3, provide details in (11)

1.	Will any other person or persons: (a) Have trading authorization in this account?	No	Yes
	(b) Guarantee this account?	No	Yes
	(c) Have a financial interest in such accounts?	No	Yes
2.	Do any of the signatories have any other accounts or control the trading in such accounts?	No	Yes
3.	Does client have accounts with other Brokerage firms? (Type______________)	No	Yes
4.	Is the account (a) discretionary or (b) managed	(a)	(b)
	Insider Information		
5.	Is client a senior officer or director of a company whose shares are traded on an exchange or in the OTC markets?	No	Yes
6.	Does the client, as an individual or as part of a group, hold or control such a company? (______________________)	No	Yes

(7)

(a) General Documents	Attached	Obtaining
– Client's Agreement		
– Margin Agreement		
– Cash Agreement		
– Guarantee		
– Other		

(b) Trading Authorization Documents:	Attached	Obtaining
– For an Individual's Account		
– For a Corporation. Partnership, Trust, etc.		
– Discretionary Authority		
– Managed Account Agreement		

(8) INVESTMENT KNOWLEDGE: Sophisticated / Good / Limited / Poor/Nil

ACCOUNT OBJECTIVES
Income ___ %
Capital Gains
Short Term ___ %
Medium Term ___ %
Long Term ___ %
100%

ACCOUNT RISK FACTORS
Low ___ %
Medium ___ %
High ___ %
100%

EST. NET LIQUID ASSETS (Cash and securities less loans outstanding against securities) A
PLUS
EST. NET FIXED ASSETS (Fixed assets less liabilities outstanding against fixed assets) B
EQUALS
EST. TOTAL NET WORTH (A + B = C) C
APPROXIMATE ANNUAL INCOME FROM ALL SOURCES D
EST. SPOUSE'S INCOME E

(9) Bank Reference: Name / Branch / Refer to / Accounts
Bank credit check-acceptable? Yes / No
Or Credit Bureau cheack-acceptable? Yes / No
Above credit checks considered unnecessary Explain in (11)

(10) Deposit and/or Security Received
Initial Order / Buy / Sell / Solicited / Unsolicited / Amount / Description

(11) I.A. Signature
Designated Officer, Director or Branch Manager's Approval
Date:
Date of Approval
Comments:

Revised April 26, 1994

Source: Canadian Securities Course Textbook *(Toronto: Canadian Securities Institute, August 1998), p. 12-8.*

Objectives

Portfolio objectives are always going to centre on return and risk because these are the two aspects of most relevance to investors. Investors seek returns, but must assume risk in order to have an opportunity to earn the returns. The best way to describe the objectives is to think in terms of the return-risk trade-off developed in Chapter 1 and emphasized throughout the text. Expected return and risk are related in an upward-sloping manner.

We know from Chapter 7 that investors must think in terms of expected returns, which implicitly or explicitly involves probability distributions. The future is uncertain, and the best that investors can do is to make estimates of likely returns over some holding period, such as one year. Because the future is uncertain, mistakes are inevitable, but this is simply the nature of investing decisions. Estimates of expected returns must be made regardless of the uncertainties, using the best information and investment processes available.

The issue of the life cycle of investors fits into this discussion because of its impact on the individual investor's risk and return preferences. The conventional approach is to think in terms of the risk/return trade-off as discussed throughout this text. This is shown in part (a) of Figure 21-3.

Alternatively, the life cycle approach can be depicted as shown in part (b) of Figure 21-3. Here we see four different phases in which individual investors view their wealth, although it is important to note that the boundaries between the stages are not necessarily clear-cut and can require years to complete. Furthermore, an individual can be in several of these stages at the same time. The four phases are:

1. *Accumulation Phase*. In the early stage of the life cycle, net worth is typically small, but the time horizon is long. Investors can afford to assume large risks.
2. *Consolidation Phase*. In this phase, involving the mid-to-late career stage of the life cycle when income exceeds expenses, an investment portfolio can be accumulated. A portfolio balance is sought to provide a moderate trade-off between risk and return.
3. *Spending Phase*. In this phase, living expenses are covered from accumulated assets rather than earned income. While there is still some risk-taking, the emphasis is on safety, resulting in a relatively low position on the risk/return trade-off.
4. *Gifting Phase*. In this phase, the attitudes about the purpose of investments change. The basic position on the trade-off remains about the same as in Phase 3.

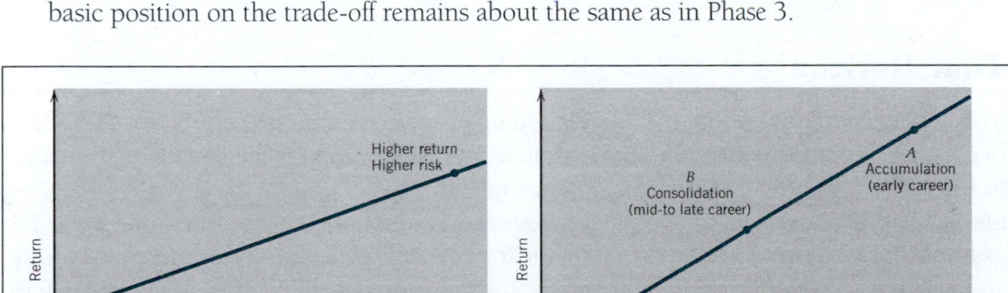

Figure 21-3
Risk/Return Position at Various Life Cycle Stages

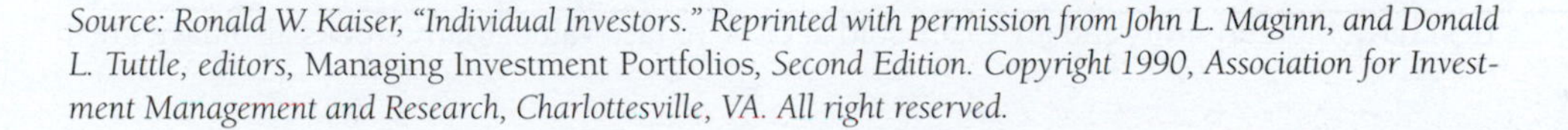

Source: Ronald W. Kaiser, "Individual Investors." Reprinted with permission from John L. Maginn, and Donald L. Tuttle, editors, Managing Investment Portfolios, *Second Edition. Copyright 1990, Association for Investment Management and Research, Charlottesville, VA. All right reserved.*

Inflation Considerations

An investment policy statement often will contain some statement about inflation-adjusted returns because of the impact of inflation on investor results over long periods of time. For example, a wealthy individual's policy statement may be stated in terms of maximum after-tax, inflation-adjusted total return consistent with the investor's risk profile. Another investor's primary return objective may be stated as inflation-adjusted capital preservation, perhaps with a growth-oriented mix to reflect the need for capital growth over time.

Inflation is clearly a problem for investors. The inflation rate of over 12 per cent in 1981 had a horrific impact on investors' real wealth. But even with a much lower inflation the damage can be substantial. It can persist steadily, eroding values. At a 3 per cent inflation rate, for example, the purchasing power of a dollar is cut in half in less than 25 years. Therefore, someone retiring at age 60 who lives to 85 and does not protect him- or herself from inflation will lose half their purchasing power over the years.

Contrary to some people's beliefs, common stocks do not always provide an inflationary hedge. In fact (as discussed in Chapters 13 through 17), high levels of inflation tend to have an adverse affect on stock market returns due to the upward pressure it exerts on interest rates, although the affect is usually less severe for stocks than for bonds. For example, inflation exceeded 12 per cent in Canada in both 1974 and 1982 and the returns on the TSE 300 Composite Index in those years were −25.93 per cent and −10.25 per cent respectively. Obviously being fully invested in stocks would have only accelerated the deterioration in wealth in those years. The converse is also true — low levels of inflation are good for stock prices. For example, a contributing factor to the strong stock market performance in Canada in 1995 (14.53 per cent return) and 1996 (28.35 per cent) was the historically low and steady rates of inflation of 1.75 and 2.17 per cent respectively.

Constraints and Preferences

To complete the investment policy statement, these items are described for a particular investor as the circumstances warrant. Since investors vary widely in their constraints and preferences, these details may vary widely also.

Time Horizon

Investors need to think about the time period involved in their investment plans. The objectives being pursued may require a policy statement that speaks to specific planning horizons. In the case of an individual investor, for example, this could well be the investor's expected lifetime. In the case of an institutional investor, the time horizon could be quite long. For example, for a company with a defined-benefit retirement plan whose employees are young, and which has no short-term liquidity needs, the time horizon would extend several decades.

Liquidity Needs

As noted in Chapter 2, liquidity is the ease with which an asset can be sold without a sharp change in price as the result of selling. Obviously, cash equivalents (money market securities) have high liquidity and are easily sold at close to face value. Many stocks also have great liquidity, but the price at which they are sold will reflect their current market valuations, which can vary substantially.

Investors must decide how likely they are to sell some part of their portfolio in the short run. As part of the asset allocation decision, they must decide how much of their funds to keep in cash equivalents.

Tax Considerations

Unlike some institutional investors, individuals must consider the impact of taxes on their investment programs. Taxes are an important issue because of the differential tax rate, with capital gains and dividends being taxed at a rate lower than ordinary income so that the interest income from bonds is taxed at a higher rate than capital gains or dividend income. Furthermore, the tax laws in Canada are continually changing, making it difficult for investors to forecast the tax rate that will apply in the future. Refer to Appendix 2-A at the end of Chapter 2 for a detailed discussion of the Canadian tax environment.

In addition to the differential tax rates and their changes over time, the capital gains component of security returns benefits from the fact that tax is not payable until the gain is realized. This tax deferral is, in effect, a tax-free loan that remains invested for the benefit of the taxpayer.

Retirement programs offer tax sheltering whereby any income and/or capital gains taxes are avoided until such time as the funds are withdrawn. Investors with various retirement and taxable accounts must grapple with the issue of which type of account should hold stocks as opposed to bonds. This is important because bonds generate higher current income in the form of interest payments, which are taxed at a higher rate than capital gains or dividend income.

Legal and Regulatory Requirements

Investors must obviously deal with regulatory requirements growing out of both common law and the rulings and regulations of provincial and federal agencies. Individuals are subject to relatively few such restrictions, unlike institutions, such as pension funds that must comply with several legal and regulatory requirements.

With regard to fiduciary responsibilities, one of the most famous concepts is the Prudent Man Rule.[4] This rule, which concerns fiduciaries, goes back to 1830, although it was not formally stated until more than 100 years later. Basically, the rule states that anyone, in managing assets for another party, shall act like people of "prudence, discretion and intelligence" act in governing their own affairs.

The important aspect of the Prudent Man Rule is its flexibility because interpretations of it can change with time and circumstances. In the past, this standard was applied to individual investments rather than the portfolio as a whole, which violates all of the portfolio building principles we learned earlier. Most legislation today requires that plan assets be diversified and that the standards being applied under the act be applied to management of the portfolio as a whole, which affords institutional investors more flexibility in performing their fiduciary duties.

[4] This discussion is indebted to "Portfolio Management: The Portfolio Construction Process," in John L. Maginn and Donald L. Tuttle, editors, *Managing Investment Portfolios*, Second Edition (Charlottesville, VA: Association for Investment Management and Research, 1990).

Unique Needs and Circumstances

Once formulated, the investment policy is an operational statement. It clearly specifies the strategies to be taken to try to achieve the investor's goals, or objectives, given the preferences of the investor and any constraints imposed. While portfolio investment considerations are often of a qualitative nature, they help to determine a quantitative statement of return and risk requirements that are specific to the needs of any particular investor.

Investors often face a variety of unique circumstances. For example, a trust established on their behalf may specify that investment activities be limited to particular asset classes or even specified assets. Or an individual may feel that their lifespan is threatened by illness, and wish to benefit within a certain period of time.

EXAMPLE: ESTABLISHING AN INVESTMENT POLICY

To illustrate the application of the investment management process, consider a question from the Level I CFA Examination.[5] The answer is contained in a succinct but sufficient form.

A. Outline a generalized framework that could be used to establish investment policies applicable to all investors.

B. List and briefly discuss five differences in investment policy that might result from the application of your Part A framework to:

1. The pension plan of a young, fast-growing consumer products company
2. The modest life insurance proceeds received by a 60-year-old widow with two grown children.

Answers:

A. FRAMEWORK

Objectives	**Constraints**
Return	Time horizon
Risk	Liquidity needs
	Tax considerations
	Legal/regulatory issues
	Unique needs and circumstances

B. APPLICATION DIFFERENCES

	Pension Fund	**Widow's Portfolio**
Return	Total return objective	Income-oriented objective with some inflation protection
Risk	Above-average capacity; company bears risk	Somewhat below-average capacity indicated; widow bears risk; safety important
Time horizon	Long term; infinite	Medium term

[5] The question and answer are taken from Question 8 of the 1989 Level I Examination. Reprinted in *I: The CFA Study Guide, 1991* (Charlottesville, VA: The Institute of Chartered Financial Analysts), pp. 165 and 173. Used with permission.

Liquidity	Low; cash flow accrues	Probably medium to high; no reinvestment likely
Tax	Tax-exempt	Income taxes paid on most investment receipts
Legal/regulatory	Government regulated	Prudent Man Rule applies
Unique needs and circumstances	Cash flow reinvested; opportunity for compounding	Widow's needs are immediate and govern now; children's needs should be considered in future planning

DETERMINE AND QUANTIFY CAPITAL MARKET EXPECTATIONS

Forming Expectations

The forming of expectations involves two steps:

1. *Macro-expectational factors*. These factors influence the market for bonds, stocks, and other assets on both a domestic and international basis. These are expectations about the capital markets.
2. *Micro-expectational influences*. These factors involve the cause agents that underlie the desired return and risk estimates and influence the selection of a particular asset for a particular portfolio.

Rate of Return Assumptions

Most investors base their actions on some assumptions about the rate of return expected from various assets. Obviously, it is important for investors to plan their investing activities on realistic rate of return assumptions.

As a starting point, investors should study carefully the historical rates of return available from a variety of sources (some of which were discussed in Chapter 6). We know the historical mean returns, both arithmetic and geometric, and the standard deviation of the returns for major asset classes such as stocks, bonds, and bills.

Having analyzed the historical series of returns, there are several difficulties in forming expectations about future returns. For example, how much should investors be influenced by recent stock market returns, particularly when they are unusually good returns?

EXAMPLE: HISTORICAL RATES OF RETURN ON TSE 300

The cumulative gain on the TSE 300 Index for 1995–97 period was 68.2 per cent. The annual returns for these years were 14.53 per cent, 28.35 per cent, and 14.98 per cent, representing an arithmetic average return of 19.29 per cent, approximately 1.6 times the annual average return on the TSE 300 over the 1924–1997 period of 12.07 per cent.

Do investors form unrealistic expectations about future returns as a result of such activity? Over the 1924–97 period there were 19 years where the return on the TSE 300 Index was negative or on average about once every four years. In addition, many observers believe that stock returns tend to "revert toward the mean" over time — that is, periods of unusually high returns tend to be followed by periods of lower returns (although not necessarily losses), and the opposite is also true. It is interesting to note that following the high returns in the 1995–97 period, the 1998 return on the TSE 300 was negative 3.19 per cent.

Investors should recognize some key points about the historical data as they form expectations about future rates of return. The equity risk premium is often defined as the return on a stock index (such as the TSE 300 Index) minus the return on riskless assets (such as Government of Canada T-bills or Government of Canada bonds). The expected equity risk premium to be used in this calculation is based on the arithmetic mean of equity risk premiums and not the geometric mean because this is an additive relationship. As stated in the Ibbotson Associates *Yearbook*, "...the arithmetic mean is correct because an investment with uncertain returns will have a higher expected ending wealth value than an investment that earns, with certainty, its compound or geometric rate of return each year."[6]

A second key point that investors should recognize in thinking about expected rates of return, and the returns they can realistically expect to achieve, is that common stock returns involve considerable risk. While the annual average compound rate of return on Canadian common stocks for the period 1924–98 period, according to the TSE 300 data, was 11.82 per cent, that does not mean that all investors can realistically expect to achieve this historical rate of return. For example, as mentioned above, 20 out of the 75 one-year TSE 300 returns were actually negative. In addition, returns over longer periods of time such as five or 10 years, were often well below this average. For example, the average return on the TSE 300 over the 1990–94 period was a mere 5.6 per cent.

The message from this discussion is that, based on the known history of stock returns, the chance that an investor will actually achieve some compound rate of return over time from owning common stocks may not be as high as he or she believes. Common stocks are risky, and expected returns are not guaranteed. Investors must be cognizant of this fact in determining the role common stocks will play in their overall investment plan.

CONSTRUCTING THE PORTFOLIO

Having considered the objectives and constraints and formed capital market expectations, the next step is portfolio construction and revision based on the policy statement and capital market expectations. Included here are such issues as asset allocation, portfolio optimization, and security selection. In summary, once the portfolio strategies are developed, they are used along with the investment manager's expectations for the capital market and for individual assets to choose a portfolio of assets.

The portfolio construction process can be viewed from a broad perspective as consisting of the following steps (again, given the development of the investment policy statement and the formation of capital market expectations):

[6] Roger G. Ibbotson and Rex A. Sinquefield, Stocks, Bonds, Bills, and Inflation (SBBI), updated in *Stocks, Bonds, Bills, and Inflation 1996 Yearbook*™ (Chicago: Ibbotson Associates, 1996), p. 155. All rights reserved.

1. Define the universe of securities eligible for inclusion in a particular portfolio. For institutional investors, this traditionally has meant asset classes, in particular stocks, bonds, and cash equivalents. More recently, institutional investors have broadened their investment alternatives to include foreign securities, small stocks, real estate, venture capital, and so forth. This step is really the asset allocation decision, probably the key decision made by investment managers. The financial planning pyramid depicted in Figure 21-4, provides a useful tool for visualizing how particular types of assets would fit their investment objectives.
2. Utilize an optimization procedure to select securities and determine the proper portfolio weights for these securities.

Both of these steps are discussed in more detail as follows.

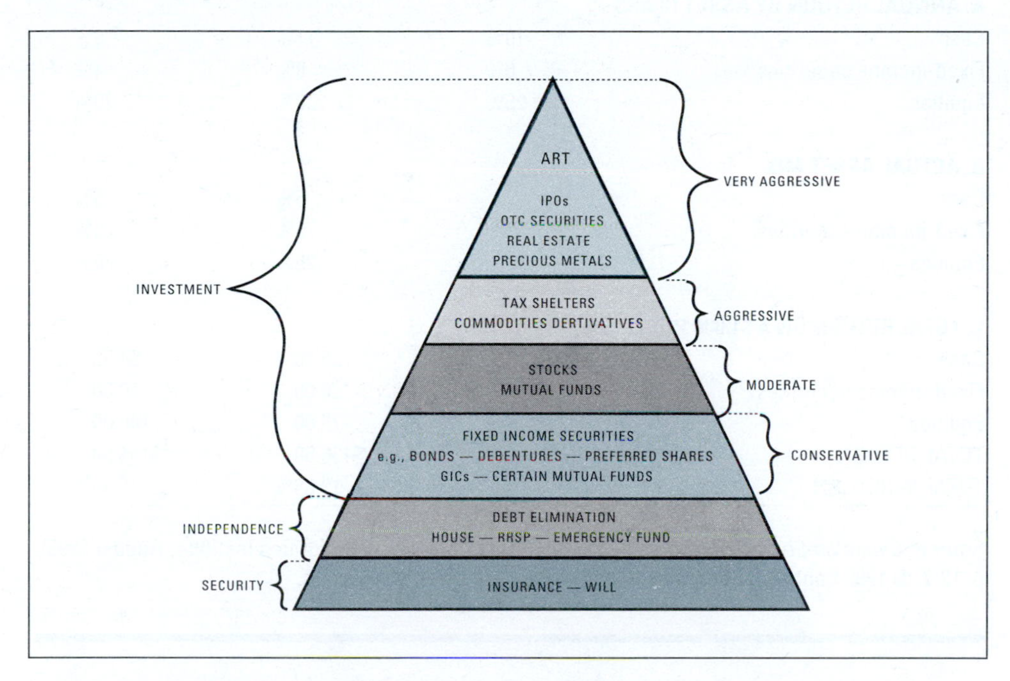

Figure 21-4
The Financial Planning Pyramid

Source: Canadian Securities Course Textbook *(Toronto: Canadian Securities Institute, August 1998), p.11-7.*

Asset Allocation

The asset allocation decision involves deciding the percentage of investable funds to be placed in stocks, bonds, and cash equivalents. It is the most important investment decision made by investors because it is the basic determinant of the return and risk taken. This is a result of holding a well-diversified portfolio, which we know is the primary lesson of portfolio management.

The returns of a well-diversified portfolio within a given asset class are highly correlated with the returns of the asset class itself. Within an asset class, diversified portfolios will tend to produce similar returns over time. However, different asset classes are likely to produce results that are quite dissimilar. Therefore, differences in asset allocation will be the key factor over time causing differences in portfolio performance. This point is demonstrated in Table 21-1, where portfolio manager Y underperforms portfolio manager X in all three asset categories (cash, fixed income, and equities), yet manager Y's overall return exceeds that of manager X due to the asset mix of the two portfolios (Y has 70 per cent in equities and 25 per cent in fixed income securities, the reverse of X).

Table 21-1

Asset Mix and Total Return

Asset Group	Index or Average	Portfolio Manager X	Portfolio Manager Y
A. ANNUAL RETURN BY ASSET CLASS			
Cash	10%	11%	9%
Fixed-income securities	6%	8%	4%
Equities	25%	30%	20%
B. ACTUAL ASSET MIX			
Cash		5%	5%
Fixed-income securities		70%	25%
Equities		25%	70%
C. TOTAL RETURN ON A $1,000 PORTFOLIO			
Cash		$5.50	$4.50
Fixed-income securities		56.00	10.00
Equities		75.00	140.00
TOTAL RETURN		$136.50	$154.50
TOTAL % RETURN		13.65%	15.45%

Source: *Canadian Securities Course Textbook* (Toronto: Canadian Securities Institute, August 1998), p. 12-7. © 1998 Canadian Securities Institute. Reprinted with permission.

The Asset Allocation Decision

Factors to consider in making the asset allocation decision include the investor's return requirements (current income versus future income), the investor's risk tolerance, and the time horizon. This is done in conjunction with the investment manager's expectations about the capital markets and about individual assets, as described above.

How asset allocation decisions are made by investors remains a subject that is not fully understood. What is known is that what investors say and what they do in deciding how to allocate assets are two different things.

According to some analyses, asset allocation is closely related to the age of an investor. This involves the so-called life-cycle theory of asset allocation. This makes intuitive sense because the needs and financial positions of workers in their 50s should differ, on average, from those who are starting out in their 20s. According to the life-cycle theory, for example, as individuals approach retirement they become more risk averse.

Table 21-2 illustrates the asset allocation decision by presenting two examples to show how major changes during life can affect asset allocation. One investor is classified as conservative and another as aggressive. They begin their investment programs and end them with different allocations, but their responses to major changes over the life cycle are similar. For example, both investors have a minimum of 50 per cent allocated to stocks at all stages of the life cycle because of the need for growth.

Table 21-2

How Major Changes Can Affect your Asset Allocation

	Conservative			Aggressive		
Asset Category	Early Career (%)	Late Career (%)	Retirement (%)	Early Career (%)	Late Career (%)	Retirement (%)
Cash	10	10	10	10	10	10
Bonds	20	30	40	0	10	10
Large-cap stocks	40	40	40	30	40	50
Small-cap stocks	15	10	5	30	20	15
International stocks	15	10	5	30	20	15

Source: Maria Crawford Scott, "How Major Changes in your Life Can Affect your Asset Allocation," *AAII Journal* (October 1995), p. 17.

Table 21-2, published in *AAII Journal*, a magazine for individual investors, is illustrative only. Different investors will choose different types of assets. Life-style changes could cause investors to move from one stage to the other, but changes in life may not cause a modification in the allocation percentages. Moreover, even among similar age groups, goals can vary substantially. Overall, asset allocation decisions may depend more upon goals than age. Thus while the life style approach may prove useful, it is not always applicable. The important point here is that all investors must make individual asset allocation decisions that will have a major impact on the investment results achieved.

It seems reasonable to assert that the level of risk aversion affects the asset allocation decision. One study examined the risk preferences of households using financial data for a large random sample of US households.[7] The definition of risk used was relative risk aversion, defined as investors' tolerance for risk as measured relative to his or her wealth level. This study found differences in relative risk aversion across three distinct categories of individuals — those 65 and older, those with very high levels of wealth, and those with incomes below the poverty level. The study also found clear patterns for asset allocation over wealth and income levels, with the proportion allocated to risky assets rising consistently with both income and wealth.

[7] William B. Riley, Jr. and K. Victor Chow, "Asset Allocation and Individual Risk Aversion," *Financial Analysts Journal* 48 (December 1992), pp. 32–37.

There are several approaches to asset allocation, some of which are described in the CSC Notes box in Chapter 14. These strategies are based on the ability to time the performance of the major financial asset categories. The most commonly referred to strategy is tactical asset allocation (TAA), which is a moderately active asset allocation approach that allows managers short-term deviations from longer-term target asset mixes to take advantage of market timing skills.

Strategic asset allocation involves adhering to a long-term mix by monitoring and rebalancing the portfolio as necessary. Integrated asset allocation represents an all-encompassing strategy that examines market conditions and investor objectives and constraints on a separate basis. Based on this analysis, the optimal asset mix is determined. The asset mix is adjusted at regular intervals, to reflect the fact that both market conditions and investor needs change through time.

Portfolio Optimization

Stated simply, portfolio construction involves the selection of securities to be included in the portfolio and the determination of portfolio funds (the weights) to be placed in each security. As we know from Chapters 7 and 8, the Markowitz model provides the basis for scientific portfolio construction that results in efficient portfolios, which are those with the highest level of expected return for a given level of risk, or the lowest risk for a given level of expected return.

MONITOR MARKET CONDITIONS AND INVESTOR CIRCUMSTANCES

Monitoring Market Conditions

The need to monitor market conditions is obvious. Investment decisions are made in a dynamic marketplace where change occurs on a continuing basis. Key macro variables, such as inflation and interest rates, should be tracked on a regular basis. Information about the prospects for corporate earnings is obviously important because of the impact of earnings on stock prices.

Changes in Investor's Circumstances

An investor's circumstances can change for several reasons. These can be easily organized on the basis of the framework for determining portfolio policies outlined above.

- *Change in wealth*. A change in wealth may cause an investor to behave differently, possibly accepting more risk in the case of an increase in wealth or becoming more risk-averse in the case of a decline in wealth.
- *Change in time horizon*. Traditionally, we think of investors aging and becoming more conservative in their investment approach.
- *Change in liquidity requirements*. A need for more current income could increase the emphasis on dividend-paying stocks or fixed-income securities, while a decrease in current income requirements could lead to greater investment in small stocks whose potential payoff may be years in the future.

- *Change in tax circumstances*. An investor who moves to a higher tax bracket may find common stocks more attractive due to the dividend tax credit, as well as the potential to defer the realization of capital gains.
- *Change in legal/regulatory considerations*. Laws affecting investors change regularly, whether tax laws or laws governing retirement accounts, annuities, and so forth.
- *Change in unique needs and circumstances*. Investors face a number of possible changes during their life, depending on many economic, social, political, health, and work-related factors.

MAKE PORTFOLIO ADJUSTMENTS AS NECESSARY

Even the most carefully constructed portfolio is not intended to remain intact without change. Portfolio managers spend much of their time monitoring and rebalancing existing portfolios. The key is to know when and how to do such rebalancing because a trade-off is involved: the cost of trading versus the cost of not trading.[8]

The cost of trading involves commissions, possible impact on market price, and the time involved in deciding to trade. The cost of not trading involves holding positions that are not best suited for the portfolio's owner, that violate the asset allocation plan, that no longer provide adequate diversification, and so forth. As discussed in Chapters 19 and 20, derivative securities provide efficient mechanisms for making portfolio adjustments without actually buying or selling underlying securities. Using derivatives may offer several advantages over direct trading in the underlying portfolio securities under some circumstances.

PERFORMANCE MEASUREMENT

The portfolio management process is designed to facilitate making investment decisions in an organized, systematic manner. Clearly, it is important to evaluate the effectiveness of the overall decision-making process. The measurement of portfolio performance allows investors to determine the success of the portfolio management process, and of the portfolio manager. It is a key part of monitoring the investment strategy that was developed based on investor objectives, constraints, and preferences.

Performance measurement is important to both those who employ a professional portfolio manager on their behalf as well as to those who invest themselves. It allows investors to evaluate the risks that are being taken, the reasons for the success or failure of the investing program, and the costs of any restrictions that may have been placed on the investment manager. This, in turn, could lead to revisions in the process.

Unresolved issues remain in performance measurement despite the development of an entire industry to provide data and analyses of *ex-post* performance. Nevertheless, it is a critical part of the investment management process, and the logical capstone in its own right of the entire study of investments. We therefore consider this issue next as a separate and concluding chapter of the text.

---

[8] This discussion is indebted to Robert D. Arnott and Robert M. Lovell, Jr., "Monitoring and Rebalancing the Portfolio," in John L. Maginn and Donald L. Tuttle, editors, *Managing Investment Portfolios*, Second Edition (Charlottesville, VA: Association for Investment Management and Research, 1990).

ILLUSTRATIVE EXAMPLES

We conclude with a couple of examples that apply some of the investment planning techniques discussed in the chapter (including the tax planning strategies discussed in Appendix 21-A at the end of the chapter). These are similar in nature to the examples presented in Chapter 12 of the CSC text.

Example One

Brigid is single, 27 years old and has a steady job in a company with a strong union and solid pension plan. She has no plans to leave her job and her current salary is $36,000 per year. It is reasonable to assume this amount will increase approximately 5 per cent per year over the next 30 to 35 years. She has never invested in RRSPs but has contributed to the Canada Pension Plan (CPP) and company pension plan for the past five years. She has recently finished paying off her student loan, and her only remaining debt is a car loan in the amount of $10,000. She rents a modest one-bedroom apartment that costs her $550 per month and feels that she can live comfortably on $1,500 a month.

a. Discuss what her primary investment objectives should focus on and what type of investment mix she should consider.

Personal Evaluation

Brigid has steady employment, with good earnings potential and an employee registered retirement plan. She has good control over her debt situation and likely has room to borrow additional funds if necessary (for investment, housing, or consumption purposes). If we assume she is adequately insured and that she has no immediate plans to purchase a house, it is reasonable to assume that she is in a position to start investing for retirement. Given the fact that she has quickly paid off her student loan and has not borrowed a great deal of additional funds, it may be reasonable to assume she has a fairly conservative attitude toward managing her finances. In addition, the fact that she has not invested in RRSPs at all suggests that she may not be an extremely knowledgeable investor. Alternatively, it may signal that she is extremely conservative and wished to pay off her debt first, even at the expense of foregoing the tax deduction benefits associated with RRSP contributions.

Investment Objectives

Her primary investment objective should be growth, since she should generate more than sufficient income in the coming years to satisfy her cash flow requirements, and since retirement is some years away. Her secondary objectives would be tax minimization and safety since she is likely to be in the moderate-to-high tax bracket in the coming years, and since she appears to have a fairly conservative attitude toward managing her finances.

Investment Strategy

Brigid's first move should be to take full advantage of her available RRSP contribution limit, which should be substantial due to the carry-over amounts available from previous years. This will minimize her tax obligations and the funds placed in RRSPs should be primarily invested in growth equities to satisfy her primary investment objective of growth. In order to maintain sufficient portfolio diversification, and in light of her apparent conservative disposition, she may want to maintain 5 to 10 per cent in money market funds and an additional 10 to 20 per cent in fixed income securities. Once she has exhausted her RRSP contribution limits, she may want to invest additional funds into more aggressive equity funds with long-term growth potential, since capital gains will only be realized when the shares are sold, and given the preferential tax treatment associated with any dividends received in the interim.

Example Two

Brennan and Angela have been married for 25 years and their children, Jason and Siobhan, are grown and on their own. Angela and Brennan are both 53 years old and have been teaching high school at the same school for the past 30 years. They both earn $62,000 per year, and they plan to retire in five years. Each of them has invested $3,000 per year in RRSPs for the past 20 years, allocating approximately 20 per cent to money market funds and the remaining 80 per cent to growth equity funds. They have both also contributed to the CPP and teachers' pension plan for the past 30 years. They recently finished paying off the mortgage on their home, which they plan to live in upon retirement and their only remaining debt is a car loan in the amount of $20,000. They feel they can live comfortably on $2,800 a month after retirement.

a. Does there appear to be any opportunities for this couple to reduce taxes by using "income splitting" strategies? Briefly explain.

No, they both earn the same amount now and likely will until retirement, therefore, they are probably in the same tax bracket. In addition, they both have contributed about the same amount to registered plans, hence their income (and tax brackets) will remain virtually identical upon retirement.

b. Identify and briefly discuss what their primary investment objectives should focus on and identify any secondary objectives you feel are relevant.

They are both in the peak earnings stage of their life cycle and preservation of capital should be their primary objective, since they plan on retiring in the near future. Since they are in a high tax bracket, tax minimization should be a secondary objective.

c. Prescribe and justify an appropriate investment mix for this couple.

They should begin adjusting their asset mix toward safer securities. Many mixes are possible. For example, an appropriate target might be 40 per cent cash (money market instruments), 30 per cent fixed income securities, and 30 per cent equities (primarily blue chip stocks).

d. Recommend two options available to them if they decide to deregister their RRSPs immediately upon retirement.

They could use the proceeds to purchase a life annuity with a guaranteed term or a fixed term annuity that provides benefits to age 90. Alternatively, or coincidentally, they could purchase a Registered Retirement Income Fund (RRIF) which provides annual income to age 90 or for life. These strategies avoid paying tax on the full amount, which would occur if it were withdrawn upon deregistration of the plan.

SUMMARY

This summary relates to the learning objectives provided on page 681.

1. **Discuss why portfolio management should be considered a process.**
   Portfolio management should be thought of as a process that can be applied to each investor. It is continuous, systematic, dynamic, and flexible. The portfolio management process can be applied to each investor to produce a set of strategy recommendations for accomplishing a given end result.

2. **Describe the steps involved in the portfolio management process.**
   The entire process consists of:
   - Developing explicit investment policies, consisting of objectives, constraints, and preferences
   - Determining and quantifying capital market expectations
   - Constructing the portfolio
   - Monitoring portfolio factors and responding to changes
   - Rebalancing the portfolio when necessary
   - Measuring and evaluating portfolio performance.
3. **Assess related issues such as asset allocation.**
   The portfolio construction process can be thought of in terms of the decisions with regard to asset allocation decision and the portfolio optimization. Asset allocation is the most important investment decision made by investors. Some of the more common approaches to asset allocation include tactical, strategic and integrated.

KEY TERM

Investment policy

REVIEW QUESTIONS

1. What is meant by the portfolio management process?
2. Why is asset allocation the most important decision made by investors?
3. Explain the difference between tactical and strategic asset allocation.
4. Must each investment management firm be organized the same way in order to carry out the investment process?
5. What are some of the differences between individual investors and institutional investors?
6. What is meant by the investment policy?
7. How can the investment policy be thought of as an operational statement for investment managers to follow?
8. How does a well-specified investment policy help institutional investors?
9. In forming expectations about future returns from stocks, to what extent should investors be influenced by the more recent past (e.g., the previous 15 years) versus the history of stock market returns from 1924 to 1998?

PREPARING FOR YOUR PROFESSIONAL EXAMS

Special Note to CSC Students

Ensure that you have read and understood the following topics:*

Portfolio management as a process, pp. 682–685
Formulate an appropriate investment policy, pp. 685–691
Determine and quantify capital market expectations, pp. 691–692
Constructing the portfolio, pp. 692–696
Monitor market conditions and investor circumstances, pp. 696–697
Make portfolio adjustments as necessary, p. 697
Performance measurement, p. 697
Illustrative examples, pp. 698–699
Appendix 21-A: Basics of Tax Planning, pp. 704–706

Reading these CSC-related topics should provide you with additional understanding of CSC material. However, it should not be seen as a substitute for reading the CSC textbook itself, which is the basis for the CSC exam.

CSC REGISTRATION QUESTIONS

The Canadian Securities Institute issued the following sample questions in the 1997 CSC registration package as a means for students to self-assess their understanding of CSC-related material.

1. The _________ approach to asset allocation involves rebalancing to return the mix to its strategic long-run position.
2. A self-employed person who did not belong to a pension plan and had earned income of $40,000 could contribute what maximum annual dollar amount to an RRSP in 1995?

PAST CFA EXAM QUESTIONS

The following question was asked on the 1989 CFA Level I examination:

1. a. Outline a generalized framework that could be used to establish investment policies applicable to all investors.
   b. List and briefly discuss five differences in investment policy that might result from the application of the framework you outlined in part (a) to:
      1. The pension plan of a young, fast-growing consumer products company; and
      2. The modest life insurance proceeds received by a 60- year-old widow with two grown children. (Note: you may find a matrix format helpful in organizing your answers to part [b]).

The following question was asked on the 1991 CFA Level I examination:

2.a. List the objectives and constraints that must be considered in developing an investment policy statement.

b. Explain why the asset allocation decision is the primary determinant of total portfolio performance over time.

c. Describe three reasons why successful implementation of asset allocation decisions is even more difficult in practice than in theory.

The following question was asked on the 1990 CFA Level I examination:

3. You are being interviewed for a junior portfolio manager's job at Progressive Counselors, Inc., and are eager to demonstrate your grasp of portfolio management basics.

a. Portfolio management is a process whose four key steps are applicable in all investment management situations. List these four key steps.

An endowment fund has a conservative board of trustees. The board establishes an annual budget that relies on gifts as well as investment income. Gift income is unpredictable, ranging from 10 to 50 per cent (averaging 30 per cent) of annual spending over the past 10 years. If the gift component of any year's total income falls short of this average level, the shortfall is met from liquidity reserves.

b. List and briefly discuss the objectives and constraints that must be considered in developing an investment policy statement for this endowment fund.

The following two questions were asked on the 1996 CFA Level II examination:

4. **Introduction**

The following information is available on two US-based accounts managed by Omega Trust Company.

Account 1: The Foote Family

Dr. and Mrs. Sheraton Foote are both 35 years old and have a combined annual income of $250,000. They are both professionals and intend to remain childless. They pay a marginal income tax rate of 40 per cent on dividends, interest, and realized capital gains, and dislike paying taxes. Their managed account, which Mrs. Foote inherited, is just over $1,000,000 in value. The Footes do not expect to use the principal or income from their managed account until their planned retirement at age 65. Any funds remaining at their death will be left to Hope Ministries.

Account 2: Hope Ministries

Hope Ministries is a tax exempt charitable organization that was established to provide financial assistance to homeless people. The foundation's charter requires that all income earned from its endowment fund must be used in operations; any increase in the value of the principal of the endowment fund, whether realized or not, must be retained in the endowment fund. Hope currently requires $90,000 annual income from its $1,500,000 endowment fund.

The Omega Trust Company uses the CAPM in managing investment portfolios, combining US Treasury bills (as a proxy for the risk-free rate) and co-mingled funds having differing characteristics. A summary of prevailing expectations for selected capital markets and for each of Omega's co-mingled funds are outlined in Table 21-3.

Table 21-3

Omega Trust Company Investment Choices

Investment	Expect Return	Beta
US Treasury bills (risk-free rate)	4.0%	0.0
S&P 500 (the equity market portfolio)	12.0%	1.0
Fund A (aggressive equity)	16.5% (including 1.0% from dividends)	1.7
Fund B (diversified equity)	13.0% (including 3.0% from dividends)	1.1
Fund C (global bond)	8.0% (including 8.0% from interest)	0.5

Use the Introduction and Table 21-3 to answer the following questions about the Foote Family.

a. Create and justify an investment policy statement for the Foote Family based solely on the information provided. Be specific and complete as to the objectives and constraints.

b. Create and justify an asset allocation for the Foote Family portfolio, considering both the requirements of the policy statement created in part (a) and the returns that are required by the prevailing security market line. Use only the three co-mingled funds (A, B, C) shown in Table 21-3.

Assume the Footes have received an additional $350,000 from a new inheritance and invested in a broadly-diversified portfolio of small-capitalization stocks having a 12 per cent expected return and a beta of 1.4. They are considering borrowing an additional $150,000 at an interest rate of 8 per cent to increase this investment to $500,000.

c. Explain the effect of the borrowing on the expected return on the $350,000 inheritance. Show any calculations.

d. State whether the borrowing is appropriate for the Footes. Justify your statement with reference to the investment policy statement you created in part (a).

5. Use the introduction from above and Table 21-3 to answer the following questions about Hope Ministries.

a. Create and justify an investment policy statement for Hope Ministries based solely on the information provided. Be specific and complete as to the objectives and constraints.

b. Create and justify an asset allocation for the Hope Ministries portfolio, considering both the requirements of the policy statement created in part (a) and the returns which are required by the prevailing security market line. Use only the three co-mingled funds (A, B, C) shown in Table 21-3.

APPENDIX 21-A

BASICS OF TAX PLANNING

Taxes and Taxation Issues

Proper tax planning should be a significant part of all financial plans, however, it should not be the sole or overriding objective. The best tax advantages are usually gained by planning early and often, allowing a reasonable time for the plan to produce the desired results. Legitimate tax avoidance entails: full utilization of allowable deductions; conversion of non-deductible expenses into deductible expenditures; postponing receipt of income; splitting income with other family members; and selecting investments which provide a better after-tax yield.

Tax Deferral Plans

The principle of tax deferral plans is to reduce taxes paid during high income (and high tax bracket) years by deferring payment until retirement, when one's income (and tax bracket) will be lower. Total contributions to tax-assisted retirement savings plans are limited to 18 per cent of earned income to a maximum dollar amount of $13,500 from 1996 to 2002.

The amount contributed to registered pension plans (RPPs) and deferred profit sharing plans (DPSPs) is called the pension adjustment or PA. These reduce the allowable contributions to an RRSP by a taxpayer, as discussed in the CSC Notes box in Chapter 3. Carry-forward provisions enable the taxpayer to make up deficient contributions in subsequent years. Registered pension plans (RPPs) are trusts that are registered with Revenue Canada that are established by the employer to provide employees with retirement benefits. Both employer and employee make contributions.

Another form of tax deferral plan is the use of Registered Retirement Savings Plans (RRSPs), which were discussed in the CSC Notes box in Chapter 3. RRSPs allow annual tax-deductible contributions up to allowable limits, and the income earned on the plan is tax-free as long as it remains in the plan, provided the plans are registered with Revenue Canada and meet the 80 per cent Canadian content requirement. A married taxpayer may contribute to an RRSP in the name of a spouse only to the extent that it does not use the maximum contribution to their own plan. It does not affect the contribution limits of the spouse.

An RRSP holder may deregister the plan at any time, but it is mandatory at age 69. Available options are:

1. Withdraw the full lump sum amount, which is fully taxable
2. Use the proceeds to purchase a life annuity with a guaranteed term or a fixed-term annuity that provides benefits to age 90
3. Purchase a Registered Retirement Income Fund (RRIF) which provides annual income to age 90 or for life
4. Amend the plan to allow transfer of funds to another RRSP or RPP to defer taxation until ultimate withdrawal of funds

5. Combinations of the above options. Upon death, remaining benefits on an annuity or RRIF can be transferred to a spouse or child, or else the value is included in the deceased's income in the year of death and is fully taxable.

RRIF holders must withdraw and pay income tax on a set fraction of the total assets in the fund (the annual minimum amount). The annual fraction is determined by a formula designed to provide benefits for a desired term, however, the owner may choose to accelerate payouts. A taxpayer may own more than one RRIF and they may be self-directed.

Registered Education Savings Plan (RESP) contributions are not tax deductible, but income earned on these plans is not taxable. The beneficiary of the plan will be taxed upon withdrawal of funds, provided they are enrolled in qualifying educational programs. Previous to 1997, the investment income earned on these plans would be lost if the beneficiary did not pursue higher education, however, that year's federal budget changed the rules applying to RESPs making them more attractive to investors. In particular, even if the beneficiary does not attend school, the earned income need not be lost since the contributor can now transfer the amount to an RRSP, provided they have room. Alternatively, they can withdraw the funds directly, and pay the required tax on the income.

In addition, the 1997 budget doubled the annual contribution limit to $4,000 from $2,000, and has allotted government grants of 20 per cent of the contributions made to the plan, to a maximum of $400.

Other Tax Avoidance Strategies

Transferring income to family members can trigger attribution rules that pass the tax consequences back to the transferor. Exceptions to attribution may occur:

1. When the property or assets are transferred at fair market values or by way of a loan at fair market rates, where the interest is actually paid within 30 days of year end
2. When the transfer was an outright gift, and if it can be shown that tax avoidance was not the main purpose of the transaction
3. Business income, rather than property income, is generally not subject to attribution.

Despite the forgoing, there exist certain opportunities to split income to reduce taxes payable:

1. Have the higher income spouse pay the bills, while lower income spouse invests more at a lower tax rate
2. The higher income spouse can loan investment funds to the lower income spouse at prescribed rates, which would result in the taxation of the net investment income over interest paid at the lower tax rates
3. Direct discharge of a spouse's debts is not subject to attribution
4. It may be advantageous to report dividends as income of the taxpayer rather than the spouse if the dividend income would reduce the marital tax credit
5. Transfer of capital losses, by selling the asset to a spouse who then sells it to obtain a capital loss
6. Payment of debts by way of a gift

7. Splitting CPP income — must split both plans and be agreed to by both parties
8. Asset swaps at fair market value are allowed, so the higher tax bracket spouse may trade income generating assets for non-income generating assets at fair market values
9. Salaries for legitimate services rendered to spouses from proprietorships are deductible
10. Gifts are not subject to attribution.

CHAPTER 22

EVALUATION OF INVESTMENT PERFORMANCE

LEARNING OBJECTIVES

After reading this chapter, you will be able to

1. Outline the framework for evaluating portfolio performance.
2. Use measures of return and risk to evaluate portfolio performance.
3. Distinguish between the three composite measures of portfolio performance.
4. Discuss problems with portfolio measurement.
5. Explain issues in portfolio evaluation such as performance attribution.

CHAPTER PREVIEW

This chapter explains what is involved in evaluating investment performance. First, we establish a framework for evaluating portfolio performance that includes a discussion of the Association for Investment Management and Research's (AIMR) Performance Presentation Standards. We then focus on the composite measures of portfolio performance developed by Sharpe, Treynor, and Jensen. We conclude the chapter with a look at some of the problems with performance evaluation and other issues such as performance attribution.

THE BOTTOM LINE

We have now discussed, in an organized and systematic manner, the major components of the investing process. One important issue that remains is the bottom line of this investing process: evaluating the performance of a portfolio. The question to be answered is this: Is the return on a portfolio, less all expenses, adequate to compensate for the risk that was taken? Every investor should be concerned with this issue because, after all, the objective of investing is to increase or at least protect financial wealth. Unsatisfactory results must be detected so that changes can be made.

Evaluating portfolio performance is important whether an individual investor manages his or her own funds or invests indirectly through investment companies. Direct investing can be time consuming and has high opportunity costs. If the results are inadequate, why do it (unless the investor simply enjoys it)? On the other hand, if professional portfolio managers (such as those at mutual funds) are employed, it is necessary to know how well they perform. Other things being equal, if manager A consistently outperforms manager B, investors will prefer manager A, and if neither one outperforms an index fund, investors may go elsewhere. The obvious point is that performance has to be evaluated before intelligent decisions can be made.

Portfolio evaluation has changed significantly over time. Prior to the mid-1960s, evaluation was not a major issue, even for investment firms, but in today's highly competitive money-management environment it is. By September 1998 there were over 1,000 Canadian mutual funds (excluding money market funds) with approximately $300 billion in assets under management. That is approximately 12 times the money under management as of December 1990, which attests to the growth in these investments throughout the 1990s. In the US there are currently over 8,000 mutual funds managing more than $3 trillion. The pension fund universe is even larger. In addition to these money managers, trusts, discretionary accounts, and endowment funds have portfolios that must be evaluated.

Because of all this complexity, evaluation techniques have become more sophisticated, and the demands by portfolio clients more intense. The broad acceptance of modern portfolio theory has also changed the evaluation process and how it is viewed. In this chapter we discuss the evaluation of portfolio performance, with an eye to understanding the critical issues involved and the overall framework within which evaluation should be conducted. We also review the well-known measures of composite portfolio performance and the problems associated with them.

FRAMEWORK FOR EVALUATING PORTFOLIO PERFORMANCE

When evaluating a portfolio's performance, certain factors must be considered. We discuss below some of the obvious factors that investors should consider and outline the performance presentation standards recently recommended by the Association for Investment Management and Research (AIMR), which will play a prominent role in performance evaluation in the future.

To illustrate our discussion about comparisons, assume that in 1998 the GoGrowth mutual fund earned a total return of 20 per cent for its shareholders. It claims in an advertisement that it is the number one performing mutual fund in its category. As a shareholder, you are trying to assess GoGrowth's performance. What can you say?

Some obvious factors to consider are: risk levels, time periods, appropriate benchmarks, constraints on portfolio managers, as well as other considerations.

Differential Risk Levels

The risk-return trade-off underlies all investment actions, but with the information we have, we can say relatively little about GoGrowth's performance. Return and risk are opposite sides of the same coin, and both must be evaluated if intelligent decisions are to be made. But we know nothing about the risk levels of this fund, and therefore we can say little about its performance. After all, to achieve this 20 per cent return its managers may have taken twice the risk of comparable portfolios.

Given the risk that all investors face, it is totally inadequate to consider only the returns from various investment alternatives. Although all investors prefer higher returns, they do not like the accompanying higher risk. To evaluate portfolio performance properly, we must determine whether the returns are large enough given the risk involved. If we are to assess performance carefully, we must evaluate performance on a risk-adjusted basis.

Differential Time Periods

It is not unusual to pick up a publication from the popular press and see two different mutual funds of the same type — for example, aggressive equity funds or balanced funds — advertize themselves as the number one performer. How can this be? The answer is simple. Each of these funds is measuring its performance over a different time period. For example, one fund could use the 10 years ending December 31, 1998, while another fund uses the five years ending December 31, 1998. GoGrowth could be using a one-year period ending on the same date or some other combination of years. Mutual fund sponsors can choose any time period they wish in promoting their performance and funds can also define the group to which comparisons are made. And, to present themselves in the best light, they often stress those periods of highest performance.

Although it seems obvious when one thinks about it, investors tend not to be careful when making comparisons of portfolios over various time periods. As with the case of differential risk, the time element must be adjusted for if valid performance of portfolio results is to be obtained.

Appropriate Benchmarks

A third reason why we can say little about the performance of GoGrowth is that its 20 per cent return is meaningful only when compared to a legimitate alternative. Obviously, if the average-risk fund or the market returned 25 per cent in 1998, and GoGrowth is average, we would find its performance unfavourable. Therefore, we must make relative comparisons in performance measurement, and an important related issue is the benchmark to be used in evaluating the performance of a portfolio.

The essence of performance evaluation in investments is to compare the returns obtained on some portfolio with those that could have been obtained from a comparable alternative. The measurement process must involve relevant and obtainable alternatives; that is, the **benchmark portfolio** must be a legitimate alternative that accurately reflects the objectives of the portfolio owners.[1]

Benchmark Portfolio
An alternative portfolio against which to measure a portfolio's performance.

An equity portfolio consisting of TSE 300 stocks should be evaluated relative to the TSE 300 Composite Index or other equity portfolios that could be constructed from that index, after adjusting for the risk involved. On the other hand, a portfolio of small capitalization stocks should not be judged against the benchmark of the TSE 300 Index, but against a small-cap index such as the Nesbitt Burns Canadian small-cap index, or the recently introduced S&P/TSE Small Cap Index (which contains the 180 smallest TSE 300 stocks and is replacing the TSE 200). Similarly, a predominantly mid-cap fund should be compared with an index such as the new S&P/TSE Mid-Cap Index, which consists of 60 mid-cap stocks from the TSE 300. If a bond portfolio manager's objective is to invest in bonds rated A or higher, it would be inappropriate to compare his or her performance with that of a junk bond manager.

Even more difficult to evaluate are equity funds that consist of some mid-cap and small stocks as well as many from the TSE 300. Comparisons for this group can be quite difficult.

EXAMPLE: BENCHMARKING CANADIAN EQUITY MUTUAL FUNDS

Most of the largest equity funds underperformed the TSE 300 Composite Index for the three-year period ending September 30, 1998. For example, 100 companies categorized as Canadian equity mutual funds had returns below the three-year 9.4 per cent annual return on the TSE 300 Total Return Index, while only 45 had returns above this amount. The median return for these funds over this period was 7.9 per cent and the average annual return was 7.8 per cent. Why? Generally, these funds held more small- and mid-cap stocks than are in the TSE 300 Index, and such stocks underperformed the large-caps in those years. In addition, most of these funds hold some percentage of their total assets in cash equivalent securities, unlike the TSE 300 Index, which is a truly "all stock" portfolio.

The TSE 300 Index has been the most frequently used benchmark for evaluating the performance of Canadian institutional portfolios such as those of pension and mutual funds. However, many observers now agree that multiple benchmarks are more appropriate to use

[1] For a discussion of benchmarks, see Jeffrey V. Bailey, "Evaluating Benchmark Quality," *Financial Analysts Journal* 48 (May–June 1992), pp. 33–39.

when evaluating portfolio returns for reasons such as those described in the example above. Customized benchmarks also can be constructed to evaluate a manager's style that is unusual. For example, in addition to several small-cap and mid-cap indexes (some of which were mentioned above), new indexes designed to accommodate portfolio managers' "styles" have been developed, such as the Russell 100 Growth Index and the Russell 100 Value Index.

Constraints on Portfolio Managers

In evaluating the portfolio manager rather than the portfolio itself, an investor should consider the objectives set by (or for) the manager and any constraints under which he or she must operate. For example, if a mutual fund's objective is to invest in small, speculative stocks, investors must expect the risk to be larger than that of a fund invested in TSE 300 stocks, with substantial swings in the annual realized returns.

It is imperative to recognize the importance of the investment policy pursued by a portfolio manager in determining the portfolio's results. In many cases, the investment policy determines the return and risk of the portfolio. For example, authors Brinson, Hood, and Beebower found that for a sample of pension plans the investment policy accounted for approximately 94 per cent of the total variation in the returns to these funds.[2] This obviously leaves little variation to be accounted for by the manager's skills.

If a portfolio manager is obligated to operate under certain constraints, these must be taken into account. For example, if a portfolio manager of an equity fund is prohibited from selling short, it is unreasonable to expect the manager to protect the portfolio in this manner in a bear market. If the manager is further prohibited from trading in options and futures, nearly the only protection left in a bear market is to reduce the equity exposure.

Other Considerations

Of course, other important issues are involved in measuring the portfolio's performance. It is essential to determine how well diversified the portfolio was during the evaluation period, because, as we know, diversification can reduce portfolio risk. If a manager assumes non-systematic risk, we want to know if he or she earned an adequate return for doing so.

All investors should understand that even in today's investment world of computers and databases, there do not exist any precise universally agreed-upon methods of portfolio evaluation. As we will see below, investors can use several well-known techniques to assess the actual performance of a portfolio relative to one or more alternatives. In the final analysis, when investors are selecting money managers to turn their money over to, they evaluate these managers only on the basis of their published performance statistics. If the published "track record" looks good, that is typically enough to convince many investors to invest in a particular mutual fund. However, the past is no guarantee of an investment manager's future, as discussed in Chapter 10 and demonstrated in the Real-World Returns box in that chapter. Short-term results may be particularly misleading.

[2] Gary P. Brinson, Randolph Hood, and Gilbert L. Beebower, "Determinants of Portfolio Performance," *Financial Analysts Journal* 42 (July/August 1986), pp. 39–44.

AIMR's Presentation Standards

Performance Presentation Standards (PPS) Minimum standards for presenting investment performance as formulated by Association for Investment Management and Research (AIMR).

The Association for Investment Management and Research (see Appendix 1-A), based on years of discussion, has issued minimum standards for presenting investment performance.[3] These **Performance Presentation Standards (PPS)** are a set of guiding ethical principles with two main objectives:

1. To promote full disclosure and fair representation by investment managers in reporting their investment results.
2. To ensure uniformity in reporting in order to enhance comparability among investment managers.

Some aspects of the standards are mandatory and others are recommended. Table 22-1 summarizes many of the key points of most relevance to this discussion. We will encounter some of these points as we consider how to go about evaluating portfolios.

Table 22-1

AIMR's Performance Presentation Standards

Requirements

1. **Total return** — must be used to calculate performance
2. **Accrual accounting** — use accrual, not cash accounting for fixed-income and all other securities that accrue income
3. **Time-weighted rates of return** — to be used on at least a quarterly basis and geometric linking of period returns
4. **Cash and cash equivalents** — to be included in composite returns
5. **All portfolios included** — all actual discretionary portfolios are to be included in at least one composite
6. **No linkage of simulated portfolios with actual performance**
7. **Asset-weighting of composites** — beginning-of-period values to be used
8. **Addition of new portfolios** — to be added to a composite after the start of the next measurement period
9. **Exclusion of terminated portfolios** — excluded from all periods after the period in place
10. **No restatement of composite results** — after a firm's reorganization
11. **No portability of portfolio results**
12. **All costs deducted** — subtracted from gross performance
13. **10-year performance record** — minimum period to be presented
14. **Present annual returns for all years**
15. **Convertible and other hybrid securities** — must be treated consistently across and within composite
16. **Asset-only returns** — must not be mixed with asset-plus-cash returns
17. **Leverage** — return results must be calculated on both an actual basis and a restated all cash basis

There are additional requirements for international portfolios, for real estate, and for venture and private placements. In addition, performance presentations must disclose several items of information, such as a complete list of a firm's composites, whether performance results are gross or net of investment management fees, and so on.

Source: Reprinted with permission from *Peformance Presentation Standards*, Second Edition. Copyright 1997, Association for Investment Management and Research, Charlottesville, VA. All rights reserved.

[3] *Performance Presentation Standards*. Second Edition. Charlottesville, VA: Association for Investment Management and Research, 1997.

RETURN AND RISK CONSIDERATIONS

Performance measurement begins with portfolio valuations and transactions translated into rate of return. Prior to the introduction of the performance measures in 1965 (discussed later in this chapter), returns were seldom related to measures of risk. In evaluating portfolio performance, however, investors must consider both the realized return and the risk that was assumed. Therefore, whatever measures or techniques are used, these parameters must be incorporated into the analysis.

Measures of Return

When portfolio performance is evaluated, the investor should be concerned with the total change in wealth. As discussed throughout this text, a proper measure of this return is the total return (TR), which captures both the income component and the capital gains (or losses) component of return. This is the measure reported by investment funds in Canada, as required by security regulators such as the Ontario Securities Commission. It is also required by the AIMR, as shown in Table 22-1.

In the simplest case, the market value of a portfolio can be measured at the beginning and end of a period, and the rate of return can be calculated as

$$R_p = \frac{V_E - V_B}{V_B} \tag{22-1}$$

where V_E is the ending value of the portfolio and V_B is its beginning value.

This calculation assumes that no funds were added to or withdrawn from the portfolio by the client during the measurement period. If such transactions occur, the portfolio return as calculated, R_p, may not be an accurate measure of the portfolio's performance. For example, if the client adds funds close to the end of the measurement period, use of Equation 22-1 would produce inaccurate results because the ending value was not determined by the actions of the portfolio manager. Although a close approximation of portfolio performance might be obtained by simply adding any withdrawals or subtracting any contributions that are made very close to the end of the measurement period, timing issues are a problem.

Dollar-Weighted Returns

Traditionally, portfolio measurement consisted of calculating the **dollar-weighted rate of return (DWR)**, which is equivalent to the internal rate of return (IRR) used in several financial calculations. The IRR measures the actual return earned on a beginning portfolio value and on any net contributions made during the period.

Dollar-Weighted Rate of Return (DWR)
Equates all cash flows, including ending market value, with the beginning market value of the portfolio.

The DWR equates all cash flows, including ending market value, with the beginning market value of the portfolio. Because the DWR is affected by cash flows to the portfolio, it measures the rate of return to the portfolio owner. However, because the DWR is heavily affected by cash flows, it is inappropriate to use when making comparisons to other portfolios or to market indexes, a key factor in performance measurement.

EXAMPLE: CALCULATING THE DOLLAR-WEIGHTED RATE OF RETURN

An equity portfolio is worth $10,000 at the beginning of the year. After six months the portfolio pays a dividend of $100 and the investor contributes $300 more to the portfolio. Just before the contribution and dividends, the portfolio was worth $10,050. At the end of the year, the investor receives $100 in dividends and withdraws an additional $150 from the portfolio, which has an ending value of $10,700 after the withdrawal has been made.

To solve for the DWR, we equate the present value of the contributions and the beginning market value, with the present value of withdrawals, cash receipts, and the ending portfolio value, and solve for the corresponding discount rate, as shown below:

Present value (Beginning wealth + Contributions)
= Present value (Cash distributions + Withdrawals + Ending wealth)

$$10{,}000 + \frac{300}{(1 + r)} = \frac{100}{(1 + r)} + \frac{150}{(1 + r)^2} + \frac{100}{(1 + r)^2} + \frac{10{,}700}{(1 + r)^2}$$

which reduces to

$$10{,}000 + \frac{200}{(1 + r)} = \frac{10{,}950}{(1 + r)^2}$$

Solving by financial calculator, we find $r = 3.65$ per cent, which is a six-month return; the annual effective return is: $(1 + .0365)^2 - 1 = 0.0743$ or 7.43 per cent.

Time-Weighted Returns

Time-Weighted Rate of Return (TWR)
Measures the actual rate of return earned by the portfolio manager.

The **time-weighted rate of return (TWR)** typically is calculated for comparative purposes when cash flows occur between the beginning and the end of a period. TWRs are unaffected by any cash flows to the portfolio; therefore, they measure the actual rate of return earned by the portfolio manager.

Calculating the TWR requires information about the value of the portfolio's cash inflows and outflows. To compute the TWR, we calculate the return to the portfolio immediately prior to a cash flow occurring. We then calculate the return to the portfolio from that cash flow to the next, or to the end of the period. Finally, we link these rates of return together by computing the compound rate of return over time. In other words, we calculate the rate of return for each time period defined by a cash inflow or outflow, and then calculate a compound rate of return for the entire period. If frequent cash flows are involved, substantial calculations are necessary.

EXAMPLE: CALCULATING THE TIME-WEIGHTED RATE OF RETURN

For the above example, the corresponding TWR would be:

For period one (the first six months) $r_1 = \dfrac{10{,}050 - 10{,}000 + 100}{10{,}000} = 1.50\%$

For period two (the next six months) $r_2 = \dfrac{10{,}850 - 10{,}350 + 100}{10{,}350} = 5.80\%$

So the annual return (based on the geometric average) over the entire period is:

$$r = [(1.0150)(1.0580)] - 1 = 0.0739 \text{ or } 7.39\%$$

Notice that this value differs from the DWR of 7.43%.

Which Measure to Use?

As the examples above illustrate, the dollar-weighted return and the time-weighted return can produce different results. While the difference above is not drastic due to the simplistic nature of the examples, at times these differences are substantial. The time-weighted return captures the rate of return actually earned by the portfolio *manager*, while the dollar-weighted return captures the rate of return earned by the portfolio *owner*.

For evaluating the performance of the portfolio manager, the time-weighted return should be used because he or she generally has no control over the deposits and withdrawals made by the clients. The objective is to measure the performance of the portfolio manager independent of the actions of the client, and this is better accomplished by using the time-weighted return. As we can see in Table 22-1, the Performance Presentation Standards require that returns be computed using the TWR approach.

The use of total returns and the TWR approach is required by Canadian mutual funds, according to the Ontario Securities Commission. In particular, they determine total returns based on the change in net asset value of the fund (as defined in Chapter 3). They require that "the indicated rate[s] of return [are] the historical annual compound total return[s] including changes in [share or unit] value and reinvestment of all [dividends or distributions] and [do] not take into account sales, redemption, distributions or optional charges or income taxes payable by any securityholder that would have reduced returns." Dividends or distributions are to be assumed "reinvested in the mutual fund at the net asset value per security of the mutual fund on the reinvestment dates during the portfolio measurement period." In addition, fees and other charges "are assumed to be paid in proportion to the length of the performance measurement period."[4]

[4] Ontario Securities Commission Web site: <http://www.osc.gov.on.ca>.

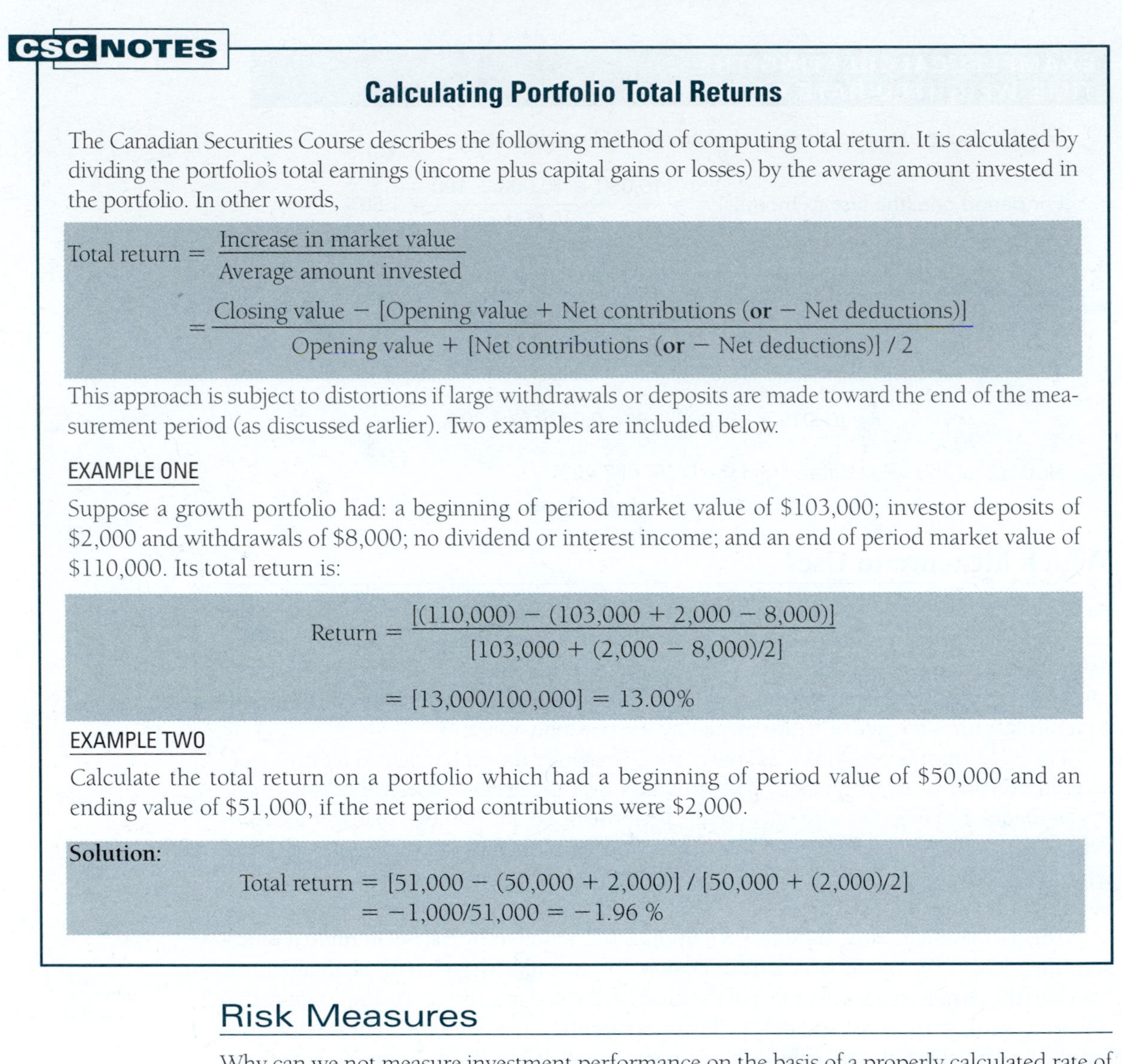

CSC NOTES

Calculating Portfolio Total Returns

The Canadian Securities Course describes the following method of computing total return. It is calculated by dividing the portfolio's total earnings (income plus capital gains or losses) by the average amount invested in the portfolio. In other words,

$$\text{Total return} = \frac{\text{Increase in market value}}{\text{Average amount invested}}$$

$$= \frac{\text{Closing value} - [\text{Opening value} + \text{Net contributions } (\textbf{or} - \text{Net deductions})]}{\text{Opening value} + [\text{Net contributions } (\textbf{or} - \text{Net deductions})] \,/\, 2}$$

This approach is subject to distortions if large withdrawals or deposits are made toward the end of the measurement period (as discussed earlier). Two examples are included below.

EXAMPLE ONE

Suppose a growth portfolio had: a beginning of period market value of \$103,000; investor deposits of \$2,000 and withdrawals of \$8,000; no dividend or interest income; and an end of period market value of \$110,000. Its total return is:

$$\text{Return} = \frac{[(110{,}000) - (103{,}000 + 2{,}000 - 8{,}000)]}{[103{,}000 + (2{,}000 - 8{,}000)/2]}$$

$$= [13{,}000/100{,}000] = 13.00\%$$

EXAMPLE TWO

Calculate the total return on a portfolio which had a beginning of period value of \$50,000 and an ending value of \$51,000, if the net period contributions were \$2,000.

Solution:

$$\text{Total return} = [51{,}000 - (50{,}000 + 2{,}000)] \,/\, [50{,}000 + (2{,}000)/2]$$
$$= -1{,}000/51{,}000 = -1.96\ \%$$

Risk Measures

Why can we not measure investment performance on the basis of a properly calculated rate of return measure? After all, rankings of mutual funds are often done this way in the popular press, with one-year, three-year, and five-year returns shown. Are rates of return, or averages, good indicators of performance?

As stated in Chapter 1 and restated above, we must consider risk when making judgments about performance. Differences in risk will cause portfolios to respond differently to changes in the overall market and should be accounted for in evaluating performance.

We now know that the two prevalent measures of risk used in investment analysis are total risk (as measured by standard deviation) and systematic or market risk (commonly measured by beta). The standard deviation for a portfolio's set of returns can be calculated easily with a calculator or computer and is a measure of total risk.

Any number of software programs can calculate beta. However, we must remember that betas are only estimates of systematic risk, with respect to a chosen market proxy such as the

TSE 300 Index. Betas can be calculated using weekly, monthly, quarterly, or annual data, and each will produce a different estimate. Such variations in this calculation could produce differences in rankings that use beta as a measure of risk. Furthermore, betas can be unstable, and they change over time.

RISK-ADJUSTED MEASURES OF PERFORMANCE

Based on the concepts of capital market theory, and recognizing the necessity to incorporate both return and risk into the analysis, three researchers — William Sharpe, Jack Treynor, and Michael Jensen — developed measures of portfolio performance in the 1960s. These measures are often referred to as the **composite (risk-adjusted) measures of portfolio performance**, meaning that they incorporate both realized return and risk into the evaluation. These measures are often still used, as evidenced by Morningstar, a well-known source of mutual fund information, reporting the Sharpe ratio.

Composite (Risk-Adjusted) Measures of Portfolio Performance Portfolio performance measures combining return and risk into one calculation.

The Sharpe Performance Measure

William Sharpe, whose contributions to portfolio theory have been previously encountered, introduced a risk-adjusted measure of portfolio performance called the **reward-to-variability ratio (RVAR)** based on his work in capital market theory.[5] This measure uses a benchmark based on the ex post capital market line.[6] This measure can be defined as

Reward-to-Variability Ratio (RVAR) Sharpe's measure of portfolio performance calculated as the ratio of excess portfolio return to the standard deviation.

$$\text{RVAR} = [\overline{\text{TR}}_p - \overline{\text{RF}}] / \text{SD}_p = \text{Excess return/Risk} \tag{22-2}$$

$\overline{\text{TR}}_p$ = the average TR for portfolio p during some period of time (we will use annual data)
$\overline{\text{RF}}$ = the average risk-free rate of return during the period
SD_p = the standard deviation of return for portfolio p during the period
$\overline{\text{TR}}_p - \overline{\text{RF}}$ = the excess return (risk premium) on portfolio p

The numerator of Equation 22-2 measures the portfolio's excess return, or the return above the risk-free rate. (RF could have been earned without assuming risk.) This is also referred to as the risk premium. The denominator uses the standard deviation, which is a measure of the total risk or variability in the return of the portfolio. Note the following about RVAR:

- It measures the excess return per unit of total risk (standard deviation)
- The higher the RVAR, the better the portfolio performance, since excess return (which investors desire) is in the numerator and risk (which investors dislike) is in the denominator
- Portfolios can be ranked by RVAR.

[5] W. Sharpe, "Mutual Fund Performance," *Journal of Business* 39 (January 1966), pp. 119–138.
[6] Sharpe used it to rank the performance of 34 mutual funds over the period 1954–63.

As an example of calculating the Sharpe ratio, consider the data for five Canadian equity mutual funds for the three-year period from November 1, 1996 to October 31, 1998, which were chosen randomly for illustrative purposes only: **AIC Diversified Canadian (AI)**, **Altamira Equity (AL)**, **Investors Canadian Equity (I)**, **Royal Canadian Equity (R)**, and **Templeton Canadian Equity (T)**. Table 22-2 shows annual fund returns, the standard deviation of these returns, the beta for the fund, the average return for the TSE 300 Index for those years, and the average yield on 30-day government T-bills, which proxy for RF. On the basis of this data, Sharpe's RVAR can be calculated using Equation 22-2, with the results reported in column two of Table 22-3.

Table 22-2

Return and Risk Data for Five Canadian Equity Mutual Funds
November 1, 1996 to October 31, 1998

Mutual Fund	Average Return (%)	Standard Deviation (%)	Beta
AIC Diversified Canadian	36.40	18.18	0.87
Altamira Equity	3.01	21.64	1.04
Investors Canadian Equity	7.24	19.79	0.97
Royal Canadian Equity	12.03	16.76	0.84
Templeton Canadian Equity	12.99	12.57	0.63
TSE 300	13.75	18.05	
RF (30-day T-bills)	5.19		

Table 22-3

Risk-Adjusted Measures for Five Canadian Equity Mutual Funds
November 1, 1996 to October 31, 1998

Mutual Fund	RVAR	RVOL (%)	Jensen's Alpha (%)*
AIC (AI)	1.72	35.87	23.76
Altamira (AL)	−0.10	−2.10	−11.08
Investors (I)	0.10	2.11	−6.25
Royal (R)	0.41	8.14	−0.35
Templeton (T)	0.62	11.59	1.91
TSE 300	0.47	8.56	

*Jensen's differential return measure is discussed below.

Based on these calculations, we see that two of these five funds — AIC and Templeton —outperformed the TSE 300 Index on an excess return-risk basis during this period, although the average return exceeded that for the TSE 300 for only one fund (AIC). Since this is an ordinal (relative) measure of portfolio performance, different portfolios can easily be ranked on this variable. Using only the Sharpe measure of portfolio performance, we would judge the portfolio with the highest RVAR best in terms of *ex post* performance. The RVAR value for the appropriate market index has also been calculated and used for comparison purposes.

As we can see, two funds — AI and T — have RVAR ratios that exceed the RVAR of 0.47 for the TSE 300 for the period. While the average return of 36.40 per cent for AI was well above the average TSE 300 return of 13.75 per cent, the average return for T was actually below that of the TSE 300, at 12.99 per cent. However, T's standard deviation was well below that of the TSE 300 (12.57 versus 18.18 per cent), hence its Sharpe ratio exceeded that of the TSE 300 Index.

Sharpe's measure for these funds is illustrated graphically in Figure 22-1. The vertical axis is rate of return, and the horizontal axis is standard deviation of returns. The vertical intercept is RF. As Figure 22-1 shows, RVAR measures the slope of the line from RF to the portfolio being evaluated. The steeper the line, the higher the slope (RVAR) and the better the performance. The arrows indicate the slope for the TSE 300 Total Return Index and for AIC, the fund with the greatest slope.

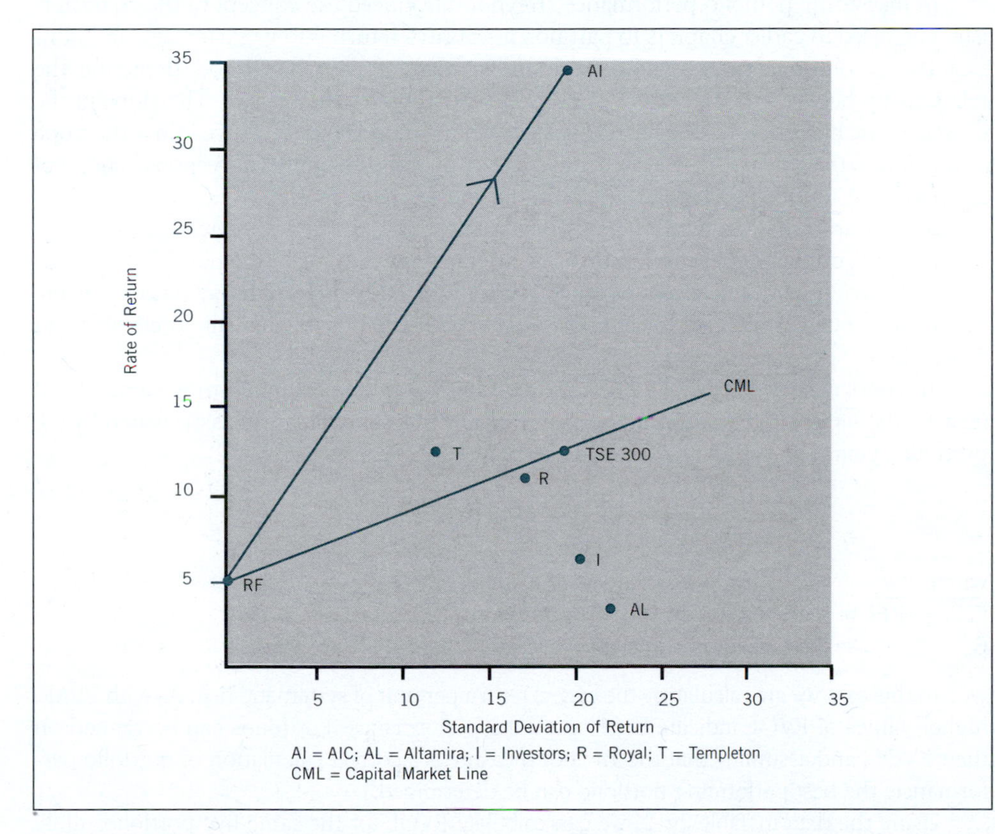

Figure 22-1
Sharpe's Measure of Performance (RVAR) for Five Mutual Funds, November 1996 – October 1998

Because of their superior risk-adjusted performance, AIC and Templeton have the largest slopes, whereas the slopes for the other funds are lower than that of the TSE 300 Index. Because the RVAR for AI and T is greater than the RVAR for the market measure (in this case the TSE 300), these portfolios lie above the capital market line (CML), indicating superior risk-adjusted performance. The other three lie below that line, indicating inferior risk-adjusted performance.

In Figure 22-1 we are drawing the CML when we plot the market's return against its standard deviation and use RF as the vertical intercept. Based on the discussion in Chapter 9, all efficient portfolios should plot on this line, and an investor with the ability to borrow and lend at the rate RF should be able to attain any point on this line. Of course, this is the *ex post* and not the *ex ante* CML.

The Treynor Performance Measure

Reward-to-Volatility Ratio (RVOL)
Treynor's measure of portfolio performance calculated as the ratio of excess portfolio return to beta.

At approximately the same time as Sharpe's measure was developed (the mid-1960s), Jack Treynor presented a similar measure called the **reward-to-volatility ratio (RVOL)**.[7] Like Sharpe, Treynor sought to relate the return on a portfolio to its risk. Treynor, however, distinguished between total risk and systematic risk, implicitly assuming that portfolios are well diversified; that is, he ignores any diversifiable risk. He used as a benchmark the *ex post* security market line.

In measuring portfolio performance, Treynor introduced the concept of the characteristic line, used in earlier chapters to partition a security's return into its systematic and nonsystematic components. It is used in a similar manner with portfolios, depicting the relationship between the returns on a portfolio and those of the market. The slope of the characteristic line measures the relative volatility of the fund's returns. As we know, the slope of this line is the beta coefficient, which is a measure of the volatility (or responsiveness) of the portfolio's returns in relation to those of the chosen market index.

As we learned in Chapter 8, characteristic lines can be estimated by regressing each portfolio's returns on the market proxy returns using either raw returns for the portfolios and raw proxy returns, or by using excess portfolio returns and excess market proxy returns (where the risk-free rate has been subtracted out). The latter method is theoretically preferable and is used here.

Treynor's measure relates the average excess return on the portfolio during some period (exactly the same variable as in the Sharpe measure) to its systematic risk as measured by the portfolio's beta. The reward-to-volatility ratio is

(22-3)
$$\text{RVOL} = [\overline{\text{TR}}_p - \overline{\text{RF}}] / \beta_p$$

where
$[\overline{\text{TR}}_p - \overline{\text{RF}}]$ = average excess return on portfolio *p*
β_p = the beta for portfolio *p*

In this case we are calculating the excess return per unit of systematic risk. As with RVAR, higher values of RVOL indicate better portfolio performance. Portfolios can be ranked on their RVOL, and assuming that the Treynor measure is a correct calculation of portfolio performance, the best performing portfolio can be determined.

Using the data in Table 22-2, we can calculate RVOL for the same five portfolios illustrated and for the TSE 300, which has a beta of 1.0 by definition. These calculations indicate that only two funds — AIC (AI) and Templeton (T) — outperformed the market on the basis of their excess return/systematic risk ratio. The other three funds had RVOL ratios lower than the TSE 300. Once again, although T had a lower average return than the TSE 300, its beta of 0.63 was low enough to compensate for this smaller return (at least over this time period).

[7] J. Treynor, "How to Rate Management of Investment Funds," *Harvard Business Review* 43 (January–February 1965), pp. 63–75.

Figure 22-2 illustrates the graph of the Treynor measures in a manner similar to Figure 22-1 for the Sharpe measures. In this graph we are viewing the *ex post* security market line (SML). Again, two funds plot above the line — AI and T — and the other three plot below. Once again, if we were to draw lines to each fund's return-risk point, the steepest line would be the one drawn to AI, which has the largest slope and represents the best risk-adjusted performance.

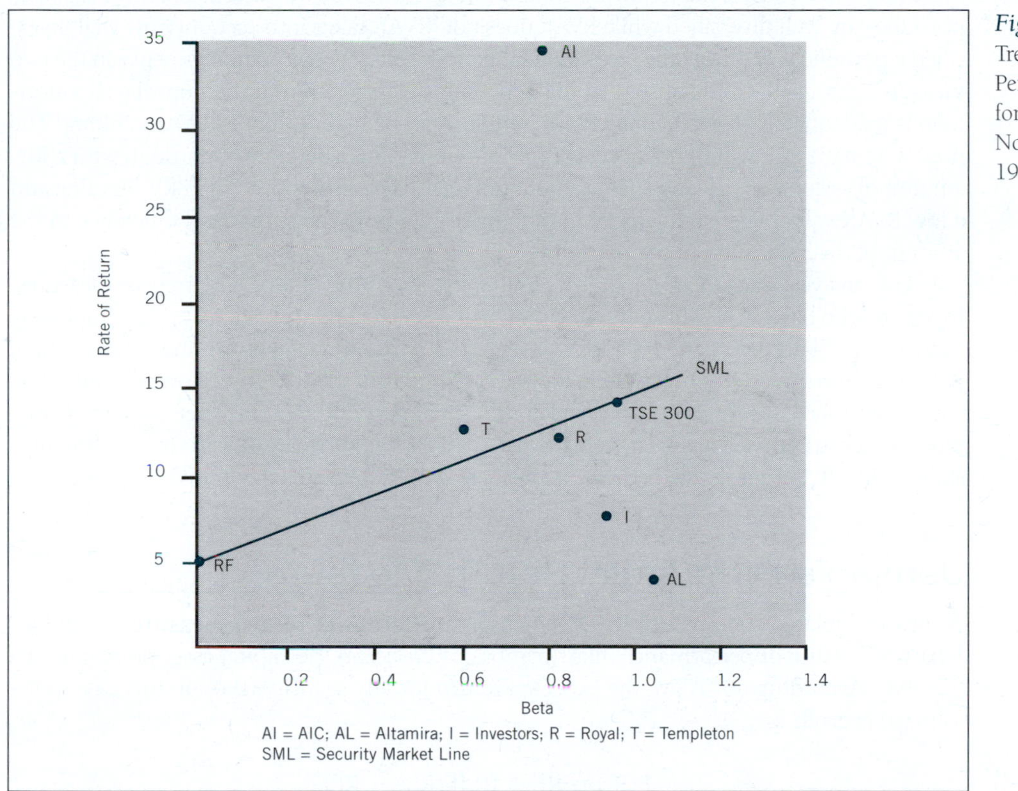

Figure 22-2
Treynor's Measure of Performance (RVOL) for Five Mutual Funds, November 1996–October 1998

The use of RVOL, of course, implies that systematic risk is the proper measure to use when evaluating portfolio performance; therefore, it implicitly assumes a completely diversified portfolio. (Similarly, the use of RVAR implies that total risk is the proper measure to use when evaluating portfolios.) As we now know, systematic risk is a proper measure of risk to use when portfolios are perfectly diversified so that no non-systematic risk remains.

Comparing the Sharpe and Treynor Measures

When should RVAR be used and when RVOL and why? Actually, given the assumptions underlying each measure, both can be said to be correct. Therefore, it is usually desirable to calculate both for the set of portfolios being evaluated. The choice of which to use could depend on the definition of risk. If an investor thinks it correct to use total risk, RVAR is appropriate; however, RVOL is appropriate for systematic risk.

What about the rankings of a set of portfolios using the two measures? If the portfolios are perfectly diversified — that is, the correlation coefficient between the portfolio return and the market return is 1.0 — the rankings will be identical. For typical large, professionally managed portfolios, such as broad-based equity mutual funds, the two measures often provide identical, or almost identical, rankings as was the case in our example above.

As the portfolios become less well diversified, the possibility of differences in rankings increases. This leads to the following conclusion about these two measures: RVOL assumes portfolios are well diversified while RVAR does not. RVAR takes into account how well diversified a portfolio was during the measurement period. Differences in rankings between the two measures can result from substantial differences in diversification in the portfolio. If a portfolio is inadequately diversified, its RVOL ranking can be higher than its RVAR ranking. The non-systematic risk would not affect the RVOL calculation. Therefore, a portfolio with a low amount of systematic risk and a large amount of total risk could show a high RVOL value and a low RVAR value. Such a difference in ranking results from the substantial difference in the amount of diversification of the portfolio.

This analysis leads to an important observation about the Sharpe and Treynor measures. Investors who have all (or substantially all) of their assets in a portfolio of securities should rely more on the Sharpe measure because it assesses the portfolio's total return in relation to total risk, which includes any non-systematic risk assumed by the investor. However, for those whose portfolio constitutes only one (relatively) small part of their total assets — that is, they have numerous other assets — systematic risk may well be the relevant risk. In these circumstances, RVOL is appropriate because it considers only systematic or non-diversifiable risk.

Differential Return Measure (Alpha)
The measure of portfolio performance calculated as the difference between what the portfolio actually earned and what it was expected to earn given its level of systematic risk.

Jensen's Differential Return Measure

A measure related to Treynor's RVOL is Jensen's **differential return measure** (or alpha). Jensen's measure of performance, like Treynor's, is based on the capital asset pricing model (CAPM). According to CAPM, the expected return for any security (i) or, in this case, portfolio (p) is given as

(22-4)
$$E(R_p) = RF + \beta_p\,[E(R_M) - RF]$$

with all terms as previously defined.

Notice that Equation 22-4, which covers any *ex ante* period, can be applied to *ex post* periods if the investor's expectations are realized, on average. Empirically, Equation 22-4 can be approximated as Equation 22-5.

(22-5)
$$R_{pt} = RF_t + \beta_p\,[R_{Mt} - RF_t] + e_{pt}$$

where
R_{pt} = the return on portfolio p in period t
RF_t = the risk-free rate in period t
R_M = the return on the market in period t
e_{pt} = a random error term for portfolio p in period t
$[R_{Mt} - RF_t]$ = the market risk premium during period t

Equation 22-5 relates the realized return on portfolio p during any period t to the sum of the risk-free rate and the portfolio's risk premium plus an error term. Given the market risk premium, the risk premium on portfolio p is a function of portfolio p's systematic risk — the larger its systematic risk, the larger the risk premium.

Equation 22-5 can be written in what is called the risk premium (or, alternatively, the excess return) form by moving RF to the left side and subtracting it from R_{pt}, as in Equation 22-6:

$$R_{pt} - RF_t = \beta_p [R_{Mt} - RF_t] + e_{pt} \tag{22-6}$$

where
$R_{pt} - RF_t$ = the risk premium on portfolio p

Equation 22-6 indicates that the risk premium on portfolio p is equal to the product of its beta and the market risk premium plus an error term. In other words, the risk premium on portfolio p should be proportional to that on the market portfolio if the CAPM model is correct and investor expectations were generally realized (in effect, if all assets and portfolios were in equilibrium).

A return proportional to the risk assumed is illustrated by Fund Y in Figure 22-3. This diagram shows the characteristic line in excess return form, where the risk-free rate each period, RF_t, is subtracted from both the portfolio's return and the market's return.[8] Equation 22-6 can be empirically tested by fitting a regression for some number of periods. Portfolio excess returns (risk premiums) are regressed against the excess returns (risk premiums) for the market. If managers earn a return proportional to the risk assumed, this relationship should hold. That is, there should be no intercept term (alpha) in the regression, which should go through the origin, as in the case of Fund Y in Figure 22-3.

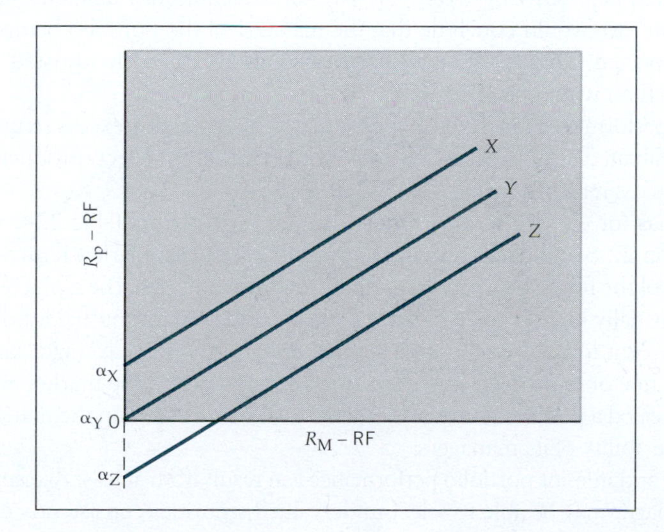

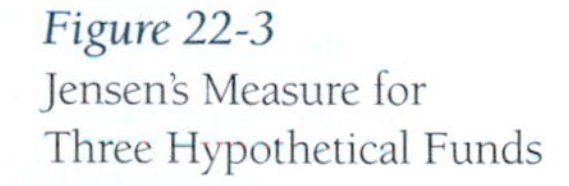
Figure 22-3
Jensen's Measure for Three Hypothetical Funds

Given these expected findings, Jensen argued that an intercept term, alpha, could be added to Equation 22-6 as a means of identifying superior or inferior portfolio performance. Therefore, Equation 22-6 becomes Equation 22-7 where α_p is the alpha or intercept term:

$$R_{pt} - RF_t = \alpha_p + \beta_p [R_{Mt} - RF_t] + e_{pt} \tag{22-7}$$

[8] This version is usually referred to as a characteristic line in risk premium or excess return form.

The CAPM asserts that equilibrium conditions should result in a zero intercept term. Therefore, the alpha should measure the contribution of the portfolio manager since it represents the average incremental rate of return per period beyond the return attributable to the level of risk assumed. Specifically:

- If alpha is significantly positive, this is evidence of superior performance (illustrated in Figure 22-3 with portfolio X, which has a positive intercept)
- If alpha is significantly negative, this is evidence of inferior performance (illustrated in Figure 22-3 with portfolio Z, which has a negative intercept)
- If alpha is insignificantly different from zero, this is evidence that the portfolio manager matched the market on a risk-adjusted basis (as in the case of portfolio Y).

Note that Equation 22-7 can be rearranged to better demonstrate what α_p really is. Rearranging terms, Equation 22-7 becomes, for the sample time period:

(22-8)
$$\alpha_p = (\overline{R}_p - \overline{RF}) - [\beta_p (\overline{R}_M - \overline{RF})]$$

where the bars above the variables indicate averages for the period measured.

Equation 22-8 states that α_p is the difference between the actual excess return on portfolio *p* during some period and the risk premium on that portfolio that should have been earned, given its level of systematic risk and the use of the CAPM. It measures the constant return that the portfolio manager earned above, or below, the return of an unmanaged portfolio with the same (market) risk.

As noted, this difference can be positive, negative, or zero. It is important to recognize the role of statistical significance in the interpretation of Jensen's measure. Although the estimated alpha may be positive or negative, it may not be significantly different (statistically) from zero. If it is not, we would conclude that the manager of the portfolio being evaluated performed as expected. That is, the manager earned an average risk-adjusted return, neither more nor less than would be expected given the risk assumed.

Jensen's performance measure can be estimated by regressing excess returns for the portfolio being evaluated against excess returns for the market (in effect, producing a characteristic line in excess return form).

The alphas for the five mutual funds that are presented in Table 22-3 were estimated using Equation 22-8 and using averages for portfolio returns, market returns, and the risk-free rate. Two of the funds — AI and T — showed positive alphas. The alpha of 23.76 per cent for AIC is unusually high, relative to those typically observed for mutual funds. If significant, the 23.76 per cent for AIC would indicate that this fund, on the average, earned an annual risk-adjusted rate of return that was close to 24 per cent above the market average. In other words, AIC earned a positive return attributable to factors other than the market, presumably because of the ability of its managers.

Superior and inferior portfolio performance can result from at least two sources. First, the portfolio manager may be able to select undervalued securities consistently enough to affect portfolio performance. Second, the manager may be able to time market turns, varying the portfolio's composition in accordance with the rise and fall of the market. Obviously, a manager with enough ability may be able to do both.

A Comparison of the Three Composite Measures

The Sharpe measure, which uses the standard deviation, evaluates portfolio performance on the basis of both the portfolio's return and its diversification. Treynor's measure considers only the systematic risk of the portfolio and, like Sharpe's, can be used to rank portfolios on the basis of realized performance. Although the Sharpe and Treynor measures rank portfolios, they do not tell us in percentage terms how much a fund outperformed (or underperformed) some benchmark.

Like the Treynor measure, Jensen's alpha uses beta as the measure of risk. Jensen's measure was not designed for ranking portfolio performance, but it can be modified to do so. The Jensen and Treynor measures can produce, with proper adjustments, identical relative rankings of portfolio performance.[9]

If a portfolio is completely diversified, all three measures will agree on a ranking of portfolios. The reason for this is that with complete diversification, total variance is equal to systematic variance. When portfolios are not completely diversified, the Treynor and Jensen measures can rank relatively undiversified portfolios much higher than the Sharpe measure can. Since the Sharpe measure uses total risk, both systematic and non-systematic components are included.

PROBLEMS WITH PORTFOLIO MEASUREMENT

Using the three risk-adjusted performance measures just discussed to evaluate portfolios is not without problems. Investors should understand their limitations and be guided accordingly.

These measures are derived from capital market theory and the CAPM and are therefore dependent on the assumptions involved with this theory, as discussed in Chapter 9. For example, if the T-bill rate is not a satisfactory proxy for the risk-free rate, or if investors cannot borrow and lend at the risk-free rate, this will have an impact on these measures of performance. An important assumption of capital market theory that directly affects the use of these performance measures is the assumption of a market portfolio that can be proxied by a market index. We have used the TSE 300 Index as a market index, as is often done. However, there are potential problems.

Richard Roll has argued that beta is not a clear-cut measure of risk.[10] If the definition of the market portfolio is changed, the beta can change. This could, in turn, change the rankings of portfolios. In addition, if the proxy for the market portfolio is not efficient, the security market line (SML) used may not be the true SML. When portfolios are plotted against an incorrect SML, benchmark errors can occur.

Although a high correlation exists among most of the commonly used market proxies, this does not eliminate the problem that some may be efficient but others are not. This relates to Roll's major point (mentioned in Chapter 9) that using a market portfolio other than the

---

[9] Jensen's alpha divided by beta is equivalent to Treynor's measure minus the average risk premium for the market portfolio for the period.

[10] R. Roll, "Ambiguity When Performance Is Measured by the Securities Market Line," *Journal of Finance* 33 (September 1978), pp. 1051–1069; "Performance Evaluation and Benchmark Error, Part I," *Journal of Portfolio Management* 6 (Summer 1980), pp. 5–12, and Part II, 7 (Winter 1981), pp. 17–22.

"true" one does not constitute a test of the CAPM. Rather, it is a test only of whether or not the chosen market proxy is efficient. According to Roll, no unambiguous test of the CAPM has yet been conducted. This point should be kept in mind when we consider the Treynor and Jensen performance measures, which are based on the CAPM.

The movement to global investing increases the problem of benchmark error. The efficient frontier changes when foreign securities are added to the portfolio. The measurement of beta will be affected by adding foreign securities. Given that a world portfolio is likely to have a smaller variance than the TSE 300 Index, any measure of systematic risk is likely to be smaller.

A long evaluation period is needed to successfully determine performance that is truly superior. Over short periods, luck can overshadow all else, but it cannot be expected to continue. According to some estimates, the number of years needed to make such an accurate determination is quite large. As we saw in Table 22-1, the Performance Presentation Standards stipulate at least a 10-year performance record.

Theoretically, each of the three performance measures discussed should be independent of its respective risk measure. However, over the years some researchers have found a relationship between them. In some cases the relationship was negative, and in others it was positive. It can be shown that a fundamental relationship does exist between the composite performance measures and their associated risk measure.[11] Given an empirical CML, the relation between Sharpe's measure and the standard deviation can be instantly derived. Similarly, given an empirical SML, the relationship between Jensen's and Treynor's performance measures and beta can be deduced. The only other variable needed to do these calculations is the mean market return for the period.

OTHER ISSUES IN PERFORMANCE EVALUATION

Monitoring Performance

Evaluation of managed portfolios should be a continuous process using some of the techniques discussed above. In addition, a monitoring process should evaluate the success of the portfolio relative to the objectives and constraints of the portfolio's owners.

Performance Attribution

Performance Attribution
A part of portfolio evaluation that seeks to determine why success or failure occurred.

Most of this chapter has considered how to measure a portfolio manager's performance, but portfolio evaluation is also concerned with the reasons why a manager did better or worse than a properly constructed benchmark with complete risk adjustment. This part of portfolio evaluation, called **performance attribution**, seeks to determine, after the fact, why a particular portfolio had a given return over some specified time period and, therefore, why it succeeded or failed.

Typically, performance attribution is a top-down approach; it looks first at the broad issues and progresses by narrowing the investigation. Its purpose is to divide the total performance of a portfolio into specific components that can be associated with specific decisions made by the portfolio manager.

[11] J. Wilson and C. Jones, "The Relationship Between Performance and Risk: Whence the Bias?" *Journal of Financial Research* 4 (Summer 1981), pp. 109–117.

Performance attribution often begins with the policy statement that guides the management of the portfolio. The portfolio normally would have a set of portfolio weights to be used, but if the manager uses a different set, this will account for some of the variation in the results. In effect, we are looking at the asset allocation decision referred to in Chapter 14. If a manager chooses to allocate portfolio funds differently than the weights that occur in the benchmark portfolio, what are the results?

After this analysis, performance attribution might analyze sector (industry) selection and security selection. Did the manager concentrate on, or avoid, certain sectors, and if so what were the results? Security selection speaks for itself.

Part of this process involves identifying a benchmark of performance to use in comparing the portfolio's results. This "bogey" is designed to measure passive results, ruling out both asset allocation and security selection decisions. Any differences between the portfolio's results and the bogey must be attributable to one or more of these decisions made by the portfolio manager.

Another way to think about performance attribution is to recognize that performance different from a properly constructed benchmark comes from one or both of these sources:

- Market timing
- Security selection.

Techniques are available to decompose the performance of a portfolio into these two components.[12]

Can Performance Be Predicted?

The objective of performance evaluation is to measure the performance of a portfolio and its manager over a certain time period. Having assessed how well a portfolio manager has performed over the past, is such information valuable in predicting future portfolio performance? As discussed in Chapter 10, most studies suggest that the correlation between past relative performance and future performance is weak. For example, the correlation coefficients for the average returns for a five- or one-year period with average returns for the subsequent corresponding period, are quite low, usually less than 0.20. Therefore, past relative returns do not successfully predict future returns.

SUMMARY

This summary relates to the learning objectives provided on page 707.

1. **Outline the framework for evaluating portfolio performance.**
Evaluation of portfolio performance, the bottom line of the investing process, is an important aspect of interest to all investors and money managers. The framework for evaluating portfolio performance consists of measuring both the realized return and the differential risk of the portfolio being evaluated, determining an appropriate benchmark portfolio to use to compare a portfolio's performance and recognizing any constraints that

[12] R. Henriksson, "Market Timing and Mutual Fund Performance: An Empirical Investigation," *Journal of Business* 57 (January 1984), pp. 73–96.

the portfolio manager may face. AIMR has issued a set of Performance Presentation Standards designed to promote full disclosure by investment managers in reporting their investment results and help ensure uniformity in reporting.

2. **Use measures of return and risk to evaluate portfolio performance.**
The time-weighted, as opposed to the dollar-weighted, return captures the rate of return actually earned by the portfolio manager. Total returns are used in the calculations. The two prevalent measures of risk are total risk (standard deviation) and systematic risk (beta). The most often used composite measures of portfolio performance are those of Sharpe, Treynor, and Jensen, which bring return and risk together in one calculation.

3. **Distinguish between the three composite measures of portfolio performance.**
The Sharpe and Treynor measures can be used to rank portfolio performance and indicate the relative positions of the portfolios being evaluated, while Jensen's measure is an absolute measure of performance. Both the Sharpe and Treynor measures relate the excess return on a portfolio to a measure of its risk. Sharpe's RVAR uses standard deviation, whereas Treynor's RVOL uses beta. Since RVAR implicitly measures the lack of complete diversification in a portfolio and RVOL assumes complete diversification, portfolio rankings from the two measures can differ if portfolios are not well diversified. The Sharpe measure is more appropriate when the portfolio constitutes a significant portion of an investor's wealth, whereas the Treynor measure is more appropriate when the portfolio constitutes only a small part of that wealth. Jensen's differential return measures the difference between what the portfolio was expected to earn, given its systematic risk, and what it actually did earn. By regressing the portfolio's excess return against that of the market index, alpha can be used to capture the superior or inferior performance of the portfolio manager. Based on capital market theory, alphas are expected to be zero. Significantly positive or negative alphas indicate above or below average performance.

4. **Discuss problems with portfolio measurement.**
The composite measures are not without their limitations and problems. The problems associated with capital market theory and the CAPM carry over to performance measurement. One problem in particular is the market portfolio, which can not be measured precisely. Failure to use the true *ex ante* market portfolio may result in different betas and different rankings for portfolios because of benchmark error.

5. **Explain issues in portfolio evaluation such as performance attribution.**
Performance attribution is concerned with why a portfolio manager did better or worse than an expected benchmark. It involves decomposing performance to determine why the particular results occurred.

KEY TERMS

Benchmark portfolio
Composite (risk-adjusted) measures of portfolio performance
Differential return measure (alpha)
Dollar-weighted rate of return (DWR)
Performance attribution
Performance Presentation Standards (PPS)
Reward-to-variability ratio (RVAR)
Reward-to-volatility ratio (RVOL)
Time-weighted rate of return (TWR)

ADDITIONAL RESOURCES

Some of the problems in performance measurement are discussed in:
Ferguson, Robert. "The Trouble with Performance Measurement." *The Journal of Portfolio Management.* (Spring 1986), pp. 4–9.

A short discussion of performance measurement can be found in:
Good, Walter. "Measuring Performance." *Financial Analysts Journal.* (May-June 1983), pp. 19–23.

The relationships among the composite measures are explained in:
Wilson, Jack, and Jones, Charles. "The Relationship Between Performance and Risk: Whence the Bias?" *Journal of Financial Research.* (Summer 1981), pp. 109–117.

REVIEW QUESTIONS

1. How can one construct a characteristic line for a portfolio? What does it show?
2. Explain why the steeper the angle, the better the performance in Figures 22-1 and 22-2.
3. Outline the framework for evaluating portfolio performance.
4. What role does diversification play in the Sharpe and Treynor measures?
5. In general, when may an investor prefer to rely on the Sharpe measure? the Treynor measure?
6. Explain how Jensen's differential return measure is derived from the CAPM.
7. In theory, what would be the proper market index to use?
8. Do the Sharpe and Jensen measures always produce the same rankings of portfolio performance?
9. Explain how the three composite measures of performance are related to capital market theory and the CAPM.
10. How does Roll's questioning of the testing of the CAPM relate to the issue of performance measurement?
11. Illustrate how the choice of the wrong market index could affect the rankings of portfolios.

PREPARING FOR YOUR PROFESSIONAL EXAMS

PAST CFA EXAM PROBLEM

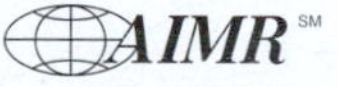

1. An analyst wants to evaluate portfolio X, consisting entirely of US common stocks, using both the Treynor and Sharpe measures of portfolio performance. The table below provides the average annual rate of return for portfolio X, the market portfolio (as measured by the Standard & Poor's 500 Index), and US Treasury bills during the past eight years.

	Average Annual Rate of Return	Standard Deviation of Return	Beta
Portfolio X	10%	18%	0.60
S&P 500	12	13	1.00
T-bills	6	n/a	n/a

n/a = not applicable

a. Calculate both the Treynor measure and the Sharpe measure for both Portfolio X and the S&P 500. Briefly explain whether portfolio X underperformed, equaled, or outperformed the S&P 500 on a risk-adjusted basis using both the Treynor measure and the Sharpe measure.

b. Based on the performance of portfolio X relative to the S&P 500 calculated in (a), briefly explain the reason for the conflicting results when using the Treynor measure versus the Sharpe measure.

PROBLEMS

1. Consider the five funds shown below:

	α	β
1	2.0	1.0
2	1.6*	1.1
3	3.5	0.9
4	1.2	0.8
5	0.9*	1.20

* Significant at the 5% level.

a. Which fund had the lowest market risk? The highest?

b. According to Jensen's alpha, which fund(s) outperformed the market?

2. The following data are available for five portfolios and the market for a recent 10-year period:

	Average Annual Return (%)	**Standard Deviation (%)**	β_p
1	14	21	1.15
2	16	24	1.1
3	26	30	1.3
4	17	25	0.9
5	10	18	0.45
TSE 300	12	20	
RF	6		

a. Rank these portfolios using the Sharpe measure.

b. Rank these portfolios using the Treynor measure.

c. Compare the rankings of portfolios 1 and 2. Are there any differences? How can you explain these differences?

d. Which of these portfolios outperformed the market?

3. Annual total returns for nine years are shown below for eight mutual funds. Characteristic lines are calculated using annual market returns. The *ex post* values are as follows:

Fund	(1) R_p(%)	(2) σ_p(%)	(3) α_p	(4) β_p
A	17.0	20.0	7.53	0.88
B	19.0	17.8	11.70	0.65
C	12.3	25.0	3.12	0.83
D	20.0	24.5	9.00	1.00
E	15.0	17.4	6.15	0.79
F	19.0	18.0	10.11	0.83
G	8.6	19.0	−1.37	0.91
H	20.0	21.5	9.52	0.93

where

R_p = mean annual total return for each fund
σ_p = standard deviation of the annual returns
α_p = the constant of the characteristic line
β_p = the slope

Using an 8.6 per cent risk-free return:

a. Calculate Sharpe's RVAR for each of these eight funds, and rank the eight funds from high to low performance.

b. Calculate Treynor's RVOL for each fund and perform the same ranking as in part (a).

4. Given the following information:

Period	Market	RF	Portfolio 1	Portfolio 2
1	0.12	.07	0.14	0.16
2	0.10	.07	0.18	0.20
3	0.02	.08	0.06	0.04
4	0.20	.08	0.30	0.26
5	0.16	.07	0.21	0.21
6	−0.03	.08	−0.04	−0.06
7	−0.05	.07	−0.04	−0.01
8	0.13	.07	0.14	0.12
9	0.30	.08	0.28	0.32
10	−0.15	.09	−0.20	−0.25

a. Rank the portfolios on RVAR.

b. Rank the portfolios on RVOL.

c. Rank the portfolios on alpha.

d. Which portfolio had the larger beta?

e. Which portfolio had the larger standard deviation?

f. Which portfolio had the larger average return?

g. How are the answers to (d), (e), and (f) related to the results for the composite performance measures?

5. Given the following information for three portfolios for a six-year period:

Period	Market	RF	Portfolio 1	Portfolio 2	Portfolio 3
1	0.10	.05	0.15	0.16	0.17
2	0.02	.06	0.09	0.11	0.13
3	0.20	.08	0.26	0.28	0.18
4	0.30	.09	0.34	0.36	0.42
5	−0.04	.08	−0.02	−0.03	−0.16
6	0.16	.07	0.16	0.17	0.17

Answer (a) through (c) without doing the calculations.

a. Which portfolio would you expect to have the largest beta?

b. Which portfolio would you expect to have the largest standard deviation?

c. Which portfolio would you expect to rank first on the basis of RVAR?

d. Determine the rankings of the three portfolios based on RVAR and on RVOL.

e. Which portfolio had the largest alpha?

f. Which portfolio exhibited the best performance based on the composite measures of performance?

6. The following information is available for two portfolios, a market index, and the risk-free rate:

Period	Market Return	RF	Portfolio 1	Portfolio 2
1	0.10	.06	0.10	0.20
2	0.12	.08	0.12	0.24
3	0.20	.08	0.20	0.40
4	0.04	.08	0.04	0.08
5	0.12	.08	0.12	0.24

a. Without doing calculations, determine the portfolio with a beta of 1.0.

b. Without doing calculations, determine the beta of portfolio 2.

c. Without doing calculations, what would you expect the alpha of portfolio 1 to be?

d. What would you expect the RVAR and RVOL to be for portfolio 1 relative to the market?

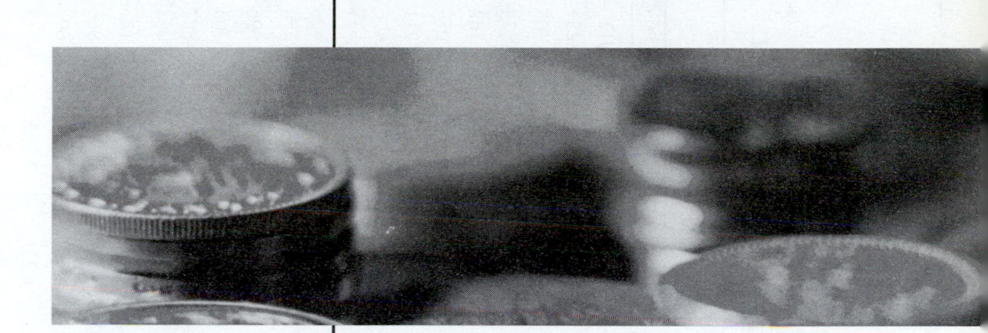

APPENDIX
Tables

TABLE A-1

Compound (Future) Value Factors ($FV_{R,N}$) for $1 Compounded at R Per Cent for N Periods $FV_{R,N} = (1 + R)^N$

N	R = 1%	2%	3%	4%	5%	6%	7%	8%	9%	10%	11%	12%	13%
1	1.01	1.02	1.03	1.04	1.05	1.06	1.07	1.08	1.09	1.1	1.11	1.12	1.13
2	1.02	1.04	1.061	1.082	1.103	1.124	1.145	1.166	1.188	1.21	1.232	1.254	1.277
3	1.03	1.061	1.093	1.125	1.158	1.191	1.225	1.26	1.295	1.331	1.368	1.405	1.443
4	1.041	1.082	1.126	1.17	1.216	1.262	1.311	1.36	1.412	1.464	1.518	1.574	1.53
5	1.051	1.104	1.159	1.217	1.276	1.338	1.403	1.469	1.539	1.611	1.685	1.762	1.842
6	1.062	1.126	1.194	1.265	1.34	1.419	1.501	1.587	1.677	1.772	1.87	1.974	2.082
7	1.072	1.149	1.23	1.316	1.407	1.504	1.606	1.714	1.828	1.949	2.076	2.211	2.353
8	1.083	1.172	1.267	1.369	1.477	1.594	1.718	1.851	1.993	2.144	2.305	2.476	2.658
9	1.094	1.195	1.305	1.423	1.551	1.689	1.838	1.999	2.172	2.358	2.558	2.773	3.004
10	1.105	1.219	1.344	1.48	1.629	1.791	1.967	2.159	2.367	2.594	2.839	3.106	3.395
11	1.116	1.243	1.384	1.539	1.71	1.898	2.105	2.332	2.58	2.853	3.152	3.479	3.836
12	1.127	1.268	1.426	1.601	1.796	2.012	2.252	2.518	2.813	3.138	3.498	3.896	4.335
13	1.138	1.294	1.469	1.665	1.886	2.133	2.41	2.72	3.066	3.452	3.883	4.363	4.898
14	1.149	1.319	1.513	1.732	1.98	2.261	2.579	2.937	3.342	3.797	4.31	4.887	5.535
15	1.161	1.346	1.558	1.801	2.079	2.397	2.759	3.172	3.642	4.177	4.785	5.474	6.254
16	1.173	1.373	1.605	1.873	2.183	2.54	2.952	3.426	3.97	4.595	5.311	6.13	7.067
17	1.184	1.4	1.653	1.948	2.292	2.693	3.159	3.7	4.328	5.054	5.895	6.866	7.986
18	1.196	1.428	1.702	2.026	2.407	2.854	3.38	3.996	4.717	5.56	6.544	7.69	9.024
19	1.208	1.457	1.754	2.107	2.527	3.026	3.617	4.316	5.142	6.116	7.263	8.613	10.197
20	1.22	1.486	1.806	2.191	2.653	3.206	3.87	4.661	5.604	6.727	8.062	9.646	11.523
21	1.232	1.516	1.86	2.279	2.786	3.4	4.141	5.034	6.109	7.4	8.949	10.804	13.021
22	1.245	1.546	1.916	2.37	2.925	3.604	4.43	5.437	6.659	8.14	9.934	12.1	14.714
23	1.257	1.577	1.974	2.465	3.072	3.82	4.741	5.871	7.258	8.954	10.026	13.552	16.627
24	1.27	1.608	2.033	2.563	3.225	4.049	5.072	6.341	7.911	9.85	12.239	15.179	18.788
25	1.282	1.641	2.094	2.666	3.386	4.292	5.427	6.848	8.623	10.835	13.585	17	21.231
30	1.348	1.811	2.427	3.243	4.322	5.743	7.612	10.063	13.268	17.449	22.892	29.96	39.116
35	1.417	2	2.814	3.946	5.516	7.686	10.677	14.785	20.414	28.102	38.575	52.8	72.069
40	1.489	2.208	3.262	4.801	7.04	10.286	14.974	21.725	31.409	45.259	65.001	93.051	132.782
45	1.565	2.438	3.782	5.841	8.985	13.765	21.002	31.92	48.327	72.89	109.53	163.98	244.641
50	1.645	2.692	4.384	7.107	11.467	18.42	29.457	46.902	74.358	117.39	184.56	289.00	450.735

TABLE A-1

Compound (Future) Value Factors ($FV_{R,N}$) for $1 Compounded at R Per Cent for N Periods (Continued) $FV_{R,N} = (1 + R)^N$

	R =												
N	14%	15%	16%	18%	20%	22%	24%	25%	30%	35%	40%	45%	50%
1	1.14	1.15	1.16	1.18	1.2	1.22	1.25	1.25	1.3	1.35	1.4	1.45	1.5
2	1.3	1.323	1.346	1.392	1.44	1.488	1.538	1.563	1.69	1.823	1.96	2.103	2.25
3	1.482	1.521	1.561	1.643	1.728	1.816	1.907	1.953	2.197	2.46	2.744	3.049	3.375
4	1.689	1.749	1.811	1.939	2.074	2.215	2.364	2.441	2.856	3.322	3.842	4.421	5.063
5	1.925	2.011	2.1	2.288	2.488	2.703	2.932	3.052	3.713	4.484	5.378	6.41	7.594
6	2.195	2.313	2.436	2.7	2.986	3.297	3.635	3.815	4.827	6.053	7.53	9.294	11.391
7	2.502	2.66	2.826	3.185	3.583	4.023	4.508	4.768	6.275	8.172	10.541	13.476	17.068
8	2.853	3.059	3.278	3.759	4.3	4.908	5.59	5.96	8.157	11.032	14.758	19.541	25.629
9	3.252	3.518	3.803	4.435	5.16	5.987	6.931	7.451	10.604	14.894	20.661	28.334	38.443
10	3.707	4.046	4.411	5.234	6.192	7.305	8.594	9.313	13.786	20.107	28.925	41.085	57.665
11	4.226	4.652	5.117	6.176	7.43	8.912	10.657	11.642	17.922	27.144	40.496	59.573	86.498
12	4.818	5.35	5.936	7.288	8.916	10.872	13.215	14.552	23.298	36.644	56.694	86.381	129.746
13	5.492	6.153	6.886	8.599	10.699	13.264	16.386	18.19	30.288	49.47	79.371	125.25	194.62
14	6.261	7.076	7.988	10.147	12.839	16.182	20.319	22.737	39.374	66.784	111.12	181.61	291.929
15	7.138	8.137	9.266	11.974	15.407	19.742	25.196	28.422	51.186	90.158	155.56	263.34	437.894
16	8.137	9.358	10.748	14.129	18.488	24.086	31.243	35.527	66.542	121.71	217.79	381.84	656.841
17	9.276	10.761	12.468	16.672	22.186	29.384	38.741	44.409	86.504	164.31	304.91	553.67	985.261
18	10.575	12.375	14.463	19.673	26.623	35.849	48.039	55.511	112.45	221.82	426.87	802.83	1477.892
19	12.056	14.232	16.777	23.214	31.948	43.736	59.568	69.389	146.19	299.46	597.63	1164.1	2216.838
20	13.743	16.367	19.461	27.393	38.338	53.358	73.864	86.736	190.05	404.27	836.68	1687.9	3325.257
21	15.668	18.822	22.574	32.324	46.005	65.096	91.592	108.42	247.06	545.76	1171.3	2447.5	4987.885
22	17.861	21.645	26.186	38.142	55.206	79.418	113.57	135.52	321.18	716.78	1639.8	3548.9	7481.828
23	20.362	24.891	30.376	45.008	66.247	96.889	140.83	169.40	417.53	994.66	2297.8	5145.9	11222.74
24	23.212	28.625	35.236	53.109	79.497	118.20	174.63	211.75	542.80	1342.7	3214.2	7461.6	16834.11
25	26.462	32.919	40.874	62.669	95.396	144.21	216.54	264.69	705.64	1812.7	4499.8	10819.	25251.17
30	50.95	66.212	85.85	143.37	237.37	389.75	634.82	807.79	2619.9	8128.5	24201.	69348.	191751.1
35	98.1	133.17	180.31	327.99	590.66	1053.4	1861.0	2465.1	9727.8	36448.	130161.	444508.	
40	188.88	267.86	378.72	750.37	1469.7	2847.0	5455.9	7523.1	36118.	163437.	700037		
45	363.67	538.76	795.44	1716.6	3657.2	7694.7	15994.	22958.	134106.	732857.			
50	700.23	1083.6	1670.7	3927.3	9100.4	20796.	46890.	70064.	497929.				

TABLE A-2

Present Value Factors ($PV_{R,N}$) at R Per Cent for $1 Received at the end of N Periods $PV_{R,N} = \left[\frac{1}{(1+R)^N}\right]$

N	R = 1%	2%	3%	4%	5%	6%	7%	8%	9%	10%	11%	12%	13%
1	.990	.980	.971	.962	.952	.943	.935	.926	.917	.909	.901	.893	.885
2	.980	.961	.943	.925	.907	.890	.873	.857	.842	.826	.812	.797	.783
3	.971	.942	.915	.889	.864	.840	.816	.794	.772	.751	.731	.712	.693
4	.961	.924	.888	.855	.823	.792	.763	.735	.708	.683	.659	.636	.613
5	.951	.906	.863	.822	.784	.747	.713	.681	.650	.621	.593	.567	.543
6	.942	.888	.837	.790	.746	.705	.666	.630	.596	.564	.535	.507	.480
7	.932	.871	.813	.760	.711	.665	.623	.583	.547	.513	.482	.452	.425
8	.923	.853	.789	.731	.677	.627	.582	.540	.502	.467	.434	.404	.376
9	.914	.837	.766	.703	.645	.592	.544	.500	.460	.424	.391	.361	.333
10	.905	.820	.744	.676	.614	.558	.508	.463	.422	.386	.352	.322	.295
11	.896	.804	.722	.650	.585	.527	.475	.429	.388	.350	.317	.287	.261
12	.887	.788	.701	.625	.557	.497	.444	.397	.356	.319	.286	.257	.231
13	.879	.773	.681	.601	.530	.469	.415	.368	.326	.290	.258	.229	.204
14	.870	.758	.661	.577	.505	.442	.388	.340	.299	.263	.232	.205	.181
15	.861	.743	.642	.555	.481	.417	.362	.315	.275	.239	.209	.183	.160
16	.853	.728	.623	.534	.458	.394	.339	.292	.252	.218	.188	.163	.141
17	.844	.714	.605	.513	.436	.371	.317	.270	.231	.198	.170	.146	.125
18	.836	.700	.587	.494	.416	.350	.296	.250	.212	.180	.153	.130	.111
19	.828	.686	.570	.475	.396	.331	.277	.232	.194	.164	.138	.116	.098
20	.820	.673	.554	.456	.377	.312	.258	.215	.178	.149	.124	.104	.087
21	.811	.660	.538	.439	.359	.294	.242	.199	.164	.135	.112	.093	.077
22	.803	.647	.522	.422	.342	.278	.226	.184	.150	.123	.101	.083	.068
23	.795	.634	.507	.406	.326	.262	.211	.170	.133	.112	.091	.074	.060
24	.788	.622	.492	.390	.310	.247	.197	.158	.126	.102	.082	.066	.053
25	.780	.610	.478	.375	.295	.233	.184	.146	.116	.092	.074	.059	.047
30	.742	.552	.412	.308	.231	.174	.131	.099	.075	.057	.044	.033	.026
35	.706	.500	.355	.253	.181	.130	.094	.068	.049	.036	.026	.019	.014
40	.672	.453	.307	.208	.142	.097	.067	.046	.032	.022	.015	.011	.008
45	.639	.410	.264	.171	.111	.073	.048	.031	.021	.014	.009	.006	.004
50	.608	.372	.228	.141	.087	.054	.034	.021	.013	.009	.005	.003	.002

TABLE A-2

Present Value Factors ($PV_{R,N}$) at R Per Cent for $1 Received at the end of N Periods (Continued) $PV_{R,N} = \left[\frac{1}{(1+R)^N}\right]$

N	R = 14%	15%	16%	18%	20%	22%	24%	25%	30%	35%	40%	45%	50%
1	.877	.870	.862	.847	.833	.820	.806	.800	.769	.741	.714	.690	.667
2	.769	.756	.743	.718	.694	.672	.650	.640	.592	.449	.510	.476	.444
3	.675	.658	.641	.609	.579	.551	.524	.512	.455	.406	.364	.328	.296
4	.592	.572	.552	.516	.482	.451	.423	.410	.350	.301	.260	.226	.198
5	.519	.497	.476	.437	.402	.370	.341	.328	.269	.223	.186	.156	.132
6	.456	.432	.410	.370	.335	.303	.275	.262	.207	.165	.133	.108	.088
7	.400	.376	.354	.314	.279	.249	.222	.210	.159	.122	.095	.074	.059
8	.351	.327	.305	.266	.233	.204	.179	.168	.123	.091	.068	.051	.039
9	.308	.284	.263	.225	.194	.167	.144	.134	.094	.067	.048	.035	.026
10	.270	.247	.227	.191	.162	.137	.116	.107	.073	.050	.035	.024	.017
11	.237	.215	.195	.162	.135	.112	.094	.086	.056	.037	.025	.017	.012
12	.208	.187	.168	.137	.112	.092	.076	.069	.043	.027	.018	.012	.008
13	.182	.163	.145	.116	.093	.075	.061	.055	.033	.020	.013	.008	.005
14	.160	.141	.125	.099	.078	.062	.049	.044	.025	.015	.009	.006	.003
15	.140	.123	.108	.084	.065	.051	.040	.035	.020	.011	.006	.004	.002
16	.123	.107	.093	.071	.054	.042	.032	.028	.015	.008	.005	.003	.002
17	.108	.093	.080	.060	.045	.034	.026	.023	.012	.006	.003	.002	.001
18	.095	.081	.069	.051	.038	.028	.021	.018	.009	.005	.002	.001	.001
19	.083	.070	.060	.043	.031	.023	.017	.014	.007	.003	.002	.001	
20	.073	.061	.051	.037	.026	.019	.014	.012	.005	.002	.001	.001	
21	.064	.053	.044	.031	.022	.015	.011	.009	.004	.002	.001		
22	.056	.046	.038	.026	.018	.013	.009	.007	.003	.001	.001		
23	.049	.040	.033	.022	.015	.010	.007	.006	.002	.001			
24	.043	.035	.028	.019	.013	.008	.006	.005	.002	.001			
25	.038	.030	.024	.016	.010	.007	.005	.004	.001	.001			
30	.020	.015	.012	.007	.004	.003	.002	.001					
35	.010	.008	.006	.003	.002	.001	.001						
40	.005	.004	.003	.001	.001								
45	.003	.002	.001	.001									
50	.001	.001	.001										

TABLE A-3

Future Value Annuity Factors ($FVA_{R,N}$) for $1 Compounded at R Per Cent for N Periods $FVA_{R,N} = \left[\frac{(1+R)^N - 1}{R}\right]$

	R =												
N	1%	2%	3%	4%	5%	6%	7%	8%	9%	10%	11%	12%	13%
1	1	1	1	1	1	1	1	1	1	1	1	1	1
2	2.01	2.02	2.03	2.04	2.05	2.06	2.07	2.08	2.09	2.1	2.11	2.12	2.13
3	3.03	3.06	3.091	3.122	3.152	3.184	3.215	3.246	3.278	3.31	3.342	3.374	3.407
4	4.06	4.122	4.184	4.246	4.31	4.375	4.44	4.506	4.573	4.641	4.71	4.779	4.85
5	5.101	5.204	5.309	5.416	5.526	5.637	5.751	5.867	5.985	6.105	6.228	6.353	6.48
6	6.152	6.308	6.468	6.633	6.802	6.975	7.153	7.336	7.523	7.716	7.913	8.115	8.232
7	7.214	7.434	7.662	7.898	8.142	8.394	8.654	8.923	9.2	9.487	9.783	10.089	10.405
8	8.286	8.583	8.892	9.214	9.549	10.897	10.26	10.637	11.028	11.436	11.859	12.3	12.757
9	9.369	9.755	10.159	10.583	11.027	11.491	11.978	12.488	13.021	13.579	14.164	14.776	15.416
10	10.462	10.95	11.464	12.006	12.578	13.181	13.816	14.487	15.193	15.937	16.722	17.549	18.42
11	11.567	12.169	12.808	13.486	14.207	14.972	15.784	16.645	17.56	18.531	19.561	20.655	21.814
12	12.683	13.412	14.192	15.026	15.917	16.87	17.888	18.977	20.141	21.384	22.713	24.133	25.65
13	13.809	14.68	15.618	16.627	17.713	18.82	20.141	21.495	22.953	24.523	26.212	28.029	29.985
14	14.947	15.971	17.086	18.292	19.599	21.015	22.55	24.215	26.019	27.975	30.095	32.393	34.883
15	16.097	17.291	18.599	20.024	21.579	23.276	25.129	27.152	29.361	31.772	34.405	37.28	40.417
16	17.258	18.639	20.157	21.825	23.657	25.673	27.888	30.324	33.003	35.95	39.19	42.753	46.672
17	18.43	20.012	21.762	23.698	25.84	28.213	30.84	33.75	36.974	40.545	44.501	48.884	53.739
18	19.615	21.412	23.414	25.645	28.132	30.906	33.999	37.45	41.301	45.599	50.396	55.75	61.725
19	20.811	22.841	25.117	27.671	30.539	33.76	37.379	41.446	46.018	51.159	56.939	63.44	70.749
20	22.019	24.297	26.87	29.778	33.066	36.786	40.995	45.762	51.16	57.275	64.203	72.052	80.947
21	23.239	25.783	28.676	31.969	35.719	39.993	44.865	50.423	56.765	64.002	72.265	81.699	92.47
22	24.472	27.299	30.537	34.248	38.505	43.392	49.006	55.457	62.873	71.403	81.214	92.503	105.491
23	25.716	28.845	32.453	36.618	41.43	46.996	53.436	60.893	69.532	79.543	91.148	104.60	120.205
24	26.973	30.422	34.426	39.083	44.502	50.816	58.177	66.765	76.79	88.497	102.17	118.15	136.831
25	28.243	32.03	36.459	41.646	47.727	54.865	63.249	73.106	84.701	98.347	114.41	133.33	155.62
30	34.785	40.568	47.575	56.085	66.439	79.058	94.461	113.28	136.30	164.49	199.02	241.33	293.199
35	41.66	49.994	60.462	73.652	90.32	111.43	138.23	172.31	215.71	271.02	341.59	431.66	546.681
40	48.886	60.402	75.401	95.026	120.8	154.76	199.63	259.05	337.88	442.59	581.82	767.09	1013.704
45	56.481	71.893	92.72	121.02	159.7	212.74	285.74	386.50	525.85	718.90	986.63	1358.2	1874.165
50	64.463	84.579	112.79	152.66	209.34	290.33	406.52	573.77	815.08	1163.9	1668.7	2400.0	3459.507

TABLE A-3

Future Value Annuity Factors ($FVA_{R,N}$) for $1 Compounded at R Per Cent for N Periods (Continued) $FVA_{R,N} = \left[\frac{(1+R)^N - 1}{R}\right]$

	R =												
N	14%	15%	16%	18%	20%	22%	24%	25%	30%	35%	40%	45%	50%
1	1	1	1	1	1	1	1	1	1	1	1	1	1
2	2.14	2.15	2.16	2.18	2.2	2.22	2.24	2.25	2.3	2.35	2.4	2.45	2.5
3	3.44	3.472	3.506	3.572	3.64	3.708	3.778	3.813	3.99	4.172	4.36	4.552	4.75
4	4.921	4.993	5.066	5.215	5.368	5.524	5.684	5.766	6.187	6.633	7.104	7.601	8.125
5	6.61	6.742	6.877	7.154	7.442	7.74	8.048	8.207	9.043	9.954	10.916	12.022	13.188
6	8.536	8.754	8.977	9.442	9.93	10.442	10.98	11.259	12.756	14.438	16.324	18.431	20.781
7	10.73	11.067	11.414	12.142	12.916	13.74	14.615	15.073	17.583	20.492	23.853	27.726	32.172
8	13.233	13.727	14.24	15.327	16.499	17.762	19.123	19.842	23.858	28.664	34.395	11.202	49.258
9	16.085	16.786	17.519	19.086	20.799	22.67	24.712	25.802	32.015	39.696	49.153	60.743	74.887
10	19.337	20.304	21.321	23.521	25.959	28.657	31.643	33.253	42.619	54.59	69.814	80.077	113.33
11	23.045	24.349	25.733	28.755	32.15	35.962	40.238	42.566	56.405	74.697	98.789	130.16	170.995
12	27.271	29.002	30.85	34.931	39.581	44.874	50.895	54.208	74.327	101.84	139.23	189.73	257.493
13	32.089	34.352	36.786	42.219	48.497	55.746	64.11	68.76	97.625	138.48	195.92	276.11	387.239
14	37.581	40.505	43.672	50.818	59.196	69.01	80.496	86.949	127.91	187.95	275.3	401.36	581.859
15	43.842	47.58	51.66	60.965	72.035	85.192	100.81	109.68	167.28	254.73	386.42	582.98	873.788
16	50.98	55.717	60.925	72.939	87.442	104.93	126.01	138.10	218.47	344.89	541.98	846.32	1311.682
17	59.118	65.075	71.673	87.068	105.93	129.02	157.25	173.63	285.01	466.61	759.78	1228.1	1968.523
18	68.394	75.836	84.141	103.74	128.11	158.40	195.99	218.04	371.51	630.92	1064.6	1781.3	2953.784
19	78.969	88.212	98.603	123.41	154.74	194.25	244.03	273.55	483.97	852.74	1491.5	2584.6	4431.676
20	91.025	102.44	115.38	146.62	186.68	237.98	303.60	342.94	630.16	1152.2	2089.2	3748.7	6648.513
21	104.76	118.81	134.84	174.02	225.02	291.34	377.46	429.68	820.21	1556.4	2925.8	5436.7	9973.77
22	120.43	137.63	157.41	206.34	271.03	356.44	469.05	538.10	1067.2	2102.2	4097.2	7884.2	14961.65
23	138.29	159.27	183.60	244.48	326.23	435.86	582.63	673.62	1388.4	2839.0	5737.1	11433.	22443.48
24	158.65	184.16	213.97	289.49	392.48	532.75	723.46	843.03	1806.0	3833.7	8032.9	16579.	33666.22
25	181.87	212.79	249.21	342.60	471.98	650.95	898.09	1054.7	2348.8	5176.5	11247.	24040.	50500.34
30	356.78	434.74	530.31	790.94	1181.8	1767.0	2640.9	3227.1	8729.9	23221.	60501.	154106.	383500.1
35	693.57	881.17	1120.7	1816.6	2948.3	4783.6	7750.2	9856.7	32422.	104136.	325400.	987794.	
40	1342.0	1779.0	2360.7	4163.2	7343.8	12936.	22728.	30088.	120392.	466960.			
45	2490.5	3585.1	4965.2	9531.5	18281.	3497.1	66640.	91831.	447019.				
50	4994.5	7217.7	10435.	21813.	45497.	94525.	195372.	280255.					

TABLE A-4

Present Value Annuity Factors ($PVA_{R,N}$) at R Per Cent Per Period for $1 Received per Period for Each of N Periods $PVA_{R,N} = \left[\frac{1 - \frac{1}{(1+R)^N}}{R}\right]$

	R =												
N	1%	2%	3%	4%	5%	6%	7%	8%	9%	10%	11%	12%	13%
1	0.990	0.980	0.971	0.962	0.952	0.943	0.935	0.926	0.917	0.909	0.901	0.893	0.885
2	1.970	1.942	1.913	1.886	1.859	1.833	1.808	1.783	1.759	1.736	1.713	1.690	1.668
3	2.941	2.884	2.829	2.775	2.723	2.673	2.624	2.577	2.531	2.487	2.444	2.402	2.361
4	3.902	3.808	3.717	3.630	3.546	3.465	3.387	3.312	3.240	3.170	3.102	3.037	2.974
5	4.853	4.713	4.580	4.452	4.329	4.212	4.100	3.993	3.890	3.791	3.696	3.605	3.517
6	5.795	5.601	5.417	5.242	5.076	4.917	4.767	4.623	4.486	4.355	4.231	4.111	3.998
7	6.728	6.472	6.230	6.002	5.786	5.582	5.389	5.206	5.033	4.868	4.712	4.564	4.423
8	7.652	7.325	7.020	6.733	6.463	6.210	5.971	5.747	5.535	5.335	5.146	4.968	4.799
9	8.566	8.162	7.786	7.435	7.108	6.802	6.515	6.247	5.995	5.759	5.537	5.328	5.132
10	9.471	8.983	8.530	8.111	7.722	7.360	7.024	6.710	6.418	6.145	5.889	5.650	5.426
11	10.368	9.787	9.253	8.760	8.306	7.887	7.499	7.139	6.805	6.495	6.207	5.938	5.687
12	11.255	10.575	9.954	9.385	8.863	8.384	7.943	7.536	7.161	6.814	6.492	6.194	5.918
13	12.134	11.348	10.635	9.986	9.394	8.853	8.358	7.904	7.487	7.103	6.750	6.424	6.122
14	13.004	12.106	11.296	10.563	9.899	9.295	8.745	8.244	7.786	7.367	6.982	6.628	6.302
15	13.865	12.849	11.938	11.118	10.380	9.712	9.108	8.559	8.061	7.606	7.191	6.811	6.462
16	14.718	13.578	12.561	11.652	10.838	10.106	9.447	8.851	8.313	7.824	7.379	6.974	6.604
17	15.562	14.292	13.166	12.166	11.274	10.477	9.763	9.122	8.544	8.022	7.549	7.120	6.729
18	16.398	14.992	13.754	12.659	11.690	10.828	10.059	9.372	8.756	8.201	7.702	7.250	6.840
19	17.226	15.678	14.324	13.134	12.085	11.158	10.336	9.604	8.950	8.365	7.839	7.366	6.938
20	18.046	16.351	14.877	13.590	12.462	11.470	10.594	9.818	9.129	8.514	7.963	7.469	7.025
21	18.857	17.011	15.415	14.029	12.821	11.764	10.836	10.017	9.292	8.649	8.075	7.562	7.102
22	19.660	17.658	15.937	14.451	13.163	12.042	11.061	10.201	9.442	8.772	8.176	7.654	7.170
23	20.456	18.292	16.444	14.857	13.489	12.303	11.272	10.371	9.580	8.883	8.266	7.718	7.230
24	21.243	18.914	16.936	15.247	13.799	12.550	11.469	10.529	9.707	8.985	8.348	7.784	7.283
25	22.023	19.523	17.413	15.622	14.094	12.783	11.654	10.675	9.823	9.077	8.422	7.843	7.330
30	25.808	22.396	19.600	17.292	15.372	13.765	12.409	11.258	10.274	9.427	8.694	8.055	7.496
35	29.409	24.999	21.487	18.665	16.374	14.498	12.948	11.655	10.567	9.644	8.855	8.176	7.586
40	32.835	27.355	23.115	19.793	17.159	15.046	13.332	11.925	10.757	9.779	8.951	8.244	7.634
45	36.095	29.490	24.519	20.720	17.774	15.456	13.606	12.108	10.881	9.863	9.008	8.283	7.661
50	39.196	31.424	25.730	21.482	18.256	15.762	13.801	12.233	10.962	9.915	9.042	8.304	7.675

TABLE A-4

Present Value Annuity Factors ($PVA_{R,N}$) at R Per Cent Per Period for $1 Received per Period for Each of N Periods (Continued) $PVA_{R,N} = \left[\frac{1 - \frac{1}{(1+R)^N}}{R}\right]$

N	R = 14%	15%	16%	18%	20%	22%	24%	25%	30%	35%	40%	45%	50%
1	0.877	0.870	0.862	0.847	0.833	0.820	0.806	0.800	0.769	0.741	0.714	0.690	0.667
2	1.647	1.626	1.605	1.566	1.528	1.492	1.457	1.440	1.361	1.289	1.224	1.165	1.111
3	2.322	2.283	2.246	2.174	2.106	2.042	1.981	1.952	1.816	1.696	1.589	1.493	1.407
4	2.914	2.855	2.798	2.690	2.589	2.494	2.404	2.362	2.166	1.997	1.849	1.720	1.605
5	3.433	3.352	3.274	3.127	2.991	2.864	2.745	2.689	2.436	2.220	2.035	1.876	1.737
6	3.889	3.784	3.685	3.498	3.326	3.167	3.020	2.951	2.643	2.385	2.168	1.983	1.824
7	4.288	4.160	4.039	3.812	3.605	3.416	3.242	3.161	2.802	2.508	2.263	2.057	1.883
8	4.639	4.487	4.344	4.078	3.837	3.619	3.421	3.329	2.925	2.598	2.331	2.109	1.922
9	4.946	4.772	4.607	4.303	4.031	3.786	3.566	3.463	3.019	2.665	2.379	2.144	1.948
10	5.216	5.019	4.833	4.494	4.192	3.923	3.682	3.571	3.092	2.715	2.414	2.168	1.965
11	5.453	5.234	5.029	4.656	4.327	4.035	3.776	3.656	3.147	2.752	2.438	2.185	1.977
12	5.660	5.421	5.197	4.793	4.439	4.127	3.851	3.725	3.190	2.779	2.456	2.196	1.985
13	5.842	5.583	5.342	4.910	4.533	4.203	3.921	3.780	3.223	2.799	2.469	2.204	1.990
14	6.002	5.724	5.468	5.008	4.611	4.265	3.962	3.824	3.249	2.814	2.478	2.210	1.993
15	6.142	5.847	5.575	5.092	4.675	4.315	4.001	3.859	3.268	2.825	2.484	2.214	1.995
16	6.265	5.954	5.668	5.162	4.730	4.357	4.033	3.887	3.283	2.834	2.489	2.216	1.997
17	6.373	6.047	5.749	5.222	4.775	4.391	4.059	3.910	3.295	2.840	2.492	2.218	1.998
18	6.467	6.128	5.818	5.273	4.812	4.419	4.080	3.928	3.304	2.844	2.494	2.219	1.999
19	6.550	6.198	5.877	5.316	4.843	4.442	4.097	3.942	3.311	2.848	2.496	2.220	1.999
20	6.623	6.259	5.929	5.353	4.870	4.460	4.110	3.954	3.316	2.850	2.497	2.221	1.999
21	6.687	6.312	5.973	5.384	4.891	4.476	4.121	3.963	3.320	2.852	2.498	2.221	2.000
22	6.743	6.359	6.011	5.410	4.909	4.488	4.130	3.970	3.323	2.853	2.498	2.222	2.000
23	6.792	6.399	6.044	5.432	4.925	4.499	4.137	3.976	3.325	2.854	2.499	2.222	2.000
24	6.835	6.434	6.073	5.451	4.937	4.507	4.143	3.981	3.327	2.855	2.499	2.222	2.000
25	6.873	6.464	6.097	5.467	4.948	4.514	4.147	3.985	3.329	2.856	2.499	2.222	2.000
30	7.003	6.566	6.177	5.517	4.979	4.534	4.160	3.995	3.332	2.857	2.500	2.222	2.000
35	7.070	6.617	6.215	5.539	4.992	4.541	4.164	3.998	3.333	2.857	2.500	2.222	2.000
40	7.105	6.642	6.233	5.548	4.997	4.544	4.166	3.999	3.333	2.857	2.500	2.222	2.000
45	7.123	6.654	6.242	5.552	4.999	4.545	4.166	4.000	3.333	2.857	2.500	2.222	2.000
50	7.133	6.661	6.246	5.554	4.999	4.545	4.167	4.000	3.333	2.857	2.500	2.222	2.000

TABLE A-5

Cumulative Normal Distribution

d	$N(d)$	d	$N(d)$	d	$N(d)$
−3.00	.0013	−1.42	.0778	−0.44	.3300
−2.95	.0016	−1.40	.0808	−0.42	.3373
−2.90	.0019	−1.38	.0838	−0.40	.3446
−2.85	.0022	−1.36	.0869	−0.38	.3520
−2.80	.0026	−1.34	.0901	−0.36	.3594
−2.75	.0030	−1.32	.0934	−0.34	.3669
−2.70	.0035	−1.30	.0968	−0.32	.3745
−2.65	.0040	−1.28	.1003	−0.30	.3821
−2.60	.0047	−1.26	.1038	−0.28	.3897
−2.55	.0054	−1.24	.1075	−0.26	.3974
−2.50	.0062	−1.22	.1112	−0.24	.4052
−2.45	.0071	−1.20	.1151	−0.22	.4129
−2.40	.0082	−1.18	.1190	−0.20	.4207
−2.35	.0094	−1.16	.1230	−0.18	.4286
−2.30	.0107	−1.14	.1271	−0.16	.4365
−2.25	.0122	−1.12	.1314	−0.14	.4443
−2.20	.0139	−1.10	.1357	−0.12	.4523
−2.15	.0158	−1.08	.1401	−0.10	.4602
−2.10	.0179	−1.06	.1446	−0.08	.4681
−2.05	.0202	−1.04	.1492	−0.06	.4761
−2.00	.0228	−1.02	.1539	−0.04	.4841
−1.98	.0239	−1.00	.1587	−0.02	.4920
−1.96	.0250	−0.98	.1635	0.00	.5000
−1.94	.0262	−0.96	.1685	0.02	.5080
−1.92	.0274	−0.94	.1736	0.04	.5160
−1.90	.0287	−0.92	.1788	0.06	.5239
−1.88	.0301	−0.90	.1841	0.08	.5319
−1.86	.0314	−0.88	.1894	0.10	.5398
−1.84	.0329	−0.86	.1949	0.12	.5478
−1.82	.0344	−0.84	.2005	0.14	.5557
−1.80	.0359	−0.82	.2061	0.16	.5636
−1.78	.0375	−0.80	.2119	0.18	.5714
−1.76	.0392	−0.78	.2117	0.20	.5793
−1.74	.0409	−0.76	.2236	0.22	.5871
−1.72	.0427	−0.74	.2297	0.24	.5948
−1.70	.0446	−0.72	.2358	0.26	.6026
−1.68	.0465	−0.70	.2420	0.28	.6103
−1.66	.0485	−0.68	.2483	0.30	.6179
−1.64	.0505	−0.66	.2546	0.32	.6255
−1.62	.0526	−0.64	.2611	0.34	.6331
−1.60	.0548	−0.62	.2676	0.36	.6406
−1.58	.0571	−0.60	.2743	0.38	.6480
−1.56	.0594	−0.58	.2810	0.40	.6556
−1.54	.0618	−0.56	.2877	0.42	.6628
−1.52	.0643	−0.54	.2946	0.44	.6700
−1.50	.0668	−0.52	.3015	0.46	.6773
−1.48	.0694	−0.50	.3085	0.48	.6844
−1.46	.0721	−0.48	.3156	0.50	.6915
−1.44	.0749	−0.46	.3228	0.52	.6985

TABLE A-5

Cumulative Normal Distribution (Continued)

d	*N(d)*	*d*	*N(d)*	*d*	*N(d)*
0.54	.7054	1.18	.8810	1.82	.9556
0.56	.7123	1.20	.8849	1.84	.9671
0.58	.7191	1.22	.8888	1.86	.9686
0.60	.7258	1.24	.8925	1.88	.9699
0.62	.7324	1.26	.8962	1.90	.9713
0.64	.7389	1.28	.8997	1.92	.9726
0.66	.7454	1.30	.9032	1.94	.9738
0.68	.7518	1.32	.9066	1.96	.9750
0.70	.7580	1.34	.9099	1.98	.9761
0.72	.7642	1.36	.9131	2.00	.9772
0.74	.7704	1.38	.9162	2.05	.9798
0.76	.7764	1.40	.9192	2.10	.9821
0.78	.7823	1.42	.9222	2.15	.9842
0.80	.7882	1.44	.9251	2.20	.9861
0.82	.7939	1.46	.9279	2.25	.9878
0.84	.7996	1.48	.9306	2.30	.9893
0.86	.8051	1.50	.9332	2.35	.9906
0.88	.8106	1.52	.9357	2.40	.9918
0.90	.8159	1.54	.9382	2.45	.9929
0.92	.8212	1.56	.9406	2.50	.9938
0.94	.8264	1.58	.9429	2.55	.9946
0.96	.8315	1.60	.9452	2.60	.9953
0.98	.8365	1.62	.9474	2.65	.9960
1.00	.8414	1.64	.9495	2.70	.9965
1.02	.8461	1.66	.9515	2.75	.9970
1.04	.8508	1.68	.9535	2.80	.9974
1.06	.8554	1.70	.9554	2.85	.9978
1.08	.8599	1.72	.9573	2.90	.9981
1.10	.8643	1.74	.9591	2.95	.9984
1.12	.8686	1.76	.9608	3.00	.9986
1.14	.8729	1.78	.9625	3.05	.9989
1.16	.8770	1.80	.9641		

INDEX